Money, Prices, and Policy

Money Prices and Policy

Walter W. Haines
Professor and Chairman
The Department of Economics
University College of Arts and Science
New York University

Second edition

McGraw-Hill Book Company
New York / St. Louis / San Francisco
Toronto / London / Sydney

Money, Prices, and Policy

Printed in the United States of America.

Library of Congress Catalog Card Number 65-26479
25525

2 3 4 5 6 7 8 9 0 HD 7 3 2 1 0 6 9 8 7 6

Preface

Polonius. What do you read, my lord?
Hamlet. Words, words, words.

Hamlet
Act II, scene 2, line 195

When I first started writing this book, my major purpose was to provide an introduction to money and banking that would be clear and readable for student and layman alike. Its success in this respect has been heartening, and revision provides an opportunity not only to update, but also to make the material conform even more closely to the needs expressed by its users. The most important of these changes are listed below.

The book's orientation, however, remains the same; in examining the role that money plays in a modern economy, its ultimate objective is to add to an understanding of monetary policy and its effect on both national income and the standard of living of the individual. Policy, however, rests on the twin foundations of institutions and theory, and both of these, in turn, are illuminated by history as well as by current developments. The book, then, has four themes: history, institutions, theory, and policy. They overlap so extensively that only in the broadest sense can they be considered separate approaches. In each area it is hoped that this book makes a real contribution in presentation.

Although the present moment is always most important to those who live in it, it is the heir of the past and the father of the future. Any attempt to restrict a history of money to the confines—both geographic and temporal—of the United States loses not only a measure of the wider panorama of experience, but also much of the excitement of money's colorful past. On the other hand, however, the past is no substitute for the present, and at all points I have tried to bring all information up to the latest date available and to suggest where future material may be found.

Commercial and central banking institutions must necessarily form the core of any book on money, but the financial intermediaries, once thought to be rather peripheral, are becoming increasingly important in the money market and can no longer be ignored. They are given three chapters to themselves and enter the discussion at numerous other points.

Theory is the result of past experience and the base of future policy. In the theoretical sections I have been especially careful to be as lucid as possible. Without avoiding controversy, I have concentrated on those areas of theory where there appears to be greatest agreement among economists. In the process I have found it fairly easy to integrate the best of both classical and modern theory, for they complement each other in most essentials. In approaching national income theory I have used a pictorial rather than an algebraic presentation (although equations cannot be completely omitted), for experience shows that this is easier for the student to grasp and that it forms a sound foundation on which more complex concepts can be built.

Policy is presented not only from the point of view of historical development and official pronouncement, but also as a field of continuing controversy that will occupy an important place in public debate for some time to come. The gold drain, "operation twist," the increased emphasis on growth, proposals for revamping the Federal Reserve structure or operation, and other less orthodox ideas are examined in an attempt to emphasize that change is inevitable and that a course in money and banking today is useful for the future only if it prepares the student to keep abreast of his times and use his knowledge in the solution of new problems as they arise. Even some of the problems discussed in the first edition have now become outdated.

The questions and bibliography at the end of each chapter are also directed toward this end. Hopefully, the bibliographies will encourage the reader to get acquainted with important literature in the field and to form the habit of looking for answers in the proper place. The questions are not mere memory testers, but are designed to get the student to use the information he has acquired and to correlate it with material from other areas. Most of them cannot be answered merely by turning back a few pages, and the answers to many will vary with the individual's orientation and philosophy. In this sense they resemble the real-life questions with which we all wrestle.

Revisions. For those who have used the book before, the following should prove a useful guide to the differences that will be encountered in this edition.

Chapters 1 and 2 of the first edition have been combined into a single Chapter 1 and have been shortened somewhat.

Since users have not been happy with the unorthodox postponement of the material on monetary standards and systems, this information has been moved forward. The material of Chapter 18, on monetary standards, has been incorporated into Chapters 2, 5, and 6; and Chapter 19, on the United States monetary system, is now Chapter 3.

The discussion of bank liquidity and portfolio management, formerly in Chapter 7, has been substantially enlarged and appears as a new Chapter 10.

The material of Chapter 14, on credit and finance, has been expanded and separated into two chapters: Chapter 4, Credit and Credit Instruments, and Chapter 16, The Money and Capital Markets.

Perhaps the most important change is the introduction of a completely new Chapter 30, which discusses the Hicks-Hansen theory of interest rate and income determination as well as other refinements of monetary, income, and price theory.

Chapters 31 and 32, on Federal Reserve policy, have been combined as Chapter 32.

Throughout the book figures have been brought up to 1964 and 1965. A fair amount of space is now given to the United States' adverse balance of payments and its effects on monetary policy, including such matters as international liquidity, gold movements, new international monetary arrangements, the abandonment of bills only, and the development of new types of banking instruments in response to rising interest rates.

Use. Although the book is designed for a one-semester course, most instructors will probably not want to try to cover everything in such a course. The wide array of topics provides considerable flexibility by permitting the instructor to build his program around the basic area and to choose from among the others those which he wants to emphasize. For this reason a number of chapters are relatively self-contained and may be omitted without interfering with the core of the traditional course in money and banking. Many students will find it worthwhile to read these chapters on their own. Practical suggestions for such treatment are given on pages xix and xx.

On the other hand, the coverage of topics is adequate for most two-semester courses, giving time for deeper penetration and for outside reading, whether in the form of a book of readings, selections from the bibliographies, or materials available—frequently without cost—from the Federal Reserve System and other organizations.

Some teachers may wish to rearrange the order of presentation, particularly by assigning Chapter 32, on Federal Reserve policy, immediately after Chapter 13 or 14, which cover Federal Reserve controls. There is no reason why this may not be done.

All this material has been classroom-tested. It has also benefited from numerous and sometimes detailed suggestions from a large number of readers, among whom, without any intention of slighting others, I should especially like to thank Harlan Smith, of the University of Minnesota. My wife has read the entire manuscript from the point of view of the neophyte and was good enough to say that she found it not only understandable but also interesting. If others have the same experience, the book will have served its purpose well.

Walter W. Haines

Contents

Part Six. Monetary Theory

Part Seven. National Income Theory

Part Eight. Monetary Policy

List of Tables

List of Figures

Suggestions for a One-semester Course

Course A, emphasizing institutions:

1 The nature of money
3 The monetary system of the United States
4 Credit and credit instruments
8 Commercial bank operations
9 Principles of credit expansion
10 Liquidity and portfolio management
11 Development of the Federal Reserve System
12 Federal Reserve operations
13 Federal Reserve controls
14 The bank reserve equation
15 The current banking situation
16 The money and capital markets
17 Consumer finance
18 Business credit
21 The value of money
22 Money and business fluctuations
23 Theories of the value of money
24 Transactions and cash balances
25 The income approach
26 The income-creating process
27 The role of expectations
31 Aims of monetary policy
32 Federal Reserve policy
33 Critique: The bases of monetary policy
34 Critique: The tools of monetary policy

Course B, emphasizing theory:

1 The nature of money
3 The monetary system of the United States
4 Credit and credit instruments
5 The origins of modern banking

6 Early banking in the United States
7 State and national banking
8 Commercial bank operations
9 Principles of credit expansion
11 Development of the Federal Reserve System
12 Federal Reserve operations
13 Federal Reserve controls
21 The value of money
22 Money and business fluctuations
23 Theories of the value of money
24 Transactions and cash balances
25 The income approach
26 The income-creating process
27 The role of expectations
29 The rate of interest
30 Money, income, prices, and production
31 Aims of monetary policy
32 Federal Reserve policy
33 Critique: The bases of monetary policy
34 Critique: The tools of monetary policy
35 Fiscal policy

Money, Prices, and Policy

Part One
Money
and Credit

Chapter 1 The Nature of Money

He that wants money, means, and content is without three good friends.

As You Like It
Act III, scene 2, line 25

This book on money, prices, and policy is concerned with everyday matters that touch us all very closely. It deals with familiar concepts, but as we study them more carefully, we are likely to find that they are more complex than we thought. Casual acquaintances have many unsuspected qualities, and surface appearances often hide as much as they reveal. Our task, then, is to probe the mystery of the familiar.

Money. Money can hardly be called an unknown phenomenon. Every one of us has some in his pockets. We know where it comes from even though we may sometimes be a little baffled as to where it all goes. We know it well enough to call it by many pet names: lettuce, dough, sheckles, fish, brass, cabbage, moola, chink, rhino, ducats, tin. We know that we never have enough of it; at the same time we may realize vaguely that it is possible for a nation as a whole to have too much of it. Most important, we know that as long as we have money we can buy anything (or almost anything) we want, anywhere, any time.

Money talks; and when it talks, it doesn't plead—it commands. "If money goes before, all ways do lie open."[1] This universal acceptability of money appears to give it a desirability above all other things. "All anyone needs to know about money," it has been said, "is how to make some."

[1] Shakespeare, *Merry Wives of Windsor,* Act II, scene 2, line 177.

Yet no one wants money. In this day and age, when money is merely a token, no one except the miser desires money for its own sake. We can't eat it, wear it, ride on it, or cut the grass with it, and even in that oft-pictured use for lighting cigarettes it is not as efficient as a match. We don't want money; we want its power to command goods, that mysterious force that lets us buy a refrigerator or a trip to Europe and give nothing but a few pieces of paper in exchange.

What marvelous pieces of paper! Do we really know what they are or where their power comes from? Have we even had the curiosity to read what is printed on them? What is money? Why does it have value? And what value does it have?

Prices. The value of money, like the value of anything else, is the quantity of other things that can be obtained in exchange for it. How much we can get for a dollar depends, of course, on the prices of the things we want to buy. Prices are another economic phenomenon that everybody knows about. Our very standard of living is dependent upon two sets of prices between which we are held as in a vise: the price of the services (usually labor) that we sell (our income) and the price of the goods that we wish to buy. We would be very happy to have the price of the first raised and that of the second lowered.[2]

Prices are no secret. We know that milk is, perhaps, 26 cents a quart, a subway ride 20 cents, and a color television set $300. But a few years ago milk was 23 cents, the subway was a nickel, and color television $1,000. What has happened to prices; why can't they stay where they belong? To what extent are price changes due to technology or competitive conditions in a particular industry, and to what extent are they due to monetary causes—to changes in the value of money itself?

Policy. We know that the value of money does change because we have heard people talking of a "50-cent dollar" and referring to the fact that the price level (whatever that is) has doubled since the beginning of the war.[3] "Inflation" some people call it, and others call it less printable names. We may also have heard vague references to the Great Depression of the thirties, when the problem was not inflation but deflation, falling prices, curtailed production, layoffs, breadlines, the tightened belt, and idle factories. This was a dismal period in which almost all measures of economic activity hit rock bottom except for unemployment and business failures, which were at an all-time high. Did falling prices mean too little money, just as rising prices mean too much? To what extent was money responsible for the inter-

[2] A friend of mine expressed what is probably true of most of us when he said, "If my income were raised $1,000 a year, I could afford to live in the manner in which I am now living."

[3] We may even have heard the old wheeze that it was no problem for George Washington to throw a silver dollar across the Rappahannock because dollars went further in those days.

war depression or the postwar boom? To what extent can money be controlled in order to prevent a repetition of violent swings in the economy?

In the field of policy we probably know that the Federal Reserve System is supposed to control the money in the economy so that it doesn't get out of adjustment. The newspapers talk of monetary policy, automatic stabilizers, unemployment insurance, deposit insurance, tax reduction, public works, and the burden of the national debt. What policies would be effective in promoting stabilization of the economy and why?

These are the questions that this book is written to try to answer. While nobody knows all the answers, there are certain principles on which most economists are agreed, and basic to all of them is an understanding of what money is, what it is not, and precisely how it functions in our present economy. In spite of the fact that everybody knows something about money, there is much that most people do not know—and, in fact, much that they do "know" that just isn't true.

Why Is Money Important?

Money is characteristic of nearly every highly developed civilization, and we might almost say that it is necessary to such development. Occasionally Socialists have suggested that money is an invention of the capitalists and that its purpose is to exploit the people, but even socialism does not emphasize this theory today. It is more common among all varieties of critics to call for a better use of money than to advocate its abolition. Even the Soviet Union, which one tried to abolish money, found from bitter experience that it was practically impossible to get along without it.

Money and Trade. Money is essential to a high level of trade. One of the simplest ways to examine the importance of money is to imagine the difficulties that would arise in the normal course of events if there were none.

The Disadvantages of Barter. Suppose you are a shoemaker and receive, as wages, five pairs of shoes a week. With these you must obtain all the other things you want. Trying to barter your shoes, you would soon find that there were several problems involved:

1. In the first place, it is obvious that there must be a value placed on shoes in terms of everything else for which shoes exchange. We have already tacitly assumed that a pair of shoes is worth one-fifth of a week's labor. It may also be worth 200 chocolate bars, 10 pounds of butter, 2 opera tickets, a hat, or one-twentieth of a refrigerator. Each item must have a ratio of exchange with every other article. The possible number of exchanges in a modern economy—and hence the number of ratios that would have to be known—is fantastic.

2. Suppose you want a hat. Not only do you have to find a hatter, but the hatter has to want shoes. This is what economists refer to as *double coinci-*

dence of wants. If the hatter wants butter or an overcoat, the two of you still can't make a trade. Either you must look for another hatter, who wants shoes, or else you must find a dairyman who is willing to give you 10 pounds of butter for a pair of shoes so that you can take the butter to the hatter to get a hat. (And if at this point the hatter says that he wants 12 pounds of butter for a hat, you will probably throw the butter in his face and go and invent money.)
3. The third disadvantage of barter arises when you try to get a chocolate bar. Suppose you are lucky enough to find a confectioner who wants shoes. A pair of shoes is worth 200 chocolate bars, but what would you do with that many? On the other hand, it won't help to cut your shoes into 200 pieces. The only thing to do is to take the chocolate bars and hope to be able to barter those you don't want for something else. By this time you have spent so much time trying to exchange your shoes for the things you want that you don't have any time left to make more shoes.

Barter is obviously a possible method of trade, but it is hardly an efficient one. The introduction of money solves all these problems. Since all goods are valued in terms of the monetary unit, there are only as many ratios as there are goods. Since money is acceptable by everyone, double coincidence of wants is unnecessary. Since money is divisible into small fractions, we can buy the smallest things with it as well as the largest.

Specialization and the Extent of the Market. The use of money simplifies enormously the problems of trade and therefore makes possible a tremendous increase in the volume of transactions. In exchange for our labor or the use of our land or capital we are paid in money, the universal medium of exchange. By a simple money payment we can satisfy our wants from an almost infinite array of goods provided for our selection from the ends of the earth. This vast extent of trade in turn makes possible the minute specialization of labor that is characteristic of industrial countries the world over, a specialization that permits the efficiency on which our high standard of living is based.

Consider, for example, the family automobile. Without the far-flung network of producers who bring together steel, glass, rubber, plastics, asbestos, lacquer, tires, batteries, carburetors, headlights, and foam-rubber seats, it would be impossible to think of producing an automobile except perhaps a crude, handmade affair turned out by the most laborious methods. That whole intricate network of suppliers is held together by money payments.

Money and Economic Coordination. Not only does money bind together the various parts of the economic system, but it also regulates those parts and coordinates them in a relatively smooth-working unit. We are all aware of maladjustments in the economy—bottlenecks in steel, perhaps, or an oversupply of cotton. These are prominent because they are exceptions to the general effectiveness with which the economy usually works. Did you ever pause to wonder how it is that no matter what you want there is almost always someone there to supply it? Should you want a haircut or a can of caviar, a can opener or a dishwasher, a trip to Dallas or a recording of the "St. Louis Blues," you don't generally have far to look. Why is it that everything you want is there in the proper amount? The answer is money.

Suppose that for some reason people decided that they didn't want white shirts, but everybody clamored for purple shirts. The price of white shirts would fall; the price of purple shirts would rise. Producers would have less incentive to make white shirts and more to make purple, and the result would be just what people wanted: an increase in the availability of purple shirts. Each consumer casts his vote for a product in terms of the number of dollars he is willing to spend on it. And producers, other things (primarily costs) being equal, produce those goods with the most dollar votes.

Similarly in the field of labor. If people want fewer blacksmiths, the wages of blacksmiths fall, and blacksmiths are induced to become auto mechanics. If there are too few engineers, the wages of engineers rise, and more students take up engineering. The whole intricate web of an extremely complex economy is thus held together by the relatively automatic operation of the money-price system.

Although money carries on this task of coordination with a minimum of conscious direction, it is not impossible for a barter economy to achieve a fairly high level of development by other means. Many forms of tribal organization, the greater part of the structure of feudalism, the medieval monasteries, the economy of Egypt prior to the sixth century B.C., much of the history of China, and the very complex culture of several of the ancient civilizations in the Americas all attest to the possibility of a relatively high level of achievement in a nonpecuniary society. Perhaps a short description of the economy of the Incas in Peru will give an indication of the nature of such a society.

The Nonmonetary System of the Incas. The Incas, with a widespread empire covering most of the coast and highlands of western South America at the time of Pizarro's conquest in 1532, represent one of the highest forms of civilization achieved in the New World prior to its colonization by Europeans. The Inca architecture, while not elaborate, was a masterpiece of engineering, their roads rivaled those of the Romans, their government was a marvel of ingenuity, and at least one writer maintains that their fabrics have not been surpassed before or since. Yet the Incas had no monetary system of any kind.

Their society might be described as an autocratic-theocratic socialism. The Inca was not only the supreme ruler, but also the high priest of their religion, which was Sun worship. All land belonged to the Inca, but he graciously divided it into three parts: one part for himself, one part for the Sun, and the third part for the *ayllu,* or tribe, which was the basic social group. The *ayllu* in turn apportioned the land among its members for their use, enough to each family to maintain it in comfort.

The foundation of the economy was agriculture. In addition to providing its own food, each family made its own clothes and engaged in various handicrafts: basketry, weaving, pottery, and metalwork. The family was normally self-sufficient except for its supplies of cotton and wool, and these were distributed to the people from the state warehouses. These warehouses were filled by tribute exacted of each family.

Tribute was rendered in the first place by agricultural labor in the fields of the Inca, of the Sun, and of those unfortunates who could not themselves work: the widows, orphans, aged, sick, and those absent on state business. Tribute also consisted of other types of work according to a complicated set of regulations which provided for all the needs of the government to be filled by labor instead of taxation.

Thus each family owed certain duties to the state, and in return the state saw to it that the people were never in want and were provided with those things that they could not provide for themselves.

Although the Indians were tied very closely to the land and could not leave it under normal circumstances, they did not have a right to the land as did the serf in medieval England. The *ayllu* could redistribute the land at any time. Or, for purposes of colonization, particular individuals or households could be sent by the Inca anywhere in the empire. The good of the community came first, and individuals had to submit to whatever the Inca thought was best for the whole nation.

The coordination of the Inca economy, therefore, was achieved by a master plan, a most intricate and well-executed plan of a highly despotic though paternalistic government. "The eye of the central power was upon them, and the never-failing brain, beneficent though inexorable, provided for all their wants, gathered in their tribute, and selected their children for the various occupations required by the State, according to their several aptitudes."[4]

Money and Freedom. One basic fact about such a nonpecuniary culture stands out. In the absence of money any highly developed civilization must rely on an intensive organization in which each individual fits into his own appointed place without any alternative open to him. There are two ways such organization may be maintained. One is by complete dictatorship, where each person produces what he is told and consumes what he is given. The other is by a complete acceptance by the whole society of a pattern of life that each person slips into without deviation, where habit (after initial organization) takes the place of directives. Most nonpecuniary societies tend to combine these two methods in varying degrees. But in Egypt in the sixth century B.C. the system was so ancient and so thoroughly organized (having already lasted for a thousand years) that the Pharaoh himself seems to have been a captive of tradition and law, thus becoming as much a slave to his position as his vassals were to theirs.

[4] Sir Clements Markham, *The Incas of Peru* (E. P. Dutton & Co., Inc., New York, 1910), pp. 168–169. See also Garcilasso de la Vega, *First Part of the Royal Commentaries of the Yncas,* trans. by Sir Clements Markham (The Hakluyt Society, London, 1869–1871).

Whatever the form of organization, the result of the absence of money is a lack of freedom and of individuality. While a monetary civilization may also limit freedom of choice, money at least provides the *possibility* of freeing man from his shackles. Liberty is perhaps the greatest of the advantages of money.

When I am paid in money and buy with money, I have freedom of choice of goods. I don't have to consume what I am given. If I don't like beef, I can eat pork; or I can be a vegetarian in peace, or even starve myself in order to go to the opera every night.

I have freedom of choice of job and can go where wages are highest or other attractions greatest. I can quit a job I don't like and look for another. I can take two jobs if I can stand it, or I can go without working at all, at least temporarily. I can start work as an errand boy at the age of fourteen, or I can go to college and train to become a lawyer, or an archeologist, or an educated bum.

I have freedom of movement because I am not tied to the land or to a particular job. If I don't like the city, I can move to the country; if I don't like the country, I can move back to the city. If I want to work in Los Angeles, nothing stops my going there. These are very great gains.

Freedom is important not only for the individual, but for society as well. Where individuals are free to move, they are most likely to be drawn to those occupations and regions where their contribution is highest, thus enhancing the economic efficiency of the community. The dynamic force in such a social structure also aids progress. The inventor and the innovator are given free reign. They can marshal resources with money—whether their own or borrowed funds—in the hope of providing new and desirable products. The heavy hand of tradition can be shrugged off more easily by men with the freedom and mobility that money provides.

Without money, freedom may be possible at a very low standard of living. Without money, a relatively high standard of living may be obtained without freedom. Only with money are *both* freedom and affluence possible.

The Form of Money. We use dollars so often that sometimes we think they are synonymous with money. But money may take, and in the past has taken, very different forms from the one we are accustomed to. Many proposals for social reform which suggest the elimination of "money" really mean the elimination of the form of money we know and the substitution of a different kind (as, for instance, Robert Owen's "labour tickets"). The basic meaning of money is the subject of our next chapter.

The Drawbacks of Money

Although money makes freedom possible, it certainly doesn't make it inevitable. After all, money is simply a tool for the facilitation of trade; it isn't a panacea for all ills. In fact one of the drawbacks of money is that sometimes it seems so important that people think it has more power than it actually has.

Some people worship this power, like the miser gloating over his pile of coins. Some ride roughshod over their neighbors in order to amass vast amounts of the almighty dollar. Still others, shunning the productive activity of industry, attempt to make their fortune by the manipulation of monetary instruments, even though their actions may result in chaos in the underlying productive process. Some of the most colorful, if least edifying, chapters in United States business history are concerned with the struggle for financial control of corporations, corners in the stock market, the juggling of corporate structures, watered stock, pyramiding of holding companies, and other monetary maneuvers.

Money *can* be manipulated, not only by individuals but also by governments. Through the ages debasement of the currency has piled up untold miseries for nation after nation. It is precisely because money is so important that interference with its smooth operation may have far-reaching effects on the economy. Lenin paid tribute to the power of money when he suggested that the best way to ruin a capitalist economy was to debauch its currency.[5] Macaulay, referring specifically to the closing years of the seventeenth century, spoke eloquently of the evils of unsound money: "It may well be doubted whether all the misery which had been inflicted on the English nation in a quarter of a century by bad kings, bad ministers, bad Parliaments, and bad judges, was equal to the misery caused in a single year by bad crowns and bad shillings."[6]

The Veil of Money. One of the difficulties with money is that we take it so much for granted. Pigou speaks of it as "a veil behind which the action of real economic forces is concealed."[7] In some cases the concealment is so effective that we forget that there are any real economic forces there at all. Sometimes we seem to feel that it is money that produces goods, not men and machines. In the latter part of the nineteenth century the Populists thought that if the quantity of money were only increased, everyone would be better off. But what would people do with the extra money if there were no more goods to buy? Today it is sometimes suggested that a nation may push the cost of a war onto "unborn generations" by issuing bonds to pay for the war. In financial terms this may be partially true, but those who present this point of view often forget that no matter where the money comes from, the planes, the ammunition, and the uniforms are produced by today's machines and today's workers.

[5] John M. Keynes, *Essays in Persuasion* (Harcourt, Brace & World, Inc., New York, 1932), p. 77.

[6] Thomas Babington Macaulay, *The History of England from the Accession of James II* (Everyman's Library, E. P. Dutton & Co., Inc., New York, 1906), vol. III, p. 391.

[7] A. C. Pigou, *The Veil of Money* (Macmillan & Co., Ltd., London, 1949), p. 18.

Although money is extremely useful in facilitating production and trade, it cannot by itself produce a single shoestring. Material well-being is improved by producing more goods, never by simply increasing the money supply.

Say's Law. Again, however, we must be careful not to go to the other extreme of suggesting that money has no influence on the economy at all except as a catalyst. The idea that money is neutral was quite common among the classical economists of the nineteenth century. They thought of money as oil in the machinery: it made for smoother, more efficient operation but did not change the mechanical process. Adam Smith compared money to "a highway, which, while it circulates and carries to market all the grass and corn of the country, produces itself not a single pile of either."[8]

Half a century later, John Stuart Mill stated the classicist's concept of the neutral role of money even more clearly:

> It must be evident, however, that the mere introduction of a particular mode of exchanging things for one another by first exchanging a thing for money, and then exchanging the money for something else, makes no difference in the essential character of the transactions. . . . There cannot, in short, be intrinsically a more insignificant thing, in the economy of society, than money; except in the character of a contrivance for sparing time and labour. It is a machine for doing quickly and commodiously, what would be done, though less quickly and commodiously, without it: and like many other kinds of machinery, it only exerts a distinct and independent influence of its own when it gets out of order.
>
> The introduction of money does not interfere with the operation of any of the Laws of Value laid down in the preceding chapters. The reasons which make the temporary or market value of things depend on the demand and supply, and their average and permanent values upon their cost of production, are as applicable to a money system as to a system of barter. Things which by barter would exchange for one another, will, if sold for money, sell for an equal amount of it, and so will exchange for one another still, though the process of exchanging them will consist of two operations instead of only one.[9]

This notion that under a monetary system goods exchange just as they would in the case of barter is also the basic assumption behind Say's famous law of markets.[10] According to Say, supply creates its own demand, for whenever a producer comes to market with a product to sell, the money he receives from the sale is purchasing power that he will use to buy someone else's goods.

Under barter this must be the case. If I come to the market with a pair of shoes that I have made, the shoes represent a supply of goods offered for

[8] Adam Smith, *An Inquiry into the Nature and Causes of the Wealth of Nations,* ed. by Edwin Cannan (Modern Library, Inc., New York, 1937), p. 305.

[9] John Stuart Mill, *Principles of Political Economy,* ed. by W. J. Ashley (Longmans, Green & Co., Ltd., London, 1909), pp. 487–488.

[10] Jean Baptiste Say, *A Treatise on Political Economy,* trans. from 4th ed. of the French by C. R. Prinsep, 5th Amer. ed. (Grigg and Elliott, Philadelphia, 1832), pp. 76–79.

exchange. But I cannot get rid of these shoes except by trading them for some other article, say, a hat. So my supply of shoes equals my demand for a hat. If I cannot find someone who will barter a hat for my shoes, neither my supply nor my demand finds a proper outlet. My desire to get rid of the shoes and my desire to acquire a hat are both frustrated, perhaps because there are too many shoes already on the market. This represents misdirected production—but not overproduction (in the sense of more goods than people want). There are both too many shoes (excess supply) *and* too few hats (deficient supply). The market is unbalanced but not glutted.

Sand in the Machinery. While Say's law is necessarily true under barter, money introduces an entirely new dimension into exchange, that is, time. If I sell shoes for money and buy a hat with the proceeds, I have engaged in indirect barter. Money has simply facilitated trade. But suppose I sell my shoes, take the money home, and put it under the mattress. My supply of shoes has found an outlet. But I have demanded nothing in return. I have completed only half of the barter process. The seller of hats can't find a buyer. I have the money to buy his hat, but I don't want to do so. I have hoarded; I have withdrawn money from the stream of commerce and have thereby depressed the market.

For Say's law to hold true, money must continue to circulate. Withholding of purchasing power can truly lead to depression. The hatter can't sell his hats; he lays off workers. The ex-workers can't buy steak; the butcher's income falls along with that of the farmer who raises cattle. They buy less, and we have started on a general spiral of falling purchases, falling production, falling income. Perhaps money is only oil in the machinery, but if the oil is removed, the machinery may grind to a halt.

There is another possibility. In a modern monetary economy it is possible for me to go to market and buy a hat without ever having produced shoes. If my credit is good, I can borrow money from the bank, money that didn't exist before.[11] Without selling anything, I have purchasing power to buy goods. If I'm the government, I can simply print the money. In either case, I buy my hat and the hatter has purchasing power. But what will he buy? In a barter economy he would have "bought" my shoes. But here I didn't produce any shoes. The money he holds came onto the market without any goods behind it. It is new money added to the total already being used to purchase goods. If the hatter tries to buy something with this new money, he adds to the existing demand; and with no corresponding increase in supply, all that this additional purchasing power can do is to push prices up. The increased money is absorbed in higher prices. And so the economy is off on inflation, with too much money chasing too few goods.

[11] The alchemy by which the banks produce money out of nothing is the major topic of Part Two of this book.

The evils of these swings in the economy are well known. Fundamentally they fall into two categories:

1. Any shift in price levels redistributes income and wealth. This is particularly true as between debtors and creditors. When price levels are falling, the debtor repays his obligation in money that will buy more than the money he borrowed. He pays back greater purchasing power than he received. If prices are rising, he repays his debt in money that will buy less than it did when he borrowed it. The creditor receives less purchasing power than he lent. Other groups are affected as well. Anyone whose income fluctuates little (pensioners, to take one obvious example) can buy more when prices fall, less when they rise. But businessmen lose sales in a falling market, and profits tumble; when everything is going up, business does well.

2. Even more important than these shifts in distribution of income is the fact that depression means idle men, idle machines, idle resources, and fewer goods for everybody. Not only does national income fall, but idleness has its corrosive effects on personality, and social unrest frequently leads to drastic suggestions for reform, which in some cases might be even worse than the disease they were intended to cure. Inflation, on the other hand, is usually associated with full employment; but, if carried too far, it may disrupt the delicately balanced economic machinery and lead to less production rather than more. More serious is the fact that inflation carries within it the seeds of depression. The chief danger of inflation, therefore, is that it will not be stopped except by plunging the country into depression. Neither inflation nor depression is a healthy state for the economy.

In these movements, both up and down, money is an active participant. Of course, money does not act of its own volition. Behind the withdrawal of money in the first example lay my desire to hoard. Behind the increase in the second case lay my desire to borrow and the bank's willingness to lend. If we want to understand business cycles, we must find out *why* hoarding or money creation takes place, and this is a long story, some chapters of which are still not fully understood. Enough has been said to indicate that money plays an important role in business fluctuations and that it cannot be ignored.

The economy does not operate in precisely the same way under a monetary system as it does under barter. In fact the business cycle as we know it could not exist under barter. Business activity might fluctuate because of changes in the weather, wars, or new discoveries; there might be destruction, pestilence, or famine; but the phenomenon we generally think of as a business cycle could not occur.

Even John Stuart Mill, in the passage quoted earlier, hints that money is not quite as neutral as would appear on first glance when he says that money "only exerts a distinct and independent influence of its own when it gets out of order." The trouble is that money seems to be perennially out of order. In almost any period of history one can find a vast volume of literature suggesting ways for correcting the problems presented by the improper functioning of money. The preface of almost any book on money will explain the mess things are in. Surely if money is continually getting out of joint, we haven't learned as much as we need to know about how to control it, and it certainly isn't neutral.

Money: Bane or Blessing?

Perhaps our discussion of business cycles gives the impression that money is a curse we would do well to dispense with. If the reader feels that way, he should reread the section "Money and Freedom." The difficulty here, as in so many areas of life, lies in striking a balance between extremes. Money is not all-important; neither is it unimportant. Money is not an evil, nor is it an unmixed blessing.

Probably the best way to put money in focus is to realize that it is a tool. A tool helps us do a job more effectively. Sometimes it may be clumsily built so that it is awkward to use, or does the job badly, or even causes harm to the user. Sometimes a tool may be used for purposes for which it was not intended, as when a man runs amuck with a meat cleaver. Fire is one of the greatest of man's inventions, but unless properly controlled it destroys our homes and kills our children. Similarly money may be misused by the individual or mismanaged by the economy as a whole. Properly handled it may indeed be a blessing.

We might think of this book as an instruction manual on the use of money, showing what it is, what it does, and how it may be controlled. But with one caution. We are not yet sure of all the answers. There are areas still shrouded in mystery, and the changing conditions under which money is used are so numerous that it is impossible to give any simple solution to every conceivable problem. A driver's manual may tell us how to operate a car and lay down general rules of safe driving, but it cannot tell us what to do in every situation that might confront us on the road.

The monetary mechanism is much more complex than an automobile. It is no wonder that it may sometimes run into difficulties. In this book we will first describe the mechanism of the monetary machine (monetary institutions). Then we will examine the principles on which the machine operates (monetary theory). Finally we will look into some driving techniques, both good and bad (monetary policy).

Money as a Medium of Exchange

Money is so familiar that for purposes of general conversation there would be no necessity for defining it. But since we will be talking about money for a long time now, perhaps it will be just as well to review some fundamentals.

The most striking characteristic of money is that it facilitates trade by pro-

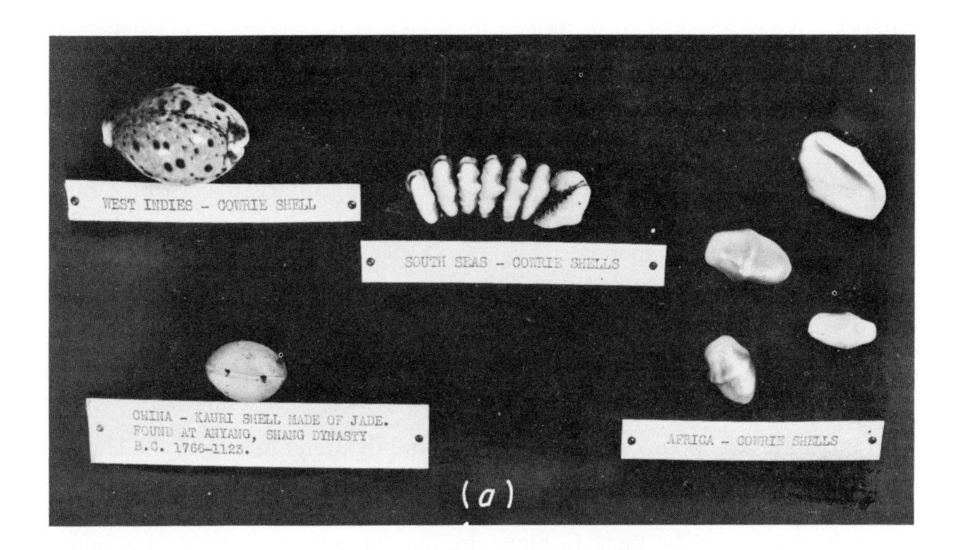

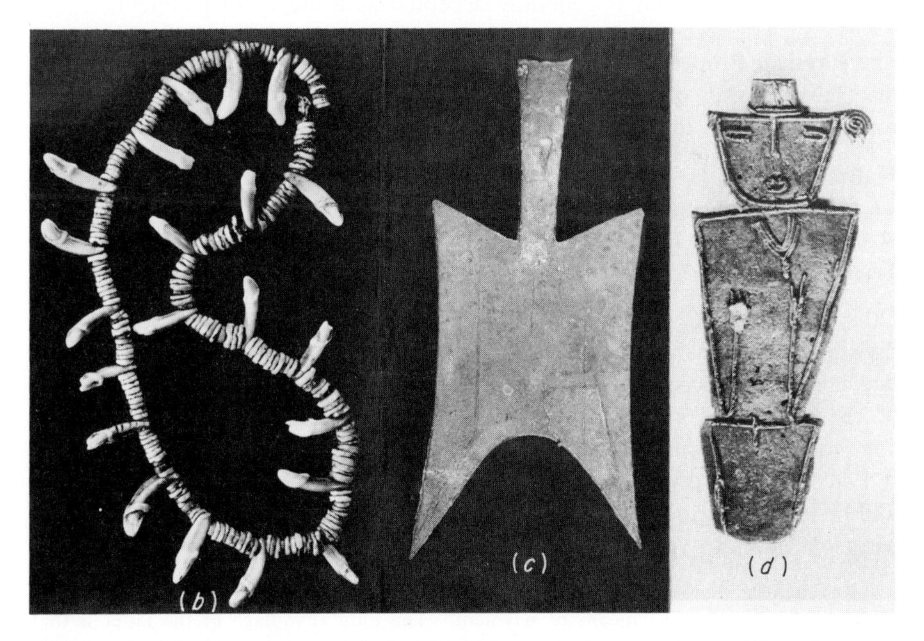

Figure 1-1. Primitive money. (*a*) Cowries. These shells were (and still are) a very common form of money in primitive societies. (*b*) Dogs' teeth from the Solomon Islands. (c) Spade money of China, about 2000 B.C. (*d*) Aztec money of wrought gold, pre-Columbian era. *(Courtesy of the Chase Manhattan Bank Museum of Moneys of the World, New York.)*

viding a medium which everyone is willing to accept in exchange for goods or in payment of debts. This universal and obvious function is so basic that money may best be defined in terms of its use. *Money is anything that is generally accepted as a means of payment.*[12] General acceptability is the only criterion. What physical form money may take is unimportant and depends, in any particular instance, on the customs and usages of the community. In the United States today we are accustomed to think of money in terms of certain coins, paper bills, and "money in the bank" (checking accounts). These are the things we habitually accept in payment of debts or in exchange for goods. But if people somewhere else are willing to accept red brick dust as a medium of exchange (as they do in some places in Kenya), then for them red brick dust is money.

What is money in one community may not be money somewhere else; it may not have been money even within this community in the past; it may cease to be money tomorrow. But as long as it is generally accepted—as long as it is normally used as a means of payment—it is doing the job of money, and it is money.

Franc notes are money in France; they certainly aren't money in the United States. Continental currency was money in the United States during the Revolutionary War; it is not money now. Fashions in money change, though generally more slowly than fashions in hats; function remains the same. Money is anything that is generally accepted as a means of payment.

The Physical Properties of Money. Many writers have attempted to examine the characteristics of money in terms of its physical attributes. One acrostic, for instance, says that the substance used for money must be:

Material
Useful
Scarce
Transferable

Other writers add such properties as portability, durability, homogeneity, divisibility, cognizability, and stability of value.[13] However, as long as a particular article is acceptable, it doesn't matter what it is made of, and a survey of the history of money shows a remarkable diversity among the various commodities that have been used.

Paul Einzig lists 172 objects used as money in primitive societies alone, and he is the first to admit that the list is far from complete.[14] These materials run from adzes to yarn, from human skulls to woodpecker scalps, from bread

[12] It is a little more common among economists to speak in terms of a "medium of exchange" rather than a "means of payment." The only advantage of the latter is that it includes transactions—such as payment of debts, gifts, and so on—that are not strictly exchanges. For practical purposes the two phrases are interchangeable.

[13] See, for instance, W. Stanley Jevons, *Money and the Mechanism of Exchange* (D. Appleton & Company, Inc., New York, 1896), chap. 5.

[14] Paul Einzig, *Primitive Money* (Eyre & Spottiswoode (Publishers), Ltd., London, 1948), pp. 507–509; see also pp. v–vi.

to jam, from rats to elephants, from pigs' jawbones to whales' teeth, from coal to ivory, from wine to women (but not including song). Among the items included, milk is probably the least durable, cannons the least portable. The "living money" (cattle, slaves, buffaloes, etc.) is neither homogeneous nor divisible. Even gold is not too clearly recognizable from base alloys. And as for stability of value, no one has yet devised a money with that attribute. Clearly money may take the widest variety of forms.

In some respects the most commonly used money in the United States today is the strangest of all. Checking accounts are neither material nor useful, and in terms of physical limitations they are not even scarce. Paper currency is material only in the sense that it consists of a piece of paper, but the paper itself is of no significant value. Such a currency would be incredible to the primitive native accustomed to using shells for money.

An Excursion to Yap. Perhaps it will enable us to get a better perspective on our own folkways if we examine one of these "primitive" monetary systems. One of the most curious still in use is that of the island of Yap, one of the Caroline Islands in the western Pacific. While Yap uses a number of kinds of money—shells, dyestuffs, coconuts, tobacco, and mats—its principal money is *fei*. The *fei* consists of large stones in the shape of a wheel with a hole in the center so that they may be carried on a pole. These stones range in size from enormous pieces 12 feet in diameter to "small coins" 1 foot or less across. They are made of a type of limestone not found on Yap itself, and hence they must be quarried and brought by canoe and raft from Guam and Palau. They have no known use except as money. Yet even foreign traders are willing to accept them because they may be used to obtain any other goods on the island.

Figure 1-2. Stone money (*fei*) of the island of Yap. (*Courtesy of the Chase Manhattan Bank Museum of Moneys of the World, New York.*)

Although this stone money is still used on Yap, modern currency is not unknown. The Spaniards, who first claimed possession of the island, attempted to introduce Spanish currency. When Germany purchased the Caroline Islands in 1899, it replaced Spanish currency with its own. Japan acquired a mandate over the territory as a result of World War I, with a similar shift in currency. And finally, after World War II, the United States was given the Carolines as a trust territory. In each case the islanders preferred their own money to the paper and coin of the foreigner. Our experience in trying to make United States dollars legal tender on Yap is somewhat humbling. Informed of the proposed substitution of dollars for Japanese yen, a Yap chief remarked: "First Spanish money no good, then German money no good, now Japanese money no good. Yap money always good!"[15] And so it is.

But lest we think that although it is good, it is probably also cheap—as we might think of shells and pebbles and feathers as cheap—let us reflect on the fact that museums cannot afford to purchase large specimens for display. One authority reports that a stone "a foot in diameter costs about seventy-five U.S. dollars. A stone man high is worth many villages and plantations, and a stone two men high is beyond price."[16]

Cigarettes and a World War. Another type of money that might be called primitive even though it was first used in fairly recent times is the cigarette. Particularly during World War II the scarcity of cigarettes was so great that almost any soldier with a cigarette ration could buy goods from fellow soldiers or native civilians with this highly acceptable medium. Even a nonsmoker was willing to accept cigarettes because he knew he could pass them on. In many areas prices were regularly quoted in cigarettes, and in Siam (now Thailand) at the end of the war such prices were even printed in newspaper advertisements.

Although the use of cigarettes was almost universal among the armed forces as a supplement to whatever other currency was in use, this type of monetary system reached its highest development in the prisoner-of-war camps, where there was no other currency. In these camps barter originated from the fact that prisoners received essentially the same rations even though tastes differed. Some preferred jam to chocolate and were willing to barter with those of opposite tastes. In particular, nonsmokers were willing to give cigarettes for food, while heavy smokers would give almost anything for cigarettes, even to the point of malnutrition.

[15] *Life,* Apr. 25, 1949, p. 100. A more extended account of the same incident is told by Walter Karig in *The Fortunate Islands: A Pacific Interlude* (Holt, Rinehart and Winston, Inc., New York, 1948), pp. 195–197; reprinted in Charles R. Whittlesey, *Readings in Money and Banking* (W. W. Norton & Company, Inc., New York, 1952), pp. 1–2. See also William H. Furness III, *The Island of Stone Money* (J. B. Lippincott Company, Philadelphia, 1910).

[16] Willard Price, *Japan's Islands of Mystery* (William Heinemann, Ltd., London, 1944), p. 80; quoted in Einzig, *op. cit.,* p. 52.

Gradually cigarettes became the commonly accepted medium of exchange, prices were quoted in cigarettes, and a regular price system developed. Services as well as commodities were sold for cigarettes; middlemen appeared, taking advantage of differences in prices from time to time or in various parts of the camp; and regular stores were established, all using cigarettes as currency. Radford tells us that in one camp "there was a coffee stall owner who sold tea, coffee or cocoa at two cigarettes a cup, buying his raw materials at market [cigarette] prices and hiring labor to gather fuel and to stoke; he actually enjoyed the services of a chartered public accountant at one stage. After a period of great prosperity he overreached himself and failed disastrously for several hundred cigarettes."[17]

The Monetary Unit as a Standard of Value

Although money's primary function is as a medium of exchange, any mention of prices suggests another monetary function: that of a standard of value or unit of account. The value of any object is its ability to command other goods in exchange. Thus under barter we suggested a case in which a pair of shoes had a value of 200 chocolate bars, 10 pounds of butter, and so on. All goods can be valued in terms of everything for which they can exchange.

When we take any one commodity and decide to use it as the *standard* in terms of which all other goods shall be measured, then we have a monetary unit; and we call the value of any object in terms of the standard its *price.* Thus the *value* of a pair of shoes (or rather one of its many values) may be 2 opera tickets, although its *price* is $10—the dollar being a monetary unit.

We have the same problem in measuring value that we have in any other kind of measurement. The length (or weight or volume) of various objects may be stated in terms of all other objects, or it may be compared with a common standard. Thus a robin may be five times as long as a caterpillar or one-twentieth as long as a Ford. We find it more convenient to establish a standard unit of length and say that a robin is 10 inches long. Thus the length of anything may be stated in terms of a single denominator, just as the value of anything may be stated in terms of its price.

There is, however, a difference between the *monetary unit,* which measures the price of goods, and *money,* which is a means of buying them. The difference is somewhat similar to that between a standard of measurement, such as a foot, and an instrument of measurement, such as a ruler. A ruler may have a length of 1 foot, but so does my shoe, the *Columbia Encyclopedia,* and acoustical ceiling tile. None of these, including the ruler, is a standard

[17] R. A. Radford, "The Economic Organization of a P.O.W. Camp," *Economics,* New Series, vol. 13, no. 48 (November, 1945), p. 194. See also Paul Einzig, "The Cigarette Standard," *The Banker* (September, 1945); and G. B. Clarke, "The Experiment," *Clare Market Review* (Summer, 1946), pp. 29–31.

of measurement. Similarly, a dollar bill may have a value of $1, but so does a pound of steak, a movie admission, and a necktie. None of these, including the dollar bill, is a standard of value. Money buys goods; the monetary unit measures their price. The monetary unit is an abstract concept; money is a physical substance.

We tend to confuse these two because a dollar bill is always worth a dollar (at least within our memory). If we go back into history, however, we will discover that money and the monetary unit were not always the same thing. In fact the monetary unit or unit of account seems to have existed in many areas before money was used as a medium of exchange. In Egypt a given weight of copper (sometimes called the *deben*) appears to have been the standard of value in terms of which all other things were measured even in the period when barter was common. Thus "an ox was purchased for a hundred and twenty *deben;* payment included an ornamental stick worth twenty-five *deben,* a simpler stick worth twelve *deben,* eleven jugs of oil worth ten *deben,* etc."[18] Later gold developed as an actual medium of exchange while copper for a time still served as a unit of account. At this period a man's stock of gold would be valued at so many *deben* of copper.

We don't have to go back to Egypt to find this distinction. In Britain today the guinea is quite frequently used as a monetary unit, prices being quoted in guineas in many cases rather than pounds. Yet there is no money precisely corresponding to the guinea (which was last coined in 1813).[19]

Another example of the separation of money and the monetary unit can be found here in the United States during and immediately following the Civil War. Until that time the Federal government had issued no money except gold and silver coins (with minor coins for small change). In 1863, to finance the war, the government issued its first paper money, the greenbacks, which were not redeemable in gold or silver and which in fact had no backing at all. Because they were irredeemable, people were less willing to accept greenbacks than metallic coin. As a result, the value of greenbacks fell relative to that of coin. Thus if a storekeeper quoted a price of $10 in gold for a particular article, a person who wanted to pay in paper bills might have to give him fifteen. In other words, a dollar bill was not worth a dollar in gold, though both circulated together.

In spite of these exceptional cases in which money and the monetary unit have gone their separate ways, it is generally true that they are tied so closely together as to be differentiated only with difficulty. It is for this reason that many writers do not distinguish between the two and speak of the functions of money as including that of a standard of value.

The monetary unit serves a function almost as important as the medium of exchange. Without a standard of measurement the price system would disappear; accounting would become a practical impossibility. A store's

[18] Einzig, *Primitive Money,* p. 203.

[19] The guinea is the equivalent of 21 shillings, while the pound contains 20 shillings.

balance sheet, for instance, would list as assets 3 counters, 1 display rack, 6 dozen shirts, 50 neckties, and so on. Without a monetary unit they couldn't be added together because they can't be expressed in terms of a common factor. With a monetary unit the job is easy: the dollar values of each item are simply added to obtain a dollar total.

Without a monetary unit the liability side would be just as bad, no balance could be struck, and the businessman wouldn't have much idea what his financial position was. Income statements would be no better, and whether a business had made a profit this year would be anyone's guess.

The implications of the lack of a price system are so manifold that many others could be added by anyone who cares to think over his own use of the pricing mechanism that we take for granted: What would a store be like without prices? How would you buy insurance? Or save? Or borrow?

A Fluctuating Standard. A standard of value is a tremendously useful instrument. But every such standard thus far devised has been very weak and unstable compared with our physical standards. A yard is a precisely determinable distance, defined by law as 3600/3937 of a meter, which in turn is "the length of exactly 1 650 763.73 wavelengths of the radiation in vacuum corresponding to the unperturbed transition between the levels $2p_{10}$ and $5d_5$ of the atom of Krypton 86."[20]

This is quite an improvement over the original concept of a yard as the distance between Henry VIII's nose and his thumb, or of the foot as we are told it was once "scientifically" determined:

> To find the length of a rood in the right and lawful way and according to scientific usage you shall do as follows: Stand at the door of a church on Sunday and bid sixteen men to stop, tall ones and small ones, as they happen to pass out when the service is finished; then make them put their left feet one behind another and the length thus obtained shall be a right and lawful rood to measure and survey land with, and the sixteenth part of it shall be a right and lawful foot.[21]

Unsatisfactory as such a standard would be for our surveyors or engineers today, it is infinitely better than any monetary standard ever devised. A rise in the general level of prices means that the dollar is worth less; a fall in prices means the value of the dollar has risen. Prices in the United States have been fairly stable compared with those of other countries, and yet prices fell 25 per cent from 1929 to 1933 and then doubled from 1933 to 1951. This would be similar to a 12-inch ruler that expanded to 16 inches at one time and shrank to 8 inches at another. If our physical measurements showed such erratic behavior, we should probably go mad, as Alice in Wonderland almost did when she couldn't control her size. Yet, while our monetary gyrations

[20] E. A. Mechtly, *The International System of Units: Physical Constants and Conversion Factors* (National Aeronautics and Space Administration, Washington, 1964), p. 3.

[21] Jacob Koebel, *Geometrei* (1536); quoted in George F. Warren and Frank A. Pearson, *Gold and Prices* (John Wiley & Sons, Inc., New York, 1935), p. 267.

have had some very serious consequences for the economy, we seem to have managed to get along, though not as well as we might with a more stable standard of value.

These fluctuations in our monetary unit correspond fairly closely to the general ups and downs of business that we call the business cycle. They present a problem to which a great part of our analysis of monetary theory and monetary policy will be devoted.

Other Functions of Money

So far we have examined money as a means of payment and the monetary unit as a standard of value. Each of these functions has a corollary. Because money is a medium of exchange, it also serves as a store of generalized purchasing power. Because the monetary unit is a standard of value, it also serves as a standard of debt.

A Store of Generalized Purchasing Power. The holder of money normally considers that it is part of his wealth, though it would be more accurate to think in terms of assets rather than wealth. Money has value, just as securities or furniture or a house has value. But the value of money is a special kind of value because it can be used at any time to acquire any other asset. It represents generalized purchasing power.

Any other kind of wealth or claim to wealth must be turned into money before it can be exchanged for something else. Some forms of nonmoney—such as listed securities—may be turned into ready cash with a minimum of inconvenience. Other forms—such as houses—can be sold only with extended effort. Money can be used for direct payment, without the necessity of converting it into something else first.

Money, because it is readily acceptable, has two collateral advantages as a store of assets. Because it can be used to buy goods at any time, it is possible for individuals to postpone purchases to some later date rather than use all their income to obtain goods immediately. And because money is accepted anywhere within the area where it circulates, it is a convenient device for carrying assets from place to place. It is less cumbersome than most goods at the same time that it is always exchangeable for whatever is needed.

The use of money as an asset is particularly important in periods when its value is rising, that is, when prices are falling. If money is expected to buy more tomorrow than it can today, we will be better off if we hold on to our money so we can buy a larger quantity of goods in the future. If, on the other hand, the price level is rising, the convenience of having a store of generalized purchasing power may be more than offset by the gradual erosion of its value. In such periods people will try to get rid of money as fast as possible in exchange for real wealth.

A Standard of Debt. Money may be used to pay for a purchase at the time the merchandise is received, but it is also possible to obtain goods against a promise to pay in the future, that is, by a debt. Debt is simply credit looked at from the other side. *Credit is the present acquisition of anything of value*—goods, securities, money, etc.—*in exchange for a promise to return an equivalent at some future time.* Credit can exist in a nonmonetary economy. If I borrow a cup of sugar from a neighbor, I have received credit in the form of a cup of sugar and am in debt to my neighbor for that amount. In a monetary economy most debts are stated in terms of the monetary unit. If I buy a $50 suit on credit, I don't owe the store a suit; I owe it $50.

Money itself can be acquired on credit. I may borrow $100 from the bank in exchange for a promise to pay back $110 a year from now. The credit is in money, while my obligation to repay is stated in terms of the monetary unit. In this case a question might be raised as to the equivalence of my present acquisition of $100 in exchange for a promise to repay $110. This question lies at the center of the whole problem of interest rates. Everyone agrees that a bird in the hand is worth two in the bush, and a dollar that I can spend today is worth more than a dollar I can't spend until a year from now. Just how much more is a matter that cannot be generalized. In the example above, the bank and I have obviously agreed that $1 today is the equivalent of $1.10 next year. If I thought it was worth less than that (say, $1.05), I wouldn't have borrowed the money at 10 per cent interest.

In our present economy credit is so universal that it plays a dominant role in almost all kinds of transactions. And it is in this area of credit that the worst features of a fluctuating standard of value show up. If I borrow $100 in exchange for a promise to repay the same amount plus interest at some future date, there is an underlying assumption that the value of $100 remains unchanged for the life of the contract. If prices rise in the interval, the money I pay back is worth less—it will buy fewer goods—than the money I borrowed. The creditor is cheated because the standard of value in which the debt is measured has shrunk. It is as if the cup in which sugar is measured became smaller between the time I borrowed the sugar and the time I returned it.

Similarly, if the price level falls, then I must return more purchasing power than I originally borrowed (in addition to the interest). The cup has gotten larger. Fluctuations in the standard of debt thus tend to redistribute wealth between debtors and creditors, sometimes in one direction, sometimes in another. A stable monetary standard would avoid this difficulty. The question is how it can be achieved.

The Monetary Revolution

Money and Wealth. We suggested a little earlier that money would generally be considered by its owner to be a form of wealth. In an economy in which money was a commodity—whether rice or beads or gold—there would be no need to challenge this attitude. Wealth consists of stocks of scarce commodities. If a man owns rice, he owns a valuable commodity. He may hold it primarily because it is money, but he could eat it if he wished. Certainly somewhere down the line, after more or fewer exchanges, it *will* be eaten and will add to the enjoyment of its final consumer. Many forms of money, such as beads, may be worn for ornament and are enjoyed at the same time that they serve as a store of purchasing power. It is for this reason that some countries today mint coins with holes in the middle so that they may be strung and worn. This is one case where one can eat his cake and have it too.

When money has become, as it has in most of the civilized world, simply a token (coins that are worth less than their face value, paper bills, and bank credit), it has ceased to be wealth and becomes merely a claim to wealth. As we pointed out before, one cannot eat a dollar bill or wear it or ride on it. It is a symbol of wealth, a means of acquiring wealth, but not wealth itself.

This is quite clear if we shift our attention from the individual to society as a whole. As long as money is a commodity, an increase in the total money in circulation means more goods (rice or beads or gold) that can be used to satisfy wants. An increase in paper money means no such thing. It simply typifies an increase in counters used for playing the game, not an increase in the prizes available. In a rice system a man may create money by growing rice. This raises the standard of living of the community. If a government creates money by printing pieces of paper or if a bank creates money simply by increasing its promises to pay depositors, the economy is no better off than it was before.

The tendency to mistake money for wealth is another aspect of the money illusion. It persists partly because it was once true. But drastic changes in the nature of money have altered its role. If we are to understand the nature of money today, it is necessary to adjust our thinking to current conditions, not to those of years ago.

Money Is Accepted because It Is Accepted. A further problem associated with this new role of money is the difficulty of understanding just why money has value. Rice has value because people want it to eat; beads they want to wear; gold they use for ornaments or for utensils. Paper currency and bank deposits have no use. If they weren't money, they would be wastepaper. What gives them value?

Sometimes it is suggested that the government confers value on them because it issues them, accepts them, or requires citizens to accept them. The journals of history, however, are full of the failures of attempts on the part of governments to bolster the value of currencies in which the people had lost confidence. George Washington, to take a single example, denounced those who refused to accept at full value the bills of the Continental Congress as "pests to society and the greatest enemies we have to the happiness of America. I would to God that some one of the more atrocious in each state was hung in gibbets upon a gallows five times as high as the one prepared by Haman."[22] Yet the Continental currency, to which he was referring, could not gain the confidence of the people and continued to fall in value until it became the epitome of worthlessness: "Not worth a Continental." It lost value because people lost faith in it.

Conversely, money today has value because people *have* faith in it. If tonight everyone should dream that dollars were worthless, and if they all believed in dreams, tomorrow dollars would have no value at all. No one would accept them. Money is acceptable because it is acceptable. Except for commodity money (such as silver coin) it has no other value.

Questions for Thought and Discussion

1. If money will buy practically anything, does this mean that it is the most valuable thing in the world?

2. Make a list of things that money will not buy.

3. How valuable is a dollar bill? Has it always had this value?

4. Marx said that workers were "wage slaves," chained to their need to earn a money income. Do you think this is true?

5. Can you draw a blueprint of an economy that does not need money?

6. Is a counterfeit dollar bill money?

7. When John gives Sam a jackknife in exchange for sixty marbles, is the knife money? Are the marbles?

8. Are Italian lire money? Are Confederate dollar bills money?

9. If a storekeeper refused to take the dollar bill you offered him and said it was worthless, what would be your reaction?

10. What makes paper money valuable?

11. When we say that a man is worth $10,000, do we mean that he has that much money in his pocket or in his bank account?

12. Can you explain clearly the difference between money and the monetary unit of account?

13. If the value of the monetary unit varies so widely over time, why don't we use something more accurate?

Selected Bibliography

Angell, Norman: *The Money Mystery: An Explanation for Beginners,* J. M. Dent & Sons, Ltd., Publishers, London, 1936.

Cole, G. D. H.: *What Everyone Wants to Know about Money,* Alfred A. Knopf, Inc., New York, 1935.

[22] Quoted by Horace White, *Money and Banking,* 5th ed. (Ginn and Company, Boston, 1914), p. 95.

Coulborn, W. A. L.: *A Discussion of Money,* Longmans, Green & Co., Ltd., London, 1950.

Crowther, Geoffrey: *An Outline of Money,* rev. ed., Thomas Nelson & Sons, London, 1948.

Crutchfield, James A., Charles N. Henning, and William Pigott: *Money, Financial Institutions and the Economy: A Book of Readings,* Prentice-Hall, Inc., Englewood Cliffs, N.J., 1965.

Del Mar, Alexander: *The Science of Money,* 2d ed., Effingham Wilson, London, 1896.

Ederer, R. J.: *The Evolution of Money,* Public Affairs Press, Washington, 1964.

Federal Reserve Bank of New York: *Money: Master or Servant?* 1955.

Federal Reserve Bank of Richmond: *Readings on Money,* 1963.

Groseclose, Elgin: *Money: The Human Conflict,* University of Oklahoma Press, Norman, Okla., 1934.

Helfferich, Karl: *Money,* trans. from the German by Louis Infield, 2 vols., The Adelphi Company, New York, 1927.

James, F. Cyril: *The Economics of Money, Credit, and Banking,* 3d ed., The Ronald Press Company, New York, 1940.

Jevons, W. Stanley: *Money and the Mechanism of Exchange,* D. Appleton & Company, Inc., New York, 1896.

Marshall, Alfred: *Money, Credit, and Commerce,* Macmillan & Co., Ltd., London, 1921.

Ritter, Lawrence: *Money and Economic Activity: A Selection of Readings in the Field of Money and Banking,* 2d ed. Houghton Mifflin Company, Boston, 1961.

Robertson, Dennis H.: *Money,* Pitman Publishing Corporation, New York, 1948.

Smith, Warren L.: *Readings in Money, National Income, and Stabilization Policy,* Richard D. Irwin, Inc., Homewood, Ill., 1965.

Withers, Hartley: *The Meaning of Money,* 6th ed., John Murray (Publishers), Ltd., London, 1937.

Sources of Current Information. The *Federal Reserve Bulletin* (monthly) contains a large volume of current statistics on money, banking, and the economy in general, as well as articles of current interest. It is frequently used in conjunction with a text to bring the material up to date. Other useful sources of information are listed below.

Bank for International Settlements, Basel, Switzerland:
Annual Report

Board of Governors of the Federal Reserve System, Washington:
Annual Report
Banking and Monetary Statistics (1943)
Digest of Rulings

The Federal Reserve Act (as amended)
Federal Reserve Bulletin (monthly)
Federal Reserve Charts on Bank Credit, Money Rates and Business (monthly, with an annual historical supplement)
Regulations
Rules of Organization and Rules of Procedure

Bureau of the Census, Washington:
Historical Statistics of the United States, Colonial Times to 1957 (1960)
Statistical Abstract of the United States (annually)

Comptroller of the Currency, Washington:
Annual Report

Director of the Mint, Washington:
Annual Report

Federal Deposit Insurance Corporation, Washington:
Annual Report

Federal Reserve banks of each district:
Annual Reports
Monthly Bulletins

International Bank for Reconstruction and Development, Washington:
Annual Report

International Monetary Fund, Washington:
Annual Report
Balance of Payments Yearbook (annually)
International Financial News Survey (weekly)
International Financial Statistics (monthly)

Joint Economic Committee, Washington:
Economic Indicators (monthly)

National Association of Supervisors of State Banks:
Proceedings (annually)

The New York Times or a similar newspaper with comprehensive coverage

Office of Business Economics, Washington:
Survey of Current Business (monthly, with special supplements)

Secretary of the Treasury, Washington:
Annual Report
Treasury Bulletin (monthly)

United Nations (Columbia University Press, New York):
Monthly Bulletin of Statistics
World Economic Report (annually, with separate regional supplements)

United States Congress, Washington:
Various committee documents, hearings, and reports, especially those of the Senate Committee on Finance, Senate Committee on Banking and Currency, House Committee on Banking and Currency, and Joint Economic Committee

Chapter 2
The Evolution of Money and Monetary Standards

And Abraham weighed to Ephron the
silver, which he had named in the
audience of the sons of Heth,
four hundred shekels of silver, current
money with the merchants.

Genesis 23:16

One outstanding fact about money is that it has taken innumerable forms and is still in the process of evolution. The money that we use today is the result of a long development that is by no means completed. In fact, today the form of money seems to be changing more rapidly than at any period in its history. Between the time this book was written and the time you read it, the monetary system of this country will have changed.

The kind of money we now use can be understood only in terms of its growth. Just as a psychiatrist cannot comprehend the behavior of a patient until he knows something of his background, so some of the peculiarities of money are incomprehensible except in the light of its earlier history. Nor can we hope that a description of our current monetary machinery will be adequate for the future. Tomorrow's monetary system will be an older and a different system, but like today's it will have its roots in the past.

An examination of that past is complicated by the great diversity of monetary practices. We can here draw only some of the broad outlines, primarily of our Western experience, hoping thereby to illustrate the more important tendencies and some of the underlying principles.

The Origin of Money

Money was not given to man, like the apple, in the Garden of Eden, nor was it invented, like canasta. It arose out of the needs of society, and it developed and changed as those needs themselves grew and shifted. Although exchange itself is not necessary in a society in which each family is fully self-sufficient, almost every society of which we have historical records had both some process of exchange and a standard of value. Early societies merely chose some commonly used object as a general standard in terms of which all other goods were valued or "priced." Sometimes the monetary standard was also used as a medium of exchange; in other cases it served only to fix the value of goods that were bartered against one another.

The Pacific islands and parts of the Americas seem to have shown a preference for shells, beads, and other articles of adornment. Throughout most of Europe and Asia, as well as in parts of Africa, animals have played the most important role because of the significance of flocks and herds to a pastoral people. Evidence of the use of cattle as the common denominator of value can be found in dozens of primitive cultures: Homeric Greece, Persia of the Zend-Avesta, India of the Rig-Veda, Abraham's Mesopotamia, ancient Egypt, Gaul, primitive Italy, Britain, and Ireland. In China the buffalo takes the place of the cow, while certain Siberian tribes valued everything in terms of reindeer as late as the nineteenth century.

At least two modern words attest this origin of a monetary standard. "Pecuniary" is derived from *pecus,* the Latin word for "cattle," while "fee" comes from the Old English *feoh* (cognate to the German *vieh*), also meaning "cattle."

Even today we can find cattle serving as a standard of value. Among the Dinka, a pastoral people of the Southern Sudan who measure wealth in cattle and goats, a recent traveler reports that "a reasonably sound wife cost about 40 head of cattle, with perhaps a few goats and chickens thrown in."[1]

Yet cattle had several basic disadvantages as money, and there is no evidence that such use was ever very widespread. Part of the difficulty lay in the difference in value between particular specimens. A further problem was that because of their high value and complete indivisibility, they couldn't be used in small transactions. In all societies where cattle were used, therefore, we find other subsidiary articles serving a similar function for smaller exchanges. Here again they must be articles in common use, whether for food, clothing, adornment, or tools: such things as sheep, rice, fish, cloth, skins, shells, rings, axes, hoes, or fishhooks. These were the small change, and several varieties might be used simultaneously at a fixed ratio with cattle and with one another.

Metals as Money. Out of this welter of dissimilar objects metallic ones gradually emerged as more suitable for monetary uses than others. Fishhooks, rings,

[1] John M. Goddard, "Kayaks down the Nile," *National Geographic Magazine,* vol. 107, no. 5 (May, 1955), pp. 713–714.

or simple bars of metal out of which other objects could be made achieved priority in early monetary systems. The metals most frequently used were copper (or bronze), gold, silver, and iron, probably in that order, although the use of all four can be traced back as far as 1000 B.C.

Metals fulfill better than almost any other object the fundamental requirements of a commodity money. In addition to being material, useful, scarce, and transferable they are almost completely homogeneous, highly durable, easily portable, and divisible into any size. In time their use became almost universal.

In some cases the metallic money developed as a stylized symbol of some implement or adornment which had itself performed earlier the function of a medium of exchange. Thus we have Chinese hoes that are obviously too thin for working the ground, bent pieces of gold wire bearing tangible evidence of their evolution from fishhooks, knives without cutting edges, and rings of various kinds that are too small to be worn (see Figure 2-1).

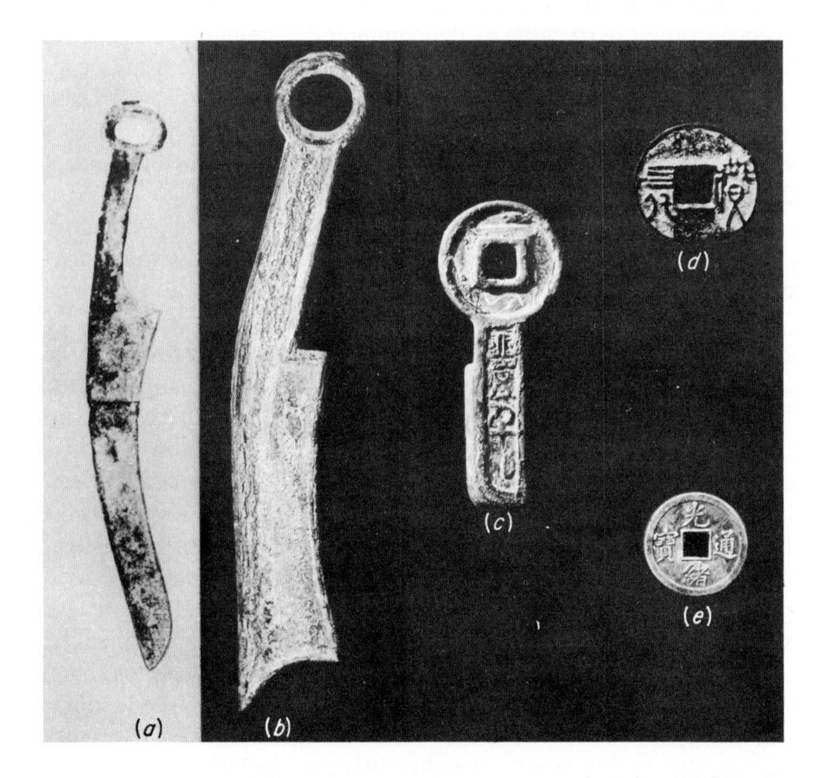

Figure 2-1. The development of Chinese "cash." Bronze knives, an early form of money in China (*a*), became stylized between the seventh and third centuries B.C. and lost their cutting edge (*b*). By the beginning of the first century, the blade had shrunk to merely symbolic size (c) and soon disappeared entirely (*d*). Today the only additional change is the result of more refined minting techniques (e). (*Courtesy of the American Numismatic Society, New York.*)

In other cases bars of metal were introduced of a standard weight equal to the value of an ox. So closely related is the development of money to the development of weight standards that a number of currencies are named after their original weight: the British pound, the French livre, the German mark, the Italian lira, the shekel, and the talent, among others.

The Development of Coinage

For hundreds of years after its introduction, metallic money passed current simply by reason of its shape or its weight. It bore no mark to establish its value. Anyone accepting such money had to determine its value for himself, either by eye or by weighing upon the scales. In addition he had to judge its purity, an even more difficult process known as *assay*. This could be done with acid, but the process was somewhat difficult, and many people found it easier to assume the purity of the metal.

Merchants and others who dealt continually with money were not so sanguine, and among them ingots passed strictly by weight and assay. At some point (some say at Lydia in the seventh century B.C.) one of them decided that if he punched some identifying mark on each ingot as he assayed it, then when such an ingot again passed through his hands, he would recognize his mark and avoid the job of reassay (see Figure 2-2). These were the first coins, for *a coin is a piece of metal the value of which is certified upon its face.*

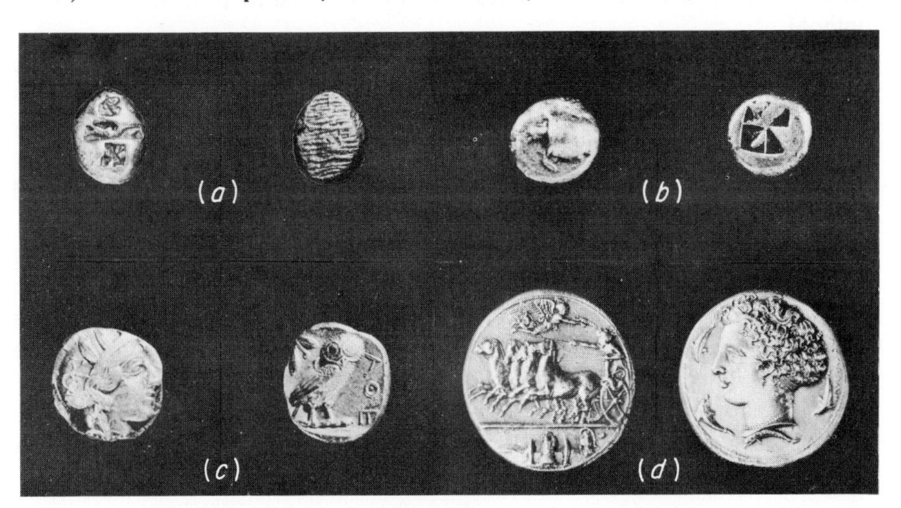

Figure 2-2. Early coins. (*a*) The earliest coin known, an electrum stater of Lydia, thought to date from the time of Gyges, 700–637 B.C. The obverse shows three incuse punch marks, while the reverse is striated. Electrum is a natural alloy of gold and silver. (*Courtesy of the British Museum, London.*) (*b*) Stater of Aegina, seventh century B.C., one of the first silver coins. (c) Silver tetradrachm of Athens, 525–430 B.C. It is easy to see why these were known as *owls*. (*d*) Decadrachm of Syracuse, 412 B.C. Minting techniques had reached a high level by this time, and in beauty of design this silver coin can hardly be excelled. (*Courtesy of the Chase Manhattan Bank Museum of Moneys of the World, New York.*)

These coins were first produced by private merchants for their own use. Others who had faith in the merchant's word might accept them at face value (the value stamped on their face), but it was possible for unscrupulous people to cut off a part of the metal without disturbing the punch mark. Those who accepted such coins by tale (count) rather than by weight did so at their own peril. Soon the designs of coins were extended to cover the whole face (obverse and reverse) in order to reduce the extent of *clipping,* but this type of fraud was not finally stopped until the seventeenth century, when *milling* (serrating) the edges of coins was introduced so that a piece could not be cut anywhere without affecting the design.

Even then it was possible to *sweat* coins by shaking them together in a leather bag so that the metallic dust that rubbed off could be collected and remelted. It is not profitable to do this with today's coins, but there are many other ways of tampering with the value of money, as we will see.

Government Coinage. Money does not depend on government; it is a natural outgrowth of the needs of the community. Nor did the government invent coinage; it was the child of private enterprise. Governments did, however, take over this task from the merchants at a very early date, and in the past two thousand years coinage has become almost a government monopoly. Private coinage has reappeared on a number of occasions—gold miners produced their own coins in California, for instance, during the gold rush of the last century (see Figure 2-3)—but it has not achieved more than a temporary foothold.

The state has seen fit to suppress private coinage for two contradictory reasons. The first was to provide a uniform, readily recognizable, and honest system of coins. When coins are accepted at face value without testing their weight or purity, a new opportunity for the unscrupulous appears. If the person who puts his stamp on the ingot is not thoroughly honest, he may well obtain a profit by certifying a higher value than the coin actually contains. Face value depends on faith in the issuer. Where the issuer is not worthy of faith, coinage deteriorates. While it is an exaggeration to say that "the system of free private coining became everywhere a system of false coining,"[2] it cannot be denied that the temptation was always there. Presumably the government could avoid this difficulty by taking over the job itself.

Unfortunately the second reason for the state to take over coinage was precisely the fact that in this way it could preempt for itself the profits that might otherwise accrue to dishonest private coiners.

Debasement. The record of government coinage is certainly a dismal recital of broken faith. *Debasement,* which is the *reduction in the real value of a coin below its face value,* seems to have been the normal state of affairs. Governments throughout history have had trouble balancing their budgets. How easy it would be to reduce the amount of silver in a coin, replace it with some

[2] E. Babelon; quoted in Arthur R. Burns, *Money and Monetary Policy in Early Times* (Alfred A. Knopf, Inc., New York, 1927), p. 78.

Figure. 2-3. Fifty-dollar gold coin, 1851. In spite of the inscription it was not an official coin, but was privately minted in California during the gold rush. (*Courtesy of the Chase Manhattan Bank Museum of Moneys of the World, New York.*)

cheaper substance, and thereby produce more coins from a given amount of silver. How easy, how common, and what a fraud!

Such debased coins could not circulate for long at their old value, however. As the public became aware of the deception, the value of the coins fell. The king's stamp on the face did not *give* value to the coin; it merely *certified* value. If the certificate was false, it could not keep the value of the coin above its real worth. In fact, even if the trickery was undetected, the value of the coins would fall by reason of their overissue. The value of money, like the value of anything else, depends at least partly on its scarcity. If money becomes more plentiful, its value will fall relative to other goods; each coin will buy less.

Gresham's Law. Another consequence of debasement was that as less valuable coins were issued, the older, more valuable coins disappeared from circulation. If two coins have the same nominal value but are of different weight, people will pass the worse one on to their neighbors in trade and keep the more desirable one for hoarding or melting down into bullion. This tendency of bad money to drive good money out of circulation is known as Gresham's law, after Sir Thomas Gresham, Queen Elizabeth's Chancellor of the Exchequer, who is supposed to have first stated it.[3] Its application to a

[3] Actually Aristophanes suggested the principle two thousand years earlier in *The Frogs:*

Yea for these, our sterling pieces, all of pure Athenian mould,
All of perfect die and metal, all the fairest of the fair,
All of workmanship unequalled, proved and valued everywhere
Both among our own Hellenes and Barbarians far away,
These we use not; but the worthless pinchbeck coins of yesterday,
Vilest die and basest metal, now we always use instead.

Trans. by B. B. Rogers, *The Harvard Classics* (P. F. Collier & Son Corporation, New York, 1909), vol. 8, p. 440.

debased currency is the first of three manifestations of the general tendency which we will have occasion to examine.

Metallic Standards

Money does not need legal sanction to perform its function, but since the early entry of government into the issuance of coins in the pre-Christian era, government has continued to play a prominent role in monetary management. Private issue of coins has been a rarity, and everywhere it is assumed that the government has the right and the obligation to regulate the monetary system. Thus our own Constitution declares that "Congress shall have Power . . . to coin Money [and] regulate the Value thereof."

As money itself has become more complicated, so has the task of government in this area. Here we will examine only that part of its task that relates to its designation of the monetary standard—the country's definition of its standard money.

Commodity Money. In money's younger days there was never any question of legal status. What was accepted as money depended entirely upon the desire of the community. Money was simply a commodity with certain characteristics that enhanced its general acceptability. Its value was determined in precisely the same way as that of any other commodity. In fact money had no special value as money. It had value as a commodity, and because of this people desired it for its own sake, not primarily because of its ability to exchange for other goods.

The value of cattle was their ability to give milk or pull a plow. The value of rice was its nourishment. The value of iron was its usefulness in implements. The value of gold was its ornamental desirability. A commodity was money, and money was a commodity with very little to distinguish it from other commodities.

Even coins were originally no more than standardized pieces of a metallic commodity. The entry of government into the monetary arena involved simply the certification of the weight and purity of the metal contained in these coins. It thus took over a task that others had already performed in a private capacity and gave wider acceptability to coins because of the greater influence that it wielded. Early government money was still commodity money. Its value was still determined by the value of the monetary metal of which the coin was made. The government added nothing to this value except to give it a common label.

One additional effect of government coinage was the fact that it tended to standardize the monetary material. A particular metal (in some cases two metals) was used by the sovereign for most coinage, and this metal thereby achieved a special position. It came to be identified more and more closely with money until it was no longer primarily a commodity that had monetary uses but rather was primarily money with incidental commodity uses. It became the *monetary standard* of the country.

Silver as a Standard Money. Several metals have been standard money in ancient times, but the first to achieve widespread use was silver, with gold a close second. The first coins known, those of Lydia in the seventh century B.C. (see Figure 2-2), were made of electrum, an alloy of gold and silver found in a natural state in that area of Asia Minor. Coinage spread rapidly to Greece, where silver was the predominant metal, although gold served also on sporadic occasions. Greek monetary history is peculiarly free of debasement with two spectacular exceptions under Solon and Dionysius.

Roman money was predominantly silver with an added touch of bronze in the early period and gold at the end. The denarius was originally one-sixth of an ounce of silver 99 per cent pure, but by A.D. 270 it had been debased to one-seventh of an ounce containing only 2 per cent silver.

After the collapse of Rome (ascribed by some to the debasement of its currency, though this was more likely a symptom rather than a cause of weakness) and the general eclipse of monetary institutions, we find in the medieval period the reemergence of silver. The most important example was the British pound, which in its initial form was literally a pound of standard (sterling) silver, too large to be coined itself but divided into 240 pennies (see Figure 2-4). The French livre was also a pound of silver, and this identity of British and French standards at the time of Charlemagne (ninth century) represents one of the early international monetary systems. Unfortunately it did not last because both currencies soon depreciated but at different rates.

Figure 2-4. Early English coins. (*a*) London penny of the reign of Aethelred II (979–1016). No coin of a larger denomination was struck until 1257. (*b*) Shilling of Henry VIII (1544–1547). Although nominally silver, this coin was little more than copper with a silver wash. As the silver wore off, the copper showed through, a fact that gave Henry the nickname "Old Coppernose." (*Courtesy of the American Numismatic Society, New York.*)

Other European countries also developed a silver standard at one time or another, and several countries in other parts of the world have abandoned it only quite recently. Of these the most important are Mexico, China, and India.

The Rise and Decline of Bimetallism. Although silver emerged as a primary monetary metal in many countries, it seldom held the stage for long all by itself. In fact one of the reasons for debasement has been a shortage of silver relative to the desire for a monetary medium. If there wasn't enough of one monetary metal to do the work, might not a second metal be found to lighten the task? Gold has usually been the metal to fill this role. Its use in conjunction with silver gave rise to *bimetallism,* which is a monetary system in which two metals are used side by side with an official ratio of exchange established between them.

In addition to broadening the monetary base, bimetallism has other advantages, the most important of which is its ability to provide coins of reasonable size for both large and small values. Thus early Roman monetary history shows the principal coin to be the *as,* composed of 1 pound of copper. The awkwardness of using such money for sizable transactions led to the introduction of the silver denarius in 269 B.C. At the time of its introduction this coin was the legal equivalent of 10 *asses*. Later the gold aureus was added to the system, and for awhile the three metals were used together.

The difficulty with bimetallism arises from the fact that in a free market the relative values of the two metals tend to change over time, while their respective weights as coins are defined by law. Unless the legal parity is constantly shifted to match the values in the market, one type of coin will be worth more (relative to its face value) than the other. The bad money (worth less as a metal than the law says it is worth as a coin) will continue to circulate as money, while the good money (worth more as a metal) will be melted down and will disappear from circulation in accordance with Gresham's law. In practice, then, a bimetallic standard becomes a monometallic standard of the overvalued (that is, the poorer) metal.

This difficulty has plagued all attempts at bimetallism. Yet in spite of its problems bimetallism has a long history. It became the most common type of monetary system in Europe in the eighteenth and nineteenth centuries and, indeed, has been the monetary system of the United States throughout the greater part of our existence as a nation.[4] Finally, however, the disadvantages became too great to maintain the system, both here and abroad. A number of international conferences toward the close of the nineteenth century attempted to devise an acceptable bimetallic standard, but fluctuations in the relative prices of gold and silver were too great to provide any basis of agreement, and the bimetallic standard was gradually abandoned.

[4] The history of bimetallism in the United States, detailed in Chap. 6, illustrates admirably the operation of Gresham's law with respect to such a standard.

The "Universal" Gold Standard. As the Western world turned from bimetallism it adopted gold, and this movement, although fairly recent, has apparently enshrined gold in a special sanctuary where it is often worshiped with a fervor hard to understand.

So enchanted has mankind become with the thought of the yellow metal that the impression sometimes persists that the gold standard is the only true and proper standard and that it can be traced back to a time whereof the memory of man runneth not to the contrary. This is a myth that history will not support. Gold is a new contender in the realm of standard money, and the universal gold standard—if it is not indeed somewhat of a figment of the imagination—can at best be said to have held a short reign over monetary affairs.

The first country in the world to adopt a gold standard in the modern sense was Great Britain. The year was 1821. Britain abandoned gold temporarily from 1914 to 1925 and permanently in 1931. Its brief reincarnation, however, was on a somewhat modified basis that some students would be a little loath to class as a pure gold regime. By any definition gold's most faithful adherent bowed to its sway for a total of less than one hundred years.

Portugal, the second country to adopt gold, took the step in 1854. Germany joined in 1871, and other European countries followed during the last quarter of the nineteenth century and the first decade of the twentieth. All belligerents in World War I except the United States fled from gold in 1914[5] and readopted it for short periods in the postwar era. The United States was on the gold standard from 1900 to 1933. Many countries have never adopted gold.

In spite of its brief stay, however, the gold standard made many friends and has managed to capture an ideological place as the best of metallic (and, some people feel, of all) monetary standards. It therefore deserves special mention.

A pure gold standard is a monetary system in which a nation (1) defines its currency as a given weight of gold, (2) provides convertibility at par between gold and all other forms of currency, and (3) permits free movement of gold both at home and abroad. There are three basic variants of the gold standard: gold coin, gold bullion, and gold exchange. There are also innumerable ways in which a country may maintain some monetary tie to gold without subscribing to the gold standard as above defined. Under most of these variants (many of them in existence today) the country defines its currency in terms of gold but does not provide convertibility and may restrict gold movements. We will refer to these forms under the general designation of gold reserve standards, although many names, some of them quite uncomplimentary, have been used to describe particular systems of this type.

Gold Coin Standard. The gold coin standard is the "pure" form, and generally speaking this is the variety that existed prior to 1914. In addition to the

[5] From 1917 to 1919 gold exports from the United States were under almost complete embargo, but convertibility was maintained domestically.

requirements listed in our definition, the gold coin standard requires that a nation provide gold coins for general use.

Under these conditions, gold serves the two functions of any commodity money: it is a commodity, and it is money, and the two uses are interchangeable. Since gold bullion can be changed into coin at the mint, and since gold coin can be melted down by anyone into bullion, the value of gold coin must be equal to the value of gold for other uses. Since the gold standard requires that the government maintain convertibility between gold coin and all other forms of currency, any form of money can be transferred into gold at par, and therefore the value of all types of currency must be equal to the value of an equivalent weight of gold. Thus between 1837 and 1933 the dollar was defined as 23.22 grains of fine (that is, pure) gold. During this period the price of 23.22 grains of fine gold must have been $1, and a $10 bill must have had the same value as 232.2 grains of gold since it could be exchanged for an eagle ($10 gold piece), which had this weight.

The primary advantage of the gold coin standard is that as long as the coins are not debased (and metallic debasement has not been a problem in recent times), the value of the whole monetary system is tied directly to the value of gold. If gold did not fluctuate in value, the purchasing power of money would also be stable.

Looked at from another angle, the gold standard restricts the quantity of currency that the government can issue to some "reasonable" amount and therefore prevents runaway inflation. As long as gold can be gotten for paper at a fixed ratio, the purchasing power of the paper must be equal to the purchasing power (or the inherent utility) of the equivalent amount of gold. If an increase in the issue of paper currency reduces its value below this point, people will turn their paper in to the Treasury for gold. Since the stock of gold that the government holds is finite, and since it cannot therefore afford to hand out gold indefinitely to those who ask for it, any such run on the Treasury would force the government to restrict its issue of paper currency. As one modern advocate of gold has put it, the gold standard provides a network of golden wires by which the public controls the Treasury's issue of currency.

The major disadvantage of the gold coin standard lies in the fact that gold does not remain stable in value, and any fluctuation in the value of gold tends to be transmitted to the value of money. Thus the general price level depends at least partly on gold-mining costs and the demand for wedding rings. The downward drift of prices in this country from 1865 to 1896 is generally attributed to the growing world shortage of the precious metals, while the upward movement from 1896 to 1914 was at least partly based on new gold discoveries in Alaska and South Africa.

On the other hand, when the public becomes less attached to gold coin, and the link between gold and other currencies becomes weaker, large fluctuations in prices are possible within the limits of the gold standard. The United States managed to hang onto gold during World War I, but prices more than doubled from 1914 to 1920, and then by 1932 they fell further than they had risen. The simple fact that we were on a gold coin standard was not sufficient to prevent these fairly serious changes in the value of money.

Another disadvantage—which cannot really be laid to the door of the standard itself—is the fact that many governments under pressure choose to abandon the gold standard rather than adopt the restrictions that its proper functioning would require. Since the gold standard is the result of a simple act of the legislature, it can be altered or abolished just as easily. This is what happened in most countries during World War I and again in the Great Depression.

Gold Bullion Standard. In the interval between these two catastrophes, most nations managed to struggle back to gold, but generally on an altered basis. The change was due partly to a widespread shortage of gold and partly to changed habits of the population. Several countries found it neither necessary nor expedient to put gold coin back into circulation and adopted instead the gold bullion standard. Under this system coins are no longer minted, and convertibility is restricted to transactions in bullion. The government stands ready to buy and sell gold at a fixed price but only in standard bars, whose value at the present time is $14,000 each.

Thus gold disappears as a medium of exchange in common transactions, although it may be used in larger deals, particularly in international trade, where gold is really the only money for final settlement of accounts. The gold bullion standard removes gold from the touch of the ordinary individual, and it is interesting to note how docilely he accepted this basic move from a commodity to a paper money.

Gold Exchange Standard. Another refinement of the gold standard introduced in the twenties in order to conserve gold and to aid those nations whose stock of it was quite low was the gold exchange standard. This goes even further than the gold bullion standard by providing that the government may redeem its paper currency at its own option *either* in gold bullion *or* in foreign exchange on a gold-standard country, usually England or the United States. Thus a central bank of a gold-exchange-standard country, when asked to redeem its currency, could do so with a check drawn on the Bank of England. Since this check could be used to obtain gold from England, it was as good as gold. But as long as it was as good as gold, there was usually no point in getting gold for it. The check itself could be used in international payments as readily as gold. The gold exchange standard was a practical recognition of the use of paper representing pound or dollar deposits as an international medium of exchange. It pushed gold even further into the background.

Paper Standards

Meanwhile, as implied above, paper money had been introduced side by side with coin, and the gold standard did not mean that gold was the only money but merely that it was the standard money into which anyone could change his paper notes (or silver or other coins) whenever he wished. Whether paper money was issued by banks or by governments,[6] the amount that could be issued depended entirely on the willingness of the public to accept this paper instead of *specie* (metallic coins or bullion of full value), and in the early days of paper money this willingness was fairly low. Familiarity with paper increased its acceptability and hence the amount that could be issued. Throughout this development, however, paper money was clearly a substitute for the underlying metal.

The governmental issue of paper came fairly late in the history of this country. The Constitution gives Congress the power to "coin Money," but for many years it was felt that "coin" did not mean "print" and that the issue of paper money was thus constitutionally prohibited. It was the pressure of the Civil War that broke down this argument. Except for the emergency period of the war, however, government paper money, like private paper money, was a representation of the underlying metal. Anyone who wanted specie ("real money") could get it on demand. This is the essence of a metallic standard.

There have been many periods in history when a nation has been forced to suspend redemption of its paper currency temporarily: the Bank Restriction in England, the Civil War issue of greenbacks, the experience of most countries during World War I, and numerous others. In each of these cases both paper currency and full-bodied metal coins circulated side by side but at different values. The country was theoretically still committed to a gold standard, and it was expected that this would be reintroduced as soon as possible.

The Great Depression, however, produced a new set of circumstances in almost all Western countries under which they not only suspended redemption but also withdrew all full-bodied coins from circulation. The result was a paper standard *in place of* a metallic one.

Gold Reserve Standard. Most of these countries continued to define their currency as a given weight of gold and still considered gold their basic monetary stock. But nobody could get it. This is a strange gold standard indeed. The United States, for instance, defines a dollar at the present time as $13\frac{5}{7}$ grains of fine gold. This is mathematically equivalent to the well-known price of gold of $35 per ounce. Yet if I were to take my dollar to the Treasury, I couldn't get gold for it unless I obtained a license, and these licenses are issued only under special circumstances. I am not even permitted to hold gold (except for nonmonetary uses subject to regulation). At the same time the government holds some $15 billion worth of gold, which it considers to be the monetary base of the economy. Some ramifications of this strange situation are examined in the following chapter. Suffice it to say here that while technically the dollar is based on gold, in actual practice the dollar is based on the dollar. We are essentially on a paper standard with a gold reserve of questionable significance. The same is true of almost all the nations of the world today.

[6] The origin of paper money is traced in Chap. 5, and its development in the United States in Chap. 6.

Under these circumstances money is fiduciary; that is, it does not itself have any intrinsic value, nor is it redeemable in anything that has. Its acceptability rests solely on the faith of the people in the money and perhaps to a certain extent on their faith in the government. But paper money is as good as any other *as long as people continue to accept it.*

Pure Paper Standard. There is, indeed, no necessity for a currency to maintain any tie to gold (or any other commodity) at all. As long as money is acceptable, nothing else matters. A number of countries have experimented with a pure paper standard from time to time, and Canada was on such a standard from 1950 to 1962. Under a paper standard the value of the currency depends exclusively on what people are willing to give in exchange for it, and this in turn depends pretty much on the quantity of dollars issued in relation to the work that people want dollars to do, a subject that we will examine in detail in Part Six. If the government were to issue too many dollars, their value would fall, and the country would suffer from inflation. If there were too few, a money stringency would develop, and the value of money would rise.

A pure paper currency must be intelligently managed if it is to fulfill its work most effectively and without dislocation. *If properly managed,* a paper currency may be even better than a gold currency because it is not subject to the erratic and undesirable fluctuations in the value of gold itself. If not properly managed, a paper currency can destroy the faith of the nation and may finally cease to be money because no one will accept it. Unfortunately history is replete with examples of badly managed paper currencies.

Kinds of Money

Although commodity money, used for centuries, took many forms, it was essentially a rather simple phenomenon. With the development of higher forms of money, the situation has become more complicated, and we frequently find different types of money existing side by side. A brief classification of these varieties of money may be helpful in our understanding of what modern money is and is not. Currency may be classified along three different lines.

Legal Tender and Optional Money. Good money circulates freely as a medium of exchange without regard to its legal status, but when governments take over money, they are frequently not satisfied to let things take their natural course. They are rather inclined to say that anyone *must* accept their money. This gives rise to the concept of *legal tender, which is any money that must by law be accepted in satisfaction of a debt.*

The penalty for nonacceptance of legal tender has varied considerably. In the United States failure to accept legal tender merely prevents the creditor from charging any further interest on the debt or from levying any other kind of penalty. At other times and places such failure might result in the forgiveness of the debt or in a fine or imprisonment of the creditor. Indeed the French Revolutionary government in 1793 decreed the death penalty for trading paper assignats at less than their face value or for "having asked, before a bargain was concluded, in what money payment was to be made."[7] Even this threat of violent punishment was unable to maintain the value of a currency that was being issued in grossly exaggerated amounts, and within a few years the assignats had depreciated to one-thousandth of their original value.

The law may force a creditor to accept payment in a doubtful currency if it denies him the use of the courts to collect any other, but it is almost impossible to force a man to sell his goods for "money" that he does not trust. His alternatives are to hold onto the goods or to resort to barter. If people have no faith in the "money," the law cannot coerce them into believing in it. Trust is a tender plant that does not thrive in an atmosphere of force. The very fact that extreme penalties are invoked for failure to accept a currency is itself evidence that that currency is *not* generally acceptable.

It it is acceptable, it needs no legal tender law. Federal Reserve notes were not legal tender in this country prior to 1933. They were *optional money,* which people could accept or not as they chose. Yet during the twenties these notes represented the most common form of currency in circulation, and rare indeed was the person who would turn down a Federal Reserve note and say, "Give me a gold certificate instead." Most people didn't even know the difference between the two. Checks are not legal tender, but they account for over 90 per cent of all current payments. Technically, all currency in the United States today is legal tender, but few people know this, and even fewer care.[8]

Full-bodied and Token Money. Full-bodied money is that which has just as much value as a commodity as it has as money. All money was originally full-bodied, and even when debasement lowered the metallic content of a coin below its face value, the public soon caught on and valued the coin at its reduced worth. A token, on the other hand, is not worth its face value except as money. Gold coins, when they were in circulation, were full-bodied. Paper bills are obviously token money, as are most modern coins. Silver dollars, after almost one hundred years as tokens, became full-bodied again in 1963 as the result of a sudden rise in the market price of silver, but they have practically disappeared from circulation. In most of the world there is no full-bodied money in circulation, and nobody seems to care very much.

[7] See Andrew Dickson White, *Fiat Money Inflation in France* (Appleton-Century-Crofts, Inc., New York, 1933), pp. 42–43.

[8] Not even the experts agree as to whether coin is full legal tender or only limited legal tender, that is, legal tender in limited amounts: up to 25 cents for pennies and nickels and $10 for subsidiary silver (cf. *U.S. Code,* Title 31, secs. 459, 460, and 462). The law is obscure, and no definitive court case has ever been taken on this point. The story is told of one individual who protested a traffic fine of $13.50 by paying it with 1,348 pennies—and making the clerk count it three times before shelling out the other 2 cents. This, of course, is precisely what a limited legal tender law is designed to prevent.

Definitive, Convertible, and Nonconvertible Money. The distinction involved in these three types of money has become almost academic. Definitive money is the kind in which the monetary system is defined. Thus under a gold standard, gold coin would be definitive money.

Convertible money is money that may be converted into definitive money by legal right. Gold certificates (under the gold standard) are clearly convertible, while all other currency is convertible in practice as long as the gold standard remains intact. As long as conversion is possible, the distinction between definitive and convertible money doesn't mean much.

Nonconvertible money cannot be converted into standard money. Since definitive money (our currency is still defined as gold) doesn't exist in this country, all currency is nonconvertible. Here again, it doesn't seem to worry most people.

Summary. If history teaches us anything about the nature of money, it is that our original definition of it is absolutely fundamental. Money is anything that is generally acceptable as a means of payment. It doesn't matter what the form; it doesn't matter what the standard; it doesn't matter what the legal terms used—except as these may affect acceptability.

Money can exist without a government. A government can create money only if the people approve. The government may create "money" of which the people do not approve, but their objection will take the form of refusing to accept it in exchange for real wealth except at a depreciated value. Then the monetary system may degenerate into a shambles from which it will emerge only when someone produces a money in which people have faith.

Questions for Thought and Discussion

1. Why did the American Indians not use cattle as money?

2. Why are metals more satisfactory as money than cattle? Than rice? Than diamonds? Than pebbles? Why is gold more satisfactory than iron?

3. Is a coin issued by a merchant worth more or less than a similar coin issued by a government? Why?

4. Would you be happier if you could use full-bodied gold coins for monetary transactions rather than dollar bills or checks?

5. Is it any more logical to base a monetary system on the quantity of gold produced than it would be to base it on the quantity of wheat or coal?

6. Does the tendency to push gold further and further into the background as a monetary material indicate a deterioration of monetary morals?

7. In what respects is paper money an improvement over commodity money? In what respects is it inferior?

8. If Congress were to repeal all legal tender laws, what effect would this have on the conduct of business? Before you read this chapter, did you know what "legal tender" meant?

9. Does the elimination of silver from the dime and the quarter make these coins less valuable?

10. Under what circumstances would money become less valuable?

Selected Bibliography

Angell, Norman: *The Story of Money,* J. B. Lippincott Company, Philadelphia, 1929.

Brown, William A.: *The International Gold Standard Reinterpreted, 1914–1934,* 2 vols., National Bureau of Economic Research, Inc., New York, 1940.

Burns, Arthur F.: *Money and Monetary Policy in Early Times,* Alfred A. Knopf, Inc., New York, 1927.

Carlile, W. W.: *The Evolution of Modern Money,* Macmillan & Co., Ltd., London, 1901.

Del Mar, Alexander: *A History of Money in Ancient Countries,* G. Bell & Sons, Ltd., London, 1885.

Einzig, Paul: *Primitive Money,* Eyre & Spottiswoode (Publishers), Ltd., London, 1948.

Furness, William H.: *The Island of Stone Money,* J. B. Lippincott Company, Philadelphia, 1910.

Gayer, Arthur D.: *Monetary Policy and Economic Stabilization,* 2d ed., The Macmillan Company, New York, 1937.

Graham, Frank D., and Charles R. Whittlesey: *Golden Avalanche,* Princeton University Press, Princeton, N.J., 1939.

Gregory, T. E.: *The Gold Standard and Its Future,* 3d ed., E. P. Dutton & Co., Inc., New York, 1935.

Hawtrey, Ralph G.: *The Gold Standard in Theory and Practice,* 5th ed., Longmans, Green & Co., Ltd., London, 1947.

Kemmerer, Edwin W.: *Gold and the Gold Standard,* McGraw-Hill Book Company, New York, 1944.

Laughlin, J. Laurence: *The History of Bimetallism in the United States,* D. Appleton & Company, Inc., New York, 1896.

Quiggan, A. Hingston: *A Survey of Primitive Money,* Methuen & Co., Ltd., London, 1949.

Ridgeway, William: *The Origin of Metallic Currency and Weight Standards,* Cambridge University Press, London, 1892.

Shaw, W. A.: *The History of Currency, 1252 to 1894,* 3d ed., G. P. Putnam's Sons, New York, 1896.

Spahr, Walter E.: *The Case for the Gold Standard,* Economists' National Committee on Monetary Policy, New York, 1940.

Walker, Francis A.: *International Bimetallism,* Henry Holt and Company, Inc., New York, 1896.

White, Trumbull (ed.): *Silver and Gold, or Both Sides of the Shield: A Symposium of the Views of All Parties on the Currency Question,* Publishers' Union, New York, 1895.

Whittlesey, Charles R.: *International Monetary Issues,* McGraw-Hill Book Company, New York, 1937.

Chapter 3
The Monetary System of the United States

For this they have engrossed and pil'd up
The canker'd heaps of strange-achieved gold.

The Second Part of King Henry VI
Act IV, scene 5, line 69

Much ink has been spilled in an attempt to describe the kind of standard on which the United States bases its current monetary system. In the preceding chapter we referred to it as a gold reserve standard. More specifically it might be called a domestically inconvertible, international gold bullion standard. Rather than try to name the system, however, it would be better to examine how it operates. Names can often be misleading.

The Effective Money Supply

Since gold no longer circulates in the United States, our description had better start not with gold but with those parts of the system that are visible. What is actually used as money? Today we have two basic kinds of money: currency and checking accounts. These are the things that are generally accepted in payment of obligations.

Currency. Currency includes all coin and paper money issued by the government and by banks. But not all currency in existence is part of the effective money supply, that is, purchasing power in the hands of the public. Some money is held by the monetary authorities themselves. This must first be subtracted from the total issued in order to determine the amount available to the public to spend. There are two adjustments:

1. Currency held by the issuers (the Treasury and the Federal Reserve banks). When one of these agencies holds its own obligations, it is similar to a man holding his own IOU. Such currency may exist, but it has no signficance for the economy.

2. Currency held by commercial banks. While banks do not create actual currency today, they are merchants of money. Their cash in vault is not so much purchasing power as it is part of their stock-in-trade. Moreover, a bank's potential purchasing power is not limited to its cash, for it can itself create money, as we will see in Chapter 8. Cash held by a bank, therefore, is in a different category from cash held by the rest of us.

If we subtract these cash holdings of monetary agencies, we get the figure we want, currency outside banks:

Currency outstanding
less currency held in the Treasury and by Federal Reserve banks
equals currency in circulation

Currency in circulation
less vault cash
equals currency outside banks

Table 3-1. Currency in Circulation and the Effective Money Supply for Selected Years

Figures for June 30; Millions of Dollars

Type of currency	1900	1914	1929	1933	1939	1945	1950	1960	1964
Coin:									
Gold coin	611	325	81	34	0	0	0	0	0
Silver coin	142	230	328	285	403	913	1,135	1,789	2,469
Minor coin	26	57	115	113	155	292	361	549	736
Treasury paper:									
Gold certificates	201	1,026	935	265	72	52	41	30	*
Silver certificates	408	479	387	361	1,454	1,652	2,177	2,128	1,708
Treasury notes of 1890	75	2	1	1	1	1	1	1	*
United States notes	318	338	262	269	266	323	321	318	321
Treasury-accepted paper:									
National bank notes	300	715	653	920	186	120	86	56	162†
Federal Reserve bank notes	0	0	4	126	26	527	274	100	
Federal Reserve paper:									
Federal Reserve notes	0	0	1,693	3,061	4,484	22,867	22,760	27,094	32,338
Total currency in circulation	2,081	3,172	4,459	5,434	7,047	26,746	27,156	32,065	37,734
Less vault cash‡	750	1,639	820	673	1,042	1,649	1,971	3,765	4,714
Currency outside banks	1,331	1,533	3,639	4,761	6,005	25,097	25,185	28,300	33,020
Plus demand deposits, adjusted	4,420	10,082	22,540	14,411	27,355	69,053	85,040	107,800	120,311
Effective money supply	5,751	11,615	26,179	19,172	33,360	94,150	110,225	136,100	153,331

* Included in figure for Treasury-accepted paper.
† Includes gold certificates and treasury notes of 1890.
‡ Vault cash is computed here as the difference between currency in circulation and currency outside banks.
Sources: Board of Governors of the Federal Reserve System, ***Banking and Monetary Statistics*** (1943), pp. 34-35, 408-409; ***Federal Reserve Bulletin***, vol. 31, no. 9 (September, 1945), p. 917; vol. 32, no. 9 (September, 1946), p. 1033; vol. 36, no. 9 (September, 1950), p. 1202; vol. 37, no. 9 (September, 1951), p. 1152; vol. 46, no. 9 (September, 1960), p. 1019; vol. 46, no. 10 (October, 1960), p. 1138; vol. 50, no. 9 (September, 1964), p. 1157; vol. 50, no. 10 (October, 1964), p. 1287. Detail may not add to totals because of rounding.

If we wish to examine statistics for the various kinds of currency that make up this total, however, it is necessary to use data for currency in circulation since banks do not record the particular kinds of cash that they hold in vault. Table 3-1 shows currency in circulation by type, as well as the total for currency outside banks, for selected years since 1900. This table provides some interesting insights into the general growth of the money supply, the relative importance of particular types of currency, and various shifts in emphasis that have occurred. Let us examine each item separately.

Gold Coin. Gold coin, which had been a basic constituent of our money supply since coinage was established in 1792, was withdrawn from circulation by act of Congress in 1933. Owners of gold coins were required to turn them over to the government in exchange for other currency. Since that time the holding of gold coin has been illegal except in coin collections.

While gold coin was in use, the standard denomination was the eagle, worth $10. Coinage included double eagles, half eagles, and quarter eagles, with a very limited number of $1, $3, and $50 pieces.[1]

Silver Coin. The standard silver dollar, the second half of our original monetary system, still survives and has the same weight of pure silver (371.25 grains) as was first specified in the act of 1792. Since the silver dollar is 9⁄10 fine, its total weight (including 10 per cent of copper alloy) is 412.5 grains. Silver dollars, however, have not been minted since 1935, and a large number of those technically "in circulation" are actually in hoards or numismatic collections.

Silver half-dollars, quarters, and dimes (all 9⁄10 fine) were last minted in 1966. Other silver coins produced in the past are trade dollars, 20-cent pieces, half dimes, and 3-cent pieces.

Minor Coin. The half-dollar is now a quasi-silver coin, containing 40 per cent silver and 60 per cent copper. Quarters and dimes are sandwiches, with cupronickel faces (of the same composition as the nickel) and pure copper cores. Nickels, interestingly enough, are only 25 per cent nickel, with the rest copper. Pennies are pure copper, but in the past they have been minted of nickel, bronze, zinc-steel, and copper-zinc. Minor coins, of course, are worth much less as bullion than they are as coins.

Gold Certificates. Gold certificates, originally issued as a means of saving wear and tear on gold coins and on pocketbooks, are backed 100 per cent by gold. They are therefore mere warehouse receipts, promising gold coin to the bearer on demand. Like gold coin, the certificates were withdrawn in 1933 and cannot be held by private individuals. The amount now in circulation represents bills which have been lost, destroyed, or exported or which rest in collections and attic trunks. The decrease in the figures from year to year

[1] For a description of all coins issued by the mint from 1793 to 1963, see *Domestic Coin Manufactured by Mints of the United States* (Government Printing Office, 1964).

reflects the fact that people sometimes clean their attics and turn in their long-lost hoards. The Treasury will redeem them if the owner can give a satisfactory explanation of why he didn't turn them over in 1933, when he was supposed to.

Gold certificates are now held legally only by the Federal Reserve banks. For this use some $13 billion worth is outstanding—but not in circulation.

Silver Certificates. Until 1963 silver certificates represented almost our total supply of $1 bills, nearly half of our $5 bills, and a scattering of other denominations. Like gold certificates they are warehouse receipts, fully backed by silver. Their nature is described on their face, which bears the legend: "This certifies that there is on deposit in the treasury of the United States of America one dollar in silver payable to the bearer on demand."

In 1963 Congress decided to replace silver certificates in circulation with Federal Reserve notes. Silver certificates will therefore gradually disappear from our money supply, and the silver backing behind them will no longer be needed.

Treasury Notes of 1890. These were issued only briefly under the Sherman Silver Act. They are unique in that they have not only 100 per cent silver backing but a partial gold backing as well. These notes are being retired, and there is only a nominal amount in circulation, presumably in collections or lost.

United States Notes. Originally issued as a fiat currency during the Civil War, they were later redeemed in small amounts until 1878, when Congress decreed that their issue should remain fixed at the amount then outstanding ($347 million). This law has never been altered, and as old notes wear out, they are replaced with new ones. The year-to-year changes in the amount in circulation, therefore, represent changes in the amounts held by the Treasury and the Federal Reserve, not in the amount issued. Almost all $2 bills are United States notes, as are a fair number of $5 bills. United States notes are sometimes found in other denominations.

The Treasury maintains a gold reserve of $156 million against United States notes, but holders cannot get gold for their notes, and since the total amount outstanding is prescribed by law, the reserve seems to serve no useful purpose.

National Bank Notes. These notes, issued by national banks against security of government bonds deposited with the Treasury, have not been issued since 1935. In that year the Treasury called for redemption the last of the United States bonds bearing the note-issuing privilege, thus withdrawing the only collateral against which national bank notes could legally be issued. At the same time the Treasury required national banks with notes outstanding to pay into the Treasury sufficient funds to retire all notes. The Treasury thus assumed the liability of redeeming notes that are still in circulation. These notes are retired as fast as the public will give them up.

Federal Reserve Bank Notes. The Federal Reserve *bank* notes, which have had a checkered career, should not be confused with Federal Reserve notes. Federal Reserve *bank* notes were provided for in the Federal Reserve Act to take the place of national bank notes, whose gradual retirement the act contemplated. They were to have the same backing as the national bank notes (that is, government bonds) and in all other respects were similar except for the issuing bank. They thus differed from Federal Reserve notes, which were at that time backed by commercial paper and gold.

In practice the history of Federal Reserve bank notes is one of emergency. Three times they have been issued in sizable amounts followed by a period of gradual retirement. The right of the Federal Reserve banks to issue these notes was revoked in 1945, and, like national bank notes, they will gradually disappear from circulation.

Federal Reserve Notes. Federal Reserve notes are by far the most important component of our currency, representing some 85 per cent of currency in circulation, and their importance is growing as other forms of paper money are retired. They are issued by the twelve Federal Reserve banks under conditions described in greater detail in Chapter 12.

Summary. The current importance of the various types of currency is indicated in the following simplified summary:

Silver and minor coins account for payments under $1.
United States notes provide us with $2 bills (and some $5 bills).
Federal Reserve notes provide the rest of our current circulating currency.
Gold certificates are held only by Federal Reserve banks.
All other currency is being retired.

Lawful Money, Legal Tender, and All That. Paper money has become such a common part of our experience that most of us never bother to question what sort of an animal it really is. How many of us have ever stopped to read the very interesting legends appearing on a $5 Federal Reserve note, for instance? It says there: "The United States of America will pay to the bearer on demand five dollars." What is "five dollars"? What will we get if we demand "five dollars"?

Another portion of the bill seems to answer this question: "This note is legal tender for all debts, public and private, and is redeemable in lawful money at the United States Treasury or at any Federal Reserve bank." We knew the note was legal tender—all currency issued in the United States is legal tender. So we have to accept it in payment of debt, and in return the government promises to redeem it in lawful money—whatever that is. If we did a lot of research we might find that national banks were required to hold lawful money as reserves against their notes or deposits. But nowhere in the law is the term defined. Does anyone know what it is?

A gentleman named A. F. Davis decided that he wanted to find out. He sent a $10 Federal Reserve note to the Treasury and asked for "$10.00 in lawful money." By return mail, without explanation, came two $5 United States notes (which promise no redemption at all except that "the United States will pay the bearer Five Dollars"). On further prodding the Treasury broke down enough to say:

> You are advised that the term "lawful money" has not been defined in federal legislation. It first came into use prior to 1933 when some United States currency was not legal tender but could be held by national banking associations as lawful money reserves. Since the Act of May 12, 1933, as amended by the Joint Resolution of June 5, 1933, makes all coins and currency of the United States legal tender and the Joint Resolution of August 27, 1935, provides for the exchange of United States coin or currency for other types of such coin or currency, the term "lawful currency" no longer has special significance.[2]

So "lawful money" has no special significance, and that's what the government gives you. If this legal sidestepping means anything at all, it is that all legal tender is lawful money. Thus a Federal Reserve note is redeemable in itself. It is as if I gave you an IOU for $5 and promised that any time you wanted payment I would give you a nice new clean IOU—in a different color ink if you liked.

The moral of this tale is not that Federal Reserve notes are no good. Rather it is the same old truism: the value of money depends entirely on people's faith in it, and as long as they have faith in a piece of paper, then that paper is money and has the value that people ascribe to it no matter what it says. In the United States people are willing to accept irredeemable paper money, and so it *is* money. If you don't think yours is worth any more than a scrap of paper, just send it to me—I'll pay the postage.

It is true, of course, that in practice all United States currency is interchangeable, so that the holder of paper can get silver for it not only from the Treasury, but at any bank. But this is a matter of courtesy, not a right. And while coins are necessary and useful for small transactions, practically no one prefers them solely because of their higher intrinsic value. The question of what the government promises to give in exchange for its paper bills is therefore academic.

The new $1 Federal Reserve notes avoid even the pretense of redeemability. All they say is: "The United States of America. One dollar. This note is legal tender for all debts public and private." That's it. Take it or leave it. No one

[2] The complete exchange of correspondence is printed in *American Affairs,* April, 1948, p. 88, and reproduced in Arthur D. Gayer, C. Lowell Harriss, and Milton H. Spencer, *Basic Economics* (Prentice-Hall, Inc., Englewood Cliffs, N.J., 1951), pp. 347–349.

seems to mind, however, and these notes, although they excited some curiosity when they were first introduced in 1964, have taken their place without further question among the other forms of currency.

No one would question the propriety of including all the various forms of currency in the money supply. They clearly fit our definition of money in terms of acceptability. Because currency is universally acceptable, we call it *common money.*

Checking Accounts. But if paper money is a far cry from commodity money, how much further are demand deposits (bank deposits subject to check), which are not even paper, but only a ledger account in the bank's books. Many people would never consider these money at all. Are they generally acceptable? A consumer goes into a store where he is not known, and he is perfectly well aware that he cannot make payment by check. His personal check just isn't good in many cases.

A check is not as readily used as currency because it will not normally be accepted unless the person receiving it has faith in the maker—faith that he has an account in the bank, that it has at least as much money in it as the check calls for, that he has used a proper signature on the check, and that he will not ask the bank to stop payment on the check before it is paid. In spite of these qualifications, however, more than 90 per cent of the dollar volume of all payments in the United States is by check. Most of these payments are made by business firms to suppliers, to employees, to stockholders, and so on, while the individual has a tendency to make a larger proportion of his payments in cash. Consumers, however, are using checks in an increasing number of transactions—for utilities, professional bills, charge accounts, insurance premiums, and so on.

Certainly if the economy as a whole transacts nine-tenths of its business through checking accounts, we must admit that they are generally acceptable as a means of payment. We must recognize also that they are not universally acceptable, as currency is. Although they are money, they are a slightly different kind from dollar bills, and we call them *particular money.*

One technicality arises at this point over the difference between checks and checking accounts. A checking account is money; a check is not. A check is merely evidence of a transfer of money. When someone gives me a check, he is telling his bank to transfer ownership of his bank balance to me. I accept the check because it transfers this bank balance, but it's the balance I want, not the check. The significance of this point appears when we look at the quantity of money. The quantity of currency consists of all those coins and bills in the hands of the public. This is the community's purchasing power in cash. Their purchasing power in terms of bank accounts is not the quantity of checks in existence at any moment of time (a figure which we have no means of ascertaining) but rather the total of their checking account balances. The total in my account represents the money (other than cash) which I have to spend. My writing a check is simply the process of spending it.

Demand Deposits, Adjusted. In Table 3-1 we have listed checking accounts as part of the money supply under their technical title, "demand deposits, adjusted," a figure that shows the portion of bank deposits that represents purchasing power in the hands of the public. The process of deriving this figure is as follows:

Gross deposits (demand and time)
less interbank deposits and cash items in process of collection
equal net deposits

Net deposits
less United States government balances at commercial and savings banks
equal deposits, adjusted

Deposits, adjusted
less time deposits (adjusted) at commercial and savings banks
equal demand deposits, adjusted

The purpose of each of these subtractions from gross deposits is to eliminate a nonmonetary component of the total. Since interbank deposits represent deposits of monetary agencies whose purchasing power does not depend on their bank balances, these are subtracted from the total. Cash items in process of collection represent double counting: the amount of such checks has been added to the payee's balance but has not yet been subtracted from the drawer's account. This double counting must be eliminated. United States government balances, again, represent accounts of a money-creating authority whose purchasing is not restricted by such accounts. Finally, time deposits, which are not money, must also be excluded from the final figure.

The result—demand deposits, adjusted—is the total that the nongovernmental, nonbank public has available to spend from its checking accounts.

The total money supply of the country then consists of cash plus checking accounts in the hands of the public, technically called *currency outside banks plus demand deposits, adjusted.* The importance of checking accounts in the total is clear from Table 3-1. It is for precisely this reason that we combine a study of money with a study of banking. The commercial banks, through their power to create money in the form of bank deposits, play a vital role in the monetary affairs of the country, and they will occupy much of our attention throughout this book.

Changing Monetary Relationships. The table shows also how some of our major types of money have changed in magnitude over time. The decline in gold coin and gold certificates is a natural result of the abandonment of a gold coin standard. But even prior to 1935 we find that the use of gold coin was passing out of vogue. From 1900 to 1929, for instance, a doubling of total currency in circulation was accompanied by a drop in gold coin of almost 90 per cent. This is a dramatic indication of growing indifference on the part of the public to hard money. Gold coin simply wasn't as easy to use as paper currency.

Silver and minor coin have generally tended to grow at about the same rate as total currency, and although there have been some minor fluctuations (why, for instance, did both kinds of coin decline from 1929 to 1933 while the total money supply was growing?), the total of silver and minor coin has remained between 5 and 10 per cent of total currency in circulation. Silver certificates have fluctuated more widely but have in general also grown with the money supply. With their replacement by Federal Reserve notes in 1964, they will gradually disappear.

The stability of United States notes is due to the peculiarity of the law, while the disappearance of treasury notes of 1890 and national bank notes reflects their retirement. Federal Reserve bank notes show clearly their erratic history, while Federal Reserve notes show a spectacular rise to a point of unrivaled preeminence at the present time. They were intended as an elastic currency, and they have certainly stretched.

Vault cash, though reasonably stable in absolute amount, shows a remarkable proportionate drop when compared either with currency in circulation or, more pertinently, with demand deposits, adjusted. In 1900 vault cash was 36 per cent of currency in circulation and 17 per cent of demand deposits. In 1964 the comparable figures were 12 and 4 per cent. This is one evidence of (1) the more effective organization of the banking system, whereby cash is more rapidly obtained (from the Federal Reserve) if needed, and (2) the smaller demand on the part of customers for cash, reflecting in turn both greater confidence in banks and an increased use of checkbook money.

The figures illustrate also the tremendous growth in the total money supply, which by 1964 was more than twenty-five times its 1900 level. This growth is related to three factors: (1) the growth in population, (2) the increase in production per capita, and (3) the rise in prices.

The relation of the quantity of money to price levels and business activity will concern us through most of the remainder of this book. Only one comment appears pertinent at this point. While complete figures would show clearly the fluctuations in money supply that accompany fluctuations in business activity, even the few figures here given show the Great Depression in stark outline. From 1929 to 1933 the total money supply fell from $26 billion to $19 billion—a $7-billion drop. This was not due to any contraction of currency, which actually rose by $1 billion. Rather it was due to a fall in bank deposits of $8 billion, as the following summary figures (in billions of dollars) indicate:

	June 30, 1929	*June 30, 1933*	*Change*
Currency outside banks	3.6	4.8	+1.2
Demand deposits, adjusted	22.5	14.4	−8.1
Effective money supply	26.1	19.2	−6.9

In a sense it might be said that this drop in money supply *is* the Depression. Not that it caused the Depression, but simply that it illustrates the forces at work: less money, less purchasing power, lower sales, lower prices, sinking profits, reduced production, unemployment, lower income.

The threefold rise in effective money supply during the war also tells a story, this time of rapidly rising output and not quite so rapidly rising prices. Only after the war was over did this increase in monetary circulation have its full effect on prices.

Money is an important adjunct to business and plays a prominent role in its fluctuations, both up and down.

Near-money

Although currency and checking accounts are the only money in the United States today, there are a number of other things that act *almost* as if they were money. I may think of my savings account or my Series E savings bonds as readily available purchasing power. All I have to do to get money for them is to go to the bank and withdraw my savings account or redeem my savings bonds, and I know I can do this at any time.[3] These assets may be almost as good as cash in my pocket, and the more I have of them, the less I feel I need in cash. If some unexpected expense comes up, I can withdraw money from my savings account to meet it. If I don't have such an account, I had better keep more cash (or more in my checking account) to meet emergencies.

All this means, however, is that some assets are highly liquid; that is, they can be turned into money rapidly and without loss of value. The more liquid an asset is—and savings accounts and savings bonds are the most liquid of the nonmoneys—the more nearly it resembles money. But money itself is 100 per cent liquid. It is instantly available for any expenditure, day or night, Sundays, Mondays, or holidays. Perhaps we might score savings accounts as 99 per cent liquid. The difference between them and money, however, is not unimportant. Savings accounts cannot be used to make payments; they must be turned into something else—money—first. And as a practical matter this can't be done at two o'clock in the morning to pay a poker debt or at the Fourth of July picnic to buy a hamburger. For these things only money will do.

Liquidity is entirely a matter of relativity. It refers to the *speed* and *certainty* with which assets can be turned into cash. Savings accounts and savings bonds may be immediately turned into cash (during banking hours) at a price that is guaranteed in terms of dollars. Treasury bills (especially those issued for a period of 91 days) can be sold at any time in an active securities market, but at any particular moment the price may not be as high as that originally paid for them. If, however, one wishes to wait to maturity (which

[3] Savings banks are permitted by law to require notice of withdrawal of up to two months, but in practice they never do.

cannot be more than three months), he is sure of receiving full face value. Because maturity is always so near, the price cannot fluctuate by any very great amount. Such securities are only slightly less liquid than savings bonds.

Other government securities can also be sold without delay, but because they have longer to run before they are redeemed, their price may fluctuate more from their face value, and, on the other hand, the owner must wait longer to be certain of receiving that value.

Corporate bonds are more risky than government bonds, and hence their fluctuation in price may be greater and their liquidity is lower. Another notch down the liquidity ladder would be preferred stocks, then common stocks, with great variation as between securities of different corporations.

Most commodities, because they do not have as active a market as securities do, are harder to sell in a hurry or at full price. Some are less liquid than others. Among the least liquid are houses or, even worse, specialized factories that can be used for only one purpose. Some of these perhaps cannot be sold for any price, but most will find a buyer if the owner is willing to (1) wait long enough or (2) accept a low enough price. These two characteristics of speed and certainty of price are clearly alternatives when it comes to relatively illiquid assets. We do not say that a house is illiquid solely because it takes a long time to sell. I will guarantee that your house can be sold tomorrow—if you are willing to accept a few dollars for it. If you want a reasonable price, however, you may have to wait years.

All assets are a store of value. All of them are to a certain extent substitutes for money in this respect. How good a substitute depends on how high they stand on the liquidity scale. Some of those at the top are a very close substitute for money as a store of readily available purchasing power. But none of them can serve as a medium of exchange. Assets that are highly liquid may be called *near-money,* but they are not money. Currency and checking accounts are money, but not savings accounts, savings bonds, or other less liquid assets.

The Status of Gold

In some respects the first part of this chapter tells all that needs to be known about our monetary system. It describes those forms of money we actually use and gives some idea of the relative importance of each. Since gold is no longer used, it is not money. Yet it still holds a very important place in the system and is the center of continuous controversy. What is its precise status?

Gold and the Law. The Gold Standard Act of 1900 defined the dollar as 25.8 grains of gold $9/10$ fine, equal to 23.22 grains of fine gold. This made an ounce of gold worth $20.67. Our currency maintained this relationship to gold until the bank holiday in 1933 occasioned a series of Executive orders that cut us adrift by requiring that all gold coin, gold bullion, and gold certificates be turned in to the Federal Reserve banks. Since that period no one has been permitted to hold gold except under treasury regulations. These allow the holding of gold coin in collections, gold jewelry or other manufactured articles, gold in its natural (unrefined) state, not more than 50 ounces of gold legitimately used in industry, and not more than 50 ounces in the form of gold scrap. The Federal Reserve banks may also acquire gold for settlement of international balances. All other uses require a treasury license. The purpose of these regulations is obviously to permit the use of gold for almost all purposes *except* that of money.

In spite of this removal of gold from ordinary circulation, the dollar is still based on gold. The Thomas amendment, which was—rather inappropriately —a rider to the Agricultural Adjustment Act (May 12, 1933), gave the President the power to devalue the dollar by not more than 50 per cent. This he did by proclamation on January 31, 1934, defining the dollar as 15$\frac{5}{21}$ grains of gold $\frac{9}{10}$ fine, equivalent to 13$\frac{5}{7}$ grains of fine gold. This can be translated into the familiar price of gold of $35 an ounce (480 grains). The law under which this action was taken specifies that the gold dollar so defined "shall be the standard unit of value, and all forms of money issued or coined by the United States shall be maintained at a parity with this standard and it shall be the duty of the Secretary of the Treasury to maintain such parity."[4] The manner in which he is to maintain parity between paper currency that circulates and gold that does not is nowhere specified. In practice it is done by offering to buy or sell gold in standard bullion bars for the settlement of international trade balances.

What is the legal status of gold? The very act that makes it the basis of our monetary system prohibits its use as money. Although it does not refer directly to our coinage, a Swiss court decision throws a rather penetrating light on this anomaly. It seems that in 1952 two gentlemen were engaged in the interesting process of "minting" English sovereigns (gold pounds) and other gold coins, which they sold to hoarders at a premium of some 20 per cent above the price of gold bullion. The coins themselves were of full weight and standard fineness. Arrested for counterfeiting, they were released by the Swiss Federal Court on the grounds that counterfeiting is an unauthorized manufacture of money, and since gold coins are no longer money, they cannot be counterfeited. The men involved were therefore not counterfeiters, but simply entrepreneurs producing a product for sale. Thus has gold fallen to the same level as potatoes. While such a decision may be unique, and has in fact been contradicted in other cases, it has a certain ironic reality about it.

Not content to leave this lucrative business to private enterprise, at least four countries have attempted to meet the demand for gold themselves. There is a persistent rumor that the Bank of France has been minting its own gold Napoleons, with fictitious dates, for sale on the black market. The British Treasury, more openly, has been minting sovereigns for sale to authorized

[4] Act of May 12, 1933, 48 Stat. 53, Title III, chap. 25, sec. 43.

dealers in the London gold bullion market. This is legal since Britain, unlike the United States, does not prohibit the holding of gold. The Bank of England was selling sovereigns in 1958 at about $9.25 each (equivalent to $39 an ounce), yielding a neat profit.

Italy has attacked the problem in a different way by issuing commemorative medals of gold to be sold by the Treasury at a premium. They have no face value and are not legal tender, but they are of standard weight and fineness. West Germany is minting ducats depicting the head of Queen Elizabeth II, "suitable for hoarding."

It is possible that these various actions are preliminary to restoration of some kind of legal gold coin standard, although the current demand is primarily for hoarding rather than for use. It is therefore similar to the hoarding of diamonds, of land, or of any other article whose value may be expected to rise. And the price of gold *will* rise in terms of any currency that is devalued, for devaluation these days means that a government offers a higher price in its own currency for a given amount of gold (or for other currencies based on gold). So those people who trust gold more than their currency will tend to hoard, and hoarding is therefore most common in countries where faith in the currency is weak. Gold yields no interest, and those who hold it will benefit only if their currency actually is devalued.

Gold and the Quantity of Money. Gold is not money, but it still functions as reserves for our monetary system. And there are many people who think that in such a role it sets limits to the expansion of our money supply. Federal Reserve banks, for instance, must keep a gold reserve equal to 25 per cent of their Federal Reserve notes in circulation. But such notes are not redeemable in gold, and the quantity of them in circulation is, as we will see later, determined by the desires of the public rather than by the amount of gold that the Reserve banks have.

In the past there has been another, even stronger link between the money supply and gold. Prior to 1965 the Federal Reserve banks had to keep a 25 per cent gold reserve against their deposit liabilities also. Since these deposit liabilities are the reserves of member banks and determine how much credit they can extend, there was in the earlier period a theoretical relation between the gold stock and the quantity of demand deposits, the largest component by far of the money supply.

But the weakness of the argument that the quantity of gold is intended to limit the quantity of money was clearly exposed when Congress removed the gold requirement against Federal Reserve deposits in 1965 precisely because the dwindling gold stock threatened to restrict the money supply. And although the requirement was retained against Federal Reserve notes, there is no question but that this also will be eliminated whenever there is any danger of its becoming effective. We simply cannot afford to hamstring monetary policy by tying it too closely to so capricious a bellwether as the gold stock.

Gold and the Value of Money. Sometimes a gold reserve is said to have its greatest merit not in its restriction of the quantity of money, but rather in the fact that gold gives value to money. It is certainly true that money in its early days was simply a commodity, and its monetary value was the same thing as its commodity value. But that was a long time ago. What is the relation today between the value of money and the value of gold?

Does money have value because it is backed by gold—because by law a dollar is "worth" $\frac{1}{35}$ of an ounce of gold? Rather it is the other way round. *Gold has value because it is used as a monetary reserve.* If governments decided that they no longer wished to hold gold as backing for their currencies, who would want gold and for what purpose? It is unexcelled for filling teeth; it is pretty and therefore has considerable use in jewelry; and perhaps if it were cheap enough, it might find many industrial uses. But at current prices the major use of gold by far is for monetary hoards.

According to the Bank for International Settlements, at no time since 1946 have industrial (that is, nonmonetary) uses taken as much as 20 per cent of the annual output of gold. On the average from 1951 to 1958, $1,048 million worth of gold was made available each year. Of this amount $547 million went into government gold reserves, $320 million went into private hoards, and $181 million was used for all other purposes.[5]

If we assumed that governments no longer bought gold for reserves and that in consequence gold lost its attraction for private hoarders, what would have happened to this $867 million of gold absorbed by monetary uses (government reserves and private hoards) in these years? And if we assumed further—perish the thought!—that governments decided to sell the $40 *billion* of gold they now hold, and individuals disgorged the $12 billion estimated to reside in hoards, what an utter collapse in gold prices would occur!

Monetary gold now in existence equals forty years' production at current rates and over 250 years' industrial use at current rates. If this tremendous stock were thrown on the market, even gradually, could gold possibly be worth more than a fraction of its current price?

It has been well said that the dollar is not on a gold standard—gold is on a dollar standard.

Gold and Confidence. In spite of all this, gold *does* serve a function; in fact it serves two functions. The first is its magical ability to give people confidence in the currency. Most people are completely unaware of the legal or the economic aspects of gold as a monetary reserve. But they do know that the dollar is backed by gold (they may even think that it is backed 100 per cent), and the symbol of Fort Knox is a very heartening one to somebody who doesn't understand very much about money.

[5] Bank for International Settlements, *Twenty-ninth Annual Report, 1958–1959* (Basle, Switzerland), pp. 166–170; averages computed by the author. All figures exclude the U.S.S.R. and associated areas, for which information is lacking, except that Soviet gold *sales* are included in production figures. Dollar estimates of industrial uses of gold have not been prepared by the Bank since 1958.

Because confidence promotes acceptability, this psychological advantage of a gold reserve is a very real one. We might point out (very quietly so as not to disturb anyone's peace of mind) that it doesn't really matter whether the gold is actually there or not as long as people *think* it is. If our gold stock had all disappeared into the bowels of the earth during an earthquake or had been surreptitiously spirited away to the South Seas, it wouldn't matter one iota *as long as no one knew about it.* Our monetary system would remain just as sound as it is today, dollar bills would be accepted just as readily, and commerce would continue without pause.

But as soon as the news leaked out, what a howl would arise. It would be a national calamity. Faith in the currency would be destroyed, and it is hard to predict precisely what the result would be. There are some people who worry about whether the gold really is there. The Daughters of the American Revolution passed a resolution at their annual convention in 1952 asking for a congressional committee to count the gold, and a bill to carry out this policy was actually introduced into Congress but never passed.

Perhaps someday our memory of gold may become so hazy that we won't care whether it backs our money or not, but until that day arrives, gold does give us some confidence in our currency.

Gold and International Trade. The second real function that gold fulfills is as an international medium of exchange. In international trade gold is the only real money, the only thing that is generally accepted in final settlement of claims. Thus a gold stock represents international purchasing power in the same way that dollar bills represent domestic purchasing power.

To the extent that we own gold, we can buy foreign goods without paying for them with our own goods. That is, we could enjoy an import balance equal to our gold stock. To a certain extent that is exactly what we have been doing for several years. Our gold stock fell gradually from $23.2 billion in 1952 to $22.8 billion in 1957 and then rapidly to less than $14 billion in 1965. This loss of more than $9 billion represented gold used to make payments to foreign nations that we could not make in any other way. Although the drop was exceptionally large and raises a number of questions with regard to both monetary policy and international trade (which we will discuss later), it meant basically that gold was being used as international purchasing power in the way in which it is intended to be used.

The Status of Silver

The United States has a long history of silver agitation and silver legislation, the effect of which during the last century has been primarily to subsidize the mining of the white metal. In 1963 the last monetary ties to silver were broken when Congress passed a law which (1) repealed the requirement that the Treasury buy all newly mined domestic silver at 90½ cents an ounce, (2) repealed the 50 per cent tax on profits made from trading in silver and thus made possible the reestablishment of a free silver market, and (3) provided for the gradual replacement of silver certificates by Federal Reserve notes over a ten-year period. The elimination of silver certificates will free the silver used as backing for these notes, and the government can either use it for new coins or sell it to industry, whose demand for silver has risen significantly.

This demand is so great, in fact, that it has pushed the price of silver up to $1.29 an ounce, at which price a silver dollar is worth as much in bullion as it is worth as money. This is the first time that the silver dollar has been full-bodied money since 1873, and a number of companies have found it cheaper to buy silver from the Treasury at the monetary price than to buy it in the open market. The dwindling silver stock held by the government induced Congress in 1965 to substitute base-metal coins for the formerly silver half-dollar, quarter, and dime. Although the dollar remains legally as a silver coin, there is little likelihood that any silver dollars will be minted in the foreseeable future, for they would undoubtedly disappear almost immediately into hoards or the melting furnace.

Questions for Thought and Discussion

1. Why are savings deposits not counted as part of the effective money supply?

2. Why are treasury cash and government deposits not counted as part of the effective money supply?

3. Add to Table 3-1 a column for the latest figures you can find (try the *Federal Reserve Bulletin*). Can you explain any differences between these figures and the ones given for 1964?

4. If you can't get anything but another bill for a Federal Reserve note, does this mean that the whole thing is a hoax? Are Federal Reserve notes money?

5. If paper bills and government securities are alike merely promises of the government to pay other bills in exchange, what is the significant difference between the two? Does this difference have any implications for government fiscal and monetary policy?

6. Our discussion of money has indicated that it has changed fairly drastically over the past century. Can you think of ways in which our money might be improved in the future? Does our current monetary system fulfill its basic functions in the best possible manner?

7. What happened to the $7 billion of the effective money supply that disappeared between 1929 and 1933?

8. Have you ever handled a gold coin? Does this fact help explain at least partly why your attitude toward gold may be different from that of older persons who grew up in an economy that used gold for day-to-day transactions?

9. Some people object to the infringement on personal freedom inherent in the prohibition against holding gold. Does the law actually prohibit anyone from holding gold? Can you buy gold if you want it?

10. Would there be any serious disadvantages in the repeal of all legislation interfering with the use of gold?
11. Do you think there really is any gold in Fort Knox? On what evidence?
12. What are the advantages of holding gold as against holding other assets (money, securities, real estate)? What are the disadvantages? Would gold be hoarded if it were not a monetary metal?
13. If countries are able to carry on domestic trade without the use of gold, might it be possible to carry on international trade without the use of gold? What would be used in its place?

Selected Bibliography

Breckinridge, S. P.: *Legal Tender,* The University of Chicago Press, Chicago, 1903.
Carothers, Neil: *Fractional Money,* John Wiley & Sons, Inc., New York, 1930.
Dunne, Gerald T.: *Monetary Decisions of the Supreme Court,* Rutgers University Press, New Brunswick, N.J., 1960.
Leavens, Dickson: *Silver Money,* Principia Press, Bloomington, Ind., 1939.
Linderman, H. R.: *Money and Legal Tender in the United States,* G. P. Putnam's Sons, New York, 1877.
Mann, F. A.: *The Legal Aspects of Money,* 2d ed., Oxford University Press, London, 1953.
Nussbaum, Arthur: *Money in the Law: National and International,* Foundation Press, Brooklyn, N.Y., 1950.
Olivecrona, Karl: *The Problem of the Monetary Unit,* The Macmillan Company, New York, 1957.
Taussig, F. W.: *The Silver Situation in the United States,* G. P. Putnam's Sons, New York, 1893.
Westerfield, Ray B.: *Our Silver Debacle,* The Ronald Press Company, New York, 1936.
Young, Ralph A.: *The New Monetary System of the United States,* National Industrial Conference Board, Inc., New York, 1934.

Chapter 4
Credit and Credit Instruments

Three thousand ducats for three months, and Antonio bound. . . . He is sufficient. . . . I think I may take his bond.

The Merchant of Venice
Act I, scene 3, line 9

Our historical survey shows clearly that money started its life as a commodity but that it has progressed inexorably if gradually to the status of a credit instrument. Dollar bills are promises to pay; bank checks are orders by a depositor to his bank to transfer "money" from his account to someone else's. This "money in the bank," in turn, is merely a promise of the bank to honor checks. Neither cows nor gold coins are sophisticated enough to do the work of money in our complicated society, and our modern credit money is aided in its task by a multitude of credit arrangements.

The Nature of Credit

The whole industrialized economy of the United States is built solidly on the base of credit. Take credit away and no wheel would turn, no mill would operate. The influence of credit is so pervasive that we take it for granted just as we take the air for granted. But the one is just as essential to economic well-being as the other is to physical health.

Credit and Faith. Credit is essentially faith. The word itself is derived from the Latin *credo*—"I trust." The business definition of credit may be stated in more specific terms: *Credit is the present acquisition of anything of value (money, commodities, or services) in exchange for a promise to return an equivalent at some future time.*

If this definition is interpreted broadly, it should be evident that practically every business transaction involves an element of credit. Each of the following activities represents a credit transaction:

1. Jones borrows $100 for three months.
2. Smith buys a refrigerator on the installment plan.
3. Brown uses his charge account to buy a suit.
4. The ABC Corporation sells bonds to investors.
5. John's Drugstore receives merchandise from a wholesaler on open-book account.
6. Williams works for the XYZ Company in exchange for an (implied) promise of the company to pay him on payday.
7. Johnson buys a train ticket in exchange for the railroad's promise to deliver him to his destination.
8. Green pays tuition in exchange for an education to be delivered (?) during the course of the semester.
9. Carson uses electricity, a bill for which is submitted at the end of the month.
10. Simons pays a month's rent in advance.
11. Mrs. Burns borrows a cup of sugar from her neighbor with the understanding that she will return it later. (Many so-called "loans" in this area are really gifts; "May I borrow a cigarette" frequently implies no promise to pay it back.)
12. Bradley lends money to his bank by depositing cash to his account.
13. Carey helps Mitchell plant his oats with the understanding that Mitchell will help Carey bring in his hay.
14. Gordon mails a check with his order for a book.

Even where a customer buys merchandise for cash, he is making payment with a credit instrument: a promise on the part of the government to pay the bearer of the paper bill something. It is therefore almost impossible to think of any business transaction short of pure barter in which the element of credit is completely absent. Faith turns the wheels of industry and commerce.

In common usage the word "credit" is more restricted in its meaning than some of the above examples would indicate. If one can get either money or goods now in exchange for money or goods in the future, there are four possible credit combinations:

Money now for money later
Goods now for money later
Money now for goods later
Goods now for goods later

In business practice only the first two of these are normally thought of when credit is mentioned, and we will confine our further discussion to this more limited use of the term. In this sense credit is the present acquisition of anything of value in exchange for a promise to make an equivalent *money payment* at some future time.

The question of what constitutes an equivalent payment is one that cannot be determined by formula but must be left to the parties to decide for themselves. It is generally agreed that if one borrows money, an equivalent payment is not the identical amount borrowed, but rather this sum plus interest. When one borrows goods, the equivalent payment may be either the purchase price of the goods or such a price plus interest or a service charge. The parties should agree as to what the equivalent is before credit is extended, or a lawsuit may be part of the price.

Credit and Debt. One interesting thing about credit is that it cannot exist without debt. They are the two sides of the same transaction. As the lender extends credit, the borrower goes into debt. Credit is the present acquisition, while debt is the promise to make future payment. A creditor cannot exist without a debtor any more than a seller can exist without a buyer.

Sometimes the statement is heard that credit is good but debt is bad. This is about as intelligent as saying that the inside of a cup is more useful than the outside. Undoubtedly both borrowing and lending are unwise under certain circumstances; they are highly desirable under others.

Credit Standing. Credit rests on trust. Because the creditor is giving up something of value in exchange for a mere promise of the debtor to make payment, the person extending credit must have faith in both the *ability* and the *willingness* of the borrower to fulfill his promise.

If I lend money to Jones, who is incompetent, he may well squander the money in unwise ventures. And though Jones may be as honest as the day is long and suffer the torment of the damned because he is unable to keep his word, all his soul's agony doesn't get my money back for me. If, on the other hand, I lend to Smith, a clever scoundrel who is able to turn my money into a fortune for himself, this also will profit me naught if he is unscrupulous enough to want to defraud me and astute enough to find ways of doing it. I can pursue him in the courts (if I can find him), but this is a long, an uncertain, and a costly process.

Therefore any lender wants to make reasonably sure of the *credit standing* of a potential borrower before he gives him credit. Credit standing is usually thought of from the point of view of the borrower; it is his ability to obtain credit. But his ability to borrow is simply the other side of the lender's willingness to lend. And this is based on the creditor's estimate of how good his chances are of getting repayment.

Some creditors examine the creditworthiness of a potential borrower very carefully. What is his past record of payment of obligations? How adequate are his assets compared with his liabilities? Is the venture on which he is embarked well conceived? Is he capable of carrying through the project successfully? Or, if the loan is to a consumer, is his income sufficient in size to permit repayment, and is it likely to continue? Is he well established in the community and not likely to leave in the middle of the night? Commercial banks are usually very strict in their credit evaluation. Other lenders, particularly some retailers selling on credit, are willing to accept the credit standings of customers almost literally at face value—"he has an honest face."

Naturally, the more careful the credit examination, the less likely the creditor is to suffer loss. But even the most careful lenders cannot be completely protected against mistakes, and even the most careless usually find that their loss ratio is fairly small. It is one of the strengths of our economy that most people do meet their obligations and that the faith that credit represents is usually justified.

Types of Credit

We have already indicated that credit may take a great many forms. The major differences can be emphasized by classifying credit in several different ways.

By Source. In terms of the type of lender, credit may be:

1. Individual
2. Mercantile
3. Finance
    a. Commercial banks
    b. Financial intermediaries

Individual credit covers those occasional loans made by individuals or organizations outside of the ordinary course of business. This includes loans between friends as well as the purchase of securities by consumers, nonfinancial corporations, and other institutions (such as universities) with surplus funds on which they want to earn interest.

Mercantile credit is extended by businesses whose primary object is the sale of goods and for whom credit is an adjunct to such sale. This would include retail charge accounts, end-of-month billing by utilities and professional men (such as doctors), open-book sales by one business to another, and installment sales where the dealer himself extends the loan to the purchaser. Mercantile credit finances almost all sales from one business to another as well as a growing volume of sales to consumers.

Finance credit refers to all loans made by institutions for whom lending money is a basic part of their operations—banks, finance companies, savings and loan associations, credit unions, life insurance companies, and so on. Finance credit may be subdivided into commercial bank credit, where the funds lent are newly created by the bank, and all other finance credit, where the lending agency merely acts as intermediary for passing on the savings of others.

By Use. Just as we can distinguish among the lenders, so we can classify loans according to their use by the borrowers:

1. Consumer
2. Government
3. Business
  a. Commercial
  b. Investment

Consumer credit is obtained by an individual in order to buy goods for himself or to pay his own bills, not in the course of business. One of the distinguishing characteristics of consumer credit is that the loan does not give rise to an equivalent ability to repay. Repayment of a consumer loan can come only from the individual's income. To this extent the loan provides him with purchasing power now by mortgaging his future income and reducing purchasing power at the time of repayment.

Government credit represents borrowing by the government in order to make up the difference between tax receipts and expenditures. Like consumer credit, government credit does not lead to increased ability to pay and can be repaid only out of future tax receipts at a time when they exceed expenditures.

Unlike consumer and government loans, business loans are self-liquidating. They directly increase the ability of the borrower to repay because they are put to work in his business and thus (unless he has miscalculated) directly increase his income.

Commercial loans represent borrowing for circulating capital needs. When a retailer uses credit to buy inventory that he expects to sell in a short time, or when a manufacturer buys raw materials that will soon become finished goods that he can sell, this is commercial credit. The sale of the goods gives the business the funds with which to repay the loan with interest and (unless something has gone wrong) some profit. The commercial bank is so named because its primary function was originally conceived to be the provision of commercial credit.

Investment credit is obtained for fixed capital purposes—the provision of plant and equipment. Here again, though it takes longer for the machinery to pay for itself, the product turned out with the aid of the capital equipment will in time return the original cost of the investment and thereby provide the means for repayment of the loan.

By Usance. Usance (or tenor) refers to the length of time that a debt has to run before repayment. Here classification simply draws arbitrary lines between short-term and long-term loans. Recent terminology has introduced the concept of intermediate loans, while some loans must be paid on demand. The result is a fourfold classification:

1. Demand (terminable at the option of either the lender or the borrower)
2. Short-term (less than one year)
3. Intermediate (one to five years)
4. Long-term (more than five years)

In the field of government finance the original maturity is indicated by the name of the instrument:

1. Short-term:
   a. Treasury bills
   b. Certificates
2. Intermediate: notes
3. Long-term: bonds

While bills and certificates are both short-term debts, bills are issued on a fairly regular basis every week and are sold at auction to the highest bidders (those willing to take the lowest interest return). Certificates are issued irregularly and frequently fall due on tax dates, and the Treasury determines the interest rate in advance, hoping to find enough buyers at the rate set. Notes and bonds also have the interest rate set in advance by the Treasury. The use of certificates has been declining; none were issued in 1964.

By Collateral. Credit may also be classified on the basis of whether or not the borrower is required to deposit with the lender some article of value, or the title to it, in order to guarantee repayment. On this basis loans are classified as (1) *secured* or (2) *unsecured.*

Collateral would include securities, jewelry, mortgages on real estate, and chattel mortgages on other property such as automobiles or furniture. In the event of default the lender could sell the collateral to reimburse himself. Loans are generally secured (that is, collateral is required) when the lender is somewhat uncertain of the credit standing of the borrower and wishes to make repayment less risky. The majority of loans are unsecured.

Credit Instruments

The creditor-debtor relationship involves a contract between the two parties. This agreement may be formal or informal. It normally takes one of four forms:

1. Parole credit
2. Open-book credit
3. Promissory note
4. Bill of exchange

Parole Credit. Some debt is incurred simply on the oral promise of the borrower. When I borrow $10 from Joe, I may merely tell him I will pay him next week. The law considers this a perfectly valid and enforceable contract *provided its existence can be proved.* But an oral contract depends entirely on the memory and honesty of the parties to it unless witnesses can be found, and therefore parole credit, more than any other, requires complete confidence in the integrity of the borrower.

Open-book Credit. Open-book credit represents a notation on the books of a seller that he has sold merchandise worth a certain amount to Jones and that Jones, therefore, owes him this amount. In some cases of open-book credit Jones has signed a sales slip certifying that he has received the merchandise and implying his willingness to pay for it. In other cases the buyer is not a party to the written record, and in these instances open-book credit is little better than parole credit; although the seller can produce his books, he cannot show any evidence that the buyer has agreed with the entries. Much merchandise is sold under both types of open-book credit.

Promissory Notes. In transactions where such informal arrangements are not sufficient to satisfy the creditor a promissory note is customarily used. Promissory notes (along with bills of exchange) are *negotiable instruments,* a group of claims given very special legal status. In order to qualify for such status a negotiable instrument must conform strictly to the legal requirements. By law a promissory note is

1. an unconditional promise
2. in writing,
3. signed by the maker,
4. promising to pay a specified sum of money
5. to the order of a specified individual or to bearer
6. at a specified or determinable time.

A simple IOU is a promissory note of sorts, even though it may not conform entirely to these criteria. If its intent is clear, it can be enforced in the courts. But such a promise will not be *negotiable* unless it meets precisely the definition above. The simplest form of negotiable promissory note is shown in Figure 4-1.

Although a promissory note may say a great deal more than the one illustrated—and some run to a full page or more of fine print—it cannot say less and still be negotiable.

This note is in writing (part handwriting, part printing, either of which satisfies the law), signed by Henry R. Madison, who is the *maker* and also the *payer.* He is promising to pay $1,000 to the order of Richard A. Newton (the *payee*) on November 7, 1966. On this note the due date is written in, but this is not necessary since it can be determined by adding sixty days to Sep-

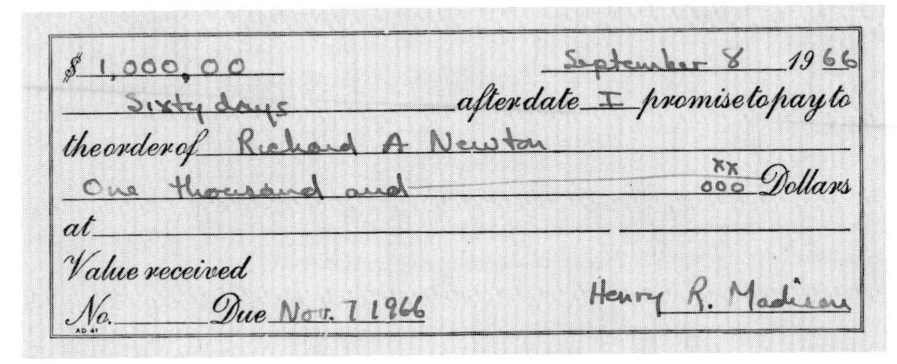
$ 1,000.00 September 8 1966
Sixty days after date I promise to pay to
the order of Richard A Newton
One thousand and xx/000 Dollars
at
Value received
No. Due Nov. 7 1966 Henry R. Madison

Figure 4-1. Simple promissory note.

tember 8. Nor need the other spaces be filled. Some notes are payable on demand. The fact that this money is payable *to the order of* Newton means that Newton may order it paid to someone else if he wishes. This is how a note is negotiated, a process that we will discuss in a moment. As another possibility the note could have been made payable *to bearer,* which means that anyone who holds the note on the due date may claim payment, and ownership is transferred by merely handing it to someone else, who now becomes the bearer.

Most formal evidences of debt are notes. Paper money is in the form of a demand note payable to bearer; a $10 Federal Reserve note says, "The United States of America will pay to the bearer on demand ten dollars." When a bank makes a loan, it requires the borrower to sign a promissory note payable to the bank. Installment contracts have at their heart a promissory note in which several payments are specified, each falling due at a different time. Corporate bonds and government securities are simply promissory notes, while even bond coupons are miniature promissory notes for the amount of the interest due.

Negotiability. The special status held by promissory notes (and bills of exchange) arises from the Uniform Negotiable Instruments Act enacted by all states in this country and by the major trading countries of the world in more or less the same general form. These laws, whose origins can be traced back several centuries, evolved from the desire for a form of asset that could be readily transferred from one owner to another with a minimum of risk. The general law concerning transfer of property states quite clearly that no individual can transfer to another person property rights that he himself does not possess. This introduces considerable uncertainty into transactions where legal rights of ownership are not clearly known.

For example, suppose Brown steals a horse from Adams. Obviously the horse does not belong to Brown, although he has (unlawful) possession of it. Suppose Brown sells this horse to Campbell. Although Campbell paid good money in good faith for the horse, he does not own it. Since Brown didn't own it, he cannot transfer ownership to anyone. If Adams comes along and claims his horse, Campbell is compelled to return it since Adams is the rightful owner, and Campbell is out both the purchase price and the horse—unless he can find Brown and sue him.

Under the Negotiable Instruments Act, however, a purchaser of a negotiable instrument (technically a *holder in due course*) may acquire a greater title than the person from whom he bought it, provided he bought it in good faith without knowledge of any deficiency in the title of the seller. Thus if Adams owned a promissory note payable to bearer, and Brown stole it and sold it to Campbell without Campbell having any way of knowing it was stolen, Campbell will receive full title. If Adams turns up and claims that the note is his, the law will back up Campbell, and in this case it is Adams who has to find Brown and sue him if he wants redress.

This means that a purchaser of a negotiable instrument has complete legal protection in his ownership as long as his purchase was in good faith. This facilitates greatly the use of such instruments in commerce. Imagine the difficulty that would arise if you had to check the legitimacy of the claim of every former owner of a dollar bill before you could be certain that it was legally yours!

Title to a negotiable instrument is transferred by simple delivery if it is payable to bearer or by endorsement and delivery if it is payable to order. There are two general types of endorsement and several restrictive ones. If the payee (the person to whose order the instrument is payable) simply writes his name on it, this is *endorsement in blank,* and it makes the instrument payable to bearer. It may then be transferred further by delivery without endorsement. Instead of endorsement in blank the original payee may endorse it "pay to the order of ———" and then his signature. This gives the new payee all the rights of the initial payee, and he can collect it when due or negotiate it further as he wishes. In either case he must endorse it before passing it on.

Of the restrictive endorsements perhaps the most common is "for deposit only," frequently used on checks. This makes the check useless to anyone who might obtain it illegally since it can be used only for deposit to the account of the endorser. All checks deposited by mail should be so endorsed for safety.

Bills of Exchange. A check, however, is not a promissory note. It belongs in another category of negotiable instruments: bills of exchange. A bill of exchange, as defined by law, is

1. an unconditional order
2. in writing,
3. signed by the drawer,
4. ordering a specified individual
5. to pay a specified sum of money
6. to the order of a specified individual or to bearer
7. at a specified or determinable time.

The chief difference between a promissory note and a bill of exchange is that the former is a promise, while the latter is an order. The most common form of bill of exchange in domestic use is the bank check, illustrated in Figure 4-2.

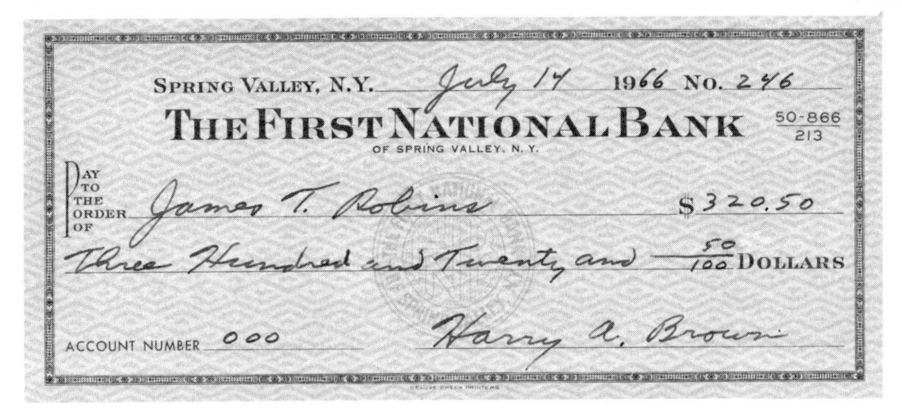
SPRING VALLEY, N.Y. July 14 1966 NO. 246
THE FIRST NATIONAL BANK 50-866/213
OF SPRING VALLEY, N. Y.
PAY TO THE ORDER OF James T. Robins $320.50
Three Hundred and Twenty and 50/100 DOLLARS
ACCOUNT NUMBER 000 Harry A. Brown

Figure 4-2. Bank check. *(Courtesy of the First National Bank of Spring Valley, N.Y.)*

Note that in a bill of exchange there are three parties: the *drawer,* Brown, who is ordering the *drawee,* the First National Bank of Spring Valley (also called the payer) to pay the *payee,* Robins. In a bill of exchange there must be some relationship between the drawer and the drawee that the bill itself does not show; that is, the drawer must have some right to order the drawee to make payment. In a bank check the relation is that of the depositor to his bank. The bank has promised to honor the depositor's checks, and so he is writing one on his account.

Bills of exchange are frequently used also in international trade where the drawer is an exporter ordering the drawee, an importer in another country, to pay for merchandise which he has bought. Further examination of this type of bill will be deferred to Chapter 36.

If you compare the bank check with the list of requirements mentioned in the definition of a bill of exchange, it may seem that one of them—a specified or determinable time—is not present. In any other kind of bill of exchange, the time of payment would be specified in the same way that it is on a promissory note, but in the bank check the time is by invariable custom *on demand.* In spite of the fact that the time is not stated, therefore, it is determinable. A check must be honored by the bank on which it is drawn as soon as it is presented for payment.

Interest Rates: The Cost of Credit

Since a bird in the hand is worth two in the bush, a price is usually charged for providing something of value today in exchange for a promise of payment sometime in the future. This is interest, the cost of acquiring credit.

Figure 4-3. Steel check. This odd specimen demonstrates that as long as the basic requirements of a bill of exchange are met, the other attributes of a check do not matter. It represents the first prize in a welding contest and was produced by welding on a steel plate, 1 by 2 feet in size. The check was duly honored by the Cleveland Trust Company and was canceled with machine-gun bullets. *(Courtesy of the Chase Manhattan Bank Museum of Moneys of the World, New York.)*

The interest rate, unlike any other price, is not normally stated as so many dollars and cents but as a proportion of the value of the thing borrowed. Even when stated as a dollar sum (as, for instance, a 50-cent service charge on a deferred payment), this amount is relatively meaningless unless it is related to the principal of the loan. Interest is a percentage. But there is considerable confusion over the meaning of the percentage.

Interest as a Time Rate. Interest is not a simple ratio; it is a time rate and must take into account the time period involved. If I borrow $100 and pay back $105, the $5 premium I pay is obviously 5 per cent of the $100 borrowed. If I have borrowed the money for one year, the cost is 5 per cent *per year*. But if I borrowed it for only one month, the cost is 5 per cent *per month*, or 60 per cent per year. While both of these payments may be spoken of as 5 per cent interest, such a use of the word in the second case is highly misleading unless it is qualified. In a technical sense *the rate of interest always means the rate per year* unless otherwise specified. When a small-loan company charges 2½ per cent per month, the interest rate is 30 per cent.

Interest and Discount. Although for a large number of loans the interest charge is added to the principal as in the preceding examples ($100 borrowed plus $5 interest equals $105 returned), many lenders, particularly commercial banks, *deduct* the interest from the amount given to the borrower. On a $100 loan they will subtract $5, giving the borrower $95 and asking him to repay $100. The interest *cost* is the same in both cases, but the interest *rate* is different. In the first case the interest rate is 5 per cent ($5 for the use of $100). In the second the interest rate is 5.26 per cent ($5 for the use of $95). In this second case we would call 5 per cent the *discount rate* rather than the interest rate because it is deducted (discounted) from the face of the note before the borrower gets his money. Whenever an interest charge is stated as a discount rate, the true interest rate is somewhat higher than the nominal figure quoted.

Service Charges. Another way in which the interest rate may be understated is through the addition of charges which are actually a part of the cost of borrowing but which are stated separately. Thus I may borrow $100 at 5 per cent "interest" but have to pay a $2 service charge in addition. In this case (assuming the duration of the loan to be a year) I am actually paying 7 per cent interest.

In many cases when goods are sold "on time" the extra cost of not paying cash is indicated in the difference between the cash price and the time price either with or without an additional "interest" charge. This difference is obviously part of the interest cost.

It should be clear that an accurate measure of the real interest rate paid for the use of money can be obtained only by finding the precise proportion between the amount of funds actually received by the borrower (or the net cash price of the merchandise received) and the *total* amount paid for the use of the funds. This payment must then be translated into the rate per *year* if a different payment period is involved.

Amortization. Even when we have done this, we may not be at the end of the process. The most difficult problem in the determination of the annual interest rate occurs when the loan is paid back in installments. If I borrow $100 at 8 per cent "interest" and repay the loan (including interest) in 12 monthly installments of $9 each, it is obvious that I have not had the use of the full amount for a year. Therefore I am not paying $8 for the use of $100 for a year, but rather for the use of $100 for one month, of $91 for another month (after I have made the first $9 payment), of $82 for a month, and so on. In reality I have had the use of only half of the $100 averaged over the full-year period; more in the earlier months, less in the later. The actual interest rate is therefore not 8 per cent, but something close to double that amount.

The Interest Rate Formula. Because it is not immediately apparent how to reduce the payment in our last example to an annual rate, and because the greater part of all consumer loans are actually of this type, it is convenient to have a formula that can be applied to any kind of loan in which equal repayments are made at regular intervals. While there are several such formulas, differing slightly in refinement, the simplest and most commonly used is

$$i = \frac{2MC}{P(N + 1)}$$

where $i =$ true interest rate

$M =$ length of payment period divided into a year, without regard to number of payments actually made (where payments are monthly, $M = 12$; where they are weekly, $M = 52$; where they are quarterly, $M = 4$)

$C =$ total dollar amount of charges paid for the loan

$P =$ amount of credit actually received (principal)

$N =$ number of repayment installments made

Many bank loans are made at 6 per cent "interest," which is in reality a discount, and with 12 monthly payments. On a $100 loan $6 would be deducted in advance, the borrower would receive $94, and he would repay $100 in 12 installments. The actual interest rate can be easily determined by the following formula:

$$i = \frac{2 \times 12 \times 6}{94 \times (12 + 1)} = 11.78 \text{ per cent}$$

This, in fact, is a general case that may be summarized as a rule of thumb: at x per cent discount with repayment in 12 monthly installments, the true interest rate is approximately $2x$ per cent.[1]

Let us take another, slightly more complicated example from an actual case. A merchant sells goods worth $40. He requires a 20 per cent down payment ($8) and charges a $3 service charge for carrying the $32 balance. Payment must be made at the rate of $5 per month, and since the total payment is $35, this means seven installments.

$$i = \frac{2 \times 12 \times 3}{32 \times (7 + 1)} = 28.13 \text{ per cent}$$

Except for the fact that they are normally discounts (which slightly understate the rate), most published interest rates of *business* loans are true interest rates, correctly adjusted for the time element. Interest rates on mortgages are also true interest rates. In the field of consumer credit, however, utter confusion reigns, and all published rates should be taken with a whole handful of salt until they have been refined by means of the formula given above.

In 1960 Senator Douglas and nineteen colleagues introduced into Congress a bill that would require installment sellers and other lenders to state clearly not only the actual interest charge involved in each credit transaction, but also the true annual rate of interest. One objection to the bill raised by businessmen was that the installment credit field, in particular, was so chaotic that even the lenders themselves couldn't determine what rate of interest they were charging. Although hearings have been held sporadically, the bill had still not reached the floor of Congress by 1965.

Interest Yield and the Price of Securities. There is still another way in which interest rates may be confusing. When an interest rate is printed on a bond (or

[1] This generalization understates the true rate of interest for discounts of more than 7½ per cent, the understatement becoming progressively greater as the discount rises.

other similar security), it is stated as a percentage of the *face value.* A $1,000 bond with a stated interest rate of 3 per cent pays $30 per year interest. This is actually a 3 per cent interest yield *if* the purchaser of the bond pays $1,000 for it. But if he can buy such a bond at, say, $800, then it should be clear that he is earning $30 a year for a loan of $800, and this is not 3 per cent but $30/$800 = 3¾ per cent. In addition, if he holds the bond to maturity, he will receive the full $1,000 principal, which represents $200 more than he paid for it. What percentage return this $200 represents depends on the length of time the bond has to run until maturity.

If it is repayable within one year, the $200 represents an additional 25 per cent, or a total (with the $30 interest payment) of 28¾ per cent. If, on the other hand, the bond has twenty years to run, then the $200 represents an average of $10 per year appreciation in value of the investment, and the annual interest yield might appear to be $30 + $10/$800 = 5 per cent. On the other hand, this calculation assumes that the $10 is actually received each year rather than in a lump sum at the end of the period. The mathematical calculations necessary to adjust for the fact that the appreciation is not received annually are fairly complicated, and it is easier in cases of this kind to look up the answer in published bond yield tables, which have been prepared specifically to provide such information in readily readable form. In this particular case the bond table shows that the actual yield is slightly more than 4½ per cent.[2]

In one respect the foregoing example tackled the problem backward, for it *assumed* that the bond could be bought for $800. Why should such a bond sell for so low a price? For one thing, it is possible that the issuer has run into difficulties, so that purchasers have some doubt about his ability to repay the bond; that is, the risk may have increased. But even with no change in risk, such a situation will occur naturally if interest rates in general rise.

When the bond was issued, 3 per cent was apparently the proper interest rate for securities of this type. But now, perhaps ten years later, the interest rate structure has risen, and new bonds of the same type are being issued at 4½ per cent. This means that anyone buying a newly issued bond for $1,000 will receive $45 a year in interest. No one then will pay $1,000 for a bond that yields only $30 per year. How much will he pay for such a bond? He will pay that amount which will yield him (including interest and appreciation of

[2] The following equation can be used as a rough rule of thumb to approximate the interest yields shown in a bond table:

$$\frac{\text{Interest per year (in dollars)} + \dfrac{\text{appreciation to maturity (in dollars)}}{\text{number of years to maturity}}}{\dfrac{\text{Purchase price} + \text{maturity price}}{2}}$$

In our example this turns out to be

$$\frac{\$30 + \dfrac{\$200}{\$20}}{\dfrac{\$800 + \$1{,}000}{2}} = \frac{30 + 10}{900} = 4.44 \text{ per cent}$$

principal, taking into account the fact that he won't receive the appreciation until maturity) the same 4½ per cent being offered on new bonds. What that price will be can be determined from the bond tables, and a glance at the tables shows that this is $803.50.

Although this example is couched in the language of computation, it illustrates a basic relation between changes in the interest rate structure and changes in the prices of securities. A rise in interest rates in our example pushed the price of securities down. In the alternative case a fall in interest rates would raise the prices of earlier-issued securities. This is simply because an investor will not accept a lower yield when he buys an old security than he can get on a new one. Since the old security pays a fixed dollar amount, its yield can rise only if its price falls. Similarly its yield will fall as its price rises. Hence if interest rates in general are falling, buyers will attempt to buy the old securities with their higher dollar returns until this increased demand forces up the price of the old securities to the point where their yield is equal to that of the present interest rate structure of new securities. Mathematically, interest yield and security prices move in opposite directions.

Compounding. One further refinement of interest rate calculations may be mentioned briefly. The interest rate formula is based on the theory that interest is payable at the end of the payment period. I lend $100 and get back $106 at the end of the year, indicating a simple interest rate of 6 per cent. But if I get back $3 in six months plus $103 in twelve, I have the opportunity of lending the $3 for six months and earning interest on that as well (9 cents if the interest rate is 6 per cent).

We speak of interest as being *compounded* when it is paid on the interest as well as on the principal of a loan, and this is the normal practice for savings institutions. Our example shows that $100 at 6 per cent interest compounded semiannually yields $6.09 for the year; the true interest yield is thus 6.09 per cent. Similarly if 6 per cent interest is compounded quarterly, the yield rises to 6.14 per cent; compounded monthly, it becomes 6.17 per cent; and compounded daily (as at some savings and loan associations), it would be 6.19 per cent.

Questions for Thought and Discussion

1. What is the difference between credit, credit standing, and credit instrument?

2. Can you think of any transaction you have carried on within the past year that did not involve credit or a credit instrument?

3. John Wanamaker once said that a businessman should always be in debt since he ought to be able to earn more in his business than the going interest rate. Is this sound advice?

4. Why is business credit self-liquidating while consumer credit and government credit are not?

5. Is it safe for businessmen to sell goods on open-book account without getting the customer's signature on the sales slip? Why is so much business carried on in this manner?

6. Suppose I wrote a note promising to pay $10 to the order of Joe White when (if?) he got married. Would this be a negotiable instrument?

7. Suppose I wrote a note promising to pay $10 on June 10, 1965, "to Tom Beck only." Would this be a negotiable instrument?

8. Since a bank check is merely an order to the bank to pay a certain sum of money, what is to prevent me from writing such an order on a bank in which I have no account?

9. If you have borrowed money or purchased goods on the installment plan recently, compute the true rate of interest you were charged.

10. Suppose you buy a car worth $3,000. The dealer accepts your old car, worth $1,050, as down payment. He adds $450 to your bill for the premium on insurance. You make monthly payments of $87.25 for thirty-six months. What is the true rate of interest you are paying?

Selected Bibliography

American Bankers Association: *Savings Interest: Methods and Procedures for Computing and Paying Interest on Savings Accounts,* New York, 1964.

American Institute of Banking: *Negotiable Instruments,* New York, 1947.

Ettinger, Richard P., and David E. Golieb: *Credits and Collections,* 5th ed., Prentice-Hall, Inc., Englewood Cliffs, N.J., 1962.

Green, T. F., Jr.: *Practical Summary of Negotiable Instruments,* Longmans, Green & Co., Inc., New York, 1938.

Robinson, Roland I. (ed.): *Financial Institutions,* 3d ed., Richard D. Irwin, Inc., Homewood, Ill., 1960.

Wyatt, John W., and Madie B. Wyatt: *Business Law,* 2d ed., McGraw-Hill Book Company, New York, 1963.

See also references listed under Chapters 16 and 29.

Part Two
Banking

Chapter 5
The Origins of Modern Banking

Thou oughtest therefore to have put money to the exchangers, and then at my coming I should have received mine own with usury.

Matthew 25:27

Our discussion of money in the preceding chapters has concentrated mostly on currency, the easiest part of the money supply to see and understand. We did point out, however, that bank deposits are part of the money supply also and that banks are important monetary institutions. If we go back now and follow the development of the banking process, it will help us to understand the banking system as it exists today.

Early Banking Operations

Like coinage, banking as we know it was never invented; it developed out of the needs of the times. Lending, even at interest, predates money itself, for commodities can be lent; the Code of Hammurabi (about 1900 B.C.) deals with debts and mortgages. Even when lending became an organized activity, it was often a sideline to some other business, as was the later acceptance of deposits. Money changing was perhaps the first full-time banking occupation; it arose from the need for some machinery for exchanging the multitude of different coins issued by both prince and merchant.

These banking functions were known in the pre-Christian era. But while the use of coins in Europe declined significantly after the fall of Rome, banking functions disappeared utterly. As the Western world emerged from the wreckage of the Roman Empire, monetary institutions were slowly re-created in response to the needs of a newly awakened commerce. Merchants reintroduced coinage, monarchs again preempted the right of both coinage and debasement, the requirements of a new economic activity called forth institutions designed to facilitate payment, and a new monetary system arose and developed to meet the demands of the times.

The institutions that we find in this early period were hardly banks as we know them today. Frequently their monetary operations were offshoots of some other activity. Only gradually were these pursuits combined into a special business. Even today our financial machinery is composed of many diverse, often overlapping agencies, still adapting themselves to the shifting patterns of commerce and industry. Any history of banking shows a kaleidoscopic picture of infinite variety and change. Here we can examine only a few of the highlights.

Monks and Templars. Among the earliest financial operations in post-Roman Europe were those carried on incidentally by religious orders. Because of their own great wealth and their immunity from sacrilegious depredations, the monasteries had emerged as early as the tenth century as important centers of finance, particularly on the European continent. They accepted articles of value (whether money or goods) for safekeeping and frequently acted as paying agents and trustees.

These functions were also performed by the rising militant religious orders, whose names are normally associated with the Crusades but who also loom large in financial history. The Knights Templars, in particular, were the most important financial power in Europe during the thirteenth century. They accepted for safekeeping the wealth of both kings and merchants. They acted as fiscal agents for the kings of France, collecting taxes and making payments as directed. Out of their vast wealth they made loans to prince and peasant, and they sometimes acted as guarantor of loans made by others. When Philip IV of France dissolved the order in 1307, he erased a debt to the Temple of over ½ million gold livres. Aided by their vast network of temples stretching across Europe, they were able to transfer funds by receiving money at one office and paying it out at another without the necessity of shipping the actual coin. They also effected book transfers between merchants in the same city who kept accounts with the Temple. Unquestionably the Knights Templars laid the foundation for much of the subsequent development of banking.

Jews and Lombards. Although the religious orders did make loans, church law put a damper on lending activity by banning usury, which in those days meant any interest charge. The church, looking primarily at loans to the poor, felt that interest meant profiting from the misfortunes of others. Yet the church could not eliminate the desire for loans. The individual impoverished by misfortune or prodigality, the merchant desiring to finance a trading expedition, the monarch with an empty treasury and a war to fight—all looked to a lender for aid. And lenders were found to meet the need. Some were outside the pale of the church and not subject to its laws; some were granted special immunity by the church itself; and others operated in defiance of the ban on usury.

Jews had always been active in what little commerce existed, and as both trade and money developed, it was natural for them to branch out into money changing and moneylending. Their activities covered all the mercantile towns of Europe, but their rapid rise and even more abrupt fall are illustrated most clearly in the case of England.

William the Conqueror, anxious to attract their wealth and talent, gave Jews special privileges, allowing them to charge as much as 45 per cent interest—while collecting from them vast taxes and borrowing freely. In the thirteenth century, however, the political climate changed, others were found who would do the work more cheaply, and the royal protection was withdrawn. Gradually the Jews were subjected to greater and greater persecution, until in 1290 they were ordered to leave the country under penalty of death.

The place of the Jews was taken by the Lombard bankers, financiers from various parts of Italy who extended their operations throughout Europe and in the process gave their name to a financial street in London and for a time to the very process of banking itself. The Lombards achieved their success by reason of papal indulgence. Through their widespread net of offices they acted as collection agents for church funds destined for Rome. In return for this service they were exempted from the ban on usury and made loans to merchants and kings as well as to the Pope himself until they in time also lost their special position to others.

The Great Financiers. As trade and wealth grew, so did the size and scope of lending operations. The power of money was making itself felt as never before, and money was eagerly sought after on almost any terms. Ehrenberg says of the period of the Renaissance: "Never since the time of the Roman empire had everything been so easily bought with money: the highest ecclesiastical and worldly dignities, the blood of men, the honour of the greatest ladies, and eternal salvation itself."[1]

To meet this great need for money many financial houses arose, obtaining funds originally from their own private fortunes. The names of several of these families are writ large on medieval and Renaissance finance. The Bardi and the Peruzzi belong to the Lombards. Their place was taken in Italy by the Medici and the Strozzi. William de la Pole, in England, and Jacques Coeur, in France, were briefly important. Germany produced the Fuggers and the Rothschilds, the latter carrying on the family tradition even to the present day. Of these great financial dynasties the Medici are undoubtedly the most picturesque, combining banking with romance, political skulduggery, and murder. But the Fuggers, whose very name suggests the plodding, lackluster German, wielded more economic power in their day.

[1] Richard Ehrenberg, *Capital and Finance in the Age of the Renaissance* (Harcourt, Brace & World, Inc., New York, 1928), p. 25.

The Fuggers started building their fortune as weavers as early as 1367. Then they became merchants, dealing in spices and cloth. As their wealth grew, they extended their activities into mining and by 1492 had acquired sufficient capital to extend loans to the Holy Roman Emperor. During the next century their rise and fall were spectacular.

> The Fuggers, thanks to judicious loans to Maximilian, had acquired enormous concessions of mineral property, farmed a large part of the receipts drawn by the Spanish Crown from its estates, held silver and quicksilver mines in Spain, and controlled banking and commercial businesses in Italy, and, above all, at Antwerp. They advanced the money which made Albrecht of Brandenburg archbishop of Mainz; repaid themselves by sending their agent to accompany Tetzel on his campaign to raise money by indulgences and taking half the proceeds; provided the funds with which Charles V bought the imperial crown, after an election conducted with the publicity of an auction and the morals of a gambling hell; browbeat him, when the debt was not paid, in the tone of a pawnbroker rating a necessitous client; and found the money with which Charles raised troops to fight the Protestants in 1552. The head of the firm built a church and endowed an almshouse for the aged poor in his native town of Augsburg. He died in the odor of sanctity, a good Catholic and a Count of the Empire, having seen his firm pay 54 per cent for the preceding sixteen years.[2]

But the luck of the firm ran out in 1557, when the Hapsburgs defaulted on their debts, and the Fuggers started a long decline into oblivion.

Transfer of Funds. While the financiers were developing the loan business, other important banking developments were taking place among the merchants. Many of these centered on the improvement of arrangements for transferring funds. Payment could always be made by delivery of coins, but for large sums or over long distances this was distinctly inconvenient. The multitude of devices which arose to ease the burdens of transfer almost defy description.

Bills of Exchange. At the heart of many transfers lies the *bill of exchange,* which is essentially an order by one person to another, requiring him to make payment to a third. The bank check is a modern bill of exchange.

The bill of exchange probably existed in Roman times; it was certainly used extensively in the Middle Ages. When an Amsterdam citizen of the twelfth century wanted to make a payment to someone in England, he could buy from the Knights Templars a bill drawn on the London Temple payable to that person. A merchant who was owed money by a foreign debtor could draw a bill of exchange against him and sell it to a traveler who wanted money in the foreign city. Thus the merchant was paid his debt and the traveler obtained money at his destination without the risk of carrying coin with him.

[2] R. H. Tawney, *Religion and the Rise of Capitalism* (Harcourt, Brace & World, Inc., New York, 1926), p. 79; quoted by permission.

Bills of exchange were also used domestically. At the great international fairs such as those at Leipzig and Lyons, merchants, wishing to carry as little cash as possible from fair to fair, would often settle their purchase with bills of exchange, the seller drawing a bill on the buyer for the amount of the sale, dating the bill to fall due at the next fair. At that time payment might be made or the bill offset by others calling for payment in the opposite direction. Elaborate machinery was devised for offsetting debts against each other by means of book transactions without the need for using cash except for the settlement of net balances.

Bourses. Among the institutions developed to facilitate the handling of both foreign and domestic bills of exchange the great bourses—especially those at Antwerp and Lyons—were the most important. Just as the fairs brought together the buyers and sellers of commodities, so the bourses brought together the buyers and sellers of bills. The provision of an organized market at which such instruments could be traded made it a great deal easier to match the financial needs of merchants and others who had occasion to transfer funds.

Later the bourses became centers for the flotation of government debt, which was by this time too large to be handled by a single financial house. The bourses also operated as channels through which other loans were placed, and as securities of private companies entered the picture, the bourses took on many of the aspects of a modern stock exchange. The bourses had developed into well-established financial institutions by the middle of the sixteenth century.

Banks of Deposit. Although their contribution to the evolution of banking was relatively minor, a few words should be said about the great banks of deposit (giro banks), whose primary task lay in the provision of a sound currency. While coinage was widespread at this period, its very universality presented numerous problems. Coinage in England and in a few other countries was fairly centralized in the king. But the Italian cities, the German states, and many principalities of various descriptions all issued their own coin. Any trade between these areas was hampered by the multiplicity of monetary systems. In addition, even coins of the same monarch were often of different weights or fineness as a result of normal wear, clipping, or imperial debasement.

The consequent confusion gave rise to money changers and, in a more organized market, to giro banks. The giro banks accepted silver coins for deposit on the basis of their weight rather than their face value, issued their own bank credit in exchange for these coins, and kept a 100 per cent silver reserve against their credits so that deposits could be withdrawn at any time in the stated weight of silver. Their sole purpose was to provide a medium of exchange that would be more stable than the silver coins themselves, for their deposits were uniform in value and not subject to abrasion or debasement.

Giro banks were established in Venice, Genoa, Amsterdam, Nuremburg, and Hamburg. The Bank of Amsterdam (Amsterdamsche Wisselbank), founded in 1609, was the most noted, and for a while its bank money was used for payments not only in Amsterdam but also in many of the trading centers of Europe. Unfortunately the Bank, in great secrecy, made loans to the city of Amsterdam out of its silver reserve, thus reducing its stock of coin below the value of its outstanding obligations. When this was discovered, public confidence in the Bank was lost, and it finally dissolved in 1820.

By this time the improvement of the coinage had made giro banks less necessary, and one by one they passed into history, the last to go being the Bank of Hamburg. This bank remained true to the 100 per cent reserve principle to the end and was finally closed by government decree as part of the general revision of the German monetary system in 1874.

The Goldsmiths

None of the institutions so far mentioned, important as they all were in the financial development of Europe, was a bank in anything approaching the modern sense. Many of the operations they introduced have been taken over by banks, but the essence of commercial banking—the creation of money—was not part of their work. The development of this vital banking process is illustrated most clearly by the history of the goldsmiths.

Goldsmiths, or jewelers, have existed since earliest times and carried on their work throughout the known world. (One of their number, Benvenuto Cellini, carved a permanent place for himself by adding writing to his other talents.) In the seventeenth century, and particularly in England, some of them added a number of sidelines to their trade that eventually turned them into the first full-fledged bankers.

The goldsmith combined two characteristics that laid the groundwork for his role as banker, both of them growing out of the fact that only a man of wealth could afford the raw materials of the jeweler's craft. In the first place, because he was a man of substance the goldsmith was frequently asked for loans by his friends, his business associates, and even his king.[3] Second, because he continually had large quantities of valuable merchandise in his shop he had of necessity provided himself with the means of keeping his valuables safe from the itching fingers of others. In consequence he was able, on occasion, to rent space in his vault to merchants or others who wished to obtain security for large sums of money.

Deposits. Like the monasteries, the goldsmith first accepted boxes locked and sealed by their owners, redelivering the same unopened chest. Later it became more common for customers to deposit certain sums of money, receiving a receipt, which might read something like this:

[3] One interesting sidelight of history is that Johann Fust, a goldsmith of Mainz, lent Gutenberg the money needed to complete the printing of the first Bible.

October 31, 1611

This certifies that I have received from George Merchant two hundred gold sovereigns, repayable to him on demand.

(signed) Joe Smith

This is basically a warehouse receipt, but of a special type. It didn't matter whether George got back the same 200 pieces he turned over or some other pieces. The worth would be the same. In other words he could not claim that any particular coins were his (as he could if he had left a sealed box). He could require only that the goldsmith pay him *some* 200 sovereigns. He had, in fact, lost title to his coins and had become the creditor of the goldsmith on a demand loan. The goldsmith obtained ownership of the coins and could do with them as he wished as long as he was prepared to pay any claimant on demand. Without this distinction between deposit and safekeeping, banking as we know it would be impossible.

Clearing. Now suppose George, with this receipt in his pocket, went to the market and found some Italian pottery worth £200 that he wanted to buy. He might say to William Potter, "I'll take these goods, but I don't have their price with me. Hold them for me a few minutes while I go down to the smith's to get the money."

"Oh," says Bill, "you keep your money with Joe Smith? So do I. If you carted the gold down here, I would only have to lug it back again. Why don't you just write him a note asking him to transfer it to my account and save us all trouble?"

So George would write a note to the goldsmith, asking him to pay the 200 sovereigns to William Potter instead of to himself. Thus originated the modern check (see Figure 5-1). Its use reduced the need to carry large sums of bulky coin.

Bank Notes. It became even easier to transfer funds when the goldsmiths began to make receipts payable to the bearer and to issue them in standard denominations. The depositor would receive several notes of small denominations rather than a single receipt for the amount of his deposit and could make payments of whatever size he desired merely by handing the paper over to his creditors. The notes might then read:

July 29, 1657

This is to certify that I have on deposit five gold sovereigns, payable to the bearer on demand.

(signed) Joe Smith

Goldsmiths' notes similar to this circulated widely in England in the latter part of the seventeenth century (see Figure 5-2). Such notes are direct forerunners of the bank notes common in this country as elsewhere in the nineteenth century and are near relatives of our present-day paper money.

As people became accustomed to them, goldsmiths' notes passed readily

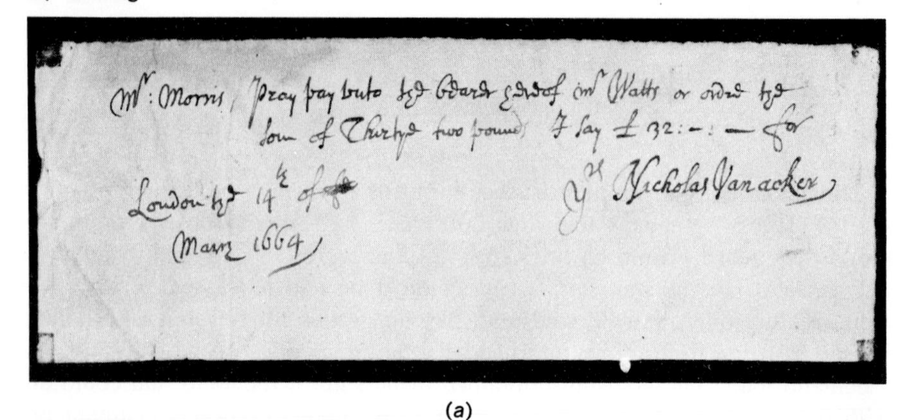

(*a*)

(*b*)

Figure 5-1. Two early checks. (*a*) "Mr. Morris. Pray pay unto the bearer hereof Mr. Watts or order the som of Thirtye two pounds. I say £32:–:– for Y[our] se[rvant] Nicholas Vanacker. London the 14th of March 1664." (*Courtesy of the Chase Manhattan Bank Museum of Moneys of the World, New York.*)
(*b*) "Mr. Thomas Ffowles. I desire you to pay unto Mr. Samuel Howard or order upon receipt hereof the sum of nine pounds thirteene shillings and sixe pence and place it to the account of Yor Servant Edmond Warcupp. 14 Augt 1675. £9:13:6d. Ffor Mr. Thomas Ffowles Gouldsmith at his shop between the two temple gates, Ffleete streete." The endorsement on the back reads: "Rcd in full of this bill the sume of nine pounds thirteen shillings sixpence. Saml. Howard." (*Courtesy of the Library of the Institute of Bankers, London.*)

from hand to hand in substitution for the gold or silver that they represented. Thus paper bills, like coinage, were developed not by governments but by private individuals casting around for ways to improve the means of carrying on trade. Since merchants and others found this paper convenient for making payments, it became money, generally accepted as a medium of exchange.

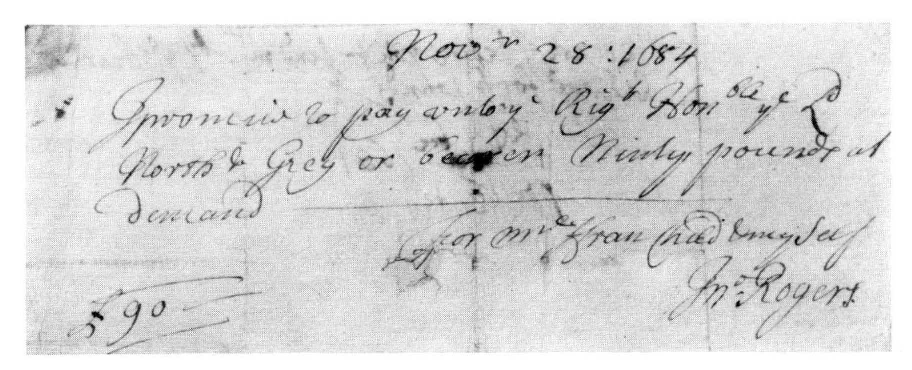

Novr 28: 1684
I promise to pay unto ye Rig^t Honble ye L^d
North & Grey or bearer Ninety pounds at
demand
for Mr Fran Child & my Self
Jno Rogers
£90

Figure 5-2. A goldsmith's note. This is one of the earliest examples still in existence. It reads: "November 28: 1684. I promise to pay unto ye Rig[h]t Hon[ora]ble ye L[or]d North & Grey or bearer Ninety pounds at demand. £90. for Mr. Fran[cis] Child & myself, Jno. Rogers." *(Courtesy of Glyn, Mills & Co., London.)*

Money Creation. The goldsmith was now heavily engaged in two activities that were destined to merge into the modern bank: lending and acceptance of deposits. Up to this point in our narrative these activities were separate. The goldsmith loaned his own funds; he accepted deposits only for safekeeping and maintained a 100 per cent reserve against all his outstanding notes. His notes therefore merely represented the gold in his vault and circulated in place of it.

But suppose one day Harry Hooper came into Joe Smith's shop and said, "I have a bill for supplies for my barrel factory, and I need £50 to pay it. How about a loan for 60 days?"

Joe replied sadly, "I'm sorry, Harry. I'd like to do it, but I'm a little short of funds myself." But then he thought an evil thought. He had £10,000 worth of gold and silver coin that belonged to his depositors. Of course he had to pay this amount whenever the depositors asked for it—*but they never all came in at once.* As some asked for coin, others were depositing more, and there was *always* a fairly large stock of coin in his vaults. Who would know if he lent £50 to Harry? "Sure, Harry, I think I can manage it." And he gave him £50 of his customers' coin, to be repaid—with interest—in two months.

At this precise instant fractional-reserve banking was born. While lending was common prior to this period, loans had always been made from the lender's own funds. Here for the first time a banker has created money out of thin air. Harry has 50 sovereigns which he didn't have before; the original owner of these sovereigns has a goldsmith's note representing them, which he can use to make payments just as readily as if he had the coins themselves. The same 50 sovereigns are thus being used as purchasing power by two separate individuals.

Let's go back over the effect which the goldsmith has had on the community up to this point. Suppose that originally the community had a metallic coin circulation of £60,000:

Money supply: £60,000 coin

Now assume that people deposit £10,000 in coin in exchange for the goldsmith's notes. The total circulation has not changed at all. Gold has been removed from circulation to the safety of the goldsmith's vaults, while its place is taken by the newly issued notes that pass as money in its stead:

Money supply:	£50,000	coin
	10,000	goldsmith's notes
	£60,000	

Goldsmith's reserve against notes: £10,000 coin

When the goldsmith lends Harry Hooper 50 sovereigns from his reserve, the paper circulation remains the same, but the coin circulation is increased by this £50 taken out of storage:

Money supply:	£50,050	coin
	10,000	goldsmith's notes
	£60,050	

Goldsmith's reserve against notes: £9,950 coin

The goldsmith has increased the money supply by £50. He has created money. And he has done it by reducing his reserve below the level of notes outstanding against it.

As a matter of fact there is no particular reason why the goldsmith must give Harry coin. If goldsmiths' notes are generally acceptable, Harry can use them to pay his bill. So all the goldsmith really has to do is to write another note for £50, certifying that there is that amount on deposit (which there is not), and lend this to Harry. This is a different method of creating money, but the result is similar:

Money supply:	£50,000	coin
	10,050	goldsmith's notes
	£60,050	

Goldsmith's reserve against notes: £10,000 coin

In both cases the effective money supply has been increased by £50. In both cases the smith has created money by reducing his coin reserve below the amount of notes owed to his customers. In both cases he is engaged in fractional-reserve banking.

The essence of fractional-reserve banking lies in the creation of more demand liabilities (which circulate as money) than the banker would be able to pay *if all creditors asked for payment at the same time*. The quantity of goldsmiths' notes that can be issued against a given reserve depends entirely on the actual desire of noteholders to redeem them in coin. This desire depends in turn on the temper of the times, and the goldsmith attempts to estimate it on the basis of past experience. If not more than half of his customers have ever come in asking for redemption at one time (before others have come in to make new deposits), the goldsmith can afford to keep only half of his deposits in coin—plus some additional amount as a margin of safety. Putting the matter another way, he can afford to issue notes (by loan or otherwise) in an amount equal to approximately twice his gold reserve. If no more than 10 per cent of his creditors ask for coin at the same time, he may presumably lower his reserve to 10 per cent, creating notes up to ten times his reserve.

But heaven help him if he underestimated! Suppose he had a 50 per cent reserve, but suddently people wanted more coin for some reason and demanded it in excess of his stock. He would be bankrupt. In this early period he would very likely be tarred and feathered or even drowned in the nearest millpond. This sudden desire on the part of noteholders to get their money back is referred to in modern terms as a *run on the bank*. Pepys's diary records the first such run known, when the defeat of the British fleet by the Dutch at Chatham (1667) led to a general rush to obtain gold.

The calculation of the amount of money which a goldsmith may lend on the basis of a given reserve becomes both a science and an art. Those who keep too large a reserve lose the opportunity of earning interest on a larger note circulation. Those who keep too small a reserve suffer failure on the day of retribution. There is no formula for finding the magic number. Only experience, wisdom, and perhaps a little good luck can give the answer. And of course the figure changes as conditions change. Fifty per cent reserves were too low in the early days of fractional-reserve banking; two per cent in cash seems adequate at most times for banks in our highly developed financial market in the United States today.

The banker-goldsmiths illustrate perfectly the basic principles of commercial banking and the money-creating function. Their development, like that of most institutions, was a slow one, but they gradually emerged into the forefront of monetary institutions, finally giving up their original goldsmith craft and turning their attention exclusively to finance. After the Great Fire (1666) burned Goldsmiths' Row, they moved into Lombard Street, thus inheriting the location as well as much of the business of the Lombards. The time was ripe for the development of banking on a larger, more highly organized, and less individual scale. New forms, new institutions emerged, but the basic principles of the goldsmiths remain even to this day.

The Chartered Banks

Important as they were in pioneering a new field, the goldsmiths were soon overshadowed by the growth of corporate banking and in particular by the great chartered banks.

The Bank of Sweden. The first of these, the Bank of Sweden, owes its origin to John Palmstruch, head of the Swedish Merchants' Guild, who obtained a government charter for a loan and credit bank in 1656. Palmstruch was well acquainted with the public giro banks, but he considered that their maintenance of a 100 per cent reserve was unduly conservative and reduced the usefulness of the bank. He seems to have gone to the opposite extreme.

The Bank was started with very little capital, and it issued *notes of credit* (certificates of deposit) considerably in excess of its reserves. In this respect it followed the example of the goldsmith in lending notes to merchants without having a proper regard for a reasonably safe reserve ratio. The flood of easy money swamped the market, put inflationary pressure on prices, and led to a loss of faith in the bank notes and a run on the Bank. As a consequence the Bank was forced to suspend payment, and in 1668 it was thoroughly reorganized under state control.

For a while it operated with a 100 per cent reserve, but in 1701 it embarked upon another period of expansion, making large loans not only to private borrowers but also to the government. By 1745 its reserves of coin had fallen to 8 per cent of its liabilities, and again it suspended redemption of its notes. Their value fell lower and lower, until they were finally redeemed in 1776 at 50 per cent of their face value, and the Bank was reorganized for the second time.

Gresham's Law Again. Here we have another example of Gresham's law. When an irredeemable paper currency exists side by side with a metallic currency, people will always try to make payment with the paper and will hoard the coin. Bad money drives out good, as the depreciating paper circulates and the coin disappears. Since coin is no longer used in payment, prices are quoted in terms of paper notes, and the increasing issue of these notes pushes prices up in an inflationary spiral.

This story of the overissue of paper currency has been repeated monotonously in monetary history throughout the world. In the case of the Bank of Sweden the institution involved was a bank, but as governments have taken over the issue of paper money, they have done the same thing. Depreciation has replaced debasement of the coinage as the device by which a government attempts to increase its stock of money in order to finance expenditures for which it cannot raise sufficient taxes.

The Bank of England. The forces leading to the creation of the Bank of England in 1694 were of a different nature from those which led to the commercial scheme of Palmstruch. That bank owes its existence almost solely to the financial straits of the British government. Pressed by war with France, Parliament agreed to a proposal advanced by William Patterson, a Scotch adventurer, under which he promised to lend the government £1.2 million at 8 per cent interest (an incredibly low rate for a government accustomed to paying 40 per cent to the goldsmiths) in exchange for a bank charter.

Since the Bank's capital equaled the amount of its loan to the government, it was in the interesting position of starting life with a portfolio of government bonds but no cash. It could, however, issue bank notes against its government securities, accept deposits, and make loans. These were activities in which the goldsmiths were already engaged, and the only distinguishing characteristics of the Bank of England were the limited liability provided by its charter and its portfolio of government securities. In its early days the Bank was actually weaker than many of the private bankers who flourished in London, and within two years of its birth it was in serious trouble. In 1696 its cash reserve (which included goldsmiths' notes as well as coin) was only 6 per cent of its note circulation, and in consequence of a run it was forced to suspend payment of its notes, which immediately started to circulate at a discount.

The Bank remained in business, however, and in 1697 new legislation increased its capital, reduced the interest on the government debt to 6 per cent, and gave the Bank a partial monopoly by providing that no other company *of more than six persons* could issue demand notes. While this did not affect the operation of the individual goldsmiths or even small partnerships, it did prevent the establishment of other large banks. It also made the Bank in effect the exclusive banker for the government, thus giving it a source of deposits and other financial business which was not available to other bankers.

In spite of its privileged position the Bank rested on very shaky financial grounds, since its primary business represented simply the refunding of the government debt. For thirty years it tottered precariously on the brink of failure. Its influence on the business affairs of the community was very slight, and what there was did not extend beyond London, leaving the banking needs of the rest of the nation to be filled as best they might by the "country bankers," who grew in great profusion. Even in London the goldsmiths and small-shopkeepers-turned-bankers continued to flourish, accepting deposits, making loans, and issuing bank notes, some of them hardly worth the paper they were written on.

Only gradually did the Bank of England emerge as the major London bank. An important factor in its success was its ability, more by good luck than good management, to weather the storm created by the collapse of the South Sea Bubble, the English version of the great Mississippi Bubble.

The Mississippi Bubble

John Law, of Lauriston, son of a Scotch goldsmith, was perhaps the most colorful of the world's financiers. A man of wit, imagination, and daring, he was well educated, widely traveled, and thoroughly acquainted with the financial institutions of his time. Like Palmstruch he felt that the Bank of Amsterdam was unduly conservative. He believed that a paper currency was of great value to business and could never cause inflation as long as it was issued to meet the needs of trade.[4] His proposals were rejected in England and Scotland, but in Paris he was better received.

France at that time was on the verge of bankruptcy; its coinage and *billets d'état* (paper currency issued by the crown) were in a chaotic state. The French Regent jumped at Law's promise to restore prosperity to France, and in 1716 Law was granted letters patent for an incorporated bank that was to have a monopoly of note circulation. The bank had a modest capital subscribed one-quarter in coin and three-quarters in depreciated *billets d'état* at face value. In spite of this rather dubious device of stock watering, the bank achieved almost instantaneous success.

It accepted bullion in exchange for its own notes, which were stated in terms of a fixed weight of silver (like the Bank of Amsterdam), and although it maintained only a fractional reserve, its notes (Figure 5-3) were fully con-

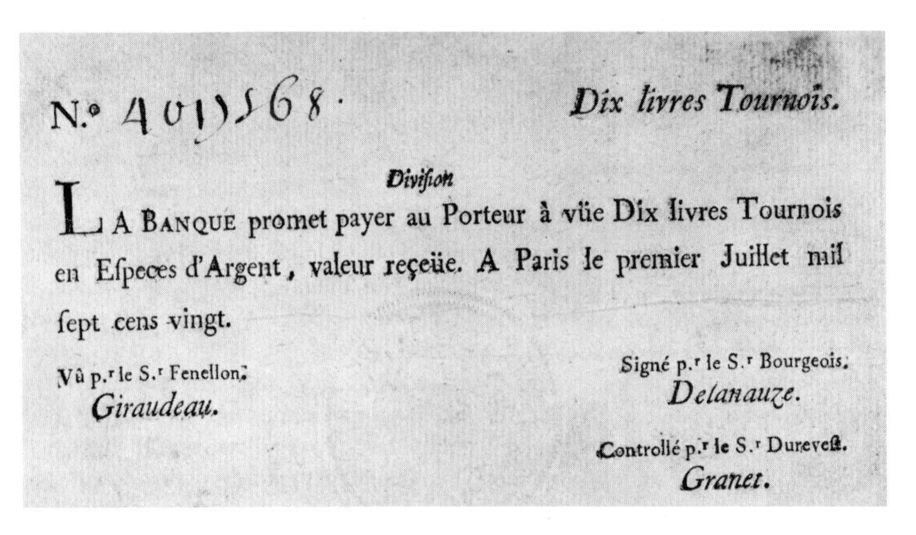

Figure 5-3. Note issued by John Law's bank. The pertinent part of the note reads: "The Bank promises to pay to the bearer on demand ten silver livres of Tours, value received. Paris, July 1, 1720." (*Courtesy of the Chase Manhattan Bank Museum of Moneys of the World, New York.*)

vertible into specie. It lent these notes on good security at a rate of interest of 6 per cent, thus (like the Bank of England) providing money at a fraction of the cost of borrowing from established lenders, where 30 per cent was a minimum charge. In addition Law directly encouraged various forms of commerce and industry by proposals for improving efficiency.

[4] This belief, which has dominated much monetary thinking even as late as the twentieth century, is known today as the *real-bills doctrine*. As long as merchants borrow only enough to finance the inventories of goods that are flowing through their hands, the new money extended as loans will be equaled by the new goods which the merchants hold. With a simultaneous increase in both the money supply and the supply of commodities, says the doctrine, there will be no upward pressure on prices. The real-bills doctrine is examined in more detail in Chap. 11.

The results of a sound currency, available credit, and restored confidence were truly spectacular. "Nothing could be more extraordinary than the restoration of prosperity caused by the foundation of Law's Bank in 1716. It is probably one of the most marvelous transitions from the depths of misery to the heights of prosperity in so short a space of time in the annals of any nation. And if Law had confined himself to that, he would have been one of the greatest benefactors any nation ever had."[5] Such were the benefits of a sound banking system for a nation that had never known it.

But Law's ideas were too magnificent to stop with mere banking. He established the Compagnie d'Occident, whose stated purpose was colonization of the Mississippi Valley but whose real object was to buy government bonds. Soon he obtained for his company a monopoly of the whole foreign commerce of France. Then in succession the company took over the operation of the mint, the farming of the public revenues, the salt taxes, the tobacco monopoly, and finally the whole public debt, for which it was to receive 3 per cent interest.

With each additional success of the Compagnie, the public's enthusiasm for buying its shares rose. As his system grew, Law created more bank notes to finance not only its business operations, but also the rapidly rising speculative fever for its stock. The whole process of stock selling was new and little understood. It seemed to smack of magic rather than arithmetic, for it promised to make a man rich overnight! At the height of the frenzy in 1720, shares were selling at thirty-six times their face value.

Then the bubble burst. Apparently the wiser of the speculators realized that such a ridiculous price rise could not continue. In attempting to dispose of their shares they unsettled the price, and others realized for the first time that what goes up can also come down. The spell was broken. As prices tumbled, it became apparent that the tremendous volume of notes of the Royal Bank, used primarily to finance stock transfers, was now redundant. Bank notes, too, fell in value, and every attempt on the part of the government to support them only demonstrated how weak they were. Bank notes were made legal tender and were given preference in payment of taxes; coins were debased and then withdrawn completely from circulation; and holding, carrying, and exporting gold, silver, and even jewels were forbidden in order to prevent persons from turning their notes into more tangible forms of wealth.

Nothing availed. Frenchmen refused to accept paper as they lost faith in it. The panic grew, even as the speculative frenzy had grown. A commission appointed to investigate the Royal Bank found that against its note issue the Bank held less than 2 per cent in gold and silver coin and less than 10 per cent in all assets combined! In the ensuing run on the bank a dozen people were trampled to death, and Law barely escaped from a crowd bent upon lynching him. The Bank collapsed, and though the government slowly brought some semblance of order out of the utter chaos of financial values, the experience was so thoroughly distasteful that no other bank was chartered in France

[5] Henry Dunning MacLeod, *The Theory and Practice of Banking*, 5th ed. (Longmans, Green & Co., Ltd., London, 1893), vol. 2, p. 254.

for over fifty years. Thus ended France's first experience with a major inflation.

Was the whole scheme, then, a fraud and a deception? The answer is clearly "no." Many of Law's ideas were truly brilliant. His recognition of the importance of credit and of commerce, his reform of taxes, his provision of loans at reasonable rates—these were of great value. But he made the common error of mistaking money for wealth. Because Law's vision was grandiose, his energy inexhaustible, he compounded the error into a more colossal fiasco than a lesser man could have done. The inflationists are ever with us; may we never have another with the power of Law!

The South Sea Bubble

While Law's system was at its height, the contagious fever of speculation swept across the English Channel and engulfed Britain in a similar if somewhat milder outburst.

The South Sea Company was established in 1711 to engage in trade with Spanish America. When news of Law's success in government finance reached London, the South Sea Company, hoping to emulate his success, offered to take over the whole British government debt (some £30 million) at 5 per cent interest, and for this "privilege" offered the government a premium of £3½ million in four annual installments. The Bank of England, annoyed that this upstart should be able to muscle in on such a supposedly lucrative field, offered £5 million. The South Sea Company countered by raising its offer to £7½ million, and—fortunately for the Bank of England—this offer was accepted by Parliament. The company accordingly issued stock to raise the necessary funds, and speculative fever carried the price of the stock to thirteen times its face value in only three months.

The example of the South Sea Company led many other promoters to seize the opportunity to issue stock on both legitimate and illegitimate schemes, many not even bothering to acquire letters patent. One author lists 185 of these get-rich-quick companies formed in the single year 1720. They include such interesting ventures as "Melting Sawdust and Shavings into Deal Boards of any length and free from Knots," "Insurance from Death by drinking Geneva [Holland gin]," and "Curing Herrings a la mode de Hagun Mogun."[6]

The beginning of the end came when the South Sea Company, unhappy over this competition, got a court order against companies issuing stock without legal authority. The collapse of the stock of these companies created public distrust of all stock, and that of the South Sea Company fell with all the rest.

In the general liquidation several banks that had an interest in the South Sea Company failed, but the Bank of England, smarting from its initial inabil-

[6] William John Lawson, *The History of Banking,* 1st Amer. ed. (Gould and Lincoln, Boston, 1852), pp. 117–119.

ity to bid the national debt away from the company, had remained completely aloof from the affair. After the collapse, therefore, the Bank was able to help in picking up the pieces of the disaster, lent money to the South Sea Company itself after the water had been squeezed out of its stock, and in general saved London from the total failure that had engulfed Paris. Its ability to come through this crisis unscathed marked the real emergence of the Bank of England as London's most powerful bank and started it along the road to becoming the world's first central bank.

The Development of British Banking

This road was neither short nor clearly marked. At no time was it planned to make the Bank of England a central bank; the very concept of a central bank was completely unknown. Rather, the Bank just grew along lines that appeared natural at the time. We have already noted the three advantages which it had over its competitors:

1. It had limited liability.
2. It was the only joint stock company that could issue notes (although individual bankers or partnerships not exceeding six persons could do so).
3. It was the repository for government funds.

Gradually London bankers (goldsmiths who had outgrown their earlier jewelry business, as well as newer entrants into the field) found it convenient to keep their idle funds with the Bank of England, and since these balances were payable in currency on demand, such deposits could be considered part of their readily available reserves. Country bankers, of whom there were a large number in the rural areas and provincial towns, also found it convenient to maintain correspondent deposits with one of the London banks (not necessarily the Bank of England). This enabled them to make remittances to London and also to obtain funds by means of bills of exchange drawn on their city correspondents. Although bank checks as we know them were not common among ordinary individuals (the greater part of the banking business still consisted of note issue, not deposit accounts), they were developing as a means of making payments between correspondent banks.

The Bank Restriction. By the end of the eighteenth century the British banking system had become fairly well knit. Country banks maintained balances with London bankers, who in turn kept reserves with the Bank of England, which therefore became the ultimate source of cash for the country as a whole whenever an emergency induced people to demand specie rather than paper.

Such emergencies arose in 1763, 1772, and 1783, and they were promptly and efficiently met by the Bank. The Napoleonic Wars, however, presented even graver difficulties, aggravated by inept government policies. The government, unwilling to pay for the war by taxation or even by public loans, borrowed heavily from the Bank of England against the advice of that institution. The result was a serious inflation, which in turn led to lack of confidence in the currency and a desire to turn paper into specie. This desire led to panic in 1797, when it was rumored that Napoleon's forces were about to invade England. The resultant bank run was channeled from all parts of the country to the Bank of England. Faced with this drain on its resources, the Bank turned to the government for help, which was given in the form of an Order in Council prohibiting it from redeeming its obligations in "cash" (specie). Thus the government "restricted" the Bank from redeeming its notes. The Bank continued to issue notes, but they became an irredeemable paper currency, which nevertheless continued to circulate side by side with gold and silver. As the crisis subsided, business improved in spite of the restriction.

Although the Bank could well have resumed specie payments within a short time, the government saw fit to continue the restriction. This left the Bank with no adequate means of determining the proper volume of loans. Formerly an outflow of coin would have signaled the need to contract credit, and an inflow would have indicated the possibility of expansion. In the absence of this barometer the Bank decided to meet all legitimate demands for loans on the theory that as long as the money was used in trade an overexpansion was impossible.[7] The result was a significant increase in bank notes placed in circulation. At the same time prices tended to edge upward, rising 50 per cent between 1797 and 1810.

The exact relation between these two facts was not clearly understood at the time, although as early as 1809 David Ricardo (then relatively unknown) had suggested that an overissue of irredeemable paper currency would inevitably lower its value, that is, raise prices.

The Bullion Report. The government, itself wondering why the value of gold had risen relative to that of paper, appointed a committee to examine the problem. The ensuing Bullion Report (1810) was a brilliant analysis of the relation of the quantity of money to the price level:

> An increase in the quantity of the local [paper] currency of a particular country, will raise prices in that country exactly in the same manner as an increase in the general supply of the precious metals raises prices all over the world. By means of the increase of quantity, the value of a given portion of that circulating medium, in exchange for other commodities, is lowered; in other words, the money prices of all other commodities are raised, and that of Bullion with the rest. In this manner, an excess of the local currency of a particular country will occasion a rise of the market price of gold above its mint price.[8]

[7] The real-bills doctrine again.

[8] Quoted in Edwin Cannan, *The Paper Pound of 1797–1821* (P. S. King & Staples, Ltd., London, 1919), p. 17.

In practical terms the committee blamed the price rise on the Bank of England's overissue of paper money but suggested that proper management of a paper currency was too much to expect of "any man or set of men." It recommended, therefore, that specie payments be resumed as a control over the supply of bank notes.

Although the Bullion Report was officially rejected by Parliament, it started a public debate on the proper role of the Bank of England that lasted for thirty years and more. It also made the Bank of England more cautious in extending loans and helped pave the way for resumption of specie payments, which began on a partial basis in 1816 and on a full basis in 1821.

In order to carry out redemption, the Bank discovered that it was first necessary to reduce the volume of outstanding notes sufficiently to bring the market price of gold down to the mint price, or else everyone would desire gold for notes as soon as it was possible to obtain it. Thus experience proved one of the major contentions of the Bullion Report, which both the Bank and the government had denied, namely, that overissue of paper currency lay at the root of England's monetary troubles.

With resumption of specie payments in 1821, England went back to a metallic standard, but not quite the one she left in 1797. The old standard was bimetallic, in which gold and silver had equal importance. In 1821 silver was dropped as a standard metal, and England was the first country in the world to adopt a gold standard, a step that was not followed by any other country for fifty years.

The Banking and Currency Controversy. The questions that the Bullion Report raised about the proper volume of paper currency were not answered by resumption of specie payments but continued as a subject of debate in the press, pamphlets, and Parliament, though the precise nature of the arguments shifted as banking practices changed.

One of the important changes was the more thorough transformation of the Bank of England into a central bank, still without deliberate intention and without legal prescription. It was the sole fiscal agent of the government and the only important issuer of bank notes in London, and it had come by practice to hold the metallic reserves of much of the banking system. Changes in law permitted the establishment of joint stock banks (provided they did not issue notes) and at the same time gave the Bank of England the right to open branches throughout England. Both actions tended to strengthen the banking structure. They also helped lay the basis for the extension of deposit banking, the only form of banking in which the joint stock banks could engage.

The country was feeling its way toward a sound banking structure based on the still fairly new concepts of a paper currency and even newer checking accounts. At the same time industrialization, with its growing pains, was subjecting the country to the unhappy experience of boom and collapse that had not yet been christened a "business cycle." It was natural that people should wonder what relation there was between the recurrent crises and the operation of the banks, particularly since financial stringency was the most apparent aspect of the problem.

In particular the railroad boom and subsequent panic of 1837 led to heated controversy over the role of bank notes in dislocating the economy. This controversy gave rise to two schools of thought, the proponents of which went after each other hammer and tongs. Both agreed that the gold standard was the best monetary system and that the quantity of money should be based on gold, but there all similarity stopped. The fundamental disagreement was over the very concept of what constituted money.

Currency School. The currency school insisted that only bank notes and coin were money. Deposits were not money, but a form of capital. They were not a medium of payment and hence could not affect the value of money. On the other hand, the overissue of notes against a fractional reserve of gold increased the money supply unnecessarily and led to inflation. The currency school believed that these inflationary pressures would be eliminated if the quantity of money were limited to the amount of gold held by the issuing bank. They therefore advocated a return to the early system of the goldsmiths with a 100 per cent reserve in gold.

Banking School. The banking-school position was both more varied and more extensive than this and cannot be compressed into a single generalization. Its advocates suggested that money was needed to finance trade and that an increase in general business activity would necessarily require more money, regardless of the size of the gold stock. They also insisted that checking accounts were money just as surely as currency was, an interpretation that is today universally accepted. While check payments at that time were limited almost exclusively to transactions between businessmen, they nevertheless represented an important part of the total monetary function and could not be ignored. The banking school also maintained that an increase in currency was more likely to be a *result* rather than a cause of price increases. Thomas Tooke, for instance, suggested the following chain of events: (1) Borrowing by merchants resulted in an increase in their deposit accounts and in their check payments; (2) the increase in payments raised the price of goods the merchants bought, and they in turn charged their customers more; and (3) in order to meet these higher prices the public had to withdraw bank notes from the banks, thus increasing the amount of currency in circulation.[9] The banking school concluded, therefore, that it was much more important to control bank lending policies (which the currency school felt to be unimportant) than to attempt to limit the quantity of currency. They were not, however, sure just what form this control should take.

[9] Thomas Tooke, *An Inquiry into the Currency Principle, the Connexion of the Currency with Prices, and the Expediency of a Separation of Issue from Banking* (Longman, Brown, Green, and Longmans, London, 1844).

Bank Charter Act of 1844. While the basic arguments of the banking school sound convincing today, they carried little weight at the time. The currency school completely carried the day when Parliament passed the Bank Charter Act of 1844. This revision of the charter of the Bank of England separated the Bank into two parts. The issue department had sole responsibility for the issue of bank notes but under extremely strict regulations. It could issue £14 million of notes without any backing other than government securities. All other notes could be issued only against a 100 per cent gold reserve. Thus the quantity of Bank of England notes could fluctuate only as a consequence of gold movements into or out of the Bank. The banking department carried on all other activities of the Bank, including accepting deposits and making loans. These activities were completely unregulated.

The act also provided that no bank or banker could issue bank notes in excess of the amount in circulation in 1844. If any bank gave up its issue, the Bank of England could add two-thirds of the amount given up to its fiduciary (unbacked) circulation. Thus the Bank of England gradually achieved a complete monopoly of bank notes but under a rigid formula.

That this was not the solution to the problem of business fluctuations became immediately apparent in the wave of speculation that ensued, leading to the economic collapse of 1847. In spite of this failure and in spite of continuing controversy and investigations into the causes of fluctuations, no significant additional changes were made in the charter of the Bank until it was nationalized in 1946, and even then operating procedures were not altered.

With such a thoroughly rigid currency system (modified periodically and temporarily in time of emergency), England would have been in a financial straitjacket, unable to grow industrially, if the currency school had been right in its evaluation of the role of demand deposits. But because the act left demand deposits alone, they developed rapidly as the basis of much of England's monetary structure. The fact is that the Bank Charter Act of 1844 was an anachronism. It attempted to regulate the money supply by regulating currency at precisely the time when currency was becoming a minor part of that supply.

We will not follow British financial history to the present time, but by 1844 much of its present structure was already clearly outlined. We have seen enough of its development to understand many of the principles involved in monetary evolution and to lay the foundation for a more extensive investigation of the monetary system in the United States.

Questions for Thought and Discussion

1. How many of the banking functions described in this chapter are carried on by your own commercial bank? Does it do anything not mentioned here?

2. If your friend Joe lends you $5, is he a bank?

3. Is there any significant difference between the money changers of the ancient world and modern foreign exchange banks?

4. Why do we say that the goldsmith created money even when he lent coin from his reserves?

5. Since the goldsmith's obligations to make payment exceeded his reserves, does this mean that deposits with him were unsafe? Is the same true of a commercial bank today that holds only a fractional reserve against its deposits?

6. Look up (in the *Federal Reserve Bulletin*) the total deposits of all commercial banks in the United States today. Now look up the amount they hold as cash in vault. Are you surprised?

7. What is the relationship between the creation of money and fractional-reserve banking?

8. How was it possible for notes of the French Royal Bank to fall from a premium of 10 per cent above gold in 1719 to practical worthlessness in 1720 even though there was no basic change in their nature or backing?

9. What was Law's fundamental mistake, and how do you think he might have avoided it?

10. Does the issue of paper currency always lead to an inflationary spree? Why or why not?

11. Why do you think the currency school refused to classify demand deposits as money? Why do we insist that they are money?

Selected Bibliography

Andreades, A.: *History of the Bank of England,* 3d ed., Staples Press, Ltd., London, 1935.

Ashton, T. S., and R. S. Sayers (eds.): *Papers in English Monetary History,* 2d ed., Clarendon Press, Oxford, 1954.

Cannan, Edwin: *The Paper Pound of 1797–1821,* Staples Press, Ltd., London, 1919.

Clapham, Sir John Harold: *The Bank of England,* 2 vols., The Macmillan Company, New York, 1944.

Conant, Charles A.: *A History of Modern Banks of Issue,* 5th ed., G. P. Putnam's Sons, New York, 1915.

Corti, Count Egon Caesar: *The Rise of the House of Rothschild, 1770–1830,* trans. from the German by Brian Lunn and Beatrix Lunn, Garden City Books, New York, 1927.

Crick, W. F., and J. E. Wadsworth: *A Hundred Years of Joint Stock Banking,* Hodder & Stoughton, Ltd., London, 1937.

deRoover, R.: *The Rise and Decline of the Medici Bank, 1437–1494,* Studies in Business History No. 21, Harvard University Press, Cambridge, Mass., 1963.

Dunbar, Charles F.: *Chapters on the Theory and History of Banking,* 2d ed., G. P. Putnam's Sons, New York, 1901.

Ehrenberg, Richard: *Capital and Finance in the Age of the Renaissance,* trans. by H. M. Lucas, Harcourt, Brace & World, Inc., New York, 1928.

Feavearyear, A. E.: *The Pound Sterling: A History of English Money,* rev. by E. V. Morgan, Oxford University Press, Fair Lawn, N.J., 1963.

Goddard, Thomas H.: *General History of Banking Institutions in the United States and Europe,* H. C. Sleight, New York, 1831.

Hoggson, Noble Foster: *Banking through the Ages,* Dodd, Mead & Company, Inc., New York, 1926.

James, F. Cyril: *The Economics of Money, Credit, and Banking,* 3d ed., The Ronald Press Company, New York, 1940, chaps. 7 to 10.

Kerr, Albert Boardman: *Jacques Coeur: Merchant Prince of the Middle Ages,* Charles Scribner's Sons, New York, 1927.

Lawson, William John: *The History of Banking,* 1st Amer. ed., Gould and Lincoln, Boston, 1852.

Martin, John Biddulph: *"The Grasshopper" in Lombard Street,* The Leadenhall Press, London, 1892.

Oudard, George: *John Law: A Fantastic Financier, 1671–1729,* Jonathan Cape, Ltd., London, 1928.

Richards, Richard D.: *The Early History of Banking in England,* Frank Cass and Co., London, 1958.

Streider, Jacob: *Jacob Fugger the Rich,* trans. by Mildred L. Hatsough, The Adelphi Company, New York, 1931.

Sumner, William Graham (ed.): *A History of Banking in All the Leading Nations,* 4 vols., The Journal of Commerce and Commercial Bulletin, New York, 1896.

Usher, Abbott Payson: *The Early History of Deposit Banking in Mediterranean Europe,* Harvard University Press, Cambridge, Mass., 1943.

van Dillen, Johannes Gerard: *History of the Principal Public Banks,* Publications of the International Committee for the Study of the History of Banking and Credit, Martinus Nijhoff, The Hague, 1934.

Viner, Jacob: *Studies in the Theory of International Trade,* Harper & Row, Publishers, Incorporated, New York, 1937, chaps. 3 to 5.

Chapter 6
Early Banking in the United States

Confusion now hath made his masterpiece!

Macbeth
Act II, scene 3, line 72

In broad outline the early history of money in the United States is scarcely different from that in other communities. The relatively late development of this country meant that many of our early monetary institutions were imported from Europe as part of the baggage brought over by immigrants. Settlers, carrying small amounts of coin of their own countries, had at least some money to use in transactions among themselves. They met Indians who had money in the form of wampum (Figure 6-1). Though both these kinds of money changed hands on a limited scale, trade with the Indians took place mostly through barter. Barter, even among colonists, was encouraged by what seems to have been a continuous shortage of coin, and barter in turn led to the development of money commodities indigenous to the several colonies.

In Massachusetts beaver skins were used almost from the landing of the *Mayflower* as a common medium of exchange, and within a few years they were declared to be legal tender in payment of debts. Corn was made legal tender in 1631,[1] and for fifty years corn, beaver skins, and British coins circulated side by side as money. Later additions included musket balls, wheat, rye, barley, peas, and dried fish. At one time "pin money" was just that; pins were actually used as small change. Other commodities were also used on occasion.

[1] "It is ordered that corne shall passe for payment of all debts at the usual rate it is solde for, except money or beaver be expressly named." From an order of the General Court of Massachusetts, quoted in Joseph B. Felt, *An Historical Account of Massachusetts Currency* (Perkins & Marvin, Boston, 1839), p. 16.

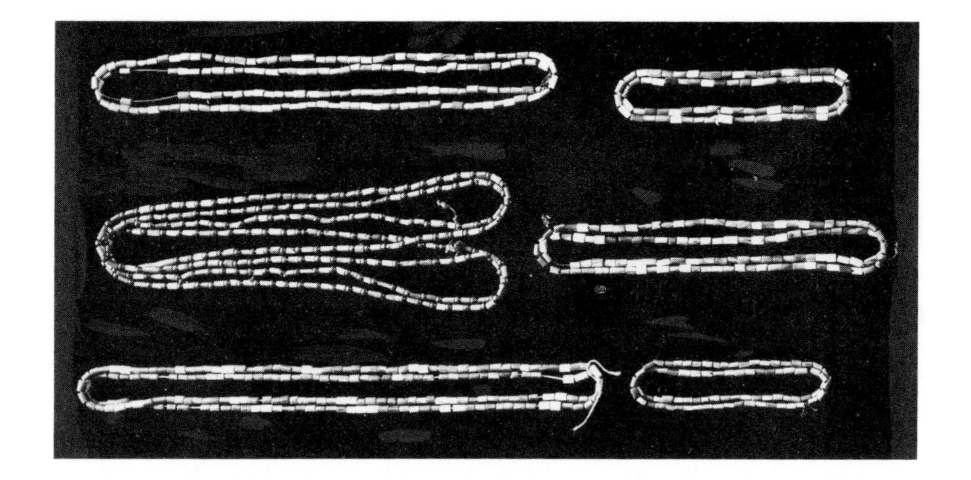

(*a*)

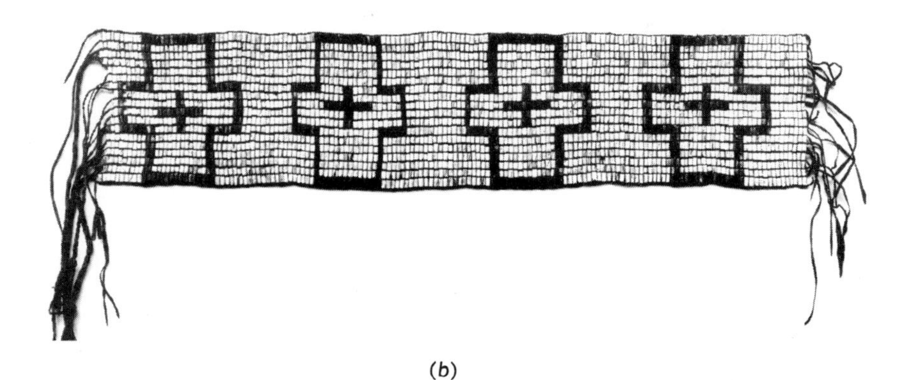

(*b*)

Figure 6-1. Wampum. (*a*) Wampum was frequently strung on sinew threads. It could be worn as an ornament, thereby serving at the same time as a medium of exchange and a badge of wealth and position. These strings are from the Penobscot and Passamaquoddy Indians. (*b*) Wampum was also used for ceremonial purposes and as a record book. The belt pictured here was presented by the Delaware Indians to William Penn at the Treaty of Shackamaxon, 1683, "the only treaty never sworn to and never broken." The white background symbolizes peace; the cruciform enclosures designate lands ceded to the Quakers. (*Courtesy of the Museum of the American Indian, Heye Foundation, New York.*)

Early records show that:

The term bills of students at Harvard College were for many years met by the payment of produce, live stock, meat, and "occasionally with various articles raked up from the family closets of student debtors." One student, later president of the college, in 1649 settled his bill with "an old cow," and the accounts of the construction of the first college building include the entry, "Received a goat 30 s. plantation of Watertown rate, which died."[2]

In Virginia the common money was tobacco, and this was made legal tender in 1619; however, as its production increased, its value in terms of coin declined. In Carolina rice was legal tender, while Tennessee and Kentucky used deer and raccoon skins as money.

Early Coin and Currency

Coin. Coin, almost exclusively silver, was never completely absent from the colonies. Both immigrants and exports brought some in. Because much of the trade was with the Spanish colonies, the greater part of the metallic circulation consisted of Spanish pieces of eight, containing eight *reals* and commonly referred to by the colonists as *Spanish milled dollars* (see Figure 6-2).[3] However, even when dollars were used in the settlement of debts, the predominantly English background of the colonists led them to reckon their accounts in pounds, shillings, and pence. Thus it was common for the unit of account and the medium of exchange to differ. In the early days the Spanish dollar was worth four shillings, sixpence in general trade. Later it rose to seven shillings, sixpence.

Portuguese coins also circulated fairly generally, and one colony, Massachusetts, set up its own mint in 1652. Here pine tree shillings were coined for a number of years (see Figure 6-3), but since none of the colonies had silver mines, the metal had to be imported.

In fact, coin tended constantly to disappear from circulation because the great need of the colonists for all sorts of goods led them to use what coin they had to pay for imports—goods being more needed than money.

Colonial Bills of Credit. This shortage of coin induced the colonies, like many

[2] Davis Rich Dewey, *Financial History of the United States,* 7th ed. (Longmans, Green & Co., Inc., New York, 1920), p. 19.

[3] In 1516 a rich silver mine was discovered in Joachimsthal (the Valley of St. Joachim) in Bohemia. A large number of silver coins were minted here and called Joachimsthalers. This was shortened to thalers, and the term, with its variants, including *dollar,* was later applied to other coins of a similar size. The Spanish dollar is the lineal ancestor of our present currency.

Figure 6-2. Spanish milled dollar, or eight-real piece. This is the famous "piece of eight," often cut into parts for small change. It was the most common coin in circulation in the American colonies, and our dollar is patterned after it. The quarter piece shown here represents two bits (that is, two reals); hence the slang name for our quarter. These coins continued to be legal tender in this country until 1857. (*Courtesy of the Chase Manhattan Bank Museum of Moneys of the World, New York.*)

others before them, to experiment with paper money in the form of "bills of credit." These schemes were of two varieties: unbacked bills issued by governments to meet their pressing expenses, and notes issued by governments or by others against land as security.

Figure 6-3. Pine tree shilling, Massachusetts, 1652. This first coin struck in the colonies is of silver. (*Courtesy of the Chase Manhattan Bank Museum of Moneys of the World, New York.*)

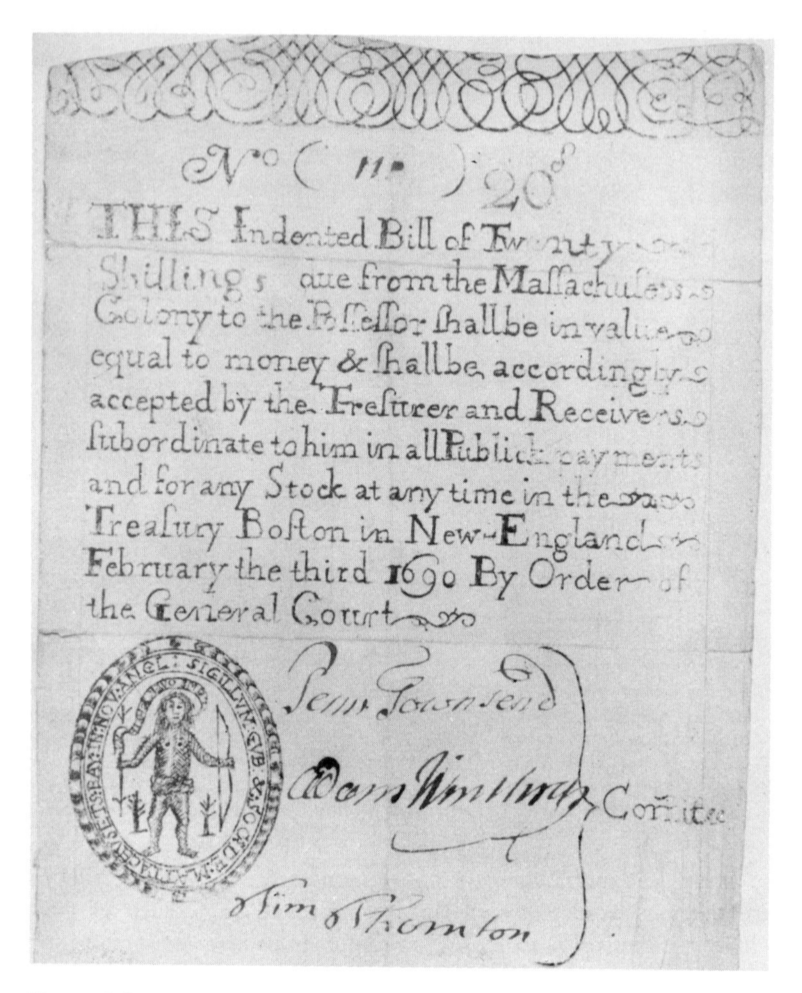
No (11) 20s

THIS Indented Bill of Twenty Shillings due from the Massachusetts Colony to the Possessor shall be in value equal to money & shall be accordingly accepted by the Tresurer and Receivers subordinate to him in all Publick payments and for any Stock at any time in the Treasury Boston in New-England February the third 1690 By Order of the General Court

Penn Townsend

Adam Winthrop } Comitee

Tim Thornton

Figure 6-4. Massachusetts bill of credit issued in 1690, the first paper money in the New World. (*Courtesy of the Massachusetts Historical Society, Boston.*)

In 1690 Massachusetts sent an expedition to storm Quebec, hoping to pay the soldiers from the resulting booty. When the army returned, defeated and clamoring for pay, the government, having no funds, printed £40,000 in bills of credit for the purpose. These bills were promises to pay but without any period specified (see Figure 6-4).

Because Massachusetts for twenty years provided for redemption of these bills within a year of issue out of tax revenues and kept the total outstanding quite small, they circulated during this period at a par with coin. Gradually, however, the temptation to take the easy way to pay debts prompted not only Massachusetts, but all the other colonies as well, to issue bills of credit in such large quantities that they could not be redeemed. Although most bills were

Five Shillings. [No.3328]

THis Indented Bill of *Five Shillings*, due from the Colony of New-York to the Poſſeſſor thereof, ſhall be in value equal to Money, and ſhall be accordingly accepted by the Treaſurer of this Colony, for the time being, in all publick Payments, and for any Fund at any time in the Treaſury. Dated, New-York 31ſt of *May*, 1709. by order of the Lieut. Governour, Council and General Aſſembly of the ſaid Colony.

(*a*)

(*b*)

Figure 6-5. Colonial bills of credit. (*a*) New York, 1709, and (*b*) Pennsylvania, 1755. (*Courtesy of the Chase Manhattan Bank Museum of Moneys of the World, New York.*)

later made legal tender (at least for some purposes), they gradually depreciated in value compared with coin. Before quoting a price to customers a merchant would want to know what form payment was to take. If in bills, he would quote a higher price than if payment was to be in coin.

By 1748 the Massachusetts bills were worth one-tenth of their face value. About the same time Rhode Island bills were worth 4 per cent of their face value, while New Hampshire bills became completely worthless by 1771. Other colonies fared somewhat better (New York bills apparently never fell below 75 per cent of their face value), but in all of them the general tendency was the same. The clamor for cheap money and the complaint of scarce money (we would call it "tight money" today) prevailed upon the legislatures to put out more and more paper to "help business" as well as to balance the budget. The resultant inflation was inevitable, and as prices rose, even the greatly increased quantity of money seemed to be too little in the opinion of the easy-money adherents. "More money," they cried. Never did they seem to learn that money is not wealth.

As if the government issue were not bad enough, various "bank" schemes were advanced for lending funds at low rates of interest. In this period a "bank" was simply a device (often without separate organizational structure) for issuing paper bills. In almost all these plans the paper was issued against land collateral on the assumption that paper money could not be overissued if it was backed by real value—and what was more real than land?

One major difficulty with this thesis lay in the fact that land, while it is real enough, is completely illiquid, so that bills issued against it were irredeemable. In addition they bore no relation to the job that money has to do, that is, to buy goods. These bills suffered further from the fact that, unlike government bills, they were not even supported by the power to tax.

In spite of these defects, "banks" were established by the dozens—some set up by private individuals and others under public authority—and the issue of bills continued to increase as debtors clamored for more money and lower interest rates in order to enable them to pay off their debts more easily. The resultant erosion of values played hob with ordinary commercial and manufacturing pursuits, but the lure of easy money was too seductive to resist. The British government attempted both directly and through the colonial governors to suppress the issue of paper with only partial success. The resentment which this interference aroused in the colonists was an important factor in the final break with England.

Continental Currency. If the colonial bills of credit were bad, the Revolution made matters even worse. The financial needs of the war were great; there was no central government with power to levy taxes; and the former use of bills to finance government had made the citizenry extremely reluctant to submit to taxation by the individual colonies.

In order to help pay for the war, the Continental Congress first issued bills of credit in June, 1775, in the amount of 2 million Spanish milled dollars.

Figure 6-6. Continental currency. *(Courtesy of the Chase Manhattan Bank Museum of Moneys of the World, New York.)*

Another 4 million were issued later the same year, and the total reached 15 million before the Declaration of Independence was signed. The issues followed one another in increasing volume until by 1779 they totaled $242 million, not much by today's standards, but a prodigious sum at that time. The more money the Continental Congress issued, the higher prices rose; the higher prices rose, the more money was needed to meet expenses; the more money was needed, the more was issued—and so on in a vicious spiral.

Various devices were adopted in an attempt to keep prices from rising and to punish anyone who refused to accept the Continental currency at face value, but they were uniformly unsuccessful. One contemporary observer writes:

> The fatal error, that *the credit and currency of the Continental money could be kept up and supported by acts of compulsion,* entered so deep into the mind of

Congress and of all departments of administration throughout the States, that no considerations of justice, religion, or policy, or even experience of its utter inefficiency could eradicate it; it seemed to be a kind of obstinate delirium, totally deaf to every argument drawn from justice and right, from its natural tendency and mischief, from common sense, and even common safety. . . . It is not more absurd to attempt to *impel faith* into the heart of an unbeliever by *fire* and *faggot*, or to whip love into your mistress with a *cowskin*, than to force *value* or *credit* into your money by *penal laws*.[4]

But the wheels of the printing press ground on inexorably. In 1780 the Congress officially recognized the depreciation that had occurred by declaring the bills worth only one-fortieth of their face value. Within a year they had fallen to 500 for 1, and by 1781 they were "not worth a Continental." In 1790 Congress offered to redeem them in 6 per cent bonds at the rate of 1 cent on the dollar, but by that time most of them had been thrown away as worthless.

Of this chapter of monetary history the same writer says:

[The Continental currency] *polluted the equity* of our laws, turned them into *engines of oppression and wrong;* corrupted the *justice of our public administration;* destroyed the *fortunes* of thousands who had most *confidence* in it; enervated the *trade, husbandry, and manufactures* of our country; and went far to *destroy the morality* of our people.[5]

We have suffered *more* from this than from *every other* cause of calamity: it has killed *more* men, pervaded and corrupted the choicest interests of our country *more*, and done *more* injustice than even the arms and artifices of our enemies.[6]

Government Coinage

Yet this debacle had one fortunate result, and that was a lasting revulsion against the excesses of paper money. The Constitution therefore provided that no state should "coin Money; emit Bills of Credit; make any Thing but gold and silver Coin a Tender in Payment of Debts." And the Federal government itself refused to issue any form of paper money until the Civil War. As far as government money is concerned, therefore, for seventy years after Washington's inauguration it consisted solely of gold and silver full-bodied coins along with minor coins for small change.

In 1792 our first coinage law provided for a standard dollar weighing 371.25 grains of fine silver. This was the basis of our monetary system. The particular weight chosen was determined upon as the average weight of Span-

[4] Pelatiah Webster, *Strictures on Tender-acts* (Philadelphia, 1780), reprinted in *Sound Currency*, vol. 3, no. 11 (May 1, 1896), pp. 1, 4. Italics in the original.

[5] Pelatiah Webster, *Political Essays on the Nature and Operation of Money, Public Finances and Other Subjects* (Joseph Crukshank, Philadelphia, 1791), pp. 175–176n. Italics in the original.

[6] *Ibid.*, p. 51.

ish silver dollars then circulating in the colonies.[7] Thus both the name and the metallic content of our first national currency were taken from Spanish coins.

In addition to the silver dollar the law also provided for a gold *eagle,* worth $10 and containing 247.5 grains of fine gold—or 24.75 grains of gold per dollar. This established a mint ratio between gold and silver of 371.25:24.75, or 15:1.

Both gold and silver were to enjoy *free coinage, which is the right of an individual to bring bullion to the mint and to receive an equivalent amount of gold or silver coin.*[8] This meant that bullion and coin were completely interchangeable. Anyone with bullion could bring it to the mint to be coined. Anyone with coins could melt them down into bullion. Gold and silver coins were also interchangeable since anyone with a gold eagle could get ten silver dollars for it, and vice versa. Thus gold bullion could be converted into silver bullion through the mint at the legal ratio of 15:1.

Gresham's Law. On world markets, however, the price of gold was nearer 15.3 times the price of silver and tended to rise. Thus silver was overvalued at the mint—worth more by law than it was worth in trade. In accordance with Gresham's law the bad (overvalued) money drove out the good, and gold disappeared from circulation. An ounce of gold coin, which was worth only 15 ounces of coined silver, could be sold in the market as bullion for 15.3 ounces of silver. So the more valuable gold was hoarded or exported to pay foreign debts, while the less valuable silver was taken to the mint to be coined and used for domestic transactions.

In 1834 Congress attempted to remedy the situation by altering the ratio to 16:1. It is interesting to note that the definition of the silver dollar was retained, while the content of the gold dollar was reduced to 23.20[9] grains fine. This medicine, however, was too strong, for the market ratio was still not above 15.5:1. As a result, silver was the undervalued metal at the mint and tended to disappear from circulation except for old, worn coins whose weight had fallen below their market value. New, full-weight silver coins were hoarded or exported, and gold coins became the common circulating medium.

This produced a shortage of small-denomination coins, which was remedied only in 1853, when Congress reduced the weight of the half-dollar, quarter, dime, and half dime by 7 per cent to the equivalent of 345.6 grains of fine silver per dollar. At the same time free coinage of these coins was abolished,

[7] See Alexander Hamilton, *Report on the Establishment of a Mint* (Washington, 1792).

[8] Free coinage is not necessarily gratuitous. "Free" refers to the *right* to have bullion coined freely. Sometimes a charge, called *brassage,* is made for the cost of minting and of the alloy in the coins since pure gold (or silver) is too soft to be handled without heavy wear and must be hardened with a small proportion of some other metal. The United States (since 1837) has minted coins $\frac{9}{10}$ fine (that is, 90 per cent gold, 10 per cent alloy). Sometimes a charge more than sufficient to cover the cost is levied; this is called *seigniorage* and yields a profit to the mint.

[9] Raised to 23.22 in 1837.

and they became tokens—worth in bullion less than than their face value. This made it unprofitable to melt them down.

The silver dollar itself enjoyed free coinage until the "crime of '73," a general revision of the coinage laws in which the standard silver dollar was omitted from the list of official coins.[10] A heavier *trade dollar* (378 grains of fine silver) was specified in its place. This dollar was of approximately the same weight as the Mexican dollar, which was much used in trade with the Far East, and it was thought that the trade dollar would compete more favorably with Mexican dollars in foreign trade. It was not intended for domestic use, although it did circulate on a limited scale.

Our monetary system continued to be defined in terms of both silver and gold, but the elimination of the standard silver dollar from the monetary system created a *limping standard,* neither the full bimetallic standard of the past nor yet a monometallic gold standard.

Silver Legislation. Meanwhile the downgrading of silver gave rise to a loud and prolonged outburst of public indignation, and it was blamed both for the fall in the price of silver (which occurred almost immediately) and for the gradual deterioration in the general price level over the following two decades. This agitation was insufficient to reenthrone silver as a coequal with gold, but it did produce the first of a long succession of specific bills to "do something for silver."

The Bland-Allison Act (1878), which started out to restore the bimetallic standard, was modified in the Senate to provide only that the silver dollar should again be coined at the old weight and that the Treasury should buy between $2 million and $4 million worth of silver per month for this purpose. The silver dollar was restored to legal tender status, but free coinage was not provided. At this time the price of silver had fallen in world markets from $1.29 an ounce (the official mint price) to a little over 90 cents. The silver dollar was therefore no longer worth a dollar in bullion and became only a token coin.

Vast amounts of silver dollars were coined under this law. In 1878 alone three times as many silver dollars were turned out as had been minted in the whole period 1793–1873, and this production continued at an even higher rate until 1890. The public, however, had no use for this much silver, and the coins piled up in the mints.

In 1890 the Sherman Silver Act replaced the Bland-Allison Act, but the changes were technical. Large purchases of silver continued, gold coin (full-bodied while silver was only token) tended to disappear from circulation, and there was some fear that the United States was headed for a silver standard.

The Sherman Silver Act was repealed in 1893 in spite of strong protests by the silver miners, the Populists, many of the farmers, and inflationists in general, and the uproar that this caused turned the presidential election of 1896

[10] At the same time foreign coins, many of which (both gold and silver) had been made legal tender by various acts of Congress, were declared to be no longer legal tender.

almost entirely into a battle between silver and gold. William Jennings Bryan, running on a "free-silver" platform, was defeated, and the country formally closed the chapter on bimetallism with the Gold Standard Act of 1900.

By this time most European countries had already abandoned bimetallism as unworkable. A number of international conferences toward the close of the nineteenth century had attempted to devise an acceptable bimetallic standard, but fluctuations in the relative prices of gold and silver precluded any possibility of agreement.

The lessons of history, both in this country and elsewhere, show quite plainly that a functioning bimetallic standard is a practical impossibility except for the shortest periods of time. It will work only as long as the mint parity is precisely equal to the market ratio of the two metals, and since the latter is free to fluctuate, only the barest chance can maintain such equality for long. In practice, then, a bimetallic standard becomes a monometallic standard of the overvalued (that is, the poorer) metal. For practical purposes the standard money in the United States was silver from 1792 to 1834 and gold from 1834 on, although we did not legally adopt a gold standard until 1900.

The First Banks

While these changes were taking place in our coinage system, coins themselves were giving way to an increasing use of paper money. In the first instance this was provided by private banks, just as the goldsmiths produced the first paper currency in England. Banking institutions of the type known today did not exist in this country prior to the Revolution but sprang up quite rapidly thereafter.

Bank of North America. The first bank on this continent worthy of the name (and the third in the world, being preceded only by the Bank of Sweden and the Bank of England) was the Bank of North America, established in 1781 by the Continental Congress and still in existence.[11] The Bank was proposed by Robert Morris. Its capital was originally subscribed by the Continental Congress, but within two years this stock was sold to the public.

The operations of the Bank were identical with those of the goldsmiths. It received deposits of silver coin, giving the depositor its own paper bank notes, payable on demand. Since it found it necessary to maintain only a fractional reserve in silver in order to redeem those notes turned in by holders, it was able to make loans, both to businessmen and to the government, by issuing more notes than it had silver. By careful management it avoided the inflationary excesses of former colonial money-issuing schemes, and it was able at all times to redeem such notes as were presented. Thus its notes were well received and circulated at a par with coin even at a time when the Continental currency was sinking into worthlessness. In fact the Bank of North America

[11] Having merged with what is now the First Pennsylvania Banking and Trust Company, Philadelphia.

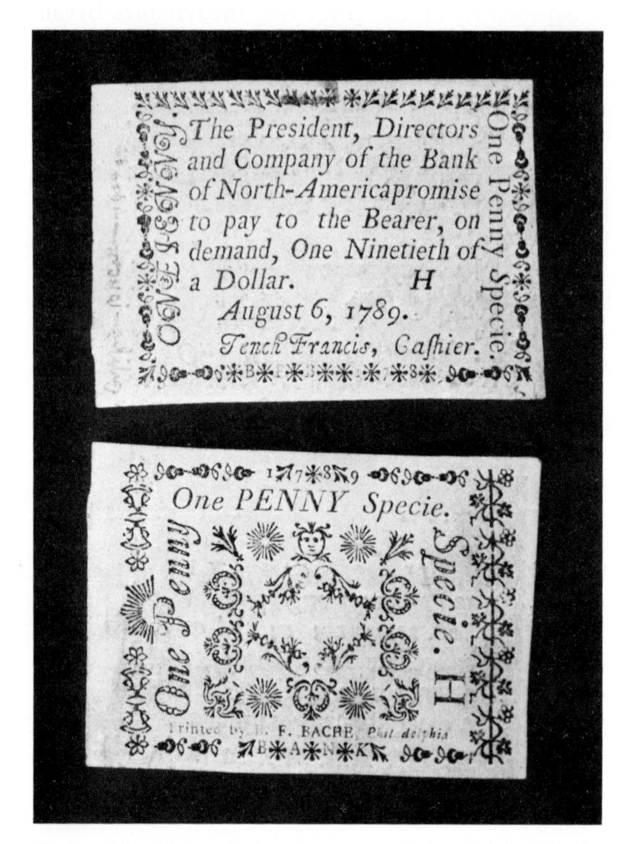

Figure 6-7. Note of the Bank of North America. This note represents a British penny, not a cent as we know it. Since the Spanish dollar was worth seven shillings, sixpence (90 pence) at this time, one penny was one-ninetieth of a dollar. (*Courtesy of the Chase Manhattan Bank Museum of Moneys of the World, New York.*)

may be said to have established for the first time a sound American monetary and banking system. The Bank not only aided in financing the closing years of the Revolutionary War, but also set sound standards for short-term loans to merchants.

There was, however, some question whether the Continental Congress had the power to incorporate a bank, and after a period of some confusion the Bank of North America obtained a charter from the state of Pennsylvania, under which it operated until it joined the national banking system in 1864.

Although Congress had suggested that the states create no other banks, this advice went unheeded, and within a decade similar institutions had been chartered in Massachusetts, New York, Maryland, and Rhode Island, all patterned after the Bank of North America. Other banks followed in fairly rapid succession under both state and private control.

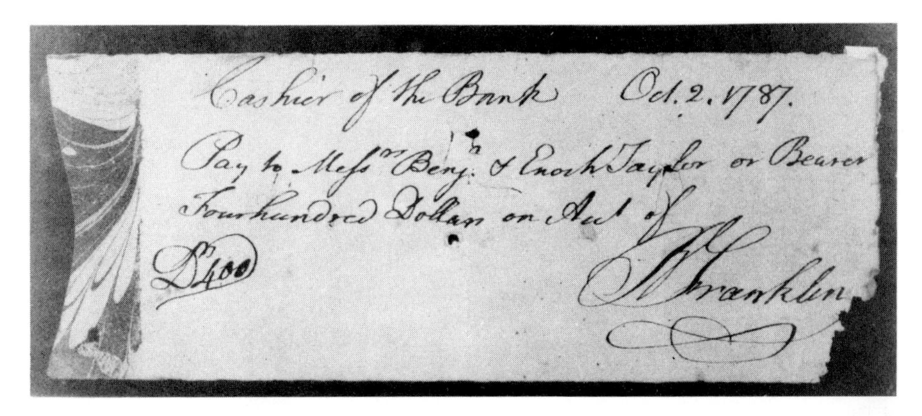

Figure 6-8. Check drawn on the Bank of North America by Benjamin Franklin. It is directed simply to the "Cashier of the Bank" because at that time there was only one. Personal checks were exceedingly rare in this early period. (*Courtesy of the Chase Manhattan Bank Museum of Moneys of the World, New York.*)

Bank of the United States. Meanwhile Congress created the Bank of the United States, and this, with its successor, the Second Bank of the United States, dominated the financial machinery of the country for forty years. We will examine these two national banks before coming back to the trials and tribulations of the growing multiplicity of local banks which continued to operate at the same time.

Alexander Hamilton, the first Secretary of the Treasury, desired a nation-wide bank that would carry on central bank functions as well as the type of lending operations undertaken by the Bank of North America. Unable to induce that institution to broaden its scope under a renewed Federal charter, he persuaded Congress to establish the Bank of the United States.

This bank, which began business in 1791 with a twenty-year charter, was capitalized at $10 million, of which $2 million was subscribed by the Federal government and $7 million by foreigners—an indication of the scarcity of capital in this country. The government paid only one-tenth of its share immediately, promising to pay the remainder in nine annual installments. This device of subscribing to capital with its own promissory notes was highly questionable. As one critic said:

> If the stockholders of a bank are debtors to it and not creditors of it, it is a swindle. They take something out where they have put nothing in. They are not lending a surplus of their own; they are using an engine by which they can get possession of other people's capital. They print notes which have no security and make the public use them as money. They bear no risk of their own operations, but throw all the risk on others while taking in all the gain.[12]

[12] William Graham Sumner, "A History of Banking in the United States," in *A History of Banking in All the Leading Nations* (Journal of Commerce and Commercial Bulletin, New York, 1896), vol. 1, p. 33.

Figure 6-9. "Church money," Troy, N.Y., 1792. Governments and banks were not the only issuers of currency, but such private notes are quite rare. (*Courtesy of the Chase Manhattan Bank Museum of Moneys of the World, New York.*)

Yet the example here set was copied many times by other early banks selling stock to impecunious individuals in exchange for a promise to pay later. Although the Bank of the United States managed to escape any serious consequences of this impairment of its capital, other banks were not so fortunate and suffered severely, even to the point of bankruptcy.

The Bank had its head office in Philadelphia and set up branches in eight of the more important money centers. It issued notes (which could not exceed its capital), made loans, transferred funds from one branch to another, accepted on deposit some two-thirds of the funds of the Federal government, and acted as both paying and receiving agent for the government. Perhaps its greatest contribution was the provision of a paper currency that passed at par throughout the country. At the same time the Bank refused to accept payment in notes of other banks that were not paying specie. It thus put pressure on weak and fraudulent banks and established high standards of currency acceptability for the whole nation.

In spite of its manifest accomplishments the Bank had many enemies: those who resented its insistence on prompt payment of debts; those of low credit standing, who smarted under their inability to obtain loans; the inflationists, who disliked the monetary stability the Bank promoted; the state banks, who feared its competition; those who felt Congress had no constitutional right to establish a bank in the first place; and those who feared the domination of foreign stockholders (even though they could not vote). This strangely assorted group of opponents was able to defeat the renewal of the Bank's charter in 1811 by the narrowest of margins: 65 to 64 in the House and 17 to 17 in the Senate.

This piece of utter stupidity on the part of Congress had dire consequences. The vacuum created by the dissolution of the Bank was filled by a veritable avalanche of state banks. The four state banks in existence in 1791 had increased to eighty-eight by 1811, while 120 more were chartered in the next three years. Most of these were financial weaklings, unable to stand up under the stress of the War of 1812, when most of them suspended payments, "after which the country wallowed in irredeemable paper for several years."[13]

Second Bank of the United States. This intolerable situation was relieved by the creation of the Second Bank of the United States in 1816 along lines similar to those of the first. Its capital was increased to $35 million and the number of branches to twenty-five. It was given an exclusive charter for twenty years.

The career of the Second Bank was not as uniformly successful as that of its predecessor. It experienced considerable difficulty in its first three years as a result of serious mismanagement and outright fraud on the part of several of its officers. Loans were seriously overextended, specie tended to flow out of the bank, stockholders failed to pay installments due on their stock, and the president and the cashier of the Baltimore branch embezzled more than $1 million.

Langdon Cheves accepted the task of cleaning up this mess in 1819, and by the time Nicholas Biddle began his brilliant but erratic administration as president in 1823, the Bank had overcome its earlier difficulties and had reestablished the sound banking structure that was characteristic of the First Bank. In the process, however, it had gained the enmity of many state banks by its attempts to force them to redeem their notes in specie.

This precipitated the "bank war," in which the Second Bank, Biddle, and the National Republicans were pitted against the state banks, Jackson, and the Democrats. Jackson in particular—representing the debtor class and the West—objected to the monetary aristocracy of the Bank as well as to its conservative lending policies. He felt that the monopoly exercised by the Bank was undemocratic and should be abolished, and he felt that an expansion of currency circulation based on a continually increasing issue of paper money would benefit the country, particularly on the trans-Allegheny frontier, where money tended to be quite scarce.

In this struggle the manifest usefulness of the Bank would undoubtedly have won the day except for a series of very questionable political moves on the part of Biddle. He antagonized the Secretary of the Treasury by telling him not to meddle in the Bank's affairs. When Henry Clay opposed Jackson in the election of 1832 on a platform that included renewal of the Bank's charter, Biddle threw all the Bank's weight into the election in an attempt to support Clay. When Clay lost, it is alleged that Biddle tried to apply pressure on Jack-

[13] Horace White, *Money and Banking*, 5th ed. (Ginn and Company, Boston, 1914), p. 264.

son by restricting loans in order to "starve the country into submission."[14] It is certain that he handled some of the Bank's fiscal operations in a manner that was not only aggravating to the government but at times also illegal. The result was to harden Jackson's opposition to the Bank and to alienate even some of its friends. In a direct retaliatory gesture Jackson directed that all government deposits be removed and placed in state banks, the so-called "pet banks."

The Bank could still have served as an important institution without the government deposits, but at this juncture Biddle lost his head completely and embarked upon a highly questionable program of lending large sums on doubtful projects and stock speculations. When the national charter expired in 1836, the Bank obtained a charter from the state of Pennsylvania by a bribe of more than $2½ million. As a state bank it continued its unsound policies until 1841, when it crashed ignominiously in a cloud of broken fortunes.

The Bank's final excesses had two rather interesting side consequences. They made the country extremely skeptical of the benefits of a nationwide bank, so that even today we have not returned to a single central bank. Second, they discredited Philadelphia, the seat of the Bank, as a money center and aided tremendously in the growth of New York banks, which had stuck to conservative banking practices throughout the period of the Second Bank's inflationary zeal and were thus able to survive the storm of its collapse in much the same way as the Bank of England rode out the South Sea Bubble. Except for Nicholas Biddle, Philadelphia might still be the monetary heart of the United States.

Questions for Thought and Discussion

1. What do you think might have been some of the disadvantages of making rice legal tender?
2. Why was it relatively easy for full-bodied silver coins to circulate outside the country that issued them?
3. Why is land a poor collateral for bank notes?
4. Why would people refuse to accept at par money that had been issued by their own government, such as the Continental currency?
5. Explain Gresham's law in your own words and give a detailed example of its operation.
6. In what ways is paper currency more satisfactory than metallic coin?
7. From what you now know of the effect of government on money, would you say that its influence has been helpful or harmful? Why?
8. If you had been President Jackson, what would your attitude have been toward the Second Bank of the United States?

[14] Walter Buckingham Smith, *Economic Aspects of the Second Bank of the United States* (Harvard University Press, Cambridge, Mass., 1953), p. 149.

9. Why is it impossible for everyone to get rich simply through the issue of more money?

Selected Bibliography

Bullock, Charles L.: *Essays on the Monetary History of the United States,* The Macmillan Company, New York, 1900.

Cable, John Ray: *The Bank of the State of Missouri,* Columbia University Studies in History, Economics and Public Law, vol. 102, no. 2, whole no. 232, Columbia University Press, New York, 1923.

Catterall, Ralph C. H.: *The Second Bank of the United States,* The University of Chicago Press, Chicago, 1903.

Chaddock, Robert E.: *The Safety Fund Banking System in New York, 1829–1866,* Publications of the National Monetary Commission, Government Printing Office, 1910.

Dewey, Davis R.: *State Banking before the Civil War,* Publications of the National Monetary Commission, Government Printing Office, 1910.

———: *Financial History of the United States,* 12th ed., Longmans, Green & Co., Inc., New York, 1934.

Felt, Joseph B.: *An Historical Account of Massachusetts Currency,* Perkins and Marvin, Boston, 1839.

Gibbons, J. S.: *The Banks of New-York: Their Dealers, the Clearing House, and the Panic of 1857,* D. Appleton & Company, Inc., New York, 1859.

Gouge, W. M.: *A Short History of Paper Money and Banking in the United States,* T. W. Ustick, Philadelphia, 1833.

Gras, Norman S. B.: *The Massachusetts–First National Bank of Boston, 1784–1934,* Harvard University Press, Cambridge, Mass., 1937.

Hammond, Bray: *Banks and Politics in America from the Revolution to the Civil War,* Princeton University Press, Princeton, N.J., 1957.

Hepburn, A. B.: *History of Currency in the United States,* rev. ed., The Macmillan Company, New York, 1924.

Holdsworth, John T.: *The First and Second Banks of the United States,* Publications of the National Monetary Commission, Government Printing Office, 1910.

Kinley, David: *The Independent Treasury of the United States and Its Relations to the Banks of the Country,* Publications of the National Monetary Commission, Government Printing Office, 1910.

Knox, John Jay: *A History of Banking in the United States,* Bradford Rhodes & Company, New York, 1900.

Lanier, Henry Wysham: *A Century of Banking in New York, 1822–1922,* Doubleday & Company, Inc., Garden City, N.Y., 1922.

Lewis, Lawrence: *A History of the Bank of North America,* J. B. Lippincott Company, Philadelphia, 1882.

Lunt, Dudley C.: *The Farmers Bank, 1807–1957,* The Farmers Bank of the State of Delaware, Wilmington, 1957.

McKay, George L.: *Early American Currency,* The Typophiles, New York, 1944.

Nettels, Curtis P.: *The Money Supply of the American Colonies before 1720,* The University of Wisconsin Press, Madison, Wis., 1934.

Nevins, Allan: *History of the Bank of New York and Trust Company, 1784 to 1934,* New York, 1934. (Privately printed.)

Nussbaum, Arthur: *A History of the Dollar,* Columbia University Press, New York, 1957.

Phillips, Henry, Jr.: *Historical Sketches of the Paper Currency of the American Colonies,* W. Elliot Woodward, Roxbury, Mass., 1865.

Scott, Kenneth: *Counterfeiting in Colonial America,* Oxford University Press, Fair Lawn, N.J., 1957.

Smith, Walter Buckingham: *Economic Aspects of the Second Bank of the United States,* Harvard University Press, Cambridge, Mass., 1953.

Studenski, Paul, and H. E. Krooss: *The Financial History of the United States,* 2d ed., McGraw-Hill Book Company, New York, 1963.

Sumner, William G.: *A History of the American Currency,* Henry Holt and Company, Inc., New York, 1874.

Taus, Esther R.: *Central Banking Functions of the United States Treasury, 1789–1941,* Columbia University Press, New York, 1943.

U.S. Congress, House Committee on Banking and Currency: *Federal Banking Laws and Reports: A Compilation of Major Federal Banking Documents, 1780–1912,* 1963.

White, Horace: *Money and Banking, Illustrated by American History,* 5th ed., Ginn and Company, Boston, 1914.

Chapter 7
State and National Banking

What a tide of woes
Comes rushing on this woeful land at once!

. . .

How shall we do for money for these wars?

The Tragedy of King Richard II
Act II, scene 2, line 98

While the government was attempting, without permanent success, to establish a nationwide branch banking system under the Banks of the United States, other banks continued to operate within the various states.

State Banking

We have already seen that state banks were doing business as early as 1781. Although these banks had competed with the two Banks of the United States, they operated at a serious disadvantage in many respects, and in 1830 the value of the combined assets of the 329 state banks then doing business was only three times that of the Second Bank. With the transfer of the government deposits to Jackson's pet banks and with the collapse of the Second Bank, the state banks grew prodigiously. By 1863 they had increased almost fivefold in number and sixfold in assets. Yet at no time in this period was our financial system as strong as it had been during the best days of the First Bank of the United States.

Banking Chaos. Banking was still somewhat of a mystery and a very alluring one. People realized that banks made money by lending their own bank notes to borrowers, but since bank notes were themselves debts of the bank (payable in specie on demand), it appeared that the bank earned interest on its own debt. What a way to get rich! Banking therefore seemed to be the most profitable type of speculative venture.

Banking was easy too. All you had to do to become a bank was to get a charter from the state legislature, and if the lawmakers were reluctant, a little bribery could often do the trick. Armed with the charter, a printing press, and perhaps a modicum of specie to pay those few individuals who were distrustful enough to ask for redemption of your notes, you set up your bank, printing bank notes and lending them on good collateral at 6 per cent interest. The more notes you could keep in circulation, the more interest you could earn. Redemption of notes, on the other hand, depleted your stock of specie.

All sorts of devices were used to discourage the redemption of notes. The most common was establishing the head office of the bank in an inaccessible location but putting the notes into circulation in a large city, perhaps by means of a floating branch office. This made it almost physically impossible for a holder to claim redemption, since he could do so only over the counter of the main office. The "wildcat banks" were so named because they were located so far from civilization that their only neighbors were wildcats. Banks also issued postdated notes—which were promises to pay specie at some future date rather than on demand—but since this restriction was usually printed in type too small to read readily, the public was all too often unaware of it until they tried to redeem the notes.

The deplorable condition of banking is illustrated by an amusing sidelight recorded in the police records of the time. In 1837 four men were discovered in the garret of a New York house busily printing bank notes. Arrested as counterfeiters, they indignantly proved that they were a legal bank, one of the men being president and a second, cashier.

Under the circumstances it is not surprising that bank failures were prevalent. No knowledge of banking was necessary to start in business, and for the most part the states provided no supervision of the banks. In fact it is often suggested that instead of the states controlling the banks, the banks controlled the states.

It should not be inferred that all banks were of this fly-by-night character. New England had early established a relatively sound banking structure, and many well-run banks could be found in the larger cities, particularly along the Eastern seaboard. But the prevalence of incompetent and fraudulent banks produced something close to chaos in the monetary circulation of the country. It must be remembered that at this period the Federal government issued no currency except coins; all paper money consisted of bank notes, so that anyone using money at all was inevitably confronted with the circulating notes of banks, good and bad.

The bank notes circulating in any area could be classified in several different categories: (1) notes of sound local banks, circulating at par; (2) notes of sound banks in distant cities, circulating at a slight discount because of the physical difficulty of presenting them for redemption at the bank of issue; (3) notes of banks which were in danger of insolvency or which had suspended

Figure 7-1. Early state bank note. The Bank of Missouri was among the sounder banks of this period. Note that the signatures of the officers are in ink. *(Courtesy of the Chase Manhattan Bank Museum of Moneys of the World, New York.)*

specie payments, circulating at a discount that varied with the chance of getting full or partial repayment through the reopening of the bank or through a claim on the bank's assets in liquidation; (4) notes of fraudulent banks, usually worthless but accepted by unsuspecting people; (5) counterfeits of legitimate notes, as well as notes on nonexistent banks and legitimate notes with forged signatures.

The difficulty of dealing with a paper currency issued by a thousand or more individual banks, each with several denominations and often several issues of the same denomination, plus perhaps an equal number of fraudulent and counterfeit issues can well be imagined. The wonder of the situation is that business could be carried on at all with such a monetary system—or lack of system. One of the necessary periodicals for every merchant was a *Banknote Reporter,* of which there were half a dozen, listing the various counterfeits as well as the current discount on notes of banks in difficulties. Thus when a customer offered a dollar bill in payment for goods, the seller would check the *Reporter* to see whether that particular note was worth a dollar, 93 cents, or perhaps nothing at all. The only way to be certain of the value of your money was to accept only specie, and many contracts required such payment. It was hardly an ideal system.

The Suffolk Banking System. Throughout the period prior to the Civil War a number of attempts were made to remedy one or another of the defects of the banking structure. The first of these was carried out by the banks in New England under the leadership of the Suffolk Bank of Boston. Since the notes of country banks circulated in Boston at a discount, they tended, according to Gresham's law, to remain in circulation while the notes of Boston banks were presented to the bank of issue for redemption. In order to eliminate this discount the Suffolk Bank agreed to redeem the notes of any New England bank that arranged to keep with it a redemption fund for the purpose. In order to force banks into the system the Suffolk Bank would accumulate notes of noncooperating banks and send them to the bank of issue for payment in inconveniently large amounts.

This strategy worked well enough to bring almost all the New England banks into the arrangement by 1825, and thereafter New England had one of the soundest currencies in the country. No bank could produce an excessive amount of notes because redemption was too easy and continually tested the bank's solvency. It is estimated that the complete issue of any bank was presented for redemption, either at the bank of issue or at the Suffolk Bank, on the average of once every five weeks.

The Safety Fund System. Another device to maintain the value of bank notes was New York's Safety Fund System, essentially an insurance scheme. Established in 1829, the Safety Fund provided that each bank in the state should pay a yearly assessment of ½ per cent of its capital into a common pool until the contributions equaled 3 per cent of its capital. The fund was to be used to pay bank creditors (both depositors and noteholders) of failed banks when they could not otherwise collect the full value of their claims. When such a payment depleted the fund, further contributions were to be made by solvent banks.

After an auspicious start the fund was severely shaken by the failure of eleven banks from 1840 to 1842. As payments from the fund in this period exceeded its total assets, the state made a loan to the fund, which was eventually repaid, but the scheme showed an inherent weakness too great to allow complete recovery.

The fund served a useful purpose and would have been sufficient to meet all claims of noteholders if its provisions had not been extended to protect depositors as well. One of its disadvantages, given the temper of the times, was that it gave a sense of false security to both the banks and their noteholders and thus actually encouraged overexpansion of note issue.

Free Banking. Another innovation was the free banking principle, introduced by Michigan in 1837 and soon copied by other states. Prior to that time no bank (or any other business) could obtain a corporate charter except through a specific act of the state legislature. This procedure gave rise to many possibilities of favoritism and other abuses.

The Bank of New York, for instance, was owned by Federalists, who, because they controlled the state assembly, were in a position to prevent any other group from obtaining a charter. In 1799 Aaron Burr managed to get a charter for a water company with an obscure clause permitting it to use any capital not needed for the waterworks "in the purchase of public or other stocks, or in any other moneyed transactions or operations not inconsistent with the laws and constitution of the State of New York."[1] Although the

[1] Quoted in Allan Nevins, *History of the Bank of New York and Trust Company, 1784 to 1934* (New York, 1934), p. 31. (Privately printed.)

Manhattan Company, so chartered, did actually supply some water until 1842, its real purpose was achieved through the Bank of the Manhattan Company,[2] which was thus enabled to compete with the Bank of New York, but only by such a ruse.

In other cases banks obtained charters by political pressure or outright bribery. This corruption and favoritism, coupled with the cry of monopoly, created considerable public disgust and led to the proposal that anyone ought to be able to start a bank provided he met certain prescribed qualifications. The Michigan act of 1837 set up such a system and provided, for the first time, for state supervision of banks.

In New York the Equal Rights Party (or Locofocos) adopted the principle of every man a banker as a major plank in its platform and, joining with the Whigs, carried the state in 1837. They promptly enacted a similar free banking law, which provided that any group of individuals could form a bank by petitioning the state comptroller. The bank could issue notes only to the amount of Federal or state bonds or real estate mortgages deposited with the comptroller. While the state did not guarantee such notes, the collateral in the hands of the comptroller was theoretically sufficient to pay all noteholders in case of default.[3] In addition, banks were required to maintain a specie reserve equal to 12½ per cent of their note circulation, the first example of reserve requirements in this country.

There was a rush to take advantage of the new law. Within a year and a half 134 incorporations were requested, although only seventy banks actually commenced business. Similar laws were also passed in sixteen other states. Unfortunately this experiment in "democratic" banking proved no more satisfactory than the previous "autocratic" method. The difficulties were many. Again the presumed safeguards of the system provided a false sense of security. Most "bankers" had no knowledge of the business, and there was no effective limit on the inflationary pressure of an expanding note issue. Many states did not even require a specie reserve, while those that did found widespread evasion. " 'Gold and silver,' complained a perplexed commissioner, 'flew about the country with the celerity of magic; its sound was heard in the depths of the forest, yet like the wind, no one knew whence it came or whither it was going,' although a shrewd guess would have been that it was going from a bank that had already been examined to one that was due to be inspected on the morrow."[4]

No wonder that the country suffered from a continuous succession of bank failures and that complaints over the chaotic nature of the currency situation were incessant.

[2] Merged in 1955 with the Chase National Bank to form the Chase Manhattan Bank.

[3] The free banks were not included in the Safety Fund System, which applied only to the older chartered banks.

[4] F. Cyril James, *The Economics of Money, Credit, and Banking,* 3d ed. (The Ronald Press Company, New York, 1940), p. 184; the enclosed quotation is from C. A. Beard and M. R. Beard, *The Rise of American Civilization* (The Macmillan Company, New York. 1930), vol. 1, p. 685.

The Independent Treasury

The situation was so bad that the Federal government itself refused to trust the banks at all after Jackson's brief experiment with pet banks. With some exceptions the government required that all taxes be paid in specie and in turn made its payments also in coin. In order to handle its funds after the collapse of the Second Bank of the United States and the failure of so many of the pet banks, the government established the Independent Treasury (1840), which consisted of a number of subtreasuries in various parts of the country. These treasury branches received taxes and made disbursement for government account. They were, in fact, simply vaults for the storage of government funds (coin) between their receipt and expenditure.

State Banking and the Civil War

Such was the primitive banking and fiscal system under which the country labored up to the period of the Civil War. It was an era of monetary chaos and of experimentation by a country that stressed rugged individualism, a country strong in imagination and energy but poor in available capital and full of untried ideas as to how to obtain it painlessly. We were a new society, awkward in growing up, learning for ourselves the hard way.

The emphasis was on quantity of money rather than quality. It is true that too little money may make it difficult to carry on trade and that some of the frontier regions suffered from such a shortage of money, which was alleviated when banks were organized to care for these needs. But too much money is just as bad as too little, although the tendency in many areas was to feel that if a little money was good, more must necessarily be better. The inevitable result was deterioration of the monetary system. General suspension of specie payments occurred in 1814, 1818, 1837, 1841, and 1857, and local difficulties were even more frequent. It was a period of irresponsibility, bank failures, monetary fraud, speculation, and confusion. The country grew, economically as well as geographically, but it was in spite of the monetary system, not primarily because of it.

These monetary difficulties were aggravated by the Civil War. Although the country as a whole had recovered remarkably well from the depression of 1857, the government finances were in poor shape. The Federal deficit for fiscal 1858 was $27 million, the largest in our history up to that date; it was due primarily to a serious drop in customs revenue. Though the government attempted to put its affairs in order by cutting expenditures, it could not make ends meet and had to borrow large sums in the market.

As the crisis developed, borrowing became more and more difficult. By December, 1860, the Treasury was forced to pay 10 per cent interest in order to attract investors, and by the time Lincoln assumed office in March, 1861, the public treasury was almost as bare as Mother Hubbard's cupboard. In its attempt to obtain funds to meet the rapidly mounting expenses of the war (government expenditures rose from $67 million in fiscal 1861 to $1,298 million in 1865),[5] the government adopted a great number of expedients, of which two permanently changed the monetary structure of the country: the issue of paper currency and the creation of the national banking system.

Paper Currency

Prior to 1861 the banks had a monopoly on the issue of paper money. In that year the Treasury, having no funds with which to make payments, first issued demand notes payable in specie and receivable by the government in payment of all taxes. The specie reserves of the banking system were fast dwindling, however, and on December 30 the banks suspended specie payments on their own notes. The government followed suit, and the country was left again to wallow in the morass of an irredeemable paper currency. The government was faced with the dismal prospect of having to accept in taxes the multitude of disreputable bank notes of the weak and fraudulent banks as well as the sound notes of the better banks. Gold and silver coins were still the only legal tender, but for most purposes they were unobtainable.

United States Notes. Congress attempted to remedy this situation by authorizing the issue of $150 million of United States notes in February, 1862, and by making them legal tender, the first time that such government sanction had been conferred on a paper currency.[6] A second issue of similar size was authorized in June, and a third in March, 1863, bringing the total to $450 million. At the same time, legal tender quality was conferred upon a small amount of postage currency and fractional currency (paper bills in denominations of less than a dollar introduced to alleviate a shortage of small coins—see Figure 7-2) and a larger volume of short-term interest-bearing notes, which were intended to pass as currency.[7]

The United States notes, commonly called "greenbacks," were legal tender; that is, creditors were required to accept them in payment of debt. But they

[5] In 1865 the interest on the public debt alone was greater than total Federal expenditures four years earlier.

[6] Their legal tender quality had two exceptions: they were not receivable for payment of customs and were not to be used for paying interest on the national debt. The latter provision arose from the general reluctance of people to buy securities (private as well as governmental) unless they contained a "gold clause," specifying payment in specie rather than merely in "dollars." The former guaranteed the government a source of specie to meet its obligations. Since tariffs were the government's main source of revenue, this meant that the government required other people to accept greenbacks while avoiding taking them itself in most cases.

[7] Interest-bearing treasury notes that were receivable for taxes had been issued on a number of occasions and are sometimes classed as currency. In spite of their limited legal tender quality, however, they bear more resemblance to bonds than to money.

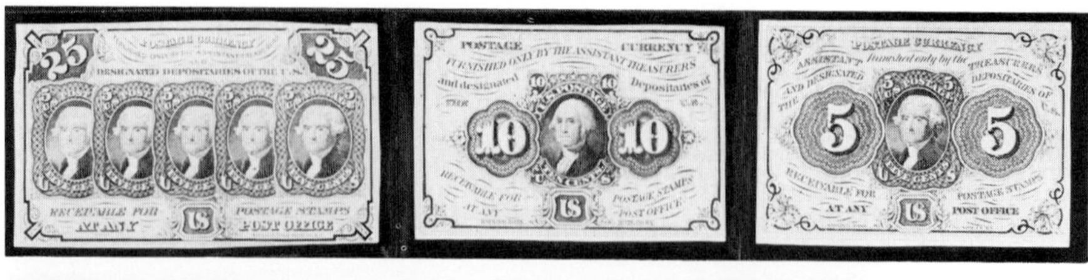

Figure 7.2 Civil War small change. Fractional currency notes were commonly called *shinplasters.* All these, incidentally, are still legal tender. *(Courtesy of the Chase Manhattan Bank Museum of Moneys of the World, New York.)*

were not redeemable in anything at any specified time. While it was obviously the intent of the government to redeem them in specie as soon as possible, memories of previous defaults, particularly the repudiation of the Continental currency, raised the question of whether redemption would ever take place. The natural result of this uncertainty was skepticism as to whether a dollar greenback was worth a dollar.

Although the Legal Tender Act required a creditor to accept greenbacks in payment of old debts, it could not force a seller to accept greenbacks for goods, since his alternative was to refuse to make a sale. He would accept greenbacks only at a depreciated value in terms of specie. Thus gold and silver represented the monetary unit of the country, while paper currency was the predominant medium of exchange. During the most dismal days of the war greenbacks sank to a value of 36 cents in terms of specie. That is, an article that could be purchased for one silver dollar would require $2.85 in greenbacks.

Actually specie tended to disappear from circulation in accordance with Gresham's law, except for import and export trade. A gold exchange was established in New York at which gold (including coin) was bought and sold for paper money in much the same way that wheat is traded on the Chicago

Board of Trade, its price varying with changes in the expectation of redemption of the paper in specie.

For three years following the war the government reduced somewhat the quantity of paper in circulation by selling bonds for greenbacks. From 1875 to 1878 some greenbacks were returned in exchange for specie. These two circumstances brought the amount outstanding down to $347 million. At that point Congress declared that no more greenbacks would be taken out of circulation and that all those redeemed should be reissued. (To this day there is precisely this amount of United States notes outstanding.) The notes were still, however, irredeemable except at the option of the Treasury.

Meanwhile the government had been accumulating a larger and larger stock of gold, and as full convertibility became more and more likely, the premium on gold gradually declined. On December 17, 1879, it disappeared entirely, and the gold exchange was closed for lack of any work to do. On the following New Year's Day the Treasury offered to redeem any and all greenbacks in gold, and thenceforth they were fully convertible into specie. Banks which had been keeping two different accounts for customers, one in paper and one in gold, now merged them into a single dollar account. Once again we had a single monetary system instead of two different moneys circulating side by side but at varying values in relation to each other.

Fortunately the paper currency of the Civil War did not follow the path of Continental currency into worthlessness,[8] but rather was able to prove itself finally "as good as gold." Having realized the usefulness of a paper currency and having won from the Supreme Court—after a long battle and by a 5 to 4 decision—the right to make paper money legal tender,[9] the government never again reverted to a simple coin system, and several other types of paper currency took their place beside the greenbacks.

As early as 1863 Congress had authorized the issue of gold certificates (with a 100 per cent gold backing), but the power was not used until 1866. The first silver certificates (with a 100 per cent silver backing) were placed in circulation in 1878, and in 1890 a temporary paper currency, the treasury notes of 1890 (also backed by silver), was introduced. Both the greenbacks and notes of private banks, however, continued to form a significant part of the monetary system, though bank notes took on a different meaning with the passage of the National Bank Act.

The National Bank Act

This act was another war measure, and though it played a significant role in curing the worst abuses of the banking situation of the time, its most impor-

[8] Confederate currency issued by the Southern states during the Civil War did, however, repeat almost precisely that unfortunate history.

[9] *Legal Tender Cases,* 12 Wallace 457 (December, 1870), which reversed the decision in *Hepburn vs. Griswold,* 8 Wallace 603 (December, 1869).

tant function in the eyes of many who voted for its passage was that it would help finance the Civil War by providing an additional market for the sale of government bonds. Fortunately the war did not last long enough to test this fiscal effect to any great extent, but the other provisions of the act were of continuing significance.

The first National Bank Act was passed in 1863, but it was so badly drawn that it was of little effect and was replaced the following year by a completely revised statute which marks the practical beginning of the national banking system and which is, with later amendments, still the basis of that system.

The act established the office of Comptroller of the Currency in the Treasury Department. To be appointed by the President for a five-year term, the Comptroller was to charter, examine, and supervise national banks, which were now to be established for the first time under a Federal incorporation law.

National Banks. A national bank could be established, either from scratch or by transfer from state charter, by any group of not less than five persons who fulfilled certain specified conditions. Charters were provided by the Comptroller, ran for twenty years, and permitted the institution to do a general banking business.

The Secretary of the Treasury was permitted to deposit government funds in the new national banks, thus giving them an immediate source of large deposits. They did not, however, replace the Independent Treasury System, which remained in operation side by side with the banks until 1921, when it was abandoned as duplicative of the work done by the Federal Reserve.

Capital. The minimum capitalization of a national bank was $50,000 for banks in cities of less than 6,000 population,[10] $100,000 in cities between 6,000 and 50,000, and $200,000 for banks in larger cities. The capital had to be at least 50 per cent paid in, with the rest provided in five months or less. This was not an ideal arrangement, but it was a great improvement over some of the long-term stock notes then in vogue.

Each bank was required to apply 10 per cent of its profits to surplus until surplus reached 20 per cent of capital. In order to give added protection to the creditors of the bank, the stockholders were made subject to double liability: if the bank failed, each stockholder could be required to pay in an additional sum of money equal to his original stock contribution if this was necessary in order to pay creditors in full. The provision for double liability was dropped in 1937, but by that time the capital provisions had been changed to require that 120 per cent of the par value of stock be paid in by stockholders, thus providing the bank with an initial 20 per cent paid-in surplus, and in addition that 10 per cent of profits be carried to surplus until surplus

[10] From 1900 to 1933 banks in cities with less than 3,000 population could be started with only $25,000 capital.

reached 100 per cent of capital. In this way double liability is provided gradually by accumulations in surplus, but the stockholder can no longer be dunned for an additional cash contribution.

In order to remedy some of the abuses of bank lending power, national banks were forbidden to make loans on the basis of their own stock as collateral, nor can a national bank make loans to any one individual (with certain exceptions) in excess of 10 per cent of its capital and surplus. This limitation is still on the books and frequently restricts quite severely the ability of a bank to meet the needs of large borrowers.

Bond Purchases. Each national bank was required to buy government bonds of not less than $30,000 or one-third of its paid-in capital, whichever was greater. It was this proviso which was expected to create an additional market for government bonds during the Civil War. In 1874, when the crisis had passed, an amendment provided that no bank need purchase more than $50,000 worth of bonds, and in 1882 the minimum was reduced to one-quarter of capital. With the establishment of the Federal Reserve in 1913, this requirement was removed completely.

Notes. The bonds that the national banks purchased were deposited with the Treasurer of the United States, who issued to the banks national bank notes equal to 90 per cent of the value of the bonds deposited. (In 1900 this was changed to permit issue of notes up to the full value of the bonds.) Banks could obtain additional notes by buying and depositing more bonds than the minimum, but in no case could they get more than the amount of their capital.

The act provided for a uniform currency for all national banks, since the actual printing was done by the Bureau of Printing and Engraving (the bank paying for the plates and the Treasury for the printing). It thus reduced the danger of counterfeiting and the confusion of multitudinous kinds of notes. At the same time it provided both collateral, in the form of government bonds, and a reserve (as we will see in a moment). In this way it was felt that the issue of currency would be adequately regulated and inflationary pressures kept in bounds.

Each national bank was required to accept the notes of others, and they were redeemable in lawful money at the bank of issue and at the Treasury. The notes were not full legal tender but were acceptable by the government for all payments except customs duties and could be used by the government for all payments except interest on the public debt (which had to be made in specie).

Reserves. The act further regulated the issue of notes, as well as deposit liabilities, by requiring that each bank maintain a specified reserve against both notes and deposits. The amount of this reserve depended on the size of the city in which the bank did business. For central reserve cities (New York was the only city in this category originally; later Chicago was added) the reserve had to be 25 per cent in lawful money in the vaults of the bank.[11] For reserve cities (originally sixteen of the larger cities) the reserve was also 25 per cent, but only one-half of this had to be in lawful money. The rest could be kept on deposit with New York banks. For all other banks, designated today by the strange nomenclature "country banks," the reserve was 15 per cent, of which two-fifths had to be in lawful money, while the rest could be held on deposit with New York or reserve city banks.

This geographical discrimination was, in fact, nothing more than a recognition of normal banking practices of the time. The banks in the smaller cities relied on money-center banks to hold their excess funds for them and at the same time to perform functions that the smaller banks outside the main markets could not carry out. Since banks did, in fact, maintain balances with these reserve city banks, the law simply made it possible for them to count a reasonable amount of such deposits as part of their legal reserves. New York, being in the unique position of supremacy, had no higher level with which balances were kept. As we will see, this interlocking reserve structure had serious weaknesses, but these were not clearly recognized when the act was passed.

In 1874 the reserve against notes was abolished, and in its place each national bank was required to maintain with the Treasury a redemption fund equal to 5 per cent of its note issue. The reserve against deposits remained unchanged.

Taxes. In order to meet the expenses of supervision of the system, a 1 per cent per year tax was levied against the total outstanding note issue of each bank, plus a ½ per cent tax against deposits and that portion of capital not invested in government bonds. The tax against deposits and capital was repealed in 1883.

More important than the tax on national bank notes was the tax levied on state bank notes by an amendment in 1865. It had been hoped that the advantages of a national charter would induce practically all state banks to join the national system. The stricter requirements for a national bank were, on the contrary, a threat to the rather haphazard existence of many state banks, and the shift to national charters was very slow. In order to speed up the process Congress levied a 10 per cent tax on notes issued by state banks after July 1, 1866. Since no bank could earn as much as 10 per cent by lending notes, the tax was obviously confiscatory and a classic case of the dictum that the power to tax is the power to destroy.

The immediate result was a rush of state banks into the national fold. If they could not issue notes, their business was gone. In a single year almost three-quarters of the state banks abandoned their state charters.

A Uniform Currency. This abolition of state bank notes was in itself a re-

[11] Lawful money is a somewhat obscure concept, as already noted (Chap. 3). At this time it appears to have meant all currency except national bank notes.

markable reform. Gone were the spurious issues of nonexistent banks; the questionable issues of corner shaving shops; the confusion over thousands of shapes, sizes, and designs of bills; the heyday of "every man his own counterfeiter." While there were still hundreds of banks issuing notes, these were all of the same size, shape, color, and general design. They were all redeemable by the Treasury and were in effect guaranteed by the government bonds serving as collateral. They had their defects, as we will see in a later chapter, but they were infinitely superior to the chaos they replaced.

Even the Federal Reserve System failed to supplant the national bank notes, which reached their greatest circulation in 1933. In 1935, however, the last government bonds that could be used as collateral for these notes were paid off and retired, so that no new national bank notes have been issued since that date, and notes outstanding have been redeemed as rapidly as they have been turned in by the public.

The Growth of Deposit Banking

The great rush of state banks to obtain national charters in order to replace their now impossibly expensive state bank notes with national bank notes had almost accomplished the objective of bringing all banks into one fold when certain astute state bankers realized that there was another satisfactory alternative and that the stampede had been unduly precipitate.

Was it necessarily true that the lending of notes was the only important way in which a bank could earn money? What about deposits? Even in 1865 deposits were larger in amount than notes outstanding. And while deposits had previously been mainly the result of customers giving up specie or bank notes, the banks now realized—almost for the first time—that it was possible to *lend a deposit* just as previously they had loaned bank notes. Simply crediting a borrower with an account against which he could draw checks was as satisfactory as paying him in bills when he borrowed. It was far easier and less expensive as well. Although the practice of making payments by check was then not very widespread, it had become sufficiently well established to make such a plan feasible.

A few state banks, therefore, hung onto their charters and concentrated on expanding the checking business. Their efforts were so successful that gradually the state banks recaptured a dominant position in the financial structure, and even the national banks began to rely less on notes and more on deposits. Table 7-1 shows this changing pattern of bank activities by detailing note and deposit liabilities of both types of banks by years from 1862 to 1865 and by decades thereafter.

Today there are twice as many state as national banks, although the state banks handle slightly less in total deposits. It should not be concluded, however, that national banks are uniformly larger than state banks. Seven of the fifteen largest banks in the United States are state banks. Nevertheless, the *average* national bank is larger than the average state bank.

In 1844 the British Bank Charter Act accepted the contention of the currency school that bank deposits were not money, and it attempted to regulate the monetary system by control over bank notes alone. Twenty years later we followed almost precisely the same outmoded patterns. It is true that the National Bank Act recognized the existence of deposits and placed the same reserve requirements against them as against notes. Nevertheless it assumed that destroying the power of a bank to issue notes must necessarily destroy the bank itself, and thereby it ignored the potentiality of deposit business, and this precisely at the time when deposits were just beginning to come into their own. In fact the act actually encouraged the growth of deposit banking.

Table 7-1. Number, Deposits, and Notes of National and State Banks for Selected Dates, 1862 to 1964

Deposits and Notes in Millions of Dollars

Year (June 30)	National banks			State banks*		
	Number	Deposits	Notes	Number	Deposits	Notes
1862	—	—	—	1,492	357	184
1863	66	10	—	1,466	494	239
1864	467	147	26	1,089	233	150
1865	1,294	614	132	349	75	48
1870	1,612	706	291	325	70	45
1880	2,076	1,085	318	1,279	1,137	—
1890	3,484	1,979	126	4,717	2,598	—
1900	3,731	3,621	265	8,696	3,171	—
1910	7,138	7,254	675	17,376	7,390	—
1920	8,024	17,159	688	22,267	19,523	—
1930	7,247	23,235	649	16,432	28,032	—
1940	5,164	33,014	—	9,370	27,232	—
1950	4,971	82,430	—	9,175	61,415	—
1960†	4,542	116,178	—	8,951	97,669	—
1964	4,702	155,978	—	8,967	128,924	—

* Data prior to 1900 are estimates which do not provide complete coverage but which include savings and other noncommercial banks; later figures include only commercial banks.
† June 15.
Sources: Adapted from U.S. Bureau of the Census, *Historical Statistics of the United States, Colonial Times to 1957* (1960), pp. 626–632; *Federal Reserve Bulletin*, vol. 46, no. 12 (December, 1960), p. 1361; vol. 50, no. 12 (December, 1964), p. 1556.

Table 7-1 details the eclipse of bank notes. Deposits, which had been only two times the amount of notes in circulation in 1862, had increased to six times notes in 1880 and thirty-two times in 1900. Deposit banking had by that time established itself securely. This is the kind of banking that we take for granted today. We should bear in mind, however, that the widespread use of bank checks is less than a hundred years old in this country and scarcely older in England. It is a relatively new addition to our monetary system and is still in the process of refinement. As time goes on, we find new and better ways to carry on the monetary transactions of the community, but the chances are that we will never achieve a perfect system of money or of banking. Changes elsewhere in the business world are continually calling for improvements in the way in which payments are made, and the banking system is continually adjusting itself to new conditions.

Banking Control

Although the National Bank Act brought about a tremendous improvement in our financial machinery, it failed in one of its important objectives: to provide a unified control over all banks. Instead of supplanting state banks, it merely superimposed a new set of institutions on the old. As a result we have a dual banking system in which state and national authorities compete in the regulation of their separate institutions. It is still a matter of some discussion whether this is desirable or not; but one thing is certain: the dual system was not planned that way. It is an accident of history, growing out of the failure of the National Bank Act to eliminate state banks.

Even within the national banking structure government control was originally somewhat limited. The major areas of regulation concerned bank notes along with—almost accidentally—the establishment of reserve requirements against deposits. The former rapidly lost most of their practical significance, while the latter were insufficient to meet the needs of the time.

To a great extent this failure to come to grips with basic problems was due to a lack of understanding of the way in which money affects the rest of the economy and to a belief that very little in the way of control was really needed. The ideas of the currency school were still dominant: regulate the quantity of currency so that it follows the same pattern as a fully metallic coin system would, and all will be well. At the same time the classical economists were telling us that money had no real effect on the underlying economic transactions of the community. If it had no effect, it wasn't very important.

This point was hotly disputed by many, and the closing years of the nineteenth century were filled with monetary agitation. Yet no major change was made in our banking laws until the Federal Reserve was established in 1914. By that time the continuing parade of financial crises had finally convinced almost everyone that money *was* important and that greater efforts were needed to achieve a really effective monetary system.

The Federal Reserve Act helped, but it too showed flaws and has been amended from time to time as conditions changed and our understanding of money improved. It is still in the process of evolution.

Before we enter upon that chapter of our monetary history, however, we need to interrupt our historical narrative long enough to take a closer look at the nature of the banking mechanism that had emerged by the beginning of the twentieth century. The deposit banking of that period differed only in detail from that which we know today, and a closer scrutiny of how deposit banking works will help our understanding of the meaning and nature of modern efforts at monetary control.

Questions for Thought and Discussion

1. If you had been able to control the banking structure between the Revolution and the Civil War, what changes would you have made?

2. Do you ever read the dollar bills that are paid to you? How do you know that they are worth anything? Would you have been more inclined to read the bank notes used in, say, 1850?

3. Why does central convertibility, such as provided by the Suffolk Banking System, increase the value of bank notes?

4. Why is a bank not completely safe if it holds "Federal or state bonds or real estate mortgages" equal to the amount of its note issue?

5. Would it have been possible for an individual to refuse to accept anything except specie in payment of debt, as the Federal government did? What would happen if everyone did this?

6. When greenbacks were originally issued with no backing and no convertibility, why did they have any value at all?

7. If a person pays $25 (in paper bills) to buy $10 (in gold coin), which is the money? Which is the standard of value?

8. Compare the provisions of the National Bank Act with those of the New York Free Banking Act.

9. Do you draw any conclusions from the fact (Table 7-1) that the number of banks fell 50 per cent from 1920 to 1960?

10. Why is a 1 per cent tax on bank notes merely a source of revenue, while a 10 per cent tax is prohibitive?

11. Is the bank (or banks) in your neighborhood a national or a state bank? Does it make any difference in your evaluation of the bank's soundness?

12. Do you know of any recent developments in making payments that are even more efficient than ordinary checks? Is it possible that checks may become obsolete?

Selected Bibliography

Barnett, George B.: *State Banks and Trust Companies since the Passage of the National-Bank Act,* Publications of the National Monetary Commission, Government Printing Office, 1911.

Barrett, Don C.: *The Greenbacks and Resumption of Specie Payments,* Harvard University Press, Cambridge, Mass., 1931.

Davis, Andrew McFarland: *The Origin of the National Banking System,* Publications of the National Monetary Commission, Government Printing Office, 1910.

Friedman, Milton, and Anna Jacobson Schwartz: *A Monetary History of the United States, 1867–1960,* Princeton University Press for the National Bureau of Economic Research, Princeton, N.J., 1963.

Knox, John Jay: *United States Notes,* 3d ed., Charles Scribner's Sons, New York, 1894.

Mitchell, Wesley Clair: *A History of the Greenbacks,* The University of Chicago Press, Chicago, 1903.

Morris, Henry C.: *The History of the First National Bank of Chicago,* R. R. Donnelley & Sons Company, Chicago, 1902.

Noyes, Alexander Dana: *Forty Years of American Finance,* G. P. Putnam's Sons, New York, 1909.

Unger, I.: *The Greenback Era: A Social and Political History of American Finance, 1865–1879,* Princeton University Press, Princeton, N.J., 1964.

See also references listed under Chapter 6.

Chapter 8 Commercial Bank Operations

Go, presently inquire, and so will I,
Where money is.

The Merchant of Venice
Act I, scene 1, line 184

What is a bank, and what does it do?

There are many kinds of banks: savings banks, commercial banks, investment banks, giro banks, industrial banks, central banks. But in the next two chapters we will concern ourselves with only one of these—the commercial bank. Most of the time we will refer to it simply as a "bank," but it should be clearly understood that when we speak of a bank without any identifying adjective, we always mean a commercial bank. In fact we mean something even narrower than that. Today many so-called commercial banks are really department stores of finance: accepting deposits (both demand and time), making loans, acting as trustees, underwriting municipal securities, holding custody of valuables, acting as brokers, operating safe-deposit vaults, and performing many other services. While all these activities are legitimate and useful, we will be concerned for the moment with only a part of them, and *by "bank" we shall mean exclusively that part of a bank dealing with commercial banking functions.*

Commercial banking concerns itself with the receipt, creation, and transfer of demand deposits for the accommodation of the general public.[1] Our special concern with this particular type of banking arises from the fact that demand deposits are the only form of money used in this country

[1] In the past, commercial banks also issued notes as an addition to, or a substitute for, deposits. This is no longer permitted in the United States.

not created by the government. Commercial banks, then, fulfill a unique function. Other banks may be quite useful as intermediaries between borrower and lender, speeding individuals' savings on their way into productive channels, but only the commercial bank can create money that wasn't there before or destroy that which was.

Commercial Bank Functions

Our definition indicates that commercial banks have three primary functions, all of them revolving around demand deposits. These basic functions are:

1. *Receipt.* The bank accepts money from a depositor in the form of cash or checks and thereby incurs the obligation of repaying an equal sum on demand. The depositor may have several reasons for wishing to hold his money in the form of deposit credits rather than cash: the relative safety that "money in the bank" affords from the hazards of theft, fire, or accidental loss; the convenience of making payments by check; the prestige and added credit standing that a bank account gives; the various auxiliary services that a bank may provide for its customers; or the desire to establish a relationship on which future loans may be based. Of these, the ability to use the checking facilities of the bank is ordinarily the most important.

2. *Creation.* In addition to receiving deposits the bank may also create deposits by making loans of various kinds. In exchange for the borrower's promise to pay the bank at some specified future time, the bank gives him the right to draw checks against the bank immediately. This is the money-creation function.

3. *Transfer.* Although a depositor has the right to withdraw cash any time he wishes, he ordinarily asks the bank (by means of a check) to make payment to someone else, and these checks are frequently deposited in a bank other than the one on which they are drawn. This requires the transfer of credit not only from one depositor to another but also from one bank to another. This process—called *clearing*—has become a highly complicated but exceedingly efficient part of bank operations. Without it the use of checks would be of relatively little importance.

Each of these functions will be analyzed in detail.

The Balance Sheet

While we do not plan to examine banking operations from the point of view of the bank officer—since we are primarily interested in monetary principles and public policy rather than in bank administration—nevertheless we will spend some time on specific details of individual transactions. To do so we will use the bank balance sheet to show precisely what happens in each case. A discussion of general principles often leaves one with rather fuzzy notions of what is being presented, while an examination of actual cases usually provides a little clearer light in which to see the sharp outlines. For this purpose at least a rudimentary knowledge of a few accounting fundamentals is necessary.[2]

In order to keep the explanation as simple as possible, all our material can be put in the form of balance sheets. A balance sheet is a summary of the financial position of a corporation (or any other economic unit) at a specific point in time. It is an instantaneous snapshot that records the value of everything the business owns and the size of all debts the business owes. Most corporations draw up a balance sheet as of the close of business on December 31. Some provide balance sheets semiannually, quarterly, or even monthly. Because of the nature of its operations, a bank often prepares a balance sheet daily. A balance sheet may be drawn up at *any* instant of time, say, at 10:37 this morning, and in fact the larger banks do keep a sort of rough running balance sheet, recording on it the results of all major transactions as they occur.

A balance sheet is always prepared in two sections. In one section (normally at the left or at the top) is recorded the value of all assets, that is, everything the corporation owns. This would include such things as cash, accounts receivable, securities owned, inventories of both materials and finished goods, and plant and equipment. The total assets represent the value of the company to its creditors and owners; that is, someone has a claim to this total value.

A statement of the claims is listed in the second part of the balance sheet (at the right or bottom). First come the claims of the creditors, those who have a specific and legal debt owed to them by the business. These debts constitute the liabilities. Listed here would be such things as accounts payable, taxes payable, bonds payable, and (for a bank) deposits. Each of the creditors represented by these liabilities has the right to demand payment from the business under the terms of his claim.

Then come the claims of the owners. The owners have a residual right to everything that is left. An owner does not have a legal claim against his own business—a stockholder cannot sue his corporation for the "value" of his stock—but certainly any value that the corporation has over and above that needed to pay its debts belongs to the owners. This residual ownership is called *net worth* (or *stockholders' equity* or *capital accounts*).[3]

[2] Any reader acquainted with accounting procedures can skip this section and go on to "Getting Started."

[3] In bank statements net worth is generally not stated separately from liabilities. The net worth items, however, are the same as those for any other corporation and include capital, surplus, undivided profits, and, sometimes, reserve for contingencies. Adding these items together yields total net worth; the rest of the "liabilities" represent liabilities due creditors. Some banks differ slightly in another matter of terminology by speaking of their assets as "resources."

Because net worth is defined as the value of a business over and above the claims of its creditors, we may state it algebraically:

$$\text{Net worth} = \text{assets} - \text{liabilities}$$

Or, with a little rearrangement:

$$\text{Assets} = \text{liabilities} + \text{net worth}$$

This fundamental accounting principle is known as the *balance sheet equation.* It indicates why the balance sheet must always balance (as long as the firm's accountants can add). Any increase in assets that is not offset by an increase in liabilities must result in an equal increase in the residual claims of owners. Or, to put the matter more broadly, any change anywhere in the balance sheet must be precisely offset by an equal change in some other item. An increase in cash, for instance, may result from a decrease in accounts receivable (if a customer pays his bill) or from an increase in notes payable (if the firm borrows from a bank), or it may represent an increase in net worth (if the cash received is a gift or if it is the result of earned profits).

In our examination of bank operations we will trace this dual effect of each transaction on the bank's balance sheet.

Getting Started

Let us take an imaginary bank and trace its growth and operations from the very beginning. Suppose we wish to start a new bank in Crossroads, Ohio. Because banking is controlled by law, we must first obtain from the Comptroller of the Currency (for a national bank) or from the state superintendent of banks (for a state bank) authority to organize the bank, indicating that there is a need for this additional banking service in Crossroads and that the proposed bank appears to be reasonably sound. We will assume that our bank obtains a state charter.

With our charter in hand we sell stock to those who wish to join our venture as part owners. Suppose we sell 500 shares of stock at $120 each, receiving $60,000 in cash. Half of the proceeds we use to build and equip our modest banking offices. Our balance sheet now looks like this:

Crossroads Bank

Assets		*Liabilities*	
Cash	30,000		
Banking house	30,000	*Net worth*	60,000
	60,000		60,000

Obviously our stockholders are our first source of funds, but from here on they play a minor role in bank operations.

Deposits

With our bank building complete, we hold a gala opening celebration, giving cigars to the men, orchids to the ladies, and a ball-point pen to everyone who opens an account. Suppose this inducement succeeds in bringing in $100,000 worth of demand deposits. Various people give the tellers $100,000 in cash in exchange for a notation in a passbook and a book of blank checks. We have now acquired more cash in exchange for a demand liability called *deposits.* Both sides of our balance sheet have risen. (The figures in parentheses show the change from the previous balance sheet.)

Crossroads Bank

	Assets			*Liabilities*	
Cash	130,000	(+100,000)	Deposits	100,000	(+100,000)
Banking house	30,000		*Net worth*	60,000	
	160,000			160,000	

What is the precise nature of this transaction? We speak of a *depositor* giving the bank something called a *deposit,* and yet we find that this deposit appears on the bank's balance sheet as a liability. Shouldn't a deposit be an asset for the bank? The answer is that the word "deposit" is used in two meanings which are almost diametrically opposed, and this confusion has led to a great deal of difficulty in understanding just what is happening. When a customer "makes a deposit," he gives the bank cash or its equivalent, and *the bank gives him a deposit credit.* The deposit which a person has "in the bank" is not the cash that he gave it nor any other cash that the bank might hold. It is the right of the individual to draw checks against his account. A *demand deposit is the obligation of a bank to pay a certain sum of money to a specified individual (the depositor) on demand.*

A deposit, therefore, is the promise that the bank gives the depositor in exchange for the cash he "deposits."[4] The cash is an asset; the deposit is a liability. The depositor is a creditor of the bank, having lent it cash, and he can claim repayment at any time.[5]

Interbank Deposits. Just as individuals wish to maintain deposit accounts with commercial banks because of the services that such accounts provide, so banks themselves often hold deposit accounts with other banks for the same reason.

Our Crossroads Bank is a very small institution in a very small town, and our facilities are limited. What do we do if one of our customers deposits a check drawn on a bank in Chicago? Certainly we can't send someone to Chicago to collect it. Or what if a customer wants to buy or sell foreign exchange? We have neither the facilities nor the knowledge to accommodate

[4] Deposits may also arise from other types of transactions to be examined shortly.

[5] Of course a deposit is an asset *for the depositor.* This is simply an illustration of the fact that every debt is somebody else's credit.

him. As a small bank, relatively inexperienced in the intricacies of banking, we may want advice on banking policy or an analysis of economic prospects to guide our lending activities. Perhaps we wish to make investments in a financial center or to have a place where we can go for loans if we get into trouble. We may need a large bank to join with us in lending to a customer who requests a loan that is simply too big to handle with our limited resources. Or we may need access to big-city brokerage facilities if some of our customers ask us to help them buy or sell securities. Perhaps we want to take advantage of the automated procedures made possible by the use of a big bank's computer system.

All these needs can be met by associating our bank with a bank in a larger city, which, in turn, will have contacts in still larger centers. So we become a *correspondent* of the First National Bank of Columbus by making a deposit there. Suppose we send $80,000 of cash to our Columbus correspondent for deposit to our credit.

Crossroads Bank

Assets			*Liabilities*	
Cash	50,000	(−80,000)	Deposits	100,000
Due from banks	80,000	(+80,000)		
Banking house	30,000		*Net worth*	60,000
	160,000			160,000

"Due from banks" means that the Columbus bank owes us $80,000. It has promised to honor our demands upon it up to that amount. (The Columbus bank will, of course, record this as a liability.)

We can send out-of-town checks to Columbus for deposit to our account; we can draw checks on Columbus to pay our bills if we wish; and because we have established this relationship, the Columbus bank will perform for us a number of services that we are too small and too isolated to perform for ourselves.

If we wished to join the Federal Reserve System, we would become a correspondent ("member" is the word normally used in this case) of the Federal Reserve Bank of Cleveland. Except for certain technical obligations involved, membership in the Federal Reserve is essentially a correspondent relationship, with the Federal Reserve bank performing a great number of valuable services for its members.

Correspondent relationships are quite extensive in our system of unit banking. Every bank except the very largest will have an account in at least one, sometimes several, larger banks, and the big-city banks may have hundreds or even thousands of country correspondents who maintain balances with them. A large bank may have deposit liabilities, therefore, not only for the account of the general public but also for other banks and, as we will see in a moment, for the government as well. These are the three major groups of depositors.

In addition to these three types of demand deposits, most banks also accept time (or savings) deposits. These are deposits against which checks cannot be written, for the withdrawal of which the bank may demand up to two months' prior notice, and on which interest is paid. In theory at least they represent funds for which the depositor has no current use and which he therefore intends to leave in the bank for a fairly long period of time. As stated previously, these are not a part of the bank's *commercial* activity, and until we get to Chapter 17, we will not discuss them further. As used in this and the following chapter, "deposits" refer to "demand deposits."

Loans and Investments

While a bank is very happy to accept deposits, in one important sense this is not the primary objective of the bank. The servicing of deposits is not generally a paying proposition even when charges are levied against the depositor. The greater part of a bank's income is received from interest on loans. It is also in the process of lending that the paramount social signficance of banking lies.

Commercial Loans. Jones owns a hardware store and wants to increase his inventory in anticipation of Christmas sales, but he doesn't have the funds to buy additional merchandise. So he goes to the Crossroads Bank and asks for a loan of $5,000. If the bank is satisfied that Jones is a good credit risk, it will probably grant his request.

First it will require that Jones make out a promissory note in which he agrees to make repayment at a specified time, probably not later than three months in the future. The bank will list this note as an asset; it is a debt due to it that will be collected in cash or its equivalent on the due date.

What does the bank give in exchange? The bank *could* give Jones cash: five hundred $10 bills or perhaps five $1,000 bills. For some purposes—such as to meet a payroll—cash might be desired by a borrower, but this is not the common case. Jones wants to pay his suppliers, and here checks are more satisfactory than cash. So the bank grants him a deposit credit of $5,000. It gives him a passbook with the notation in it that $5,000 has been credited to his account, and it provides him with sufficient blank checks to meet his needs.

Jones is now a depositor-creditor of the bank. How did he get that way? He didn't "make a deposit." All he did was give the bank an IOU. In exchange the bank created for him a deposit account. Where did the bank get the money to lend? The answer is quite clear: the bank didn't get the money from anywhere; it simply created it out of a little ink on a ledger sheet. Jones now has "money in the bank." He has $5,000 worth of purchasing power that he didn't have when he went into the bank. Nobody had it; it didn't exist. The total purchasing power of the community has been raised by $5,000 by the simple process of the bank's agreeing to honor Jones's checks for that amount. This is the process by which banks create money. On the balance sheet it looks simple enough: Jones's IOU will be listed under loans and discounts as an asset, and deposits will rise by the same amount.

Crossroads Bank

Assets			*Liabilities*	
Cash	50,000		Deposits	105,000 (+5,000)
Due from banks	80,000			
Loans and discounts	5,000	(+5,000)		
Banking house	30,000		*Net worth*	60,000
	165,000			165,000

Interest and Discount. The bank, of course, is not going to lend Jones $5,000 today in exchange for a promise to pay $5,000 in three months. It is granting him an important privilege: money today against a promise to pay money in the future. For this privilege the bank will charge interest. This may be computed in either of two ways. It may be added to the amount that Jones has to pay back, or it may be subtracted from the amount he gets. In the first instance the charge would be called *interest,* and the process of lending would be referred to as a *loan.* In the second case the charge would be called *discount,* and the process of lending would also be referred to as a *discount.* Thus the difference between loans and discounts (as assets) or between interest and discount (using income terms) is simply one between collection of the charge at the end of the period and collection at the beginning. If Jones borrows $5,000 at 4 per cent interest for three months, he receives $5,000 and repays $5,050. (Interest of 4 per cent on $5,000 for one year would be $200; for three months it is $50.) If he borrows the same amount at 4 per cent discount, he receives $4,950 and repays $5,000.

In either case the bank gets an asset worth $50 more than the deposit liability that it incurs. How is this discrepancy accounted for on the balance sheet? To the extent that the $50 represented pure profit, it would appear as an increase in net worth (assets have risen by $50 more than liabilities). But the bank has expenses as well as income, and most of the $50 will go to pay employees' salaries and other operating costs and hence will not appear on the balance sheet at all (if payments equal receipts, there is no change in either assets or liabilities). Our numerical examples will ignore these factors of income and expense for the sake of mathematical simplicity.

The phrase "loans and discounts" on the balance sheet gives rise to another slight terminological hurdle. A loan is not what the bank gives the borrower. What the bank gives the borrower is a deposit. What are called "loans" on the balance sheet are the promissory notes of borrowers, which the bank will collect on the due date. These promissory notes are frequently referred to as *commercial paper.* They are obviously assets.

Government Securities. The businessman is not the only one who borrows from commercial banks. While the Federal government does not actually approach a bank to negotiate a loan, it does issue securities, many of which are purchased by banks. The process of lending to the government is similar to that of lending to business. The bank subscribes to a certain portion of a new issue of securities, the securities (which are promissory notes of the government) are delivered to the bank, and the bank credits the Treasurer of the United States with a deposit.

In technical detail the government account is handled somewhat differently from an individual deposit,[6] but in underlying principle it is just the same. The bank has received an IOU of the government promising to pay a certain sum of money at a future date, and in turn the bank has given the government its promise to pay a similar sum on demand. The bank has created money for the government in the form of bank deposits which did not previously exist. If we assume that our bank buys $20,000 worth of government securities, our balance sheet becomes:

Crossroads Bank

Assets			*Liabilities*		
Cash	50,000		Deposits:		
Due from banks	80,000		Individuals	105,000	
Loans and discounts	5,000		United States government	20,000	(+20,000)
Government securities	20,000	(+20,000)			
Banking house	30,000		*Net worth*	60,000	
	185,000			185,000	

In addition to buying newly issued securities directly from the government, banks may also buy securities on the open market, that is, from some previous holder who wishes to dispose of them. Although this might also result in a new deposit for the seller of the securities, the mechanics of the market are such that the bank is more likely to buy such securities for cash or its equivalent (usually a check drawn on its Federal Reserve account, on a correspondent, or on itself). Suppose the Crossroads Bank bought $10,000 worth of such securities in the open market, paying for them with a check drawn on its Columbus correspondent. The result would be:

Crossroads Bank

Assets			*Liabilities*	
Cash	50,000		Deposits:	
Due from banks	70,000	(−10,000)	Individuals	105,000
Loans and discounts	5,000		U.S. government	20,000
Government securities	30,000	(+10,000)		
Banking house	30,000		*Net worth*	60,000
	185,000			185,000

Other Loans and Investments. There are a number of other types of loans and investments that banks may make, but none of them introduces any new principle of banking. Loans may be made on real estate (mortgages), to brokers or others for financing stocks and bonds, or to consumers for install-

[6] This will be discussed in Chap. 12.

ment purchases or to pay medical or other bills. Banks may buy securities issued by state or local governments or by corporations. In each case the bank's acquisition of the asset must be offset by some other item on the balance sheet: usually by an increase in its deposit liabilities; sometimes by a decrease in its cash or "due from banks." The nature and relative importance of the various kinds of bank assets are discussed in more detail in Chapter 10.

Clearing

The third function of the commercial bank—transfer of deposits—is actually the biggest job in terms of manpower. When a depositor in the Crossroads Bank mails a check to a department store in Columbus or deposits a dividend check drawn on a bank in Chicago, he assumes that the first will be charged against his account and the second added to it without giving the matter a moment's thought. His assumption is justified not because the process is simple but because the banking system has devised some very ingenious and efficient machinery for handling this complicated task.

The process by which deposit credits are transferred through the banking system may be considered at three different levels, depending on whether the bank in which the check is deposited is (1) the same bank on which it was drawn, (2) a different bank in the same city, or (3) in a different city.

Intrabank Clearing. If Sam Green writes a check on his account in the Crossroads Bank and gives it to William Smith, who deposits it to his account in the same bank, clearing is simplicity itself. The bank deducts the amount of the check from the account of Green and adds it to the account of Smith. There is no change in the total amount owed to depositors by the bank; it simply owes less to Green and more to Smith.

Intracity Clearing. The process is more complicated when Green draws a check on the First National Bank and Smith deposits it in the Second National Bank, even when these banks are in the same city. Second National gives Smith deposit credit; that is, it increases its deposit liabilities by the amount of the check (say, $100). In exchange it has received a check from Smith worth $100. This will appear at the moment on the balance sheet under "cash items in process of collection." How can the $100 be obtained? Second National can't deduct it from Green's account because Green doesn't have an account there. Somehow Second National must obtain the funds from First National, which can then charge the amount against Green.

In the early days of banking this was done by sending a messenger to First National with the check and collecting cash from the teller. Second National then had $100 in cash to offset its increase in deposits. First National had lost $100 in cash and had charged Green's account accordingly. To send a messenger to every bank on which checks were drawn, however, was obviously an inefficient procedure. In order to facilitate such transfers, the first clearing house in this country was established in New York in 1853, and others have followed in all large cities. In some cases clearing houses have also been established for counties or other larger units.

The *clearing house* is a membership association composed of all (or almost all) the banks in a given city. Its primary purpose is to provide physical facilities and a set of rules to expedite the clearing of claims among members. At a designated hour every banking day (in New York three times a day), each bank sends to the clearing house all checks that it holds drawn on other clearing-house members. These claims are then exchanged among the banks and a balance drawn up. A hypothetical case using only token figures is shown in Table 8-1.

Table 8-1. Hypothetical Clearing-house Settlement

Amounts in Dollars

Owed to \ Owed by	A	B	C	D	Total owed to	Net balance	
						Credit	Debit
A		21	6	14	41	3	
B	23		8	12	43		7
C	4	10		6	20		1
D	11	19	7		37	5	
Total owed by	38	50	21	32	141	8	8

If A and B were to offset their claims against each other of $21 and $23, respectively, this total debt could be settled by a payment of $2 from A to B. But while A owes B $2, it has net credits with C of $2 and with D of $3. Bank A therefore has a net credit with the clearing house as a whole of $3. Similarly D has a credit of $5, while B and C owe $7 and $1, respectively. Instead of direct settlement between each pair of banks, the clearing can be accomplished by B and C paying the clearing house a total of $8, which can then be distributed between A and D. This sum of $8 would suffice to settle claims totaling $141.

Even this amount does not need to be paid in cash. A number of alternative methods have been used in the past for making clearing-house settlements, but today the most common procedure is to make all payments by means of the balances which the banks maintain in the Federal Reserve bank of the district. The manager of the clearing house certifies the clearing statement to the Federal Reserve bank, and the Federal Reserve then credits the deposit account of A $3 and that of D $5 and charges the account of B $1 and that of C $7. A member with an adverse clearing balance (owing more than it is owed) loses deposit credits with the Federal Reserve ("due from banks"), while a bank with a net excess of claims on the clearing house increases its reserves.

Intercity Clearing. A clearing house functions by bringing its members together each day. Its operation, therefore, is limited to a geographical area that is small enough to make such daily meetings feasible. Over wider areas this device will not work. How does our Crossroads Bank collect a check drawn on a bank in Columbus or Chicago?

Before the advent of the Federal Reserve the only way in which this could be done was by presenting the check to the bank in question either in person or by an agent. Since distance made the cost of the first prohibitive for most checks, collection was accomplished through correspondents. This is one reason for the tremendous growth of correspondent relationships, and even today, when most checks can be collected easily through the Federal Reserve, many are still sent through the old correspondent channels.

In order to collect out-of-town checks, our Crossroads Bank may send them for collection to the First National Bank of Columbus, its correspondent. In exchange for an increase in its deposits due to the persons who originally deposited these checks, the Crossroads Bank receives an increase in its own account (due from banks) at the First National. If the check is drawn on another Columbus bank, the First National can collect it through the Columbus clearing house. If it is drawn on a Chicago bank, First National will send it to its Chicago correspondent, and it will be collected through the Chicago clearing house. If the check is drawn on a bank in Keokuk, Iowa, it will probably go to Chicago anyway and from there perhaps to Des Moines before final collection from Keokuk. At each step in the process credit is given through changes in the correspondent's bank balance.

While the vast net of correspondent relationships made it possible to send a check through channels for collection anywhere in the United States, the procedure was often roundabout, time-consuming, and expensive. In addition some banks charged exchange fees for paying checks presented from out of town, so that the depositor could not be credited with the full face value of his check. Banks which make such charges are known as *nonpar banks.*

One of the original purposes of the Federal Reserve was to improve this process of clearing out-of-town checks, and today it handles the great bulk of such collections. It clears checks not only for its members, but also for nonmembers who are willing to keep a deposit balance with the Federal Reserve bank of their district large enough to cover normal clearing activity. Such *nonmember clearing banks* are not subject to any of the requirements of the Federal Reserve System except that they must pay all checks at par; that is, they cannot impose an exchange charge.[7]

To use Federal Reserve clearing our Crossroads Bank would have to maintain a deposit with the Federal Reserve Bank of Cleveland, either as a member

[7] Member banks and nonmember clearing banks are permitted to make a *collection* charge covering the costs of handling checks, but not an *exchange* charge, which is an arbitrary fee imposed only against checks presented for payment through the mails rather than over the counter. Many banks which do not use Federal Reserve clearing machinery still charge for exchange. Most of these banks are in the South and the upper Middle West.

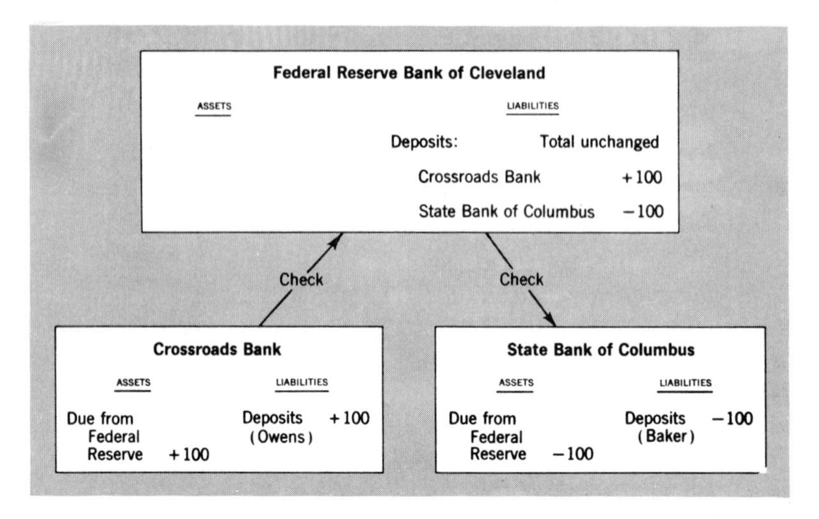

Figure 8-1. Intradistrict Federal Reserve clearing.

or as a nonmember clearing bank. Crossroads would then send its out-of-town checks to the Reserve bank.[8] Once the checks are received by the Federal Reserve bank, they are handled for clearing in two different ways, depending on whether the check is drawn on a bank within the same Federal Reserve district or one outside the district.[9] In our example checks drawn on Columbus and Chicago represent the two possibilities.

Suppose George Baker has drawn a check for $100 on the State Bank of Columbus and sent it to Harry Owens, who has deposited it in the Crossroads Bank. The Crossroads Bank has sent the check for collection to the Federal Reserve Bank of Cleveland. The Federal Reserve will credit the account of Crossroads, charge the account of the State Bank, and remit the check to the latter. This means that Crossroads has increased its reserve account (due from Federal Reserve) by $100, while the State Bank has suffered a reduction in its account with the Federal Reserve. As State Bank receives the check, it charges it against the original drawer, Baker, and its deposit liabilities go down by the same amount as its assets. The transaction is summarized in Figure 8-1, which shows only *changes* in the various balance sheets.

The Federal Reserve Bank of Cleveland is able to complete this transaction by simple book entries because both banks carry deposit accounts with it. If the two banks are located in different districts, one more step is necessary.

Interdistrict Clearing. Suppose Ralph Scott has drawn a check for $100 on the Loop Bank of Chicago and sent it to Robert White, who has deposited

[8] No bank is required to use the Federal Reserve if it prefers to clear through its other correspondents.

[9] There are twelve individual Federal Reserve banks, each serving a specified geographical area.

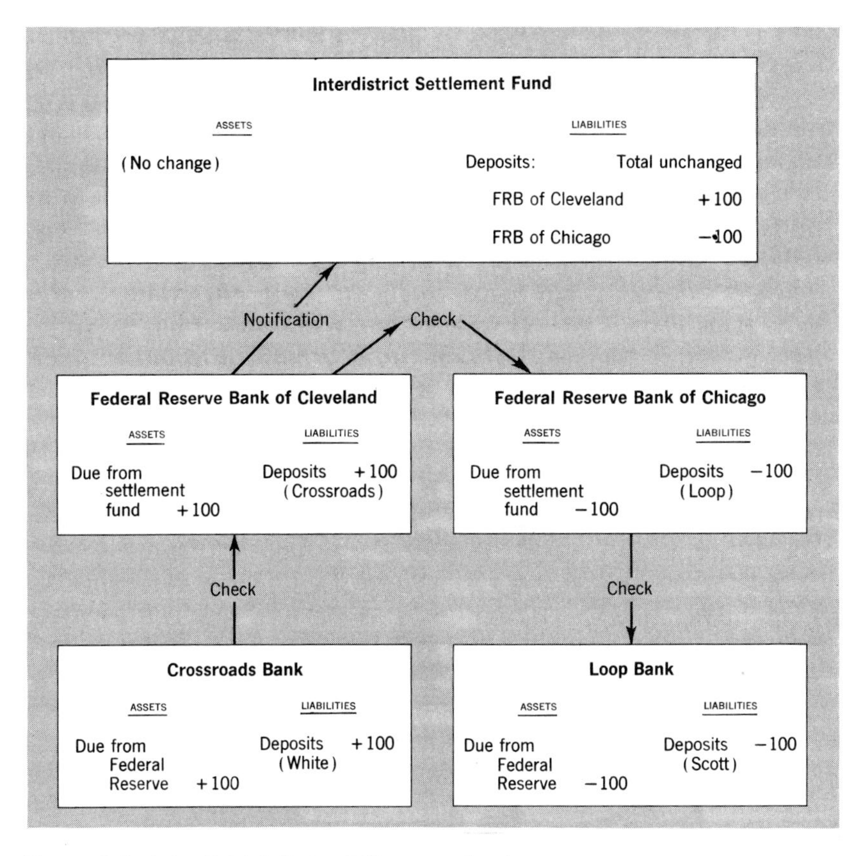

Figure 8-2. Interdistrict Federal Reserve clearing.

it in the Crossroads Bank. When Crossroads sends this check to the Federal Reserve Bank of Cleveland, that bank cannot charge the account of the Loop Bank because the latter carries its account with the Federal Reserve Bank of Chicago, not with the Federal Reserve Bank of Cleveland.

In order to provide for exchanges of this sort between districts, the Federal Reserve System has set up a special fund in Washington under the control of the Board of Governors of the Federal Reserve System called the Interdistrict Settlement Fund. Each Federal Reserve bank is required to deposit with the settlement fund an amount of gold certificates sufficient to cover its clearing operations with other Federal Reserve banks. The settlement fund is a kind of bank whose only assets are gold certificates and whose only liabilities are deposits for each of the twelve Federal Reserve banks. Through these deposits it is possible to transfer credits between the various Federal Reserve districts.

When the Crossroads Bank sends its check drawn on the Loop Bank to the Cleveland Federal Reserve, the latter credits the account of the Crossroads Bank as it did in our previous case. Then it does two things: it sends the check to the Federal Reserve Bank of Chicago, and it notifies the Interdistrict Settlement Fund that Chicago owes it $100[10] (see Figure 8-2). The settlement fund then charges the account of the Chicago Federal Reserve Bank and credits the account of Cleveland. Meanwhile the Federal Reserve Bank of Chicago has received the check and charged it against the Loop Bank, which in turn charges the account of Scott.

By this simple process of book entries, checks may be cleared anywhere in the country. If any Federal Reserve district is suffering a net movement of funds out of the district, this will be felt in terms of a continuous reduction of its balance with the Interdistrict Settlement Fund. The balance may be restored by depositing more gold certificates with the fund. On the other side of the picture the Federal Reserve bank of the district that is gaining funds will find its balance with the settlement fund growing larger than is needed for current transactions, and it can withdraw gold certificates from its account. In other words, if there is a net movement of check payments from New England to California, the Federal Reserve Bank of Boston will lose gold certificates, while the Federal Reserve Bank of San Francisco will gain them. It is in this manner that a shift in basic monetary resources follows a shift in funds evidenced by check payments.

Further examination of the operation of the Federal Reserve will be deferred until Part Three, while we go back and examine the social implications of the creation of deposits. An understanding of the nature of clearing is necessary as a background for that explanation.

Questions for Thought and Discussion

1. When a bank's assets equal its liabilities plus net worth, does this mean that the bank isn't making any profit? What does it mean?

2. Explain in your own words why a deposit is a bank's liability and a loan is a bank's asset.

3. If the making of a loan increases a bank's deposit liabilities, what happens when the loan is repaid?

4. Show the effect on a bank's balance sheet of a withdrawal of cash by a depositor.

5. If a bank's major expenses occur in connection with clearing checks of depositors, why does it not charge depositors the full cost of this service?

6. If the Columbus Trust (in which the Crossroads Bank has a correspondent balance) receives a check drawn on Crossroads, how would that check most easily be cleared? How does this affect the Crossroads Bank's balance sheet?

7. Show the effect on the balance sheet of the Liberty Bank of Boston of a purchase by it of $1,000 worth of corporate bonds, paid for by an officer's

[10] Actually each bank reports only once a day the total of all its claims against each of the other Federal Reserve banks.

check drawn on itself, deposited by the seller in the Back Bay Bank, and cleared through the Boston Clearing House.

8. Can you think of ways in which clearing-house balances might be settled other than by credits on the books of a Federal Reserve bank?

9. Trace the machinery for clearing a check drawn on the Nob Hill Bank in San Francisco by Charles Deere and deposited by Arthur Maine in the Peach Street Trust Company in Atlanta.

10. If you were to buy a book from France, would you be able to pay for it with your personal check drawn on a United States bank? If so, how would it be cleared?

Selected Bibliography

American Bankers Association: *The Commercial Banking Industry,* Prentice-Hall, Inc., for the Commission on Money and Credit, Englewood Cliffs, N.J., 1962.

American Institute of Banking: *Bank Administration,* New York, 1952.

———: *Principles of Bank Operations,* New York, 1956.

Crum, Lawrence L.: *Time Deposits in Present-day Commercial Banking,* University of Florida Press, Gainesville, Fla., 1964.

Edwards, Gurden: *How Banks Lend,* American Bankers Association, New York, 1939.

Federal Reserve Bank of Chicago: *Modern Money Mechanics: A Workbook on Deposits, Currency, and Bank Reserves,* 1961.

Federal Reserve Bank of New York: *Essays in Money and Credit,* 1964.

Federal Reserve Bank of Philadelphia: *Exercises in the Debits and Credits of Bank Reserves,* 1955.

Finney, K.: *Interbank Deposits: The Purpose and Effects of Domestic Balances,* Columbia University Press, New York, 1958.

Foster, Major B., et al.: *Money and Banking,* 4th ed., Prentice-Hall, Inc., Englewood Cliffs, N.J., 1953.

Jones, Thatcher C.: *Clearings and Collections: Foreign and Domestic,* Columbia University Press, New York, 1931.

Kniffin, William H.: *Practical Work of a Bank,* 9th ed., Bankers Publishing Company, Cambridge, Mass., 1948.

———: *How to Use Your Bank,* 2d ed., McGraw-Hill Book Company, New York, 1949.

Nadler, Marcus S.: *Time Deposits and Debentures: The New Sources of Bank Funds,* C. J. Devine Institute of Finance, New York University, New York, 1964.

Chapter 9
Principles of Credit Expansion

There is something in this more than natural, if philosophy could find it out.

Hamlet
Act II, scene 2, line 392

The commercial banking mechanism—the process of creating deposits by making loans—is so important that we need to examine it in some detail. The principles, already touched on in our discussion of the goldsmiths,[1] require further elaboration.

Goldsmiths and the First National Bank

The operations of the banker-goldsmith and those of the First National Bank of Anytown today are essentially the same. The goldsmith was issuing notes that were payable in specie (gold or silver) on demand. Against these notes he maintained a reserve of the precious metals sufficient to pay as many of these notes as he thought would be presented for redemption at any one time. While some holders of notes were asking for coin, others were depositing specie in order to obtain the convenience of notes. So his stock of metals fluctuated up and down, but at no time was he required to pay out the value of all his outstanding notes at once. Experience had demonstrated that he could work with a *fractional reserve*.

If the goldsmith did not have to maintain a 100 per cent reserve against his notes, he could issue more notes than he had specie and lend them to others at interest. Each time he made a loan he created money: he increased the purchasing power of the community by providing the borrower

[1] See Chap. 5.

with a means of payment (goldsmiths' notes) that previously had not existed. This is the essence of commercial banking.

A demand deposit is simply a new mechanical twist to the process. Today a bank no longer issues bank notes. It creates money, not in the form of a piece of paper promising payment of specie on demand against presentation of the note, but in the form of a promise (usually only implied) to pay currency (specie being no longer normally used in this country) on demand against a written order (a check) drawn by the depositor against the bank. The mechanism has changed; the principle is identical.

Bank Credit as Money

Modern banks create money by making loans in the form of credits to the borrower's checking account. Banks cannot create rice or beads or gold. They cannot even mint coins. If people required these things as money and would accept no other, commercial banking could not exist. Moneylending could exist. An individual or group, such as the Fuggers, could accumulate a store of wealth and lend part of it to others. But the Fuggers didn't create money. Their loans gave the borrower purchasing power only to the precise extent that the lender gave up purchasing power. Money was transferred from one person to another without changing the total amount in the community.

Where money is rice, a farmer can create money by raising rice, but a farmer isn't a bank. Where money is gold, a miner can create money by digging gold out of the ground, but a miner isn't a bank. Where money is a commodity of any kind, additional money can be had only by productive effort equal to that needed to produce any other commodity of equal value. But where money consists of promises, anyone whose promise will be acceptable can create money simply by making a pledge.

When a community finds generally acceptable the written promise of a bank to pay specie, then the bank can create money by printing bank notes and placing them in circulation. When a community finds generally acceptable the unwritten promise of a bank to pay currency against checks, then the bank can create money by issuing demand deposits. Our monetary system today uses predominantly a money that is only a bank's word.

The Process of Money Creation. When a businessman obtains a loan, he gives the bank his own promissory note payable at some specified future date. What he receives in return is a credit to his account against which he can now write checks. The bank has increased its liabilities (deposits) at the same time that it has increased its assets (loans or, more explicitly, promissory notes). Since its liabilities are money, the monetary stock of the community has been increased.

Sometimes one runs into a banker who denies this. He says that all he does is lend his reserves and that he certainly can't lend more than his depositors have given him. In a very superficial sense he has a point,[2] but fundamentally he is quite wrong and will not find support even among the majority of his fellow bankers.

Let us take the simplest possible case. Suppose I have a $10 bill. I walk into the Crossroads Bank and hand this bill to the teller. He makes a notation of a $10 deposit in my passbook, and I go my way. The bank's balance sheet would show the effect of this transaction as follows (recording only the *changes* that would occur as a result of this particular transaction):

Crossroads Bank

Assets		*Liabilities*	
Cash	+10	Deposits	+10

What has happened to the quantity of money? As far as I am concerned, nothing. I walked into the bank with $10 in cash; I walked out with $10 in deposit credit. I have substituted one form of money for another, but I have not altered the total quantity at all. I still have $10 that I can spend any time I want to by writing a check.

What about the bank? The bank has added $10 to its cash, but this is precisely offset by its monetary obligation of $10. More important from an analytical point of view, the vault cash of the bank (this $10 bill) is not considered part of the effective money supply. It is true that the bank *could* use this currency to buy stationery or to pay its clerks, but (1) this is not the usual way in which a bank makes payments, and (2) the amount of goods or services that a bank can buy bears no direct relation to the amount of cash it holds. When a bank makes payment, it usually does so by issuing an officer's check drawn on itself. If this check is redeposited in the same bank, it results in an increase in deposit liabilities, not a reduction in cash. If it is deposited in another bank and comes back to the Crossroads Bank through clearing, it will normally result in a reduction in the Crossroads Bank's deposit in some correspondent (perhaps the Federal Reserve Bank of Cleveland), but again not in cash.

Your purchasing power and mine are limited to the amount of money we actually possess. But a bank can create money, and therefore the amount that it holds at any time is not a limitation on its buying power. So we do not normally count cash in vault of a commercial bank as part of the money supply. It is more in the nature of an inventory; cash is a commodity in which banks deal. It bears a certain resemblance to the shirts on the haberdasher's shelves. The customer considers shirts something he can wear. The haberdasher would not think of them as part of his wardrobe but only as something he can sell. Similarly the bank considers its vault cash not purchasing power but part of its stock-in-trade.

Under this interpretation, therefore, my $10 bill turned over to the bank

[2] A partial justification for such a position is given later in this chapter.

doesn't give the bank any more money. Neither the bank nor I have increased our purchasing power, and the money supply has not changed.[3]

Suppose now that Brown comes into the Crossroads Bank and wants to borrow $10. The bank takes his promissory note and gives him a $10 deposit credit.

Crossroads Bank

Assets		*Liabilities*	
Loans and discounts	+10	Deposits	+10

Brown walks out with $10 he didn't have when he came in. Does anybody have any less? Obviously not. Certainly the bank hasn't lent Brown *my* money; I still have my right to draw checks up to $10. Nobody else has $10 less. Brown has $10 that didn't exist before. The money supply has risen by $10 as a result of the bank's lending activity. It has created $10.

Take an even stronger case. Suppose that instead of giving Brown a deposit credit, the bank hands him the very same $10 bill I had just deposited.

Crossroads Bank

Assets		*Liabilities*
Cash	−10	(no change)
Loans and discounts	+10	

Exactly the same conclusion follows. Brown walks out with $10 more than he had. I have no less. Since we agreed that the bank didn't gain money when it put $10 in the till, it can't lose money when it pays it out. It is money in the hands of the nonbank public that is important. And money in the hands of the public has increased by the $10 Brown now has. Thus a commercial bank creates money when it makes a loan even when it hands the borrower cash.

We should emphasize again that it is not *my* $10 the bank has loaned. My $10 is the right I have to draw checks in that amount. The $10 bill is what I gave the bank in exchange for that right. It is no longer mine. Whatever the bank does with the cash, I still have $10 worth of deposits, and this the bank cannot under any circumstances deprive me of. In other words, "money in the bank" is not cash nor any other asset that the bank may hold against its liabilities; it is the liabilities themselves. Money in the bank is not *in* the bank, nor is it even money from the bank's point of view. It is the bank's obligation to pay money.

The two alternative forms in which a borrower may obtain a loan—cash or deposit credit—are completely interchangeable. If he were given cash but preferred a deposit, he could take the cash to the teller's window and deposit

[3] Even if we reject this explanation and wish to consider cash in the till as part of the money supply, we still must conclude that the bank can create money. On this basis, since I have the same amount of money I had and the bank has $10 more, then obviously the money supply has risen by $10. Under this interpretation the bank creates money every time it issues a deposit credit.

it. If he received a deposit credit but preferred cash, he could write a check for the amount of the deposit and cash it. Therefore whether he gets cash or a deposit is a matter of convenience. While there may be cases in which cash is desired, most business borrowers prefer deposits, and so the majority of bank loans take this form.

Monetization of Debt. When Jones borrows $5,000 from the Crossroads Bank, two things happen. He gives the bank his IOU for $5,000 payable in 90 days, and the bank gives him its promise to honor his checks up to that amount whenever he writes them. All that has transpired is that Jones has given the bank his debt and accepted the bank's debt in return. A simple exchange of debts. Yet Jones is willing to pay interest in order to make such an exchange. Why?

Because the bank's debt is money and his debt is not. With the bank's debt (through the medium of a check) he can pay his bills; with his own debt he cannot. Jones may be able to *postpone* payment of claims against him by giving his own promissory note to suppliers or others, but he cannot *settle* his bills that way.

Bank credit is a very special kind of debt that does settle bills, that is accepted in payment, that is, in short, money. So this exchange of debts between Jones and the Crossroads Bank represents the *monetization of debt.* Jones has written an IOU, and the bank has turned that IOU into money by exchanging its own debt for it.

Often the phrase "monetization of debt" is used to describe the process by which Federal Reserve banks create reserves for their member banks by a similar process of lending. But reserves are not money. What the Reserve banks are doing is simply *making it possible* for the banks to create money; the real monetization of debt occurs when the commercial bank makes a loan.

Destruction of Money. So far we have concentrated solely on the creation of money. The other side of the coin is that a bank can destroy money as well. This is done when a bank reduces its assets, such as when loans are paid off or securities sold.

Three months ago Jones borrowed $5,000. He received a deposit credit for that amount and immediately spent it for the purchase of inventory. Now the time has come to repay this loan. What is Jones going to do? Actually it is more a case of what he has been doing. Over the past three months he has been selling the merchandise he bought with the loan, and as it was sold he deposited the proceeds of the sale in his bank account. Unless his calculations were wrong, the sale of the goods has resulted in receipts sufficient to cover all his expenses, pay the loan with interest, and leave a little over for profit.

In other words, at the end of three months his bank account has risen by more than $5,000. When the loan falls due, he writes a check against his account, gives it to the bank, and receives his canceled note as evidence that the loan has been repaid. The bank has a check payable to its own order and drawn on Jones's account. The bank pays itself by canceling $5,000 of its own deposit liability to Jones. The total effect of repayment of the loan on the bank's balance sheet is as follows:

Crossroads Bank

Assets		*Liabilities*	
Loans and discounts	−5,000	Deposits	−5,000

The entries are precisely the opposite of those entered when the loan was originally made. When making payment, Jones walked into the bank with $5,000 in his deposit account. He walked out without it. Nobody got the $5,000; it simply disappeared. The community's purchasing power has dropped by $5,000. The bank has reduced its liabilities, which the community uses as money, and so the bank has destroyed that much money.

Any operating bank will be making loans and investments and receiving repayments continually. For the most part we would expect that the new loans and the repayments would about cancel each other. If they do, then the bank is neither adding to, nor subtracting from, the money supply. If new loans exceed repayments, deposits are growing, and the bank is creating money, net. If repayments exceed loans, deposits are shrinking, and the bank is destroying money.

Deposits and Fractional Reserves

If a bank had to maintain a 100 per cent reserve against its deposit liabilities, if it had to have currency or its equivalent equal to every cent it owed its depositors, bank creation of money would be impossible. When I deposit a $10 bill, a 100 per cent reserve would require that the bill be kept in the till to back the bank's liability to me. The bank couldn't lend that $10 bill to a borrower. It couldn't give the borrower a deposit credit either, for the additional deposit would have to be backed with currency, and where would the additional currency come from? If the $10 bill backs my deposit, it cannot at the same time back somebody else's. A bank may exist under such circumstances, but it becomes primarily a warehouse plus, perhaps, a very useful device for facilitating payments through the clearing machinery. In its early days the Bank of Amsterdam was exactly such a warehouse, and a highly valuable function it performed; but it did not create money.

Reserves and Experience. When the goldsmith first ventured into fractional-reserve banking, he did so with great caution. How much reserve did he have to keep? Was 90 per cent sufficient, or did he need 95 per cent? While such figures may sound ridiculously high, it was only as the result of many years of experience, many decades of gradual lowering of reserve ratios, that we have reached the low reserve percentages of modern banking.

What reserve a goldsmith or a bank must maintain for safety has always been a matter of experience. No generalization on this score can be made. In a society in which specie is the normal medium of exchange and bank notes and deposits are used only sparingly, any individual acquiring a bank note may wish to turn it into metal immediately because he does not know or trust the paper. In such a community 50 per cent might be too small a reserve. As the economy becomes more and more accustomed to bank money, such money becomes a larger and larger part of the circulating medium, redemption is asked for less frequently, and a lower reserve is possible.

Reserves and Law. In some countries, such as Spain, a bank may keep any amount of reserves that its own business judgment dictates. In others, such as the United States, the government has seen fit to make certain requirements. Originally these reserve requirements were imposed because the government didn't think the banks had enough sense to maintain sufficient safety if left to their own devices. This was true, for instance, of the free banking system in New York, with its requirement of government bonds as collateral against bank notes. It was also the reason for the reserve requirements of the National Bank Act and the original Federal Reserve Act.

Such reserve provisions contain one joker, however. If rigidly enforced they may protect the bank's creditors somewhat in case of failure of the bank, but they do not provide cash in an emergency. As long as the law requires a certain reserve to be maintained at all times, that sum cannot be used to pay depositors. The bank, then, must maintain *in addition* to the legal reserve a sum sufficient to meet normal withdrawal demands.

Today legal reserves are no longer thought of primarily as safety devices. Rather they are the means through which the money supply is controlled. As we will see, the size of the reserve that any bank must maintain determines the extent to which that bank may create money.

Deposit Expansion on Four Planes

The relation between reserves and the ability of a bank to extend credit (create money) can be simplified by examining this relation under several different situations, both imaginary and real.

A Monopoly Bank in a Noncash Society. Let us imagine a closed economy having no business relations with the outside world. In this society there is only one bank, the Alpha Bank. A long time ago this society used coins as money, but gradually all these coins were deposited with the Alpha Bank in exchange for deposits; the current generation has never even seen them, but they are dutifully carried on the bank's balance sheet. All transactions in this community are settled by means of bank checks, and no cash is ever used.

Suppose that at the moment we visit this community the Alpha Bank's balance sheet looks as follows (we will use very low numbers for simplicity, and anyone may add as many zeros to each item as he wishes):

Alpha Bank

Assets		*Liabilities*	
Cash	10	Deposits	100
Loans	90		
	100		100

How much more can this bank lend? Suppose I ask for a loan of $10; could I get it? $20? $100? $1,000? $3 billion? The answer is that in our hypothetical case there is no limit at all to the amount that the bank can lend. Suppose it lent me $100. The balance sheet would become:

Alpha Bank

Assets		*Liabilities*	
Cash	10	Deposits	200
Loans	190		
	200		200

I have $100 that I didn't have before. I write checks against this deposit to pay my creditors. They deposit the checks in the Alpha Bank, which charges my account and credits theirs. The bank owes someone else instead of me, but its balance sheet as a whole does not change.

Precisely the same thing would be true if the bank loaned me, or any combination of individuals, $1,000 or $3 billion. Since by assumption deposits are the only money in the community, no one would ever try to "redeem" a deposit in cash. The bank, therefore, will never be asked to pay out assets. All it will ever have to do is transfer liabilities. For this it needs no reserves at all, and the $10 cash on the balance sheet serves no practical purpose.

Under such conditions credit creation can approach infinity. This may not be desirable from the point of view of public policy. Indiscriminate credit expansion will unquestionably lead to a serious inflation. This is, as a matter of fact, why we have legal reserve requirements today. But in the absence of any reserve requirements, whether legal or customary, a bank *can* create any amount of money it wishes.

A Monopoly Bank with a Currency Drain. Let us change the assumptions of our case a little. Take another isolated community with a single bank, the Beta Bank. In this community checks are used, but there are still some transactions for which cash is more convenient. Assume that the Beta Bank has the same balance sheet as the Alpha Bank in our first case:

Beta Bank

Assets		*Liabilities*	
Cash	10	Deposits	100
Loans	90		
	100		100

How much can this bank lend? Here, we regret to say, the answer is indefinite. We don't know. The answer depends entirely on what the experience of this bank has been concerning the desire of depositors to obtain cash. This desire, in turn, will depend on the structure of the society, the relative advantages and disadvantages of using cash as against checks, the faith of the community in the bank, and the stability of the economy. It is also subject to change over time, so that an adequate reserve at one time may be inadequate (or much more than adequate) at another. Past experience plus a little prudence to take account of unforeseen changes will indicate what a safe cash reserve would be.

If the bank felt that 10 per cent was a desirable reserve ratio (which is a little more than British banks commonly carry today), then it could not make any loans at all, for its reserves are just 10 per cent now. If it felt that 2 per cent reserves were sufficient, it could expand its loans and deposits by $400. Then its balance sheet would show:

Beta Bank

Assets		*Liabilities*	
Cash	10	Deposits	500
Loans	490		
	500		500

Reserves here are 2 per cent of deposits.

If, on the other hand, it felt that perhaps 50 per cent reserves were prudent, then it would have to let its loans run off until deposits dropped back to $20.

The higher the required reserve, the less the bank's ability to create money; with a 100 per cent reserve the bank could create no money at all. The lower the required reserve, the greater the bank's ability to create money; with a zero reserve requirement the bank could create money without limit.

A Competitive Bank in a Large System. These conclusions are based partly on the fact that the banks in our examples are the only banks in their communities. Does the same conclusion hold true with respect to a bank that is only one among many? To what extent can banks in the United States today expand credit? Actually there are two parts to this question, and they must be kept separate. Much confusion over the credit-creating powers of banks arises from a failure to distinguish between the power of a single bank acting alone and the power of the banking system with all banks acting together.

First the single bank. To what extent can one bank out of the thousands in the United States expand deposits? This is the problem that is faced by a bank's lending officer every day. Given his bank's current balance sheet position, how much can he prudently lend?

Suppose our Crossroads Bank, which we last examined at a very early stage of its growth, has developed to the point where its balance sheet looks as follows:

Crossroads Bank

Assets		*Liabilities*	
Cash and due from banks	200,000	Deposits	1,000,000
Loans and discounts	350,000		
Securities	520,000		
Banking house	30,000	*Net worth*	100,000
	1,100,000		1,100,000

"Cash and due from banks" is the heading usually used in published bank statements to include cash in vault, balances with correspondents, and balances with the Federal Reserve bank. Historically most bankers would consider all of them reserves—funds immediately available. Legal definitions of reserves may be more limited, but since we are here concerned with principles rather than law, we will simply refer to "cash and due from banks" as "reserves."

Under deposits we include all deposits due on demand, whether to individuals and businesses, governments, or other banks. As noted before, we are not here concerned with time deposits.

Given this balance sheet, how much can the Crossroads Bank lend? The significant items are its deposits and reserves, $1,000,000 and $200,000, respectively. Even these figures, however, are insufficient to provide the answer. We have already learned that one key fact always necessary to a decision of this kind is the percentage reserve requirement. Whether reserves are required by law, by experience, or by a combination of the two, our banker will know at any time what proportion of his deposits he has to maintain in the form of reserves. We will call this proportion his "required reserve" without regard to whether it is required by law or by custom. Let us assume that the Crossroads Bank has a required reserve of 20 per cent. Remember that this is merely an assumption and that the actual figure for any bank at a particular time might be considerably higher or lower than this.

With deposits of $1,000,000 and a required reserve of 20 per cent, the Crossroads Bank would have to maintain total reserves of $200,000. Since it has precisely that figure, it cannot afford to make any additional loans at all. To make a loan means to create an equivalent amount of deposits, and this would reduce the reserve proportion below 20 per cent.

Let us assume, then, that a depositor comes in and deposits $10,000 in cash. Leaving out those items that do not immediately concern us, the significant figures on the bank's balance sheet would become:

Crossroads Bank

Assets		*Liabilities*	
Reserves	210,000 (+10,000)	Deposits	1,010,000 (+10,000)

Assuming a 20 per cent reserve requirement, required reserves against $1,010,000 would be $202,000. The bank therefore has *excess reserves,* over and above those required, of $8,000:

Reserves		210,000
Required (20 per cent of 1,010,000)	202,000	
Excess	8,000	

Our analysis of the Beta Bank might lead us to believe that with excess reserves of $8,000 and a reserve requirement of 20 per cent our Crossroads Bank could create additional loans and thereby additional deposits of $40,000. Another way of looking at it would be to suggest that $210,000 of reserves would support $1,050,000 of deposits. While this would be true of the Beta Bank with a 20 per cent reserve ratio, it is definitely *not* true of the Crossroads Bank. The difference between the two is that the Beta Bank had a monopoly and knew that all checks drawn on it must be deposited back with it. All payments made by the Beta Bank (except for cash demanded by depositors, which we have taken care of in the required reserve) would then be cleared on the books of the bank itself without any change in its total assets or liabilities.

The Crossroads Bank is not in such a favorable position. It is one of many thousands of banks in the United States, and it knows that most checks drawn on it will find their way to depositors in other banks and will be presented to the Crossroads Bank for payment through the clearing machinery. The Crossroads Bank will then have an *adverse clearing balance* and will lose part of its reserve to other banks. The Beta Bank never had this problem.

Suppose the Crossroads Bank *did* lend $40,000 to one or more borrowers. The immediate result would be:

Crossroads Bank

	Assets		*Liabilities*
Reserves	210,000	Deposits	1,050,000 (+40,000)
Loans and discounts	390,000 (+40,000)		

But businessmen don't borrow money simply to increase their bank balances. They borrow in order to pay bills or to buy goods. A borrower, therefore, must normally be expected to write checks against his account up to, or almost up to, the full amount of his loan. In this case borrowers write checks for $40,000. These checks are deposited in other banks. The other banks present them to Crossroads through clearing, and Crossroads loses $40,000 of reserves. What is the result?

Crossroads Bank

	Assets		*Liabilities*
Reserves	170,000 (−40,000)	Deposits	1,010,000 (−40,000)
Loans and discounts	390,000		

The bank's deposit liabilities have fallen by $40,000, but so have its reserves. And $170,000 of reserves is less than 17 per cent of deposits of $1,010,000. The bank has fallen below its required reserve ratio.

No bank can take the chance that this will happen, and in order to avoid the possibility, every bank follows one very simple, practical, down-to-earth rule concerning the amount of loans it can safely make at any particular time: *Never lend more than the amount of excess reserves.*

Let us revert to the position of Crossroads before we assumed the $40,000 loan. Its excess reserves were $8,000. This is the maximum that a prudent banker would lend under the circumstances:

Crossroads Bank

	Assets		*Liabilities*
Reserves	210,000	Deposits	1,018,000 (+8,000)
Loans and discounts	358,000 (+8,000)		

Suppose now that the borrower draws checks in the amount of $8,000 and that these checks are deposited in other banks and come back to the Crossroads Bank for payment through clearing:

Crossroads Bank

	Assets		*Liabilities*
Reserves	202,000 (−8,000)	Deposits	1,010,000 (−8,000)
Loans and discounts	358,000		

Here there is no problem. The bank still has its 20 per cent reserve.

There are two assumptions that lie behind the banking rule that limits new loans to the amount of excess reserves: (1) that new borrowers will wish to use *all* the amount borrowed and (2) that *all* the checks so drawn will be deposited in other banks. Some writers have suggested that in actuality neither of these assumptions may be strictly true. If the borrower writes checks to an amount less than that borrowed or if some of the checks are redeposited in the lending bank, then the bank will not lose reserves to the full amount of the loan. Under these circumstances the bank could afford to lend more than its excess reserves.[4]

[4] In some cases banks require borrowers to maintain in their deposit accounts some proportion of any loan as a *compensating balance.* In effect this means that the borrower is not really obtaining the full amount of the loan. If, for instance, a bank requires a 20 per cent compensating balance to be kept for the duration of the loan, a borrower who needs $10,000 must borrow $12,500 in order to have the use of the needed sum. In this case the bank knows that 20 per cent of the "loan" cannot be checked out, and the nominal value of "loans" may exceed excess reserves. The precise amount can be determined by the so-called Phillips formula:

$$x = \frac{c}{kr + (1 - k)}$$

where x = amount that may be loaned
c = excess reserves
k = proportion of loan required to be kept as compensating balance
r = required reserve ratio

Thus, with $8,000 in excess reserves, a 20 per cent required reserve, and a 20 per cent required balance, a bank might safely lend $9,524. This formula, however, cannot be used if the potential borrower already has a deposit balance that can be counted toward the required compensating balance.

The difficulty with this position is that there is no way for the bank to know whether it has this extra margin or not. In most cases it probably won't lose reserves to the full amount of the loan, but it is always possible that it might. A banker is not in the gambling business; he can't afford to take any more risk than necessary. He has to gear his actions to the worst that might reasonably be expected to happen. It is *possible* that a loan will result in an equal loss of reserves, and simply as a matter of business prudence, therefore, the banker limits himself to lending an amount that he knows is safe. That amount is the amount of his excess reserves.

Actually, if the full loan is *not checked out,* the banker hasn't lost anything except a little time. Suppose the man who borrowed $8,000 writes checks in the amount of only $7,000, of which $2,000 is redeposited in the Crossroads Bank. The bank, then, loses only $5,000 through clearing. After presentation of these checks for payment, its balance sheet will read:

Crossroads Bank

Assets			*Liabilities*
Reserves	205,000 (−5,000)	Deposits	1,013,000 (−5,000)
Required 202,600			
Excess 2,400			

The bank is now in a position to lend an additional $2,400, representing excess reserves that it still has. *Now* it knows that the original loan has not meant a loss of reserves of the full amount. *Now* it knows that it still has excess reserves, and now it is safe to make an additional loan equal to its current excess reserves. But because it can't count on this turn of events, it would not have been safe to have loaned $10,400 in the first instance.

The Banking System as a Whole. This matter of reserves staying within the bank brings us to the closely related problem of credit expansion for the banking system as a whole. No individual bank can afford to lend more than its excess reserves, but the banking system as a whole can lend up to several times that amount. How is this possible?

Fundamentally, it is possible because reserves that are lost by one bank through an adverse clearing balance are obviously gained by some other bank. The second bank, therefore, has additional reserves against which it can afford to increase loans. If the banking system as a whole moves upward together, each bank continuing to lend as long as it has excess reserves, then the banking system has the same power of credit expansion as a monopoly bank.

Our last example showed the beginning of such a process. Let's review the basic facts. The Crossroads Bank received a $10,000 cash deposit. This resulted in excess reserves, which permitted the bank to lend $8,000. The key changes in its balance sheet are as follows:

Crossroads Bank

Assets			*Liabilities*	
$10,000 *is deposited:*				
Reserves		+10,000	Deposits	+10,000
Required	+2,000			
Excess	+8,000			
$8,000 *is loaned:*				
Reserves		unchanged	Deposits	+8,000
Loans		+8,000		
$8,000 *is withdrawn through clearing:*				
Reserves		−8,000	Deposits	−8,000
Loans		unchanged		

We have assumed that checks have been written for the full amount of the loan and deposited in other banks. Let's call these banks collectively "bank A." These banks (bank A), having received $8,000 of deposits in the form of checks written on the Crossroads Bank, collect these checks through clearing and thereby increase their reserves by $8,000. To the extent that some of these checks are redeposited in the Crossroads Bank, we can simply say that this bank is represented in our collective bank A. If we assume, for simplicity, that all banks have the same 20 per cent reserve requirement, their new deposits of $8,000 require additional reserves of $1,600, leaving this "second generation" of banks $6,400 of excess reserves.

(Collective) Bank A

Assets			*Liabilities*	
Reserves		+8,000	Deposits	+8,000
Required	+1,600			
Excess	+6,400			

We are assuming, of course, that bank A had no excess reserves prior to its receipt of the new $8,000. Since any individual bank can lend up to the amount of its excess reserves, bank A can make new loans of $6,400. This will initially increase its deposits by this amount, but as the borrowers write checks that are presented for payment, the deposits will fall back to their previous level, and bank A will lose $6,400 of reserves. The following changes in bank A's balance sheet show the effect of both of these transactions, differentiated by the symbols (*1*) and (*2*):

Bank A

Assets		*Liabilities*	
Reserves	—6,400 (*2*)	Deposits	+6,400 (*1*) —6,400 (*2*)
Loans	+6,400 (*1*)		

What bank A loses, other banks (call them collectively "bank B") will gain.

Bank B

Assets			*Liabilities*	
Reserves		+6,400	Deposits	+6,400
Required	+1,280			
Excess	+5,120			

Bank B can now make loans of $5,120, which will be checked out and deposited in other banks, called collectively "bank C."

Bank B

Assets		*Liabilities*	
Reserves	—5,120 (*2*)	Deposits	+5,120 (*1*)
Loans	+5,120 (*1*)		—5,120 (*2*)

Bank C

Assets			*Liabilities*	
Reserves		+5,120	Deposits	+5,120
Required	+1,024			
Excess	+4,096			

This type of merry-go-round can continue through the banking system. Each bank that receives checks drawn on a preceding bank increases its reserves as well as its deposits. It must hold the necessary required reserves against the new deposits and can lend an amount equal to the excess reserves, which in our example would be 80 per cent for each bank (the total reserve produced by the new deposits minus the required reserve that the bank must retain). If we were to follow this process until the original excess reserve of the Crossroads Bank of $8,000 were exhausted, we would find that the banking system had been able to create $40,000 of new money in the process. This is summarized in Table 9-1.

The initial deposit of $10,000, representing an increase in *total* reserves of $10,000, resulted in a total expansion of deposits of $50,000. Thus with a 20 per cent reserve requirement (one-fifth), *deposits* can expand by five times the *total* new reserves.

Looked at from another (more significant) point of view, the initial increase of $8,000 in *excess* reserves permitted the banking system to expand loans (and thereby create deposits) to the extent of $40,000. Thus with a 20 per cent reserve requirement, new *loans* can expand by five times the *excess* reserves.

The difference between *created deposits* of $40,000 and *total new deposits* of $50,000 is the $10,000 *received deposit* that started off the expansionary process.

Again to change our point of view, the total balance sheet of the banking system shows an increase in deposit liabilities of $50,000 and an increase in assets of $50,000, of which $10,000 is reserves (resulting from the cash deposit) and $40,000 is loans.

Table 9-1. Deposit Expansion by the Banking System
Assuming a 20 Per Cent Reserve Requirement

Banks	New deposits received	Required reserves against new deposits	Loans made (deposits created) on basis of excess reserves
Crossroads Bank	$10,000	$ 2,000	$ 8,000
Bank A	8,000	1,600	6,400
B	6,400	1,280	5,120
C	5,120	1,024	4,096
D	4,096	819	3,277
E	3,277	656	2,621
F	2,621	524	2,097
G	2,097	419	1,678
H	1,678	336	1,342
I	1,342	268	1,074
First ten banks	$44,631	$ 8,926	$35,705
Banks J to ∞	5,369	1,074	4,295
Total, all banks	$50,000	$10,000	$40,000

While this is a special case assuming a required reserve of 20 per cent, the principle can be extended to any reserve requirement. The general rule is that *the banking system as a whole can create deposits to an amount equal to x times its excess reserves, where x is the reciprocal of the reserve requirement.* With a 20 per cent (one-fifth) requirement, banks can create deposits equal to five times their excess reserves. If reserve requirements were 10 per cent (one-tenth), loans could be expanded by ten times the excess reserves. With a 30 per cent (three-tenths) requirement, deposits could be created to $3\frac{1}{3}$ times excess reserves. With a 100 per cent requirement, deposits could be created only to the extent of the excess reserves themselves.

In practice reserve requirements differ from bank to bank, so that no simple figure can be used to show the credit-creation multiplier for the system as a whole, but a rough average will give a general idea of the magnitude involved.

In speaking of this multiple-deposit creation by the banking system, we must remember that the individual bank, although it is a participant in the process, cannot bring it about alone. If other banks do not wish to expand in step with the new deposits they receive, the expansion will not progress to the extent indicated in our hypothetical case. The example shows the limits that *might* be reached if every dollar of excess reserves were put to work. In actual practice it is not likely that such perfect coordination would occur.

Another point that we might note, which is a source of some confusion, is that for practical purposes each bank in the chain creates deposits for *some other* bank. The normal effect of a loan by bank A in the amount of $6,400 is not a permanent increase of its own deposits, but rather a loss of that amount of reserves to bank B. To bank B this looks like any other deposit that increases its reserves. Bank B then creates an additional loan of $5,120, which in turn results in loss of reserves of that amount from bank B to some other bank.

The individual banker, as only one link in the whole chain, may not see the complete process. As far as his individual part is concerned, perhaps he may be excused for feeling that he does not create deposits. All he does, he maintains, is lend reserves that have resulted from someone's depositing checks drawn on other banks. In fact he doesn't even lend the whole amount, he says, but only that portion (80 per cent in our example) over and above his required reserve. "Utterly absurd," the banker may say, "this tommyrot about me creating money! All I do is lend assets just as any other financial institution does."

This attitude is the result of a mirage. We have already seen that even if the credit-creating process went no further than a single loan—even if the bank lent cash—the result is more money in circulation than there was before. And for the banking system as a whole the process can go much further. No single bank in a multibank system can create deposits to a multiple of its excess reserves, but working together (not in collusion but simply with the same object guiding each of them) banks as a whole can do so.

Practical Limits to Deposit Expansion

Perhaps it will be well to tie together our material on bank creation of money by looking at the practical limitations on deposit creation in the United States today on the basis of the principles worked out above. Only a few details need to be added.

Legal Reserves. About half of our banks (holding some 85 per cent of all commercial bank assets) are members of the Federal Reserve System and are subject to its reserve requirements. The law states that for these banks legal reserves shall consist of deposits with the Federal Reserve banks plus the amount of cash held in vault. In common usage the phrase "legal reserve requirements" refers to these provisions of the Federal Reserve.

We must remember, however, that all banks are not subject to these requirements. Nonmember banks are regulated by their respective state laws, which vary from state to state. All states except Illinois have such requirements, and all these laws permit banks to count cash in vault and sums due from other banks (correspondent balances) as legal reserves. A few also permit certain securities to be included. Whether subject to Federal or state regulations, the bank must maintain reserves, in whatever form is specified, at least equal to the legal requirement.

Customary Reserves. In addition to reserves required by law, all banks must have some reserves that can be used as working balances. Member banks usually maintain some "excess" reserve with the Federal Reserve banks in order to have funds through which clearing can be carried out, money transfers made, and so on. Small member banks probably wish to maintain some minimum balance with one or more correspondent banks, which cannot be counted as legal reserves. All banks need some extra cash to meet withdrawals. Legal reserves cannot be used for this purpose because to do so would bring the reserves below the required percentage. Just as an individual or firm usually has some minimum below which he doesn't want his bank balance to fall for fear of being "caught short," so banks are not easy if their reserve balance is too close to the legal limit.[5]

Customary reserves, therefore, must be held in addition to legal reserves. How much any bank considers it necessary to hold in this category depends on its own experience. Because banks are so dissimilar in size, location, legal status, type of customer, and so on, the proportion of deposits held in customary reserves undoubtedly varies considerably from bank to bank. There is some indication that *on the average* customary reserves (reckoned as a percentage of deposits) may include a little more than 1 per cent in cash, plus considerably less than 1 per cent in deposits with the Federal Reserve (in excess of legal requirements), plus an indeterminate amount that may run from 0 to 10 per cent in deposits in other banks.

Whatever the amount, banks must add customary reserves to legal reserves before they can compute excess reserves against which they can afford to lend. And it is the reciprocal of this total reserve requirement that would indicate the maximum possible expansion of the banking system.

Currency Drain. In our earlier example all the reserves that bank A lost were gained by bank B, but in practice this may not be the case, for some reserves may be drained away from the banking system.

When a borrower obtains a loan from a bank, he may withdraw part or all of it in cash. If the cash is used, say, to pay employees who in turn deposit it in another bank, the result will be the same as if the other bank received reserves through clearing. If, however, the borrower (or anyone else) withdraws currency that stays in circulation, this is a subtraction from the reserves of the banking system, and its ability to expand deposits further is correspondingly reduced. If, for instance, the $8,000 originally lent by the Crossroads Bank were *all* withdrawn in cash and kept in hand-to-hand circulation, deposit

[5] New York and Chicago banks have always been exceptions to this generalization. Because of their extensive facilities and their proximity to the money market they can balance their Federal Reserve accounts more precisely; in times of "tight money" they may walk a tightrope along the very edge of their legal requirements. Recently, as facilities for dealing in the federal-funds market have been extended by money-market banks to their correspondents, there has been a substantial decrease in excess reserves even of the smaller banks. From the end of World War II until 1960 "country" banks had maintained reserves that averaged close to 10 per cent higher than required by law. By 1965, however, their excess reserves had fallen to less than 4 per cent of their required reserves, or less than ½ per cent of their deposits.

expansion would stop right there; no other bank would acquire excess reserves against which it could make loans. If one-fourth of it were kept in circulation, then bank A would receive only $6,000, and its ability to expand would be limited accordingly.

Although only 10 per cent of all payments are made by using cash, approximately one-fifth of the total money supply is in the form of currency. This figure has varied from time to time, but there has almost always been a tendency for currency to increase as demand deposits increase. The greater monetary volume of business necessitates more pocket money as well as more checkbook money. If the total quantity of money is expanded by bank creation of deposits, some of the available reserves will undoubtedly be siphoned off into the hands of the public. To the extent that this occurs, the deposit-expansion multiplier will be less than the reciprocal of the required reserve ratio.

Gold Drain. A somewhat similar effect is produced if the monetary expansion of the economy leads to an increase of imports, so that part of the increased purchasing power is acquired by foreign exporters. Without going into the intricacies of foreign trade at this point we may simply suggest that under these circumstances there will be a tendency for the country to ship gold to those foreigners who hold dollar claims, and this loss of gold will also reduce the amount of reserves available to support expansion.

Ability to Lend and Actual Loans. If these various factors could all be given numerical values—which is not possible in practice—we could arrive at a definite figure for the ability of the banking system to expand deposits under given circumstances. This figure would change as legal requirements, the attitudes of the banks, and the habits of the community changed.

About all we can say with certainty is that under any conditions we have known in the United States, the banking system could create deposits to the extent of *some multiple* of its excess reserves. Since the Federal Reserve was formed in 1914 this multiple has probably not been less than 3 or more than 10.

But even if we knew how much banks *can* expand credit, we still wouldn't know how much they *will*. A bank is not compelled to expand, and whether it will or will not utilize the power inherent in excess reserves depends on a number of factors, which can be summed up in two general categories:

1. In order to make loans the bank must find customers who wish to borrow. If businessmen don't want to borrow, or if no one wishes to sell securities, obviously loans cannot be made, and excess reserves will not be used as a base for increased deposits.

2. Even though borrowers appear, the bank may be reluctant to lend. This may be due to a lack of faith on the part of the bank in the individual soundness of the prospective borrower. The bank can't lend to everyone who wants money; it will try not to make loans that it thinks are likely to be defaulted.

Or perhaps the bank has lost faith, not in the individual borrower, but in the general business situation. It may feel that business conditions are so critical that no loans except the very soundest should be made, or it may desire to hold an exceptionally large amount of excess reserves in order to satisfy its desire for liquidity. If it fears a "run," it is likely to wish to have extra funds immediately available and therefore may not want to whittle away its excess reserves.[6] For any of these reasons the *ability* of a bank to lend is not the same as its *willingness* to lend.

Historically we find that the very low level of bank lending in the period of the thirties was not due to any legal restrictions on reserves. From the end of 1933 to the end of 1941, member banks had very substantial reserves in excess of the legal requirement. During most of 1934 and 1935 total reserves were almost double those required by law. Banks do not always expand as much as they can.

As we close this chapter we should remind ourselves that deposit creation is a two-way street. We have emphasized the principles of credit expansion because they are fairly complicated. The principles of credit contraction are simplicity itself. If a bank wants to contract credit by making no new loans as old loans mature and by selling its securities, there is no limit to its power. It can reduce its earning assets—and thereby its created deposits—to zero. It would then cease, for all practical purposes, to be a commercial bank. While such extreme contraction is highly unlikely, less drastic contraction of credit from time to time is as normal a part of our economy as expansion. It was primarily such periodic fluctuations in credit that led to the establishment of the Federal Reserve System, whose basic function is to control them in the interest of the economy as a whole.

Questions for Thought and Discussion

1. When you lend me $10, have you created money? When a personal loan company lends me $10, has it created money? When I borrow $10 on my insurance policy, has the insurance company created money? Where does the money come from in each of these cases?

2. How would you go about determining the total amount of money created by banks?

3. When a bank pays its clerks in cash, does this increase money (purchasing power) in circulation?

4. If a bank can pay its bills with checks drawn on itself, does this mean that it can spend any amount of money it wants to?

[6] This case could be considered one in which the reserve requirements of the bank have risen, not in the legal sense, but in the sense that, times being what they are, the bank considers a higher reserve ratio necessary for prudent operation. Under this interpretation the reserves which are excess from a legal point of view are not excess from the bank's operational point of view.

5. In the case of the Alpha Bank, do you think people would continue to prefer checks to cash even if the bank began to create deposits in astronomical quantities?

6. What would the balance sheet of the Beta Bank look like if it decided it needed a 50 per cent reserve and reduced the volume of its loans sufficiently to achieve this result?

7. What would happen to a bank if its depositors suddenly wanted to withdraw more cash than the bank had in its till? Than it had on deposit with the Federal Reserve and other banks?

8. If money is checked out of a bank that has a required reserve of 22 per cent and deposited in a bank that has a required reserve of 18 per cent, how does this affect the ability of the banking system to create money?

9. If money is withdrawn from a demand deposit and put into a savings deposit, how does this affect the ability of the banking system to create money?

10. Why can the banking system create money to some multiple of excess reserves while a single bank cannot?

11. Illustrate with balance sheet examples the limits to credit expansion of a banking system with $1,000 excess reserves and a 10 per cent reserve requirement.

12. Why do legal reserves not represent the total reserves that banks need to maintain? If there were no legal requirements, would a bank let its reserves drop to zero?

13. Are there any causes other than an increase in total money supply that would cause a currency drain from the banking system?

14. What is the relationship between the large excess reserves of banks in the thirties and the state of the economy at that time? Were banks the cause of our failure to come out of the Depression?

15. The Constitution gives Congress the power "to coin Money, regulate the Value thereof, and of foreign Coin." Does this mean that it is unconstitutional for banks to create money?

16. Do you think it is desirable for commercial banks to have the power to create money? What good and what ill effects does this have on the economy?

Selected Bibliography

See references listed under Chapter 8.

Chapter 10
Liquidity and Portfolio Management

My ventures are not in one bottom trusted
Nor to one place; nor is my whole estate
Upon the fortune of this present year.

The Merchant of Venice
Act I, scene 1, line 42

We now have an overall view of the role of commercial banking in the economy. We have examined the principles that lie behind the creation of money and the mathematical significance of reserves in limiting that expansion. But the actual operation of the banking system is something more than a mathematical model; it is the result of individual actions taken continually by individual banks. The ways in which these banks respond to particular circumstances will determine not only whether an expansion takes place but also through what channels it takes place and what its effects on the economy will be. Banks may also contract credit even though their reserves are adequate. A closer look at the problems of bank operation is therefore in order.

One way to approach this study is to examine a consolidated balance sheet for all commercial banks. Such a balance sheet for December 31, 1964, is shown in Table 10-1. It is obtained by adding together the balance sheets of all commercial banks doing business in the United States on that date, a total of 13,761.

Capital

First let us look at the bottom of the balance sheet. The item called "capital, surplus, and undivided profits" represents the stockholders'

Table 10-1. Assets and Liabilities of All Commercial Banks, December 31, 1964

	Billions of dollars			*Per cent of total*		
Assets						
Cash and due from banks:						
Currency and coin		4.5			1.3	
Reserves with Federal Reserve banks		17.6			5.1	
Due from other banks		15.1			4.4	
Cash items in process of collection		23.3	60.5		6.7	17.4
Loans and discounts:						
Commercial and industrial loans		60.2			17.4	
Loans to farmers		7.5			2.2	
Loans on securities		8.4			2.4	
Real estate loans		43.7			12.6	
Consumer loans		39.8			11.5	
Loans to banks		3.5			1.0	
Loans to other financial institutions		10.9			3.1	
Other loans		5.2			1.5	
Less valuation reserves		(3.6)	175.6		(1.0)	50.6
Securities:						
U.S. government:						
Bills	13.4			3.9		
Certificates	0.0			0.0		
Notes	19.0			5.5		
Bonds	30.6	63.0		8.8	18.2	
States and localities		33.5			9.7	
Other securities		5.3	101.8		1.5	29.3
Other assets			9.0			2.6
Total assets			346.9			100.0
Liabilities						
Deposits:						
Demand:						
Individual and business	135.7			39.1		
U.S. government	6.5			1.9		
State and local government	13.5			3.9		
Interbank	17.9			5.2		
Certified and officers' checks	6.0	179.6		1.7	51.8	
Time:						
Individual and business	116.6			33.6		
U.S. government	0.3			0.1		
State and local governments	9.8			2.8		
Interbank	0.8	127.5	307.1	0.2	36.8	88.5
Borrowings			2.7			0.8
Other liabilities			9.3			2.7
Total liabilities			319.1			92.0
Net worth						
Capital, surplus, and undivided profits			27.8			8.0
Total liabilities and net worth			346.9			100.0

Source: Adapted and partially computed from *Federal Reserve Bulletin*, vol. 51, no. 6 (June, 1965), pp. 842, 846, 847. Detail may not add to totals because of rounding.

equity in the bank—the amount that stockholders invested when the bank was first started plus earnings that have been left in the bank as plowed-back profits. This item is sometimes called "capital and surplus" or more frequently simply "capital accounts."

Since assets exceed liabilities by the amount of the capital accounts, this net worth represents the cushion of safety provided by the owners of the bank for the depositors. If the bank should fail, the depositors will be paid first, and only if there is anything left over will the stockholders receive payment. This basic principle holds true for any corporation. But although a manufacturing concern may have a ratio of net worth to assets of 60 or 75 or 90 per cent, banks on the average have a ratio of only 8.0 per cent, as shown in the table.

Bank supervisory agencies have sometimes indicated that they feel that such a ratio is unduly low, and they have put pressure on banks to raise it. Consequently many banks plow back sizable portions of their earnings into surplus, but deposits have grown so rapidly at the same time that the net effect on the capital-assets ratio has been minor. It is true that a ratio of 8 per cent is low by historical standards (in the early days of the National Bank Act the ratio was over 30 per cent). Nevertheless, with the introduction of deposit insurance (which we will discuss in Chapter 15), the function of capital accounts as a cushion for depositors has lost much of its significance, and the present ratio does not appear to be dangerous.

Deposits

With the exception of a relatively insignificant amount of borrowings and "other liabilities" (such things as unpaid bills, accrued taxes, and similar items), the whole remainder of the liabilities and net worth side of the bank's balance sheet consists of deposits—amounts owed by the bank to its depositors which it has promised to pay them on demand or after a brief period of time. It is the relatively large volume of its deposit liabilities (88.5 per cent of total assets), plus the fact that these deposits must be paid almost at once if customers request it, that makes the operation of a bank such a ticklish business.

Demand Deposits. Table 10-1 shows the distribution of demand deposits among individuals, government units, and other banks. Table 10-2 provides additional data on the breakdown of these deposits among individual and business owners. These data are not strictly comparable with those in Table 10-1 since they pertain to 1961 and the figures cover only insured banks, but they do provide useful information.

Table 10-2 shows that individuals held over forty-six million checking accounts, and since there were approximately fifty-four million households in the United States in 1961, this suggests that 85 per cent of our households

Table 10-2. Demand Deposit Accounts of Individuals, Partnerships, and Corporations, January 25, 1961

Estimates for Insured Commercial Banks

	Number		Amount	
	Millions of dollars	Per cent of total	Billions of dollars	Per cent of total
Corporate business	2.3	3.9	49.5	45.4
Noncorporate business	4.0	6.8	14.7	13.5
Nonprofit organizations	3.0	5.1	5.3	4.8
Farm operators	2.8	4.8	4.1	3.7
Individuals — personal	46.2	79.2	32.4	29.7
All other	0.1	0.2	3.1	2.8
Total	58.4	100.0	109.0	100.0

Source: *Federal Reserve Bulletin*, vol. 47, no. 4 (April, 1961), p. 405. (This is the last survey of ownership of demand deposits published.)

keep a checking account.[1] These individual accounts add up to almost 80 per cent of all private demand deposits by number, but less than 30 per cent in terms of the dollar amount. This is hardly surprising since it means that the individual account is usually pretty small compared with business accounts. Corporations held only 4 per cent of the number of accounts, but 45 per cent of the dollar total; their average balance is much larger. Noncorporate business held 13.5 per cent of the dollar amount. Other depositors are relatively small when measured in terms of either numbers or amount.

If we combine the pertinent information from Tables 10-1 and 10-2, we find that business (both corporate and noncorporate) holds close to half of all demand deposit balances. Both on its liabilities side and (as we will see later) on its assets side, the bank is closely concerned with the activities and with the fluctuations of business.

Certified and Officers' Checks. The last item under demand deposits requires a bit of explanation. A *certified check* is a check which is drawn by a depositor on his account and on which the bank has certified that the check is in order and will be paid. When a bank certifies a check, it immediately subtracts the amount from the depositor's account and puts it into a separate account out of which the check will be paid.

An *officer's check* is a check drawn by the bank on itself, which it uses to pay for purchases or other debts. Sometimes an officer's check (or, as it is variously called, a *cashier's check*) is written at the request of a customer and sold to him at its face value plus a service charge. As soon as the check is written, the bank records it as a liability that must be paid on presentation.

Time Deposits. Although we have defined commercial banking as that part of banking activity having to do with demand deposits, there is hardly a bank

[1] Since some people probably had more than one account, the actual percentage may be somewhat lower than this figure.

in the United States that does not accept time deposits as well. And since banks do not provide separate accounts for the demand side of their business except in a few states where this is required by law,[2] any attempt to analyze the practical operation of a bank must include a look at the whole balance sheet. The assets of the bank are related to the whole of the bank's liabilities, not to any specific part of them, and one cannot therefore ignore the fact that time deposits are a very large part of the bank's business.

There are three types of time deposits, each carefully defined by law:

1. A *savings deposit* may be made only by an individual or nonprofit association. The bank has the right to require a savings depositor to give thirty days' notice of his intention to make any withdrawal, but in practice such notice is never required.

2. A *time certificate of deposit* (CD) is a deposit evidenced by a negotiable certificate stating the amount of the deposit and the date on which it will be repaid to the depositor or to anyone to whom he sells the certificate. A CD cannot be issued with a repayment date earlier than thirty days from the date of deposit, and it cannot be redeemed prior to the date stated. Time certificates are sometimes used by corporations who have temporarily idle funds which they will not need until some known date in the future. After having dropped almost into oblivion, CDs were revived in the high-interest market of the early sixties, and their use has increased rapidly.

3. A *time deposit, open account,* is any time deposit other than the two specified above. The bank *must require* the holder to give at least thirty days' notice of intention to withdraw it. These deposits are used primarily by corporations, who cannot open savings accounts. Most banks do not encourage corporate time deposits, and their amount is probably small.

Time deposits differ from demand deposits in two primary respects, directly related to each other. A depositor cannot draw a check against a time deposit; he must present the passbook and make a withdrawal. Thus he can turn his time deposit *into* money readily, but the deposit *is not* money. Any deposit against which a check can be written—that can be spent as money—is by definition a demand deposit.

On the other hand, time deposits pay interest, while demand deposits do not. Maximum rates that may be paid by commercial banks are prescribed by the Federal Reserve. The maximum rates permitted as of May, 1965, are as follows:[3]

	Per cent
Demand deposits	0
Savings deposits	4
Other time deposits payable in ninety days or more	4½
Other time deposits payable in less than ninety days	4

[2] California, Connecticut, Massachusetts, Rhode Island, and Texas require that the assets, liabilities, and capital accounts of a savings department be segregated from the rest of the bank's operations.

[3] The rates paid by savings banks on deposits or by savings and loan associations on shares are not controlled by Federal law; they may be subject to state restrictions.

From the point of view of the bank, time deposits are more desirable than demand deposits because (1) they are more likely to be long-term deposits not subject to sudden withdrawal, and they therefore present less threat to the bank's ability to meet claims of depositors, and (2) they are less costly to maintain because they do not require check-clearing facilities. On the other hand, of course, they do require the payment of interest; this is the price the bank must pay for borrowing on a longer-term basis. And when interest rates are high, time deposits may indeed be quite volatile. If an individual has an excess balance in his checking account that he does not expect to use for a month or two, he is tempted to shift this amount into a savings account while it's not needed and then shift it back again when it is. Since banks do not in fact require notice of withdrawal, he doesn't even lose any substantial amount of liquidity by so doing.

With many banks paying 4 per cent interest, they have indeed found that there has been a noticeable shift out of demand deposits into time deposits. So in many cases they are paying interest on what are, for all practical purposes, demand deposits. If they refuse to pay such high interest rates, however, they may lose the deposits entirely to savings banks or savings and loan associations. Similarly if they don't go along with the desire of corporations to obtain time certificates of deposit at an attractive interest rate, the corporations often withdraw their funds and buy short-term government securities. In this respect banks find that their attempt to attract funds must reckon with a rather highly competitive market.

Assets

Against its time deposits the bank holds three major types of assets: cash, loans, and investments. Each of these represents a sizable portion of its total portfolio.

Cash and Due from Banks. Cash in vault (currency and coin) is the bank's basic stock-in-trade, immediately available to meet the requests of its customers. Almost as readily available are deposits with other banks (either the Federal Reserve banks or other commercial banks with which it holds correspondent balances). These deposits, payable on demand, can be withdrawn at any time in cash. Or, more commonly, they are used as clearing balances, being drawn down when the bank faces an adverse clearing balance and built up when the tide of clearing moves in its favor.

Cash items in process of collection are checks that have been deposited with a bank but that have not yet been paid by the bank on which they were drawn. They represent funds that the bank will obtain as soon as the checks are cleared.

Commercial Loans. Commercial loans are almost the largest item among the bank's assets, which is hardly surprising. A commercial bank is so named because its original purpose was to provide loans for the carrying out of commerce. Merchants who needed funds to buy inventory could obtain short-term loans from the bank and could then repay these loans from the sale of the goods bought with the help of the loan. Generally it was felt that a merchant could turn over his inventory in at least three months, so the traditional loan of this kind is for 90 days. Loans to farmers have some of the same quality, since they presumably enable the farmer to meet his bills while his crop is maturing. He is then expected to repay the loan from the sale of the crop. But because of the more lengthy process of crop production, agricultural loans have traditionally been made for periods up to six months.

The Real-bills Doctrine. This doctrine, to which we have referred several times in our history of banking, is a formal justification for this activity of banks. It says that the proper quantity of money is the amount that is just sufficient to equal the quantity of goods currently available in the market (at current prices). If the economy is static, presumably the proper quantity of money is constant. If the economy expands, more money is needed to finance the additional goods. If banks lend to merchants an amount exactly equal to the additional quantity of goods (inventories) that they are buying, then the quantity of goods and the quantity of money will remain in balance; the proper quantity of money is created automatically. This is the real-bills doctrine.[4]

Stated negatively, the real-bills doctrine says that if banks make loans only for commercial purposes, then the quantity of money cannot expand to an undesirable extent and inflation cannot take place. By the same token, banks should *not* finance fixed capital—plant, equipment, and other assets that do not result in additional goods on the market until some time in the future. Only when goods are ready for sale should new money be made available.

From the point of view of the bank, real-bills loans provide a high degree of safety. Since the merchant has the goods actually in stock, he can easily repay the loan from the proceeds of the sale of these goods. The loan is therefore self-liquidating.

Although there is a good deal of truth in the real-bills doctrine, it is not foolproof. For one thing, the money created by the loan is not tied directly to the goods but is simply put into the money stream. It may then go on to finance a number of transactions while the goods still lie on the shelf. The fact

[4] The name "real bills" is a British term arising from the fact that in Britain the seller of merchandise frequently arranged to get payment by drawing a bill of exchange on the buyer, ordering him to pay the amount due at some future date. This bill was then discounted by the seller at his bank. The bank in effect made a loan on the basis of the bill as collateral. These bills were drawn against sales of real goods in existence; hence, "real bills." In the United States we speak more commonly of "self-liquidating paper," although this is a somewhat broader term.

that the merchant has bought the goods does not mean that he will necessarily find a market for them.

Another difficulty arises from the fact that as an expanding economy approaches the physical limits of production, prices tend to rise. Thus the *value* of goods that merchants may want to finance on purely real-bills terms will rise even though the *quantity* does not. The economy "needs" more money not because there are more goods but because there is inflation. Creating loans on a real-bills basis under these conditions will in turn produce more inflation.

Further, money is general purchasing power, and it cannot be restricted to the use for which it was ostensibly borrowed. Suppose, for instance, that a businessman has in the past been financing his own current purchases without relying on bank credit. Then he wants additional money to add a new wing to his store. By borrowing on a commercial loan he frees his own funds to put into the expansion of plant, certainly not a commercial use. He may even use the funds for purely speculative activity.

Finally, there is no way of telling whether businessmen will in fact ask for just the amount of loans that will equal the new goods coming to market, nor is there any assurance that banks will grant precisely this amount.

The real-bills doctrine is therefore no longer held in high esteem, either by economists or by bankers. Commercial and industrial loans account for only 17.4 per cent of banks' total assets, even though this category includes a number of loans that would not fit the real-bills doctrine. Many 3-month loans are renewed constantly from quarter to quarter and are never paid off, so that they become in effect long-term loans. Some industrial loans are made frankly for long-term capital purposes. *Term loans,* with a maturity of more than 1 year and sometimes as long as 10 years, have become increasingly important in bank portfolios since the thirties, and at the present time about one-third of bank loans to business are on a term basis. Many term loans must be repaid in installments, but even with this condition they are relatively illiquid and obviously do not conform to the real-bills doctrine.

Other Loans. Table 10-1 shows that real estate and consumer loans are two other very important areas of bank lending. Real estate loans are almost the antithesis of the real-bills doctrine. They are long-term, sometimes for as long as 30 years, and because they have no ready secondary market, they are highly illiquid. The Depression of the thirties, when the bottom dropped out of the real estate market, put many banks in serious trouble because of their mortgage loans, and the government had to bail them out by taking over many such loans through the Home Owners Loan Corporation. As long as business conditions are good, however, real estate loans pay well, and if they are insured by the FHA or the VA (see Chapter 19), they are quite safe.

Loans to consumers are of shorter term, usually one year but sometimes as long as three. They are completely non-self-liquidating since they do not increase the consumer's ability to repay and he must take the money for repayment out of his income. Such loans, however, carry high rates of interest, and the experience of the banks has been that they are quite safe on the average.

The volume of other types of loans is relatively small; in most cases the classifications are self-explanatory, and we will not discuss them further here.

Valuation Reserves. Valuation reserves, however, require a word of explanation. They are essentially reserves for bad debts. Some loans (the bank obviously doesn't know which ones, or it wouldn't make them) are bound to be defaulted as businesses or individuals find themselves in a position where they simply can't pay. The bank estimates the amount of anticipated bad debts, usually as a percentage of total loans outstanding, and *subtracts* this amount, under the heading "valuation reserves," from the total of its loans.

Securities. When a bank buys securities, it engages in a transaction that is almost the same as a loan, with one basic difference. A loan is the result of a personal relationship between the bank and its customer. The bank personally examines the credit standing of the customer, and the terms of each loan are worked out in negotiation between the bank and its client. Frequently the relationship is a continuing one in which the bank feels some sense of obligation to take care of the needs of the borrower as long as his credit standing remains satisfactory. It usually holds his loan until maturity.

It buys securities, however, on the open market without any personal relationship with the issuer. In such an impersonal market it buys whenever it has excess funds or wants to balance its portfolio in some particular way, but without any sense of obligation to the issuer. Similarly, if it needs funds, it has no compunction in selling securities at any time.

By far the largest security holdings are of government obligations, especially those of the Federal government. Banks held no certificates on December 31, 1964 (there were none outstanding on that date), but they held sizable amounts of short-term bills as well as the longer-term notes and bonds. There is an active market in government securities, and banks can sell them readily at any time. Such securities are therefore highly liquid. Their interest yield, however, may be relatively low.

The bonds of state and local governments (often called *municipals*) are not as liquid as those of the Federal government (often called *governments*), but they are relatively safe, and their income is tax-exempt. In addition, banks sometimes like to hold them as a matter of public relations.

Corporate bonds are held in relatively small amounts. Usually these are bonds of public utilities, which are considered quite safe and which pay a higher rate of interest than government securities. Banks have not held corporate stocks in any significant amount since the twenties. In fact the bank regulatory agencies, by direct prohibition or by moral pressure, limit the type and amount of stocks (and even of corporate bonds) that banks may hold.

Other Assets. About half of the item called "other assets" consists of bank buildings, equipment, and furnishings needed to carry on business. The rest is miscellaneous claims of a technical nature that need not concern us.

Portfolio Management

The balance sheet shows that banks hold a large variety of assets. Some of them earn no interest at all, such as currency and coin, reserves, deposits with other banks, and bank premises. Some loans are made at very low interest rates, while others earn more. A survey of seventy-one banks in 1963 showed that their average return on installment loans was 8.6 per cent, on real estate loans it was 5.5 per cent, and on investments it was 3.1 per cent.[5] Why this great diversity of assets with different earning power?

Part of the answer lies in the fact that the bank cannot make loans unless borrowers want them, while it is under a certain amount of pressure to comply with any reasonable request from a good customer. The greater part of the answer, however, arises from the bank's need to balance somewhat conflicting objectives: liquidity, safety, and income.

Portfolio management is the science (or the art) of balancing the various types of assets in the bank's portfolio in such a way as to maximize income without incurring the danger of insolvency. The main concern of portfolio management grows out of the fact that although the bank must be prepared to pay any depositor instantly, the only instant asset (cash) earns no income at all, and the higher interest rates normally are found on loans which are somewhat risky (such as installment loans) or which do not mature for fairly long periods of time (mortgages).

Primary Reserves. Since almost all liabilities of a bank are payable on demand, either by law (demand deposits) or by practice (savings deposits), the bank must be prepared to make such payments at any time in any amount that could conceivably be asked for by its depositors. To be absolutely safe a bank would have to carry 100 per cent reserves in cash so that every last depositor could be paid even if they all asked for their money at once. In practice banks have discovered that this degree of safety is not necessary and that a very much smaller fraction will suffice to meet any foreseeable demand. But some reserve is essential. Part must be in currency and coin so as to be instantaneously available; another part may be in deposits with other banks, available on demand but taking a little time to collect. The bank's *primary reserves* then consist of cash and due from banks.

Cash in Vault. Currency and coin are actually all the bank has immediately on hand to meet withdrawals. It is therefore little short of astounding that

[5] Federal Reserve Bank of New York, *Functional Cost Analysis: Comparative Study, 71 Banks, 1963–1962.*

banks as a whole hold less than 1½ per cent of their assets in cash. The uninitiated would probably think that this was completely unsafe. Don't more depositors than this withdraw their funds at one time? The answer is clearly "no." As a matter of long experience the banks have found that this small amount provides a substantial margin of safety. As some depositors are withdrawing, others are depositing, and the net turnover of cash is remarkably small.

Reserves with the Federal Reserve Banks. Although we will discuss reserve requirements in more detail in succeeding chapters, we have already indicated that members of the Federal Reserve System keep correspondent balances with the Federal Reserve bank of their district. These balances consist of two parts: *required reserves,* which the bank must keep according to law, and *working reserves,* which are excess reserves above the legal requirement that the bank keeps for much the same purpose as it keeps a cash reserve. Since legal reserves must be maintained (within narrow limits, to be discussed in Chapter 13), only the excess reserves can be used for clearing checks or for withdrawing additional cash when the bank thinks this is needed. Excess reserves are also incredibly low. In 1965 they averaged only $0.5 billion, or little more than 0.1 per cent of member banks' total assets. This figure, small as it is, must be a reasonable working balance for the member banks, or they wouldn't keep it so low.

Due from Other Banks. Banks also maintain correspondent balances with other commercial banks. For nonmember banks these balances can usually be counted as part of the reserves required by state law. For other banks they are part of the working balances and are used for carrying out interbank clearing operations and for other purposes. If a particular bank needs additional cash, it can obtain some by withdrawing it from the bank in which it holds a correspondent account. This, however, would merely shift cash from one bank to another; it is therefore not a way in which the banking system as a whole can obtain additional cash if needed.

Collection Items. Although cash items in process of collection appear on the balance sheet as part of "cash and due from banks," they are not properly a part of reserves. At the same time that bank A is collecting these claims against banks B, C, and D, those banks are also presenting claims against bank A. Bank A is likely to have to pay out in clearing approximately the same amount it receives, and its net position is not going to improve. No bank can count on cash items in process of collection as a source of funds to meet depositors' claims.

It is interesting to note that collection items amounted to $23.3 billion, while there was only $4.5 billion in cash in till (and $0.4 billion in member banks' excess reserves in the Federal Reserve) with which to pay them. This shows not that the banking system is in a shaky condition but that the clearing process can handle a large amount of claims with only a very minor net payment from one bank to another.

Since reserves, though necessary, are nonearning assets, a bank will always strive to keep its reserves at as low a level as is consistent with safety and with whatever laws may govern the bank's operations. It will attempt to keep the amount of collection items as low as possible by speeding them through the collection machinery, but otherwise it has no control over the size of this figure.

Secondary Reserves. One way of keeping cash at a minimum is to have available certain assets which earn interest but which are readily convertible into cash at short notice, that is, assets that have high liquidity or moneyness. These stand as a secondary line of defense in case unexpected demands are made on the bank by its depositors. They can be sold to acquire the needed funds.

There is no precise definition of secondary reserves, for liquidity is purely a matter of relativity (as pointed out in Chapter 3). The most important secondary reserves are unquestionably treasury bills, especially those with a maturity of ninety-one days. Not only do they enjoy an active market, where sales can be made almost instantaneously, but since they are payable within a very short time, their price cannot fluctuate very much from par. They therefore fulfill admirably the requirements of liquidity: they can be turned into cash rapidly and at a known value.

Other assets that might be considered secondary reserves by some banks at some times are bank acceptances (bills of exchange that a bank has promised to pay, usually within less than three months),[6] short-term high-grade municipal bonds, call or demand loans, and possibly even three-month commercial loans, although their liquidity is somewhat questionable. Longer-term government securities may sometimes be thought of as secondary reserves because of their highly organized market and lack of ultimate risk, but if a government bond has a long time to run to maturity, its price may be subject to substantial fluctuation for several reasons. The easiest case to see is the one in which all banks are experiencing difficulties at the same time. If they all try to sell government securities (or any other asset), who is going to buy unless the price falls to a level that makes the purchase attractive? But at lower prices the sale of securities results in a loss.

For assets of this type, liquidity really means *shiftability:* the possibility of finding someone else who is willing to give up cash for the security. In a normal market, shiftability of government securities is high, but if everyone is trying to get out from under at the same time, there may be no one to whom they can be shifted without loss.

Borrowing. Although it is not even an asset, much less a form of reserves, the ability to borrow is an important element in a bank's portfolio manage-

[6] Bank acceptances are discussed in detail in Chap. 36.

ment. Banks may borrow from other banks and frequently do, particularly on a one-day basis. The most highly organized form of interbank lending is the federal-funds market. The term *federal funds* refers to the reserve balances held by a member bank with its Federal Reserve bank. If a bank has excess reserves, it may lend them to a bank whose reserves are deficient. The normal "purchase" of federal funds means that bank L (the lending bank) gives bank B (the borrowing bank) a check drawn on bank L's reserve account, which bank B can deposit to its reserve account immediately. Bank B pays for this by giving bank L an officer's check drawn on itself. Bank L will put this check through clearing the next day and thereby receive payment. The result is that bank B gets the use of the funds for a single day. There is a brisk and almost continuous trade in federal funds. On occasion banks also lend to each other for longer periods and on more formalized terms.

Alternatively, member banks may borrow from the Federal Reserve bank for periods up to fifteen days. While lending between banks can be done only when some banks have excess funds, borrrowing from the Federal Reserve can be done even if all banks are in difficulty at the same time. Although such borrowing is generally confined to short and unusual periods, the fact that the possibility exists makes it practical for banks to carry smaller amounts of reserves than would otherwise be needed.

Call and Demand Loans. It is sometimes suggested in popular treatments of banking that a bank can improve its reserve position by calling loans. While this used to be possible in some cases, it is less so now, for the nature of the loan market has changed over time. The old *call loan,* made for a period of one day and automatically renewed until either the borrower paid or the bank called it, has disappeared. In its place is the *demand loan,* which superficially looks like the same thing. It is made on stock collateral primarily to brokers—as the call loan was—and it is technically payable on demand. But it is rare today for a bank to demand payment. What the bank does when it wants to discourage demand loans is raise the interest rate. Since the loan is renewable daily, the interest rate is not fixed for more than one day in advance. In this way a higher interest rate may *induce* a borrower to make repayment, but it does not *compel* him to do so. Even demand loans, however, are made by a small number of banks in major financial markets, and they do not represent a significant part of normal bank operations (they are part of "loans on securities" in Table 10-1).

Commercial Loans. Not only do the most liquid of the secondary reserves (treasury bills and bank acceptances) carry a relatively low rate of interest, but they also do not represent the type of activity that commercial banks were established to provide. Commercial loans are one step down the liquidity scale and one step up the interest ladder. They represent the largest single (and the traditional) type of bank lending. Because they are normally repayable within ninety days, the bank doesn't have its assets tied up for long periods. But, as already indicated, there is a growing tendency for banks to make term loans and to permit renewal of other loans. In this regard they are responding to the requests of business, which in many cases wants to plan its financing for some time into the future and would prefer not to have to work within the schedule of the traditional three-month commercial loan. Some bankers have expressed concern over this trend, but there is no evidence so far that it has seriously undermined the safety of the banking business. It has certainly changed its nature.

Other Loans. Along with the trend toward longer commercial and industrial loans has been the growth of real estate and consumer loans. Real estate loans have long been granted by commercial banks, although they represent almost the extreme of illiquidity. They are normally long-term and difficult to sell in the best of times. A good part of the "frozen assets" of banks that failed or almost failed in the thirties consisted of mortgages. Experience showed that, given time to thaw out, most of them were perfectly good investments. But liquid they were not. Perfectly good assets in the long run do not help a bank much when it needs cash today to meet the demands of its depositors. On the other hand, mortgages carry a higher interest rate than most business loans. Particularly if a bank has substantial amounts of time deposits, which it expects depositors to consider as long-run savings, it is likely to feel that at least part of its funds can be tied up in high-income low-liquidity loans on real estate.

Loans to consumers carry even higher rates and are more liquid than mortgages. On the other hand, the bookkeeping cost of processing these relatively small loans with their monthly payments is somewhat higher per dollar of loan than the cost of processing most other types. Banks first started making consumer loans on a substantial scale in the thirties, when business borrowers were few and far between. They are now actively pushing this type of business.

Maturity Distribution. Even if a considerable portion of a bank's assets are fairly illiquid, the bank has one partial means of protection. If loans are spaced in such a way that some are constantly falling due each day, even though the loans are themselves illiquid, their repayment as they mature will provide a steady flow of funds into the bank. The same is true, in a smaller way, of loans that are repaid in regular monthly installments, and this is the normal method of repayment for real estate and consumer loans. A part of portfolio management, therefore, is to space the various assets so that they provide an even maturity distribution.

Summary. These are the problems that the bank must consider when determining what amount of each type of asset it should keep in its portfolio. The bank that stays too liquid may lose money because its income is too low, while one that is not liquid enough may be forced into bankruptcy when it cannot meet the demands of its depositors.

Adjustment to Changing Conditions

How does a bank adjust its portfolio to meet changing conditions in the economy or in its own position? The ways in which banks react to an increased demand for loans or to increased reserves or to changes in the interest rate structure will have significant effects on the economy. Since monetary policy acts primarily through the channels of bank lending, it is well to know what banks are likely to do in particular circumstances. This is portfolio management in action.

Decreased Reserves. Suppose that banks find that their reserve ratio (the proportion of deposits held in the form of primary reserves) has suddenly fallen to a dangerously low level. This could occur for any of three reasons: (1) overexpansion of loans has raised the level of deposits relative to reserves; (2) a reduction of reserves has occurred because of an adverse clearing balance, perhaps because the monetary authorities are attempting to restrict credit;[7] (3) the required reserve ratio has risen, either because of a change in the law or because the bank decides that for safety it must hold a larger working reserve.

Suppose, for instance, that deposits are $100,000, while reserves are $18,000. This means that the (actual) reserve ratio is 18 per cent. Suppose further that the bank wishes (or is legally required) to maintain a reserve ratio of 20 per cent. This can be done either by reducing deposits to $90,000 or by raising reserves to $20,000. What steps will the bank take?

In the short run, at least, it is usually much easier to raise reserves than to reduce deposits. If the deficiency is expected to be purely temporary, the bank will probably borrow federal funds, provided the interest rate on such loans is below the discount rate.[8] If federal funds are scarce, the bank will probably borrow from the Federal Reserve. In either case the proceeds of the loan will be received in the form of an increase in the bank's reserve account. Even if the deficiency is expected to last, borrowing may be used to give the bank time to adopt other measures. Loans, however, carry an interest cost. If the interest rate on federal funds (or the Federal Reserve discount rate) is low, borrowing may be attractive. The higher the rate, the more inducement there is for banks to find other methods. In any case, since loans must be repaid, they are not a permanent solution to the problem.

For the longer-run solution the bank will probably turn to its secondary reserves. By selling government securities, particularly treasury bills, it adds to its reserves. Such a sale, however, has two consequences. In the first place it adds to the supply of securities on the market and therefore tends to depress

[7] The ways in which they do will concern us in Chaps. 12 and 13.

[8] In 1965 the rate on federal funds remained fairly consistently at ⅛ per cent above the discount rate, as banks found that the federal-funds market could be counted on to provide a somewhat continuous source of funds, while borrowing from the Federal Reserve is restricted to more or less emergency circumstances.

their price—slightly if only one or a few banks are affected, significantly if all banks are trying to obtain reserves at once. This drop in price of securities *is* a rise in the interest yield; the bank's attempt to gain reserves therefore raises interest rates. Second, as the bank disposes of secondary reserves, its liquidity falls. Unless it was overly liquid in the first place—had more secondary reserves than it really wanted—it is likely to look around for some means of replacing these secondary reserves.

Here it has two basic choices. It can sell long-term securities, or it can reduce its loans outstanding. The sale of government securities is always possible, but whether it is attractive or not depends on the interest rate. If interest rates are rising, this means that the market price of securities will be falling (as we saw in Chapter 4), and securities can probably be sold only at a loss. The more banks are involved in the attempt to regain liquidity this way, the larger the supply of securities offered for sale and the lower their price will fall (the higher their interest yield will rise).

The alternative of reducing loans may involve even more problems. It is, in the first instance, a slow process. Except for demand loans, which are relatively unimportant for most banks, all loans specify not only a date for repayment but also the rate of interest (or discount). The bank has no right to ask for repayment before the due date, nor can it raise the interest charge to induce earlier repayment. All it can do is wait for the maturity date to roll around. If its loans are spaced evenly over time, some loans will be falling due today, some more tomorrow, and so on. If the bank stops making new loans, the normal repayment of old loans will gradually reduce its deposits.

When a bank attempts to reduce the volume of new loans that it grants, it may do so in either of two ways. Most obviously, it may raise the interest rate that it charges customers. This may discourage borrowers, just as an increase in cost of any other resource may discourage prospective purchasers. On the other hand, as we will see later, businessmen may be so optimistic about the future prospects of business that a small rise in the cost of borrowing is insignificant compared with the profit they expect to derive from expansion. Some marginal borrowers may be discouraged, but perhaps most will not.

The second way, therefore, in which banks may try to reduce loans is by rationing, that is, by looking more carefully at the qualifications of prospective borrowers and refusing to make some loans that they previously would have been glad to make. Under these conditions borrowers who are willing to pay the current rate of interest simply cannot get loans. This is what is referred to as a *tight-money market*. Normally credit rationing and rising interest rates go together.

Whichever method the bank uses to reduce the volume of loans, it has to take into consideration the reactions of its regular customers. Many businessmen expect that the bank will, almost automatically, grant any loan they request for legitimate reasons. Others are accustomed to loans being renewed regularly, and their plans would be upset by the bank's failure to take care of them. The bank normally respects these attitudes on the part of its customers and frequently will bend over backward to avoid cutting down on a certain portion of its loans. In rationing loans it will probably refuse to lend to new customers rather than to old, and even when it raises interest rates, it may do so selectively.

Because the bank is striving to regain lost liquidity, it is especially anxious to shorten the average length of loans, and for this reason new mortgages may be particularly restricted. Consumer loans may also be discouraged. And the portfolio of long-term securities may be reduced in spite of a capital loss on the sale of these assets. On the other hand, these are the best-paying assets that a bank has, and if it has to cut down on them, it therefore has additional incentive to raise interest rates on the loans that it continues to make.

The net effect of all these reactions of the bank to a need to improve its reserve ratio is a reduction in the availability of all types of bank loans and a rise in interest costs in a wide area, from federal funds through treasury bills to long-term securities and bank loans of all kinds. But the effect may be felt more strongly in some areas than in others, depending on the bank's specific reaction, on the composition of its portfolio before the change, on its assessment of relevant changes elsewhere in the economy, on the reaction of the business community, and on the importance both banks and others place on the need for liquidity.

If, for instance, banks have abnormally large holdings of government securities, as they did in the period immediately after World War II, they may simply sell these without any reduction in loans at all. If their portfolio is well balanced, the reduction in earning assets may be fairly evenly spread over all categories, with perhaps some lag in the adjustment of loans. If the bank's liquidity position is very weak (small amounts of both primary and secondary reserves), the effect on business loans is likely to be both more immediate and more drastic.

Increased Demand for Loans. To take a different case: if a bank, starting from a reserve position that is considered satisfactory, faces an increase in the demand for loans, particularly from its good customers, it may well feel that at least some of the requests should be granted. To do so, however, increases its deposits and reduces its reserve ratio. It is then in the same position already described; how will it restore the ratio? The bank *may* simply let the ratio decline, but this reduces its liquidity in the vital area of primary reserves and may in fact bring them below the legal requirement.

If it sells secondary reserves, it shifts the liquidity problem somewhat; its first line of defense is bolstered, but its second line is weakened. Its safety as well as its liquidity is impaired, for the new loans are certainly riskier than cash and almost certainly riskier than short-term government securities, although they are likely to produce more income. The bank may wish to improve overall liquidity by selling long-term securities, but it can improve its safety only if they are nongovernment obligations. Sale of corporate bonds, however, may involve the bank in loss. Possibly it can improve safety by getting rid of some loans to brokers. It can improve both safety and liquidity by reducing mortgages or consumer loans, but this is almost certain to reduce income as well since these are generally higher-interest loans.

Whichever way it turns there are some disadvantages as well as advantages. The art of portfolio management involves weighing these different alternatives and deciding which presents the best long-run advantage to the bank.

Increase in Reserves. What happens if a bank finds itself with substantial excess reserves? We won't follow this case through in detail because for the most part it is simply the opposite of the case of deficient reserves. It differs in one respect, however. If banks have deficient reserves, they *must* borrow, sell securities, or reduce loans. If banks have surplus reserves, they *may* repay borrowing, buy securities, or expand loans.

If banks are not in debt, if avaliable securities carry a very low interest yield or are of a type that appears too risky, and if acceptable borrowers are not asking for loans, a bank may simply hold on to any additional reserves that it might acquire. This is sometimes referred to as the *liquidity trap:* additional funds or potential funds are absorbed in increased liquidity without becoming available in the economic marketplace. One device for expanding the economy by encouraging bank lending is to provide banks with excess reserves (as we will see in more detail in Chapter 13). But if banks wish neither to lend nor to buy securities, they will use the additional reserves simply as a source of greater liquidity, and the monetary pressure toward expansion is trapped before it can become effective.

Questions for Thought and Discussion

1. How does it happen that the total assets of all commercial banks (Table 10-1) exactly equal their liabilities plus net worth?

2. Why do bank regulatory authorities care how much net worth ("capital") a bank has?

3. In its published statements, why is a bank likely to include "due from banks" as part of "cash assets"? Is this related to our definition of money?

4. Would it be desirable for banks to return to a policy of making loans only on a real-bills basis?

5. Should banks be prohibited from making mortgage or term loans?

6. Why does a bank have to worry about liquidity at all?

7. Do you as an individual have problems of liquidity similar to those of commercial banks?

8. Why is shiftability an important part of liquidity? If there were a general run on all banks in the United States, where would the banking system obtain the funds necessary to pay depositors?

9. Why is the ability to borrow almost as important a part of liquidity as secondary reserves? Under what circumstances might it be even more important?

10. In order to be completely safe, why doesn't a bank keep all its assets in cash?

11. Why should a bank's attempt to increase its liquidity raise interest rates generally?

12. When its reserves fall, why does a bank resort to credit rationing when it could increase its income by raising interest rates charged borrowers?

Selected Bibliography

American Bankers Association: *Investment Fundamentals,* New York, 1962.

———: *Banking and Monetary Developments and Their Application to Bank Asset Management,* New York, 1963.

Einstein, Major B.: *Managing the Bank's Investment Portfolio,* First National Bank in St. Louis, St. Louis, Mo., 1962.

Hodgman, Donald R.: *Commercial Bank Loan and Investment Policy,* Bureau of Economic and Business Research, University of Illinois, Urbana, Ill., 1963.

Lyon, Roger A.: *Investment Portfolio Management in the Commercial Bank,* Rutgers University Press, New Brunswick, N.J., 1960.

Phillips, Chester Arthur: *Bank Credit,* The Macmillan Company, New York, 1920.

Prochnow, Herbert V., and Roy A. Foulke: *Practical Bank Credit,* 2d ed., Harper & Row, Publishers, Incorporated, New York, 1963.

Reed, Edward W.: *Commercial Bank Management,* Harper & Row, Publishers, Incorporated, New York, 1963.

Robinson, Roland I.: *The Management of Bank Funds,* 2d ed., McGraw-Hill Book Company, New York, 1962.

Welfling, Weldon: *Bank Investments,* American Institute of Banking, New York, 1963.

Part Three Central Banking

Chapter 11 Development of the Federal Reserve System

No sooner knew the reason but they sought the remedy.

As You Like It
Act V, scene 2, line 41

Having gotten a firmer notion of just what a modern bank is and how it operates, we are now ready to resume our historical survey, which we left at the end of the nineteenth century. By 1900 the national banking system was well established, although over two-thirds of the 12,500 banks in the country had state charters. National bank notes had replaced state bank notes but constituted less than 15 per cent of the currency in circulation, the largest element of which was gold coin. Bank deposits, while twenty times greater than they had been in 1864, were less than 4 per cent as large as they are today.

Panic and Reform

Not all was perfect in the banking world of this period. Serious questions had been raised about the adequacy of the circulating medium as a result of the gradual but continuous fall in the price level that had been going on since the close of the Civil War.[1] This fall in prices affected particularly the farmers, who found their incomes falling and the burden of their debts increasing, and much popular agitation was aroused in favor of cheap money—that is, more money. Because the currency was tied so

[1] The fall in prices is shown graphically in Fig. 22-1.

closely to gold at that time and because it was believed that the shortage of money was therefore linked to the failure of the gold supply to expand as rapidly as business required, much of the discontent centered on the gold standard. The epitome of this feeling was expressed by William Jennings Bryan's famous thrust: "You shall not press down upon the brow of labor this crown of thorns; you shall not crucify mankind upon a cross of gold."[2] But additional gold discoveries alleviated the stringency somewhat, and business conditions improved substantially in the closing years of the nineteenth century.

By 1900 the country seemed to be in fine shape. Although criticisms were directed at particular aspects of banking, although the machinery for transfer of funds between cities left something to be desired, although there was some fear over the concentration of bank reserves in New York, although currency stringencies did develop from time to time, nevertheless the general feeling was one of complacency. Business had never been so good, and though some reformers suggested the need for changes, they were voices crying in the wilderness. No one listened; everyone was too busy making profits.

The Panic of 1907. This attitude of complacency soon gave way to panic on a large scale. Elements of overexpansion in the banking system were evident in 1906. In that year the Secretary of the Treasury proposed greater government regulation of the money market, and the American Bankers Association appointed a currency commission to study the problem, but no action followed.

In the spring of 1907 the "rich man's panic" hit the stock market with declines greater than any previously experienced. In October, after substantial recovery, the stock market fell again, and the panic spread to the banking system. Ten New York banks were forced to close their doors in a single week, and others, faced with runs not only from their local depositors but also from their correspondent banks all over the country, restricted cash payments. Many other banks throughout the country, unable to obtain cash from their New York accounts, followed suit. The demoralization of the monetary system and the difficulty of obtaining loans forced many businesses into liquidation, with repercussions on the whole economy that lasted well into 1908.

The Aldrich Committee. The deficiencies of the banking system could no longer be ignored. Congress passed the Aldrich-Vreeland Act in 1908, which, among other things, created a National Monetary Commission, composed of nine senators and nine representatives, to "inquire into and report to Congress at the earliest date practicable, what changes were necessary or desirable in the monetary system of the United States or in the laws relating to banking and currency. . . ."[3] Senator Aldrich was appointed chairman of this commission, and it may not be amiss to note in passing that its membership included H. M. Teller and H. D. Money.

[2] Address before the Democratic National Convention, July 8, 1896.

[3] Act of May 30, 1908, 35 Stat. 546, sec. 18.

The "earliest date practicable" turned out to be January 8, 1912, when its final report was submitted. The reason for the delay was the extreme thoroughness with which the commission tackled its assignment. In addition to ordinary hearings it delved into the history of banking back to the origins of the United States as well as the development and operation of banking and central banks in all major countries. It collected voluminous statistics, compilations of laws, and views of European and American bankers and others interested in finance. It was a thoroughgoing and in most respects highly competent survey of the whole banking problem.

Shortcomings of the National Banking System

The report of the National Monetary Commission begins with an enumeration of the defects of the country's banking system of that period. The commission listed seventeen deficiencies. The major ones may be grouped under five headings: currency, clearing, reserves, credit, and control.

Inelastic Note Issue. Currency occupied a more important place in financial discussion of this period than demand deposits, and in fact it was the inability of banks to pay out currency in the panic of 1907 that caused a good deal of the distress. It was generally felt that our currency was too inelastic to meet changes in business conditions both seasonal and cyclical. The biggest seasonal influence on hand-to-hand circulation was the moving of crops in the fall, when large amounts of currency were needed by farmers to pay harvesting workers and to repay bank loans contracted in the spring, while at the same time others needed funds to buy the agricultural output. The business cycle, with its fluctuations in the level of general business activity, brought changes in the demand for currency from year to year.

Yet there was no provision in our monetary system of this period to meet these seasonal or cyclical swings. One writer describes this condition very aptly:

> A physician would probably say that what primarily ails our currency system and causes panics and desperate stringencies is something akin to *arteriosclerosis*. The veins and arteries of credit, which in order to function properly ought to be elastic and contractile like rubber, are hard and brittle as glass. When subjected to unusual strain they can yield but little and are very liable to rupture, and when once stretched they are apt to remain over-enlarged.[4]

A glance at the composition of our currency in this period, as shown in Table 11-1, will indicate why this was so.

[4] A. Piatt Andrew, "The Essential and the Unessential in Currency Legislation," in *Questions of Public Policy,* Addresses delivered in the Page Lecture Series, 1913, before the senior class of the Sheffield Scientific School, Yale University (Yale University Press, New Haven, Conn., 1913), p. 62; quoted in Chester Arthur Phillips, *Readings in Money and Banking* (The Macmillan Company, New York, 1921), p. 673.

Table 11-1. Currency in Circulation, June 30, 1910

Millions of Dollars

Gold coin	591
Silver coin	208
Minor coin	46
Gold certificates	803
Silver certificates*	483
United States notes	335
National bank notes	684
Total	3,149

* Including $4 million of treasury notes of 1890
Source: Adapted from Board of Governors of the Federal Reserve System, *Banking and Monetary Statistics* (1943), p. 408. Detail does not add to total because of rounding.

Gold and silver coin were limited by the production of the mines or import from abroad, the latter in turn depending on the nature of our foreign trade. Minor coin was insignificant in amount. Gold certificates and silver certificates were backed 100 per cent by metal and hence were limited in the same way as gold and silver coin. As for United States notes, a congressional act of 1878 required that the amount issued be kept at a constant level.

This leaves only national bank notes, and because of the conditions under which they were issued these also failed to provide flexibility. National bank notes were backed 100 per cent by government bonds, and the quantity of notes issued depended, therefore, on the quantity of bonds that banks were able and willing to hold. From 1880 to 1891 the government operated at a surplus sufficient to pay off over half the national debt, and during this period national bank notes also declined by more than half. In the decade from 1900 to 1910 the quantity of notes would have dropped even further except for two unusual circumstances: (1) Starting in 1900 new government bonds were issued at an interest rate of 2 per cent, too low to attract most nonbank investors, so that by 1910 national banks held over two-thirds of the total national debt as security for notes. (2) During this period the government reissued bonds that could have been retired out of current surplus, specifically for the purpose of avoiding a drop in note issue that would have inevitably followed repayment of any substantial part of the debt. In other words, the government issued bonds not because it needed the money but because the public needed the currency that could be issued by national banks against bonds as collateral.

Although this device made possible a gradual growth in the quantity of bank notes, it was not a satisfactory method from the point of view of sound finance, and it did nothing to ease the problems of inelasticity over the shorter periods. Currency stringency in the fall was especially noticeable. Not only was it difficult for the rural areas to obtain funds, but to the extent that they succeeded, they depleted the currency of the cities and therefore merely shifted the burden.

Inefficient Transfer System. Although clearing houses had been established by 1900 in most large cities, the collection of out-of-town checks still involved the cumbersome, expensive, and inefficient process of collecting through correspondents. Many banks charged high fees for collection, and in order to avoid these charges checks were often sent by much more circuitous routes than necessary. In one famous case a check drawn on a bank in Sag Harbor, New York, was deposited in Hoboken, New Jersey, 93 miles away. It traveled 1,233 miles and through eleven banks as far away as Boston and Albany before finally being paid at Sag Harbor.[5]

The cost and difficulty of check clearing between regions was so great that in many instances sellers or others to whom payments were due would refuse to accept checks drawn on out-of-town banks. Thus a New York manufacturer would quote prices, not in dollars, but in "New York funds." This meant either cash or a check drawn on a New York bank, which could be collected through the clearing house. Since the out-of-town customer didn't have a deposit in New York, he could not use his own check but had to buy a bank draft from a bank that had a correspondent in New York, much as if he were making payment to a foreign country.

In addition to the fee that the purchaser of such a draft had to pay, he might also have found, particularly during financial panic, that New York dollars were more expensive (or perhaps cheaper) than his own dollars. On November 16, 1907, for instance, $1,000 in New York funds cost $1,005 in Philadelphia, $1,001 in Chicago, $1,007 in St. Louis, and $997 in New Orleans. On August 12, 1893, another period of panic, the same amount in New York exchange cost $1,002 in Boston, $985 in Philadelphia, and $970 in Chicago.[6] The difference in rates depended on whether banks had more reserves in New York than they wanted (so that they were willing to dispose of them cheaply for cash in hand) or whether their New York balances were already low and they did not wish to deplete them further except at a premium.

In foreign payments our machinery was just as deficient. The primary instrument used in making international payments is a bill of exchange usually drawn upon a bank and accepted by it.[7] London banks had perfected this device to the point where it was a highly effective instrument, while in the United States the law actually prohibited incorporated banks from accepting bills. As a result almost all our foreign trade was financed through London banks and practically none of it through our own financial system.

Inadequacies of the Reserve Structure. The third great difficulty of the national banking system was the ineffective use of reserves. The United States

[5] The route was Hoboken→New York City→Far Rockaway, L.I.→Port Jefferson, L.I.→Albany→Tonawanda, N.Y.→Boston→New York City→Riverhead, L.I.→Long Island City→Sag Harbor.

[6] O. M. W. Sprague, *History of Crises under the National Banking System,* Publications of the National Monetary Commission (Government Printing Office, 1910), pp. 291, 204.

[7] A process we will consider further in Chap. 36.

was at this time the only country in the world that required banks by law to maintain a specified proportion of their deposit liabilities in cash or on deposit with other banks. In spite of this presumed safeguard, our banks were not immune to the difficulties associated with a run. The very fact that reserves could not legally be reduced below the requirement meant that in an emergency they could not be used. We have, then, the spectacle of a New York bank with over 20 per cent of its deposit liabilities in cold cash right in the vault having to close its doors during a run because this was below the minimum that the law said must be kept intact to ensure the soundness of the bank!

Under the National Bank Act there were plenty of reserves in the country. The *cash* held by national banks in this period averaged between 10 and 15 per cent of deposits for the nation as a whole. But each bank had to hang on to its own reserve. Reserves could not be brought together to meet a particular run at the place where it developed, nor could they be used even to help the bank that held them. In actual practice some banks did attempt to meet a crisis by reducing reserves below the legal requirements, and in most cases the Comptroller of the Currency tacitly ignored such violations. The basic system, however, was defective, and attempts to meet an emergency by ignoring the law simply illustrated how unsatisfactory the law itself was.

Although deposits in correspondent banks could be counted as part of legal reserves, the attempt on the part of banks to translate these deposits into cash tended to spread the fire. If banks in Pennsylvania, for instance, were experiencing difficulty, the country banks would call on their correspondents in Philadelphia and Pittsburgh for cash. These banks in turn would call on their New York correspondents. Where would the New York banks get funds? They couldn't use their legal reserves of 25 per cent cash. Their next most liquid assets were call loans, loans made primarily to stockbrokers for carrying securities and subject to call by the bank at any time. As one New York bank attempted to obtain funds by exercising its right to call, the brokers, needing funds to make payment, would try to refinance by borrowing from other banks, thus just shifting the burden. If all banks were calling loans, the broker could get money only by selling securities, and if this pressure were general, the vast amount of securities dumped on the market could lead only to a precipitate decline in stock prices and further panic.

Thus the pyramiding of reserves in New York didn't provide a rational means of mitigating a crisis but rather tended to channel any major disturbance anywhere in the country to New York, where it exploded instead of being eased.

Primitive Credit System. The nature of reserve requirements had another unfortunate result. Since there was no flexibility in requirements, and since, in addition, there was no place where a bank could acquire additional reserves when business was growing, the quantity of bank credit based on loans was almost as inelastic as the quantity of currency. Since reserves are unprofitable, banks tried to keep their deposits as high as their reserves would allow. If the economy expanded and more credit was called for, the banks could not respond. To increase loans they would need excess reserves. And for these there was no place to turn.

The primary difficulty facing a bank that wanted additional reserves, whether as a source of loans or to meet withdrawals, was the general illiquidity of the banking system. Except for call loans in New York the earning assets of banks were almost impossible to turn into cash on short notice. Few short-term securities were available, while government bonds, normally quite salable, were tied down as collateral for bank notes and hence could not be used. The largest group of assets was loans and discounts, but whereas Europe had developed financial instruments whereby commercial loans were embodied in bills of exchange that could be discounted and rediscounted so that any bank wishing to obtain quick funds could sell its bills in a highly organized bill market, the United States frowned on such measures. Our commercial loans were tied up in promissory notes that did not have a good market because they represented a very personal relationship between the borrower and his banker. Under these conditions a bank could be highly solvent but thoroughly illiquid. If it had the misfortune to be the object of a run in spite of complete soundness, it had nowhere to turn to obtain help.

Illiquidity of assets had another unfortunate result. Since most assets couldn't be turned into cash anyway, bankers paid less attention to the soundness of the loans they made. This tendency was strongly reinforced by rigid reserve requirements, which turned the banker's attention from the *quality* of his loans to the *quantity* of his cash.

The picture was not entirely black, for clearing houses, cooperative associations that they were, did provide some help to members in emergencies. The banks in the clearing house often pooled their resources to make loans to members in distress. This help, however, had its limitations. It was not always forthcoming as rapidly as might be desired and obviously was limited to the larger cities, and even the clearing houses ran into difficulties when all banks in the city were in trouble.

Lack of Coordination. Finally, the banking system suffered from the absence of any semblance of coordinated policy. The National Bank Act had envisioned all banks under the single authority of the Comptroller of the Currency. This hope was not fulfilled, and in 1910 only 7,138 out of 24,514 banks had a national charter. The rest were subject to forty-six different state regulations, some relatively effective, others only nominal.

Even the national banks, although they were subject to uniform requirements and similar examinations, could hardly be said to be coordinated. Within very broad limits each bank did pretty much as it pleased. There was no agency whose primary purpose was to provide direction for the monetary system, no one to cope with the problem of insufficient currency or inelastic credit, no one to help banks in an emergency or to mobilize the resources of the banking system to meet a crisis, no one to bring some sort of order into the chaotic conditions of a thoroughly decentralized system.

It is perhaps not too much to say that the United States did not have a banking system at all; it had an agglomeration of 24,000 banks going their 24,000 separate ways with a minimum of cooperation through correspondent relationships and clearing-house associations and with no unifying purpose except the individual profit of the individual bank. The results, as the panic of 1907 had clearly demonstrated, were thoroughly unsatisfactory.

Background of the Federal Reserve System

In order to correct these deficiencies of the banking system, the National Monetary Commission proposed to set up a new agency, a National Reserve Association, which was essentially a voluntary association of banks. It would issue its own notes, hold deposits for those banks that joined, and make loans to them against acceptable collateral. In spite of (or perhaps because of) strong support by leading bankers and the Republican party, the bill met much opposition from the general public and from the Democratic House of Representatives and was never brought to a vote.

Meanwhile the House Committee on Banking and Currency, under the chairmanship of Carter Glass, was already at work on a different kind of bill. The Glass bill was strongly opposed by the banking community, but after some compromise it emerged on December 23, 1913, as the Federal Reserve Act.

While differing in some important details from the National Reserve Association plan, the Federal Reserve System as established had the same objectives and many of the same functions. One fundamental difference was the reduced influence of bankers in the administration of the system and the substitution of a completely government-appointed board at the top. In this respect the Federal Reserve approached more nearly the concept of a central bank. To have called it a central bank, however, would probably have ensured its defeat, for these words in 1912–1913 signified a degree of government interference with private enterprise that the nation was unwilling even to consider. In fact, while the Federal Reserve had some central banking attributes, it differed significantly from any central bank then in existence. It was a typically American solution to a typically American problem.

Foreign Central Banking. Central banking at this period was well established in Europe and even in Japan and had been studied in detail by the National Monetary Commission. The Bank of Sweden had been founded in 1656, the Bank of England in 1694, and the Bank of France in 1800. Even the German Reichsbank, a relative newcomer, was almost forty years old. Although we studied these examples before setting up our own Reserve, we did not copy any of them because both our financial machinery and our philosophical leanings had taken their own distinct form.

In most European countries there were a few large private banks, many with branches scattered over the whole country. Clearing, mobilization of reserves, and even a degree of centralized control were functions carried out by individual banks or by easy cooperation among a few, often on an informal basis. Discount markets were so well established that credit could be obtained from the market without recourse to any central agency.

The function of foreign central banks, then, was primarily to provide and control the issue of currency. In most countries the use of checks was relatively undeveloped, and notes represented the major means of payment. Only in Britain, where checking facilities were even more important than in the United States, was this not the case, and even the Bank of England was primarily a bank of issue.

In most cases the central bank was privately owned, with a degree of government control that ranged all the way from negligible with regard to the Bank of England to almost complete in the case of the Reichsbank. European central banks were not exclusively bankers' banks but dealt as well with the general public. The Bank of France, for instance, was the largest commercial bank in the country with some six hundred branches. Far from limiting itself to the large transactions that we associate with central banking, the bank reported that at the head office alone in 1889 there were over twenty thousand loans on the books in the amount of 10 francs ($1.93) or less.[8]

The degree of control exercised by these central banks was generally small. The financial markets were not in need of much coordination of the central bank variety, and their ability to weather financial storms with less crisis than was common in the United States was due as much to their structure as to the existence of a central bank.

United States Banking Philosophy. Our examination of the development of banking in the United States has already indicated quite clearly not only that our banking structure was quite different from that of Europe but also that the difference was the result of a contrasting philosophy.

Individualism. Our attitude toward banking has always leaned strongly toward the unit banking principle, that is, a large number of small independent banks. Supporting this attitude is our heritage of rugged individualism, the pioneer spirit of an open country. Anyone should be able to try his hand at banking as well as at anything else he wanted to do. There should be no privileged class given a monopoly by the state.

At the same time, and for somewhat the same reasons, we have objected to bigness—to big business and, particularly, to big banking. In order to counter any tendency for a few banks to monopolize the financial structure of the economy, the country has seen fit to cling to the small bank and to restrict severely the growth of individual banks.

Many of the ills of our system resulted from this fractionalization of the

[8] Horace White, *Money and Banking,* 5th ed. (Ginn and Company, Boston, 1914), p. 389.

banking structure. But the country believed that these ills were of less moment than the disaster of a banking monopoly. A great deal of thought went into the development of a coordinating mechanism that would produce some order in this system but still prevent any banking group or political body from exercising monopoly power.

The result, the Federal Reserve System, is a delicately balanced mechanism with both private and government participation, providing as much of a system of checks and balances as the Federal government itself. At the same time the predominantly private part of the system, the Federal Reserve banks themselves, are split into twelve separate units. This serves the purpose of providing local direction for the solution of local problems and of permitting each Reserve bank to adapt its policies to the peculiarities of a relatively small geographical area. It also represents an attempt to build a bulwark against a single agency that could be dominated by "Wall Street."

Even with these safeguards against concentration of power, it is doubtful whether the Federal Reserve would have been acceptable except for the fact that it was assumed that most of the work of the System would be almost automatic without a great deal of discretion by administrators.

This was particularly true of the issue of notes, one of the hottest political controversies of the day. Although it was universally recognized that a flexible currency was necessary, there was much fear that elasticity might lead to overissue. The framers of the act felt that this tendency could be eliminated by providing safeguards based on two commonly accepted theories of central banking: the automatic gold standard and the real-bills doctrine. These concepts were the outgrowth of nineteenth-century thought, and while the twentieth century has generally repudiated them, it is necessary to understand their importance at the time the Federal Reserve was established, for they are two of the cornerstones on which its structure rested.

The Automatic Gold Standard. This standard assumed that each country based its currency on gold and did not restrict gold movements. Under these conditions the price levels of all countries that adhered to the standard were related to one another through the gold value of their respective currencies. If prices in any one country tended to rise compared with prices of its neighbors, the country with the higher prices would find its (high-priced) exports declining and would tend to export gold to pay for the goods it was buying from the relatively low-price countries. If a country lost gold, the quantity of money would necessarily contract, and this in turn would tend to bring prices back down to equilibrium. Countries gaining gold, on the other hand, would experience an increase in currency as well as a rising price level.

Thus a country's gold stock, currency, and price levels were interconnected, and all the central bank had to do to achieve stability was maintain a specified gold reserve against its note issue. By requiring a 40 per cent reserve of gold against notes, the Federal Reserve Act relieved the authorities of any necessity for exercising independent judgment on this score.

The Real-bills Doctrine. To provide double protection against inflation and at the same time to ensure that there would be enough money available, the framers of the act counted on the real-bills doctrine. If banks lent only against real bills, they argued, then the quantity of money would expand as output increased, but there could be no overcreation of loans.

In order to encourage banks to stick to lending against real bills, the Federal Reserve Act provided that the Reserve banks could make loans to banks only on the basis of "eligible commercial paper," which represented loans by the banks to finance real commercial transactions. In addition, Federal Reserve notes could be issued only against suitable commercial paper as collateral. In both these respects, therefore, the assumption was that automatic safeguards were provided against undesirable increases in the money supply, and here again the Federal Reserve was relieved of any need for active intervention.

Curing the Ills of the National Banking System

Since the Federal Reserve was established to remedy the defects found in the National Banking Act, it is pertinent to discuss its original operations in terms of the same five areas already singled out: currency, clearing, reserves, credit, and control. We are speaking here of the original functions of the system; some of these are still vitally important, while others have been altered to some degree by subsequent legislation.

An Elastic Currency. The Federal Reserve Act did not affect any type of currency already in circulation, but it did add another to the mélange. Federal Reserve notes could be issued by each of the Federal Reserve banks against a gold reserve of 40 per cent *plus* 100 per cent collateral in the form of commercial paper. The purpose of the collateral requirement was to make Federal Reserve notes, which rapidly became the dominant type of currency, responsive to the needs of business. The more transactions business carried on, the more businessmen borrowed, the more commercial paper was created, the more banks replenished reserves by borrowing from the Federal Reserve banks, the more commercial paper the Reserve banks had, and the more notes they could issue. If business was dull, bank loans would be paid back, banks would reduce their loans from the Federal Reserve, and the Federal Reserve note issue would have to contract. The note issue was to be not only elastic, but automatically elastic.

Nationwide Clearing. We have already described the Federal Reserve clearing mechanism. Although banks still wish to clear some of their checks through correspondents, where the process is fairly direct, the Federal Reserve has practically eliminated circuitous routing, expensive collection, and exchange charges.

In the foreign field the prohibition against bank acceptances has been removed, and the Federal Reserve has actively encouraged this kind of business. Although progress was slow in the early days, the growth of the United States as a world financial power has been partly the cause and partly the result of an expanding foreign exchange market in New York.

Mobilizing Reserves. Reserve requirements appear to be similar on the surface to those of the National Bank Act, but one big change has been introduced. Since all member banks must keep reserves on deposit with the Federal Reserve, the funds so deposited create a central pool of assets for the Federal Reserve. As a result of this centralization, reserves can be mobilized and used to help any bank in trouble. That is, any bank in difficulties may borrow reserves from the Federal Reserve. Reserves are no longer useless in an emergency.

A Developed Credit System. Not only does the Federal Reserve have custody of the pool of member bank reserves, but it has also established standards under which it will make loans. Because the Federal Reserve will discount acceptable commercial paper, any bank is liquid to the extent that it holds such paper as the result of making loans that satisfy the Federal Reserve regulations. While the United States has never developed the kind of a bill market that exists in Europe (primarily because we have found that sales on open account are as safe as, and less cumbersome than, sales financed by domestic bills of exchange), rediscount with the Federal Reserve serves the same purpose as far as the bank is concerned.

Centralized Control. The Federal Reserve Board was originally intended to exercise some powers of coordination over the banking system, but these were rather limited, and operations were expected to be fairly automatic. This is seen in the fact that in most respects the individual Federal Reserve banks were more powerful than the Federal Reserve Board in Washington. Over the years this has changed, partly by shifts in emphasis within the system, but even more significantly through legislation. This is perhaps the most important way in which the Reserve has developed over the years.

Growth of the Federal Reserve

Before examining in detail the various operations of the Federal Reserve System it may be well to review briefly the chaotic period through which it has come and to see how its various powers have been altered to meet new situations.[9]

Getting Down to Work. The Federal Reserve started operations in November, 1914, when the world had already embarked upon World War I, and problems of monetary management were of acute importance. As the Federal Reserve

[9] A discussion of the use of these powers (monetary policy) may be found in Chap. 32.

translated the provisions of law into concrete actions, it rapidly became apparent that there were flaws in the blueprint that needed correction. No less than thirteen of the thirty sections of the act had been revised by the end of the war, one of them four times. Most of these changes were minor, but three were of considerable significance: two struck directly at the real-bills doctrine, and the third made important changes in reserve requirements.

Real Bills. The real-bills doctrine was incorporated in the original act in two ways. Banks could borrow from the Federal Reserve only by rediscounting promissory notes that arose from short-term loans financing the movement of goods in trade, and Federal Reserve notes had to be secured 100 per cent by these rediscounts.

In 1916 banks were permitted to borrow on their own promissory notes with collateral of either "eligible paper" (real bills) *or* government securities. This made government securities more acceptable to banks because they could be used as a source of loans. It also meant that the Reserve System was in effect sanctioning an increase in the money supply based on a government deficit. Although this was not the purpose of the change, which was considered simply an improvement in technique, it was a long step away from the real-bills doctrine.

The following year the provision for backing of Federal Reserve notes was modified to permit the use of gold as both reserves *and* collateral. The requirement became 40 per cent in gold plus 60 per cent in commercial paper *or* gold. Thus the total requirement was reduced from 140 per cent to 100 per cent, and at the same time the link between commercial transactions and the quantity of currency was slightly loosened.

Reserves. The first draft of the Federal Reserve bill had suggested that all legal reserves be kept on deposit with the Federal Reserve banks. This raised a tremendous howl from the bankers, who protested this encroachment on established correspondent relationships. In order to placate the bankers the act as passed provided a rather involved formula whereby part of the reserve was to be held in the form of vault cash, part in the Federal Reserve banks, and part in correspondent banks, with the last portion gradually decreasing. Because it was felt that the mobilization of reserves under the Federal Reserve would reduce the need for such large amounts as had been required by the National Bank Act, the total reserve requirements were reduced for each class of banks, and a new category of time deposits was recognized, for which reserve requirements were lowered still further.

In 1917, in an effort to reduce complexity and to strengthen the Federal Reserve by increasing its resources, banks were required to carry *all* their reserves with the Federal Reserve banks. As partial compensation for the decision to disallow cash in vault as legal reserves, the reserve requirements were further reduced. A comparison of these requirements is given in Table 11-2.

In one respect this action had regrettable consequences. The new requirements gave banks sizable excess reserves. Since we were at war and the demand for loans was heavy, this increased lending power was immediately put to work and resulted in considerably more inflationary pressure than

Table 11-2. Legal Reserve Requirements, 1863, 1913, and 1917
Per Cent of Deposits

Type of deposit	National Bank Act, 1863	Federal Reserve Act, 1913	Amendment of 1917
Demand deposits:			
Central reserve cities	25	18	13
Reserve cities	25	15	10
All other (''country'')	15	12	7
Time deposits	Same as demand	5	3

would otherwise have been possible. This was by no means the only reason for the inflation that occurred in this period, for wars have always been noted for their disrupting effect on the monetary system. Reduced reserve requirements were simply one factor along with an inflow of gold, the increasing demand for loans on the part of foreign governments trying to obtain funds to purchase war materiel, a growing government debt (particularly after we entered the war), and all the other pressures of an economy working under forced draft. Suffice it to say that the theories of stability based on an automatically controlled money supply were one of the early casualties of the world conflagration.

Internal Control. Perhaps the most important change in the Federal Reserve System in this period was one not of law, but of procedure. The law provided that three of the nine directors of each Federal Reserve bank were to be appointed by the Federal Reserve Board and that one of these, designated the Federal Reserve agent, should be chairman of the board of directors. Although not specifically stated, it was assumed that the Federal Reserve agent should be the operating head of the bank and, as an appointee of the Federal Reserve Board, should provide the link through which the scattered parts of the system would be coordinated.

The Federal Reserve banks thought differently. They confined the activities of the Federal Reserve agent to those specifically spelled out by law and appointed, as the operating head of each bank, a governor of their own choosing. Not content with this gesture of independence toward the Federal Reserve Board, they went further and established a Conference of Governors, an informal assembly of the governors of the twelve banks, which rapidly became more important in a practical sense than the Federal Reserve Board itself. Under the leadership of Benjamin Strong, governor of the Federal Reserve Bank of New York, a thoroughly competent banker and devoted public servant, this conference tackled many knotty problems of Federal Reserve operation and provided a higher degree of coordination among the districts than was contemplated in the original act. Many procedures worked out by the conference were later incorporated into law.

Peace, Prosperity, and Disaster. Although the decade of the twenties witnessed considerable improvement in Federal Reserve operating techniques, particularly in the area of open-market operations, it called forth little in the way of banking legislation. While a large number of banks failed in this period (5,209 from 1922 to 1929), each failure seemed to be a rather isolated case, for the economy as a whole was buoyant. In fact it was frequently stated that as long as the Federal Reserve was there as watchdog of the economy, another major crisis was impossible.

The crash of 1929 shattered these illusions, and Congress passed eleven laws in three years, 1930 to 1932, attempting to bolster the banking system. The most important were the establishment of the Reconstruction Finance Corporation (1932), which was authorized to aid banks by making special loans to those in distress, and the Glass-Steagall Act (1932), which permitted Federal Reserve banks to use government securities as collateral behind Federal Reserve notes. Prior to this period there had been a significant decline in the amount of rediscounting with the Federal Reserve banks, as a result of which the banks held smaller amounts of commercial paper and had been forced to use an increasing amount of gold as collateral for their notes over and above the 40 per cent required by law. This act permitted them to substitute government securities for gold and thus averted an impending currency shortage.

These measures were insufficient to provide long-run solutions. The developing financial crisis in Europe, the high point of which was England's abandonment of the gold standard in September, 1931, could not help affecting this country, and the banking system—its underpinnings sorely shaken by its own excesses in the preceding boom, by the stock market fiasco, by the downfall of foreign financial machinery, and by the general feeling of gloom that pervaded the country—collapsed into utter ruin in the early morning of March 4, 1933.

At twenty minutes after four on that morning, Governor Lehman of New York proclaimed a bank holiday, which spread like wildfire over the nation, so that as President Roosevelt rode to his inauguration at noon amid festive banners and grim faces, there was not a single state in the union that had not either closed or otherwise restricted its banks. The next day a proclamation by the President of the United States made the holiday universal. Never in the history of the country had such utter chaos devastated our financial machinery. This was more than a panic; it was complete paralysis. The system devised after such careful study to prevent precisely this situation was impotent. The very worst had occurred.

Slowly the country began to pick up the pieces. Almost immediately banks were given the power, if they were able, to provide cash for "medicine, other necessities of life, distress relief and other essential purposes," but this was just a drop in the bucket. The Emergency Banking Act, passed nine hours after Congress convened on March 9, started major salvage operations. Gradually banks that could demonstrate their soundness were allowed to open, but in some cases it took months to iron out their affairs, and by the end of the year almost three thousand of them had failed to open.

Revamping the Federal Reserve. Putting the Federal Reserve back on a new, more solid base was a longer process. There was never any question about its financial soundness, and, in fact, the Federal Reserve banks opened before any private banks were permitted to do so; but the original design had shown fatal flaws, and monetary architects worked for two years to build a better structure, providing first the somewhat tentative Banking Act of 1933 and then the more far-reaching Banking Act of 1935. These two acts produced drastic changes in both the operation and the philosophy of the system. In the cumulative process of change, four of the original cornerstones of the Federal Reserve were removed.

Real Bills. The principle of the real-bills doctrine, moribund in 1914, was completely dead even before the 1929 collapse. Banks could borrow from the Federal Reserve on their own note, using as collateral commercial paper, government securities, or any other collateral that the Federal Reserve was willing to accept. Banks *were* making many kinds of loans that did not fall under the heading of self-liquidating paper. The Glass-Steagall Act gave final, official recognition to this fact by permitting the substitution of government securities for commercial paper as collateral behind Federal Reserve notes. The quantity of commercial paper ceased, therefore, to have any relation to the quantity of currency.

Gold. The worldwide gold standard had collapsed almost as soon as the Federal Reserve was organized. When nations that had abandoned gold during World War I drifted back to it in the twenties, the gold standard to which they returned was not the unregulated, automatic gold standard of the prewar period. Even this modified standard suffered almost complete oblivion as a result of the Great Depression, and in 1933 the United States joined the great parade away from gold. Along with a change in the definition of the dollar, gold was completely withdrawn from circulation, so that the relation between money in circulation and gold became tentative at best. Gold still remained as required reserves against Federal Reserve notes and deposits, but when World War II gave rise to a fear that this might not permit enough of a monetary expansion to finance the war, the requirements were reduced (1945) to 25 per cent. Thus the link between gold, money, and prices has been further loosened, and it appears today to be little more than a technicality.

Automatic Operation. The idea that the problems concerned with the currency could be solved by providing a rigid framework within which automatic correctives would operate to maintain a balanced money supply necessarily gave way as the automatic criteria themselves disintegrated. If we cannot rely on the real-bills doctrine and the gold-standard "rules of the game," then human decision becomes more important. Many years ago Walter Bagehot said that "money will not manage itself." If money must be managed by men, then these men must have the authority and the tools to do a proper job.

One of the major tools given to the Federal Reserve System in 1935 was the power to change reserve requirements within the limits of the rates set in the 1917 amendment as a minimum and twice those figures as a maximum. This was a change in basic philosophy as well as a change in technique. Reserves up until this time had been considered a safety device to protect the bank's depositors (or in earlier years the bank's noteholders) from the consequences of a run. Gradually the realization spread not only that the original purpose was not very well implemented in practice but also that reserves played a much more vital role in an entirely different direction. As we have already seen, the size of the required reserve is one of the very important determinants of how much credit a bank can extend. Therefore changing the reserve requirement is a potent method of controlling the degree of deposit creation available to the banks. By putting this power in the hands of the Federal Reserve Board, Congress gave them an additional weapon for credit control.

Decentralization. In 1913 the fear of monopoly had led to the creation of twelve Federal Reserve banks with only nominal coordinating power in the hands of the central Federal Reserve Board. But we discovered the hard way, through a nationwide catastrophe, that the country was so thoroughly bound together by ties of commerce that an attempt to give each geographical area a degree of autonomy was unsound. Even the Reserve banks recognized this in their attempt to coordinate policy through the Conference of Governors.

The Banking Act of 1935, facing this issue squarely, raised the status of the Federal Reserve Board and, as a symbol of the change, bestowed upon it the longer title of Board of Governors of the Federal Reserve System. At the same time it gave legal recognition to the executive officer that had been introduced into the Reserve banks, changing his title from governor to president and providing that his appointment must be approved by the Board of Governors.

The Board of Governors was given complete power to make changes in reserve requirements within the legal limits, was given majority representation on a new Open Market Committee with complete authority over all open-market operations of the System, and obtained greater power over changes in discount rates.

As a result the System has come more and more to resemble a strong central bank. It still does not have control over all banks, but even in areas where it lacks legal authority its influence is not unimportant. By reason of public support and bankers' respect it has often been able to guide banking policy where it had no specific power to compel. It is no more perfect than any other human institution is perfect, and changes in the economy still require adaptation to new conditions, but we have come a long way since the panic of 1907.

Postwar Progress. The slow revival from the Depression was hastened by the second world holocaust, and the problems of the war and postwar readjustment have taxed the powers of our whole economy. The Board of Governors, with its expanded powers, has been gravely tested. On the whole, though mistakes have been made, the System has shown its ability to adjust to the times and has gained a good deal of valuable experience.

In 1959 an amendment to the Federal Reserve Act altered reserve requirements in two respects: (1) It made it possible for member banks to count vault cash as part of the legal reserves, a privilege that had been abolished in 1917, and (2) it provided for the abolition of the central reserve city classification, thus putting New York and Chicago banks in the reserve city category. Although both changes reduced the effective reserves that banks must carry, the primary purpose behind the changes was to reduce inequities among banks.

A change in the reserve requirements of the Federal Reserve banks themselves was introduced in 1965, when the gold reserve requirement against the deposit liabilities of the Federal Reserve banks was abolished in order to free additional gold for use in international transactions. The 25 per cent gold reserve against Federal Reserve notes, however, was retained.

Undoubtedly the law will continue to change as altered conditions and increased experience suggest improvements. Meanwhile we are now ready to examine in much greater detail the structure and operation of the Federal Reserve System as it exists today.

Questions for Thought and Discussion

1. Trace the steps by which a demand for more currency helped cause a stock market collapse in 1907. Would the same chain of events occur today?

2. The original Federal Reserve Act was written in the belief that the money supply should increase as business expands. Does the same belief motivate the Federal Reserve authorities today?

3. Why was the original act more concerned with an elastic currency than with elastic bank deposits?

4. If we returned to the old gold standard, would the threat of inflation be eliminated?

5. If you had been a member of Congress in 1913, do you think you could have developed a better central banking system than the Federal Reserve? What changes would you have made?

6. Why has the banking system in the United States developed along such different lines from those of other banking systems?

7. Trace the development of reserve requirements in the United States in terms of both philosophy and law.

8. If the Federal Reserve System were being newly established at the present time, do you think it would be broken up into twelve districts?

9. Is there still a threat of "Wall Street domination" of our banking system? What about the threat of political domination?

10. Do you believe that the real authority of the Federal Reserve should be vested in the Board of Governors or in the individual Federal Reserve banks?
11. In 1928 people were saying that we would never have another depression because the Federal Reserve had been designed to prevent such a thing. People are saying similar things today. Are they right?

Selected Bibliography

Bach, George Leland: *Federal Reserve Policy-making,* Alfred A. Knopf, Inc., New York, 1950.

Board of Governors of the Federal Reserve System: *The Federal Reserve Act as Amended through December 31, 1956,* 1957.

———: *The Federal Reserve System: Purposes and Functions,* 5th ed., 1963.

Burgess, W. Randolph: *The Reserve Banks and the Money Market,* 3d ed., Harper & Row, Publishers, Incorporated, New York, 1946.

Federal Reserve Bank of Boston: *The Federal Funds Market: Its Origin and Development,* rev. ed., 1964.

Federal Reserve Bank of New York: *The Federal Funds Market,* 1959.

———: *The Treasury and the Money Market,* 1954.

Federal Reserve Bank of Philadelphia: *Fifty Years of the Federal Reserve Act,* 1964.

Harding, W. P. G.: *The Formative Period of the Federal Reserve System,* Constable & Co., Ltd., London, 1925.

Hawtrey, Ralph G.: *A Century of Bank Rate,* Longmans, Green & Co., Ltd., London, 1938.

Kemmerer, E. W., and Donald L. Kemmerer: *The ABC of the Federal Reserve System,* 12th ed., Harper & Row, Publishers, Incorporated, New York, 1950.

McKinney, George W., Jr.: *The Federal Reserve Discount Window,* Rutgers University Press, New Brunswick, N.J., 1960.

Madden, Carl H.: *The Money Side of "the Street,"* Federal Reserve Bank of New York, 1959.

Meek, Paul: *Open Market Operations,* Federal Reserve Bank of New York, 1963.

Nadler, Marcus: *New Tools for Credit Control,* C. J. Devine Institute of Finance, New York University, New York, 1964.

Prochnow, Herbert V. (ed.): *The Federal Reserve System,* Harper & Row, Publishers, Incorporated, New York, 1960.

Sprague, O. M. W.: *History of Crises under the National Banking System,* Publications of the National Monetary Commission, Government Printing Office, 1910.

Warburg, Paul M.: *The Federal Reserve System: Its Origin and Growth,* 2 vols., The Macmillan Company, New York, 1930.

Willis, H. Parker: *The Federal Reserve System,* The Ronald Press Company, New York, 1923.

Chapter 12 Federal Reserve Operations

Join we together for the public good.

The Second Part of King Henry VI
Act I, scene 1, line 200

The Federal Reserve System as it stands today is the result of a process of change and growth that has, among other things, doubled the length of the Federal Reserve Act. In the process of legal amendment, sometimes under the pressure of emergency, many loose ends have appeared that have never been properly tied together. Many suggestions have been made for improvements in the act, frequently by the Board of Governors itself. Growth in our understanding of monetary phenomena has proceeded hand in hand with growth in our economy, and both have tended to make certain provisions of the act obsolete. In spite of this, however, the Federal Reserve System is much stronger and much more effective today than it was forty, twenty, or even ten years ago.

Federal Reserve Structure

The Federal Reserve System has three levels of organization somewhat in the nature of a pyramid. At the bottom are the member banks. They own and control, within limits, the Federal Reserve bank of their district, which stands at the next higher level. On top of the pyramid and exercising control over the whole system is the Board of Governors. These three layers will each be examined in turn, but first a look at the regional nature of the system is in order.

Regional Organization. For Federal Reserve purposes the United States has been divided into twelve districts, as shown in Figure 12-1. In each district there is a Federal Reserve bank, and in most districts there are one or more branches established for the purpose of increasing the ease of access to Federal Reserve facilities.

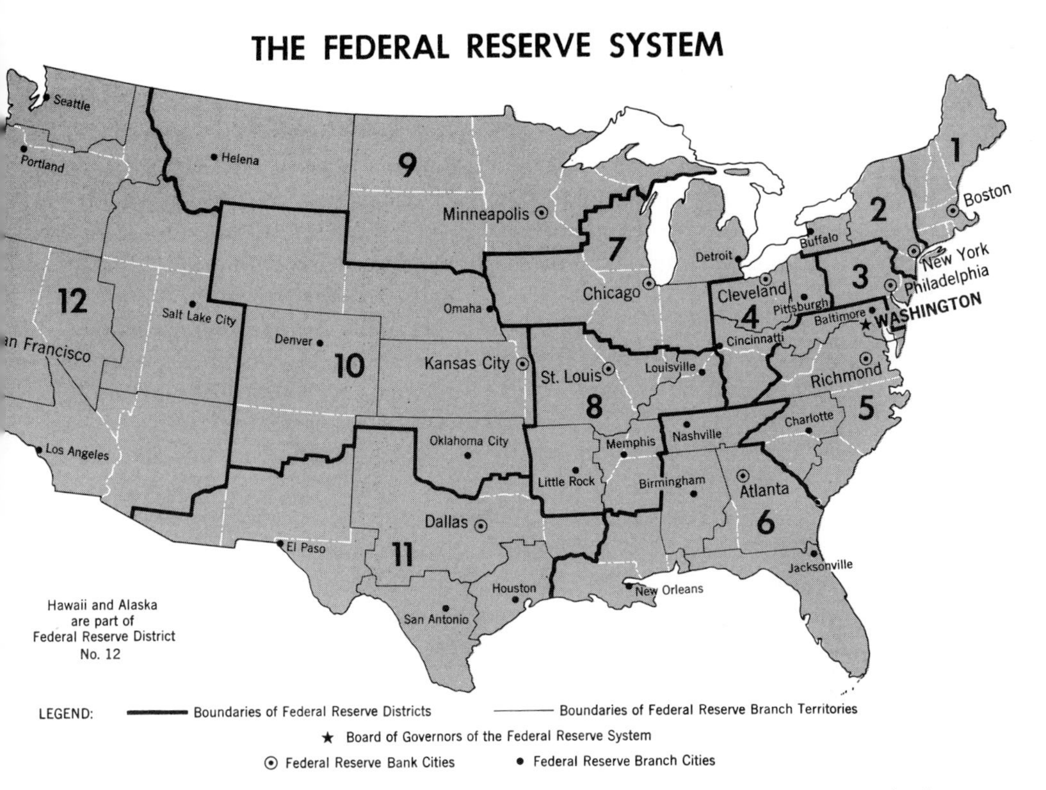

Figure 12-1. Boundaries of Federal Reserve districts and their branch territories. *(Adapted from Federal Reserve Bulletin.)*

Although it was hoped that the districts might be fairly equal in financial strength, this proved impossible. The Federal Reserve Bank of New York has assets of almost \$15 billion, while the Federal Reserve Bank of Minneapolis has only slightly over \$1 billion. Yet cutting the size of the New York district wouldn't help much since banks maintaining head offices in the New York City financial district alone represent almost one-sixth of the nation's banking assets. On the other hand, the map of the Federal Reserve districts shows at a glance that the Federal Reserve banks of Minneapolis, Kansas City, and Dallas, three of the four smallest banks, serve wide geographical areas, which could hardly be extended without further reducing the local nature of the banks.

Although increasing technological developments in transportation and communication have drawn the country much closer together in the last fifty years, and although the increasing power of the Board of Governors of the Federal Reserve System has reduced somewhat the local autonomy of the Federal Reserve banks, there is still much feeling that this regional structure works better than the concentrated authority of a single central bank would.

Member Banks. The law requires that all national banks join the Federal Reserve System, while state banks that can fulfill the requirements are invited to do so. At the present time not quite half the banks in the United States are members, but these banks account for 83 per cent of the total commercial banking business of the country as measured by size of demand deposits. In other words, the larger banks have joined the system, while the smaller banks make up the bulk of nonmembers. One of the commonest reasons why state banks do not join the system is that their capital is too small to meet the minimum requirements for membership. Another reason why some banks have not joined is that they are unwilling to give up the lucrative exchange charges that they levy on checks presented for payment from out of town, charges that member banks are forbidden to exact. Table 12-1 shows the distribution of member and nonmember banks both by number and by size of deposits.

Because of the number of nonmember banks it is erroneous to think of the banking system of the United States as being entirely under the jurisdiction of the Federal Reserve System. However, in the sense that member banks account for 83 per cent of the banking business of the country, the Federal

Table 12-1. All Banks in the United States by Classes, December 31, 1964

Class of bank	Number		Deposits, billions of dollars: Demand		Time	
Commercial banks:						
Member banks:						
National	4,773		98.7		71.0	
State	1,452	6,225	52.7	151.4	33.4	104.3
Nonmember banks:						
Insured	7,262		26.8		22.6	
Noninsured	274	7,536	1.4	28.2	0.6	23.2
Total commercial banks		13,761		179.6		127.5
Mutual savings banks:						
Insured	327		0.3		42.4	
Noninsured	178		*		6.4	
Total savings banks		505		0.3		48.8
Grand total, all banks		14,266		180.0		176.3

* Less than $50 million.

Source: *Federal Reserve Bulletin*, vol. 51, no. 9 (September, 1965), pp. 1296–1297. Detail may not add to totals because of rounding.

Reserve System can certainly be considered the predominant type of banking organization. Even nonmember banks feel some of the weight of its actions, in some cases directly and in others because of its influence on the total monetary structure.

Membership in the Federal Reserve System involves both rights and obligations. The rights include (1) the ability to borrow from the Federal Reserve when necessary, (2) the use of Federal Reserve facilities for clearing checks and transferring funds, (3) the right to acquire currency at any time by drawing a check against Federal Reserve balances, (4) the receipt of information and advice provided by the System, and (5) a share in the ownership and control of the Federal Reserve bank of the district.

The obligations that a bank incurs include (1) maintenance of a reserve deposit with the Federal Reserve in an amount prescribed by the Board of Governors, (2) compliance with various regulations of both law and administrative ruling concerning bank operations, and (3) subjection to examination and general supervision by Federal Reserve authorities.

A nonmember bank does not escape these obligations entirely, for it is subject to similar requirements set up by state law. In many cases, however, state law is less rigorous than its Federal counterpart.

Federal Reserve Banks. A bank joins the Federal Reserve System by applying to the Board of Governors. If approved, it must subscribe to an amount of stock of the Federal Reserve bank of its district equal to 6 per cent of its own capital and surplus. One-half the price of this stock must be paid in, and the remainder is subject to call by the Board of Governors. In practice no such call has ever been made, and it does not appear that any ever will be. Banks do not even carry the unpaid portion of their stock as a contingent liability, and for practical purposes we may say that the member bank subscribes to Federal Reserve stock in an amount equal to 3 per cent of its capital and surplus. This amount is adjusted annually if the bank's capital or surplus changes. On the paid-up portion of this stock the Federal Reserve bank pays cumulative dividends of 6 per cent per year. Stock is not issued to anyone else, nor can any member bank own more than the prescribed amount.

The member banks exercise control over their Federal Reserve bank through their election of six of its nine directors. Three of these (class A directors) are bankers; the other three (class B directors) must be actively engaged in commerce, agriculture, or some other industrial pursuit but must not be officers, directors, or employees of any bank.

For purposes of electing directors the banks in each district are divided into three size groups consisting of large, medium, and small banks. These groups are not equal either in number of banks or in size of total assets, but represent something of a compromise between these two concepts. In 1954, out of about 6,700 member banks, some 700 (10 per cent) were included in the "large" category, about 2,500 (38 per cent) in the "medium," and 3,500 (52 per cent) in the "small." In each district each of these groups elects one class A and one class B director. This type of representation is designed to afford a voice to the bankers (class A) and to their customers (class B) and to recognize the interests of banks of various sizes.

Three directors (class C) are appointed by the Board of Governors, and these also must not be officers, directors, or employees of any bank. The class C directors are the "public directors" and, with those of class B, provide a majority of nonbankers on the board.

One of the class C directors is designated by the Board of Governors as Federal Reserve agent and chairman of the board. Although originally intended to be the executive officer of the Federal Reserve bank, the Federal Reserve agent now performs only the statutory duties of overseeing the collateral behind Federal Reserve notes (a fairly routine function) and of making certain reports to the Board of Governors.

The board of directors of each Federal Reserve bank (not to be confused with the Board of Governors of the Federal Reserve System) has the responsibility for determining policy for the bank. To carry out the daily operations of the bank they appoint a president and first vice-president (who must be approved by the Board of Governors) and other officers and employees.

The Federal Reserve banks, in spite of their ownership and majority control by commercial banks, are quasi-governmental institutions operated in the public interest. Although they make a profit, profit is not their objective. It is rather the inevitable result of the nature of their work in carrying out policies designed to strengthen the banking system. Many activities of the Federal Reserve banks are available free to member banks and even to the general public.

Most of the income of the Federal Reserve banks is earned from interest on loans made and securities held. After the operating expenses of the bank have been met and the 6 per cent dividend paid on stock, part of the remainder is added to surplus, and the rest is paid to the United States Treasury. The proportion so paid has undergone several changes over the years. At the present time it represents all net earnings (earnings after expenses and dividends) not needed to maintain the surplus of each Federal Reserve bank at a level equal to its subscribed capital (twice its paid-in capital).[1]

The legal basis for this payment has been the subject of considerable debate. The general rationale behind it is that since the Federal Reserve banks are not operated for profit, since dividends to stockholders are limited to 6 per cent, and since the law provides that in case of liquidation all surplus remaining after payment of debts and the par value of stock shall become the property of the United States, there is no reason why the Treasury should not receive immediately the benefit of all funds not needed to ensure the stability of the System.[2] In the period from its founding through 1964 the Federal Reserve has shown the following disposition of its earnings:[3]

[1] See *Federal Reserve Bulletin,* vol. 46, no. 1 (January, 1960), p. 24.

[2] See *Federal Reserve Bulletin,* vol. 33, no. 5 (May, 1947), pp. 518–519.

[3] Adapted from Board of Governors of the Federal Reserve System, *Annual Report, 1964,* p. 233.

	Per cent
Operating expenses	23
Dividends	4
Surplus	4
U.S. Treasury	69

Each of the twelve Federal Reserve banks is a separate corporate entity. While there is a great deal of coordination and collaboration among them both directly and under the overall supervision of the Board of Governors, there is no mingling of funds or sharing of operating responsibility. Each bank is thus a local organization staffed by local men and responsive to the needs and opinions of its own district. It is in this way that the framers of the Federal Reserve Act hoped to adjust the System to the differing industrial development, the varying importance of agriculture, the disparities in interest rates, and the varieties of banking practice that characterized the heterogeneous regions of the United States.

The Board of Governors. Over all this diversity, however, there was to be superimposed a common objective and an integration of nationwide credit policies. This integration is provided in the Board of Governors of the Federal Reserve System. The Board of Governors consists of seven members appointed by the President of the United States with the advice and consent of the Senate. No two governors can represent the same Federal Reserve district, and the composition of the Board is to be representative of financial, agricultural, industrial, and commercial interests. Governors are appointed for fourteen-year terms, cannot be reappointed, and cannot be removed from office except for cause. It was hoped that in this way the Board, although political appointees in the first instance, would be as far removed from day-to-day politics as possible. Currying favor could not result in reappointment, nor could unpopular actions lead to dismissal.

In technical details this system has not worked as smoothly as planned, primarily because a governor may be reappointed if he has not served a full fourteen-year term, and by reason of death or resignation many unexpired terms have arisen to be filled with short-term appointments. Thus Marriner Eccles was appointed in 1936 for a term of four years, was reappointed in 1940 to fill another unexpired term of four years, and was then reappointed in 1944 for a full fourteen-year term—but resigned in 1951. In spite of technical difficulties, however, the Board has appeared to be cognizant of its public responsibilities and for the most part has kept clear of political entanglements.

The President appoints one member of the Board as Chairman and another as Vice-chairman, each for a period of four years, subject to reappointment. The Board appoints a staff to aid it in its work, the expenses of which are borne by assessments on the Federal Reserve banks.

Originally intended as a rather weak coordinating agency, the Board of Governors was granted ever greater powers as time went by. It now has most of the powers of a central bank (in fact more than some central banks) and might be considered, at the risk of oversimplification, the policy-making body of the system, while the Federal Reserve banks are the operating arms.

Open Market Committee. Even in policy, however, the Board does not have sole jurisdiction. One of its most important functions is shared jointly with the Federal Reserve banks in the Federal Open Market Committee. This committee is composed of twelve members: the seven members of the Board of Governors plus five presidents of the Federal Reserve banks. The president of the Federal Reserve Bank of New York is a permanent member of the committee, and the presidents of the other eleven Reserve banks serve in rotation.

The Federal Open Market Committee has only one official function. It determines open-market policy for the whole System, a task that will be examined in detail in Chapter 13. It is significant that a majority of the Committee consists of the Board of Governors, thus indicating the preeminence of the Board in this matter of major policy. In practice most decisions of the Committee are unanimous.

Federal Advisory Council. When the Federal Reserve Act was passed, the bankers felt that they, through the Federal Reserve banks, could manage the monetary system adequately by themselves. They opposed the creation of the Board of Governors and feared that a government-appointed board would not understand the problems of banking. As a concession to this point of view the Federal Advisory Council was established. The Council consists of one banker elected by each Federal Reserve bank. Its primary purpose is to confer with the Board of Governors on policy questions in order to make sure that the banking point of view is taken into consideration. It can also call for information and make recommendations on any banking matter, but it has no power to act.

There are also two other advisory bodies of minor importance: the Conference of Agents, composed of the Federal Reserve agents from each of the Federal Reserve banks; and the Conference of Presidents, similarly constituted.

The interrelations of the various parts of the system are shown in Figure 12-2. This chart also indicates the seat of responsibility for the four major controls which the System exercises over the economy. These controls will be described in detail in Chapter 13.

The Federal Reserve Balance Sheet

We have examined the skeleton of the Federal Reserve System—the way it is put together. But a skeleton isn't a person. In this section we will continue our study by taking up the muscles, the banking processes through which actions are carried out. The following two chapters will be devoted to the brain, the conscious direction of policy for the purpose of achieving certain ends. A study of Federal Reserve personality will have to wait until Chapter

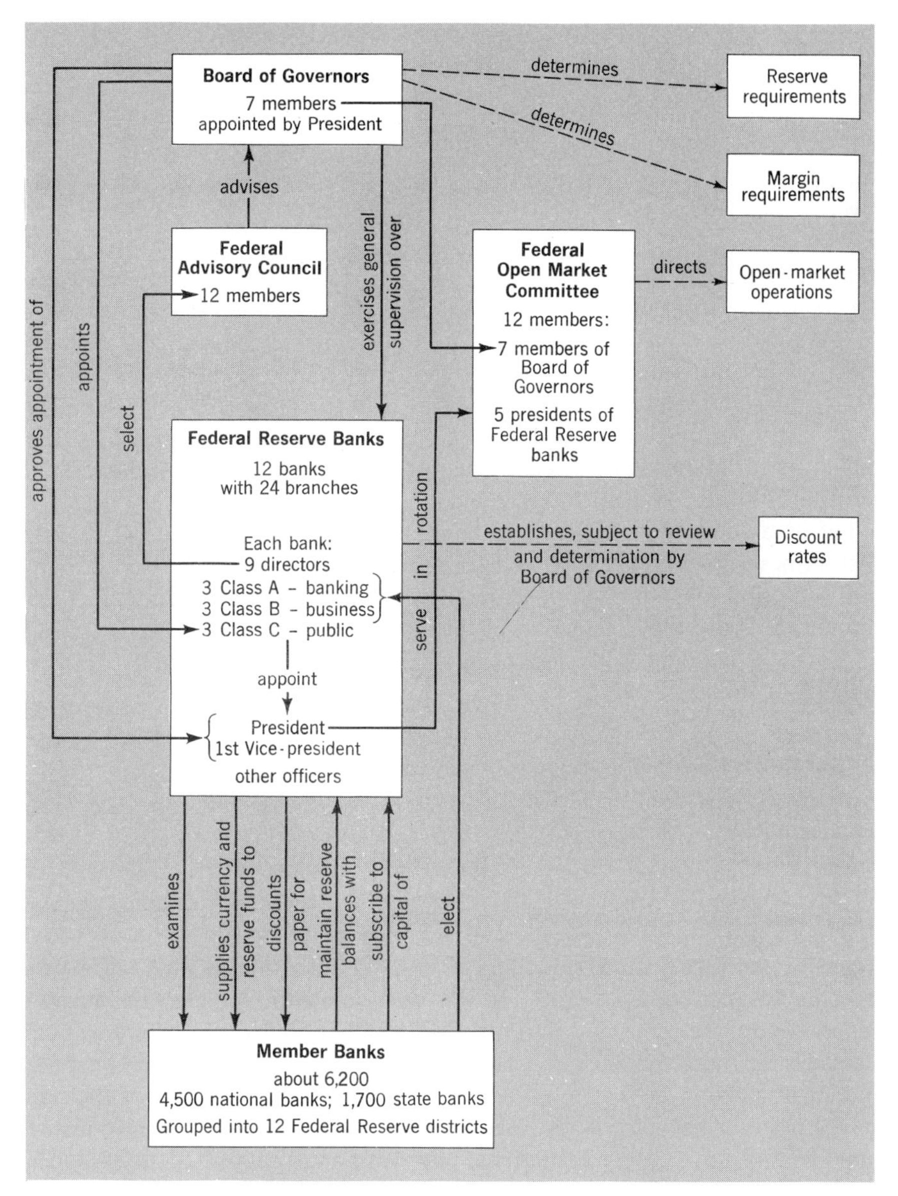

Figure 12-2. Organization and functions of the Federal Reserve System. *(Adapted from Board of Governors of the Federal Reserve System, "The Federal Reserve System: Purposes and Functions," 1954, pp. 82-83.)*

32, when we will have a more complete understanding of the environment within which the System operates.

The basic operating mechanism of the System is the individual Federal Reserve bank. Its functions are similar to those of an ordinary commercial bank except that its customers are primarily banks and the government and that it retains the right of note issue, which commercial banks no longer have. Since it is simply a bank of a different kind, the Reserve bank's activities can be traced in the same way we used for our analysis of the commercial bank, that is, by their effect on the balance sheet of the bank. For purposes of illustration we will consider a mythical Federal Reserve Bank of Metropolis, covering the Thirteenth Federal Reserve District.

Capital. Originally capital stock had to be paid for in gold or gold certificates, but today any form of money is acceptable. Since the banks were formed in the days when gold was an important part of the money stream, and since the effect of this provision, reinforced by the terms of the Gold Reserve Act of 1934, was to concentrate all gold certificates in the hands of the Federal Reserve banks, our examples will assume (as was the case historically) that capital subscriptions as well as early deposits resulted in the acquisition of gold certificates by the Federal Reserve bank.

Let us assume that the member banks of the Thirteenth Federal Reserve District have combined capital and surplus of $100 million. They must therefore subscribe to $6 million of Federal Reserve stock and pay in half of that amount. Suppose that $1 million of this amount is used by the Reserve bank to provide a building. (The figures on all our balance sheets will be stated in millions of dollars.)

Federal Reserve Bank of Metropolis

Assets		*Liabilities*	
Gold certificates	2		
Bank premises	1	*Net worth*	3
	3		3

Deposits. As with commercial banks, the stockholders are the first but not the most important source of funds. In this case, however, the stockholders and depositors are the same, for not only must member banks subscribe to capital, but they must also maintain a deposit in the Federal Reserve bank equal to a certain proportion of their own deposits. This is the major part of their required reserve. They are likely in addition to maintain a little extra to provide some leeway for clearing operations. Suppose banks deposit $500 million in gold certificates and another $10 million in other kinds of cash, say, silver certificates and coin.

Federal Reserve Bank of Metropolis

Assets		*Liabilities*	
Gold certificates	502 (+500)	Deposits, member banks	510 (+510)
Other cash	10 (+10)		
Bank premises	1	*Net worth*	3
	513		513

It is through these reserves of member banks that the Federal Reserve exercises its greatest control over credit expansion and contraction. Reserves are also the device through which clearings, both of the Federal Reserve and most clearing houses, take place.

Nonmember Deposits. In addition to the deposits of member banks the Federal Reserve also holds clearing balances for nonmembers who wish to use the Federal Reserve clearing machinery. These are large enough to cover only the normal clearing needs of each individual bank, but otherwise they are identical with member bank deposits.

Loans and Investments. Federal Reserve banks may make loans and buy securities, but the type of customer and the method of operation are somewhat different from those of commercial banks. These differences arise primarily from two distinguishing characteristics of the Reserve System already noted. Since the Reserve banks are not motivated by the desire for profit, their loan and investment policy is directed solely toward the accommodation of business and the stabilization of the economy and not toward net return. In portfolio management the conflict between liquidity and income that besets commercial banks plays no part in Federal Reserve decisions.

In the second place, because the Federal Reserve is a bankers' bank, its primary dealings are with commercial banks and with the money market itself rather than with the general public.

Discounts and Advances. The Federal Reserve System had as one of its original purposes the provision of financial aid to banks, and it was assumed in the early days that rediscounts for banks would constitute the major earning asset of the Federal Reserve banks. When a bank rediscounted commercial paper, it simply turned over to the Federal Reserve bank promissory notes that its own customers had given in exchange for deposit credit. The Federal Reserve deducted the discount charge and credited the borrower's deposit account with the balance.

This was the classical rediscount, which was supposed to gear both bank credit and the quantity of Federal Reserve notes to business borrowing. Banks, however, have turned increasingly to borrowing on their own promissory notes with government security as collateral.[4] This is a much simpler process for several reasons: (1) The precise amount and period of the note may be suited to the bank's convenience instead of conforming to the amounts and maturities of commercial paper held. (2) Since the Federal Reserve banks frequently act as custodians for government securities owned by member banks, a minimum of paper work is involved in using these securities as collateral for notes. (3) The bank avoids having to endorse commercial paper, thus showing the original borrower that the bank had used his paper for its own loan.

[4] Banks may also borrow on notes secured by commercial paper or—at a rate of interest ½ per cent higher than the discount rate—by any other collateral acceptable to the Federal Reserve bank.

Almost all loans to member banks today, therefore, are made against the note of the bank itself and are called *advances,* to distinguish them from discounts of commercial paper. The member bank writes its own IOU promising to pay the Federal Reserve a specified sum at a specified future date. Along with this note the bank turns over to the Federal Reserve bank sufficient collateral, almost always government securities. In exchange the Federal Reserve bank, after deducting the discount charge, credits the member bank's deposit account (reserve) with the balance. Advances seldom exceed fifteen days and are frequently made for as short a period as three days.

Let us assume that member banks borrow $20 million from the Federal Reserve Bank of Metropolis. For simplicity we will ignore the discount charge (which would be handled precisely the same way as in the case of a commercial bank making a loan to a businessman) and assume that the bank receives the full amount of its note as a deposit credit.

Federal Reserve Bank of Metropolis

Assets			*Liabilities*		
Gold certificates	502		Deposits, member banks	530	(+20)
Other cash	10				
Discounts and advances	20	(+20)			
Bank premises	1		*Net worth*	3	
	533			533	

The result of this process is to give the member bank additional reserves, either to build up a deficiency or to produce excess reserves against which additional loans can be made or currency withdrawn.

Other Loans. During the Depression the Federal Reserve banks were given authority to make loans directly to industrial or commercial business in exceptional circumstances. Such industrial advances were never a large part of Federal Reserve activities, and the power to make them has now been removed.

The Federal Reserve banks are permitted to make loans to foreign monetary authorities on the security of gold collateral and to the general public against United States securities. The latter type of loan is practically nonexistent. Some few foreign loans have been made.

Securities. The Federal Reserve Act permits the Federal Reserve banks to buy and sell securities of the United States, bank acceptances, certain obligations of states and localities, and bills of exchange. In practice the banks have limited themselves almost exclusively to dealing in the first two classes of securities, and since 1932 government securities have far outweighed bank acceptances in importance.

The law requires that all purchases of government securities (and bank acceptances as well) be on the open market except that the Federal Reserve may hold not in excess of $5 billion of government securities purchased directly from the Treasury. This latter power has been used very sparingly, in small amounts, and usually for a period of only a few days to finance the Treasury without disturbing the money market immediately prior to major tax payment dates.[5] With this minor exception the Federal Reserve banks cannot buy securities newly issued by the Treasury. They can buy only securities that are already in the hands of some member of the public who now wishes to dispose of them. Sales are also made on the open market, but of course the Federal Reserve is entitled to receive payment from the Treasury for any securities it holds at maturity.

Purchase and sale of government securities, known as *open-market operations,* are currently under the complete control of the Federal Open Market Committee. No Federal Reserve bank engages in open-market operations on its own initiative, and all operations are conducted by the Federal Reserve Bank of New York (under the direction of the Open Market Committee) for the account of all twelve Federal Reserve banks. The use of open-market operations as a control device is treated more fully in the following chapter. Here we wish to concentrate solely on the mechanics of the operation and will use a single Reserve bank for illustrative purposes.

Purchase of Government Securities. Suppose the Federal Reserve Bank of Metropolis is going to buy $25 million worth of government securities of a certain kind. How does it go about the task? Basically it does just what you and I would do. Remember that we are not buying a new issue from the Treasury, but rather an issue already in the hands of the public. We would go to a broker and place an order; the broker in turn would go to a government-bond house and buy the securities for our account. The Federal Reserve, operating on a much larger scale, doesn't have to go through a broker but deals directly with a bond house.

The government-bond house is the key to the whole operation. These dealers in government securities—there are less than twenty of them in the country—specialize in the purchase and sale of such securities. They always hold a portfolio of issues that they are willing to sell from or add to by purchase. They make an active market at all times by offering either to buy or to sell, whichever their customers wish, and they make their profit by the difference, usually very small, between buying and selling price. They have extensive communication systems through which they constantly keep in touch with potential buyers and sellers, and they are thus able to adjust their price quotations to changes affecting any part of the market for government securities.

The Federal Reserve Bank of Metropolis in our case would call several bond dealers to compare prices quoted by different ones and would then place

[5] From 1955 to 1964 the Federal Reserve bought securities directly from the Treasury only once (1958) and held them only two days (see Board of Governors of the Federal Reserve System, *Annual Report, 1964,* p. 227).

an order for $25 million worth of securities. The bond house would deliver the securities and would receive in exchange a check drawn by the Federal Reserve bank on itself. The dealer would deposit this check in his own bank, say, the First National, and receive deposit credit. The bank, in turn, would deposit the check in its reserve account at the Federal Reserve. The result of this transaction would be to increase the Federal Reserve bank's holdings of government securities and increase its deposit liabilities to member banks.

Federal Reserve Bank of Metropolis

Assets			*Liabilities*		
Gold certificates	502		Deposits, member banks	555	(+25)
Other cash	10				
Discounts and advances	20				
Government securities	25	(+25)			
Bank premises	1		*Net worth*	3	
	558			558	

Because open-market operations are so important as a credit-control device, it is desirable to show also the changes in the balance sheets of the other principals in this transaction. In the case of the bank and the bond house we will not try to present a complete balance sheet, but only those items affected by the bond purchase.

First National Bank

Assets		*Liabilities*	
Due from Federal Reserve bank (reserves)	+25	Deposits (government-bond house)	+25

Government-bond House

Assets		*Liabilities*	
Government securities	−25		(No change)
Due from banks	+25		

This process of Federal Reserve purchase of government securities has increased the bank's reserves and thus its ability to make loans. The government-bond house has increased its bank balance, thereby increasing its purchasing power, in exchange for securities.

The increased demand for securities by the Federal Reserve will have a tendency to push up their prices. This will be reflected in the quotations of the bond house, and this higher price will probably induce some holders—individuals, banks, insurance companies, or other corporations—to sell some securities from their portfolios. The ultimate effect is a depletion in the security holdings of the public and an increase in the security holdings of the Federal Reserve, with the government-bond dealer acting as intermediary. The Federal Reserve has bought government securities and in the process put additional money in the hands of the public and additional reserves in the hands of the banks.

Sale of Government Securities. The sale of securities on the open market is simply the reverse of the above procedure. Suppose that at some later date the Federal Reserve decides to sell $10 million worth of bonds. Again the government dealers are contacted, a price is obtained, and the securities are transferred to the dealer. He gives the Federal Reserve bank a check written on his own bank. In the process of clearing, the Federal Reserve bank deducts this check from the account of the bank on which it is drawn and sends the check to this bank, which in turn deducts it from the account of the bond house.

Federal Reserve Bank of Metropolis

Assets			*Liabilities*		
Gold certificates	502		Deposits, member banks	545	(−10)
Other cash	10				
Discounts and advances	20				
Government securities	15	(−10)			
Bank premises	1		*Net worth*	3	
	548			548	

First National Bank

Assets		*Liabilities*	
Due from Federal Reserve bank (reserves)	−10	Deposits (government-bond house)	—10

Government-bond House

Assets		*Liabilities*
Government securities	+10	(No change)
Due from banks	−10	

The result of this sale of government securities has been to reduce the reserves of member banks and to reduce the funds in the hands of the public while increasing their holdings of securities.

Federal Reserve Notes. The Federal Reserve banks are authorized to issue Federal Reserve notes against a collateral that consists of 25 per cent gold and an additional 75 per cent in gold, government securities, or commercial paper. Because of the reduction in the amount of commercial paper held by the Federal Reserve banks, the collateral today consists almost exclusively of gold and government securities.

Federal Reserve notes are printed by the Bureau of Printing and Engraving of the United States Treasury and delivered to the Federal Reserve agent at each bank. He holds them in a special vault until the bank wants to issue them. At that time the bank gives the Federal Reserve agent the requisite collateral and receives the notes.

A Federal Reserve bank, of course, cannot force currency into circulation but simply stands ready to provide it when member banks call for it. Suppose the First National Bank needs $5 million worth of currency to meet the payroll requirements of several of its depositors. When a bank wants currency, it does exactly what you and I do when we want currency. It writes a check against its bank account (in the Federal Reserve) and cashes it.

Suppose the bank needs $1 million in coin and $4 million in bills (almost all bills in the United States are Federal Reserve notes). The Federal Reserve Bank of Metropolis receives the check drawn by the First National Bank and charges it to that bank's account. It then reduces its cash holdings by $1 million in coin and gives up $4 million worth of its Federal Reserve notes.

Federal Reserve notes are a liability of the Federal Reserve bank that issued them, and they are interchangeable with the bank's deposit liabilities. As far as the $4 million is concerned, the Federal Reserve bank has merely exchanged one form of liability (notes) for another form (deposits).

Federal Reserve Bank of Metropolis

Assets			*Liabilities*		
Gold certificates	502		Deposits, member banks	540	(−5)
Other cash	9	(−1)	Federal Reserve notes	4	(+4)
Discounts and advances	20				
Government securities	15				
Bank premises	1		*Net worth*	3	
	547			547	

If the First National Bank, on the other hand, had an excess of cash in its vaults, it would deposit some of it in the Federal Reserve, thus increasing its reserves (the Federal Reserve bank's deposits) and decreasing the quantity of Federal Reserve notes in circulation.

Clearing. The clearing activities of the Federal Reserve represent one of its most important services to member banks. The fundamental process of clearing has already been described in Chapter 8. There is one aspect of clearing, however, that needs further clarification. This is the concept of "float."

Float. Float is a rather mysterious word, but mathematically it is a fairly simple concept. It is the difference between "deferred availability cash items" on the liabilities side of the Reserve bank balance sheet and "cash items in process of collection" on the assets side.

We have already seen that when a commercial bank receives a check for deposit, it lists it initially under "cash items in process of collection." The Federal Reserve does the same. But the Reserve does not immediately credit the account of the bank that deposited the check (a commercial bank may not give a depositor immediate credit either). Rather it gives the depositing bank "deferred availability" for a certain number of days as indicated in a schedule that represents the length of time that the Reserve feels it *ought* to take to collect the check involved. Only at the expiration of this period is the depositing bank given reserve credit. The use of a specified time schedule simplifies bookkeeping and lets the depositing bank know precisely when it can count its deposit as reserves. A Federal Reserve bank normally gives immediate deposit credit for checks that are cleared through the local clearing house, but it defers credit for not more than two business days for checks drawn on out-of-town banks.

If all checks were actually collected in the time indicated on the deferred availability schedule, there would be no float, since checks would be collected and credited to the depositing bank's account at the same time. If checks are delayed in collection, however, the Reserve bank credits the reserve account of the depositing bank according to schedule, thereby reducing deferred availability items before the corresponding uncollected cash items are actually turned into cash. This represents credit extended by the Federal Reserve to its member banks, for the depositing bank is given the use of funds before the Federal Reserve has received them.

Suppose on a Monday the Hanover Bank deposits two checks in the Federal Reserve Bank of New York: one for $100 drawn on a Detroit bank (one-day availability) and one for $300 drawn on a Des Moines bank (two-day availability). As of Monday credit for both would be deferred:

Federal Reserve Bank of New York

Assets		*Liabilities*	
Cash items in process of collection	+400	Deferred availability cash items	+400

On Tuesday Hanover automatically gets credit for the Detroit check. Suppose, however, that bad flying weather delays collection of this check:

Federal Reserve Bank of New York

Assets		*Liabilities*	
Cash items in process of collection	No change	Deposits (Hanover)	+100
		Deferred availability cash items	−100

At this point uncollected cash items total $400, but deferred availability cash items are only $300, giving a float of $100. This is the value of the Detroit check credited to the Hanover Bank, although it has not been collected.

On Wednesday Hanover automatically gets credit for the Des Moines check. Assume also that both checks are collected. The whole transaction has been completed, and float disappears. The changes on Wednesday would be:

Federal Reserve Bank of New York

Assets		*Liabilities*	
Due from Interdistrict Settlement Fund	+400	Deposits (Hanover)	+300
		Deferred availability cash items	−300
Cash items in process of collection	−400		

As the example illustrates, float is by its nature a very temporary matter for any individual transaction, but with thousands of checks constantly passing through clearing, there is almost bound to be some float at any point in time.

Fiscal Agency Operations. In the nineteenth century the government carried out its fiscal operations through the Independent Treasury System, and most government receipts and payments were handled in cash. With the growth of deposit banking, and more particularly with the development of the Federal Reserve clearing mechanism, the concept of the Independent Treasury—already expensive and frequently a destabilizing influence on the money supply in the hands of the public as cash flowed into or out of the government coffers—was abandoned. Since the final closing of the subtreasuries in 1921 the Federal Reserve has acted as fiscal agent for the government and has handled almost all the government's finances with some help from the rest of the banking system. Most government payments are made by means of checks drawn on the Federal Reserve.

Tax and Loan Accounts. It would be possible for the government to keep all its funds in the Federal Reserve banks, deposit all receipts in the Treasury's account, and draw all checks on this account. Such a procedure has one very serious drawback. The government does not receive its funds smoothly over time, but rather in large lumps at periodic tax dates or at the time of a large bond issue. Around April 15, for instance, the procrastinators (and that includes about all of us) get their income tax returns in. Similar humps come at the end of each of the quarterly payment periods for corporation taxes.

If all these payments were made to the Federal Reserve, the result would be to draw large sums of money out of the banking system and put them in the Federal Reserve. Banks would lose large quantities of reserves, and money would become scarce because so much of it was tied up in the Reserve banks. Only gradually as the government spent this money would it come back into commercial banks. This alternation of feast and famine was one of the disadvantages of the Independent Treasury, and it would be incredibly worse now with the greatly increased magnitude of government transactions.

In order to obviate this problem the Treasury keeps in the Federal Reserve banks only a sufficient balance to meet current expenditures. The rest of its funds are kept on deposit with regular commercial banks that can qualify as special depositories, of which there are about eleven thousand. Each special depository is permitted to maintain deposits for the Treasury in the form of a tax and loan account.

Credits are made to the tax and loan account from a wide variety of transactions: (1) the purchase by the bank of newly issued government securities; (2) the sale by the bank (as agent) of newly issued government securities to its customers; (3) withheld taxes (income, old-age insurance, and railroad retirement) and excise taxes paid to banks for deposit to the account; and (4) "large" checks (the definition of "large" fluctuating from time to time) given the Treasury in payment of individual and corporate income taxes and returned to the bank on which they are drawn for credit to the account. Thus a large part of the government's receipts flow into the commercial banks, while the remainder go directly to the Federal Reserve banks.

The Treasury makes all payments, however, by means of checks on its Federal Reserve balance. When that account (it is, of course, twelve different accounts, one in each Federal Reserve bank) gets low, it is necessary to replenish it by transferring funds from the tax and loan accounts. This is done by means of the *call.* Banks are divided into three classes depending on the size of their treasury balances, those with the largest amounts being subject to call most frequently. Calls may be as infrequent as once a month or as frequent as every day. Whenever a call is made on any group, each bank in the group must transfer a certain percentage, say 25 per cent, of the total in its tax and loan account to the Federal Reserve bank of its district. This is done by authorizing the Federal Reserve to deduct this amount from the member bank's reserve account. The effect is the same as if the Treasury wrote a check on its tax and loan account in each bank and deposited the checks in its Federal Reserve account. The paper work involved in a call is much less complicated.

Suppose a Treasury call had the effect of requiring banks in the Thirteenth Federal Reserve District to transfer $12 million to the Federal Reserve Bank of Metropolis. Its balance sheet would then become:

Federal Reserve Bank of Metropolis

Assets		*Liabilities*		
Gold certificates	502	Deposits, member banks	528	(−12)
Other cash	9	Deposits, U.S. Treasury	12	(+12)
Discounts and advances	20	Federal Reserve notes	4	
Government securities	15			
Bank premises	1	*Net worth*	3	
	547		547	

The Treasury can now write checks against its Federal Reserve account to meet expenses. When these checks are deposited in the recipients' accounts, they will be sent to the Federal Reserve for credit by the bank in which they are deposited. This will cause a reverse flow of deposits; the Treasury's account will be charged the amount of the checks, and the banks will be credited with a similar amount of reserves. Thus the banks will get back the reserves they lost because of the call. As long as the Treasury's calls approximately balance its current expenses, the effect of treasury receipts and outpayments will not be seriously disturbing to bank reserves.

Foreign Operations. The Federal Reserve Bank of New York acts as the agent for the whole Federal Reserve System in relations with foreign banks.

In these transactions all the Federal Reserve banks share. That is, if the Federal Reserve Bank of New York receives deposits from foreign central banks or international agencies, these deposits will be divided among all the Reserve banks in proportion to their size. As correspondent of foreign banks, the Federal Reserve provides many services associated with the financing of foreign trade as well as many intergovernmental financial transactions.

It is obvious that the Federal Reserve cannot handle any transactions except in dollars. It cannot promise to pay in marks, or francs, or lire because it doesn't have any and cannot create any. Foreign banks, therefore, can obtain deposits in the Federal Reserve only by shipping gold (which will be accepted for deposit at $35 per ounce and then turned over to the Treasury in exchange for gold certificates) or by acquiring a dollar balance from someone else. For instance, when the United States government paid its subscription to the International Monetary Fund, it did so by transferring to the Fund a portion of its own balance at the Federal Reserve. Or a foreign bank may obtain a claim against a United States commercial bank in payment for goods exported to the United States. The foreign bank could transfer this deposit to the Federal Reserve by writing a check against the commercial bank and depositing it in the Federal Reserve. The Federal Reserve would then owe the domestic bank less and the foreign bank more.

Let us illustrate two of these transactions simultaneously by assuming that a foreign central bank ships $5 million worth of gold to the Federal Reserve Bank of Metropolis and at the same time deposits a check drawn on a member bank in the amount of $2 million.

Federal Reserve Bank of Metropolis

Assets			*Liabilities*		
Gold certificates	507	(+5)	Deposits, member banks	526	(−2)
Other cash	9		Deposits, U.S. Treasury	12	
Discounts and advances	20		Deposits, foreign	7	(+7)
Government securities	15		Federal Reserve notes	4	
Bank premises	1		*Net worth*	3	
	552			552	

The Aggregate Balance Sheet. The various transactions that we have discussed constitute the major operational functions of the Federal Reserve banks. If we were to take each of the twelve Federal Reserve banks and add together their various assets and liabilities, we would get an aggregate statement of condition such as that shown in Table 12-2 for December 31, 1964.

While there are a considerable number of items even on a simplified balance sheet such as this, one significant fact is apparent at once. Only four are of any real magnitude. This is particularly true if we realize that "deferred availability cash items" is essentially an offset to "cash items in process of collection," and for some purposes it would be more appropriate to show only the net item—float—as an asset. In this case float, swelled by the year-end logjam in check collection, is $2,606 million.

Table 12-2. Statement of Condition of the Twelve Federal Reserve Banks Combined, December 31, 1964
Millions of Dollars

Assets		
Gold certificates		15,075
Cash on hand:		
Federal Reserve notes of other banks	684	
Other cash	146	830
Discounts and advances		186
Bank acceptances		94
U.S. government securities:		
Bills	6,044	
Certificates	0	
Notes	25,188	
Bonds	5,274	
Held under repurchase agreement	538	37,044
Cash items in process of collection		8,984
Bank premises		102
Other assets		552
Total assets		62,867
Liabilities		
Federal Reserve notes		35,343
Deposits:		
Member bank reserves	18,086	
U.S. Treasurer	820	
Foreign	229	
Other	321	19,456
Deferred availability cash items		6,378
Other liabilities		642
Total liabilities		61,819
Net worth		
Capital paid in	524	
Surplus	524	
Other capital accounts	0	1,048
Total liabilities and net worth		62,867

Source: Adapted from *Federal Reserve Bulletin*, vol. 51 no. 1 (January, 1965), p. 127.

Only four items are larger than this, and all are very much larger. These are "gold certificates," "government securities," "Federal Reserve notes," and "member bank deposits." It is a simplification but hardly an exaggeration to suggest that the combined balance sheet of the twelve Federal Reserve banks might be summarized for many purposes as follows:

Twelve Federal Reserve Banks

Billions of Dollars

Assets		*Liabilities*	
Gold certificates	15	Member bank deposits	15
Government securities	35	Federal Reserve notes	35
Other	10	Other	10
	60		60

There is one figure on the balance sheet for December 31 that needs to be taken with a grain of salt. Because commercial banks usually publish their balance sheets on that date (and also at the end of the other quarters) and because they consider it somewhat degrading to have any debt appearing on these published statements, they will move heaven and earth to pay off their debt to the Federal Reserve (discounts and advances) on this one date, although they may have sizable debts outstanding on December 30 and may borrow again on January 2. This sprucing up of the published balance sheets is known as *window dressing* and is almost universal.

Thus the figure for discounts and advances on December 31, 1964, is $186 million. But it averaged $535 million for the week ending December 30 and was back up to $337 million on January 6. Even these larger figures, however, are small relative to the four major items on the balance sheet.

These four figures indicate the most important activities of the Federal Reserve banks as operating institutions. They do not, however, show the total impact of the System on the economy. A great part of that impact stems from the power that the Federal Reserve has to control credit expansion, and to this subject we now turn.

Questions for Thought and Discussion

1. It has been said that permitting banks to elect directors of the Federal Reserve banks is like having the railroads run the Interstate Commerce Commission. Is this analogy valid?

2. It is sometimes suggested that the Federal Reserve is not independent *of* the government but independent *within* the government. What is the distinction here, and how is it achieved? Would it be better if the Federal Reserve were more directly under the control of the President?

3. In view of both the rights and the obligations of membership, if you ran a bank would you want it to join the Federal Reserve System?

4. What is the difference between a discount and an advance, and why is the latter more frequently used?

5. Why are Federal Reserve notes liabilities of the Federal Reserve banks while United States notes are assets?

6. If an airline strike delays the transit of checks, what is the effect on float?

7. Explain clearly why float represents a loan by the Federal Reserve banks to members.

8. Show by means of balance sheets how the deposit by the Federal government of a tax check directly in its Federal Reserve account reduces the reserves of the bank on which the check was drawn. How does the use of tax and loan accounts eliminate this problem?

9. Show the effect on the Federal Reserve balance sheet of the payment by the United States of its subscription to the International Monetary Fund.

10. Find a current statement of condition of the Federal Reserve banks (in the *Federal Reserve Bulletin* or the Friday *New York Times* or other financial paper) and compare it with Table 12-2. What important changes have occurred? Do you have any idea why?

Selected Bibliography

See references listed under Chapter 11.

Chapter 13
Federal Reserve Controls

You must confine yourself
within the modest limits of order.

Twelfth Night
Act I, scene 3, line 8

In terms of the physical volume of work that the Federal Reserve banks carry out, the greater part of their operations are fairly routine: receiving and paying out cash, clearing checks, and handling the issue and redemption of government securities as agent of the Treasury.

In 1964 the twelve Federal Reserve banks received and counted over nine billion pieces of currency and coin worth $35 billion. They cleared over five billion checks worth $1,600 billion. They transferred $4,000 billion worth of funds other than by check.[1] They handled over two hundred million government securities worth $750 billion. Their total monetary transactions, therefore, exceeded $6 trillion.[2]

In spite of the almost incomprehensible size of these transactions and in spite of the tremendous value they are to the banking community in facilitating financial operations, this work is not the most important function of the Federal Reserve System today in the field of policy. Its most significant task is the maintenance of stability in the economy to the extent that this can be done through control of the quantity of money. The System is, of course, only one agency among many whose job it is to try to keep the economy on an even keel, but it is one of the most important.

As aids in accomplishing this task the Federal Reserve has several quite different tools at its disposal. Sometimes it uses one, sometimes another, sometimes several at once.

[1] Primarily transfers of funds by wire for the account of member banks.

[2] Board of Governors of the Federal Reserve System, *Annual Report, 1964,* p. 234.

1. Control over excess reserves
   a. Reserve requirements
   b. Discount rates
   c. Open-market operations
2. Indirect controls
   a. Bank relations
   b. Publicity
   c. Voluntary credit restraint
3. Direct controls
   a. Margin requirements
   b. Consumer credit controls
   c. Mortgage credit controls

Of these controls only six can currently be used. Items 2*c*, 3*b*, and 3*c* have been utilized in the past, and power to use them may again be given to the Federal Reserve; but at present authority in these three areas has expired.

In this chapter we are concerned primarily with technique. In Chapter 32 we will examine Federal Reserve policy as it has operated in specific situations.

Control over Excess Reserves

We have already seen that the size of excess reserves is the basic determinant of the ability of banks to expand credit. A single bank can create deposits in an amount equal to its excess reserves, while the banking system, if it pulls in unison, can create deposits to some multiple of excess reserves depending on the required reserve ratio. Control of excess reserves can therefore mean control over the capacity of the banking system to create money. If excess reserves are eliminated, expansion can be stopped; if excess reserves are created, expansion can proceed.

Excess reserves represent the difference between total reserves and required reserves. Therefore excess reserves can be increased by increasing total reserves or by reducing required reserves. Similarly excess reserves can be reduced by reducing total reserves or by increasing required reserves. Of the three major tools of Federal Reserve policy, one (changes in reserve requirements) affects required reserves, while the others (discount rate and open-market operations) affect total reserves.

The Impact of Reserve Policy. When excess reserves are increased, the bank faces no basic problem unless it is where to find additional customers. But when reserves are decreased, it is forced to adjust its position to conform with the law, and such an adjustment may be both difficult and slow. How much time does a bank have in which to take the necessary action?

We need to realize, in the first place, that the ax is not likely to fall suddenly. In the case of changes in reserve requirements the bank is normally given prior notice of a week or so in order to provide time for it to adjust its accounts. While open-market operations and changes in discount rate are not announced in advance, their impact is much less severe. Further, a bank has the privilege of averaging its reserves over a period of time; no bank has to maintain required reserves at each instant. For city banks reserves are averaged weekly. This means that a bank can, and many banks often do, have deficient reserves during several days of the week provided they have enough excess reserves on the remaining days to bring the average for the whole week up to the required level. With special permission from the Federal Reserve bank a city bank whose reserves fall below the requirement for the whole week may be permitted a second week to achieve the average required. Country banks are required to average their reserves over a two-week period, and this may be increased to four weeks by special dispensation. Thus banks have some time in which to adjust to changed conditions.

Even if a bank fails to maintain its average reserve at the required level, the immediate penalty is simply an interest charge on the deficiency at a rate 2 per cent higher than the current discount rate. Naturally no bank wants to be put in such a position, not only because of the cost, but also because of the stigma that attaches to such a penalty. If a bank persists in its failure to maintain reserves, it may be removed from membership in the Federal Reserve. Such action has never been necessary.

Within these limits, however, a bank must maintain its reserves at the required percentage of deposits. As we saw in Chapter 10, it may adjust its position through any one or any combination of the following actions:

It may raise its actual reserves:

By borrowing federal funds
By borrowing (discounting) from the Federal Reserve
By liquidating secondary reserves (primarily short-term government securities)
By selling other assets (primarily long-term government securities)

It may reduce loans (and thereby deposits):

By calling demand loans (a seldom-used procedure)
By letting old loans mature and cutting down on new loans:
  By raising interest rates
  By credit rationing

Having made this digression into the reaction of a bank to changes in its reserve position, let us return to an examination of the tools of control used by the Federal Reserve to cause such changes.

Changes in Reserve Requirements. Changes in reserve requirements serve a double purpose. In the first place they affect excess reserves directly. If banks have no excess reserves and hence are unable to make new loans at all, a reduction in reserve requirements will free excess reserves and permit expansion. If banks are lending freely because of substantial excess reserves, an increase in requirements will soak up some of the excess and slow down the expansion.

Second, reserve requirements are the fulcrum around which other credit policy is made effective. Not only do changes in the requirements alter the excess reserves held by banks, but they change also the credit-expansion multiplier. If required reserves are 10 per cent, excess reserves of $100 can be expanded by the banking system into $1,000 of deposits. Under a 5 per cent required reserve the same excess reserves could result in $2,000 of new deposits, while a 20 per cent requirement would permit only $500 of expansion.

The Board of Governors was given the power to change reserve requirements in 1935. At that time the limits within which such changes could be made were the requirements specified by the amendment of 1917 (see Table 11-2) at the lower extreme and twice these amounts at the upper. In 1948, at the height of the postwar boom, Congress gave the Board temporary power to raise requirements even higher than these maxima, but this power expired the following year. In 1959 in an attempt to reduce inequalities among banks Congress provided for the elimination of the central reserve city classification, and New York and Chicago consequently became reserve cities. Simultaneously the Board of Governors was authorized to set requirements for reserve city banks as high as 22 per cent (from a previous maximum of 20 per cent). The same law also provided that banks could count vault cash (as well as deposits in their Federal Reserve bank) as part of the legal requirement. Table 13-1 shows the maximum and minimum rates as well as the requirements in effect as of May 1, 1965, for each group of banks.

The power to change reserve requirements is the strongest power that the Federal Reserve has. Under most conditions it is too strong, for a rise in reserve requirements of only one percentage point applied to all classes of banks

Table 13-1. Member Bank Reserve Requirements

Per Cent of Deposits

Type of deposit and class of bank	Minimum permitted by law	Maximum permitted by law	In effect May 1, 1965
Demand deposits:			
Reserve city	10	22	16½
Country	7	14	12
Time deposits:			
All banks	3	6	4

wipes out $1½ billion in excess reserves. Such a meat-ax approach may be too blunt when a surgeon's scalpel is all that is needed.

The first use by the Board of its new powers was an attempt to sop up large excess reserves created by substantial gold inflows into the United States in the middle thirties. Between 1936 and 1937 requirements were raised in three steps from the minimum to the maximum then permitted. The contraction that followed this action was much more severe than the Board had anticipated, and subsequent changes have been much more moderate. Required reserves have been raised only once since 1951: in 1960 the requirement for country banks was raised 1 percentage point in a technical move intended to offset the liberalizing effect of letting them count vault cash among their legal reserves.

Open-market Operations. We already have a pretty good idea of open-market operations—how they are carried out, their effect on banks' ability to lend, and at least some of the reasons for their use. When the Federal Reserve System, on decision of the Federal Open Market Committee, buys government securities in the open market, it puts additional reserves in the hands of banks. Other things remaining the same, this makes it possible for banks to expand deposits. By selling securities the Federal Reserve reduces bank reserves and therefore puts pressure on banks to reduce loans or at least to decrease the rate of expansion.

The Development of Open-market Operations. The philosophy behind open-market operations, like that behind reserve requirements, has changed significantly over the years. Although the original act gave each bank power to buy and sell government securities, there is no mention of using this power as a control device, and it was probably intended primarily as a means of acquiring earning assets. Nor was there any provision for coordination of such operations among the Reserve banks.

It early became evident that open-market operations did affect credit conditions throughout the country and that their effects did not stop at district lines. After experiments with several methods of cooperative action, the Banking Act of 1935 finally gave to the newly constituted Federal Open Market Committee sole authority to determine open-market operations for the entire system.

In the process of change it also became evident that open-market operations were both flexible and highly effective as a tool of credit control, and today they have become the most important, though not the most spectacular, of Federal Reserve controls. They can be used in any amount, large or small, as frequently or infrequently as necessary, and they can be reversed instantaneously to meet new conditions without undesirable repercussions on business confidence.

The Open Market and Treasury Finance. It has already been made clear that open-market operations mean dealing with government-bond houses, that is, with the general public rather than with the Treasury itself. Nevertheless, the effect of Federal Reserve policy on the Treasury cannot be ignored. This is true of Federal Reserve policy in general, since any rise or fall in interest rates will affect the ease with which the Treasury can sell new security issues to the public. The effect is most direct with regard to open-market operations since these involve Treasury securities themselves.

Suppose, by way of example, an extreme case in which the Federal Reserve by tremendous sales of certain long-term government bonds forced their market price down from 100 (per cent of par) to 90 (per cent of par). Prior to this action a $1,000 bond could be bought at face value, and, supposing it carried a 3 per cent rate of interest, would yield $30 a year to the holder. After the price had fallen to 90, the same bond, still paying $30 a year, could be bought for $900. But a return of $30 on an investment of $900 indicates a yield of 3.33 per cent.[3] As the purchase price falls, the interest yield rises. If bonds already on the market yield 3.33 per cent, the Treasury would be unable to sell new bonds of a similar character unless they carried a comparable interest rate. New long-term financing is therefore going to cost the Treasury approximately 3.33 per cent interest instead of 3 per cent. Federal Reserve policy has raised the cost of Treasury borrowing.

While the example is extreme, the principle is quite real. Any attempt on the part of the Federal Reserve to restrict credit, thereby tending to raise interest rates, hits the Treasury in the pocketbook by making its borrowing more expensive. It is easy to see, therefore, why the Treasury and the Federal Reserve may not see eye to eye on the need for credit restraint—and particularly open-market sales.

Discount Rates. We have already studied the machinery through which member banks borrow from the Federal Reserve banks. The price charged for such loans is the discount rate. This rate applies either to rediscounts of commercial paper or to advances made to banks on their own promissory note secured by eligible commercial paper or by government securities. Each Federal Reserve bank sets its own discount rate, and, as with open-market operations, the original act did not emphasize the control nature of this device. It specifically stated that discount rates "shall be fixed with a view to accommodating commerce and business." In the early days this seemed to mean that when bank reserves were pinched as business expanded, it was the duty of the Reserve banks to ease the discount rate in order to provide additional credit. This is almost the opposite of credit control as we see it today.

It was further assumed that differing economic conditions in various sections of the country would normally lead to different rates in the various districts. As time has gone on, the increased efficiency of communications has reduced considerably the financial differences between regions, and a national policy now appears to be more desirable than it was in 1913.

Each Federal Reserve bank still has the power to set discount rates, but the rate in each case is subject to "review and determination" by the Board of

[3] Ignoring for arithmetic simplicity the appreciation of the bond from $900 when purchased to $1,000 at maturity. If this consideration were included, the yield would be even higher.

Governors so that the Board has the power of veto over any change in the rate. The Banking Act of 1935 further provided that each Federal Reserve bank must establish the rate every fourteen days. This does not mean that the rate must be changed, but it does give the Board the power to veto any rate, including the old one, each two weeks, and thus in effect it gives the Board the power to veto not only a change but also the existing rate.

In practice changes in discount rates are fairly extensively discussed among the various banks and within the Federal Open Market Committee in order to arrive at a general agreement as to the desirability of a particular level of rates. As a result it is now quite unusual for any Federal Reserve bank to have a different discount rate from that of any other except for brief periods while adjustments are being made.

Over the years the use of the discount rate has also changed in other, more important ways. It was originally thought that banks would be borrowing more or less continually from the Federal Reserve and that as a consequence (1) the discount rate would represent the primary source of income of the Reserve banks, and (2) changes in the discount rate would be the primary means by which the Federal Reserve would influence the market.

In the thirties, as bank loans declined and excess reserves piled up, banks found very little need to borrow, and discounts dropped to practically nothing. As discounting fell into disuse, the banking fraternity developed an aversion to the practice, and a trend of thought arose, partly fostered by the Federal Reserve, to the effect that it was a sign of weakness for a bank to be in debt to the Reserve. Discounts therefore remained at a very low level even throughout the boom during the war and the immediate postwar period. This development marked the decline of discount rate changes as a major instrument of Federal Reserve policy. If banks don't borrow, raising or lowering the cost of borrowing is a rather futile gesture. At the same time the Reserve banks purchased larger amounts of government securities through open-market operations, and these securities now provide their major source of income. There has been a moderate increase in discounting since the war, particularly in the tight-money markets of the early fifties, but the practice has never regained the importance it enjoyed in the twenties.

Even when discounts are negligible, however, a change in the discount rate performs a function, which can best be explained as psychological. Upward revisions in discount rate are a form of notice to bankers that the Federal Reserve feels credit expansion is progressing too rapidly and that maybe it is time to apply the brakes a little. Reductions suggest that further expansion might be desirable. Because bankers have developed a fairly high degree of confidence in the integrity and competence of the Federal Reserve, they have often heeded these signals even though they were not currently borrowing funds. To the extent that this may have been the function of discount rates, it puts them almost in the same category as other devices of the Federal Reserve System that do not directly affect reserves but that operate through bankers' attitudes toward lending policies.

Moral Suasion

The phrase "moral suasion" has been used to describe the twilight zone where control comes more from suggestion than from specific action. This rather vague term covers a wide area of somewhat diverse situations of which the common denominator is predominantly the fact that compliance is voluntary rather than compulsory.

Bank Relations. The most intimate relations of the Federal Reserve banks are with their member banks, and this contact gives rise to a number of opportunities for putting monetary policy on a more personal basis than the technical instruments of credit control allow.

Examination. Each Federal Reserve bank has the right, and indeed the obligation, to examine every member bank. In practice the Federal Reserve banks do not examine national banks but merely accept the report of the national bank examiners, who work for the Comptroller of the Currency. With regard to state banks the Federal Reserve examiners usually examine the bank jointly with the state bank examiners.

The purpose of bank examination is the maintenance of a sound banking system primarily through the minimization of bank failures. The examination not only evaluates the bank's assets but also appraises the quality of management. In the process of examination, which may take from three days to over two months, the examiners, among many other things, check the bank's loans with regard to the adequacy of collateral, credit standing of the borrower, and so on, and classify loans which seem to be below standard. In this connection the examiners may also discuss with the bank's directors the broader question of credit policy, particularly if the examiners feel that the bank has been making too many loans of one kind or to one type of business or that the bank seems to be overextending itself generally. Conversely the examiners might also discuss the situation if they feel that the bank has been too timid in making loans and thus is not meeting the legitimate needs of the community. This type of discussion, which is only a small part of the total task of examination, is primarily advisory rather than compulsory and is geared to the needs of the individual bank. However, it will naturally be related to the general credit situation at the time and often helps to bring banks into step on overall credit policy.

Visitation. In addition to the formal examination, whose objectives and procedures are fairly well standardized, the Federal Reserve banks also conduct a program of bank visitation, sending representatives periodically to each member bank. These conferences have several purposes:

1. Helping the bank with specific problems it may have
2. Explaining Federal Reserve policy to the bank

3. Attempting to get full cooperation with policy objectives
4. Gathering information on economic activity in the bank's area

This program is completely voluntary, but it is estimated that 80 to 90 per cent of member banks give full cooperation to the Federal Reserve in these matters of moral suasion.

Credit Rationing. Credit rationing goes somewhat beyond the purely voluntary aspects of moral suasion, but it does include, as part of the process, an attempt to induce the bank involved to adopt different policies.

No member bank has the *right* to borrow from the Federal Reserve. This is a privilege that the Federal Reserve bank can deny to any member for any reason that it deems sufficient. The Federal Reserve bank may therefore refuse discount accommodation to banks which it feels are not using their credit-creating powers properly. The Reserve bank can deny loans on the grounds that the collateral is unacceptable (although this can hardly be done when government securities are offered) or, more commonly, on the basis that the funds borrowed would not be used for proper purposes. The primary reasons for refusing funds would be that the bank was making excessive loans for speculation in stocks, real estate, or commodities, but any other practices considered detrimental to sound credit conditions might also be taken into account.

As discounts have dwindled in importance, this right to deny loans to banks has also become less significant. In any case the Reserve banks would prefer to accomplish their objectives without resorting to such drastic action. It is often, however, the very banks that are expanding unwisely that need to borrow, so that there is still some use for this discretionary power.

Publicity. Many central banks, the Bank of France being an outstanding example, maintain a practice of complete silence with regard to their operations and policy objectives. The Federal Reserve does not follow this tradition, believing that an informed public not only is better able to appreciate the need for central bank operations but also may aid in the work of the system by its own monetary actions as well as by intelligent support of the kind of legislation that will encourage sound monetary development.

The law requires that minutes of the Board of Governors and of the Open Market Committee be published, but the system goes far beyond this rather technical detail in an effort to carry its story to the public.

The Board of Governors publishes the monthly *Federal Reserve Bulletin,* containing statistics, new laws and rulings, a summary of business conditions, and informative articles on the state of the economy and on various problems of the monetary system. It also publishes for free distribution a 300-page book, *The Federal Reserve System: Purposes and Functions,* as well as numerous other materials. The Board also compiles and publishes many sets of statistics dealing not only with monetary conditions but also with business in general. The best-known of the latter is the index of industrial production.

Each Federal Reserve bank publishes a monthly review of credit and business developments and makes available a large number of pamphlets, many of them written for the layman and others on a more technical level, describing all aspects of the monetary system and of Federal Reserve operations. In addition the Federal Reserve banks invite the public to tour their buildings and send out speakers, often fortified with films or flannel-board presentations, to explain either general Federal Reserve activities or the particular policies currently being implemented.

No one can be quite sure how effective all this diverse publicity is in aiding Federal Reserve policy in any particular instance. It is certain, however, that it tends to raise the level of understanding, not only of the lay public, but also of the bankers. It makes people more cognizant of the importance of money and of monetary policy, and it has thus developed considerable knowledge of, and support for, Federal Reserve policy.

Voluntary Credit Restraint. An interesting experiment in the field of moral suasion was introduced during the expansion that occurred as a result of the Korean conflict. Under the powers given him by the Defense Production Act of 1950, the President delegated to the Board of Governors the power to encourage and coordinate voluntary agreements among financial institutions to restrain credit expansion. Accordingly a National Voluntary Credit Restraint Committee was formed, with Oliver Powell, of the Board of Governors, as chairman and with representatives from commercial banks, investment banks, life insurance companies, mutual savings banks, and savings and loan associations. Under the national committee were regional and local committees.

The purpose was to formulate a uniform policy concerning what types of loans were reasonable and what were not and, through the local committees, to persuade banks and other financial institutions to refuse to make loans that were not essential to the defense effort but whose effect would be simply to add to inflationary pressures. As the title indicates, the whole program was voluntary, and no one had any power to prevent an institution from making any loan it wanted to. It was effective, however, in channeling funds away from speculative or competitive uses into more productive ones.

There are three reasons why it was generally successful: (1) Bankers were anxious to cooperate with the defense effort and to try to gear their individual operations to what they believed to be the best interests of the country. (2) Bankers had someone else to blame when customers complained about being refused accommodation. "I'm sorry. I'd be glad to let you have it, but 'the committee' says no." (3) As long as compliance was fairly universal no banker had to fear that a customer whom he turned away could go across the street and get the same loan from someone else. This was the major advantage of having uniform standards.

The most spectacular success of this program was in the refusal of investment bankers to handle state bonds issued for the purpose of paying a veterans' bonus,[4] which would have put more money in the hands of consumers without increasing production at all. At the same time this very success cost it public support. As inflationary pressures eased, the program was suspended in May, 1952, after it had been in operation a little more than a year.

In spite of its limited experience and many complaints from those who couldn't get loans, this type of control is considered to have been quite successful as a device for allocating loans to the most important uses in a period when credit as a whole had to be expanded to meet a national emergency but when it was desirable to prevent inflationary forces from arising in nonessential areas.

Direct Controls

Another group of controls under the supervision of the Board of Governors concerns itself not with control of credit in general, but with control over particular kinds of credit, which, it is assumed, are either less desirable or less responsive to a tightening of the general money market. These controls do not operate through the reserve position of member banks but rather are general restrictions applying to all loans of a particular type regardless of whether the lender is a member bank, a nonmember bank, or some other kind of lending agency.

Margin Requirements. The only one of these powers that the Board of Governors has at the present time is that over margin requirements. This refers to the amount that may be loaned "for the purchase or carrying of securities." Its primary purpose is to reduce stock market speculation by requiring the purchaser of securities to provide a substantial part of the purchase price in cash.

The history of margin requirements goes back to the experience of the twenties, when prices in general were fairly stable but stock prices shot up spectacularly. Banks played a major part in this rise, for by 1929 loans on securities amounted to almost half of total bank loans outstanding.

With only general credit-control powers, any major attempt on the part of the Federal Reserve to restrict credit in the stock market would have resulted in restriction elsewhere in the economy as well and might have sent wholesale and retail prices down disastrously. Thus the Federal Reserve felt impotent to interfere in the obviously explosive stock market boom.

In 1934, in order to correct this situation for the future and to single out stock credit for selective control without affecting the rest of the credit structure, the Board of Governors was given the power to set margin requirements. *Margin* is the percentage of the purchase price of a security that a purchaser

[4] Under the program a total of sixty-seven state and local issues for various purposes were postponed "voluntarily."

must put up in cash. Thus when margin requirements are 75 per cent, the purchaser must pay three-quarters of the price in cash and can get a loan for a maximum of one-quarter of the price. If margin requirements are put at 100 per cent, no one can borrow at all for the purpose of buying securities.

The power was given to the Board not by the Federal Reserve Act, but by the Securities and Exchange Act. The act makes it unlawful for "any person" to extend credit in contravention of the Board's margin requirements, and the regulations cover specifically brokers and dealers (Regulation T) as well as banks (Regulation U). In this way the Board of Governors can restrict the amount of credit going into stock speculation directly, regardless of the source.

The Board initially set margin requirements at 40 per cent, permitting 60 per cent of the price of a security to be borrowed. During World War II margins were raised to 50 per cent, to 75 per cent, and in 1946 to 100 per cent, where they stayed for a year. Since that time the requirement has fluctuated within the limits of 50 per cent and 90 per cent. This is a far cry from the situation in 1928–1929, when, in the absence of any legal restriction, cash margins were frequently as low as 10 per cent.

While there has been much grumbling over margin requirements, it seems reasonable to believe that they have restrained somewhat the excesses of stock speculation that would have been the inevitable result of a continuing high level of prosperity in the postwar period. No one believes that margin requirements themselves can prevent a stock market boom or the subsequent collapse, but wisely used they should cushion the worst evils of both movements.

Consumer Credit. There is no current authority to control consumer credit. Such authority was originally given to the Board of Governors by a presidential Executive order in 1941 under the War Powers Act. Under the Defense Production Act of 1950 this power was specifically provided for by law, but the authority was repealed in 1952, and this form of control no longer exists.

The most important aspect of consumer credit control was the restriction of installment sales. Regulation W prescribed the minimum down payment and the maximum repayment period for such loans. Maxima and minima differed for various types of consumer goods and were changed from time to time. At one period, for instance (1952), the down payment for automobiles had to be at least one-third of the purchase price, and the balance had to be fully paid within eighteen months; home improvements could be purchased with a 10 per cent down payment and three years to pay. At another time, charge accounts and single-payment consumer loans were included in the restrictions. These regulations, like margin requirements, applied to all lenders, not only banks.

The wartime reason for consumer credit control was to restrain consumer purchases in order to channel resources into war production. Later the argument was raised that consumer credit, like stock market credit, is a particularly unstabilizing type of borrowing that is not adequately affected by general credit restraint. The debate still continues over the desirability of controls that single out consumer credit as specially in need of restriction; Congress has sporadically considered giving the Federal Reserve standby powers to regulate consumer credit whenever it appears necessary, but it has not done so.

Mortgage Credit. Real estate activity is another area where special powers have been given to the Federal Reserve in the past. Under the authority of the Defense Production Act of 1950, the President gave the Board of Governors the duty of establishing minimum down payments and maximum periods of repayment for various kinds of loans on real estate other than those issued or guaranteed by the Federal government. The Housing and Home Finance Administration had jurisdiction over the latter, and in practice this agency adopted restraints similar to those set up by the Board. Here, as in other selective controls, the power to limit credit terms (Regulation X) applied to all lenders, not merely member banks.

The power to regulate real estate credit was restricted in 1952 and expired in 1953. Experience with such control was brief, and there is not much pressure for reviving it.

Tax and Loan Accounts

It would be well at this point to suggest that tax and loan accounts may be used as instruments of credit policy, but by the Treasury rather than the Federal Reserve.

To the extent that the Treasury holds money in these accounts it is permitting the banks to retain reserves. As soon as calls are made on the accounts, the bank must release to the Federal Reserve an equal amount of reserves. Calls, therefore, make credit tighter. The Treasury, then, can put pressure on the money market by increasing the amount of its calls on tax and loan accounts and relieve such pressure by reducing its calls. The Treasury may also ease the credit market by increasing the number of types of payments that can be credited to tax and loan accounts.

In actual practice the Treasury has attempted to maintain its Federal Reserve balance at about as low a working level as it feels is safe, calls are instituted almost exclusively to build this balance up to working strength as it is depleted by government payments, and credit policy has not been a consideration in Treasury activities. In fact, these accounts were set up primarily to remove the effect of Treasury receipts and disbursements from the money market so that they would *not* cause changes in credit tightness. The control potential, however, is there.

The Interrelationship of Controls

Although any one of the Federal Reserve controls can be used separately, it is much more likely that several of them will be used in combination. In 1938, for instance, when reserve requirements were raised by 14 per cent, the authorities recognized that this would hit some banks much harder than was desirable. Simultaneously, therefore, the Reserve went into the market to buy government securities, thereby making it easier for banks to sell secondary reserves to meet the new requirement. The second action softened the effect of the first.

On the other hand, the Reserve can reinforce the effect of a rise in reserve requirements by raising the discount rate and engaging in open-market sales at the same time. Banks are thereby discouraged both from borrowing the additional reserves needed (particularly since the federal funds rate will probably rise along with the discount rate) and from selling securities since the Federal Reserve is depressing their price. Banks are therefore almost forced into the alternative of reducing loans. If margin requirements are also raised, this will shift the scarce funds away from speculation into more constructive channels, and such a shift can be further promoted by moral suasion, particularly in the areas of bank examination and bank supervision.

On the upward side also a combination of actions is likely to be more effective than a single one. A drop in reserve requirements plus open-market purchases not only provides banks with additional excess reserves but, by reducing interest rates, also makes borrowing more attractive to the banks' customers. Publicity may further induce a more optimistic attitude on the part of prospective borrowers.

Although we are not prepared to go into detail at this point, it is well to bear in mind that the Federal Reserve is by no means the only government agency that affects the money supply, liquidity, and the interest rate structure. The Treasury in particular exerts an important, sometimes a major, influence. As the most important borrower in the nation it cannot help but affect the money market by its debt management policies—the type of securities it issues, the interest coupon and other conditions it attaches to its securities, the timing of its borrowing activities, its use of advance refunding (a fairly new technique of offering security holders the option of turning their bonds into new issues before the ones they hold mature), and so on. Some sort of correlation between Treasury and Federal Reserve actions is necessary if the policy actions of either are to be effective.

We will have a good deal more to say about these policy issues after we have laid a firmer basis in monetary theory.

Questions for Thought and Discussion

1. In early 1957 interest rates and the volume of bank loans both increased. Does this mean that the higher interest rates induced more people to borrow?

2. Check (in the *Federal Reserve Bulletin* or elsewhere) the current reserve requirements for member banks. If they differ from those given in the text, does this suggest anything about changes in the state of the economy?

3. Where would you find figures on reserve requirements for nonmember banks in your state? Are they subject to change by some administrative body?

4. Are open-market operations desirable when they increase the Treasury's cost of borrowing?

5. What is the current discount rate for the Federal Reserve bank of your district? Does it differ from that of any other Federal Reserve bank?

6. If banks were required to hold 100 per cent reserves, would there be any way in which the Federal Reserve could influence expansion or contraction of credit?

7. To what extent would a loss of confidence in the Federal Reserve on the part of bankers reduce the effectiveness of credit control?

8. In what ways are margin requirements and consumer credit control similar? In what ways are they different?

9. Do consumer credit or real estate credit controls reduce the total volume of credit outstanding or only its distribution among borrowers?

10. Review the classification of Federal Reserve credit-control powers. Which are no longer available for use?

Selected Bibliography

See references listed under Chapter 11.

Chapter 14 The Bank Reserve Equation

There take an inventory of all I have
To the last penny.

The Life of King Henry VIII
Act III, scene 2, line 452

Although moral suasion and direct control do help in the whole process of credit control, the main instruments, as we have seen, are those that affect bank reserves. The Federal Reserve, through its open-market operations and discount rate policy, has a significant influence on reserves. But there are other influences, outside the control of the System, that may also affect the ability of the banking system to create credit.

The best way to examine the interrelations of all these forces is in terms of the bank reserve equation, which shows all the sources of funds for the economy as a whole and all the uses to which they may be put, including their use as bank reserves. The bank reserve equation is derived by adding to the balance sheet of the combined Federal Reserve banks those operations of the Treasury that directly affect the monetary circulation. In the preceding chapters we have examined most of the items involved in the equation, and a brief rundown of its components will serve as a summary of the effect on reserves (and hence on the ability of banks to create money) of much that has already been explained at greater length.

Sources and Uses of Funds

The bank reserve equation—under the title "Member Bank Reserves, Federal Reserve Bank Credit, and Related Items"—appears first in the array of useful statistics presented regularly in the *Federal Reserve Bulletin*. The data for December 31, 1964, are shown in Table 14-1, which is essentially a balance sheet of the "monetary system."[1]

Table 14-1. The Bank Reserve Equation, December 31, 1964
Millions of Dollars

Factors supplying reserve funds			
F.R. bank credit outstanding:			
U.S. government securities:			
Bought outright	36,506		
Held under repurchase agreement	538	37,044	
Discounts and advances		186	
Float		2,606	
Bank acceptances		94	39,930
Gold stock			15,388
Treasury currency outstanding			5,405
Total sources			60,723
Factors absorbing reserve funds			
Currency in circulation			39,619
Treasury cash holdings			612
Deposits with F.R. banks (other than member bank reserves):			
Treasury		820	
Foreign		229	
Other		321	1,370
Other Federal Reserve accounts			1,036
Member bank reserves with Federal Reserve banks			18,086
Total uses			60,723
Member bank reserves and borrowings*			
Total reserves:			
Deposits with Federal Reserve banks		18,338	
Currency and coin		3,658	21,996
Less required reserves			21,441
Excess reserves			555
Less borrowings at Federal Reserve banks			504
Free reserves			51

* Average of daily figures for the week ended Dec. 30, 1964. Since required reserves are computed on a weekly basis, no figures are available for Dec. 31, and hence this section of the table is not strictly comparable with the preceding part.
Source: Adapted from *Federal Reserve Bulletin*, vol. 51, no. 2 (February, 1965), pp. 263, 264.

[1] Many of these figures can be compared directly with those of the Federal Reserve balance sheet of Table 12-2. As a matter of terminology, gold certificates are here called *gold stock* (since the Treasury holds the gold while the Reserve holds the certificates—a slight difference between the two representing free gold held by the Treasury as part of Treasury cash), while Federal Reserve notes have disappeared into "currency in circulation." The following equations show the technical relations between the two tables: (1) Federal Reserve notes + treasury currency outstanding + free gold (gold stock − gold certificates) = Treasury cash holdings + "cash on hand" of the Federal Reserve + currency in circulation. (2) "Other Federal Reserve accounts" = capital and surplus + "other liabilities" − bank premises − "other assets."

The total gold stock, Federal Reserve bank credit, and treasury currency are the basic ingredients of the money supply, giving rise to funds that must be held by someone. The second part of the table shows who holds them: the public (currency in circulation), the Treasury, foreigners, member banks, and others. All funds that are provided by the monetary system must be held by someone. For monetary purposes it is convenient to divide these holders into member banks (who use such funds as reserves) and all other holders (for whom funds do not constitute reserves). It is because bank reserves are so important to our monetary system and its control that we refer to these data as the *bank reserve equation.* This equation can be written:

Sources of funds = reserve uses + nonreserve uses

Or, rearranging and expanding:

Reserve uses of funds	= sources of funds	− nonreserve uses
Bank deposits with F.R.	Reserve bank credit	Currency outside banks
Vault cash	Gold stock	Treasury holdings of:
	Treasury currency	Cash
		Deposits with F.R.
		Foreign deposits
		Other deposits
		Other F.R. accounts

Among other things this restatement suggests that for the banking system as a whole, both member and nonmember deposits with the Federal Reserve are part of reserves, as is also vault cash. For nonmember banks, correspondent balances may generally be counted as reserves, and in some states certain securities may be included as well. The "Factors absorbing reserve funds" part of Table 14-1 does not give us details on these items (it does not, for instance, break currency in circulation down into vault cash and currency outside banks), and to that extent the table, though it covers the most important items, is incomplete. In the last section of the table, "Member bank reserves and borrowings," the Federal Reserve fills in the item for vault cash ("currency and coin") of member banks, but since its responsibility does not extend to nonmembers, it has not attempted to provide data for them.

Bearing in mind this slight discrepancy, we can say that as a general rule an increase in any of the sources of funds listed in the table, other things remaining the same, will increase bank reserves. A decrease in any nonreserve use (if not offset elsewhere) will similarly increase reserves.

Most of these items have already been discussed; others need a brief word of explanation.

Reserve Bank Credit. Reserve bank credit, as Table 14-1 shows, covers several kinds of operations. We have already seen how an open-market purchase (an increase in United States government securities held by the Reserve banks) increases bank reserves, and how a sale reduces reserves. This is at present the major instrument of Federal Reserve policy.

Repurchase agreements are a special device used by the Federal Reserve banks for the financing of government-bond dealers. They are technically purchases of government securities but have the effect of loans. Under a repurchase agreement the Federal Reserve bank buys securities from a bond house with the understanding that the dealer can repurchase them at the same price within a specified (usually very short) period of time. The bank charges a fee for this service that is similar to the discount rate. The Federal Reserve engages in these transactions only when it feels that funds are needed in the market to aid government-bond houses in maintaining their portfolios of government securities. The amounts involved are fairly small.

Discounts and advances represent almost exclusively loans to member banks.

Similarly float is, in effect, a loan to the banks but is not subject to Federal Reserve control since it depends primarily on fortuitous circumstances such as the weather, which may delay mail delivery of checks for collection.

Bank acceptances, arising out of foreign trade and representing basically a bank's promise to pay, are highly liquid short-term obligations with a well-organized market in New York. Purchases and sales of acceptances by the Federal Reserve have exactly the same effect on bank reserves as purchases and sales of government securities, and they are accordingly considered open-market operations.

Gold Stock. Although gold is not money at the present time in this country, it *is* the basis on which our monetary system still stands, and it represents, through gold certificates, one of the two major assets of Federal Reserve banks. As the Reserve banks acquire gold, they provide additional reserves to commercial banks. The effect is the same as when they buy securities, although the process is a little more involved. Conversely, when they lose gold, bank reserves are reduced.

There are two basic sources of gold: gold mines and foreign countries. In either case the procedure through which the Treasury acquires gold is pretty much the same. The following examples, though oversimplified, illustrate the basic effect accurately.

Suppose a foreign trader wants dollars to buy our goods. He has gold, which he can sell to the Treasury of the United States at $35 an ounce. The Treasury would make payment in the form of a check drawn on its Federal Reserve account. The trader then deposits this check in a commercial bank so that he can draw against it to pay for the goods (or he gives it to the United States exporter directly in payment of his bill, and the exporter deposits it in his bank). The bank in either case deposits the check to its own account in the Federal Reserve bank and thereby acquires reserves.

Meanwhile the Treasury, having received a given amount of gold, issues a gold certificate of equal value and deposits this gold certificate in its account at the Federal Reserve, thus replenishing its account in the amount of the check drawn against it (which it used to buy the gold). The steps in this process are illustrated by the balance sheets shown in Table 14-2.

Table 14-2. The Effect of a Treasury Gold Purchase on Bank Reserves

1. Treasury buys gold with a check on its Federal Reserve account.
2. Seller deposits check in his bank.
3. Bank deposits check in Federal Reserve, which charges Treasury's account.
4. Treasury issues gold certificates and deposits them in Federal Reserve.

United States Treasury

Assets		*Liabilities*	
Gold	+100 (*1*)	Gold certificates	+100 (*4*)
Due from Federal Reserve	−100 (*1*)*		
	+100 (*4*)		

Federal Reserve bank

Assets		*Liabilities*	
Gold certificates	+100 (*4*)	Deposits, member banks	+100 (*3*)
		Deposits, Treasury	−100 (*3*)
			+100 (*4*)

Commercial bank

Assets		*Liabilities*	
Cash items in process of collection	+100 (*2*)	Deposits (due seller of goods)	+100 (*2*)
	−100 (*3*)		
Due from Federal Reserve (reserves)	+100 (*3*)		

* The equivalent entry on the books of the Federal Reserve bank occurs in step (3).

When the Treasury buys gold from a domestic gold mine, the result is similar. The miner receives a Treasury check, which he deposits in his bank, and his bank deposits it in the Federal Reserve. The Reserve charges the check against the Treasury, which reimburses its account by the deposit of gold certificates issued against the new gold.

The effect of both kinds of gold purchases by the Treasury is thus to increase bank deposits and reserves.

When the Treasury sells gold, which under current conditions it would do only for a foreign bank, the process is repeated in reverse. The buyer pays with a check on his commercial bank; the Treasury deposits this check to its account at the Federal Reserve. The Federal Reserve charges the account of the bank on which the check was drawn, but instead of crediting the Treasury's account, it returns an equal amount of gold certificates to the Treasury to be canceled. The effect is to reduce member bank reserves.

Gold movements, while large and at times very disturbing to the monetary system, cannot be controlled for the purposes of monetary policy. As long as the Treasury stands ready to buy or sell gold at $35 an ounce, it must do so whenever any foreign central bank wishes to sell or buy. Gold purchases and sales depend primarily on gold-mining conditions and on the desire of foreigners to obtain gold for dollars, or vice versa. The latter depends to a large extent on the balance of trade of the United States, over which neither the Treasury nor the Federal Reserve has any appreciable control.

Treasury Currency Outstanding. When we speak of treasury currency, we mean that part of our money supply issued directly by the Treasury (plus a small amount of discontinued issues for which the Treasury has accepted final responsibility for payment): primarily United States notes and coin. The law requires that the volume of United States notes be kept constant, so the only changes likely to occur in treasury currency outstanding are an increase in coin and the redemption of discontinued issues. Since coin is minted only to meet the demands of the public, any new issue would be absorbed into currency in circulation. When silver certificates are redeemed, they are replaced with an equal amount of Federal Reserve notes so that their redemption causes no change in currency in circulation. There are no other discontinued issues outstanding in sufficient numbers to worry about. Changes in treasury currency outstanding, therefore, are not likely to have any effect at all on reserves.

Currency in Circulation. Having examined the sources of funds, we now turn to the various uses to which these funds may be put.

It might be assumed that currency in circulation simply equals the amount issued by the Treasury and the Federal Reserve and that its amount, therefore, is controlled by the issuing authorities. Nothing could be further from the truth. While both of these agencies may *influence* the quantity of currency in circulation, neither can actually *determine* it. The final determining authority is you—the general public. Given the total quantity of money (checking accounts plus currency), the monetary authorities cannot control the proportion of that total that people wish to hold in cash.

Suppose I decide I have too much cash in my pocket compared with the amount I have "in the bank." I go to the bank and deposit cash. The bank now has more vault cash, and if this movement of cash into the bank is at all general, the bank in turn will deposit the extra cash in its Federal Reserve account. The currency has been withdrawn from circulation. There is nothing the Federal Reserve or the Treasury can do to keep it in the hands of the public.

Suppose, on the other hand, I decide to hold more cash. I write a check on my deposit account and cash it. The bank *has* to give me cash, or it is bankrupt. In order to replenish its vault cash the bank will draw a check on its Federal Reserve account and present it for payment. The Federal Reserve bank *has* to give the bank the currency it wants, or the Reserve bank is bankrupt. Suppose it has no currency. It will simply create more Federal Reserve notes, which are, after all, the primary circulating currency of the country. It has no choice. So a demand for cash forces the Reserve to create it; it cannot refuse.

We are talking here about the quantity of *currency,* not the quantity of *money*. The monetary authorities can, and do, control the total quantity of money and hence *indirectly* the quantity of currency.

As far as the bank reserve equation is concerned, an increase in the demand of the public for cash—an increase in currency outside banks—tends to reduce bank reserves as the banks meet the demand by drawing checks against their Federal Reserve accounts. Similarly, as currency is retired from circulation, it will be deposited in the Reserve banks and will increase member bank reserve balances.

Vault Cash. Since currency in circulation includes vault cash held by banks and since the law permits this vault cash to be counted by member banks as part of their reserve requirements, a leakage of currency into circulation may not reduce the credit-creating potential of the banking system *if it ends up in the banks' tills.* On the other hand, if currency moves from banks to the public, there will be downward pressure on bank reserves even though the total currency in circulation does not change.

Treasury Holdings. To the extent that the United States Treasury holds either cash or checking accounts in the Federal Reserve, this represents a competing use, for the funds so held obviously cannot at the same time be used for bank reserves.

Cash held by the Treasury is not part of "currency in circulation." This term covers only currency in the hands of the general public, which includes the commercial banks but not the issuing authorities (the Treasury and the Federal Reserve banks). But Treasury cash holdings have the same general effect on the equation as private holdings. Treasury cash, however, is not an active factor in changing member bank reserves, for the amount held is small, and changes are primarily the result of receipts from, or payments to, the public; that is, transfers directly between Treasury cash and currency in circulation, an increase in one being offset by a decrease in the other.

More important are Treasury deposits with the Federal Reserve. When the Treasury increases these deposits (for example, by a call on its tax and loan accounts in commercial banks), this transfers funds out of member bank balances with the Federal Reserve and thereby reduces reserves. When the Treasury writes checks on its account and these checks are deposited in member banks, these banks in turn deposit the checks in their reserve accounts, thus increasing reserves.

The Treasury may hold its funds in three forms: (1) in cash, (2) on deposit with the Federal Reserve, and (3) on deposit with commercial banks. With a given amount of funds the Treasury can *reduce* bank reserves by increasing the proportion it holds in the first two categories, or it can *increase* bank reserves by raising the proportion it holds in commercial banks. It is this fact that gives the Treasury a certain amount of control over bank credit through the balances it holds in tax and loan accounts.

Foreign and "Other" Deposits. When a foreign central bank obtains a check written on a United States commercial bank and deposits this to its credit in the Federal Reserve, the process of clearing will result in a reduction in the reserves of the bank on which the check was drawn and an increase in foreign deposits with the Federal Reserve. When the foreign central bank draws on its account to make payments to United States exporters, such checks will be deposited in the exporters' commercial bank and will then be credited to that bank's reserve account. Such operations depend primarily on the international payments position of the United States and are not subject to monetary control.

The "other" deposits with the Federal Reserve consist mainly of balances held by nonmember clearing banks. If a check drawn on a member bank is deposited in a nonmember clearing bank, the member bank loses reserves, while the nonmember bank gains a Federal Reserve deposit, which, as a matter of fact, can be counted as reserves for that bank under all state laws. Such a transfer of accounts, therefore, does not actually alter the ability of the *banking system* as a whole to expand credit, but it does reduce the ability of *member banks* to do so. Changes in this item are very small and can be ignored for most purposes.

Other Federal Reserve Accounts. This item too can be ignored for practical purposes. It represents the net value of miscellaneous Federal Reserve assets, liabilities, and capital accounts not listed separately. The figure is fairly stable over time.

Member Bank Reserves and Borrowings. As we already know, total reserves (deposits with the Federal Reserve banks plus currency and coin in vault) less required reserves yield excess reserves. A small amount of excess reserves (*legally* excess, that is) is necessary to give the bank a margin for clearing purposes. The statistics suggest that this margin may be in the neighborhood of $300 million to $400 million at the present time. Any amount over this gives the banks the power to create additional credit.

The final figures in Table 14-1 show that although banks held $555 million in excess reserves in the last week of December, 1964, they were in debt to the Federal Reserve banks for almost as much. Thus they had *free reserves* (the amount of excess reserves they would have had if they had paid back their debt to the Federal Reserve) of only $51 million. If banks have borrowed from the Federal Reserve banks more than the amount of their excess reserves, they are said to have *net borrowed reserves* (that is, free reserves are negative). Net borrowed reserves are normally a sign of tight money, since they indicate that member banks have had to borrow substantial amounts to replenish reserves depleted by a high level of lending.

Another measure of the tightness of money that has been developed only recently is the *basic reserve position.* This subtracts from excess reserves not only the sums borrowed from the Federal Reserve banks, but also federal funds borrowed. This procedure recognizes the fact that the federal funds market is an alternative source of reserves for banks whose reserve position would otherwise be deficient. While by far the greater part of federal funds transactions are between one bank and another, so that the *net* amount of funds available to the banking system as a whole from this source is almost nil, certain groups of banks—particularly those in the large money markets who maintain their reserve positions extremely close to the legal limit—may well be net borrowers.

Table 14-3 shows, for the week ending December 30, 1964, the basic reserve position of the forty-six banks for which the Federal Reserve provides statistics. It is significant not only that the basic reserve position of these banks is negative by $1,145 million, a fairly large figure for this small number of banks, but also that their net borrowings of federal funds considerably exceeded their borrowings from the Federal Reserve banks. The demand for federal funds in this period was so great that some large banks, apparently for the first time, were paying more than the discount rate to obtain them.

Table 14-3. Basic Reserve Position of Forty-six Selected Banks for the Week Ended December 30, 1964

Average of Daily Figures; Millions of Dollars

Excess reserves	62
Less borrowings at F.R. banks	309
Free reserves	−247
Less net interbank federal funds transactions	898
Basic reserve position	−1,145
Basic reserve position as per cent of average required reserves	11.8

Source: Adapted from *Federal Reserve Bulletin*, vol. 51, no. 2 (February, 1965), p. 266.

Summary. A review in capsule form of the various major groups of items affecting member bank reserves may be helpful. Table 14-4 shows each item with a brief comment on its absolute (dollar value) importance in the bank reserve equation and an indication of its significance as a device for carrying out monetary policy objectives.

It is clear that several causes of changes in bank reserves are not subject to control by the monetary authorities. Frequently, therefore, Federal Reserve policy is directed toward canceling out the influence of some disturbing force in order to prevent undesirable changes in bank reserves. This can be as important as precipitating desirable changes. For instance, a temporary increase in float may be offset by an equivalent sale of government securities.

Table 14-4. The Bank Reserve Equation and Monetary Policy

Sources of funds

Federal Reserve bank credit:

U.S. government securities. Most important source of funds. Most important instrument of credit policy (open-market operations).

Securities held under repurchase agreement. Quite small. Used as a special type of control to affect funds in the hands of government-bond dealers.

Discounts and advances. Minor source of funds. Controlled by discount rate.

Float. Changes may be fairly large but depend on fortuitous circumstances (such as weather). Not subject to control.

Acceptances purchased. Very small but may be used as an instrument of control in a manner similar to purchase and sale of government securities.

Gold stock. Important source of funds. Changes are mainly the result of foreign trade developments not subject to monetary control.

Treasury currency outstanding. Moderately important as a source of funds. Tendency is to grow gradually over time without significant short-run fluctuations. Not used as an instrument of control, although it could be.

Uses of funds

Currency in circulation. Most important use of funds. Subject to desire of public to hold cash and can be controlled only indirectly.

Treasury cash holdings. Relatively small (was fairly large during World War II). Could be used as control device by the Treasury but has not been.

Deposits with Federal Reserve banks (other than member bank reserves):

Treasury deposits. Relatively small. Could be, and for short periods sometimes is, a fairly important controlling (or disturbing) influence. Normally the policy of the Treasury has been to keep changes to a minimum.

Foreign deposits. Relatively small. Changes are mainly the result of foreign trade developments not subject to monetary control.

Other deposits. Relatively small. Changes are insignificant; not subject to control.

Other Federal Reserve accounts. Relatively small. Changes are insignificant; not subject to control.

Member bank deposits. Important use of funds. These are considered the object of monetary policy since (along with a small amount of vault cash) they determine the ability of member banks to create deposits.

A loss of gold could be counteracted by purchasing securities or even by lowering reserve requirements. An understanding of the push and pull of the various forces acting on the monetary system as they are shown in the bank reserve equation is necessary to an appreciation of the constant vigilance necessary on the part of the Federal Reserve in order to maintain an even balance in the economy.

The Bank Reserve Equation in Practice

Perhaps an illustration of these forces may make the equation more realistic. Table 14-5 shows changes in the major factors in the equation for five selected periods. The first two and the last show data for fairly extended periods during which major changes were occurring in our basic monetary structure. The other two illustrate changes that can occur in briefer periods as a result of more temporary influences. It should be noted, however, that the particular periods shown were chosen because of the magnitude of the changes that occurred; they are not typical or average situations.

The first period is one in which foreigners, attempting to find a safe haven for their wealth and harassed by inflation, devaluation, and debt repudiation in their own countries, sent large sums of gold to this country in order to

Table 14-5. Changes in the Bank Reserve Equation for Selected Periods

Billions of Dollars

	Dec. 31, 1934, to Dec. 31, 1941	Dec. 31, 1941, to Dec. 31, 1945	Dec. 31, 1948, to Mar. 31, 1950	Mar. 31, 1950, to Mar. 31, 1951	Dec. 31, 1957, to Dec. 31, 1963
Sources of funds:					
Reserve bank credit	−0.1	+22.7	−6.0	+6.1	+10.6
Gold stock	+14.5	−2.7	*	−2.4	−7.3
Treasury currency	+0.7	+1.1	*	*	+0.4
Total sources	+15.1	+21.2	−6.0	+3.7	+3.8
Uses of funds:					
Currency in circulation	+5.6	+17.4	−1.2	+0.1	+5.9
Treasury cash and deposits	−0.1	+0.2	−0.1	+0.1	*
Foreign and other deposits	+1.2	−0.1	−0.1	+0.2	−0.1
Other Federal Reserve accounts	+0.1	+0.2	+0.2	*	+0.1
Total nonreserve uses	+6.8	+17.7	−1.2	+0.3	+5.8
Member bank reserve deposits	+8.4	+3.5	−4.8	+3.4	−2.0
Total uses	+15.1	+21.2	−6.0	+3.7	+3.8

* Less than $50 million.

Sources: Computed from Board of Governors of the Federal Reserve System, *Banking and Monetary Statistics* (1943), pp. 376, 377; *Federal Reserve Bulletin*, vol. 37, no. 4 (April, 1951), p. 400; vol. 44, no. 9 (September, 1958), p. 1072; vol. 50, no. 2 (February, 1964), p. 179. Detail may not add to totals because of rounding.

obtain dollar assets. During part of this period the Treasury attempted to "sterilize" incoming gold by adding it to its cash holdings rather than putting it into the monetary gold stock—that is, it did not issue gold certificates against the new gold—but this practice was soon abandoned and does not show in our figures. A small part of the increased funds that resulted from the gold inflow was absorbed by foreign deposits in the Federal Reserve. A larger portion was offset by an increase in currency in circulation due to a growing population and increased business activity, particularly in the latter part of the period. More than half the gold inflow, however, found its way into bank reserves. Federal Reserve credit in this period changed by an insignificant amount—open-market operations were quite small and discounts practically nonexistent. As we have seen, the Federal Reserve did take steps in 1936 and 1937 to counteract part of this increase in reserves by raising reserve requirements drastically. This meant that the rise in actual reserves did not represent an equivalent increase in excess reserves, a factor that our table does not show.

The war period, 1941–1945, illustrates the tremendous expansion potential inherent in the monetary system. In order to finance the war the Federal Reserve made available almost $23 billion of credit. A small part of this was eaten up in an outflow of gold. The greater part was absorbed in a doubling of currency in circulation; the war prosperity meant that people were carrying more money in their pockets. Some of the increase in Federal Reserve credit, which resulted almost entirely from purchases of government securities, found its way into member bank reserves. This increase in reserves, coupled with substantial excess reserves held by banks at the beginning of the period, permitted them to expand credit significantly in order to meet the needs of the government for funds to buy war materiel as well as the needs of business for funds to expand production to provide the materiel. Part of the increased credit was wasted in inflation, a problem always associated with wars.

The second and third periods covered in our table illustrate cases in which the effect of changes in Federal Reserve credit was felt more directly by bank reserves—in one case downward and in the other upward. During 1949 and the first three months of 1950, Federal Reserve credit fell $6 billion. A little over $1 billion of this drop was offset by a fall in currency in circulation, but the rest resulted in a reduction of reserves.

In the succeeding twelve-month period Federal Reserve credit expanded by an almost identical amount. In this case currency in circulation changed little, but a gold outflow of $2½ billion absorbed part of the increase, while reserves rose by the amount of the remaining $3½ billion.

The last period is one in which the United States was losing gold at the rate of more than $1 billion a year as a result of an adverse balance of payments on our international account. This gold loss was more than offset by a very substantial increase in Federal Reserve credit, almost all of it through the purchase of government securities. A small increase in treasury currency reflected the slowly growing demand for coin. These three forces together produced a rise in sources of funds of $3.8 billion for the six-year period. But this increase was more than absorbed by a demand for currency in circulation, so that member bank reserve deposits *fell* by $2.0 billion.

These examples show the importance of Federal Reserve credit, of gold flows, and of currency in circulation in affecting member bank reserve balances. They also indicate the relative unimportance of other items in the equation, at least in the long run. But for periods of a few days or weeks we would find that Treasury deposits or other items might exert a fair degree of pressure on the reserve situation. For these shorter periods we would also find it helpful to break down Federal Reserve credit into its components in order to get a more detailed view of what was happening.

Table 14-6 gives this type of analysis for the two weeks ending June 20 and June 27, 1956. In the first week the most remarkable occurrence was the unusually large increase in float. This fortuitous increase much more than offset a fairly large increase in Treasury deposits plus moderate rises in other deposits and other Federal Reserve accounts. The result was a significant increase in bank reserves. The sale of securities by the Federal Reserve was undoubtedly intended to offset part of the upward pressure of float, while the discounts by member banks very likely occurred before they realized how much their reserves would be increased anyway. One indication of this is their attempt the following week to reduce discounts in spite of falling reserves.

In this second week the Federal Reserve was still selling securities to reduce the unexpected increase in reserves, while float dropped back toward a more normal level. Treasury deposits still rose, but this was more than offset by drops in foreign and other deposits. At the same time a moderate drop in

Table 14-6. Changes in the Bank Reserve Equation for Selected Weeks

Millions of Dollars

	Week ending June 20, 1956	Week ending June 27, 1956
Sources of funds:		
Reserve bank credit:		
U.S. government securities	−24	−15
Discounts and advances	+17	−8
Float	+537	−138
Gold stock	+2	+1
Treasury currency	0	0
Total sources	+532	−160
Uses of funds:		
Currency in circulation	−1	−56
Treasury cash	−5	+7
Treasury deposits	+137	+35
Foreign deposits	−1	−34
Other deposits	+18	−27
Other Federal Reserve accounts	+16	+2
Total nonreserve uses	+164	−73
Member bank reserve deposits	+367	−86
Total uses	+532	−160

Source: Computed from *Federal Reserve Bulletin*, vol. 42, no. 9 (September, 1956), p. 943.

currency in circulation aided bank reserves, which fell considerably less than float.

The specific weeks chosen here for illustration do not have any particular significance. They merely show the interplay of the various factors in the equation and indicate how the Federal Reserve adapts its policy to day-by-day conditions in the money market. Bank reserves are of central importance in the monetary system, and the bank reserve equation throws considerable light on the level of bank reserves and the forces that influence them.

Determinants of the Money Supply

Before we leave the area of money mechanics it may be well to summarize the forces affecting the money supply as a whole, remembering that in this chapter we have emphasized those that affect bank reserves, which are not themselves directly a part of the money supply at all. We have already seen that the amount of currency in circulation is determined entirely by the public. If people want more cash, they can withdraw it from the banks by writing checks against their accounts. If they wish to hold less, they will deposit it in their bank accounts. The desire to hold currency is itself influenced by many things: income, expenditure patterns, availability of credit, and faith in the banking system, among others. The most important determinant in the short run, however, is the total money supply, for people generally hold some rough proportion of their total money in currency and the rest in checking accounts.

The major part of the total money supply consists of bank deposits subject to check. This quantity is determined most directly by the commercial banks. They can expand it within the limits of whatever reserve requirements are applicable. They cannot expand, however, unless businessmen (or government or consumers) are willing to borrow. Expansion, therefore, is contingent on a desire on the part of the economy to go into debt to increase its business activity. To that extent banks are restricted by the general desires of the community.

On the other hand banks are also restricted by their legal reserve requirements. Here the Federal Reserve enters the picture. It can permit an expansion of credit, or it can force a contraction through its various powers of control.

The total money supply, therefore, depends on a number of interrelated factors and involves not only the banks and the Federal Reserve but also businessmen, government, and the man in the street. Many of these forces will show up in the bank reserve equation; others will appear only on the balance sheets of commercial banks. Table 14-7 summarizes these factors under three headings, with the items listed in each section roughly in order of their importance. Although the table uses the language of a rise in the money supply, a fall would naturally occur as a result of a reversal in the direction of any of the factors.

Table 14-7. Determinants of the Money Supply

Currency in circulation or bank reserves (or both)* will rise if:
- The Federal Reserve banks increase their assets (Federal Reserve bank credit)
- The gold stock increases
- The Treasury issues additional currency
- Treasury cash holdings or deposits with the Federal Reserve banks increase
- Foreign deposits with the Federal Reserve banks fall
- "Other" deposits with the Federal Reserve banks fall
- Other Federal Reserve liabilities fall

Given the volume of total reserves, excess reserves will rise if:
- Reserve requirements are lowered
- Time deposits are shifted to demand deposits
- Demand deposits are shifted from banks with higher reserve requirements to banks with lower requirements (as from reserve city banks to country banks)

Given excess reserves, demand deposits (adjusted) will rise if:
- Banks increase their assets (make more loans)
- Treasury deposits in commercial banks fall (are shifted to private accounts)
- Time deposits fall (are shifted to demand deposits)
- Foreign accounts in commercial banks fall (are shifted to domestic accounts)
- Other bank liabilities fall

* Although currency and demand deposits are both components of the money supply, a shift from one to the other is likely to change the total. For instance, a deposit of cash in a bank reduces currency in circulation but will raise the total money supply if the bank increases its loans on the basis of the reserves thus obtained.

Questions for Thought and Discussion

1. What would be the net effect on member bank reserves of each of the following:

a. An inflow of gold, which the Treasury sterilized by not issuing gold certificates against it?

b. The transfer of funds from a nonmember bank to the Treasury?

c. An increase in bank borrowing from the Federal Reserve for the purpose of meeting an outflow of cash into circulation?

d. A net clearing balance out of nonmember banks into member banks?

e. The payment by the government of clerks' salaries by checks drawn on the Federal Reserve?

f. A Treasury call on tax and loan accounts?

g. The sale by the Federal Reserve of government securities?

h. The purchase by a member bank of newly issued government securities?

i. An increase in legal reserve requirements?

2. Look up "Member Bank Reserves, Reserve Bank Credit, and Related Items" in the *Federal Reserve Bulletin* and analyze the changes that occurred during the last week shown; during the last year shown; between 1929 and 1933.

3. Differentiate the following concepts: reserves, excess reserves, free reserves, and basic reserves.

Selected Bibliography

American Institute of Banking: *Utilizing the Weekly Federal Reserve Statement,* New York, 1938.

Federal Reserve Bank of New York: *Bank Reserves: Some Major Factors Affecting Them,* November, 1953.

Federal Reserve Bank of Philadelphia: *Weekly Financial Barometers: How to Interpret Reports of Member Banks and the Federal Reserve Banks,* October, 1959.

Chapter 15 The Current Banking Situation

But since the affairs of men rest still incertain,
Let's reason with the worst that may befall.

Julius Caesar
Act V, scene 1, line 96

Our summary of banking thus far has thrown some illumination on the dim origins of banking, on its growth in wisdom and stature, on the major operations that a commercial bank performs, on the principles by which a bank extends credit, and on the operation of the Federal Reserve System. There are many peculiarities of bank operations that have been alluded to only briefly, and others that have not been touched on at all. The function of this chapter is to draw together some of the most important aspects of present-day banking that have, up to here, been lost in the shuffle.

Unit Banking

The most peculiar aspect of banking in the United States is its fragmentation. At the end of 1964 we had 13,761 independent commercial banks. This figure is only 1,000 less than it was thirty years ago, and it is currently rising at the rate of about 15 per month. We are still a unit banking nation. No other country is blessed with so many banks per capita as we, though several of them have more banking *offices* per capita. This occurs because other countries in the main have a few large banks with many branches. There are only sixteen commercial banks in Great Britain, and of these only five are considered large. But these sixteen banks operated some thirteen thousand branches in 1964, which is an average of one banking office for each 4,000 inhabitants. Canada, with eight chartered banks, had 5,496 branches at the end of 1962, or an average of one banking office for each 3,300 people.

In the United States, by contrast, less than one-sixth of the banks operate any branches at all. The total number of commercial banking offices in the United States in 1964 was 27,685, or an average of one banking office for 7,000 people.

Unit Banking Tradition. The unit banking principle in this country is based on both tradition and law. The emphasis on free enterprise and rugged individualism affirms the right of everyone to become a banker. This right has been modified to some extent in recent times as various supervisory agencies have been established in an attempt to produce a sound banking system. But our tradition has been that anyone with the capital and the desire to establish a bank should be allowed to do so as long as the safety of the public is protected.

Part of the rationale behind this open system of banking has been the belief that here as elsewhere in the economy competition must be preserved. There is a deep distrust in the American mind of the monopolistic banker even in the terribly fragmented system we now have. "Wall Street" is the symbol, if not the substance, of the fear of too much monetary power in too few hands.

While there are only sixteen banks in England today, this was not always the case. In 1825 there were 554 private banks, and many more were formed under the act of 1826, which permitted the establishment of joint stock banking. Then the pendulum swung the other way toward amalgamations and mergers. This trend has been blocked in the United States not only by public sentiment, but also by three very different types of legislation.

Branch Banking Laws. The greatest bar to branch banking results from the various laws governing the operation of branches. Eighteen states, predominantly in the Midwest and Great Plains, prohibit any bank from carrying on business in any place except its head office. Here branch banking is nonexistent. Sixteen states, such as New York, permit branches only within the same city, county, or other contiguous geographical area. Sixteen states, of which California is the outstanding example, permit branches anywhere in the state. But no state bank may operate branches in another state.

One indication of the temper of the times is the fact that over the years branching privileges have gradually been extended in one state after another. In 1960 the New York legislature enlarged the districts within which branches could be established, and Illinois is considering the desirability of permitting branches for the first time, a move strongly endorsed by the Chicago banks.

As for national banks, their position was originally not clear. The National Bank Act neither prohibited nor authorized branches. It was assumed that lack of authorization implied prohibition, but in 1923 the Comptroller of the Currency ruled otherwise and permitted the operation of branches under certain restricted circumstances. The McFadden-Pepper Act of 1927 wrote these provisions into law, and the Banking Act of 1933 completed the process by permitting national banks to establish branches under the same conditions as applied to state banks in the state involved. Thus national banks and state banks are now both controlled by the state law in each particular state as far as branches are concerned. These various restrictions on the operation of branches have made it impossible to establish nationwide or even regional banks and in general have restricted the growth of strong individual banks.

Bank Mergers. The second limitation on bank growth has been the requirement of Federal law as well as most state laws that any merger (and in many cases the establishment of branches) must be approved by the chartering agency. While this has not prevented consolidation, it has restrained it to a certain extent. The Bank Merger Act of 1960 was an attempt on the part of Congress to provide a definitive procedure for approval of mergers to replace what had been a somewhat chaotic situation. No insured bank may merge with, or acquire the assets of, another without prior written consent of the appropriate Federal agency: the Comptroller of the Currency for a national bank, the Board of Governors for a state member bank, or the Federal Deposit Insurance Corporation for a nonmember insured bank. In each case the agency involved must request an advisory opinion from each of the other two agencies and from the Attorney General, but it is not bound to follow this advice. Noninsured banks are not covered, and control, if any, over their merger is therefore left to the states. Similarly the state may prevent the merger of nonnational banks even if the Federal agency approves.

Whether the Bank Merger Act has in practice clarified the situation or complicated it further is hard to say. There is no doubt that the required procedures have uncovered a good deal of disagreement among the agencies, some of it acrimonious. A sizable number of mergers have been approved under the act's provisions, but several requests have been blocked as well, and an unknown number may have been discouraged from making application.

Antitrust Laws. The third difficulty centers on the antitrust laws, which have always been a potential threat to extensive bank expansion. In 1952 the threat became an actuality when the Federal Reserve succeeded in breaking up the holding company relationship between the Transamerica Corporation and the Bank of America. Then starting in 1962 the Department of Justice brought several successful suits against bank mergers that had been previously approved by the appropriate banking authorities, and the dissolution orders have been upheld by the Supreme Court. Whether it is physically possible to break up the merged banks into their original components is a thorny economic and legal problem which has not yet been solved and with which the courts are still wrestling. But the very threat of such a suit, brought under either the Sherman Antitrust Act or the Clayton Antitrust Act, can significantly dampen the ardor of any bank executive contemplating a corporate marriage.

Unit Banking Results. The result of both tradition and law has been the proliferation of small banks, most of them engaged in a purely local business. Some states permit banks to start with a capital of $10,000, which is hardly sufficient to set up a corner delicatessen. Such a bank, limiting its loans to 10 per cent of its capital, could lend no more than $1,000 to any one borrower! The *average* capital *and surplus* of all commercial banks in the United States, raised considerably by the inclusion of the huge metropolitan banks, is only $1,000,000—enough to make a maximum single loan, on the average, of $100,000. The average capital and surplus of nonmember banks (which include half the banks in the country) is only $340,000. Almost two-thirds of the banks in the United States have *deposits* of less than $2,000,000.[1] If all these 9,000 banks were added together, their *combined* deposits would be less than those of either the Bank of America (California) or the Chase Manhattan Bank in New York.

These small banks scattered throughout the country cannot possibly serve the best interests of their areas. They are too small to be efficient, to make the size of loan needed in many cases even by local business, to provide a full complement of banking services, to diversify their investments, and in some cases even to be honest.

Bank Failures

It is no wonder that the United States has been visited with the worst plague of bank failures ever known anywhere. When bank failures are mentioned, many people immediately think of the holocaust of 1933, when the problem was so acute that a national bank holiday was necessary to give time to clear up the debris and put the banking system back into some kind of working order. But while 1933 represented paralysis, the whole history of banking in this country bears witness to endemic sickness.

Prior to 1934 incomplete reports show that at least two banks had failed in every year since even partial statistics were first compiled in 1864. Since 1900 the annual number of failures had never fallen below 47; since 1920 it had never fallen below 367. In fact as we went into the new era of prosperity, presumably unequaled anywhere any time, the banking system seemed to disintegrate. From a peak of 30,456 commercial banks in operation in June of 1921 the ranks were decimated as by a plague. There were 505 failures in 1921, 367 in 1922, and so through the decade, with a maximum of 976 in 1926. During the height of prosperity, 1922 to 1929, 5,209 banks suspended operation with a total estimated loss to depositors of $500 million. In the next four years 9,106 banks failed, adding $1,336 million to depositors' losses. In these twelve years more banks failed than currently exist in this country.

[1] One insured bank that failed in 1936 had total deposits of only $5,088.

One can search through the annals of history in vain to find any banking system that has turned in such a miserable record as this.

The tide turned in 1934. The most vulnerable banks had already been removed from the scene, and more stringent supervision prohibited banks from reopening after the national bank holiday unless they were in reasonably sound condition. Changes in the law prevented some of the gross abuses that had previously weakened the system:

1. Banks were prohibited from engaging in the underwriting of securities, a process that had frequently led to a bank's having to hold in its portfolio doubtful securities that its underwriting department had been unable to sell.

2. Banks were prohibited from paying interest on demand deposits, a process that had developed as a result of competitive attempts to lure deposits away from other institutions. Not only was such a practice costly, but it induced banks to invest in highly speculative loans and securities in order to attempt to earn enough income to pay such interest.

3. The Federal Reserve was given power to administer margin requirements, thus forcing an improvement in the collateral behind security loans.

4. The Federal Reserve was given broader authority to make advances to member banks on the basis of collateral previously unacceptable, thus permitting help to a bank that was basically sound but temporarily in distress.

5. The Federal Deposit Insurance Corporation was established. This will be described in more detail shortly.

The net result of these actions, plus a more cautious attitude on the part of bankers who had been burned once, was to strengthen considerably the underpinnings of the whole banking system. The improvement, however, did not achieve perfection. From 1934 to 1942, 488 banks were closed because of financial difficulties.[2] Since that time the number of failures has averaged more than four banks per year. The record is better than it was, but it is not good. If we should ever have the misfortune to go through another serious depression, there is no certainty that banks will not again start dropping by the wayside like flies, probably not by the thousands, as in the thirties, but perhaps by the score.

Such a situation would be intolerable anywhere else. In Canada, for instance, there hasn't been a bank failure since 1923. Mass failures are characteristic of a unit, rather than a branch, banking system.

Through the years numerous devices have been tried to correct this appalling situation. Such attempts have taken two directions: the strengthening of banks in order to prevent failure, and the protection of the bank's creditors against the consequence of failure.

In the first category are many institutions already discussed: state regulatory agencies, the National Bank Act, and the Federal Reserve Act. More will be said about the current status of bank regulation in a moment, but first let us examine the other arm of the attack—deposit insurance.

[2] Not including an even greater number of voluntary liquidations.

Deposit Insurance

Several individual states had attempted to insure bank notes prior to the Civil War. The Safety Fund System was perhaps the most successful of these, but even this device ran into financial difficulties.

Following the panic of 1907 eight Western states adopted plans for the insurance of bank deposits.[3] The experience with these plans was also not encouraging. All failed before 1930 because the tide of bank failures produced losses greater than the insurance funds were able to pay. This history of failure has been cited frequently as proving the impracticability of deposit insurance, and certainly the record is depressing. All these cases, however, show a somewhat common pattern that points to basic weaknesses in the plans used:

1. All the states involved were agricultural states that were especially hard hit by the agricultural depression that started in 1921 and lasted to a certain extent throughout the whole decade of the twenties. In some cases over one-third of the banks involved failed within the period.

2. Because the plans were in each case limited to a single state, geographical and even industrial diversification was impossible.

3. National banks were not included in the schemes, and these banks tended to be the stronger institutions. In the two states where participation was voluntary, the stronger state banks refused to participate, while in the other six states some of the stronger state banks avoided the plan by taking out national charters. In other words, only the weaker banks were insured.

4. Deposit insurance was not coupled with high standards of supervision. On the contrary, it tended to lull banks into a sense of false security and to encourage unsound banking practices.

5. The plans were in several cases badly conceived and based on inadequate premiums.

The Federal Deposit Insurance Corporation. In view of the unfortunate experience with state insurance, the establishment of the Federal Deposit Insurance Corporation created some misgivings among those who felt that it would suffer the same fate. The FDIC, however, was basically much stronger than the ill-fated state plans. It was nationwide, thereby achieving both geographical and industrial diversification of the areas covered. By requiring participation of all member banks of the Federal Reserve it automatically included the stronger banks in its coverage. And perhaps most important, the FDIC was coupled with relatively strong supervisory control over a banking system from which the weaker banks had already been weeded out.

The FDIC was established on a temporary basis by the Banking Act of 1933 and was made permanent in 1935. It is a government corporation whose

[3] Oklahoma (1908), Kansas (1909), Nebraska (1909), Texas (1909), Mississippi (1914), South Dakota (1915), North Dakota (1917), Washington (1917).

original capital was provided by the Treasury ($150 million) and the twelve Federal Reserve banks ($139 million). As the corporation has grown and achieved financial strength, it has paid back the whole amount of this capital with interest at 2 per cent, and it is now a mutual insurance fund. The FDIC is managed by a board of directors consisting of the Comptroller of the Currency and two additional members appointed by the President of the United States.

All members of the Federal Reserve System are required to become members of the FDIC. Other banks are encouraged to do so, and although they must meet certain minimum standards, the corporation has been fairly lenient in interpreting these requirements. Currently only 274 commercial banks in the United States are not members, and these noninsured banks hold less than one-half of 1 per cent of total deposits of commercial banks.

Each insured bank pays an insurance premium of $1/12$ per cent of its total deposits. The FDIC insures each depositor up to a maximum of $10,000. It is estimated that this maximum fully covers 98 per cent of all *depositors*, but only 57 per cent of all *deposits*. The disparity arises from the fact that almost all depositors have small balances, while a very few large corporations with deposits in the millions represent a considerable part of the total dollar volume of deposits.

One of the functions of the FDIC is to prevent failures if possible. Its powers of supervision and examination may help in this objective, although in this area its efforts overlap the work of other Federal and state regulatory agencies.

When a bank gets into difficulties, the FDIC has two methods of protecting depositors. One is to arrange with some other insured bank to take over the accounts of the insolvent bank. In such a case the sound bank accepts *all* the deposit liabilities of the failing bank and such assets as are acceptable to it, while the FDIC makes available an amount of cash equal to the difference between these two amounts and in return receives the other assets of the failing bank, which it then proceeds to liquidate. The advantage of this procedure is that all depositors are paid in full even though they may have deposits in excess of the insured maximum. It also provides for continuity of banking services.

If no bank wishes to take over, the failing bank is put into receivership, and the FDIC pays cash to its depositors up to the amount of insurance. As the bank's assets are liquidated, the FDIC is reimbursed to the extent of the funds realized, and at the same time depositors with accounts in excess of $10,000 receive a pro rata share on the uninsured portion of their deposits.

Table 15-1 shows the experience of the FDIC up until 1964 with regard to both types of operation. Actually the *current* record is considerably better than the table suggests, for of the total of 454 cases in which banks required FDIC assistance, 395 occurred prior to 1944.

It is clear that the FDIC has reduced substantially the loss to depositors,

Table 15-1. Experience of the Federal Deposit Insurance Corporation, 1934–1964

	Banks merged with FDIC aid	Banks suspended and insurance paid
Number of banks	182	272
Number of depositors	1,034,733	481,735
Number of depositors receiving payment in full	1,034,733	469,012
Per cent	100.0	97.4
Total deposits	$466,527,000	$191,161,000
Amount paid to depositors	$466,527,000	$181,680,000
Per cent	100.0	95.0
Disbursements by FDIC*	$198,074,000	$142,601,000
Less recoveries by FDIC*	$185,020,000	$120,256,000
Net loss by FDIC	$ 13,054,000	$ 22,345,000
Loss as a per cent of total deposits	2.8	11.7

*Including estimated additional disbursements and recoveries after 1964.
Source: Federal Deposit Insurance Corporation, *Statement of Operations: Annual Report, 1964, Part One* (1965), pp. 11, 12. Loss percentage computed by the author.

and this has been done at a relatively small cost. In fact, the losses of the FDIC have been so small that considerable complaint has been raised against the size of its assessments, which for the most part go simply to raise the surplus of the Corporation. These complaints led to a change in the law in 1950 that provides that 60 per cent of the net assessment (after payment of expenses, losses, and additions to reserves) should be returned to the member banks as a refund on their premium payment.

Currently there is also a complaint over the fact that assessments are levied against *total* deposits, while deposits over $10,000 are not covered by insurance. It has been suggested that insurance coverage of 100 per cent would not significantly increase the losses of the FDIC, particularly as long as it continues the policy of promoting mergers to forestall insolvency. Full protection might also strengthen the whole banking system by reducing the incentive of large depositors to withdraw funds in excess of $10,000 when they fear a bank may be in trouble. A further strengthening of the system, it is argued, could be obtained with little difficulty by requiring *all* banks to join the insurance scheme.

While the FDIC has worked quite well, it must be remembered that it has not had to deal with a general collapse of the banking structure such as occurred in the thirties. But it may be that the greatest contribution of the FDIC is in forestalling such a panic rather than in reimbursing depositors after a collapse has occurred. If depositors know that their money is safe, they have no cause to start a run on a bank that is rumored to be in temporary difficulties. In the absence of a run many a bank, now dead, would have been able to pull itself together to weather the storm of the Depression.

Bank Regulation

As the government at both state and Federal levels has attempted from time to time to mend the holes in the banking fabric, what has emerged is a patchwork of regulations of various kinds with much less coordination among them than might be desired.

Of the 13,800 banks in the United States, 9,000 are chartered by the individual states. Each of the fifty states has its own banking laws, stating the conditions under which a bank may obtain a charter and controlling the investing activity of the bank, the limitations on its ability to operate branches, the reserves it must keep (for nonmember banks), and the manner of examination. No individual bank, of course, is subject to more than one state jurisdiction, but for the country as a whole this means fifty differing sets of regulations with little coordination among them.

All national banks are chartered by the Comptroller of the Currency and are subject to his regulations as well as Federal law. This means a fifty-first set of rules.

All national banks are also subject to the jurisdiction of the Federal Reserve, and all state member banks fall under the dual authority of the Federal Reserve and their state authorities.

In addition both national banks and state members, as well as nonmember insured banks, come under the surveillance of the FDIC.

This complex web of authority is shown in Figure 15-1. In addition to these agencies that have primary responsibility for bank supervision there are other agencies that make rulings affecting banks in particular aspects of their operation. These include the Treasury, Securities and Exchange Commission, Department of Labor, Federal National Mortgage Association, Federal Housing Administration, Veterans Administration, and the Anti-Trust Division of the Department of Justice.

For the most part the various agencies have established a working relationship where their functions overlap, and this reduces somewhat the duplication of function. For instance, the Federal Reserve does not examine national banks but leaves that job to the national bank examiners, who work for the Comptroller of the Currency. The Federal Reserve and the state bank examiners examine state member banks jointly. Similarly the FDIC and the state examiners examine nonmember insured banks jointly, while the FDIC leaves the examination of member banks to the Comptroller and the Federal Reserve.

On occasion, however, considerable friction can develop. When James J. Saxon became Comptroller of the Currency in 1962, he brought to that office not only a number of new, sometimes controversial, ideas, but also a vigorous personality and an impatience with delay and interference. As a result he frequently clashed head on with other governmental agencies and particularly with the Board of Governors. To take two examples out of many: He issued a ruling that national banks could accept savings deposits from corporations, a practice prohibited by the Federal Reserve. The Board promptly warned the

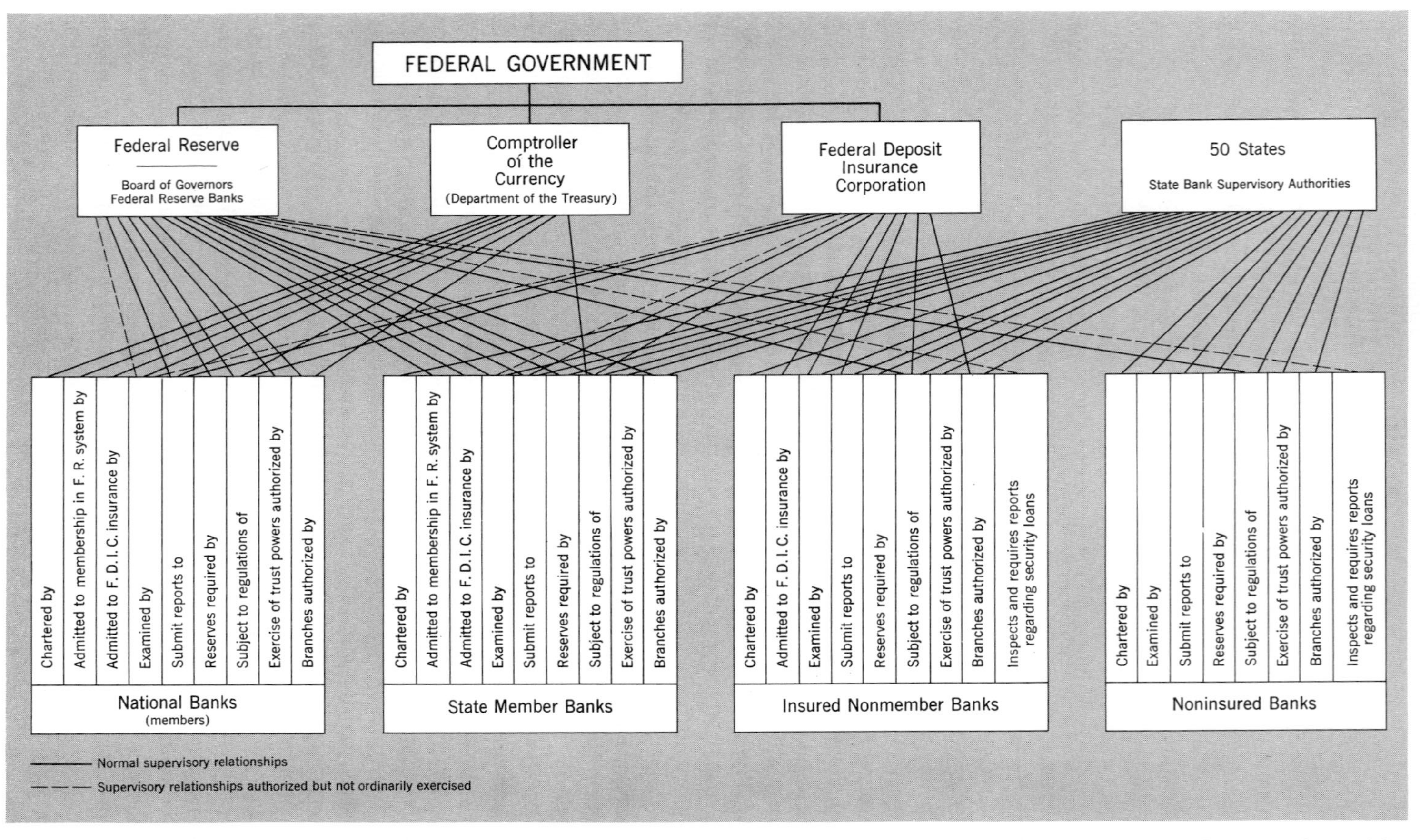

Figure 15-1. Supervision of the commercial banking system. *(Adapted from Board of Governors of the Federal Reserve System, "Supervision of the Commercial Banking System: Principal Relationships," 1947.)*

banks that the Comptroller had no authority to make such a ruling and that any national bank accepting such a deposit would be deemed to be acting illegally. For bank reports required as of September 30, 1963, the Comptroller unilaterally reduced the amount of information to be furnished by national banks, preventing the Federal Reserve from obtaining certain data needed to prepare the continuing series of statistics on bank operations. Although the President intervened at one point to call for consultation in areas of mutual concern, the situation did not improve.

In light of this and other problems, the question may be raised as to whether more effective supervision might not be obtained by simplification of the administrative structure. Suggestions, some of which might have far-reaching consequences, include extension of Federal Reserve membership to include all banks, subordination of the FDIC to the Federal Reserve, placing the Federal Reserve under the Treasury, putting the Secretary of the Treasury and the Comptroller back on the Board of Governors, and requiring all banks to obtain a national charter.

Our Dual Banking System. The last suggestion, in particular, is certain to raise intense opposition, for many people feel that one of the great strengths of our banking system lies in its dual nature: a bank may take out either a national or a state charter and may change from one to another if that appears desirable. Thus national banks have been known to change to state institutions because state limitations on the size of loans to individual customers are less stringent, because they felt that the national bank examiners were too strict, or because state banks were permitted to make loans denied to national banks. Similarly under certain circumstances state banks have moved over to a national status in order to be able to issue national bank notes, in order to avoid state insurance schemes, because they felt that holding company legislation favored national institutions, because approval of mergers was easier to obtain from the Comptroller of the Currency, or because they thought a national charter conveyed greater prestige. This ability to move from one system to the other is often considered an important freedom, which would be abridged if only one chartering authority existed.

On the other hand, the desirability of similar institutions existing side by side but governed by differing regulations may be questioned. In particular the threat of losing banks has frequently deterred the national banking authorities and perhaps less frequently the state banking authorities from becoming more strict in their regulations. Perhaps our banking system would be sounder and more efficiently organized if this competition in laxity were ended and a single set of requirements substituted. The question is one that frequently enters public discussion.

Branch Banking

The unit banking system in this country and the reasons for its development have already been mentioned. Many economists and some bankers feel that a branch banking system (a few banks with many branches such as exist in Canada and Great Britain) would be much more efficient.

The primary advantage of branch banking is the reduction in failures. There are several reasons for this. A larger bank has more capital.[4] It is able to obtain more competent top personnel to set general policy. It is less likely to be swayed in the direction of unwise loans by the "friendly pressure" of small-town loyalties. It can diversify its assets both geographically and by industry; it is therefore less vulnerable to local depressions. It can mobilize the resources of the whole institution to meet a run or other difficulty in a particular branch.

In addition, the large bank is able to operate branches with limited facilities in communities that are too small to support the whole apparatus of an independent marble-fronted palace complete with president and six vice-presidents. The branch of a larger bank can make larger loans than would be permitted to, or desirable for, an independent bank of the same size (as the branch). Funds can be channeled from branches where they are in surplus to areas where investment opportunities exceed the financial resources of the community.

Incidentally (all heat of argument to the contrary notwithstanding), both logic and experience indicate that this flow of funds is normally away from the large city and into the smaller town. This flow has a tendency to equalize interest rates throughout the country. Canada, with its branch banking system, shows much less variation in interest rates between the industrial East and the agricultural Midwest than the United States. In this country a high level of saving keeps interest rates low on the Eastern seaboard, while Western banks must charge higher rates because they are short of funds.

The New York State Banking Department reported in 1964 that loan rates were lower at the large New York City banks than at the smaller upstate banks, that they paid higher interest rates on savings, that they offered more liberal terms on auto and mortgage loans, and that they provided more services but that their charges for checking accounts were higher and that they made fewer unsecured loans.[5] The report concluded that expansion of the large banks into the rest of the state would generally benefit the public.

These advantages are so great that many attempts have been made to achieve some of the benefits of branch banking in spite of the tradition and the law limiting it.

Bank Mergers. While there has always been some tendency toward consolidation of banking facilities in this country, the merger movement increased in tempo following World War II. In the decade 1953–1962, a total of 1,669

[4] Of all FDIC-insured banks suspended (not absorbed by other banks), 45 per cent had capital of *less* than $25,000. Only 7 per cent had capital of more than $100,000.

[5] New York State Banking Department, *Branch Banking, Bank Mergers, and the Public Interest,* New York, 1964.

banks were absorbed by merger.[6] In most of these cases the absorbed banks have continued to operate as branches. By this method several New York City banks, for instance, have each obtained one hundred or more branches. The same process, on a smaller scale, is going on all over the country, but in each case the effect is limited by the various state laws restricting the area in which branches may be opened.

Group and Chain Banking. One way to get around branch banking laws is through group and chain banking, which are similar in their purpose and effects. Chain banking describes a situation where two or more banks are controlled (usually through major stock ownership) by a single individual. Group banking is a similar situation where control is exercised by a holding company.

While chain and group banking do not permit the mingling of funds of the various banks involved, they do provide a degree of centralization of management. They also permit the concentration, either in one bank of the group or in a service organization, of many bank operations that can be most effectively handled on a larger scale than by the single bank. These would include such things as foreign exchange operations, management of investment portfolios, purchasing of supplies, training of personnel, and so on.

In 1956 Congress passed the Bank Holding Company Act, the primary purpose of which was to control the expansion of bank holding companies by prohibiting them from obtaining banks outside their own state (unless the acquisition is approved by the state), by requiring Federal Reserve approval for any new bank acquisitions, and by prohibiting them from holding nonbank subsidiaries. In actual practice the act seems to have stimulated interest in the expansion of group banking. This is partly due to loopholes in the law itself. To a greater extent it results from the fact that the law ended uncertainty as to what Congress was going to do; and because it spelled out fairly completely the procedure by which holding companies might acquire banks, it has induced several banks to examine the possibilities of joining forces with others through the use of holding company affiliates.

At the end of 1964 there were 54 bank holding companies registered with the Federal Reserve. They controlled 460 banks with 1,839 banking offices in 32 states and with total deposits of $25.0 billion. The largest of these is Firstamerica Corporation, a new company formed in 1958 to take over controlling interest in all the banks then owned by Transamerica Corporation, which was required by the Bank Holding Company Act to separate its banking from its nonbanking affiliates and which elected to dispose of its banks. Firstamerica thus acquired a total of 23 banks with 322 banking offices in 11 Western states and with deposits exceeding $3 billion. The second largest group is the Marine Midland Corporation of New York, closely followed by

[6] See "Changes in Banking Structure," *Federal Reserve Bulletin*, vol. 49, no. 9 (September, 1963), pp. 1191–1198.

the Northwest Bancorporation and the First Bank Stock Corporation, both with headquarters in Minneapolis.

As long as branch banking is restricted there will undoubtedly continue to be interest in devices such as group banking which promise at least some of the advantages of greater banking concentration. Nationwide branch banking is probably inevitable in this country, though it may be a very long time in coming.

Department Store Banking

Another aspect of banking that bears some examination is the proliferation of services offered by a single banking institution. So far we have limited our discussion of banking to commercial banking in the strict sense—the provision of checking accounts and those services directly associated with them. In practice there is probably no bank in the country that limits itself to this area.

For some years the old distinction between a "bank" and a "trust company" has been meaningless. Every large bank has a trust department,[7] while there is only one trust company in the United States that does not accept deposits.

In addition to its trust business the average "commercial bank" accepts time or savings deposits, makes consumer and real estate loans, provides safe-deposit boxes, and acts as a broker for securities. The large city banks go even further. Their business may include foreign exchange transactions, security analysis, underwriting of municipal securities, industrial research, "term" loans to business, and many other specialized transactions. Their trust business will include pension trusts and corporate trust activities, such as registry and transfer of stock certificates.

While such diversification of activity is often of advantage to bank customers, who can thus meet all their financial needs by dealing with a single institution, it does present certain difficulties.

To the extent that the bank branches out into long-term loans it intensifies the problem of liquidity discussed in Chapter 10. This has been a basic trend in current banking. Not only are banks making long-term mortgage loans and consumer loans with maturities of one and two years, but they are also making more "term" loans—loans to business of a year or more. In addition there is a growing tendency for short-term commercial loans to slip into the long-term category through continued renewal. This retreat from the real-bills doctrine, already evident when the Federal Reserve was formed in 1914, has continued at an accelerated pace. The question may be raised as to whether commercial banks today are primarily short- or long-term lenders.

Commercial bank involvement in the stock market in the twenties led to legislation requiring the separation of commercial banking from the under-

[7] The nature of the trust business will be examined in Chap. 18.

writing of securities. The banks, however, continue to be concerned with securities in their activities as brokers, trustees, security analysts, investment managers, and corporate trust agents. They may also act as underwriters of municipal securities. In this area also there is considerable discussion of the propriety of a commercial bank, whose primary concern is the creation of money, engaging so extensively in areas concerned with capital financing.

There has also been much comment over whether the close association between big business and the banks that provide much of its finance is desirable. Cries of Wall Street domination of business are frequently heard, and interlocking directorates are decried. The volume of literature on both sides of the question is voluminous and does not permit an easy judgment of the issues or even a brief summary of the divergent points of view. All we can do here is call attention to the controversy.

Only one fact can be stated with certainty. Whatever the merits or defects of our present banking system, that system will never remain static. The history of banking is a story of adaptation to new needs, of development of new techniques. In some cases the results have been unsatisfactory, and these undesirable methods have been abandoned or prohibited by law. In other cases the change has been a great improvement, but this in turn may be later superseded by an even better method. This process of change is continuous. We know that it will not stop, that the banking system of tomorrow will be significantly different from the one we know today. But we cannot foresee with clarity what form these changes will take. Only by constant vigilance can we ensure that the new system will be more satisfactory than the one it replaces. Novelty is not desirable for its own sake, nor is the timeworn pattern necessarily best for today.

Questions for Thought and Discussion

1. What accounts for the large number of bank failures in such a "normal" year as 1926?

2. What do you think would happen if bank failures at some future period exhausted the resources of the FDIC?

3. How does the FDIC prevent (*a*) bank failures and (*b*) loss to depositors?

4. In what ways could the efficiency of the banking structure be improved, in your opinion, by changing the machinery of bank supervision?

5. If a town has only a single bank, does this represent monopoly? Would it be better for the town if the bank were split in two? What difference would it make if the bank were a branch of a larger bank rather than independent?

6. What does your state law say about the operation of bank branches? Does the resulting pattern of banks serve the communities of the state as well as might be possible?

7. Would you favor a law permitting national banks to establish branches in any state?

8. Are group and chain banking more or less monopolistic than branch banking?

9. What problems arise from the proliferation of services under the roof of a single bank? Would it be better if each of these services were provided by a separate institution?

10. Is the dual banking system desirable or undesirable? Why?

Selected Bibliography

Alhadeff, David A.: *Monopoly and Competition in Banking,* University of California Press, Berkeley, Calif., 1954.

Backman, Jules: *The Bank Holding Company Act,* C. J. Devine Institute of Finance, New York University, New York, 1963.

Cartinhour, Gaines Thomson: *Branch, Group and Chain Banking,* The Macmillan Company, New York, 1931.

Chapman, John M., and Ray B. Westerfield: *Branch Banking,* Harper & Row, Publishers, Incorporated, New York, 1942.

Commission on Money and Credit: *Money and Credit,* Prentice-Hall, Inc., Englewood Cliffs, N.J., 1961.

Edwards, Franklin R.: *Concentration and Competition in Commercial Banking: A Statistical Study,* Federal Reserve Bank of Boston, 1964.

Federal Deposit Insurance Corporation: *Annual Reports.*

Fischer, Gerald C.: *Bank Holding Companies,* Columbia University Press, New York, 1962.

Hall, George R., and Charles F. Phillips, Jr.: *Bank Mergers and the Regulatory Agencies: Application of the Bank Merger Act of 1960,* Board of Governors of the Federal Reserve System, 1964.

New York State Banking Department: *Branch Banking, Bank Mergers, and the Public Interest,* New York, 1964.

Robb, Thomas Bruce: *The Guaranty of Bank Deposits,* Houghton Mifflin Company, Boston, 1921.

U.S. Congress, House Committee on Banking and Currency: *Bank Holding Companies,* 1963.

Part Four
Financial Intermediaries

Chapter 16
The Money and Capital Markets

Answer me,
In what safe place you have bestowed my money.

The Comedy of Errors
Act I, scene 2, line 77

Although we have spent considerable time examining the activities of commercial banks, we need to recognize that they are only one type of institution among many engaged in lending. We must now broaden our point of view and survey the whole panorama of financial institutions, whose operations provide funds when and where they are needed anywhere in the economy.

Money and Saving

The primary function of commercial banks is to create money. In this they differ fundamentally from all other financial institutions. The latter—ranging from savings banks to the stock market to pawnbrokers—have as their basic purpose facilitating the flow of funds from ultimate lenders to ultimate borrowers. Some of these institutions use their own funds. Some collect savings from many individuals and lend these funds to others. Some obtain funds from other institutions in large amounts and retail these sums to smaller borrowers. Others maintain a channel through which funds may flow more freely from one institution to another. Some do not handle funds at all but merely provide advisory services or other facilities to the market.

There are two basic sources of funds: newly created money and saving (see Figure 16-1). We have examined in detail how commercial banks create money. We also know that governments can create money by printing paper bills. This latter source of money is much frowned upon in this country, and indeed in most developed countries, and there is no need to consider it further at this point.

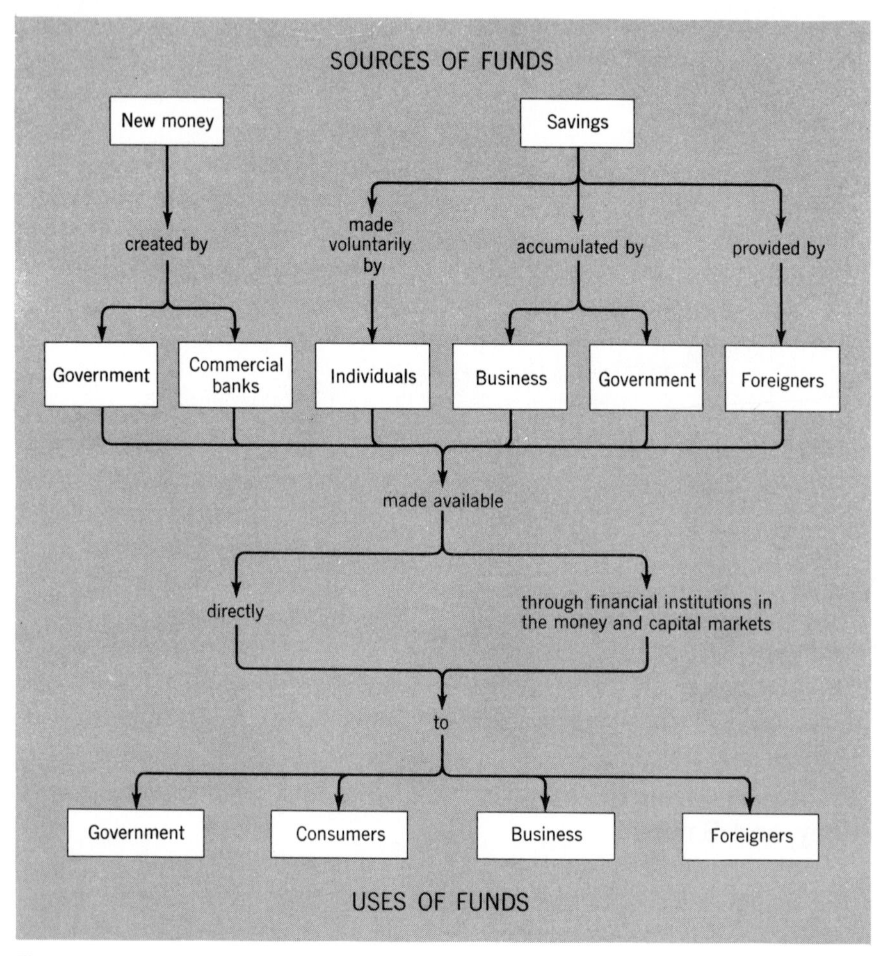

Figure 16-1. Sources and uses of funds.

With these two exceptions, *there is no ultimate source of funds available to borrowers except the savings of individuals.*[1] These savings may appear, however, in four forms:

1. Individuals may make their money available voluntarily.

[1] Even bank credit and fiat paper money represent "forced saving," that is, reduced consumption due to higher prices. This problem will be analyzed in greater detail when we come to monetary theory.

2. A business may save from its own income, such as when a corporation withholds earnings from stockholders in order to plow them back into the business. Such saving is done by the business on behalf of its owners. Although they never see the funds, they have saved in the sense that their purchasing power is reduced by the amount of profit they otherwise would have received as income, while the value of their stock is (at least theoretically) increased by the growth of the company.
3. The government may provide funds that it has collected in taxes, thereby saving on behalf of the public at large. (If the government lends borrowed money, it is acting as a financial intermediary rather than as a source of funds.)
4. Foreigners may provide funds in the market, but here again these must originate in the saving of the nationals of that country.

In each of these cases the individual is the ultimate source of saving.

On the borrowing side, the people who use funds may be grouped in the same four basic categories: individuals (consumers), business, government, and foreigners. Not only do the same groups appear on both sides of the market, but fairly frequently the same person or organization is borrowing and lending at the same time. The same consumer who is putting money aside in his savings account charges his purchases at the department store. The same corporation that just obtained funds through a new bond issue will buy treasury bills with a portion of these funds not immediately needed. The Federal government not only is a constant borrower but also has established a number of lending programs to aid particular sectors of the economy.

Channels through Which Funds Flow

Not only may an individual be on both sides of the market at the same time, but he may also provide as saver the very funds he uses. The owner of a drugstore may use his personal savings to expand his inventory. A corporation that buys machinery with plowed-back earnings is using its own stockholders' funds for the direct acquisition of capital assets. Funds in the Old Age and Survivors Insurance Trust Fund (social security) are used to purchase government securities, which means basically that the government is accumulating public savings with one hand and using them with the other.

In some cases funds are loaned directly from saver to borrower without going through a financial institution. Loans between individuals are one example. Credit accounts financed out of the savings of a business are another. A corporation purchase of a newly issued government bond involves a direct transaction between the business and the government.

In most cases, however, the transfer of funds from savers to users requires the professional services of one or more financial institutions specializing in the details of particular types of transactions. When a consumer buys a corporate bond, he normally does so from an investment banking syndicate (if it is a new issue) or through a broker (if it is already outstanding). A corporation wishing to buy an outstanding government bond does so through a bond house. If it has excess funds, it may make them available to a bank by purchasing time certificates of deposit, and the bank then does the lending. Individuals normally put their savings into a savings institution of some kind, which in turn seeks out borrowers. The number of institutions aiding in these and other types of transactions is quite large. Even the commercial banks, while they create money through their demand deposit activities, are also intermediaries in terms of their savings accounts, trust activities, investment services, and so on.

Financial Markets

A financial intermediary, then, is an institution that transmits, or aids in the transmission of, funds between those who supply them and those who wish to use them. The financial marketplace includes both the financial intermediaries and the money-creating activities of commercial banks, as well as the technical facilities used by these institutions to carry on their work.

This market is a single market in the sense that it deals in one basic commodity: money. At the same time it is a very fragmented market in the sense that the transactions with which it deals are extraordinarily diverse. A savings deposit, a corporate bond, a bank acceptance, and a home mortgage are all claims to money, but they serve very different purposes and are not easily interchangeable. The elements of unity and diversity make it a very difficult market to describe and even more difficult to classify.

Mercantile and Finance Credit. To take one example: We have distinguished, in Chapter 4, between mercantile credit (provided by a dealer to his customer) and finance credit (provided by an institution specializing in finance). In most discussions of financial intermediaries the former is not even mentioned, and indeed the transaction may well take the form of a direct loan from a business saver to a consumer-user without involving an intermediary. Yet it makes little difference to the buyer whether the purchase of his new car is financed by the dealer or by a commercial bank. If it is financed by the dealer in the first instance, he in turn will usually borrow the funds from a bank or other agency. In that case the dealer is certainly transmitting funds in much the same way as other financial intermediaries do. Even if the dealer uses his own funds, he is transmitting savings (his own) to borrowers, and this act makes it unnecessary for the buyer to go elsewhere for funds. His effect on the financial markets therefore cannot be ignored. Does it matter much whether General Motors uses its own corporate savings directly to finance purchases of its customers or whether it sets up a subsidiary (General Motors Acceptance Corporation) to do the same thing? Yet by convention GM is not a financial intermediary, while GMAC is.

The examples could be multiplied indefinitely. The point is that any classification of financial markets is subject to considerable overlapping and lack of clear-cut demarcations. Yet only by attempting to outline differences among various types of activity can we get a notion of what the market actually does, and indeed how complex it really is.

Market Structure. Figure 16-1 has already indicated some of the complexities involved. Commercial banks have a special position in the market because they can create funds—although it is also true that they must have sufficient reserves to make it possible to do so, and for these reserves they depend upon deposits from the public. Other financial institutions depend entirely upon savings, and they must attract these savings by offering money instruments designed to meet the various needs of different types of savers. At the other end, the needs of borrowers differ substantially also, and so the intermediaries must be prepared to make loans available in a form satisfactory to their customers. It is primarily the continuing attempt to meet these varying and changing needs of both savers and borrowers that has given rise to the proliferation of both institutions and instruments in the market. The market was never planned; it has developed new devices to meet new requirements, sometimes dispensing with institutions no longer needed but more frequently adding additional ones to the already complex array.

There is something in the market for everybody. Various instruments have differing maturities, differing principal sums, differing collateral, differing repayment conditions and legal protections, differing liquidity and salability, differing availability, and, in consequence of all these differences, differing interest rates. The details of a number of the most important instruments will be the subject of our next three chapters, while a more detailed analysis of interest rates will be found in Chapter 29.

Open and Negotiated Markets. Within the market structure itself a number of distinctions can be seen. One such distinction is that between open-market credit and negotiated credit. *Open-market* credit comprises instruments issued in standardized form for purchase and transfer by anyone through more or less established and widespread channels. It includes stocks, bonds, government securities, open-market commercial paper, and similar instruments. The liquidity of open-market instruments is relatively high, although price changes for long-term bonds or for corporate stock may be considerable.

When the details of a particular transaction are worked out individually between the borrower and the lender, the credit is said to be *negotiated.* The details are tailored to the needs of both borrower and lender, and the terms therefore may well differ from one such transaction to another. This would be true of bank loans, mortgages, most consumer loans, and privately placed security issues, among others. The relationship is a somewhat personal one and depends, to a certain extent at least, on the direct knowledge that the parties have of each other. Generally when credit is negotiated, the lender expects to keep the loan in his portfolio until its maturity. If he wishes to dispose of his claim by sale to others, he may find it difficult and costly to do so.

A somewhat different category, for which there is no generally accepted name, consists of standardized instruments that are not readily salable, such as savings deposits, savings and loan shares, and credit union shares. The relation between borrower and lender is not basically a personal one, and there is no specified time period to the loan. The lender cannot transfer title to anyone else, but he can (under most circumstances) withdraw his funds at any time.

Primary and Secondary Markets. Since open-market instruments are both sold by the borrower and resold by the holders, there are two somewhat distinct markets involved: borrowers obtain funds on the *primary market;* lenders dispose of their holdings in the *secondary market.* When a corporation sells a new issue of stock, it does so through an investment underwriter, who sells it to the public. This is a primary market. Holders of such stock may dispose of it to others through the stock exchange. This is a secondary market. Open-market credit, by definition, has well-developed secondary markets. There are some secondary markets for negotiated instruments such as mortgages (for instance, through the government's Federal National Mortgage Association), but for the most part secondary markets for negotiated credit are either rudimentary or nonexistent. The extensive development of secondary markets for a wide range of credit instruments is one of the characteristics of a highly developed financial system.

Money and Capital Markets. The most common distinction of all is that between the money market and the capital market, based primarily on the time the instrument has to run to maturity. The arbitrary line between the two is drawn at one year.

The *capital market,* then, deals in instruments with more than one year to run or without a redemption date (such as stocks). The *money market* concerns itself with short-term instruments.

In technical discussions, however, the money market is defined more narrowly than this as the market dealing in highly liquid short-term instruments. These would include treasury bills, open-market commercial paper, bank acceptances, federal funds, and certain short-term debentures, particularly those issued by commercial banks. In this sense mercantile credit, bank loans, and other short-term negotiated credit without developed secondary markets would not be counted as money market instruments, regardless of their maturity.

The money market has a very special importance for financial institutions in general, for it is through this market that they can adjust readily any discrepancy between funds available and demands of borrowers. We have already discussed this role in connection with bank reserves. If a bank finds itself short of reserves, it may borrow federal funds or sell treasury bills or bank acceptances (or its own debentures), all through the money market. In the absence of such a market it would have much less flexibility and would be able to adjust much less readily to changes in business conditions or in the requirements of its customers.

The same thing is true of other institutions as well. Bond houses, stock brokerage firms, and even life insurance companies have been known to borrow federal funds, while other intermediaries can obtain additional funds by issuing short-term debentures (promissory notes). On the other hand, temporarily surplus funds can be put to work by using them to buy various short-term instruments, such as treasury bills, time certificates of deposit, and so on. The money market is therefore a kind of balance wheel, shifting money from one institution with a temporary shortage of borrowers to another with a temporary shortage of funds.

Stocks and Bonds. We should perhaps pause to remind ourselves that although we started talking about credit, we have included in our discussion stocks and shares, which are not credit instruments at all. A bond is a credit instrument; its holder is a creditor of the company and has a legal claim to certain stated payments of principal and interest. A stock is a certificate of ownership; its holder is a part owner of the company and has no legal claim for payment of any sum at any time. He is entitled to dividends *if declared* and to a pro rata share in the net proceeds of the dissolution or sale of the company, but to nothing else.

It is therefore incorrect to speak of a stock certificate as a credit instrument, of the stock market as a credit intermediary, of the stockholder as a lender, or of the issuing company as a borrower. The stockholder, however, is a *source of funds,* the company is a *user of funds,* the stock market is a *financial intermediary,* and the stock certificate is a *financial instrument.* With these cautions in mind, we may perhaps be forgiven for a certain amount of oversimplification in talking of credit markets and financial markets as if they were the same thing.

The Functions of Intermediaries

Theoretically it would be possible for potential borrowers to seek out potential lenders (or vice versa) without the need for financial intermediaries. If Jones needs $10,000 to build his house and can find Smith, who has $10,000 that he would like to lend for twenty years at 5 per cent interest, they would both appear to be better off than if Smith deposited his money in a savings bank at 4 per cent and Jones borrowed it from the bank at 6 per cent. Why should the intermediary be able to siphon off 2 per cent simply for bringing the two together?

For one thing, that is by no means all the bank does. The services performed by intermediaries fall into several different categories (in the following list the mortgage activities of savings banks are used as illustrations, though similar examples could be devised for most of the intermediaries):

1. They provide a central market to which both lenders and borrowers may come. Jones doesn't know where to find Smith; the savings bank is always there.

2. They build up small sums into large ones. Smith may have only $100 to lend; the savings bank puts his funds together with those of other savers to make Jones's $10,000.

3. They provide greater assurance to the small saver. Smith may not trust Jones. If he puts his money into the savings bank, he is sure of repayment no matter what happens to Jones's loan.

4. They provide safety through diversification. Jones may go bankrupt, but the savings bank, by spreading its loans out among many people and many different types of investments, will suffer loss on only a minute portion of its total loans.

5. They provide safety through expert management. Not only is the savings bank able to investigate Jones's credit standing more carefully than Smith could, but it is also in a stronger position to take actions that will safeguard its loan if Jones should get into financial trouble or try to evade payment.

6. They tailor their own obligations to the desires of the ultimate lenders. Smith may not want his money tied up for twenty years. With a savings account he can get it back whenever he wants to. If he wants different terms, he can find other institutions that issue instruments that meet his requirements.

7. They tailor the conditions of their loans to the desires of the borrowers. Jones may want to make monthly payments, whereas Smith doesn't want the bother of having to look for a new borrower as every payment is made. The savings bank not only can accept monthly payments but would much prefer to do so in order to improve its maturity distribution.

8. They provide geographic mobility for funds. If Smith is in Boston and Jones is in Seattle, the savings bank can (generally through other intermediaries) channel the funds from east to west.

9. They provide a competitive market. Because there are so many intermediaries competing with one another and because their activities receive considerable public attention, they tend to provide a somewhat similar rate structure for similar types of loans. This reduces the possibility of an inexperienced saver or borrower being exploited.

10. They provide liquidity. If Smith lends Jones money on a mortgage and then finds himself in need of funds, he may experience great difficulty in trying to sell the mortgage or otherwise get his money out. Because of their standardization and the reputation of the issuers, most claims on financial institutions that are not directly redeemable (as a savings account is) have a secondary market in which they can be sold with relatively small loss. Some institutions have as their primary purpose the establishment of such a market (the stock exchange, for instance).

Financial Intermediaries and Monetary Control

The financial intermediaries provide a large variety of services, catering to the needs of the market, but they also present some problems. The most important of these arises from the fact that their very complexity makes them difficult to control in the interests of stability. The Federal Reserve System has developed an extensive array of devices for controlling the creation of credit by commercial banks and has accumulated a fair amount of experience in using these tools. The financial intermediaries, on the other hand, are subject to a patchwork of state (and a few Federal) restrictions, which have no overall plan and which are intended primarily to provide greater safety for the individual customer rather than stability of the economy as a whole. The monetary authorities have generally felt that by controlling the quantity of money—and the commercial banks are the only nongovernmental agencies that can create or destroy money—they have done their job. The financial intermediaries have been free to go their own way.

At the risk of anticipating material that will come in later chapters on theory and policy, we need to realize that the financial intermediaries can have an important effect on the flow of money even though they cannot change its amount directly. To take one of the simpler examples: If Green puts money in a savings bank, this is an alternative to keeping it in some other form. If his savings account is an alternative to holding the money in cash under the mattress, then the savings bank, by lending out the funds Green provides, puts the money into active use. The total money supply is unchanged, but a portion of it has been taken out of dead storage and put to work. The effect on the economy is the same as if that quantity of money had been newly created.

The same thing happens, strangely enough, if Green transfers money from a checking account. Although the *initial* effect is to reduce both the deposits and the reserves of the commercial bank in which Green holds his checking balance, the money will be lent by the savings bank and will almost certainly end up in the checking account of the borrower or of the person to whom he makes payment. Thus both deposits and reserves will be replaced, and the commercial banking system will be unaffected except for the transition period. Meanwhile Green's formerly idle deposits have been activated. If the savings bank keeps the money in its till without lending it out, there will be a depressing effect on the monetary system, but the same would hold true if any consumer, business, or other institution hoarded funds.

If Green deposits in his savings account money that he otherwise would have made available to some other intermediary or borrower, the direction of the use of the funds may be changed without there being any basic change in the amount available to the economy as a whole. He may buy government bonds, for instance, while the savings bank would have lent the money on mortgage. The question here is not centered on the total money supply but on its distribution among alternative uses.

One of the basic functions of the financial community is to channel funds into one use rather than another, since there are never enough funds to satisfy all potential borrowers. At least a part of this function is performed through the medium of the interest rate. If the interest on Series E savings bonds is higher than the rate paid by savings banks, money will tend to flow to the government. A rise in savings bank dividend rates will probably shift the flow in the other direction. To a certain extent, however, the various parts of the market are not completely fluid, and various factors may hinder the immediate response of investors to a change in the interest rate pattern.

There may also be a certain amount of rationing on the part of the intermediaries. When more borrowers apply at current rates than can be accommodated with the available funds, the intermediaries may choose to lend to particular borrowers and refuse others on various grounds but without raising the interest rate, which would exclude just those unwilling to pay the higher rate.

Rationing of scarce funds, whether through the interest rate or otherwise, is a necessary function of the market. A number of critics, however, have raised the question as to whether it is desirable to leave the nonbank sector of the market almost completely free of controls aimed at stabilizing the market while at the same time restricting the commercial banks fairly extensively. Should not at least the total supply of credit available from the financial intermediaries be regulated?

Actually the intermediaries do not completely escape the effects of monetary control. For one thing, a number of them depend to a greater or lesser extent on commercial banks for their operating funds (brokers and sales finance companies, for instance, are two of the important customers of the banks), and to this extent any restriction of bank credit hits them directly. For another, the open-market operations of the Federal Reserve, while primarily intended to affect the reserves of banks, almost inevitably affect also the volume of government securities held by intermediaries. Further, almost all Federal Reserve controls operate through changes in the interest rate, and this in turn cannot fail to affect the whole financial marketplace. Still many people feel that the importance of the financial intermediaries has not yet been given sufficient weight in conscious direction of policy. More of this later.

The Nongovernmental Financial Marketplace

In the following three chapters we will describe in detail a number of the most important financial intermediaries. Since each of these is essentially a channel through which funds flow on their way from savers to borrowers, it is possible to examine any one in terms of where it fits into that flow. Does it get its funds directly from individuals and, if so, under what circumstances? Does it get funds from some other institution that in turn has gotten them from savers? Or does it merely provide an auxiliary service to the financial community? If it makes loans, to whom, for how long, and under what conditions?

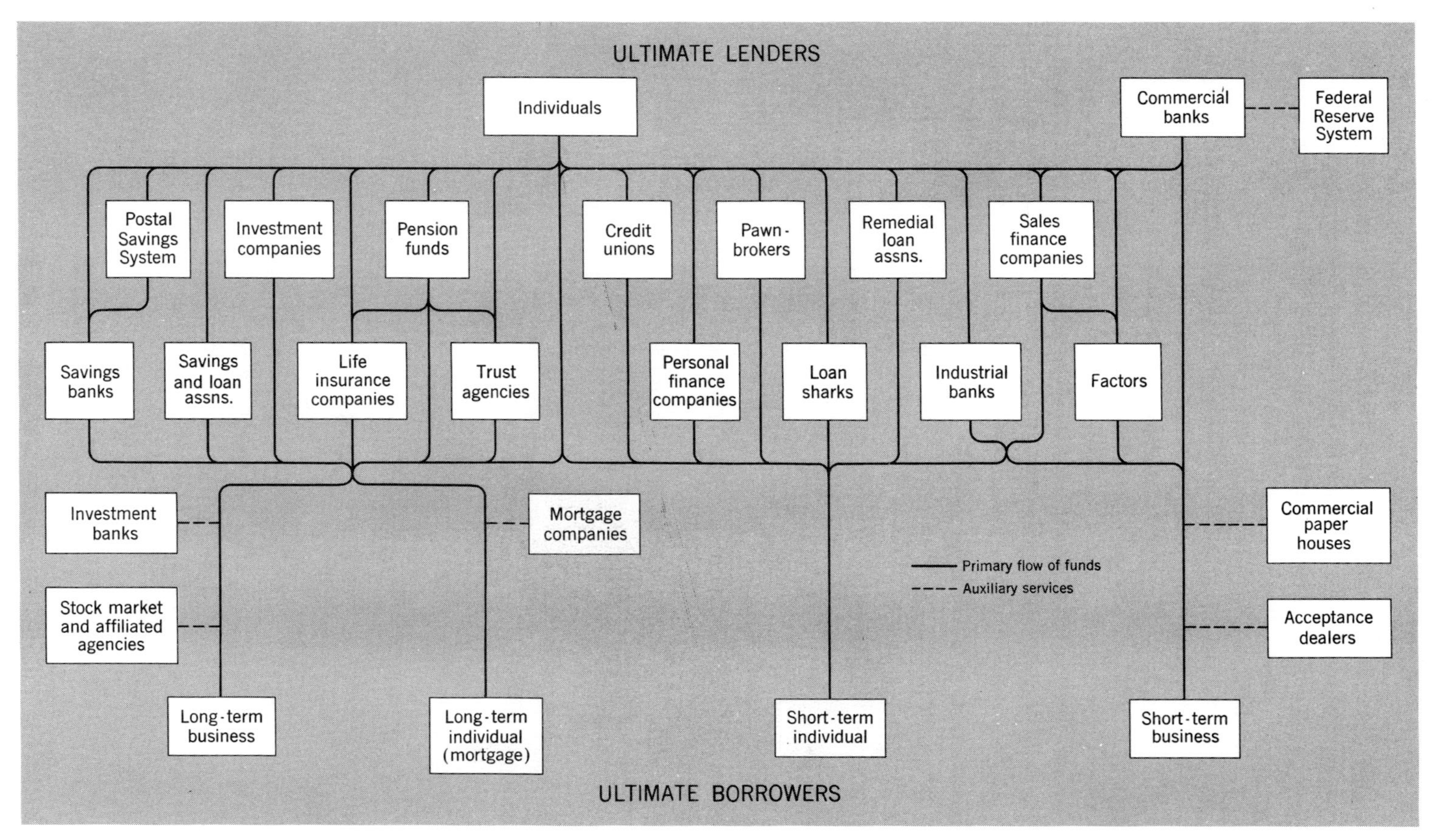

Figure 16-2. The nongovernmental financial marketplace.

The basic operation of any intermediary can be judged from three factors: (1) From whom does it get its funds? (2) What instrument does it offer in exchange for funds? (3) What kinds of loans does it make? The internal organization of the institution may help to round out its personality, but it is much less significant in terms of its effect on the economy.

A simplified picture of the major nongovernmental institutions in the financial market is shown in Figure 16-2. In the diagram many minor or highly technical agencies have been omitted, as have some interrelations among those institutions shown. Loans to or from foreigners also have not been included. In magnitude they are of considerably less importance than domestic loans, though their effect on the international balance of payments may be considerable and will be discussed in Part Nine.

The Government as a Financial Agency. A major omission, in the interests of simplification, is that of government, which would appear on both sides of the market: as a borrower and as a lender. The Federal government is by far the largest borrower in the country today, and state and local governments also borrow large sums. Almost all institutions shown in the chart lend to the Federal government through the purchase of securities, and many of them also supply funds to other levels of government.

On the lending side the state and local governments are relatively unimportant, while the Federal government has established a vast array of lending agencies, particularly in the fields of real estate and agricultural credit. A separate chart showing this activity is given in Chapter 19.

We should emphasize in conclusion that government lending agencies are no exception to the rule that loanable funds must come from savings. The funds that are provided by government agencies either are themselves borrowed from some other source or come from tax revenues. The latter case would simply be a form of involuntary saving, the taxpayer being the unwilling saver. He is forced to reduce his consumption by the amount of the taxes used to make loans to others.

Questions for Thought and Discussion

1. In what sense is it correct to say that there is no ultimate source of funds available to borrowers except the savings of individuals?
2. In what respect is your local appliance dealer a financial intermediary? Your telephone company? Your doctor?
3. In the pure sense a commercial bank is not a financial intermediary, while the First National Bank of Anytown is. Explain.
4. Why have secondary markets for negotiated credit remained relatively undeveloped? What might be some of the difficulties encountered if your bank tried to dispose of a promissory note you had given it?

5. If money is homogeneous, why are there different markets in which it is lent and borrowed? Why are there so many kinds of financial intermediaries?
6. Is there any basic difference between a financial intermediary such as a savings bank and, say, a real estate broker in the way in which they act as go-betweens?
7. How does the interest rate function as a rationing device?

Selected Bibliography

Commission on Money and Credit: *Private Capital Markets,* Prentice-Hall, Inc., Englewood Cliffs, N.J., 1964.

———: *Private Financial Institutions,* Prentice-Hall, Inc., Englewood Cliffs, N.J., 1964.

Cook, Gilbert, et al.: *Financial Institutions: Their Role in the American Economy,* Simmons-Boardman Publishing Corporation, New York, 1962.

Goldsmith, Raymond W.: *Financial Intermediaries in the American Economy since 1900,* Princeton University Press for the National Bureau of Economic Research, Princeton, N.J., 1958.

Moulton, Harold G.: *Financial Organization and the Economic System,* McGraw-Hill Book Company, New York, 1938.

Nadler, Marcus, Sipa Heller, and S. S. Shipman: *The Money Market and Its Institutions,* The Ronald Press Company, New York, 1955.

Prochnow, Herbert, et al.: *American Financial Institutions,* Prentice-Hall, Inc., Englewood Cliffs, N.J., 1951.

Robinson, Roland I.: *Money and Capital Markets,* McGraw-Hill Book Company, New York, 1964.

Chapter 17 Consumer Finance

Falstaff: *What money is in my purse?*
Page: *Seven groats and twopence.*
Falstaff: *I can get no remedy against this consumption of the purse: borrowing only lingers and lingers it out, but the disease is incurable.*

The Second Part of King Henry IV
Act I, scene 2, line 266

Consumer finance falls into two separate—in fact opposite—categories, depending on whether the particular consumer is able to pay his bills or not. If he can, and has something left over, he wants to know where he can keep it not only safely but productively. Consumer savings form the foundation on which the vast physical plant and equipment of this country has been built. Every cent that went into the purchase of business assets of every description came from the savings of consumers in one way or another. But the individual consumer is not conscious of this. He knows only that he has some extra money. He can keep it in cash or in his checking account and be perfectly liquid. Having spending money instantly available has obvious advantages, but such funds earn no income. In order to put his money to work he can buy securities and perhaps make a killing—or lose his shirt. Or he can find a safer, more conservative savings institution that will pay him a small but continuous income for the use of his funds. It is primarily the institutions serving this last need that will be examined in this chapter.

But our consumer may not be fortunate enough to have idle funds. He may find his expenses exceeding his income, and far from having excess money to lend, he may himself need financial aid. For him consumer finance refers to those agencies that are willing to lend him money. Perhaps he expects to get credit free or even to raise his standard of living by borrowing—after all, the advertisers have been assiduous in convincing us that we can get something for nothing. More frequently he knows that it costs something to borrow, but he probably has no real idea of how much. Perhaps it doesn't matter: he has to have funds regardless of cost. In other cases he might be shocked into living within his income if he realized how much of his purchasing power buys only carrying charges.

Actually consumers cannot be neatly classified as either borrowers or lenders. Almost all of them have some savings (if only in old-age assistance or industrial pension accounts). Similarly almost all consumers receive credit of one kind or another (if only from their doctor and the electric company). The same person who holds government savings bonds buys his car on the installment plan. Most consumers, therefore, are interested in both savings and credit institutions.

Savings Institutions

Savings institutions provide consumers with a relatively safe place to put their savings to work. They may also make loans to consumers, but the man in the street thinks of them more frequently in their savings than in their lending aspect.

In the broad sense savings institutions comprise all those intermediaries on the left side of Figure 16-2 that are shown as making long-term loans to business or to individuals, plus credit unions, which appear on the short-term lending side.

Mutual Savings Banks. Benjamin Franklin advised his fellow countrymen that "a penny saved is a penny earned." Yet if they followed his suggestion, they had no place to keep their savings except under the mattress. At that time, and for fifty years more, almost the only financial institutions were commercial banks whose basic function was note issue. For the most part they did not even accept demand deposits, let alone savings.

The thrifty Scots, as one might guess, first developed the idea of the modern savings bank. This was in 1810, and six years later similar institutions were set up almost simultaneously in Boston, New York, and Philadelphia. These early banks, and others that followed, were established by groups of public-spirited citizens whose sole objective was to encourage thrift among the poorer people. Mutual savings banks were, and have continued to be, philanthropic and nonprofit in nature. As a public service the original founders contributed the funds necessary to start the bank, and these banks, therefore, have no capital stock and no stockholders to benefit financially from their operation. They are run solely for the benefit of their depositors.

From their introduction in 1816 savings banks spread rapidly throughout the northeastern section of the country, primarily in the larger industrial centers. As other thrift institutions developed, their expansion slowed down, and none has been started recently. Of the 505 mutual savings banks currently in operation, 65 per cent (327) are in New England, another 25 per cent (125) in New York, and the remaining 10 per cent almost entirely in New Jersey (21), Pennsylvania (7), and Maryland (6), with a scattering in eight other states.

The trustees under whose direction a savings bank operates constitute a self-perpetuating board. Members serve for life, and upon death their successors are chosen by the surviving members. The board represents a public trust; the law classifies savings banks as trustees, and their operations are strictly regulated in order to assure a high degree of safety for the depositors' funds.

Mutual savings banks receive deposits only from individuals and nonprofit associations. Most states limit the amount that any one depositor may have on deposit. In New York, for instance, this maximum is $15,000. The bank has the right to require advance notice of sixty days if the depositor wishes to withdraw part or all of his funds, but in practice this notice is universally waived.

By far the greater part of the savings banks' funds are invested in real estate mortgages. Savings banks also buy fairly substantial amounts of United States government securities and corporate bonds. Recently the banks have been investigating the feasibility of owning real estate developments outright and of investing in commercial paper and personal loans. While these areas may be expanded in the future, they currently represent a minute fraction of savings bank assets. A comparison of the financial operations of savings banks and other savings institutions is shown in Table 17-1.

The income that a savings bank receives from loans and investments, after expenses and allocation to surplus and reserves, is distributed to depositors as dividends on their deposits. Since savings banks are mutual institutions, the amount available as dividends to depositors depends on the earnings record of the bank. Banks paid dividend rates of 4 to 5 per cent in the twenties. During the Depression the rate fell to around 2 per cent, but it rose again along with other interest rates in the fifties. Dividends on deposits are not guaranteed in advance; they are paid only when declared by the board of trustees.

Mutual savings banks may join the Federal Deposit Insurance Corporation if they wish, but their greater safety and very low failure rate have made insurance less necessary for them than for the commercial banks. Even during the worst days of the Depression, when almost ten thousand commercial banks closed, only fourteen mutual savings banks were suspended. In New York, however, pressure by the banking commissioner has forced all mutual savings banks in that state to join the FDIC. For the country as a whole, almost two-thirds of the banks have taken out insurance.

Savings Departments in Commercial Banks. Most commercial banks accept not only savings deposits of individuals, but also time deposits of corporations. The latter differ from savings deposits in that the law *requires* a bank to wait sixty days before permitting withdrawals from time deposits while *permitting* a bank to ask for notice of savings withdrawals. In the past most banks did not encourage corporate time deposits, but since 1960 there has been a substantial increase in the volume of time certificates of deposit issued to corporations as banks have aggressively sought additional sources of funds. As Table 17-1 shows, the commercial banks hold a considerably larger volume of savings deposits than mutual savings banks do. There are, after all, over thirteen thousand commercial banks scattered throughout the country, while 500 savings banks serve only 18 states.

Because the savings department of a commercial bank is only part of its operations and its funds are not separated from the other assets of the bank,[1] it is not possible to say just how these particular funds are used.

There are also in the country a few stock savings banks, whose operations are similar to those of the savings department of a commercial bank except that they stand alone as separate institutions. They are included in the statistics as commercial banks.

Postal Savings System. The Postal Savings System was established by Congress in 1910 to provide a safe depository for the funds of small savers who did not trust banks or for whom savings facilities were not readily accessible. Depository post offices accept deposits in round dollar amounts to a maximum of $2,500. Withdrawals may be made on demand at the office at which the account is kept. Interest is paid at the rate of 2 per cent per year. In recent years the funds deposited have been invested predominantly in government bonds.

In terms of the volume of funds handled, the Postal Savings System has been relatively unimportant. At its high point in 1947 the System held only $3.5 billion, and the total has declined steadily since then. The availability of savings bonds in small denominations and the safety provided bank deposits by the FDIC has led to considerable opposition to continued government operation of the System.

Savings Bonds. While savings bonds may not properly be called an "institution," they certainly bear more resemblance to savings deposits than they do to the general securities market. Unlike any other security, savings bonds may be redeemed at any time at a known price. The money put into savings bonds, in other words, can be "withdrawn" on demand.

The most popular of the savings bonds are the Series E bonds, first issued

[1] Except in California, Connecticut, Massachusetts, Rhode Island, and Texas, where the law requires that the assets, liabilities, and capital of a savings department be segregated from the rest of the bank's operations.

Table 17-1. Operations of Major Savings Institutions, December 31, 1964

Billions of Dollars

Institution	Savings represented		Assets[a]					
	Form	Amount	Cash	U.S. government securities	Other securities	Mortgages	Other loans	Other assets[b]
Mutual savings banks	Deposits	48.8	1.0	5.8	5.5	40.3	0.7	0.9
Commercial banks	Time deposits[c]	126.7			(Not available)			
Postal savings system	Deposits	0.4	*	0.4				*
U.S. savings bonds	Outstanding	49.7			(Not applicable)			
Life insurance[d]	Policy reserves	95.4	1.5	5.6	70.3	55.2	7.1	9.8[e]
Insured pension funds	Policy reserves	25.3						
Savings and loan associations	Share capital	101.8	4.0	7.0	1.2	101.3		5.8
Credit unions	Share capital	8.2		0.4	0.9		7.0	1.0
Closed-end investment companies[f]	Net assets	2.3	0.1		2.1			0.1
Mutual funds	Net worth	29.1	1.3[g]		27.8[h]			*
Fire, marine, and casualty insurance companies	Assets	36.7	1.4	5.9	25.4	0.1	*	3.8
Trust accounts in commercial banks	Trust funds	155.8	1.7	11.9	133.0			9.2
Noninsured pension funds	Assets	51.9	0.9	3.1	42.7	2.7		2.5
Old-age and survivors insurance	Assets	19.1	1.4	17.8				*
Railroad retirement trust fund	Assets	3.7	0.1	3.6				*
Other U.S. government pension funds[i]	Assets	17.0	0.2	16.8				*
State and local government pension funds[j]	Assets	29.9	0.5	12.0	16.0	1.0		0.4
Unemployment insurance trust fund	Assets	7.4	*	7.4				*
U.S. veterans' life insurance	Assets	5.9	*	5.8				*
Charitable foundations[k]	Assets	14.5			(Not available)			
Colleges and universities[l]	Endowment funds	3.7			(Not available)			

* Less than $50 million

[a] Assets may exceed savings by the amount of liabilities not shown.

[b] May include other categories listed but for which no separate figure is available for the particular institution.

[c] Excluding interbank deposits. There is no acceptable way of allocating the assets of commercial banks between their demand and time deposits.

[d] Not including insured pension fund reserves, listed separately below.

[e] Includes $4.5 billion of real estate held directly.

[f] These and the following institutions are discussed in Chap. 18.

[g] Cash, U.S. government securities, and short-term bonds.

[h] By subtraction; all other assets of such companies are negligible.

[i] Predominantly for civil service employees.

[j] Distribut on of assets estimated on the basis of 1957 data.

[k] A summary of balance sheets for various dates from 1960 to 1963.

[l] 1955–1956 school year.

Sources: Adapted and partly estimated from *Federal Reserve Bulletin*, vol. 51, no. 9 (September, 1965), pp. 1293, 1294, 1306, 1307, 1310; *Report of Operations of the Postal Savings System, 1964*, p. 3; *Life Insurance Fact Book, 1965*, pp. 37, 62, 70; *1965 Savings and Loan Fact Book*, p. 90; *International Credit Union Yearbook, 1965*, pp. 13, 16; Investment Company Institute, "Closed-end Investment Company Securities, Fourth Quarter, 1964" (mimeographed); Investment Company Institute, "The 1964 Mutual Fund Statistical Record" (mimeographed); *Best's Fire and Casualty Aggregates and Averages, 1965*, pp. 54, 154, 214, 216; *National Banking Review*, vol. 2, no. 4 (June, 1965), p. 490; Securities and Exchange Commission, "Private Noninsured Pension Funds, 1964," Statistical Series, no. 2053 (mimeographed); *Annual Report of the Secretary of the Treasury on the State of the Finances, 1962–1963*, p. 641; *Treasury Bulletin*, February, 1965, pp. 15–18; "Employee-retirement Systems of State and Local Governments," *U.S. Census of Governments, 1957*, vol. 4, no. 1, p. 12; *The Foundation Directory*, 2d ed., 1964, p. 17; *Biennial Survey of Education in the United States, 1954–1956* (1959), chap. 4, sec. II, p. 10.

(as Series A) in 1935. They were known at that time as "Baby Bonds" because they were available in denominations as low as $25 in contrast with the normal $1,000 face value of other government (and corporate) bonds.

Series E bonds are sold at a discount of 25 per cent: a $25 bond (maturity value) costs $18.75; a $100 bond costs $75. The bond matures in seven years and nine months, at which time its appreciation amounts to a compound interest rate of 3¾ per cent. If it is cashed before maturity, however, the interest rate is less, rising gradually from nothing for bonds redeemed during the first six months to the maximum of 3¾ per cent if held for the full period. This redemption value at a graduated scale of interest has the double advantage of giving the holder the right to obtain cash should he need it at any time but of still providing an inducement for him to hold the bond as long as possible in order to benefit from a higher rate of interest in the later years.

Series E bonds are sold only to individuals and are not transferable. No more than $10,000 face value may be purchased in any one year. Many persons buy them through a regular payroll savings plan whereby the employer automatically deducts a specified amount from the worker's salary each payday and applies it to the purchase of bonds. Similarly a bank, if requested, will automatically deduct a given amount monthly from a customer's account to purchase bonds for him.

Another type of savings bond, Series H, is similar to Series E except that it pays its interest by check semiannually on a graduated scale designed to approximate the interest that accrues on Series E bonds. Redemption is at face value but only on one month's notice.

Life Insurance. Many people do not think of life insurance companies as savings institutions, but in fact they hold more consumer savings than any other type of organization. The ordinary policyholder sometimes thinks of his premium as merely buying a service—protection. Yet only part of the premium goes for protection, while the rest is credited to his account and can be withdrawn at any time (by letting the policy lapse).

This is true of all life insurance policies except term insurance. Term life insurance represents a policy under which the company will pay the face value if the insured dies within the term of the contract.[2] If the insured is alive at the end of the period, the policy has been completely fulfilled. Term insurance is similar to fire insurance. If your house doesn't burn during the fire insurance policy period, the company owes you nothing. In the same way term insurance is temporary insurance, and the premium buys protection for only a specified period.

Life insurance differs from all forms of property insurance in that the hazard insured against (death) is certain to occur. The only question is: When? It would be possible to provide continuous insurance, which would

[2] Term policies may be written for a one-year period but are more usually written for five, ten, fifteen, or twenty years.

finally result in payment of the claim, by purchasing a series of term policies until death occurred. Since the chance of death increases with age, the premium would rise as the insured grew older. Thus $1,000 of one-year term insurance might cost perhaps $6 at age 20 and $6.05 at age 21, the premium rising gradually to $8.60 at age 40, $29 at 60, $140 at 80, and $1,000 at 99.[3] If the company uses the common "1941 Commissioners Standard Ordinary Table of Mortality," it assumes that everyone dies by age 100, and it will pay the face value of the policy on the insured's hundredth birthday even if he is still alive; therefore the premium at age 99 is not for a risk at all, but for a sure thing.

Most people don't like the prospect of this rising cost and prefer what is called a *whole-life policy*.[4] With such a policy the premium is much higher in the earlier years but remains at the same level for the whole life of the insured. While a one-year term policy may cost about $6 per $1,000 of insurance at age 20, a whole-life policy at the same age will cost about $15. What happens is that $6 of the whole-life premium covers the risk and is used to pay the claims of policyholders who die in their first policy year. The other $9 goes into the policy reserve, or "cash value," of the policy.[5] But since this $9 already belongs to the policyholder, he is actually buying only $991 of protection. In the second year he again pays $15. Again $6 (roughly) is risk premium, while his policy reserve is now $18 plus interest on the first $9 for one year. Thus he is buying less than $982 of protection. In this way throughout the life of the policy he is building up savings that will be returned to his beneficiary as part of the face value of his policy when he dies, the rest of the payment being taken out of the pool of risk premiums paid by all policyholders.

This process is illustrated in Figure 17-1, which shows how the actual amount of risk that the company must insure against is reduced as the policy reserve grows through both the addition of the nonrisk portion of each premium and the accumulation of compound interest. Thus at age 50 the figure indicates that the policy reserve has grown to $335, and the amount of insurance protection is only $665.

The policy reserve (cash value) belongs to the policyholder. It is his savings. A whole-life policy guarantees that at all times the amount of this savings plus the amount of insurance protection will equal $1,000. Thus savings and insurance are combined in a single policy.

Because of the savings feature, life insurance companies hold large sums for their policyholders. The greater part of these funds is invested in corporate

[3] In practice insurance companies generally refuse to write term insurance for anyone over 65.

[4] Or an endowment policy, which operates on the same principle but pays the face value if death occurs prior to a certain age (say, 65) or on that birthday if death has not occurred sooner. Technically a whole-life policy is an endowment at age 100.

[5] Figures are rough for simplicity. They ignore expenses and other niceties of insurance operation.

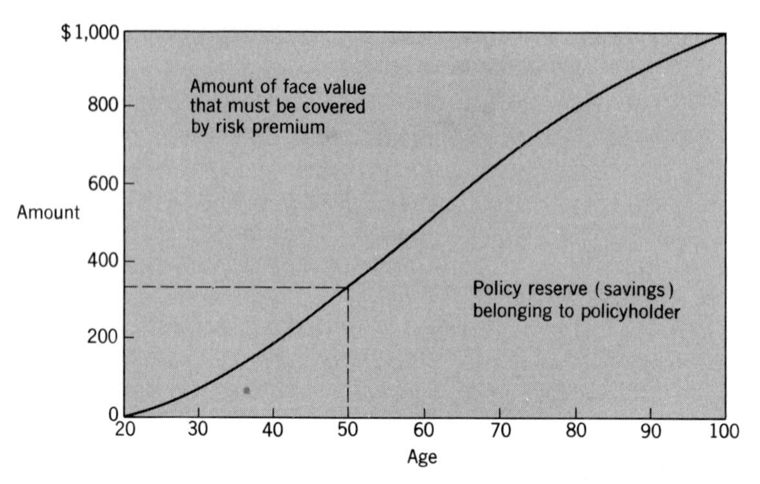

Figure 17-1. The savings and risk components of a whole-life insurance policy issued at age twenty.

bonds. Another large part goes into mortgages. Government securities were held in fairly large amounts in the past, but the trend since the war has been to reduce holdings of government securities in order to invest larger amounts in private business. Small sums go into corporate stocks. Some funds are lent back to policyholders on the security of the cash value of the policy. Recently insurance companies have ventured into other areas in order to earn a higher return. One of these is direct construction and operation of large-scale apartment developments. Another is the purchase and lease of stores and other business properties. A third has been the rental of freight cars to railroads. Such activities have not yet become an important part of the total assets held by life insurance companies.

Savings and Loan Associations. The savings and loan association is a mutual thrift institution. It had its origin well over one hundred years ago in the desire on the part of consumers to obtain housing without waiting until their individually accumulated savings would equal the purchase price. Mortgage money in those days was practically unobtainable. The answer was a device by which a group of neighbors pooled their resources in order to make loans to themselves. The procedure can best be illustrated by an example.

Suppose ten people each wanted a $10,000 house but could afford to save only $1,000 a year. This meant that they would each have to wait ten years before obtaining a house. But if the ten put one year's savings together, they would have enough to build one house. They could form an association in which each member agreed to pay $1,000 a year for ten years. Each year one member, chosen by lot or otherwise, would be able to borrow sufficient money to build his house. At the end of ten years all members would have houses, and most of them would have them sooner than would otherwise be possible. Those members who obtained loans and thereby got their houses sooner would have to pay interest on the borrowed funds and thus reimburse the others for waiting.

More recently, and particularly in the period since World War II, this original concept has undergone considerable modification, but the fundamental purpose of the savings and loan association still remains. It is a mutual organization into which members place their excess funds, which are then used to make mortgage loans to others.

It should be emphasized that these associations do not, and by law cannot, accept deposits.[6] It is in this respect that they differ fundamentally from savings banks. When a member "puts money into" a savings and loan association, he is purchasing stock. In most associations today stock certificates as such are not issued, and the transaction is entered in a passbook in much the same way that a deposit might be entered by a bank. The similarity is further enhanced by the fact that a member may purchase any fractional part of a share of stock that he wishes; that is, he may make payment of any amount toward the purchase of a share.

Since the member does not desposit money, he obviously cannot withdraw it. What he does when he wants cash is to ask the association to repurchase whatever number of shares or fractional part of a share is equal to the sum he wishes to obtain. The association will do this on request as long as sufficient funds are available, but it is not legally obligated to do so since the member is not a creditor, but a stockholder. If the association cannot spare funds for the repurchase of stock, the member wanting cash will put his name on a waiting list, and his request will be honored (in whole or in part, depending on the bylaws of the association) when funds are available and those ahead of him on the list have been paid. In some states there is a limit to the length of time the association may take to meet such requests; in others there is not. During the dark days of the Depression some members had to wait years to obtain funds.

Most associations are insured by the Federal Savings and Loan Insurance Corporation, a government agency similar to the FDIC, which protects members against loss of their investment through failure of the association. Such insurance, however, means that they will get their money eventually. It does not provide for them to get it immediately since a stockholder cannot force an association into bankruptcy in the same way that a bank depositor (who is a creditor) can if his demand for funds is not met. A commercial bank must pay its demand depositors on demand. A savings bank must pay its savings depositors within sixty days. A savings and loan association must pay its members whenever it has sufficient funds.[7]

[6] A few states, including California, Ohio, and Texas, do permit associations to accept deposits in addition to their other activity, but this is the exception.

[7] New York in 1958 provided that any association not honoring a request for repurchase within sixty days would be taken over by the Superintendent of Banks, but this provision is quite unusual, and the law is still the subject of controversy.

Savings and loan associations invest their money almost exclusively in home mortgages, except for a small amount held in cash or invested in government bonds. In this sense they still keep very closely to their original purpose and are, in the singleness of their aim, one of the least complicated of financial institutions.

Savings and loan associations are chartered under both state and Federal law. Operation of both types is similar. Members elect a board of directors who in turn determine the policies of the association.[8] Since there are no stockholders other than the members, the net earnings of the association, after payments into reserves and surplus, are paid to members in the form of a dividend on their stock investment. This dividend, like any other, is payable only as earned and declared. It cannot be determined or guaranteed in advance. Generally the rate is slightly higher than interest rates paid by mutual savings banks, reflecting the savings and loan association's smaller degree of liquidity.

Federal associations must join the Federal Savings and Loan Insurance Corporation and the Federal Home Loan bank of their district.[9] State associations may join both, and in practice most have done so. The most important function of the Federal Home Loan banks is to make loans to associations against mortgages as collateral. Not only does this permit an association to make more loans than would be possible out of its own funds, but it also provides a certain amount of liquidity if cash is needed to meet demands of members who wish their shares repurchased.

The savings and loan associations are the fastest-growing thrift institutions in the country. Unfortunately they frequently create the impression that they are savings banks, and it is entirely possible that many of their members are under the misapprehension that they are making deposits when in reality they are purchasing stock. How much of their growth may be due to this misunderstanding is impossible to say.

Credit Unions. A credit union is a mutual thrift association organized under either state or Federal charter in which members place their savings by purchasing stock. Each member has one vote in electing directors and establishing policy. The credit union lends to its members on their own note, either secured or unsecured, generally for a short period of time. In some states they make mortgage loans, and sometimes they invest in the shares of savings and loan associations. Their basic difference from the latter institutions is in the smaller size and shorter maturity of their loans.

The law requires that all the members of a credit union have a common bond, which may be occupational (workers in the same plant), organizational

[8] In some states, notably California, Ohio, and Texas, it is possible to establish a proprietary savings and loan in which permanent investors receive a special type of stock that carries all voting rights. There are some five hundred of these proprietary associations in the United States.

[9] These agencies are discussed in more detail in Chap. 19.

(members of a church, lodge, consumers' cooperative, etc.), or residential (residents of a particular community). Most credit unions are occupational. The credit union is basically a self-help association. Officers and directors often serve without pay, though in larger credit unions full-time professional help is necessary. The neighborliness of the members is one of the important factors counted on to eliminate bad-debt losses, since the borrower-member doesn't want to let his associates down.

Income comes almost exclusively from interest on loans. After expenses are met and payments made into reserves, the member-shareholders are paid a dividend on the value of their shareholdings.

Most credit unions have banded together in a federation known as Credit Union National Association (CUNA), which operates as a clearing house for information, collects statistics, and carries on an educational program. Although the absolute volume of their loans and capital is quite small, credit unions are growing rapidly at the present time.

Other Savings Institutions. The other institutions shown in Table 17-1 will be discussed in greater or lesser detail in the following two chapters.

Consumer Credit

As we have seen in the preceding section, most consumer savings institutions also make loans to consumers, primarily in the area of mortgage credit. There are a number of additional institutions providing consumer credit of various kinds. Table 17-2 summarizes the major types of consumer credit outstanding in 1964.

Charge Accounts. Charge accounts are among the earliest forms of consumer credit and are indeed so common that we might tend to overlook them. When we buy "on the cuff," the merchant is in effect lending us the purchase price of the goods we buy. The traditional form of charge account permits the customer to buy whatever he wants, and a bill is sent at the end of the month. Payment is expected within ten days. If purchases are evenly spaced over the month, and if payment is reasonably prompt, charge account credit runs for an average of about twenty-five days. Recently there has been some tendency for stores to lengthen the period of payment to three months. In other cases the ordinary charge account has been replaced to some extent at least by "revolving credit" and other installment forms of credit.

Since there is frequently no stated charge for the privilege of using a charge account, it appears to the consumer that this type of credit is costless. Unfortunately this is an illusion. The merchant must meet three costs when he extends credit: (1) the clerical expense of keeping records, sending bills, and so on; (2) the risk of loss through nonpayment, usually a small but positive figure; and (3) the interest cost the merchant must pay to obtain funds to

Table 17-2. Consumer Credit by Type of Credit and Lender, December 31, 1964

Billions of Dollars

Lender	Installment credit					Noninstallment credit				Total credit
	Auto-mobile	Other consumer goods	Repair	Personal loans	Total	Single pay loans	Charge accounts	Service credit	Total	
Commercial banks	12.8	3.4	2.4	5.4	23.9	5.5	0	0	5.5	29.4
Sales finance companies	8.7	3.9	0.1	2.0	14.8	0.1	0	0	0.1	14.9
Consumer finance companies	0.5	0.1	0.1	4.4	5.1	0.1	0	0	0.1	5.2
Credit unions	2.2	0.9	0.8	3.2	6.5	0.6	0	0	0.6	7.0
Other financial				1.1	1.7	0.1	0	0	0.1	1.8
Department stores	0	3.9	0	0	3.9	0	0.9	0	0.9	4.8
Furniture stores	0	1.2	0	0	1.2					
Household appliance stores	0	0.3	0	0	0.3	0	4.8	0	4.8	8.2
Automobile dealers	0.4	0	0	0	0.4					
Other retail outlets	0	1.7	0	0	1.7					
Credit cards	0	0	0	0	0	0	0.6	0	0.6	0.6
Service credit	0	0	0	0	0	0	0	4.6	4.6	4.6
Total	24.5	15.3	3.5	16.1	59.4	6.5	6.3	4.6	17.4	76.8

Source: Adapted and partly estimated from *Federal Reserve Bulletin*, vol. 51, no. 9 (September, 1965), pp. 1322–1323; *International Credit Union Yearbook, 1965*, pp. 11–12; National Consumer Finance Association, *1965 Finance Facts Yearbook*, pp. 50–51. Detail may not add to totals because of rounding.

carry on his business while customers aren't paying for goods. In order to reimburse himself for these expenses, the seller must add to the price of the goods he sells. Usually this higher price is paid by both cash and credit customers, so that the credit cost is divided between those who use it and those who don't. In a growing number of cases the lower prices charged by "cash-and-carry" stores have forced credit stores to differentiate between their own cash and credit customers by quoting a cash price and a "time price." If the latter is payable over a period of months, however, it differs somewhat from the traditional charge account and becomes an installment purchase.

Service Credit. Similar to charge accounts is service credit extended by doctors, electric companies, and others who bill their customers at the end of the month. In these areas the extension of credit is almost universal, and the cost necessarily is included in the price, but since everyone pays on the same basis, the cost is equitably distributed.

Universal Credit Cards. In the fifties there was an explosion in consumer credit that led to the development of the "universal" credit card. Such organizations as Diners' Club, the American Express Company, Hilton Hotels, and many large city banks now issue credit cards that are accepted by a great number of restaurants, hotels, travel agencies, and stores. All purchases under the card are charged through a single bill submitted monthly. Most of these plans (except for the banks) charge the holder an annual fee of $5 or $6, but there are no interest charges as such. Member institutions honoring such cards, however, pay 4 to 7 per cent of the accounts charged, to reimburse the central organization for billing and collection costs. There have been complaints from some sellers about this cost, and there is some indication that prices are being raised to cover it. Finding themselves unable to raise prices in a weak market, some hotels are reported to have gone into bankruptcy at least partly because of the added expense of carrying charge accounts, while on the other hand several of the universal credit card sponsors have lost substantial sums of money on their operations.

The Development of Consumer Loans. The above types of credit are extended by sellers of commodities and services as a normal sideline to their primary selling activities. They represent mercantile credit, and the credit is subsidiary to the sale. Other agencies that specialize in credit make cash loans to consumers either as part of a general financial business or as a highly specialized service. Until fairly recently this field was occupied almost exclusively by the loan shark and the pawnbroker.

Loan Sharks. Our historical survey touched on the fact that the medieval church frowned on the charging of interest. This prohibition was based primarily on the fact that most loans in this period were made to people in distress, and it was felt that interest simply increased the misery of those unfortunate ones who needed help. Even when the growth of business borrowing showed the productivity of business capital and hence justified interest charges, interest on consumer loans was still considered unethical. The moneylenders who dared to incur opprobrium by attempting to meet the needs of consumers in financial distress operated on the periphery of society and charged high rates to compensate both for the high risk of such loans and for the ostracism associated with this kind of business. In later days when interest became more respectable, legal limits were set on the amount that could be charged. At these rates no legitimate lender could afford to make consumer loans, and the loan shark, operating outside the law, had to raise his rates even higher to cover the added risk of arrest.

The development of small-loan laws and the consequent growth of legitimate consumer finance agencies have tended to drive the loan shark out of business. He still operates on a small scale, however, and it is not impossible to find among the city slums some benevolent friend of the poor who is willing to lend $10 today on practically no security in exchange for $20 next week. This yields a modest return of 100 per cent per week, or 5,200 per cent per year. This is an extreme case, and many loan sharks operate on rates of 120 to 480 per cent (10 to 40 per cent per month). Because such contracts are illegal, the loan shark cannot collect through the courts, but his methods of collection are usually remarkably effective and just as illegal as the interest charge.

Pawnbrokers. The history of the pawnbroker is as old as that of the loan shark and arises from the same set of conditions. The pawnbroker avoids usury by the expedient of buying and selling. He purchases some article of value (called the pledge) at a fraction of its real worth and agrees to sell it back to the original owner within a specified time at a specified price, somewhat higher than the price paid. If the owner does not reclaim the pledge within the given period, the pawnbroker can sell the article and thus reimburse himself. Since he pays only a small part of the value of an article, there is little chance of his being unable to sell it for a sufficient sum to cover his costs.

Although this transaction is not strictly a loan, the principle is similar, and interest may be computed by treating the difference between purchase price and specified redemption price as an interest charge. Thus if a pawnbroker buys an article for $10 and agrees to sell it back within six months for $12, the interest charge is $2 for a six-month loan. This is 20 per cent for six months, or 40 per cent per year.

Since the pawnbroker runs almost no risk and since his business is legal, his charges are considerably less than those of the loan shark. Even so his rates, when expressed as an interest charge, usually run from 24 to 120 per cent per year.

Most states have passed special laws covering pawnbrokerage. These regulate the charges he may make as well as other details of this kind of business.

Small-loan Laws. It became clear early in this century that the growing needs of consumers for funds were not being reasonably met by loan sharks and pawnbrokers, while other lending agencies could not afford to make loans of this kind within the legal rates of interest permitted by the various state usury laws. Agitation to revise these statutes was spearheaded by the Russell Sage Foundation, which was organized in 1907. The foundation prepared a Uniform Small Loan Law as a model for the states to follow, and today most states have some form of small-loan law on the books. This law exempts institutions operating under its provisions from the restrictions of the usury law but provides for licensing and regulating them. The fundamental principle of such laws is that the only way to make adequate credit available to consumers is to permit consumer credit agencies to charge higher rates to compensate them for the higher cost of this kind of business.

The precise limitations written into the statute vary somewhat from state to state. The most lenient terms permit an interest charge of 3½ per cent *per month* on the unpaid balance on loans not exceeding $500. In most cases a lower interest rate is prescribed for large loans than for small ones. Thus New York permits a charge of 2½ per cent per month on the first $100, 2 per cent on the next $200, and ½ per cent on the next $200. The rate of interest charged is the true rate on the unpaid balance and cannot be padded by other charges or fees. The maximum rate, therefore, for the smallest loans in New York is a true 30 per cent per year. In some states the rate may be as high as 42 per cent.

Remedial Loan Associations. The first institutions founded under these laws were the remedial loan associations, a semiphilanthropic type of consumer loan agency whose aim was to make loans at as low a cost as possible. In size these associations have never been important. Their major contribution has been their pioneering in a previously unknown area of finance; they were responsible for demonstrating the soundness of this concept of consumer credit and thus attracting other agencies into the field.

Consumer Finance Companies. The most important such agency is the consumer finance company, which achieved considerable growth in the twenties and has been expanding ever since. There are now some three thousand consumer finance companies (also called *personal finance companies*) in the United States, although the greatest volume of business is done by a half dozen national companies with branches or subsidiaries throughout the country. These companies obtain funds from the issue of their own stock, to a limited extent from the issue of bonds, and to a greater degree from fairly continuous borrowing at short term from commercial banks.

Funds are lent to consumers for periods ranging from eight months to two years. In almost all cases the loans are amortized by monthly payments. Loans may be made on the collateral of chattel mortgages on automobiles or furniture, but since the seizure and sale of such collateral are awkward, expensive, and destructive of goodwill, the companies prefer to rely on the financial standing and character of the borrower. The greater part of their loans are therefore unsecured. Experience has shown this faith in the integrity of the consumer to be well founded, and the high interest charges are based more on the cost of doing business than on a high bad-debt loss.

Industrial Banks. Industrial banks originally arose from the same need and at about the same time as consumer finance companies. The first one was started at Norfolk, Virginia, in 1910 by J. Arthur Morris for the purpose of making consumer loans to industrial workers. Until recently many banks operating according to his principles were called Morris Plan banks. As the plan spread, many states enacted special legislation for the incorporation of industrial banks, while in other states they operate under the small-loan or general banking laws.

Originally most loans were made on cosigner notes (usually with two cosigners required) and the remainder on some kind of collateral. While interest charges varied considerably, a typical rate was 6 per cent discount plus a 2 per cent "commission" or service fee. Repayments were made weekly over a 50-week period. Thus on a note for $100 the borrower would receive $92 and repay $2 per week for 50 weeks. This gives an effective interest rate of 17.7 per cent.[10] Originally the funds for such loans came predominantly from capital.

As time went on, industrial banks became more and more like commercial banks. They now lend to small businesses as well as to consumers, sometimes at rates quite comparable with those of commercial banks. The comaker note has declined in importance and has been replaced by unsecured or collateral loans. Weekly payments have given way to monthly payments. Additional funds have been obtained from the public through the sale of thrift certificates and through the acceptance of savings deposits and even checking deposits. Membership in the Federal Reserve and the Federal Deposit Insurance Corporation is permitted. For practical purposes industrial banks are now usually classified as commercial banks, and many of them are hardly distinguishable as a separate species.

Credit Unions. Credit unions have a background very similar to that of the previous two institutions. They first arose in New Hampshire in 1909 as an attempt by consumers themselves to fill the need for consumer credit, but here again they owe much of their early growth to the enthusiasm of one man, Edward A. Filene, and the Credit Union National Extension Bureau, which he organized.

We have already examined the basic operation of credit unions and shall pause here only to mention that their interest rates are regulated by special laws governing them. The Federal law and most state laws permit a true inter-

[10] $i = \dfrac{2 \times 52 \times 8}{92 \times (50 + 1)} = 17.7$ per cent

est rate of 1 per cent per month—12 per cent per year. Some charge as little as 6 per cent per year. The typical credit union loan is in the neighborhood of $100 to $500.

Commercial Banks. The commercial banks are newcomers in the consumer finance field. Their early preoccupation with the real-bills doctrine of self-liquidating commercial loans, plus their belief that the consumer was a poor credit risk, prevented their making any effort to explore this field. Two developments changed their minds. One was the record of success turned in by the other consumer credit agencies in the twenties, and the other was the lack of demand for business loans during the Depression years. In order to use their available funds, commercial banks started experimenting with consumer loans, and today they make close to one-third of all personal installment loans and practically all consumer loans repayable in one lump sum.

Commercial banks are highly conservative in their choice of consumer borrowers, setting high credit standards and conducting a fairly rigorous credit investigation. In addition they generally require that a prospective borrower have a steady income from a good job and that his total borrowing from all sources not exceed a reasonable proportion of his income.

Partly as a result of careful selection, which reduces both bad-debt losses and collection costs, and partly because of their ability to spread overhead over the whole of their operations, commercial banks are able to charge lower rates of interest than most other consumer lenders. A typical bank rate is 6 per cent discount on a one-year amortized loan (11.8 per cent interest), while at one time certain New York banks were offering a discount as low as 3.33 per cent on collateral loans and 3.83 per cent on noncollateral loans (6.4 per cent and 7.4 per cent interest, respectively).

As consumer credit became big business throughout the country, many banks inaugurated in 1959 a revolving credit account, in which the consumer is granted a line of credit against which he can write checks whenever he wants to, repaying one-twelfth of the amount borrowed each month. The interest charge on the unpaid balance (true interest) is approximately 1 per cent per month, the maximum permitted by law on this kind of loan in many states. The great advantage to the consumer is that he may obtain a line of credit in advance, which is always ready when needed but for which he pays nothing until it is actually used.

Installment Purchases. Although many of the consumer loans discussed above are repaid in installments over a period of time and thus are properly called "installment credit," this term is more commonly used by consumers to refer to credit that is extended by or through a seller to help finance the purchase of goods, primarily automobiles and household appliances. The "installment plan" as a means of enabling a customer to acquire durable goods before he is able to pay for them in full—a practice that developed extensively in the twenties along with the automobile and the radio—has become solidly entrenched as an American institution with its "a dollar down and a dollar a week." Installment purchases account for over half of all consumer credit outstanding, the greater part appearing in the financing of automobiles.

Generally speaking an installment contract represents a promissory note of the purchaser against which the automobile or other merchandise is security. This may take the form of a chattel mortgage, where the merchandise is collateral for the loan, or of a conditional sales contract, where the seller continues as the actual owner of the merchandise until final payment is made.[11] In either case the goods can be repossessed and sold if payments are not kept up, although dealers try to avoid this drastic step if possible.

There are two characteristic ways by which installment sales may be financed: the dealer may hold the contract himself until it is paid, thus financing the credit out of his own resources (whether owned or borrowed), or he may sell the contract to a specialist in finance. The second method is almost universal in automobile sales, while the first is more common with respect to other merchandise.

Department, furniture, and jewelry stores, accustomed to charge accounts and with installment sales forming a relatively small part of total sales, are generally in a position to finance such sales themselves. In cases of this kind the cost of financing is often hidden in the price of the merchandise, as it is with charge sales, but more and more commonly the finance charge is stated separately in order to match the cash price against that of competitors who do not offer credit. In the latter case the interest rate can be computed for any particular purchase by means of the formula already used. Any generalization about such rates is impossible because of the great variation from one transaction to another. One New York store that advertises its installment-purchase plan charges rates that vary with the type of article purchased from 6 per cent for pianos to 17 per cent for clothing. A large mail-order house charges from 13 per cent to 35 per cent depending on the size of the initial balance. Unquestionably both lower and higher rates could be found.

Sales Finance Companies. When installment sales contracts are sold by the dealer to a specialist in finance, the purchaser may be either a commercial bank or a sales finance company, with about half of the business going to each. Sales finance companies are specialized institutions that provide funds to dealers to carry inventories and to consumers to purchase goods. It is the latter with which we are here concerned. Some sales finance companies specialize in automobile paper, some in nonautomobile paper, and some in both. There are three large national companies (General Motors Acceptance Corporation, Commercial Credit Company, and C.I.T. Financial Corporation),

[11] This aspect of the transaction is emphasized in Great Britain, where installment contracts are called *hire-purchase* agreements. The consumer is renting the article in question by making monthly payments. When these payments equal a stated sum, they become full payment for the purchase of the article. Similar arrangements are sometimes made in this country with respect to typewriters and other goods.

several regional companies, and some twenty-five hundred local companies. These companies pay cash to the dealer for his installment contracts and collect from the customer. The funds that they advance are obtained from their own capital and from bank borrowing.

The amount of interest that a consumer pays for automobile installment credit not only varies widely, but frequently cannot even be determined because the finance charges are lumped together with other costs, including insurance, accessories, and even freight and taxes. An investigation by the New York State Committee to Study Installment Sales revealed that *usual* effective rates of interest for automobile installment financing in 1948 ranged from 31.5 to 52.1 per cent and in one case reached 529 per cent. Since that time it appears that rates have been drastically reduced, partly as a result of legal pressure.

Because no actual *money* is lent in installment buying, the service charges are not legally considered interest and therefore are not subject to the usury laws. In order to protect buyers from unconscionable charges, several states have enacted specific laws limiting this finance charge. In New York, for instance, the law now provides a maximum *charge* per year (not the *rate,* which would be approximately twice as high) of 7 per cent for new automobiles, 10 per cent for cars up to three years old, and 13 per cent for older cars. For other types of merchandise the maximum charge is 10 per cent for balances up to $500 and 8 per cent for balances over that amount. Other interesting provisions of the law require that the finance charges be stated separately, that a partial refund of service charges be made if payment is completed before the due date, and that the contract carry a warning against failure to read the whole contract and against signing a contract with blank spaces.

Generally when a car or other collateral is repossessed and resold, the seller must return to the debtor any amount received over and above the balance due plus the costs of repossession. However, repossession does not relieve the debtor of his legal obligation for his note, and if the car cannot be resold for enough to pay the debt plus the costs of repossession, the seller can still sue him for the balance. In practice repossession represents a very small fraction of installment sales, but it can be both embarrassing and costly to the consumer when it does occur, as the cartoons are fond of pointing out.

Residential Mortgage Finance. Technically, mortgage finance does not belong in a discussion of consumer credit since by convention a house is considered capital rather than a consumer good and the owner a landlord even when he lives in the house himself. However, the average homeowner is likely to consider himself a consumer rather than a businessman.

There are no statistics available on the distribution of mortgages between owner-occupants and owners who rent their property to others. About all that we can say here is that, lumping both groups together, total residential mortgages outstanding are approximately $200 billion—more than 2½ times the volume of consumer credit. Of the total, roughly one-half is provided by savings and loan associations, one-quarter by life insurance companies, one-eighth by commercial banks, and one-eighth by savings banks. Although the figures for the different lending institutions are not precisely comparable, Table 17-3 gives a general idea of the distribution of home mortgages among the various lenders and the different types of mortgages for 1964.

Table 17-3. Home Mortage Loans Outstanding,* December 31, 1964
Billions of Dollars

Type of lender	Total	FHA	VA	Conventional
Commercial banks†	28.9	7.3	2.7	18.9
Mutual savings banks†	36.5	12.3	11.1	13.1
Life insurance companies‡	50.9	11.5	6.4	33.0
Savings and loan associations§	101.3	4.9	6.7	89.7
Federal National Mortgage Association§	4.4	3.0	1.4	0.0
Total, all institutions¶	197.7	38.3	30.4	129.0

* Note that the class of mortgage included varies from one institution to another (see following footnotes). The figures are therefore not strictly comparable and will not add up to the totals for all institutions, which are derived from different data.
† Residential mortgages.
‡ Nonfarm mortgages.
§ Total mortgages.
¶ Mortgages on nonfarm one- to four-family residences.
Source: *Federal Reserve Bulletin*, vol. 51, no. 5 (May, 1965), pp. 729–731.

Interest rates on mortgage loans are always stated as true rates. They have not varied greatly from a range of 4 to 7 per cent. The low rate is attributable partly to the nature of the collateral, but even more to the fact that these loans are relatively large and therefore the expense of making and carrying them is small relative to the amount of money lent.

The High Cost of Consumer Credit. We have seen both why and how consumer interest rates vary from the rate the businessman has to pay. Table 17-4 presents in a ready form for comparison typical rates for particular types of lending agencies. Caution must be used in interpreting the table, however, for interest rates vary so much from case to case and from time to time that all figures in the table can be taken only as rough approximations.

The average consumer could probably save money if he learned a little about how to compare interest rates and then shopped around to get the lowest rate. For instance, it is sometimes possible to get a bank loan on automobile collateral at half the cost of financing a car through a sales finance company. Similarly our table indicates that the pawnbroker and loan shark should be shunned like the plague. Unfortunately, people who are unable to qualify for loans elsewhere often use these lenders as a last resort.

In most cases the consumer simply has no idea of how much interest he is paying. In some cases he isn't even interested in the price of merchandise he buys on the installment plan—as long as the monthly payments are reason-

Table 17-4. Common Interest Rates for Various Kinds of Consumer Loans

Type of loan	Typical method of stating charges	Actual rate of interest for charge shown in second column, per cent per year	Normal range of actual rates, per cent per year
Charge accounts and service credit	No charge	*	3–7†
Life insurance loans	5% on unpaid balance	5	4–6
Mortgage loans	5% plus ½% insurance	5.5	4–7
Commercial banks	6% discount	11.8	7–20
Credit unions	1% per month	12	6–18
Industrial banks	6% discount plus 2% commission	17.7	12–34
Installment sales	$160 finance charge (on $1,500 unpaid balance)	19.7‡	6–50
Personal finance company	2½% per month	30	24–42
Pawnbrokers	$10 purchase price $12 redemption price	40§	24–120
Loan sharks	20% per month	240	120–1200

* Included in sales price of product.
† Estimated cost to the retailer.
‡ Assuming one-year repayment.
§ Assuming redemption in six months.

able. A recent study of the National Bureau of Economic Research shows not only that startlingly few consumers know what interest rate they are paying on consumer loans, but also that those who are aware of the rate pay a significantly lower rate than those who are not. These differences are greater, the smaller the loan. The survey, taken among some sixteen thousand subscriber members of Consumers Union (a group with a relatively high educational background), showed that only 5 per cent of the respondents who had borrowed less than $500 on installment purchases could say with reasonable accuracy what true interest rate they were paying; this group actually paid an average of 12.1 per cent. Another 6 per cent of the borrowers were able to state the finance charge but not the true rate; these paid an average of 17.1 per cent. The remaining 89 per cent could not report even the charge with any accuracy; their average rate was 30.8 per cent.[12]

The total cost of consumer credit is enormous, although precise figures are impossible to obtain. Not counting mortgages, consumer credit in the United States at the present time amounts to more than $1,500 per family. Assuming an average interest rate of 15 per cent (a fairly conservative estimate), the average family pays $225 a year in interest alone. It is sobering to realize that if this average family postponed purchases until it was able to pay for them (which is, of course, not always possible) and then put the *interest* saved into

[12] F. Thomas Juster and Robert P. Shay, *Consumer Sensitivity to Finance Rates: An Empirical and Analytical Investigation* (National Bureau of Economic Research, Inc., New York, 1964), p. 55.

a savings bank at 4 per cent per year compounded annually, their bank balance in forty years would be over $22,000.

Perhaps it is worth this price to get things a year or two sooner; perhaps the pressure of repayments has made the income earner work harder and has thereby increased his income; perhaps if credit were not used, the interest saved would be squandered on unessentials—or perhaps the problem was simply never looked at in this light. Consumers are not noted for their close scrutiny of the relations between costs and benefits.

Questions for Thought and Discussion

1. Why is the premium for an endowment insurance policy payable at age sixty-five higher than one for a whole-life policy?

2. Why do you think postal savings have never been very important in this country, although they are major savings institutions in several foreign countries?

3. Compare the advantages (including convenience, safety, and interest return) of the various savings institutions. If you had $1,000 in savings, where would you prefer to put it? Would you make the same choice if your savings were $10 per week?

4. If credit unions lend only to their members, why do they charge any interest at all?

5. Is it possible for consumers to raise their standard of living in the short run by buying on the installment plan? In the long run?

6. What limits does your state place on interest charged by consumer finance companies? By installment sellers? By other types of lenders?

7. What are the primary agencies making mortgage loans? Do they get their funds from essentially the same place? Why don't commercial banks make more mortgage loans?

8. How is it possible for interest rates charged consumers to vary so much from one lender to another? Why don't borrowers all go to the cheapest source?

9. Considering your own credit standing, where do you think you could get a loan at the lowest interest?

10. Check the figures for consumer and mortgage loans in a current issue of the *Federal Reserve Bulletin*. Have there been any significant changes?

Selected Bibliography

American Bankers Association: *Credit Unions,* New York, 1958.

———: *Savings and Loan Associations,* New York, 1958.

Caves, Richard C.: *Some Credit Cost Comparisons,* Consumer Research Institute, San Francisco State College, San Francisco, Calif., 1964.

Chapman, J. M., and F. W. Jones: *Finance Companies: How and Where They*

Obtain Their Funds, Columbia University Graduate School of Business, New York, 1959.

Cox, Reavis: *Economics of Consumer Credit,* The Ronald Press Company, New York, 1949.

Credit Union National Association: *International Credit Union Yearbook,* Madison, Wis. (annually).

Croteau, John T.: *The Economics of the Credit Union,* Wayne State University Press, Detroit, 1963.

Goldsmith, Raymond W.: *A Study of Savings in the United States,* 3 vols., Princeton University Press, Princeton, N.J., 1955–1956.

Hardy, Charles O. (ed.): *Consumer Credit and Its Uses,* Prentice-Hall, Inc., Englewood Cliffs, N.J., 1938.

Horne, H. Oliver: *A History of Savings Banks,* Geoffrey Cumberlege, Oxford University Press, London, 1947.

Institute of Life Insurance: *Life Insurance Fact Book,* New York (annually).

Juster, F. Thomas, and Robert P. Shay: *Consumer Sensitivity to Finance Rates: An Empirical and Analytical Investigation,* National Bureau of Economic Research, New York, 1964.

Kelsey, R. Wilfred, and Arthur C. Daniels: *Handbook of Life Insurance,* Institute of Life Insurance, New York, 1949.

Kendall, Leon T., for the United States Savings and Loan League: *The Savings and Loan Business,* Prentice-Hall, Inc., for the Commission on Money and Credit, Englewood Cliffs, N.J., 1962.

Life Insurance Association of America: *Life Insurance Companies as Financial Institutions,* Prentice-Hall, Inc., for the Commission on Money and Credit, Englewood Cliffs, N.J., 1962.

McCracken, Paul W., James C. T. Mao, and Cedric V. Fricke: *Consumer Instalment Credit and Public Policy,* Bureau of Business Research, University of Michigan, Ann Arbor, Mich., 1965.

National Association of Mutual Savings Banks: *Annual Reports,* New York.

———: *Mutual Savings Banking: Basic Characteristics and Role in the National Economy,* Prentice-Hall, Inc., for the Commission on Money and Credit, Englewood Cliffs, N.J., 1962.

National Consumer Finance Association: *The Consumer Finance Industry,* Prentice-Hall, Inc., for the Commission on Money and Credit, Englewood Cliffs, N.J., 1962.

Neifeld, M. R.: *Cooperative Consumer Credit with Special Reference to Credit Unions,* Harper & Row, Publishers, Incorporated, New York, 1936.

Phelps, Clyde William: *The Role of the Sales Finance Companies in the American Economy,* Commercial Credit Company, Baltimore, 1952.

Smith, Paul F.: *Consumer Credit Costs, 1949–59,* Princeton University Press, for the National Bureau of Economic Research, Princeton, N.J., 1964.

United States Savings and Loan League: *Savings and Loan Fact Book,* Chicago (annually).

See also references listed under Chapter 16.

Chapter 18
Business Credit

So far as my coin would stretch; and where it would not, I have used my credit.

The First Part of King Henry IV
Act I, scene 2, line 61

Since commercial banks were not designed to serve consumers' needs, it is not surprising that special institutions were developed to fill the gap. Even in the field of short-term business finance, however, commercial banks do not have a monopoly of loanable funds, while investment credit has traditionally been an area in which commercial banks are not prominent.

Commercial Credit

While commercial banks are still by far the most important source of short-term business loans, several other agencies have entered the field, in some cases lending their own funds, in others acting as intermediaries between the commercial banks and ultimate borrowers. Two of these institutions also lend to consumers, and in this role have already been discussed.

All the institutions discussed in this section obtain funds from their own capital, while most of them also borrow more or less heavily from commercial banks.

Industrial Banks. The business lending activities of the industrial banks are so similar to those of commercial banks that they need no further discussion. Their main distinction lies in the fact that they are especially adapted to making small loans to small business, and in some states the size of loan they may make is limited by law. Interest charges on such loans are similar to those on consumer loans of the same size.

Sales Finance Companies. While financing the consumer is the main function of sales finance companies, many of them have found that the dealer is similarly in need of funds to carry his inventory prior to its sale. This is particularly true in the automobile field, where manufacturers traditionally require the dealer to pay for cars as soon as they are delivered. While a dealer may use his own funds for this purpose or may borrow from a commercial bank, the sales finance companies specialize in financing automobiles on a wholesale as well as a retail basis.

Such financing of dealers' stocks is normally done by means of a short-term loan which is retired by a single payment rather than in installments and which carries an interest rate much lower than the one charged consumers.

The finance company pays the manufacturer directly, thereby obtains legal ownership of the cars, and releases them to the dealer on a trust receipt (which means that the dealer is holding the merchandise in trust for the finance company, which is the legal owner). Less frequently the cars are stored in a public warehouse, and the finance company holds the warehouse receipt. When the cars are sold, the trust (or warehouse) receipt is released to the dealer against payment of the loan. The dealer can pay his debt to the finance company either in cash or by turning over an equivalent amount of his customers' installment contracts. In the latter case the loan originally made to the dealer is automatically transferred into a loan to the consumer.

Increasingly, but still on a small scale, sales finance companies have also gone into the financing of machinery and equipment purchased by farmers, manufacturers, or other businessmen. These loans are long-term and as such belong more properly in the category of investment credit.

Sales finance companies have also gone into factoring, a type of finance in which several other lenders participate. A small amount of this business is done by the sales finance companies directly, and a very much larger part by wholly owned subsidiaries.[1]

Factoring. The term *factor* has at least two different meanings. Originally a factor was either a principal or an agent who sold goods on a commission basis. He was particularly important in the cotton trade. Frequently he found that he had to finance both the planters from whom he bought and the mills to which he sold. As the commercial factor declined in importance, the name was attached to the financial operations that he inaugurated, and today it has an even more restricted meaning than this. In today's finance a factor is a lender who finances accounts receivable.

Factoring is most common in the textile field, but it is expanding into many

[1] Two of the five largest factors in the country are subsidiaries of C.I.T. Financial Corporation, and another is a subsidiary of Commercial Credit Company.

other industries ranging from fertilizer to furniture. It is associated almost exclusively with the financing of manufacturers and wholesalers.

The factor advances money to a seller against the security of his accounts receivable. Sometimes these receivables are pledged as collateral for the loan; sometimes they are purchased outright. Sometimes the relationship between factor and borrower is a permanent one, sometimes temporary. While the various possibilities are combined in different ways, two primary patterns predominate.

Old-line Factors. The "old-line factor"—who, far from being obsolete, is growing in importance—operates under a continuing agreement with his client under which he assumes both credit and collection functions. He investigates the credit standing of prospective purchasers, buys all accounts receivable as they arise, sends bills to his client's customers in his own name, takes full responsibility for the collection of bills, and assumes all risk of credit loss. He operates, in other words, as if he were the credit department of his client and in that role provides many specialized services in addition to lending money.

The service charge, which reimburses the old-line factor for the credit and collection costs plus bad-debt losses, ranges from ¾ to 4 per cent of all accounts handled. In addition there is a customary interest charge of 6 per cent per year on uncollected balances, representing the amount of money actually advanced by the factor.

Nonnotification Factoring. The other major type of factoring, now frequently referred to as *commercial financing,* involves a loan to a seller against the pledge of accounts receivable as collateral. In this case the customers are usually not notified of the transaction and pay their bills as usual to the seller. He must then turn these payments over to the factor until the debt is extinguished. The seller remains responsible for the complete credit and collection function as well as bad-debt losses. Generally the factor will advance only 70 to 80 per cent of the value of the receivables in order to protect himself against the inability of the seller to collect the full value of his accounts. Since the factor does not deal with the borrower's customers directly, he must rely entirely on the credit standing of the borrower himself.

Usually this type of financing is used by a firm on a noncontinuing basis when it needs funds for some special purpose and is unable to obtain an ordinary loan from a commercial bank. It is therefore frequently a last resort for a business that is of relatively poor credit standing, and the interest rate is likely to be high, ranging from 12 to 24 per cent. In some cases the pledging of receivables has been the last desperate effort of a dying company to stave off bankruptcy, although it should not be assumed that all such financing falls into this category.

Commercial Paper Houses. Although most businesses wishing to borrow from a commercial bank deal directly with an individual bank, there are many firms whose needs are so great that no single bank can provide sufficient funds or who wish to borrow in distant markets where interest rates are lower than they are locally. In other countries such needs would be met easily by a large branch banking firm. But under our unit banking system, some different machinery is needed to provide mobility of funds to meet these needs. The commercial paper house provides such facilities.

A company wishing to borrow, say, $10 million for a short period (not over six months) will issue a series of promissory notes in standard denominations of not less than $5,000 each, payable to itself and endorsed in blank. The commercial paper house, a specialist in finding buyers for this kind of paper, will undertake to sell the notes to various banks and other institutions who have excess funds to invest at short term. For this service the commercial paper house charges ¼ per cent commission.

To distinguish this type of operation from the commercial paper arising from ordinary bank loans, it is frequently referred to as *open-market commercial paper,* but in other cases only the context will tell which is meant.

Because this kind of open-market paper can be disposed of in the most advantageous market, because it is normally issued only by substantial firms, and because the commercial paper house investigates the issuer carefully (although it does not guarantee the paper), interest rates tend to be fairly low. Unlike some bank loans, which may be renewed, open-market commercial paper is always paid at maturity.

The three large sales finance companies obtain most of their funds through open-market commercial paper, but they sell directly to the banks without using the facilities of the commercial paper house. Their financing requirements are so large that they represent a very important influence in the money market, and their paper carries its own designation: *finance paper.*

One important characteristic of open-market commercial paper in general, and of finance paper in particular, is that the interest rate is set not by the lending bank, but by the issuing corporation (usually in consultation with the commercial paper house). In this and other respects open-market paper has most of the characteristics of a bond except that it is short-term. Of course, if the rate is set too low, buyers will be unwilling to purchase, and the corporation will be unable to obtain the needed funds.

Since there is a ready market for commercial paper, it represents a very liquid asset, and small banks unable to make direct loans to large corporations are usually glad to invest in it.

Acceptance Dealers. Another agency in the short-term open market is the acceptance dealer, who specializes in bank (or bankers') acceptances. Acceptances are obligations of the large foreign exchange banks, generally with a maturity of three months or less. Because of its importance in international trade, London is still the primary market for bank acceptances, but the New York market is growing rapidly.

Acceptance dealers (they are called *bill brokers* in England) are the core of this market. They buy acceptances from those who wish to obtain funds and sell them in turn to others who have funds to lend. They will usually have a portfolio of acceptances that they are offering for sale, but generally they depend for their income more on the difference between their buying and selling rates than on the interest earned on acceptances held.

Because accepting banks, who are responsible for the payment of these instruments, are large institutions with the very highest credit standing, the rate of interest on bank acceptances is usually about the lowest rate on any kind of security, at times even falling below the rate on United States treasury bills. Acceptances are highly liquid, and the largest purchasers are commercial banks. Manufacturing corporations with temporarily excess funds on hand are increasingly entering the acceptance market as buyers.

Currently the Federal Reserve is engaging in open-market purchases and sales of bank acceptances on a small scale after an absence from the market for two decades. This activity tends to encourage the growth of the market for acceptances.

Investment Credit

While commercial credit meets the needs of business for short-term (circulating) capital, there are also many institutions ready to finance long-term (investment) capital requirements. Although there is some overlapping, the investment market is for the most part a very different market from the consumer finance or the commercial credit market. In some respects it is a simpler market since it involves essentially only two types of instrument: stocks and bonds.

Stocks and Bonds. While business may obtain some long-term funds by direct negotiation with individual lenders, as, for instance, on mortgages, the greater part of such funds are obtained by the issue of stocks or bonds, some of which are privately placed but most of which are offered to the general public.

We have already noted the significant difference between stocks and bonds, the former evidencing a share in the ownership of the business and the latter representing a creditor's claim. There are certain classes of preferred stock that look somewhat like bonds, as well as certain junior participation bonds that look very much like stock, but these instruments are of relatively minor importance and will not concern us further.

Important as the distinction is between stocks and bonds, the two together comprise the genus "securities" and are dealt in more or less indiscriminately by the various investment institutions. We will not differentiate further between them in this chapter.

Investment Banks. Investment banks are not banks, nor do they normally provide investment funds. They are essentially specialists in the distribution of corporate securities. It is possible for a corporation to sell its own securities. This is obvious in the case of the small corporation where one family or a few friends are the only stockholders. Even a large corporation can sell securities directly to the public through a sales staff or by mail. But just as a homeowner wanting to sell his house usually goes to a real estate broker, so a corporation wishing to sell securities usually goes to an investment banker.

The investment bank performs three functions at three different levels, frequently calling in others to assist in the third or even the second stage. These functions are investigation, underwriting, and distribution. When an investment bank is asked to handle a new issue of securities, its first job is to *investigate* the financial status of the company, its prospects, the purposes for which the funds are to be used, and any other factors bearing on the soundness of the proposed issue. If it feels that the issue is justified, it will, in consultation with the management, determine the price or interest rate at which the securities will be offered to the public. As an alternative to this kind of direct negotiation, several investment banks may investigate independently and bid against one another for the privilege of handling the issue. Such competitive bidding is common for the issues of municipalities and public utilites.

Once the terms are agreed upon, the investment bank will *underwrite* the issue, either alone or with other investment banks joined together in an underwriting syndicate. Underwriting means a guarantee that the issue will be sold on the specified terms. If the whole issue is not sold, the underwriter must pay the issuing corporation anyway and is free to hold the unsold securities or to dispose of them in any way that it can. When the syndicate includes more than one member, each one underwrites a stated percentage of the total issue and will be responsible for that proportion of any unsold securities. For its guarantee each participant receives an underwriting commission.

The third step is *distribution.* A single investment bank or underwriting syndicate may sell through its own corps of salesmen. Usually a larger group of banks, stockbrokers, and others is invited to participate in order to achieve as wide a distribution as possible. Each participant receives a selling commission for those securities he sells. A seller who is not an underwriter, however, incurs no obligation for unsold securities unless he has agreed to purchase them.

Suppose a new bond issue is priced to sell to the public at 99 (per cent of par value, that is, $990 for each $1,000 bond). Members of the selling group will pay perhaps 98 for it. The underwriting syndicate may pay 96, while the investment bank that originated the issue may pay the corporation 95. Thus a seller earns $10 for each bond sold, plus $20 for his portion of the underwriting (if any), while the originating investment bank receives an additional $10 for its investigation services. In most cases the spread would be less than this, but it could also be more.

When a new issue is sold in this manner, or in any other, *it is never sold through the stock market.* Rather it is sold directly by salesmen to ultimate purchasers: banks, insurance companies, trustees, corporations, and individuals. Not until an issue of securities is already in the hands of the public and is properly "seasoned" can it be listed on a stock exchange.

Stock Exchanges. A stock exchange is a membership association that provides physical facilities and a set of rules under which its members can trade specified ("listed") securities among themselves. Contrary to some popular notions, a stock exchange never buys or sells securities itself. Similarly, corporations never sell their own securities on the exchange. Sales are made by members of the exchange either out of their own portfolios or for the accounts of their clients who wish to dispose of securities previously acquired. Purchases are made by members for their own portfolios or for their customers. A large number of members are brokers who execute orders for the general public. Other members are specialists in particular stocks, who help to maintain an orderly market for these issues. Two firms specialize in odd-lot transfers: purchase or sale of blocks of less than 100 shares. A few members buy and sell only for their own accounts. Among all these members stocks are sold to the highest bidder or bought from the lowest asker on the principle of an auction market.

A stock exchange is a nonprofit association and meets its expenses by annual assessments on the members, who are in turn reimbursed for the most part through the commissions they receive from their customers. The New York Stock Exchange has 1,366 members, and a new member can be admitted only by buying the "seat" of a retiring or deceased member. The exchange is managed by a board of governors, which is responsible to the membership.

The New York Stock Exchange is by far the largest in the country, with over twenty-seven hundred different securities listed for trading, including both stocks and bonds of most of the major United States corporations. More than three-fourths of all stock exchange transactions take place on this one exchange, with the remaining business carried on through a dozen other exchanges located throughout the country, some of them extremely small.

While the stock exchanges do not themselves provide a market through which corporations can issue new securities, they nevertheless facilitate the financing of large corporations whose securities may be expected to be listed, since an investor is more likely to be willing to buy securities if he knows that there is an active market in which he can dispose of them if he wishes. The exchanges thereby increase the liquidity of those securities that are listed.

Over-the-counter Markets. Only a relatively small number of the total securities issued by United States corporations (and governmental units) are listed on the exchanges. The securities of all small corporations and some of the larger ones are traded only over the counter. Banks and insurance companies, for instance, traditionally do not have their stocks listed. The over-the-counter market—more accurately designated as an over-the-phone market—has no physical existence. It represents the informal arrangements by which brokers and dealers in particular securities keep in touch with each other.

If John Jones wants to buy ten shares of Astral Lighting Corporation, he calls his broker just as he would if he wanted ten shares of General Motors. The broker will know one or more dealers who "make a market" in Astral. This means that they are ready at any time either to buy or to sell shares of Astral at a price. The broker will call several of these dealers on the phone and place an order with the one who quotes the lowest "asking" price. If Jones wanted to sell, his broker would similarly find the dealer in Astral who quotes the highest "bid" price. The difference between an individual dealer's bid price and his ask price represents his source of income on this type of business.

So far we have mentioned several agencies that facilitate the exchange of securities, and perhaps it will help to summarize the work of each of them:

Investment banks provide for the distribution of new securities.
Stock exchanges provide facilities for trading listed (old) securities.
Over-the-counter dealers stand ready to buy or sell those (unlisted) securities in which they specialize.
Government-bond dealers specialize in government securities.
Specialists help maintain an orderly market in selected securities on the stock exchange.
Odd-lot dealers facilitate the transfer on the stock exchange of small blocks of stock.
Brokers execute orders for the general public.
Many firms act in two or more of these capacities.

Mortgage Companies. A final service auxiliary that needs brief mention is the mortgage company, although this takes us away from the securities market.

Because many of the institutional holders of mortgages—savings banks and life insurance companies—are concentrated in industrial centers, particularly in the Northeast, whereas mortgage funds by their nature are needed all over the country, the mortgage company has taken on the task of middleman between borrower and lender in this field.

The function of mortgage companies is to originate and service mortgages for institutional lenders. They may make mortgage loans out of their own funds in the hope of being able to sell them later, but in most cases they act as agents of the institutional lenders, processing mortgages in amounts requested by these institutions. They deal primarily in FHA-insured and VA-guaranteed mortgages since these are fairly standardized and reduce the risk for the ultimate lender in carrying on mortgage lending at a distance.

The value of these companies is in facilitating the placement of institutional funds in areas that would otherwise find mortgage loans hard to get. By increasing the geographical fluidity of mortgage funds they help in equalizing interest rates in various sections of the country.

Investors. The institutions so far discussed in this section are not themselves sources of funds for investment needs; they simply facilitate the issue and transfer of securities. The actual lenders[2] are those individuals and institutions that hold securities in their portfolios. Wealthy, and even not-so-wealthy, individuals have traditionally been the primary source of investment funds as they use their savings directly in the purchase of stocks and bonds. Increasingly, however, other financial intermediaries are entering the field, and this shift in investment patterns has had significant effects on the market, not all of which are clearly known.

Nonprofit institutions with endowment funds are important investors, particularly universities and philanthropic foundations. Nonfinancial corporations are a source of capital for their subsidiaries and sometimes hold other securities for their investment value. Commercial banks hold small amounts of securities, and the role of savings banks and insurance companies has already been mentioned. Their activity in the market is expanding, but the great growth in institutional investors has occurred in investment companies and trust funds.

Investment Companies. An investment company is a corporation that holds securities of other corporations (or governmental units) for the purpose of earning an income. It thus differs in purpose from a holding company, which is a corporation that holds stocks of other corporations for the purpose of control. While an investment company may vote the stock it owns, thus exercising a certain amount of control, this is not its primary objective, and it does not normally own a controlling interest in any corporation.

The investment company provides the small investor with two advantages that he cannot normally obtain by purchasing securities directly: diversification and expert management. One of the first rules of stock investment is not to put all your eggs in one basket. Because even the best company in the best industry may run into bad luck or bad management, the investor is well advised to buy stock in many companies in various industries and in different sections of the country. Most investors also wish to hold bonds as well as a reasonable cash backlog for greater liquidity. For the man with limited funds such diversification is impossible. But by buying as little as one share in an investment company he becomes part owner of the whole cross section of securities owned by that company.

In addition he has hired the expert management of the company to look after his investments and to decide when and what to buy or sell. The dividends that he receives represent the earnings of the investment company on its portfolio, including capital gains as well as interest and dividends.

Not all investment companies invest in a true cross section of securities. Some specialize in bonds, others in preferred stocks or in speculative stocks; some even specialize in particular industries such as railroads or missiles, but this destroys the basic objective of diversification.

Nor should it be assumed that an investment company is by definition safe.

[2] Stretching the term "lenders" somewhat to include stockholders as well as bondholders.

Experience with such companies in the late twenties and thirties was very dismal indeed. The stock market collapse, coupled with bad management in some cases and outright fraud in others, put many an investment company into bankruptcy. The bitter fruits of experience plus more effective government supervision have weeded out the worst abuses, but some investment advisers still look on the investment companies with a wary eye.

Closed-end Companies. There are two basic plans under which investment company stock is issued. The closed-end company operates in the same manner as a regular corporation with regard to stock. It issues a specified amount of stock at one time through an investment bank. This stock is then listed on a stock exchange or sold over the counter. A new purchaser can obtain stock only from an old holder at a price determined by supply and demand on the market.

Mutual Funds. Open-end companies, or mutual funds, are more numerous than the closed-end type. The mutual fund has no specified amount of stock outstanding but stands ready at all times to sell its stock directly to new purchasers. The price of the stock at any specific time is determined by a mathematical formula: it is the book value of the stock (found by dividing the fund's current net worth by the number of shares outstanding) plus a "loading charge," or commission, which is usually in the neighborhood of 7 to 9 per cent. The price, therefore, fluctuates with the market value of the securities held by the fund.

The stock of a mutual fund is not transferable and therefore cannot be sold on an exchange or over the counter. The fund will buy back its own stock at any time, paying the book value of the stock as of a time several days (the precise period varying from one fund to another) *after* the repurchase. In other words, a stockholder wishing to get out must sell his stock back to the fund before he knows what price he will get for it. The interval of time is provided to protect the fund in a period of rapidly falling prices and to give it the opportunity to dispose of certain assets if necessary in order to obtain cash with which to pay the stockholder.

Fire, Marine, and Casualty Insurance Companies. Although they are not generally put in the same category, the non-life insurance companies share many of the characteristics of the investment companies. The sheer volume of their financial operations gives them substantial assets, which they invest in a cross section of securities designed to combine safety and a certain degree of liquidity with reasonable earnings. In aggregate size they exceed mutual funds and closed-end investment companies combined.

Trustees. A *trustee* is an individual or institution who manages the funds of someone else (the *trustor*) for the benefit of either the trustor or someone whom he has named (the *beneficiary*) under the terms of a written understanding (the *trust agreement*). The arrangement is sometimes referred to as a *fiduciary relationship,* and the trustee is also called a *fiduciary.*

There are two basic types of personal trust agreement: living trusts and testamentary trusts. A *living trust* is set up by an individual to operate during his lifetime. Its primary purpose is to relieve the trustor of the day-to-day paper work associated with the investment of his funds and to put the management of his affairs into the hands of someone in whose judgment he has more faith than he has in his own. A *testamentary trust* is set up by will and involves the management of the estate of the deceased. Its purpose is to protect the heirs of the trustor. Frequently the two are combined, a living trust becoming a testamentary trust on the death of the trustor.

The trust agreement may specify in great detail the precise actions that the trustee may take, listing the securities to be bought and sold, the way in which the proceeds shall be reinvested or distributed, and so on. Since this negates one of the primary purposes of the trust—the skilled management of the trustee—it is more common to give the trustee considerably more discretion in the exercise of his judgment. The trustee then uses the trust funds in whatever way he thinks will best achieve the broad purposes of the trust within the limits imposed by the trust agreement.

Trust Companies. The origin of trusts may be traced back many centuries. In the early period the trustee was almost always an individual or group of individuals, and even today many trusts are handled on this basis. But the advantages of perpetual life and more expert management that may be obtained through the use of a specialized trust institution have led to the rise of corporate trustees. The United States Trust Company in New York City (chartered 1853) was the first institution in this country to specialize in the trust business, and it was followed by the establishment of many trust companies in the latter part of the century. Over the years, however, the trust companies have extended their activities into the acceptance of deposits and other banking business, while at the same time the larger commercial banks have added trust departments. The two institutions have thus grown so close together that today the difference between them is nominal, and banking statistics put them in the same classification. Some twenty-eight hundred commercial banks in the United States operate trust departments.

The trust department has its own special existence and is connected only vaguely with the other operations of the bank. The funds that it handles belong to the individual beneficiaries of each trust and are not part of the bank's general assets. Each trust represents a separate agreement and must be handled by itself. The trust officer in charge of a particular trust is essentially the alter ego of the trustor and acts in all respects for him alone.

The trustee is reimbursed for his services by a fee that is based on the total size of the fund, on its income, and on the size of payments made out of it. Since this fee is limited by law and is generally a very small percentage of the amount of funds handled, most banks can accept small trusts only at a loss.

A small fund has the further disadvantage of lack of diversification. Many trust departments do not like to accept trusts of less than $25,000.

Commingled Trusts. The commingled trust, or common trust fund, was devised to get around these disadvantages and to give the benefits of trust management to the person who has a small estate. With the permission of the participant the commingled trust provides for the merging of the funds of several individual trustors into a single fund in which each shares in proportion to his original contribution. The commingled trust thus occupies an intermediate position between the individual trust and the investment company. Its advantage over the latter lies primarily in its flexibility plus the fact that the trustee will make payments out of the fund in any way that the trustor has specified.

Pension Funds. Almost unknown twenty-five years ago, private pension plans have shown a spectacular growth in the postwar period as they have become one of the most important fringe benefits for which labor has fought. Their total assets rose from $2 billion in 1940 to $77 billion in 1964 (see Table 17-1). Designed to provide retirement income, private pension plans now cover 25 million workers, or one-third of the total labor force.

The funds are financed through regular contributions by the employer, the employee, or both. These sums are accumulated throughout the working life of the employee and paid out according to the terms of the agreement under one of three plans:

1. Some pension funds are handled by life insurance companies. The contributions are paid to the insurance company as premiums on annuities payable to the workers. While the precise terms of the annuities will be specifically tailored to the needs of the particular pension plan, there is no fundamental difference between such plans and the annuities regularly sold to individuals. The insurance company will merge these funds with its other assets and invest them in the same way as other funds.

2. In some cases pension plans are handled by a trust company or trust department of a commercial bank (or even by a life insurance company) under a trust agreement. Except for significant differences in magnitude, such trusts do not differ from individual trusts already discussed. The agreement may contain any terms that are satisfactory to the company providing the pension plan and also to the bank, with consent in most cases required of the union or other representatives of the beneficiary employees.

3. In a number of cases the control of pension funds is left entirely in the hands of the company or of a committee representing both management and labor. Some funds in this category are invested wholly or predominantly in the securities of the company concerned. In other cases investments are diversified in the same way as might be done by a bank trustee.

In each of these cases the pension plan operates through established machinery and does not represent a new financial intermediary. Pensions are discussed separately primarily because of their relative newness and their tremendous impact on financial markets. They represent a significant increase in compulsory saving on the part of the economy, which in turn makes large sums of money available for business (or government) borrowing.

In 1964, for example, noninsured pension funds increased their net holdings of corporate stocks by $2.2 billion, an amount substantially greater than the $1.2 billion of stocks newly issued during the year. Their net purchases of corporate bonds amounted to $1.6 billion, which was more than 20 per cent of such bonds issued. These funds therefore represent a sizable new element in the economy, the effects of which are not yet thoroughly understood.

Other Trust Funds. Financial arrangements are in a constant state of flux, and our understanding of the importance of particular changes always lags somewhat behind the changes themselves. We may add here only that welfare funds established by employers or unions are another growing pool of assets and that governments are expanding their role in the pension and welfare field. Government trust funds in this area include those for old-age and survivors insurance; railroad employees' retirement; Federal, state, and local pension plans; unemployment insurance; and veterans' life insurance. The money in most of these funds is not available to business at the present time, but suggestions have been made that it might be used to finance home building and other types of private activity.

Charitable foundations are also expanding rapidly, but little is known about their investment policies.

Internal Financing. Another growing force in the investment market that should be mentioned—although its significance lies in the *absence* of any financial intermediary—is internal financing. Increasingly corporations are providing funds for capital expenditure out of their own operations. For this there are two quite different sources.

Depreciation allowances are a form of corporate saving that provide for the replacement of plant and equipment as it wears out. While such funds cannot finance new growth, they are an important element in the total demand for capital goods.

A second form of corporate saving comes from reinvested earnings—profits plowed back into the business instead of being paid out as dividends to stockholders. This represents forced saving on the part of the corporation's owners since they must forgo present income in exchange for an increase in the book value of their stock. The significance of this practice is that it allows the corporation to acquire funds without going to the capital market and without subjecting its decisions to the judgment of independent investors.

The relative importance of these two methods of financing is indicated in Table 18-1, where they are compared with the volume of new capital obtained by the issue of securities.

Table 18-1. Sources of Long-term Funds Available to Corporations, 1964
Billions of Dollars

Depreciation allowances			55.7*
Reinvested earnings:			
Profits before tax	64.8		
Less profits tax liability	27.6		
Profits after tax		37.2	
Less dividends		17.2	
Undistributed profits			19.9
Sale of securities:			
Bonds	10.9		
Stock	3.1		
Gross proceeds		14.0	
Less expenses, retirement of old issues, etc.		2.8	
Net new money			11.2
Total available funds			86.8

* Includes noncorporate business.
Source: *Federal Reserve Bulletin*, vol. 51, no. 9 (September, 1965), pp. 1315, 1336, 1337. Detail may not add to totals because of rounding.

Questions for Thought and Discussion

1. What is the basic difference between the instruments used for commercial and for investment credit?
2. Why is there such a large number of different financial intermediaries? Wouldn't it be simpler to combine them into a few basic institutions?
3. It is sometimes said that the record of investment companies is little better than the average of good stocks. Is this a good reason for a small investor to avoid the investment companies?
4. Why has there been such a tremendous rise in trust and pension funds in the last twenty years? Does this have anything to do with our rising standard of living? Does it have any effect on the prices of securities?
5. Do you see any advantages or any dangers in the growing ability of corporations to obtain funds through internal financing?
6. Why are stocks not considered credit instruments?

Selected Bibliography

American Institute of Banking: *Trust Business,* New York, 1946.
Bullock, Hugh: *The Story of Investment Companies,* Columbia University Press, New York, 1959.
Colean, Miles L., for the Mortgage Bankers Association: *Mortgage Companies: Their Place in the Financial Structure,* Prentice-Hall, Inc., for the Commission on Money and Credit, Englewood Cliffs, N.J., 1962.

Federal Reserve System: *Financing Small Business,* Report to the Committee on Banking and Currency and the Select Committee on Small Business, U.S. Congress, Apr. 11, 1958.

Harbrecht, Paul T.: *Pension Funds and Economic Power,* The Twentieth Century Fund, New York, 1959.

Investment Company Institute: *Management Investment Companies,* Prentice-Hall, Inc., for the Commission on Money and Credit, Englewood Cliffs, N.J., 1962.

Klaman, Saul B.: *The Postwar Rise of Mortgage Companies,* Occasional Paper 60, National Bureau of Economic Research, Inc., New York, 1959.

Machlup, Fritz: *The Stock Market, Credit, and Capital Formation,* trans. by Vera C. Smith, The Macmillan Company, New York, 1940.

New York Stock Exchange: *New York Stock Exchange Yearbook,* New York (annually).

Phelps, Clyde William: *The Role of Factoring in Modern Business Finance,* Commercial Credit Company, Baltimore, 1956.

Willis, H. Parker, and Jules I. Bogen: *Investment Banking,* rev. ed., Harper & Row, Publishers, Incorporated, New York, 1936.

See also references listed under Chapter 16.

Chapter 19 Government Credit Agencies

Neither have I money, nor commodity
To raise a present sum: therefore go forth;
Try what my credit can in Venice do.

The Merchant of Venice
Act I, scene 1, line 179

Our discussion of the financial marketplace up to this point has concentrated on nongovernmental financial institutions. The government itself is both a borrower and a lender as well as a guarantor of loans. Practically all financial institutions and many nonfinancial corporations and individuals purchase government securities of one kind or another. The Federal government is, in fact, the largest borrower in the country by a wide margin, and state and local governments also issue sizable amounts of securities. Table 19-1 shows the widespread importance of the Federal government as a borrower by indicating not only the kinds of securities outstanding, but also the amount of each held by different classes of owners.

The government is both an ultimate borrower in the sense that it must obtain funds from the public in order to defray its own expenses (by far the most important reason for borrowing) and also a financial intermediary when it or any of its financial agencies borrow for the purpose of making loans to others. The government may also use tax revenues for the latter purpose. Whichever way government lending agencies obtain their funds, the ultimate lenders are individual citizens, either as taxpayers or as lenders to the government.

In some cases states, and even localities, have set up loan agencies for specific purposes. These are generally of two types: loans to victims of calamity (such as flood or unemployment) to enable the borrower to get

Table 19-1. United States Government Debt by Ownership and Type of Security, December 31, 1964

Billions of Dollars

Holder	Total debt	Public issues: Marketable: Bills	Notes	Bonds	Convertible bonds	Nonmarketable bonds	Savings bonds	Special issues	Other*
All holders	318.7	56.5	59.0	97.0	3.0	2.3	49.7	46.1	5.1
U.S. government agencies and trust funds	60.6								
Federal Reserve banks	37.0								
Commercial banks	63.7								
Mutual savings banks	5.7								
Insurance companies	11.1								
Other corporations	19.7								
State and local governments	21.6								
Individuals	68.1								
Foreign and international	16.7								
Other†	14.5								

* Non-interest-bearing debt (including notes held by the International Monetary Fund, matured debt, United States notes, national bank notes, Federal Reserve bank notes, and savings stamps) and guaranteed securities.

† Includes savings and loan associations, dealers and brokers, nonprofit institutions, and corporate pension funds.

Source: *Federal Reserve Bulletin*, vol. 51, no. 5 (May, 1965), p. 720.

a new start and loans to businesses to induce them to settle in a particular area. We will not examine these lending activities further because of the great diversity of jurisdictions and the relatively minor nature of the total sum involved.

The Federal government, on the other hand, has become a major lender. Although its loans are made by a large number of different agencies, the greater number are concentrated in two fields: agriculture and real estate. In addition the Federal government makes miscellaneous loans to business and a rather large volume of loans to foreign countries. The various agencies involved are diagramed in Figure 19-1, which shows the major government loan agencies as of 1965. It must be remembered that Congress frequently changes its mind concerning the desirability of particular programs, and as a result new agencies are created, and old ones altered or discontinued. In many cases operations are shifted from one agency to another without basic change in the nature of the program. This chart is therefore more likely than most to become obsolete in a short time.

The government has entered the credit field only in response to what it felt was a need that was not adequately being met by private financial institutions. Most of the agencies now operating were established during the Depression of the thirties, when the shortcomings of the financial system were most apparent. Some now appear to be firmly established on a permanent basis, some have already fallen by the wayside, and others are still subject to debate as to their desirability, and their life therefore hangs in the balance.

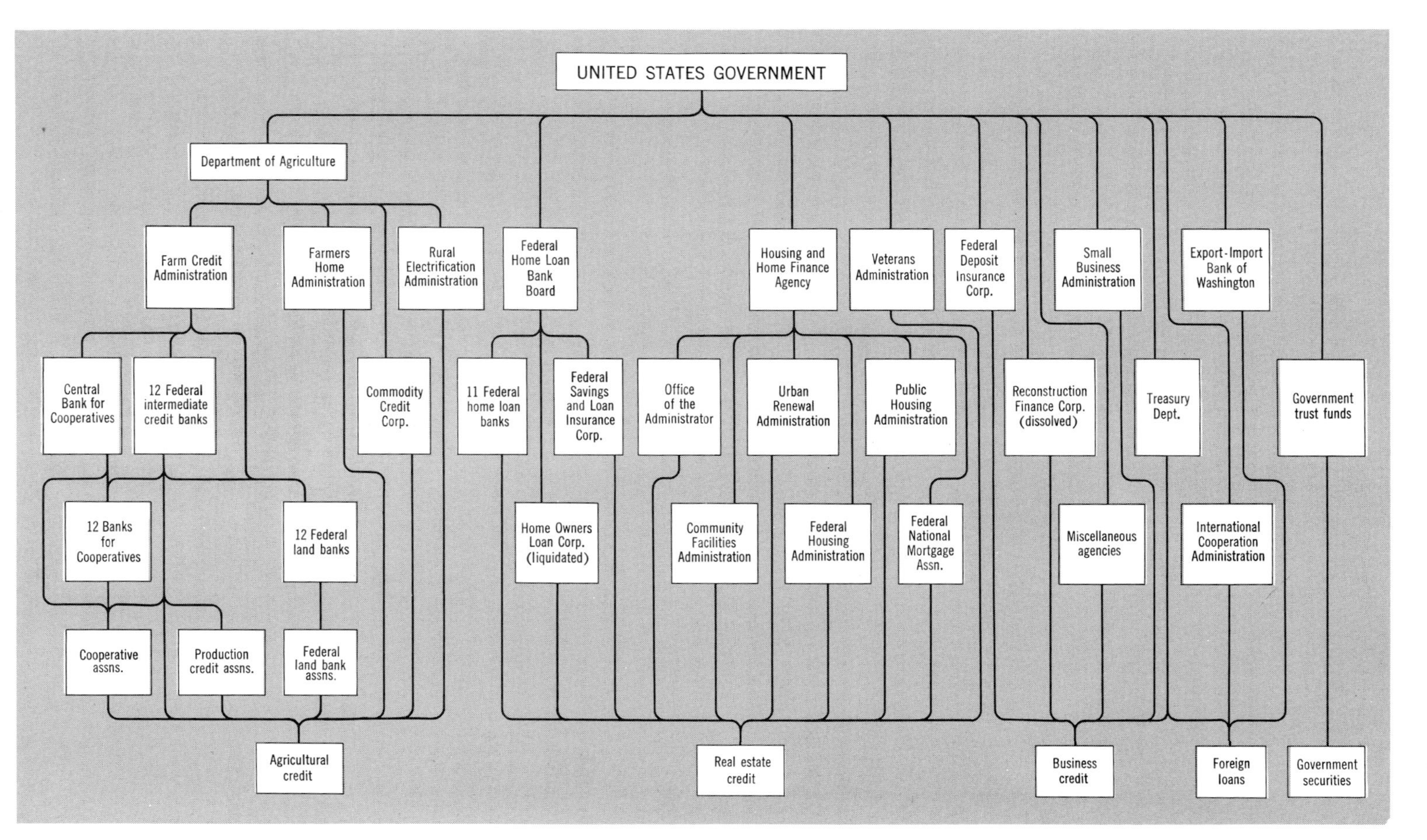

Figure 19-1. Federal government credit and credit-insurance agencies.

Agricultural Credit

Farmers have always been at somewhat of a disadvantage in obtaining loans. Their operations are so small, their income so uncertain, and their needs so large and sometimes so long-term that on the whole commercial banks have been a little reluctant to lend to any except the most solidly established farmers, and even for them interest rates have been fairly high. The government's Farm Credit Administration is designed to remedy this situation. It is composed of a group of agencies that will lend on long-, intermediate-, and short-term bases. The system originated piecemeal as needs became urgent. The Federal Land banks were established in 1916, the intermediate credit banks in 1923, and the production credit corporations and banks for cooperatives in 1933. Other agencies with specialized tasks have been added to the system at various times.

Banks for Cooperatives. The Central Bank for Cooperatives makes loans to large national and regional cooperative associations. The twelve banks for cooperatives—one of which is located in each of the farm credit districts (patterned somewhat along Federal Reserve lines but with different boundaries)—make loans to smaller associations. These banks provide funds to a cooperative association in which farmers band together for marketing farm products or for purchasing farm supplies on a joint basis. Loans are made against commodities held by the association, as well as for operating-capital purposes and for the acquisition of market facilities. The activity of these banks has not been very great.

Production Credit Corporations. There are twelve regional production credit corporations, set up along the same geographical lines as the banks for cooperatives. These corporations supervise some five hundred local production credit associations, which are voluntary organizations of farmers who purchase stock in, and elect the directors of, the association. The purpose of the associations is almost exclusively to provide short-term credit to member farmers for any legitimate need connected with farm operation. Loans are generally made for a period of less than a year, though some loans for capital improvement may have a maturity of up to seven years. The association obtains its funds primarily by discounting the notes it receives from its borrowers with the Federal intermediate credit bank of the district.

Federal Intermediate Credit Banks. The twelve Federal intermediate credit banks are a source of funds for several other agencies. In addition to discounting notes of production credit associations, they provide funds (generally by discounting paper arising from loans) for the banks for cooperatives, Federal Land banks, commercial banks that make loans to farmers, agricultural credit corporations, livestock loan companies, farmers' cooperatives, and other institutions of this sort. Most of their discounting is on paper with less than a year's maturity, but some notes run up to seven years. They obtain funds mainly from the sale to the public of their own short-term debenture bonds.

Federal Land Banks. The twelve Federal land banks, on similar district lines, make long-term loans against first mortgages on farm property. They operate through national farm loan associations, which own all the stock of the land banks. The loan associations are in turn owned by member borrowers, each buying an amount of stock equal to 5 per cent of his loan. Loans may not exceed 65 per cent of the value of the farm or ranch. They are made not only for the purchase of property, but for any legitimate agricultural use. Interest is charged at the rate of 5 to 6 per cent. Funds are obtained by the land banks through the sale of their own bonds to the public. Since the land banks do not use government funds, they are sometimes not included among the government lending agencies, but their organizational connection with the Farm Credit Administration would seem to qualify them for such inclusion.

Farmers Home Administration. The Farmers Home Administration was established in 1946 as a successor to the Farm Security Administration and the Resettlement Administration. Its primary objective is to aid in the maintenance, rehabilitation, and improvement of the family-size farm, and in order to achieve this goal it not only makes loans to farmers but also provides planning services for its borrowers.

Loans are made for almost any legitimate need of the farmer, including the purchase or improvement of a farm; purchase of livestock, machinery, and supplies; construction and repair of farm homes; and even meeting farm family living needs. The Administration also insures mortgage loans made by private lenders. Interest ranges from 3 to 5 per cent, and the repayment period is from one to forty years depending on the type of loan. Loans are usually made through the county agent's office[1] and are supervised by a committee of three local residents. The Farmers Home Administration is also responsible for supervising the disaster loan program of aid to farmers who are victims of flood, drought, or other catastrophe.

Rural Electrification Administration. In 1935 it was stated that Sweden had electricity in a larger proportion of its pigpens than the United States had in its farmhouses. The Rural Electrification Administration was established in that year in an attempt to rectify the situation. The REA encourages the development of central power stations and distributing lines in areas where no such service is available. It will make loans of up to 100 per cent of the cost of construction of electrical facilities, with preference given to public agencies and cooperatives. Loans may be made for a maximum of thirty-five years and are currently subject to a 2 per cent interest charge. In addition to

[1] Nearly all agricultural counties in the country have a county agent at the county seat; he is responsible for the many activities of the Department of Agriculture and the state agricultural services at the local level.

financing, the REA provides engineering, financial, and legal advice. The low interest rate has been the subject of considerable debate since the government must itself pay more than this to get the funds that it lends.

The REA also makes funds available through power distributors for financing the wiring of individual farms and the purchase of electrical equipment and, interestingly enough, plumbing supplies. In 1949 the scope of REA was extended to include telephone organizations. It has been estimated that in its first quarter-century of existence the REA made loans that provided 1½ million miles of electrical transmission lines, which brought electricity to almost five million families.

Commodity Credit Corporation. The CCC is a government corporation with its own board of directors and a capital of $100 million. It is authorized to borrow up to $14.5 billion to meet the cost of its programs. Its primary activity at the present time is agricultural price support. The CCC makes "nonrecourse" loans to farmers against stored crops that Congress has included in the support program. These loans are made at a price determined by the Secretary of Agriculture within limits set by Congress. They frequently exceed the market price of the commodities (this being the purpose of support), and if the farmer doesn't want to repay the loan, the CCC merely takes title to the crop. Fundamentally this is an indirect device for buying crops from the farmer in order to reduce the amount coming to the market. Although technically a loan is made, it is not expected that such loans will be repaid.

The CCC also makes bona fide loans for the construction of farm storage facilities. The amount of this type of financing is not great.

Summary. The loans outstanding under the various Department of Agriculture activities total over $15 billion, of which $3 billion represent "loans" of the CCC. A breakdown of these loans by categories is shown in Table 19-2 along with other government lending activities. In spite of the number of government agencies engaged in providing credit to farmers and the variety of their programs, government loans today represent only one-third of total agricultural credit extended by all lenders.

Real Estate Credit

The government first went into the real estate mortgage business during the Depression in order to bail out homeowners who were unable to keep up payments on their mortgages. Later the emphasis shifted to the stimulation of additional home building, both public and private. Except for the incidental activities of the Veterans Administration in the field of veterans' housing, the government's real estate activities are concentrated in two agencies: the Federal Home Loan Bank Board and the Housing and Home Finance Agency. These in turn have jurisdiction over a number of constituent agencies.

Table 19-2. Loans Outstanding of Federal and Federally Sponsored Agencies, December 31, 1964
Millions of Dollars

Federal agencies:				
Loans to agriculture:				
Rural Electrification Administration		3,956		
Farmers Home Administration:				
Farm mortgage loans	1,029			
Other loans	705	1,734		
Commodity Credit Corporation:				
Crop, livestock, and commodity loans	2,802			
Storage facilities and equipment loans	44	2,846	8,536	
Loans on real estate:				
Federal Housing Administration		169		
Federal National Mortgage Association		2,511		
Federal Savings and Loan Insurance Corporation		133		
Housing and Home Finance Administrator		82		
Public Housing Administration		1		
Veterans Administration:				
Mortgage loans	1,242			
Other loans	556	1,798	4,694	
Loans to industry:				
Maritime loans: Commerce Department		114		
Area Redevelopment Fund, Commerce Department		78		
Defense production loans: Interior, Treasury, and Defense Departments		33		
Small Business Administration		902		
Other		40	1,167	
Loans to education:				
Health, Education, and Welfare Department:				
Loans to institutions	6			
Loans to students	471	477		
Housing and Home Finance Administrator:				
College housing loans		1,824	2,301	
Loans to states and territories:				
Housing and Home Finance Administrator		407		
Other		319	726	
Foreign loans:				
Agency for International Development		3,608		
Export-Import Bank		3,472		
Treasury Department		3,154		
State Department		110		
Defense Department		56		
Commerce Department		3	10,404	
Other loans:				
General Services Administration, credit sales		103		
Bureau of Indian Affairs		23	126	27,954
Federally sponsored agencies:*				
Cooperative farm credit system:				
Banks for cooperatives		757		
Production credit associations		2,533		
Federal intermediate credit banks		134†		
Federal land banks		3,516	6,940	
Federal National Mortgage Association:				
Secondary market operations			1,940	
Federal home loan banks:				
Advances to members			5,325	14,205
Total				42,159

* These are agencies that obtain funds in substantial amounts from capital subscribed by members or from securities sold directly to the public.
† Not including $2,371 million of loans to production credit associations and banks for cooperatives.
Sources: Adapted from *Treasury Bulletin*, April, 1965, pp. 132–134; *31st Annual Report of the Farm Credit Administration on the Work of the Cooperative Credit System, 1963–64*, p. 66; *Federal Reserve Bulletin*, vol. 51, no. 9 (September, 1965), p. 1314.

Home Owners' Loan Corporation. Although the HOLC has been liquidated, it deserves mention for the pioneer work that it did, with great success, during the Depression. It was organized in 1933 as an emergency agency to refinance mortgages of distressed homeowners. This it did by giving them longer and more liberal terms and by providing for monthly amortization of principal, then a relatively new technique in home loans. It obtained funds from a treasury capital subscription and by selling bonds to the public. In a three-year period it made over a million loans totaling $3½ billion. It ceased making loans after 1936 and by 1951 had sold all remaining mortgages to private financial institutions.

In view of the fact that the HOLC provided funds only to borrowers who were already in difficulty, it is interesting to note that the Corporation met all its operating expenses, paid back all bonds with interest, retired the treasury capital subscription, and returned to the Treasury on liquidation a surplus of $14 million.

Federal Home Loan Bank System. The Federal Home Loan Bank System is primarily concerned with supervision of savings and loan associations and with providing funds to them and to other mortgage lenders. In structure and in some of its operations it bears much resemblance to the Federal Reserve; it has a central Board at the top, a regional organization of eleven banks, and a foundation of member institutions.

Federal Home Loan Bank Board. The board consists of three members appointed by the President for a four-year term. It has supervisory authority over the whole system.

Federal Home Loan Banks. There are eleven banks, each with twelve or more directors. Four directors are appointed by the Federal Home Loan Bank Board, and the others are elected by the member institutions. Original capital was provided by the Treasury, but over time this subscription has been repaid, and the banks are now owned entirely by the member institutions, each of which is required to subscribe to stock in an amount equal to 1 per cent of its outstanding mortgage loans. The banks may also accept deposits from members and from Federal agencies and may sell their own bonds or debentures to the public.

Member Institutions. Membership in the Federal Home Loan bank of their district is open to savings and loan associations, savings and cooperative banks, and insurance companies. All Federal savings and loan associations are required to join, and other institutions are invited to do so. There are today some five thousand members, mostly savings and loan associations.

The Federal Home Loan Bank Board charters and supervises the Federal savings and loan associations, but the major purpose of the System is not so much control as it is financial assistance. Long-term advances to members, not exceeding ten years, are secured by first mortgages or government securities. Short-term loans of thirty days to one year are unsecured. The majority of loans are short-term.

Federal Savings and Loan Insurance Corporation. The FSLIC is also under the jurisdiction of the Federal Home Loan Bank Board. It was created in 1934 to avert the avalanche of failures of savings and loan associations. Its operation is similar to that of the FDIC, although it is a completely separate agency. It insures individual share accounts up to $10,000, charging a premium of $1/12$ per cent of the insured association's aggregate liabilities. As indicated earlier, this insurance protects the shareowner against ultimate failure of the association, but since his investment in a savings and loan association represents an owner's equity rather than a creditor's claim, the insurance cannot guarantee that he will get his money when he wants it.

The FSLIC may make loans or contributions to associations in financial difficulty, may purchase some of their assets in order to provide liquid funds, or may arrange for the merger of associations in order to forestall the insolvency of one of them. In case of actual default, payment is made either in cash or by transferring the insured member's account to another sound association in the community. The Treasury contributed the corporation's original capital of $100 million, but this amount has now been retired.

Housing and Home Finance Agency. The Housing and Home Finance Agency was created in 1947 to consolidate the work of several other agencies and in its short life has itself gone through a number of changes in structure. The Agency, under supervision of an Administrator appointed by the President, has wide powers in the field of housing, including technical research, planning, direct subsidies for public housing, and a number of different types of loans. Most lending activities are carried on by the six constituent organizations (see Figure 19-1).

Office of the Administrator. The Administrator, along with general supervisory functions, is in charge of the work of the *Voluntary Home Mortgage Credit Program.* This program, established by the Housing Act of 1954, helps obtain mortgage credit for FHA-insured and VA-guaranteed loans in areas where such credit is difficult to obtain. It is specifically charged with aid to minority groups in this regard, but it is also more generally concerned with the whole question of the adequacy of funds available for mortgage loans.

Community Facilities Administration. This agency makes loans to colleges to help finance the construction of housing for students and faculty and provides loans and advances to state and local governments for needed public works. It also provides loans to agencies building rental housing for elderly persons.

Urban Renewal Administration. This agency makes loans and grants to local public bodies for slum clearance and redevelopment as part of its extensive work in this field.

Public Housing Administration. The PHA is concerned primarily with low-rent public housing under the Public Housing Act of 1937, as amended. The act provides for Federal financial assistance to local housing authorities for construction and operation of low-rent housing in order to keep rentals within the means of low-income families. The greater part of the funds are direct grants, and only a small amount represent loans.

All the preceding programs of the Housing and Home Finance Agency are supported directly by congressional appropriation.

Federal National Mortgage Association. The Federal National Mortgage Association, familiarly known as Fanny Mae, does not itself make mortgage loans but acts rather as a purchaser of FHA-insured and VA-guaranteed mortgages that the original makers wish to sell. It thus provides a secondary market for mortgages and increases their liquidity. In this way it encourages lenders to make available more mortgage money than they would otherwise be willing to invest in this type of security. Fanny Mae will also sell mortgages from its portfolio when the market is ready to absorb them. Such sales are often made in large blocks to institutional investors. The Association also provides direct financing for special housing programs as authorized by the President or Congress.

Fanny Mae obtains funds from the sale of its own bonds to the public as well as from congressional appropriation.

Federal Housing Administration. The FHA, probably the best known of the governmental real estate credit agencies, was established in 1934 to help avoid a complete collapse of the mortgage market by insuring lenders against loss on new mortgage loans. It is not itself a lending agency, but it guarantees loans made by others.

The most important function of FHA is the insurance of mortgage loans on one- to four-family homes. The property must meet certain construction specifications of FHA and will be appraised by an FHA inspector to determine its fair value. Current terms (1965), subject to change by administrative regulation, include the following provisions:

1. Maximum mortgage coverage on a one- or two-family house is $25,000, with higher limits for multifamily dwellings.
2. For owner-occupied homes the maximum amount of the mortgage is 97 per cent of the first $15,000, 90 per cent of the next $5,000, and 75 per cent

of the value above that amount, the total value to be determined by FHA appraisal.

3. Maximum length of mortgage is thirty years. All mortgages must be amortized by regular monthly payments.

4. Maximum interest rate is 5¼ per cent plus ½ per cent FHA insurance premium.

5. Monthly payments must include funds to pay fire insurance premiums, taxes, and special assessments.

Special terms are available for replacement of homes damaged by major disasters and for homes occupied by a serviceman on active duty.

If a mortgage is defaulted, the mortgagee (lending institution) must foreclose within one year and turn the property over to FHA in return for a sum equal to the unpaid principal plus other incidental claims. The FHA will attempt to reimburse itself by sale of the property.

The FHA also insures a number of other types of loans for home improvements ("Title I loans"), cooperative housing, rental housing, trailer courts, urban renewal, housing for the elderly, nursing homes, experimental housing, and armed service housing.

Veterans Administration. Under the Servicemen's Readjustment Act of 1944 (the GI Bill of Rights) the Veterans Administration is authorized to guarantee mortgages to veterans in a manner similar to that of the FHA but on somewhat more liberal terms. Current (1965) provisions are:

1. The total amount of the mortgage is not restricted; the VA will guarantee payment up to 60 per cent of the loan, but not more than $7,500.

2. A minimum down payment is not required.

3. Maximum length of mortgage is thirty years (forty years for farms).

4. Maximum interest rate is 5¼ per cent.[2]

Most World War II veterans are no longer eligible for this program, and it will be completely phased out by 1975.

One of the difficulties with the government-insured mortgage program has been that in periods of generally rising interest rates, Congress has been reluctant to raise the maximum interest rates on insured loans. As the differential between these rates and those on conventional mortgages has widened, banks

[2] In addition to its mortgage activity the Veterans Administration guarantees loans for other purposes, including farm and business loans. Only a small proportion of loans guaranteed by the VA fall in this category.

Where private lending facilities are not available, the VA makes direct loans to veterans. Almost $1 billion has been made available under this program.

and other lenders have become more and more reluctant to make these low-rate loans, and at such times VA-guaranteed mortgages in particular have become almost impossible to get.

Government-guaranteed mortgages have never reached 50 per cent of the total outstanding mortgages on one- to four-family homes (compare Table 17-3).

Business Credit

While the Federal government has made a concerted effort to tackle the special problems of finance in agriculture and real estate, its efforts in other areas have been of a more sporadic nature, limited to a few widely scattered fields where particular problems arose. For the most part business lending by the government was initiated during the Depression of the thirties and represented an attempt to get business back on its feet at a time when banks were unable or unwilling to take the necessary risks. As the need for this type of help has declined, the government has tended to withdraw its efforts.

Federal Deposit Insurance Corporation. The FDIC is one of the few permanent agencies that have developed in this area, and its work is insurance rather than lending. Its activities have already been discussed.

Reconstruction Finance Corporation. The RFC was established in 1932 for the purpose of shoring up the sagging banking structure by making loans to, and purchasing preferred stock of, commercial banks. It also made extensive loans to railroads to maintain support for their bond values in the market. Later the RFC became a jack-of-all-trades in the world of finance. It made loans to local governments for drainage, irrigation, and other self-liquidating public works. It made loans to, and provided original capital for, several other government financial agencies such as the Federal land banks, Fanny Mae, CCC, REA, and the Export-Import Bank. It has also made loans to businesses that could not obtain financing from banks. During World War II many such loans were made for construction of war plants, and in the postwar period the RFC has made loans to the victims of floods and other disasters.

Although there is no doubt that its early activities were quite useful in providing support for the financial system and in pioneering some types of lending activities that banks have now taken over, it has always been criticized as undue meddling by government in a field that many people feel should be left to private enterprise. The criticism increased after World War II, particularly as a result of one or two questionable loans, and the RFC was abolished in 1957.

Small Business Administration. The purpose of the Small Business Administration is to help the little fellow in order to maintain traditional competition. This it does through many channels: conducting research, giving advice, and making loans. The last function is carried out by the Loan Policy Board, in some respects along lines similar to those laid down by the RFC. Loans may be made for plant construction, the acquisition of machinery or supplies, or general working-capital purposes. Loans may also be made to aid victims of floods or other disasters.

In 1958 Congress encouraged regional autonomy in this area by authorizing the establishment of private investment companies to provide capital funds to small business. The Small Business Administration may make loans to these companies as well as to development companies under state or local government auspices.

Other Loans. Scattered through a number of government agencies are provisions for special types of government loans. Among these are loans made by the Bureau of Reclamation for irrigation and reclamation projects; credit by the General Services Administration to buyers of surplus property; insurance by the Maritime Administration of loans for ship construction; loans and guarantees of the Defense Department to support military production; loans made by the Veterans Administration for a number of miscellaneous purposes; loans of the Office of Education to colleges for equipment and for support of student loan programs; loans by the Bureau of Commercial Fisheries for fishing vessels and equipment; loans of the Public Health Service for construction of hospitals; loans by the Bureau of Indian Affairs to support tribal business enterprises; loans of the Office of Mineral Exploration to aid in the discovery of mineral resources; guarantees by the Department of Commerce of loans for the purchase of airplanes; and loans of the Area Redevelopment Administration to private enterprises to finance the creation of permanent employment opportunities and to communities to provide public facilities. Many of these smaller programs are quite ephemeral in nature.

Foreign Loans

Although foreign loans are sometimes considered more in the realm of politics than of economics, a brief word should be said about the fairly extensive activities of the government in this field.

Export-Import Bank of Washington. The Eximbank is another Depression concern, created in 1934 to increase the foreign trade of the United States by making loans to importers or exporters either here or abroad. Loans are made to finance trade directly or for the construction of facilities that would result in increased trade. The Eximbank obtains its funds from the Federal Treasury.

Agency for International Development. The Agency for International Development was created in 1961 as the successor to the International Cooperation Administration and its forerunners to supervise the government's various foreign assistance programs. Under its lending powers it makes loans for economic development and for supporting assistance to aid in the stabilization of foreign countries. Loans are made both to foreign governments and to private enterprises, in both dollars and foreign currencies. Currently they are made only in Latin America (under the Alliance for Progress program), Asia, and Africa. For a fee the AID will guarantee certain types of investment abroad against inconvertibility, expropriation, and war risk; under special circumstances even broader guarantee coverage is available. The money for AID programs comes from Congressional appropriation.

International Agencies. Through its membership in the Inter-American Development Bank, the International Bank for Reconstruction and Development, the International Development Association, the International Finance Corporation, and the International Monetary Fund, the government supports and participates in the lending activities of these agencies. They will be discussed in more detail in Part Nine. The Treasury and the Federal Reserve have also entered into certain lending agreements directly with foreign governments and central banks.

Government Trust Funds

In a very different category from the type of government financing so far discussed are the government trust funds, which, like private pension plans, have grown significantly in the last few decades.

The Federal government has a very large stake in pension funds through the Old Age and Survivors Insurance program as well as the Railroad Retirement Act and pension plans for its own employees (see Table 17-1). In addition most states and many municipalities have pension provisions for civil servants. Whenever these plans are funded (that is, accumulated over time rather than relying on payments out of current taxes), they represent sizable sums of money available for investment. The Federal pension and insurance programs, for instance, have assets of over $53 billion, exclusively cash and government securities. State and local plans also invest almost entirely in either Federal or local government securities.

These funds, therefore, are not available to private borrowers. In some respects they represent primarily bookkeeping transactions in which the government owes itself money. Since the funds are separately managed, however, they do exert some pressure on the government securities market, for when the government sells securities to one of its trust funds, this means that it does not have to sell them to someone else. The trust funds are therefore not entirely neutral.

There has been some discussion of the desirability of using these funds to support other sectors of the economy (for instance, by the purchase of mortgages), but so far this has not been done. Like private pension funds they represent a new influence of great magnitude in the money market whose final role has not yet been clearly defined.

On this note of slight uncertainty we will close our survey of financial institutions with a repetition of the observation that the financial marketplace is a kaleidoscope of changing patterns and colors that hardly holds still long enough to have its picture taken. Old ideas and methods must adapt themselves to new conditions, and we must be continually on the alert if we wish to keep abreast of current developments.

Questions for Thought and Discussion

The technical details of operation of the many agencies described in this chapter are undoubtedly too much for anyone not directly engaged in the field to remember in their entirety. What is important is an understanding of the general nature of government participation in the financial marketplace.

1. What are the basic areas in which the Federal government makes loans? Why has it chosen these areas rather than others?

2. Is it desirable for the government to engage in as much lending activity as it does? What Federal lending agencies do you think should be abolished? Are there other areas where you think the government should establish new lending agencies?

3. If agricultural credit extended by government agencies is only one-third of the total, does this suggest that it is not particularly important?

4. Do you think that all government lending agencies should obtain their funds from the public (by issue of bonds or capital stock) rather than from congressional appropriations?

5. If the HOLC was able to make a profit on its handling of sour mortgages, why couldn't the banks that originally made these mortgages simply have held them to maturity?

Selected Bibliography

Colean, Miles L.: *The Impact of Government on Real Estate Finance in the United States,* National Bureau of Economics Research, Inc., New York, 1950.

Commission on Money and Credit: *Federal Credit Agencies,* Prentice-Hall, Inc., Englewood Cliffs, N.J., 1963.

———: *Federal Credit Programs,* Prentice-Hall, Inc., Englewood Cliffs, N.J., 1963.

Export-Import Bank of Washington: *Semi-annual Reports*

Farm Credit Administration: *Annual Reports.*

Federal Home Loan Bank Board: *The Federal Home Loan Bank System, 1932–1952,* 1952.

Fuller, Douglas R.: *Government Financing of Private Enterprise,* Stanford University Press, Stanford, Calif., 1948.

Gilmore, Donald R.: *Developing the "Little" Economies: A Survey of Area Development Programs in the United States,* Committee for Economic Development, New York, 1960.

Harriss, C. Lowell: *History and Policies of the Home Owners' Loan Corporation,* National Bureau of Economic Research, Inc., New York, 1951.

Housing and Home Finance Agency: *Annual Reports.*

Jones, Jesse H., with Edward Angly: *Fifty Billion Dollars: My Thirteen Years with the RFC (1932–1945),* The Macmillan Company, New York, 1951.

Jones, Lawrence A., and David Durand: *Mortgage Lending Experience in Agriculture,* Princeton University Press for the National Bureau of Economic Research, Princeton, N.J., 1954.

Pugh, Olin C.: *The Export-Import Bank of Washington,* The University of South Carolina Press, Columbia, S.C., 1957.

Saulnier, R. J., Harold G. Halcrow, and Neil H. Jacoby: *Federal Lending and Loan Insurance,* Princeton University Press for the National Bureau of Economic Research, Princeton, N.J., 1958.

U.S. Congress, House Committee on Banking and Currency: *Federal Credit Programs,* 2 vols., 1964.

Part Five
Monetary Systems

Chapter 20 Foreign Banking Systems

There are more things in heaven and earth, Horatio,
Than are dreamt of in your philosophy.

Hamlet
Act I, scene 5, line 166

Our attention so far has been directed primarily to the banking system of the United States. But our economy is in many respects unique. Indeed no two nations have identical problems, and even when problems are similar, different solutions may be used. Lest we become too parochial, thinking that our system is the only reasonable one, we will do well to examine, if only briefly, a few other types of banking organizations. A look at the experience of others may also help us to rethink the desirability of the institutions that are so close to us that we have difficulty in evaluating them effectively.

Great Britain

Great Britain had developed her financial institutions to a very high level of technical perfection by the nineteenth century. Some writers even suggest that Britain's preeminence as a nation was due in good part to the facility with which her financial institutions were able, on the one hand, to assemble the small savings of the general populace so that they could be made readily available for investment and, on the other, to provide procedures by which payments, both domestic and foreign, could be made speedily, easily, and safely. It is not an accident that London was, and to a great extent still is, the financial center of the world: she was equipped to do the job better than her competitors.

Branch Banking. One of the outstanding characteristics of British banking, when compared with that of the United States, is the small number of banks. Although there are eleven London clearing banks and eighteen other banks doing a specialized or local business, by far the greater part of the commercial banking in England is carried on by the "Big Five." [1] Among them they operate over nine thousand branches throughout Great Britain. In addition to the general advantages of branch banking discussed in Chapter 15, the cohesiveness of the British system makes clearing simplicity itself. Those checks that cannot be cleared on the books of a single bank through its branch system can be handled through the London clearing house, though there are also clearing houses in other large cities that avoid the delay of sending local checks through London. There is no need for correspondents or for interdistrict clearing as we know it. Since the Bank of England is a member of the London Clearing House, all net settlements are made by entries on its books, thereby affecting the deposit accounts of the clearing banks.

One interesting practice that the British have added to check collection is the "crossed check." Such a check, identified by parallel lines across its face, cannot be cashed but must be presented for payment through clearing. Such a procedure guards against loss due to theft of checks in the mails or otherwise.

Deposits and Loans. British banks accept three kinds of deposits. Balances on *current account* are payable on demand and are similar to our demand deposits. Balances on *deposit account* are payable only on notice, normally of twenty-one days. They carry interest at a rate usually 2 per cent below the discount rate of the Bank of England. *Fixed deposits* are for longer periods and carry a higher rate of interest. They customarily involve large sums and are individually negotiated, thus differing from our savings deposits. The savings business is left to savings banks, including the Post Office Savings Bank, similar to those in the United States.

Loans by British banks differ from ours primarily in that they stick closer to the real-bills doctrine (except for their holdings of government securities). They make almost no long-term loans. They also do less negotiation of individual short-term loans, emphasizing instead the purchase of open-market bills (such as bank acceptances).

Another British practice strange to United States banks is the *overdraft*. This is a device whereby a bank will honor checks written by a customer against an account that has no balance. This can be done only within the limits of a line of credit approved by the bank in advance. It is obviously a loan, and interest is charged. It differs in the fact that the borrower incurs the obligation only at the time and to the extent that the funds are actually used, and it is repaid whenever the balance is brought back up to a positive figure. There is no fixed amount or maturity. The obvious advantage to the

[1] Barclays Bank, Lloyds Bank, Midland Bank, National Provincial Bank, and Westminster Bank.

businessman, in addition to the lack of red tape, is that he doesn't pay interest on any amount not actually used.

United States banks are just beginning to develop overdraft facilities. Banks in Boston, Philadelphia, and New York have already instituted such plans, and others are bound to follow. Strangely enough the first such arrangements were in the field of consumer rather than business loans.

Reserves. Until recently there was nothing in British law requiring banks to maintain reserves, but just like the goldsmiths or any other bank they had to have sufficient funds available to meet the demands of their depositors. Since World War II the customary level of reserves, which consist of cash in vault plus deposits with the Bank of England, has been about 8 per cent. Banks will let their reserves fall below the customary level when funds are needed to meet withdrawals, but they will not make new loans until that level is restored.

On several occasions the Bank of England, after consultation with the Treasury, has entered into informal agreements with the banks in which they have undertaken to maintain a certain amount of specified assets or to refrain from extending loans beyond certain limits, and these arrangements have had almost the force of law. In 1960, for the first time, the Bank of England required the London clearing banks to make special deposits with it, but the amount involved was only 2 per cent of gross deposits. This is perhaps the first step toward a system of regularly required reserves.

Other Banking Institutions. Partly a cause, and partly a result, of London's importance as a world financial center is her varied array of institutions specializing in international trade and its financial instruments.

Great Britain permits foreign banks to establish branches within her territory on the same terms as domestic banks. These foreign branches tend to specialize in the foreign exchange of their own countries. Particularly important in this group are the dominion and colonial banks, which maintain large offices in London. In the other direction Britain has set up specialized banks to engage in overseas trade, and several of these have branches all over the world.

Another distinctive institution is the *merchant banker,* a descendant of the old merchant adventurer, who is now highly respectable and engaged primarily in accepting bills of exchange and other related foreign exchange transactions.

The *bill broker* is a specialist in handling bills of exchange. He may act purely as a broker in executing orders for customers ("running broker") or may hold bills for his own account ("discount house"). Because of the large volume of foreign bills in London, both institutions have occupied a key place in the London money market.

The Bank of England. We have already seen how the Bank of England emerged, almost by accident, as England's most important bank and how the Bank Act of 1844 cut its operations in half by separating the issue and banking departments. The only significant legal action affecting the Bank in the past century was its nationalization in 1946, which authorized the government to buy the Bank's outstanding stock from its stockholders and consequently to appoint its directors but which resulted in no real change in its operation.

The Bank is managed by a governor, a deputy governor, and sixteen directors (collectively called the *court of directors*), appointed by the Queen. It is indicative of the small practical changes produced by nationalization that the first court appointed included the former governor, deputy governor, and thirteen of the former directors.

Except for a very few matters the law neither defines nor limits the actions of the Bank. Its position in the banking system is therefore almost exclusively the result of experience, experiment, and tradition. Under the 1946 act the Treasury is given the authority to issue directives to the Bank when it appears, after consultation with the governor, that such action is in the public interest. The Bank is also empowered to give directives to bankers for the same purpose. In practice both powers have been used sparingly, and voluntary cooperation (moral suasion) has been the general rule.

Currency. The issue department of the Bank is now the sole source of paper currency in England, while the Treasury is responsible for coin.[2] The Bank Act of 1844 allowed the Bank to issue £14 million of its own notes without any gold backing (called the *fiduciary issue*). Any notes in excess of this amount were required to have a 100 per cent gold reserve. Thus there was a fractional gold reserve against paper currency, but the fraction varied over time. As other banks gave up their note issue, the fiduciary issue of the Bank of England was increased.

During and after World War I the British government issued its own paper notes to supplement those of the Bank of England. In 1928 these were taken over by the Bank, and its fiduciary issue was raised to £260 million. At the same time the Bank was authorized to raise the fiduciary issue at any time with the consent of the Treasury. Such increases had pushed the figure to £580 million by the outbreak of World War II, at which time the Bank was required to transfer almost all its gold to the Exchange Equalisation Account.[3] This action made practically the whole issue fiduciary—backed by government bonds and a small quantity of silver—and has been followed by several increases in this unbacked issue since that time.

The position of the Bank in 1964 is shown by the balance sheet reproduced in Table 20-1. This shows clearly that although there is still a fractional gold

[2] Private banks still issue notes in Scotland and Northern Ireland. Their total amounted to £127 million in 1964.

[3] Discussed briefly in Chap. 37.

Table 20-1. Bank of England Statement, December 30, 1964
Millions of Pounds Sterling; £1 = $2.80

Issue department				
Assets		*Liabilities*		
Government debt	11.0	Notes issued:		
Government securities	2,788.0	In circulation		2,732.8
Other securities	0.7	In banking department		67.6
Coin (other than gold)	0.3			
Fiduciary-issue	2,800.0			
Gold	0.4			
	2,800.4			2,800.4
Banking department				
Assets		*Liabilities*		
Coin	0.8	Deposits:		
Notes	67.6	Public (government)		13.4
Government securities	214.7	Other		352.3
Other securities	100.8	Total deposits		365.7
		Capital	14.6	
		Rest (surplus)	3.6	18.2
	383.9			383.9

Source: Bank of England, "An Account . . . for the Week . . . ending Wednesday, the 30th Day of December, 1964."

reserve behind England's paper currency, the fraction is less than 1/50 of 1 per cent. For practical purposes it is no exaggeration to say that Britain has a pure managed paper currency whose volume is controlled entirely by the administrative discretion of the Bank of England in consultation with the Treasury.

Gold. Since the Bank of England is under no obligation to buy or sell gold against currency, there is no reason for it to have any gold at all. For international payments it is just as satisfactory, perhaps more so, to have the country's gold held by the Exchange Equalisation Account, whose primary responsibility is the orderly conduct of foreign exchange transactions.

Great Britain, unlike the United States, does not prohibit the holding, import, or export of gold. As a result the world's largest gold market is again (after an extended absence due to the war) in London. Prices, however, can hardly vary much from the official United States price, since our Treasury stands ready to buy and sell gold at a fixed price, which Britain will not do. The pound sterling does have a legal gold content, but under present regulations this means merely that foreigners (not British residents) can exchange pounds for any other currency they want at the official gold parity of the currencies involved. It does not permit them to get gold itself. In this respect Great Britain is even further from the gold standard than the United States is.

Monetary Control. The traditional instrument of monetary control in England is the discount rate, called *bank rate*. This is the rate at which the Bank of England will make loans. The Bank does not normally lend to commercial banks, however, but makes bank rate effective somewhat indirectly through the bill market.

Bill brokers hold large quantities of commercial bills and customarily borrow funds from the commercial banks in order to finance their portfolios. These loans, either on demand (call loans) or at short term, carry interest rates lower than the yield of the bills held by the brokers. This encourages them to borrow as much as possible. When banks need additional funds, they call these loans. The brokers then turn to the Bank of England for loans, paying bank rate. If the Bank of England wishes to put pressure on the market, a rise in bank rate will induce the brokers to dispose of bills in order to pay off their loans, thus tending to push bill prices down and interest rates up. The mechanism differs, but the effect is similar to a rise in discount rate by the Federal Reserve Banks.

As foreign financing in London declined as a result of depression and war, the bill brokers and other financial institutions turned more and more to treasury bills to fill the vacuum created by the disappearance of commercial bills. As the government-bill market expanded, the Bank of England increased its holdings of such bills and simultaneously stepped up its open-market operations as a supplement to control by bank rate. Open-market sales are, in fact, a device by which money can be withdrawn from the market in such a way as to force brokers "into the bank," thus making bank rate effective.

We have already mentioned Britain's slight movement toward the use of legal reserve requirements. She has also imposed direct controls sporadically, particularly on installment contracts.

British control devices are thus very similar to ours in basic principle. Perhaps the greatest difference lies in philosophy rather than mechanics, for control in Great Britain requires much less legal intervention. Banks there are more aware of the social implications of their policies, need less formal control, and are more easily influenced by what we would call "moral suasion." True, British banking is a private-enterprise operation, but it is also held to be somewhat of a public trust.

Canada

The Canadian banking system shares many similarities of both the British and United States systems, with adaptations suited to its own conditions. One measure of its effectiveness is evidenced by the fact that no Canadian bank has failed since 1923, a record better by two years than that of Britain.

The Chartered Banks. Like England, Canada has a branch banking system. There are eight chartered banks operating almost fifty-five hundred branches. The number of banks has never been large because the federal government has always had a monopoly on bank charters and has insisted on adequate capital. At no time has a bank been permitted with a capital of less than $500,000, which is ten times the amount required of a national bank in this country.

An interesting aspect of Canadian banking legislation is that charters are given for a period of only ten years. The renewal of charters requires a revision of the Bank Act, thus providing a review of the whole subject every decade.

In operation Canadian banks differ little from ours. One minor difference is that they hold a much larger proportion of "notice" (savings) deposits, amounting to considerably more than half of all business and personal accounts. Notice is in practice never required, and checks can be written against notice deposits within limitations, a practice common in the United States prior to 1933. Canadian banks make fewer real estate, consumer, and term loans than United States banks do, but their activity in all these areas is increasing.

The Bank of Canada. The Bank of Canada was not established until 1934, although several central banking functions had been exercised prior to that time by the Treasury. At its origin the bank was privately owned, but in 1938 the government became the sole owner.

In operation the Bank of Canada closely resembles the Federal Reserve System, and in fact Canada has sometimes been referred to as the "thirteenth Federal Reserve district." The Bank holds the legal reserves of the chartered banks and is empowered to change the legal ratio within the limits of 8 and 12 per cent. It discounts for the chartered banks and engages in open-market operations. It is the sole issuer of notes.

Until 1940 it was required to hold a 25 per cent gold reserve against both notes and deposits, but at that time the requirement was suspended, and its gold reserves were transferred to the Exchange Fund Account under the control of the Treasury. The Canadian currency therefore, like the British, is essentially a pure managed paper currency.

While open-market operations have been the most common method of monetary control, the small number of banks in Canada has also made it possible to rely on informal agreements, similar to moral suasion but much more effective. Discount rate policy on loans to chartered banks is similar to that in the United States, but the rate on loans to money market dealers is established weekly at ¼ per cent above the going rate for three-month treasury bills (but not more than bank rate). This rate, therefore, is no longer subject to administrative discretion as an instrument of monetary policy.

France

The three countries so far discussed all have highly developed money markets, put their major emphasis on private commercial banks, and rely extensively on the use of checks. These characteristics are by no means universal. France, while it is truly representative of nothing except itself, will serve to illustrate how an industrialized country may produce very different monetary institutions.

The Banking System. French banking, more than most, has developed haphazardly, with a minimum of government control and with a high degree of secrecy that until recently has made even a description of the system difficult. The first major piece of banking legislation enacted by France since the Mississippi Bubble was the law of December 2, 1945 (under the first de Gaulle government), which nationalized the Bank of France and the four largest deposit banks[4] and defined the scope of other banking institutions.[5] This law divides banks into three classes: deposit banks, business (investment) banks, and long- and medium-term credit banks. Each bank was required to limit its business to one of these categories.

Deposit Banks. Deposit banks may be either local or national. The national banks have extensive branch systems covering the whole of France as well as overseas offices in French colonies and foreign countries. Under nationalization they are managed by twelve directors: four appointed by the Minister of National Economy, four by the Minister of Finance, and four by the "most representative employees' unions." While public ownership of central banks is common, this nationalization of commercial banks is fairly unusual.

Not nationalized are some twenty regional banks and over two hundred small local banks, including a number of Paris banks specializing in particular types of banking operations. French banking thus combines branch banking with unit banking, public banking with private banking.

Deposit banks accept demand deposits or deposits with a term of not more than two years. The use of checks is much less common in France than in this country, for the average Frenchman likes hard money when he can get it and paper that he can at least handle when he can't get gold. The total of demand deposits in banks *of all types* is no greater than the amount of currency in circulation! As a result (and in turn partly a cause) check-clearing machinery is quite primitive.

The deposit banks provide short-term loans to French business, but the instruments used are primarily the trade bill and the overdraft. The latter

[4] Crédit Lyonnais, Société Générale pour Favoriser le Developpement du Commerce et de l'Industrie en France, Comtoir National d'Escompte de Paris, and Banque National pour le Commerce et l'Industrie.

[5] A translation of this law is provided in *Federal Reserve Bulletin,* vol. 32, no. 5 (May, 1946), pp. 483–488.

we have examined in our discussion of British banking. The trade bill arises out of a commercial transaction where the seller uses a bill of exchange to order the buyer to make payment within a specified period. When the buyer accepts the bill by signing his name to it, it becomes essentially a promise to pay, and the holder can discount it with his bank if he wants the funds immediately. Such loans are perfect examples of the real-bills doctrine.

Investment Banks. Investment banks are a type of institution unknown in this country. They accept deposits from a very restricted clientele, consisting of those with whom they have other business relations. Their basic activity is participation in, and management of, business enterprises. They help in the organization of new enterprises, provide for the sale of securities, hold securities themselves, and arrange mergers and consolidations. They also hold government securities, make commercial loans to enterprises with which they are associated (primarily through purchases of bills and acceptances), and act as correspondents for local deposit banks that want a Paris agent.

Although these banks have not been nationalized, the government appoints a commissioner to sit with the board of directors of each of the larger banks. He has the right to veto any decision contrary to the national interest.

Credit Banks. Medium- and long-term credit banks operate under strict government control, with a governmentally appointed president. Their loan activity is indicated in their title, while on the liability side they accept time deposits with a maturity of not less than two years. Most of these banks were established in the interwar period by deposit banks that could not themselves safely engage in longer-term loans. There are still only a handful of them, and they do not appear to be growing in importance.

Other Banks. There are a number of private banks, some specializing in the management of family estates, others operating as underwriters of securities or as dealers in trade bills, acceptances, and foreign exchange. None of them accept deposits.

Several hundred savings banks and fifteen thousand branches of the Postal Savings Bank accept savings deposits, which, like ours, are ordinarily withdrawable on demand. Strangely enough the post offices also accept deposits that pay no interest but against which checks may be written. These are intended for the man in the street, who normally has little relation with the commercial banks.

Other specialized institutions deal in mortgages, agricultural credit, and small loans, primarily to merchants. A large proportion of these operate as cooperatives for the mutual benefit of their members.

The government operates a small number of "funds," which act very much like banks, obtaining money from other institutions (such as the savings banks and insurance companies) or from the Treasury and making it available to public authorities, other banks, and private companies through both loans and the purchase of securities. They also handle much of the finances of the government.

The Bank of France. The Bank of France was until recently an interesting double hybrid. Established by Napoleon in 1800, it was managed jointly by the government and private stockholders. At the same time it performed both ordinary commercial banking functions and those associated with a central bank. In 1946 the private stockholders were bought out by the government, which is now the sole owner, but the Bank still continues its commercial banking activities and is, in fact, the largest commercial bank in France. It deals not only with banks, but also with business and individual Frenchmen.

The General Council, the governing body of the Bank, consists of twelve members, of whom four are ex officio heads of government funds, seven are appointed by the Minister of Finance, and one is elected by the employees of the Bank.

The Bank of France has a monopoly of note issue. It has a small gold reserve, which since 1952 has not exceeded 10 per cent of its note circulation There is no legal reserve requirement against notes, and they are not redeemable.

In its control of monetary conditions the Bank of France is aided by the fact that it deals with the vast public through its network of 650 branch offices as well as with banks. Its discount rate therefore is immediately effective since it is itself a market rate. It holds some deposits of banks, but such deposits are not part of the banks' reserves. In fact the only reserve requirement for deposit banks specifies that they hold 25 per cent of their deposits in the form of short-term government securities.

Prior to 1938 the discount rate was the only significant instrument of monetary control. Since that time various types of open-market operations have been tried, more in the area of trade bills than of government securities. This activity is hampered by a relatively undeveloped money market.

Other Control Agencies. The Bank of France is not the sole arbiter of credit policy. It shares this role with three other agencies, all of fairly recent origin.

The *Professional Association of Bankers,* ostensibly a trade association, was established by law in 1941, and membership was made compulsory for all banks. In addition to performing certain liaison and consultative functions among its members, the association makes recommendations to, and in many areas carries out decisions of, the two control bodies next described.

The *Bank Control Commission* was established at the same time as the association. The Commission includes the governor of the Bank of France and representatives of the Council of State, the Treasury, the Ministry of

Economic Affairs, the banks themselves, and bank employees. Its powers are similar to those of our regulatory agencies. The Commission, among other things, has established a liquidity ratio for the commercial banks according to which they must maintain an amount equal to 60 per cent of their short-term liabilities in the form of liquid assets. This is intended to promote sound banking practice and is not used as a means of credit control. It does, however, restrain certain types of bank expansion. It is the Control Commission (with the assistance of the National Credit Council) that oversees the nationalized banks.

The *National Credit Council,* established in 1945, has the broadest powers of all, for its primary purpose is the coordination of credit policy for the whole nation. Since its scope is broad, the Council is representative of wide interests. It consists of thirty-eight members, of whom ten represent agricultural and industrial groups, seven are proposed by labor unions, seven represent state planning agencies, seven are officials of public or semipublic financial institutions, and seven represent the other banking agencies.

This unwieldy body, designed to get everyone's viewpoint, is also intended to do everything. Its powers include bank regulation (even to the setting of minimum interest rates), issuance of directives concerning the proper distribution of credit, determination of general credit and monetary policy, preparation of banking legislation, making of decisions concerning the financing of foreign trade, and management of the nationalized banks. In several of its activities it acts jointly with other agencies already described as well as with the Treasury and other government departments concerned with economics and finance. In terms of overall credit policy it is superior to the Bank of France.

Although French banks are not subject to specific legal reserve requirements, they are even more strictly controlled by means of directives from both the Bank of France and the National Credit Council, which specify from time to time the kinds of loans that may be made, the proportion of funds that must go into government securities, rates of interest, and other details of banking operation. At times individual loans exceeding a specified sum have required approval of the Bank of France. Thus a banking system that was practically free of all control until 1945 is now among the most highly controlled in the world.

France's experience with these control devices is too short to permit a full evaluation of their usefulness. Preliminary judgment seems to indicate that they have achieved a large degree of coordination over France's traditionally heterogeneous banking structure. The currency reform that France instituted in 1959 would probably have been much more difficult, if not impossible, without them. On the other hand, they still leave much to be desired in terms of unified authority, for they represent an even more scattered array of overlapping jurisdictions than we have in the United States.

The Soviet Union

If banking in other European countries seems strange, we might be disinclined even to call the financial institutions of the Soviet Union banks. Yet money is universally needed as a means of carrying on commerce, and even a socialist economy must have some device for making payments.

Early Experience. The early Bolsheviks thought otherwise. Recognizing that interference with the normal operations of money—by debasement, depreciation, manipulations of financial instruments, and so on—caused great misery, they suggested that one of the first acts of a socialist state should be to abolish money. The experience of World War I reinforced this belief, for Russia, with an antiquated and inadequate tax system, suffered more from inflation than most belligerents, and by 1917 prices had risen ten times as high as they had been four years earlier.

When the Bolsheviks took over in 1917, they attempted to introduce a moneyless economy by requisitioning agricultural and industrial products for distribution to consumers. At the same time, presumably only on a transitional basis, the government found it necessary to meet most of its own expenses with money payments, and it printed large quantities of money in order to do so. With production falling as a result of general demoralization and much of the output not available for sale, the decline in work for money to do, coupled with a large increase in its amount, inevitably led to even further inflation, and prices shot up astronomically.

An article costing 1 ruble in 1913 would have cost 10 rubles in 1917, 80,000 rubles in mid-1921, and 60 *billion* rubles by March, 1924.[6] The government printing plants turned out notes in an endless stream even while the government was attempting to abolish money.

It didn't work, and finally the government realized that a sound currency was absolutely essential to industrial progress. An unsuccessful attempt was made to stabilize the currency in 1922. A more thoroughgoing reform was introduced in 1924, which finally succeeded in halting the price rise. Stability is still somewhat elusive, and although subsequent fluctuations have been much more moderate, inflation is a pervasive force in the Soviet Union as elsewhere. In 1947 another currency reform, fairly complicated in detail, had the practical effect of substituting a new ruble for the old at a ratio of 1:10.[7]

At the present time the currency of the Soviet Union consists of bank notes of the State Bank, treasury notes, and silver and copper coins of small denominations. The bank notes have a reserve of 25 per cent in gold, plati-

[6] See Arthur Z. Arnold, *Banks, Credit, and Money in Soviet Russia* (Columbia University Press, New York, 1937), pp. 49, 128, 187.

[7] The conversion ratio was considerably more favorable (ranging from a 1-1 to a 1-3 ratio) for holders of government bonds and savings accounts.

num, and foreign exchange, and 75 per cent in short-term securities. The treasury notes are a fiat currency without backing.

For many years the ruble was officially defined as .222168 grams of pure gold (which gave an exchange rate of four to the dollar), but all currency was completely inconvertible and could not be exported or imported. The State Bank bought gold at the fixed rate but would not sell at that price. Rubles were used very little in foreign trade, which was carried out primarily in non-Soviet currencies at arbitrary prices not necessarily related to the official gold value of the ruble. The gold definition of the ruble was therefore even more than in other countries a formal fiction without practical meaning. In 1961 a new "heavy" ruble was introduced, worth 10 old rubles but with a gold content of only 0.987412 grams and a foreign exchange value of $1.11. The more realistic exchange rate and other reforms were expected to promote greater use of the ruble in international trade.

Currency performs the same functions in the Soviet Union as it does elsewhere. Workers receive their wages in currency and buy the things they need with it. They can deposit it in savings accounts at interest. The only thing they can't do with it is use it to set up their own business. Just as in the United States, about 10 per cent of the value of all transactions takes place in currency; the rest goes through the State Bank.

Commercial Banking. In the Soviet Union there is only one commercial bank: the State Bank (Gosbank). Here is an almost perfect example of the monopoly bank in the (almost) closed economy. Its power to expand credit, however, is directly related to the overall plan, and the Gosbank is a key institution in carrying out the operations of the plan. All current payments between enterprises are handled by the Gosbank with its 5,500 offices throughout the country. The Gosbank thus can oversee all transactions through its monetary control.

All productive enterprises (except for farming and a small number of handicraft operations carried out by individuals without the aid of hired labor) are owned and controlled by the state. The objectives and operations of these facilities are set out in the master plan. The first Five-Year Plan was established in 1928, and the latest plan began in 1965. The plan is set up by the State Planning Commission (Gosplan) with the approval of the All-Union Party Congress and the Supreme Soviet of the U.S.S.R. The plan provides not only for the physical requirements of production, but also for their financing.

It is with the Credit Plan that the Gosbank is concerned. This plan places a certain amount of funds at the disposal of each enterprise. These funds, representing working capital, are in the form of deposits with the Gosbank, and practically all payments between enterprises are handled through the transfer of these deposits.

Transfers of deposits are made by *giro orders* rather than checks. A giro order, like a check, is an order on a bank to pay a specified sum of money to a particular individual, but unlike a check it is sent directly by the drawer to the bank, which then enters the credit to the account of the payee. In the Soviet Union the giro order, in addition to stating the amount of rubles involved, also indicates the nature of the transaction, thereby permitting the Gosbank to check on whether the enterprises are properly following the plan. Such orders are obviously nonnegotiable, and the facilities of the Gosbank can be used only by enterprises subject to the plan.

The State Bank has a monopoly of all short-term credit, so that an enterprise needing funds has only one place to go. Not even trade credit is permitted, and all buyers must pay for goods immediately on their receipt. The plan itself establishes the maximum amount that any enterprise may borrow. In case of emergency the limit may be exceeded, but only if the Bank approves the purpose of the loan. Loans are for short periods and carry interest rates of between 2 and 4 per cent. Even though all productive facilities are owned by the state, and interest is therefore paid by one state agency to another, the Soviet Union uses accounting devices of this kind to calculate profit and loss in an attempt to determine the relative efficiency of management.

It is clear that the Gosbank is even more than a central bank and that it has absolute control not only of the quantity of bank credit outstanding, but also of the physical operation of industry itself. It is in this sense a general overseer for the government of the whole operation of the economy.

Since enterprises do not use currency and individuals do not use demand deposits, there is no convertibility between the two types of money. The quantity of currency is therefore not determined by the demands of the public but is rather a matter of planning. The Cash Plan determines the need in terms of wages to be paid and goods available to the public, and the Gosbank merely produces, for the government, the planned amount. This currency is then provided to enterprises for wage payments and charged against their accounts.

The Bank acts also as fiscal agent for the government, receiving all taxes and making payments. It is also responsible for all foreign exchange transactions.

Money and Prices. In view of the strict and unified control that the Gosbank exercises over both currency and credit, it may seem surprising that the Soviet Union should have any trouble with inflation. There are at least two reasons: inefficiency and the exigencies of government finance.

When a firm fails to fulfill its planned output, its receipts fall below planned sales, and its balance at the State Bank is not replenished as fast as anticipated. Such an enterprise in a capitalist economy might obtain additional funds from its stockholders or might be allowed to fail. It would represent a poor risk for a bank loan. But in the Soviet Union an enterprise can hardly be permitted to fail, and while the manager might feel the wrath of the powers that be (and be retired to Siberia), the enterprise itself must be given additional funds to enable it to continue. Thus an undesired amount of credit is pumped into the economy at the same time that output is falling short of expectations.

The second problem concerns government finance. Even in the Soviet Union the government may find it impractical to operate within a balanced budget. Apparently even there the government, especially during a war, is afraid to raise taxes sufficiently to meet all expenses. The easiest course is then simply to issue more money. Throughout history wars have always bred inflation, and the Soviet Union is not immune to this universal disease.[8]

The nature of the disease is somewhat different, however. All transfers between government enterprises are carried out at prices set in the plan, and the majority of consumer goods are sold in state stores, also at prices determined by the government. Such prices bear no relation to supply and demand. Increased purchasing power therefore merely tends to empty the stores of goods. During World War II this situation was met, as in the United States, by rationing. The Soviet Union put a new twist in rationing, however, by providing fewer ration coupons than there were goods available. The excess goods were then sold in separate "commercial" stores (also operated by the state) at higher prices, sometimes several times higher, than those in the "ration" stores. In addition there have always been free markets not under government control, notably the farm markets and peasant bazaars. Frustrated purchasing power found an outlet in these free markets, and prices soared there to fantastic levels. This is the same sort of phenomenon that appears in black markets under price control, but in this case it was perfectly legal. The country had three different price structures, and only one of them was influenced by supply and demand forces. Since the currency reform of 1947 the inflationary pressures have themselves been removed, rationing has been abolished along with the commercial stores, and the differential between prices in the state stores and the free markets has been reduced significantly.

Other Financial Institutions. Long-term investment, formerly divided among four specialized institutions, is now in the hands of the All-Union Bank for the Financing of Capital Investment (Stroibank). Within the overall limitations of the plan, Stroibank provides funds not only for the fixed capital requirements of industrial and marketing enterprises, but also for farm improvements and municipal facilities. It may make long-term interest-bearing loans for these purposes, or, depending on the provisions of the plan, it may provide outright grants, which represent in effect the government's contribution to the basic capital of the enterprises involved. Since, in drawing up the plan, the government can choose between grants and loans, it is able to subsidize certain industries at the expense of others. Like the State Bank, the

[8] The Soviet government blamed the World War II inflation on counterfeit notes issued by the German army of occupation. While this may have been a factor, it could hardly have been the major one.

Investment Bank exercises strict supervision over the use of the funds it provides.

Stroibank also provides mortgage loans to industrial workers for the construction of private homes.

Savings banks are another important segment of the Soviet financial machinery. The government obtains most of its funds from taxation and the profits of state enterprises, but it also encourages saving by the general public. For this purpose the State Savings Bank has over thirty thousand offices throughout the country, operated in conjunction with post offices, railway stations, factories, and other village facilities. These banks accept savings deposits of individuals, trade unions, collective farms, and cooperatives, and at the option of the depositor the bank will either pay interest on the account or enter it in a lottery. Interest accounts pay 5 per cent on sums deposited for six months or more and 3 per cent on other sums. Lottery accounts pay no interest, but twice a year are entered in a drawing in which the winners receive prizes equal to from one-half to two times their average balance over the preceding six months. Thus does the socialist state promote equality of income!

India

All the countries so far examined have fairly well-developed economies. Many of the amenities of a complex and efficient monetary and banking system that we take for granted are absent in the less developed countries. In some banking is almost nonexistent.

India is by no means among the least-developed nations, and it is making great strides forward. But it still has a long way to go to catch up with Europe and the United States. Most of the population is engaged in agriculture, and while there is a substantial amount of cottage and small-scale industry, less than 2 per cent of the working population is employed in large-scale industry. This underlying nature of India's economy is expressed clearly in its banking structure.

Banking Institutions. Still one of the most important credit institutions in India is the village moneylender. Lending his own funds, sometimes merely as a sideline to some other business, he provides funds to farmers for both consumption and agricultural needs. Short-term loans are generally unsecured, often verbal, and carry high rates of interest. Long-term loans are made on land security. This type of lending, coupled with ignorance and poverty on the part of the borrower, leaves room for considerable abuse on the part of unscrupulous lenders, and in the postwar period many Indian states have attempted to license and control the practices of the village moneylenders.

The indigenous banker is only one step above the moneylender. His primary distinction is that he is located in a town rather than a village, and his transactions are a bit more orderly; but frequently he too is part banker, part merchant. He not only makes loans—to traders and artisans as well as farmers—but also accepts deposits and deals in local bills of exchange. Sometimes he provides funds for the village moneylender.

Because of the absence of organized banking facilities, a number of cooperative devices have been developed through which the people provide their own banking services. These cooperatives take a great number of forms. Their common characteristic is that they obtain small sums of money—usually in the form of share capital, sometimes as deposits—from their members and then lend it to other members. The small cooperatives of a given area are frequently joined together in a "central bank," which can often obtain funds from a broader area, and these funds can then be made available to the local societies. At a higher level still the state cooperative banks serve the federations as well as carrying on a more generalized banking business.

Mortgage credit is also provided by special cooperatives, not unlike our savings and loan associations in their early days. Some of these mortgage cooperatives obtain additional funds by issuing mortgage bonds or by accepting deposits.

Commercial banking, while limited pretty much to the larger towns, is growing in importance. The "scheduled banks," of which there are fewer than one hundred, are registered with the Reserve Bank of India and fall under its jurisdiction. The nonscheduled banks, although they number over four hundred, carry on a small fraction of the total commercial banking business. The Imperial Bank of India, which had been a quasi-governmental institution, was nationalized in 1955 and its title changed to the State Bank of India. It is by far the largest Indian bank, with 450 branches throughout the country, and it is charged with the task of extending its branches to areas without banking services. There are a few other fairly large banks, but the majority of banks are regional or local. Thus India, like France, combines both branch and unit banking. But with some five hundred banks and thirty-five hundred branches, India has only one banking office for every 75,000 people. That is one-tenth the saturation in the United States and one-twentieth that in Canada.

Operation of the commercial banks themselves is little different from that of their United States cousins. The greater part of their loans finance trade, while industrial loans are dominated by the cotton, jute, and sugar interests. Loans to agriculture are extremely small in spite of the importance of agriculture in the Indian economy. Investments consist mainly of government securities. Both time and demand deposits are accepted, and interest is paid on both.

In terms of savings accounts the Post Office Savings Bank, with some eleven thousand offices, is more important than all the banks put together, even though it accepts only accounts of less than 10,000 rupees ($2,100).

Central Banking. The Reserve Bank of India was founded in 1935 and nationalized in 1948. It has the sole right of note issue and, like the Bank of England, separates its issue department from its other activities. It originally had to maintain a 40 per cent reserve in gold and foreign exchange against its note issue. By 1959, however, the reserve had fallen below 20 per cent.

In many respects the Reserve Bank was patterned after the Federal Reserve, but its powers are considerably less potent. Reserve requirements apply only to the scheduled banks. The basic requirements are 5 per cent of demand deposits and 2 per cent of time deposits, and the Reserve Bank has the power to raise them to four times this minimum figure. Up to 1964 this authority had not been exercised.

The Reserve Bank lends to the scheduled banks and to the state cooperative banks and buys debentures from the mortgage banks to aid them in making long-term loans to agriculture. Its discount rate, however, has not been very flexible. It remained constant from 1935 to 1951, and since then it has been changed relatively infrequently.

The bank also engages in open-market operations, but the very limited extent of money market facilities in India, as well as the low level of reserve requirements, reduces seriously the effectiveness of such operations as a credit-control device.

Perhaps the most important part of the Bank's tasks at the present time is its effort to unify and develop the nation's banking machinery, for in spite of the many different kinds of lenders, facilities are still extremely meager by United States or European standards. Where money cannot flow readily from lender to borrower or from one part of the country to another; where there is only a limited market in which obligations of debt can be bought and sold; where the various kinds of financial intermediaries, such as bill brokers, are practically nonexistent; and where interest rates consequently tend to be high—there the flow of funds into productive investment will be hindered, and development will proceed only slowly. The improvement of financial machinery is just one of the many processes that are necessary to economic progress.

Questions for Thought and Discussion

1. Are there any aspects of the banking systems described in this chapter that you think might be advantageously adopted by the United States?

2. Why do British banks hold any reserves at all? Does 8 per cent sound sufficient?

3. If overdraft facilities were allowed businessmen by United States banks, do you think it would have any effect on interest rates?

4. Why is the post office so widely used as a savings institution?

5. With regard to central banks what is the basic difference between private ownership (common in the early days of such banks), quasi-public ownership (such as the Federal Reserve), and nationalization (now almost universal)? Which type is most effective in monetary control?

6. Why does monetary control through open-market operations require a highly developed money market?

7. Do you think the widespread membership of the French National Credit Council is the best way to assure the wisest credit policy? Would you suggest such a council for the United States? Who would you put on it? What powers would you give it?
8. Can you think of any way in which money might be eliminated from an industrialized economy?
9. What are the differences between a giro order and a check?
10. Does the Soviet banking system distribute funds more efficiently than a banking system operating in a free market? What criteria would you use in judging efficiency?
11. Why does it seem to be impossible for a government with as much authority as the Soviets have to avoid a government deficit at times?
12. Does the experience of the Soviet Union with prices during World War II suggest anything about the effects of a price-control policy that includes only some articles?
13. What steps do you think might be taken to expand banking facilities in India, particularly in the area of agriculture?
14. If the village moneylenders have been exploiting the farmers, would it be better to abolish them? What would take their place?

Selected Bibliography

Adams, Thomas F. M.: *A Financial History of Modern Japan,* Research Ltd., Tokyo, 1964.
Asfour, Edmund Y.: *Syria: Development and Monetary Policy,* Harvard Middle East Monographs, no. 1, Harvard University Press, Cambridge, Mass., 1959.
Aufricht, Hans (ed.): *Central Banking Legislation: A Collection of Central Bank, Monetary, and Banking Laws,* International Monetary Fund, Washington, 1961.
Bagehot, Walter: *Lombard Street,* 14th ed., John Murray (Publishers), Ltd., London, 1922.
Beckhardt, Benjamin H. (ed.): *Banking Systems,* Columbia University Press, New York, 1954.
Brown, C. V.: *Government and Banking in Western Nigeria: A Case Study in Economic Policy,* Oxford University Press for the Nigerian Institute of Social and Economic Research, Ibadan, Nigeria, 1964.
Chacko, K. C.: *The Monetary and Fiscal Policy of India,* Vora, Bombay, 1957.
Chlopner, Ben Sergo: *Belgian Banking and Banking Theory,* The Brookings Institution, Washington, 1943.
Dacey, W. Manning: *The British Banking Mechanism,* 4th ed., Hutchinson's University Library, London, 1962.
Davies, S. Gethyn (ed.): *Central Banking in South and East Asia,* Oxford University Press, Fair Lawn, N.J., 1960.

Dieterlen, Pierre, and Charles Rist: *The Monetary Problem of France,* King's Crown Press, New York, 1948.

Di Venuti, Biago: *Money and Banking in Puerto Rico,* University of Puerto Rico Press, Rio Piedras, 1950.

European Economic Community, Monetary Committee: *The Instruments of Monetary Policy in the Countries of the European Economic Community,* Brussels, 1962.

Firth, Raymond, and B. S. Yamey (eds.): *Capital, Saving and Credit in Peasant Societies: Studies from Asia, Oceania, the Caribbean and Middle America,* Aldine Publishing Co., London, 1964.

Fousek, Peter G.: *Foreign Central Banking: The Instruments of Monetary Policy,* Federal Reserve Bank of New York, 1957.

Gailbraith, John A.: *The Economics of Banking Operations: A Canadian Study,* McGill University Press, Montreal, 1964.

Gifford, J. K., J. Vivian Wood, and A. J. Reitsma: *Australian Banking,* 2d ed., University of Queensland Press, Brisbane, 1955.

Gunasekera, H. A. de S.: *From Dependent Currency to Central Banking in Ceylon: An Analysis of Monetary Experience, 1825–1957,* G. Bell & Sons, Ltd., London, 1962.

Harr, Luther A.: *Branch Banking in England,* University of Pennsylvania Press, Philadelphia, 1929.

Institute of Bankers: *Banking Trends in Europe Today,* a series of lectures delivered at the 17th International Banking Summer School, London, 1964.

Jamieson, A. B.: *Chartered Banking in Canada,* The Ryerson Press, Toronto, 1953.

Jucker-Fleetwood, E. E.: *Money and Finance in Africa,* Frederick A. Praeger, Inc., New York, 1964.

Karunatilake, H. N. S.: *The Variable Reserve Ratio as an Instrument of Central Bank Policy,* Central Bank of Ceylon, Colombo, 1963.

Lindholm, R. W.: *Money, Banking and Economic Development in Free Vietnam,* Cong-dan Publishing Company, Saigon, 1957.

Lutz, Friedrich A., and Vera C. Lutz: *Monetary and Foreign Exchange Policy in Italy,* Princeton University Press, Princeton, N.J., 1950.

McIvor, R. Craig: *Canadian Monetary, Banking and Fiscal Development,* St Martin's Press, Inc., New York, 1958.

Muranjan, S. K.: *Modern Banking in India,* 3d ed., Kamala Publishing House, Bombay, 1952.

Neufeld, E. P.: *Bank of Canada Operations and Policy,* University of Toronto Press, Toronto, 1958.

Newlyn, W. T., and D. C. Rowan: *Money and Banking in British Colonial Africa,* Oxford University Press, Fair Lawn, N.J., 1954.

Northrup, Mildred B.: *Control Policies of the Reichsbank,* Columbia University Press, New York, 1936.

Otsuki, T.: *The Banking System of Japan,* Ministry of Finance, Tokyo, 1951.

Patrick, Hugh T.: *Monetary Policy and Central Banking in Contemporary Japan,* Allied Publishers Private, Ltd., Bombay, 1962.

Plumtre, A. F. W.: *Central Banking in the British Dominions,* University of Toronto Press, Toronto, 1940.

Qureshi, A. I.: *Financial Institutions: National and International,* Ministry of Finance, Government of Pakistan, Rawalpindi, 1964.

Reserve Bank of New Zealand: *Money and Banking in New Zealand,* Wellington, 1963.

Sarasas, Phra: *Money and Banking in Japan,* Heath Cranton, Ltd., London, 1940.

Sayers, R. S.: *Banking in Western Europe,* Oxford University Press, Fair Lawn, N.J., 1962.

———: *Modern Banking,* 6th ed., Oxford University Press, London, 1964.

——— and W. F. Crick (eds.): *Commonwealth Banking Systems,* Oxford University Press, Fair Lawn, N.J., 1965.

Schiffer, Hubert F.: *The Modern Japanese Banking System,* University Publishers, Inc., for Loyola University, New Orleans, 1959.

Schwartz, Harry: *Russia's Soviet Economy,* Prentice-Hall, Inc., Englewood Cliffs, N.J., 1950.

Sen, S. W.: *Central Banking in Underdeveloped Money Markets,* Bookland, Calcutta, 1952.

Sithi-Amnuai, P. (ed.): *Finance and Banking in Thailand: A Study of Commercial System, 1888–1963,* Thai Watana Panich, Bangkok, 1964.

State Bank of the U.S.S.R.: *Banking in the U.S.S.R.,* Moscow, 1962.

Tamagna, Frank M.: *Banking and Finance in China,* Institute of Pacific Relations, New York, 1942.

Thorne, William J.: *Banking,* Oxford University Press, London, 1948.

van Dillen, Johannes Gerard: *History of the Principal Public Banks,* Publications of the International Committee for the Study of the History of Banking and Credit, Martinus Nijhoff, The Hague, 1934.

Wilson, J. S. G.: *French Banking Structure and Credit Policy,* Harvard University Press, Cambridge, Mass., 1957.

Part Six
Monetary Theory

Chapter 21
The Value of Money

There shall be in England seven half-penny loaves sold for a penny.

The Second Part of King Henry VI Act IV, scene 2, line 73

The first half of this book has explored the use of money as a means of payment: the ways in which money has emerged over the course of history, the current forms that money takes, and the institutions that deal in money.

But money—or, as we were careful to point out earlier, the monetary unit—is also a standard of value. It is the measuring device against which the values of all other goods are measured. Yet it is a very unreliable yardstick, for the value of money fluctuates significantly over time. Much energy has gone into the attempt to devise a money with a stable value, but so far no magic formula has been discovered. Alas, we can control machines, atoms, the bubonic plague, even interplanetary rockets, but the control of money still eludes us. This is the problem with which most of the rest of this book will deal.

Value and Price

In economics the most common meaning of value is *exchange value, the power of a good to command other goods in exchange*. The value of a pair of shoes is 1 hat or one-fifth of a suit or 5 bushels of wheat or 20 movie admissions or $10. All these represent things that the owner of a pair of shoes can get in exchange. The last is a special kind of value that is so universally used that it has its own name: price. *Price is the value of a good expressed in the monetary unit.*

While money is thus the common measure of the value of other goods, there is no common measure for the value of money. The value of a dollar is one-tenth of a pair of shoes, one-tenth of a hat, one-fiftieth of a suit, one-half bushel of wheat, or two movie admissions. But no one of these alone adequately expresses the value of money. Simply because money *is* so universal, because it can buy everything, its value is measurable only in terms of some composite of all things for which it can be exchanged.

If prices always remained the same, this difficulty in expressing the value of money would not be important. The value of money would be a vague, immeasurable concept which could not be defined but which everyone would understand in terms of the goods that he himself wanted to buy. He would know from experience what a dollar was worth. Unfortunately price changes plague us with confusion.

If the price of wheat is $2 a bushel, the value of a dollar (in terms of wheat) is ½ bushel. Suppose the price of wheat falls to $1, a drop of 50 per cent. By the same token the value of money (in terms of wheat) has doubled. The two values have changed in relation to each other, but which has moved? When you sit in a train at the station with another train beside you, and suddenly the other train changes its position, you are not always sure until you check with some stationary object whether it is your train or the other that has moved.

So in our example it is necessary to check our position with other prices before we can say with certainty whether it is the value of wheat or the value of money that has changed. If, for instance, we find that all other prices have remained the same, then we can conclude that it is the value of wheat that has changed. Not only will wheat buy fewer dollars, but it will also buy less of everything else. If, however, all other prices have been cut in half at the same time that this has happened to wheat, then we would conclude that it is the value of money that has risen. A dollar can buy twice as much of everything, while a bushel of wheat still exchanges for the same quantity of everything else except money.

But life isn't even that simple. Suppose that in the same period the price of wheat has fallen by 50 per cent, the price of hats has remained stationary, the price of movie admissions has doubled, and other prices have shown other diverse movements, as in the following example:

	Original price	*Later price*
Shoes	$10.00	$ 8.00
Hats	10.00	10.00
Suits	50.00	60.00
Wheat	2.00	1.00
Movie admissions	0.50	1.00

Our whole set of values has become scrambled. Not only have the values of most of these goods changed in relation to money, but they have also changed in relation to one another. Shoes, which used to be worth one hat, are now worth only four-fifths of a hat. While they were originally worth 20 movie admissions, they are now worth 8. While the price of shoes has fallen, they will exchange for more wheat. It is difficult to make any general statement as to what has happened to the value of shoes in general.

It is just as difficult to determine what has happened to the value of money. Has it risen or fallen? Unfortunately there is no way of answering this question with complete accuracy. The nearest approach we can make is through the use of price indexes.

Price Indexes

Any index number is at heart an *average,* a measure of central tendency. A price index, in particular, attempts to assess various price movements, to consider the relative importance of each, and to come up with a single figure that gives a reasonable summary of all of them. This is no easy task.

Index numbers differ from many averages in that they show *changes* over time rather than absolute values. They are always related, therefore, to a particular year (or average of several years) as a base, and this base is traditionally referred to as 100. If the base period is 1957–59 (currently used for most United States statistics) and a particular price index for 1963 stands at 106.7, this means that prices in 1963 were 106.7 per cent of the 1957–59 average level, or, in other words, that prices had risen 6.7 per cent since that base period. If the index rises to 108.2 in 1964, this is a further increase during the year of 1.5 percentage points, or 1.4 per cent, over the 1963 level.[1]

Such a rise represents a fall in the value of money since it now takes more money to buy the same amount of goods. A price index is the reciprocal of the value of money; if prices double, the value of money is cut in half.

The Shortcomings of Price Indexes. An index, however, must be taken with several grains of salt. It would be fully accurate only if prices never changed or if they all changed in precisely the same proportion. These are just the cases in which an index would be unnecessary since the nature of the change would be obvious. As soon as we consider the possibility of different prices moving in different directions or at different rates of speed, then the process of describing such diverse changes in a single figure is bound to be an oversimplification. The reasons are many.

Dispersion. No single figure can express fully the multitude of individual price changes—some little, some great, some up, some down—that are constantly occurring. Or, as a statistician would put it, no average adequately describes the *dispersion* of its component items. Thus if two students

[1] A rise of 1.5 points from a 106.7 base. The rise in *percentage points* is the per cent rise only if the starting point is 100. For instance, if the index in one year is 200 and the next year is 210, this is obviously only a 5 per cent rise; i.e., 10/200 = 0.05 (or 5 per cent). In the example in the text 1.5/106.7 = 0.014 (1.4 per cent).

take a test in which one makes 100 and the other 0, to say that the average (arithmetic mean) grade is 50 is a perfectly valid statement, but it obscures almost as much as it shows. To take another instance, the average family in the United States in 1960 was composed of 3.65 persons. Do you know of any family that was average?

For an example of price dispersion, let's look at the behavior of wholesale prices from November, 1962, to November, 1963, a period during which the total index remained completely stable. The index for this period along with individual figures for groups and subgroups of commodities is given in Table 21-1.

This table shows two different kinds of movement. It records changes from the average of 1957–59 (100) to November, 1962 (first column of figures), and to November, 1963 (second column of figures). A comparison of the two columns shows changes between November, 1962, and November, 1963. Even though this whole period was one of general stability, there are some marked variations in individual price categories.

The all-commodity index rose by only 0.7 per cent from 1957–59 to 1962 and was at exactly the same level one year later (although it had fluctuated slightly in the meantime, a fact not shown by the table). But eighteen of the subgroups (themselves averages of a number of different products) rose or fell by more than 10 per cent in one period or the other (see Table 21-2). Silk products rose by almost one-third in the first period but then remained virtually stable for the second. Nonalcoholic beverages rose 17.4 per cent in the first period and another 8.8 per cent in the second. Sugar and confectionery, which rose by only 2.5 per cent from 1957–59 to 1962, then shot up by 28.0 per cent in twelve months. Inedible fats and oils lost one-quarter of their value in the first period but regained more than half of the lost ground in the second. Going back to Table 21-1, at least a glimpse of the farm problem is afforded by the fact that the price of farm products as a group fell in both periods, while manufactured animal feeds rose by a total of 17.2 per cent and agricultural machinery and equipment went up by 11.5 per cent.

The only significant conclusion that can be drawn from this indigestible mass of figures is that prices vary. They vary in all sorts of strange ways. Any attempt to assess these oddly assorted movements in anything so simple as a single index number is therefore bound to suffer from inadequacy.

On the other hand, the attempt to compute an index should not be abandoned as futile. Look again at the scores of figures in Table 21-1 (themselves index numbers of many commodities making up each group) and ponder just how helpful they would be in showing what happened to prices in general in the absence of the all-commodities index, which ties them together, however inadequately. Certainly a price index is not perfect, but it is useful.

What Index to Use. In an abstract sense the value of money refers to its ability to buy *everything*. A price index designed to measure the (universal)

Table 21-1. Wholesale Prices, by Groups of Commodities, November, 1962, to November, 1963

Index Numbers of the Bureau of Labor Statistics, 1957-59 = 100

Commodity groups	Nov. 1962	Nov. 1963
All commodities	100.7	100.7
Farm products:	99.3	96.2
Fresh and dried produce	96.4	96.0
Grains	99.5	100.3
Livestock and poultry	98.3	87.9
Plant and animal fibers	97.6	99.8
Fluid milk	102.1	103.1
Eggs	112.4	102.4
Hay and seeds	106.9	117.5
Other farm products	90.1	90.7
Processed foods:	101.3	102.5
Cereal and bakery products	107.7	107.8
Meat, poultry, and fish	100.1	91.7
Dairy products and ice cream	108.0	107.9
Canned and frozen fruits, and vegetables	96.3	106.4
Sugar and confectionery	102.5	131.2
Packaged beverage materials	79.1	84.1
Animal fats and oils	92.2	93.5
Crude vegetable oils	79.8	83.8
Refined vegetable oils	88.7	84.1
Vegetable oil and products	91.8	86.6
Miscellaneous processed foods	101.2	107.8
Textile products and apparel:	100.5	101.0
Cotton products	100.7	101.2
Wool products	100.1	101.7
Man-made fiber textile products	93.6	94.4
Silk products	130.3	130.5
Apparel	101.7	102.3
Other textile products	127.8	119.0
Hides, skins, leather, and products:	107.3	103.6
Hides and skins	107.1	82.7
Leather	106.8	99.7
Footwear	108.4	108.3
Other leather products	105.0	103.4
Fuels and related products, and power:	100.7	97.9
Coal	97.7	98.3
Coke	103.6	103.6
Gas fuels (Jan. 1958 = 100)	122.3	122.7
Electric power (Jan. 1958 = 100)	102.7	101.3
Petroleum products, refined	98.6	93.8
Chemicals and allied products:	97.0	96.3
Industrial chemicals	95.9	94.2
Prepared paint	103.8	105.1
Paint materials	93.9	90.9
Drugs and pharmaceuticals	95.1	95.0
Fats and oils, inedible	75.9	90.8
Mixed fertilizers	103.1	103.8
Fertilizer materials	99.2	98.4
Other chemicals and products	99.5	99.0
Rubber and products:	93.7	94.2
Crude rubber	92.8	91.6
Tires and tubes	88.0	91.7
Miscellaneous rubber products	99.7	97.9
Lumber and wood products:	96.3	99.3
Lumber	96.3	99.5
Millwork	102.3	106.2
Plywood	91.5	92.5
Pulp, paper, and allied products:	99.1	99.4
Wood pulp	89.4	94.4
Wastepaper	96.0	91.0
Paper	102.2	102.9
Paperboard	94.1	96.6
Converted paper and paperboard	99.7	99.4
Building paper and board	96.6	95.9
Metals and metal products:	99.3	101.0
Iron and steel	98.4	100.0
Nonferrous metals	98.3	100.2
Metal containers	103.7	104.6
Hardware	103.8	104.4
Plumbing equipment	97.5	100.6
Heating equipment	92.8	92.7
Fabricated structural metal products	98.1	99.0
Fabricated nonstructural metal products	103.9	107.0
Machinery and motive products:	102.2	102.5
Agricultural machinery and equip.	109.8	111.5
Construction machinery and equip.	108.2	110.9
Metalworking machinery and equip.	109.3	110.6
General purpose machinery and equip.	103.7	104.7
Miscellaneous machinery	103.3	103.7
Special industry machinery and equip. (Jan. 1961 = 100)	102.5	104.7
Electrical machinery and equip.	98.1	97.5
Motor vehicles	100.8	99.9
Transportation equip., R.R. rolling stock (Jan. 1961 = 100)	100.5	100.5
Furniture and other household durables:	98.6	98.1
Household furniture	104.1	104.8
Commercial furniture	102.5	103.1
Floor coverings	96.8	97.9
Household appliances	93.1	91.2
Television, radios, and phonographs	90.4	87.8
Other household durable goods	102.9	103.4
Nonmetallic mineral products:	101.6	101.3
Flat glass	96.6	101.0
Concrete ingredients	103.3	102.9
Concrete products	102.8	101.4
Structural clay products	103.4	103.5
Gypsum products	105.0	106.1
Prepared asphalt roofing	89.4	87.4
Other nonmetallic minerals	102.4	101.4
Tobacco products and bottled beverages:	104.5	107.5
Tobacco products	102.2	105.9
Alcholic beverages	101.5	100.9
Nonalcoholic beverages	117.4	127.7
Miscelleneous products:	109.8	110.9
Toys, sporting goods, small arms	101.2	101.0
Manufactured animal feeds	114.9	117.2
Notions and accesories	98.7	99.1
Jewelry, watches, photo equipment	104.4	103.5
Other miscellaneous products	101.7	101.4

Source: *Federal Reserve Bulletin*, vol. 50, no. 1 (January, 1964), pp. 102–103.

Table 21-2. Price Changes of Selected Groups of Commodities*

Commodity groups	Percentage rise (+) or fall (−) in price	
	1957–59 base to November, 1962	November, 1962, to November, 1963
Silk products	+30.3	+0.1
Other textile products	+27.8	−6.9
Gas fuels	+22.3	+0.3
Nonalcoholic beverages	+17.4	+8.8
Manufactured animal feeds	+14.9	+2.0
Eggs	+12.4	−8.9
Hides and skins	+7.1	−22.8
Sugar and confectionery	+2.5	+28.0
ALL COMMODITIES	+0.7	0.0
Livestock and poultry	−1.7	−10.6
Canned and frozen fruits, and vegetables	−3.7	+10.5
Wood pulp	−10.6	+5.6
Prepared asphalt roofing	−10.6	−2.2
Refined vegetable oils	−11.3	−5.2
Tires and tubes	−12.0	+4.2
Crude vegetable oils	−20.2	+5.0
Packaged beverage materials	−20.9	+6.3
Fats and oils, inedible	−24.1	+19.6

* This table contains all subgroups from Table 21–1 that varied by more than 10 per cent in either period.
Source: Computed from Table 21–1.

value of money, therefore, should theoretically include *all* the things for which money is used; not only all commodities, but services, wages, real estate, securities, and other things as well.

Such an index is almost impossibly difficult to compute. An attempt was made by Carl Snyder, whose general price index for the United States for the years 1860–1938 is well known. Even his index, however, was simply a combination in a single figure of several specialized indexes. As finally revised it had twelve components whose (somewhat arbitrary) weights in the composite index are indicated in the following list by their percentage values:

	Per cent
1. Industrial commodity prices at wholesale	10
2. Farm prices at the farm	10
3. Retail food prices	10
4. Rents	5
5. Other cost-of-living items	10
6. Transportation costs	5
7. Realty values	10
8. Security prices	10
9. Equipment and machinery prices	10
10. Hardware prices	3
11. Automobile prices	2
12. Composite wages	15
Total	100

It is not only easier, but for most purposes more useful, to concentrate on the specialized indexes themselves rather than on such a broad concept as a general price level. The two best-known indexes in the United States cover only a part of the price spectrum. They are the wholesale price index and the consumer price index, both computed by the Bureau of Labor Statistics. It is the wholesale index that we have already examined in Table 21-1. As its title indicates, it measures only prices paid by business, whether for raw materials, semifinished goods, or finished goods moving in the channels of trade. It is therefore of particular use to those concerned with business costs. It doesn't tell the final consumer much about what *he* has to pay.

This latter job is done by the consumer index, which measures the price of commodities and services at retail. Even here, however, a good deal of caution is needed in using the index, for its coverage is more limited than its short title might indicate. Technically "the Consumer Price Index is a measure of the average change in prices of goods and services customarily purchased by families of *wage earners and clerical workers living in cities* of the United States." [2]

In other words, it is not intended to measure *all* retail prices. It does not cover goods generally purchased only by more wealthy families, nor does it measure prices in rural areas. But even if you belong to a wage-earning family in a city, you can't assume that if the consumer price index rises 2 per cent, your cost of living has risen by the same amount. This would be true only if yours were a perfectly average family. And who is average? Perhaps the index rises because of an increase in the cost of automobiles or of rent. But you aren't in the market for an automobile and own your own home. The price of pork has risen, but you've switched to beef instead. Subway fares went up in New York, but you live in Omaha. You've just bought a sailboat, but this price isn't included in the index. No index can measure *your* cost of living unless you compute it yourself.

Wholesale and consumer prices are not the only ones for which specialized indexes are computed. The farm parity program of the Federal government depends on indexes of the prices farmers receive for their crops, on the one hand, and of the prices they have to pay for materials, labor, and so on, on the other. For many purposes an index of wages is desired. A stock average, such as the Dow-Jones, is essentially an index of a very specialized kind, covering prices of certain stocks.

All these indexes are useful, but no one of them is intended to measure the general value of money. Each measures the value of money *in a particular use*—for producers' goods, for consumers' goods, for labor services, for stocks. While the various indexes frequently move in the same general direction, they do not always do so. No one of them, therefore, can tell us what is happening to money in the economy as a whole.

[2] U.S. Department of Labor, *The Consumer Price Index,* Bulletin 1140 (1953), p. 2. Italics added.

Sampling. Once we have determined what purpose our index is to serve and therefore what kind to use, we are faced with another difficult choice. Precisely what price quotations are to be included? There are literally millions of kinds of goods sold in the United States. But clerical costs alone require that only a fairly limited number be included in any index. Which? An intelligently chosen sample would include (1) those that are most important and (2) those that can fairly be said to represent a larger group. The selection, however, is never an easy one.

The consumer price index uses prices for only 400 goods that are assumed to make up a typical "market basket" bought by the families the index is intended to cover. The wholesale price index uses 2,200 commodities, but even these represent a small proportion of the total.

The problem of which price quotation to obtain is of similar magnitude, particularly for the consumer index. The same commodity sells at different prices in different cities, in different parts of the same city, and in different types of stores almost next door to one another. Are we interested in prices charged by the supermarket or the neighborhood grocer; by the high-class specialty shop, the department store, or the discount house; by a service or cash-and-carry store or mail-order house?

The consumer price index is based on prices obtained in forty-six cities and from all kinds of stores averaged together. But if you shop the discount markets exclusively, your individual cost of living may not be adequately described by the published index.

Errors in Data. Closely related to the problem of obtaining proper samples is the fact that the prices obtained by survey may be different from prices actually paid by purchasers. Special sales, hidden discounts, and other variations from stated prices raise problems of this type.

Even more disconcerting is the difficulty of obtaining comparable figures for past periods when data were not systematically collected at the time. The wholesale price index was started in 1902, but what if we want to compare present prices with prices prior to that time? A great deal of research has gone into an attempt to obtain from business records, contemporary documents, letters, and other sources as many price quotations as possible for earlier periods, and on the basis of this evidence the index has been carried back as far as 1749. The further back one goes, however, the scarcer the facts are and the less reliable the index. The so-called "index" for 1749, or even 1800, is little more than an educated guess—but still better than no knowledge at all.

Weighting. Suppose we have decided on our index and our sample and have collected data as accurate as possible. Our job is still not done. How are we to process these many figures to obtain a single index? How do we combine the price of shoes and ships and sealing wax? Do we simply add them together and divide by three?

We could, but the result would be a statistical monstrosity. It assumes that each of these items has an equal impact on the economy, that a rise in the price of shoes is precisely as important as a similar rise in the price of sealing wax. This we know is not so. We must find some way of giving numerical value to the greater significance of shoes.

This is done by *weighting,* multiplying the price of each item by a figure that measures its relative importance. The weight most commonly used represents the quantity sold in some base period. Thus if 100,000 pairs of shoes are sold in the base year as against 1,000 sticks of sealing wax, the price of shoes will be weighted 100 times as heavily in the index. The difficulty of obtaining figures for weights, however, introduces one more problem, for sales figures are more difficult to obtain than prices, while changes in taste patterns may rapidly make the weighting system obsolete.

There is, in addition, considerable debate over the "proper" mathematical procedure to use in the actual calculation of the figures. Irving Fisher, in his monumental work *The Making of Index Numbers,*[3] examines 134 different formulas for the calculation of index numbers and discards most of them as seriously deficient in one way or another. His "ideal formula," on the other hand, is so burdensome to compute that for practical purposes it simply can't be used.

The basic difficulty is that an index number is a synthetic hybrid that does not exist in nature. Any formula for deriving it inevitably has a certain air of artificiality that cannot be completely removed. The full complexities of the mathematics are far beyond the scope of this book, but the appendix to this chapter goes a little more deeply into some of the basic considerations of both weighting and computational problems.

Changes over Time. If we are to measure changes in prices alone, it is necessary that the prices that we quote apply to *identical* goods, for if quality changes over time, then a different price may simply mean a different product rather than a change in the value of money.

In 1933 I could buy a Plymouth coupe for $495, f.o.b. factory. Does the fact that a Plymouth today lists at over $2,000 mean that the price of automobiles has quadrupled? Or is it simply that today's Plymouth is four times as much car? Or is it a combination of both, and in what proportion? Is today's prepared cake mix the equivalent of yesterday's plain flour? What about television, frozen foods, automatic dishwashers, stereo records, and the thousands of other things that didn't exist thirty years ago?

Similar questions arise as we consider what happens when the relative importance of particular items alters because of changes in purchasing patterns. When we use base-year weights, we must (for mathematical reasons) stick to the same weights for the life of the index. If we don't, changes in weights will show up as if they were changes in prices. But how well does the index meas-

[3] Irving Fisher, *The Making of Index Numbers* (Houghton Mifflin Company, Boston, 1922).

ure significant price changes during a period when iceboxes, formerly a reasonably significant part of the consumer's market basket, pass out of prominence; as people buy less flour and more bakery products, less potatoes and more beef? These are changes that can be accounted for only by a complete revision of the index at frequent intervals, a long and costly process. But to keep an index up to date it must be done.

The consumer price index was first computed on a 1913 base. It later was moved to 1926, later still to the 1935–39 average, then to 1947–49, and then to 1957–59. It will be changed again before too long. In each case the new index is "spliced" to the old at overlapping years so that some degree of continuity is obtained. It is not a perfect method, but there is no perfect method. The patterns of our economy shift so rapidly that we cannot for long work with old methods of measuring them. The further away from its base period an index gets, the less accurate it becomes.

In spite of all these problems, price indexes are extremely useful devices, telling us infinitely more than we could glean from the raw data. But we must not be misled by the apparent accuracy of an index number stated to the first decimal place. Someone has said that statistics is the science of stating an uncertainty with precision. Always the uncertainty is there, partially obscured by the figures. Index numbers must be treated with care and understanding; so treated they yield a great deal of useful information.

United States Price Levels

As long as we bear in mind their limitations, particularly for earlier periods, it is quite instructive to look at the picture that available price indexes paint of the value of money in the United States. Figure 21-1 charts the course of wholesale prices since 1720 and of consumer prices since 1820. Table 21-3 gives the numerical values for these two series in the more recent period since 1913 along with figures for another index, the implicit price deflators for gross national product, which go back only to 1929.

A number of interesting facts are apparent from even a cursory examination of these data, some of them contrary to common concepts of what has happened to prices over the years.

Wholesale Prices. Let's look at wholesale prices first. It is immediately obvious that they mark dramatically the major wars in which this country has engaged. The Revolution, the War of 1812, the Civil War, and both world wars produced startling increases in wholesale prices. Almost as characteristic is the subsequent collapse of prices, a phenomenon associated with each war except the last.

Another impression that might be gathered from a cursory glimpse of Figure 21-1 is that there has been a general tendency for prices to rise over time. Prices in the 1950s were five times as high as they were in the 1720s. Does this describe accurately the trend of prices over the whole two centuries? The

Table 21-3. Prices in the United States, 1913 to 1964

Year	Wholesale price index (1957-59 = 100)	Consumer price index (1957-59 = 100)	Implicit price deflator for gross national product (1958 = 100)
1913	38.2	34.5	
1914	37.3	35.0	
1915	38.0	35.4	
1916	46.8	38.0	
1917	64.3	44.7	
1918	71.7	52.4	
1919	75.8	60.3	
1920	84.5	69.8	
1921	53.4	62.3	
1922	52.9	58.4	
1923	55.1	59.4	
1924	53.6	59.6	
1925	56.6	61.1	
1926	54.8	61.6	
1927	52.3	60.5	
1928	53.0	59.7	
1929	52.1	59.7	50.6
1930	47.3	58.2	49.3
1931	39.9	53.0	44.8
1932	35.6	47.6	40.3
1933	36.1	45.1	39.3
1934	41.0	46.6	42.2
1935	43.8	47.8	42.6
1936	44.2	48.3	42.7
1937	47.2	50.0	44.5
1938	43.0	49.1	43.9
1939	42.2	48.4	43.2
1940	43.0	48.8	43.9
1941	47.8	51.3	47.2
1942	54.0	56.8	53.0
1943	56.5	60.3	56.8
1944	56.9	61.3	58.2
1945	57.9	62.7	59.7
1946	66.1	68.0	66.7
1947	81.2	77.8	74.6
1948	87.9	83.8	79.6
1949	83.5	83.0	79.1
1950	86.8	83.8	80.2
1951	96.7	90.5	85.6
1952	94.0	92.5	87.5
1953	92.7	93.2	88.3
1954	92.9	93.6	89.6
1955	93.2	93.3	90.9
1956	96.2	94.7	94.0
1957	99.0	98.0	97.5
1958	100.4	100.7	100.0
1959	100.6	101.5	101.6
1960	100.7	103.1	103.3
1961	100.3	104.2	104.6
1962	100.6	105.4	105.7
1963	100.3	106.7	107.1
1964	100.5	108.1	108.9

Source: See Figure 21-1; also *Survey of Current Business*, vol. 45, no. 8 (August, 1965), pp. 52–53.

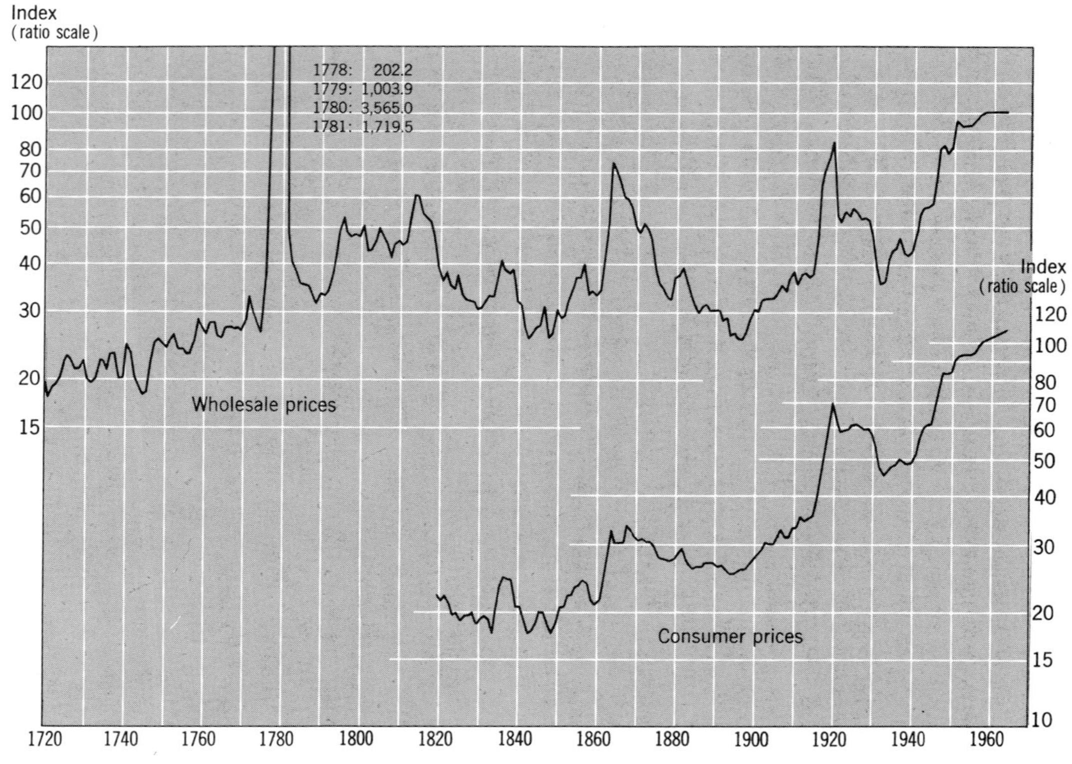

Figure 21-1. Wholesale and consumer prices in the United States, 1720 to 1964 (1957–59 = 100). (U.S. Bureau of Labor Statistics, "All Commodities Wholesale Price Index, 1957–59 = 100," mimeographed; "Index of Estimated Cost of Living in U.S., 1820 to 1913," mimeographed [converted to 1957–59 base by the author]; "Consumer Price Index U.S.: All Items, 1913 Forward—Series A," mimeographed; *Federal Reserve Bulletin*, current issues.)

answer is a qualified "no," for there is some indication that both the beginning and the end of the period are somewhat unusual. If, for instance, we confine our examination to the period from 1800 to 1940, we get a very different picture. (Just block off the two ends of the graph and see what this does to the long-run trend.) To point out that the index in 1940 was 4.5 percentage points lower than it was in 1800 doesn't mean very much since the two years are chosen pretty much at random, but it would seem significant that the average index for the period 1800–1820 was almost exactly the same as the average for 1920–1940.[4] The whole picture that emerges for the nineteenth century and the early part of the twentieth is definitely *not* one of rising wholesale prices.

To change our frame of reference, suppose we look at the period from 1932 to 1958. This is a time of rapidly rising prices, with the wholesale index almost tripling in the period. Is this indicative of a new long-run trend that has just started recently? There are many who say it is. If so, what happened in 1958? The wholesale price index has remained within three-tenths of 1 percentage point of its 1958 level in each following year. Is *this* a new long-term trend? The answer is a secret guarded by the future itself.

But let us look again at the whole record. What does it show? Essentially a series of cycles that cannot be attributed to wars alone, although the peak of each cycle occurs during or shortly after a war. Yet prices generally started rising many years before the war and continued falling for a decade or more afterward. The dates of the turning points are shown in Table 21-4.

Table 21-4. Turning Points of Wholesale Price Cycles

	Preceding low	High	Following low
Revolutionary War	1750	1779	1791
War of 1812	1791	1814	1849
Civil War	1849	1864	1897
World War I	1897	1920	1932
World War II	1932	?	?

Source: See Figure 21–1.

The pattern indicated in this table is quite clear—until we come to World War II. Then something happened. Never before have prices failed to fall substantially within three years of the end of a war. Is it this change in pattern, among other considerations, that leads many economists to suggest that the cycle is broken, that the price collapse that has followed every previous war will not again occur? Are they right? There is no way of telling.

We do know some reasons for the behavior of prices in recent decades. The

[4] The averages for the two periods were 1800–1820, 49.5; 1920–1940, 49.1. It is true that the former period includes the War of 1812, but the latter period includes 1920, the peak year of World War I prices.

beginning of the war pushed prices up as expected until the government stepped in with price controls and forced a temporary slackening in the upward pace. When controls were removed in 1946, the delayed reaction set in. Wartime incomes, which couldn't be spent during the war because of price control and rationing, were now put actively to work. Prices climbed. Three years later it appeared that these inflationary forces had spent themselves. But prices didn't decline far, nor for long. Nor is it possible to blame the Korean conflict for all of the upsurge in 1950 since prices actually started up in January, five months before the hostilities started. And while the war undoubtedly added pressure to the upward movement, there has been no significant downturn since its conclusion. We appear to be moving approximately sideways on a plateau higher than we have ever reached before.

No one knows quite why. Nor can anyone say for certain that we will not sometime have the props pulled out from under us and start down the roller coaster. It is, of course, the job of monetary and fiscal policy to prevent such a catastrophe. Only time will tell whether they will succeed.

What else of interest does our chart show? Among other things, a very intriguing reaction of prices to the prosperity of the 1920s. What happened to wholesale prices during the boom? Not much of anything. They moved up and down somewhat from year to year, but they certainly didn't rise the way they might have been expected to. In 1928 the index stood precisely where it had been in 1922, having fallen from a high in 1925. In 1929 it fell even further. For the whole boom period it showed essentially a sidewise movement. Prosperity, even boom, without inflation—an interesting historical record.

Consumer prices. If we turn our attention to the consumer price index, we discover a pattern very similar to that of wholesale prices but somewhat muted. Consumer prices seem to move more sluggishly, but otherwise they resemble wholesale prices. The war years are clearly shown. They trace the same sidewise movement in the period of prosperity from 1922 to 1929.

In one major respect, however, consumer prices differ from wholesale. There is no substantial period when consumer prices have not edged upward. Even if we end our survey in 1940, we find the consumer price index significantly higher than in any period prior to World War I, twice as high as in the mid-nineteenth century.

Why do consumer prices rise more in the long run than wholesale prices? One reason is the difference in the nature of the goods involved. Most manufacturers have been able to maintain the (low) price of their products in spite of a rapid rise in wage rates. They can do so because of improvements in technology that permit greatly increased output per man-hour. To get these goods to the consumer, however, requires a distributive network (of which the retail store is only the final link) where it is not nearly as easy to introduce labor-saving devices. As wages rise, distributive costs cannot be kept down by technological improvements as effectively as manufacturing costs.

Closely related is the fact that a large and growing part of consumer expenditures is for services, where labor is again the greatest cost and where the economies of machines are not as readily available.

In addition it is undoubtedly true that part of the increase in the index is a matter of inherent defects of measurement, for it is almost impossible to prevent increases in quality from showing up as increases in prices. Autos are better than they used to be—hence more expensive. Instead of bulk foods we buy them prepackaged, frozen, precooked. To the extent that we are getting better quality, some of the rise in prices is fictitious. On the wholesale level, since so many of the goods involved are fairly standardized raw materials, this problem is less significant.

In view of these problems the rise in the consumer price index from 1958 to 1964 needs some interpretation. During this period the wholesale index was stationery, while the consumer index was rising at the rate of 1¼ per cent per year. It is perhaps not fanciful to suggest that this small rise measures improvements in quality rather than a price change per se. If so, it is erroneous to speak of continuing inflation in this period. Even without such an interpretation the rise is small by historical standards.

Implicit Price Deflators. Another type of price index, which comes closer to the concept of a universal measure, is the series called *implicit price deflators for gross national product*. The gross national product (GNP) is the money value of all production in the country in a given year, and its total depends on both physical output and the price level.[5] In order to eliminate the effects of price changes, a second series is computed called *GNP in constant dollars.* The computation is exceedingly complex. Basically it involves adjusting each individual series in the total by an appropriate price series or price index. Thus the value of shoe production is adjusted by an index of shoe prices in order to obtain a measure of changes in the volume of shoe output. When all such items, as adjusted, are added together, the resulting GNP in constant dollars presumably measures what GNP would have been if there had been no price changes since the base year. Since GNP in current dollars (the original series) includes the influence of price, dividing the current dollar series by the constant dollar series should tell us what happened to prices in the meantime. This is the implicit price deflator (*implicit* because it is implied by the comparison of the corrected and uncorrected GNP figures, but not calculated directly).

The implicit price deflators are pretty close to being all-inclusive, and it might therefore be thought that they would provide a much better indication of the general behavior of prices than either the wholesale or the consumer index. However, because of difficulties, both theoretical and practical, in deriving the figures, their accuracy is generally considered to be not as great as that of the other series.

On the other hand, the general behavior of the GNP price deflator series is

[5] A further discussion of GNP will be found in Chap. 26.

not significantly different from that of the other price indexes, as Table 21-4 shows. In the past decade, in particular, the deflator has risen at a rate only very slightly greater than the rise in consumer prices of 1¼ per cent per year. Since consumer expenditures are by far the largest part of GNP, it is not surprising that the two indexes should be reasonably comparable, but the GNP deflator is pushed up somewhat more rapidly by a rather substantial increase in the cost of government purchases of goods and services, whose prices have risen faster in the past ten years than those of any other major component of GNP.[6]

These are some of the relationships shown by an examination of prices over the past 200 years. It will be our task in the next several chapters to examine more critically and in greater detail why price levels move as they do.

The Effects of Price-level Changes

But why worry about changes in the price level? What difference does it make that the value of money is not the same today as it was yesterday? Who cares? I do. You do. Everybody does, whether he realizes it or not. Price changes affect not only the distribution of income and wealth, but also even the level of production, the standard of living, and the amount of employment.

Strangely enough it is not fluctuations in the value of money as such that do the damage. It is not the fact that price levels change that bothers us, but rather that when they do, individual prices do not all move together.

If *all* prices moved at precisely the same rate, any variation would make absolutely no difference to anybody. By "all prices" we mean not only prices of commodities, but also such things as wages, prices of real estate, and the value of securities, pension rights, and other debts. Suppose, for instance, that the country woke up one morning and found that all prices had doubled overnight. The price of everything I buy has doubled, but so has my income. I'll receive twice as much on my investments, but I'll have to find twice as much to pay off the mortgage. The value of money has shrunk, but such a change would make no more difference than if the physical size of the dollar bill had been cut in half.

Redistribution of Income. The difficulty of a fluctuating price level arises from the fact that some prices move when others don't, or else they move more rapidly. If retail prices rise faster than wages, the wage earner is squeezed into a lower standard of living. If wages rise more than the price of his product, the employer is likely to be caught with reduced profits. If some wages rise more steeply than others, the lucky workers push themselves up ahead of

[6] For the individual components of the series, see the source cited for the table. An explanation of the computation of the figures is given in Department of Commerce, *National Income, 1954 Edition: A Supplement to the Survey of Current Business* (U.S. Government Printing Office, 1954), pp. 155–158.

those less fortunate. If the cost of things the government buys rises faster than taxes, the government runs into an unexpected deficit.

Anyone who depends on an income that moves sluggishly is likely to find himself with a falling real income as prices rise, and his salary won't stretch over the increased cost of living. But when prices fall, he's in clover (provided he can hang onto his job). His salary is not likely to be cut, and he finds he can buy more goods with the same income. For other people, particularly those dependent upon profits, income may fluctuate more than prices. As prices rise, their incomes rise even faster, and their real standard of living goes up. In depression their income falls drastically, perhaps even to zero, and they are worse off even if prices fall somewhat. Workers subject to cyclical unemployment would also be in this category.

Inflation, then, tends to redistribute income from those with sticky incomes to those with rapidly increasing incomes. Deflation favors those with sluggish incomes over those whose incomes fall rapidly.

The problem is one of lags; some prices are stickier than others. Some are completely fixed. The most important fixed prices are debts—all kinds of debts, from dollar bills to bank accounts to bonds, insurance policies, and pension funds.

Debtors and Creditors. Because debts are fixed in monetary value, debtors gain and creditors lose when prices rise. The value of money (in terms of which the debt is defined) has fallen, so the debtor pays—and the creditor has to accept—a lower real value in payment.

Suppose I borrow $100 from Jones for a year at an interest rate of 5 per cent. Jones is willing to give up his right to use $100 now in order that he may have a larger amount ($105) to spend a year later. But suppose prices rise 5 per cent during the year. This means that when I pay back $105, that amount of money will buy precisely the same goods as $100 would have bought a year earlier. In real terms Jones gets back precisely what he lent. He has been cheated out of his interest. He has given up the use of his money and run the risk of my not repaying him without receiving any real benefit from what he has done. I have received the use of his money at no real cost at all. If prices had risen by 10 per cent, Jones would actually have been paying *me* $5 for using *his* money.

Suppose I figure that I ought to have $20,000 in life insurance in order to protect my wife when I die. So I buy that size policy. Perhaps I pay premiums for twenty years, and at my death she collects $20,000 only to discover that it will buy only half as much as it would have when I took out the policy because prices have doubled in the meantime. As a creditor of the insurance company I (or rather my wife) have been defrauded by inflation. The same thing would be true if I had put my money in a savings account or government bonds or any other type of fixed dollar investment.

On the other side of the picture the debtor gains by being able to pay off his debt in depreciated dollars.

If prices are falling, the reverse is true: debtors lose and creditors gain (at least if they don't find their claims uncollectable). Suppose that Farmer Brown, looking at the high price of wheat in 1920 ($2.50 a bushel), decided he could afford to increase his production by buying additional wheat land. So he bought land worth $2,500, borrowing the money on a mortgage, which he figured he could pay off in a couple of years from the proceeds of 1,000 bushels of wheat. But by the end of 1921 the price of wheat had fallen below $1 a bushel. At that price it would take 2,500 bushels to pay off the mortgage. No wonder farmers were having trouble in the twenties, for Farmer Brown is fairly typical of the farm community in that period.

Inflation, then, tends to redistribute wealth from creditors to debtors. Deflation tends to shift it from debtors to creditors.

Gain Plus Loss Equals Loss. Although some people gain and others lose no matter which way prices are moving, it should not be thought that the gains necessarily counteract the losses. In a depression particularly, there is a net loss. As prices fall, wealth and income are shifted away from debtors and from people whose incomes are more volatile than other prices. But in addition they are shifted away from creditors *if* debts are defaulted and from people with normally sticky incomes (salaried employees) *if* they lose their jobs. Misery is widespread, and only a fortunate few are better off.

The basic reason for this net loss is that in a period of falling prices and depression (which usually, but not always, go together), total output falls for the economy as a whole, and there are therefore fewer goods to go around. On the other hand, it is possible that an inflation that gets out of hand may also result in decreased production as uncertainty plagues business and it appears more profitable to indulge in speculation than in production. In those periods when production is maintained, changes in the price level only redistribute income without changing its total. And of course if output rises, *average* income must go up even though some people may be worse off.

As the above discussion may suggest, both money and prices are inextricably bound up with general business conditions, prosperity, depression, growth, and stagnation. Our concern with money can hardly stop short of an analysis of the whole range of business fluctuations, and to that subject we turn in the next chapter.

Appendix: Construction of a Price Index

Anyone seriously interested in economics should strike up more than a nodding acquaintance with statistics. Economics is based on facts, not fancy, and most useful economic facts are in the form of statistics—a mathematical condensation of raw data that is much easier to digest than the original mass of figures. In order to use statistics intelligently the economist must have some knowledge of the pitfalls inherent in their compilation. It was a statistician trying to substitute facts for opinions who said, "Statistics don't lie"— and a realist who had been through the ropes before who added, "But liars use statistics." They may, in fact, even compile them. Statistics can be dangerous if not handled properly or if their precise meaning is not clearly understood.[7]

Perhaps we should not be cynical enough to agree that a statistician is a man who draws a mathematically precise line from an unwarranted assumption to a foregone conclusion, but we should nevertheless maintain a healthy skepticism concerning any statistics unless we understand how they were computed and by whom. Our examination of the pitfalls of index numbers in the preceeding sections of this chapter should help. An excursion into the purely mathematical difficulties may give us further insight.

Average of Relatives. Suppose we obtain the following information concerning the price of bread and milk (assuming for our example that these are the only two items to be included in a price index) for the years 1776 and 1777. P stands for price, and the subscripts refer to the years.

	P_{76}	P_{77}
Bread (loaf)	\$0.10	\$0.20
Milk (quart)	0.20	0.10

Prices have moved in opposite directions. Bread has doubled; milk has been cut in half. How do we arrive at an average? One of the simplest ways of combining these figures into an index is by computing *relatives* for each product and then averaging these relatives. A relative is obtained by choosing some year as a base year, arbitrarily setting the price of each product in that year equal to 100, and then computing the relative change from the base year to the year for which the index is to be compiled (called the *given year*).

Thus if we choose 1776 as the base, the relative for both bread and milk will be set at 100 for that year. In 1777 bread has doubled; its relative for that year is 200. Milk, whose price is only 50 per cent of the 1776 figure, will have a relative of 50 for 1777. To obtain an average (arithmetic mean) of these figures, they are added and the sum divided by 2. Thus:

	P_{76}	*Relative*$_{76}$ (*base* 76)	P_{77}	*Relative*$_{77}$ (*base* 76)
Bread (loaf)	\$0.10	100	\$0.20	200
Milk (quart)	0.20	100	0.10	50
		2|200		2|250
Price index		100		125

This index says that prices in general rose 25 per cent from 1776 to 1777. But did they?

[7] For an amusing journey into the use and abuse of statistics see Darrell Huff, *How to Lie with Statistics* (W. W. Norton & Company, Inc., New York, 1954).

Suppose we use precisely the same figures but decide to consider 1777 our base year instead of 1776. In other words, we set prices of each product equal to 100 in *1777* and compute their relative prices for 1776 on that base.

	P_{76}	$Relative_{76}$ (*base* 77)	P_{77}	$Relative_{77}$ (*base* 77)
Bread (loaf)	$0.10	50	$0.20	100
Milk (quart)	0.20	200	0.10	100
		2|250		2|200
Price index		125		100

The same prices, the same index formula. All we have done is shift the arbitrary base, and we discover that instead of rising 25 per cent from 1776 to 1777, prices have fallen 20 per cent (from 125 to 100)!

There must be something wrong with the method! There is indeed. As any statistician knows, the arithmetic mean is a questionable character and has to be watched carefully, or he'll put something over on us. The arithmetic mean has a built-in tendency to overstate—to give undue emphasis to large figures. The doubling of price from 10 to 20 gives a relative of 200 (100 points more than the base), while cutting it in half from 20 to 10 (which is precisely the same movement in the opposite direction) gives a relative of 50 (only 50 points less than the base). Averaging these two together will emphasize the 100-point rise more than the 50-point fall. So no matter which year we use as base, the given year shows a higher index than 100. We'd better look for a more reliable formula.

Unweighted Aggregate. One way of avoiding the difficulties of an average is to use an aggregate. The aggregate is based on the concept of the market basket. It compares, for the two years, the total cost of buying all the products to be included in the index. It adds up the prices for each year, takes the ratio between these totals, and multiplies by 100 (to make the answer comparable to the standard index of 100 for the base year). The formula for this process is

$$\frac{\Sigma p_1}{\Sigma p_0} 100$$

which reads, "the sum of prices in the given year divided by the sum of prices in the base year, the answer multiplied by 100." For our example the process is:

	P_{76}	P_{77}
Bread (loaf)	$0.10	$0.20
Milk (quart)	0.20	0.10
Aggregate	$0.30	$0.30

$$\text{Index}_{(1777 \text{ on base } 1776)} = \frac{30}{30} \times 100 = 100$$

With this formula no matter which year we choose as a base the ratio between them remains the same. The index is therefore consistent with regard to direction. The answer also appears more reasonable—more in line with what we would probably have thought the index should be from looking at the original figures.

In spite of its reasonable appearance, however, this index is also seriously defective. It is called an *unweighted* aggregate because we have not considered the relative importance of the two products. At least we have not done this deliberately. But our very failure to do so provides weights of a sort, for a truly unweighted aggregate is a mathematical impossibility. In this case we have unconsciously weighted a loaf of bread and a quart of milk equally.

Such unconscious weighting varies with changes in the unit we use in pricing our goods, though this may be entirely unintended. Suppose we had priced a *pint* of milk instead of a quart, assuming a pint to cost just half as much. We get an entirely different index.

	P_{76}	P_{77}
Bread (loaf)	$0.10	$0.20
Milk (pint)	0.10	0.05
Aggregate	$0.20	$0.25

$$\text{Index}_{(1777 \text{ on base } 1776)} = \frac{25}{20} \times 100 = 125$$

This index makes it appear that prices have risen by 25 per cent, although the basic price relations are precisely the same as in our last example, which told us that prices hadn't changed at all. The difference is that this second example gave milk (which fell in price) less weight than it had in the first example by using a pint as the unit of measurement rather than a quart. Since all indexes are weighted either by chance or design, it would be better to do the job intelligently.

Weighted Aggregate. All weighted aggregates are computed by multiplying each price by some measure of importance and then adding these weighted prices together to obtain the aggregate. The simplest weight to use is the quantity of the product purchased in the base year. This is easy to understand. It carries the idea of the market basket to the realistic point of computing the total cost not of a basket containing one of each item, but of a basket containing precisely the amount of each item that people actually bought in the base year. In the base year this is the total cost of actual purchases; in the given year it is the total cost of an identical market basket.

This base-weighted aggregate is the method used by the Bureau of Labor Statistics in computing both the wholesale and the consumer price indexes at the present time. Its formula is

$$\frac{\Sigma p_1 q_0}{\Sigma p_0 q_0} 100$$

where q_0 = quantity of each article bought in the base year.

Suppose we assume that in 1776 consumers bought 100 loaves of bread and 60 quarts of milk. These two figures are the weights by which we multiply prices in both years.[8]

	q_{76}	p_{76}	$p_{76}q_{76}$	p_{77}	$p_{77}q_{76}$
Bread (loaf)	100	\$0.10	\$10.00	\$0.20	\$20.00
Milk (quart)	60	0.20	12.00	0.10	6.00
Aggregate			\$22.00		\$26.00

$$\text{Index}_{(1777 \text{ on base } 1776)} = \frac{26}{22} \times 100 = 118.2$$

According to this index prices have risen by 18.2 per cent from 1776 to 1777. Compared with our first example of an unweighted aggregate, this shows more of a rise because our analysis of purchasing habits has shown that bread is actually more important in the market baskets of our hypothetical community than milk, and bread is the commodity whose price has risen. If we had found that milk was more important, our computations would have shown a drop in the general price level because we would have been giving more mathematical weight to the fall in price than to the rise. (Try computing your own index with consumption figures reversed—60 for bread and 100 for milk. You should get 86.2 as the index for 1777.)

Although this index seems to solve all our problems, and although it is actually used by the BLS, it still has one serious flaw. It requires the use of base-year quantities throughout the life of the index until the whole method of computation is reworked on a new base. As we know, this is an oversimplified assumption. Tastes change; people buy more of this product, less of that. Even price changes themselves are likely to lead to decreased consumption of higher-priced goods and increased use of cheaper ones. So the assumption inherent in a base-weighted aggregate—that quantities bought remain constant—simply isn't true.

We ought, then, to adjust our weights as buying habits change. But we cannot use the base-year weights in the base year and the given-year weights in the given year, for this would mean that changes in the index would result *both* from price changes *and* from quantity changes. We wouldn't be measuring the price changes for a given market basket; we would be measuring instead the total amount paid for an entirely different market basket. The result wouldn't be a price index at all, but a value-of-total-product index, and that's not what we want.

For mathematical reasons, then, our weights must remain the same even

[8] In actually carrying out the arithmetical computations the BLS goes at the job in a somewhat different manner. The results are identical with those illustrated here.

though people change their consumption patterns. This is one of the built-in difficulties of an index number that cannot be entirely removed. Two formulas, however, have been suggested to overcome this problem partially. Both attempt to combine base-year weights and given-year weights by averaging.

Marshall-Edgeworth Formula. The simpler of these formulas, developed by Alfred Marshall and Francis Edgeworth, uses as a weight the arithmetic mean of the two quantities, one for the base year and one for the given year:[9]

$$\frac{\Sigma p_1(q_0 + q_1)}{\Sigma p_0(q_0 + q_1)}$$

Except for the averaging of weights this formula is identical with the one we have just computed.

Fisher's Ideal Formula. Irving Fisher, as a result of his study of index numbers, developed a formula that has fewer defects than any other. He called it the *ideal formula:*

$$\sqrt{\frac{\Sigma p_1 q_0}{\Sigma p_0 q_0} \times \frac{\Sigma p_1 q_1}{\Sigma p_0 q_1}}$$

Although this formula looks formidable, it is fairly simple in fundamental concept. If we take it apart, we see that the first fraction is simply the base-weighted aggregate we have already examined. The second fraction is precisely the same except that it uses given-year weights instead of base-year weights. These two indexes, one based on base-year quantities and the other on given-year quantities, are then averaged by what is called a *geometric mean,* which is more accurate than an arithmetic mean. Instead of adding the two numbers and dividing by 2, it calls for multiplying them together and extracting the square root. Its great advantage is that it avoids the upward bias of the arithmetic mean.

The ideal formula obviously involves more extended mathematical computation than any other formula we have examined. In addition it shares one serious disadvantage with the Marshall-Edgeworth formula. Both require the collection of data on purchases for every year for which the index is to be computed. In practice this is an impossible task. Figures for quantities are much more difficult to obtain than prices, and not only would their collection cost an inordinate amount of money, but it would also involve a greatly increased amount of time, so that the index would not be available for many months after the period to which it referred.

[9] Logically the formula would appear as

$$\frac{\Sigma p_1 \dfrac{q_0 + q_1}{2}}{\Sigma p_0 \dfrac{q_0 + q_1}{2}}$$

The 2s, however, cancel out, yielding the simpler form.

Since price indexes are valuable tools of current policy, it is highly desirable to have them available as rapidly as possible. For this reason as well as on the grounds of cost, no current index uses these theoretically more accurate formulas. The error introduced by confining ourselves to the use of a base-weighted aggregate is a small price to pay for its more rapid availability and cheaper cost, particularly if the base period is moved up frequently enough so that the base-weight quantities are never seriously behind the purchase patterns of the times.

Questions for Thought and Discussion

1. Do you know of anything the price of which has not changed for years? Has the value of such a good remained constant?

2. Does the wholesale price index measure the value of money in general? Does any price index?

3. If candy bars continue to sell for a nickel but their weight is reduced, is this a change in price? (Price of what?)

4. Wholesale prices as a whole showed no rise during the twenties. Do you know of any groups of prices that rose significantly in this period?

5. Does the low point reached by wholesale prices in 1897 have any connection with the silver controversy in this country?

6. If one man said that prices rose 5 per cent from 1962 to 1963, while another said they fell 5 per cent, would you conclude that one of them was a liar? (See Table 21-2.)

7. Look up the data for the wholesale and consumer price indexes for the past ten years. Can such changes as have occurred be related to changes in general business conditions?

8. Can you think of any reasons why the particular commodities shown in Table 21-2 as especially volatile should show greater price flexibility than others such as motor vehicles, industrial chemicals, or iron and steel?

9. Why do you think consumer prices change more sluggishly than wholesale prices?

10. If the BLS consumer price index rises 5 per cent at the same time that you get a 5 per cent raise, will you be better or worse off?

11. If I lend money at 5 per cent interest during a period when prices are falling 5 per cent per year, what is the real rate of return that I am earning?

12. Why does the Institute of Life Insurance refer to inflation as the "cruelest tax of all"? Why should they be more concerned about it than, say, the National Association of Security Dealers?

Selected Bibliography

Cannan, Edwin: *Money: Its Connexion with Rising and Falling Prices,* 8th ed., Staples Press, Ltd., London, 1935.

Fisher, Irving: *The Making of Index Numbers,* Houghton Mifflin Company, Boston, 1922.

Huff, Darrell: *How to Lie with Statistics,* W. W. Norton & Company, Inc., New York, 1954.

Mills, Frederick C.: *The Behavior of Prices,* National Bureau of Economic Research, Inc., New York, 1927.

———: *Prices in Recession and Recovery: A Survey of Recent Changes,* National Bureau of Economic Research, Inc., New York, 1936.

———: *Prices in a War Economy: Some Aspects of the Present Price Structure of the United States,* National Bureau of Economic Research, Inc., New York, 1943.

———: *The Structure of Postwar Prices,* National Bureau of Economic Research, Inc., New York, 1948.

———: *Statistical Methods,* 3d ed., Holt, Rinehart and Winston, Inc., New York, 1955.

Mitchell, Wesley C.: *The Making and Use of Index Numbers,* U.S. Bureau of Labor Statistics Bulletin 284, 1921.

National Bureau of Economic Research, Price Statistics Review Committee: *The Price Statistics of the Federal Government,* New York, 1961.

Suits, Daniel B.: *Statistics: An Introduction to Quantitative Economic Research,* Rand McNally & Company, Chicago, 1963.

U.S. Department of Labor: *The Consumer Price Index,* Bulletin 1140, 1953.

———: *A Description of the Revised Wholesale Price Index,* ser. no. R2067, 1952.

Chapter 22 Money and Business Fluctuations

This sickness doth infect
The very life-blood of our enterprise.

The First Part of King Henry IV
Act IV, scene 1, line 28

Although it is necessary to an understanding of money's role in the economy to explore the fundamental nature of business fluctuations, we should recognize that a single chapter is far too short to do full justice to a subject that many volumes have failed to describe completely. Our task here must be limited to brushing in only some of the starkest outlines.

Business Fluctuations

If business activity continued at a steady pace, rising gradually as population dictated and technology allowed, many economic problems would disappear. But one of the most obvious facts of economic life is that all is not smooth. Business fluctuates; that can be seen from an examination of almost any statistical series describing the course of business: prices, production, employment, bankruptcies, profits, inventories, investment, and a host of others.

Figure 22-1 summarizes the fluctuations of fourteen of these business indicators since World War I ended.[1] If we tried to carry our figures further back, we would discover that many statistics simply don't exist for

[1] The data are plotted on semilog paper so that an equal vertical distance shows equal *percentage* changes rather than equal absolute changes. A rise in production from 30 to 60 occupies the same vertical distance as a rise from 60 to 120 since both cases represent a doubling of output. Thus the rate of increase (or decrease) of any series can be directly compared with that of any other by means of the slopes of the respective curves. Wherever the slope of any series is greater than the slope of another, the first is rising (or falling) at a faster rate.

earlier periods. No other index goes back as far as the one we have examined for wholesale prices. Estimates for industrial production have been pushed back to 1860,[2] but the earlier figures are somewhat shaky. Simon Kuznets has made estimates of gross national product back to 1869,[3] and even earlier (though somewhat questionable) estimates have been made, but the Department of Commerce series was not started until 1929. While employment figures are shown in census data as early as 1820, annual figures date only from 1900, while accurate information on *un*employment is not available prior to 1929.

The forty-five years covered in the table are sufficient to indicate clearly the erratic nature of business. The data show two fundamental relations: (1) Most of the economic indicators *tend generally* to move in the same direction (except for unemployment, which for obvious reasons moves inversely). (2) There are, nevertheless, differences in movement clearly discernible within the general pattern. For instance, wholesale prices seem to move faster and further than retail prices, while the prices of primary commodities (basic raw materials) are even more volatile. These differences among price movements persist over the years and seem to be part of a general pattern.

In other cases differences between series appear at one point or another, but not consistently over time. Construction contracts fell in 1928, when the rest of business was booming; they missed the depression of 1938, dropping instead during the war. Wholesale prices, which usually rise with production, failed to do so in the twenties and the sixties.

If we used less general figures than the aggregates shown, this diversity would be even more pronounced. Just as individual prices may vary considerably from the average, so the production of particular commodities may diverge from the general index. Thus shoe factories may be running at half speed while chemical plants are pushed to capacity. There may be similar variations among regions. Textile towns of New England may fail to share in general prosperity, or a new plant in Seattle may stir a frenzy of activity there while the economy generally feels the effect of a slump. In Michigan, so dependent on the automobile for its work, unemployment reached almost 20 per cent of the work force in 1958, when the national average was only 8 per cent.

There are long-run shifts in activity as well. The difference between freight carloadings and electric power output is striking. While both show the effects of business ups and downs, power output has increased fortyfold in the past forty-five years, while carloadings today are less than they were in 1919. The railroad has felt the increased competition of newer methods of transport at the same time that more and more uses have been found for electricity. For electricity, recessions have usually brought a slowing down of the rate of increase rather than an actual decline.

[2] Edwin Fricky, *Production in the United States, 1860–1914* (Harvard University Press, Cambridge, Mass., 1947).

[3] Simon Kuznets, *National Product since 1869* (National Bureau of Economic Research, Inc., New York, 1946).

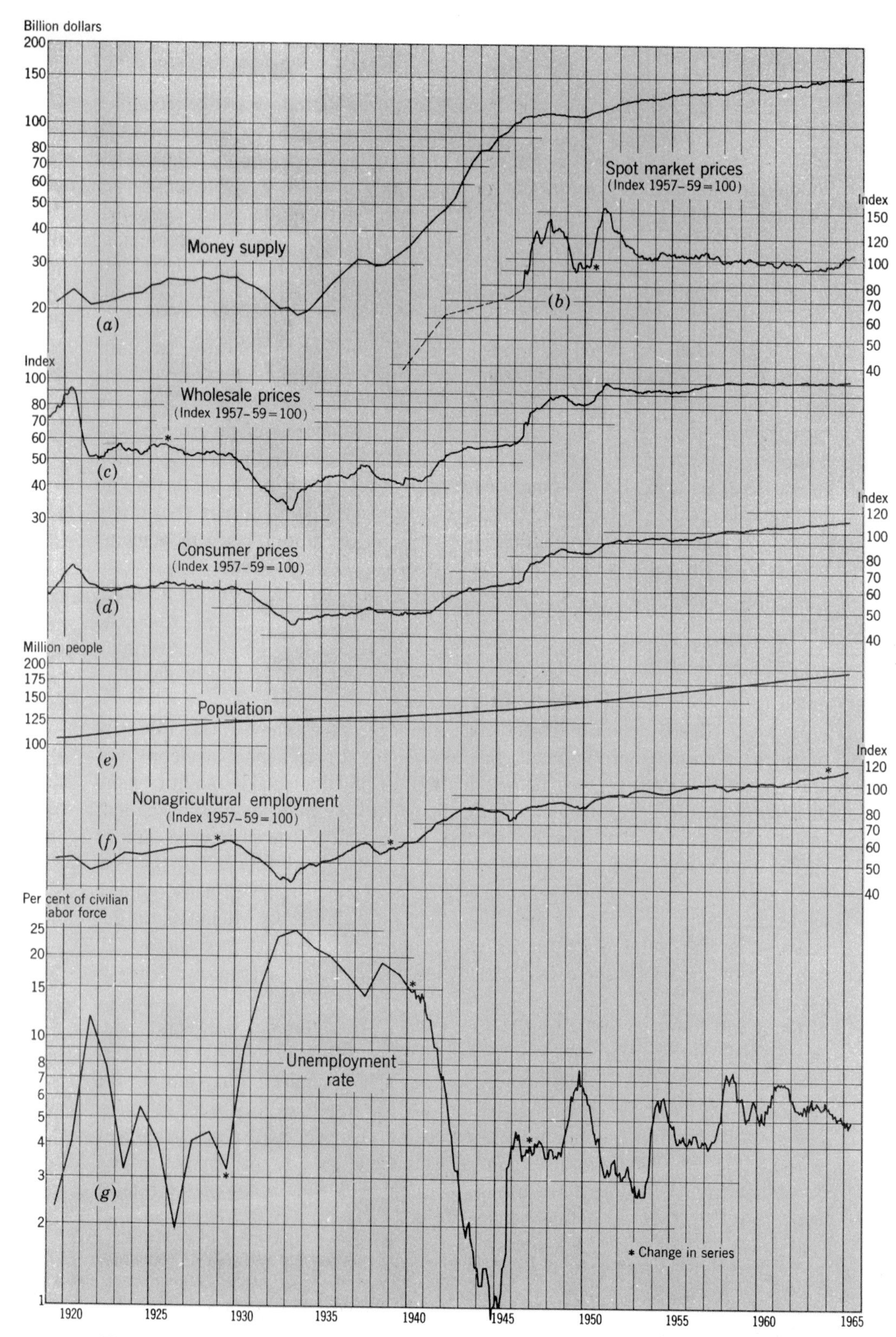

Figure 22-1. Caption on page 412.

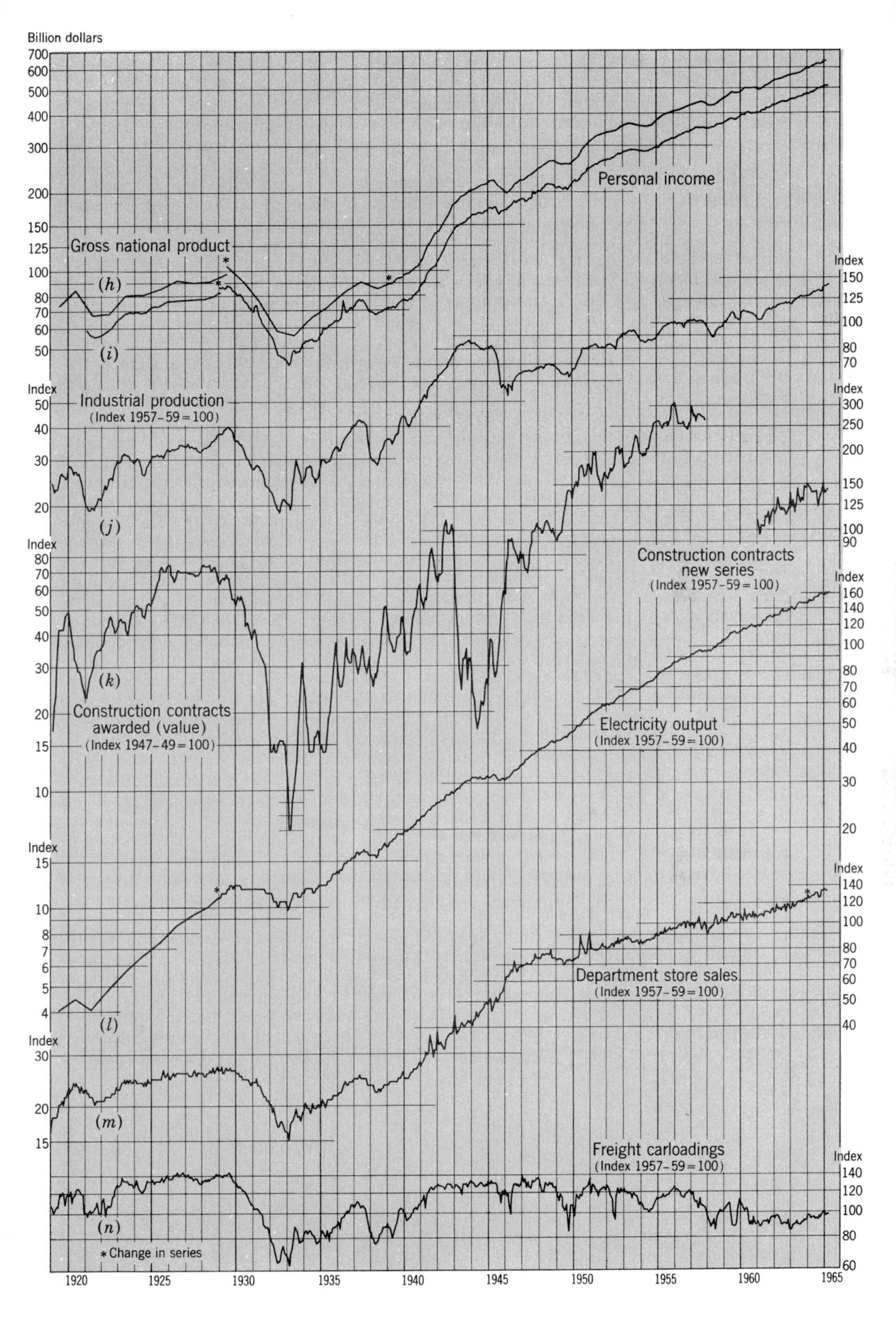

Billion dollars
Personal income
Gross national product
(h)
(i)
Industrial production
(Index 1957–59 = 100)
(j)
Construction contracts
new series
(Index 1957–59 = 100)
Construction contracts
awarded (value)
(Index 1947–49 = 100)
(k)
Electricity output
(Index 1957–59 = 100)
(l)
Department store sales
(Index 1957–59 = 100)
(m)
Freight carloadings
(Index 1957–59 = 100)
(n)
* Change in series
Index
1920
1925
1930
1935
1940
1945
1950
1955
1960
1965

Figure 22-1. Selected indexes of business activity, 1919 to 1965. (*a*) **Money supply** [demand deposits, adjusted, plus currency outside banks]: Board of Governors of the Federal Reserve System, *Banking and Monetary Statistics,* pp. 34-35; *Federal Reserve Bulletin,* vol. 34, no. 9 [September, 1948], p. 1135; vol. 46, no. 2 [February, 1960], p. 134; current issues. (*b*) **Spot market prices:** U.S. Bureau of Labor Statistics, "Revised Daily Index of Spot Market Prices, June 1946–December 1951 and Selected Dates," mimeographed; "Daily Index Numbers of Spot Market Prices, Monthly Average Indexes," mimeographed; "Daily Spot Market Prices and Indexes, Weekly Summary," current issues, mimeographed. (*c*) **Wholesale prices:** U.S. Bureau of Labor Statistics, "All Commodities Wholesale Price Index, 1957–59 = 100," mimeographed; *Federal Reserve Bulletin,* current issues. (*d*) **Consumer prices:** U.S. Bureau of Labor Statistics, "Consumer Price Index—U.S.: All Items, 1913 Forward—Series A," mimeographed [converted to 1957–59 base by the author]; *Federal Reserve Bulletin,* current issues. (e) **Population:** U.S. Bureau of the Census, *Statistical Abstract of the United States: 1964,* p. 5; *Survey of Current Business,* current issues. (*f*) **Nonagricultural employment:** *Federal Reserve Bulletin,* vol. 45, no. 8 [August, 1959], p. 1028; Board of Governors of the Federal Reserve System, "Indexes of Total Employment in Nonagricultural Establishments," mimeographed; U.S. Bureau of Labor Statistics, "Seasonally Adjusted Index of Employees in Nonagricultural Establishments," mimeographed; *Federal Reserve Bulletin,* current issues [1947–49 indexes converted to 1957–59 base by the author]. (*g*) **Unemployment rate:** Stanley Lebergott, "Annual Estimates of Unemployment in the United States, 1900–1954," in *The Measurement and Behavior of Unemployment* [Princeton University Press, Princeton, N.J., for the National Bureau of Economic Research, 1957], p. 215; U.S. Bureau of Labor Statistics, "Unemployment Rates, Old Definitions, March 1940–December 1946, Seasonally Adjusted," typewritten; "Labor Force, Employment and Unemployment, January 1947 to date" [June 30, 1959], mimeographed; *Federal Reserve Bulletin,* current issues. (*h*) **Gross national product** [at annual rates]: Simon Kuznets, *National Product since 1869* [National Bureau of Economic Research, Inc., New York, 1946], p. 51; U.S. Office of Business Economics, *National Income, 1954 Edition,* pp. 224-225; *U.S. Income and Output* [1958], pp. 118, 120-121; *Federal Reserve Bulletin,* current issues. (*i*) **Personal income** [at annual rates]: U.S. Bureau of the Census, *Historical Statistics of the United States, 1789–1945,* p. 328; U.S. Office of Business Economics, *National Income, 1954 Edition,* pp. 238-241; *U.S. Income and Output* [1958], pp. 148-149; *Business Statistics, 1963 Edition,* p. 7; *Survey of Current Business,* current issues. (*j*) **Industrial production:** Board of Governors of the Federal Reserve System, *Industrial Production, 1957–59 Base,* p. S-148; *Federal Reserve Bulletin,* current issues. (*k*) **Construction contracts awarded** [thirty-seven Eastern states, 1919 to 1957]: Board of Governors of the Federal Reserve System, "Index of Construction Contracts Awarded," mimeographed; *Federal Reserve Bulletin,* current issues. New series [forty-eight states, 1961 to 1965]: *Federal Reserve Bulletin,* current issues. [All construction contract figures are based on data of F. W. Dodge Company, a Division of McGraw-Hill, Inc.] (*l*) **Electricity output:** *Federal Reserve Bulletin,* vol. 42, no. 10 [October, 1956], pp. 1063-1065; current issues [1947–49 data converted to 1957–59 base by the author]. (*m*) **Department store sales:** *Federal Reserve Bulletin,* vol. 37, no. 12 [December, 1951], p. 1490; current issues [1947–49 data converted to 1957–59 base by the author]. (*n*) **Freight carloadings:** Board of Governors of the Federal Reserve System, "Index of Freight Carloadings, 1935–39 Average = 100," mimeographed; *Federal Reserve Bulletin,* current issues [1935–39 and 1947–49 data converted to 1957–59 base by the author].

If we examine carefully a large number of data for business activity—those presented in Figure 22-1 as well as many other series of various kinds—we discover that there are four different types of movement:

1. *Secular trend*—a long-term, persistent movement in one direction or another.

2. *Business cycles*—more or less regularly recurring fluctuations around the long-term trend. A business cycle is characterized chiefly by the fact that it seems to affect simultaneously most parts of the economy and particularly the economic aggregates (such as prices, production, employment, and income). By general agreement no such movement is called a business cycle unless it runs more than a year from peak to peak (or trough to trough).

3. *Seasonal variations*—movements in specific indexes that recur regularly at the same period each year. They differ from one series to another.

4. *Random or sporadic fluctuations*—a catchall for erratic movements that don't seem to fit adequately into any of the above categories. Their causes may be nontypical and nonrecurring and are often not even known. Because there is little in the way of generalization that can be said about random fluctuations, we will not examine them further.

Secular Trend. One of the most striking facts shown in Figure 22-1 is that all but two of the series rise over the whole period shown, regardless of what they may do from year to year. This is secular trend, a basically continuous movement of a statistical series in the same direction over a period of time much longer than the business cycle. Unemployment shows no appreciable trend at all, while for freight carloadings the trend may be slightly downward. Other activity, such as surrey production or railroad construction in this century, would show a pronounced downward trend.

In an expanding economy aggregate figures for production, employment, and income will always show an upward trend. This is what we mean by the growth of the economy.

Let's take industrial production as an illustration. This is a figure very commonly used as a measure of growth. In the period covered by the chart, production has risen fivefold. Why? One reason is the increase in population, which has not quite doubled. Obviously more people need more shoes, more soap, more saxophones. So significant is this relationship that production figures are frequently computed on a per capita basis—output divided by the number of people.

Production, however, has risen much faster than population, and per capita output has gone up almost threefold. This is due primarily to technological improvements, which have increased our ability to turn out goods. Productivity per worker has increased as more and better capital equipment and more efficient methods are introduced. This is the rise in the standard of living for which the nation is always striving and which it has been quite successful in achieving.

This general upward movement, then, is the secular trend of production. Other indexes will show trend patterns based on conditions peculiar to each series. When we are studying business cycles, it is frequently desirable to try to eliminate the effect of trend in order that the cyclical pattern may appear more clearly. The simplest way to do this is to estimate the trend by drawing a line through what appears to be the middle of the data. Such a trend line for industrial production is shown in the top half of Figure 22-2. For some series a fitted trend line of this sort might not be straight; a curve or a broken line might describe the data more accurately. In the case of industrial production (as plotted on semilog paper) a straight line does very well. This implies that production—though interrupted by cyclical ups and downs—has grown at a relatively constant long-run rate, a rate of approximately 3¾ per cent per year.[4] Quite obviously the rate has been much larger at certain times and negative at others, but this is the average for the whole period shown.

There might, indeed, be some question as to whether this trend most adequately describes the data, for it is clear that there are sizable deviations from the line we have drawn. The largest of these, however, occurred during the Depression of the thirties, which was obviously a cyclical phenomenon, not a change in long-term direction. The war pushed production in the other direction, but here again the large deviation from trend was temporary, and since the war we seem to have gotten back into almost the same pattern that existed in the twenties.

Once the trend line has been drawn, we can restate the original figures in terms of their deviation from trend, thus showing the data "corrected for trend." This is done by dividing the actual figure for each month by the value of the trend line for that month as read from the graph. Thus in March, 1940, the trend was precisely 50, while the original index of production was 40.2. Dividing 40.2 by 50 gives a figure of 0.804 (or 80.4 per cent), which means that in this month production was 19.6 per cent below "normal."[5] In March, 1959, with the trend at 100, actual production was 104.8, or 4.8 per cent above the trend. The deviations from trend for the whole period are shown in the lower half of Figure 22-2.

While the upward trend of industrial production is based primarily on increases in labor force and productivity, other series may show very different secular movements. A particular industry may grow, decline, and die—such as trolley-car production—thus showing a reversing trend. Other industries may slow down for long periods of time and then pick up again as new outlets for the product are developed.

The trend of employment is based primarily on population growth but is altered somewhat by changes in the ages at which people start to work or retire and by the extent to which women normally work.

Long-term trends in gross national product (GNP) would be similar to those for production (with some modifications based on the inclusion of farm

[4] The actual slope of the trend line in Fig. 22-2 is 3.7 per cent per year. Others might draw it slightly differently.

[5] The word "normal" must be taken with a grain of salt since the trend line is drawn somewhat arbitrarily. Although it seems reasonable, it is not really normal in an objective sense (if there is such a thing as objective normality).

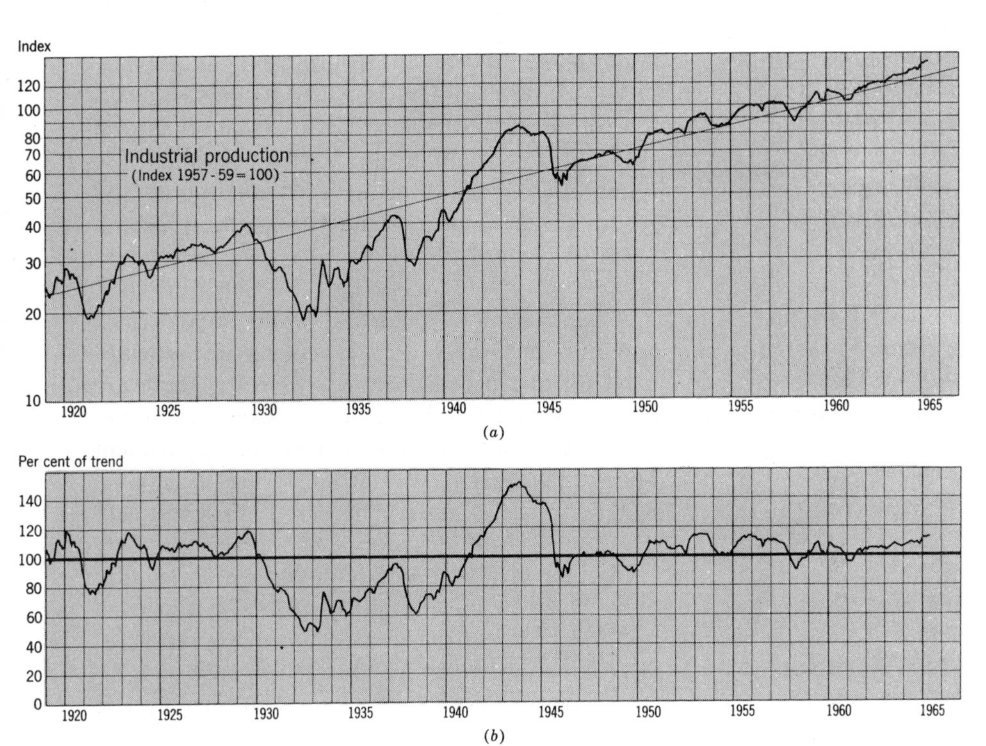

Figure 22-2. Trend in industrial production, 1919 to 1965. (*a*) Original data, 1957–59 = 100 (from Figure 22-1), with trend line fitted by the author; plotted on semilog paper to show equal percentage changes as equal distances. (*b*) Deviations from trend; trend = 100; plotted on regular graph paper.

production, mineral extraction, services, government purchases, and other items not covered by industrial production) if the price level remained constant, since GNP is simply the monetary value of total output. In order to express GNP in "real" rather than in monetary terms, the figures are sometimes "deflated," that is, adjusted for price changes, as discussed in the preceding chapter.

For instance, GNP in 1964 was $628.7 billion in current (1964) dollars. But since prices in 1964 were 108.9 per cent of their level in 1958 (the year used as the base for deflated GNP figures), the value of GNP in 1964 expressed in terms of 1958 dollars can be obtained by dividing $628.7 billion by 1.089.[6] The resulting figure, $577.6 billion, is the amount that GNP presumably would have been in 1964 if prices had remained constant between 1958 and 1964.

[6] Technically the process of deflation does not use any standard price index. Instead each component part of GNP is deflated by its own appropriate price index before the components are added together to form the total.

The secular trend of GNP stated in constant dollars shows the rise in real output of the economy. This figure can also be divided by population to show per capita changes. Figures for GNP in current dollars (uncorrected) combine both real changes and price changes without distinguishing between them.

There is no fundamental reason why price indexes should show a secular trend, although for the period we are examining they seem to do so. As we saw in Chapter 21, the trend for the nineteenth century, at least for wholesale prices, could be considered either a straight line or a slow oscillation up and down. For monetary policy both the cyclical movements and the trend are important considerations.

Seasonal Variation. Although business activity tends to move for long periods in the same direction, there are also very short-term movements in particular types of business activity that tend to recur regularly every year. These are seasonal variations. Even industrial production has a slight seasonal variation, but it is more obvious in other series, such as employment and department store sales, or in particular lines of production, such as lumbering or canning.

Employment rises significantly during the summer because both supply and demand for labor rise. College students and others enter the work force only in the summer at the same time that the number of jobs rises in agriculture and the resort industry. As a result employment is likely to rise in June even though we may be moving into a depression. Department store sales rise dramatically in November and December regardless of the general state of business. If they rise *less than usual,* business is deteriorating. Only if they rise *more than usual* do they indicate a business upturn.

Because seasonal factors are both misleading if ignored and relatively easy to recognize, almost all business series where seasonal factors are important are adjusted for seasonal variation before publication. This is a process similar to that for removing trend except that the original figures (or, less frequently, figures already adjusted for trend) are compared with the seasonal pattern for the particular series rather than with a trend line.

Figure 22-3 shows both original and seasonally adjusted figures for employment and department store sales. The sawtooth pattern of unadjusted figures and the relative smoothness introduced by adjustment are readily apparent.

All the series in our earlier Figure 22-1 have already been adjusted for seasonal variation where any seasonal pattern is apparent. They have not, however, been adjusted for trend. In most cases this latter process could be carried out roughly but adequately by drawing a pencil line through the center of the data. Since the seasonal variation has already been removed, the deviations of the figures from such a trend line would represent business cycle or random fluctuations.

The Business Cycle. The business cycle, as already suggested, is a general movement of aggregate business activity up and down around the secular trend, such fluctuation requiring more than a year for the complete cycle. This is not an ideal definition and is not nearly as explicit as we might desire. The

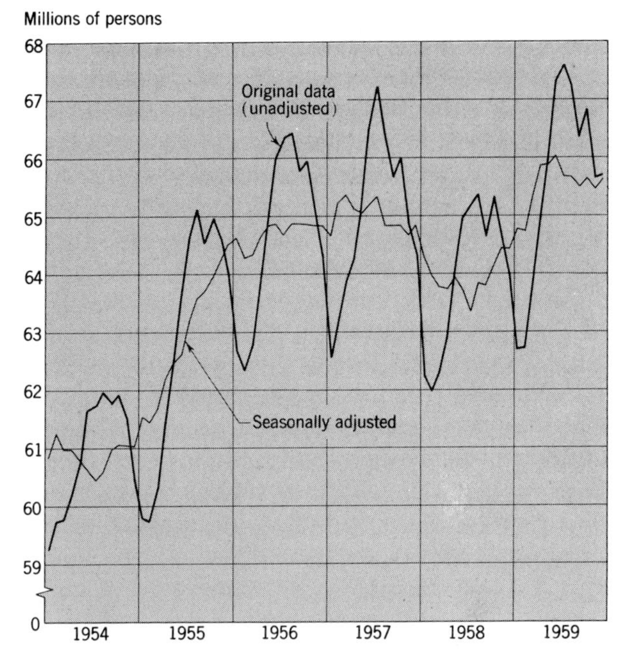

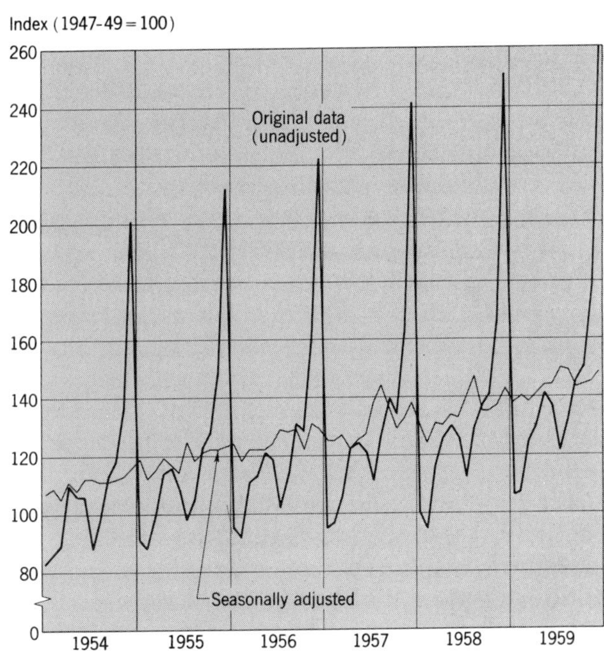

Figure 22-3. Seasonal variation in employment and department store sales, 1954 to 1959. (*a*) Employment; (*b*) department store sales. (*U.S. Bureau of Labor Statistics, "Total Employment," mimeographed; "Total Employment* [*New Definition*] *Seasonally Adjusted,"* typewritten; *Federal Reserve Bulletin, current issues.)*

unfortunate fact is that business cycles are such complex phenomena, and they take so many shapes, that they can't be pinned down to our complete satisfaction. In view of these diversities many economists question even the use of the term "cycles," maintaining that it implies more regularity than exists. As long as we recognize the diverse nature of the fluctuations, however, there is an advantage (and little harm) in sticking to the traditional terminology.

Business activity is not a homogeneous concept that can be measured in terms of inches or tons. When Joe says, "Business is good," he usually means *his* business. Bill's firm may have just failed—which is hardly good for Bill.

The key to the problem lies in the fact that the business cycle is a movement of business in *general.* Not necessarily all of it, but most of it. Yet while a true and complete picture of a cycle could be obtained only by examining the data for all kinds of business activity, it is difficult for the mind to comprehend simultaneously the large number of indexes involved. For practical purposes a compromise may suffice, in which a first approximation to the problem is obtained by using a single index that is widely inclusive. Such a picture is presented in Figure 22-4.

The data plotted on this chart are essentially those for per capita industrial production with both seasonal variation and trend removed. For the earlier years (prior to 1901), for which aggregate production figures are simply not available, Leonard Ayres, the compiler, resorted to an extremely complex series of statistical procedures in order to approximate production figures. In spite of the care with which this work was done, nothing can really take the place of complete original data. The data for the early years covered in this index, therefore, just as in the case of the wholesale price index, must be taken with several grains of salt. Nevertheless, it is the best we can do if we want to achieve historical perspective in a single series.

In spite of its shortcomings the chart reveals quite clearly (and no amount of further documentation would contradict it) that business cycles are not a simple alternation of prosperity and depression in a recurring pattern of constant design. Production moves up and down, but in no recognizable rhythm. Sometimes it fluctuates rapidly without wandering very far from normal, as from 1867 to 1870. Sometimes it moves sharply up and down in a short period, as in 1924. Sometimes it remains depressed for a long period but without falling much below 90 per cent of normal, as from 1874 to 1879. Never has it fallen so low or stayed in the cellar so long as in the Great Depression of the thirties, from which we were dragged only by the tremendous government expenditures of the war.

Not only do timing and extent of movement vary, but the direction of movement is frequently unclear. What appears to be the start of a recovery, as in 1932, sometimes peters out before it gets very far. Even when we had definitely passed the turning point in 1933 (as we can see by hindsight), the upward thrust was not continuous; it was interrupted several times by fairly severe setbacks. Even the peak of 1937 was submerged below the normal level instead of pushing above the line.

This makes it difficult to say when a peak or a trough actually occurs. The problem is compounded by the fact that other series (say, employment or bank loans outstanding) reach turning points at different times.

The National Bureau of Economic Research, an outstanding independent research organization that has devoted the greater part of its efforts since its founding in 1920 to intensive examination of business cycle facts, has tried, by an examination of all variables simultaneously, to set up "reference dates"

Table 22-1. Business Cycles in the United States, 1854 to 1964

Monthly reference dates		Duration in months		
Peak	Trough	Expansion	Contraction	Full cycle
	December 1854			
June 1857	December 1858	30	18	48
October 1860	June 1861	22	8	30
April 1865	December 1867	46	32	78
June 1869	December 1870	18	18	36
October 1873	March 1879	34	65	99
March 1882	May 1885	36	38	74
March 1887	April 1888	22	13	35
July 1890	May 1891	27	10	37
January 1893	June 1894	20	17	37
December 1895	June 1897	18	18	36
June 1899	December 1900	24	18	42
September 1902	August 1904	21	23	44
May 1907	June 1908	33	13	46
January 1910	January 1912	19	24	43
January 1913	December 1914	12	23	35
August 1918	March 1919	44	7	51
January 1920	July 1921	10	18	28
May 1923	July 1924	22	14	36
October 1926	November 1927	27	13	40
August 1929	March 1933	21	43	64
May 1937	June 1938	50	13	63
February 1945	October 1945	80	8	88
November 1948	October 1949	37	11	48
July 1953	August 1954	45	13	58
July 1957	April 1958	35	9	44
May 1960	February 1961	25	9	34
Average duration, 26 cycles		29.9	19.1	49.0
Median duration		25.5	15.5	43.5

Source: Geoffrey H. Moore, *Measuring Recessions*, Occasional Paper 61 (National Bureau of Economic Research, Inc., New York, 1958), p. 260. The last three dates were furnished by the Bureau directly to the author. Average and median duration computed by the author.

for the peaks and troughs of all cycles since 1854. These are given in Table 22-1. They have also been indicated on the chart of business activity (Figure 22-4). With minor exceptions[7] they conform closely with the turning points of

[7] The notable exceptions are December, 1858; April, 1865; December, 1867; June, 1899; and October, 1945.

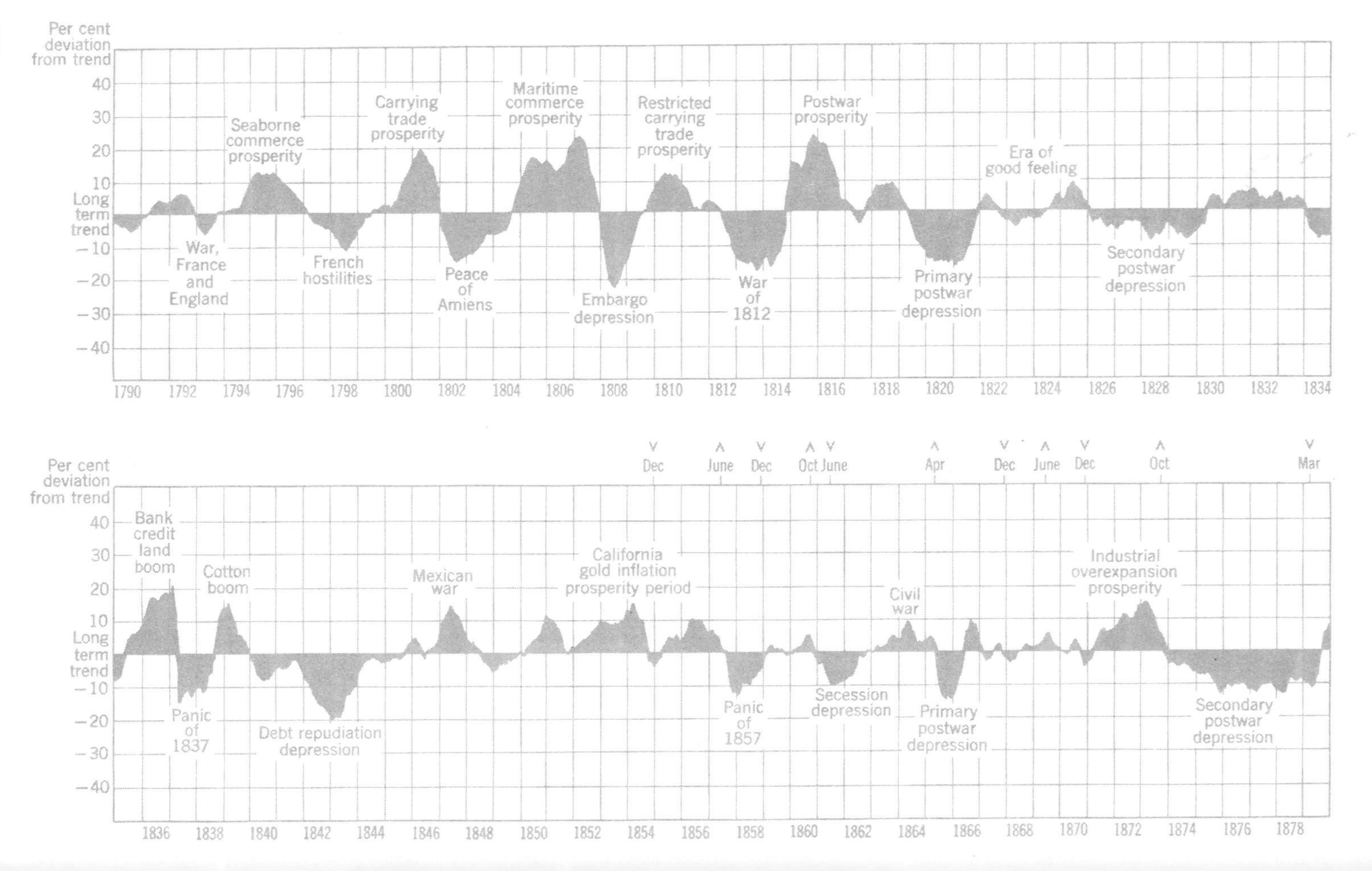
Per cent deviation from trend
40
30
20
10
Long term trend
−10
−20
−30
−40
War, France and England
Seaborne commerce prosperity
French hostilities
Carrying trade prosperity
Peace of Amiens
Maritime commerce prosperity
Embargo depression
Restricted carrying trade prosperity
War of 1812
Postwar prosperity
Primary postwar depression
Era of good feeling
Secondary postwar depression
1790 1792 1794 1796 1798 1800 1802 1804 1806 1808 1810 1812 1814 1816 1818 1820 1822 1824 1826 1828 1830 1832 1834
Dec June Dec Oct June Apr Dec June Dec Oct Mar
Bank credit land boom
Panic of 1837
Cotton boom
Debt repudiation depression
Mexican war
California gold inflation prosperity period
Panic of 1857
Secession depression
Civil war
Primary postwar depression
Industrial overexpansion prosperity
Secondary postwar depression
1836 1838 1840 1842 1844 1846 1848 1850 1852 1854 1856 1858 1860 1862 1864 1866 1868 1870 1872 1874 1876 1878

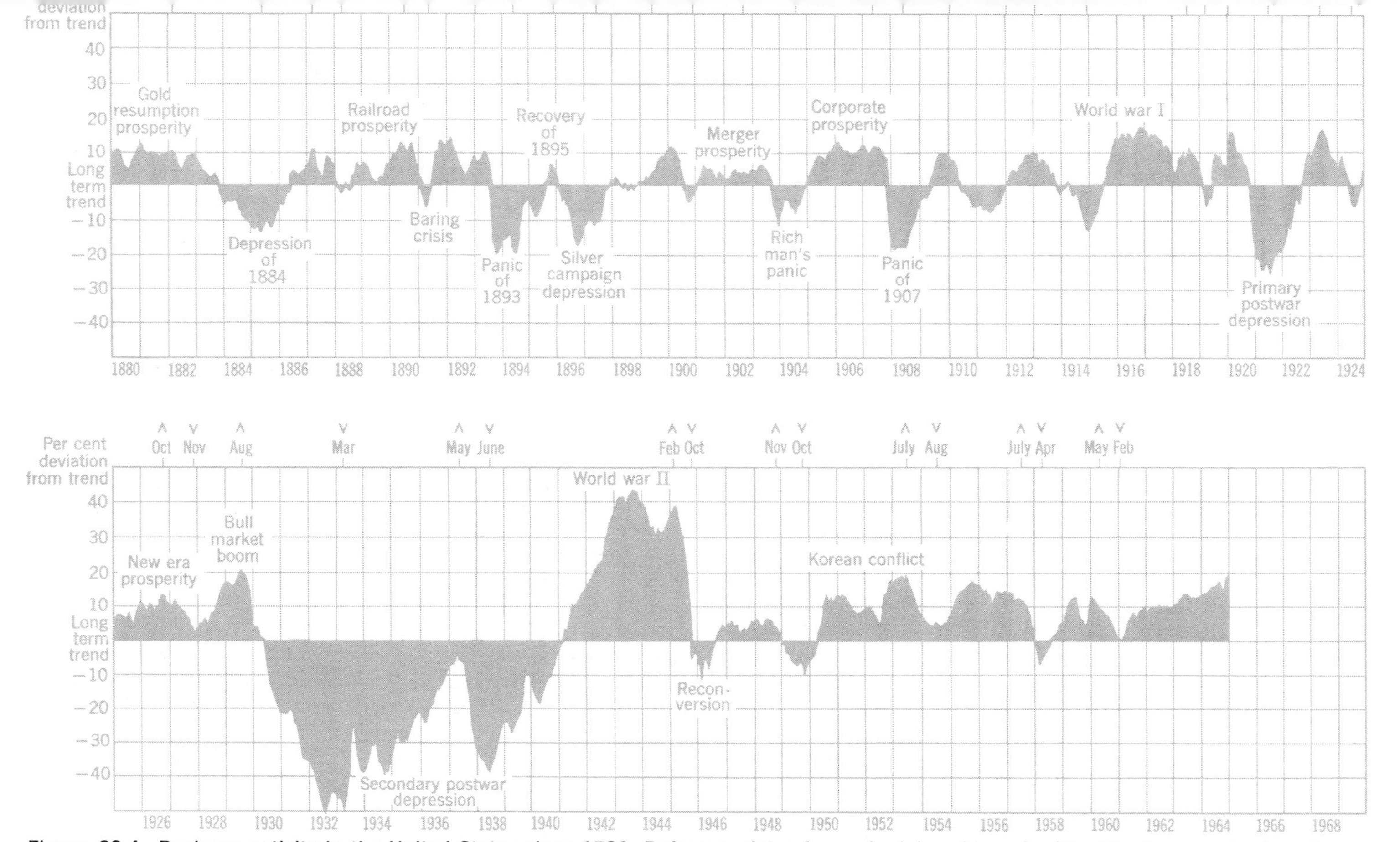

Figure 22-4. Business activity in the United States since 1790. Reference dates for peaks (Λ) and troughs (V) of business cycles have been added by the author from Table 22-1. *(Courtesy of the Cleveland Trust Company, Cleveland, Ohio.)*

industrial production, though from what has already been said about diversity it is obvious that complete conformity could scarcely be expected.

These reference dates give us some basis for measuring the length of cycles. Measured from trough to trough the twenty-six cycles from 1854 to 1961 vary from two to eight years in length. The arithmetic mean is slightly over 4 years, and the median is 43½ months. In duration, as in other aspects, no two cycles are alike.

This brief examination of the nature of business cycles only begins to tell the story of their variation. They vary not only in terms of effects, but in terms of causes as well. It is awkward to discuss them in generalities or to speak of a "normal" cycle. A "normal" cycle is pretty much on a par with a "normal" eccentric. There isn't any such animal. Nevertheless business cycles usually do have a great deal in common. The details differ, but there is a core of similarity. Although highly individualistic, each cycle is a member of the same species, and the basic characteristics that seem to recur in most cycles may be considered reasonably typical of the species as a whole.

The business cycle, since it has no beginning and no end, cannot be said to start at any point. It represents a continuous alternation of prosperity, recession, depression, and revival, each contributing to the next phase. The causes of each particular movement lie not only in the factors of the moment, but also in maladjustments created in the preceding phase or even in some previous cycle.

The Great Depression of the thirties, for instance, owed its severity to a great number of factors going back a decade or more, many of them directly or indirectly related to World War I. Among them are:

1. General depression in agriculture, which started in 1921 and was never satisfactorily cured. The problem arose partly from overexpansion of farm production during the war and the difficulty of readjusting to new conditions at lower prices in the face of overhanging mortgages and too many farmers on the land.
2. The satisfaction of backlogs of demand that were created during the war and were gradually whittled down during a decade of high production. This was most obvious in the field of housing, where the backlog was filled by 1926 or 1927, with a consequent decline in construction activity before the rest of the economy felt the pinch.
3. The development of new industries after the war, particularly automobiles and electrical appliances. These fed originally on a broad new market, but when practically everyone had a radio, replacement demand was insufficient to support production at the former rate.
4. The growth of consumer credit, which fed the boom with new purchasing power. When incomes dropped, those who were still paying off last year's debts had less available to buy this year's goods.
5. The unsoundness of the banking structure, a legacy of over a century of inadequate banking supervision. When the financial debacle occurred, the

domestic situation was aggravated by international financial problems based to a large extent on complications resulting from postwar reparations payments.

6. The stock market boom, which gave rise to a false optimism based on rising prices rather than sound underlying conditions. Any failure of stock prices to continue upward at an accelerating rate was a cause for pessimism.

7. An unsound structure of industrial development based partly on the enthusiasm engendered by a booming stock market, partly on an overestimation of potential markets, and partly on unsound credit expansion.

These are but a few of the problems. Among other things they indicate that one of the primary reasons why this depression was so bad was that downswings in several sectors of the economy happened to coincide. The agricultural cycle does not conform closely to industrial activity. If agriculture is in good shape, it will help to modify the severity of an industrial decline. But if agriculture is already in the doldrums, it will have a depressing effect on the rest of the economy.

The same is true of real estate activity, which seems to work on a much longer cycle than other business activity. Construction helped to keep the economy from falling flat on its face in 1924 and 1927, as did a backlog of demand for other durable goods. Once construction turned down, the rest of the economy lost an important buoying influence.

Another case in point is the banking crisis. This did not touch off the downturn. It was rather the result of collapse in other sectors. But when widespread bank failures did appear in 1932 and 1933, they seriously shook the confidence of business, already at a low ebb, and made recovery that much more difficult.

A business cycle, as we have already noted, is composed of many aspects of business. When some are going up and others down, the economy as a whole isn't too badly off. When they all go down at once, the result is disastrous.

Just as the basis for the Great Depression lay in many forces already existing in the previous prosperity, so the process of business retrenchment lays the groundwork for future expansion. The weakest firms fail, and their assets pass into the hands of others more capable. Overcapacity is whittled down by the simple process of wearing out of equipment over time. Water is squeezed out of stock values. A backlog of new inventions accumulates, and these can be drawn on once the upswing starts. The overhanging burden of debt is reduced by default and negotiation. Consumers, having felt the pinch of austerity for a while, are ready to buy as soon as their income permits. The force of each factor varies, of course, from one cycle to another.

Each cycle thus has its own personality based on its particular place in the flow of history. Nevertheless, as we have already suggested, there are common characteristics of most cycles that make it not too unreasonable to try to describe a "typical" cycle. This we will attempt to do.

The "Typical" Cycle

Since a cycle does not really begin at any particular point, our examination must simply choose a convenient place for breaking in. Let's say we are at the bottom of a depression.

Business in the Doldrums. Everything is low: production, prices, employment, sales, money supply, income, inventories—and spirits. Strangely enough the last may be most important, for what happens to the economy depends on what businessmen think about the future prospects of their business. If business was bad this year, entrepreneurs may expect it to be even worse next year. If so, they will cut back their purchases and production, and things will actually get worse. On the other hand, regardless of how bad business is this year, if the managers think it will be better next year, they will plan for better times, and this is likely to produce the upturn they expected.

We're speaking here of businessmen as a group. No single individual can think the nation into prosperity, nor does a businessman usually consider the effects of his action on the economy. But if all producers start expanding output, they hire more employees, and the extra pay in workers' pockets provides an expanded market for their goods.

Optimism. It is optimism, then, that breaks the gloom of economic inactivity, optimism that starts the nation moving upward. But to say that optimism is the cause of revival doesn't take us very far. Why do businessmen become optimistic? To answer that question fully would almost be a course in business cycles all by itself. Very briefly, here are a few possibilities (there are many others):

1. Inventories, which were excessive, have been worked down to a more satisfactory level, so that distributors are more apt to reorder from manufacturers, thus encouraging increased production.
2. Consumers who have postponed the normal replacement of their cars or refrigerators because conditions were bad and the old ones *could* be used for a while longer now decide that these items are past further repair. This means higher sales, one of the best producers of optimism there is.
3. The same thing may happen to manufacturers who finally have to replace decrepit machinery that they had been nursing along beyond normal useful life. This produces new orders for machinery makers.
4. Entrepreneurs may feel that a new invention may sell well even though business in general is bad.
5. New technological processes may reduce costs to a point where the product can be marketed at a price consumers won't pass up.
6. Producers, foreseeing eventual recovery ("We can't stay down here forever"), may want to get the jump on competitors by building that new factory or increasing inventories *now* while costs of materials, wage rates, interest, and so on, are low.
7. Consumers, having limited their consumption in the early days of the

depression in order to provide a nest egg against future unemployment, may find that things aren't as bad as they feared. They may then start spending more freely.

8. The government may spread purchasing power by increased payments to the unemployed, by works projects, or by other increases in spending. A war almost inevitably raises the level of economic activity for this reason.

9. Lower taxes similarly stimulate private spending.

10. The failure of many firms often makes it possible for others to purchase their physical assets at bargain prices, thus making production possible at lower overhead costs.

11. The gradual repayment of overhanging debts will put debtors in a more liquid position and therefore make them more ready to spend. Even bankruptcy may permit the bankrupt to start afresh.

12. Banks with excess reserves may encourage business to borrow for expansion purposes through lower interest rates, new types of lending contracts, or more ready availability of funds. The monetary authorities can aid in this direction by easing controls.

13. It is even possible that optimism may be induced by changes in the weather or by subtle environmental changes that we do not yet understand. Jevons's attempt to blame business cycles on sunspots appears to be rather unscientific, but the whole influence of environment cannot simply be written off; we don't know enough about it.

In broad terms these various possibilities (except for the last) fall into two groups: (1) sales rise, thus stimulating business, or (2) firms increase production in anticipation of greater sales at some time in the future. The statistics seem to indicate that the latter predominates, for investment plans (as measured by new incorporations, by construction contracts awarded, and by new securities issues) normally start upward before production or sales indexes.[8]

The Upward Push. The start of the revival occurs when a sizable number of businessmen decide that they will expand production, whether to meet orders already received or to anticipate expected future orders. Increased output means hiring more workers (or lengthening the workweek of those already employed), buying more raw materials and supplies, perhaps ordering more machinery, or even building a new factory.

All these mean spending money. If the firms involved don't have idle funds of their own to put to work, they must borrow the money from others, in many cases from commercial banks. In the latter case the total money supply rises as the banks create new deposits. If they put idle funds to work, this increases the velocity with which money circulates in the economy; the same quantity of money does more work. In any event money is an important part of the process. Producers must have money before they can spend it, and statistics corroborate the fact that changes in monetary phenomena tend to precede changes in production and other physical aspects of business.

[8] Wesley C. Mitchell, *What Happens during Business Cycles: A Progress Report* (National Bureau of Economic Research, Inc., New York, 1951), pp. 265, 305.

Regardless of where business gets the money, the spending of it gives a lift to the economy. If it is used to buy materials or machinery, it means sales for the suppliers. A new factory gives work to the construction industry. Higher payrolls mean more money in the pockets of consumers, and since many of these workers were formerly unemployed, it doesn't take much imagination to see them in the stores on Saturday, buying that new dress for Mary or a sirloin steak for a celebration. Thus consumer goods industries see their sales rising too.

The initial upsurge is now spreading out through the economy. If it was very small to start with, it may become so thin that its upward push is unnoticeable. If it is sufficiently large, however, it is likely to affect the business expectations of many (not necessarily all) of the firms that receive the increased income. They in turn will buy more materials, hire more workers, borrow more money, and so add their upward push to the economy.

Thus while some producers gave an initial fillip to the economy by increasing their business expenditures, the consequent rise in income and in purchases by consumers induces other producers to expand *their* productive facilities. This in turn further raises employment, income, and consumption. Unless some depressing factor intervenes to reverse this movement, the economy is off on an upward spiral of rising prosperity.

Maladjustments in the Economy. Hopefully this upsurge will last for a long time, but it is probable that it cannot go on forever, and it is certain that in the past it never has. Table 22-1 indicates that the average revival lasts only 2½ years. Why? There are any number of reasons, but some of the most important are inherent in the nature of the upswing itself.

First we should remember that not all sectors of the economy are necessarily benefiting from the general improvement. There are always backwaters that, for reasons of their own, do not feel, or do not yield to, the upward pressures. These pockets of unemployment and depressed activity act as a drag on the rest of the economy and may pull it down if its momentum is not great enough to overcome their influence.

Other forces develop as the revival progresses.

Prices. As we have seen, the upswing requires either an increase in the money supply or an increase in its turnover. At the beginning this increased purchasing power may be balanced by increased sales out of inventory or by the increase in physical production. As the upswing continues, however, prices are likely to feel the upward pressure too. As demand rises, as production grows, as unemployment dwindles, bottlenecks appear. Certain facilities or supplies or labor skills are in short supply and cannot be increased as rapidly as the need for them grows. Their prices are forced up as prospective purchasers vie with each other for their possession.

Even without specific bottlenecks sellers may feel that the increased demand represents a good time to lift prices up from the (perhaps unprofitable) levels of the depression onto a more normal plane.

In the early stages of revival the price rise is likely to increase business optimism and add to the improvement of business conditions. Higher prices are encouraging to business for several reasons: (1) Profit margins may increase because prices of finished goods frequently rise faster than the costs of production, particularly such things as depreciation, rentals, and often wage rates (though with the growing strength of labor unions the last advantage seems to be disappearing); (2) businessmen are frequently debtors, owing money both to banks and to bondholders, and rising prices lighten the burden of their debts; (3) rising prices are usually associated with "good business" and increased sales; and (4) rising prices also mean that if a businessman makes a mistake in calculating his costs or the sales possibilities of his product, the general business expansion may cover up his errors.

But there are difficulties connected with price rises as well. Because of the highly heterogeneous nature of the pricing process from one industry to another, because of the varying impact of rising demand, and because of the differing supply situations, price movements will not be at all uniform. Wholesale prices tend to move more freely than consumer prices; raw materials more than finished goods; nondurables more than durables; prices in competitive industries more than prices in more closely controlled industries; prices of stocks more than prices of bonds; wages of hourly rated employees more than salaries of yearly rated personnel.

The impact of price changes will thus create stresses within the economy that may make it vulnerable to other disturbing influences. For instance, some businessmen whose costs are rising faster than the prices of their products will find themselves in a squeeze that may discourage further expansion. Speculation may be encouraged at the expense of more soundly conceived projects. Unpredictable shifts in the demand for products or in the utilization of resources may occur. At some point the price rise may discourage purchases by those who think prices have gone too high, and then we find goods "pricing themselves out of the market." If spending stops rising, the whole bubble may burst.

Saving. Another reason why buying may fail to expand at its former pace is that people have caught up on their backlogs of demand. They have replaced the old refrigerator and car and have bought a new TV, washing machine, and hi-fi set, and now they decide they had better start saving a little more. Savings are necessary and useful to the economy, and if the extra savings are made available to businessmen to help them finance the expansion, they may add to the upward push. But at the same time money saved is money not spent, and any increase in saving necessarily detracts from sales and is a drag on the upward movement. If the savings are hoarded, the drag is doubled, for purchasing power disappears from active circulation and is effectively lost.

Money and Credit. Since the upward movement inevitably requires some means of financing, bank credit normally plays a very significant role in the process. But banks can expand only so far. As excess reserves disappear and as banks find their liquidity impaired, they become more cautious, interest rates rise, and credit is rationed. Funds may then cease to be readily available for further expansion. It is of course possible for the monetary authorities to ease credit, and if the upswing continues along healthy lines, this probably will be done. But by the time the economy reaches full employment, inflation has undoubtedly already set in, and the authorities are likely to feel that since additional money cannot add to physical output but only to the price rise, further extension of credit is undesirable. This will be particularly true if borrowers appear to be using large amounts of newly created funds for speculative purposes. The general tightness of money may adversely affect some legitimate production projects and add to difficulties imposed on expansion-minded businessmen by higher prices of materials, higher wages, and other problems.

Inventories. Another factor in both the rise and the subsequent collapse may be the behavior of inventories. Inventories are usually low in a depression. As recovery commences, they drop still further, for the first impact of rising demand for any product reduces the stock of it on distributors' shelves. The retailer depletes his stock in order to meet the demands of his customers. In order to replenish it he orders more from wholesalers, who in turn order more from manufacturers, who increase their output. But the process takes time, and for a while sales are likely to exceed production, and inventories decline. As the pace of output is increased, this decline will be stopped and then reversed as sellers "fill up the pipelines." In the later part of the upswing, therefore, inventories are likely to increase.

This adds to the improvement in business, for production is kept at a level higher than current consumption by the amount being added to dealers' stocks. But what happens when inventories are built up to the desired level? Without any slackening in the demand on the part of ultimate buyers, orders reaching the manufacturer drop off. If there are other weaknesses in the economy, this may be sufficient to touch off a recession. This happens so frequently that a number of our minor recessions have been christened "inventory recessions" in honor of their major cause.

Plant Expansion. A somewhat similar effect may occur in terms of investment in plant and equipment. As sales rise, many firms may find it necessary or desirable to expand their productive facilities, particularly if they foresee a continued rise in demand in the future. The result is further work for construction companies and machinery suppliers. But a time may come when so much new plant has been built that there is little need for further expansion, and the construction industry finds its jobs declining even though the rest of the economy shows no dip. But unemployment here will show up in falling sales elsewhere, and so the economy may be pulled down.

At the same time the opening of new plants may have other undesirable effects, particularly if the firms that built them overestimated the size of the demand. A large volume of new goods may be turned out only to sit on the shelves for lack of purchasers, and this also will have a depressing effect.

Summary. We have mentioned these four factors at some length because they are cited prominently in certain business cycle theories, and they seem to be important in many business downturns. On particular occasions, however, other forces may be even more important. We may list some of these briefly along with a summary of those already discussed:

1. Prices may be so high that consumers and producers may hold off buying in anticipation of a fall.
2. Consumers, having been on a spending spree, may decide they had better start saving a little more, which means buying less.
3. Liquidity is reduced and credit becomes tighter, making it more difficult to finance further expansion.
4. Merchants find that they have overestimated and built up excessive inventories, which they now wish to reduce.
5. Manufacturers, having built new plants, see no further need to expand at this time.
6. Producers, building plants against an expected demand, may have overestimated and find themselves unable to sell the output of the expanded facilities.
7. Rapid increases in costs may have cut down the market for particular goods or have reduced the profit on them.
8. Consumers have stocked up on durable goods, and replacement demand is insufficient to maintain the former rapid rate of sales.
9. Government may decrease its expenditures or raise taxes sufficiently to discourage business.
10. Firms that started on a shoestring in a period of overoptimism may find they can't make a go of it. Their failure may have serious repercussions for their creditors.
11. A general expansion of consumer purchases on credit may finally peter out against the impossibility of borrowing indefinitely more and more.
12. Uneven expansion of different areas of the economy may produce strains or bottlenecks that undermine an already maladjusted structure of industry.
13. An attempt to push expansion beyond full employment will almost inevitably put strains on the price structure.
14. The mere failure of expansion to continue at an accelerating pace may disappoint businessmen.

While any of these causes, and many others, may help cause a downturn, the last suggests that if nothing else does the trick, the structure will eventually fall of its own weight. This may be too drastic a judgment, but history shows that no expansion in the last century has in fact lasted more than seven years, and only six managed to exceed three years. Something has kept us from expanding indefinitely.

The Downward Spiral. Whatever the cause, or causes, the downturn is based on pessimism, just as the upturn thrived on optimism. Businessmen see diminished prospects of profit. They scale down production plans, shorten the workweek, lay off workers. The economy slips into recession.

As business falls, so does financial activity. Businessmen no longer have need for new funds. Bank loans are repaid and the money destroyed. Funds lie idle for lack of productive employment. The fall in financial activity does not cause the drop in business, but it accompanies it—in fact it precedes it. In his analysis of business cycles, Mitchell discusses thirty-four comprehensive measures of activity. Eight of these generally fall before the rest of the economy, and seven of the eight are financial: bond prices, bond sales, stock prices, stock sales, new corporate security issues, New York City bank debits, and Snyder's index of deposit activity (the eighth item is construction contracts let).[9]

These statistics do *not* demonstrate that it is movements in the financial field that *cause* business cycles. Rather they suggest that fundamental forces at work in the economy show themselves most rapidly in the financial marketplace.

Whatever the forces, financial or otherwise, that cause the economy to tip over the brink of recession, it is clear that the ride downward represents the same spiral in reverse as the trip upward. Pessimism and "loss of confidence" take over. Profit prospects seem dimmer, and businessmen cut down on their expansion plans. The drop in building activity puts construction workers on the unemployment rolls. The drop in machine orders brings a slowdown to the machine producers, less steel is needed, and so on through the economy. Payrolls drop, consumers are forced to buy less, and this in turn makes retailers gloomy. They try to cut overhanging inventories, which accelerates the drop in orders reaching manufacturers. This results in more cutback in production, more layoffs, more decline in income and spending—and hence in production.

Meanwhile the burden of debt incurred during the prosperity phase presents its own problems. Businessmen no longer need additional cash to expand output. They tend to pay back their bank loans. There is less money in circulation, just as there are fewer payments to be made because of the general drop in business activity.

Many firms find that the glorious prospects that induced them to borrow have evaporated. Pressed for repayment, they attempt to raise cash by lowering prices. Some go into bankruptcy, and their stocks are disposed of at distress sales. Some lucky ones are able to buy up factories, equipment, and inventories at these advantageous prices and by thus lowering costs are able to pass on reductions to their customers. Others lower prices to meet competition or simply because they can't find buyers at the old prices. Some try to keep up prices and find their sales dropping instead.

[9] *Ibid.*, p. 32.

Optimism Again. No depression lasts forever. Gradually the forces of gloom spend themselves, and one area or another of the economy moves upward again. We are back at the point where we originally broke into the cycle. There is nothing to add here except a reminder that this is not the "beginning" of a cycle. We don't end one cycle and begin another. We simply move continuously from prosperity to recession to depression to revival to prosperity in a never-ending process. The seeds for revival are contained in depression, just as the seeds of recession are inherent in prosperity. Perhaps a greater feeling of that continuity would be obtained if we went back, with the events of the downturn fresh in mind, and reread "The Upward Push," which continues logically from this point.

Conclusion. In conclusion we would repeat, for it is vitally important, that this description of a "typical" business cycle is of necessity oversimplified. It does not describe *any* business cycle completely, and it is wholly inadequate to describe some. Physicists may reduce the universe to a single equation, but man's psychological reactions are apparently more complex than physical laws and refuse to be marshaled in neatly documented array.

Questions for Thought and Discussion

1. Would you expect to find the same seasonal variation in toy production as in bathing suit output?

2. Is there any seasonal movement in the quantity of currency outside banks? (See *Federal Reserve Bulletin.*)

3. Is it possible to predict the future course of any statistical series (such as department store sales) by means of extrapolating the long-run trend shown in the past?

4. Can you illustrate from your own experience disparities among various types of business activity over the course of a business cycle?

5. Can you explain why construction contracts awarded fluctuate so much more widely than industrial production?

6. Table 22-1 compares cycles on the basis of duration. Would it be possible to construct a similar table to compare their amplitude? What measure would you use?

7. Why are optimism and pessimism so important in influencing business activity?

8. What other causes not here listed can you think of that might help cause a revival or a decline in business activity?

9. Would it be possible to have business cycles as we know them in a nonmonetary economy? In a purely agricultural economy? In a fully socialized economy?

10. Can you conceive of conditions under which prosperity would continue indefinitely?

11. What is the general state of business at the present moment? What factors are (or have been) important in producing this particular state of business?

Selected Bibliography

American Economic Association: *Readings in Business Cycles,* Richard D. Irwin, Inc., Homewood, Ill., 1965.

Burns, Arthur F., and Wesley C. Mitchell: *Measuring Business Cycles,* National Bureau of Economic Research, Inc., New York, 1946.

Clark, John J., and Morris Cohen: *Business Fluctuations, Growth, and Economic Stabilization: A Reader,* Random House, Inc., New York, 1963.

Gordon, Robert Aaron: *Business Fluctuations,* 2d ed., Harper & Row, Publishers, Incorporated, New York, 1961.

Haberler, Gottfried: *Prosperity and Depression,* 3d ed., League of Nations, Geneva, 1941.

Hansen, Alvin H.: *Business Cycles and National Income,* W. W. Norton & Company, Inc., New York, 1951.

——— and Richard V. Clemence: *Readings in Business Cycles and National Income,* W. W. Norton & Company, Inc., New York, 1953.

Kuznets, Simon: *Economic Change: Selected Essays in Business Cycles, National Income, and Economic Change,* W. W. Norton & Company, Inc., New York, 1953.

Mitchell, Broadus: *Depression Decade, 1929–1941,* Holt, Rinehart and Winston, Inc., New York, 1947.

Mitchell, Wesley C.: *Business Cycles: The Problem and Its Setting,* National Bureau of Economic Research, Inc., New York, 1927.

———: *What Happens during Business Cycles: A Progress Report,* National Bureau of Economic Research, Inc., New York, 1951.

Saulnier, Raymond J.: *Contemporary Monetary Theory,* Columbia University Press, New York, 1938.

Soule, George: *Prosperity Decade: From War to Depression, 1917–1929,* Holt, Rinehart and Winston, Inc., New York, 1947.

Chapter 23
Theories of the Value of Money

Find out the cause of this effect,
Or rather say the cause of this defect,
For this effect defective comes by cause.

Hamlet
Act II, scene 2, line 101

We have seen that price changes play an important role in business activity. But price changes may be of two different kinds: changes in individual prices and changes in the whole price level. It is the latter with which we are primarily concerned here.

Any individual price may move because of changes in demand or supply. Demand may shift as a result of changes in tastes of consumers, changes in the price of other goods, movements in consumer income or in income distribution, the impact of advertising, or other factors affecting the consumer's desire to buy a particular product. Supply may shift because of changes in cost brought about by new techniques, wage negotiations, movements of raw material prices, or tax repercussions. These various factors push some prices up and others down.

Even while such price movements are occurring continuously, however, it is possible for the value of money to remain constant; as long as price increases offset decreases, the price index will not change. Such stability is fairly unusual, and in practice the value of money itself is subject to considerable fluctuation; the whole price structure moves up or down. What causes such movements?

The answer to this question is far from simple. Although it has attracted considerable attention for over a century, we still do not know as much as we would like about the problem. Many theories of the value of money have been advanced, criticized, and defended, and the discussion still goes on. Research and analysis have disclosed a great number of factors affecting the value of money. Some theories have proved more reasonable than others and have withstood better the tests of time and changed conditions, but the "ultimate" theory has not yet been devised.

At one time it was thought that monetary forces were simple to understand, and the earliest theories are correspondingly uncomplicated. We now realize that modern society is a complex of interrelated forces and that money is not merely a passive agent whose only task is to facilitate the exchange of goods. On the contrary, the way money is handled can seriously affect the whole operation of the economy in many ways: some obvious, some more obscure, some undoubtedly not yet even guessed at.

The objective of this and the following chapters is to trace our growing fund of knowledge about the way money works. Approximately in the order of their historical development we will examine several approaches to monetary theory:

1. Commodity theory
2. State theory
3. Equation of exchange
   a. Quantity theory
   b. Transactions and cash-balances approaches
4. Income approach
5. Flow-of-funds approach

The commodity, state, and quantity theories are rather in disrepute today, but they still have enough followers to warrant examination, if only to point out the pitfalls that they present to the unwary. It is significant that the more modern concepts are not designated as theories. They are ways of looking at the problem which provide much valuable insight but which cannot be said to give complete answers to monetary questions.

The Commodity Theory

The commodity theory is by all odds the easiest way to look at money. It says that money is essentially a commodity like any other and that its value is similarly determined by supply and demand—the cost of producing it and the desire people have for it in its nonmonetary uses. Not only is this concept simple, but it also accurately describes the value of money in its earliest forms. A cow has a value that is determined by the fact that it is a cow. It is used as money precisely because it has this value, and its worth as money is its worth for milk, for meat, or as a draft animal. Take away its monetary use, and it is still as valuable as it ever was. Take away its nonmonetary use, and it is worthless.

The same thing can be said for almost all the primitive forms of money—

fishhooks, beaver skins, beads, rice, or whatnot. Their monetary value was their commodity value.

But times change, and a theory that was true of a historical system many years ago does not necessarily describe new conditions. Gradually the monetary commodity has moved further and further away from its original use. The first step in the process is an increased demand for the money commodity. In a particular community there will be a given demand for fishhooks for fishing. But if people start carrying fishhooks without any intention of using them on a line but rather because they can be used in exchange for other goods, then the demand for fishhooks has increased. To the ordinary demand is added a monetary demand. This greater demand, as elementary economics teaches us, tends to raise the value of fishhooks. Thus the value of commodity money tends to rise above its commodity value alone.

This change occurs so slowly that it is almost impossible to trace. There is no point at which we can say with certainty, "Here the commodity theory ceases to be valid." So some people cling by habit to the old theory even though it is clear that we have long since crossed that invisible dividing line.

Certainly a dollar bill does not derive its value from the commodity value of the paper. Yet one sometimes hears the argument that the paper still represents gold—that it is still something like a warehouse receipt, in spite of the fact that a holder of currency can't get gold for it and that our gold reserve is only a small fraction of our total money supply.

Warren and Pearson, the most recent apostles of the commodity theory, marshaled vast collections of statistics to demonstrate that prices do depend on the value of gold. Consequently they felt that the value of the dollar depended on the amount of gold legally equal to a dollar and that "by reducing the weight of gold in the dollar, any desired price level can be established."[1] That is, the higher the price of gold (in dollars), the higher the price of everything else (in dollars).

Strange as it may seem, this theory influenced our monetary policy in 1933–1934. The reasoning went something like this: Prices today (1933) are some 40 per cent lower than they were in 1926. In 1926 we had prosperity. If we can raise prices to their 1926 level, we will again have prosperity. How do we raise prices by two-thirds?[2] Raise the price of gold by that amount. And that's just what we did. The devaluation of the dollar in 1933–1934 reduced its gold content by slightly over 40 per cent and thereby raised the price of gold from $20.67 to $35 an ounce. The Depression was solved.

But was it? Prices rose gradually from their low levels of 1932. But they started rising before devaluation and continued rising rather slowly thereafter. There is no indication that devaluation itself had any significant influence on that rise. It was not until October, 1942, that prices, as measured by the BLS wholesale price index, finally climbed up to their 1926 average. In the mean-

[1] George F. Warren and Frank A. Pearson, *Prices* (John Wiley & Sons, Inc., New York, 1933), p. 371.

[2] If prices were 100 in 1926, a 40 per cent drop would lower them to 60. To raise them 40 points back to 100 requires an increase of two-thirds (40/60).

time hundreds of other factors were working to bring us out of the Depression. No specific one can be singled out as *the* cause of recovery. Devaluation undoubtedly had some effect on prices, particularly with regard to imports, for it meant that more dollars had to be paid to obtain the same amount of foreign goods. But even this is only indirectly related to the value of gold.

The whole experience of this period tends to demonstrate the inapplicability of the commodity theory of money under current conditions. The value of today's paper money must come from some other source.

The State Theory

Another school believes that this value comes from the government. The state theory of money says that the value of money lies exclusively in the laws that create and govern it. "The soul of currency is not in the material of the pieces, but in the legal ordinances which regulate their use."[3]

It is certainly true that the modern state has a great deal to do with money. It can create money, presumably in any amount that it wishes. It can charter other institutions, such as commercial banks, and give to them the power to create money. Then it can regulate this issue within whatever limits it deems desirable. In addition it can give wider acceptability to money by agreeing to receive it for all taxes or other payments, by redeeming some forms of money in other types (convertibility), and by placing its guarantee or implied guarantee on money and thus increasing the faith of the populace in what otherwise might be unacceptable paper. And finally it may require that creditors accept particular kinds of money in payment of debt (legal tender) or even provide that goods must be sold for a given amount of money (price control).

In these various actions there are three fundamental ways in which the government affects the value of money:

1. It may improve the general acceptability of money by increasing people's confidence in it.
2. It can at least attempt to determine the value of money directly by legislating individual prices.
3. It can influence the quantity of money in circulation and hence its value.

In none of these respects, however, does the state have absolute power. Fundamentally money is not what the state says it is. Money is what people are willing to accept. Although the state may influence that willingness, it cannot compel it. If the state introduces something which it calls money but doesn't do the work of money satisfactorily, it won't be accepted as money. People will devise some other means of carrying on payments: scrip, for instance, or book transfers, or even barter.

Even legal tender laws do not make a particular instrument money, as we have already seen. If the law requires creditors to accept in payment some-

[3] George Friedrich Knapp, *The State Theory of Money,* abridged ed., trans. by H. M. Lucas and J. Bonar (St Martin's Press, Inc., New York, 1924), p. 2.

thing in which they have no faith, they may have to submit in those cases in which they cannot induce debtors to make more satisfactory payment by nonlegal means. But under such circumstances no new debts will be contracted, and no new sales will be entered into except in ways that avoid the legal requirement of an unacceptable means of payment. Legal tender quality can do almost nothing to add to the acceptability of an unwanted money; it is not necessary for a money that is acceptable without it.

Price-control laws fall in the same general category, although here the sweep of the law is broader. But it is certainly not an absolute power. If the law says I cannot sell goods except at a given price, I have three alternatives: to sell at that price, not to sell at all, or to break the law. In any given situation, undoubtedly all three actions will be taken by different sellers. We know that price control instituted during World War II had all these effects. There were large numbers of legal sales, but the total amount of products brought to market was less than it would have been at higher prices, and the black market flourished fairly openly in spite of the fact that patriotic motives associated with the war induced many people to accept controls that they would not have tolerated in normal times. History is replete with similar examples.

That leaves the power to influence the value of money by controlling its quantity. Here we are on much firmer ground. The state in almost all instances has either issued money itself or regulated those who have issued it, and it influences the amount of money in the community in a number of ways. But this power—to control value by controlling quantity—assumes a relation between the two that we have not yet demonstrated. In fact it assumes most modern monetary theory. It suggests that while the state may be the instrument through which the quantity may be regulated, it is quantity itself that controls value.

In other words, while governments may *influence* the value of money, they cannot *decree* it. Any attempt to do so must inevitably break down eventually in the face of forces more powerful than the state itself—the forces of supply and demand.

The United States Congress has seen fit to define a dollar as $15\frac{5}{21}$ grains of gold, $\frac{9}{10}$ fine. This sets the price of gold at $35 an ounce, and this attempt at price control over a single commodity, gold, has been fairly successful since the government stands ready to buy and sell gold (at least in large amounts and for certain purposes) at that price. This does not mean that the government has decreed the value of the dollar. All it has done is decree the price of gold, which is something else again.

Other prices are free to fluctuate and have in fact done so over a wide range. Nor can it be said that these movements have been caused by deliberate government action. The rise in prices after the last war, for instance, was largely the result of various government programs, but it was not intentional. It was an unwanted side effect. The government in fact *wanted* to keep prices down, but it either didn't know how or was unable to discipline itself sufficiently to accomplish its price objective. *Wanting* stable prices is not enough; *legislating* stable prices won't work. Only intelligent—often unpopular—

action can possibly bring about stability. There is no easy way, and the path of history is strewn with the wrecks of governments that fell afoul of the siren's isle of inflation.

The Equation of Exchange

The value of money doesn't depend on the material out of which it is made, nor on the authority that issues it, nor on the laws concerning it. A dime is only one-tenth as valuable as a paper dollar, although its "commodity" value is higher. A bank check drawn on a private bank circulates side by side with a note of the Federal Reserve Bank of Dallas. What do these various forms of money have in common? Certainly neither material nor issuer. Their common denominator is the fact that they all represent claims on goods designated in a certain number of "dollars." Taken all together these claims add up to the total purchasing power of the nation, the most significant aspect of which is its quantity.

The value of money, like the value of saucepans, is determined by supply and demand—the number of dollars there are and the amount of work for them to do. Money has value because it is scarce. Scarcity, however, is relative. What might be considered scarcity of money today would have been a tremendous oversupply 100 years ago. Scarcity must be measured in terms of the uses for money, in terms of the things available for it to buy. One common definition of inflation emphasizes this point: "too much money chasing too few goods"—prices rise because of a reduction in the relative scarcity of money.

This is the key to the quantity theory of money as well as modern modifications of that theory involving the transactions and cash-balances approaches. All these rely on the *equation of exchange,* which is itself not a theory at all, but a statement of fact.

Because the problem of measuring the value of money involves heterogeneous aggregates (the many diverse things for which money is demanded), it is difficult to conceive of supply of, and demand for, money in terms of ordinary price diagrams. The equation of exchange solves this problem by expressing the forces involved in a simple but comprehensive form.

The equation of exchange has been used in one guise or another for over two hundred years, and, though some economists today feel that it is a bit old-fashioned, the relationships that it shows are as true in the modern world as they ever were. The equation of exchange (which, in common with all supply-demand concepts, refers to a specified period of time) is

$$PT = MV$$

where P = general price level
T = *physical* volume of transactions (sales) during the period
M = quantity of money in circulation
V = velocity of circulation of money (number of times an average dollar changes hands during the period)

The equation of exchange is a truism, valid under all conditions. It says simply that the value of goods sold (PT) is equal to the amount of money paid for them (MV).

At the level of the individual transaction, at least, this is surely self-evident. Suppose I go to the grocer for five loaves of bread (t). I give him a dollar bill (m), and of course I give it to him only once (v). Assuming he gives me no change, it is clear that bread sells for 20 cents a loaf (p).

$$p \times t = m \times v$$
$$\$0.20 \times 5 = \$1 \times 1$$

Suppose the grocer takes the same dollar bill and buys 4 quarts of milk. The milkman in turn uses the same bill to pay a $1 movie admission. These transactions, along with my purchase of bread, are summarized in Table 23-1.

Table 23-1. Illustration of the Equation of Exchange

		p ×	t =	m ×	v
5 loaves of bread	@ $0.20	$0.20	5	$1.00	1
4 quarts of milk	@ 0.25	0.25	4	1.00	1
1 movie admission	@ 1.00	1.00	1	1.00	1
$PT = MV$		$0.30 ×	10 =	$1.00 ×	3

When we try to combine these individual transactions in order to obtain the equation for the whole economy, we find that we can't simply add them together. For instance, our example specifically states that the *same* dollar bill was used in all three transactions. The total quantity of money used must therefore be only $1 and not $3. But it is equally clear that this dollar changed hands three times: from me to the grocer, from the grocer to the milkman, and from the milkman to the movie house. Thus we see that velocity, which appears to have no significance for the single transaction (where it is always one), is actually an important element in the total. The same *quantity* of money may do more monetary work if it moves more rapidly.

On the other side of our aggregate it is possible to add the physical volume of transactions, although the result is a strange conglomeration of diverse items: ten units of bread, milk, and movie admissions mixed together. Whatever this hybrid animal may signify, it is conceptually possible to determine its average price. This cannot be done by adding the separate prices together nor yet by dividing this sum by 3. As we have seen in our examination of index numbers, a usable index must *weight* each price by its relative importance, which is indicated in this case by the number of units sold. Thus the price of bread (20 cents) is multiplied by its weight (5), and this product ($1) is added together with the similar (price times weight) products of milk and movie admission, and the total so derived is then divided by the sum of the weights (10), as shown in Table 23-2.

The result is an average price of 30 cents, much nearer to the price of

Table 23-2. Derivation of an Average Price

	p	q	pq
Bread	$0.20	5	$1.00
Milk	0.25	4	1.00
Movie admissions	1.00	1	1.00
		10	$3.00

$$\frac{\Sigma pq}{\Sigma q} = \frac{\$3.00}{10} = \$0.30$$

bread and milk than to the cost of movie admissions because purchase patterns in our example indicate that these two products are much more important to the economy in terms of amounts sold.

As the astute student will recognize at once, the mathematical process of computing a weighted price (P) is precisely the same as that of dividing MV ($3) by T (10). In other words

$$P = \frac{MV}{T}$$

which is simply an alternative way of stating the equation of exchange. As we said, the equation is a truism.

While the equation of exchange can be given numerical values for any period of time similar to those indicated in Table 23-2, there is little purpose to be served by using absolute figures for P and T because of the heterogeneous nature of the transactions involved. To say that the average price of cans of peas, tons of steel, shares of General Motors stock, subway fares, and tennis rackets is $7.31 is about as meaningless a statement as a statistician can make.

Fortunately we are not really interested in the *level* of prices, but rather in *changes* in that level. This can be measured by index numbers rather than by absolute magnitudes. Thus we know from the equation of exchange that an increase in M, for instance, must be associated with a decrease in V or an increase in T or P (or some combination of these), since from any given level taken as a starting point no factor in the equation can change without an equivalent change in some other factor or factors.

V and T Are Not Identical. Confusion very frequently arises in attempting to distinguish between V and T. Both are rates. T is the rate of sale of goods. V is the rate of turnover of money. It is not surprising that those who meet the equation for the first time sometimes conclude that if money is spent more rapidly, then more goods must be bought. But this does not necessarily follow. Money may be spent more rapidly simply because there is less of it. Or increased velocity may raise prices without increasing the *number* of goods sold. Thus a change in V may be associated with a change in M or P or T (or some combination).

Table 23-3 shows in a highly simplified form the ways in which various

Table 23-3. Hypothetical Changes in the Equation of Exchange under Highly Simplified Conditions

Week	Money held at beginning of week by: Business	Money held at beginning of week by: Worker	Paid by business in wages	Spent by worker on goods	$PT = MV$ (weekly basis)	Factors in equation changed from preceding case
Case 1. Assume: Economy consisting of a single worker earning $10 per week, paid every four weeks; produces ten schmoos a week and buys them all at $1 each; total money in existence, $40.						
1	40	0	40	10	$1 \times 10 = 40 \times \frac{1}{4}$*	—
2	10	30	0	10		
3	20	20	0	10		
4	30	10	0	10		
	(cycle returns to week 1)					
Case 2. Assume: Worker strikes and gets $20 per week; employer pays him every two weeks and raises price to $2.						
5	40	0	20	20	$2 \times 10 = 40 \times \frac{1}{2}$	*P, V*
6	20	20	0	20		
	(cycle returns to week 5)					
Case 3. Assume: Employer loses $20 down the drain; decides to pay worker weekly.						
7	20	0	20	20	$2 \times 10 = 20 \times 1$	*M, V*
	(repeats)					
Case 4. Assume: Worker doubles his productivity to twenty schmoos a week; employer cuts prices back to $1; worker buys all twenty schmoos.						
8	20	0	20	20	$1 \times 20 = 20 \times 1$	*P, T*
	(repeats)					
Case 5. Assume: Employer finds $20 again; doubles wages and prices simultaneously.						
9	40	0	40	40	$2 \times 20 = 40 \times 1$	*P, M*
	(repeats)					
Case 6. Assume: Worker doubles his productivity; employer doubles wages, obtaining new money from a bank loan, but doesn't raise prices; worker buys all forty schmoos a week.						
10	80	0	80	80	$2 \times 40 = 80 \times 1$	*T, M*
	(repeats)					
Case 7. Assume: Worker decides to work only half as long, lowering his production to twenty schmoos; his wages fall to $40, and employer pays him $80 every two weeks.						
11	80	0	80	40	$2 \times 20 = 80 \times \frac{1}{2}$	*T, V*
12	40	40	0	40		
	(cycle returns to week 11)					

* It takes four weeks for all the $40 to be spent by the worker; thus only one-fourth of it turns over per week.

combinations of factors in the equation may change under certain assumed conditions. For simplicity it is assumed that the economy concerned consists of only one individual working for a nonhuman employer, and the data for the equation of exchange are based only on the sale of the finished product. The table is designed to show *possible* situations and should not be interpreted as suggesting that any one of these conditions is normal. As we shall see shortly, it is more common for all four factors to move together than for some to remain constant while others change. But it is erroneous to assume that changes in V and T (or any other pair) must *necessarily* go together.

Transactions and Income Forms of the Equation. Since the individual transactions on which the equation of exchange is based are themselves statements of equality ($pt = mv$), it follows that no matter how we add them together, the total ($PT = MV$) must also be an equality. We might consider only transactions in coal, for instance, or only transactions taking place on Mondays. As long as factors in the equation referred to the same thing, the result would still be a truism.

The most commonly used form of the equation is very broad, and is called the *transactions equation.* It refers to the *general* price level (the prices of everything for which money is spent) and to the *total* transactions of the economy of whatever kind (sales of commodities, services, real estate, securities, labor, and so on). PT, then, is the total monetary value of all transactions in the economy. Velocity in such an equation is *transactions velocity,* the number of times on the average that dollars are spent for any purpose.

The *income equation,* however, is equally useful. Here P is (roughly) the *retail* price level, T is the volume of sales to *ultimate users,* and PT is the value of the final product only—a concept numerically less than total transactions primarily because it excludes sales between businesses. It is essentially the same as income, and V in such an equation becomes *income velocity.* While transactions velocity is the number of times money changes hands within the period, income velocity is the number of times money moves *from one income recipient to another.* Thus if I give a dollar to the grocer, who pays it to the baker, who turns it over to the miller, who pays it to a worker in wages, the transactions velocity is 4, while the income velocity is only 1 (from me to the worker, through several intermediate steps that aren't counted since they represent business receipts but not income).

In order to differentiate this equation from the more usual transactions form, we add the subscript $_y$ to all terms (except money)[4] to indicate that they refer to income concepts.

$$P_y = \frac{MV_y}{T_y}$$

[4] Since a particular piece of money can be used for any purpose, it is impossible to separate money used to pay income from money used in other ways. Hence we say that money is used less frequently to pay income (that is, its velocity for this purpose is less), not that there is less of it.

where P_y = price level at point of final sale
V_y = income velocity of money
T_y = physical volume of sales to final users (primarily at retail)

Statistical Verification. Since the equation is necessarily true, it follows that if we could obtain statistical data for the various components, they would show a numerical equality. Unfortunately, the data are not all available in a usable form. The quantity of money is an easily obtainable figure, and price indexes have been computed both for the general price level and for consumer prices, which, rough as they are, provide fairly useful tools of comparison.

Data on transactions are more difficult to come by. Indexes of industrial production are available, but this represents only a portion of total transactions, and while certain other types of transactions are fairly closely linked to industrial production, others are not: agricultural production, securities sales, and real estate transfers, to name a few.

Figures on velocity are similarly elusive. There is simply no way of telling how frequently a dollar bill changes hands. For bank deposits some rudimentary figures are available in the ratio of bank debits (checks charged against customers' accounts) to total deposits. These series, in addition to lack of full coverage, suffer from the fundamental defect that many checks do not represent real transactions. When a depositor writes a check in order to withdraw cash, his account is debited, but no transaction has occurred. Similarly when he buys securities, he normally sends a check to his broker in payment. His broker in turn may draw his own check to pay the seller's broker, who similarly draws a check to pay his customer. Bank debits in this case would be three times the actual amount of the transaction.

It *is* possible to derive figures for velocity but only through the use of the equation of exchange itself, not independently. We know, for instance, what total income is (P_yT_y). We also know the quantity of money (M). This leaves only one unknown (V_y). Thus personal income in 1964 was $495.0 billion, while there was $153.5 billion of money in circulation.[5] Income velocity, then, was

$$\frac{495.0}{153.5} = 3.2$$

This means that each dollar passed through the pockets of 3.2 consumers during the year; or, saying the same thing another way, it took almost four months for money to travel from one consumer's pocket to another's. Considering the speed with which money leaves your pocket and mine, this sounds as if business must hang on to it for a long time. Whether it's business or consumers who are responsible, the fact is that money travels more slowly than many people would guess.

[5] Demand deposits, adjusted, plus currency outside banks on June 29, seasonally adjusted.

The same approach can be used to obtain an approximation of transactions velocity, though deficiencies in our ability to measure the total value of transactions make the result somewhat tentative. Estimates of total nonfinancial transactions run more than four times as high as personal income. This means that on the average money goes through three businessmen's hands on its way from one consumer to another. On this basis, transactions velocity for nonfinancial transactions would come to slightly more than 12, indicating a turnover of funds about once a month. Including financial transactions would add an unknown amount to the velocity figure.

These examples are illustrative only. They refer to a specific year, and velocity, like any other factor in the equation, varies over time.

The Quantity Theory

The equation of exchange is a truism that does no more than state an algebraic relation. Unfortunately it is sometimes confused with another concept, the quantity theory of money. The quantity theory is a belief concerning the cause-and-effect relationship among the factors of the equation, and (in its crude form, at least) it is in considerable disrepute among economists because it tends to oversimplify the problem to the point of being incorrect.

The quantity theory, which can be traced back to Locke and Hume and followed through Adam Smith, Ricardo, and Mill, suggests that in the equation of exchange changes in V and T can safely be ignored, while changes in P are passive. This makes M the villain of the piece. In its simplest and least defensible form the quantity theory states that price varies directly and proportionately with the quantity of money in circulation. This means that a 50 per cent increase in the quantity of money would raise prices by 50 per cent.

Irving Fisher, who gives the most complete formulation of the theory, is careful to hedge his statement so that it is technically correct and in fact little more than a verbalization of the equation of exchange. "The level of prices," he says, "varies directly with the quantity of money in circulation, *provided the velocity of circulation of that money and the volume of trade which it is obliged to perform are not changed.*"[6]

In other words, if M changes while V and T do not, then P must. This is perfectly correct on the given assumptions. But Fisher goes on at great length to demonstrate that this is the *normal case* and that in fact V and T do not change much over time except in periods of "transition."

This obscures a basic problem, since the economy is almost continually in a state of transition—moving either up or down. If V and T move only slowly over the long run, as they appear to do, they also move fairly rapidly over the period of the business cycle. Since the business cycle is one of our most per-

[6] Irving Fisher, *The Purchasing Power of Money* (The Macmillan Company, New York, 1911), p. 14. Italics added.

sistent and embarrasing economic problems, short-run movements deserve more attention than quantity theorists are disposed to give them.

The quantity theory is correct in saying that the quantity of money is an important factor in determining prices. It is wrong in saying that it is the *only* important factor. The significance of V and T will be examined in the next chapter, but first a word about another area in which some quantity theorists go wrong.

The Relation between Currency and Demand Deposits. Fisher's book was written in 1911, at a time when checking accounts were beginning to achieve prominence in monetary payments but before they had reached the importance they have today. Older quantity theorists thought of money as consisting of currency only. Fisher could not ignore demand deposits; neither was he prepared to lump them together with currency. As a compromise he subdivided money into its two components and treated them separately. Thus he writes the equation of exchange

$$PT = MV + M'V'$$

where M = quantity of currency
V = velocity of circulation of currency
M' = quantity of bank (demand) deposits
V' = velocity of circulation of bank deposits

Since MV (in the equation that we discussed originally) equals $MV + M'V'$ (in Fisher's), this does not change the equation in any way except to provide a bit more detail.

But in discussing causal relationships between M and M' Fisher falls into an error that arises from the relatively primitive knowledge in that period concerning the role of demand deposits. He felt that the quantity of currency determined the quantity of deposits, so that "normally the effect of doubling money [currency] in circulation (M) is to double deposits (M') because under any given conditions of industry and civilization deposits tend to hold a fixed or normal ratio to money in circulation. Hence the ultimate effect of a doubling in M is the same as that of doubling both M and M'."[7] The implication is that if the Treasury increases the number of dollar bills, then the public will increase their demand deposits proportionally.

As we have seen in Chapter 14, this is not what actually happens in our present monetary system. There *is* a tendency for currency and bank deposits to rise and fall together, as Figure 23-1 shows, but this does not prove Fisher's point. Although the Treasury and the Federal Reserve can "issue" more currency, they can't keep it in circulation unless people want to hold it. A rise in people's desire to hold currency is normally a result of the same basic causes as a rise in bank deposits, namely, an increase in business activity.

In fact, if anything, the causal connection between currency and deposits is

[7] *Ibid.*, p. 151.

the opposite of that envisioned by Fisher. Banks expand their loans in times of prosperity, thereby increasing bank deposits. This results in an increase in the monetary value of business transactions, which in turn means that people require more currency to make day-to-day purchases. This is the "cash drain" that banks must meet when the banking system as a whole is expanding. The increase in currency follows the bank expansion; it doesn't cause it.

This is the general tendency. But as Figure 23-1 indicates, it does not

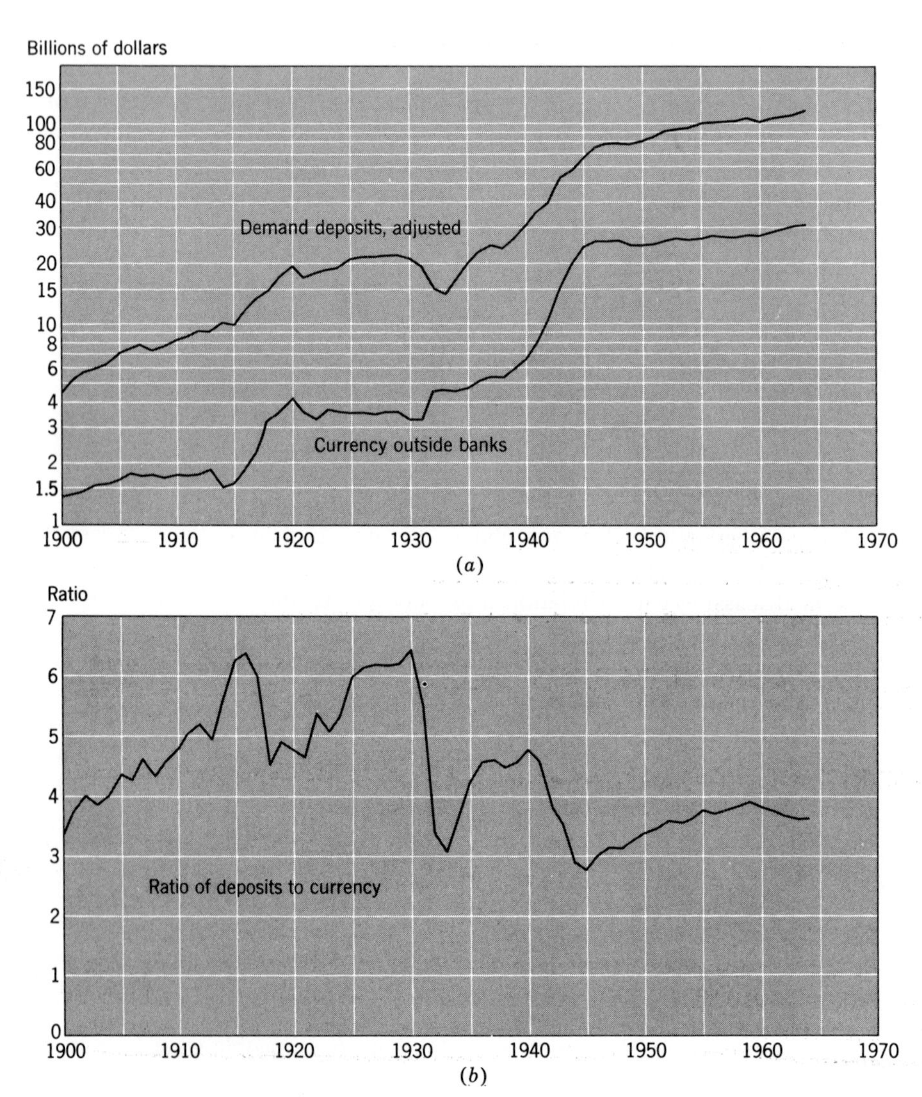

Figure 23-1. Demand deposits and currency, 1900 to 1964 (end-of-June figures). (*a*) Demand deposits, adjusted, and currency outside banks (semilog chart: equal vertical distances show equal *percentage* changes). (*b*) Ratio of demand deposits, adjusted, to currency outside banks (regular chart: equal vertical distances show equal *absolute* changes). *(U.S. Bureau of the Census, "Historical Statistics of the United States, Colonial Times to 1957," p. 646; Federal Reserve Bulletin, current issues. Ratio computed by the author.)*

always hold true. There have been a number of times when currency and demand deposits moved in opposite directions. Most of the cases involved only minor shifts, but the Great Depression showed a very striking diversity of movement. Deposits fell by 35 per cent from 1929 to 1933, while currency outside banks *rose* by 30 per cent. This phenomenon is easily explainable in terms of growing public distrust of banks and a consequent desire of individuals to hold their money in their own pockets rather than in the form of a bank promise to pay. This historical incident, however, thoroughly disproves the thesis that an increase in currency will cause a proportional increase in demand deposits. It also suggests that we should not take for granted a fixed relationship between M and M'.

The figures seem to indicate that as banking became more commonly accepted as a payments mechanism in the early part of the century, the proportion of their funds that people kept in checking accounts gradually increased. With some dislocations caused by World War I, this trend is fairly clear up to 1929. The crash seriously reduced the banks' portion of the total money supply, and World War II reduced it still further. More recently demand deposits have increased very slowly relative to cash. Even today, however, the ratio of demand deposits to currency is lower than it was at any time from 1902 to 1931, a phenomenon that is a little difficult to explain in view of the growing popularity of checking accounts.[8]

While there are advantages for some purposes in examining these two kinds of money separately, as Fisher did, it is more common in most discussions of the equation of exchange to think of the quantity of money as a single entity, recognizing that bank deposits constitute the bulk of the supply and that they are probably much more important in a causal sense than the amount of cash. That is precisely why banking takes such a prominent place in any study of money.

Conclusion of the Crude Quantity Theory. The basic conclusion of the quantity theory in its crude form is that the quantity of currency determines the quantity of demand deposits and that the two of them together determine the price level. Conceptually, then, the price level could be controlled by printing more (or less) currency. This is much too simple and too mechanical an explanation.

A Sophisticated Quantity Theory. It would be unwise, however, to throw the quantity theory away completely. While the relation between money and prices is not as rigid as the crude theory suggests, it is nevertheless indisputably true that *there is a tendency* for prices to move in the same direction as the money supply. A number of modern economists use the term "quantity theory" to mean not the mechanistic variety of Fisher but this more realistic

[8] Phillip Cagan has examined this phenomenon in some detail. He suggests that the cash ratio depends primarily on interest rates and income tax rates (the higher the tax rate, the more currency is desired to hide transactions). See *The Demand for Currency Relative to Total Money Supply,* Occasional Paper 62 (National Bureau of Economic Research, Inc., New York, 1958).

description of a flexible relationship. They feel that attacks on the quantity theory are sometimes interpreted as suggesting that there is no causal relationship at all between money and prices, and they wish to counter this obviously false conclusion by pointing out that, properly qualified and carefully interpreted, there is an important grain of truth in the theory.

Two of the most prominent contemporary quantity theorists are Milton Friedman[9] and Don Patinkin.[10] Both emphasize that the effect that a rise in the money supply is likely to have on prices depends to a large extent on the attitude of individuals toward the amount of money they wish to keep on hand (which in turn operates through V). Friedman stresses the importance he ascribes to these money balances in his very definition of what he considers the quantity theory to be: "The quantity theory is in the first instance a theory of the *demand* for money."[11] His attempt to show that this demand is relatively constant over time (and that V is therefore also constant) is a key to his conclusion that money does affect the price level. His analysis (and that of Patinkin) is a far cry from Fisher's. It is indeed a form of the cash-balance approach to money, which will be discussed in the following chapter.

Questions for Thought and Discussion

1. If Congress were to raise the price of gold to $50 an ounce, what effect would this have on the general price level?

2. To what extent is the acceptability of bank checks based on faith in the government?

3. If gold coins were in circulation, would they give commodity value to the rest of the currency?

4. What kinds of action are likely to destroy faith in a paper currency?

5. If the government decreed that match covers were legal tender at 5 cents each, would they become money? What value would they have?

6. Suppose Congress declared that beefsteak was legal tender at 20 cents a pound; would anyone pay his debts with it?

7. Why is the attempt to legislate a high value for money (such as by price control) doomed to failure in the long run?

8. The quantity of money in this country doubled from 1914 to 1924. What happened to prices (Table 21-3)? Why?

9. In 1923 velocity of circulation of currency in Germany rose phenomenally. At the same time the physical volume of transactions fell. How is this possible?

10. "If more goods are produced, costs of production and hence selling prices

[9] Milton Friedman (ed.), *Studies in the Quantity Theory of Money* (The University of Chicago Press, Chicago, 1956).

[10] Don Patinkin, *Money, Interest, and Prices,* 2d ed. (Harper & Row, Publishers, Incorporated, New York, 1965).

[11] Friedman, *op. cit.,* p. 4.

must necessarily rise." Comment on this statement in terms of the equation of exchange.

11. Why is transactions velocity so much higher than income velocity?

12. Why would an increase in bank deposits tend to raise the quantity of currency outside banks?

Selected Bibliography

Dean, Edwin (ed.): *The Controversy over the Quantity Theory of Money,* D. C. Heath and Company, Boston, 1965.

Fisher, Irving: *The Purchasing Power of Money,* The Macmillan Company, New York, 1911.

Friedman, Milton: *Studies in the Quantity Theory of Money,* The University of Chicago Press, Chicago, 1956.

Hawtrey, Ralph G.: *Currency and Credit,* Longmans, Green & Co., Ltd., London, 1930.

Hegeland, Hugo: *The Quantity Theory of Money: A Critical History of Its Historical Development and Interpretation and a Restatement,* Elenders Boktrycheri Aktiebolag, Goteborg, Sweden, 1951.

Knapp, Georg Friedrich: *The State Theory of Money,* St Martin's Press, Inc., New York, 1924.

Laughlin, J. Laurence: *The Principles of Money,* Charles Scribner's Sons, New York, 1903.

Newlyn, W. T.: *Theory of Money,* Oxford University Press, London, 1962.

Niebyl, Karl H.: *Studies in the Classical Theories of Money,* Columbia University Press, New York, 1946.

Patinkin, Don: *Money, Interest, and Prices,* 2d ed., Harper & Row, Publishers, Incorporated, New York, 1965.

Vickers, Douglas W.: *Studies in the Theory of Money, 1690–1776,* Chilton Company—Book Division, Philadelphia, 1959.

Warren, George F., and Frank A. Pearson: *Gold and Prices,* John Wiley & Sons, Inc., New York, 1935.

Wicksell, Knut: *Lectures on Political Economy,* trans. by E. Classen, vol. II, *Money,* Macmillan & Co., Ltd., London, 1934.

Chapter 24 Transactions and Cash Balances

How little you know about the age you live in if you fancy that honey is sweeter than cash in hand.

Ovid: Fasti
Book I, line 191

The quantity theory starts from the equation of exchange,

$$P = \frac{MV}{T}$$

and ends with the conclusion that changes in M cause changes in P. This is all right as far as it goes; it simply doesn't go far enough. Over the course of time V and T are are not constant, nor are they necessarily proportional to each other. On the other hand, P is not entirely passive either, and price changes themselves may affect not only the supply of money, but the velocity and the volume of transactions as well. We need to examine all these forces.

The Level of Transactions

The volume of trade is a complex variable, affected by three major groups of forces in the economy, which may be summarized as follows:

1. The factors of production
   a. Size and nature of the population (labor)
   b. Natural resources (land)
   c. Accumulated capital
   d. Technological knowledge

2. The structure of industry
   a. Nature of distribution
   b. Degree of industrial integration
   c. Relative freedom of trade
   d. Monetary machinery
3. The state of business
   a. Consumer purchasing patterns
   b. Business confidence

The Factors of Production. Many of these forces are self-explanatory. A larger population provides both a market and a labor force for increased output. The age distribution of the population also affects production. In the United States at the present time our growing crop of babies at the one end and increasing longevity at the other combine to provide a smaller proportion of workers in the total population. Reducing the workweek also lowers the output to be expected from a given work force. It indicates that we put a growing value on leisure compared with goods.

In addition to labor, the basic factors of production include natural resources and capital. The larger and more varied a country's endowment of either, the larger its production is likely to be.

Technical knowledge, including managerial ability, is also necessary to the productive process, and the "state of the arts" is thus an important determinant of output. Yankee ingenuity is frequently given much of the credit for our high standard of living, though our liberal endowment of natural resources and energetic population are certainly important contributors. In fact much of the vaunted "Yankee" ingenuity itself seems to be attributable to first-generation Italians, Irish, and Poles.

The Structure of Industry. These factors affect the level of production, but production itself does not uniquely determine the volume of transactions. Production, though it is closely related to transactions, is not at all the same thing. In an economy in which everyone was self-sufficient there would be no exchange regardless of the level of output. If all goods were sold directly by producers to consumers (and assuming no transactions in such things as real estate and securities and no inventory accumulation), then production and transactions would be identical.

In the United States, as in most countries, the distributive process is more complicated than that. On the one hand goods usually reach consumers only after passing through the hands of wholesalers and retailers and perhaps other distributors, while on the other the producer buys his supplies and components from other manufacturers, who in turn buy raw materials from others, and so on.

To take one highly simplified example: Suppose the Harris Hat Company produces 10,000 hats a year. It buys its raw materials from the Ferris Felt Company and sells its products to Dan Dealer, who sells in turn to Smith

Stores, who sell to the consumer. The 10,000 hats represent 40,000 transactions:

Ferris Felt sells 10,000 felts to
Harris Hat, which sells 10,000 hats to
Dan Dealer, who sells 10,000 hats to
Smith Stores, who sell 10,000 hats to
Consumers

Although specialization tends to multiply transactions, the process may be reversed by integration. Suppose, for instance, that Harris merges with Ferris. What formerly was a sale of felt now becomes only an internal transfer on the books of the company from the felt department to the hat department. This eliminates 10,000 transactions, though the same number of hats is produced and sold. If Harris then buys out Dan Dealer, another 10,000 transactions disappear.

The volume of transactions may also be affected by other influences. Governments may interfere with the movement of goods or even with their production, as by tariffs, farm-production quotas, and so on. Interference with trade reduces T; increased freedom of trade raises T.

Efficient monetary machinery also encourages trade. The existence of some type of monetary system is taken for granted these days, but some countries have gone through monetary upheavals in which confidence in the monetary system was severely undermined and trade was handicapped. The more efficient the means for making payments, the easier it is to carry on business and the greater the volume of trade will be.

The State of Business. While any of the foregoing forces can change T in the long run, they all act sluggishly. Natural resources are relatively fixed; the population grows fairly slowly, and its work habits do not shift drastically from one year to the next; additions to capital in any one year are small compared with the total accumulation; technical progress, while continuous, cannot change productive processes overnight; distributive, industrial, and financial structures change gradually; and patterns of trade freedom are fairly well established. As far as these causes are concerned, then, we should not expect T to produce much change in the equation of exchange except over extended periods of time.

This is essentially the position of the early quantity theorists. What they ignore is the short-run significance of the third group of factors: consumer purchasing patterns and business confidence. Here lies the crux of the business cycle. For if consumers stop buying or businessmen stop producing, the effect on the economy may be drastic. The physical factors of production set the limit on how much we *can* produce at any particular time, but they do not determine how much we *will* produce, and unfortunately the record shows that we frequently fail to live up to our potential.

During a depression production falls significantly. When businessmen become pessimistic, the bottom drops out of the economy, and in this decline changes in T can be extremely important. In fact T can decline even more than production, for if consumers won't buy, then goods already produced pile up on the shelves of manufacturers or distributors. Although produced, they aren't sold.

Suppose, to revert to our recent example, that the integrated Harris Hat Company finds that it can't sell all its 10,000 hats (already produced) to Smith Stores because customers aren't buying hats. Imagine the following case:

Harris Hat	sells 9,000	hats, adds	1,000	to inventory
Smith Stores	sell 8,500	hats, add	500	to inventory
	17,500			

Under normal circumstances the production of 10,000 hats would have led to transactions involving 20,000 hats. Here we find only 17,500 transactions, although production has not fallen—yet. It soon will, however, for Harris isn't in business to build up its inventory. If hats won't sell, Harris will make fewer hats. It lays off workers, who in turn can buy fewer hats as well as fewer other things, and the whole economy is off on a downward spiral.

It should be clear, then, that T is not only a variable, but a significant variable. It cannot be relegated to the position of an innocent and well-behaved bystander, as the quantity theorists suggest.

For the sake of completeness we should add that although the above discussion concentrates on transactions in goods, T includes more than that, since it must encompass everything for which money is paid. The value of transactions in such things as securities and real estate is considerably smaller than that of transactions in goods, but it is even more volatile. There are times, such as in the boom market of the late twenties, when failure to consider the impact of real estate and security sales would give the observer a seriously distorted picture of the total economy.

The factors affecting T deserve much more attention than we have paid them, but since they are exhaustively treated in other economics courses, we only mention them here to round out the picture and pass on to more strictly monetary problems.

Velocity and Hoarding

Fisher recognized a number of causes for shifts in V over time[1] but believed that all of them occurred slowly. He did not recognize the possibility of velocity having any significant effect on either prices or general business conditions in the short run.

In order to correct this omission several writers have emphasized the role of velocity by making it the center of attention. Alfred Marshall and D. H.

[1] Irving Fisher, *The Purchasing Power of Money* (The Macmillan Company, New York, 1911), p. 79.

Robertson looked at the problem from the point of view of cash balances, while Keynes has tackled it only slightly differently in his development of liquidity preference concepts. These two approaches overlap, and we will draw from both of them in an attempt to provide a unified picture.

Both approaches attack the determination of velocity indirectly rather than frontally. Instead of asking, "What determines the speed with which money is handed around?" they ask, "What determines the desire of people to hold money—to keep it from circulating?" These two questions represent two ways of looking at the same phenomenon, as we will see presently.

When dealing with velocity, we need to remember that the equation of exchange may take two major forms: the transactions form and the income form. In the first, PT is the total value of all transactions, and V is the *transactions* velocity of money, the number of times money changes hands within the period. In the second, P_yT_y is the value of sales to ultimate users, and V_y is the *income* velocity of money, the number of times money passes from one income recipient to another.

Most of the literature on velocity and cash balances is concerned with income velocity, but the same approach can be used to examine transactions velocity with proper modification in the meaning of the terms.

The Marshallian *K*. Alfred Marshall first examined the concept of cash balances in detail. He suggested that "there is some fraction of their income which people find it worth while to keep in the form of currency."[2] (It is clear from his argument that by "currency" he really meant money—"ready purchasing power.") This fraction is designated by the symbol k.[3] For each person k is the proportion of his annual income that he keeps (on the average) in a monetary form.

$$k = \frac{m}{y}$$

where m = average cash balance (currency plus checking accounts) of the individual

y = annual income of the individual

Suppose Green earns $5,000 a year, keeps an average balance in his checking account of $450, and usually has about $50 in his wallet (and his wife's purse).

$$k = \frac{m}{y} = \frac{500}{5{,}000} = \frac{1}{10}$$

Green's average cash balance, then, is one-tenth of his annual income.

[2] Alfred Marshall, *Money, Credit, and Commerce* (Macmillan & Co., Ltd., London, 1923), p. 45.

[3] Not to be confused with the Keynesian multiplier (see Chap. 27), which uses the same symbol k. Although symbolized by the same letter, these concepts are completely different.

This concept can be applied to the nation as a whole by adding up the amounts of money normally held by each individual and the total incomes of those individuals. Then for the aggregate,

$$K = \frac{M_c}{Y_c}$$

where $M_c =$ quantity of money held by consumers
$Y_c =$ (aggregate) personal income
In this sense K would be the quantity of money that the average citizen holds, expressed as a percentage of his income.

For instance, in 1964 consumers (including nonprofit organizations) held \$73.6 billion in demand deposits and currency, while personal income totaled \$495.0 billion.

$$K = \frac{M_c}{Y_c} = \frac{73.6}{495.0} = 0.149, \text{ or } 14.9 \text{ per cent}$$

In that year, individuals on the average held almost one-sixth of their annual income (two months' income) in money.

Consumers, however, are not the only holders of cash. In fact the statistics show that businesses hold more than half of the total. In its most common use K relates (total) money in circulation to net national product (which is somewhat larger than personal income but comes closer to measuring the net output of the economy). The psychological meaning of such a concept is a little hazy, but its practical significance is great. We will call this relation K_y, which is the proportion of its national product that a country desires to hold in cash.

In 1964, when net national product was \$573.0 billion, the quantity of money (currency outside banks plus demand deposits, adjusted) was \$153.5 billion. Thus

$$K_y = \frac{M}{Y} = \frac{153.5}{573.0} = 0.268, \text{ or } 26.8 \text{ per cent}$$

This means that the total supply of money held by the economy was slightly more than one-quarter of its income, enough to buy three months' product.

If a country holds one-quarter of its annual income in cash, then its annual income is four times the quantity of money. This is the same as saying that money must have an income velocity of 4. Our cash-balance approach is therefore simply a device for looking at velocity of circulation of money from the back door.

Ignoring some of the niceties of precise definition, net national product is the final output of the economy available for sale. This is the same thing as P_yT_y in the income form of the equation of exchange. But if

$$K_y = \frac{M}{Y}$$

while $$Y = P_y T_y$$

and $$P_y T_y = MV_y$$

then $$K_y = \frac{M}{P_y T_y} = \frac{M}{MV_y} = \frac{1}{V_y}$$

In other words, the income K is the reciprocal of the income velocity of circulation. This is simple common sense. The larger the proportion of their income that people hold in money (K_y), the more slowly money turns over (V_y). Any reduction in their cash balances speeds up monetary circulation. Anything that induces people to hoard slows down V_y.

So we can study V by looking at K, and it is a bit easier to think of the rather concrete problem of how much money people hold than it is to try to grasp the more abstract terms of how rapidly money is transferred. Or, as Robertson would put it, we can train our binoculars more carefully on money sitting than we can on money on the wing.

The Transactions *K*. In addition to the income K, we can consider also a transactions K, which differs from it only in detail. Since businesses, as well as consumers, hold money, and since they hold it for reasons that are more nearly related to their receipts than to national income, it may help to think of K_t as the proportion of total *receipts* (business as well as personal) that people wish to hold in the form of money. Then

$$K_t = \frac{M}{R}$$

where R is the annual monetary receipts of the community, which is equal to its total sales of commodities and services. So defined, R is nothing more than the monetary value of total transactions, that is, PT. Therefore the transactions K is the reciprocal of the transactions V.

Hoarding and the Goods Value of Money. It can be seen that K is essentially the propensity to hoard—the desire to hold a certain proportion of one's income in cash. We should bear in mind, however, that it is stated as a fraction, not as a specified amount. This is at least partly because money is desired not for itself, but for what it will buy. A given quantity of money has no meaning until we translate it into the quantity of goods that it will buy. In fact Robertson defines K as the proportion of *real* national product that people wish to have enough money on hand to buy.[4] This suggests that a doubling of all prices would not change K. People would merely want to hold twice as much money against twice as much income, and the ratio would not be altered. The quantity of goods represented by the enlarged stock of cash would be the same. Or, to state it a third way, the increased quantity of money simply offsets the decreased value of each dollar, and *real balances* are unaltered.

[4] D. H. Robertson, *Money* (Pitman Publishing Corporation, New York, 1948), p. 180.

It is also true that an increase in real balances (K) may occur with no change in the quantity of money held, provided income falls. For then the same stock of money would be a larger *proportion* of income. We will have occasion to refer to this principle in Chapter 27.

Liquidity Preference

Since V and K are simply different ways of looking at the same thing, they are both caused by the same forces. What are they?

Marshall suggested that the amount of money an individual wants to hold depends not only on his income, but also on his "property" (assets). But these are not the only factors affecting such decisions, and, indeed, different people may be influenced by different motives. In this connection we need to realize that most cash is held not by consumers, but by businesses. Much of the remainder is in the hands of wealthy individuals. In considering the motives for holding cash, therefore, we must include factors affecting General Motors and Gloria Vanderbilt as well as those affecting you and me.

What then determines K? Or to put the same question in the more modern terminology introduced by Keynes:[5] What lies behind *liquidity preference, the desire to hold a portion of one's assets in the form of money?* Money itself is barren. Since it is of no value to eat, wear, or hit a golf ball with, it is obvious that it is not desired for itself.

Cash balances are idle purchasing power that might have been used to buy consumer goods for personal enjoyment or might have been put to work (through the purchase of securities or directly in a business) to earn more money. Holding money is an alternative to using it and therefore involves a cost, measured by either the pleasure or the profit foregone. No one would keep his assets in cash unless there were powerful reasons—reasons strong enough to make it worth giving up the interest that the money might be earning.

There are four basic motives for liquidity preference: transactions, precautionary, convenience, and speculative. These in turn are based on a number of forces affecting both consumers and businessmen. The following summary will serve as a starting point for our discussion:

1. Transactions motive
   a. Level of income or receipts
   b. Degree of specialization
   c. Frequency and timing of receipts and expenditures
   d. Speed with which payments may be made (e.g., check clearing)
   e. Availability of credit
2. Precautionary motive
   a. Size of assets

[5] John Maynard Keynes, *The General Theory of Employment, Interest and Money* (Harcourt, Brace & World, Inc., New York, 1936), pp. 165–174.

   b. Availability of insurance
   c. Expectations as to future income or receipts
   d. Availability of credit
   e. Efficiency and safety of financial institutions in making interest-earning assets available (liquidity of assets)
3. Convenience motive
   a. Cost and effort involved in obtaining interest-earning assets
4. Speculative motive
   a. Expectations as to future prices and interest rates

Transactions Motive. The transactions motive refers to the need to have money on hand to meet ordinary and anticipated expenditures.

Income. Since money is used to buy goods, the amount which anyone holds at any time is related at least partly to the quantity of goods he intends to buy. This in turn is influenced by his income.

The importance of income is emphasized in the cash-balance equation itself, for K is defined as a fraction of income. A change in actual cash balances proportional to a change in income does not alter K. But it is entirely possible that people will actually wish to hold a different *proportion* in cash as their income level changes. If, for instance, expenditures do not rise as fast as income (that is, savings become a larger proportion of higher income levels), the proportion of cash needed will decline relative to income.

In the case of business firms the level of expenditures is related to the size of the business and of its receipts.

Degree of Specialization. If a man's income were all in the form of physical commodities (if, for instance, he were completely self-sufficient, producing all the things he consumed), he would need no money. Hence the desire for cash rises as specialization increases. Conversely, integration of industry reduces the volume of cash transactions and thereby reduces the need for business as a whole to hold money.

Frequency of Receipts and Expenditures. If a man's income were paid to him in equal installments every minute of every day and if his expenditures were likewise evenly spaced over time, he would need a minimum of cash in reserve. He could pay it out literally as fast as it was received. When he is paid once a week, however, he must see that he has enough to last him through the week. He can't spend it all on the first day. Suppose he has no reserve funds and spends one-seventh of his wages each day. He would have seven-sevenths of his weekly pay on payday (say, Friday), six-sevenths on Saturday, five-sevenths on Sunday, and so on. On the average he would have half a week's pay in his pocket—more at the beginning of the week; less at the end. If his pay period is lengthened to a month, he would have to keep much more cash on the average. He would start off on payday with a whole month's pay, and not until a week before the next payday rolled around would he be down to a week's pay. The shorter the pay period, therefore, the less the need to hold cash.

A similar situation concerns expenditures. If expenditures come in large doses, cash must be available to meet them when they fall due. If the month's rent must be paid immediately after payday, it reduces immediately the amount of money the tenant holds. If it comes due just before payday (unlucky tenant), then money must be held all month against that payment. For larger payments, such as insurance or a new sofa, money may have to be put aside for several months in advance. Corporations, whose receipts are frequently rather evenly spaced over time, may have to build up funds to meet large payments such as a monthly payroll, taxes, or quarterly dividends.

Speed with Which Payments Are Made. When I pay the grocer cash on the barrelhead, he has immediate use of the money. But if I pay a distant creditor by check, the money involved is immobilized until he gets the check (speed of the mails) and is able not only to deposit it but to get actual availability of the funds (speed of clearing plus bank practice with regard to availability). The faster the mails and the clearing machinery, the lower the nation's cash balances need to be.

Availability of Credit. To the extent that I can buy on credit, I need less cash in hand. It is theoretically possible to imagine a person who charges everything. On payday he settles all his bills and goes on piling up a new set for next payday. Such an individual would have practically no need for cash balances at all. His suppliers, however, would still have to meet their obligations even though they don't themselves get paid until the end of the month. So, unless they also get credit, they would have to accumulate cash to meet their expenditures while receipts were not coming in. If they receive credit, this need disappears also. A growth of credit facilities in general tends to reduce the amount of money held by the community as a whole.

Much business borrowing is seasonal. The business carries less cash than is needed to meet *all* its regular expenses, relying on its borrowing capacity to tide it over the slack period. Farmers, for instance, seldom keep sufficient cash from their fall sales to carry them through the whole year to the next harvest. Instead they borrow in the spring to meet heavy expenditures for seed, fertilizer, and so on, and the loans are repaid when the crops are sold.

Precautionary Motive. The precautionary motive refers to the desire to hold sufficient funds to meet unexpected expenditures. The transactions motive pertains to the known, the normal rhythm of income and outgo; the precautionary motive concerns the unknown. These unexpected payments may be the result of either emergencies or exceptional opportunities. The motorist carries enough money for gas, tolls, meals, and other anticipated expenses, but if he is wise, he also carries extra cash in case of breakdown. The businessman maintains a sufficient bank balance to meet his bills even if customers fail to pay as promptly as usual or to replace a broken show window.

Less pressing, but more rewarding, are those occasions when a little extra cash may enable Mary to snap up that bargain in dresses she runs into. It may enable the businessman to take advantage of a manufacturer's closeout. Thus holding money may be a means of saving money. On the other hand, the person who figures his expenditures too closely may find himself continually in difficulties because those extra expenditures he didn't count on reduce his cash balance below the level needed for ordinary transactions and thus throw out of kilter his whole expenditure pattern.

Size of Assets. The amount that anyone *wants* to hold for emergencies is not the only factor determining the size of precautionary balances, however. The amount that any person *can* hold in cash depends at least partly on how large his total assets are. He may want to keep an adequate bank balance, but if he never manages to save that much in the first place, his intentions won't create the dollars. Generally, the larger a person's (or firm's) assets, the larger the amount of money held.

Availability of Insurance. Insuring against emergencies is an alternative to holding cash to pay for them. I may have less money in the bank because I know that the day I die the insurance company will provide a check to pay for the funeral. I may carry less cash in my pocket because if my car breaks down, the insurance company will pay the towing fee.

Expectations as to Future Income. One common emergency that people do their best to provide against is unemployment. If an individual is fairly certain of the continuance of his job, this may not be a serious threat, and very little may be laid aside to take care of it. The higher the uncertainty, the more an individual may want to have laid aside for that rainy day. The same thing holds true of expectations concerning any other kind of uncertainty regarding future income. Governmental initiative in providing unemployment insurance and old-age pensions, as well as the growing volume of private unemployment payment plans, have reduced this uncertainty somewhat.

Businessmen, too, face similar problems. If their receipts are subject to wide fluctuations, they will need more cash on hand than if their receipts are steady and predictable.

Availability of Credit. For meeting emergencies, as well as for ordinary transactions, the availability of credit may reduce the need for holding money.

Borrowing, however, has some disadvantages of its own in addition to the interest cost. The firm with a line of credit may know that it can borrow whenever it wants to, but not all businesses (and even fewer consumers) are able to arrange for such facilities. And it may be precisely when a firm needs money most that it finds it most difficult to borrow. This would be true, for instance, if the bankruptcy of a principal debtor should not only leave a firm short of cash, but also undermine its whole financial structure. Severe sickness lowers a consumer's credit standing just when he needs extra funds.

It is in any case unwise to be borrowing every time some small emergency arises. In fact one of the best recommendations for obtaining a loan is a sizable cash balance. This high credit standing may well be the most important reason for holding a comfortable bank balance. The balance itself is available to meet small contingencies, while the confidence it inspires makes it simpler to borrow for the large emergencies.

Financial Institutions. The primary disadvantage of cash balances is that they are barren; they yield no interest. To a certain extent it is possible to kill two birds with one stone by holding some emergency funds not in cash, but in liquid assets such as savings accounts, government bonds, or other securities. Whether such assets will serve for this purpose depends on their degree of liquidity, including both availability and certainty of value. It also depends on whether the interest rate that can be earned is high enough to make it worthwhile to give up the absolute liquidity of cash.

Frenchmen are noted for keeping their emergency funds in the form of gold buried in the backyard because they don't trust their financial institutions. In the United States we have developed an elaborate array of instruments for monetary investment of almost every variety with regard to both safety and marketability. This has significantly reduced the need for large sums of cash on hand.

A savings account or a savings bond is just about as good as money. If an individual has a comfortable amount in these assets, he needs less in his pocket to meet that unexpected illness or to save up against the purchase of a new car.

Because of the high liquidity of these forms of savings, a few writers speak of them as money. They argue that an increase in savings deposits, for instance, has the same effect on the price level as an increase in checking accounts. This is probably true, to a limited extent at least, but we don't need to call savings accounts money to explain the effect. An increase in savings balances reduces the need to hold so much cash. Thus K falls, V rises, and this tends to raise prices (other things remaining the same). Savings balances have this effect not because they are money but because they are a very good money substitute. Other types of investments do the same job in only a slightly less effective way. This is, in fact, the very essence of liquidity: how rapidly and safely an asset can be turned into money in case of need. The higher the liquidity, the more the asset involved acts like money. In all cases of near-money, however, the effect on prices is through V rather than through M. In this respect the very availability of credit may have somewhat the same effect as its actual creation since it tends to increase V.

Business finds similar high liquidity in treasury bills and in time certificates of deposit.

As we move down the scale of liquidity, earning assets become less and less satisfactory as a substitute for cash, for the possibility increases that at the time the funds are needed the asset cannot be sold except at a loss. This is particularly true of stocks and to a lesser extent of bonds, even marketable government bonds. In 1960 some marketable treasury bonds were selling at less than 80 per cent of par because the rise in interest rates had reduced the attractiveness of those bonds issued in former years at lower rates.

There is, therefore, some disadvantage in counting on liquid assets to meet all emergencies and an incentive to hold cash even though it means forgoing some interest return. The two motives of liquidity and income pull in opposite directions.

It is, of course, possible to sell almost any asset if it is necessary, but the sale of physical assets may be difficult and is almost certain to reduce the efficiency of the business or the standard of living of the consumer. Thus it wouldn't make sense for a firm to sell part of its machinery to meet a business obligation, or for a man to sell his car to pay a traffic fine. These are *operating assets,* and only in the direst circumstances are they normally available as a source of cash.

Convenience Motive. Sometimes money is held simply because it is too much trouble to do anything else with it. For some people financial institutions are not handy, and in many cases knowledge of the available opportunities may be lacking. For some types of securities, brokers' fees or other costs may reduce the attractiveness of the yield, particularly when funds are available for only a short (or unknown) period of time, while taxes further cut down the net return.

Many financial institutions are devising ways to make their services more convenient by increasing the number of offices, providing mail facilities, and so on. The level of interest rates is important too, for the higher the rate, the greater the incentive to overcome inertia and put money to work in income-earning assets.

Speculative Motive. The speculative motive refers to the desire to hold cash in order to take advantage of an anticipated fall in prices, whether of goods or securities. This is speculative in the sense that the holder is hoping for an increase in the value of the money he holds, and it depends on his expectations as to future prices and interest rates.

If people think prices will rise, they will prefer to hold less money since the value of money is falling. If prices are expected to fall, money becomes more valuable and is a desirable asset to keep.

The case of interest rates is just the opposite since interest rates move inversely to the price of securities. Why buy a bond at today's low interest return if you expect interest rates to rise tomorrow? An anticipated rise in interest rates, therefore, will induce people to hold more cash until it occurs (or until the expectation fades).

If they anticipate a price fall, not only will people refrain from buying securities that they feel are overpriced, but they are also likely to sell the ones they hold in the hope of buying them back at a lower price in the future. Thus they accumulate speculative balances of cash.

When prices are expected to rise, nobody will hold money for speculative purposes. People may, in fact, reduce their precautionary balances below normal levels in order to get rid of as much as possible of the money that is falling in value. In a severe inflation even transactions balances may be sacrificed to the desire to get rid of money while it is still worth something. What does it matter if we won't have enough money to last out the week? By the end of the week it will be worthless anyway.

Although this contraction of working balances might be called a reduction in the transactions motive (or in the precautionary motive, as the case may be), it is more realistic to speak of it as a negative speculative balance.[6] When all the money in the speculative balance has been used, money is "borrowed" from the precautionary or transactions balances in order to buy goods (whose value is expected to rise) with money (whose value is expected to fall).

Changes in the speculative motive can produce drastic effects on K, and thus on the velocity of circulation, and in this way can significantly affect national income, prices, and production. The factors influencing transactions and precautionary balances are fairly stable in the short run and are likely to change only slowly over time. Such things as basic income and expenditure patterns and the structure of the financial machinery are not likely to shift rapidly. But expectations as to future prices can be highly volatile.

A person's views as to what prices are going to do next week can be influenced by too large a number of forces to be cataloged. They include even such noneconomic factors as how much sleep the individual got the night before or the state of the weather. Of course no single individual can move the economy alone, but if he is in an influential position (particularly if he is responsible for hiring or firing a large number of workers or placing or canceling large orders), he can change the thinking as well as the actions of many others and so set off a chain reaction that can have significant consequences.

Active and Passive Balances. Individuals do not consciously divide their cash into its four component parts. There is, even in theory, much overlap among the categories. In fact some economists do not recognize the convenience motive, counting such balances rather as part of precautionary funds. Many people meet emergencies out of transactions balances and then either readjust their subsequent ordinary purchases or borrow or liquidate some earning assets to acquire cash.

In spite of this fuzziness around the edges, it is important economically to distinguish between the four types of balances because the money in each behaves differently.

Money held for transactions is *active* money. The dollar in your pocket that will be used to buy dinner tonight is temporarily resting, but it will soon be on its way again.

Money in precautionary balances, however, is effectively out of the moneyflow until some emergency actually arises. The dollar you keep as "mad money" in your shoe may never see the light of day; it is off on a long rest

[6] It is somewhat analogous to the practice of selling stocks "short" when their price is expected to fall.

cure and just isn't employed as *current* purchasing power. The same is true of convenience balances. They will stay where they are until occasion arises to spend them or until the interest rate rises far enough to lure them out of hiding. Both of these are *passive* balances.

Some economists suggest that passive balances are not even part of the effective money supply and should not be counted in M. There is no need to go to this extreme, however, for as long as they are at rest their velocity is 0, and their effect on income is similarly nonexistent. Any quantity of M multiplied by a zero V acts precisely like a zero quantity of M. There is this important difference, however: passive balances become active the instant their owner wants to spend them without any action on the part of the monetary authorities such as would be needed to create additional money.

Speculative balances have some of the characteristics of both active and passive accounts. They are temporarily passive, waiting for the anticipated price fall to materialize. Once the fall occurs, they become completely active, and there is no tendency to try to build them up again as there would be for precautionary balances depleted by emergency.

Statistically it is impossible to separate these various accounts, since they are made up of the same dollar bills and the same deposit credits. Conceptually the precautionary balance is the minimum level of cash that a person holds regularly: the $10 he always keeps in a separate compartment of his wallet plus the $300 minimum bank balance below which he writes checks only when absolutely necessary; or the $10,000 that the firm considers a necessary cushion and below which it starts to take special steps to conserve funds or to borrow.

The difference between this minimum and the average amount actually held would represent the transactions balance. Any unusual increase in total funds might then be considered speculative, though it may be a convenience balance or a transactions balance being built up for a large purchase.

Considerable research is currently being done in an attempt to analyze these differing balances, and the results may tell us a good deal about the way money is used, about K, and about the velocity of circulation.

The Stability of V. The above analysis suggests that K (and therefore V) is likely to change over both the long run (such as by the growth of near-money) and the short run (such as by changes in price expectations). Unless such changes are precisely offset by identical changes in T (and there is no reason to assume that they should be), the price level *cannot* move proportionally to the quantity of money.

Modern quantity theorists would generally agree in basic principle with the list of forces affecting the public's demand for money, but they are likely to insist, along with Fisher, that the actual effect of such forces is quite small and that K does in fact remain remarkably stable. Although Friedman, for instance, spells out specifically a number of factors influencing the demand for money, he states his conclusion in unqualified terms:

> There is perhaps no other empirical relation in economics that has been observed to recur so uniformly under so wide a variety of circumstances as the relation

between substantial changes over short periods in the stock of money and in prices; the one is invariably linked with the other and is in the same direction; this uniformity is, I suspect, of the same order as many of the uniformities that form the basis of the physical sciences. And the uniformity is in more than one direction. There is an extraordinary empirical stability and regularity to such magnitudes as income velocity that cannot but impress anyone who works extensively with monetary data.[7]

Yet his own data hardly bear out such a statement, and his historical analysis contradicts it. He refers, among other cases, to the "unprecedented collapse in the velocity of money from 1929 to 1932" and notes that "the most distinctive feature of the postwar period . . . is the sharply rising trend in the velocity of money."[8] The apparent contradiction undoubtedly lies in Friedman's tendency to think of stability in terms of the long-run trend moving at a more or less constant *average* rate (as did Fisher) while ignoring the short-run variations that are important for considerations of business cycle fluctuations.

Figure 24-1 illustrates movements of velocity on an annual basis since 1915. Monthly or quarterly figures would undoubtedly show a much more

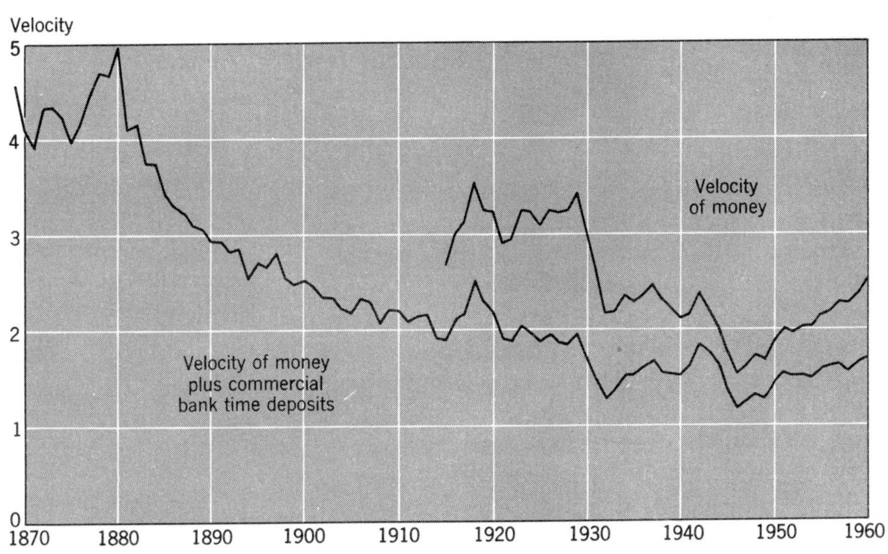

Figure 24-1. Income velocity of money, 1869 to 1960. Money income divided by (*a*) the stock of money (currency in circulation plus demand deposits) and (*b*) the stock of money plus time deposits of commercial banks. Figures for demand deposits are not available separately for the period prior to 1915. *(Milton Friedman and Anna Jacobson Schwartz, "A Monetary History of the United States, 1867–1960," A Study of the National Bureau of Economic Research, Princeton University Press, Princeton, N.J., 1963, p. 774.)*

[7] Milton Friedman, *Studies in the Quantity Theory of Money* (The University of Chicago Press, Chicago, 1956), pp. 20–21.

[8] Milton Friedman and Anna Jacobson Schwartz, *A Monetary History of the United States, 1867–1960* (*A Study of the National Bureau of Economic Research,* Princeton University Press, Princeton, N.J., 1963), p. 639. See also the graphs of velocity, pp. 640–641.

erratic pattern. In the light of these data it would be unwise to ignore movements in V as important elements in an understanding of the equation of exchange.

The Influence of Prices

So far in this chapter we have indicated that transactions and velocity must be included as important variables in the equation of exchange. But one more blow must be struck at the quantity theory, for prices are not the exclusively dependent, passive variable that the quantity theory assumes. A rise in prices, from whatever cause, will in turn cause changes elsewhere in the economy. There are, in addition, those who maintain that price increases may arise independently and may force an increase in the money supply. This is a relatively new argument that runs in terms of the cost push. We will examine these two different problems in turn.

The Effects of Price Changes. Since movements of the general price level affect the distribution of both income and wealth, it is hardly surprising that they will seriously affect the operation of the economy. If prices rise, what happens to T, M, and V?

Transactions. One of the determinants of the level of transactions is the state of business confidence, and prices are an important ingredient of confidence. Since a rise in prices makes businessmen more optimistic, one of its primary effects is to encourage a higher level of output. Such expansion is possible only if the economy is operating at less than full employment, but under those circumstances the rising profit expectations produced by higher prices will raise production, employment, and probably investment in plant and equipment.

A price rise may also induce people to sell assets formerly held off the market in anticipation of just such an appreciation of their value. This would be particularly true of securities, but it might apply also to inventories of commodities in the hands of dealers or speculators. All these involve a rise in the physical volume of transactions.

Money. As prices (and production) rise, the very fact that businessmen are trying to expand output means that they must borrow additional funds for financing. At least part of these funds is likely to come from commercial banks, thus increasing the money supply.

A higher price level is also likely to mean that distributors, holding a more valuable inventory, need more working capital, which may also be obtained from commercial banks. Consumers, too, may borrow more to finance current high-level consumption or to pay skyrocketing bills.

Velocity. The most important short-run influence on velocity is the expectation of price changes, and price changes themselves are likely to affect expectations. But the effect may not be identical under all conditions. When prices start rising from the low level reached during a depression, the expectation may be that they will continue to rise for a while. If so, buyers will rush out to get goods before their prices go up, and velocity will rise.

As prices continue to climb, however, there may be a tendency to think that this movement can't go on for ever. Prices are thought to be "too high," and the inevitable collapse is expected. If this is the case, then buyers will postpone purchases. Velocity will fall—and this in turn will help to bring about the very price decrease that was anticipated.

When such a determination not to buy until prices come down becomes widespread, it is often referred to as a *buyers' strike,* but it is certainly unorganized, and its very existence is hard to document. It is easy enough to tell when sales are declining, but it is not always clear why.

A fall in prices would produce opposite effects to a rise. Businessmen become pessimistic, cut production, and borrow less. For a while the price drop may be expected to continue, and velocity will fall as buyers hold off for even lower prices. As the fall continues, prices get so low that buyers don't think they will fall further, and they start buying in order to beat an anticipated rise.

The change in prices themselves is certainly not the only factor influencing expectations, but it is an important one. And its influence on V, coupled with its effect on T and M, makes it an important contributing cause of changes throughout the economy.

Demand Pull. The classical analysis assumes that whatever effect price changes may have, they are themselves the result of changes in money, velocity, or both. This is known as *demand pull.* In terms of the equation of exchange the movement of the economy upward from depression might be described (in an oversimplified fashion) as follows:

1. Businessmen decide to expand production.

2. In order to do so they need to spend additional funds for labor, raw materials, and so on.

3. This money comes from:

a. Their own idle funds (V rises)

b. Selling securities to others who use idle funds to buy them (V rises)

c. Borrowing from commercial banks (M rises)

4. This money is paid to factors of production (of which labor is the best example), who now have more purchasing power (demand rises).

5. Although the new products for which the workers have been paid are not yet finished or available for sale (especially if the initial expansion is in plant and equipment that takes a long time to complete), transactions will rise because sellers are willing to reduce their inventories in order to meet the increased demand for goods. Thus the initial effect of a rise in M (or V) is likely to be on T rather than P.

6. Better business conditions induce more businessmen to start expanding production, borrowing more money, paying more workers—resulting in further increases in demand and in sales.
7. Eventually prices will begin to feel the pressure. Inventories near depletion, or bottlenecks appear in the productive process. Since demand is strong, it is easy to let prices be pulled up (the demand pull).
8. The rise in P has two effects. It increases optimism and thereby adds to the desire to increase production. It is also likely to influence liquidity preference, increasing V. Thus the spiral is accelerated. Everything is going up, each of the factors interacting on the others, each being simultaneously cause and effect.
9. Eventually we reach the physical limits of output within the current state of technology and available resources. Production rises only slowly, while M, P, and (perhaps) V continue to rise more or less rapidly. Beyond this point inflation brings no further increase in T.
10. At some point (either before or after step 9) the economy breaks down. Businessmen lose their confidence, cut back production (T falls), borrow no more, and pay back old loans (M falls). Perhaps V has already fallen. The spiral reverses itself.

In explaining these movements we certainly can't say that money is the *cause* of the upswing (or downswing). But it is equally certain that it is a vital part of the process. The sequence of events is:

1. Decision to increase production
2. More money created through loans (or increased velocity)
3. Higher purchasing power
4. Higher prices

The increased demand resulting from increased money supply pulls up prices.

Cost Push. There is a tendency today for some economists to cast this picture in a different form. Their approach does not depend on the state of the business cycle and is most frequently used to explain why prices rise even when demand is falling. The argument (again in a simplified form) goes as follows:

1. Labor unions are powerful enough to win a rise in wages even when it is not justified by increased demand for the product or by increased productivity.
2. This rise in costs pushes prices up since employers are unable or unwilling to absorb it in reduced profits.
3. Since demand is unchanged, fewer goods are sold at the higher price (T falls), and production is cut back, creating unemployment.
4. Since the economy cannot tolerate sustained unemployment, the government will be forced to try to bolster the economy by pumping in additional purchasing power. The consequent deficit will be financed by the sale of secu-

rities to the general public, who will use idle funds to purchase them (V rises), or, more likely, by sale to the banks, who will create additional money (M) for the purpose.
5. This will raise demand, which in turn will increase production and employment.

In the cost push the sequence of events is:

1. Higher wages
2. Higher prices
3. More money injected through government action to support the higher prices without unemployment

Higher costs push up prices, and the higher prices are then validated by an increase in the money supply.

The cost-push concept gathered its most ardent support during the fifties, when it was felt that somehow control over the price level had been lost. In the moderate but sustained upswing of the early sixties, price increases were smaller, and consequently less emphasis was placed on the cost-push doctrine.

Conclusion. Both demand-pull and cost-push explanations can be phrased in terms of the equation of exchange. This is not surprising since the equation is necessarily true under all circumstances, and any theory that contradicts the equation must therefore be false. But the two explanations differ markedly from each other and from the simple quantity theory in the way in which they explain causal relationships among the factors. Other theories might present still further possibilities. The equation cannot tell us which is right. For this we need factual evidence from the economy itself. Indeed it is likely that both demand pull and cost push have some elements of truth (as does the quantity theory). Further light on this problem, including the role of government—here only briefly mentioned—can be obtained by a more extensive analysis of the various sectors of the economy, such as is provided by national income theory.

Questions for Thought and Discussion

1. How does the growth of do-it-yourself projects affect the volume of transactions?
2. How does an improvement in monetary machinery tend to increase the volume of business activity?
3. If K is simply the reciprocal of V, why do we bother to talk about it at all?
4. Would a corporation executive with a long-term contract hold a greater or smaller cash balance than an odd-job man who didn't know where the next job was coming from? What conflicting motives are involved?

5. How do actual (as distinguished from anticipated) changes in interest rates affect liquidity preference?
6. If you knew that prices were going to rise, would you be inclined to buy bonds? Stocks? Real estate? Would you save more? Borrow more?
7. Does all money in circulation actually circulate? What about passive balances?
8. Is it possible for cost push to raise prices without an increase in the quantity of money? Without a change in *any* other factor in the equation of exchange?
9. Which of the factors in the equation of exchange cause changes in others? Which are the result of changes in others? Is it possible to establish a modern theory on the basis of the equation as simple as the quantity theory?

Selected Bibliography

American Economic Association: *Readings in Monetary Theory,* McGraw-Hill Book Company, New York, 1951.
Berle, Adolf A., and Victoria J. Pederson: *Liquid Claims and National Wealth,* The Macmillan Company, New York, 1934.
Chandler, Lester V.: *An Introduction to Monetary Theory,* Harper & Row, Publishers, Incorporated, New York, 1940.
Gurley, John G., and Edward S. Shaw: *Money in a Theory of Finance,* The Brookings Institution, Washington, 1960.
Hart, Albert Gailord, and Peter Kenan: *Money, Debt, and Economic Activity,* 3d ed., Prentice-Hall, Inc., Englewood Cliffs, N.J., 1961.
Keynes, John Maynard: *A Tract on Monetary Reform,* The Macmillan Company, New York, 1923.
———:*A Treatise on Money,* 2 vols., St Martin's Press, Inc., New York, 1930.
Lindahl, Erik: *Studies in the Theory of Money and Capital,* Holt, Rinehart and Winston, Inc., New York, 1939.
Marget, A. W.: *The Theory of Prices,* 2 vols., Prentice-Hall, Inc., Englewood Cliffs, N.J.: 1938.
Marshall, Alfred: *Money, Credit, and Commerce,* St Martin's Press, Inc., New York, 1923.
Money, Trade, and Economic Growth, Essays in Honor of John H. Williams, The Macmillan Company, New York, 1951.
Robertson, Dennis H.: *Essays in Monetary Theory,* Staples Press, Ltd., London, 1940.
———: *Money,* 4th ed., The University of Chicago Press, Chicago, 1959.
Thorp, Willard L., and Richard E. Quandt: *The New Inflation,* McGraw-Hill Book Company, New York, 1960.

Part Seven
National Income Theory

Chapter 25 The Income Approach

What pile of wealth hath he accumulated
To his own portion! and what expense by the hour
Seems to flow from him! How, i' the name of thrift,
Does he rake this together?

The Life of King Henry VIII
Act III, scene 2, line 108

Our examination of theory has so far concentrated on the value of money as evidenced by the level of prices. This type of analysis occupied the attention of most monetary economists of the nineteenth and early twentieth centuries. More recently, however, there has been an almost universal growth of interest in another type of theory centering on national income, its level, and the ways in which it is earned and spent. Although attempts at this type of analysis can be traced back almost to the dawn of economics,[1] it has been only since the publication of Keynes's *The General Theory of Employment, Interest and Money* in 1936 that such attention has become widespread. Today the concepts of national income analysis are household words among economists, businessmen, government officials, and even the general public, although they are not always thoroughly understood.

Recognition of their importance has resulted in an accumulation of national income statistics, which are available in great detail as compiled by the Office of Business Economics of the Department of Commerce.[2] These data are frequently used as a gauge of business conditions. They require, however, a little care in interpretation.

[1] Both the mercantilists and the physiocrats were thinking essentially in terms of the wealth and income of the whole nation. Because of errors in their theories Adam Smith approached the problem from a different angle, and the national income viewpoint was submerged for over a century.

[2] See U.S. Office of Business Economics, *National Income, 1954 Edition* (1954), and *U.S. Income and Output* (1958), both supplements to the *Survey of Current Business.* Summaries are published regularly in the *Federal Reserve Bulletin.*

For one thing, national income figures represent values. They cannot, therefore, be interpreted directly as a measure of *real* output. They are, rather, the monetary value of that output, P_yT_y, and vary with changes in either prices or production.

In the second place, the phrase "national income" is used in more than one meaning, and many a heated argument over the size of national income in a particular year has turned out to be founded on nothing more substantial than semantic differences.

The Meaning of National Income

In its broadest and most commonly used sense, national income refers to *any* measure of the aggregate output produced by the residents of a given nation, or of the income received by them, in a given period. In its *technical* meaning national income refers specifically to one such measure: the aggregate income earned from current production.

Under the broad concept there are several subclassifications, of which five are of sufficient importance to merit special consideration: gross national product, net national product, national income, personal income, and disposable personal income.

Gross National Product. Gross national product (GNP) is the market value of all commodities and services produced by an economy in a given period of time (usually one year). It includes not only the products of business, but also the output of government in the form of national defense, police protection, schools, roads, etc. It is important to note, however, that GNP is not synonymous with the aggregate value of transactions. Transactions measure *exchanges,* while GNP measures *production.* A single commodity, which obviously can be produced only once, may, however, be exchanged several times.

Final Value of Product. There are two ways to avoid the double counting that would arise from adding together all the sales of a single product. One is to count only the *final* value of the product, which would normally be the sales price at the point of final sale. For consumers' goods this would be the retail price. For capital equipment (but not supplies, raw materials, or semifinished goods, which enter into a finished product sold later) it would be the price at which the equipment was sold to its final user.[3] This is referred to as *gross investment.* Government services, since they are not sold and hence have no price, are counted at cost. Production for sale to foreigners (exports) is offset by that part of foreign output that we buy (imports), with only the net difference counted as part of national product. GNP, then, is composed of these items:

[3] Goods that have not been sold to their final user within the period (e.g., radios in the manufacturer's warehouse) are counted at their inventory value.

Personal consumption expenditures
Gross private domestic investment
Net exports of goods and services
Government purchases of goods and services

The actual figures for 1964 are shown in Table 25-1.

Table 25-1. Gross National Product, 1964
Billions of Dollars

Personal consumption expenditures:			
Durable goods		58.7	
Nondurable goods		177.5	
Services		162.6	398.9
Gross private domestic investment:			
Residential structures		27.5	
Nonresidential structures		21.1	
Producers' durable equipment		39.4	
Change in business inventories		4.8	92.9
Net exports of goods and services:			
Exports		37.0	
Imports		−28.5	8.6
Government purchases of goods and services:			
Federal:			
National defense	49.9		
Other	15.4	65.3	
State and local		63.1	128.4
Gross national product			628.7

Source: *Survey of Current Business*, vol. 45, no. 8 (August, 1965), p. 8. Detail may not add to totals because of rounding.

Two items require brief explanation. As a statistical convention, houses are classified as business expenditures (investment) whether they are owned by landlords as rental property or occupied by their owners. All other purchases by consumers for their own use are considered consumption expenditures. This classification is arbitrary and open to some debate, but it is the way the figures are currently computed.

Second, government purchases of goods and services means just that. It does not include government transfer and interest payments (which we will examine later) and is therefore less than government expenditures by the amount of these payments.

Of the four categories contributing to GNP, two represent private investment: one domestic and one foreign. Combining these two, we find that GNP arises from three sectors of the economy as follows:

Consumption:	+	Government:	+	Investment:	= GNP
Personal consumption expenditures		Government purchases of goods and services		Gross private domestic investment Net exports of goods and services	

Value Added. The second method of avoiding double counting is to include only "value added" at each step of the productive process. Value added represents the income received by a firm from the sale of its product (regardless of who the purchaser is) minus the payments made to other *firms* for raw materials, supplies, and other current expenses.

Table 25-2. Hypothetical Example of Production and Value Added

	Purchases from other firms	Other expenses	Sales	Value added
Farmer:				
Purchases	0			
Farmhand, wages		81		
Farmer, net return		19		
Wheat			100	100
Miller:				
Wheat	100			
Employees, wages		170		
Miller, net return		30		
Flour			300	200
Baking corporation:				
Flour	300			
Employees, wages		241		
Bondholders, interest		24		
Depreciation expense		89		
Property taxes		93		
Corporate profits		103		
Bread			850	550
Grocer:				
Bread	850			
Clerk, wages		89		
Owner of store, rent		29		
Grocer, net return		32		
Bread			1,000	150
	1,250	1,000	2,250	1,000

A highly simplified example is shown in Table 25-2. It assumes that the farmer buys nothing from other firms and that the miller, baker, and grocer buy no supplies or materials except wheat, flour, and bread, respectively. The value added by the farmer, since he has no purchases, is equal to his sales. The miller, having bought wheat for \$100 and sold flour for \$300, has added \$200 to the original value of the wheat. This \$200 represents the earnings of himself and his workers. And so on down the list.

The first conclusion that we may draw from this table (oversimplified though it may be) is that the total sales value of a product is the sum of the values added at the successive stages of its manufacture and distribution. The \$1,000 receipts of the grocer from final sale of bread to consumers is the same as the aggregate value added by the farmer, the miller, the baker, and the grocer himself. Thus our two different methods of computing gross national product are mathematically identical.

It is also apparent that value added is identical with the total expenses (including profit) of all producers other than payments to supplying firms. GNP can be examined, then, in terms of the sum of these payments, which can be subdivided into three categories: depreciation, indirect business taxes, and income earned by the factors of production. This breakdown is given in Table

Table 25-3. Hypothetical Gross National Product and Its Components

Gross national product		1,000
Less depreciation	89	
Net national product		911
Less indirect business taxes	93	
National income		818
Wages	581	
Proprietors' income (nonfarm)	62	
Farm proprietors' income	19	
Rental income	29	
Corporate profits	103	
Interest	24	

25-3, which shows also the primary differences between GNP, net national product, and national income in its technical sense. These figures are simply rearranged and summarized from the payments recorded in Table 25-2.[4]

From what we have just said it is clear that the $1,000 spent for bread by consumers goes to pay the various factors of production, the taxes of government, and the current cost of using capital goods (depreciation). Money spent for goods flows through business to income recipients, who are then in a position to spend it again. This circuit flow of money is the primary concern of this chapter, and we will return to it shortly.

Net National Product. The difference between GNP and net national product is depreciation, as indicated in Table 25-3. GNP includes the production of durable producers' equipment as well as consumers' goods. Much of this equipment is not a net addition to the economy but merely replaces machinery worn out during the period. If we subtract depreciation, which measures the cost of this wear and tear, the result is a better measure of the *net* output of the economy.

National Income. Part of the cost of this product, however, represents payments to government that never become earnings of any factor of production.

[4] The figures chosen for our example are such that if the decimal point is moved one place to the left, the result is the percentage distribution of GNP in 1964. Thus depreciation in that year was 8.9 per cent of GNP, while indirect business taxes were 9.3 per cent, and so on.

Indirect business taxes—any taxes not directly related to income, including primarily property, excise, sales, and franchise taxes—are a cost of production which must be included in the price of the product but which are not part of anyone's income. If we subtract these from net national product,[5] the result is national income, the total income earned by all factors of production for their part in producing the commodities and services turned out by the economy in a given period of time. Table 25-3 indicates the various forms that this income takes: wages, proprietors' and rental income, corporate profits, and interest.

Personal Income. Although national income represents income *earned* in production, it does not represent income actually *received* by individuals. Some income that is earned is not received, while some that is received is not earned. In the first category there are three major subdivisions:

1. Undistributed corporate profits (corporate saving or plowed-back earnings) represent that part of the profits of a corporation that technically belongs to the stockholders but that is not actually paid to them. They increase the stockholders' equity but do not increase their immediate purchasing power.
2. Corporate profits taxes represent that part of the profits of the corporation (and thus of the stockholders) that is turned over to the government without the stockholders' ever laying hands on it.
3. Contributions for social insurance similarly represent earnings that are turned over to the government without being received by the workers.[6]

On the other side of the coin are payments made to individuals who have not earned them for productive effort in the current period (although they may have earned the right to them by productive activity in some prior period). Principal payments of this type are old-age and unemployment insurance payments, veterans' benefits, and relief payments. These are called *transfer payments* to distinguish them from income proper, since they represent a transfer of purchasing power without a similar increase in the quantity of goods available. By tradition, interest on the public debt (net interest paid by government) is also treated in the same manner as a transfer payment. It is *not* included in the value of government services as part of GNP, but it is obviously received by individuals. The underlying assumption is that those who lend money to the government are not aiding the productive activity of the economy.[7]

If then, starting with national income, we subtract corporate saving, corporate profits taxes, and contributions for social insurance and add transfer

[5] Along with three other minor adjustments not worth worrying about at this point.

[6] Personal income taxes, even though withheld from the worker's pay envelope, are treated differently. It is assumed that the worker actually receives this amount and then makes his payment to the government.

[7] It is often argued that most money lent to the government has been for the purpose of fighting wars and has therefore been already blown up; it cannot then be productive at the present time regardless of the lender's previous (and present) sacrifice of the use of the funds.

payments (including government interest), we obtain personal income, the income actually received by individuals (and nonprofit associations) in the economy.

Disposable Personal Income. Although personal income represents the purchasing power individuals in the economy receive, it is not the amount over which they have complete control. The government claims a portion, whether we will or no. Disposable personal income is what is left after personal taxes have been paid, and this we may use as we see fit. In terms of broad categories, disposable personal income may be used for personal consumption expenditures or personal saving.

Summary. The interrelationships among these various concepts of national income can be summarized in terms of the actual figures for 1964 as shown in Table 25-4. Among other things this tabulation shows that GNP can be broken down into the individual components in the right-hand column. Or, putting it the other way around, we can obtain GNP by adding up these components (subtracting transfer payments, which are not included in GNP). These items can be grouped in three broad categories: consumption, taxes, and saving:

Consumption:	+	Taxes:	+	Saving:	= GNP
Personal consumption expenditures		Personal taxes		Personal saving	
		Social insurance taxes		Undistributed corporate profits	
		Corporate profits taxes		Depreciation	
		Indirect business taxes			
		Less transfer payments			

It might be well at this point to compare this equation with the one given earlier that shows how GNP is built up of consumption, government purchases, and investment. The two equations show how the same GNP can be looked at either as the sum of products produced or as the sum of incomes generated in that productive process.

The significance of these relationships among income, consumption, taxes, saving, government purchases, and investment lies at the heart of what we call "national income analysis."

The Circuit Flow of Money

We have seen that expenditures by consumers, purchases by government, and investment by business flow into income, which in turn is directed into consumption, taxes, and saving. Thus money moves through the economy in a continuing stream, carrying on the nation's business without being used up

Table 25-4. Relation of Gross National Product and Its Components, 1964
Billions of Dollars

Gross national product	628.7	
Less depreciation		55.7
Equals net national product	573.0	
Less indirect business taxes		58.0
minor adjustments*		0.6
Equals national income	514.4	
Less undistributed corporate profits†		19.7
corporate profits taxes		27.6
social insurance taxes		27.8
Plus transfer payments‡		(55.7)
Equals personal income	495.0	
Less personal taxes		59.2
Equals disposable personal income	435.8	
Less personal outlays		409.5
Equals personal saving		26.3
Total (subtracting transfer payments)		628.7

* Business transfer payments (2.3); statistical discrepancy (—0.5); current surplus of government enterprises less subsidies (—1.2).
† Including inventory valuation adjustment: corporate profits (64.8) and inventory valuation adjustment (—0.3) less corporate profits tax liability (27.6) and dividends (17.2).
‡ Government transfer payments (34.2); net interest paid by government and by consumers (19.1); business transfer payments (2.3).
Source: *Survey of Current Business*, vol. 45, no. 8 (August, 1965), pp. 28-33.

in the process. This circuit flow of money is essential to the operation of any pecuniary society. It is similar to the flow of blood through the body as it is collected into the heart from the network of veins and passes out again through the various arteries to do its essential work.

Much as a medical text might diagram the circulatory system of the body, we may show a similar circulatory diagram of the money stream. While the analogy is not perfect, we may think of consumers as the heart of the economic system, collecting money from their various sources of income and putting this money back into the economy through various channels. This is the basic outline of the circuit flow of money.

The concept of such a circuit flow may be diagramed in many different ways, depending somewhat on the particular part of the economic process being investigated. Here we will deal with a very much simplified type of flow that concentrates on the essential components of national income already examined. In this analysis we will not always be completely explicit as to which concept of national income we are using, but the concepts are interchangeable with proper modifications in the definitions of their components.

Throughout the rest of this chapter we will build up our version of the circuit flow piece by piece. It may help the reader to know where we are going if he glances briefly at the completed model in Figure 25-1 (page 491) before tackling the assembly instructions that follow.

The Disposition of Income. At the outset it is probably simplest to think in terms of personal income, since this is the concept most clearly identified with the consumer. Here, then, is the consumer—the collective consumer representing all consumers in the country—receiving income that he can utilize in various ways. What does he do with his money?

Taxes. Over the first portion of his income he has no choice. The government stretches out its hand and decrees that a certain amount must be paid in taxes, which represent any involuntary payment made to the government.

Consumption. After he has made provision for the government, the consumer is free to dispose of the rest of his income as he sees fit. The greater part will be spent for consumption; that is, the purchase of commodities and services for personal use (including, of course, the use of family and friends with whom one shares). In this meaning consumption must be distinguished from two other common uses of the same word.

Consumption in this sense does not include any business purchase or business use. Some statistics, particularly for raw materials, include under "consumption" all purchases of any kind from the original producer or middleman. Thus "cotton consumption" represents primarily the purchase of raw cotton by textile mills for further processing. On the other hand, some businessmen speak of the "consumption" (that is, depletion) of stocks of raw materials or supplies. In national income analysis consumption does not have either of these connotations. To consume, one must be a consumer interested in satisfying his own wants.

A differentiation must also be made between consumption in the monetary sense and consumption in the psychological sense. Economists frequently define consumption as the *use* of goods to satisfy personal wants. This definition concentrates on the underlying psychological motivation of the economy: human satisfaction. Without detracting one iota from this basic concept, we suggest that from the standpoint of *moneyflows* the actual use of consumers' goods is irrelevant. At the moment that I buy a can of pears I put money into the hands of the grocer to compensate him and all other factors of production engaged in making cans of pears available, and at the same time I induce the pear industry to continue to produce in order to replace the can I bought. Whether I eat the pears today or next year, feed them to the goldfish, or lose them down a manhole may affect my personal enjoyment, but it does not affect the course of the money I have already spent. For monetary economics, therefore, the important transaction is the purchase rather than the use of consumers' goods.

Saving. After the consumer has paid his taxes and bought what goods he wishes, he has something left over (or perhaps he hasn't!), which we call *saving.* Again the definition is important because the word is used in so many different ways. In income analysis *personal saving is all income (after taxes) that is not spent on consumption.* Algebraically:

Saving = income − taxes − consumption

Saving, then, is a residual. If my income is $5,000 and I pay $1,000 in taxes and buy $3,400 worth of consumers' goods, my saving is $600. It is also clear that if my income and taxes remain the same but I spend $4,300 on consumption, then my saving is *minus* $300. This is *dis*saving.

	Case 1		*Case 2*	
Income		$5,000		$5,000
Less taxes	$1,000		$1,000	
consumption	3,400	4,400	4,300	5,300
Equals saving		$ 600		−$ 300

Dissaving, which means living beyond one's income, is possible under several circumstances:

1. If an individual has accumulated assets in the past (money, securities, etc.), he may draw on these past accumulations to pay for his present expenses; he may use his past saving to offset his present dissaving. This would be the situation of anyone living on an annuity, collecting an endowment policy, and so on.

2. If an individual can borrow, he may increase his expenditures now by promising to devote his future income to repayment of the debt; he may dissave now by agreeing to save in the future. Obviously he *must* save in the future since he cannot pay the debt unless his expenditures on other things are less than his income.

3. A person may be able to obtain funds from someone else who is willing to give him the money outright; he is able to dissave by inducing someone else to save on his behalf. But while an individual can dissave in this manner, a nation as a whole cannot (except through foreign gifts) since the dissaving of one individual is canceled (in the aggregate) by the saving of the other.

The nation as a whole can dissave in any one period by using up its past accumulation of savings or by borrowing abroad. In the United States personal saving was negative in both 1932 and 1933.

The definition of saving does not mention the forms that saving may take. All disposable income not consumed is saved whether it is hoarded, put into a savings account, used to buy securities, put into one's own business, or whatnot. It may make a considerable difference to the economy what form saving takes, but it is saving regardless of the form.

There are, then, three possible uses of income, no more. This can be shown diagrammatically:

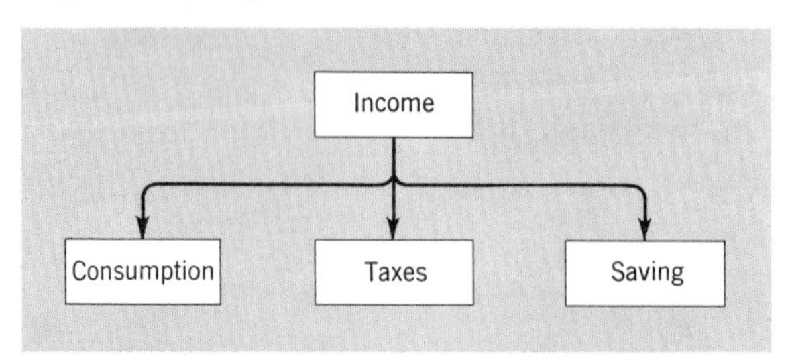

We should perhaps emphasize that consumption and taxes are expenses—once the goods have been bought or the taxes paid, the money is gone—while saving gives rise to an asset (called savings) in the form of cash, securities, and so on. It is because of this embodiment of saving in asset form that it is possible to dissave, that is, to reduce the stock of one's savings.

Income to Income. Now what happens to the money that is funneled into these three channels? For the most part it comes right back again as income for someone else.

Domestic Consumption. As we have already seen, when I buy a loaf of bread, every cent I spend eventually becomes income for someone engaged in the productive process. The blood put into circulation by the heart goes through the body, carries on its business, and returns to the heart.

Sometimes the chain of payments from consumer to eventual income recipient (who is also a consumer looked at from a different angle) may be a long one. In our bread example the maximum was five steps: consumer to grocer to baker to miller to farmer to farmhand. The money that became the profit of the grocer went through only one step, the wages of the grocer's clerk through two, and so on. In actuality the number of steps could greatly exceed the five of our example, for we have not considered the many possibilities of interbusiness payments for capital goods, raw materials, supplies, and services. But eventually all money spent must become income of some factor of production, and the circuit is closed.

But though the payment for bread represents the ultimate source of income for the farmhand, we must not assume that he has to wait until the bread is sold before he is paid. His pay is advanced out of the farmer's circulating capital, which is then reimbursed from the sale of wheat. The wheat, in turn, is paid for out of the miller's circulating capital, and so on. This is why circulating capital is necessary to the orderly flow of production. But the circulating capital is not itself the source of income; it merely advances income payments until the product can be sold. The consumer is the only ultimate source of income as he buys the output of industry.

Imports and Exports. All consumption expenditures become income of somebody, but all the funds may not flow to income recipients in the United States. If I buy a pound of coffee, part of my dollar goes to buy raw coffee from Brazil. This becomes income of the Brazilian exporter, Brazilian coffee workers, etc., and is withdrawn from the United States income stream.[8] All payments for imports become, initially at least, income for foreigners.

We must divide consumption, therefore, into two components: domestic consumption and imports, imports representing that portion of the price of United States purchases that is paid to foreigners.

[8] It should be clear that only that part of the coffee purchase that actually goes to foreigners is included in imports. The rest is domestic consumption.

While imports thus represent a deduction or a leakage from national income, this is at least partially compensated for by exports. Exports represent sales to foreigners, who pay for the goods out of their income. The proceeds earned by exports become income for our own workers in the export industries. This is just the reverse of the import case.

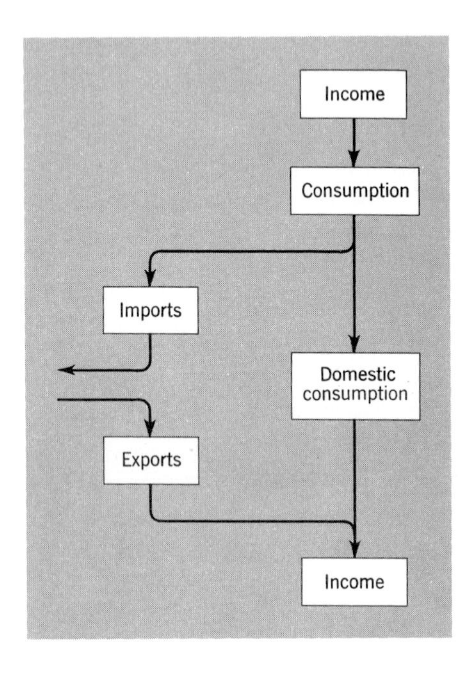

If imports and exports (on current account)[9] always balanced, we would not have to pay any attention to this area of our flow, for we could simply treat imports as interbusiness payments, all of which would come back as receipts for exports. But they may not balance, and if imports are larger than exports, then the foreign sector will represent a leakage from the circuit flow. Or if we have an export balance, this provides an addition to (or injection into) the circuit flow. How such a difference is possible we will examine later.

Taxes and Government Expenditure. The money that is paid in taxes has an effect similar to that of money used for consumption to the extent that government uses tax receipts to pay its bills. Government expenditure means payments to government clerks, purchases from business, and so on. Here again, either directly or indirectly, everything spent by the government becomes income for someone in the economy.

[9] A fuller examination of some of the details of the foreign balance must wait until our section on international monetary relations.

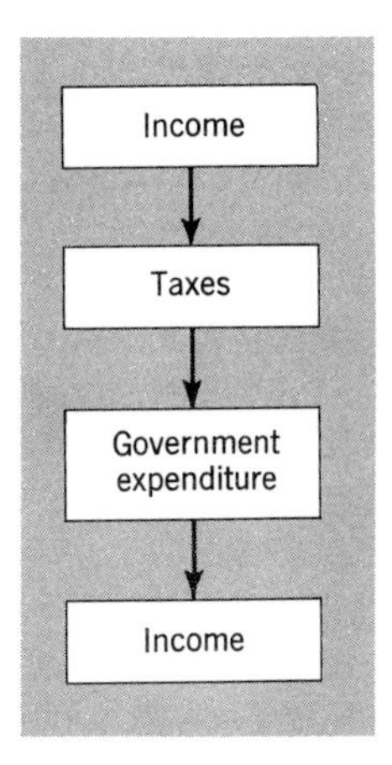

But taxes and government expenditures may not be equal. If the government pays out more than it takes in (government deficit), there is a net addition to the circuit flow; if it takes in more than it pays out (government surplus), there is a net reduction in the flow. Further discussion of this disparity must also wait for a few pages.

Saving and Investment. What becomes of the money channeled into saving? Does it also flow through the economy and become income? It may or may not, depending on whether it goes into investment or hoarding.

Investment. Investment is another word that has a technical meaning in national income analysis that is different from its common meaning. It is unfortunate that the word has this dual personality, and it is vitally important, if confusion is to be avoided, that its special use in income analysis be thoroughly understood. Here *investment* (more accurately, domestic investment) *is an increase in the physical assets (real capital) of business.*

First, investment can be carried out only by *business.* A consumer cannot invest (except when he buys a house, and in this role he is considered a businessman). Even when he buys durable goods, such as a refrigerator, he is consuming, not investing. All businessmen, as individuals, are consumers, but their business activity is in a separate sphere from their consumption. If a businessman makes a particular purchase for the purpose of increasing his direct satisfaction, he is acting as a consumer, and the purchase is consumption; if the purchase is for the purpose of increasing the income of his business, it is investment.

Second, investment applies only to *physical* (real) assets. Investment would include the purchase of machinery or raw materials, or the building of a plant. It does not include the purchase of securities or any other monetary asset; this is what would be meant by "investment" in financial circles, but *not* in national income analysis. Here investment has to do only with real wealth, not claims to wealth.

Third, investment is an *increase* in such assets. While assets may be increased by purchase, they may also be increased by production. A manufacturer may increase his physical assets by taking raw materials worth, say, $100, spending money to hire labor and pay other expenses involved in the manufacturing process, and thereby creating finished goods worth, say, $250. This represents an increase in physical assets of $150 and is investment of that amount.[10]

The value of the firm's physical assets, while it is increased by purchase and production, is decreased by sale. A sale, therefore, is *dis*investment (negative investment); it reduces the firm's physical assets by exchanging them for monetary assets. Depreciation would also represent disinvestment, since it measures the wearing out of equipment. Net investment, then, for a particular period may be either positive or negative, depending on the total effect of the continuous process of investment-disinvestment over the period. To take a simple example: A retailer invests when he buys merchandise for inventory; he disinvests when he sells it. Assuming his other physical assets (building, fixtures, delivery trucks, etc.) remain fixed over the year, if he started the year with $1,000 worth of inventory and ended it with $1,200 worth of inventory, he has invested $200 during the year. If, however, in addition to this change in inventory his other physical assets have depreciated $500 without replacement, then he has disinvested $300 ($200 increase in inventory, more than offset by $500 decrease in other physical assets).

When a business buys assets, the payments become income of the factors of production that produced them, just as in the case of the consumer's purchase of bread. When a firm *produces* assets, the increase in value is measured by the costs involved, that is, by payments to employees and other factor payments. Investment thus results in income in the same way that consumption does. To the extent, then, that saving is used to finance investment, the funds flow through the circuit unchecked.

Hoarding. But all saving is not necessarily channeled into investment. Some funds may lie idle in the pockets or checking accounts of consumers or in the vaults of financial intermediaries. Some saving, in other words, is hoarded. *Hoarding is defined as any part of saving not used for investment.* Sometimes the consumer himself hoards. Sometimes he makes his money available to financial institutions, who fail to pass it on to businessmen, but if at any point the flow of saving is interrupted so that it does not reach investment, the result is hoarding.

Saving, then, may be either invested or hoarded.

Just as saving gives rise to an asset, which we call *savings* (with an *s*), so the process of hoarding results in a pool of hoards. These hoards represent liquid purchasing power which is currently not being used but may be subsequently dishoarded when the funds are used for any purpose: consumption, taxes, or investment. Thus hoarding, like saving and investment, may be either positive or negative.

[10] Although we are speaking of physical assets, their value can obviously be measured only in monetary terms. Although polishing a diamond reduces its weight, the result is an increase in its real asset value.

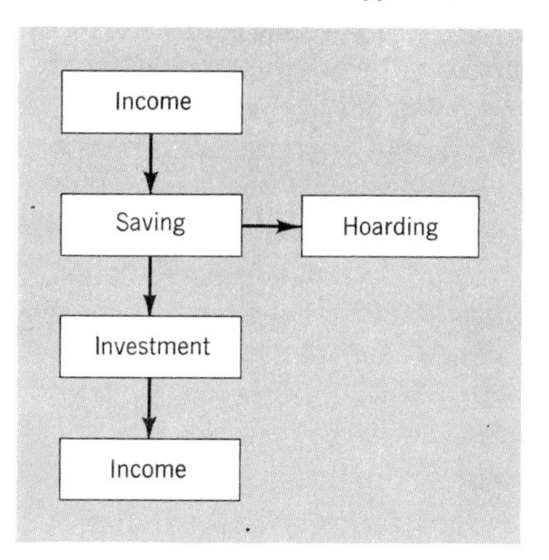

The Uses of Saving. When the ordinary consumer thinks of the uses of saving, he is not likely to consider the two uses we have discussed here. He is accustomed to thinking in terms of more specific actions. The funds that he has not used for consumption or taxes may be lying in his pocket or checking account. Or he may have put them in a savings bank or other savings institution, bought securities (new or old, private or government, domestic or foreign), bought a house, or—if he is in business for himself—financed additional inventory or bought new machinery.

There are essentially eight different types of transactions here, and each may be analyzed with reference to its effect on investment and hoarding:

1. Savings may be held in the form of currency. This is obviously hoarding. I may intend to use the money in my pocket to buy supper tonight, but as long as it is in my pocket, it is hoarded. It will be dishoarded (and dissaved) at supper time. For a given period (such as a year) hoarding represents the net addition to hoards (positive or negative).

2. Savings may be held in the form of a balance in a checking account. This again is hoarding. If I deposit cash or its equivalent in the bank, the asset that the bank receives may provide the reserves *on the basis of which* it may extend loans to be used for investment. *But* it is obvious that a bank cannot lend my deposit, since this is the bank's liability to me, not an asset. The bank creates *new* deposits when it makes a loan. My checking account, therefore, is hoarded.

3. Savings may be deposited in a savings institution. These institutions are intermediaries between consumers and investors, taking the savings of the former and lending them to the latter. When businessmen borrow, the savings are used for investment. But it is possible that some of the savings (usually a small part) are not lent out, but remain in the institution. To this extent the savings would be hoarded. When a customer puts his savings in a savings account, he is turning over to the institution the decision as to whether his savings will be lent for investment purposes or will be hoarded. In normal circumstances it would be assumed that most of the funds would find their way into investment.

4. Savings may be used to buy securities that are *newly issued* by a business firm. Most of these funds will be used for investment purposes, since this is usually what the firm borrowed the money for. But it may keep part of them in cash or bank balances, which represent hoarding. If the new issue is for purposes of refunding, the results are similar to those discussed in case 6.

5. Savings may be used by an individual owner of a business directly to increase the physical assets of his own business. These funds are obviously used for investment.

6. Savings may be used to purchase old securities already in someone else's hands. This would, in the nature of the case, include all purchases on the stock exchanges as well as most over-the-counter purchases. Here we have a more complicated situation, for essentially the purchase is a transfer of funds from buyer to seller. What happens to the funds depends entirely on the seller's decision. He may use the proceeds of the sale to buy a radio. In this case the buyer's saving is balanced by the seller's dissaving (his purchase is made with funds not received as current income, but from the sale of previously accumulated assets), and the net result is an increase in consumption. He might use the funds to pay his taxes. Or he might keep them in savings: in cash (hoarding), in a savings account, in a direct investment in his own business, or in any other form that savings may take. In other words, he can use the funds for any purpose for which income can be used. Thus the purchase of old securities may, but is not likely to, result in investment.

7. Savings may be channeled into the purchase of newly issued government securities. The government would be borrowing only if its expenditures were exceeding its receipts. In such a case the government is dissaving, and the saving of individuals offsets the dissaving of the government. This concept of saving will be examined in more detail in the next chapter. Suffice it to say here that this use of saving results in income through the medium of government expenditures and therefore is part of a continuous flow of funds.

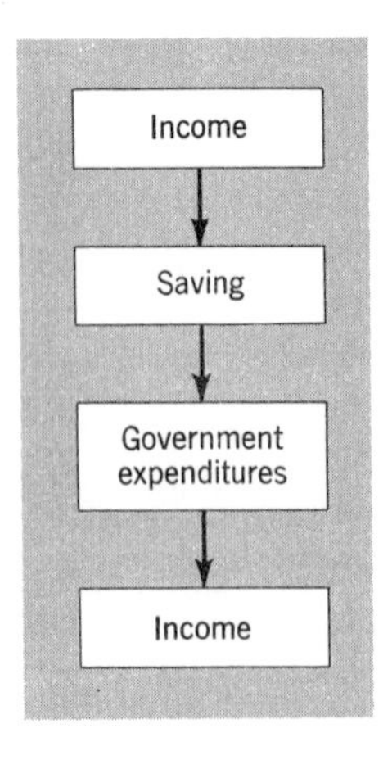

8. Savings may be used to purchase foreign assets (including such short-term assets as foreign bank balances, bank acceptances, and gold, as well as foreign stocks, bonds, and physical assets located abroad). This is the other side of our discussion of imports and exports. If we sell more (exports) than we buy (imports), we can do so only if we lend the foreigners the difference or if they sell assets (securities, gold, or direct investments) that they had previously accumulated. Either of these would be considered foreign investment, which is defined as the excess of exports over imports,[11] or (which amounts to the same thing) as the increase in net foreign debts owed to us.

If we use our savings to buy foreign securities, we are providing funds with which foreigners will buy our exports, which in turn provide income for people working in our export industries. Similarly if foreigners sell assets that they had formerly accumulated, they obtain funds from United States savers, and these funds are in turn used to buy United States exports. Savings used for foreign investment continue through the circuit flow (via the foreign country) and return as income for our workers in the export industries.[12]

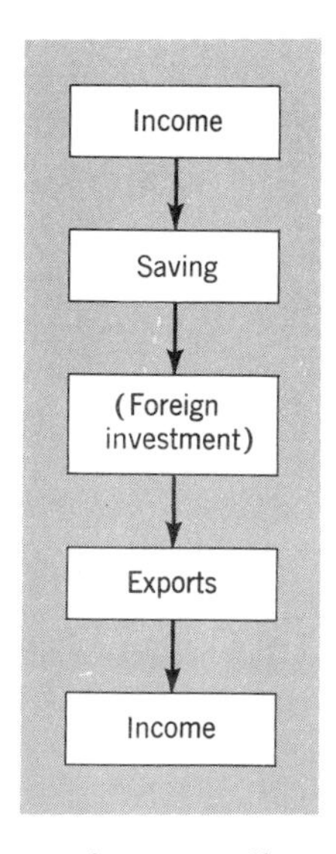

Foreign investment, like domestic investment, may be negative as well as positive. An import balance means that we are reducing our holdings of foreign assets in order to buy more goods than we are selling.

This survey of the uses of savings indicates that the part of saving that is channeled into domestic investment, into government expenditures, and into foreign investment results in an equal amount of income. But that part of saving that is hoarded does not result in income. It is idle purchasing power withheld from the economy, and it represents a leakage from the circuit flow.

Money Creation. While hoarding is thus a leakage, it is possible to inject into

[11] On current account. See Chap. 38 for further discussion of this point.

[12] Another way of putting this is to say that imports plus foreign investment equals exports.

the stream new money that does not originate in income. While a businessman may tap savings in order to provide funds for investment, the commercial bank is another source of such funds, particularly for working capital. When a commercial bank makes a loan, it is not acting as a middleman to pass on the savings of a consumer. It is creating money that did not exist before and that obviously, therefore, did not come out of anyone's income. The borrower uses this money to pay his workers, to buy raw materials, and so to create income, not out of consumption, taxes, or saving, but out of money newly injected into the flow.

The government can also use this source of funds to finance a deficit. By selling securities to the commercial banks, it obtains money that did not formerly exist and that it can now add to the income stream. In fact the government could simply print the money if it wished, though this method of augmenting the circuit flow is presently frowned upon.

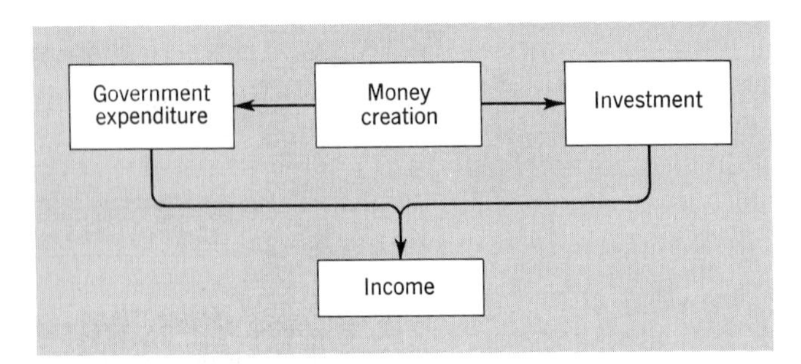

Money can also be destroyed. When bank loans are paid back, total money in the form of checking accounts is reduced. Generally the borrower has obtained the funds needed to repay the loan from the sale of his product. He has therefore disinvested (reduced his inventory by sale) to the extent of the repayment. The reduction of money therefore generally proceeds parallel with disinvestment.

Or the government may pay back its obligations, which means that its taxes have exceeded its expenditures so that it has a surplus out of which repayment can be made.

In either case (disinvestment or reduction of government expenditure) the effect of repayment of bank loans (destruction of money) is a reduction in income. Thus, while creation of money is an injection into the circuit flow, destruction is a leakage out of it.

The Circuit Flow as a Whole. We are now in a position to put together the various elements of the circuit flow in a single complete diagram, as shown in Figure 25-1.

While this diagram shows all the major relationships, it is not by any means exhaustive. It is intended to give the general picture without being cluttered up with all conceivable types of transactions. A few of the more important possibilities omitted for the sake of simplicity are the following:

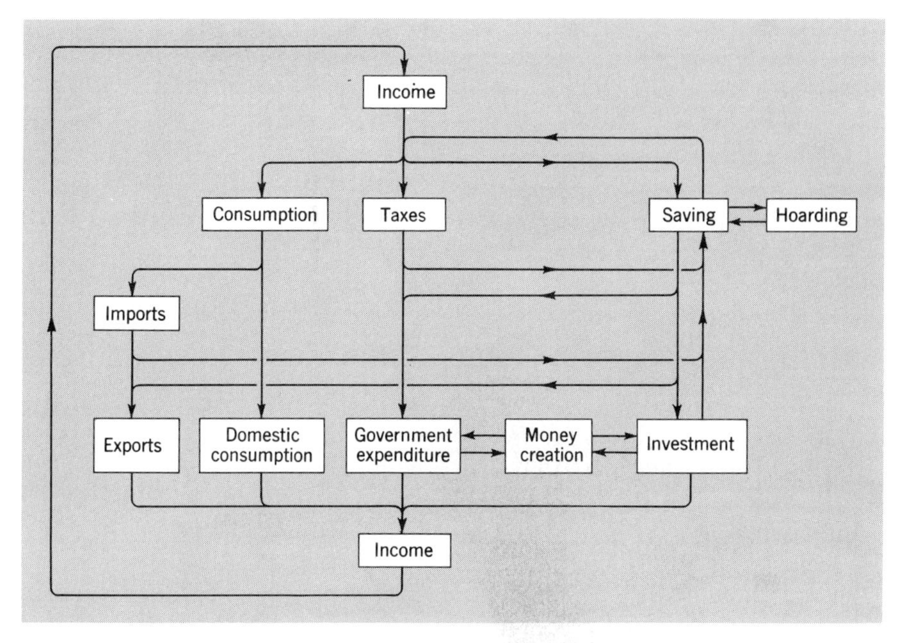

Figure 25-1. The circuit flow of money.

1. Business pays taxes, may save by plowing back earnings, and may hoard by holding cash on hand. If we consider that business does this on behalf of its ultimate owners (individual proprietors or stockholders), we may say that these ultimate owners as consumers are doing it indirectly. But we must not lose sight of the fact that consumers and businesses act for different reasons, so that saving by a corporation arises from different motives and takes a different form from personal saving by its stockholders.
2. When consumers borrow from commercial banks, new money is injected into consumption rather than into business or government. The effect, however, is the same, namely, a rise in income.
3. Not all imports go into consumption; some may represent investment goods or government purchases. Government operations have been an important factor in the international balance since our entry into World War II.
4. The many interrelationships among businesses and the great diversity of forms of business are impossible to indicate on a diagram of this type. The great danger of any aggregate approach is that it tends to make us forget the individual transactions that make up the total as well as the varied individual reactions to any specific situation. This danger we must constantly guard against, for no statistical total can ever adequately convey the many complexities of which it is composed.

The Circuit Flow Is a Spiral. There is one aspect of the circuit flow that cannot be shown in two dimensions. Although the income earned by the factors of production is the same income that consumers allocate among consumption, taxes, and saving and that in turn flows through the business system to come out again as earned income, the whole process takes place over time. The income earned today is spent and becomes someone else's income in a subsequent time period. In other words, the circuit flow is not a circle, but a spiral, each circuit moving forward in time.

Perhaps an even better way to look at it is the one with which we started. The flow of money is similar to the circulation of blood, which is simultaneously coursing through all parts of the body. It all goes through the heart (income), but some of it takes longer to come back (from the legs, for instance) than the rest. The heart may beat faster or more slowly, thereby affecting the general speed with which the blood moves, but the velocity in particular areas is also affected by local conditions (as when a tourniquet is applied at some point). The body may lose blood through a cut or gain it by transfusion, but once the blood supply is sufficient to do the work it has to do, there is nothing to be gained by adding more.

All this is similar to the continuous but complex coursing of money through the economy. In fact, complicated as the body is, it is a fairly simple mechanism compared to a modern industrial society. It is inevitable, therefore, that any attempt to draw a picture of the monetary circulation must be only a first approximation to the actual operation of the economy.

Questions for Thought and Discussion

1. Given the following sales and expenditure figures from the accounts of a firm making matches, calculate the value added by the firm:

Purchases of raw materials	25
Payment for electricity	3
Payment to an advertising agency	5
Wages	40
Interest on bonds	7
Sales of matches	85

2. Why are corporate income taxes considered part of national income (in its technical meaning), while indirect business taxes are not?

3. Why are earnings plowed back by corporations into the business considered part of the (national) income accruing to the stockholders of the corporation? Why are they not counted as part of personal income?

4. If all goods produced represent equivalent payments to the factors of production, is it possible for aggregate income to be too small to buy the output of industry?

5. Given the following figures, draw up a table showing the numerical value of all five measures of national income:

Consumption	256
Personal taxes	35
Social insurance taxes	11
Corporate profits taxes	22
Indirect business taxes	33
Government transfer payments	16
Personal saving	17
Undistributed corporate profits	10
Depreciation	32

6. When a consumer buys a refrigerator, is this investment? Is it a physical asset for the consumer? Would he include it on his balance sheet if he drew one up? How does it differ from a factory machine?

7. By statistical convention we do not include the increase in physical assets of government (dams, post offices, etc.) in investment. Is this logical? Do they represent real wealth of the community?

8. If a business reduces its inventory, where does that fit in the circuit flow?

9. Illustrate dishoarding by an example.

10. Why does borrowing by a consumer represent a claim against future saving?

11. Is it possible for an individual to make available for investment (lend) in any one year more than he saves in that year? How? If I buy a government bond for $1,000, must I have saved all that amount the same day I buy it?

12. Why is it necessary to consider the circuit flow of money in terms of a specified time period? Why can it not be thought of as an instantaneous picture?

Selected Bibliography

Chandler, Lester V.: *An Introduction to Monetary Theory,* Harper & Row, Publishers, Incorporated, New York, 1940.

Dahlberg, Arthur O.: *National Income Visualized,* Columbia University Press, New York, 1956.

Day, A. C. L., and Sterie T. Beza: *Money and Income,* Oxford University Press, Fair Lawn, N.J., 1960.

Dernburg, Thomas F., and Duncan M. McDougall: *Macro-economics: The Measurement, Analysis, and Control of Aggregate Economic Activity,* McGraw-Hill Book Company, New York, 1960.

Halm, George N.: *Monetary Theory,* 2d ed., McGraw-Hill Book Company, New York, 1946.

Hansen, Alvin H.: *Monetary Theory and Fiscal Policy,* McGraw-Hill Book Company, New York, 1949.

——— and Richard V. Clemence: *Readings in Business Cycles and National Income,* W. W. Norton & Company, Inc., New York, 1953.

Harrod, Roy F.: *The Trade Cycle,* Oxford University Press, Fair Lawn, N.J., 1956.

Hawtrey, Ralph G.: *Capital and Employment,* Longmans, Green & Co., Ltd., London, 1939.

Keynes, John Maynard: *The General Theory of Employment, Interest and Money,* Harcourt, Brace & World, Inc., New York, 1936.

Kuznets, Simon: *Economic Change: Selected Essays in Business Cycles, National Income, and Economic Growth,* W. W. Norton & Company, Inc., New York, 1953.

Morgan, Theodore: *Income and Employment,* 2d ed., Prentice-Hall, Inc., Englewood Cliffs, N.J., 1952.

Robinson, Joan: *Introduction to the Theory of Employment,* The Macmillan Company, New York, 1937.

Ruggles, Richard: *An Introduction to National Income and Income Analysis,* McGraw-Hill Book Company, New York, 1949.

Shoup, Carl S.: *Principles of National Income Analysis,* Houghton Mifflin Company, Boston, 1947.

Vandermeulen, Alice (John), and Daniel Carlson Vandermeulen: *National Income Analysis by Sector Accounts,* Prentice-Hall, Inc., Englewood Cliffs, N.J., 1956.

Chapter 26
The Income-creating Process

Remuneration! O! that's the Latin word
for three farthings:

Love's Labour Lost
Act III, scene 1, line 143

The circuit flow of money, like the equation of exchange, shows certain relationships within the economy and is thus a useful tool of analysis. It does not indicate cause and effect, but it helps us look in the right places and points out some errors to avoid. National income analysis takes two forms: an examination of the historical record and an attempt to assess the effect of particular changes in the future. We will examine the first of these uses in this chapter and the second in the chapter following.

***Ex Post* Is a Picture of the Past.** Examination of past historical events we refer to as *ex post* analysis. The past is on the record, and in this country at least a large volume of statistical data gives us a pretty clear picture of how the economy has acted. We know, for instance, that personal income in 1964 was $495.0 billion and gross private domestic investment was $92.9 billion. How does the circuit flow help us interpret these figures?

Saving and Investment

It would be possible to examine the circuit flow in the form in which it appears in Figure 25-1, but for clarity of initial exposition it is easier to simplify it still further by two assumptions, which may be relaxed at any time without interfering with the basic argument. We will assume:

1. That imports equal exports, so that the amount of money flowing into consumption (domestic consumption plus imports) is exactly equal to the income produced from domestic consumption plus exports. This allows us to eliminate the foreign sector as an area of special attention; all consumption flows into income, whether directly or through foreign channels.
2. That taxes equal government expenditure, so that the amount taken in taxes flows unaltered into income through government payments. Since this eliminates the government as an area requiring special attention, it is convenient purely as a matter of exposition to redefine consumption (temporarily) to include taxes along with consumption proper. This may be defended even as a matter of nomenclature by suggesting that taxes represent (fundamentally though indirectly) consumption of government services.

Our simplified circuit flow then becomes:

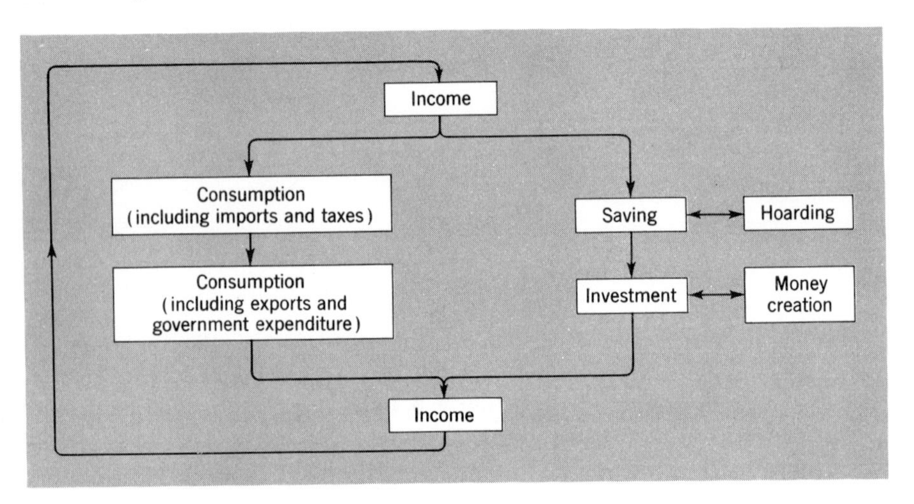

Since *ex post* analysis refers to a given period of time, it is obvious that the income at the top of the diagram (income used) is the same as the income at the bottom (income received). For this reason it may be more useful to cut the diagram in half and reassemble it top to bottom in this manner:

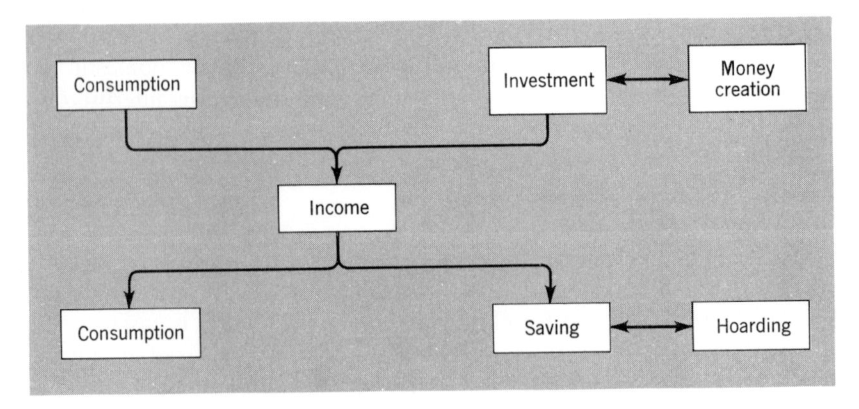

The top half of this revised diagram shows the source of income: it was earned by producing commodities and services for consumers (export, domestic, and government) or for investors. The bottom half shows how this same income was used: it was spent on consumption (imports, domestic goods, and taxes), or it was saved. Remembering that for the moment we are including both the foreign sector and the government sector in consumption, we can translate our diagram into algebra:

$$Y \text{ (earned)} = C + I_d$$
$$Y \text{ (spent)} = C + S_p$$

where Y = income
C = consumption
I_d = investment (domestic)
S_p = saving (private)

Since income earned and income spent in any one period of time must be the same thing,

$$C + I_d = C + S_p$$

or

$$I_d = S_p$$

In other words, saving is equal to investment.

Many people find it difficult to believe this equality of saving and investment, which lies at the heart of much income analysis. Yet it is incontrovertibly true. The skeptics fall into four main groups:

1. Those who object to the definitions of saving and investment. It is true that different definitions might very well lead to different conclusions. It is also true that definitions are arbitrary. Ours are no more right (or wrong) than any other. But they are convenient, and they are standard in this field. To object to the definitions, therefore, only confuses the issue. What we have said is that the excess of income over expenditures for consumption goods (which we have decided to designate by the word "saving") is equal to the increase in the physical assets of business ("investment"). This can be proved.

2. Those who forget that we are speaking exclusively of *ex post* quantities—statistical sums for a given past period. It is perfectly true that the desire to save on the part of consumers may differ markedly from the desire to invest on the part of businessmen. This is a vitally important subject, to which we will devote all of Chapter 27. But however much anticipations may differ, *realized* saving must equal *realized* investment.

3. Those who say that while this may be true under the simplified assumptions made here, it is not true when these assumptions are relaxed and we consider government deficits or net foreign investment. While the introduction of the foreign and government sectors will require a slight change in terminology, it will not alter the underlying principle. This problem will be explored later in this chapter.

4. Those who don't understand algebra sufficiently to accept its conclusions or who have a vague, restless feeling that while saving and investment may be equal algebraically, this is true only in an unrealistic mathematical sense, and in real life it just isn't so.

In order to satisfy these dissenters let us examine the whole problem in more realistic terms. National income consists fundamentally of a flow of goods produced during a period of, say, one year. Let us imagine all these goods stacked in one huge pile—real national income. From this pile consumers buy and remove what they want for their own consumption. What is left is, by definition, saving—that part of income not consumed. Those goods that still remain in the pile must belong to business since they have not been bought by consumers. Since they are part of this year's production, they didn't exist at the beginning of the year. They have therefore been added to the (physical) assets of business during the year. This is our definition of investment. Saving equals investment.

Any addition to physical assets can come about only as a result of consuming less than has been produced, that is, by saving. People may *wish* to save less (or more) than businessmen *wish* to invest, but if so, one or the other group must be disappointed because an inequality between saving and investment *ex post* is just as impossible as it is for two bodies to occupy the same space at the same time—in spite of the number of automobiles that have tried it!

Hoarding and Money Creation. At this point you may be tempted to say, "Yes, I understand all that. But if saving and investment are equal, then there cannot be any hoarding." Not so. We did not say that all saving goes into investment. Nor that all investment comes from saving. Part of saving may be hoarded; part of investment may come from newly created money. It follows, then, that if some saving is hoarded, this must be precisely offset by an equal injection of new money into investment.

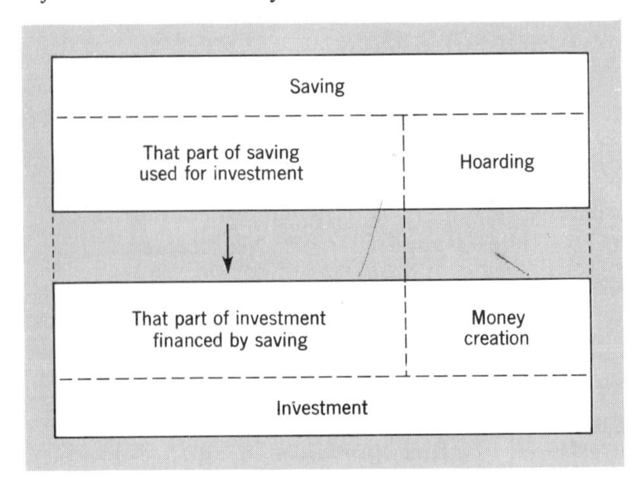

The strange (and perhaps unpalatable) conclusion is that hoarding (that is, the addition to hoards) equals money creation.[1] This can be demonstrated both algebraically and logically.

Let us look first at the algebra. Saving can be used in only two ways, investment or hoarding. Therefore

$$S_p = S' + H$$

where S' = that part of saving used for investment
H = hoarding
Similarly, investment funds can come from only two sources: saving or new money. Then

$$I_d = S' + M$$

where M = money creation
Since it has already been demonstrated that

$$S_p = I_d$$

therefore $$S' + H = S' + M$$

or $$H = M$$

The same conclusion may be shown logically. As a first step let us drop briefly our investigation of flows and look instead at stocks, that is, hoards rather than hoarding, and money in circulation rather than money creation. In what form are hoards held? They represent money income that has not been spent either for consumers' goods or for producers' goods (investment).[2] If hoards represent money received as income but not yet spent, they must still be held in the form of money. In other words, all hoards consist of money.

Similarly, all money in existence must be hoarded. Obviously all money belongs to someone at every moment of time. It cannot remain ownerless. But if someone holds it, it must represent income that has not yet been spent (for either consumption or investment); that is, it must represent hoards. Suppose that I have just received my pay and am on my way to the grocery store for the week's food purchases. The money in my pocket is hoarded until the moment I pay the grocer. At the moment I hand it over to him I have consumed that portion of my income (spent it on consumption goods) and am no longer hoarding. But at this precise moment the grocer starts hoarding; he has received money which he has not yet spent. As soon as he uses the money, say, to pay wages to his clerk, he is no longer hoarding, but the clerk

[1] The negative proposition is of course also true: dishoarding equals money destruction.

[2] Income received in kind does not change the argument, since it is considered consumed at the moment of receipt and therefore cannot be saved or, of course, hoarded.

is. Thus all money is at any moment hoarded by someone or other, whether a consumer or a business firm. But if all hoards are in the form of money while all money is in hoards, then the two must be identical.

Although the argument so far is in terms of stocks, it is easy to translate into the flow concept with which we are primarily concerned. If hoards and money are always equal at every point in time, then any increase in one must of necessity be balanced by an exactly equal increase in the other; any decrease in one must equal the decrease in the other. If hoards and money in existence at the beginning of the period were equal at $100 million and at the end of the period were equal at $110 million, then obviously the addition to hoards (hoarding) must have equaled the addition to money (money creation), each being $10 million.

It should be emphasized that this, as in the saving-investment case, is a purely formal, *ex post* equality. It does not imply that if people *want* to dishoard, the money necessarily disappears. Nor, in broader terms, does it imply that any leakage from the flow in the form of hoarding will have no effect on the economy because the seepage in the form of new money will exactly offset it. On the contrary, *attempts* to hoard or dishoard may affect the economy very seriously, a problem that will be examined in detail in the following chapter. We only suggest that, in practice, nobody can hoard more money than there is. It is, however, possible to speed up the circulation of money so that while the same amount of money is hoarded at any one instant, more business is transacted over a given period of time because the money circulates faster. This is the concept of velocity, which has already been discussed and to which we will return later.

The Government and Foreign Sectors. We are now ready to relax our initial simplifying assumptions concerning the equality of taxes and government expenditures on the one hand and the equality of imports and exports on the other. Suppose neither of these sectors is in balance. Doesn't this completely change our conclusions? No, it does not. All that it requires is a more detailed examination and some minor adjustments in terminology.

Let us return to our complete diagram of the circuit flow (Figure 25-1) and turn it upside down as we did the simpler diagram.

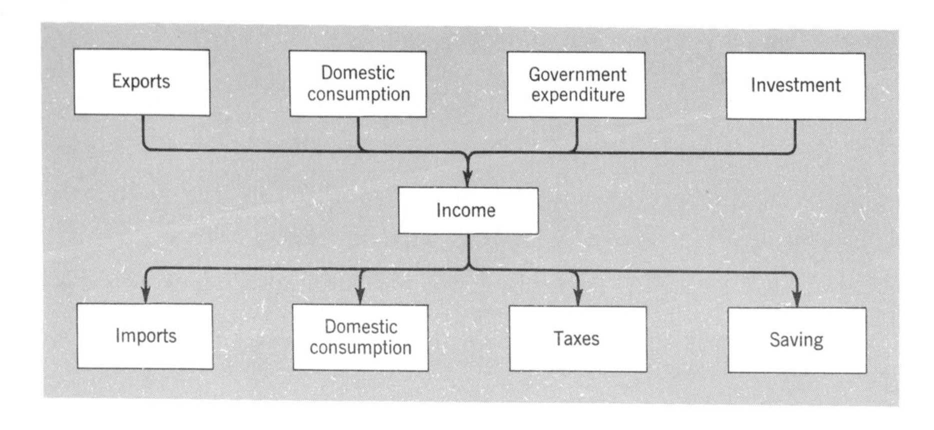

The top half of the diagram shows the sources of income: it was earned by producing commodities and services for domestic consumers, for export, for government, or for investors. The bottom half shows how income was used: it was spent on imports, domestic consumption, or taxes; or it was saved.[3] So far our only change has been to list explicitly several items that we lumped together with consumption previously. Now we can state each of these factors separately in our income equations:

$$Y \text{ (earned)} = C_d + Ex + G + I_d$$
$$Y \text{ (spent)} \;\; = C_d + Im + T + S_p$$

where C_d = domestic consumption
Ex = exports
Im = imports
G = government expenditure
T = taxes

Since income earned and income spent are the same thing,

$$C_d + Im + T + S_p = C_d + Ex + G + I_d$$

Rearranging the two sides of the equation,

$$(C_d - C_d) + S_p + (T - G) = I_d + (Ex - Im)$$

Or, dropping $(C_d - C_d)$,

$$S_p + (T - G) = I_d + (Ex - Im)$$

In order to emerge from this morass of symbols it is desirable to give a name to each of the quantities within parentheses. The quantity $T - G$ is what is normally called the *government surplus*. Here we refer to it as *government saving,* defined as the excess of government tax receipts over government expenditure. It is similar to private saving, which also represents the excess of receipts (income) over expenditures (consumption). Or we might say that the taxpayer is being forced to save because the government takes his money but (to the extent of the surplus) does not spend it. If government expenditures exceed receipts ($T - G$ being negative), the government is operating at a deficit. In this case the government is dissaving, just as an individual does when he lives beyond his income.

The quantity $Ex - Im$ is our export surplus, and this we call *net foreign investment*. It is defined as the excess of exports on current account over

[3] For simplicity the diagram leaves out hoarding and money creation. The more extended analysis with which we are here concerned makes no changes whatever in the conclusions we have already reached concerning these two items.

imports on current account.[4] This means that foreigners are buying more of our merchandise and services than they are selling to us. How can they pay for the excess goods? Without going into the intricacies of foreign finance at this point, we may say that they obtain these needed dollars by borrowing from us.[5] In other words, we make "investments" (in the monetary sense) in these foreign countries. While this differs somewhat from our concept of domestic investment as an increase in *physical* assets, it does result in an increase in *foreign* assets, that is, in claims against foreign real wealth. Domestically we cannot count *claims* against wealth as investment because we count the wealth itself, and we don't want to count twice. But since we do not count foreign wealth, it is justifiable to count claims against it as investment (net foreign investment). If imports exceed exports ($Ex - Im$ being negative), we have net foreign disinvestment, which is the same as an import surplus.

Using these definitions our equality becomes private saving plus government saving equals domestic investment plus net foreign investment:

$$S_p + S_g = I_d + I_f$$

where S_g = government saving ($T - G$)
I_f = net foreign investment ($Ex - Im$)

We might then speak of total saving as including both private and governmental varieties and of total investment as including both domestic and foreign investment. Then

$$S = I$$

where S = total savings ($S_p + S_g$)
I = total investment ($I_d + I_f$)

Total saving equals total investment.

It must be borne in mind that the magnitudes involved in this last equation are not the same as those in our original equation, $S_p = I_d$. That equation concerned itself only with private saving and domestic investment, and it is correct only if both foreign trade and the government budget are in balance. Our totals here are broader and represent a more general case than our first presentation. The equation $S = I$ holds true whether the government budget

[4] Technically, the current account includes gifts to foreigners in addition to merchandise and services. Net foreign investment (net exports on current account) therefore differs from $Ex - Im$ (net exports of goods and services) by the amount of gifts sent abroad (personal and government transfer payments to foreigners). This leads to some slight discrepancies in Tables 26-2 and 26-3 (column 9 of Table 26-2 and column 5 of Table 26-3 on the one hand, and columns 2 and 7 of Table 26-3 on the other) in figures that would otherwise appear to be identical; but since such gifts are relatively small, we have ignored them in the present discussion. For further explanation of this point see Chap. 38, especially Table 38-4.

[5] Or by liquidating past loans to us or by shipping gold. All these transactions are handled in a similar manner in the international accounts.

is balanced or not, whether foreign trade is balanced or not. It does not depend on any qualifying assumptions whatsoever. It rests solely on an understanding of the definitions (what is meant by total saving and total investment) and an *ex post* analysis.

Saving actually achieved *cannot* exceed investment. It is impossible for a nation as a whole to refrain from using all the output of the economic machine without the unused portion accumulating in the form of real wealth. Investment actually achieved *cannot* exceed saving. It is impossible for a nation to increase its stock of real wealth unless it refrains from consuming a portion of its output.

Saving and Investment in the United States

So far we have demonstrated the equality of saving and investment in both algebraic and logical terms. Another way of facing the problem is in terms of actual statistics. Figures for 1964 are shown in Table 26-1. A few comments on the items listed may be helpful.

Personal saving is that part of income *actually received* that is not spent for taxes or consumption. All the other items in private saving represent income earned but not actually received.

Business saving is net income earned by firms that has not been paid out to stockholders or other owners of the business. It represents saving by the firm on behalf of its owners. Such saving takes three forms:

Table 26-1. Gross Saving and Investment Account, 1964
Billions of Dollars

Private saving:			
Personal saving		26.3	
Business saving:			
Capital consumption allowances	55.7		
Undistributed corporate profits	19.9		
Corporate inventory valuation adjustment	−0.3	75.4	
Statistical discrepancy		−0.5	101.2
Government saving (surplus)			−2.4
Gross saving and statistical discrepancy			98.7
Domestic investment:			
Residential structures		27.5	
Nonresidential structures		21.1	
Producers' durable equipment		39.4	
Change in business inventories		4.8	92.9
Net foreign investment			5.8
Gross investment			98.7

Source: *Survey of Current Business*, vol. 45, no. 8 (August, 1965), pp. 25, 41. Detail may not add to totals because of rounding.

1. *Capital consumption allowances* (primarily depreciation) are saving only in the gross sense. They represent that portion of the sale price of the product not paid to any factor of production or in taxes. They thus represent funds available to the business and are customarily used to invest in replacement machinery. In order to derive *net* saving and investment, capital consumption allowances are subtracted from both private saving and domestic investment.
2. *Undistributed profits* are the item most commonly associated with corporate saving. They represent corporate profits minus profits taxes and dividends to stockholders and are frequently referred to as *plowed-back earnings.*
3. *Inventory valuation adjustment* is a technical device to remove artificial changes in corporate profits introduced by price movements. Its effect is to reduce profits when they are inflated by rising prices of inventories and to raise profits unduly depressed by falling values of inventories. It can be thought of as part of undistributed corporate profits.

The *statistical discrepancy* is an unfortunate item that arises from the inadequacy of present techniques for estimating the various components of national income. When the figures for GNP are added together[6] and capital consumption allowances and indirect business taxes subtracted, the same figure should be obtained as when the components of national income are added together.[7] However, because of the extreme complexity of the economy and the difficulty of obtaining accurate estimates for some of these components, a discrepancy arises between these two, similar to the error of closure on a rough survey map. Since we know that the two should be identical, we close the gap in our statistical measurements by assigning a value to the difference and carrying this figure on the books as the statistical discrepancy. We do not know precisely where the discrepancy arose (if we did, it wouldn't be a discrepancy), and including it under saving is, therefore, an arbitrary device. It must, however, be included somewhere, and there appears to be no better place to put it.

Someone might object at this point that if the statistical discrepancy were not included, saving would *not* equal investment. In a sense this is true. The figures themselves do not prove the equality of saving and investment. That equality has been proved in two other ways. The figures do show a very marked similarity between saving and investment, and in view of the hundreds of thousands of different figures that must be combined in order to obtain the national income accounts it would be unusual indeed to expect complete accuracy. The statistical discrepancy has never exceeded 1½ per cent of GNP, and as our statistical methods improve it has tended to decline on the average. In 1964 it was less than $\frac{1}{10}$ per cent. It should be noted further that the discrepancy is not *computed* as the difference between saving and investment estimates; it is computed as the difference in national income estimates as calculated by two different methods.

[6] Personal consumption expenditures, gross private domestic investment, net exports of goods and services, and government purchases of goods and services.

[7] Compensation of employees, income of unincorporated enterprises, rental income, corporate profits, and net interest.

The remaining items in Table 26-1 conform very closely to concepts we have already introduced and need no further comment.

While the figures for 1964 give us an idea of the magnitude of saving and investment for one recent year, it is also desirable to see how they have changed over time. Table 26-2 shows the major components of saving and investment for each year since 1929, when the current Department of Commerce series was started.

This table shows *net* saving and investment. The last column, which is not properly a part of the table itself, gives the figures for capital consumption allowances. If these are added to (1) net corporate saving, (2) net saving (and net investment), and (3) net new fixed capital, the corresponding *gross* figures are obtained.

One aspect of this table worthy of note is that in several years net saving and investment were negative for the economy as a whole. In 1932, at the depth of the Depression, the country experienced net dissaving and disinvestment of $6.2 billion. Business spent $3.5 billion on capital goods, but depreciation amounted to $7.4 billion, resulting in a net *decrease* in capital equipment of $3.9 billion. In addition there was a drop in inventories of $2.5 billion and a very small net foreign investment of $0.2 billion. As a result we used up in this one year $6.2 billion worth of goods that we had produced in preceding years. To this extent we were living from our wealth rather than from income. This is the real meaning of dissaving: less wealth at the end of the period than at its beginning.

We financed a small part of World War II by this process of living on past accumulations. We used up capital equipment faster than we replaced it in each of the three years from 1942 to 1944, disinvested on foreign account in the four years from 1942 to 1945, and reduced the inventories on our shelves during the last three of them. In spite of the fact that private saving was larger in this period than it has ever been, before or since, it was still not sufficient to finance the tremendous government deficit that the war produced. War is a voracious user of resources, and although production doubled between 1939 and 1943, industry was still unable to produce currently enough to meet the needs of the country. So we called on our stock of accumulated wealth, disinvesting a total of $15.0 billion in 1942–1945.

Then after the war we increased investment at a rapid rate (1) to replace stocks and machinery used up during the war, (2) to catch up on the normal increase in equipment, which had been postponed during the war and to some extent during the preceding depression, and (3) to meet the new demands of a rapidly growing economy.

National Product in the United States

In order to make these figures on saving and investment more meaningful, it may be useful to examine how the other components of net national product have behaved over time. We have chosen net national product (NNP) for

Table 26-2. Net Saving and Investment, 1929–1964
Billions of Dollars

Year	Saving				**Net saving (and net investment)**	Investment			*Capital consumption allowances*
	Personal saving	Net business saving	Statistical discrepancy	Government saving		Net new fixed capital	Change in inventories	Net foreign investment	
1929	4.2	3.3	0.7	1.0	**9.1**	6.6	1.7	0.8	*7.9*
1930	3.4	0.7	−0.8	−0.3	**3.0**	2.6	−0.4	0.7	*8.0*
1931	2.6	−2.5	0.7	−2.9	**−2.0**	−1.1	−1.1	0.2	*7.9*
1932	−0.6	−4.2	0.3	−1.8	**−6.2**	−3.9	−2.5	0.2	*7.4*
1933	−0.9	−3.7	0.6	−1.4	**−5.4**	−4.0	−1.6	0.2	*7.0*
1934	0.4	−1.6	0.5	−2.4	**−3.1**	−2.8	−0.7	0.4	*6.8*
1935	2.1	−0.4	−0.2	−2.1	**−0.5**	−1.5	1.1	−0.1	*6.9*
1936	3.6	−0.3	1.2	−3.1	**1.4**	0.2	1.3	−0.1	*7.0*
1937	3.8	0.6	—	0.3	**4.7**	2.1	2.5	0.1	*7.2*
1938	0.7	0.7	0.6	−1.8	**0.3**	0.1	−0.9	1.1	*7.3*
1939	2.6	1.1	1.3	−2.2	**2.9**	1.6	0.4	0.9	*7.3*
1940	3.8	3.0	1.0	−0.7	**7.1**	3.4	2.2	1.5	*7.5*
1941	11.0	3.2	0.4	−3.8	**10.8**	5.2	4.5	1.1	*8.2*
1942	27.6	4.7	−1.1	−31.4	**−0.2**	−1.7	1.8	−0.2	*9.8*
1943	33.4	6.0	−2.0	−44.1	**−6.7**	−3.9	−0.6	−2.2	*10.3*
1944	37.3	6.1	2.5	−51.8	**−6.0**	−2.9	−1.0	−2.1	*11.0*
1945	29.6	3.9	4.0	−39.5	**−2.1**	0.6	−1.3	−1.4	*11.3*
1946	15.2	4.6	0.1	5.4	**25.3**	14.3	6.4	4.6	*9.9*
1947	7.3	8.0	0.9	14.4	**30.6**	22.2	−0.5	8.9	*12.3*
1948	13.4	13.5	−2.0	8.5	**33.4**	26.8	4.7	1.9	*14.5*
1949	9.4	13.1	0.3	−3.2	**19.7**	22.2	−3.1	0.5	*16.6*
1950	13.1	11.1	1.5	7.9	**33.5**	29.0	6.8	−2.2	*18.3*
1951	17.3	11.9	3.3	5.8	**38.3**	27.8	10.3	0.2	*21.2*
1952	18.2	12.0	2.2	−3.8	**28.5**	25.6	3.1	−0.3	*23.2*
1953	18.3	10.4	3.0	−6.9	**24.9**	26.5	0.4	−2.1	*25.7*
1954	16.4	11.0	2.9	−7.0	**23.2**	25.2	−1.5	−0.4	*28.1*
1955	15.8	14.8	2.1	2.7	**35.4**	29.9	6.0	−0.5	*31.5*
1956	20.6	13.7	−1.1	4.9	**37.5**	31.3	4.7	1.6	*34.1*
1957	20.8	12.2	—	0.7	**34.3**	29.4	1.3	3.4	*37.1*
1958	22.3	10.5	1.6	−12.5	**21.8**	23.5	−1.5	−0.1	*38.9*
1959	19.1	15.4	−0.8	−2.1	**31.6**	29.2	4.8	−2.3	*41.4*
1960	17.0	13.4	−1.0	3.7	**33.1**	27.8	3.6	1.7	*43.4*
1961	21.2	13.4	−0.7	−4.3	**29.5**	24.4	2.0	3.1	*45.2*
1962	21.6	16.3	0.5	−2.9	**35.5**	27.0	6.0	2.5	*50.0*
1963	20.5	16.3	−0.7	1.2	**37.3**	28.4	5.7	3.2	*52.8*
1964	26.3	19.7	−0.5	−2.4	**43.0**	32.4	4.8	5.8	*55.7*

Source: Adapted from *Survey of Current Business*, vol. 45, no. 8 (August, 1965), pp. 24, 25, 40, 41. Detail may not add to totals because of rounding.

our illustration rather than the more common GNP because net investment has more significance from the point of view of the long-term growth of the country than gross investment. It is the *addition* to our capital equipment that provides for growth; mere replacement keeps us where we are.

In order to correlate the statistics with theory we will place the figures in the mold of the circuit flow. In the process we will make one concession to the statistics by using only net foreign investment rather than its two basic components: exports and imports.

In its NNP form the circuit flow includes the following components:

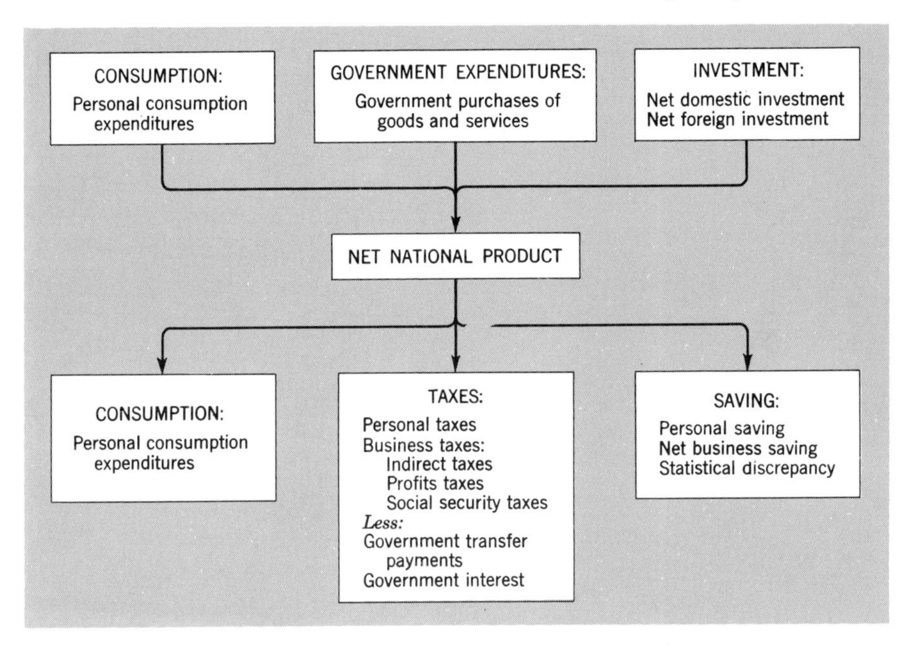

This form is the same one with which we are familiar. Only one further comment is necessary. Since government transfer and interest payments are not part of NNP, they cannot be included as part of the government contribution to that product. But since they are actually paid to persons in the economy, they can be most readily thought of as deductions from the total tax bill, that is, as rebates to taxpayers in general.

Using the categories indicated in our diagram, the figures for NNP are presented in Table 26-3 for each year since 1929.

This table shows quite clearly the great fluctuations in income and its components over time. While NNP is by no means the only measure of business activity, these fluctuations are essentially what we call the business cycle. In the Depression of the thirties we see that all the components of national product had fallen from their 1929 highs. We can trace the partial recovery by 1937, the depression of 1938, the great upsurge during the war, and the continually rising level since. The minor recessions of 1949, 1954, 1958, and 1961 are apparent in some of the figures but not all.

Table 26-3. Net National Product, 1929–1964

Billions of Dollars

Year	Personal consumption	Government purchases of goods and services	Investment		**Net national product**	Personal consumption*	Taxes				Saving			
			Net domestic investment	Net exports of goods and services			*Personal*	*Business*	*Less government transfer payments*†	Net	*Personal*	*Business*	*Statistical discrepancy*	Net private
1929	77.2	8.5	8.4	1.1	**95.2**	77.6	*2.8*	*8.5*	*−1.7*	9.5	*4.2*	*3.3*	*0.7*	8.1
1930	69.9	9.2	2.3	1.0	**82.4**	70.2	*2.7*	*8.1*	*−1.8*	8.9	*3.4*	*0.7*	*−0.8*	3.3
1931	60.5	9.2	−2.2	0.5	**68.0**	60.7	*2.0*	*7.5*	*−3.1*	6.4	*2.6*	*−2.5*	*0.7*	0.8
1932	48.6	8.1	−6.4	0.4	**50.7**	48.8	*1.6*	*7.3*	*−2.5*	6.4	*−0.6*	*−4.2*	*0.3*	−4.5
1933	45.8	8.0	−5.6	0.4	**48.6**	46.0	*1.6*	*7.7*	*−2.6*	6.7	*−0.9*	*−3.7*	*0.6*	−4.0
1934	51.3	9.8	−3.5	0.6	**58.2**	51.5	*1.8*	*8.7*	*−3.1*	7.4	*0.4*	*−1.6*	*0.5*	−0.7
1935	55.7	10.0	−0.5	0.1	**65.4**	55.9	*2.1*	*9.3*	*−3.4*	8.0	*2.1*	*−0.4*	*−0.2*	1.5
1936	61.9	12.0	1.4	0.1	**75.4**	62.1	*2.4*	*10.5*	*−4.1*	8.9	*3.6*	*−0.3*	*1.2*	4.5
1937	66.5	11.9	4.6	0.3	**83.3**	66.7	*3.5*	*11.9*	*−3.1*	12.3	*3.8*	*0.6*	—	4.3
1938	63.9	13.0	−0.8	1.3	**77.4**	64.1	*3.4*	*11.6*	*−3.8*	11.2	*0.7*	*0.7*	*0.6*	2.1
1939	66.8	13.3	2.0	1.1	**83.2**	67.0	*3.0*	*12.3*	*−4.2*	11.2	*2.6*	*1.1*	*1.3*	5.1
1940	70.8	14.0	5.6	1.7	**92.2**	71.0	*3.3*	*14.5*	*−4.4*	13.4	*3.8*	*3.0*	*1.0*	7.8

1941	80.6	24.8	9.7	1.3	**116.3**	80.8	4.1	20.9	−4.0	21.0	11.0	3.2	0.4	14.6
1942	88.5	59.6	—	—	**148.1**	88.6	7.1	25.5	−4.3	28.3	27.6	4.7	−1.1	31.2
1943	99.3	88.6	−4.5	−2.0	**181.3**	99.6	19.7	29.5	−4.8	44.4	33.4	6.0	−2.0	37.4
1944	108.3	96.5	−3.9	−1.8	**199.1**	108.6	21.2	30.0	−6.5	44.6	37.3	6.1	2.5	45.8
1945	119.7	82.3	−0.6	−0.6	**200.7**	120.2	23.2	30.0	−10.1	43.1	29.6	3.9	4.0	37.4
1946	143.4	27.0	20.7	7.5	**198.6**	144.1	20.7	30.2	−16.2	34.7	15.2	4.6	0.1	19.9
1947	160.7	25.1	21.7	11.5	**219.1**	161.4	23.6	33.2	−15.3	41.5	7.3	8.0	0.9	16.2
1948	173.6	31.6	31.5	6.4	**243.0**	174.2	23.3	35.7	−15.0	44.0	13.4	13.5	−2.0	24.8
1949	176.8	37.8	19.1	6.1	**239.9**	177.3	20.8	35.2	−16.2	39.8	9.4	13.1	0.3	22.8
1950	191.0	37.9	35.7	1.8	**266.4**	191.5	23.6	45.1	−19.3	49.3	13.1	11.1	1.5	25.7
1951	206.3	59.1	38.1	3.7	**307.2**	206.7	32.5	52.3	−16.8	68.0	17.3	11.9	3.3	32.5
1952	216.7	74.7	28.7	2.2	**322.3**	217.1	37.9	51.9	−16.9	72.9	18.2	12.0	2.2	32.3
1953	230.0	81.6	26.9	0.4	**338.9**	230.4	39.6	54.7	−17.6	76.7	18.3	10.4	3.0	31.7
1954	236.5	74.8	23.7	1.8	**336.8**	237.0	37.3	52.4	−20.1	69.5	16.4	11.0	2.9	30.3
1955	254.4	74.2	35.9	2.0	**366.5**	354.8	40.8	59.6	−21.4	79.0	15.8	14.8	2.1	32.7
1956	266.7	78.6	35.9	4.0	**385.2**	267.2	45.6	63.3	−23.7	85.3	20.6	13.2	−1.1	32.6
1957	281.4	86.1	30.8	5.7	**404.0**	282.0	49.3	66.3	−27.0	88.6	20.8	12.7	—	33.5
1958	290.1	94.2	22.0	2.2	**408.4**	290.6	49.2	65.5	−31.3	83.4	22.3	10.5	1.6	34.4
1959	311.2	97.0	33.9	0.1	**442.3**	311.8	54.1	74.8	−32.1	96.8	19.1	15.4	−0.8	33.7
1960	325.2	99.6	31.4	4.1	**460.3**	325.7	60.2	79.6	−34.6	105.2	17.0	13.4	−1.0	29.5
1961	335.2	107.6	26.5	5.6	**474.9**	335.6	62.0	82.6	−39.3	105.4	21.2	13.4	−0.7	33.9
1962	355.1	117.1	33.0	5.1	**510.4**	355.6	67.7	89.3	−40.6	116.4	21.6	16.3	0.5	38.4
1963	373.8	122.6	34.1	5.9	**536.5**	374.4	72.7	95.6	−42.3	126.0	20.5	16.3	−0.7	36.1
1964	398.9	128.4	37.2	8.6	**573.0**	399.5	71.7	101.0	−44.6	128.1	26.3	19.7	−0.5	45.4

* Plus personal transfer payments to foreigners.
† Not including government transfer payments to foreigners. Transfer payments to foreigners (personal plus governmental) equal the difference between net foreign investment and net exports of goods and services.
Source: Adapted from *Survey of Current Business*, vol. 45, no. 8 (August, 1965), pp. 24, 25, 29-33, 40, 41. Detail may not add to totals because of rounding.

Table 26.4. Gross National Product in Current and Constant Dollars, 1929–1964

Year	GNP in billions of current dollars	Implicit price deflator (1958 = 100)	GNP in billions of 1958 (constant) dollars
1929	103.1	50.6	203.6
1930	90.4	49.3	183.3
1931	75.8	44.8	169.2
1932	58.0	40.3	144.1
1933	55.6	39.3	141.5
1934	65.1	42.2	154.3
1935	72.2	42.6	169.6
1936	82.5	42.7	193.0
1937	90.4	44.5	203.3
1938	84.7	43.9	193.0
1939	90.5	43.2	209.4
1940	99.7	43.9	227.2
1941	124.5	47.2	263.7
1942	157.9	53.0	297.8
1943	191.6	56.8	337.2
1944	210.1	58.2	361.3
1945	212.0	59.7	355.4
1946	208.5	66.7	312.6
1947	231.3	74.6	309.9
1948	257.6	79.6	323.7
1949	256.5	79.1	324.1
1950	284.8	80.2	355.3
1951	328.4	85.6	383.4
1952	345.5	87.5	395.1
1953	364.6	88.3	412.8
1954	364.8	89.6	407.0
1955	398.0	90.9	438.0
1956	419.2	94.0	446.1
1957	441.1	97.5	452.5
1958	447.3	100.0	447.3
1959	483.7	101.6	475.9
1960	503.8	103.3	487.8
1961	520.1	104.6	497.3
1962	560.3	105.7	530.0
1963	589.2	107.1	550.0
1964	628.7	108.9	577.6

Source: *Survey of Current Business*, vol. 45, no. 8 (August, 1965), pp. 24-27, 52, 53.

Prices versus Production

Before going any further we should pause to remember that national income is the monetary value of output. National income can rise either because of an increase in real goods produced or because of a rise in prices. The figures that we have been looking at do not tell us whether the changes are real or monetary. As we know, prices fluctuate considerably over time, generally falling in depression and rising in prosperity. In particular, prices tend to shoot up during a war, and since World War II they have not come down from their high levels. Figures for the monetary value of output (or its components) therefore tend to exaggerate swings in the production of real goods, and they may even obscure such movements.

Since we can eat or wear only real goods and not money, it is often more useful to obtain a measure of the real value of output instead of its monetary value. But since we cannot add together locomotives, apples, and haircuts, a true picture of real output is hard to obtain. We can approximate such a measure by "deflating" the monetary value of GNP by a price index.[8] The method by which this is done was described in Chapter 21. The results for the period from 1929 to 1964 are given in Table 26-4, which shows GNP both in current dollars (as usually presented) and in constant dollars of 1958 purchasing power. The price index involved in the deflation, which is a composite one, is also shown.[9]

While the limitations of the data must be borne in mind, the deflated figures of this table certainly give a better indication of real output than the unprocessed data alone. The table shows, for instance, that GNP in current (undeflated) dollars was six times as high in 1964 as it was in 1940. In the same period, however, prices more than doubled. *Real* output, therefore, rose less than threefold, not sixfold. The rest of the rise in the monetary figures is accounted for by price increases.

While comparable deflated series for other measures of income are not readily available, they would give roughly similar results, showing, in particular, that real income did not fall as much in the Great Depression nor rise as much in the war and postwar period as the monetary data would indicate.

Questions for Thought and Discussion

1. Can you think of any way in which income may be earned except by producing goods for consumers, export, government, or business investment? Remember to distinguish between income and transfer payments.

2. If saving equals investment and income earned equals income spent, does this mean that national income can never rise or fall?

3. Do you really believe that saving equals investment as here defined? Can you prove it to yourself?

4. Explain the equality of saving and investment in the following *ex post* situation:

[8] Although this kind of adjustment is traditionally called "deflation," in periods of falling prices the result would be to inflate the current dollar figures. Perhaps the use of the word "deflation" implies a subconscious belief that rising prices are more normal (or at least more common) than falling prices.

[9] Because of the manner in which GNP is deflated it would not be proper to attempt to deflate any other measure of national income by applying this price index.

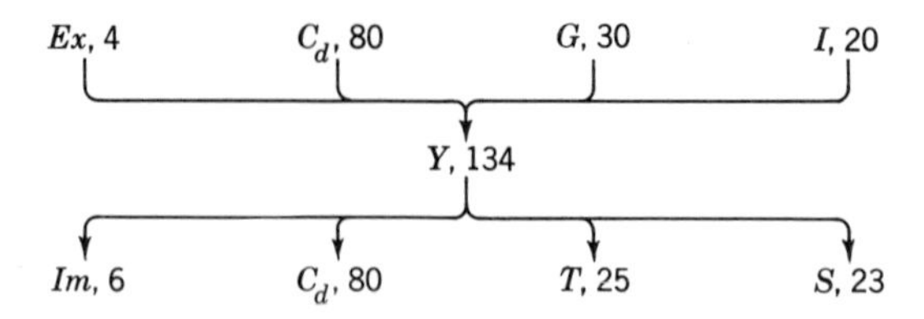

5. Can you think of the mechanism by which equality of saving and investment is brought about? (It is the subject of the next chapter.)

6. What is the difference between saving and savings? Between hoarding and hoards?

7. In what sense are capital consumption allowances saving? Do they normally flow into investment? Can they be hoarded?

8. If we aggregated, for the nation as a whole, all assets and liabilities of all persons and firms, what would happen to monetary assets (claims against others) and liabilities (claims due to others)?

9. If we aggregated the national product accounts for all countries in the world, what would happen to net foreign investment?

10. A comparison of Tables 26-2 and 26-3 suggests that net saving (and net investment) tends to rise and fall in pretty much the same way as net national product except during the war years (figures by quarters would show even greater similarity). Why do you think this is the case?

11. It has been suggested that GNP is a good measure of the ability of a nation to fight a war, while NNP is a better indication of its long-run potential. Why is this?

12. Can you see any relation, statistical or conceptual, between the equation of exchange and the circuit flow of money?

Selected Bibliography

U.S. Office of Business Economics: *National Income, 1954 Edition,* 1954.

———: *U.S. Income and Output,* 1958.

See also references listed under Chapter 25.

Chapter 27
The Role of Expectations

O! that a man might know
The end of this day's business ere it come;
But it sufficeth that the day will end,
And then the end is known.

Julius Caesar
Act V, scene 1, line 123

The preceding chapter examined national income exclusively in terms of statistical, *ex post* relationships. This skeleton framework tells us *what* happened; it doesn't tell us *why*. All economic activity is the result of the reactions and decisions of individuals in the economy, whether businessmen, consumers, or government officials. In order to put flesh and blood on our skeleton, then, we need to look at the human motivations that make the economy tick.

***Ex Ante* Is an Expectation of the Future.** The past is a matter of record; the future is a matter of expectation. Yet it is actions taken in anticipation of the future that make the economy what it is, and by examining these expectations we get considerable insight into the reasons for changes in national income and its components. This is *ex ante* analysis, an examination of what people expect to happen in the future. Thus *ex ante* saving is the amount consumers hope to save next month; *ex ante* investment refers to business plans for expansion, not the expansion that has already been carried out.

It is these plans and expectations for the future that shape the economy. An employer lays off workers when he *anticipates* that sales are going to be low. An innovator does not start producing widgets because widgets *have* been doing well, but because he thinks they *will* do well. If everyone thinks business is going to boom and starts making preparations for the avalanche of sales, the increased income generated by this rise in output will produce that avalanche of sales.

So *ex ante* analysis is the one that really matters. Of course past performance is one important element in any calculation of the future, but if the past were all that counted, we ought to be able to extrapolate any boom—or any depression—into infinity. The dynamic nature of the economy is to a large extent the result of human calculations, moods, and whims, and while we know less than we would like about what causes human behavior, we know enough to provide us with some basic principles of economic action.

Expectations and Discrepancies

Statistically (*ex post*) we know that saving must equal investment, hoarding must equal money creation, goods sold are the same as goods bought, income received is the same as income paid out. But there is no reason why anticipations in any of these areas should coincide.

Decisions to save and to invest, for instance, are usually taken by two entirely separate groups of people and for different motives. Saving is done primarily by consumers, investment by businessmen. And while businessmen are consumers when they get home from the office, their decisions to invest bear no necessary relationship to their decisions, as consumers, to save. The directors of Widgets, Inc., do not decide to spend $500,000 on plant expansion because they individually are expecting to save that sum from their personal incomes. And of course most consumers are not businessmen at all and couldn't invest if they wanted to. Since savers and investors are functionally different groups, it would be a strange coincidence if their decisions should be identical. So *ex ante* saving may differ greatly from *ex ante* investment.

Similarly individuals will not necessarily wish to hoard the same amount that banks are expecting to lend or businessmen to borrow from banks. Consumers may plan to buy more or less than businessmen expect to sell. Income earners may anticipate more or less income than businessmen plan to pay. Only by chance would such expectations coincide.

It is primarily from this disparity of expectations that changes in the income flow arise. Since we know that, for example, saving must equal investment after all the cards are down, any difference in expectations between savers and investors must inevitably lead to surprises for one group or both. If consumers expect to save $30 billion and businessmen expect to invest $40 billion, something has to give. Business cannot accumulate wealth in excess of consumers' abstention from consumption. Our circuit flow will be helpful in examining what will happen in a case of this kind.

Before proceeding with this explanation we should point out one limitation of the circuit flow, or indeed of any simplified device, in explaining anticipations and surprises. The circuit flow necessarily implies a given period of time during which all factors remain unchanged. It assumes, for instance, that consumers decide on January 1 that they will save x dollars this year (or this month, or this week). In reality, the man who puts his New Year's resolution in this form is rare indeed. And even those who make resolutions are supposed to have broken them all by the end of the second week. In fact both consumer decisions and business decisions are being made, reconsidered, implemented, revised, and abandoned all the time. Any attempt to capture this constant flux on anything so stable as the printed page is doomed from the beginning to being only the roughest of approximations. Yet even this rough approximation will give us some idea of the underlying forces in the economy. A numerical example, though it suggests an unreal degree of exactitude, will help to illustrate the principles involved. None of the numbers has any absolute meaning in itself; it is the direction of movement that is important.

If Saving Exceeds Investment. Let us assume that the circuit flow has a three-month duration, that is, that it takes three months for income earned by consumers to pass through the hands of business and become income again. Let us also assume that all decisions are made on the first day of the quarter and are adhered to (as nearly as possible) throughout the quarter. For the moment we will confine our attention to consumers and businessmen, leaving an examination of the role of government for later. Let us further assume that we stand at the threshold of 1961. The last quarter of 1960 is over and shows the following *ex post* results for the quarter (all figures expressed in billions of dollars):

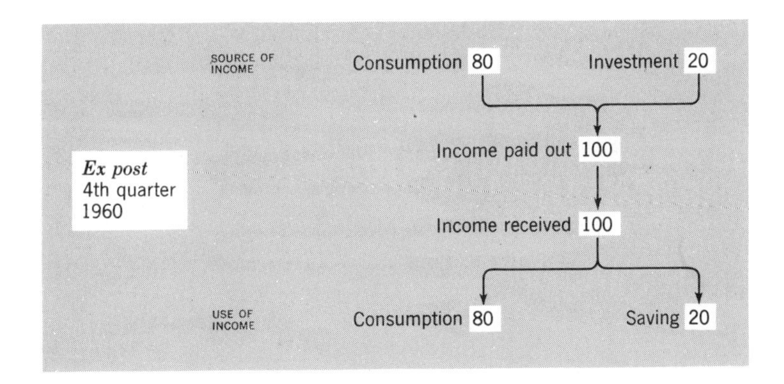

Let us assume that consumers, for some reason, decide to save more in the first quarter of 1961 but that businessmen expect conditions to remain unchanged. In other words, business anticipates paying 80 to the factors of production for producing consumer goods and another 20 to factors of production making producer goods: a total of 100. But consumers, expecting income to remain at 100, plan to shift their disposition of it to purchases of consumer goods of 75 and saving of 25. Our *ex ante* diagram becomes:

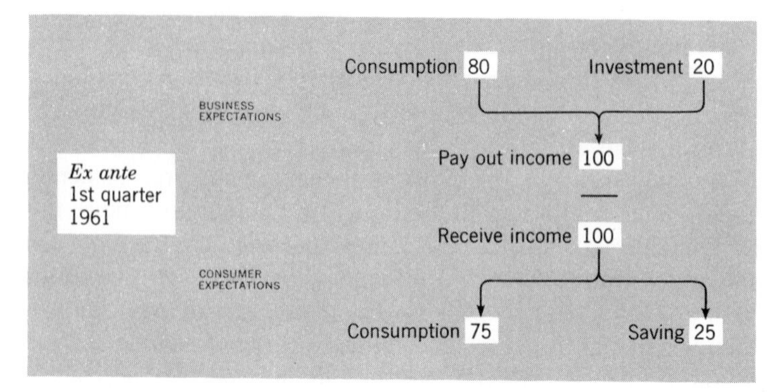

The Role of Inventories. Under conditions as here assumed obviously someone must be disappointed: business expects to sell 80 of goods, while consumers plan to buy only 75. But business can't sell goods that aren't bought. In the first instance it is the consumer who wins. He buys 75, and the storekeeper is left holding the bag with 5 in inventory that he had expected to sell. In other words, 5 of goods that were intended for sale to the consumer remain unsold on the self, increasing the physical assets held by business by 5 more than planned. This is unanticipated (and indeed unwanted) investment in inventories. Added to the investment voluntarily carried out by business (as indicated in their expectations) it makes a total investment in the quarter of 25: 20 planned and 5 unplanned. *Ex post* saving necessarily equals investment, in this case because businessmen were disappointed in their investment anticipations.

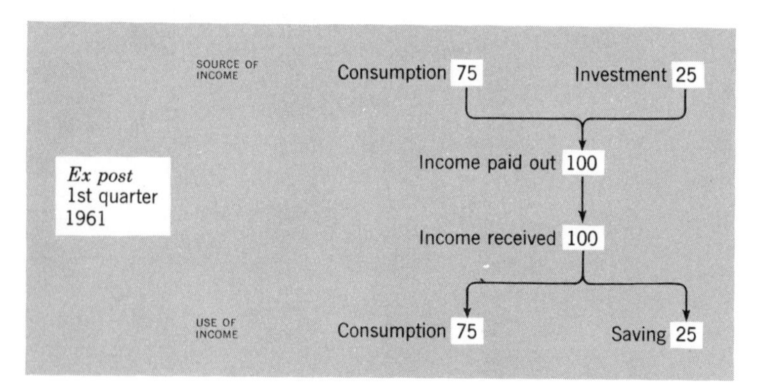

Excess Inventories Lead to Reduced Production. While this *ex post* situation indicates a formal balance, as indeed it must, it is not an equilibrium situation. Businessmen did not *want* to invest 25, and they will plan to reduce investment in the next quarter for two reasons: (1) Since they have 5 of unwanted inventories, they will try to *disinvest* by disposing of these. (2) If 20 was a reasonable level of investment for sales of 80, sales of 75 would call for a lower level of investment. The retailer does not need as large an inventory to support a lower level of sales, nor does the manufacturer need to expand his capacity as his sales drop off.[1] In common business terms, retailers, seeing sales decline, attempt to reduce inventories by cutting orders from wholesalers; wholesalers react by ordering less from manufacturers; and manufacturers cut production by reducing the work force or the length of the workweek. In the process businessmen count on paying out less in wages and other factor payments, thus reducing income.

Let us assume that *ex ante* investment for the second quarter drops relatively moderately to 18, while business adapts itself to the new lower level of sales of 75. That is, business is now attempting to produce only 75 for sale to consumers and 18 for investment purposes, therefore expecting to make total factor payments of 93. While this revision of plans is taking place in the minds of businessmen, consumers have not heard the sad news (we are standing at the threshold of the second quarter, where plans have been made but no action taken), and they continue merrily planning as before, their anticipations for the second quarter remaining the same as they were for the first.

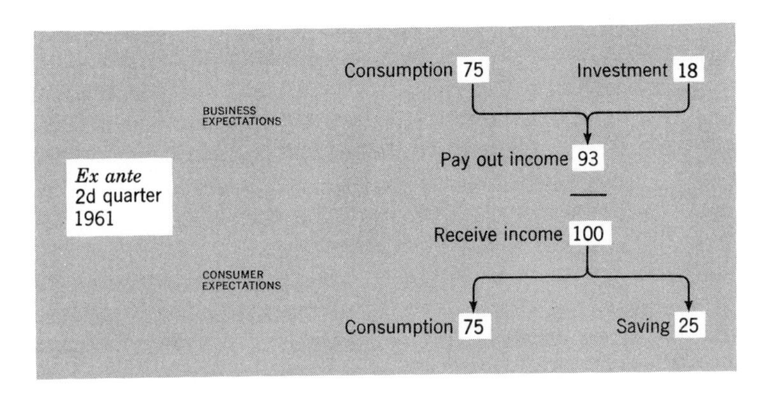

Reduced Production Lowers Income, Consumption, and Saving. Here again someone is going to be disappointed. Income recipients cannot take home any more than they are paid. Since business will pay only 93, this is all consumers have to use. They must therefore cut their spending, their saving, or both. Let us assume that they cut both. But to the extent that they cut consumption, businessmen are going to be unhappy too, since they were planning to sell 75 of goods. They cannot sell more than consumers buy, inventories are again raised just when business was hoping to get them cut, undesired investment continues to add to planned investment, and a deep sense of gloom settles down on everyone.

[1] Theoretically, if sales are dropping, there is no need to expand plant capacity at all or to increase inventories (voluntarily). On the contrary, depreciation might exceed replacement, and inventories would probably be reduced. In this case investment would be negative. For the economy as a whole, however, some firms are likely to be expanding even though sales in general are falling, and except in unusual cases net investment for the entire nation is positive. Negative investment would change the figures in the analysis here given but would not change the general tenor of the argument.

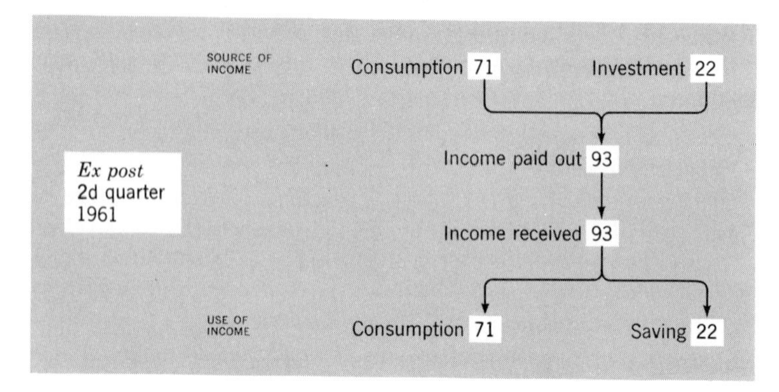

The Downward Spiral in Full Swing. Businessmen again attempt to cut back surplus inventories. By this time, however, they have probably come to the conclusion that business is likely to "get worse before it gets better," and they may therefore expect to sell even less than they did the previous quarter. Consumers also may become more pessimistic regarding the future and may anticipate a further decline in income.

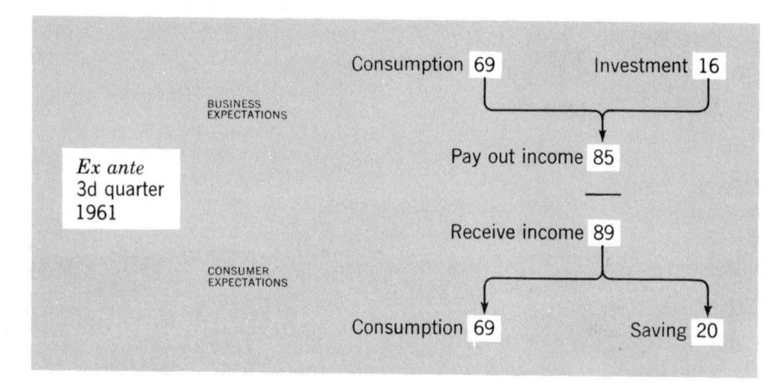

But things are even worse than consumers expected. Income has fallen below the lower level they anticipated, and they must therefore reduce consumption expenditures and saving even further. This means that sales will also fall below expectations of businessmen.

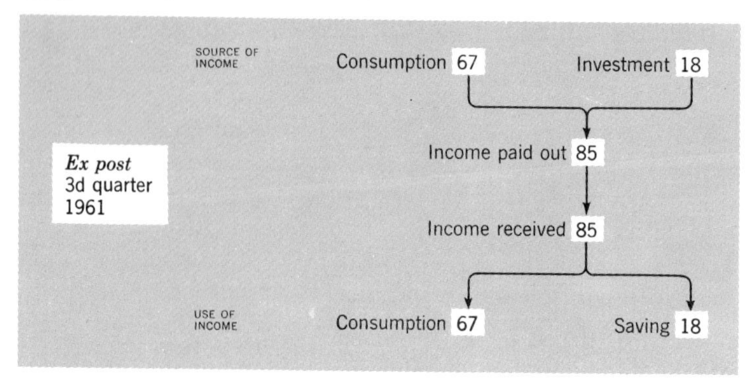

Discrepancies between expectations and realizations are now being reduced, but they are not yet eliminated, and so again we can expect a further cutback in production and hence in income.

Equilibrium at Reduced Income. This downward drift might continue for some time, but it must end somewhere. To bring our numerical example to a close, let us assume that now business and consumers plan in terms of equality for the next quarter. It should be noted that it is not inevitable that equilibrium will be reached in any particular case. Equilibrium is here *assumed,* not predicted.

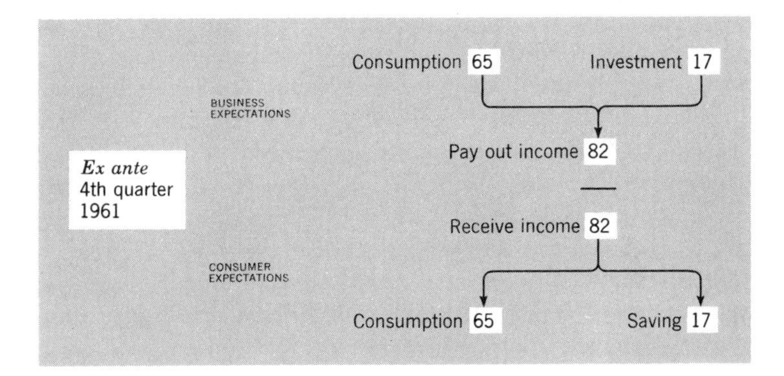

Since consumers plan to buy just the amount businessmen expect to sell, no one will be disappointed. The *ex post* results will be the same as the *ex ante* anticipations.

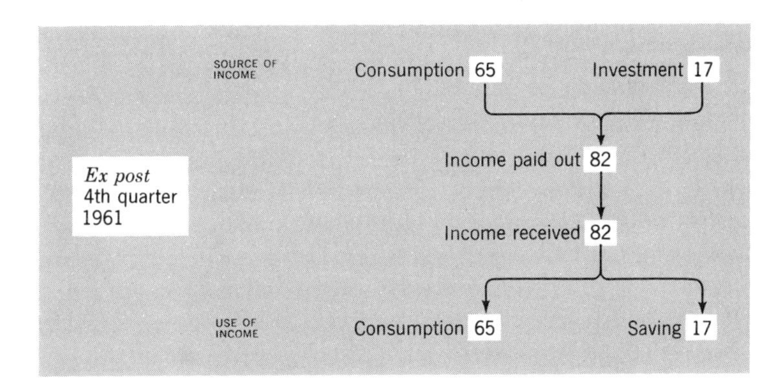

This equilibrium would continue until some change in expectations of either consumers or producers again sets in motion a similar chain of events leading either to a further fall or to a rise in income.

The Paradox of Thrift. While the new position is an equilibrium position in that it contains within itself no force tending to change it, it is obvious that it represents a considerably lower national income than the one from which we started. This lower income results from the fact that in the first quarter of 1961 consumers tried to save more than businessmen wished to invest. This example is an illustration of a general rule: starting from a given level of income *if ex ante saving exceeds ex ante investment, national income tends to fall.*

The particular form of our example is the well-known "paradox of thrift." Given the level of income, if consumers attempt to save more (without an offsetting decision of businessmen to invest more), the result will be (1) lower national income and (2) lower achieved saving because of the lower income (out of which people will save less).

While our numerical example shows the paradox of thrift at work, the underlying forces can be stated in another, more commonsense way. Suppose I decide to save $10 that I otherwise would have used to buy shirts. My saving has risen by $10. But the haberdasher's income has gone down by the same amount. Unless he decides to reduce his saving by $10, his consumption must fall also. If he does save $10 less, then society has saved exactly as much as before—$10 more for me, $10 less for him—and total saving is unchanged. It is likely, however, that he will consume less as a result of his drop in income—not necessarily $10 less, but *some* less. If the drop in his income induces him to refrain from buying, say, a $7 book, then the bookseller's income has dropped $7, and total national income is $17 lower. If the bookseller decides not to buy a $5 opera seat, national income has dropped a total of $22. And so on down the line, each reduction in spending pushing national income still lower.

Out of this reduced income people will save less. The haberdasher has saved $3 less (his spending dropped only $7 as his income fell $10), the bookseller has saved $2 less (income down $7, spending down $5), and so it goes through the economy. An attempt on my part to save $10 has lowered national income by more than $10, and out of this lowered income other people will save less.

If Investment Exceeds Saving. But this is the gloomy side of the picture. The upswing can be just as vigorous as the downswing, and historically our economy has tended to move two steps upward for every one it falls back. The upward movement may be illustrated by the circuit flow in the same manner as the downward.

Starting from the position of equilibrium we have just reached for the fourth quarter of 1961, let us assume that businessmen become more optimistic about the future. Some new development promises a big consumer market: perhaps flying manhole covers offer a potential new means of transportation for the average citizen. Without expecting an immediate rise in consumer expenditure, business decides to build plants and other equipment to produce this new product, that is, to increase investment. Consumers, however, have not yet changed their outlook.

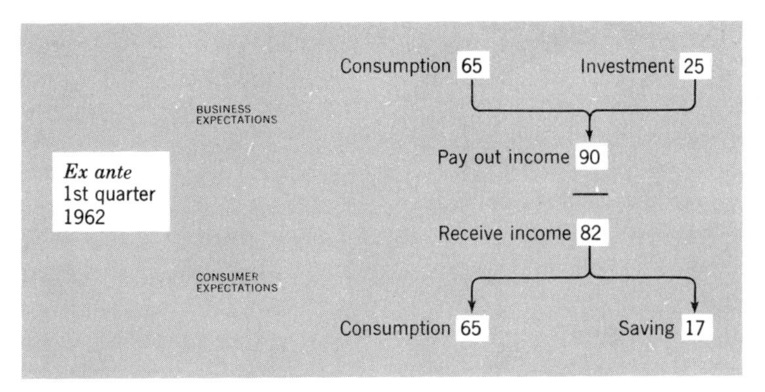

Increased Investment Raises Income. New workers must be hired to build the plant, to provide the building materials, to make the machinery, to produce the steel. Employment rises; consumers have more to spend than they anticipated. They happily go out and spend it—not yet for flying manhole covers, which are still not on the market, but for shoes, steaks, and vacuum cleaners. This creates additional business for the sellers of consumer goods generally, so that they also are pleasantly surprised. In order to make these larger sales they must draw down their inventories, that is, disinvest. This involuntary (but encouraging) disinvestment on the part of retailers will partially offset the increased investment of aviation firms, so that the immediate result is less net investment than planned. Some goods that business planned to keep as assets (inventories) are siphoned off instead into consumption.

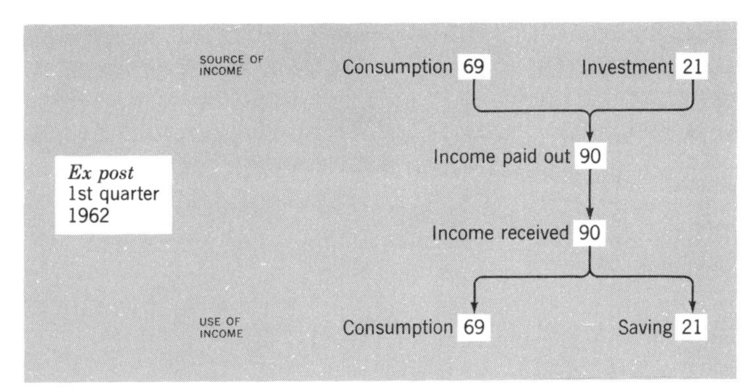

Increased Income Raises Consumption and Investment. This increased buying spreads optimism among sellers. They plan not merely to replenish depleted inventories, but to increase them in order to maintain a traditional ratio between inventories and sales. This means more orders given to wholesalers, which are passed on in turn to manufacturers, who hire more labor to produce shoes, steaks, and vacuum cleaners, and who may even decide to increase their productive facilities. Thus anticipated investment rises to even higher levels than it reached in the second quarter. It is quite clear, as a general rule, that increased consumption tends in this manner to increase investment, just as increased investment increases income.

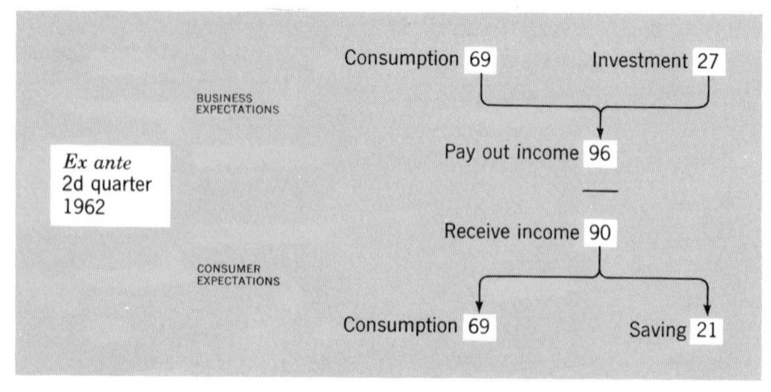

The Upward Spiral. The increase in employment and income now induces consumers to purchase even more than before. The attempt by business to replace inventories provides the purchasing power (by its effect on production) with which consumers buy even more goods, thus tending to reduce inventories. So *ex post* disinvestment in inventories again tends to draw investment down below its anticipated level.

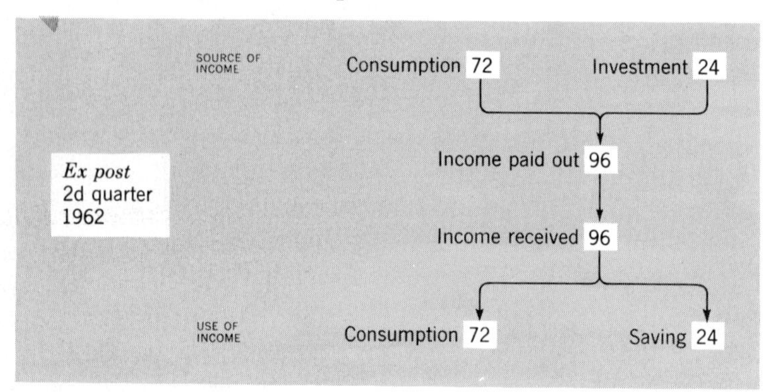

Now we have clearly embarked on a cumulative upswing. This may go on for some time, but for purposes of shortening our example we will draw it to a rapid close. Let us assume that both businessmen and consumers, seeing this upward trend, expect it to continue—business anticipating still higher consumption and consumers foreseeing still higher income.

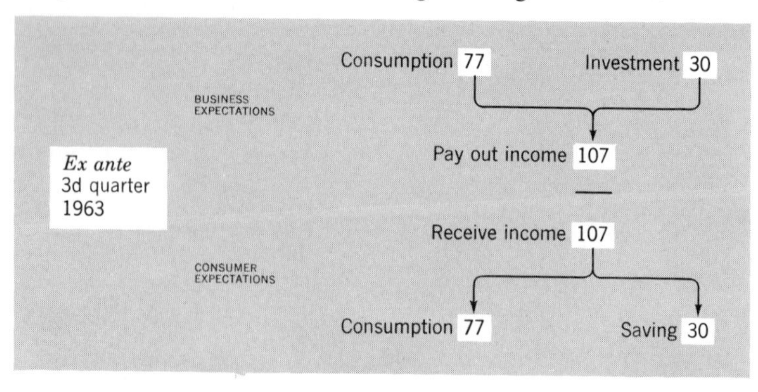

Now, since expectations of the two groups are identical, there is no reason for any further change. Consumers and business have both correctly gauged the overall state of the economy, facts will conform with anticipations, and we have reached a new equilibrium at a higher level of activity. *Ex post* third quarter 1962 will be the same as *ex ante,* and so perhaps there is no need to repeat the figures.

This equilibrium would continue until some change in expectations tended again to push the economy either up or down. It is an equilibrium at a considerably higher income level than the depressed condition from which we started in the fourth quarter of 1961. This higher level has been achieved through an increase in investment, which raised income and in turn raised consumption and saving.

This example also illustrates a general principle: from a given level of income *if ex ante saving is less than ex ante investment, national income tends to rise.*

In this particular example additional purchasing power pumped into the flow by businessmen trying to expand output was the force raising income and consumption. Exactly the same results would follow a desire on the part of consumers to consume more (that is, to save less). It matters not where the initial movement occurs—whether with producers or consumers. The only thing that matters is the disparity between them. If consumers try to save less than business expects to invest, income will rise. Another way of putting the same thing is to say that if consumers are trying to buy more than business anticipates selling, income will rise: business becomes optimistic and expands investment, and we are on the way up.

The Ephemeral Nature of Equilibrium. Although we left our example at the point of equilibrium, it is necessary to point out that such a state cannot last very long, if indeed it is ever actually reached. Conflicting forces are continually at work in the economy, and it would be quite unusual for business and consumer expectations to coincide for more than the very briefest period. And yet it is only when such a coincidence does occur that national income can stay at a given level. This may be stated as a third general rule: *if ex ante saving equals ex ante investment, national income tends to remain stable.* But while *ex post* saving always equals *ex post* investment, it is most unusual for the *ex ante* concepts to be equal.

Multiplier and Accelerator. In both of these examples the reader has probably noticed that an initial (fairly small) difference between saving and investment expectations has led to a change in national income that was several times the initial disparity. On the downswing a discrepancy of 5 led to a drop in national income of 18. On the upswing a difference of 8 led to an increase in national income of 25. While these are only illustrative examples and there is nothing sacred about the numbers used, nevertheless this particular tendency of national income to change by more than the initial push that is given to it is a well-established fact. There are a number of factors that help bring about this result. Two of them are important enough to be given names of their own: the multiplier and the accelerator.

The Multiplier. The multiplier concerns the direct relationship between investment and income. Suppose investment rises by $100. This raises income by $100 immediately because business is spending money for capital goods, and this money finds its way into the pockets of those who produce these goods. The consumers who get this additional income will not normally stash all of it away somewhere. They will spend at least part of it, say, $50. Spending $50 puts this amount into the income stream to become income for someone else, thus raising income by another $50, or a total of $150. The new recipients of $50 will spend, say, $25, which becomes income, for a total of $175, and so on. If each income recipient spends half of any addition to his income, the eventual result will be to raise national income by $200, or twice the original increase in investment. In tabular form the process is shown in Table 27-1.

Table 27-1. Hypothetical Example of the Multiplier

Assuming that Consumers Spend One-half of Any Increase in Income

Period	Original increase in investment	Out of increased income consumers spend	Raises income by
1	$100.00		$100.00
2		$ 50.00	50.00
3		25.00	25.00
4		12.50	12.50
5		6.25	6.25
6		3.12	3.12
7		1.56	1.56
8		0.78	0.78
9		0.39	0.39
10		0.20	0.20
11		0.10	0.10
12		0.05	0.05
13 to ∞		0.05	0.05
Total	$100.00	$100.00	$200.00

In this case the multiplier is 2. An initial investment of $100 has raised income by $200, $100 of which is the original investment, the other $100 being induced consumption due to the rising income. If consumers had spent a larger fraction of their income, the rise in national income would have been even greater. For instance, if they had spent three-quarters of their income, the multiplier would have been 4, and an initial investment increase of $100 would have raised national income by $400, with induced consumption of

$300. The concept of the multiplier is in line with our circuit flow analysis. The greater the consumption, the larger the amount of money that moves through the business sector, and the greater the income will be.[2]

The Accelerator. While the multiplier concerns the effect that investment will have on income, the accelerator expresses the effect that consumption will have on investment. Like the multiplier, the accelerator may be studied in terms of extended mathematical equations, but it is fundamentally a very simple idea. The accelerator suggests that an increase in consumption will cause an increase in investment (perhaps larger, percentagewise, than the rise in consumption). This is plain common sense. If businessmen see business improving, if sales are going up, they will expand their inventories in order to be sure of being able to serve customers, they will buy more machines to produce more goods, and maybe they will build more factories to meet the increased demand. True, their investment decisions are based on what they expect to be able to sell tomorrow, but nothing makes businessmen more optimistic than booming sales today.

No Wonder It's a Spiral. When we put the multiplier and accelerator together we can see why a boom feeds on itself. A relatively small injection of new investment increases income, which raises consumption, which not only raises income even more (multiplier), but at the same time also induces further new investment (accelerator), which raises income, and so on—until the economy is pushed up to full employment or else develops bottlenecks, stresses, and strains tending to bring about a precarious balance, easily subject to collapse.

A slight downward push, and unfortunately both the multiplier and the accelerator go to work in reverse. A drop in either consumption or investment begins the process, and we are on the skids. Reduced investment reduces income, which reduces consumption, which reduces both income and investment, and so on down until someone somewhere becomes a little more optimistic, consumption reaches a point where it can't reasonably fall any more, or some outside event sparks the return to brighter days.

[2] Multiplier analysis has developed a great deal of technical terminology and mathematical manipulation. The marginal propensity to consume, the starting point for the multiplier, is defined as the proportion of any increase in income that one will spend on consumption. Given the marginal propensity to consume (C_m), the multiplier (K) may be derived by means of the formula $K = \frac{1}{1 - C_m}$. In our example consumers spent half of their increase in income. The marginal propensity to consume is therefore ½, and $K = \frac{1}{1 - \frac{1}{2}} = 2$. If the marginal propensity to consume were ¾, $K = \frac{1}{1 - \frac{3}{4}} = 4$. Some economists suggest that the multiplier in the United States is about 3; others say it is 2. In actuality, however, patterns of consumer behavior vary so widely from time to time, particularly over swings of the business cycle, that any attempt to suggest a fixed multiplier is to state an extreme uncertainty with precision.

Hoarding and Velocity of Circulation

Having looked at a simple example showing the effect of expectations on national income, we are now in a position to go back and pick up some of the loose ends of our analysis. One of these relates to hoarding. Our numerical examples have made no attempt to examine hoarding because it brings in a third variable: time. By assuming an artificially fixed three-month period for our circuit flow, we ruled out the possibility of examining any variation of this time interval. This omission we must now correct.

When we looked at the circuit flow from the historical point of view, we demonstrated that *ex post* hoarding equals money creation. We can hoard \$100 only if \$100 is created. Yet common sense as well as economic analysis tells us that *hoarding takes money out of circulation and therefore reduces income, while the injection of new money must increase income.* But if new money goes only into hoards, then national income, it might be assumed, cannot possibly change. Since national income obviously does change, it might appear that there is something wrong with our analysis. The apparent contradiction here might be called the paradox of hoarding, and it is just as significant as the paradox of thrift.

The Paradox of Hoarding. We have already seen that what people *try to do* is not necessarily what they achieve. People as a whole cannot hold more money than there is, but they can try. And whereas hoarding cannot exceed money creation, the *attempt to hoard* will definitely affect national income.

In order to examine this effect it is necessary to realize that the circuit flow does not occupy a fixed period of time. The period involved is the average length of time it takes for money to travel from the pockets of income recipients through the business world and back to consumers' pay envelopes. This period may be anything from a few days (under hyperinflation) to a year or more. Just how long it will be depends on the propensity to hoard of the nation as a whole.

We should recall at this point both the equation of exchange and the Marshallian K. In its income form the equation of exchange is

$$P_yT_y = MV_y$$

If T_y is real national income and P_y is the price at which these goods sell, then, as we have seen,

$$P_yT_y = Y = MV_y$$

In other words, national income for any year represents the quantity of money in circulation multiplied by the number of times this money is circulated from one income recipient to another during the year.

Suppose that the quantity of money in circulation is \$100 billion. Suppose further that it takes three months, on the average, for this money to circulate ($V = 4$). Then national income is $400 billion (each dollar does $4 worth of work during the year, so $100 billion must do $400 billion worth of work). Suppose then that people attempt to hoard more but that there is no change in the quantity of money in circulation.

Jones attempts to hoard; that is, he holds on to his money longer. This means that since he is holding more money, he is spending less; his purchases drop, and the income of Smith, who normally sells to him, falls. But let us assume that Smith too wants to hoard. In spite of a reduced income he also attempts to hold onto money longer. This reduces the income of Brown, and so on down the line. The effect of this mass attempt to keep money from slipping through the nation's collective fingers slows down the velocity of circulation of money to, say, four months. What has happened to national income? It has fallen to $300 billion, for each dollar is now doing the work of only three during a year instead of four. But there has been no hoarding in fact. (Remember that hoarding is a flow: an increase in hoards.) The nation still holds the same $100 billion. It can't hold any more than this because there isn't any more. In spite of the absence of hoarding in the *ex post* sense, the attempt to hoard has forced national income down.

There has, however, been hoarding in a psychological sense. Robertson defined K as "the proportion of real national income which people wish to have enough money on hand to purchase."[3] People feel that they are hoarding when K rises. And in our example K has done just that. Our original assumption was that national income was $400 billion, with cash of $100 billion. Then

$$K = \frac{100}{400} = \frac{1}{4}$$

As national income fell to $300 billion without any change in the quantity of money, K rose:

$$K = \frac{100}{300} = \frac{1}{3}$$

In other words, the *proportion* of its annual income that the nation holds in cash has risen—not because the amount of cash has risen, but because the level of income has fallen. People feel that they have increased their hoards, and in the process they have pulled income down. It is in this sense that hoarding is a leakage from the circuit flow.

This leads us to a conclusion that should perhaps have been obvious from the beginning: people are more important than statistics. Expectations are more important as causal forces in business fluctuations than observed data. In determining the course of the economy it is not what has happened that is important, but what people expect to happen and what they plan for the

[3] D. H. Robertson, *Money* (Pitman Publishing Corporation, New York, 1948), p. 180.

future. It is for this reason that we have recently added to our arsenal of statistics, surveys on investment plans of business and buying plans of consumers. And now abide *ex post* and *ex ante,* and the greater of these is *ex ante.*

To return to our analysis. The injection of new money can be examined in the same frame of reference as the one we have just used to investigate hoarding. Let us start from the initial position we used in that example: $M = \$100$ billion, $V = 4$, $Y = \$400$ billion, $K = 1/4$. Suppose, then, the banks create an additional $50 billion by lending money to business borrowers. This money, like any other, must be hoarded, so that hoarding (additions to hoards) is $50 billion. If, however, national income were to remain the same, hoarding in the psychological (as well as the statistical) sense must rise.

$$K = \frac{150}{400} = \frac{3}{8}$$

People would hold a larger amount of cash and a larger proportion of their income in cash. But there is no reason to suppose that they *want* to hold more. Their tendency, therefore, is to spend this additional money. As they spend it they thereby push income up, for if $150 billion circulates as rapidly, on the average, as $100 billion did previously (once every three months), national income on an annual basis must rise to $600 billion ($150 billion times 4). At this point K will have returned to its original value,

$$K = \frac{150}{600} = \frac{1}{4}$$

and people will be hoarding the *same proportion* of a higher income. This is exactly what we would expect. An injection of new money into the economy *does* tend to raise national income in spite of the fact that every cent of it must be hoarded.

The most common, almost intuitive, reaction to a first acquaintance with the *ex post* equality of saving and investment or of money creation and hoarding is to reject these equalities as contrary to common sense and known behavior. Such a reaction is understandable. The equalities are formal, and while thoroughly correct, they do not make much sense unless rounded out with an examination of *ex ante* forces in action.

Government Saving and Foreign Investment

So far our examples have used a simplified framework in which government and international trade are pushed into the background. We have assumed that the government budget is in balance (government saving is zero) and that exports equal imports (foreign investment is zero). We know from our discussion in the preceding chapter that both of these sectors may affect national income, but we also learned how to integrate them into the circuit flow.

Total saving includes government saving (the government surplus) in addition to private saving. Total investment includes foreign investment (the export balance) as well as domestic investment. In dropping our simplifying assumption that all decisions are taken by consumers and businessmen (for domestic investment only), we have simply to add the decisions of government as they affect government saving (or dissaving) and of businessmen as they affect foreign investment (or disinvestment).

If private saving plus government saving, *ex ante,* exceed domestic investment plus foreign investment, then national income will tend to fall. If private saving plus government saving fall short of domestic investment plus foreign investment, then national income will tend to rise.

For some countries that depend strongly on foreign trade, such as Great Britain, foreign investment may be an important factor in determining national income, but for the United States it is a small figure compared to the total.[4] Further discussion of the effects of international forces will be taken up in Part Nine.

Government saving can be extremely important. Negative government saving in 1944 exceeded $51 billion, or almost 25 per cent of GNP. A government deficit of this magnitude—or even of considerably smaller size—can have a tremendous impact on the economy. The wartime deficits are one major cause of the rise in national income, both real and monetary, that occurred during the forties, although there were other important factors as well.

Other things remaining the same, government saving (surplus) tends to lower national income just as private saving does. Similarly, government dissaving (deficit) tends to raise national income just as investment does. These effects can be traced through the circuit flow in the same way we have used for the private sector. We will treat them in more detail when we come to fiscal policy.

The Circuit Flow and Economic Policy

In conclusion let us summarize some of the things we have learned about the circuit flow so that we may put it in proper perspective.

Like the equation of exchange, it is basically a mathematical concept which shows the relationships among certain variables but which does not in itself say anything about cause and effect. It tells us, for instance, that if income rises, then taxes or consumption or saving or some combination of the three *must* rise. But it doesn't tell us *which.* And even if we determine which—on the basis of statistical evidence existing independently of the circuit flow—the

[4] In 1947 it reached a peak of 4 per cent of GNP, but in each year since 1948 it has equaled less than 1 per cent (positive or negative) of GNP.

flow diagram will never help us determine *why*. In this chapter we have examined some of the theories of national income analysis. For instance, economists are reasonably sure that an increase in consumption will tend to induce businessmen to increase investment, but this is not *inevitable,* and the circuit flow itself does not prove this—or any other—theory.

Similarly, it is entirely neutral with regard to policy decisions. It does *not* show that a government deficit is necessary to achieve full employment; in fact it doesn't say anything about full employment at all. It indicates that a government deficit, other things remaining the same, will tend to raise national income, but it does not tell us (1) whether other things will, in fact, remain equal, (2) how much rise in income a given deficit will produce, (3) whether this is the *best* way to raise national income, or (4) whether, indeed, a rise in national income is desirable.

This last point is quite important. A rise in national income is one of those positively charged concepts that many people take for granted as always good. A moment's reflection indicates the dubious nature of this clean bill of health. National income is the monetary value of commodities and services produced during a given period. It has two dimensions: it is (1) the real goods produced (2) measured in terms of their price. While anyone is generally better off with more roast beef, he is obviously no better off if he has to pay more for the same amount. In order to determine the desirability of rising national income, then, it is necessary to know the rise in each of its components, and about this the circuit flow is also silent.

No theory, no equation, can adequately cover everything, and it is for this reason that we have examined several ways of looking at the role of money in the economy. Because the national income approach answers some questions that remained unanswered before, it has partially eclipsed not only earlier monetary theory, but price theory as well. This is unfortunate, for income analysis is complementary to monetary analysis, not a substitute for it. There is no contradiction between the two types of theory; their difference lies in their emphasis, and each has its own area of usefulness.

The primary advantage of the equation of exchange is that it explicitly separates prices from production in examining total income. The primary advantage of the circuit flow is that it explicitly separates the effect on income of various segments of the economy: consumers, business, government, and foreign trade. It also emphasizes the channels through which money flows, pinpointing, for instance, the desirability of directing saving into useful outlets in investment rather than into hoarding. The two approaches, taken together, give a more complete and helpful picture of the whole economy than either one by itself.

Yet when it comes to policy, all the economics we can bring to bear on a problem is still insufficient to provide an answer, for any solution must consider political and sociological ramifications as well. There is frequently more difference of opinion over whether a particular policy is desirable than over whether it will be effective. Hitler achieved full employment in Germany, but we would hardly wish to adopt his tactics for this purpose. Economic actions cannot be taken out of their context, and each individual must decide for himself, frequently on noneconomic grounds, whether he approves of particular proposals. Economic analysis alone can never say what is best for the country.

Even in terms of economic effects, since our knowledge is imperfect, mistakes may frequently be made. But this should not deter us from attempting to achieve as satisfactory an economic climate as we can. Driving a car is a hazardous business, but that doesn't keep many people home. A knowledge of the dangers involved in driving a car or steering the economy can help to avoid errors and to improve our chances of getting where we want to go as expeditiously and safely as possible. And in the economy as in driving, safety is preferable to speed. Driving off the edge of a cliff may be the fastest way to get to the bottom of the hill, but it is not generally recommended. Drastic government action (as under a dictatorship) might be the fastest way to achieve a high national income, but if it wrecks desirable institutions or basic freedoms in the process, the results will not be worth the cost.

Questions for Thought and Discussion

1. Are there any clearly describable conditions under which consumer and business anticipations would be equal?

2. If an attempt to save lowers national income as well as actual saving, why do people do it? Would it help to tell them not to?

3. What is likely to happen to saving (*ex post*) if the nation attempts to consume more?

4. Is a rise in inventories a sign of good business or of bad? Does it matter whether the rise is planned or unplanned?

5. Given the following *ex ante* expectations, what is likely to happen to national income?

a. Business expects to spend 70 for production of consumer goods and 20 on investment.

b. Consumers expect a disposable income of 85, out of which they will spend 70 on consumer goods and save 15.

c. Government plans to collect taxes of 15 and to make expenditures of 20.

6. If investment raises income, which raises consumption, which raises investment, why does the upward spiral ever stop? In reverse, why does a downward spiral ever stop?

7. Why is an increase in consumption (*ex ante*) likely to have the same kind of effect on the economy as an increase in investment (*ex ante*)?

8. Why is the psychological propensity to hoard more important than the actual amount of hoarding?

9. Why should an increase in government expenditure (without a change in tax receipts) tend to raise income?

10. Explain the significance of the following series of equalities:

$$C + G + I_d + I_f = C + T + S_p = Y = P_y T_y = M V_y = \frac{M}{K}$$

11. Why is it not possible to use the multiplier to tell us precisely how much added investment (for instance) is needed to raise national income by a given amount?

12. Is a rise in national income always desirable?

Selected Bibliography

See references listed under Chapter 25.

Chapter 28 The Flow of Funds

And how his audit stands who knows save heaven?

Hamlet
Act III, scene 3, line 82

While national income statistics emphasize the importance of saving and investment, they do not provide much detail on their composition, particularly with regard to the forms that saving may take. Yet it makes a difference whether the consumer puts his saving into savings and loan shares (thereby limiting their use almost exclusively to mortgages) or buys stock of a mutual fund or United States savings bonds. It matters not only with regard to the area of the economy receiving the use of these funds, but also in terms of the liquidity that the particular assets provide for their holders. It similarly makes a difference whether a corporation issues stocks or bonds, and whether it holds idle funds in cash or treasury bills.

Data on all kinds of financial transactions have long been available, but not until 1959 was a current series established that tied them all together in a consistent picture of total saving and investment and its components. The work on this project was inaugurated by Morris Copeland[1] and then taken up by the Federal Reserve, which made several fairly drastic

[1] Morris Copeland, *A Study of Moneyflows in the United States* (National Bureau of Economic Research, Inc., New York, 1952).

revisions in both concepts and method before starting regular publication of current statistics on the flow of funds.[2]

In contrast with the Keynesian development, work on the flow of funds did not originate as a theory, but as an accounting procedure, with the hope that it might provide information on which a theory might be built. So far the theoretical implications of the data are both meager and tentative. There is no doubt, however, that this approach has great potentialities and in time will become one of the cornerstones of both monetary and business cycle theory.

Here, as with previous approaches, we should emphasize that the flow of funds is an accounting truth whose validity cannot be challenged. Theories that might be derived from it, on the other hand, must necessarily be subject to question until their accuracy can be tested.

Flow-of-funds Accounting

The fundamental principle underlying flow-of-funds accounting is that every person (or institution) engaging in a transaction can enter that transaction on his books by a double entry.[3] When Jones buys a book, for instance, he (1) obtains a book and (2) gives up money in exchange. Further, there are always two parties to any transaction; when Jones buys his book, the bookseller at the same time (3) gives up a book and (4) receives money. Since each records his part of the transaction as two entries, both together account for four entries. Thus flow-of-funds accounting is quadruple-entry bookkeeping applied to all transactions in the economy.

Transactions. Transactions are divided into three major groups:

1. Current nonfinancial
2. Capital nonfinancial
3. Financial

For some purposes it is useful to combine these groups. This may be done in two ways: current (item 1) versus capital (items 2 + 3); or nonfinancial (items 1 + 2) versus financial (item 3).

Current Nonfinancial Transactions. Current transactions represent the great bulk of all economic transfers. In terms of the circuit flow we should classify

[2] For earlier methods and data see Board of Governors of the Federal Reserve System, *Flow of Funds in the United States, 1939–1953* (1955); "Summary Flow-of-funds Accounts, 1950–1955," *Federal Reserve Bulletin,* vol. 43, no. 4 (April, 1957), pp. 367–385; and the statistical summaries, *Federal Reserve Bulletin,* vol. 43, no. 10 (October, 1957), pp. 1190–1194. The new series is described in "A Quarterly Presentation of Flow of Funds, Saving, and Investment," *Federal Reserve Bulletin,* vol. 45, no. 8 (August, 1959), pp. 828–859, 1046–1062; and in "Flow of Funds Seasonally Adjusted," *Federal Reserve Bulletin,* vol. 48, no. 11 (November, 1962), pp. 1393–1407.

[3] Debit and credit in accounting terms, though we will not use that terminology here.

them as the receipt of income on the one hand and consumption and tax payments on the other. In the flow-of-funds accounts, however, the concept is both broader and narrower.

It is broader by the inclusion of *all* receipts and expenditures on current account, not only those relating to income. Thus sales receipts of firms would be included along with their expenses (wages, materials, and so on); the tax receipts of government along with payments to government workers and suppliers; and so on. The net difference between all current receipts and current payments for the economy as a whole, however, would still be equal to national saving.

The concept of "current" is narrower than the one we have used previously, however, by the exclusion from consumption of consumer purchases of durable goods. This procedure is based on the reasonable grounds that since consumer durables are assets and yield a flow of services into the future, they should be treated in the same way as machines and houses. This merely draws what must in any case be an arbitrary line at a somewhat different place. Since consumption in this treatment is reduced by the amount of consumer durables bought, saving is automatically increased by the same amount, and this increase in the numerical measure of saving is exactly equal to the increase in investment caused by the inclusion of consumer durable goods in capital transactions. This technical change in definition must be borne in mind as the data for flow of funds are examined.

Although the great bulk of transactions fall in the "current" category, the flow-of-funds accounts are not primarily concerned with this area of the economy, since it is adequately summarized in national income statistics. In the published accounts the net difference between receipts and expenditures (that is, saving) is the only item of current transactions recorded.

Capital Nonfinancial Transactions. Capital transactions represent the purchase of real assets that yield continuing services over time. They are equal to investment as already defined (the increase in physical assets of business) *plus* the purchase of consumer durables. The data are separated into four subcategories:

Purchases of consumer durable goods
Residential construction
Plant and equipment expenditures
Net changes in inventories

Since the definitions in this method of accounting add consumer durables to both the saving and investment accounts, it is true here, as in national income, that saving equals investment, though at a somewhat higher level of dollar value.

Financial Transactions. Because they are covered least adequately elsewhere, the financial flows receive most attention in the flow-of-funds accounts. Financial movements deal with the transfer of claims rather than the transfer of goods. Their scope is shown clearly in the subclassifications used:

Gold, foreign exchange, and treasury currency
Demand deposits and currency
Time and savings accounts
Life insurance and pension fund reserves
Consolidated bank items (claims between commercial and Federal Reserve banks)
Credit market instruments:
  United States government securities
  State and local government obligations
  Corporate and foreign bonds
  Corporate stock
  Mortgages on one- to four-family properties
  Other mortgages
  Consumer credit
  Bank loans not elsewhere classified
  Other loans
Credit issued on securities
Taxes payable
Trade credit
Proprietors' net investment in noncorporate businesses
Miscellaneous financial transactions

Coverage of Sectors. We are interested not only in the form that financial investment may take, but also in the effect on investment of different groups within the economy. For this purpose the economy is divided into eight sectors:

Households and nonprofit organizations
Business
State and local governments
United States government
Monetary authorities
Commercial banks
Nonbank financial intermediaries
Rest of the world

Sources and Uses of Funds. With these numerous sectors and types of transactions we can draw up a table of sources and uses of funds. Sources represent any means by which funds are obtained, that is, receipts or increases in liabilities (since borrowing is one way of getting cash). Uses of funds include expenditures or the acquisition of assets, including an increase in cash itself. The process may be most readily seen in terms of an example. We will illustrate only a few sectors and a limited number of transactions, which will be sufficient to demonstrate the principle but which will not cover all possibilities. For simplicity we will use very low figures, which might sound more reasonable if a number of zeros were added.

Suppose government clerks receive $90 in wages. From the point of view of consumers, wages represent a current receipt (source) of funds. What are they used for? Whatever the money may be spent for eventually, at the moment of receipt the use of the funds is to increase the cash balances (assets) of the workers.

	Households		Government	
	Uses	*Sources*	*Uses*	*Sources*
Current receipts (wages)		90		
Current expenditures (wages)			90	
Demand deposits and currency	90		−90	

From the point of view of the government the payment represents a current expenditure (use) of funds. At the same time the government must draw down its cash balances (reduce its assets). The flow-of-funds accounts record all four aspects of this transaction simultaneously.

The government's reduction of demand deposits and currency might logically be put under "sources" (the source of the wage payment is the government's cash balance). The convention, however, is to record all changes in assets under "uses," with a negative sign when a reduction is involved. Similarly a reduction in liabilities would be recorded as a negative source of funds.

In presenting flow-of-funds data, then, the general rule is:

1. To record as uses:
- *a.* Expenses
- *b.* Increases in assets
- *c.* (With a minus sign) decreases in assets

2. To record as sources:
- *a.* Receipts
- *b.* Increases in liabilities
- *c.* (With a minus sign) decreases in liabilities

Suppose households buy $178 worth of merchandise from business. This is the same type of transaction. Consumers draw down their balances to make a current purchase. Business firms sell goods (current receipts) and increase their cash holdings.

	Households		Business	
	Uses	*Sources*	*Uses*	*Sources*
Current receipts (sales)				178
Current expenditures (purchases)	178			
Demand deposits and currency	−178		178	

Suppose the government collects personal taxes of $52 and business taxes of $28. The entry is similar to those already shown except that the current expenditure and its related reduction in assets are split between two sectors.

	Households		Business		Government	
	Uses	*Sources*	*Uses*	*Sources*	*Uses*	*Sources*
Current receipts (taxes)						80
Current expenditures (taxes)	52		28			
Demand deposits and currency	−52		−28		80	

Suppose that business firms buy $500 worth of materials from other firms, pay wages of $190, and distribute dividends of $20. These are three separate transactions, but they can be recorded simultaneously. Wages and dividends both go to consumers and are easily combined in a single figure. Total business payments of $710 include $500 worth of payments between firms. This represents a reduction of cash balances for one firm, but an increase for another. The net effect on business balances, then, is the reduction of $210 transferred to consumers.

	Households		Business	
	Uses	*Sources*	*Uses*	*Sources*
Current receipts (wages, dividends)		210		
Current receipts (sales)				500
Current expenditures (wages, dividends, purchases)			710	
Demand deposits and currency	210		−210	

So far our examples have illustrated only current transactions plus changes in currency and deposits that usually accompany all transactions. But flow of funds is primarily concerned with capital and financial movements. Suppose that the government issues new marketable securities worth $14, that corporations issue new bonds worth $37, and that all these are bought by consumers. The government has increased its liabilities (sources) and has received cash assets (uses). Business has done the same. The purchasers increase their assets in the form of securities by reducing another asset (demand deposits and currency).

	Households		Business		Government	
	Uses	*Sources*	*Uses*	*Sources*	*Uses*	*Sources*
Demand deposits and currency	−51		37		14	
U.S. government securities	14					14
Corporate and foreign bonds	37			37		

Business now hires a contractor to build a new factory worth $34. For the contracting firm this represents a current sale (receipts), since it is in the business of producing such buildings. But for the buyer it represents not *current* purchases, but the acquisition of *capital assets*. This is an investment and is recorded, therefore, under capital nonfinancial transactions. The investing firm reduces its cash to make payment, while the contracting firm increases its cash by the same amount. For business as a whole, demand deposits and currency shows no change.

	Business	
	Uses	*Sources*
Current receipts (sales)		34
Plant and equipment	34	
Demand deposits and currency	{ 34 −34	

Households buy $40 worth of durable goods. For the manufacturers this is a current sale. For the buyers it is the acquisition of capital assets. Suppose the buyers pay $21 in cash and obtain credit from the sellers for the rest. Business bank balances rise by $21, while assets in the form of accounts due from customers rise by $19. From the point of view of the consumers they have acquired goods partly by reducing their assets and partly by increasing their liabilities.

	Households		Business	
	Uses	*Sources*	*Uses*	*Sources*
Current receipts (sales)				40
Consumer durable goods	40			
Demand deposits and currency	−21		21	
Consumer credit		19	19	

Suppose consumers buy houses worth $18 from construction firms. They obtain the full purchase price through the use of mortgages, borrowing $13 from banks and $5 from other consumers. This series of transactions can be examined in three parts: (1) Builders sell $18 worth of houses and increase their cash by that amount. (2) Buyers get $5 of the necessary cash from other consumers, who take it out of their balances. (3) The other $13 comes from commercial banks, but here the effect is different. Since banks lend by creating money rather than by reducing their cash, the money they provide represents an increase in their liabilities, not a decrease in their assets. In fact the demand deposit liabilities of the banks (plus the currency liabilities of the Federal Reserve banks and the government) *are* the cash assets of the rest of the community. The source of such funds, then, is the liabilities of the banking sector. In this sense the deposit liabilities of a bank are—for the bank—a negative cash balance. Other transactors can draw down their cash bal-

	Households		Business		Banks	
	Uses	*Sources*	*Uses*	*Sources*	*Uses*	*Sources*
Current receipts (sales)				18		
Residential construction	18					
Demand deposits and currency	−5		18			13
One- to four-family mortgages	5	18			13	

ances only when they are positive. A bank will always operate with a negative cash balance and lends by increasing its deposit liabilities.

Suppose consumers sell to banks $2 worth of government securities that they hold. The banks create credit to make the purchase (increase their deposit liabilities). For the consumer the increase in his cash is obtained at the expense of a reduction in another asset (government securities).

	Households		Banks	
	Uses	*Sources*	*Uses*	*Sources*
Demand deposits and currency	2			2
U.S. government securities	–2		2	

If, instead of selling securities, the consumer were to borrow on his own note, he would obtain cash as he does here, but with an increase in his liabilities instead of a decrease in his assets.

Assume that business pays back $12 of former bank loans that now fall due. This whole process appears negatively—it is, after all, a destruction of money. Business reduces its deposits for the purpose of paying off its liabilities. The payment reduces the deposit liabilities of the bank as it charges the firm's check against its account. At the same time the bank loses an asset—the businessman's promissory note, now paid.

	Business		Banks	
	Uses	*Sources*	*Uses*	*Sources*
Demand deposits and currency	–12			–12
Bank loans		–12	–12	

The making of a bank loan, incidentally, would be recorded in precisely the same fashion with the omission of the minus signs.

To see the effects of the flow of funds on foreign trade, assume that business buys $16 worth of imports. The entries are no different from those of any other sale except that the selling sector is the rest of the world.

	Business		Rest of world	
	Uses	*Sources*	*Uses*	*Sources*
Current receipts (sales)				16
Current expenditures (purchases)	16			
Demand deposits and currency	–16		16	

Assume finally that business sells $19 worth of goods abroad and that foreigners pay for it (1) by drawing on their bank balances (built up in the foregoing transaction) for $15 and (2) by issuing bonds, bought by United States consumers, for the remainder.

	Households		Business		Rest of world	
	Uses	*Sources*	*Uses*	*Sources*	*Uses*	*Sources*
Current receipts (sales)				19		
Current expenditures (purchases)					19	
Demand deposits and currency	–4		19		–15	
Corporate and foreign bonds	4					4

The Flow-of-funds Table. If the foregoing items represented the whole activity of our hypothetical economy for a given period, we could add them up to obtain a complete flow-of-funds account for the period in question. Such a summary is shown in Table 28-1, which gives the net totals cumulated from our twelve examples. The table is, of course, illustrative only and far from complete, but it indicates the basic form for actual flow-of-funds tables and should help in understanding the real data.

Because every transaction is entered four times, the table can be read in three ways:

1. Any individual figure shows the flow attributable to a specific sector for a specific type of transaction for the period under review. We can see, for instance, that consumers reduced their deposits by $9, or that business built $34 worth of plant, or that banks increased their deposit liabilities by $3.

2. The columns for any sector yield information on the total saving and investment and on the form of investment of that sector. Thus the net financial investment of business consists of $26 net increase in financial assets ($7 in currency and demand deposits plus $19 in consumer receivables) minus $25 net increase in liabilities ($37 of new bonds issued minus $12 of bank loans repaid). This $1 of net financial investment plus $34 of capital expenditures (plant and equipment) is the total investment of the business sector, which in turn is equal to its gross saving. Or, to take another example, the rest of the world dissaved $3. They borrowed $4 and added $1 to their cash balance.

3. By adding the rows across the table we can find the total for any type of transaction for the whole economy. The total increase in currency and demand deposits was $3, and it is not surprising that this was the amount created by banks. After all, $M = H$. Total saving (and investment) for the economy was $92. And again it is not surprising that this should equal the value of real capital expenditure. Changing the method of adding up the statistics does not alter the fact that saving equals investment in real goods.

And although the table talks about "net *financial* investment," a concept that we were at pains to reject in national income analysis, we see that for the economy as a whole, financial investment is zero. This is not an accident of the examples chosen; it is an inescapable fact. Since all financial assets of one person are liabilities of another—that is, since quadruple-entry bookkeeping records any financial transaction as a use in one sector and as a source in another—adding them together algebraically (with the liabilities counted negatively) must necessarily yield a sum of zero.

The flow of funds, in other words, does not contradict anything we have said up to this point. Rather it throws more light on aspects of the economy hitherto inadequately understood. It starts from the basic equality of saving and investment[4] and examines in considerable detail the way in which saving flows through the financial marketplace and its final use in financing real capi-

[4] The inclusion of consumer durables in the definitions of both does not alter the basic principle, and if one wanted, the statistics of the flow of funds would yield data for our earlier definitions by merely subtracting consumer durable goods from both gross saving and gross investment as given in the flow-of-funds table.

Table 28-1. Flow-of-funds Account for a Hypothetical Economy

	Households		Business		Government		Banks		Rest of the world		Total	
	U	S	U	S	U	S	U	S	U	S	U	S
A. **Current receipts**		300		789		80				16		1,185
B. **Current expenditures**	230		754		90				19		1,093	
C. GROSS SAVING (*A* − *B*)		70		35		−10				−3		92
D. GROSS INVESTMENT (*E* + *I*)	70		35		−10				−3		92	
E. **Private capital expenditure** (*F* + *G* + *H*)	58		34								92	
F. Consumer durables	40										40	
G. Residential construction	18										18	
H. Plant and equipment			34								34	
I. **Net financial investment** (*J* − *K*)	12		1		−10		0		−3		0	
J. Net acquisition of financial assets	49		26		4		3		1		83	
K. Net increase in liabilities		37		25		14		3		4		83
L. *Demand deposits and currency*	−9		7		4			3	1		3	3
M. *U.S. government securities*	12					14	2				14	14
N. *Corporate and foreign bonds*	41			37						4	41	41
O. *Mortgages*	5	18					13				18	18
P. *Consumer credit*		19	19								19	19
Q. *Bank loans*				−12			−12				−12	−12

Source: Summarized from examples in the text.

tal. The methods, definitions, and data used in national income statistics and flow-of-funds accounts are slightly different, and the results are therefore not identical, but they are in basic agreement at most points.

Flow of Funds in the United States

The actual figures for 1964 are summarized in Table 28-2.[5] This table adds two concepts not introduced in our examples:

1. Both a column and a row have been included to show statistical discrepancies arising from difficulties of obtaining complete, accurate, and compatible figures for all aspects of the economy simultaneously. If entries for all transactions were available in the form of our illustrative examples, no statistical discrepancy would appear. But when data must be pieced together from bits and scraps of available information, it is not surprising that the figures do not always balance neatly.

2. The final column, "national saving and investment," is intended to examine the national economy separately from the rest-of-the-world account. The figures for gross saving and investment in this column are the totals for all sectors minus the rest of the world. The figure for net financial investment, on the other hand, is that of the rest-of-the-world account with the sign changed—for the investment of the rest of the world in this country is *our* foreign *dis*investment. As we have pointed out, when all sectors are included, net financial investment is zero. For the national economy, however, this may not be the case. It is possible to own foreign bonds, for instance, which are an asset without a corresponding *national* liability. When all such foreign transactions are aggregated, the result is essentially the net foreign investment component of the national income accounts.[6] In other words, total national investment of $156.3 billion (line 4) is equal to the increase in physical capital of $151.6 (line 5) plus net foreign investment of $4.7 (line 10) and a rounding error of $0.1 billion.

$$I = I_d + I_f$$

The usefulness of the table lies not so much in its overall totals, for material of this sort was available in the national income accounts, but in its subtotals, in its individual items, and in the facility it provides for comparing these in a single place and on a consistent basis. The table shows—to take a few examples at random—that in 1964 consumer expenditures for durable goods

[5] Greater detail is available in supplementary tables published regularly in the *Federal Reserve Bulletin*.

[6] The difference between the figure shown here for net financial investment for the rest of the world (4.7) and the one in the national income account of Table 26-1 for net foreign investment (5.8) is the statistical discrepancy for the rest of the world (1.2) minus a rounding error (0.1). The sign for net foreign investment is positive (+) from the point of view of the United States; here the sign is negative (−) because we are looking at net financial *dis*investment on the part of the rest of the world.

Table 28-2. Summary of Flow-of-funds Accounts, 1964

Billions of Dollars

	Sector	Private domestic nonfinancial sectors										Financial sectors															
		Households		Business		State and local govts.		Total		U.S. govt.		Total		Monetary auth.		Coml. banks		Nonbank finance		Rest of the world		All sectors		Discrepancy		Natl. saving and investment	
	Transaction category	U	S	U	S	U	S	U	S	U	S	U	S	U	S	U	S	U	S	U	S	U	S	U	S		
1	**Gross saving**		98.4		61.8		−2.1		158.1		−5.0		3.4		.1		1.9		1.4		−5.8		150.6	−1.0		156.5	1
2	Capital consumption		55.8		47.0				102.8				.8				.4		.4				103.6			103.6	2
3	Net saving (1−2)		42.6		14.9		−2.1		55.3		−5.0		2.6		.1		1.5		1.0		−5.8		47.0			52.9	3
4	**Gross investment (5+10)**	102.1		58.3		−3.6		156.8		−2.9		4.3		.1		2.0		2.3		−4.7		153.5		−1.9		156.3	4
5	**Private cap. expend., net**	82.3		68.5				150.7				.9				.4		.5				151.6				151.6	5
6	Consumer durables	58.7						58.7														58.7				58.7	6
7	Residential constr.	19.5		7.5				27.0														27.0				27.0	7
8	Plant and equipment	4.0		56.2				60.2				.9				.4		.5				61.1				61.1	8
9	Inventory change			4.8				4.8														4.8				4.8	9
10	**Net financial invest. (11−12)**	19.9		−10.2		−3.6		6.1		−2.9		3.4		.1		1.6		1.8		−4.7		1.9		−1.9		4.7	10
11	**Financial uses, net**	47.3		15.4		6.2		68.8		4.7		63.5		3.4		23.2		36.9		3.5		140.5				8.1	11
12	**Financial sources**		27.4		25.6		9.8		62.7		7.7		60.1		3.3		21.7		35.1		8.1		138.6			3.5	12
13	Gold & off. U.S. fgn. exch.									−.2		*		*						.1	*	*	*				13
14	Treasury currency										*	−.2		−.2								−.2	*	.2			14
15	Dem. dep. and currency												7.4		2.6		4.8					6.9	7.4				15
16	Private domestic	7.4		−2.6		.7		5.6				.2	6.8		2.4		4.4	.2				5.8	6.8	1.0			16
17	U.S. govt.									.6			.2		.2		*					.6	.2	−.5			17
18	Foreign												.5		.1		.4			.5			.5				18

19	Time and svgs. accounts	23.9						28.8				.2	30.4					.2					30.4				19
20	At coml. banks	8.2		3.2		1.7		13.1		*		.1	14.6				14.6	.1		1.4			14.6				20
21	At svgs. instit.	15.7						15.7				.1	15.8					.1	15.8				15.8				21
22	Life insur. reserves	4.4						4.4			*		4.3						4.3				4.4				22
23	Pension fund reserves	11.6					3.5	11.6	3.5		1.3		6.9						6.9				11.6				23
24	Consol. bank items											.5	.5	.1	.4	.4	.1					.5	.5				24
25	Credit mkt. instr.	3.5	27.3	1.3	22.3	3.7	6.2	8.6	55.8	3.8	6.7	60.9	6.5	3.4		21.8	.6	35.8	5.9	.4	4.6	73.8	73.6				25
26	U.S. govt. securities	2.1		−1.5		.4		.9			6.2	4.8		3.5		−.5		1.8		.4			6.2				26
27	State and local oblig.	2.6				−.6	5.9	2.0	5.9			3.8				3.6		.2					5.9				27
28	Corp. and foreign bonds	−.7			4.0	3.5		2.8	4.0			4.6	2.6			.1	.5	4.5	2.1	.2	.9		7.6				28
29	Corp. stocks	−.6			1.4			−.6	1.4			3.8	1.7				*	3.8	1.6	−.3	−.2		2.9				29
30	1- to 4-family mortgages	.1	16.0		−.2	.4		.5	15.8	−.2		15.1	−.3			2.3		12.9	−.3				15.5				30
31	Other mortgages		1.0		9.1				10.1	.4		9.7				2.2		7.4					10.1				31
32	Consumer credit		6.9	1.4				1.4	6.9			5.5				2.8		2.8					6.9				32
33	Bank loans n.e.c.		2.6		5.0				7.6			10.0	.5	*		10.0			.5		1.9		10.0				33
34	Other loans		.8	1.4	3.0		.4	1.4	4.1	3.6	.5	3.7	2.0	−.1		1.4		2.4	2.0	.2	2.0	8.9	8.7	−.2			34
35	Open market paper			1.4	n.a.			1.4	n.a.			.5	1.5	−.1		.7		−.1	1.5	.2	.4		2.1				35
36	Federal loans		.1		.9		.4		1.3	3.5			.5						.5		1.7		3.5				36
37	Security credit	−.1	−.2					−.1	−.2			*	.1			.5		−.5	.1	*	*		−.1				37
38	To brkrs. and dealers	−.1						−.1				.2	.1			.2		*	.1	*			.1				38
39	To others		−.2						−.2			−.2				.3		−.5			*		−.2				39
40	Taxes payable				.2	*		*	.2	.2			.4				.3		.1			.2	.6	.5			40
41	Trade credit		.1	8.9	4.8		.1	8.9	5.0	.2	−.2	.2						.2				9.3	4.8	−4.5			41
42	Equity in noncorp. business	−4.1			−4.1			−4.1	−4.1														−4.1				42
43	Misc. financial trans.	.6	.2	4.6	2.5			5.2	2.6	.1	−.2	1.7	3.5		.3	.6	1.2	1.1	2.0	1.0	3.6	8.0	9.6	1.6			43
44	Sector discrepancies (1−4)	−3.8		3.6		1.5		1.3		−2.1		−.9				*		−.9		−1.2		−2.9		−2.9		.2	44

Note: U = uses of funds; S = sources of funds; n.a. = not available. Financial uses of funds represent net acquisition of assets; financial sources of funds represent net changes in liabilities.
* Less than $50 million.
Source: ***Federal Reserve Bulletin***, vol. 51, no. 11 (November, 1965), p. 1608. Detail may not add to totals because of rounding.

Table 28-3. Financial Assets and Liabilities, December 31, 1964

Amounts Outstanding in Billions of Dollars

	Sector	Private domestic nonfinancial sectors										Financial sectors												
		House-holds		Business		State and local govts.		Total		U.S. govt.		Total		Monetary auth.		Coml. banks		Nonbank finance		Rest of the world		All sectors		
Transaction category		A	L	A	L	A	L	A	L	A	L	A	L	A	L	A	L	A	L	A	L	A	L	Discrep-ancy	
1	**Total financial assets**	1305.2		292.8		73.1		1671.0		84.7		874.7		60.8		306.8		507.1		80.0		2710.5			1
2	**Total liabilities**		313.4		416.4		130.1		859.9		303.3		802.7		60.8		284.0		457.8		87.6		2053.4		2
3	Gold stock									.1		15.4		15.4						27.6		43.1			3
4	Official U.S. fgn. exch.									.1		.3		.3							.4	.4	.4		4
5	IMF position									4.1	3.3		*		*						.8	.8	.8		5
6	Treasury currency										2.8	5.2		5.2								5.2	2.8	−2.4	6
7	Demand dep. and currency												175.5		36.8		138.7					162.4	175.5	13.1	7
8	Pvt. domestic	83.8		44.7		10.0		138.5				12.4	164.6		35.1		129.5	12.4				150.9	164.6	13.7	8
9	U.S. govt.									8.6			7.9		1.4		6.5					8.6	7.9	−.6	9
10	Foreign												2.9		.3		2.6			2.9		2.9	2.9		10
11	Time and savings accounts	253.0						278.2				.9	286.1					.9				286.1	286.1		11
12	At coml. banks	94.8		15.4		9.8		120.0		.3		.2	127.2				127.2	.2		6.7		127.2	127.2		12
13	At svgs. instit.	158.2						158.2				.7	158.9					.7	158.9			158.9	158.9		13
14	Life insur. reserves	101.0						101.0			6.8		94.2						94.2			101.0	101.0		14
15	Pension fund reserves	136.6					30.6	136.6	30.6		18.4		87.5						87.5			136.6	136.6		15

16	Consol. bank items											25.7	25.7	2.8	22.9	22.9	2.8					25.7	25.7		16
17	Credit mkt. instr.	714.4	299.7	45.0	243.8	52.1	96.7	811.5	640.1	49.3	268.3	779.6	68.6	37.2		270.0	.8	472.5	67.8	29.1	36.7	1669.4	1013.7		17
18	U.S. govt. securities	76.0		18.3		22.0		116.4			266.6	137.2		37.0		66.7		33.4		13.1		266.6	266.6		18
19	State and local oblig.	36.6		2.4		5.3	93.6	44.3	93.6			49.3				33.5		15.8				93.6	93.6		19
20	Corp. and fgn. bonds	4.1			92.4	22.0		26.0	92.4			88.7	15.0			.9	.8	87.8	14.3	.9	8.2	115.7	115.7		20
21	Corp. stocks	586.5			n.a.			586.5	n.a.			83.8	29.1				n.a.	83.8	29.1	13.8	n.a.	684.1	29.1		21
22	1- to 4-family mortgages	11.2	188.1		7.3	2.8		14.0	195.5	6.0		177.7	2.2			27.0		150.7	2.2			197.7	197.7		22
23	Other mortgages		13.1		62.9				76.0	5.4		70.6				16.7		53.9				76.0	76.0		23
24	Consumer credit		76.8	18.4				18.4	76.8			58.4				29.4		29.0				76.8	76.8		24
25	Bank loans n.e.c.		12.2		60.3				72.5			89.2	9.7	*		89.2			9.7		7.1	89.2	89.2		25
26	Other loans		9.5	5.9	20.8		3.1	5.9	33.4	37.9	1.7	24.8	12.6	.1		6.5		18.1	12.6	1.3	21.4	69.7	69.1	−.7	26
27	Open market paper			5.9	1.9			5.9	1.9			16.5	7.2	.1		3.8		.7	7.2	1.3	2.6	11.7	11.7		27
28	Federal loans		.8		9.3		3.1		13.2	37.3			5.3						5.3		18.8	37.3	37.3		28
29	Security credit	1.2	8.4					1.2	8.4			15.0	7.9			8.4		6.7	7.9	.1	.1	16.3	16.3		29
30	To brkrs. and dealers	1.2						1.2				6.6	7.9			5.5		1.1	7.9	.1		7.9	7.9		30
31	To others		8.4						8.4			8.5				2.8		5.6			.1	8.5	8.5		31
32	Taxes payable				17.6	1.1		1.1	17.6	18.4			1.9				.9		1.0			19.5	19.5		32
33	Trade credit		2.3	131.5	97.5		2.8	131.5	102.6	2.7	3.4	2.5						2.5				136.7	105.9	−30.7	33
34	Equity in noncorp. business	n.a.			n.a.			n.a.	n.a.													n.a.	n.a.		34
35	Misc. financial trans.	15.3	3.0	56.3	57.6			71.5	60.6	4.5	3.4	17.7	55.4		1.1	5.5	13.7	12.2	40.6	13.7	49.7	107.3	169.1	61.7	35

Note: A = assets; L = liabilities; n.a. = not available.
* Less than $50 million.
Source: *Federal Reserve Bulletin*, vol. 51, no. 11 (November, 1965), p. 1618. Detail may not add to totals because of rounding.

($58.7 billion) exceeded the expenditures of nonfinancial business for plant and equipment ($56.2 billion). Households reduced their holdings of corporate stock by $0.6 billion while nonbank financial institutions increased theirs by $3.8 billion. The United States government increased its outstanding debt by $6.2 billion while state and local governments increased theirs by $5.9 billion. The monetary authorities increased demand deposits and currency outstanding by $6.8 billion on private domestic account, but nobody knows where $1 billion of this went ("discrepancy" column). This type of information is exceedingly useful in studying the behavior of the economy.

Financial Assets and Liabilities. Precisely the same methods that are used to show the flow of funds for a given period of time may also be used to develop a similar group of data showing the financial assets and liabilities held by the economy at a given date, also cross-classified by sector and type of transaction. This information for December 31, 1964, is given in Table 28-3. Most of the line captions correspond to those in Table 28-2, and this table can be read in exactly the same way, bearing in mind that the figures here are stocks (assets and liabilities) rather than flows (uses and sources). The difference is basically that between a statement of income and expense and a balance sheet.

Theoretical Implications

Since flow-of-funds analysis started with statistics rather than theory, and since the technique is still very much in its infancy, the theoretical implications of the material are not very well developed. As the compilers of the data say:

> While the accounts are an aid to analysis, they do not, by themselves, constitute analysis or offer automatic answers to problems. Examination of the accounts may provide some insight into the functional relations between variables, may suggest workable hypotheses, and may permit the screening out of obviously implausible hypotheses, but each user must supply his own analysis and adapt the accounts to his own purposes and methods.[7]

For the most part the material confirms the theories already discussed. In time the greater wealth of detail should point the way to relationships not yet understood.

The Discretionary Thesis. In pursuing his original work on moneyflows, Morris Copeland presented some tentative suggestions that seemed to be indicated by movements of certain parts of the flow over time. The most important of these he labeled the "discretionary thesis." It emphasizes the different ways in which discretion with regard to transactions may be exercised by different sectors. Thus any transactor may exercise more or less discretion over (1) his receipts and (2) his expenditures. Since the difference between these

[7] *Federal Reserve Bulletin,* vol. 45, no. 8 (August, 1959), p. 830.

two represents the change in his net financial assets ("loanfund balances"), he obviously also has discretion over (3) his loanfund balances.

The exercise of this discretion is not the same for all sectors of the economy. For consumers and business in general, discretion over expenditures is considerably greater than that over receipts. A consumer can decide to buy or not to buy certain goods, but his income is controlled to a great extent by the wages business is willing to pay him. Similarly business may control its expenditures by employing more or fewer workers, and so on, while its receipts are pretty well fixed by the willingness of consumers to buy its products. In both cases expenditure decisions are more likely to result from changes or anticipated changes in receipts than the other way around.

But consumers and business do not exercise their discretion over expenditures in the same way. In one sentence we may say that consumers base their expenditures on current (or past) receipts, while businessmen base their expenditures on anticipated receipts. Thus consumer expenditures rise when receipts rise and fall when receipts fall. In each case the change in expenditures seems to be less than the change in receipts, so that loanfund balances move in the same direction as expenditures. This, of course, is the familiar Keynesian consumption function: when income falls, both consumption and saving fall.

Business, on the other hand, frequently increases its expenditures without its receipts having risen because it anticipates better business in the future. This it can do only by reducing its loanfund balances (drawing down cash or borrowing). Similarly, business often reduces its expenditures more rapidly than its receipts, resulting in an increase in loanfund balances. This is the reason we spoke of business cycles as existing primarily in the anticipations of businessmen. The flow-of-funds accounts verify this thesis statistically by showing that the loanfund balances of business (particularly corporate business) tend to move in an opposite direction from its expenditures—business expands by reducing its liquid assets or by borrowing.

The government and banking sectors show even more important peculiarities in their discretionary possibilities. The government may vary not only its expenditures, but also its receipts. Thus the government's influence on flows of funds can be exercised just as effectively through its tax policy as through its expenditures.

The special position of the banking system lies in the fact that its contribution to the economy comes not from its ordinary receipts and expenditures, but rather from its effect on currency and demand deposits. It is, in fact, only through bank borrowing that the total cash balances of nonbank sectors can be increased. The banking sector is the only one that can operate with negative cash.

In addition to his discretion over the total of his loanfund balances, each transactor has further discretion over the composition of these balances, particularly over the relationship of his cash balance (demand deposits and currency) to his other financial assets and liabilities. Thus while a transactor can increase his cash balance by keeping his expenditures below his receipts, he can also increase it by selling financial assets or by borrowing. In fact such an increase in cash is likely to precede an increase in expenditures. On the other hand, his cash balance may be decreased by an excess of expenditures over receipts or by the purchase of earning assets.

In this way cash balances act as a spring providing a somewhat flexible link between nonfinancial transactions, on the one hand, and the loan and security markets, on the other. When a transactor increases his spending (assuming given receipts), he can do so in the first instance by dishoarding, that is, by drawing down his idle balances. But as the balance falls, he is more and more pressed into borrowing or selling securities. He is becoming less liquid. On the other hand, if his expenditures decrease, his cash balance grows, creating more and more pressure to turn the idle balances to more useful ends by repaying debts or buying earning assets.

Much of the new statistical information available in flow-of-funds accounts concentrates on the financial transactions associated with this transfer of cash into earning assets and back again, as well as on the shift among various earning assets. It is here that it is most helpful in filling out the circuit flow, for this area is not covered by national income analysis at all since national income concepts concern real assets, not the method of their financing.

The Role of Financial Intermediaries. The emphasis on movements within the financial markets coincides with a current tendency to pay more attention to the activities of financial intermediaries. As they grow in importance, their significance cannot be ignored. Like money itself, they are not neutral. They do not merely pass money from savers to investors, for in the process they affect the direction of the flow and undoubtedly alter the total magnitude of saving and investment as well. In this process the interest rate plays an important role, and to that subject we turn in the next chapter.

Questions for Thought and Discussion

1. Make flow-of-funds entries for the following transactions:

a. A household makes a $10 cash deposit in a savings bank.

b. A corporation sells a tractor to a farmer for $1,000.

c. A household buys $40 worth of stock in a mutual fund, which uses the money to buy corporate stock formerly held by a foreigner.

d. Business pays taxes of $100 by giving up an equal amount of maturing government securities.

e. A commercial bank lends $500 to a securities broker, who in turn lends it to a household.

2. Why do you think the Federal Reserve prefers the phrase "flow of funds" to Copeland's simpler "moneyflows"? (What about trade credit as money?)

3. Explain the meaning of the following entries in Table 28-2:

a. U.S. government, sources, trade credit, −.2

b. Commercial banks, sources, demand deposits and currency, 4.8

c. Nonbank finance, uses, corporate stocks, 3.8
d. Rest of the world, uses, time and savings accounts, 1.4
e. Households, uses, U.S. government securities, 2.1
f. All sectors, sources, 1- to 4-family mortgages, 15.5
g. Nonbank finance, uses, financial uses net, 36.9

4. How can a bank operate with a negative cash balance in the sense used in this chapter?

5. Does liquidity preference shed any light on the concept of cash balances as a flexible link between nonfinancial transactions and the loan and security markets?

6. Do you think it is important to study the shift in financial assets from one sector of the economy to another in view of the fact that such a shift does not itself produce any real goods?

7. National income accounting was developed in response to national income theory; flow-of-funds accounting came before the theory. Which approach is more fruitful?

Selected Bibliography

Board of Governors of the Federal Reserve System: *Flow of Funds in the United States, 1939–1953,* 1955.

———: *Flow of Funds Accounts, 1945–1962,* 1963.

Copeland, Morris A.: *A Study of Moneyflows in the United States,* National Bureau of Economic Research, Inc., New York, 1952.

Powelson, John P.: *National Income and Flow-of-funds Analysis,* McGraw-Hill Book Company, New York, 1960.

"A Quarterly Presentation of Flow of Funds, Saving, and Investment," *Federal Reserve Bulletin,* vol. 45, no. 8 (August, 1959), pp. 828–859.

Chapter 29 The Rate of Interest

He lends out money gratis, and brings down
The rate of usance here with us in Venice.

The Merchant of Venice
Act I, scene 3, line 45

We have spent a number of chapters exploring the value of money in the normal meaning of that phrase—its power to obtain goods in exchange. But there is another "value of money": the price paid for the use of money. Not only are interest rates important in their own right, but they are also a necessary ingredient in any complete picture of the effect of money on the economy and consequently a key factor in much monetary policy.

Interest Rate Theory

For the sake of simplicity almost all interest rate theory speaks of a single interest rate in spite of the multiplicity of actual rates. This single rate may be thought of as a "typical" rate (the rate on long-term government bonds is often used as an example), as an "average" rate (whatever that means), or as a rate "structure" that describes vaguely the whole spectrum of rates. The last cannot be given a numerical value, but it may be conceived of as relatively high at one time and low at another. Since all rates *tend* to move in the same direction, the concept of a single rate does not distort seriously the underlying situation.

The interest rate is a price, and any price is determined by supply and demand. In this case, however, we are not quite sure what it is whose demand and supply we want to measure. This confusion is partly responsible for the many theories of interest rate determination.

Classical Theory. The classical theory is the simplest, but unfortunately it has failed to stand the test of time. In this system supply is the supply of saving, while demand is the demand for investment. This can be shown in the form of an ordinary price diagram (Figure 29-1).

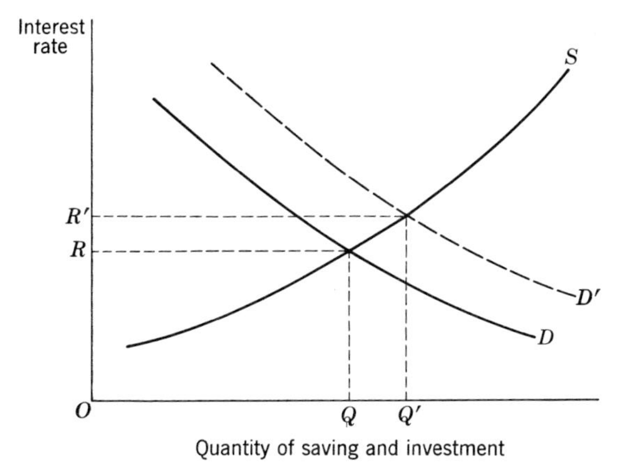

Figure 29-1. Classical theory of interest rate determination.

Here we see that at interest rate R, business plans investment of Q, while savers are willing to save precisely this same amount. Thus the interest rate brings saving and investment into equilibrium. Suppose businessmen increase their investment demand to D'. The higher demand raises the interest rate to R', and at this higher rate people are willing to save Q'. Thus the increased investment demand is satisfied with greater saving but at a higher price (interest rate).

Although this theory appears quite plausible on the surface, it fails to come to grips with all the factors involved. Like the national income theory it points to the equality of saving and investment, but where the national income theory states that they will be equated by changes in income, the classical theory says that they will be equated by changes in the interest rate. It assumes on the one hand that there are no leakages from saving (no hoarding) and on the other that there is no source of investment funds other than savers (no money creation). The implication is that as long as the interest rate is appropriate, *ex ante* saving equals *ex ante* investment, and national income is constant, presumably at the full employment level. The appearance of unemployment would represent a movement away from equilibrium that could be corrected by a shift in the interest rate. The emphasis on constant income (all other things remaining the same) makes the classical theory inapplicable under most circumstances, for it ignores the fact that a change in the quantity of investment will itself alter national income and that this in turn is likely to shift the saving curve and perhaps the investment curve as well.[1]

Loanable Funds Theory. The loanable funds theory, which is today more widely used than any other, starts from the same basic postulates as the classical theory but introduces a number of refinements for which the earlier theory had no room. It begins by examining just what it is that gives rise to interest payments. Payment is made not for saving, but for lending. Interest is paid on *loans,* from whatever source and for whatever purpose. The interest rate, therefore, is determined by the supply of, and demand for, funds in the loan market. On the supply side, then, we are interested in that portion of funds currently offered to borrowers.

Saving. An important part of these funds comes out of saving. To this extent the classical theory was right. It is not quite clear, however, that a higher interest rate increases the amount of saving. It seems evident that the aggregate saving of the economy is more dependent on the level of income and on other institutional factors than it is on the interest rate.

There are two reasons why higher interest rates may induce higher saving. The first is the obvious fact that the higher price for loanable funds may lure people to save more in order to earn this higher return. A second reason is that higher interest payments increase the income of the creditor and thus raise his *ability* to save. This effect, however, is indirect; the amount of saving responds to the higher income, not directly to the interest rate.

On the other hand, there is one major reason why the quantity of saving may vary *inversely* with the interest rate, a higher rate actually reducing the amount saved. If I decide that I need to accumlate a specified sum by a particular date, a higher interest rate will permit me to achieve my goal with a smaller current rate of saving. The final sum will be composed of more interest earnings and less saving.

To illustrate: A sum of $20,000 can be built up in 20 years by saving $722.42 per year at 3 per cent interest or by saving $576.02 per year at 5 per cent interest. In the first case $5,551.60 of the total sum of $20,000 was added in the form of earned interest. In the second case interest amounted to $8,479.60.

This principle is quite significant in the field of life insurance. The higher the interest rate on which the actuarial calculations are based, the lower the premium for a given policy, since a smaller part of the policy reserve must come out of current payments and more out of interest additions.

There are forces, then, that work both to increase and to decrease saving as interest rates rise. But a third group of forces is probably of even greater importance. These are the forces that are completely independent of interest rate changes. People save for many reasons having nothing to do with interest and would do so even if interest were zero:

[1] We will return to this problem in Chap. 30.

1. Many people save for a specific objective: for a rainy day, for old age, for their children's education, for a trip to Europe, for that little place in the country. It's nice to earn interest on these funds, but interest isn't the primary motivation.
2. A large and growing part of saving is compulsory through pension plans and the social security system. Some is semicompulsory, such as life insurance premiums, since once a policy is bought, the policyholder tries to keep up payment. The repayment of debt, which is a form of saving, is also compulsory once the obligation has been incurred.
3. There is probably some automatic saving on the part of the rich. Some people have an income that is so high that it isn't easy to spend all of it. Such people may also be more interested in the accumulation of an estate to pass on to their heirs than in interest earnings as such.
4. Consumers are not the only, nor even the largest, savers. Some business saving is undoubtedly associated with the interest rate, as when a company is deterred from borrowing by high interest charges and decides instead to plow back earnings into the business. But another large part of business saving, depreciation allowances, has no relation to interest at all. Capital consumption allowances alone are currently almost twice the magnitude of total personal saving and three times as great as other corporate saving.
5. Even the government, through its trust funds, is an important source of saving (so far used exclusively to purchase government securities), and here also the interest rate does not affect the volume of funds involved.

The cumulative weight of all these considerations seems to suggest that whatever determines the volume of saving, the rate of interest is relatively unimportant. Perhaps it plays some role, but we are not even sure whether its effect is positive or negative. In the absence of any proof to the contrary we might just as well draw the saving curve as perfectly vertical (interest-inelastic), as in Figure 29-2. This means that the same quantity of saving would be available no matter what the interest rate.

It is well to remember that saving *can* be negative. Gross saving, including depreciation allowances, never has been negative for any period for which reliable statistics are available for this country, but both personal saving and net business saving were negative in the dark days of the Great Depression (see Table 26-2).

Hoarding. Saving, however, is not the supply of loanable funds. Some savings are never loaned. While a man may be saving for that rainy day even if no interest is paid, there is no reason for him to part with the money unless the reward is high enough to overcome the loss of liquidity, the risk of loss of principal, and any costs involved.

Thus while considerable saving would occur at zero interest, no funds (with a few philanthropic exceptions) would be available for loan. The saving is hoarded. As interest rates rise, more and more people are induced to turn a larger and larger fraction of their saving into income-earning assets. This is shown by curve F_s in Figure 29-2, which indicates the quantity of loanable

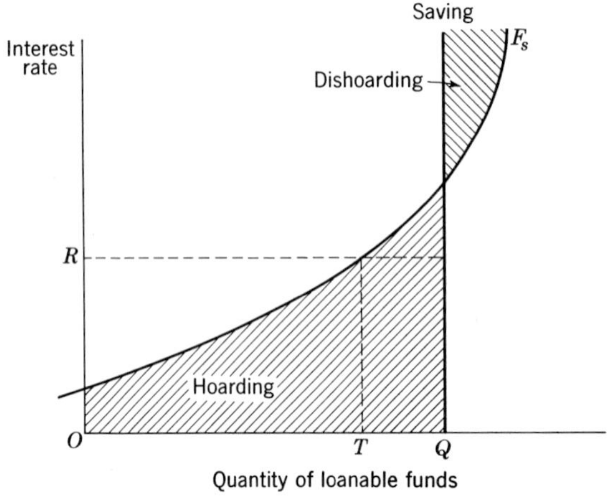

Figure 29-2. The supply of loanable funds out of saving.

funds that savers will make available. Hoarding is shown in the diagram as a subtraction from saving and is therefore measured to the left from the saving line. Thus at interest rate R, people will save OQ dollars but will hoard QT dollars and lend OT dollars.

If the interest rate rises high enough, the supply of loanable funds made available by savers will actually exceed saving. This means that people are dishoarding—putting to work cash that they had stashed away out of previous saving. Dishoarding can proceed only as long as hoards last. If, therefore, an interest rate high enough to produce dishoarding continues for any significant length of time, existing hoards will be used up, and available loanable funds out of saving will be limited to sums currently saved. The upper appendage of curve F_s is thus only a short-run possibility.

Figure 29-2 also suggests that loanable funds out of saving may be negative. This means that at very low rates "savers" may actually borrow additional funds to add to hoards in order to increase liquidity. If interest is only ½ per cent, it may be worthwhile to borrow just to maintain a larger bank balance for precautionary purposes. Or at that rate one may sell securities previously bought, thereby adding to cash more than is saved from current income.

This negative portion of the curve reminds us that almost anyone may be either a borrower or a lender and may switch from one role to the other. Many people are, in fact, both borrowers and lenders at the same time. In interest rate analysis, therefore, it is not possible to separate lenders and borrowers into clearly distinct groups as we separate, for instance, the buyers and sellers of radios.

There are two ways of handling this schizophrenic behavior of lender-borrower. One is to think of the desire to borrow as a *negative supply* of funds, as shown here by the portion of the F_s curve to the left of the vertical axis. The second method, perhaps easier to understand, is to consider such tendencies as additions to the demand for funds. Either method would lead to the same result.

Curve F_s is the supply of loanable funds out of saving. These funds may be loaned by the saver directly, as when he buys new corporate bonds. They may pass through any of the numerous financial intermediaries. Or they may be used by the saver in his own business, as with plowed-back profits. In the last case they never enter the loan market as such. They are, however, precisely balanced by an equivalent demand for investment. This flow of saving directly into investment is not completely unrelated to interest rates, though it may not produce precisely the same results that would follow if the funds did flow through the marketplace. It is not unreasonable to include such saving in the gross concept here used. A somewhat different curve would result if we subtracted saving invested by the saver himself from both the supply and the demand curves, but the final effect of using net concepts would be similar to that here discussed.

Bank Credit. We have not yet, however, shown the total supply of loanable funds. As we already know, when a businessman (or anyone else) borrows from a commercial bank, the loan does not represent a use of saving. Rather it comes out of newly created money. When banks are increasing their loans, they are producing a supply of funds in addition to the current flow out of saving. On the other hand, if repayment of bank loans exceeds the issue of new ones, then the extinguishment of loans—the destruction of money—reduces the total supply of funds below the amount supplied out of saving.

There is no conclusive evidence to suggest that the supply of new bank credit is directly correlated with interest rates. While it is true that a large volume of loans and a high interest rate usually go together, both are normally associated with a high rate of business activity, and the increased volume of loans at such times seems to be at least partly the result of an increase in demand and an attempt by banks to satisfy their customers.

It is probably also true that when banks approach the practical limit of their expansion, additional credit can be created only at a higher cost, most clearly illustrated by the bank's need to borrow reserves. Here there may be some positive correlation between interest rates and supply of bank credit. At the lower end of the scale also, since there are costs involved in any loan, a bank will probably not lend below a certain rate. Within these limits, however, banks probably are willing to lend about as much as they can with safety.

Without giving more definite dimensions to the supply of loanable funds out of bank credit, we have indicated its relation to total loanable funds in Figure 29-3. Curve F_s is the supply of loanable funds out of saving, taken from Figure 29-2. Curve F_t is the total supply of loanable funds when banks are expanding credit, and F'_t is the total when banks are contracting. When banks are neutral, the total supply is that out of saving, F_s. The diagram is intended to show direction rather than magnitude, and bank credit, either positive or negative, may be of greater relative magnitude compared with saving than the diagram suggests.

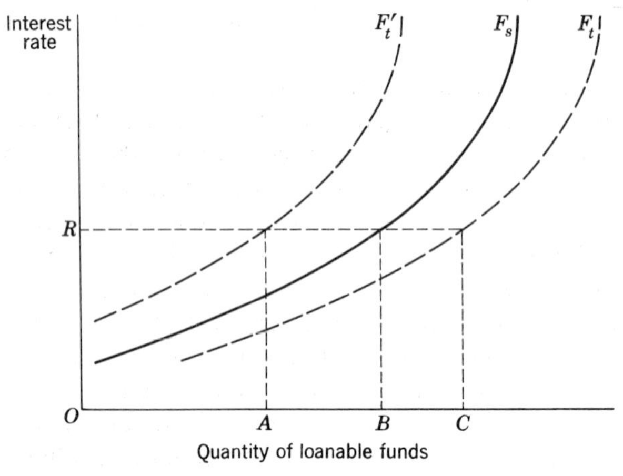

Figure 29-3. The effect of bank credit on the supply of loanable funds.

Figure 29-3 shows that at interest rate R the supply of loanable funds out of saving would be OB. If banks were expanding credit (curve F_t), they would add an amount BC to the savers' supply. Total quantity of funds available for loan would then be OC.

If, on the other hand, banks were contracting (curve F'_t), they would absorb funds equal to AB from the market, and although savers were still supplying OB, part of these funds would be used in repayment of bank loans, and the *net* amount available to borrowers would be OA.

Investment Demand. On the demand side the classicists were right in ascribing primary importance to investment, though this is not the whole story either. Fundamentally, business demand for loanable funds *is* the demand for investment, whether long-term in the form of plant and equipment or short-term in the form of inventories or current expenses involved in the production of goods.

Business demand for investment is based on marginal net revenue productivity of capital (or what Keynes called *marginal efficiency of capital*). This is the anticipated increase in total revenue that would result from a given investment expenditure after subtracting the operating costs associated with the new investment (but not including interest on the funds borrowed).

Suppose a business is contemplating purchasing a new machine costing $30,000 and estimated to last 10 years. It is expected that this machine will turn out 100,000 widgets a year, and these can be sold for 60 cents each. The cost of raw materials for this many widgets is $30,000; labor costs come to $20,000; and operating expenses, additional sales costs, and all other expenses connected with the production and sale of 100,000 extra widgets amount to $4,000. As Table 29-1 shows, this leaves the manufacturer with an expected net return of $3,000, which is 10 per cent of the cost of the machine. This is the maximum amount he can afford to pay in interest for the $30,000 needed

Table 29-1. Illustration of Marginal Net Revenue Productivity

Cost of Machine: $30,000

	First machine		Second machine	
Increase in revenue:				
100,000 widgets @ $0.60		$60,000		$60,000
Less increase in costs:				
Depreciation (one-tenth of $30,000)	3,000		3,000	
Raw materials	30,000		30,000	
Labor	20,000		21,500	
Other expenses	4,000	57,000	4,000	58,500
Marginal net revenue productivity		$ 3,000		$ 1,500
As a per cent of cost of machine		10%		5%

to buy the machine. If the interest rate is any less, he can add to his profit any difference between the 10 per cent earned on the machine and the rate he has to pay for the money. At 6 per cent, for instance, he would pay $1,800 in interest and pocket $1,200 profit.

Suppose the rate *is* 6 per cent. He will certainly borrow $30,000 and buy the machine. And if one machine is good, two should be better. But is this true? If he increases his output by another 100,000 widgets, he may have to lower his price to sell them all, he may have to pay higher wages to get additional labor, or he may find other expenses rising. Just assume he has to pay some overtime wages, raising his labor costs to $21,500, as shown in the last column of Table 29-1. This reduces his marginal net revenue productivity to $1,500, or 5 per cent of the cost of the machine. As long as the interest rate is 6 per cent, a second machine would be unprofitable, but if the rate falls below 5 per cent, a second will be bought.

At 10 per cent or less he will have a demand for loanable funds of $30,000, while at 5 per cent or less he will be in the market for $60,000. The demand for loanable funds, therefore, shows the same characteristics as any demand curve: it slopes downward to the right. At lower interest rates more funds will be demanded. This is shown in Figure 29-4*a*.

All the data in such a calculation are *estimated*. They may be based on past experience, but they must actually refer to the future. They cannot, therefore, be exact. Perhaps after taking all possibilities into consideration the businessman concludes that he *may* be able to make as much as 12 per cent, but under adverse conditions he may be able to clear only 2 per cent. Should he borrow at 6 per cent?

Here is the risk element present in all business decisions, and the answer depends on many considerations, including the state of mind of the businessman. The more optimistic he is, the higher his calculation of marginal efficiency is likely to be and the higher the interest he will be willing to pay. In a depression, on the other hand, businessmen may be so pessimistic that any expansion appears to be a losing proposition; marginal efficiency is negative, and businessmen wouldn't borrow even at a zero rate of interest.

Because interest costs are such a small part of total expenses, relatively moderate changes in other costs may be much more important in making plans than a change in the rate of interest. For certain projects the marginal efficiency of capital is so high that money would be borrowed at almost any interest rate. For others no profit can be foreseen no matter how low the rate. But there are always marginal projects where a small change in interest rates may be a deciding factor as to whether to go ahead or not.

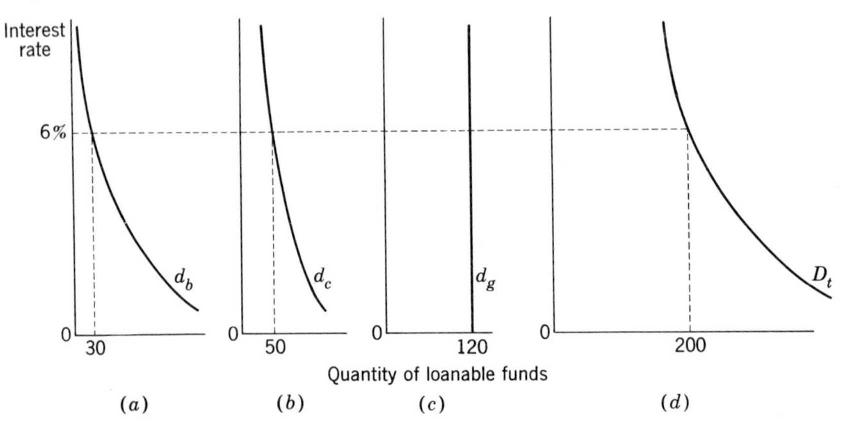

Figure 29-4. The demand for loanable funds. (*a*) Business; (*b*) consumers; (*c*) government; (*d*) total.

The quantity of investment funds demanded, in other words, *does* depend on the interest rate, but probably not to a very large degree. The demand curve is therefore likely to be interest-inelastic—a fall in interest rates (other things remaining the same) will increase the quantity of funds businessmen want to borrow, but not by as much proportionally as the change in the rate.

Consumer Demand. Business is not the only borrower of funds. Increasingly consumers have entered the market for mortgage loans, installment purchases, and loans for everything from medical expenses to airplane trips. Here the demand is determined by the psychological, often unthinking, desire of the individual to increase his consumption in anticipation of future income.

The consumer isn't quite as rational as the businessman in matters of this kind. He is more apt to borrow without paying too much attention to the interest cost. But consumers as a whole will probably borrow more at lower rates, less at higher rates, as shown in Figure 29-4*b*.

Government Demand. Traditionally, little has been said of the government in interest rate theory. But when the Federal government debt alone exceeds $300 billion, its effect on the market can hardly be ignored. There is no indication that the total volume of Treasury borrowing is determined by interest rate considerations. The government operates at a deficit either because it doesn't see how it can avoid living beyond its income (as in a war period) or because it believes a deficit is desirable as a matter of public policy (as in a depression). States and localities may pay more attention to interest rates, postponing certain projects if the rate seems too high. Such considerations probably affect a rather small proportion of government debt, and government demand for funds is therefore shown as completely inelastic in Figure 29-4*c*.

Total Demand. The total demand for loanable funds is no more than the simple addition of business, consumer, and government demand, as shown in Figure 29-4*d*. At 6 per cent, for instance, business would borrow 30, consumers would want 50, and the government demand would be 120. The total demand for funds is therefore 200.

This total demand can be plotted against total supply (curve F_t from Figure 29-3) to give the familiar supply and demand diagram of price theory (Figure 29-5). With supply at S and demand at D, the interest rate will be R. An increase in demand (D') will raise interest rates (R'), just as an increase in supply (S'), assuming the original demand, will reduce them (R''). Reduction in supply or demand will have opposite effects.

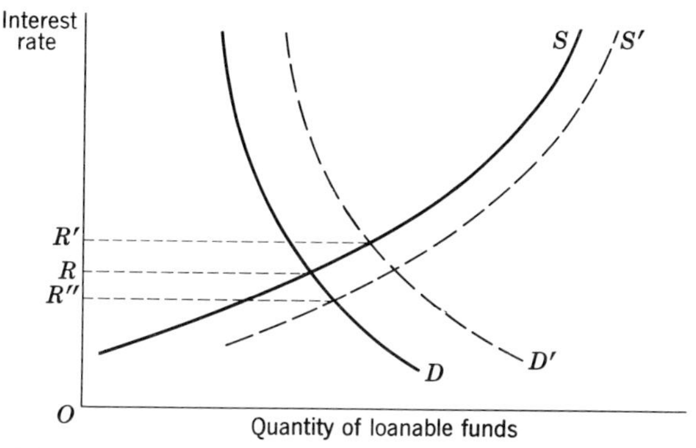

Figure 29-5. Loanable funds theory of interest rate determination.

It should not be overlooked that while we have spoken throughout of borrowers influencing the demand for funds, they do so only at the time when the loan is initially made. When loans are repaid, the sums so returned are added to the supply available to other borrowers. Repayment, therefore, must be taken into account either as a subtraction from demand or as an addition to supply. If repayments exceed new loans, then the actual amount of loanable funds in the market is negative; that is, funds flow *out* of the money market rather than into it.

Alternative Approach. Another way of examining this problem—one that recognizes that each individual may be a lender at some (high) interest rates and a borrower at other (low) rates—is to combine both supply and demand curves in a single curve such as F in Figure 29-6. This curve includes all bor-

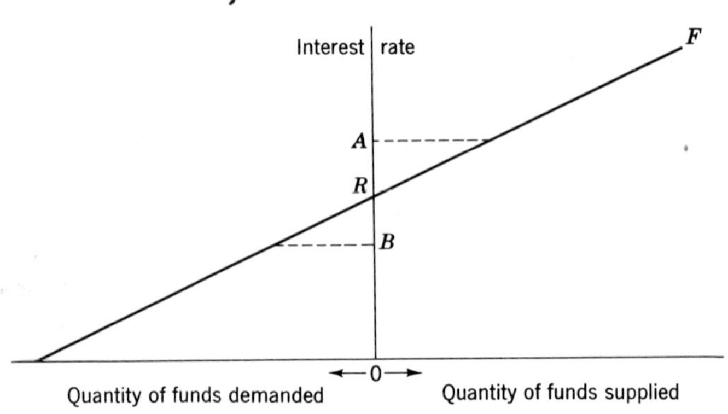

Figure 29-6. Loanable funds theory in terms of net demand or supply of funds.

rowers and lenders *except commercial banks* and shows the *net* excess of funds demanded or supplied at all interest rates.

At interest rate *A* more funds would be made available than the community as a whole wanted to borrow. Thus excess funds would flood the market, tending to force interest rates down unless commercial banks absorbed the excess funds by contracting their own loans. At interest rate *B* more people would want to borrow than could be supplied with the funds available at that rate. The demand for funds would force the rate up unless commercial banks created the additional funds wanted at that rate. At rate *R* the economy's demand for, and supply of, funds are in equilibrium: borrowers are willing to absorb precisely the quantity of funds that lenders are willing to supply.

Another way of describing this diagram is to say that if banks are neutral, the interest rate must be *R*. Some writers refer to this as the *natural* rate of interest. If banks are expanding, the rate will be forced down (say, to *B*), and the *market* rate will be below the natural rate. If banks are contracting, the rate will be forced up (say, to *A*), and the market rate will be above the natural rate.

Several economists have suggested that deviations of the market rate from the natural rate play a key role in business cycles.[2] Although the natural rate of interest is a difficult concept to work with, we do know that the expansions and contractions of bank credit are indeed significant economic variables and that they do affect the market rate of interest.

Conclusion. Before leaving the loanable funds theory we might pause to note the relation between this theory and the circuit flow of money. The right-hand side of the circuit showed saving flowing into investment and hoarding, while new money was injected into investment. Precisely the same factors appear in

[2] See Knut Wicksell, *Interest and Prices* (Macmillan & Co., Ltd., London, 1936); R. G. Hawtrey, *Currency and Credit* (Longmans, Green & Co., Ltd., London, 1928); and F. A. Hayek, *Monetary Theory and the Trade Cycle* (Harcourt, Brace & World, Inc., New York, 1932).

our interest rate analysis. Saving represents a source of funds, but it is modified by hoarding. Adding any net creation of bank credit gives the total supply of loanable funds. This in turn is absorbed into investment demand, the government's deficit, and consumer borrowing (which was mentioned briefly but never actually charted in our circuit flow).

Liquidity Preference Theory. Another approach to the theory of interest scraps the whole concept of saving-investment and looks at interest as payment for the use of *money*. While loanable funds usually take the form of money, there is nevertheless a fundamental difference between the two concepts.

When we speak of the quantity of loanable funds, we are thinking in terms of a flow of funds over a specified period of time. The supply represents funds that savers don't wish to hold and are therefore willing to lend to someone else. The demand is the demand for money as a means of exchange, not as a store of value. The borrower doesn't want money to hold; he wants to spend it.

In the liquidity preference approach, money is thought of as a stock that exists at a specific moment of time. The supply of money is not a flow into the market, but rather the physical quantity in existence. This quantity of money is produced by the monetary authorities: the Treasury, the Federal Reserve, and the commercial banks. It is presumed that this total sum is not related to the interest rate but is institutionally determined. Figure 29-7 shows this supply (M) as independent of the interest rate.

The demand for money (L) is similarly interpreted as a desire to acquire money not to spend, but rather as a store of value. This is the liquidity preference already explained in Chapter 24. Alternatively it is hoarding. It represents the keeping of money in money form.

We have already seen that liquidity preference has four components: the transactions, precautionary, convenience, and speculative motives for holding cash. And we know that the last two, at least, depend on the interest rate. The higher the interest rate, the more a person loses by keeping nonearning cash and the more he would gain by lending it to others. The lower the rate, the less is foregone by keeping idle cash and the more people will want to hold.

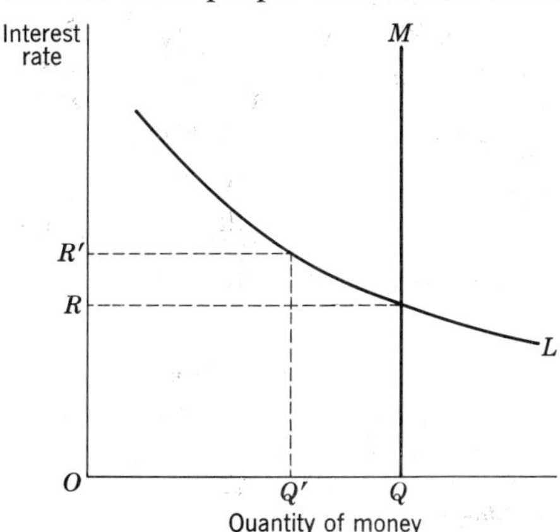

Figure 29-7. Liquidity preference theory of interest rate determination.

Similarly, the lower the rate, the greater the expectation that it is likely to rise in the future and the greater the speculative motive. As rates rise, both convenience and speculative balances are called out of hiding. The demand for money therefore slopes downward to the right as does the demand for anything else.

But the economy as a whole can hold no more money than there actually is, nor can it hold less. If the monetary authorities have provided quantity OQ (Figure 29-7), then people must hold that quantity and no other. They want to hold that amount at interest rate R. But suppose the interest rate is R'. At that rate people would prefer to hold only OQ' dollars. They will *actually be holding* OQ, since all money must be held by someone, but they *don't want to*. What do they do?

They certainly don't throw the unwanted money down the sewer. They try to exchange it for earning assets; they buy securities. This increased demand pushes security prices up. A rise in security prices, however, is the same thing as a fall in interest yields. Suppose I own a bond that pays $60 per year interest but has no specified maturity date (British consols are of this nature). When I bought the bond, the interest rate was 6 per cent. That means I paid $1,000 in order to earn $60—or 6 per cent—a year. Suppose then that the demand for such bonds increases, and the price rises to $1,200. The bond still pays $60 a year. But $60 is only 5 per cent of $1,200. The yield on the bond, which can be calculated only by dividing the dollar return per year by the purchase price,[3] has therefore fallen from 6 per cent to 5 per cent.

A corollary of this is that if the market is willing to accept a 5 per cent yield, new securities do not have to pay any more than that to find buyers. A new $1,000 bond will carry an interest coupon of only $50 a year. In other words, the increased demand for securities will lower interest rates all around.

Interest rates under these conditions will fall (in terms of Figure 29-7) from R' to R, at which rate people will no longer want to try to turn cash into earning assets, for at R they are perfectly willing to hold the quantity of money OQ that is actually in existence.

A similar process, in reverse, would take place if interest rates were lower than R. At lower rates people would want to hold more money than was available. In order to get it they would sell securities. This would force security prices down and interest yields up until R was again reached.

The liquidity preference theory also explains what happens when the supply of money is altered. If the monetary authorities take steps to contract the money supply, the M curve moves to the left, say, to Q', and the interest rate will rise then to R'. Similarly if the money supply expands, M moves to the right, and the interest rate falls.

[3] If the bond has a specified maturity date, especially if that date is fairly soon, the calculation of the yield must take into account the fact that although the holder will get $60 a year until maturity, at that date he will get back only $1,000 for a bond purchased for $1,200. The $200 loss reduces his net yield below 5 per cent. This alters the arithmetic but not the principle discussed here.

The Liquidity Trap. But how far can interest rates fall? There is nothing in Figure 29-7 to suggest any particular limit. As long as people will hold more money only at lower rates of interest, the *L* curve will decline indefinitely. But a number of writers have suggested that in fact as the interest rate falls, liquidity preference will become more and more elastic until it becomes perfectly horizontal. That is, there is some interest rate below which no further money will be lent. Any increase in the money supply beyond this point will simply add to hoards without lowering the interest rate further. This may be due to institutional factors: since there are costs involved in making loans, potential lenders will not lend unless the rate is at least high enough to cover these costs. Or it may be due to expectational factors: at some rate people will expect that the rate cannot go any lower, and for speculative reasons they would prefer to hold on to money in the hope that its value will rise.

In either case the result is that below some interest rate the demand for money is infinite. Any attempt on the part of the monetary authorities to stimulate the economy by increasing the money supply in the hope of pushing interest rates below this level is doomed to failure because all the increased money is simply hoarded; it disappears into the *liquidity trap,* the desire to increase liquidity indefinitely at this minimum rate of interest. Much has been said about the liquidity trap and its restrictive effect on monetary policy, but its existence is still subject to some dispute. The major conclusions of the liquidity preference theory do not depend on its existence.

The Problem of Income. In some respects the liquidity preference theory says much the same things as the loanable funds theory, although the point of view is different. The supply here is related to the increase in bank credit, while the demand is functionally similar to hoarding, also included in the loanable funds theory as a subtraction from saving. But just as the classical doctrine can be criticized because it omits any consideration of hoarding and bank credit, so the liquidity preference theory is incomplete because it neglects saving and investment as explicit variables. It is difficult to explain through liquidity preference, for instance, how business decisions to expand investment will raise interest rates. The loanable funds theory includes all four variables and is therefore more nearly complete. But none of the theories so far described include income as an explicit variable. Even Keynes, who gave impetus to the current study of national income theory, failed to explore the effect on interest rates of changes in income. We will examine this matter further in the next chapter.

State Determination of Interest Rates. There has been some tendency recently to simplify the issue by suggesting that these days it doesn't matter what the market does; the interest rate is determined in the final analysis by the government. Frequently the finger is pointed at the Federal Reserve as the final arbiter of interest rates; sometimes the Treasury is singled out. If this were true, it would certainly make things easier for the theorist, and this chapter would be a great deal shorter. Unfortunately such a theory does not fit the facts. The government is in a position to *influence* interest rates, and that quite strongly, but influence is not the same thing as determination.

The government operates on both sides of the market. On occasion (particularly during war periods) the government may borrow sizable sums to finance current deficits. At these times the government demand is likely to be substantially greater than that of any other individual borrower, and it therefore exerts a correspondingly large influence. But the Treasury can no more *determine* rates than Sears Roebuck or the New York Central can. True, the government sets the rate it will pay on its bonds and notes, but these rates cannot be arbitrary. They are set with other market conditions in mind and in such a way as to attract investors. If the government puts too low a rate on a new issue, nobody will buy it. If it sets too high a rate, it is throwing money away.

The rate on treasury bills is not set by the government at all, and of all interest rates on new issues, public and private, it is undoubtedly the *most responsive* to market pressures. These securities are sold every week at absolute auction to the highest bidders, that is, to those who are willing to lend the government the needed amount of cash at the lowest interest cost. Far from setting the interest rate, treasury bills are one of the most sensitive barometers of changes in market pressures for short-term securities.

If the government experiences difficulty in finding buyers for its securities, it may, with the other hand, make funds available through the operations of the Federal Reserve. This is the supply side of the market. Bank credit (whether positive or negative) is an important part of the supply, and this can be influenced (though not determined) by the Federal Reserve. This is the focal point of monetary policy, to which we will devote several chapters.

The government may also affect specific interest rates through the lending policies of its various credit agencies, but here again its influence is almost exclusively through its effect on the supply of funds available in particular markets. This reminds us that we have been talking so far about *the* interest rate, when in fact there are a great number of diverse rates that may not all move together.

The Multiplicity of Interest Rates

The number of different interest rates is legion. Treasury bills, savings bonds, marketable government bonds, corporate bonds of all kinds, the commercial bank prime rate and all its variations, bank acceptances, brokers' loans, mortgages, installment contracts, personal finance loans, factor charges, and so on, on, and on. The rate may vary from less than 1 per cent to a legal limit of 42 per cent (in some states) and considerably higher in illegal transactions. Why this wide variation?

There are two basic answers to this question. The first points out that there are several factors that influence the lender's willingness to lend and that these vary greatly from transaction to transaction. The other is that the money market in spite of the tremendous publicity it receives is still not a perfect market, that funds are not completely mobile, and that some people simply do not know what alternatives are available. These frictions may produce distortions among interest rates that are hard to explain.

Let's tackle the rational side of the market first.

Cost. Loanable funds do not have a cost of production in the same way that chairs do. Yet there are costs associated with making a loan that must be paid out of the interest return. These costs include the clerical expense of processing the loan, the maintenance of an office, investigation expenses, and so on. Some of these are overhead costs necessary for the general operation of a financial institution; others are associated with particular loans.

The administrative and clerical expense of processing a loan of $1 million may not be much more than the similar expense for a loan of $100. When stated as a percentage of the amount involved (that is, as an interest charge) the cost element in the large loan is likely to be only a small fraction of the cost of a small loan. A bank that can very profitably lend $1 million for three months at 4 per cent (interest $10,000) may well lose money on a loan of $100 at 12 per cent repayable in monthly installments over a year. The $6 income in the latter case[4] may not even pay the cost of investigation, let alone monthly handling of installments and other expenses. This is the most important reason for the higher rates charged smaller borrowers.

Table 29-2 shows how the interest rate charged by commercial banks on short-term business loans varies with the size of the loan. The cost of making the loan may not be the sole reason for the difference, since risk frequently is greater for small borrowers, but it is undoubtedly part of the reason.

Table 29-2. Bank Rates on Short-term Business Loans by Size of Loan in Nineteen Large Cities, September, 1964

	Per cent per annum
All loans	4.98
By size of loan:	
$ 1,000–10,000	5.86
10,000–100,000	5.57
100,000–200,000	5.23
200,000 and over	4.79

Source: *Federal Reserve Bulletin*, vol. 50, no. 10 (October, 1964), p. 1297.

Cost is also the primary reason for the difference that frequently arises between the interest received by savers and the amount paid by borrowers. Obviously a savings bank, for instance, would rapidly go broke if it paid its depositors the same rate it charged its borrowers.

[4] Remember what we learned in Chap. 4 about the relation between the finance charge and the interest rate.

In this respect the interest that an intermediary must pay on its own obligations is one of the costs that it must cover in making loans. The commercial bank is in a preferred position in this respect, since it does not lend other people's money but creates the money for the occasion. In this sense the cost of acquiring (creating) funds is zero as long as it has excess reserves, but at the same time it must cover the expenses of making the loan. A commercial bank may be able to make loans at 4 per cent, while a savings bank that is paying 4 per cent to its depositors couldn't possibly make ends meet at that rate.

Risk. A second element of the interest rate is the *risk premium,* an amount sufficient to cover any loss that may occur through default on the part of the borrower. Obviously a lender would not make a loan that he knew would go bad. Yet it is reasonably certain that *some* loans will be defaulted. He just doesn't know which.

He does know, however, that there are certain factors that make it more likely that default may occur, and the more of these circumstances present in an individual case, the higher the risk premium he will charge.

Table 29-3 gives some indication of differences in interest rates that are

Table 29-3. Money Market Rates and Bond Yields, September, 1964.

	Per cent per annum
Short-term rates:	
Treasury bills (3 months)	3.53
Prime bankers' acceptances (90 days)	3.75
Prime commercial paper (4–6 months)	3.89
Bond yields:	
U.S. government	4.16
Aaa corporate bonds*	4.42
Baa corporate bonds*	4.82

* Aaa and Baa are ratings given by Moody's Investors Service on the basis of their evaluation of the credit standing of the corporation and the risk inherent in the particular bonds rated. Aaa is the highest rating; Baa is intermediate.
Source: *Federal Reserve Bulletin,* vol. 50, no. 10 (October, 1964), p. 1298.

based primarily on the credit standing of the borrower. The first section, on short-term rates, indicates the high credit standing of the government compared with private borrowers, as well as the superior rating of banks compared with other businesses. The second half, showing long-term rates, reaffirms the position of the government and shows how the interest paid by corporations depends on how they are rated by professional credit agencies in regard to their safety.

Risk is dependent on so many factors, and they are so difficult to assess, that different lenders may evaluate a particular risk differently. As circumstances change, the credit standing of a particular borrower also is subject to change. Pessimism on the part of the lender without any objective change in the status of the borrower may also increase the *evaluation* of the risk.

As a rule of thumb, large enterprises usually have a higher credit standing than small; well-established businesses fare better than new ventures. It was once assumed that businessmen were better risks than consumers, but the record now shows that the consumer has proved that he too can be trusted. A loan secured by collateral is, other things being equal, less risky than an unsecured loan. In practice other things are seldom equal, and lenders usually require collateral of shaky borrowers, while lending to stable borrowers on their signature alone.

Liquidity Preference. The third element in interest represents the sacrifice involved in parting with the present use of funds: the *pure interest* (or *net interest*) that would remain even if all cost and risk were absent. The classicists were concerned almost exclusively with this pure interest component and referred to it as the reward for abstinence, the incentive that induced a person to postpone consumption in order to be able to consume more at a later date when principal would be repaid with interest. Classical theory, in other words, assumed that *time preference* was positive, that is, that people always preferred present consumption to future consumption and would therefore spend all their money in the present unless they could foresee a larger future consumption as a result of saving.

This is undoubtedly true of the very poor, whose current needs are pressing. It may also be true of the wealthy profligate, who can't seem to hang on to a penny. But in the upper-income brackets many people undoubtedly have a negative time preference after they have reached a certain level of expenditure. In other words, further purchases today seem less attractive than the use of an equivalent amount of money tomorrow. They would save regardless of the interest rate.

But they may not lend. For regardless of time preference, *liquidity preference* is always positive. Money has absolute liquidity. When it is loaned to someone else, liquidity diminishes. The resulting claim represents money to be received at some future time, but it can't be spent today. The longer the loan, the greater the sacrifice of liquidity.

Suppose I am saving for my retirement in twenty years. Since I won't need the money till then, I ought to be willing to lend it out by buying, for instance, a 20-year bond. But I am not *sure* I won't need it for twenty years. Conditions may change in the meantime. I may lose my job or need an expensive operation, or my doctor may tell me I'll never live to retire. If I make the long loan, I may find that I have miscalculated and want the money back sooner. Normally I can sell securities before maturity if I want the funds, but I have no assurance of the *price* at which I can sell them. If I have to sell on a weak market the loss of principal will offset part, perhaps even all, of the interest I have earned in the meantime.

Long-term loans are therefore less liquid than short-term, and pure interest, which appears to be primarily a payment for liquidity preference, is normally higher for long-term loans than for short-term. Thus, although all securities of the United States government presumably carry equal risk and can be obtained with no significant difference in their cost of acquisition, their interest yield tends to rise from the shorter to the longer maturities, as shown in the first column of Table 29-4.

Table 29-4. Market Yield of Government Securities, Selected Dates
Per Cent per Annum

	Week ending		
	Sept. 12, 1964	Dec. 5, 1959	May 11, 1929
3-month bills	3.52	4.50	4.98*
9- to 12-month issues	3.72	4.98	
3- to 5-year issues	4.04	4.90	†
Long-term bonds (over 10 years)	4.17	4.21	3.64

* 3- to 6-month bills and certificates.
† 3- to 5-year notes were not issued in this period.
Sources: *Federal Reserve Bulletin*, vol. 50, no. 10 (October, 1964), p. 1298; vol. 46, no. 1 (January, 1960), p. 50; vol. 15, no. 6 (June, 1929), p. 368.

This pattern is not invariable, however, as the last two columns of the same table show. In fact another set of statistics for May 11, 1929, gives an even more startling picture: although long-term bonds carried an interest rate of 3.64 per cent, stock exchange time loans (ninety-day) cost 8½ to 9 per cent, while stock exchange call loans (one-day) were made at 11.83 to 12.40 per cent.

Such an inversion of the interest rate structure usually occurs when rates are expected to fall. Consider the case, for example, in which a corporation wants to finance an expansion costing $1 million through the issue of 20-year bonds. Suppose the long-term rate is 5 per cent, but the company thinks the rate will fall to 4 per cent within a year. They would be foolish to contract a twenty-year obligation at the higher rate (total interest cost for twenty years $1 million) if they can borrow for one year even at 10 per cent interest ($100,000) and then refinance with a 19-year bond at 4 per cent ($760,000). The total interest in the second case would be $140,000 less than in the first. Under such circumstances the demand for short-term funds in a tight market may drive the rate up above the long-term rate, as our table shows.

Other Interest Rate Differentials. There are many other factors that influence rates, some of which perhaps escape attention. Many variations in rates, in fact, seem rather absurd. Why should one person earn 4¼ per cent on funds deposited in a savings bank, while his neighbor earns 3¾ per cent on an identical deposit in a commercial bank? Why should the same consumer, wanting to finance a refrigerator with a one-year loan, find a personal finance company charging 24 per cent, the dealer wanting 18 per cent, one commercial bank quoting 12 per cent, and another asking 8½ per cent? Why should a corporation seeking a loan of $100,000 find a bank in New York charging 5.0 per cent while one in Atlanta wants 5.4 per cent? Why should rates on treasury bills rise while bank acceptances fall and commercial paper remains the same?

There are many frictions in the market for funds that are responsible for such differences. One, particularly where consumers are concerned, is ignorance of alternative possibilities. Another is the fact that although the money borrowed or lent is homogeneous, the transactions are not. Each loan carries its own peculiar circumstances, and there is room for considerable difference of opinion on the part of the lender as to the risk or other factors involved.

A third, and perhaps more important, reason for what appear to be irrational disparities between different rates is that although a dollar lent in one transaction is the same as a dollar lent in another, both lenders and borrowers tend to be stratified by tradition, by temperament, sometimes by law, in such a way that a particular lender supplies funds only to a limited sector of the market, or a particular borrower never taps more than a portion of the funds available.

Thus savings and loan associations make loans almost exclusively on mortgages. Their supply of funds is unavailable to other borrowers regardless of the rate of interest elsewhere. Many intermediaries such as life insurance companies, savings banks, and trustees are forbidden by law to invest in certain types of loans. Commercial banks, because of their need for liquidity, hesitate to tie up any large amount of funds in long-term assets; they stick pretty much to the high-liquidity end of the scale. The desire to keep funds near home hinders geographical mobility, particularly in terms of international movements, though it would be a serious mistake to assume that funds *never* flow far from their source. Consumers are much more restricted geographically, in terms of both supply and demand, than business is. Consumers have also traditionally stayed away from marketable government securities, partly because dealers normally carry out transactions in large sums ($25,000 in government bonds is a "round lot") and partly because of a lack of knowledge of the field.[5]

For these and other reasons the total supply of funds is not available to *all* borrowers, nor does the total demand confront all lenders. On the other hand, it is likewise impossible to fragment the demand and supply into small components. There is, for instance, no supply of mortgage funds as distinct from loanable funds in general. Although savings and loan associations are restricted to this area, other lenders—commercial banks, insurance companies, and so on—will move funds into or out of the mortgage market as conditions change.

Institutions with a high liquidity preference supply funds mainly on short

[5] In 1959 and early 1960, however, the lure of a 5 per cent return on government bills and notes brought a large number of consumers into this market, and this may presage a change in investing patterns and hence some shift in the interest rate structure.

term, but if long-term interest rates rise sufficiently, they will shift some funds into this market. Corporations traditionally borrow short-term funds from commercial banks, but gradually they are examining certain advantages of open-market commercial paper and of factors as sources of such funds.

The funds market therefore shows evidence of fluidity and of sluggishness at the same time. It might perhaps be compared to a tank of very muddy water divided into numerous compartments by mesh screens with holes of various sizes. If pressure is put on any compartment, some of the water will move quite readily into other compartments, and some of the particles of mud won't be able to squeeze through the mesh at all, while others may find a particularly large hole. If the pressure is strong enough, the mesh itself may be broken, allowing even fuller movement.

Interest rates *tend* to move together, but with many lags and distortions. Interest rate theory therefore cannot tell us what any particular rate will be. It shows the direction of forces acting on interest as a whole, while at the same time specific circumstances may influence individual interest rates. An increased demand for funds *will* tend to raise interest rates in general even though some rates may be unaffected and others (in the exceptional case) may fall because of particular factors specifically affecting them.

The Functions of Interest Rates

Interest rates have two functions:

1. The allocation of resources between competing present needs
2. The allocation of resources between present and future consumption

Interest rates, like any other price, serve to ration scarce resources (funds) among the many people who would like to use them. In terms of business loans this means that interest rates determine the structure of industry, for the business that has the highest marginal efficiency of capital will bid funds away from others who have a lower estimate of the productivity of new investment. Production will therefore be directed into those areas where its return is likely to be highest.

It is sometimes suggested that in a socialist society interest would be abandoned. While *payment* of interest might be abolished since the government can supply whatever capital funds are needed from taxation or other sources, the *concept* of interest is needed to provide means of deciding which of the many desirable projects the government will undertake.

Even in a socialist economy the supply of funds is not unlimited. Suppose sufficient funds are available to build either a shoe factory or a hat factory, but not both. Which to choose? It is possible to toss a coin or decide on the basis of power politics or other noneconomic considerations. But if the economy is interested in maximum satisfaction, the final decision must be made on the basis of which industry has the higher marginal efficiency of capital, that is, which would be willing to pay the higher interest rate. The industry with the higher marginal net revenue productivity is the one that promises to produce the higher output for a given use of resources.

It must be admitted that in our present economy with its multiplicity of rates—some based on irrational differences—interest rates do not provide a completely accurate device for channeling money into the most useful areas. But they give a better answer than any presently known alternative.

The second function of interest rates is to allocate resources between present and future consumption. If a nation spends all its income on current expenses, it cannot add to its capital equipment. Its productivity therefore tends to remain static. Its real income next year will be the same as it is this year. If it refrains from consuming all its current income, the saving represents new capital assets, which will turn out even more goods next year, and the standard of living rises.

To what extent should consumption be postponed in order to have more pie tomorrow? Every individual answers that question for himself in terms of his own saving. The nation answers it in terms of aggregate saving.

The classicists, as we have seen, believed that the interest rate determines the amount of saving and therefore the allocation between consumers' goods and producers' goods. Today we are not quite so sure that the interest rate is wholly effective in this area. It still has some influence, however, and in a negative sense it has taken on a new meaning that the classicists never faced. When consumers borrow in order to finance current consumption, they are in effect bidding money away from businessmen who would otherwise borrow the funds. Consumer borrowing, therefore, results in larger current consumption for the community as a whole. To the extent that a high interest rate restricts consumer borrowing, it tends to increase the possibility of future consumption just as surely as when it induces increased saving.

In both saving and borrowing the insensitivity of consumers to interest rates reduces their effectivenesss as a control mechanism in allocating resources between present and future consumption, but it is not totally destroyed.

Among other things, this partial ineffectiveness of interest rates in performing their allocative function raises a number of questions about the role of interest in business fluctuations. Until we know more about the many facets of interest rate determination, as well as about its effect on business and consumer decisions, this role remains at least partially obscured. The nature and effect of interest represent one area of business cycle analysis that merits a good deal more attention than it has received.

Questions for Thought and Discussion

1. Statistics show that interest rates tend to be high in periods of prosperity, when the volume of loans is also high. Does this mean that, other things remaining the same, people will borrow more at high rates than at low rates?

2. Is it more desirable to build small plants that can produce consumer goods quickly or more extensive projects that will last longer?
3. In a depression both prices and interest rates tend to fall. Does this mean that both the yield and the market price of bonds will decline?
4. If long-term government bonds fall in price to 80 per cent of par, does this mean that people have lost faith in the ability of the government to redeem these obligations?
5. Why should some government bonds sell in the market for 104, while others sell for 99, and still others at 88? Why wouldn't everybody buy those costing 88?
6. Why would anyone lend to the government at 4 per cent if he could buy bonds of the XYZ Uranium Company paying 7 per cent? If the latter are considered too risky, why would anyone buy them at all?
7. What is the relationship between V, K, liquidity preference, saving, hoarding, national income, loanable funds, interest rates, and investment?
8. Obtain figures for a number of current interest rates of various kinds and explain the reasons for differences among them.
9. If the market interest rate were 5 per cent and the government decreed that no one could charge more than 4 per cent, what would happen?
10. If the market interest rate were 5 per cent and the government wanted to bring it down to 4 per cent without imposing an interest rate ceiling, is there any way it could do so?
11. Since financial intermediaries inevitably involve costs, why don't lenders avoid these costs by making loans directly to ultimate borrowers?
12. Why should the interest rate on commercial bank loans in New York be lower than that in Middletown? (There are at least half a dozen reasons.)
13. What is the dollars-and-cents significance of the old maxim, "The best investment is to pay off your debts"? Is this always possible, even when savings are available?
14. What is the difference between time preference and liquidity preference?
15. Could you devise a society in which interest rates were completely unnecessary?

Selected Bibliography

Allen, H. H.: *Whither Interest Rates?* Harper & Row, Publishers, Incorporated, New York, 1940.

American Economic Association: *Readings in the Theory of Income Distribution,* McGraw-Hill Book Company, New York, 1946.

Conard, Joseph W.: *An Introduction to the Theory of Interest,* University of California Press, Berkeley, Calif., 1959.

Fisher, Irving: *The Theory of Interest,* The Macmillan Company, New York, 1930.

Hahn, F. H., and F. P. R. Breckling (eds.): *The Theory of Interest Rates,* papers and summaries of discussions from the 1962 International Economic Association Conference, St Martin's Press, Inc., New York, 1965.

Hawtrey, Ralph G.: *A Century of Bank Rate,* Longmans, Green & Co., Ltd., London, 1938.

Homer, Sidney: *A History of Interest Rates,* Rutgers University Press, New Brunswick, N.J., 1963.

Koch, Karin: *A Study of Interest Rates,* Staples Press, Ltd., London, 1929.

Macaulay, Frederick R.: *Some Theoretical Problems Suggested by the Movements of Interest Rates, Bond Yields, and Stock Prices in the United States since 1856,* National Bureau of Economic Research, Inc., New York, 1938.

Riefler, Winfield W.: *Money Rates and Money Markets in the United States,* Harper & Row, Publishers, Incorporated, New York, 1930.

Robinson, Joan: *The Rate of Interest and Other Essays,* Macmillan & Co., Ltd., London, 1952.

Shaw, Edward S.: *Money, Income, and Monetary Policy,* Richard D. Irwin, Inc., Homewood, Ill., 1950.

Wicksell, Knut: *Interest and Prices,* Macmillan & Co., Ltd., London, 1936.

Chapter 30
Money, Income, Prices, and Production

Do not infest your mind with beating on
The strangeness of this business.

The Tempest
Act V, scene 1, line 246

Although we have indicated at a number of points the interrelation of monetary and real factors, of monetary and income theory, and of production and prices, it may be well to try to tie these diverse elements together more securely. Monetary theory, income theory, and price theory are, after all, merely different points of view from which to survey the field of economic activity, and although shifting our vantage point may clarify some aspects of the panorama at the same time that it obscures others, nevertheless the whole scene remains the same. Descriptions of the economy from different viewpoints will obviously vary, but they should not contradict one another. When combined, they give a more nearly complete picture than that seen from any one vantage point alone.

Interest Rates and National Income

Classical interest theory concentrates on saving and investment, emphasizing that they are equal at equilibrium. Liquidity preference theory concentrates on the money supply and liquidity preference, emphasizing that they also are equal at equilibrium. But each of these theories assumes a constant level of income.

Keynes criticized the classical theory on the grounds that the saving schedule depends on the level of income, while investment (at equilibrium) determines that level. Therefore we cannot tell what the saving schedule will be until we know what income is. We cannot know what income will be until we know the equilibrium level of investment. And this we cannot know without knowing the saving schedule. Hence an impasse. The loanable funds theory is no better in this particular respect.

Strangely enough Keynes's own solution to the interest rate problem, the liquidity preference theory, suffers from exactly the same defect. The liquidity preference schedule depends on the level of income. But the level of income depends on investment, which depends on the interest rate, which depends on liquidity preference. The difficulty is no smaller here.

The problem is not insoluble, however, but it does require introducing income into our analysis as a third dimension. We will try to show how these three-dimensional concepts can be adapted to a two-dimensional plane.[1]

Interest Determination. In Chapter 29 we showed how the classical theory explained interest rate determination in terms of the equilibrium of saving and investment. Although the loanable funds theory expanded the concepts of both saving and investment somewhat, we will ignore these additions for the time being.[2] The simplified loanable funds theory then shows the determination of the interest rate as pictured in Figure 30-1, *given the level of national*

[1] This work was pioneered by J. R. Hicks, "Mr. Keynes and the 'Classics': A Suggested Interpretation," *Econometrica,* vol. 5, no. 2 (April, 1937), pp. 147–159. The approach in this section follows more closely that of Alvin H. Hansen, *A Guide to Keynes* (McGraw-Hill Book Company, New York, 1953), chap. 7. Joseph Conard, *Introduction to the Theory of Interest* (University of California Press, Berkeley, Calif., 1959), actually uses three-dimensional diagrams to illustrate his explanation (see his chap. XI and figs. IVa to IVd).

[2] We will come back to the broader concepts later. Methodologically we may justify the simplification here as follows: *Ex post* hoarding and new money, which affect the supply of loanable funds, are equal and therefore offset each other; *ex ante* they are introduced through the liquidity preference diagram, which will be the second half of our presentation. On the demand side, consumer borrowing can be considered negative saving. This is the way it is treated in the national income accounts (Chap. 25) and also in Fig. 29-2. It is equally possible to consider government borrowing as negative government saving and to subtract this amount from private saving (along with consumer borrowing) in order to obtain a *net* (rather than a total) saving curve to be matched against investment demand.

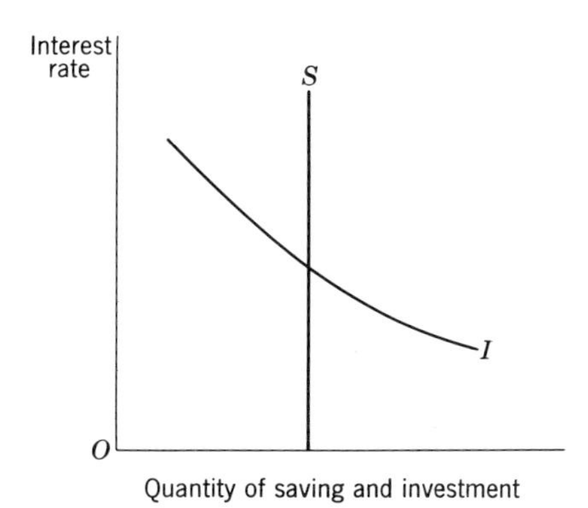

Figure 30-1. Simplified loanable funds theory of interest rate determination.

income. This diagram differs outwardly from the classical diagram (Figure 29-1) only in that it assumes that the quantity of saving does not depend on the interest rate, which means that it is interest-inelastic, or vertical.[3]

Income Determination. But this analysis assumes the level of income. How is that level itself determined? Figure 30-2 shows the first line of approach to this problem.[4]

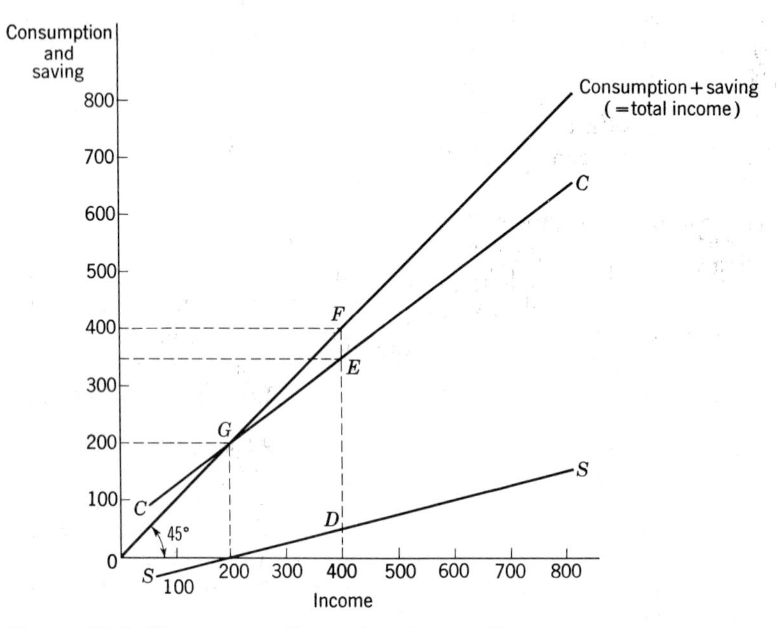

Figure 30-2. The consumption and saving functions.

In Figure 30-2 income is measured on the horizontal axis, while consumption and saving are measured on the vertical axis. Income and its components are measured in real terms—that is, prices are, for the moment, assumed to be constant. The curve *CC* is the consumption function showing, *ex ante,* how much people would spend on consumption goods at each income level. At an income of 400, for instance, the diagram suggests that they would spend 350 (point *E*).[5] If they earn 400 and spend 350, they must save 50, and this is shown on the saving function *SS* as point *D*. Since all income received must

[3] This assumption of interest inelasticity is not necessary to the basic argument. It is used here primarily because it seems to underlie the diagrams normally used in national income analysis, as we will see presently.

[4] For simplicity the diagrams used here do not consider explicitly the role of government. Government expenditures may be thought of as included in consumption (through taxes), and the government surplus, if any, is included in saving, while a government deficit would be subtracted from it, as mentioned earlier.

[5] For realism, figures can be read in billions of dollars; i.e., "400" means "$400 billion."

be used for either consumption (including government expenditures) or saving, the *CC* line and the *SS* line when added vertically must equal total income as shown in the 45° line. At an income of 400, saving is 50 (*D*), and consumption is 350 (*E*), for a total of 400 (*F*). At an income of 200, consumption is 200 (*G*), and saving is zero. At any lower income, consumption exceeds income, and saving is therefore negative.

Any *point* on *CC* can be used to show the *average* propensity to consume at that level of income. This is the proportion of income spent on consumption. At an income of 400 the average propensity to consume is

$$\frac{C}{Y} = \frac{350}{400} = .875$$

This means that 87½ per cent of income is spent at that level. At 200 the average propensity to consume is 1; that is, consumption is equal to income at that level, and saving is zero.

The average propensity to save is the proportion of income saved. At an income of 400 the average propensity to save is

$$\frac{S}{Y} = \frac{50}{400} = .125$$

Since saving plus consumption equals income, the propensity to consume (in this case .875, or 87½ per cent) plus the propensity to save (.125, or 12½ per cent) must equal 1 (or 100 per cent of income).

The *slope* of *CC* shows the *marginal* propensity to consume, which is the proportion of any *increase* in income that is spent on consumption.[6] A rise in income from 400 to 500 (an increase of 100) is accompanied by a rise in consumption from 350 to 425 (an increase of 75). The marginal propensity to consume then is

$$\frac{\Delta C}{\Delta Y} = \frac{75}{100} = .75$$

That is, 75 per cent of an increase in income will go for consumption. Conversely, 25 per cent will be saved.

Since the diagram shows *ex ante* saving at any level of income, and since we know that *ex post* saving must equal *ex post* investment, it is possible to establish what the level of income will be if we know what investment is. In Figure 30-3 all the information of Figure 30-2 is reproduced with the addition of information on investment. Curve *II* assumes that investment will be 75. Since saving (*SS*) is also 75 at an income of 500, this then must be the equilibrium income of the society, for this is the only income level at which saving and investment are equal (point *J*), as they must be *ex post*.

[6] Where *CC* is a straight line (as in these diagrams), the slope, and hence the marginal propensity to consume, is constant. If the line is not straight, the marginal propensity will change from point to point on the line.

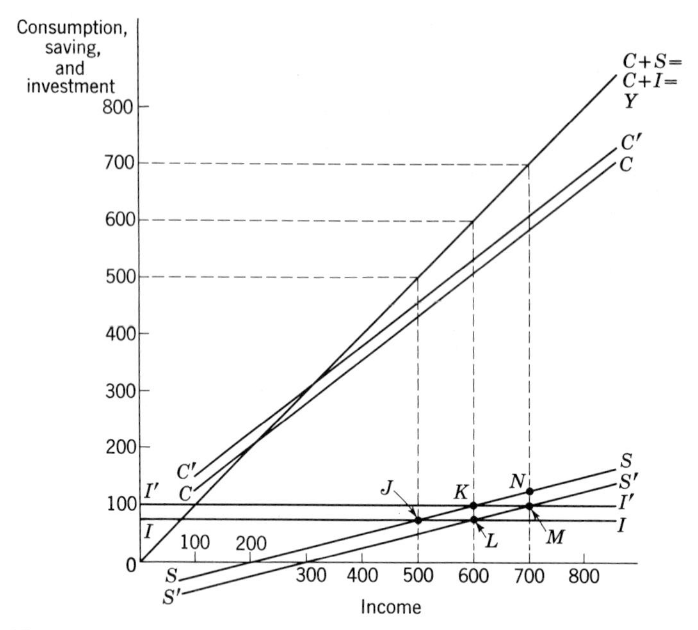

Figure 30-3. The determination of national income.

If investment were to rise to 100 ($I'I'$), income would rise to 600, as shown by the new equality of saving (SS) and investment ($I'I'$) at point K. This rise in investment of 25 (from 75 to 100) raised income by 100 (from 500 to 600), a fourfold increase. This is the multiplier effect discussed in Chapter 27.

Mathematically the multiplier is determined by the formula

$$k = \frac{1}{1 - C_m} = \frac{1}{S_m}$$

where k = multiplier
C_m = marginal propensity to consume
S_m = marginal propensity to save

In our diagram the consumption function shows a marginal propensity to consume of .75, and the multiplier therefore is

$$k = \frac{1}{1 - .75} = \frac{1}{.25} = 4$$

What this means basically is that an increase in investment ($I > S$ *ex ante*) would push up income until saving rose to the new level of investment ($I = S$ *ex post*). A marginal propensity to save of .25 means that one-quarter of any increase in income is saved. Therefore income must be raised by four times the new investment in order to lift saving (which rises one-quarter as fast as income) to the new investment level.

A similar increase in income would occur if consumption were to rise (saving to fall) by an equivalent amount. This means an increase in the average propensity to consume. Thus a rise from CC to $C'C'$ would mean a fall from SS to $S'S'$, which in turn would produce an income of 600 with an investment of 75 (intersection L) or 700 with an investment of 100 (intersection M).

The basic difficulty with this analysis lies in the fact that it ignores the effect of interest rates on investment. It assumes that investment remains fixed regardless of interest (and indeed of income). This analysis therefore cannot tell us what income will be *until* we know what interest rates are. The difficulty is similar to that of our analysis of interest rate determination. It appears that income is determined by the equality of saving and investment, *given the interest rate,* and that the interest rate is determined by the equality of saving and investment (or of the money supply and liquidity preference), *given the income level.* We need, therefore, to put these two concepts together.

The Saving-Investment Function. In Figure 30-4*a* the three saving curves S_{y_5}, S_{y_6}, and S_{y_7} show the amount of saving that would occur at three levels of income Y_5, Y_6, and Y_7. These curves assume (as do the saving curves of

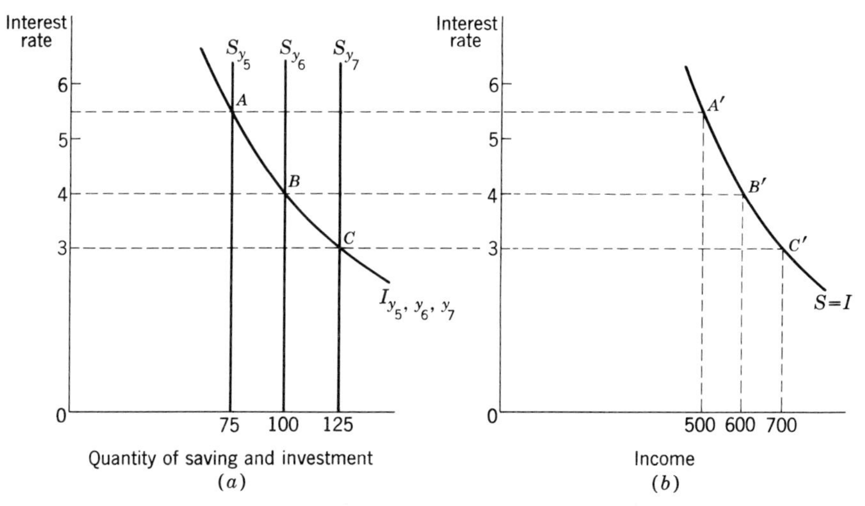

Figure 30-4. Derivation of the S=*I* curve (saving assumed to be interest-inelastic, and investment assumed to be income-inelastic).

Figures 29-2 and 30-1) that saving does not respond to changes in interest: the S curves are perfectly vertical, or interest-inelastic.[7] The diagram shows that if income is Y_5 (let's call it $500 billion, or 500 for short), saving will be 75; if income is Y_6 (600), saving will be 100; and if income is Y_7 (700), saving will be 125. These curves are, in fact, merely an extension into the interest rate dimension of the points J, K, and N on the SS curve of Figure

[7] We will examine later what happens if saving is interest-elastic.

30-3. Conversely they are an extension into the income dimension of the *S* curve of Figure 30-1.

The investment curve is identical to the *I* curve of Figure 30-1. It is labeled $I_{y_5 y_6 y_7}$ on the assumption that investment does not depend on the level of income. It is the same regardless of whether the income level is 500, 600, or 700. The curve shows, however, that investment does depend on the rate of interest and that it will be 75 (the level of the *II* curve in Figure 30-3) only if the interest rate is 5½ per cent. At this rate saving and investment are equal (point *A*, which is equivalent to point *J* on Figure 30-3) at an income of 500. If the interest rate falls to 4 per cent, investment will increase to 100, and only at an income of 600 will saving and investment be equal (point *B*, equivalent to point *K* on Figure 30-3).

Figure 30-4*b* summarizes the information of Figure 30-4*a* by eliminating the saving-investment dimension (since we can't show three dimensions adequately on paper) and substituting income on the horizontal axis. The *S=I* curve plots all points from Figure 30-4*a* for which there is an equilibrium of saving and investment. Point *A′* tells us that saving and investment will be equal[8] if the interest rate is 5½ per cent and income is 500, which is essentially what point *A* had already said. Point *B′* says that saving equals investment also at an interest rate of 4 per cent and an income of 600, as does point *B*. And so for points *C* and *C′*.

The *S=I* curve, in other words, shows every possible combination of interest rate and income at which saving and investment will be equal. Since *ex post* saving and investment *must* be equal, equilibrium must lie somewhere along the *S=I* line. But where? We don't have enough information yet to say.

Slope of the S=I Curve. Before we look for the necessary additional information, two comments are in order. First, under the assumptions so far used, the *S=I* curve must slope downward to the right; that is, all other things remaining the same, the level of income is inversely related to the interest rate. The lower the interest rate, the higher the income. The rationale of this is that only at a low rate of interest will sufficient investment be forthcoming to create a large income.

Elasticities of Saving and Investment. Second, we have used two important assumptions that may be contrary to fact: (1) that saving is interest-inelastic and (2) that investment is income-inelastic. While these assumptions may be approximately correct in some cases, they are not necessarily so. Our discussion of loanable funds indicated that some people may well save more (or possibly less) at higher interest rates. Similarly the acceleration principle says that *rising* income will raise investment, and while this is not quite the same thing as saying that *high* income will call forth high investment, nevertheless there is considerable justification for suspecting that the latter statement is

[8] It doesn't tell us *how much* saving and investment will be; to determine this we would have to go back to Fig. 30-4*a*.

also true. If we relax these two assumptions, however, we need alter only the shape of our curves, not their nature.

In Figure 30-5 the saving curves are slanted upward, showing that at any of the three levels of income Y_5, Y_6, or Y_7, a higher interest rate will call forth a larger volume of saving. Similarly there are now three investment curves,

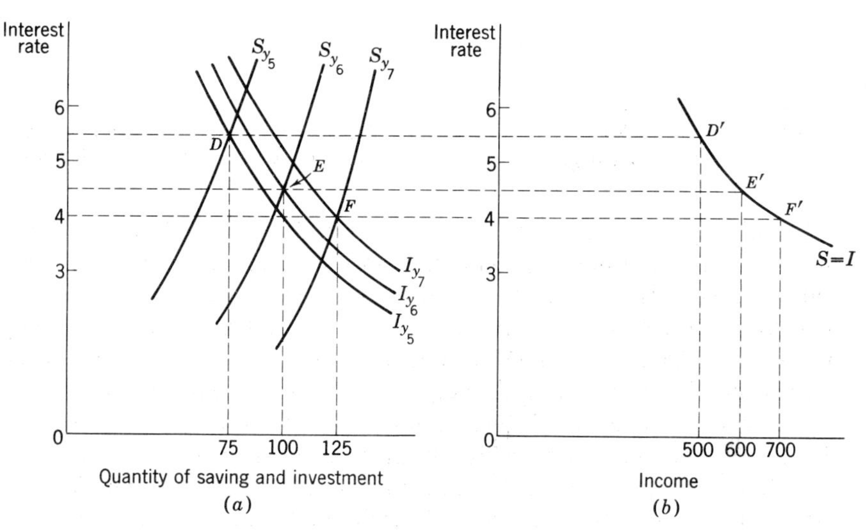

Figure 30-5. Derivation of the S=*I* curve (saving assumed to be interest-elastic, and investment assumed to be income-elastic).

each representing a different level of income. At any interest rate (4 per cent, for instance) investment is greater at income 700 than at income 600, where in turn it is greater than at income 500. Points D', E', and F' are derived exactly as in Figure 30-4 by plotting the combinations of income and interest rate for which saving and investment are equal. Note, however, that S_{y_5} must be equated with I_{y_5} (at point D) and not with I_{y_6} or I_{y_7}, which represent entirely different situations. Similarly S_{y_6} must equal I_{y_6} (point E), and so on.

The resultant $S=I$ curve is flatter (more elastic) than the one in Figure 30-4, but otherwise similar. It is flatter primarily because we are adding the accelerator effect (higher income producing larger investment) to the original multiplier effect. Hence a given fall in interest rates will produce a larger rise in income than would be true of the earlier figure.

But we have still not determined *where* along the $S=I$ line equilibrium will lie.

The Liquidity-Money Function. We can solve this problem by adding two more variables to our analysis: money and liquidity preference. In Figure 29-7 (reproduced here as Figure 30-6) we showed liquidity preference as a function of the interest rate, while the money supply was assumed to be fixed because it was institutionally determined. The level of income was assumed constant.

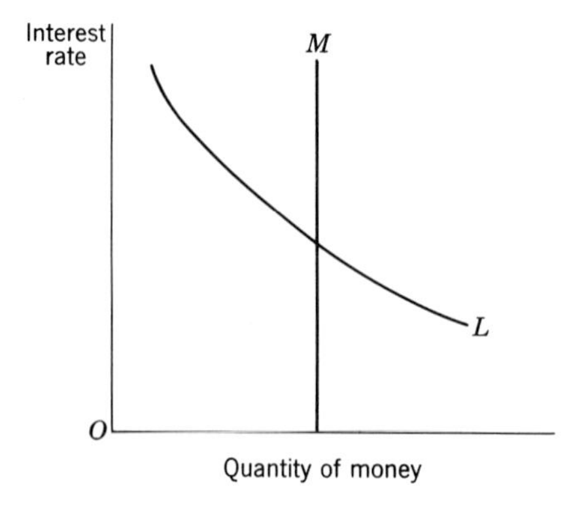

Figure 30-6. Liquidity preference theory of interest rate determination.

Liquidity preference, however, depends on the income level, particularly with regard to the transactions motive. If income rises, more goods are bought, and more cash is needed to buy them with. Figure 30-7*a* shows liquidity preference for each of three incomes as L_{y_5}, L_{y_6}, and L_{y_7}. The money supply, on the other hand, is assumed to remain constant, not only with respect to interest but also with respect to income. It is a vertical line at 150.

At higher incomes people try to hold more money (liquidity preference rises), but since they can't hold any more than there is, the only effect of their desire for larger cash balances is to push the interest rate up. As income rises from 500 to 600, for instance, liquidity preference also rises from L_{y_5} to L_{y_6}. People wish to hold more cash and try to get it by offering securities for sale. But as long as the money supply remains fixed, the larger offerings of securities merely reduce security prices, which is an increase in interest yield (see Chapter 4). Interest rates rise, therefore, from 3 to 4 per cent.

Figure 30-7*b* shows the same information with the quantity-of-money

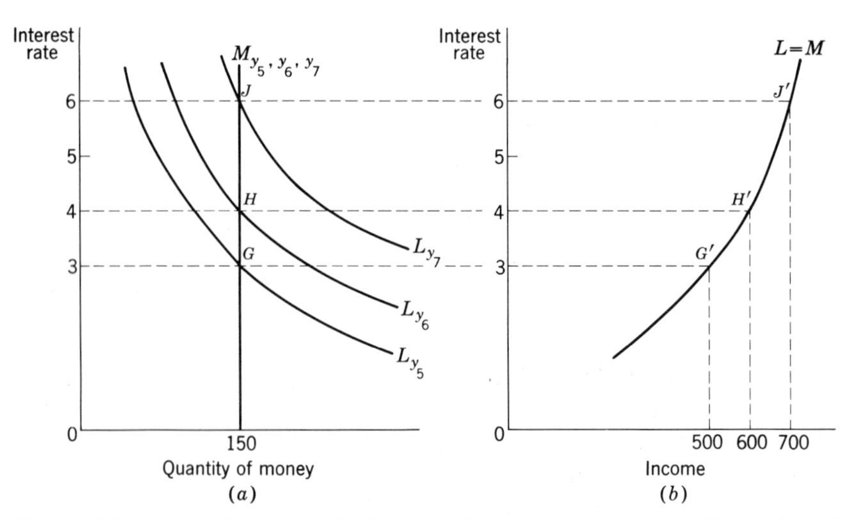

Figure 30-7. Derivation of the L=M curve (money assumed to be interest- and income-inelastic).

dimension removed and replaced by an income dimension. The points of equilibrium of Figure 30-7*a* are plotted as the $L=M$ curve. Point G' shows that the quantity of money and liquidity preference will be in equilibrium at an interest rate of 3 per cent and an income of 500 ($L_{y_5} = M_{y_5}$). The upward slope of the curve shows that higher income, by lifting liquidity preference, tends to raise interest rates.

Elasticity of Money. This diagram assumes that the quantity of money remains unchanged regardless of the rate of interest and regardless of the level of income. The first point may be approximately true. Banks no doubt would like to increase loans at higher interest rates, but a period of rising rates is likely to be one of tight money in which the monetary authorities are deliberately restricting monetary expansion. The second point, however, is contrary to both logic and statistics. As income rises (remember that we are here talking about *real* income, assuming prices constant), the greater volume of business to be done requires more money to finance it, businessmen will attempt to borrow more from the banks, and there is no reason under these circumstances why the monetary authorities should prevent an expansion. One of the original purposes of the Federal Reserve was to make possible the expansion of the currency to meet the legitimate needs of expanding trade. It is certainly true that rising output and a rising money supply have gone together historically.

Figure 30-8*a* shows this. If 125 dollars are needed for a national income of 500, then 150 dollars are required for an income of 600, and 175 dollars for an income of 700.[9] The equilibrium positions of the money supply and liquidity preference are then P', Q', and R' (Figure 30-8*b*), and the $L=M$ curve is similar to that of Figure 30-7*b* except that it is flatter, that is, more elastic.

This greater elasticity is due to the fact that at higher incomes part of the increased liquidity preference is satisfied by the larger money supply, and the upward pressure on interest rates is thereby reduced.

Equilibrium of the $S=I$ and $L=M$ Functions. We have now developed two composite functions, both of which are dependent on interest rates and income. The $S=I$ function shows that for each level of income there is only one interest rate that will produce the necessary equality of saving and investment. The

[9] This increase in the supply of money is perfectly consistent with price stability if the velocity of money remains constant, in this case at 4. In terms of the equation of exchange, at income level 500 the price level would be $\frac{125(M) \times 4(V)}{500(T)} = 1(P)$. At 600 it would be $\frac{150 \times 4}{600} = 1$. And at 700, $\frac{175 \times 4}{700} = 1$. Under these circumstances, since people wanted to hold an unvarying proportion of their (rising) incomes in cash, the liquidity preference schedule would move to the right exactly as fast as the money supply (which in this example is moving exactly as fast—proportionately—as income). This means that L_{y_6} would intersect M_{y_6} at 3½ per cent rather than at 4 per cent, and L_{y_7} would intersect M_{y_7} also at 3½ per cent. In that case the $L=M$ curve would be perfectly horizontal, and there would be no upward pressure on the interest rate.

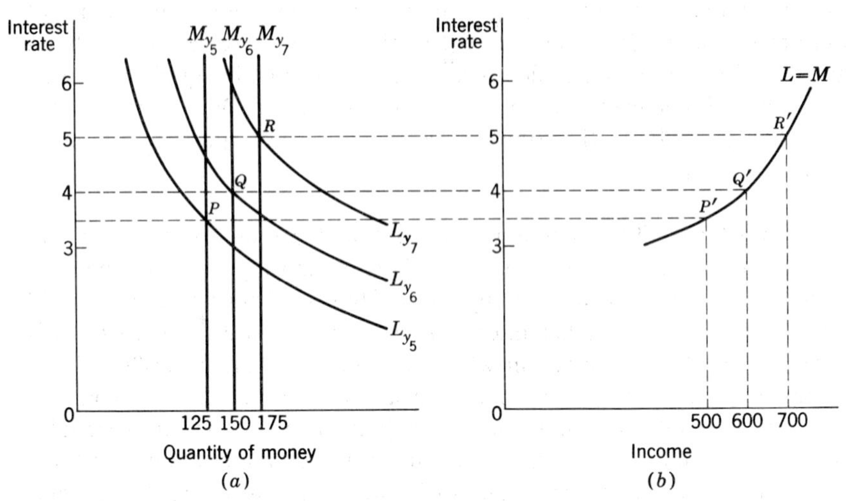

Figure 30-8. Derivation of the $L=M$ curve (money assumed to be interest- and income-elastic).

$L=M$ function shows that for each level of income there is similarly only one interest rate that will produce the necessary equality of liquidity preference and the money supply. If we put these two functions together, we find that there is only one possible combination of interest rate and income that is consistent with the equality of saving and investment and simultaneously consistent with the equality of the money supply and the public's desire to hold cash.

This is shown in Figure 30-9*b*, which merely brings together the $S=I$ and $L=M$ curves already presented in Figures 30-4*b* and 30-7*b*. Figures 30-9*a* and 30-9*c* similarly show reproductions of the underlying functions of Figures 30-4*a* and 30-7*a*, from which the $S=I$ and $L=M$ functions are derived.[10] Given these functions, the interest rate must be 4 per cent, and income will be 600 (Figure 30-9*b*). Saving and investment will be 100 (Figure 30-9*a*), and the public will hold the total stock of money in the amount of 150 dollars (Figure 30-9*c*).

This is the only possible equilibrium under the given conditions. It shows that the complete solution to the problem of interest rate determination (and simultaneously of income determination) depends on four independent variables:

1. The consumption function, which determines the saving schedule
2. The marginal efficiency of capital, which is the investment schedule

[10] We have used here the first (and simplest) forms of the two functions, partly because these are the ones most commonly referred to in economic literature. Using the more complex functions of Figs. 30-5*b* and 30-8*b* would produce no change in the fundamental nature of the graph but would permit a slightly more sophisticated interpretation.

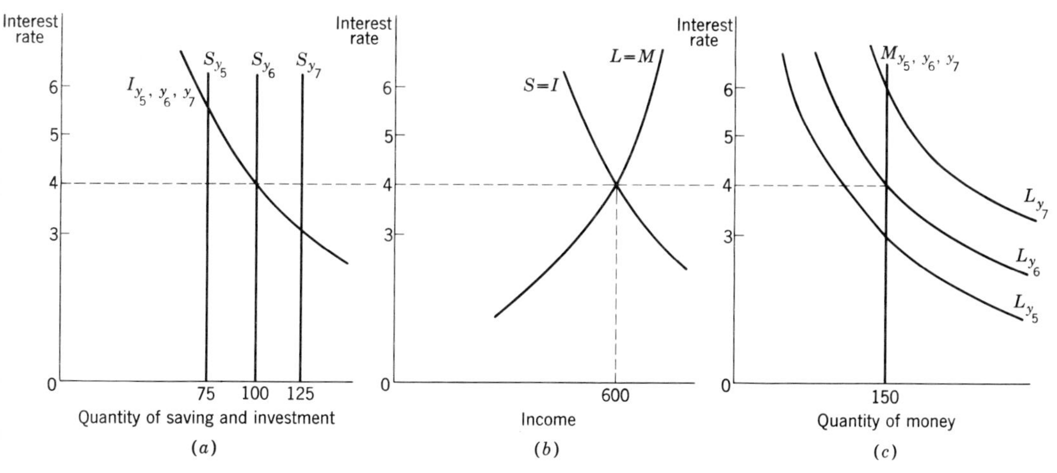

Figure 30-9. Income and interest rate determined by equilibrium of the $S=I$ and $L=M$ curves.

3. Liquidity preference
4. The money supply

If there is any change in any one of these four variables, the equilibrium will also shift, with consequent changes in both interest rates and income:

1. An increase in the desire to save moves the *S* curves to the right (that is, people will save a larger amount at every interest rate as well as at every income level). This will move the $S=I$ curve to the *left* and will lower both the interest rate and income (Figure 30-10).
2. An increase in the marginal efficiency of capital moves the *I* curve to the

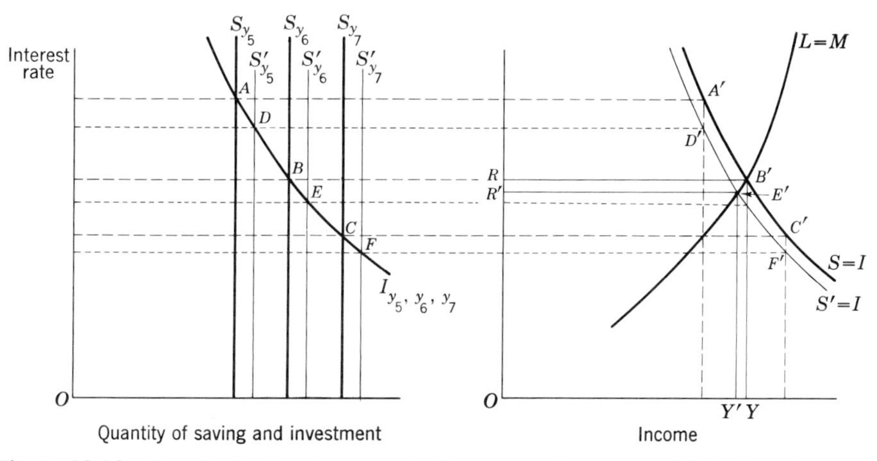

Figure 30-10. The effect of an increase in the propensity to save (S') is to reduce both interest rates (R') and income (Y').

right (businessmen decide to invest more at every interest rate as well as at every income level). This will move the $S=I$ curve to the *right* and will raise both the interest rate and income (Figure 30-11).

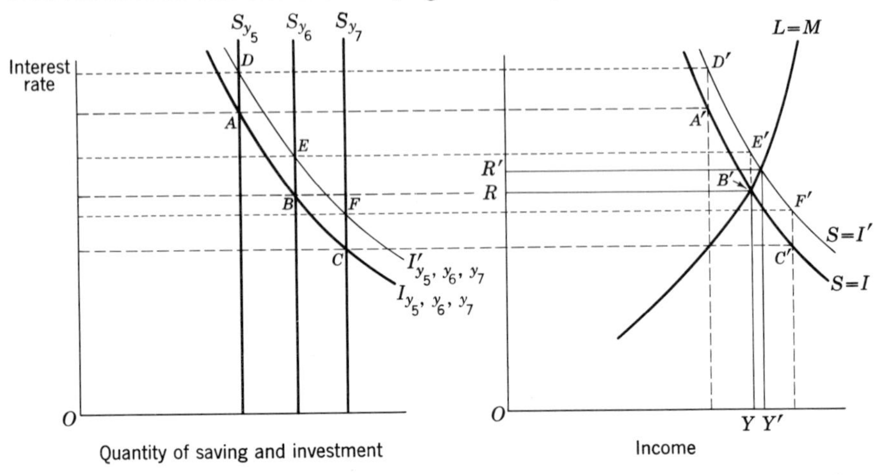

Figure 30-11. The effect of an increase in the marginal efficiency of capital (I') is to raise both interest rates (R') and income (Y').

3. An increase in liquidity preference moves the L curves to the right (people desire to hold more cash at every interest rate and at every income level). This will move the $L=M$ curve to the *left* and will raise interest rates at the same time that it lowers income (Figure 30-12).

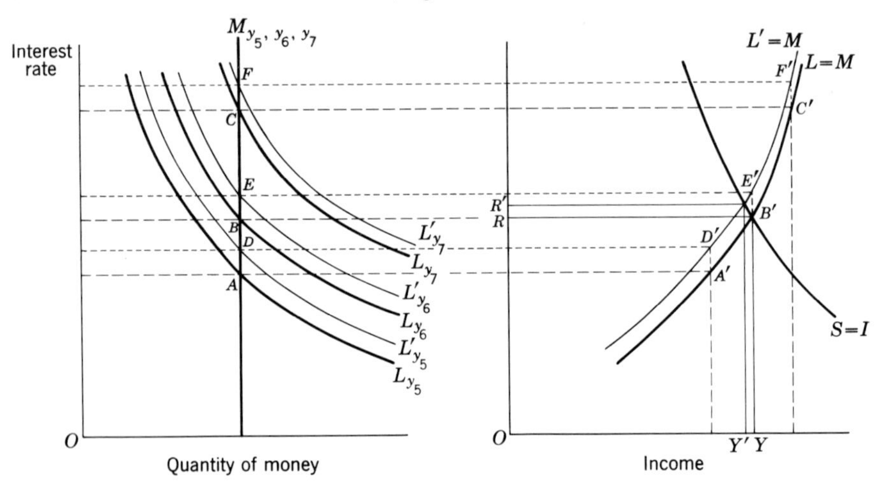

Figure 30-12. The effect of an increase in liquidity preference (L') is to raise interest rates (R') and to lower income (Y').

4. An increase in the money supply moves the M curve to the right. This will move the $L=M$ curve also to the *right* and will lower interest rates at the same time that it raises income (Figure 30-13).

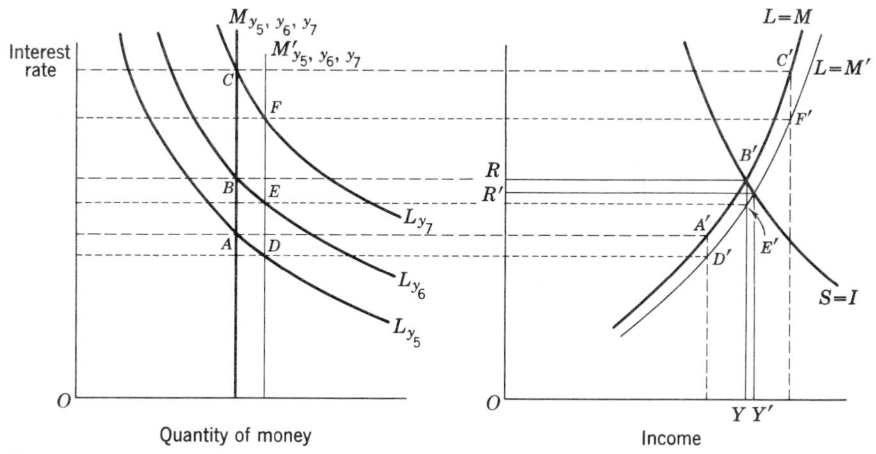

Figure 30-13. The effect of an increase in the money supply (M') is to lower interest rates (R') and to raise income (Y').

Although we have used examples of increases in each of the variables in the above discussion, analysis of decreases would follow exactly the same path but in the opposite direction in each case.

Suppose two of the variables change at the same time. What will happen can be only partly predicted, for part of the changes will offset each other. If the money supply and investment rise simultaneously, for instance, income will necessarily rise, since either one of these alone would tend to increase it. Interest rates, however, will be subject to opposing forces—the increased money supply pushing down, and higher investment pushing up. As a result the interest rate may remain the same, rise, or fall. But it cannot fall *as far* as if the money supply increased alone, nor can it rise as far as if investment increased alone.

Other combinations can be examined in much the same way.

Conclusion. Much of the analysis indicated by the equilibrium of $S=I$ and $L=M$ has already been pointed out in terms of other approaches, and we will not pursue it further here. But this graphical method serves the important purpose of tying together a number of aspects of both monetary and income theory that without it may appear to be disconnected or even contradictory.

Real Income and Monetary Income

The preceding analysis assumed prices to be constant. We were talking of real income, not money income, and so we ignored any repercussions caused by changes in price levels. To continue this type of analysis by splitting national income into its components of prices and output would require adding a fourth dimension to our diagrams, and this is beyond our power at this level. The problem has, however, already been discussed in terms of the equation of exchange ($Y = P_y T_y = MV_y$), and it is possible to approach it from this angle by making a fresh start.

Since we are interested in prices and quantities of goods produced, we can use ordinary microeconomic diagrams of the kind used to show how the price and output of shoes are determined, but generalized to include the output of all goods simultaneously. In Figure 30-14, therefore, the horizontal axis meas-

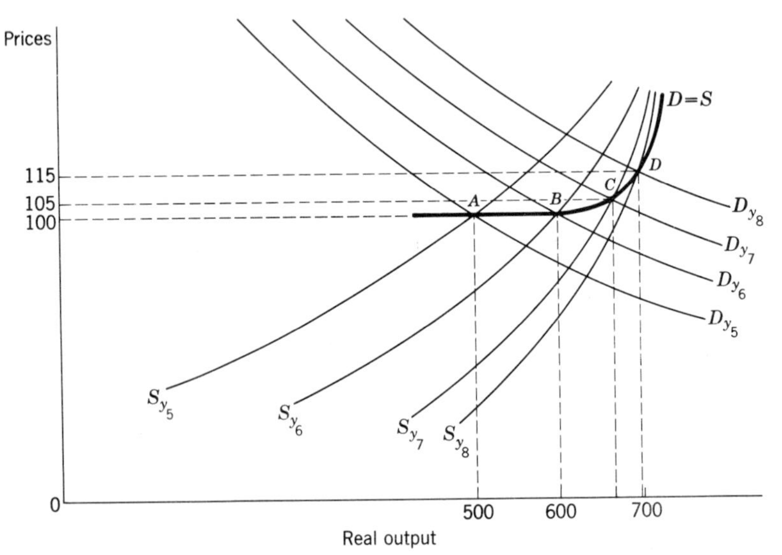

Figure 30-14. As real output rises toward capacity, there is a tendency for the price level to rise.

ures total output of the economy (similar to the quantity of shoes produced but multiplied by the total number of products), and the vertical axis is the price level (as a weighted average of all prices, including the price of shoes).

If income is Y_5, the aggregate supply schedule (S_{y_5}) is in equilibrium with the aggregate demand schedule (D_{y_5}) at a real output of 500 and a price level of 100 (point A). This can be interpreted as meaning that 500 units of output are produced and sold at $1 each, yielding a national income of $500 ($Y_5$).

As the economy expands to Y_6, the physical production schedule is pushed to S_{y_6}. This expansion in output is accompanied by an increase in employment and payrolls. With more money in their pockets, consumers are willing to spend more, and demand rises to D_{y_6}.[11] As long as supply and demand rise

[11] When talking about the case of shoes, we can draw the demand without any reference to the supply, and vice versa. But *aggregate* supply and demand curves are not independent in this sense, for the aggregate supply determines how much income will be available to consumers, and this in turn determines aggregate demand. The demand and supply curves for each income level must therefore be drawn simultaneously. The situation here is similar to that in, say, Fig. 30-5; the S_6 curve is in equilibrium with only the D_6 curve and not with the D_5 and D_7 curves, which refer to different levels of income and hence to different S curves.

by equal amounts, there will be no change in the price level. The new output of 600 units will continue to be sold at $1 each (point *B*), and monetary income will now be $600.

As production continues to increase, however, it becomes more and more difficult to push it further. Plant utilization approaches capacity; certain labor skills become scarce; overtime or second-shift work requires additional pay without a proportionate increase in output; and the physical supply curve therefore moves more slowly than the increase in demand. The result is a rise in prices.

The diagram indicates, for instance, that the effort needed to raise real output to 667 (point *C*) presses prices upward to 105. This means that 667 units are sold at $1.05 each, for a total monetary income of $700.[12] Further expansion pushes the economy even closer to full capacity (full employment), and real output rises even more slowly. As production edges up slightly to 696, prices rise to 115, yielding a monetary income of $800 (696 times $1.15).

Further small increases in output are achieved only at the cost of substantial inflation, as indicated by the *D*=*S* curve, which traces the possible equilibrium combinations of real output and prices shown by the intersections of the demand and supply curves at increasing income levels. At full employment the *D*=*S* curve should (at least theoretically) become perfectly vertical.

One of the assumptions of this analysis is that the time period is too short to introduce substantial changes in techniques. We are not trying to assert that any rise in real income *necessarily* raises prices (even in our example prices did not rise as real income increased from 500 to 600). Prices will rise only as output pushes against the limits of the country's physical capacity, and in the long run technological progress expands those limits. Our *D*=*S* curve is, in other words, a short-run curve conforming to the conditions of a business cycle upswing, not a long-run trend.

Nor is the curve likely to be the same for any two upswings. Different bottlenecks appear at different times. External conditions (wars, government controls, fads, crop conditions, and so on) as well as a host of institutional factors have their effect. Both the condition of physical plant and the speed with which it is increasing are important. If the upswing is gradual, if technology keeps pace with it, if government policy is helpful and well timed, and if a little bit of luck is thrown in, then the *ABCD* curve may in fact become horizontal, and the economy will grow at a steady pace forever. This, of course, has never happened, but there is no theoretical reason why it could not.

On the other hand, returning to the upward-sloping curve of Figure 30-14, there is some question as to whether it is reversible. If real output has reached 696 at the top of a boom and then declines, will the price level also decline? As output falls to 667, will prices drop to 105? The answer to this question is

[12] Since monetary income is real output multiplied by prices, it can be shown in Fig. 30-14 by the rectangle subtended to the axes by the intersection of the appropriate supply and demand curves, in this case S_{y_7} and D_{y_7}, which intersect at point *C*.

part of the broader problem of whether prices do in fact respond smoothly (on either the upswing or the downswing) to the ordinary forces of the marketplace, and this larger question needs to be examined first.

Institutional Effects on Prices

The institutional factors that affect prices lie outside the realm of monetary theory strictly speaking, but since both monetary theory and price theory concern themselves with prices, they cannot ignore each other. We will deal briefly, therefore, with three important nonmonetary factors affecting prices: demand conditions for particular products, cost conditions, and the institutional structure of the industry.

Demand. An increase in money—or more specifically an increase in monetary income (MV_y)—will increase aggregate demand for goods in general, but it will certainly not increase the demand for every product equally. The greatest effect is likely to be felt in luxury goods that most people were simply unable to afford previously. The demand for staple foods, such as bread, may well be unaltered. And it is even possible that the demand for some products, such as margarine, may fall as people find themselves in a position to afford more expensive substitutes. The greater the rise in demand, the greater the upward pressure on the price of the particular product affected. But even though the general price level is rising, some prices may fall.

Costs. On the supply side the number of possible differences is even larger. An industry in which there is substantial unused capacity can expand even in the short run with relatively little increase in unit costs. In fact by spreading its overhead over a larger output, it may find its total unit costs falling. Only when it runs into bottlenecks—shortages of supplies or labor, overtime payments, or pressures against the capacity of its machines—will costs tend to rise, and these bottlenecks will appear at different stages for different firms.

In the longer run, expansion of an industry requires additional plant and equipment, and here again the effect on costs depends on the individual situation. In many industries plant can be duplicated and output expanded without any significant effect on unit costs at all. These are industries of constant cost.

In other industries, particularly those which are relatively new and have not yet grown to the point where they can take maximum advantage of specialization and mechanization, increased size will yield substantial economies of scale, and costs will fall. These are industries of decreasing cost.

But all industries sooner or later run up against the pressure of the law of diminishing marginal productivity. The economies of scale disappear: management is spread too thin, and bureaucracy cuts into efficiency; raw materials become increasingly scarce; good workers are hard to find and expensive; and so on. The more closely the economy approaches full employment, the more strongly each firm feels this pinch of higher costs. But it will affect each differently and at a different phase of the expansion process.

Even firms that are not expanding at all will find their costs rising if other firms are bidding aggressively for supplies or for workers, pushing up raw material prices and wage rates.

Price Rigidity. Not only do costs respond in different ways to a general upward movement of the economy, but also there is no certainty that the price of any particular product will move at the same speed as its costs nor that it will respond rapidly to changes in demand.

Prices tend to be fairly stable in most industries in the United States, at least for short periods. They resist upward pressures for a time and then may move by fairly large jumps. When the economy is contracting, there are even greater pressures to resist downward movements of prices. The result is a situation referred to as *sticky prices, administered prices,* or *price rigidity.* It arises out of the fact that in an economy in which pure competition has almost disappeared the prices paid for most products are not determined by the market but are set by the seller.

Suppose the price of light bulbs is set at 15 cents each, as shown by curve S in Figure 30-15. The demand (D) then determines how many will be sold

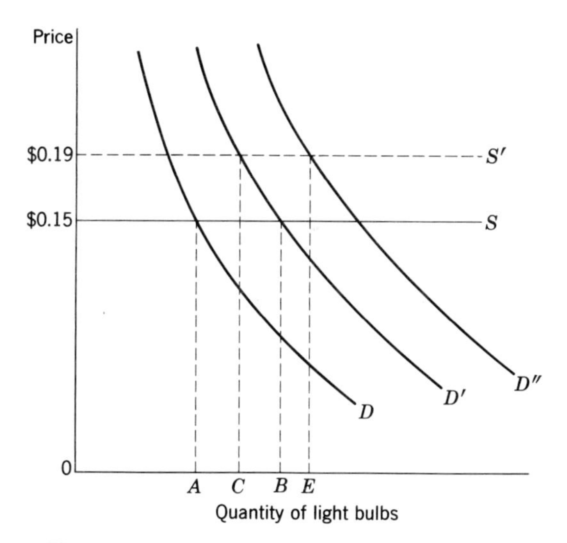

Figure 30-15. Increases in demand for light bulbs may change the price by uneven jumps.

(OA), but it doesn't determine the price. As demand increases to D', more light bulbs (OB) will be sold at the same price. This situation may continue for a while, perhaps for years, until the bulb manufacturer feels that upward pressures on price (whether from the demand or the cost side) are strong enough to justify an increase. Then the price may jump to 19 cents, which will restrict sales somewhat (OC). If demand continues to increase (D''), so will sales (OE), until again the accumulated pressures induce producers to push the price up again to some higher figure. If producers are maintaining a price of 19 cents in spite of the high demand D'', a drop of demand to D' will undoubtedly not change the price, and if demand falls further to D, the price of 19 cents may still be maintained in the hope that the reduction in demand will prove temporary.

Inertia. Price rigidity may arise from a number of underlying causes, many of which boil down to the fact that businessmen may prefer not to rock the boat. Sellers feel that established prices give an aura of respectability and strength to the consumer's image of their product, while price changes create confusion in the minds of purchasers. Changes require printing new price lists, new labels, and new catalogs; changing advertising copy and billing procedures; and so on. Price changes may also upset established distribution procedures. On the downswing lower prices may cause "chaotic conditions" in the market—which means upsetting competitors, provoking retaliation, and perhaps starting a price war. Especially when costs change by relatively small amounts, the avoidance of confusion is a strong argument in favor of standing pat.

Another reason why costs may change slowly is the long-run nature of many contracts. Leases are frequently long-term, interest on bonds already issued is fixed, depreciation is based on past acquisitions rather than current replacement cost, raw materials may be purchased on long-term contract, and wages when subject to union negotiation are frequently fixed for a year or longer. Because of union strength, wage rates go up but seldom go down, thus putting labor costs "on a ratchet." This is one of the important reasons why price increases in prosperity are relatively unlikely to be reversed in depression.

Governmental Effects on Prices. The government also may have a significant influence on prices, usually but not always in the direction of stability. Price controls, instituted in this country only during wars, are the most direct restrictions.

More recently the government has attempted to put the damper on price increases by its price and wage guideposts. Although the guideposts have only the force of moral suasion, they have been quite effective in certain key industries. The guideposts suggest that wage increases should be limited to the *average* increase in productivity *for the economy as a whole.* In any industry where productivity increases faster than the national average, the additional efficiency of the industry should be used to benefit consumers through *reduced prices.* Industries with less than average increases in productivity could then legitimately raise prices without the average price index rising. Although there have been few examples of falling prices attributed to the guideposts, it is generally thought that they have restrained both price and wage increases to some extent.

In particular instances the government has put strong pressure directly on a particular industry (steel in 1962; banks in 1964; aluminum in 1965) to rescind price increases. In these three cases in particular the move was successful.

In the area of public utilities the government regulatory agencies, both Federal and state, set prices that can be changed only by action of the agency. While the determination of fair prices must necessarily consider costs, nevertheless the final word lies with the government, and public policy undoubtedly plays a prominent role in the decision. Certainly changes are not made frequently.

With regard to wages the government sets a floor for the majority of workers in the form of the minimum wage of the Fair Labor Standards Act as amended. This in turn is likely to influence prices.

The farm subsidy program in its many and changing forms has a direct effect on the prices of farm products.

Even taxes have a significant bearing on the general price level. Business taxes are a cost of operation, a cost that is reflected more or less directly in prices. And it is interesting to note that personal taxes are now included in the computation of the consumer price index as an indication of the "purchase price" of government services.

Prices and the Equation of Exchange

With so many institutional factors involved, it is relatively easy to see that the aggregate relationships implied in the quantity theory or the multiplier analysis are not nearly as simple as the mathematical equations suggest. Even the equation of exchange and the circuit flow, truisms though they are, need to be interpreted in a fairly sophisticated way, recognizing not only changes in aggregates, but also changes among the constituents of those aggregates.

Nevertheless it is broadly true that these overall concepts do illuminate the fundamental forces at work in the economy. The quantity theory contains an important grain of truth: *in the short run and under conditions of reasonably full employment* the pressure of a sizable increase in the money supply is likely to be felt as a significant upward push on prices. Although this pressure *may* be dissipated through reduced velocity or increased transactions, it would take strong counterpressures to prevent prices from rising *approximately* in proportion to the rise in the money supply. If the economy is substantially below full employment, however (as at point A in Figure 30-14), a rise in the money supply may be part of a general upward movement of production (and hence of T) which will raise income without raising prices (point B in the same figure). Similarly as the economy grows over the long run, both production and the money supply will rise without there necessarily being any rise in prices.

Prices and the Circuit Flow

In terms of the circuit flow it may be useful to trace briefly the different effects that new money creation may have on income and its components as a result of the different ways in which the new money is injected into the economy.

If businessmen obtain bank loans to expand production with present relatively unused capacity, an increase in output (supply) will follow very quickly upon the rise in the money supply, and prices are not likely to rise. If loans are obtained for the purchase of machinery or for plant construction, the production lag is longer and the pressure on prices correspondingly greater. If banks are lending primarily to consumers, supply is not immediately affected at all, and the rise in demand puts even stronger pressure on prices, although even in this case sticky prices probably will not rise at once, as Figure 30-15 suggests.

If the government is borrowing for purposes of financing a deficit, the effect is an increase in demand (for schools or typewriters or clerks), and the initial price pressure is similar to that for consumer borrowing, although the particular products involved will be different. If the government uses the money for unemployment compensation, the increase in demand is likely to be concentrated on basic necessities such as food and clothing.

Any increase in income is likely to affect prices differently, depending on whose income is rising and what these people want to do with their money. As tastes cannot be assumed to be constant, the emphasis will shift over time. If people hoard their money, no upward pressure will be felt at all. If they consume all of it, not only is the direct effect on prices greater, but by providing no savings to finance investment they either choke off an expansion in productive capacity for lack of funds or force all such expansion to be financed by further new money creation and continued inflation. Thus, although a marginal propensity to consume of 100 per cent mathematically produces a multiplier of infinity, the consequent rise in prices *will* be greater and the increase in real output *may* be less than with a lower propensity to consume.

Conclusion. The above discussion of various possible effects on both prices and production brought about by changes in income or the money supply is no more than a cursory list. Almost every sentence could be expanded into a complete chapter, but for this we obviously have no space here. You may wish to explore further a number of the possibilities—theoretically, statistically, or historically. The mere list itself indicates how complex monetary theory is and in how many ways it overlaps ordinary microeconomic theory as well as the macroeconomic theory with which it is usually associated.

But to return to the question concerning the reversibility of the *ABCD* curve of Figure 30-14. The discussion of institutional factors has been couched in terms of a *rise* in money and income, indicating that prices are likely to respond in many cases slowly and jerkily to upward pressures. On the downswing the resistance is likely to be even stronger, for reasons already partly hinted at. Nobody likes to see his income falling, and lower prices signify falling income to the businessman just as lower wages signify falling income to the worker. Where unions are able to exert strong pressure against downward revision of wages and where employers have some control over administered prices, each price rise seems to establish a new floor from which prices may rise further but below which they drop only rarely. The result is that (with some exceptions) prices tend to rise in prosperity and remain stationary (or perhaps even continue to rise, but more slowly) in recession, producing what is commonly called the *ratchet effect*. This is one of the main reasons for concern over the possibility of built-in inflation. The nature of such concern as well as the policy actions designed to deal with it and with other monetary problems are the subject matter of Part Eight.

Questions for Thought and Discussion

1. How can consumption exceed income, as shown in Figure 30-2 for incomes below 200?
2. In Figure 30-2 why does the height of the saving line always equal the distance between consumption and the 45° line?
3. If saving always equals investment, how can the saving line in Figure 30-3 differ from the investment line?
4. From your experience, do you believe that people save more at higher levels of income or not? Is there any statistical evidence to solve this question?
5. Why would recovery from depression be easier and faster if investment and the money supply were both income-elastic?
6. Why should people wish to hold more money at higher income levels?
7. Starting from the equilibrium of Figure 30-9, what would happen to interest rates and to income if:

a. The money supply increased?
b. Interest rates fell? (Could interest rates fall as an independent causal factor?)
c. A new invention reduced the cost of production?
d. Consumers decided to buy more goods?
e. People thought prices were going to fall?
f. The marginal efficiency of capital and liquidity preference rose simultaneously?

8. If it is difficult to expand production rapidly without running into increasing costs, why don't prices rise continuously as the economy grows?
9. Would the economy be better off if wages fell on the downswing as much as they rise on the upswing, so that the ratchet effect would be avoided?
10. Doesn't the theory of competitive price say that prices move both up and down in response to the conditions of supply and demand? How then is it possible for prices to be rigid?
11. Would it be better for the government to concentrate on promoting price flexibility rather than contributing to rigidity?
12. Suppose the marginal propensity to consume is 1.2. What will happen to income?

Selected Bibliography

Ackley, Gardner: *Macroeconomic Theory,* The Macmillan Company, New York, 1961.

Bailey, Martin J.: *National Income and the Price Level: A Study in Macrotheory,* McGraw-Hill Book Company, New York, 1962.

Hansen, Alvin H.: *A Guide to Keynes,* McGraw-Hill Book Company, New York, 1953.

Hicks, J. R.: "Mr. Keynes and the 'Classics': A Suggested Interpretation," *Econometrica,* vol. 5, no. 2 (April, 1937), pp. 147–159; reprinted in American Economic Association: *Readings in the Theory of Income Distribution,* McGraw-Hill Book Company, New York, 1946, pp. 461–476.

Keynes, John Maynard: *The General Theory of Employment, Interest and Money,* Harcourt, Brace & World, Inc., New York, 1936.

McKenna, Joseph P.: *Aggregate Economic Analysis,* rev. ed., Holt, Rinehart and Winston, Inc., New York, 1965.

Patinkin, Don: *Money, Interest, and Prices,* 2d ed., Harper & Row, Publishers, Incorporated, New York, 1965.

Vickrey, William S.: *Metastatics and Macroeconomics,* Harcourt, Brace & World, Inc., New York, 1964.

Weintraub, Sidney: *A General Theory of the Price Level, Output and Income Distribution, and Economic Growth,* Chilton Company—Book Division, Philadelphia, 1959.

Part Eight
Monetary
Policy

Chapter 31 Aims of Monetary Policy

Our doubts are traitors,
And make us lose the good we oft might win,
By fearing to attempt.

Measure for Measure
Act I, scene 4, line 77

Money is not neutral. It is a contributing factor to the greatest economic problem the nation has to face: the recurrent cycle of prosperity and depression. It would be going too far to accuse money of being the *cause* of business cycles, but without money business cycles as we know them would be inconceivable. The simple exchange mechanism used in a barter economy could hardly get out of order in the way our highly complex financial machinery does.

Just as business cycles could not exist without money, so they could not exist without the industrial revolution. In an agricultural-handicraft society where every worker owns his own tools and is his own boss, unemployment cannot exist. Droughts or floods may mean starvation for many, but this is not the same type of phenomenon we experience in depression, where the problem is not *inability* to produce (we have the resources, machines, available labor, technical know-how), but the *unwillingness* to produce on the part of those who direct the wheels of industry. Nevertheless, to blame the business cycle on the industrial revolution is like blaming Thomas Edison when an electric bulb burns out.

So with money. It makes depressions possible because it makes possible the tremendous interdependence of industry that is the cause of our high standard of living and because it makes possible the intricate web of financial institutions that direct funds into their most productive channels under most circumstances. But sometimes the monetary system develops hardening of the arteries or high blood pressure. The solution is not to drain all the blood from the system, but to control its circulation.

Nor is money the only guilty party. Part of the blame lies with many other factors: business psychology, misdirected production, changing consumption patterns, misguided governmental policies, acts of God, alterations in technology, shifting population pressures, wars, and innumerable other interrelated causes. The business cycle is a strange and complex phenomenon.

The role of money, therefore, cannot be examined alone, nor can monetary policy by itself solve the problem. We will try in this and the following chapters to concentrate primarily on the monetary aspects of policy, but here as elsewhere in economics we cannot build a fence around our subject and ignore its relations with its neighbors. Precisely because the business cycle is our greatest economic problem, it must be attacked on as many fronts as possible.

What Do We Want? Apparently we aren't satisfied with what we have. The very concept of "monetary policy" suggests a device for altering the present state of things. What's wrong? What do we want monetary policy to do?

Most discussion suggests the desirability of economic stabilization. But stabilization of what? To reply "stabilization of business activity" doesn't help much unless we are clear as to what business activity means. Similarly it doesn't do much good to speak of eliminating the business cycle unless we define the business cycle in terms that can be measured.

Congress wrestled with this problem in the Employment Act of 1946, which is presumably the official statement of the aims of government policy in this field. The act says:

> The Congress hereby declares that it is the continuing policy and responsibility of the Federal Government to use all practicable means consistent with its needs and obligations and other essential considerations of national policy, with the assistance and cooperation of industry, agriculture, labor, and state and local governments, to coordinate and utilize all its plans, functions and resources for the purpose of creating and maintaining, in a manner calculated to foster and promote free competitive enterprise and the general welfare, conditions under which there will be afforded useful employment opportunities, including self-employment, for those able, willing, and seeking to work, and to promote maximum employment, production, and purchasing power.

Shorn of its qualifications this statement says that Congress thinks the goal should be maximum employment, maximum production, and maximum purchasing power. Although the precise meaning of "maximum purchasing power" is obscure, it apparently is related to the price level.

These three areas—employment, production, and prices—just about cover the field of aggregates about which the economy may be concerned. There are others, but they are all directly related to those mentioned. Thus consumption and investment are components of production, as are such subdivisions as steel output, electrical output, freight carloadings, or other industrial activities.

Final sales plus (or minus) changes in inventories also equal production, while national income is the monetary value (prices) of physical output.

Let us therefore consider production, employment, and prices.

Maximum Production

Maximum production seems highly desirable. It means all facilities adequately utilized and the highest possible standard of living.

But hold on a minute. Just what is *maximum* production? Maximum means the most possible, a situation in which *all* resources are employed to the greatest possible extent. In its literal sense maximum production could be achieved only if (to take labor resources as an example) every able-bodied man, woman, and child were employed as long as possible short of deterioration of health. Put more simply, we could certainly increase total output if the workweek were lengthened, if vacations were eliminated, and if students, retired persons, and idle women were put to work.[1]

This is certainly not what we want. As our standard of living rises, we tend to put a higher value on leisure. We want time to enjoy our gains. Part of improved status *is* the increase in leisure, although this is more difficult to measure than the goods portion of our achievements.

Everybody wants a minimum subsistence, and most people want considerably more than that; but at the same time they want other things that money can't buy, and some of these can be had only at some sacrifice of goods.

Production at a physical maximum is not therefore a desirable goal for the economy. As the Employment Act indeed suggests, what we want is maximum production *consistent with our other aspirations*. It might be more reasonable to speak of this as *optimum* production, though the change in terminology doesn't help us one iota in describing the goal in measurably precise terms.

Optimum production may be defined as the greatest output that can reasonably be achieved given the general social and organizational structure of society at the time. One important aspect of that structure in the United States today is our belief in a modified capitalistic system with the greater part of productive activity subject to conditions of a free market, a concept loosely defined as "economic freedom." Part of our belief in this kind of system stems from the feeling that it is more productive than alternative economic structures; part of it is the result of a desire for freedom for its own sake as a philosophical rather than an economic goal. Even if we could raise our output by suppressing freedom, most of us would not consider this desirable.

Another very important ingredient of the social structure is the "normal" workweek. While different individuals may want to work different hours, there is a general tendency to consider the forty-hour week fairly standard at the

[1] Some of these devices might have detrimental effects in the long run. If worked a seventy-two-hour week without vacations, people might become too tired to do as effective a job, technological progress would slow up as education declined, and so on. It is certain, however, that by a judicious increase in man-hours total production *could* be raised in the long run as well as the short.

present time. Coupled with this is the widespread acceptance of the two-week vacation, retirement at age sixty-five, and the undesirability of child labor.

Within this social and institutional structure it would seem that optimum production means the greatest output possible when everyone is working as much as he wants to. This means that optimum production is a function of technology and employment. Given full employment (a term that we will examine shortly), an increase in production can occur only through increased efficiency. When we ask for rising production, therefore, we are assuming that technology is advancing. Technological improvement has been a basic ingredient in our economy in the past, and there is no reason to expect it to stop as long as the economy is operating at a high level.

The problem comes from the other side of the picture. Given the state of technology, optimum production is possible only at full employment. It seems, in fact, that "optimum production" is another way of saying "full employment." If we achieve the latter, we will at least come close to reaching the former.

Full Employment

Full employment should presumably mean that every person who is able and willing to work has a job. For practical purposes, however, this is an impossible ideal in a free and progressive economy, and in terms of a reasonable goal of policy we must set our sights somewhat lower than that.

There are two reasons why there will always be some people unemployed. First is technological unemployment. Progress always means readjustment. New products, new techniques often make old skills obsolete. The automobile destroys the jobs of carriage makers and blacksmiths. The electric refrigerator treads on the toes of the iceman. Automation replaces the machinist. Even if the economy is running at full steam, it takes time for displaced workers to find other jobs. The automobile didn't reduce the number of jobs in the economy. It created new jobs for the factory worker, the filling station operator, and the garage mechanic. The same is true for other innovations. But the period of transition results in temporary unemployment, for the new jobs require new skills and may be in different geographical regions. But if the economy is prosperous, there will be plenty of opportunities beckoning, and it will be only a matter of time until the displaced workers find new jobs.

Since progress is continuous, there will always be some technologically unemployed. As some workers find new openings, others are being displaced. The only way to eliminate this type of unemployment in a free society would be to stop progress.

The second reason why there will always be unemployment is that in a free society one of the basic rights is the right of choice. Some workers will always be quitting because they don't like the job, they don't like the boss, they don't like the color of the washroom walls, or they just like variety. Others are being fired because the boss doesn't like them. In a prosperous economy they will be reabsorbed readily into other jobs. In fact, in boom periods workers may be more prone to quit simply because they know they can find other jobs easily. Even though the period during which any one individual is unemployed may be quite short, there are always new entrants into the pool of unemployed.[2] The only way to eliminate this kind of "voluntary" unemployment would be to revoke the right to quit as well as the right to fire.

Economists recognize the practical impossibility of achieving 100 per cent employment and use the term full employment to mean that everyone able and willing to work is employed *except* those in the groups just described. Unfortunately it is impossible to measure these groups separately, and any working definition of full employment must attempt to estimate them one way or another.

The most logical approach is that of the British, which defines full employment as a situation in which the number of unfilled jobs exceeds the number of unemployed. The assumption is that under these conditions if there were no frictions (both occupational and geographic), the unemployed could all be absorbed in available jobs. The economy is creating enough jobs, at least. The British can make practical use of a definition of this kind because they have statistics of job vacancies as well as of unemployment.

Lacking the former statistics, United States economists must take another approach. Basically this is to estimate the probable magnitude of technological and voluntary unemployment. There is some disagreement as to just what this magnitude is, but most estimates fall in the range of 3 to 5 per cent of the labor force.[3] Under this definition full employment would be a situation in which no more than 3 (or 4 or 5) per cent of the labor force is unemployed. During the war unemployment fell below 2 per cent briefly, and this situation has often been referred to as one of over-full employment. It was caused by the extraordinary pressures of all-out war production. At the close of the war the rate climbed rapidly above 3 per cent, dropped slightly below that level in 1953, but then rose again and remained in excess of 4 per cent until early in 1966. The fact that the rate refused to come down below 5 per cent from 1958 to 1964 particularly worried economists, labor leaders, and government officials.

Because unemployment not only lowers production, but also presents human problems of lowered standards of living, family disorganization, and destruction of morale and self-respect, there is almost unanimous agreement that full employment, as defined above, must be one keystone of economic stabilization.

Hidden Unemployment. Unemployment figures as generally published show only the number of workers totally out of work. They do not show those who

[2] For a statistical analysis of unemployment "turnover" see U.S. Bureau of Labor Statistics, "The Extent and Nature of Frictional Unemployment," Study Paper 6 in U.S. Congress, Joint Economic Committee, *Employment, Growth, and Price Levels* (1959).

[3] The labor force consists of those with jobs plus those unemployed (able to work and looking for jobs).

are working on short shifts. This is a form of partial unemployment often referred to as hidden unemployment. In a depression a drop in the length of the workweek accompanies layoffs. The overall reduction in hours worked is therefore greater than unemployment statistics indicate.

When we are thinking of goals for economic policy, the problem of hidden unemployment is not a major one, for as employment increases, so does the workweek, and in a period of full employment hidden unemployment also tends to disappear.

Stable Prices

Although Congress has never unequivocally listed stable prices as a goal of economic policy,[4] there is almost universal agreement that this is a second highly desirable objective. Wild gyrations of prices are highly upsetting to the economy. Not only do they produce windfall profits and losses, but they also introduce uncertainties into the market that make it difficult for business to plan ahead. They therefore reduce the total level of economic activity.

But while wide price swings are universally condemned, there is no general agreement as to the most desirable pattern of price stabilization. Three possible alternatives have their adherents, and some sort of a case can be made for each: slowly rising prices, slowly falling prices, and constant prices.

Slowly Rising Prices. Stability does not mean stagnation. It means ordered growth. Some economists believe that ordered growth in output may be promoted by a similar rise in the price level provided the rise is regular, controlled, and not too large. Paul Samuelson, for instance, in a widely used elementary economics text once said: "If price increases could be held down to, say, 2 per cent per year, such a mild steady inflation need not cause too great alarm."[5] Other writers suggest a limit of 3 per cent per year, while still others endorse the general principle without committing themselves to a specific figure.

The fundamental argument of this group is that full employment is impossible without the incentive of a rising price level and that a "mild" inflation really isn't very bad anyway.

The incentive value of rising prices comes from the fact, already discussed in Chapter 22, that increasing prices benefit the entrepreneur for several reasons:

[4] It is possible that this is what is intended in the phrase "maximum purchasing power," but it is certainly not explicit.

[5] Paul Samuelson, *Economics,* 4th ed. (McGraw-Hill Book Company, New York, 1958), p. 270. Earlier editions said "3 per cent." The sixth edition refers noncommittally to "slow price increases."

1. His profit margin may increase because of a lag in the rise of business costs.
2. If he is a debtor, he benefits by being able to pay off his debts with depreciated money.
3. Rising prices are frequently associated with "good times" and rising sales.
4. Rising prices tend to cover up mistakes in calculations he may make either as to costs or as to the market for his product. He is therefore induced to take risks he otherwise might avoid.

For these reasons the businessman is more optimistic in a period of inflation. He is more likely to expand production and hire more workers, thereby helping to create full employment.

While this is true for an inflationary period as compared with a deflationary period, *when the two alternate in uncertain rhythm,* it is by no means so clear that the same results would be achieved if prices rose at a known and controlled rate. For one thing, the arguments advanced seem to boil down to the implication that prosperity and full employment are possible only when the businessman is stimulated by a rate of profit that is increasing his share of national income. Obviously this could not continue indefinitely. But what is more important is that profit is the return to uncertainty—the reward for risk or for the particularly adroit ability to forecast an unknown future. If the future of prices could be predicted clearly, business would inevitably adjust to such certainty, and the abnormal profit possibilities would disappear.

To take just one obvious example. If prices rise 3 per cent per year, the man who borrows at 3 per cent is paying no *real interest* at all. The $1.03 he repays is exactly equal in purchasing power to the $1 he borrowed. He gains at the expense of the creditor. Who wouldn't borrow at zero interest? *But,* if everyone knows the price level will rise 3 per cent during the year, who will lend at 3 per cent nominal interest (zero real interest)? Lenders will charge 6 per cent for the same type of loan. The $1.06 the borrower returns will represent a 3 per cent real cost over and above the $1 borrowed in spite of the depreciation of money.

All contracts, wage rates, and other costs would adjust to the known rate of price rise. Wage contracts would have a built-in 3 per cent increment, as would long-term leases, contracts for sales over a period of time, and all other business arrangements. All the presumed advantages of the rising price level would disappear if the rise were predictable in advance. The only gainers would be debtors who had been lucky enough to enter into long-term contracts *before* the new policy went into effect, and they would gain at the expense of the creditors (bank depositors, insurance beneficiaries, bondholders, and pensioners) who were caught by the change.

These creditors would be hurt seriously in spite of all the protestations that the rise would be minor. A 3 per cent change doesn't sound like very much. Nobody would suffer from a rise that small. They wouldn't, wouldn't they? At 3 per cent per year prices will double in twenty-four years, quadruple in forty-eight years, octuple in seventy-two. If such a "slowly" rising price level persisted throughout your lifetime, any dollar you invested at the age of twenty (not counting interest) would be worth about 25 cents when you retired. This is not an insignificant change.

Those who advocate this policy want the advantages of two incompatible worlds: they want the businessman to benefit while no one else is hurt. This is a laudable objective, but it's impossible. *Either* the interest structure and other business practices will alter to wipe out any advantage the businessman might get, *or* creditors and others with sticky incomes will see their capital and income shrinking steadily toward worthlessness. Neither seems advantageous in the long run, and both are disturbing in the short run.

Slowly Falling Prices. A second group of economists, very small these days, suggests that a more desirable result would be obtained from stability associated with a falling price level. In this case the argument is not normally that there should be a constant rate of decrease, but rather that prices should reflect accurately the *real* cost of production. Any decrease in real costs should be passed on to consumers in lower money prices.

Technological progress means a lowering of real costs, the ability to turn out a larger quantity of goods with the same resources. This is the essence of a continually rising standard of living. In the past the greater productivity has not been passed on to consumers in lower prices; it has been given to labor in the form of higher wages (or to owners in larger profits, though these could not persist in the long run).

The argument for lower prices says that the advantages of improved technology should not accrue to the few who happen to be employed in the particular industry affected but should be spread among the whole population. If money wages remain fixed while prices go down, everybody's standard of living rises. If prices remain the same and money wages rise, the worker obviously increases his standard of living, but others—the retired, the widow living on insurance, even the worker in industries where productivity lags—receive no benefit. It is suggested that increases in general productivity are the result of social forces associated with a growing body of technical knowledge. They are not contributed by the particular workers involved (in the form of greater effort) or even by the business innovator. Society as a whole should therefore receive the benefits of such progress.

While the rate of growth in productivity is not constant, it tends to fluctuate within a fairly narrow range, and a policy of equating prices with real costs would apparently call for a price decline of perhaps 3 per cent per year.

Such a policy raises two questions, one concerning its fundamental desirability and the other concerning its practicality: (1) Is it really fair that those not engaged in production should share in the rewards of increased output? (2) Would industry continue to advance as rapidly as possible if every improvement was passed on to consumers in lowered prices without rewarding the business introducing it? The answers to these questions are not clear. This does not condemn the theory, but it means that the case for a falling price level has not been fully proved.

Most economists feel that the prospect of continual deflation would destroy the confidence and drive of business to such an extent that the economy would wallow in low gear at considerably less than either full employment or maximum efficiency.

Constant Prices. Caught between the inflationary potential of rising prices and the depression psychology of falling prices, the economy would probably do well to try to maintain a constant price level. Such stability would avoid the problems of either of the extremes and would produce certain positive advantages of its own.

1. Compared with a falling price level, constant prices will not, it is true, improve the standard of living of fixed-income groups. But neither will they depress that level. At the same time, by promoting a climate more conducive to business progress, they are more likely to raise the standard of living of the nation as a whole.

2. Compared with inflation, constant prices protect creditors against erosion of their savings. At the same time they may well provide all the incentive business needs for vigorous expansion.

One of the primary arguments for rising prices is that profit possibilities will arise from the spread between costs and prices of finished goods (see Figure 31-1*a*), thereby inducing businessmen to move ahead with production plans.

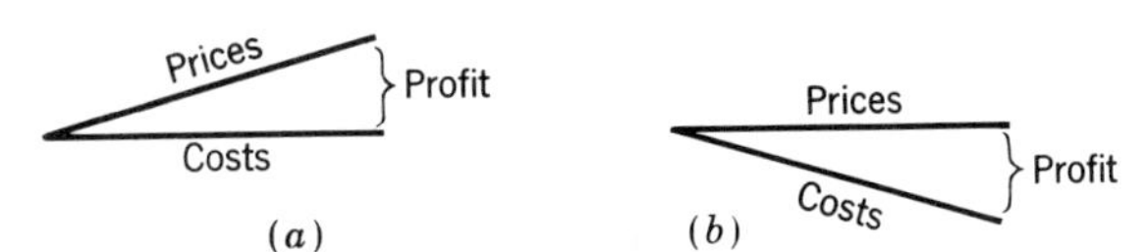

Figure 31-1. The relation between prices and costs. (*a*) Rising prices; (*b*) constant prices.

We have already suggested that in a known and predictable inflation the gap is likely to disappear, since costs will tend to rise as fast as prices. Under a 3 per cent annual price increase, for instance, labor unions will undoubtedly insist on an automatic 3 per cent per year wage increase in addition to their other demands.

In practice profit possibilities do not arise from a *general* disparity between prices and costs, but from the ability of the innovator to take advantage of some new product or process by which he is able *temporarily* to outpace his competitors. Soon his profit margin is narrowed, and the man who wants to keep ahead must find some new method that others haven't thought of. This is the essence of progress. It can't be assured by predictable inflation.

To the extent that a difference between costs and prices of finished goods does promote business optimism, a falling cost structure with a constant price level (see Figure 31-1*b*) is just as effective as constant costs and rising prices.

As real costs fall, a profit can be made at current prices. It is not suggested that this situation is any more effective than known inflation in spurring business activity but simply that it is *no less so*. In this case, as in any other, the growing gap will not be left exclusively to profits. Again labor will demand its share, and money costs will not fall continually as real costs do. It will be only the enterprising businessman able to keep ahead of his competitors who can hang onto a profit advantage.[6]

It is possible, however, that the greater simplicity of a constant price level may reduce business uncertainty and thus lead to greater activity than even a slowly rising price level.

3. Compared with either rising or falling prices a fixed level has the very great advantage of equity. We have seen how changing prices redistribute both income and wealth haphazardly between creditors and debtors. During a period of falling prices the debtor loses by having to repay a larger real purchasing power than he borrowed. The farmer especially seems hard hit both because he is chronically a debtor and because the prices of his products tend to move further and faster than the prices of industrial goods.

During inflation the creditor loses by receiving back money whose purchasing power is lower than that of the money loaned. Some, but by no means all, creditors are wealthy "capitalists," and there is some tendency for the man in the street to assume that they bear the burden of inflation and that it doesn't touch him. On the contrary, the creditor group includes many low-income savers: savings depositors, savings-bond holders, life insurance beneficiaries, and pensioners. Almost all of us fall into one or another of these groups.

A constant price level avoids these inequitable shifts in either direction. Throughout the rest of the book, therefore, when we speak of stable prices, we mean stable at a constant level, although most of the policies discussed could be used to achieve either of the other goals as well.

The Compatibility of Full Employment and Stable Prices. The importance of these two criteria has led to their general acceptance as the twin goals of economic stabilization: full employment at a reasonably stable price level. To a large extent these goals have been approved not only by economists, but also by governmental officials and a large segment of the general population. They are certainly more widely accepted than any others.

However, there are a large number of people, many economists among them, who fear that in practice it may be impossible to achieve both goals simultaneously. They feel that in fact the two are incompatible. They say, in effect, that it would be nice to go to the seashore and would likewise be nice to go to the mountains, but since we can't do both, it is necessary to choose between them.

[6] We have ignored throughout this discussion the profits of monopoly position, which continue to roll in under almost all circumstances. There is no evidence that monopolies will be stimulated any more by inflationary forces than other businesses are. Their favored position may reduce their incentive to strike out in unmapped directions under any conditions.

If a choice is necessary, the preferable course seems clear. Full employment with high production, even with inflation, seems more desirable than a stable price level with the gloom of unemployment, reduced living standards, and an economy moving ahead at half throttle.

The question is whether we do have to choose. Can't we have both? Those who feel we can't have presented the argument in many different forms, but their position may perhaps be summarized as follows: If we start from a period of unemployment, given any (presumably low) price level, and assume a business revival, the first effect will be increased production and employment. The price level may not rise immediately. But as expansion continues, bottlenecks soon appear, and prices go up. The closer we come to full employment, the harder it is to find adequate labor, the greater the scarcity of raw materials, the more problems we have with equipment breakdowns, and the greater the upward pressure on prices.

This is shown graphically in Figure 31-2. Starting from depressed condi-

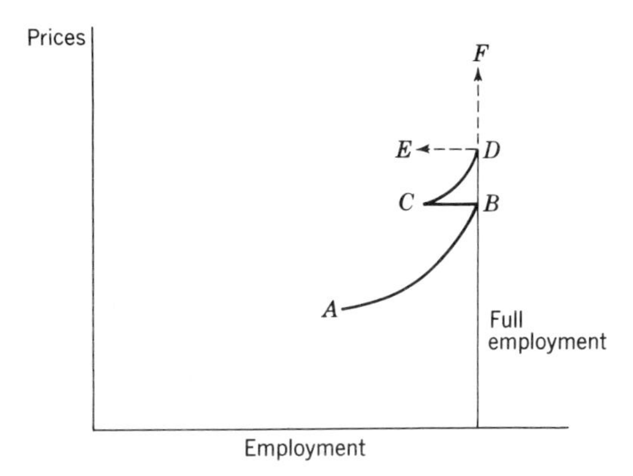

Figure 31-2. The relation between prices and employment.

tions at *A*, we reach full employment only at sharply higher prices *B*. This portion of the curve corresponds to the $D=S$ curve of Figure 30-14. If we try then to stabilize prices at this high level, we will find—so the argument goes—an inevitable tendency of employment to fall toward *C*. Full employment can then be reached at *D* only if prices are allowed to rise further. Nor can they stay at this point. To avoid a decline of employment toward *E*, prices must be pushed up continually in the direction of *F* to offset the "natural tendency" of employment to sag unless continually stimulated by new injections of price serum.

This argument is not entirely unreasonable and can call on a good deal of evidence from recent events, particularly the continuous attempt of unions to push up money wages regardless of the state of the economy. The latter tendency appears to have become so much a permanent part of union strategy that it is sometimes suggested that of three desirable goals we may be able to achieve any *two,* but not all three simultaneously: (1) full employment, (2) stable prices, and (3) economic freedom (specifically the freedom of unions to strike for higher wages). Given union pressure—the argument goes —either the price level will be forced up or the cost squeeze will result in unemployment. This is essentially the picture shown in Figure 31-2.

In spite of all this evidence, however, the case has not been fully proved, and there is considerable evidence on the other side as well. We have already seen that technological improvement can reduce real costs and give incentive to businessmen to expand while providing the possibility of raising wages without forcing prices up—provided the wage increases for the nation as a whole are no greater than the rise in productivity for the whole economy. At the same time we should recognize that implicit in this argument of incompatibility is the assumption that given freedom, labor unions will push wages higher than productivity regardless of the fact that this may cause unemployment in their own unions, a result that would occur if strict monetary controls made it impossible for the economy to find the money to pay all presently employed workers at the higher wage rates. Perhaps some unions would be that callous in the short run, but their continued disregard for the welfare of their unemployed members is hard to conceive. In any case, all the goals involved are so desirable that they are worth fighting for until we are absolutely sure that they cannot be achieved simultaneously. The evidence is not that strong yet.

On the contrary, any claim that full employment and a stable price level are incompatible is belied by history, some of it very recent. The twenties were certainly a period of full employment and general prosperity in spite of distortions of one kind or another. Yet for the whole period from 1922 to 1929 neither the wholesale nor the consumer price index rose. The whole picture has been presented in Figure 21-1. Wholesale prices, while showing variable fluctuations from year to year, moved downward for the period as a whole from 52.9 to 52.1 (1957–59 = 100). The consumer index rose from 1922 to 1926 but then fell in the next three years from 61.6 to 59.7.

A more recent, though briefer, experience of the same kind occurred in 1952–1955, when the wholesale price index fell from 94.0 to 93.2 (it had been 96.7 in 1951), and consumer prices rose less than 1 per cent from 92.5 to 93.3. True, this period included the recession of 1953–1954, but just as important as the fact that we fell into this quagmire is the fact that we came out of it with no rise in prices.

The period 1958–1964 is another example. As Table 31-1 shows, the wholesale price index remained almost completely constant during this period, which included the longest peacetime business expansion in United States history (exceeded only by the World War II expansion from 1938 to 1945). Consumer prices rose by about 1 per cent per year, but as pointed out in Chapter 21, this might be attributed primarily to an increase in quality rather than to a price increase per se. Without the stimulus of significantly rising prices, industrial production rose by almost 50 per cent in these six years. And although the unemployment rate was high throughout the period, it was lower at the end than at the beginning. It is even possible to speculate that the persistence of the upswing from 1961 to 1964 was due to the fact that it encountered no serious distortions—including distortions of the price level.

Table 31-1. Business Activity and Prices, 1958 to 1964

Year	Industrial production (1957–59 = 100)	Unemployment (per cent of civilian labor force)	Wholesale prices (1957–59 = 100)	Consumer prices (1957–59 = 100)
1958	93.7	6.8	100.4	100.7
1959	105.6	5.5	100.6	101.5
1960	108.7	5.6	100.7	103.1
1961	109.7	6.7	100.3	104.2
1962	118.3	5.6	100.6	105.4
1963	124.3	5.7	100.3	106.7
1964	132.0	5.2	100.5	108.1

Source: *Federal Reserve Bulletin*, vol. 51, no. 7 (July, 1965), pp. 1016, 1018.

Perhaps full employment and a constant price level are difficult to achieve simultaneously, but it has been done.

The Results of Inflation. Many people are willing to accept inflation if it can provide full employment because they feel it is a small price to pay. This underestimation of the destructive power of inflation arises primarily from the fact that the effects of inflation are more insidious, less obvious than the effects of unemployment. But this should not blind us to its disastrous results:

1. Inflation robs the saver. We have already seen how inflation whittles away the purchasing power of money, so that anyone who has put aside a little nest egg finds his capital evaporating.

2. Inflation discourages saving. Precisely because it robs the saver, the saver tends to decide that the game is not worth the candle. It's sort of foolish to sit and watch the value of one's monetary assets fall. Better to spend the money today while it's worth something. Because saving is necessary to investment, a general savers' strike may well reduce the country's rate of capital accumulation and hence its ability to produce in the future.

3. Inflation encourages speculation. One way a saver may avoid these untoward effects is to put his money into stocks, real estate, or other commodities rather than into fixed-value assets. In some cases this may be desirable, but it's a risky business for most small savers, who don't understand enough about the intricacies of equity finance.

4. Inflation feeds on itself. It is true that inflation encourages business, but only if the rise has not been discounted in advance. If the increase in prices is known to be at a constant rate, then all contracts will be based on future higher prices rather than current prices. The windfall gains disappear, and incentive can be reestablished only by a progressively increasing rate of increase. If prices are expected to rise at 3 per cent, only a rise of 6 per cent will give the push that would be expected from a 3 per cent rise in the absence of any anticipation of its occurrence. Then when prices are rising 6 per cent, only a 9 per cent rise will do the trick, and so on. The disadvantages of a slowly rising price level are compounded as the advance becomes more rapid. Such an acceleration of the rate is not inevitable, but if it fails to occur, many of the psychological advantages of inflation evaporate.

5. Inflation can demoralize production. While mild inflation may be a shot in the arm, runaway inflation is a sock on the jaw. As the tempo of monetary depreciation increases, people become more and more reluctant to use money or monetary assets. Long-term contracts become impossible. The market for bonds disappears. No one will part with valuable commodities in exchange for worthless money—or money that is likely to become worthless tomorrow. Barter replaces sale, and with it come all the disadvantages of a nonmonetary system. The productive process breaks down, and the only solution is a complete overhaul of the whole monetary system, including the wiping out of almost all former claims, the complete expropriation of the creditor.

Such runaway inflation is extreme, but not truly rare. This country experienced it during the Revolutionary War. The Confederate States repeated the same experience in the Civil War. Germany presented a classic example in the latter part of 1923, when prices rose as much as 2,500 per cent in one *month,* and where new marks were finally put into circulation and given in exchange for old marks at the rate of 1 new mark for every 1 *trillion* old marks.

After World War II the same kind of inflation beset many countries, Greece, China, and Hungary among them. In Budapest the cost of living index, which stood at 240 in November, 1944 (January, 1938 = 100), rose

Figure 31-3. Hungarian inflation currency, 1946. This is probably the highest denomination note ever issued in any currency, worth one hundred million *(szăzmilliŏ)* trillion pengo (*B.-pengo*), that is, one hundred quintillion pengo (100,000,000,000,000,000,000). *(Courtesy of the Chase Manhattan Bank Museum of Moneys of the World, New York.)*

to 1,076,400,000,000 by May, 1946.[7] It apparently rose another 1,000,000,-000,000,000 times in the next two months, although accurate data are not available. Obviously under conditions of this kind a price index ceases to have much meaning.

Certainly there is not much chance that the United States will ever suffer from an inflation of this kind, but we should always be on our guard against the possibility.

Even in a moderate inflation production patterns are distorted. Since business is motivated by profit, it is obvious that business decisions will have to be made on the basis of the profit potentials of rising prices. The question then may well become "How can I profit from inflation?" rather than "How can I profit from production?" It is well known that during inflationary periods many speculative ventures are started that would never appear in ordinary times. Resources are thus channeled into avenues that are economically unjustified, and these resources, in real terms, can come only from other industries that would contribute more to national output.

6. Inflation leads to depression. It would be an exaggeration to say that what goes up must come down. A price rise does not necessarily lead to an equal price fall. But inflation introduces distortions into the economy that sooner or later must be corrected. Companies that are basically unsound are bolstered by the artificial stimulus of easy money. The shift in income from one group to another disturbs the normal balance of consumption, saving, and investment. Patterns are established that are insupportable in the long run. If we are fortunate, different sections of the economy will adjust at different times, so that the economy as a whole may suffer only a "rolling readjustment," but under less auspicious circumstances a cumulation of corrective forces could produce a fairly severe depression.

Generally speaking, the greater the inflation, the more serious the maladjustments, and therefore the greater the possibility of a bust later. Inflation is not a small price to pay for full employment, and in the long run, taking the downs with the ups, it is not even clear that inflation provides more employment at all. As the chairman of the Board of Governors of the Federal Reserve System has put it: "We fight inflation partly because it is the forerunner of deflation. If I thought inflation would create jobs and prosperity, I might be for it. But I am convinced that, apart from transitory effects, the result of inflation is the destruction of jobs and prosperity."[8]

While the battle continues to rage with vocal and able adherents on both sides, I believe that the appeal of inflation as a cure for our ills is a siren song, luring us to destruction of the sound base of our productive capacity. Although full employment must always be a prime objective, we should not abandon the fight for a stable price level as well. No one assumes that we can ever achieve *complete* price stability. Some fluctuations are inevitable. But they should not be constantly in the upward direction.

[7] Rodolph Szeredas, "Inflation and Stabilization," in *Budapest on the Road to Revival* (Institute of Arts and Letters, Budapest, 1946), p. 95.

[8] William McChesney Martin, Jr., Address before the 62d Annual Convention of the Pennsylvania Bankers Association, May 4, 1956.

Economic Growth

But let's return for a moment to production. Instead of speaking of maximum production, or even optimum production, many economists today cite a "maximum sustainable rate of economic growth" as one of the basic goals of the economy. Even a high level of output, they say, isn't enough unless it's higher than it was yesterday.

The argument for growth is fairly obvious. It is growth that increases our standard of living, that permits us to achieve today what was previously impossible. Our production has risen at a compound rate of some 3 to 3½ per cent per year over the last century. Part of the increase has been absorbed by a rising population, but most of it has enabled us to live better.

Is it too much to expect that this rise will continue? Hardly. But there are many who say that the rate of increase should not be left to chance but should be a goal of national policy. We need a higher rate than in the past (5 per cent is the objective most commonly cited) in order to "accommodate the real needs of the American people for rising living standards" and to "assure the long-term maintenance of our position as the world's leading and most dynamic economy."[9]

Assuming that the economy would not reach this rate of growth of its own accord, what could be done to achieve it? As a matter of fundamental arithmetic, increased production can come only from (1) an increased number of labor hours or (2) increased productivity per worker (more goods turned out each hour). The latter in turn requires (*a*) increased capital (more machines to work with), (*b*) better machines, or (*c*) more efficient use of labor, capital, or materials.

Since nothing is produced by idle men, obviously full employment is a prerequisite to maximum growth. But once full employment is reached, increased labor can come only from lengthening the workweek or enlarging the work force by including some who do not want to work (as Britain did by a labor draft). Those who cherish freedom would be loath to see such labor controls saddled on the economy simply to achieve an artificially predetermined rate of growth. A certain amount of leisure is a part of the standard of living which many people prefer over more goods.

The road to increased capital is a less certain one. Many businessmen say that the best way to achieve it is by reducing taxes on business (the corporate profits tax in particular), but frequently this sounds too much like special pleading. There is more general agreement that price stability is needed in order to call forth the saving without which investment is impossible. To the extent that this is true, we are back to our two fundamental goals of full employment and price stability.

Better machines are primarily a matter of technological progress, and while this is more or less continuous, there may be ways in which invention, innova-

[9] Governor Nelson A. Rockefeller of New York, Speech to the Governor's Conference on Automation, Cooperstown, N.Y., June 1, 1960.

tion, and capital improvements can be encouraged. At the same time we would probably all agree that inefficiency should be combated. Yet specific proposals are often resisted: elimination of labor featherbedding, of subsidies to uneconomic businesses, of tariff protection, of racial discrimination which prevents the most effective use of labor resources. In any case most of these possibilities do not lie within the scope of monetary policy. Perhaps the most we can expect from monetary policy in this direction is that while it is being used to further our other goals, it should not interfere with growth and should aid it wherever possible.

Bearing these limitations in mind, economic growth can be added to our list of desirable economic goals.

Stability of the Dollar

In recent years a new goal has been added to the objectives of United States monetary policy: maintenance of the foreign exchange value of the dollar in terms of other currencies. Until recently we have not worried much about this because, since World War I at least, the United States dollar had been one of the strongest currencies in the world, and there was no question about the stability of its external value. As long as foreigners had an insistent demand for our commodities and services, they wanted dollars and were willing to bid strongly to get them. For several years after World War II the scramble to obtain dollars led to a dollar shortage; it was a much-wanted currency.

Since 1950, however, there has been a continuous surplus of dollars in world markets. We have been making more payments abroad than we have been receiving in return, and this "adverse balance of payments"[10] means that foreigners have (1) taken part of their excess earnings in gold and (2) built up their dollar balances, which they could use to obtain more gold in the future or which, if our goods were attractive enough, they could use to buy our products.

The adverse balance of payments became substantial in 1958, and from the beginning of that year to 1965 the United States lost $9 billion worth of gold. At the same time our short-term liabilities to foreigners exceeded $28 billion. Both the gold loss and the overhanging short-term debt pose problems for the continued international stability of the dollar. Unless our exports are attractive enough for foreigners to want to buy our goods, or unless our interest rates are high enough to induce them to hold dollar securities, further gold loss is inevitable. Since our gold stock is finite, such a loss cannot continue forever, and beyond some point it would force devaluation of the dollar. Devaluation in turn might cause something close to chaos in international markets and would certainly undermine much of the business done in foreign exchange by United States banks.

[10] The precise meaning of this phrase will be discussed in Chap. 36, which will also explore other aspects of this general problem in more detail.

One objective of economic policy is to forestall such possibilities by maintaining the strength of the dollar in world markets. This in turn means high interest rates and avoidance of inflation. Since the latter is a desirable goal in any case, no problem arises in this connection. But high interest rates may interfere with domestic policies to reduce unemployment at home. This problem of balancing external and internal stability has occupied the attention of United States policy makers for a half dozen years, and they hardly seem nearer a permanent solution now than they did at the beginning.

The whole problem of external stability is so complex that even the reasons why such stability is desirable can only be hinted at here. Yet it is necessary to bear in mind that this aim is also one of the basic objectives of the economy.

Summary. In summary, then, the major goals of monetary policy may be listed as:

1. Full employment
2. A reasonably stable price level
3. A sustainable level of economic growth
4. External stability of the value of the dollar

These goals in turn need to be pursued within the framework of a social, political, and economic structure that has other objectives of equal, or perhaps even greater, importance. Two of the most cherished of these are probably the maintenance of democracy and the maintenance of our basic freedoms. Even in the realm of economics some people would like to emphasize other desirable aims: more equitable distribution of income, conservation of natural resources, greater security, the rehabilitation of underprivileged groups, and greater mobility of resources, to name a few. Some of these are universally recognized; others are in the realm of dispute. The fact that we have ignored them in this chapter should not be interpreted to mean that they are unimportant.

Policy must always be examined in terms of all its effects, not merely in terms of its main objective. But because of the very multiplicity of these other goals it is impossible to do them justice in a book on money and banking. Here we can present only the broad strokes; the necessity for filling in the details should not be forgotten.

Questions for Thought and Discussion

1. What do you think Congress meant by "maximum employment, production, and purchasing power"?

2. Is there any way to define optimum production in terms of physical measurement? Can it be done in terms of tons' or dollars' worth of output or in terms of some kind of index number?

3. Is there any way to eliminate all unemployment?

4. How might technological unemployment be reduced?
5. Since falling prices are advantageous to all consumers, why aren't they generally considered desirable?
6. Why is inflation more acceptable to most people than depression?
7. By what means do you think technological progress might be speeded up? Is such a speedup desirable?
8. If external goals conflict with domestic ones, which should take precedence?
9. Of the following goals for the economy, which do you feel are most important and why: economic growth, economic freedom, full employment, stable prices, maintenance of the foreign value of the dollar, the right to strike, increasing leisure, rising money income, rising real income, maintenance of the *status quo?*
10. What goals, other than those discussed here, do you think are important?
11. Do you think people should work harder in order to raise their standard of living? Why don't they want to?
12. Shouldn't the economy strive for the greatest happiness of everyone? How could this be achieved?

Selected Bibliography

Alexander, Sidney S., et al.: *Economics and the Policy Maker,* Brookings Lectures, 1958–1959, The Brookings Institution, Washington, 1959.
Bach, George L.: *Inflation,* Brown University Press, Providence, R.I., 1958.
Clark, John M.: *The Wage-Price Problem,* American Bankers Association, New York, 1960.
Commission on Money and Credit: *Inflation, Growth, and Employment,* Prentice-Hall, Inc., Englewood Cliffs, N.J., 1964.
Edwards, Edgar D. (ed.): *The Nation's Economic Objectives,* The University of Chicago Press, Chicago, 1964.
Einzig, Paul: *Monetary Policy: Ends and Means,* 2d ed., Penguin Books, Inc., Baltimore, 1964.
Federal Reserve Bank of Philadelphia: *The Quest for Stability,* 1954.
Haberler, Gottfried: *Inflation: Its Causes and Cures,* American Enterprise Association, Washington, 1961.
Horvitz, Paul M.: *Monetary Policy and the Financial System,* Prentice-Hall, Inc., Englewood Cliffs, N.J., 1963.
Kurihara, Kenneth K.: *Monetary Theory and Public Policy,* W. W. Norton & Company, Inc., New York, 1950.
Reuber, G. L.: *The Objectives of Monetary Policy,* Royal Commission on Banking and Finance, Ottawa, 1962.
Royal Institute of International Affairs: *The Future of Monetary Policy,* London, 1935.
Thorp, Willard L., and Richard E. Quandt: *The New Inflation,* McGraw-Hill Book Company, New York, 1959.
See also references listed under Chapter 33.

Chapter 32 Federal Reserve Policy

The time is out of joint: O cursed spite,
That ever I was born to set it right!

Hamlet
Act I, scene 5, line 188

Money doesn't manage itself. If it is to behave, if it is to be a genuine aid to the community rather than a snare and an entanglement, there must be some means of keeping it within bounds.

There are many ways in which money is managed in the United States today, and many agencies are involved in this task, sometimes working together and sometimes at cross purposes. A partial list would include the Treasury, Congress, bank-chartering and supervisory agencies (both Federal and state), commercial banks, other financial institutions, and even the individual citizen in his own small way. But the paramount agency of control is the Federal Reserve System. What is the task that the Reserve authorities are trying to do, and how do they do the job?

These are questions that can be answered adequately only in terms of historical development, for both the powers and the objectives of the System have changed as new needs arose and as old concepts proved inadequate.

In an earlier chapter[1] we sketched briefly the major legislative changes in the Federal Reserve System as well as a number of basic changes in its philosophy. Here we will complete that picture by examining the development of policy objectives and their implementation.

[1] A review of Chap. 11 might be helpful at this point.

Mandates of Federal Reserve Policy

The Federal Reserve was intended to correct certain serious shortcomings of the National Bank Act: to provide an elastic currency, efficient clearing, centralized reserves, readily available credit for banks, and unified control of the banking system. The first four of these have been done so effectively that they are scarcely noted today—for monetary management draws attention only when something goes wrong. It is in the broader and less clearly defined area of centralized control that debate still rages. As old problems seem to be settled satisfactorily, new ones keep arising.

Since the System was established as a result of the panic of 1907, it is clear that one of its major purposes was to prevent the recurrence of such a catastrophe. But the panic of 1907 was not quite the same sort of animal as more modern depressions. Its most obvious characteristic was a shortage of funds, both credit and cash. The Federal Reserve Act reflects clearly the concern over this problem. The preamble states that it is "an Act to provide for the establishment of Federal reserve banks, to furnish an elastic currency, to afford means of rediscounting commercial paper, to establish more effective supervision of banking in the United States, and for other purposes."

An elastic currency was intended to remedy a cash shortage; rediscount would enable banks to obtain additional reserves and thereby ease a credit shortage, whereas "effective supervision" was to prevent some of the unsound banking practices that led to bank failures. These somewhat limited purposes are summed up in the phrase "accommodation to agriculture, commerce and industry," which appears (sometimes in a slightly modified form) several places in the act and crops up continually in early publications of the Federal Reserve Board. When money was needed, the Reserve was to see that it was made available.

There is nothing in the act to suggest the wider matters of general economic control that we take almost for granted today.[2] Nevertheless there was from the beginning a general feeling that the System was to encourage economic stability. Without any change in the objectives stated in the law these goals have become more clearly defined over time. In this reevaluation the Employment Act of 1946 undoubtedly played a part, although it does not specifically mention the Federal Reserve.

Today the Board of Governors sees its objectives as broadly "to help counteract inflationary and deflationary movements, and to share in creating conditions favorable to a sustained high level of employment, a stable dollar, growth of the country, and a rising level of consumption."[3]

[2] Kemmerer, for instance, assaying the Federal Reserve in 1919, makes much of its contribution to free movement of funds, facility of clearing, credit elasticity, and services to the Treasury but makes no mention of restrictive control of credit except in a footnote. Edwin W. Kemmerer, *The ABC of the Federal Reserve System,* 2d ed. (Princeton University Press, Princeton, N.J., 1919).

[3] Board of Governors of the Federal Reserve System, *The Federal Reserve System: Purposes and Functions* (1963), p. 1.

A large part of this shift in emphasis is due not to new objectives as such but rather to the growing knowledge that we have acquired concerning the business cycle itself. In the early days it was felt that a relatively automatic system built around certain simple procedures was all that was needed to assure relief from periodic crises. Now, faced with more complicated fluctuations of business, we find we need a more sophisticated road map to show us how to reach our destination, as well as a more complicated and responsive machine to negotiate the pitfalls along the way. The history of the Federal Reserve is a story of constant adaptations to new problems and to new interpretations of the role of money in the economy.

Original Concepts of Federal Reserve Policy

The tools that the Federal Reserve has at its disposal today are well known. They consist of:

1. Changes in reserve requirements
2. Open-market operations
3. Changes in discount rates
4. Moral suasion
5. Margin requirements

The first and last of these did not even exist in the original Federal Reserve Act, both having been added during the Great Depression. Moral suasion is by its nature so amorphous that it is both subject to continual change and difficult to describe historically; we will have very little to say about it in this chapter. The other two controls have been available from the beginning, but they have changed measurably in form and even more significantly in content over the years.

As we pointed out in Chapter 11, the Federal Reserve Act of 1914 was based on the idea that certain established safeguards were all that were needed to provide almost automatically for sound financial conditions. As long as banks maintained sufficient reserves for their own safety; as long as gold reserves were established for the whole system; as long as banks created money only against real bills, and the Reserve banks provided, through discount, all the reserves necessary to permit member banks to expand in this legitimate manner; as long as we had an elastic currency that would respond to the needs of business—then we were safe alike from inflation caused by overexpansion and from panic based on a shortage of currency or credit. As long as the banking system provided accommodation for business within the safeguards provided, no further control was needed.

Consequently, the tools of credit control with which the Federal Reserve was launched were relatively insignificant. The very phrase "open-market operations" was used in the act to denote purchase and sale of bankers' acceptances and bills of exchange, while dealings in government securities were mentioned among the general powers of the Reserve banks, sandwiched in between the right to "deal in gold coin and bullion" and the power "to purchase from member banks . . . bills of exchange." There is considerable evidence to suggest that operations in government securities were originally intended simply as a way in which the Reserve banks could obtain earning assets with their idle funds.

The only other control device was the right to change the discount rate. This power was granted the individual Reserve banks, subject to "review and determination" by the Federal Reserve Board.

Except for this questionable prerogative, the Board had no authority over monetary conditions other than the establishment of general rules and procedures within which the System would operate.

With these limited powers the System opened its doors for business in 1914. Almost immediately it found that the very bases of its structure were shifting. The international gold standard collapsed as the war took its toll; the real-bills doctrine gradually proved untenable in practice; and the drawing together of the various sectors of the country into a more unified whole made regional autonomy more of a liability than an asset. The controls envisioned in the original act proved insufficient, and experience developed others to take their place.

World War I

Actually the war produced less serious repercussions on the Federal Reserve than might have been expected. It resulted in several minor changes in organization and details of operation and one major change in reserve requirements. Otherwise the System proved entirely capable of aiding the Treasury in obtaining the necessary funds for the war effort and in providing the economy with an adequate financial structure.

Reserve Requirements. A primary reason why money was readily available to meet the abnormal demand caused by the war was that the Federal Reserve Act had reduced legal reserve requirements below the level specified in the National Bank Act, thereby permitting an almost automatic expansion of credit.

This situation carried such inflationary implications that the Federal Reserve Board asked Congress in 1916 for the power to raise requirements in emergencies in order to restrain undue credit creation. This request was not granted, and our entry into the war subordinated that problem to the opposite one of providing more, rather than less, funds. In 1917 a basic amendment to the act reduced requirements even further. It was this amendment that fixed the percentages at 13 for central reserve cities, 10 for reserve cities, 7 for country banks, and 3 against time deposits, although these are frequently spoken of as the "original" requirements.

Open-market Operations. That the Reserve banks did not use open-market operations as a primary credit-control device is indicated by the fact that in spite of their desire to provide funds for the government they did not buy bonds on any large scale in the war period. At the end of 1918, for instance, the twelve Federal Reserve banks combined owned only $239 million worth of government securities, although they had outstanding $1,766 million of discounts to member banks.[4]

The Reserve banks at this time acted as selling agents for the Treasury and encouraged others to buy, but they did not feel that they should inflate the currency by making large purchases themselves. In fact the Federal Reserve authorities tried to encourage the commercial banks to sell bonds to their customers in preference to buying them for their own portfolios. Thus they acted on the sound principle of trying to finance the war out of the people's savings as much as possible rather than out of bank credit.

Discount Rate. Nevertheless, as in every war, some expansion of the money supply was inevitable. Banks loaned large sums to the government as well as to industries engaged in war production. The Federal Reserve made it not only possible but relatively easy for banks to obtain the necessary reserves through extensive discounts.

All the Reserve banks began business with either a 6 or a 6½ per cent discount rate. Reductions occurred almost immediately, and by June, 1915, all banks were down to 4 per cent. Two years later all but two had dropped their rate to 3½ per cent or less. Thus the Reserve made funds available to the extent needed, while exhorting banks to restrict their loans to those contributing to the war effort.

The Federal Reserve certainly can't be credited with preventing inflation during the war, but this is a Herculean task that has never been successfully performed by any agency during any war in history.

Internal Organization. These early years also saw a shift of power away from the Federal Reserve Board to the individual Reserve banks, although this was probably not a result of the war.

The act provided that the Federal Reserve Board should designate one of the class C directors of each Reserve bank (all class C directors being appointed by the Reserve Board) to act as chairman of the board of directors and as "Federal Reserve Agent." It was intended that he be the chief executive officer of the bank, although the act does not specifically so state.

The Reserve banks seized on this omission to buttress their own position at the expense of the Board. They limited the Federal Reserve agent to the few routine tasks spelled out in the act. They then used their power to "appoint

[4] Compare these figures with those for 1945: government securities, $24,262 million; discounts, $249 million (see Table 32-1, below). For a discussion of early open-market policy see W. Randolph Burgess, "Reflections on the Early Development of Open Market Policy," *Monthly Review of the Federal Reserve Bank of New York,* November, 1964, pp. 219–226.

. . . such officers and employees as are not otherwise provided for in this Act" for the purpose of appointing a governor of their own choosing to manage the affairs of the bank. Ironically these governors were paid salaries considerably larger than those of members of the Federal Reserve Board.

The governors then proceeded to establish another extralegal institution: the Conference of Governors. By 1920 this purely voluntary but highly effective organization had become more important in practice than the Board itself. Acting as a cooperative liaison among the Reserve banks, it provided coordination of policy, which the act had not considered necessary but which experience proved to be useful and desirable. As chairman of the Conference of Governors, Governor Strong of the Federal Reserve Bank of New York became *de facto* head of the Federal Reserve System.

Postwar Readjustment

The immediate postwar period was one of financial confusion. Reconversion to peacetime activities brought a temporary decline in business, but inflationary forces soon reasserted themselves and pushed the boom on to new heights.

In an effort to aid the Treasury in keeping interest rates down, the Federal Reserve postponed any rise in discount rates, hoping that moral suasion would be sufficient to induce banks to restrain expansion voluntarily. By the end of 1919 it was clear that this policy was not effective. Discount rates were raised to 6 per cent in all banks by February of 1920, and six of the banks later boosted the rate to 7 per cent (see Figure 32-1).

By hindsight it appears that this action was ill-timed. According to the National Bureau of Economic Research the peak of the boom had already been reached in January, 1920. Higher rates, which came too late to restrain the speculative frenzy of the upswing, were just in time to prove restrictive during the collapse.

They were nevertheless retained for several months in the face of severely declining prices and a sharp drop in production and employment. According to the Federal Reserve Board this was done in order to "maintain the strength of the Federal Reserve Banks" and to "discourage applications for rediscounts for nonessential purposes." The Board felt that "the country was passing through the most acute stage of transition from wartime delirium to the more normal conditions of peace. . . . The process necessarily has been painful, but it was inevitable and unavoidable." The Board's policy therefore was to let the readjustment take place without the benefit of "artificial means or temporary expedients."[5]

The Board was apparently worried about the inflationary consequences of monetary expansion during the war and immediately afterward. "War is the most uneconomic of all processes," and it was followed by "an unprece-

[5] Federal Reserve Board, *Seventh Annual Report* (1921), pp. 1, 12.

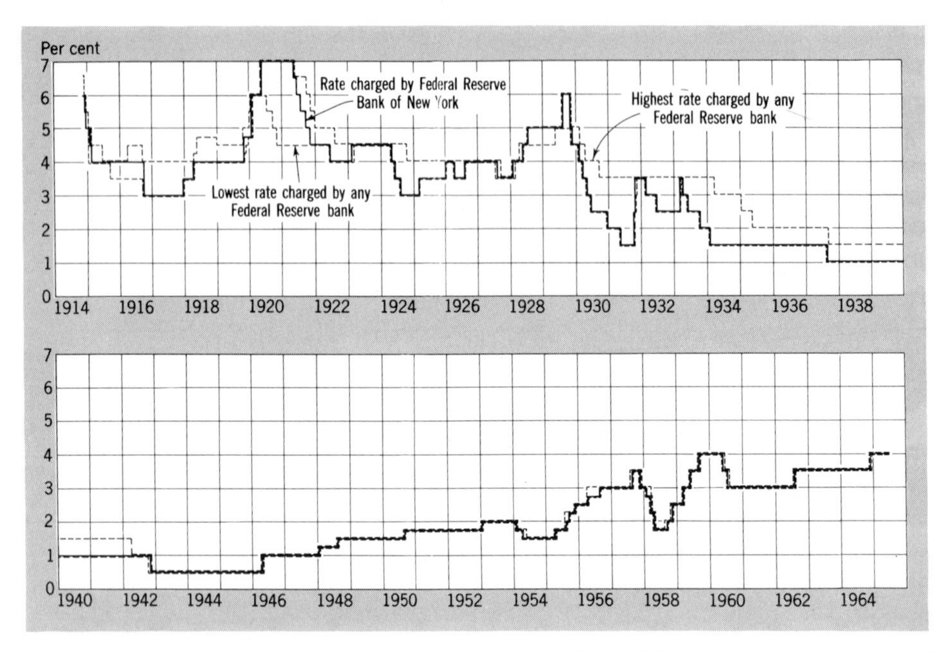

Figure 32-1. Federal Reserve discount rates, 1914 to 1965. (*Board of Governors of the Federal Reserve System, Banking and Monetary Statistics, pp. 439–442; Federal Reserve Bulletin, current issues.*

dented orgy of extravagance, a mania for speculation, overextended business in nearly all lines and in every section of the country and general demoralization of the agencies of production and distribution."[6] In the face of these speculative and inflationary forces the Board would have liked to clamp down on credit by raising discount rates (the only control device of significance at the time) in 1919, but it feared that to have done so would have interfered with the proper management of the public debt. At the same time the Board wanted to prove that the Federal Reserve System was not merely an engine of inflation, as it had been during the war. It determined, therefore, to restrain inflationary tendencies "as soon as Treasury exigencies permitted."[7] This the Board felt it could do in 1920. The fact that business was already declining was deemed irrelevant to the long-run objective of correcting the excesses of the war.

This policy seems needlessly severe. It looks as if the Board, having decided to clamp down the lid as soon as possible, refused to reconsider when underlying conditions changed. But it is at least conceivable that the readjustment fostered by such a policy, though painful at the time, may have laid the basis for sounder gains during the next few years. The depression of 1921,

[6] *Ibid.*, pp. 1, 11.

[7] *Ibid.* The situation presents interesting parallels to that in the post-World War II period.

while sharp, was fairly short, and by the middle of 1921 we were on the way up again.

Prosperity Decade

The war and immediate postwar depression of 1921 behind, the country embarked on its journey "Back to Normalcy." The tremendous expansion of the economy to meet the pent-up demand for housing and other goods in short supply during the war; the opening up of vast consumer markets for automobiles, radios, and other relatively new durable goods; the growth of consumer credit; and the needs of war-devastated countries for capital all depended on expansion of credit—and expansion we had.

Strangely enough this was not a period of inflation, as we have already seen (Table 21-3). Profits, however, were rising, for improvements in technology were reducing costs more rapidly than wage rates were increasing. The profitableness of industry gave a shove to stock prices, and once on their upward way they seemed to continue soaring on their own internal combustion, rising from a low of 54.8 in August, 1921, to a high of 237.8 in September, 1929.[8]

Booming business, stable prices, and the enticing prospect of everyone becoming a millionare on stock speculation seemed to promise a rosy future, and more than one economist who should have known better was predicting that the business cycle was a thing of the past. After all, they said, the Federal Reserve had been designed to prevent the recurrence of a crash, so there was nothing to fear. The Federal Reserve itself seemed to feel that the economy was doing nicely, thank you, and such actions as it took were relatively minor.

Discount Rate. Actually the period from 1922 to 1929 was not one of unalloyed good times, for there were clearly recognizable recessions in 1924 and 1927. These, however, were quite mild. In both cases the discount rate was lowered somewhat, but it remained within the limits of 3 and 4½ per cent until the middle of 1928, when speculative excesses finally provoked higher rates.

Here again it appears from hindsight that the Federal Reserve acted tardily. An increasing volume of speculation on the stock exchange was evident as early as 1926 and had become quite pronounced by 1927. Brokers' loans were rising even more rapidly than stock activity. But discount rates rose to only 5 per cent in 1928, and only briefly did the Federal Reserve Bank of New York impose a 6 per cent rate in August, 1929, after production had already begun to slip.

The System was aware of the threat posed by the rapid rise in both stock prices and brokers' loans. It was afraid, however, that an attempt to restrict the flow of credit into the securities market would hamper legitimate business expansion. "Low money rates may have a favorable effect on domestic business, but at the same time may stimulate speculation in securities, commodities, or real estate. High money rates, on the other hand, may exert a

[8] Standard and Poor's index of stock prices, 1935–39 = 100.

moderating influence on speculation, but at the same time may result in a higher cost of credit to all lines of business, and thus be detrimental to commerce and industry."[9]

Under the circumstances the Board felt that a rise in discount rates from 3½ per cent in 1927 to 5 per cent in 1928 was all that was justified. In support of this position they cited the rise in call money rates (for money loaned on stock collateral on a day-to-day basis), which reached 12.4 per cent in May 1929. At the same time commercial paper carried an interest rate of 6 per cent (against 4 per cent in 1927), and the rate for prime bank acceptances was at an unheard-of 5½ per cent. Under these circumstances the Federal Reserve concluded that the actions it took were as drastic as the situation called for, even though they were insufficient to put much of a damper on the boom.

The bubble burst in 1929, most spectacularly in the stock market in October, though the index of durable manufactures had started to slide in August and of nondurables in July, housing construction had reached its peak in 1925, and agriculture had never really recovered from the debacle of 1921.

The discount rate was lowered rapidly. Within three days of the stock market crash the New York bank reduced its rate from 6 to 5 per cent. Two weeks later it dropped to 4½ per cent, and by June, 1930, it had fallen in several stages to 2½ per cent, lower than it had ever been before. A year later, as recovery failed to materialize, it was down to 1½ per cent.

Open-market Operations. Although discount policy was being used in traditional ways, the decade of the twenties saw major changes in both the purpose and the organization of open-market operations.

We have seen that the purchase of government securities was originally intended as a source of earning assets for the Reserve banks and that all decisions on this matter were left to the individual banks. It was rapidly discovered that these operations could also be used to shift funds from one section of the country to another. If the Denver bank, for instance, sold bonds in New York, it meant that New York funds were obtained by Denver. The opposite would occur if Denver bought bonds in New York.

These transfers were first considered an advantageous means of evening out disparities between districts. However, they raised serious problems because they interfered with the local autonomy of the Reserve banks. When the Denver bank sold bonds in New York, it withdrew funds from the New York market, thereby making money tighter in New York. This might be undesirable from New York's point of view; it might in fact be directly contrary to the policy of the New York Reserve bank. But there was nothing in the act to prevent such operations at cross purposes.

In 1920, therefore, the Conference of Governors selected four of their number as a ponderously titled Committee on Centralized Execution of Purchases and Sales of Government Securities. This committee made recom-

[9] Federal Reserve Board, *Fifteenth Annual Report for 1928* (1929), p. 9.

mendations to the various banks in an attempt to provide some degree of uniformity in open-market policy, but it had no coercive power.

At the same time the governors recognized the significance of open-market operations as a credit-control device and suggested that such purchases and sales should be carried out "in an orderly, systematic way, not solely with regard to earnings, but with regard to the whole credit situation and to the interest of the Treasury." Open-market operations thus began to take on their present status as an important means of credit control, a role that they filled to a greater and greater extent as experience indicated the usefulness of this method of regulating the reserves of the banking community.

The governors' committee had been in operation only a year when the Federal Reserve Board, apparently in an attempt to restore some of its own prestige, substituted for this committee a new Open Market Investment Committee composed of governors of five of the banks but subject to control by the Board. Although its power was still only advisory, it was rare for a bank to refuse to participate in the operations initiated by the Committee. The actual purchase and sale were carried out by the New York bank since New York constituted the major market for both government securities and bank acceptances, the two instruments in which operations were conducted.

Later a revolt by the banks not included on the committee led to a change in both name and composition. The Open Market Policy Conference, established in 1930, consisted of all twelve governors, and the Federal Reserve Board reserved the right to give final approval to its acts. Basic policy remained unchanged.

The Banking Act of 1933 finally gave legislative approval to the conference, which was renamed the Federal Open Market Committee. Further centralization was provided by the Banking Act of 1935, which changed the composition of the committee to its present status: the seven members of the Board of Governors of the Federal Reserve System (the new name for the Federal Reserve Board) plus five presidents of the Reserve banks. The Committee was simultaneously given complete power over all open-market operations.

We should not leave this period without pointing out that the Federal Reserve made substantial advances in the details of its day-to-day operations in the twenties. Prominent among these was their success in modifying the unsteadying effects on the money market of seasonal forces, of sporadic Treasury operations, and of other temporary disturbances. It was through relatively unspectacular open-market operations that the System accomplished these results. Lack of common attention to this aspect of its work is a tribute to the effectiveness with which it was carried out.

Depression Decade

The major changes wrought in banking legislation in the thirties were the result of the failure of the Federal Reserve to prevent the greatest debacle of all time. Hadn't three years of investigation preceded the establishment of the System, investigation whose purpose was to devise a foolproof antidote for crises? There couldn't be another depression, for the Federal Reserve was there as a bulwark against collapse.

What happened? The bottom fell out!

It became obvious that automatic devices were not enough; that discount rate changes and open-market operations weren't equal to the task; even that some of the "safeguards" of the System acted less like life preservers and more like a dead weight on the economy.

Discount Rate. The New York discount rate dropped to 1½ per cent by May, 1931. But it didn't stay there long. In October it jumped in two leaps to 3½ per cent. Were inflationary forces threatening the economy? In 1931? Nothing of the sort. The Reserve was not reacting to any inflationary pressures in the domestic economy, but to a loss of gold on international account.

The deepening world financial crisis had forced Great Britain off the gold standard in September, and the spreading ripples of panic touched the United States. Foreign claimants withdrew some $400 million of gold from our reserves in October alone. The Federal Reserve reacted in the classical manner. A loss of gold must mean prices are too high (in 1931?). The rules of the game called for a restriction of the money supply and particularly for a rise in interest rates in order to attract foreign capital. This in turn would help stem the gold outflow.

The gold standard thus threw its heavy hand over the United States economy, and the needs of domestic business were sacrificed to international panic. Fortunately the inconsistency of this situation finally became quite clear, and after some vacillation the discount rate at New York fell to 1½ per cent in February, 1934, and to 1 per cent during the recession of 1937. Not until the postwar period did it rise again above this minimal level.

From 1934 to 1948 the New York discount rate was changed only three times. To a large extent this relative inactivity reflects the exigencies of depression followed by the exigencies of war. But it reflects partly a significant drop in discounts as a source of bank reserves.

At the end of 1928 discounts at all Federal Reserve banks exceeded $1 billion, the highest level since 1921. By 1934 they had fallen (irregularly) to only $7 *million,* and they stayed below $10 million from then until 1944 (see Table 32-1). When banks have large excess reserves, they certainly have no need to borrow more. This was the situation throughout most of the thirties. Business saw no profit prospects in expansion. There was therefore little need to borrow, while the few customers asking for loans were frequently considered bad credit risks by the banks.

Even in the forties, when the whole economy was running at full steam, banks, having gotten into the habit of keeping out of debt to the Federal Reserve, were extremely reluctant to discount, and today discounts remain a minor source of bank funds.

Table 32-1. Federal Reserve Bank Credit Outstanding, 1914 to 1964

December 31; Millions of Dollars

Year	Discounts and advances	Bills bought (including repurchase)	Industrial advances	U.S. government securities	Other securities	Float	Due from foreign banks	Total Reserve bank credit
1914	10	0	0	*	1	†	0	11
1915	32	24	0	16	12	†	0	84
1916	29	129	0	55	9	†	0	222
1917	660	273	0	122	5	111	0	1,171
1918	1,766	287	0	239	*	199	7	2,498
1919	2,215	574	0	300	0	201	1	3,292
1920	2,687	260	0	287	0	119	1	3,355
1921	1,144	145	0	234	*	40	1	1,563
1922	618	272	0	436	*	84	1	1,411
1923	723	355	0	134	*	27	1	1,238
1924	320	387	0	540	2	52	*	1,302
1925	643	374	0	375	3	63	1	1,459
1926	637	381	0	315	3	45	1	1,381
1927	582	392	0	617	1	63	1	1,655
1928	1,056	489	0	228	10	24	1	1,809
1929	632	392	0	511	12	34	1	1,583
1930	251	364	0	729	7	21	1	1,373
1931	638	339	0	817	31	20	9	1,853
1932	235	33	0	1,855	5	14	3	2,145
1933	98	133	0	2,437	1	15	3	2,688
1934	7	6	14	2,430	0	5	1	2,463
1935	5	5	32	2,431	*	12	1	2,486
1936	3	3	25	2,430	0	39	*	2,500
1937	10	1	18	2,564	0	19	*	2,612
1938	4	1	16	2,564	0	17	*	2,601
1939	7	0	11	2,484	0	91	*	2,593
1940	3	0	8	2,184	0	80	*	2,274
1941	3	0	10	2,254	0	94	*	2,361
1942	6	0	14	6,189	0	471	*	6,679
1943	5	0	10	11,543	0	681	*	12,239
1944	80	0	4	18,846	0	815	*	19,745
1945	249	0	2	24,262	0	578	*	25,091
1946	163	0	1	23,350	0	580	*	24,093
1947	85	0	1	22,559	0	535	*	23,181
1948	223	0	1	23,333	0	541	*	24,097
1949	78	0	2	18,885	0	534	*	19,499
1950	67	0	3	20,778	0	1,368	*	22,216
1951	19	0	5	23,801	0	1,184	*	25,009
1952	156	0	4	24,697	0	967	*	25,825
1953	28	0	2	25,916	0	935	*	26,880
1954	143	0	1	24,932	0	808	*	25,885
1955	108	28	1	24,785	0	1,585	*	26,507
1956	50	69	1	24,915	0	1,665	*	26,699
1957	55	66	*	24,238	0	1,424	*	25,784
1958	64	49	*	26,347	0	1,296	*	27,755
1959	458	75	0	26,648	0	1,590	*	28,771
1960	33	74	0	27,384	0	1,868	0	29,359
1961	130	51	0	28,881	0	2,300	0	31,362
1962	38	110	0	30,820	0	2,903	0	33,871
1963	63	162	0	33,593	0	2,600	0	36,418
1964	186	94	0	37,044	0	2,606	0	39,930

* Less than $500,000.
† Not available; deferred availability items included in deposits.
Sources: Board of Governors of the Federal Reserve System, "Total Reserve Bank Credit, 1914–1958," mimeographed; *Federal Reserve Bulletin*, current.

Open-market Operations. As the discount rate faded in importance, open-market operations took its place as the major instrument of policy. The drop in discounts following the crash was more than offset by an increase in System purchases of government securities. This increased bank reserves, and they were further boosted by a large volume of gold imports. As excess reserves were created, however, they lay idle. It wasn't that banks *couldn't* make loans, but that they didn't want to. There was little more the Federal Reserve could do. Monetary policy simply wasn't enough to bring us out of the depression. Even fiscal policy—public works, work relief, government loans, and the controversial devaluation of the dollar—proved inadequate. The economy slowly revived after 1933, but the process was long and painful.

Legal Changes in the Banking Structure. This was the period during which the most important changes in the Federal Reserve System were introduced. The economy had collapsed in spite of the safeguards that had been erected to keep us from falling off the plateau of prosperity, and new devices were obviously needed. These changes have been described in Chapter 11. They gave the Federal Reserve the power to make loans to banks on any collateral acceptable to the Reserve bank; permitted government securities to be counted as part of the backing for Federal Reserve notes; permitted the banks to make loans directly to industrial or commercial businesses unable to obtain loans elsewhere on reasonable terms; prohibited commercial banks from engaging in investment banking; gave the Federal Reserve power to prescribe minimum margin requirements on security purchases; established the Federal Deposit Insurance Corporation; removed gold from circulation; and revised the balance of Federal Reserve organization by concentrating in the hands of the newly named Board of Governors of the Federal Reserve System powers that had formerly been exercised by the individual Reserve banks.

At the same time the Board of Governors was given one more major tool of credit control: the power to alter reserve requirements, with the percentages prescribed in 1917 as a lower limit and twice that level as the upper limit. This power was conferred on a limited emergency basis in 1933 and made permanent by the Banking Act of 1935. It is interesting that this power, originally requested by the Board during the inflation of 1916, should be granted in 1933, when it was needed least. Congress was trying to do two things at the same time (with a degree of farsighted wisdom it does not always exercise): to provide emergency props to shore up the economy and, by strengthening obvious weaknesses in the banking structure, to prevent a recurrence of the excesses that had brought on the crash. It is certain that the Federal Reserve emerged from this spate of legislation with greatly increased power over the credit structure of the country.

The Use of Reserve Requirements. The Reserve also emerged from the chaos of the Depression with a realization that once the economy starts down the toboggan slide, there isn't much that monetary policy can do. The place to stop the depression is before the boom gets out of hand. Nothing else can explain the actions of the Board of Governors in raising reserve requirements in 1936 and 1937.

True, the economy was moving upward. By August, 1936, industrial production had risen to 37.3 from a low of 18.7 in 1932,[10] but it was still below the level of 1929, and the 17 per cent of the work force unemployed would have testified that the economy was still in the doldrums.

Yet it was precisely at this point that the Board used its newly acquired power and raised reserve requirements by 50 per cent. Two more increases followed in March and May, 1937, to bring the level to the maximum permitted by law (see Table 32-2). It is probably coincidental that production reached its peak in May. It is certain that over the next twelve months it fell one-third, a sharper (though shorter) decline than that which occurred between 1929 and 1933. Surely the Federal Reserve authorities cannot bear the whole blame for the collapse, but they must bear part of it.

They obviously didn't intend to bring on a recession. What, then, were they doing? Their main concern was over the large volume of excess reserves that member banks had acquired as a result of continuing and substantial inflows of gold. At the end of July, 1936, total reserves held by member banks amounted to $6,005 million, of which $2,976 million was required reserves and $3,029 million was excess. In other words member banks had more than twice as many reserves as they needed. Banks, therefore, were in a position to double their deposits if they wanted to make loans. At the same time business, although it had not fully recovered by any means, was feeling better. Looking ahead, the Federal Reserve saw the possibility of another boom and bust and wanted to remove the inflationary potential of the huge excess reserves before they were put to use too heavily.

Since reserves were twice the required amount, doubling the requirements would not, presumably, reduce the volume of loans outstanding but would merely immobilize ("soak up") reserves that weren't being used anyway.

A major difficulty arose from the fact that while banks *as a whole* had large excess reserves, all banks are not average, and some had relatively small amounts. While the increase in requirements did not affect many banks adversely, there were some that were forced to contract fairly severely.

The Federal Reserve recognized this situation by buying securities in the open market at the same time it was raising requirements. These two actions appear contradictory, but they made a good deal of sense under the circumstances. A rise in reserve requirements is a blunt instrument which hits all banks a heavy blow. Some could absorb it; for them the action accomplished its purpose of sopping up excess reserves. Others could not; their first reaction was to replenish their reserves by selling government securities. For them open-market purchases provided a market where they could sell without loss.

Unfortunately the repercussions went further than this. The gradual growth in bank loans was reversed, and a policy intended to put a mild brake on the economy helped throw it into reverse instead.

[10] Federal Reserve industrial production index, seasonally adjusted, 1957–59 average = 100.

Table 32-2. Legal Reserve Requirements under the Federal Reserve System

Per Cent of Deposits

	Demand deposits			
	Central reserve cities	Reserve cities	Country	Time deposits
National Bank Act, June 3, 1864[a]	25	25	15	Same as demand
Federal Reserve Act, Dec. 23, 1913[b]	18	15	12	5
Amendment of June 21, 1917[c]	13	10	7	3
Administrative changes by Board of Governors:[c]				
1936: Aug. 16	19½	15	10½	4½
1937: Mar. 1	22¾	17½	12¼	5¼
May 1	26	20	14	6
1938: Apr. 16	22¾	17½	12	5
1941: Nov. 1	26	20	14	6
1942: Aug. 20	24			
Sept. 14	22			
Oct. 3	20			
1948: Feb. 27	22			
June 11	24			
Sept. 16, 24[d]	26	22	16	7½
1949: May 1, 5[d]	24	21	15	7
June 30, July 1		20	14	6
Aug. 1, 11[d]	23½	19½	13	5[e]
Aug. 16, 18[d]	23	19	12	
Aug. 25	22½	18½		
Sept. 1	22	18		
1951: Jan. 11, 16[d]	23	19	13	6
Jan. 25, Feb. 1[d]	24	20	14	
1953: July 1, 9[d]	22	19	13	
1954: June 16, 24[d]	21			5
July 29, Aug. 1[d]	20	18	12	
1958: Feb. 27, Mar. 1[d]	19½	17½	11½	
Mar. 20, Apr. 1[d]	19	17	11	
Apr. 17	18½			
Apr. 24[f]	18	16½		
1960: Sept. 1	17½			
Nov. 24[g]			12	
Dec. 1	16½[h]			
1962: Oct. 25, Nov. 1[d]				4

[a] Except in central reserve cities, banks could hold a specified portion of their reserves with correspondent banks and the remainder as cash in vault.

[b] Specified portions of the total reserve could be held as cash in vault, as deposits with the Federal Reserve bank, or with correspondent banks.

[c] All reserves must be held on deposit with the Federal Reserve banks.

[d] First-of-month or midmonth dates are changes at country banks, and other dates (usually Thursdays) are at central reserve city or reserve city banks.

[e] Aug. 16 for country banks.

[f] Beginning Dec. 1, 1959, a portion of vault cash could be counted toward reserves.

[g] Beginning Nov. 24, 1960, all vault cash could be counted toward reserves.

[h] This classification was abolished effective July 28, 1962.

Sources: National Bank Act; Federal Reserve Act; *Federal Reserve Bulletin*, vol. 45, no. 12 (December, 1969), p. 1492; vol. 50, no. 9 (September, 1964), p. 1152.

The Reserve authorities learned by unhappy experience that changes in reserve requirements have drastic results.

Fortunately the depression of 1938 was short, and the levels of early 1937 were soon regained. But it was not until the United States had actually entered the war that full recovery brought unemployment down to acceptable levels.

World War II

World War II produced the same monetary problems that World War I had, but on a larger scale commensurate with greater involvement and the higher cost of modern methods of destruction. The Federal Reserve acted much more vigorously to support Treasury financial operations. Although reserve requirements were kept at the maximum legal limit (except for banks in New York and Chicago) throughout the war, discount rates were reduced (on loans backed by government securities) to ½ per cent. Even more important, however, were open-market purchases of securities.

Open-market Policy. Early in the war the Federal Reserve decided that nothing should stand in the way of an all-out effort to provide funds needed by the government to meet its unprecedented war budgets. The Reserve was concerned over the inflationary consequences, but it felt that it was impossible under the circumstances to keep the economy within bounds. Quite the contrary; its basic policy during the war was to provide a guaranteed market for all government securities that others could not absorb.

As in World War I, a concerted effort was made to obtain as much money as possible from nonbank sources. The least inflationary method of borrowing was through war bonds (now called *savings bonds*) sold to individual investors. These were nontransferable and could not even be used as collateral for bank loans, so that the money spent to purchase them came both initially and ultimately from savings.

It was the desire to tap this noninflationary source to the limit that explains the tremendous pressure to sell war bonds. It wasn't that the government couldn't have gotten the necessary funds otherwise. The government would have obtained the money somehow, even if it had to print the stuff. But selling war bonds would be much less inflationary than any alternative method of financing the deficit. The desire to sell as many war bonds as possible was therefore highly commendable, though the methods used were sometimes less than candid.

Operating in the same direction was the attempt to push sales to nonbank institutions: insurance companies, trust funds, savings banks, ordinary corporations, and others. Several bond issues were not eligible for purchase by commercial banks until some time after they had been issued. Initially the funds for these purchases had to come from savings—corporate or personal—although in time the securities might reach banks through normal market channels.

These two sources were inadequate to absorb the huge government offerings, and the next step was to persuade commercial banks to buy the rest of the securities issued. Even this was insufficient, and the Federal Reserve stood ready to take up whatever was left over.

The law prohibited the Federal Reserve from buying securities directly from the Federal Treasury,[11] but the same result was obtained by other means. When open-market operations are used for credit-control purposes, the Open Market Committee decides the amount of securities to be purchased on the basis of the quantity of funds that it thinks should be supplied to the market. The price at which the purchases are made depends on the market. During the war the situation was reversed. The authorities established the price at which securities would be bought and took all that were offered at that price.

This policy was formally inaugurated in April, 1942, when the Reserve banks announced that they would buy all 90-day treasury bills offered at a price to yield ⅜ per cent interest.[12] Later it agreed in addition to resell these bills at the same yield if the original owner wished to buy them back. The effect of this policy was to make treasury bills a form of interest-earning cash. A bank with temporarily excess reserves could buy bills and earn ⅜ per cent, knowing that the instant it needed cash it could sell them to the Reserve without loss—and buy them back again whenever it wished. This induced banks to hold more bills than they otherwise would have done, but it also meant that a bank could at any time increase its reserves in order to expand credit.

Without the same degree of rigidity the Federal Reserve extended this policy to other government securities at a graduated scale of interest yields: roughly ⅞ per cent on certificates, 2 per cent on bonds maturing in seven to nine years, and 2½ per cent on 15-year bonds. Interest rates were not permitted to rise above these levels. This meant that whenever interest yields tended to move upward (through a fall in price of securities), the Reserve stood ready to buy securities at a price corresponding to the maximum yield established by the System. These prices were universally above par, so that no bank (or anyone else) could lose by selling securities to the Reserve. The amount of reserves available to the banks under these conditions was limited only by their holdings of government securities, which were substantial.

The basic purpose of this open-end policy of purchases was to enable the Treasury to borrow whatever funds it needed at fixed (low) interest rates, thus reducing any uncertainty about the success of new Treasury issues and keeping down the cost of servicing the national debt. But it prevented the Reserve authorities from using any of the normal restraints on credit that were intended to hold a boom in check. As Federal Reserve purchases of govern-

[11] A relaxation of the general prohibition, permitting the Federal Reserve banks to hold not more than $5 billion worth of securities bought directly from the Treasury, was introduced in 1942, but this provision has never been used for general purchases. Its use has been restricted to temporary and unusual circumstances.

[12] Since bills are sold on a discount basis, the precise price that would yield ⅜ per cent would vary with the length of time to maturity.

ment securities poured new reserves into the monetary system, the resultant expansion of the money supply was vast. As Table 32-1 shows, the quantity of government securities held by the Federal Reserve banks rose from $2 billion in 1941 (a level scarcely changed from 1933) to $24 billion at the end of 1945. During the same period currency outside banks rose from $10 billion to $26 billion, and demand deposits, adjusted, almost doubled from $39 billion to $76 billion. The inflationary potential is obvious.

Direct Controls. In an attempt to provide some restraint under these conditions the Federal Reserve turned to direct controls. Speculation on the stock exchange did not appear serious in the early stages of the war, but the Board of Governors raised margin requirements to 75 per cent just in case.

Much more important was the power to control consumer credit. This authority was given to the Board of Governors by Executive order of the President in 1941 under the broad provisions of emergency war powers. Purchasing power was rising much more rapidly than the quantity of goods, putting strong pressure on prices. The Office of Price Administration (OPA), with price ceilings and rationing, attempted to resist this pressure from one direction. Consumer credit regulations were intended to restrict additional funds pumped directly into the consumer market. These regulations, prescribing minimum down payments and maximum length of the repayment period for installment loans, reduced the demand for consumer goods by keeping out of the market those who couldn't meet the terms of the regulations.

The overall effect of consumer credit control was fairly limited, but it did contribute somewhat to reducing credit expansion without imposing curbs on loans to government or business.

Repressed Inflation. The war period was one of *repressed inflation.* The inflationary pressure of an expanding money supply was evident. But instead of attacking the cause of inflation, the government confined itself for the most part to symptoms: the prices themselves. By price and (to a lesser extent) wage controls, coupled with rationing, the government made it almost impossible either for prices to rise or for people to spend all the new money that was being created. As one result, saving increased substantially, and this meant that people were accumulating a stock of readily available purchasing power that they could use as soon as the controls were removed. This occurred in 1946, and the resulting open inflation was essentially the delayed result of the increase in the money supply during the war.

Postwar Inflation

Even when the war ended, the Federal Reserve continued its support of the government bond market. The situation was similar to that in 1919. Rational credit-control policy called for restriction on the inflationary joyride, but the "exigencies of Treasury finance" seemed to require the opposite policy. The

Federal Reserve, under heavy pressure from the Treasury, failed to exercise its authority in the money market for over five years, while the value of the dollar continued to slide to the lowest point in history.

The bill rate was kept at ⅜ per cent until mid-1947, when it was allowed to drift upward to 1 per cent. Over the next two years it went even higher. Support of longer-term bonds was relaxed to a much slighter extent, and although the Reserve's total holdings of government securities did not rise in this period, their very failure to fall supported the forces of inflation. Active monetary policy would have curtailed credit as a countermeasure to the great expansion during the war. As repressed inflation broke out into the open, stability would have required a reduction in the money supply. Instead the Reserve permitted, although it certainly did not encourage, a continued expansion, as shown in Table 32-3.

This policy has been severely criticized. Even some Federal Reserve officials were not very happy with it, and the former director of the Division of Research and Statistics of the Federal Reserve has said that the excuses offered by the Board for their actions in this period were "unpersuasive."[13]

What were the considerations that induced the Federal Reserve to abdicate its role as policeman over the money supply? There were several:

1. The Reserve felt that it had induced banks to buy securities under an implied promise that it wouldn't let their price fall and that it should carry out this pledge.

2. Any substantial drop in bond prices would seriously impair the financial position of banks that held large portfolios, since they would be forced to write down the value of their assets to the new market level. Other financial institutions would be similarly affected.

3. It was feared that a drop in government security prices would be interpreted as a sign of weakness in the government itself and would impair the credit of the United States and perhaps even start a financial panic.

4. Restrictive credit policies would still leave a large residual amount of purchasing power in the hands of the public and therefore would not completely conquer inflation. "Some degree of inflation was inevitable as a result of the war."

5. The effect of restrictive credit policies might have been "to bring about a sharp downturn in business rather than merely to restrain inflation."

6. A rise in interest rates would raise the cost of borrowing by the Treasury.[14]

An analysis of these stated reasons would seem to indicate that the last was the compelling one, and the others largely excuses. The weakest are items 4 and 5, which are mutually contradictory. Together they seem to suggest that

[13] E. A. Goldenweiser, *American Monetary Policy* (McGraw-Hill Book Company, New York, 1951), pp. 200–201.

[14] Except for item 1 these reasons are given in a statement by the Federal Reserve to the Subcommittee on Monetary, Credit, and Fiscal Policies of the Joint Economic Committee of Congress, *A Compendium of Materials on Monetary, Credit, and Fiscal Policies,* 81st Cong., 2d Sess., Document 132 (1950), pp. 103–105. The two direct quotations appear in two adjoining paragraphs on p. 104.

Table 32-3. Postwar Monetary Expansion

December 31; Billions of Dollars

Year	Total Federal Reserve credit	Member bank reserves	Demand deposits adjusted	Currency outside banks	Total money supply*
1929	1.6	2.4	22.8	3.6	23.4
1933	2.7	2.7	15.0	4.8	19.8
1939	2.6	11.7†	29.8	6.4	36.2
1940	2.3	14.0	34.9	7.3	42.2
1941	2.4	12.5	39.0	9.6	48.6
1942	6.7	13.1	48.9	13.9	52.8
1943	12.2	12.9	60.8	18.8	79.6
1944	19.7	14.4	66.9	23.5	90.4
1945	25.1	15.9	75.9	26.5	102.4
1946	24.1	16.1	83.3	26.7	110.0
1947	23.2	17.9	87.1	26.5	113.6
1948	24.1	20.5	85.5	26.1	111.6
1949	19.5	16.6	85.8	25.4	111.2
1950	22.2	17.7	92.3	25.4	117.7
1951	25.0	20.1	98.2	26.3	124.5
1952	25.8	20.0	101.5	27.5	129.0
1953	26.9	20.2	102.5	28.1	130.6
1954	25.9	18.9	106.6	27.9	134.5
1955	26.5	19.0	109.9	28.3	138.2
1956	26.7	19.1	111.4	28.3	139.7
1957	25.8	19.0	110.3	28.3	138.6
1958	27.8	18.5	115.5	28.7	144.2
1959‡	29.4	18.9	116.1	29.5	145.6
1960	29.1	19.3	115.2	29.6	144.7
1961	31.2	20.1	119.2	30.2	149.4
1962	33.2	20.0	120.3	31.2	151.6
1963	36.6	20.7	124.1	33.1	157.2
1964	39.9	21.6	128.7	34.9	163.6

* Sum of preceding two columns.
† This spectacular rise in reserves with no significant rise in Reserve bank credit was primarily due to an increase in gold stock from $4.0 billion in 1933 to $17.6 billion in 1939.
‡ Beginning with 1959 data represent averages of daily figures for the month of December.
Sources: Board of Governors of the Federal Reserve System, *Banking and Monetary Statistics* (1943), pp. 375–377; *Federal Reserve Bulletin*, vol. 29, no. 3 (March, 1943), p. 227; vol. 31, no. 3 (March, 1945), p. 233; vol. 31, no. 7 (July, 1945), p. 665; vol. 36, no. 7 (July, 1950), pp. 840, 850; vol. 41, no. 7 (July, 1955), pp. 766, 774; vol. 45, no. 12 (December, 1959), pp. 1490, 1498; vol. 51, no. 2 (February, 1965), pp. 262, 274.

the Federal Reserve simply cannot exercise effective control of the monetary system because its actions would be either inadequate or overpowerful. Such an attitude is completely defeatist. It is true that Federal Reserve actions have sometimes been insufficient to prevent undesirable economic movements. On at least one occasion, as we saw in the last chapter, action has appeared to be too drastic. But to be frightened into inaction because policies may not be perfect is to deny that we can ever control our economic destiny.

The Federal Reserve under the Thumb of the Treasury. The basis of the problem in this postwar period was that the Federal Reserve was not really independent, but very much under the influence of the Treasury. It is perfectly proper for the Treasury to attempt to save the taxpayer money by borrowing at the lowest possible price. But it is not proper for the Federal Reserve, whose objectives are stable prices, full employment, and growth, to substitute for these the maintenance of an artificially low rate of interest, whether for the benefit of the Treasury or for any other reason. Yet this is what happened. The policy was usually described in terms of "maintaining an orderly market in government securities," but its results were inflation pure and simple.

Federal Reserve officials themselves were uneasy about this marriage of convenience with the Treasury, and in many minor ways they attempted to cut the ground from under inflationary forces. Margin requirements were raised to 100 per cent in 1946. Consumer credit controls were maintained except for a period in 1948 when legal authorization was withdrawn. Discount rates, which had moved to 1 per cent at the close of the war, were brought up to 1½ per cent in 1948. Gradually the Reserve lowered its support prices, as already mentioned, but not below par. The result of all these actions combined was the proverbial drop in the bucket.

In 1948 the Board of Governors twice raised the reserve requirements of central reserve city banks, the only ones not already at the maximum permitted by law (see Table 32-2). Later that year it persuaded Congress to lift the legal maximum and immediately raised all reserve requirements by 2 percentage points (1½ points for time deposits).

The results of this action demonstrated as clearly as anything could the utter ineffectiveness of any general credit restraint as long as the Reserve maintained its open-end policy of bond support. The effect of a 2-percentage-point rise in legal reserves should have been to reduce excess reserves by slightly over $2 billion. The higher requirements went into effect on September 16 and September 24. Between August 25 and September 29, Federal Reserve holdings of government securities rose by $1.8 billion, member bank holdings of government securities fell by $2.6 billion, total bank reserves rose by $2.2 billion, and *excess reserves actually rose* by $0.1 billion! The banks had simply sold enough government securities to the Federal Reserve and others on a guaranteed market to provide the increased reserves needed. Instead of contracting their loans, they actually expanded them by a billion dollars in the very month that the supposedly restrictive action was taken. Credit control simply cannot work in harness with a perpetual low-interest policy.

In 1949 the economy slipped somewhat in the first postwar recession. In this period purchases of government securities made sense, and by the time recovery suggested the need for more restrictive measures the Federal Reserve authorities seem to have steeled themselves to the necessity of breaking away from the apron strings of the Treasury. The method used turned out to be spectacular.

As recovery progressed in 1950, government interest rates returned to the same level from which they had retreated when recession struck, a level that had proved inadequate to restrain inflation. In August, 1950, with the Korean crisis already overhanging the economy, the Treasury offered a new issue of 13-month certificates at 1¼ per cent. The Federal Reserve attempted to persuade the Treasury to adopt a higher rate, but without success. The Reserve then determined to do something no central bank had ever dared before—to prevent the Treasury from selling its bonds on the market. The maneuver was highly technical. In essence it involved breaking through former support levels by selling securities from its portfolio at a lower price (higher yield) than had existed for many years. At the same time it bought all those maturing bonds and certificates that were due to be exchanged for the new issues. The effect was to raise short-term interest rates close to 1⅜ per cent, so that no one wanted to buy the new certificates at 1¼ per cent. Almost all the new certificates were therefore taken by the Federal Reserve (not by purchase but in exchange for the maturing securities that it had previously bought on the market).

For practical purposes the Treasury issue was a complete flop. An ironic footnote to the whole affair is that the securities sold by the Federal Reserve, since they were sold at lower prices than those at which they were bought, involved the Reserve in a considerable loss, amounting apparently to some $17 million. But since the greater part of the Reserve banks' net profits are paid into the Treasury, the loss was borne ultimately by the Treasury itself! It would have cost the Treasury the same amount if it had offered the certificates at 1⅜ per cent in the first place.

It took real courage for the Federal Reserve to oppose the Treasury so publicly. As Paul Heffernan summed up the situation:

> Resolved to fulfill sworn responsibilities for using certain specific powers in the interest of a stable national economy, the Federal Reserve has just transmuted the idea of central bank independence—until now a concept of theory and rhetoric—into a fact. For the first time in modern finance, a major central banking institution . . . has indicated that the "interest of the Treasury" is against the "public interest."[15]

The effect on interest rates was immediate. Within weeks all major money market rates—bank acceptances, commercial paper, demand loans, prime bank rate, and (to drive the point home) the discount rate—had risen by one-quarter or three-eighths of a point.

The effect on the tempers of Treasury officials can easily be imagined. The fight was finally taken to the President of the United States, who called in the whole Open Market Committee for a reprimand. But even that conference, unprecedented in Federal Reserve history, exploded. At its close the Presi-

[15] *The New York Times,* Sept. 10, 1950, sec. 3, p. 1.

dent issued a statement saying "that the Federal Reserve Board has given its pledge 'to maintain the stability of Government securities as long as the emergency lasts.' "[16] He followed this up with a letter saying that this meant the maintenance of support prices at existing levels.

Two days later Marriner Eccles, senior member of the Board of Governors and for a long time its chairman, denying flatly that the Committee had ever made any such promise, made public the official memorandum of the meeting with the President, approved by all members of the Board of Governors, which made no mention whatsoever of any such pledge.

A furor arose over the political implications of the President's interference with the independence of the Federal Reserve. Senator Douglas, with bipartisan support, introduced a bill in Congress the intent of which was to reaffirm that independence and to require that "the policy and actions of the Secretary of the Treasury relative to money, credit and transactions affecting the Federal debt shall be made consistent with the policies of such Federal Reserve authorities."[17]

Treasury–Federal Reserve Accord. Even before this bill was prepared, however, the Treasury and Federal Reserve had patched up their differences in the famous Accord of March, 1951. This joint statement by the two agencies declared: "The Treasury and the Federal Reserve System have reached full accord with respect to debt-management and monetary policies to be pursued in furthering their common purposes to assure the successful financing of the Government's requirements and, at the same time, to minimize the monetization of the public debt."[18]

The Accord was accompanied by an announcement of a new long-term bond bearing an interest rate of 2¾ per cent. Since this was a rise of ¼ per cent, it was obvious that the so-called compromise was actually a complete victory for the Federal Reserve's insistence on rising interest rates as a means of combating inflation.[19] This conclusion was confirmed as the Reserve gradually lowered its support prices and within a week dropped them altogether. For the first time in ten years government bonds were being sold on a free market. For the first time in ten years the Federal Reserve was free to pursue

[16] *Ibid.,* Feb. 2, 1951, p. 1.

[17] *Ibid.,* Mar. 7, 1951, p. 26.

[18] *Federal Reserve Bulletin,* vol. 37, no. 3 (March, 1951), p. 267. The announcement was issued on Mar. 4.

[19] As a face-saving device the new bond was to be nontransferable (holders could not sell it to others) and nonredeemable (holders could not get their money back from the government) prior to maturity. Holders were thus supposed to be locked in for the full twenty-nine years till maturity. The extra interest was said to be a premium for these special low-liquidity provisions. But the bond was *convertible* into 5-year notes at the option of the holder, and these notes were themselves marketable. The nonliquidity provisions thus amounted to no more than a need for two transactions (bonds into notes, then notes into cash) instead of the usual one. The nonmarketability was merely a smoke screen. Of $13½ billion of these bonds originally issued, $2 billion were actually "redeemed" (that is, converted) within a year, and by 1959 only half of the total issue was still outstanding.

its basic purpose of stabilizing the economy unhampered by artificial considerations of Treasury finance.

It should be noted in passing that none of the dire consequences predicted for a free market materialized. There was no panic. Bond prices fell, but in an orderly manner. Financial institutions experienced no noticeable difficulties. Rather they benefited by the higher interest they could now earn on their assets. Nor is there any evidence of loss of faith in government credit. Having taken the plunge, the economy found the water very much to its liking. The only serious question seemed to be: Why hadn't it been done earlier? Even the Treasury appeared satisfied with the results and adjusted its new issues to the market interest rate.

In many respects this episode is the most important in the history of central banking. The central bank had faced up to the government and won its complete independence. Whether it was the example of the Federal Reserve or whether it was spontaneous combustion, this same drama was repeated with different actors and different scenery all over the world. Central banks in England, Sweden, Germany, and dozens of other countries, fed up with the same enforced subservience to treasury policy, suddenly found their strength, broke their fetters, and began again doing the job they were supposed to do. This is the period of "resurgence of monetary policy." In some respects it was a period of painful readjustment, for muscles long unused do not readily respond to renewed activity, but it bore great hope for the future, for man's ability to control the excesses of monetary abuse.

Since the Accord

The period of the fifties was one in which the Federal Reserve perfected its techniques without any major emergency to put them to serious test. No drastic changes in general economic conditions called for corrective action. Intervals of mild inflation were interrupted by minor recessions in 1954, 1958, and 1961. Federal Reserve policy in this period has been described by its chairman as "leaning against the wind." The System acted to counter the forces of depression on the one hand and of inflation on the other, constantly on the alert to note a change in the wind and to alter course accordingly. This has required a very flexible policy and for the most part a very light touch.

Reserve Requirements. The traditional use of reserve requirements was limited to the two recessions. In each, requirements were reduced in a few small steps.

More important were changes in the law itself in 1959, which permitted member banks to count vault cash as part of legal reserves, a privilege that had been withdrawn in 1917. At the same time, the Federal Reserve raised the reserve requirement against demand deposits of country banks to 12 per cent on the grounds that these banks stood to gain most from the inclusion of cash in their reserves. The law also provided for the inclusion of central reserve city banks in the reserve city classification and raised the maximum legal reserve ratio for that classification from 20 to 22 per cent.

Open-market Operations. Open-market operations, the most sensitive of policy tools, were used from day to day and from week to week to provide stability to the money market. They were also used anticyclically, but not in large amounts. Total Federal Reserve holdings of government securities edged up irregularly from the $22 billion held immediately before the Accord to $24 billion at the beginning of 1958. Purchases since that time have been influenced heavily by the gold problem, to be discussed shortly.

Discount Rate. The discount rate has been the star performer in the fifties. Discounts, which were practically nonexistent from 1934 to 1944, picked up very slightly during the war. In 1952 they briefly approached the $2 billion mark, and since 1956 they have frequently exceeded $1 billion. This is still not very much comparatively, but it does make the discount rate somewhat more effective in cost terms, while it has never lost its psychological value.

Figure 32-2 shows better than any words how the discount rate has moved to "lean against" the forces of inflation and recession. It also shows the close correlation between the bank rate and other interest rates, though a controversy still rages over the question of whether the discount rate has preceded or followed market movements.

Obviously Federal Reserve policy (particularly when viewed by hindsight) has not been perfect, and even its supporters have frequently been critical of the timing of some of its actions in this period. For instance, much criticism has been aroused by the fact that in 1957 the discount rate was raised in August and was not reduced until November, although the economy had been moving downward since July. This is sometimes cited as a contributing cause of the 1958 recession.

Another point of some controversy was the Reserve's handling of the recession of 1958 itself. This was a period when business was unquestionably depressed. But prices continued to rise. Here we had simultaneous unemployment and inflation. Which to attack?

The record shows that the Reserve authorities took substantial steps to bolster the economy. Discount rates were reduced four times,[20] reserve requirements were reduced four times, and government securities were purchased in moderate amounts. But there is considerable indication that the Reserve moved less actively than it might have if it had not feared that stronger support might set the stage for further inflation, and as soon as the upswing began, the discount rate was raised again to prevent a desirable recovery from mushrooming into an unwanted boom.

[20] The almost instantaneous reaction of the money market to the first discount rate reduction in November, 1957, emphasized strongly the psychological significance of this tool of policy.

Government action to maintain, or to restore, high-level production and employment runs the risk of accentuating or renewing the inflationary trend, while there is serious question whether the upward price trend can be stopped without causing or at least permitting substantial curtailment of production and employment. Yet acceptance of progressive inflation would place a premium on speculative activities at the expense of constructive investment and so interfere with sustained and balanced growth, quite aside from the inequities involved.[21]

The Gold Problem

The difficulty of deciding on proper Federal Reserve policy has been aggravated since 1958 by a substantial loss of gold, associated with a continuous adverse balance of payments for the United States. The strong international position of the dollar, which had allowed us to corner $24.0 billion worth of gold—more than two-thirds of the non-Communist world's gold reserves—by 1949, began to weaken in the early fifties. By 1957 the gold reserves had slipped below $23 billion, and then the rout began. From 1958 to 1965 the United States had an adverse balance of payments (excess of foreign payments over receipts from abroad) of some $2 billion to $3 billion each year. While foreigners have used part of their increased earnings to build up their dollar balances, they have used another part to withdraw gold from the Treasury (through their central banks). As a result the United States lost $9 billion worth of gold in eight years.

This drain brought our gold stock down to $15.4 billion by the end of 1964 and reduced the gold holdings of Federal Reserve banks to 27.5 per cent of their note and deposit liabilities. With a legal gold reserve requirement of 25 per cent, the situation was distinctly disturbing. As an emergency action Congress eliminated the reserve requirement against deposit liabilities, thus freeing almost $5 billion worth of otherwise immobilized gold. But this action was not the first taken by the government to alleviate the problem, nor could it in itself improve the balance of payments. The gold drain continued through 1965, and our gold stock fell to $13.8 billion by December of that year.

Since 1958 the government as a whole has taken a number of less spectacular but more directly effective steps to ease the situation, and the Federal Reserve and the Treasury have actively participated in a series of international financial arrangements (discussed in Chapter 39) to provide both greater overall stability and more effective emergency help for currencies in difficulty. The crisis has also directly affected internal monetary policy, for both the price level and the rate of interest influence the international balance of payments.

If United States prices rise (relative to those of the rest of the world), our exports are more expensive and hence less attractive to foreigners, our balance

[21] U.S. Congress, *Joint and Supplemental Comments of the Presidents of the Federal Reserve Banks in Response to the Questionnaire of the Senate Committee on Finance*, 85th Cong., 2d Sess. (1958), p. 72.

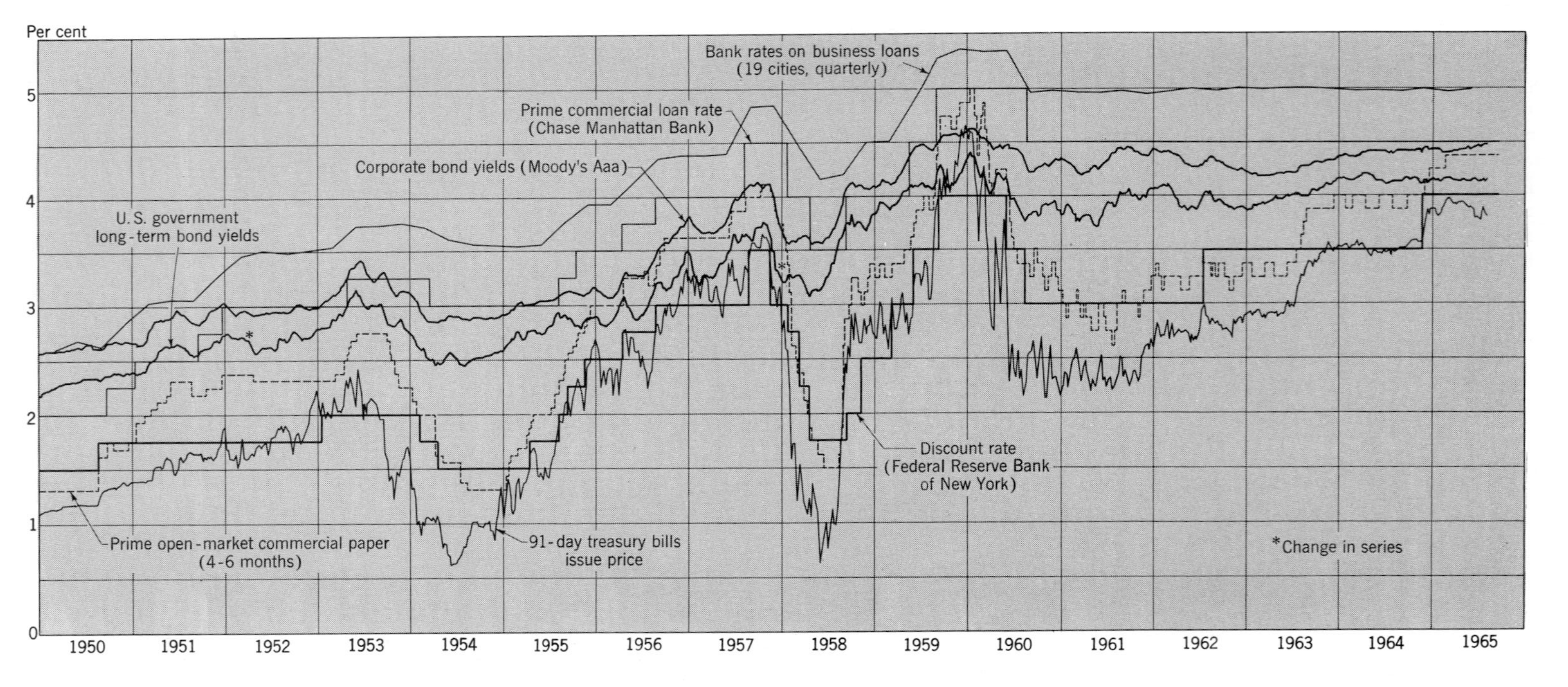
Per cent
5
4
3
2
1
0
1950
1951
1952
1953
1954
1955
1956
1957
1958
1959
1960
1961
1962
1963
1964
1965
Bank rates on business loans
(19 cities, quarterly)
Prime commercial loan rate
(Chase Manhattan Bank)
Corporate bond yields (Moody's Aaa)
U.S. government
long-term bond yields
Prime open-market commercial paper
(4-6 months)
91-day treasury bills
issue price
Discount rate
(Federal Reserve Bank
of New York)
*Change in series

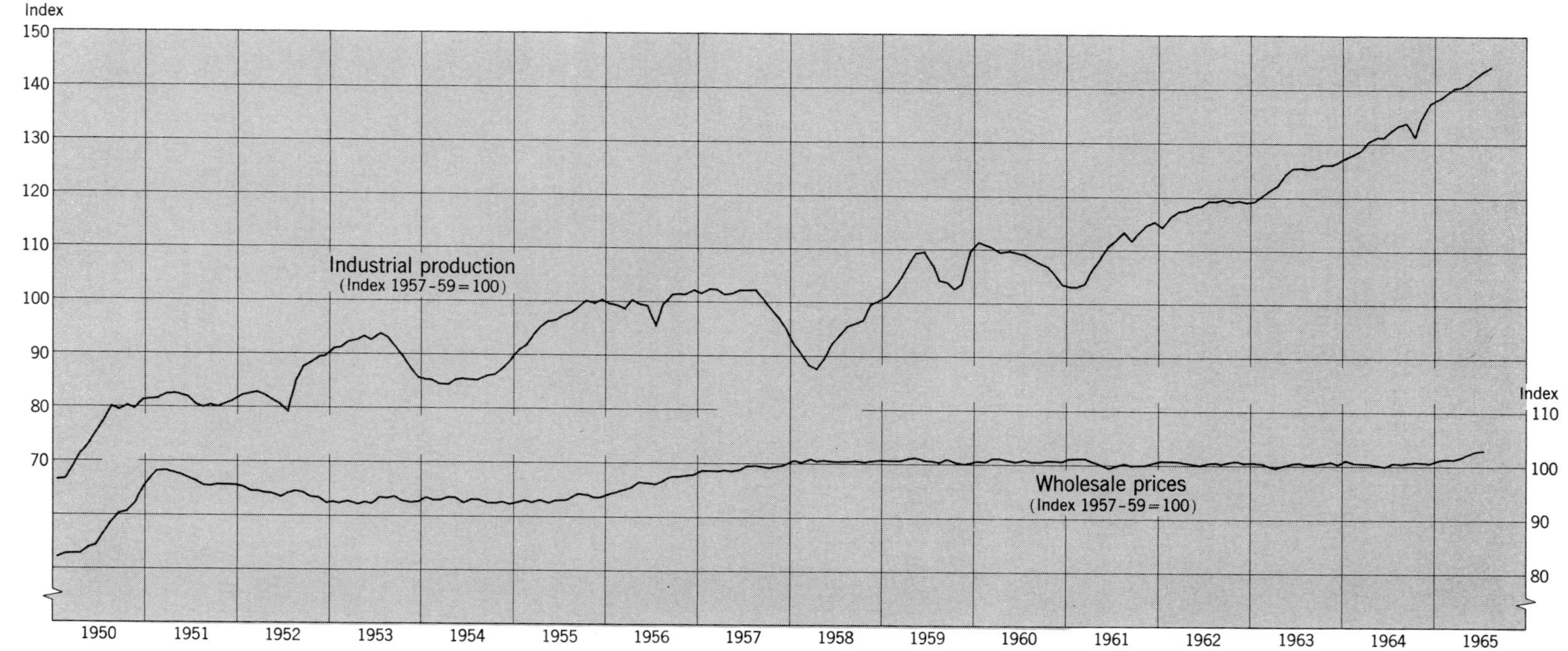

Figure 32-2. Interest rates and business indexes, 1950 to 1965. **Bank rates on business loans** (rates charged by banks on short-term loans to business, 19 cities, quarterly): *Federal Reserve Bulletin*, current issues. **Prime commercial loan rate:** Chase Manhattan Bank, Research Department; *The New York Times*, current issues. **Prime open-market commercial paper** (4–6 months): Federal Reserve Bank of New York, Research Department; *The New York Times*, current issues. **Corporate bond yields** (Moody's Aaa): *Federal Reserve Bulletin*, current issues. **U.S. government long-term bond yields:** *Federal Reserve Bulletin*, current issues. **91-day treasury bills** (issue price): *Federal Reserve Bulletin*, current issues. **Discount rate** (Federal Reserve Bank of New York): *Federal Reserve Bulletin*, current issues. **Industrial production:** Board of Governors of the Federal Reserve System, *Industrial Production, 1957–59 Base*, p. S-148; *Federal Reserve Bulletin*, current issues. **Wholesale prices:** U.S. Bureau of Labor Statistics, "All Commodities Wholesale Price Index, 1957–59 = 100," mimeographed; *Federal Reserve Bulletin*, current issues.

of payments becomes more adverse, and the loss of gold becomes more acute. This simple fact has forced the authorities to pay more attention to price stability (and thus less attention to full employment) than they otherwise might have done. This may account at least in part for both the stability of prices since 1958 and the persistence of unemployment in the 5 to 6 per cent range during the long business upswing from 1961 to 1965.

Closely correlated with this same set of conditions is the fact that low interest rates discourage foreigners from buying United States securities and similarly encourage Americans to send their money abroad, where the interest return is more attractive. The effect of both tendencies is further to aggravate the adverse balance of payments and the outward gold flow. But to raise interest rates would tend to discourage business expansion and thereby increase unemployment.

The Federal Reserve has tried to find a way out of this dilemma by a policy originally called *operation nudge* when introduced in 1961 and later referred to as *operation twist*. This policy attempts to achieve two results simultaneously:

1. *To raise short-term interest rates* on the grounds that on international markets short-term funds are the most readily affected by interest rate differentials and that higher rates will both attract such funds from abroad and reduce the flow of United States funds out of the country.

2. *To lower long-term interest rates* in the belief that these are the rates most important in business investment decisions and that low borrowing rates on bonds will encourage business to expand and will thereby stimulate employment.

In order to accomplish this twin objective the Federal Open Market Committee abandoned its bills-only policy on February 7, 1961, and began buying government securities with maturities of longer than one year. This policy had the advantage of "providing reserves to the banking system to meet the needs of the current business situation" while "avoiding direct downward pressure on short-term interest rates . . . in view of the relationship of short-term rates to the balance of payments problem."[22]

The open-market purchase of securities increases their price (by increasing demand for them) and concurrently reduces the interest yield. Buying short-term securities therefore pushes down short-term rates. This would have been the result of open-market purchases under the bills-only policy. By shifting to the long-term end of the market the Reserve avoided reducing short-term rates and succeeded (temporarily at least) in lowering long-term rates instead, thus helping to encourage borrowing in the capital and mortgage markets.

Purchases of bills were not completely abandoned, as Table 32-4 shows, but for 1961 there was a massive shift into the long-term end of the market, the first time that the Federal Reserve had intervened in this area in terms of any sizable sum since the Accord of 1951. Although there has been some drift

[22] *Annual Report of the Board of Governors of the Federal Reserve System, 1961*, p. 40.

back into the short-term market in increasing amounts, long-term purchases nevertheless continue. During this period the rate on 91-day treasury bills has moved upward from about 2.4 per cent in 1961 to 4.0 per cent in 1965 (as shown in Figure 32-2). The interest yield on long-term government bonds for the same period dropped briefly from 3.9 to 3.8 per cent and then edged upward to 4.3 per cent in 1965. It is normal for the spread between long- and short-term rates to narrow as the general level of interest rises, and it is not clear how much the abandonment of bills-only may have contributed to the narrowing in this case, but it may well have had some effect.

Table 32-4. Net Open-market Purchases of United States Government Securities by the Federal Reserve System, 1960 to 1964*

Millions of Dollars

Year	Maturing within one year	Maturing in more than one year	Total
1960			1,822†
1961	434	2,614	3,048
1962	1,285	1,824	3,109
1963	2,853	1,404	4,257
1964	4,000	1,020	5,020

* Net open-market purchases are outright gross market purchases less gross market sales. The figures do not include cash redemptions, repurchase agreements, or transactions in bank acceptances.

† Presumably all maturing within one year, since the bills-only policy was officially in effect; no statistical breakdown is available.

Sources: *Annual Report of the Board of Governors of the Federal Reserve System, 1960,* p. 117; *1961,* p. 132; *1962,* p. 152; *1963,* p. 220. *Federal Reserve Bulletin,* vol. 51, no. 2 (February, 1965), p. 269.

The Reserve authorities also used moral suasion in this period to encourage banks to solicit foreign funds, and they made minor changes in technical regulations for the same purpose. More spectacular was their reaction to the rise in the British bank rate from 5 to 7 per cent in November, 1964. In order to reduce the attractiveness of this high foreign rate, the Reserve banks raised the discount rate from 3½ to 4 per cent, five of them acting on the very day the British action was taken. Simultaneously the Board of Governors substantially increased the maximum interest that commercial banks could pay on deposits, particularly those on very short term (see Table 32-5), in the hope of attracting foreign funds and holding domestic funds that might otherwise be tempted to seek higher rates abroad.

And although these actions, taken wholly for international reasons, would normally be expected to raise interest rates generally, both Chairman Martin of the Federal Reserve and President Johnson stated emphatically that they did not expect banks to raise the rates they charged domestic borrowers. When four banks raised their prime rates, the President again expressed his view that this was contrary to public policy and would interfere with the maintenance of prosperity, and the increases were rescinded. How long banks could afford to pay higher interest for deposited funds while maintaining loan interest unchanged is an interesting point, but temporarily at least the author-

Table 32-5. Maximum Interest Rates Payable by Commercial Banks on Time and Savings Deposits

	Jan. 1, 1936	Jan. 1, 1957	Jan. 1, 1962	July 17, 1963	Nov. 4, 1964	Dec. 6, 1965
Savings deposits held for:						
One year or more	2½	3	4	4	4	4
Less than one year	2½	3	3½	3½	4	4
Other time deposits payable in:						
One year or more	2½	3	4	4	4½	5½
Six months to one year	2	2½	3½	4	4½	5½
Ninety days to six months	2	2½	2½	4	4½	5½
Less than ninety days	1	1	1	1	4	5½

Source: *Federal Reserve Bulletin*, vol. 50, no. 12 (December, 1964), p. 1546.

ities were able to manage this tricky juggling feat in the interest of reconciling the opposing pressures produced by divergent domestic and international forces.

This policy of restraint with respect to interest rates, however, could not survive the artificial stimulus given the economy by the undeclared war in Viet Nam. As the economy started to heat up, the well-known symptoms of overexpansion became evident, particularly in the wholesale price index, which rose by 2.8 per cent in the first eleven months of 1965. Interest rates on money market instruments rose in the same period by about ½ per cent. In December, therefore, the discount rate was raised to 4½ per cent. At the same time the Board of Governors raised to 5½ per cent the maximum interest that banks could pay on time deposits (other than savings deposits, for which the ceiling remained at 4 per cent). These actions came much later than seemed warranted by economic events, and in the face of strong and vocal opposition by President Johnson to such upward pressure on the interest rate structure the Federal Reserve may not feel able to pursue as stringent an anti-inflation policy as they would like, particularly if the war continues to escalate toward a world holocaust. If this occurs, it would seem that another confrontation of the administration and the Federal Reserve may be in the offing, repeating the type of wrangle that was settled temporarily by the Treasury-Federal Reserve Accord of 1951.[23]

Conclusion. In spite of these developments, however, the first fourteen years following the Accord have been a period of *relative* stability. Ups and downs, yes. But nothing like the wild gyrations of the thirties or forties. Perhaps this is just the lull before the storm. It would be foolish to extrapolate the trend into the future and to say that the business cycle has been licked. Yet it seems to have been at least temporarily moderated, and most economists feel that part of the credit should go to the Federal Reserve. On the other hand, the level of unemployment has remained uncomfortably high even in the best of

[23] If, indeed, there are any of us left to wrangle.

times, and there are those who say that our rate of economic growth has been less than it should and could have been. Some even suggest that we have had stability, such as it is, in spite of the Federal Reserve rather than because of it. Under the circumstances, therefore, it is hardly surprising that debate continues, and probably always will, over ways to improve our monetary system. To that subject we now turn.

Questions for Thought and Discussion

1. Why has no war ever been fought without inflation? Can you devise a plan by which it might be done?

2. Do you think that the reduction in the regional autonomy of the Federal Reserve banks has been desirable?

3. Why, if it was set up for just that purpose, was the Federal Reserve unable to stop the Depression of the thirties? Do you think its powers have been strengthened sufficiently to stop any future depressions?

4. Apparently the Federal Reserve has made a number of mistakes in policy over the years. Would it be better if the System were abolished?

5. Is there any way in which the government as a whole might have prevented the inflation that occured in 1945–1951? Could the Federal Reserve have done the job alone?

6. Why should there be conflict between the Federal Reserve and the Treasury?

7. When experts disagree over what policy should be followed, how can we determine who is correct?

8. Why should a deficit in our balance of international payments lead to the abandonment of the bills-only policy?

9. Are there any similarities between our present loss of gold and the gold drain of the early thirties? Do these similarities suggest any policies that should or should not be followed today?

10. What changes in the discount rate have occurred since 1965? Why?

Selected Bibliography

Achinstein, Asher: *Federal Reserve Policy and Economic Stability, 1951–57: Report to the Senate Committee on Banking and Currency,* Oct. 10, 1958.

Ahearn, Daniel S.: *Federal Reserve Policy Reappraised, 1951–1959,* Columbia University Press, New York, 1963.

Beckhart, Benjamin H.: *The Discount Policy of the Federal Reserve Banks,* Holt, Rinehart and Winston, Inc., New York, 1924.

Brown, A. J.: *The Great Inflation, 1939–1951,* Oxford University Press, London, 1955.

Burgess, W. Randolph: *The Reserve Banks and the Money Market,* rev. ed., Harper & Row, Publishers, Incorporated, New York, 1936.
———: *Inflation in the United States, 1940–1948,* Harper & Row, Publishers, Incorporated, New York, 1951.
Chandler, Lester V.: *Benjamin Strong: Central Banker,* The Brookings Institution, Washington, 1958.
Eccles, Marriner S.: *Beckoning Frontiers,* Alfred A. Knopf., Inc., New York, 1951.
Fforde, J. S.: *The Federal Reserve System, 1945–1949,* Oxford University Press, Fair Lawn, N.J., 1954.
Fousek, Peter G.: *Foreign Central Banking: The Instruments of Monetary Policy,* Federal Reserve Bank of New York, November, 1957.
Friedman, Milton, and Anna Jacobson Schwartz: *A Monetary History of the United States, 1867–1960,* published for the National Bureau of Economic Research by Princeton University Press, Princeton, N.J., 1963.
Goldenweiser, E. A.: *American Monetary Policy,* McGraw-Hill Book Company, New York, 1951.
Harding, W. P. G.: *The Formative Period of the Federal Reserve System,* Constable & Co., Ltd., London, 1925.
Hardy, C. O.: *Credit Policies of the Federal Reserve System,* The Brookings Institution, Washington, 1932.
Johnson, G. G., Jr.: *The Treasury and Monetary Policy, 1932–1938,* Harvard University Press, Cambridge, Mass., 1939.
Kemmerer, Edwin W.: *The ABC of the Federal Reserve System,* 11th ed., Princeton University Press, Princeton, N.J., 1938.
Paris, James D.: *Monetary Policies in the United States, 1932–1938,* Columbia University Press, New York, 1938.
Reed, Harold L.: *The Development of Federal Reserve Policy,* Houghton Mifflin Company, Boston, 1922.
———: *Federal Reserve Policy, 1921–1930,* McGraw-Hill Book Company, New York, 1930.
Roosa, Robert V.: *Federal Operations in the Money and Government Securities Markets,* Federal Reserve Bank of New York, July, 1956.
Warburg, Paul M.: *The Federal Reserve System: Its Origin and Growth,* 2 vols., The Macmillan Company, New York, 1930.
Willis, H. Parker: *The Theory and Practice of Central Banking,* Harper & Row, Publishers, Incorporated, New York, 1936.
Youngman, Anna P.: *The Federal Reserve System in Wartime,* National Bureau of Economic Research, Inc., New York, 1945.
See also the congressional hearings listed in Chapter 33.

Chapter 33
Critique: The Bases of Monetary Policy

And lean-look'd prophets whisper fearful change.

The Tragedy of King Richard II
Act II, scene 4, line 11

There are few who doubt that our control of monetary policy could be improved, though there is no common agreement on the precise steps to take. As in many policy matters opinions are sometimes diametrically opposed. And since we can't put the economy into a test tube to see how it would react to remedy A compared with remedy B, we will never know for certain just which proposals are most practical. But we can bring to bear on each the knowledge that we have about the operation of the economy. Theory's greatest importance lies in its ability to shed light on policy suggestions.

Is Our Aim Proper?

Even the very goals of policy are sometimes called into question. There are some who feel that the Federal Reserve shouldn't be trying to control the business cycle at all. They suggest that during a boom structural maladjustments creep into the economy. Capital investment accelerates too rapidly. Poorly conceived and poorly managed firms are able to get along, sometimes very well. The debt structure becomes topheavy. The risk factor seems to be weighted on the side of profit, without the counter-balance of loss to weed out the inefficient. Speculation is often more lucrative than sound productive effort. The depression, they say, is the inevitable consequence of former excesses. It is necessary in order to reestablish a healthy economy, to put a brake on soaring investment, to cut the debt pattern to fit the income cloth, to force uneconomic enterprises out of the market, to get inventories back to proper size, and to restore liquidity.

The burden of this case is that we can't have a boom without a bust, a spree without a hangover. It would seem, however, that this is essentially an argument for stronger controls during the upswing rather than for weaker ones on the toboggan. If the maladjustments of boom were prevented, the readjustments of depression would become unnecessary.

There are, on the other hand, those who feel that the action of the Federal Reserve in recessions has been altogether too weak. They believe that full employment is by far the most important goal of the economy, let the prices fall where they may. Such critics generally believe that the government should intervene at the first sign of a downturn regardless of the inflationary consequences. Some even suggest that the economy has an inherent tendency toward stagnation that must be countered by almost continuous expansionary policies in order to promote maximum growth. The advocates of such a policy are not impressed by objections citing the disadvantages of inflation.

This argument will probably never be settled to everybody's satisfaction, and Federal Reserve policy will consequently always be under attack from those who think it is too stringent and from those who think it is not strong enough. Meanwhile the Reserve seems committed to the watchful middle ground of compromise, for the present at least. "In principle, stable prices, business activity at high levels of production and employment, and economic growth are mutually consistent," and "too much emphasis on one objective may impair ability to achieve the others."[1] Or, as Alfred Hayes of the Federal Reserve Bank of New York put it: "It has been, and is still, our hope that high—and rising—levels of production and employment can be reconciled with stability in the value of money, and our efforts have been directed toward that combined objective."[2]

Most economists and a large number of other people seem to agree with this statement of the Federal Reserve authorities. Since a high level of employment and production is already called for by the Employment Act of 1946, it has frequently been suggested that a better balance would be achieved by adding a reasonably stable price level to that list of objectives. Although this already seems to be implied, it would avoid some confusion if it were unambiguously stated.

Is Discretionary Control Necessary?

There are some who believe that the simplest and most effective way of stabilizing the economy is to remove the need for conscious control by sub-

[1] U.S. Congress, *Joint and Supplemental Comments of the Presidents of the Federal Reserve Banks in Response to the Questionnaire of the Senate Committee on Finance*, 85th Cong., 2d Sess. (1958), p. 29.

[2] *Ibid.*, p. 72.

stituting automatic devices for administrative action. This is somewhat the same attitude that prompted the original Federal Reserve Act—the belief in automaticity—and the argument runs along similar lines. Usually the proponents of automatic control emphasize the importance of price stability as a primary goal, but they expect that a high level of business activity will also be promoted by a minimum of tinkering with the economy. Money, they say, should be controlled by law, not by human decision.

Whenever an administrator or a board must make a decision (to raise the discount rate, for example), there is always the possibility of being wrong or of being too late, or both. The two problems are interrelated, for the greatest likelihood of error arises from the need for action before all the facts are known. There are at least three significant lags in policy action:

1. Statistics take time to prepare. Figures for consumer prices, industrial production, unemployment, or national income take a month or more to compile. Some figures are available earlier, some later, but generally decisions must be made on the basis of data a month or so old.

2. Suppose these figures show a decline. Does this mean the beginning of a recession, or may it be merely a temporary setback prior to a movement to still higher levels? The economy does not move smoothly, and it frequently takes several months of statistics before a clear trend is evident. This is particularly true if different indicators are moving in opposite directions. A recession is not unmistakably clear until it is well advanced, whereas preventive measures should be taken before it starts. Decisions therefore must frequently be based on anticipations rather than facts.

3. Even when actions are taken, the results may appear slowly. If credit is restricted, for instance, banks may already have made advance commitments that keep loans expanding for awhile.

Is there any way that monetary policy can be geared *directly* to changes in the economy without having to rely on the intervention of administrative decisions? If so, the total lag could be reduced somewhat.

Back to Gold. The gold standard was in many respects such an automatic device. Some of those who once heard the clink of gold coins in their pockets lament the passing of that musical sound and suggest that our current problems arise from its absence. The argument is that just as the goldsmith couldn't issue notes in excess of his ability to redeem them when people wanted gold, so under a gold coin standard the government couldn't overissue paper money because if people began to lose faith in currency, they would demand gold coin, reducing the government's reserve and thus its ability to expand the currency.

The gold standard with provision for redemption in effect provides a system of golden wires to every individual with dollars, over which he can send messages of approval or disapproval to the central signal board. . . . This enables him to exercise some control over the use by his government and banks of the people's gold and over the amount of promises these agencies may issue. If either or both issue promises to an extent that invites lack of confidence, every individual, to the extent he has dollars, can express his lack of confidence.[3]

The author of this paragraph believes that if we returned to a gold coin standard, thus giving this form of monetary control back to the people, our basic problems would be solved. "Redeemability should bring government spending to a halt and contract it. It should result in lower taxes. It should stimulate private enterprise, savings, investment, employment, and prosperity. It should increase the safety of savings and end the depreciation of the dollar."[4]

This is a sweeping claim. Unfortunately it ignores history. The inflation in the United States during World War I (see Figure 21-1) occurred despite adherence to a completely convertible gold coin standard, at least on the domestic level. The Great Depression was not forestalled by such a standard, which was finally abandoned at the very depths of despair in 1933.

Throughout this period—whether it would have helped or not—individuals did not pull their "golden wires." Although they could get all the gold they wanted, they didn't take it. As Table 33-1 shows, the circulation of gold coin

[3] Walter Spahr, in U.S. Congress, Subcommittee on Monetary, Credit, and Fiscal Policies of the Joint Committee on the Economic Report, *A Compendium of Materials on Monetary, Credit, and Fiscal Policies* (1950), p. 361.
[4] *Ibid.*, p. 362.

Table 33-1. Gold Coin and Total Currency in Circulation, 1914 to 1932

December 31; Millions of Dollars

Year	Gold coin	Total currency
1914	320	3,032
1915	318	3,302
1916	354	3,679
1917	345	4,086
1918	215	4,951
1919	189	5,091
1920	188	5,325
1921	152	4,403
1922	136	4,530
1923	123	4,757
1924	122	4,760
1925	127	4,817
1926	122	4,808
1927	115	4,716
1928	108	4,686
1929	97	4,578
1930	81	4,603
1931	122	5,360
1932	181	5,388

Source: *Banking and Monetary Statistics* (1943), pp. 409–412.

declined progressively from 1914 to 1930 (with only two minor exceptions) come war, prosperity, and depression. From 1930 to 1932 gold circulation rose somewhat as panic resulted in hoarding. The rise in this period of $100 million is small compared with a rise of $785 million in total currency in circulation, and even smaller compared with a total gold stock of $4,026 million. Even more important is the fact that this demand for gold occurred during *deflation,* when the value of the dollar was *rising.* Its effect therefore, slight as it was, was to intensify the Depression, exactly the opposite of the task Spahr outlines for it.

It is precisely because the gold standard didn't work that more effective controls were needed. Automaticity was replaced by discretionary action. The gold-standard advocates fear this very discretion. If the quantity of money is regulated by nothing more concrete than the authority of a board, what is to prevent unscrupulous, ignorant, or weak men on such a board from permitting an infinite expansion of the currency, a runaway inflation? Nothing. The gold proponents assume that such a board *will* be unscrupulous, ignorant, or weak. Our experience with the Federal Reserve has shown that this is not necessarily true. The Reserve authorities have made mistakes, without doubt, but the record of a managed currency is no worse than that of the gold standard.

It would seem more profitable to try to perfect a discretionary system than to return to a rigid gold structure that was no better and involved an impersonality that allowed too little adjustment to changing conditions. An automatic pilot may be able to steer a straighter course than the human pilot, but it can't think and therefore can't cope with emergencies. And if it is erratic, as the gold standard was, its advantages are highly questionable and its disadvantages overwhelming.

Compensated Dollar. One of the primary disadvantages of the gold standard was that, to the extent that it controlled the quantity of money, this control was determined by mining conditions in the gold fields, not by economic conditions. The general downward drift of prices from 1872 to 1896, a fall of 50 per cent, was due primarily to a declining gold output, particularly when compared with a rapid rise in world productivity. The upturn thereafter stems from new gold discoveries and a consequent rise in gold production, which added to world monetary reserves. Why should prices be tied to such an erratic and irrelevant base?

One method of retaining a nominal gold standard but freeing the dollar from the undesirable effects of shifts in its supply (or demand) is to vary the gold content of the dollar from time to time as conditions warrant in order to maintain a stable price level.[5]

This proposal, referred to as a *compensated-dollar plan,* suggests that gold coins be withheld from circulation, their place being taken by gold certificates redeemable in gold bullion of such weight as would be officially determined from time to time. One proponent suggests daily changes; others feel that a

[5] See Irving Fisher, *Stabilizing the Dollar* (The Macmillan Company, New York, 1920).

much longer interval would be preferable. The amount of alteration in gold content would be based on changes in some representative price index. If prices fell (because of a shortage of money), the gold content of the dollar would be reduced proportionately so that more dollars could be supported on a given gold reserve. A price rise would call for opposite action.

Bills to provide for such a compensated dollar were discussed in Congress in 1922–1923 and 1925,[6] and in a sense our devaluation in 1933 was based on a modification of this principle, but there is no serious consideration of such a possibility today. It smacks too much of the discredited commodity theory of money and seems a cumbersome method of operation—trying to hang on to a gold fetish in name while abandoning it in actuality. Fisher himself recognized that this proposal would probably be insufficient to provide complete stability for the economy and suggested that the Federal Reserve should continue, and in fact increase, its discretionary policies.

Commodity-reserve Dollar. A more recent proposal, a near relative of the compensated dollar but without any tie to gold, is Benjamin Graham's commodity-reserve currency.[7] This would be a dollar (or a world currency) whose value would be defined as a specified bundle of representative basic commodities. Graham suggests, for instance, that on the basis of 1937 prices $100 might be defined as the following aggregate stock of goods:[8]

Wheat, 12 bushels
Corn, 12½ bushels
Cotton, 87 pounds
Wool, 25 pounds
Rubber, 24 pounds
Coffee, 34 pounds
Tea, 9¼ pounds
Sugar, 300 pounds
Tobacco, 16.3 pounds
Petroleum, 6.3 barrels
Coal, 3.4 long tons
Wood pulp, 204 pounds
Pig iron, 0.23 long ton
Copper, 35 pounds
Tin, 4 pounds

[6] The provisions of one such bill (the Goldsborough bill) are quoted verbatim in J. S. Lawrence, *Stabilization of Prices* (The Macmillan Company, New York, 1928), pp. 79–84.

[7] See Benjamin Graham, *Storage and Stability* (McGraw-Hill Book Company, New York, 1937) and *World Commodities and World Currency* (McGraw-Hill Book Company, New York, 1944). A similar proposal was presented by Albert G. Hart, Nicholas Kaldor, and Jan Tinbergen to the United Nations Conference on Trade and Development in 1964.

[8] Graham, *World Commodities and World Currency,* p. 45.

The government would stand ready to buy this composite group of commodities for $100 or to sell it at the same price. Thus its aggregate price could not vary from this level. There is nothing to prevent *individual* prices from changing within the group. The price of wheat could rise and the price of tin fall without altering the total. The government would not therefore control the prices of specific commodities.

When general prices rose, the government would sell the commodities, thus taking money out of circulation (just as when it sells gold or the Federal Reserve sells securities). As prices fell, the government would increase the money supply by buying. Thus the operation of the commodity-reserve proposal would automatically counteract price movements of the basic commodities included in the scheme.

Such a program would work only if the commodities chosen were reasonably representative of prices in general. Since perishable or nonstandardized commodities could not be included, the list would necessarily be limited to a relatively few basic goods, predominantly raw materials. It is hoped that the prices of finished goods would also be controlled through the prices of their raw materials, but this is not inevitable.

Another problem concerns the possibility of continued inflation. Since the government's sale of commodities assumes that it has a physical stock of them, long-continued inflationary pressure might deplete the government's reserves and bankrupt the scheme. A contrary problem is the cost of storage of large quantities of goods if the price structure needed to be supported over long periods. (Fort Knox is not cheap either.)

Perhaps the greatest advantage of the commodity reserve would appear not in its domestic, but in its international, application. In this form Graham suggests that some international agency establish a world currency on such a commodity base. In this case the emphasis would shift somewhat from stabilization of general prices to stabilization specifically of the important international raw materials included in the reserve. This, however, involves the intricate, and not entirely monetary, problem of instability in international commodity markets, a subject that we cannot examine in detail here.

The commodity-reserve scheme merits examination, but it does not promise a cure-all for price instability, and it ignores the problem of unemployment. Even if adopted, it is probable that it could not work adequately by itself. There would still be room for considerable discretionary action. In fact it may be argued that control may be more effectively exercised if it is not handicapped by the rigidities of a proposal of this nature.

A Steadily Rising Money Supply. Another plea for automaticity comes from those who see no need to tie money to a commodity, whether gold or any other, but who feel that its quantity should grow at a regular rate without regard to short-run conditions. The argument is that both population and productivity tend to rise at a relatively stable rate and that the money supply should keep pace with this growth.

One of the most impassioned pleas for this policy has been made by Professor Shaw, of Stanford.[9] His case rests on the assumption that V (or K) remains "remarkably stable" and that T (real national output) rises at a rate of 3¼ per cent per year.[10] A similar rise in M would therefore maintain a stable price level and, more important, provide sufficient funds to carry on business without undesirable shortages or gluts of the means of exchange. He suggests further that the effect of such a steady rise would be anticyclical. During a recession the drop in business, while the quantity of money continued to increase, would provide precisely the same impetus as discretionary monetary policy. In a boom the tendency of business to expand faster than normal would automatically produce tight money because the money supply, though rising, would be increasing at a slower pace than that of business.

Such a policy raises two problems. First, can we ignore changes in V over time, as well as the many interrelations among various parts of the economy that may be important but that are not evident in the aggregates? History suggests that V is quite volatile and that frequently changes in V are of more importance than changes in M itself. A discretionary policy can offset such fluctuations; an automatic policy could not.

Second, assuming such a policy to be desirable, how would it be implemented? It goes beyond present devices of encouraging or discouraging the creation of money by banks and enters the realm of direct control of the amount created. Suppose banks won't expand the money supply during a depression. How would the supply be increased? Suppose the public gives banks additional reserves by making cash deposits. How will an additional multiple creation of money be prevented? These questions suggest that the proposal requires more control than appears on the surface. It might perhaps be coupled with the 100 per cent reserve plan or with fiscal policy (both examined later), but it could hardly be introduced alone.

Extreme Proposals

While we are in the area of relatively unorthodox ideas, we may take a moment to examine several schemes that do not fit into any standard classification of monetary policy but that suggest rather drastic solutions to our financial problems.

Social Credit. The first of these is a real curiosity. The idea of social credit, originated by Major C. H. Douglas, is characterized by an intricate superstructure built on an absolutely false base. The whole scheme might be dis-

[9] Edward S. Shaw, "Money Supply and Stable Economic Growth," in The American Assembly, *United States Monetary Policy* (Columbia University, New York, 1958). A similar position has been taken by Milton Friedman. See his testimony before the Joint Economic Committee, *Employment, Growth, and Price Levels,* Hearings (1959–1960), part 4, pp. 605–637; and *A Program for Monetary Stability* (Fordham University Press, New York, 1960), especially chap. 4.

[10] Shaw, *op. cit.,* pp. 60, 54.

missed as idiotic except that it has a large following, a secretariat and its own newspaper in London, a strong political party, and an appeal that transcends reason.

The basic proposition of social credit, from which all else follows, is that purchasing power is *always* insufficient to purchase the product of industry. Not cyclically, but constantly.

The theoretical justification for this extreme statement rests on the "A plus B theorem." According to this theorem, all payments made by any "productive organisation" are divided into two groups:

Group A—all payments made to individuals (wages, salaries, and dividends)
Group B—all payments made to other organisations (raw materials, bank charges, and other external costs)

"Now the rate of flow of purchasing power to individuals is represented by A, but since all payments go into prices, the rate of flow of prices cannot be less than A + B." Purchasing power (A) is therefore insufficient to purchase the product at the established price (A + B), and a part of the product must be bought from purchasing power generated somewhere else, namely, bank credit or exports (foreigners' purchasing power), or else it remains unsold.[11]

Is it necessary to point out the fallacy? There are several ways of examining it. (1) The payments to other business firms are themselves paid out as income to the various factors of production at one stage or another. (2) Many receipts of business firms do not come from consumers but from other business firms. Thus B payments are themselves used to buy the output of industry. Consumer payments (A) plus business payments (B) equal the total output of the economy (A + B). There is no shortage here.[12]

Social credit theorists, however, insist that there is always too little purchasing power to buy the output of industry and that this can be remedied only by a National Dividend—by giving everyone a government check each month in an amount sufficient to bring the total income up to the value of goods produced. That would be a nice windfall, wouldn't it? But it couldn't increase by one iota the quantity of goods available. Its sole effect would be to raise prices. It is the purest and most blatant form of cheap money, playing on everybody's desire to get something for nothing.

The comeuppance of the movement came with success. The United Farmers' Party swept the Alberta, Canada, elections in 1935 on a social credit platform. Major Douglas himself was invited to serve as Economic Adviser to the government, but on various pretexts he declined to put his scheme to

[11] C. H. Douglas, *Credit Power and Democracy* (Cecil Palmer, London, 1920), pp. 21–22; quoted also in Philip Mairet, *The Douglas Manual* (Coward-McCann, Inc., New York, no date), p. 68; and Maurice Colbourne, *The Meaning of Social Credit* (Figurehead, London, 1935), p. 161.

[12] There is a problem, of course, if consumers don't *use* all their income; hoarding can lead to a deficiency of purchases. But this isn't what social credit is bothered about. Its proponents contend that consumers don't *have* the income.

work. The government adopted a number of unorthodox financial policies, primarily designed to lower interest rates, but never fulfilled its campaign promise to provide each citizen with a National Dividend of $25 a month. The party is still in existence, but the idea of the National Dividend has disappeared as a goal.

"Thirty Dollars Every Thursday." The desire for a monetary panacea is by no means limited to the followers of Major Douglas. Mankind is still looking for the philosophers' stone to turn lead into gold (in spite of King Midas's unedifying example of the results of success in such a search). In the Great Depression crackpot schemes sprouted like weeds.

Upton Sinclair introduced his EPIC (End Poverty in California) plan in 1934. The most popular part of his program (which included some other more reasonable proposals) was "Thirty Dollars every Thursday," which would have provided every California resident with a bonus of that amount every week in order to increase purchasing power. This was later watered down to provide payments only to aged persons to be made in the form of scrip, stamped money that would circulate only if a 2-cent stamp were placed on it each week it remained in circulation. At the end of a year the state would have received $1.04 in stamp sales. It would then redeem the scrip for cash and pocket a 4-cent profit. This is not the pure inflationary engine that simple issuance of credit money would be, since it carries a tax presumably sufficient to pay the cost. But it raises other problems of scrip money to be discussed presently. In this revised form, with a new slogan, "Ham and Eggs for Californians," the proposal was actually put on the ballot for a referendum in both 1938 and 1939, but the voters rejected it.

The Townsend Plan, widely discussed in the thirties and backed today by a nationwide network of Townsend Clubs, differs only in detail. It upped the ante to $200 a month and was to be financed by a 2 per cent transactions tax on all sales, wholesale and retail. This particular proposal would be seriously inflationary because the proposed tax would have covered only about one-fourth of the payments.[13] A modified version of the plan received fifty-six votes in the House of Representatives in 1935.

Scrip Money. The Ham and Eggers were neither the first nor the last group to suggest the use of scrip. The idea was originated by the German Silvio Gesell fifty years ago as a device for increasing the quantity of money by issuing simple paper notes that would provide for their own redemption through the sale of stamps, which must be pasted on each week to keep the scrip valid. A national government with the power to issue fiat currency would not need to resort to this roundabout stratagem, but the proposal is applicable to states, cities, or other subordinate units with no money-issuing authority. It has been tried in towns in Austria and the United States (particu-

[13] See *Economic Meaning of the Townsend Plan,* Public Policy Pamphlet 20 (University of Chicago, Chicago, 1936).

larly during the bank holiday, when other money was unavailable) and in the province of Alberta, Canada (the closest that social credit got to its National Dividend was the use of scrip to pay a dole to the unemployed).

It has not worked, for it simply isn't workable. If ordinary money circulates side by side with scrip, who will pay the extra tax to use scrip? Even if there is no other money, it may be cheaper to resort to barter or book credits. If the scrip is not acceptable in payment of taxes, it loses all sanction. If it is so acceptable, it is likely to be used for that purpose as soon as possible, and the state receives at face value scrip with only a few tax stamps affixed and for which the state has therefore received only a few cents toward redemption. This was the case in Alberta, where over half the scrip issued had been turned in to the Treasury within two months. Scrip, in other words, fails to fulfill the basic function of money: it is not generally acceptable.

Tax on Hoarding. Somewhat similar to scrip but not quite so impractical is a tax on money designed not to redeem it but to increase its velocity of circulation. Such is the "melting money" of Arthur Dahlberg. He proposed a hoarding tax of a small fraction of 1 per cent per month on both bank deposits and currency. The former would be collected from the banks (and passed on by them to depositors) on the basis of each depositor's average monthly balance. The latter would require a new issue of currency of a different color each month, and as the new issue was put into circulation, the old would become redeemable at a lower value. The idea would be to encourage people to spend their money in order to avoid the tax and thus to increase velocity. The tax would mean, in effect, that the interest rate on cash was not zero, but negative. Among other things this would tend to pull down interest rates and stimulate the economy by this means as well as by the direct effect of increased spending.

Perhaps Dahlberg's greatest contribution is to emphasize the importance of velocity in the economy and to point out that something could be done about it if this seemed desirable. The plan would involve considerable machinery for enforcement and might raise problems about the use of money substitutes, but it is not absurd. Nor is it a panacea. Since it merely *increases* velocity, it is useful only in depression. The best way to treat such a plan during prosperity, when inflation rather than deflation is the problem, would be to repeal it. All in all it seems a possible but awkward way to treat problems that might be handled more effectively in other ways.

Summary. As major alternatives to the type of monetary policy now in use these wide-ranging suggestions do not seem to offer much promise. Each of them is inflationary, and it is significant that most were originally proposed as remedies for the Depression. For a well-rounded program of control they offer little that is not already available, and if used by themselves as permanent devices, they would be downright disastrous in most cases.

It is primarily for these reasons that no proposal for a completely automatic system of monetary controls currently receives more than token support.

Who Should Administer Controls?

If we agree—and there seems to be only minor dispute on this point—that discretionary monetary controls are desirable, the question arises as to who is to administer them. Few people seem desirous of abolishing the Federal Reserve structure, but how extensive should its powers be, and to what extent should they be shared with other agencies?

The Federal Reserve and the Treasury. Since the Accord of 1951 the Federal Reserve–Treasury feud has appeared, fortunately, to be over. The experience of the forties demonstrated, apparently conclusively, that subjecting the economy to a monetary policy directed to keeping interest rates low for the Treasury was not in the interest of the economy as a whole.

Yet it must be recognized that the objectives of the Federal Reserve and of the Treasury are not identical, and it is natural that they should have different points of view.

It is perfectly proper for the Treasury to attempt to borrow money at the lowest possible interest rate; we would censure it as extravagant if it paid more than it had to. But what happens when the Federal Reserve is exerting upward pressure on rates in order to combat inflation? Something has to give. And it seems reasonable to suggest that the goals of economic stability should take precedence over a low Treasury interest cost, desirable though that may be. In fact this may, in the long run, even react favorably on interest rates themselves.

First, the short-run view. If we are in a period of full employment, the basic economic problem is a shortage of resources. Output can expand only slowly because of the physical limits of manpower, equipment, and materials. Low interest rates, particularly when bolstered by expansion of Federal Reserve credit (as by open-market purchases), encourage business (and consumers) to borrow more purchasing power and to compete with each other for scarce resources. The result cannot call forth more goods but merely pushes prices up. The resulting inflation is likely to be a high cost to pay for low Treasury interest rates.

Even for the government the total result is likely to be a higher level of expenditures, since the costs of the things it buys (including labor services) will go up along with other prices. Part of the increase will be matched by increased tax receipts as money incomes rise, but experience in other countries suggests that this rise in receipts will be less than the rise in expenditures.

If this policy is continued over a long period the result may be just the opposite of the one intended as far as interest rates are concerned. For if inflation continues, lenders may refuse to buy fixed-income securities (including government bonds) unless they are offered at a substantial interest premium. There is considerable feeling that this is what was happening in 1959. In spite of the fact that prices were not actually rising, a widespread fear that inflation was only temporarily halted seems to have induced many people to shift from bonds to stocks, thus contributing to skyrocketing stock prices on the one hand and to plummeting bond prices (and rising interest rates) on the other. If the Federal Reserve had attempted to keep interest down under these circumstances, it would have produced the inflation that was feared and thereby induced a further flight out of bonds. And with a debt of over $300 billion, the government trust funds, the Federal Reserve, and the commercial banks together are not large enough to absorb it all without help from savers and savings institutions.

To this extent the long-run goals of the Treasury rest more closely on general economic stability than might appear on the surface, and apparently the Treasury is aware of this. It still remains, however, that the Treasury is doing a different job from that of the Federal Reserve, and the question is how these two tasks may best be coordinated. There are at least five possibilities:

1. Things might be left as they are, with voluntary cooperation between the agencies. This has worked quite satisfactorily since the Accord. It assumes competent and dedicated personnel in both agencies, but this is necessary for proper administration in any case. There might still be areas in which disagreement occurred with the possibility of actions at cross purposes.

2. The Federal Reserve might be made a subagency of the Treasury. Since this would tend to subordinate stabilization policy to the exigencies of Treasury finance, such an arrangement would hardly seem feasible without a drastic reconstruction of Treasury mandates.

3. The opposite possibility would require the Treasury to secure Federal Reserve approval of all actions affecting monetary policy. Like the foregoing, this is too extreme an approach to muster much support, at least as long as relatively harmonious action can be achieved by less drastic measures.

4. An interagency coordinating committee might be established along the lines of the present National Advisory Council on International Monetary and Financial Problems, which consists of the Secretaries of the Treasury, State, and Commerce and the Chairmen of the Board of Governors and the Export-Import Bank. A similar Council on Monetary and Fiscal Policy might include the Secretary of the Treasury, the Chairmen of the Board of Governors and the Council of Economic Advisers, the Director of the Bureau of the Budget, representatives of the various government credit agencies, and perhaps others.

The advantage of such a council should be its ability to provide a forum at which mutual problems could be discussed and a consistent pattern of action agreed upon. The objections are the proliferation of administrative agencies on the one hand and the absence of any final authority to settle disputes and establish final policy on the other.

5. In order to meet this last objection a further proposal suggests that an authority superior to all these agencies be established. The Council itself could be given power to control its constituent members, or a new Department of Finance with cabinet status could be set up with ultimate authority in all matters concerning monetary policy.

Each of these possibilities has its current adherents. Inertia, if nothing else, suggests that the *status quo* is likely to be maintained for the present. Of those who advocate change, the group backing a coordinating council without enforcement powers seems to have most chance of success in the long run. A move in this direction would be most likely if serious disagreement broke out again between the Federal Reserve and the Treasury or the government credit agencies or if the country ran into another economic catastrophe.

One basic requirement of any arrangement is that it be as immune as possible from political influences concerned with the advantages of particular groups rather than of the economy as a whole. This type of independence lies at the heart of Federal Reserve organization, and it would be a mistake to interfere seriously with that basic detachment from the hurly-burly of politics. The fundamental contributions that a central bank has to offer are destroyed if it becomes merely a government department.

On the other hand, it is obviously impossible for the Federal Reserve to dissociate itself entirely from the government, for its policies affect, and are affected by, a multitude of other governmental actions. The Federal Reserve, as the phrase goes, should be independent *within* government, not independent *of* government. The ideal combination of independence and cooperation will probably never be achieved, perhaps not even defined, but it is a goal constantly to be kept in mind.

Federal Reserve Issue of Government Debt. One ingenious suggestion for avoiding the conflict of debt management and monetary policy attacks the problem from an entirely different point of view. The proposal is that the Treasury borrow all it needs directly from the Federal Reserve, which in turn would issue its own securities to the public in place of Treasury obligations.[14] This would give the Reserve complete and direct control over the terms and timing of new issues. The chief objection, of course, would be that the Treasury relinquishes its authority over an area that it has come to regard as its own. It might also bring pressure to bear on the Reserve to finance the debt by credit creation rather than by selling securities to the public, but this pressure would probably be no greater than it has been in the past and could be resisted as long as the Reserve remains independent. The suggestion merits serious consideration.

Other Government Credit Agencies. We have already discussed the vast array of government credit agencies.[15] The magnitude of their operations makes them an important force in the capital markets. At various times when the Federal Reserve has been trying to restrict credit, the Farm Credit Administration has been extending loans, and the Federal National Mortgage Association has been pouring funds into the mortgage market. At the same time that the Reserve has been putting upward pressure on interest rates, maximum

[14] George L. Bach, *Federal Reserve Policy-making* (Alfred A. Knopf, Inc., New York, 1950), pp. 219–220.

[15] See Chap. 19 for a description and Fig. 19-1 for a chart of the various agencies.

rates chargeable under FHA and VA mortgages have been kept relatively low by Congress.[16]

The conflict here is evident, and coordination is at a minimum. The very fact that credit is tight induces those who have difficulty in getting loans to lobby for governmental assistance. This makes sense in a depression when funds are hard to get because banks are afraid to lend, but it is destructive of stability when tight money is the result of a policy intended to keep the money supply within the bounds established by the productive capacity of the nation.

Most of our present Federal credit agencies were established during the Great Depression, when they filled a real need. There is some question of their role in prosperity. Surely they shouldn't become engines of inflation. There should be some method of coordinating their various lending activities with the overall monetary policy of the government. Perhaps this means more restraint on congressional delegation of powers to these agencies. Perhaps it means extension of Federal Reserve control to include other Federal lending agencies within its basic regulations. Perhaps a coordinating council would help. Perhaps some of the agencies have outlived their usefulness.

Congress. At the core of the whole conflict among government credit policies is Congress, which has ultimate authority over all of them, including the Federal Reserve itself. It must decide what powers are to be delegated and to whom. Unfortunately such decisions are frequently made on a piecemeal basis without adequate consideration of the overall implications.

In addition the government is the largest single financial unit in the country, and every receipt and expenditure has some effect on the economy. Fiscal policy is as powerful a stabilizing (or destabilizing) device as monetary policy—often more powerful. And fiscal policy in the form of appropriations and taxation can hardly be removed from Congress. The need here is obviously for congressional understanding of the requirements of anticyclical policy.

And standing behind Congress are the American people. Although congressmen may not precisely reflect the will of their constituents, they can hardly move very far away from popular opinion—or they will not long remain in office. The basic need, therefore, is for an informed public opinion ready to support rational monetary policies. Without such support all the experts in the world are useless, for they will soon be stripped of power.

The Federal Reserve and "Wall Street." Some of the preceding suggestions indicate that perhaps the Federal Reserve might do a better job if it had somewhat broader control. But there are those who maintain that it already has too

[16] There is a paradox here in that low FHA (or VA) rates, while increasing the quantity of such loans *wanted* by the public, tend to reduce the willingness of banks to make such loans, since rising rates on *other* investments become increasingly attractive. The statistics seem to indicate that low ceiling rates on mortgage loans actually restrict this type of credit during a boom, thereby being more countercyclical than normal expectations would suggest.

much power and that this power is being used for the benefit of the wrong people. The charge is often heard that the Reserve is the tool of "Wall Street." What is usually meant is that since the member banks own and control the individual Federal Reserve banks, the whole system is under bank control and is interested in enriching the bankers at the expense of the public.

These critics maintain, for instance, that a tight-money policy simply raises interest rates for the banks, increasing their profits. They ignore the fact that tight money restricts the amount that banks can lend. They ignore also the increased earnings that higher interest rates bring to savings depositors, life insurance policyholders, and other creditors, as well as the maintenance of the value of the dollar, which is the primary motivation of such policies. They give little weight to the fact that the Board of Governors consists of nonbankers appointed by the President and that the Board has been given stronger and stronger powers at the expense of the district Reserve banks.

On the other hand, their case is bolstered by the fact that bankers, by and large, favor the System and cooperate with it. It is certainly true that the System has been beneficial for the banking community: it has promoted a sounder banking structure, established such facilities as clearing machinery, provided credit in time of need, and strengthened the whole banking system by coordination of policy. But it by no means follows that what is good for bankers is necessarily bad for the general public. Everyone is benefited by stability. In fact everyone is benefited by any device that prevents bank failures or maintains high standards of banking. Certainly the nation was no better off under the chaotic conditions prior to the Civil War (or even later), when what control there was, was exercised by purely governmental agencies. Nor was it in the best of health during the Great Depression, when the banks were not doing so well either.

The Federal Reserve is not perfect, and perhaps some other completely different device would work more effectively, but in a society as complex as ours it is seldom helpful or desirable (often not even possible) to replace imperfect institutions with others which look better on paper but which are untried in practice. In terms of social institutions better results are usually achieved through remodeling rather than by tearing down the old structure in favor of a brand-new one, particularly when the old house serves our purposes fairly well and we have become accustomed to it, even to its idiosyncrasies.

Federal Reserve Structure

What remodeling might be done? In terms of organizational structure a number of suggestions have been made, many of them contradictory.

Board of Governors. Since discretionary policy is no better than the men who administer it, personnel is of prime importance. It has often been difficult to find top-notch people for the Board of Governors at the salaries the government is willing to pay, a problem that is by no means limited to the Federal

Reserve. At times the Board has for long periods functioned with only six, or even with five, members.

Perhaps a rise in salary would be more defensible here than elsewhere in the public service since it is not paid from taxes but from the earnings of the Federal Reserve banks. It seems strange that the president of the Federal Reserve Bank of New York should receive a salary several times that of the Chairman of the Board of Governors.

Some feel that the Board would achieve greater stature if its membership were reduced to five, or three, or even one. One proposal, for instance, suggests that the System should come under a single head with Cabinet status. This might also promote greater speed in arriving at decisions. On the other hand it might lessen the weight of decisions reached by a larger group and might, in addition, make it easier for political considerations to determine Reserve policy.

There seems to be general agreement that the fourteen-year term with no possibility of reappointment has not worked as planned. The Board itself has suggested a shorter term, such as six years, with reappointment possible.[17]

The Locus of Authority. Closely related to the structure of the Board is the nature of its authority. As we have seen, power within the System is distributed among the Board, the Open Market Committee, and the twelve Federal Reserve banks, with the banks gradually losing their prerogatives to the higher echelons. This division of authority is an accident of history and seems somewhat cumbersome, but many people feel that, as clumsy as it appears, it has worked well and represents a separation of powers compatible with democracy.

Others feel that more concentration would promote efficiency, but there is no agreement as to where this concentration should occur. Bankers often favor restoring all authority to the individual Reserve banks in order to provide local autonomy. Others feel that bankers already have too much control and that all decisions should be lodged with the Board of Governors. Still another group believes that all policy decisions should be made by the Open Market Committee, representing as it does both the grass-roots bank interest and experience (in the person of the Reserve bank presidents) and the public interest (by the Board of Governors).[18]

The very diversity of opinions suggests that perhaps the present arrangement is as feasible a compromise as we could expect.

Membership in the System. Perhaps more important than the structure of the Reserve System is its inclusiveness. Only half of the banks in the country are

[17] U.S. Congress, Joint Committee on the Economic Report, Subcommittee on General Credit Control and Debt Management, *Monetary Policy and the Management of the Public Debt,* Replies to Questions and Other Material (1952), part 1, pp. 301–302.

[18] A wide variety of views is presented in U.S. Congress, Subcommittee on Monetary, Credit, and Fiscal Policies of the Joint Committee on the Economic Report, *A Compendium of Materials on Monetary, Credit, and Fiscal Policies* (1950), pp. 308–313.

members of the Federal Reserve, and although nonmembers hold only 15 per cent of banking assets, they cannot be overlooked. The National Bank Act and the Federal Reserve Act both contemplated a single unified control of the whole banking structure. Neither achieved it. When the FDIC was established, it was originally intended to expand Federal Reserve control by making membership in the System a condition of insurance, but this plan was later abandoned.

Nonmember banks are not subject to supervision or examination by the Federal Reserve, they are pretty much immune to moral suasion, and they are exempt from the reserve requirements of the System.[19] We are still beset by a banking structure that defies unified control.

There are many, particularly the bankers themselves, who feel that this dual banking system is desirable. If a bank has a choice between Federal and state charter, if it can elect Federal Reserve membership or not, if it can obtain FDIC insurance or leave it alone, bankers feel that no single agency can adopt arbitrary or oppressive policies, or those banks involved will simply shift to the available alternative. Thus the dual system prevents too strict control by any agency.

Since no one likes control, it is easy to see the bankers' point. And there is certainly the possibility of abuse when power is concentrated. But the dual system may not be best suited to the promotion of the public welfare where it leads to competition in laxity. Thus the Federal Reserve in the late forties wanted the authority to raise reserve requirements above the maximum levels then in effect in order to put some restraint on inflationary forces. It feared, however, that to raise requirements for member banks alone would force many banks out of the Reserve System who wanted to take advantage of lower state requirements. It asked Congress, therefore, that all banks be required to join the Federal Reserve. This request was never granted, but the question remains open.

There are some who would go further and require all banks to take out national charters. They feel that the duplication of regulatory agencies and the confusion of fifty-one conflicting statutes do not improve the contribution of the banking system to society. In addition to the economic problems involved, this suggestion raises the highly controversial political problem of states' rights. Although the Constitution gives Congress the sole right to coin money, the states are intensely jealous of their right to establish and regulate banking agencies that create today's most important form of money.

The Patman Proposals. Congress, which has the final authority over the Federal Reserve System, is constantly reexamining its structure and operation. Congressman Wright Patman, Chairman of the House Banking and Currency Committee and long an opponent of the Reserve, has introduced a number of bills over the years that would significantly curtail its independence, and his committee has held lengthy hearings. An omnibus bill introduced by Mr. Pat-

[19] They are, of course, subject to reserve requirements set by their own respective states, but many of these are more lenient than those of the Federal Reserve.

man in 1965 includes the following provisions, many of which have been featured in earlier bills but on which action has never been taken:

The Federal Open Market Committee would be abolished, and its functions transferred to the Board of Governors.

The Chairman of the Board of Governors would serve a four-year term coterminous with that of the President, so that each President would appoint his own chairman.

The number of governors would be reduced from seven to five, and their term of office from fourteen to five years.

The stock of Federal Reserve banks would be retired, so that they would become solely agencies of the government.

Almost all income of the Federal Reserve banks would be turned over directly to the Treasury, and the operating expenses of the banks would be provided for directly in the Federal budget.

The System would be required to conform to the monetary policy laid down by the administration and to report regularly to Congress on the actions it has taken to carry out this policy.

Although there is little chance that these provisions will be enacted into law, at least as a package, the constant hearings that are held on these and similar proposals provide an excellent source of material on both the operations of, and the objections to, the Federal Reserve, for numerous witnesses from both within and without the System contribute to the printed record. And the discussion, of course, will continue.

Questions for Thought and Discussion

1. If we had been on a gold standard, would it have prevented the inflation of 1946–1951? How?

2. Why did the circulation of gold coins drop so significantly from 1914 to 1930?

3. Why wouldn't a general distribution of cash bonuses make everybody richer?

4. If social credit is complete nonsense, why do so many people support it?

5. What is the difference between the Townsend Plan and our present old-age and survivors' insurance?

6. What are the basic arguments for and against a commodity currency compared with a managed one?

7. Is there any reason why extreme proposals for monetary reform should be more numerous during depression than during boom periods?

8. Would it be possible to eliminate the danger of human error in policy decisions by requiring that specific action be taken whenever a particular index moved up or down? What index would you use?

9. By what type of agency do you think monetary controls could be most adequately administered?

10. What are the advantages and disadvantages of having a single administrator of the Federal Reserve System rather than the present arrangement of decentralized control?

11. Should all banks be required to join the Federal Reserve? Should they be required to take out national charters?

12. If you were rewriting the Federal Reserve Act, what changes would you make in the organizational structure of the System?

Selected Bibliography

Ascheim, Joseph: *Techniques of Monetary Control,* The Johns Hopkins Press, Baltimore, 1961.

Bach, George Leland: *Federal Reserve Policy-making,* Alfred A. Knopf, Inc., New York, 1950.

Barger, Harold: *The Management of Money,* Rand McNally & Company, Chicago, 1964.

Burns, Arthur F.: *Prosperity without Inflation,* Fordham University Press, New York, 1958.

Commission on Money and Credit: *Money and Credit,* Prentice-Hall, Inc., Englewood Cliffs, N.J., 1961.

———: *Impacts of Monetary Policy,* Prentice-Hall, Inc., Englewood Cliffs, N.J., 1963.

———: *Monetary Management,* Prentice-Hall, Inc., Englewood Cliffs, N.J., 1963.

———: *Stabilization Policies,* Prentice-Hall, Inc., Englewood Cliffs, N.J., 1963.

Douglas, Clifford Hugh: *Social Credit,* W. W. Norton & Company, Inc., New York, 1933.

Fisher, Irving: *100% Money,* rev. ed., The Adelphi Company, New York, 1963.

Friedman, Milton: *A Program for Monetary Stability,* Fordham University Press, New York, 1960.

Graham, Benjamin: *World Commodities and World Currency,* McGraw-Hill Book Company, New York, 1944.

Harmon, Elmer M.: *Commodity Reserve Currency,* Columbia University Press, New York, 1959.

Harrod, Roy F.: *Policy against Inflation,* St Martin's Press, Inc., New York, 1958.

Hawtrey, Ralph G.: *A Century of Bank Rate,* Longmans, Green & Co., Ltd., London, 1938.

Holtrop, Marius W.: *Monetary Policy in an Open Economy,* International Finance Section, Princeton University, Princeton, N.J., 1963.

Jacoby, Neil H. (ed.): *United States Monetary Policy,* rev. ed., Frederick A. Praeger, Inc., for the American Assembly, Columbia University, New York, 1964.

Lester, Richard A.: *Monetary Experiments: Early American and Recent Scandinavian,* Princeton University Press, Princeton, N.J., 1939.

Mintz, Lloyd W.: *Monetary Policy for a Competitive Society,* McGraw-Hill Book Company, New York, 1950.

Myers, Margaret B.: *Monetary Proposals for Social Reform,* Columbia University Press, New York, 1940.

New York Clearing House Association: *The Federal Reserve Re-examined,* New York, 1953.

Reeve, J. E.: *Monetary Reform Movements,* American Council on Public Affairs, New York, 1943.

U.S. Congress, House Committee on Banking and Currency, Subcommittee on Domestic Finance: *The Federal Reserve System after Fifty Years* (3 vols. of hearings and other materials), 1964.

U.S. Congress, Joint Committee on the Economic Report: Statements, Hearings, and Report of the Subcommittee on Monetary, Credit, and Fiscal Policies, 1949.

———: Compendium of Materials, Hearings, and Report of the Subcommittee on Monetary, Credit, and Fiscal Policies, 1950.

———: *Monetary Policy and the Management of the Public Debt,* Replies to Questions, Hearings, and Report of the Subcommittee on General Credit Control and Debt Management, 1952.

U.S. Congress, Joint Economic Committee: *United States Monetary Policy: Recent Thinking and Experience,* Hearings before the Subcommittee on Economic Stabilization, 1954.

———: *Conflicting Official Views on Monetary Policy: April, 1956,* Hearings before the Subcommittee on Economic Stabilization, 1956.

———: *Monetary Policy: 1955–56,* Hearings before the Subcommittee on Economic Stabilization, 1957.

———: *Relationship of Prices to Economic Stability and Growth,* Hearings before the Joint Economic Committee, 2 vols., 1958.

———: *Employment, Growth, and Price Levels* (10 vols. of hearings, 23 study papers, staff report, and committee report of the Joint Economic Committee), 1959–1960. See especially parts 9A and 9B, "Constructive Suggestions for Reconciling and Simultaneously Obtaining the Three Objectives of Maximum Employment, an Adequate Rate of Growth, and Substantial Stability of the Price Level."

———: *Review of the Annual Report of the Federal Reserve System for the Year 1960,* Hearings, 1961.

———: *Review of Report of the Commission on Money and Credit,* Hearings, 1961.

———: *U.S. Payments Policies Consistent with Domestic Objectives of Maximum Employment and Growth,* Report of the Subcommittee on International Exchange and Payments, 1962.

———: *The United States Balance of Payments* (3 vols. of hearings, staff materials, statements by economists and others, and report), 1963–1964.

Viner, Jacob: *Problems of Monetary Control,* International Finance Section, Princeton University, Princeton, N.J., 1964.

Yeager, Leland B. (ed.): *In Search of a Monetary Constitution,* Harvard University Press, Cambridge, Mass., 1962.

Chapter 34
Critique: The Tools of Monetary Policy

Give every man thine ear, but few thy voice;
Take each man's censure, but reserve thy judgment.

Hamlet
Act I, scene 3, line 68

Assuming that the accepted goals of monetary policy are price stability and full employment in a growing and externally stable economy and assuming that these goals will be implemented by the Federal Reserve or some similar agency, how can these objectives (or any other, for that matter) be most effectively realized? Are present control devices adequate? How might they be improved? Could others be added to advantage?

Reserve Requirements

Changes in reserve requirements are the most drastic tools in the kit of the Federal Reserve. Yet they have been a part of the general machinery of control only since 1935. And there is some question as to whether they should be used for this purpose at all. Although our own use of reserves as a control device is quite recent, it was the first in the world. Some countries, such as Spain, do not have any legal reserve requirements. Other countries do not provide any method for varying such requirements on a discretionary basis. Gradually other countries have adopted one kind or another of variable reserve requirements, particularly since World War II, but these take many forms. There is no standard basis of procedure.[1]

[1] For a description of reserve requirements throughout the world as of 1957, see Peter G. Fousek, *Foreign Central Banking: The Instruments of Monetary Policy* (Federal Reserve Bank of New York, November, 1957), pp. 102–111.

Are Reserves a Proper Tool of Control? What is the argument against the use of reserve requirements as a means of control? Partly it is an argument against any control, a plea for *laissez faire* in banking. More directly, reserves are considered an interference with the earning capacity of banks since reserves are themselves nonearning assets and at the same time restrict the ability of the bank to increase its loans.

This view, however, is distinctly in the minority, even among bankers. They recognize the benefit to the whole community, including the banks themselves, of stabilization of the economy. The significant discussion, then, is not whether reserve requirements should exist, but to what extent they should be changed and under what circumstances.

It is generally recognized that the power to alter legal reserves is a blunt instrument and for that reason may be dangerous if used indiscriminately.[2] The Federal Reserve is as aware of this as anyone.

General increases have been used during only four periods. The rise in requirements in 1936–1937 was intended primarily to offset a phenomenal rise in gold imports. Increases were instituted during the war to fight the inflationary tendencies of a tremendous government deficit; in 1948, when bond support made open-market sales inoperative; and again during the Korean conflict. These are relatively unusual circumstances, and it seems to be agreed that the use of reserve increases should be more or less limited to such conditions. Also, since a change of 1 percentage point represents a shift in required reserves of over $1 billion, the requirements have recently been altered by small amounts in order to minimize their bluntness. In addition the banks are given advance notice so that they may prepare for the change. Within these limitations control of reserves through requirements of some kind seems destined to stay for quite a while.

The Computation of Reserves. Aside from controversy over changes in requirements, there is considerable debate over the basis on which reserves are computed. Alterations in historical conditions have not been matched by adjustments in reserve practices.

Geographical Differentiation. The amount of reserves that a bank must hold depends on the size of the city in which it is located. This is a hangover from the era when correspondent balances were important primary reserves for the country banks. A bank that accepted such balances was required to hold larger reserves on the assumption that this provided a margin of safety against a run by the interior banks who owned these balances. But as we have seen, reserves do not provide liquidity since the bank cannot pay them out. They act rather as a fulcrum against which credit control can exercise leverage, and from this point of view it is not clear how geographical differentiation helps.

[2] Few would go so far as the New York Clearing House Association, which declares that "reserve requirement increases can be a vicious and destructive instrument." New York Clearing House Association, *The Federal Reserve Re-examined* (New York, 1953), p. 114.

Under the National Bank Act, moreover, the designation "reserve city bank" conferred a positive advantage on the bank in that it meant that balances held in it by correspondents could be counted as part of their legal reserves, while balances held in other banks could not. This increased the bank's ability to attract such accounts. Under the Federal Reserve Act this privilege was removed, and banks now wonder whether the distinction of being a "reserve city bank" isn't mostly illusory.

As a first step toward removal of geographical discrimination Congress in 1959 provided for the elimination of the central reserve city classification. It would seem logical to take the further step of complete geographical equalization of all banks.

There is, of course, good reason for differentiating between time and demand deposits since the latter can be created in the process of credit expansion, while the former cannot.

Security Reserves.[3] Although reserves under the Federal Reserve Act consisted solely of deposits in Federal Reserve banks until vault cash was added in 1959, other countries (and some states) permit or require certain types of securities to be held as reserves. Thus Finland, for instance, requires that banks maintain a 20 per cent reserve against demand liabilities, the reserve to consist of cash, deposits with the central bank or other banks, foreign drafts, and government securities. Austria requires a 5 per cent reserve in deposits with the central bank, plus 10 per cent in such deposits, cash, or treasury bills, plus an additional 25 per cent in these assets or government securities, other bonds, or eligible commercial paper.

In the United States the proposal for a security reserve has usually suggested that an additional reserve over and above the present legal requirement be held in government securities. One variant would limit the reserve to holdings of treasury bills.

After World War II the Federal Reserve pressed Congress for a security reserve that would require banks to hold, in addition to regular reserves, 25 per cent of their demand deposits in government securities. It was suggested that such a requirement would be similar to an increase in cash reserves while allowing the banks to earn interest on the funds involved. When the proposal was introduced, however, its primary purpose was to prevent banks from unloading government securities on the Federal Reserve at a time when the latter was supporting the government-bond market.

Security reserves are not without disadvantages, for they would not, under ordinary circumstances, restrict the total amount of bank credit. Instead they would channel it into government securities rather than into private loans. When a bank buys securities, it creates money just as when it makes a loan. A security reserve would therefore create a sheltered market for government securities, particularly if banks were restricted to specific issues. Since the banks would be forced to hold certain quantities of these obligations, it would

[3] Also called *supplementary reserves, certificate reserves,* or *secondary reserves.*

be possible for the Treasury to issue them with a lower interest rate, or even with no interest at all.

Those who feel that providing a strong market for Treasury borrowing is the most important task of the financial system may welcome this result. Others, who believe that monetary control is more significant than a low Treasury interest rate, feel that providing a specially insulated market for the government distorts the normal flow of funds and has a distinct inflationary tendency since it removes an important brake on expanded government deficits. It differs little, in fact, from printing fiat currency. As the Federal Reserve said in proposing the plan: "The authority would make it possible to limit the volume and raise the cost of private credit without necessarily increasing the interest cost to the Government on an important part of the large public debt outstanding."[4]

Since the Accord of 1951 this argument has carried much less force, and today security reserves are not frequently discussed.

Ceiling Reserves. Another method of combating inflation without altering basic reserves is to impose higher ratios (perhaps as high as 100 per cent) on all *deposits in excess* of some specified amount, which might be the amount in existence on a certain day or might be determined in some other way. Thus the penalty rate would apply only to banks that were expanding, while other banks would be in the same position they formerly were. Expanding banks could get rid of the penalty rate at any time by reducing their deposits to the base amount.

For example, suppose a particular bank was subject to a regular 20 per cent reserve requirement and held $100 million of deposits. Required reserves would be $20 million. Assume further that the Federal Reserve imposed a 50 per cent requirement on any increase in deposits above the amount held on this day. As long as the bank did not expand, its required reserves would remain at $20 million, but if it increased its deposits by $10 million, its legal reserves would rise by 50 per cent of this amount, to a total of $25 million.

This proposal has the merit of putting the burden of carrying higher reserves solely on those banks that are increasing their deposits. It has some of the deficiencies besetting any price ceiling, primarily the problem of providing equity in the initial base. A bank that happened to have made several exceptionally large loans the previous day would be in a favorable position for the future. This might be avoided by determining the base from *average* deposits over a stated period. More difficult to adjust is the position of the bank in a growing community where normal needs are rising compared with those of other communities less dynamic. If the ceiling reserves were in operation for relatively short periods, the disparities arising from such situations would probably be minor, and the very existence of such controls should help keep the inflationary period during which they were needed brief.

A variant of this proposal that attempts to avoid the question of equity

[4] *Federal Reserve Bulletin,* vol. 34, no. 1 (January, 1948), p. 16.

suggests that the penalty reserve be levied against deposits in excess of some specified multiple of capital.[5] Suppose this multiple were 10. Then a bank with $2 million capital would be subject to ordinary reserve ratios until its deposits reached $20 million. Anything above this amount would carry the penalty ratio. The bank could avoid this penalty by obtaining additional capital. A plan of this kind combines anti-inflationary pressure with a concern for the internal safety of the bank, for many banking authorities feel that banks today are operating on a dangerously slim capital for their size.

Reserves against Assets. Another proposal that attempts to put curbs specifically on those banks that are responsible for inflationary pressures is to require reserves to be held against specified *assets* (loans and securities, but not cash assets) rather than against deposits. Reserves against assets would be a substitute for reserves against deposits and in most respects would have similar results for the banking system as a whole, since the greater part of deposits arise from the loan activities of banks. The distribution, however, would be different.

A bank that received cash deposits from its customers would need to hold no reserves against them. When deposits were created by loans, however, reserves would be required, and these reserves would have to be held *even after the deposits so created were checked out.* The higher reserves therefore would affect the bank that made the loan and not the bank that received additional deposits through clearing—unless that bank also decided to expand its loans.

A number of variations of this plan are possible. It could be applied as a ceiling reserve in conjunction with the reserve against deposits. This would leave deposit reserve requirements unchanged but would add a reserve against loans in excess of those on the books in a specified base period. Or the asset reserve might be varied for specific classes of assets in order to discourage particular types of loans more than others. Reserves against loans, for instance, might be higher than those against government securities, or reserves against brokers' loans might be higher than those against eligible paper. In this way the banks would be encouraged to shift their lending activity into those areas favored by lower reserves.

The administration of such selective controls[6] would raise a number of complicated problems concerning (1) the relation between government and private borrowing (is an insulated market for government securities desirable?); (2) the pattern of interest rates on various types of loans; and (3) the competition between banks (who would be subject to control) and other lenders (who would not unless the basis of control were considerably broadened to include them). Nevertheless the proposal suggests a highly sophisti-

[5] Venezuela has a requirement of this kind. A bank must keep reserves of 15 per cent of deposits not exceeding six times its capital and surplus, and 40 per cent of all deposits over that amount.

[6] Some of the fundamental arguments for and against selective controls in general are examined at the end of this chapter.

cated means of credit manipulation that *might* work well under expert guidance. It merits further examination.[7]

Velocity Reserves. Another novel approach to the computation of reserves was suggested by Winfield Riefler in 1931. This was that reserve requirements should be based not only on the volume of deposits, but also on their velocity of circulation. In other words, reserves should be related not to M alone, but to MV, defined for this purpose as total debits to deposit accounts. The proposal is designed to meet the objection to monetary policy that it cannot directly influence velocity, which is a significant factor in the total volume of payments. If reserves were based on total deposit turnover, any increase in velocity would require larger reserves or, with a given volume of reserves, would have to be offset by a decrease in the quantity of deposits.

It is true that velocity is not under the bank's control, but that is precisely the point. The public has a hand in this inflationary business too. No device has yet been advanced for restricting velocity of circulation, but velocity reserves would provide an automatic counteraction to any increase. Conversely a drop in velocity would give banks excess reserves against which additional loans could be made. Although the proposal had the support of the Federal Reserve Board in the early thirties, little attention has been paid to it in recent years. It might be rather complex to administer, but it has no other serious faults.

The Size of Reserves. So far we have examined the base against which reserves are computed without indicating what particular ratios might be used. The very concept of the use of reserves as a tool of policy means that their level will be changed from time to time and that this level will therefore depend on the conditions of the moment. But are there limits within which these variations should take place?

A survey of legal reserves throughout the world indicates a range all the way from 0 to 100 per cent.[8] If we go back a century in United States history, we can find even greater variation, from 0 to 111 per cent,[9] but these were reserves against notes rather than against deposits. More recently the range in this country has extended from 3 (for time deposits) to 26 per cent. Are these limits satisfactory?

[7] For an evaluation of asset reserve plans see U.S. Congress, Joint Committee on the Economic Report, Subcommittee on General Credit Control and Debt Management, *Monetary Policy and the Management of the Public Debt,* Replies to Questions and Other Material (1952), part 1, pp. 481–489.

[8] The latter rate has been used in Uruguay as a ceiling reserve for deposits in excess of five times the capital structure. It was introduced in Peru in 1960 against all *increases* in reserves.

[9] No reserves were required against early bank notes, while national bank notes, when they were first introduced, had to have a backing of 111 per cent in government securities; that is, they could be issued only up to 90 per cent of the value of securities held. In a somewhat different category, the original reserve (including collateral requirements of government securities) against Federal Reserve notes was 140 per cent.

Lower Reserve Requirements. Bankers in general feel that requirements are too high. The American Bankers Association, for instance, objects to present requirements on several grounds. They "discourage membership in the Federal Reserve System and impose an unwarranted burden on member banks." They make it necessary for the Federal Reserve to hold a larger volume of government securities than would otherwise be the case (since the Reserve purchases securities to provide reserves for members). These large holdings deprive member banks of liquid earning assets. Lower rates in the future will be needed to enable banks to "accommodate the needs of our growing economy for bank credit and money."[10] At the same time the association objects to changes in requirements except to offset large gold movements or under other "highly unusual situations."[11]

On the basis of these objections the ABA recommends:

1. Eventually reduce reserve requirements for demand deposits to 10 per cent.
2. Eliminate geographical differences in reserve requirements for demand deposits.
3. Authorize the Reserve authorities to vary the reserve requirements for demand deposits over a range of 8 to 12 per cent.[12]

Recommendation 2 has been partially adopted. The proposals for reducing both the level of reserves and the discretionary power of the Reserve authorities seem based on very weak arguments. The historical increases in legal reserves have all occurred under "unusual circumstances," and although they may not have been engineered with infinite wisdom, it would appear that inflationary forces in the economy would have been much worse in the absence of such increases. While the ABA has a valid point in objecting to the use of increases for short-run credit-control purposes, significantly reducing the power to use them under any circumstances would not aid the execution of monetary policy.

Increased Reserves. On the contrary, it would appear that the limits of discretion available to the Federal Reserve are less than are needed. The problem is not pressing at this moment, but if strong inflation again threatens, particularly if it accompanies a war, the present upper limits may prove a barrier to an effective check on rising prices.

While the question of the proper level of reserves is a highly complex one, a basic consideration is whether Congress is in a better position than the Reserve authorities to determine the desirable level at any particular time. If Congress needs to restrain a possible abuse of power on the part of the Board of Governors, then there is need for some restriction on administrative action. If the Board of Governors is a responsible body, then presumably it should be able to establish legal reserves without the handicap of an arbitrary limit,

[10] American Bankers Association, *Member Bank Reserve Requirements* (New York, 1957), pp. 36–37.

[11] *Ibid.*, pp. 59–60.

[12] *Ibid.*, p. 152.

either maximum or minimum. It is usually the upper limit that is called into question, however, since inflation has been more of a problem in the last twenty years than depression. Since an upper limit ties the hands of the Board in inflation, such a limit would be welcomed by inflationists. But is this a recommendation?

100 Per Cent Reserves. There are, in fact, some who suggest that reserves should be raised to the ultimate maximum of 100 per cent. The 100 per cent reserve proposal, first discussed by Henry Simons, of the University of Chicago, was strongly espoused by the versatile Irving Fisher.[13] While he supported it with arguments derived from the quantity theory of money, it does not depend on that theory, and it has been endorsed by a large number of economists who reject the crude quantity theory.

Because it has had fairly wide acceptance, the plan has come out in a number of different modifications. Basically it would require banks to maintain 100 per cent reserves against all demand deposits. These reserves might be in cash, deposits with the Federal Reserve, deposits with other banks, specified government securities, or some other form.

The scheme is drastic and would undoubtedly produce significant changes in the structure of banks and other financial institutions, but it has a certain internal logic. Granted that control of the money supply is desirable, a 100 per cent reserve would accomplish that control most effectively and directly. Banks could no longer create money, and the total supply would therefore come from the monetary authorities. The Federal Reserve authorities would no longer *make it possible* for banks to expand in periods of depression; they would instead create the money themselves by loans (discounts) or open-market purchases of securities. This by no means suggests that the Reserve banks would become the only lenders in the economy, but rather that they would be the only ones lending newly created money. Other financial institutions (including banks) could continue to lend the savings of the public entrusted to them.

How would the plan work? Suppose the provision was that against *demand* deposits banks must hold a 100 per cent reserve in cash or deposits with the Federal Reserve or other banks. (Since time deposits are not money, they would not be included, and in fact legal reserves against time deposits might be abolished.) Before the plan went into operation the typical bank might have a balance sheet such as is shown in Table 34-1. (Adding five zeros to the figures would produce roughly the total assets and liabilities of all commercial banks as of December 31, 1964.)

When the 100 per cent reserve went into effect, this bank would have to hold $1,710,000 against its demand deposits plus a small amount of till money against its time deposits, probably not much more than 2 per cent or (roughly) $30,000. It already holds $560,000 in acceptable reserves and must get $1,180,000 more from somewhere. It could easily sell its govern-

[13] Irving Fisher, *100% Money* (The Adelphi Company, New York, 1935).

Table 34-1. Balance Sheet of Typical Bank Prior to 100 Per Cent Reserve

Assets		*Liabilities and net worth*	
Cash and due from banks	$ 560,000	Deposits:	
Loans	1,750,000	Interbank	$ 160,000
U.S. government securities	620,000	U.S. government	60,000
Other securities	380,000	Other demand	1,490,000
Other assets	90,000		
		Total demand	$1,710,000
		Time	1,270,000
		Other liabilities	140,000
		Capital accounts	280,000
	$3,400,000		$3,400,000

ment securities (to the Federal Reserve) since whatever function they perform today as secondary reserves would no longer be needed when primary reserves were equal to demand liabilities. This leaves it still short $560,000. Perhaps the least disruptive way to obtain this amount would be to borrow from the Federal Reserve with that quantity of loans as collateral. If these transactions were carried out, the balance sheet would appear as in Table 34-2.

The basic changes that have occurred are that the bank has lost $620,000 of earning assets (government securities) and has increased its liabilities by the $560,000 note to the Federal Reserve, on which it must pay interest. This spotlights the fundamental objection to the proposal: that it would reduce the earning power of banks and drive them bankrupt. This obviously could not be allowed to happen, and if the proposal led to this result, it should be rejected out of hand.

There are several ways in which such a drastic result could be avoided. One would be by imposing service charges on depositors for the various services (primarily clearing) that the banks now render free. Obviously such services are not costless. Who pays for them today? As earnings have declined over the last three decades (both because of larger nonearning reserves and

Table 34-2. Balance Sheet of Typical Bank at Advent of 100 Per Cent Reserve

Assets		*Liabilities and net worth*	
Cash and due from banks	$1,740,000	Deposits:	
Loans	1,750,000	Interbank	$ 160,000
Other securities	380,000	U.S. government	60,000
Other assets	90,000	Other demand	1,490,000
		Total demand	$1,710,000
		Time	1,270,000
		Notes payable (to Federal Reserve)	560,000
		Other liabilities	140,000
		Capital accounts	280,000
	$3,960,000		$3,960,000

because of lowered interest rates), banks have increasingly levied service charges of one sort or another. But to the extent that these charges do not cover the full cost of the service, the extra freight must be borne by borrowers, since interest is the only other significant source of bank revenue. Parenthetically we might ask whether it is fair for borrowers to pay for services rendered to depositors, bearing in mind that it is not the depositors' money that is borrowed, but money newly created by the bank.

Philosophical arguments aside, it is obviously *possible* for banks to charge the value of services directly to their depositors. Yes, some would cease to use the banks if this were done, but not many. What alternative do they have for making payments? No one else could do it cheaper. Postal money orders, for instance, are today generally more expensive than bank money orders. The banks have a very efficient, and hence cheap, clearing machinery, and no other organization could beat them on a cost basis. Some few people would revert to making all their payments in cash, but for most of us, and particularly for businessmen, this is more awkward than it is worth. Even today "special" checking accounts are increasing rapidly in popularity in spite of their cost.

Another way of supporting bank earning power would be for the Federal Reserve to pay interest on reserve deposits. One objection to the Reserve holding such a large volume of assets as it does today is based on the fact that its earnings are much larger than needed to meet its expenses. Payment of interest on reserves, while unconventional, would be fairly simple. It is not, however, generally recommended by proponents of the plan.

Another basic objection to the 100 per cent reserve proposal is that it would deprive the business community of a local source of loans. This would not be true of the procedure outlined here.[14] Our typical bank could continue to make loans with funds obtained from (1) its capital, (2) its time deposits, and (3) its borrowings from the Federal Reserve. The amount of loans outstanding is one thing that *has not changed* from the balance sheet of Table 34-1 to that of Table 34-2. As old loans were repaid, new ones could be made by shifting the collateral behind the notes payable to the Federal Reserve. The discount rate would have to be enough lower than the loan rate to cover the expense of making loans as well as the risk involved, but there is no basic reason why such a differential could not be maintained.

There would also have to be a change in attitude toward borrowing from the Reserve. Under the proposal here outlined borrowing would become normal. This carries its own particular advantage in that it means that the discount rate could continue to be used as a major instrument of policy. If the Reserve wished to expand credit, it could do so through open-market operations, putting more money directly into the hands of the public in exchange for their securities; or, by lowering the discount rate, it could induce banks to borrow in order to make loans in their own communities. The discount

[14] It does apply to some forms of the plan, where, for instance, a central monetary authority would *buy* the loans of the bank and make new loans itself.

rate would then cease to be primarily a psychological weapon and would become a real element of cost for all banks. In this way the orthodox tools of monetary control could still be used as they are today, and expansionary or contractionary pressures would be exerted without any new paraphernalia of governmental control. And the basic lending power would stay where it now is: with the local bank.

But the banks couldn't create money. If a customer deposited cash, the whole amount of that cash would have to be added to reserves. It could not be used as the basis for any multiple credit expansion. If new *time* deposits were made, the bank could lend the funds so deposited, but this would not create money. It would simply pass on the savings of the depositor to the borrower, just as savings banks and other financial intermediaries now do.

New money would be created only when Federal Reserve credit rose, primarily through a rise in either discounts or government security holdings. And the effect of increased Reserve credit would be in the ratio of 1:1, not the multiple expansion that an increase in reserves permits today. The effect of a given policy would therefore be clearly predictable, for we would no longer have the flexible relationship of the present, where banks may or may not expand credit when reserves increase.

An incidental benefit would be that bank failures would be impossible. Since the bank holds a dollar in reserves for every dollar in deposits, all depositors could not only ask for, but also get, their money any time they wanted. Similarly a withdrawal in cash would not force a contraction of loans, as it does today, since no pyramid of credit would be built on reserves.

The proposal seems both simple and logical. It does have certain disadvantages, however, not the least of which is that it *seems* revolutionary and therefore shocks the conservative feelings of most bankers and many businessmen. Although this reaction may be more emotional than logical, it is true that any major change in financial arrangements is likely to cause dislocations at the time that it is introduced.

Another objection is the fear that the added power that the plan would give to the Federal Reserve would be abused, that the Reserve might make serious mistakes, and that it might attempt to interfere with the operation of banks to the detriment of the financial machinery in general. Says the New York Clearing House Association:

> The cruel realism of the 100 per cent reserve scheme is that it means nationalization of the commercial banking system. . . . The basic error is the assumed superiority of a system in which the Government has absolute and arbitrary control over the means of payment and in insisting—the experience of a thousand years to the contrary—that commercial banking is not a proper, legitimate, and necessary area of private enterprise.[15]

Fortunately the Clearing House is knocking down not the plan, but a straw man. Certainly most proponents of the 100 per cent reserve do not wish to

[15] New York Clearing House Association, *op. cit.*, pp. 107–108.

nationalize the banking system, nor do they feel that it is not a proper area for private enterprise. They realize that money will not manage itself and feel that this is one effective way of controlling the volume of money *without* interfering with the normal operation of a commercial bank, its choice of customers, or its other basic functions. It would make commercial banks more like savings banks, but no one has suggested that savings banks are "nationalized" merely because they can't create money. One can understand the desire of commercial banks to retain their power to create money while at the same time recognizing that the history of their use of that power leaves much to be desired.

The basic question is: Shall the commercial banks control the quantity of money in the economy, or shall an independent governmental agency exercise such control? *Some* control is obviously necessary. On that everyone is agreed. The 100 per cent reserve proposal does not seem to be any more arbitrary than the powers the Federal Reserve now has.[16] For if the Federal Reserve authorities used their present powers capriciously or ignorantly, they could probably wreck the financial system. Under the 100 per cent reserve plan perhaps they could wreck it a little faster *if they tried*. Obviously any agency exercising monetary control should be competent and concerned with the public welfare. It should also have the respect and cooperation of the public. If those criteria can be met, they will probably go further toward achieving stability than any particular legal framework of operation would, whether the 100 per cent reserve plan or our present arrangements. But the 100 per cent proposal, competently administered, would provide even more effective control.

Discount Rates

In the past decade or so, discount rates have come back into their own as a major instrument of monetary policy not only in this country but also throughout the world. This increased use arises partly from the revival of monetary policy itself and partly from the fact that long-continued upward pressure on the money supply has induced banks to borrow in larger amounts from the Reserve banks, thereby giving discount rates more than a psychological significance.

The latter, however, is still important since discount rate changes give a clear clue as to what the attitude of the Reserve authorities is toward current credit conditions. Thus in 1957 as the discount rate reached 3½ per cent, it was obvious that the Federal Reserve felt inflationary pressures were dominant and needed to be combated by discount policy. At the same time its portfolio of government securities was maintained at a lower level than it had been since 1952. On November 15, the discount rate at New York and three

[16] And is less arbitrary than consumer credit and real estate credit controls, which the Clearing House favors. *Ibid.*, p. 126.

other banks was reduced to 3 per cent, and the relief of the financial community was instantaneous. The change signaled the end of tight money and the beginning of active ease. Almost overnight interest rates started dropping, as Figure 32-2 shows.

But the effect was more than psychological, for as the rate eased downward to 1¾ per cent, member bank reserve positions improved from almost half a billion dollars of net *borrowed* reserves (discounts exceeding excess reserves) to half a billion dollars of net *free* reserves (excess reserves exceeding discounts).

Another example of the impact of a discount rate change could be seen when the rate was raised from 4 to 4½ per cent on December 6, 1965. On the same day the prime rate rose from 4½ to 5 per cent, at least one savings bank raised its anticipated dividend from 4¼ to 4½ per cent, and the yield on treasury bills jumped almost ¼ per cent.

The expanded role of discount rate policy is generally approved. Differences of opinion center not on *whether* to use it, but on *when* and *how*. This is a matter of objectives rather than of tools.

Geographical Differences. Discount rates were initially expected to reflect local conditions of the individual Reserve banks, and they therefore showed considerable variation from bank to bank. As the money markets of the country have become more and more unified, geographical discrepancies have been reduced. One basic reason for this is that if the discount rate is, say 3½ per cent in Chicago, while it is 3 per cent in New York, it is possible for Chicago banks in need of funds to borrow them from New York banks at, say, 3¼ per cent, while the New York banks are borrowing from the Federal Reserve there at 3 per cent. This arbitrage is made possible by the high integration of the nation's money markets, which in turn is aided by the Reserve's own wire transfer services, over which funds can be shifted from one bank to another in a matter of minutes.

There is therefore considerable pressure on each Reserve bank to maintain the same discount rate as others in the System. Changes in rates, though officially initiated by the individual banks, are in practice discussed as a matter of general policy by the Open Market Committee, which provides a good deal of coordination. It is common for several banks to announce a change at the same time, and the rest are likely to follow within a week or two.

On occasion a bank may hold out against the trend for a while because its interpretation of current pressures differs from the consensus of the System. Thus when the rise from 3 to 3½ per cent was initiated in August, 1957, the New York bank held out for several weeks primarily, it is assumed, to indicate that it felt that a rise at this time was unwarranted. But it soon had to follow, although subsequent events have cast serious doubt on the wisdom of that increase, which occurred after the recession of 1957–1958 had already started. As Figure 32-1 indicates, we have not had since the war anything like the spread between rates that was fairly common in the twenties.

There are some who feel that local autonomy should be restored in the use of discount rates by removing the power of the Board of Governors to "review and determine" rate changes. The intention is to allow a bank to adjust its rate to local conditions, which might not be the same as those elsewhere. The idea has merit in theory, but it is doubtful whether the structure of the money markets would permit much local autonomy when funds can flow so readily from one section of the country to another. Nor would it seem desirable to attempt to interfere with this mobility, for its result is to distribute funds more evenly throughout the nation. This very mobility tends to eliminate the need for large or prolonged differentials in discount rates.

Open-market Operations

Open-market operations are the most important day-to-day tools of Federal Reserve control. They are extremely flexible in both amount and timing, are relatively unobtrusive, and affect bank operations with a minimum of disturbance. In addition to their use as a countercyclical device they are admirably suited to offsetting undesired changes in bank reserves that result from unplanned, often temporary, changes in factors in the bank reserve equation that lie outside the control of the authorities, such as changes in float, seasonal shifts in currency in circulation, or gold movements.

The only major dispute over the use of open-market operations—whether they should be used for monetary control or to support the market for government securities—has already been discussed.

A less basic question concerns the instruments that should be used for open-market operations. Traditionally most transactions have involved government securities. But of what kind? For some years following World War II the Open Market Committee limited its purchases almost exclusively to short-term issues, a decision referred to as the *bills-only* policy. It felt that because the money market for short-term securities is more fluid, such transactions are less disrupting than is the case with regard to longer-term notes and bonds.

At one time commercial banks were the main holders of treasury bills, and it was argued that operations in this end of the market therefore affected the money supply more directly than operations in longer-term securities would. Now, however, nonfinancial corporations have become the primary holders of bills (as a means of earning interest on temporarily idle funds), and this point has lost most of its weight.

Another argument is that a given change in interest rates can be achieved with less effect on the price of bills than would be the case for longer-term bonds. Thus a rise in the interest rate from 3 to 4 per cent will force down the price of a bill with 60 days to run, from $995 to $993.33. It will depress the price of a 20-year bond with a 3 per cent coupon from $1,000 to $863.25. As a result of the large swings that could result from operations in longer securities, the Reserve authorities were afraid that interference in this market, or even the possibility of interference, would create uncertainties in the minds of normal buyers and sellers and that they might be frightened away, thereby reducing the market for such securities.

In any case, the Board felt, any effect on interest rates produced by open-market operations would be transmitted rapidly through the interest rate structure to long-term securities as well (though to the extent that this is true, the force of the preceding point is dulled).

The bills-only doctrine was challenged even within the System. Allan Sproul, president of the Federal Reserve Bank of New York from 1941 to 1956, for instance, felt that there were occasions when direct operations in the longer maturities might be desirable in order to affect the flow of funds in the capital (as distinct from the money) markets. He questioned the speed with which interest rate changes are transmitted from one type of security to another, since these are frequently held by different types of institutions. When long-term funds were needed, open-market operations should provide such funds directly without the stimulation of the money supply that purchases of bills would entail. This, he felt, might be particularly true during periods of Treasury financing when support was needed to guarantee the success of the issue but otherwise it was desirable to keep money relatively tight.

The arguments are subtle and somewhat technical, but they impinge on the broader question of whether Federal Reserve policy should concern itself solely with the *total* money supply or whether it should attempt to discriminate among particular markets or types of credit. The bills-only policy suggests the former; the opponents of that policy favor the latter.[17] As has already been pointed out, the bills-only policy was abandoned in 1961 precisely because the Reserve authorities wished to keep long-term rates low while encouraging short-term rates to rise. Quite obviously such a policy discriminates in favor of the long-term borrower as against the short-term borrower (but also in favor of the short-term lender as against the long-term lender). The retreat from bills-only has not ended the argument, but there appears to be no immediate prospect of a return.

On another aspect of open-market operations it might be noted briefly that in recent years the Reserve has resumed open-market purchases of bank acceptances, a practice discontinued in the thirties. The amounts currently held are quite small.

Direct Controls

The experience of the Federal Reserve with direct controls has been somewhat erratic. Margin requirements on listed securities were provided for in the Securities Exchange Act of 1934 and have been used continuously since

[17] A discussion of the whole problem may be found in U.S. Congress, Joint Committee on the Economic Report, *United States Monetary Policy: Recent Thinking and Experience,* Hearings before the Subcommittee on Economic Stabilization, Dec. 6 and 7, 1954, pp. 15–26 and 223–230. A very detailed analysis of the technical operation of the open-market account is presented in this same publication, pp. 257–331.

then. Except among those directly connected with the stock exchanges there seems little doubt concerning the efficacy of, and the need for, such restraint.

Control over consumer and real estate credit, on the other hand, has been granted only during brief emergency periods, and a debate continues over the question of whether the Federal Reserve should be given standby authority to impose controls over consumer credit whenever the economic situation seems to call for them.

The Board of Governors itself has changed its mind over the desirability of such legislation. Following the war and during the Korean conflict the Board asked Congress on several occasions to provide such powers on a permanent basis, without success. Later, as a result of an extensive 1956 survey of consumer credit,[18] the Board reversed its position and decided that "a special peacetime authority to regulate consumer installment credit is not now advisable."[19] The problem, however, refuses to disappear and still evokes considerable attention.

Part of the argument extends well beyond the specific topic of consumer credit into the whole area of general versus selective controls: Is it better to manage only the total quantity of money and let lenders allocate this total in any way they see fit, or is it preferable to put special restrictions on those uses of credit that seem to present special problems and to encourage those uses that seem most beneficial?

The proponents of selective control in general and consumer credit controls in particular answer the second half of the question in the affirmative. They suggest that an extension of consumer credit has the same inflationary effect as any other expansion of purchasing power. At the same time it does not have the long-run advantages of business credit. Since it does not itself increase the ability of consumers to earn income, it is not self-liquidating. Its repayment depends solely on the regular income of the borrower, who, unless he renews his loans indefinitely, must cut down his purchases at the time of repayment. Looking at the same problem from another angle, consumer loans do not increase the productive capacity of the nation, as business loans do. The payment of interest on these loans is therefore a net subtraction from the purchasing power of the borrower; to the extent that he spends part of his income on interest, he can't spend it on other goods. A business loan, on the other hand, creates the income out of which interest is paid with (hopefully) a profit in addition. It therefore increases the ability of the borrower to buy other goods.

The argument runs, therefore, that consumer credit is conceptually less defensible as well as less stable than business credit. The effect of consumer credit on general business conditions is fairly obvious. During the boom an expansion of income induces consumers to borrow more heavily since they feel assured of being able to repay, while sellers are optimistic also and fre-

[18] Board of Governors of the Federal Reserve System, *Consumer Installment Credit,* 6 vols. (1957). The arguments for and against consumer credit control are summarized in part 1, vol. I, pp. 356–387.

[19] *Federal Reserve Bulletin,* vol. 43, no. 6 (June, 1957), p. 648.

quently extend easier credit terms. When a downturn comes, the obligation of consumers to repay loans cuts their spending on new goods more drastically than their income falls. Since installment credit is used primarily for the purchase of durable goods, this accentuation of cyclical swings hits that area of the economy that is most vulnerable to cyclical movements for other reasons.

While consumer credit thus aggravates the instability of the economy, it is claimed that it is not amenable to general credit controls. This stems from the insensitivity of consumers to high interest rates on the one hand and the profitability of consumer loans on the other. The method of stating (or of obscuring) interest rates on installment loans leaves consumers very much in the dark as to what they are actually paying. Buyers confronted with a published "6 per cent carrying charge" are unaware of the fact that special fees plus repayment of the loan in installments may push the actual rate well above 12 per cent. Others, pleased at an interest rate of "3 per cent," fail to read or to comprehend the significance of the next words, "per month," and therefore gladly pay 36 per cent per year.

Many buyers simply don't care about interest and will pay any amount that their pocketbooks can stand. In some cases the very price of the article is ignored, the only important figure being the monthly payment. It is not surprising, therefore, that ½ per cent increase in interest would not have much effect on consumer borrowing.

At the same time the high rates that consumers will pay often induce lenders to favor consumer loans when they have a choice. When banks, for instance, are rationing business credit because of tight money, they may at the same time be buying all the consumer installment paper offered. This, it is alleged, diverts funds from their most productive purposes when money is in short supply. As a result general controls may unnecessarily restrict business loans with little effect on consumer loans.

An analogy is often drawn with the extension of stock market credit in the roaring twenties. The Federal Reserve Board felt that such credit was reaching dangerous proportions but that any significant restriction on the total money supply would squeeze the legitimate needs of business without restraining the speculative spree. Margin requirements, unavailable in 1929, were later instituted to prevent a repetition of this situation.

A third argument for the control of consumer credit is that it would reduce the pressure toward competitive easing of credit terms that both hurts the conservative lender and increases the risk of loss to others.

The case against selective controls is equally formidable. The leading argument is the objection to the discriminatory nature of direct controls. Many people feel that they interfere with economic freedom and substitute the fallible decision of a government agency for the impersonal forces of the market. There are many facets to this belief. It is asserted, for instance, that market forces adequately allocate resources and that if consumer loans produce a higher profit margin than business loans, then these loans are conducive to higher economic satisfaction and should not be discouraged; that consumer credit helps in the long-run growth of the economy by encouraging production of consumer goods; that lenders, in touch with the actualities of the situation, are in a better position to judge the soundness of loans than a board in Washington; that the amount of paper work involved in regulation would be a severe imposition on business; and that enforcement of controls would be difficult as both borrowers and lenders chafed under what they considered unwarranted interference with their freedom.

Opponents of control also feel that consumer credit *is* amenable to general credit control since banks will restrict consumer credit along with business credit if only because they want to cater to the needs of their regular (business) borrowers. And finally they believe that the volume of consumer credit is too small to be significant as an inflationary force, representing, according to one kind of measurement, only 15 per cent of total bank loans outstanding.

While battle lines are well drawn on the issue, the conclusion is not clear, and this area of potential monetary control promises to provide material for debate for some time to come.

The problem of control of real estate credit, while somewhat similar to that of installment credit, is of much less current interest. The arguments for control are somewhat weaker. Some mortgage money is actually business credit, and even for the owner-occupant the saving in rent has some of the elements of self-liquidation. Also mortgage interest rates are much lower than those for installment credit and seem to react more like business interest rates.

On the other hand, mortgage credit can be quite a volatile element in the economy, and attempts to control it may reappear if it seems to be getting out of hand.

Financial Intermediaries

There is another area of potential control that is receiving increasing attention today: the financial intermediaries.[20] In the past the influence of the quantity theory has tended to keep monetary policy focused on the supply of money. Since the commercial banks (and the government) are the only institutions that can actually create money, they are the ones that have received most attention.

The growth of intermediaries—savings banks, savings and loan associations, insurance companies, investment companies, trust funds, and so on—has called attention to their predominant importance in many loan markets. Although they cannot create money, they can certainly affect the velocity of its circulation. This they do primarily through their effect on liquidity prefer-

[20] The discussion has been stimulated by John G. Gurley and E. S. Shaw, "Financial Aspects of Economic Development," *American Economic Review,* vol. 45, no. 4 (September, 1955), pp. 515–538. A good deal of factual information on the subject is contained in Raymond W. Goldsmith, *Financial Intermediaries in the American Economy since 1900* (published for the National Bureau of Economic Research by Princeton University Press, Princeton, N.J., 1958). See also John G. Gurley and Edward S. Shaw, *Money in a Theory of Finance* (The Brookings Institution, Washington, 1960).

ence, since savings deposits or savings and loan shares, for instance, may be good substitutes for money, particularly for precautionary motives. Conversely, if intermediaries hold onto funds, they reduce velocity. They may therefore affect the total output of the economy and the level of prices, and in the process they most certainly influence the allocation of funds as between borrowers.

All these agencies are subject to some type of control—state banking authorities, state insurance commissioners, the Home Loan Bank Board, and the Securities and Exchange Commission, among others—but this control has concentrated almost exclusively on solvency and sound business practices, with little attention paid to the overall implications of their activities.

While it is not clear precisely what controls may be most useful in molding the operations of financial intermediaries in such a way that they may contribute to growth without inflation, Gurley and Shaw suggest that our attention should be turned from a narrow concentration on "monetary control" to a more realistic consideration of "financial control."

It would be possible to establish required reserve ratios for such institutions. Since they do not create money, this would not affect the quantity of money as it does when applied to commercial banks. But high reserve ratios would require them to hold a portion of their funds idle, thus reducing velocity. Lowering requirements would then tend to increase velocity.

Alternative methods of control might be to establish selective interest rates for particular types of loans or to provide more extensive regulation of the lending practices of specific types of institutions. Or perhaps current regulations could be relaxed somewhat to permit institutions wider discretion in using their funds to increase mobility of resources. This is an area of control in which much further study needs to be done.

The Commission on Money and Credit

Because the monetary system is so complex and because it had not had a complete examination since the Aldrich Committee undertook the task in 1908–1911, considerable pressure developed during the fifties for a similar investigation of our current structure. When Congress failed to act, the Committee for Economic Development, a nonpartisan organization of liberal businessmen, with the aid of a grant from the Ford Foundation, established the Commission on Money and Credit to do the job. The twenty-five members of the Commission included many prominent businessmen and bankers and two former Federal Reserve officials. They called on a number of eminent economists both to serve on the advisory board and to contribute papers. They accumulated a mass of material on all aspects of our monetary system, which has now been published in nineteen volumes. But when their report, *Money and Credit,* was issued in 1961, it seemed that the mountain had labored and brought forth a mouse.

In many respects the report is conservative, as perhaps is inevitable when such a large group is involved. It discusses practices and problems in well-known terms and frequently in highly platitudinous generalities. It does, however, contain a number of specific conclusions, some merely reaffirming the *status quo,* while others would indeed involve substantial changes in our monetary mechanism.

The Commission confirms the three standard goals of monetary policy (the balance-of-payments problem had not become so acute at that time) and goes on to conclude "that all three goals—an adequate rate of economic growth, low levels of unemployment, and reasonable price stability—can be achieved simultaneously . . ." (p. 44).[21]

Among its major conclusions in the areas most closely connected with money and banking, the Commission recommends the following:

1. As to monetary policy:

a. Open-market operations should be "the normal or usual instrument of general monetary policy" (p. 64). It rejects the bills-only policy.

b. Discount rates should be the same for all Federal Reserve banks (p. 66).

c. "The power to change reserve requirements should be used only sparingly" (p. 67).

d. (The Commission made no recommendations concerning direct controls because it was almost evenly split on the issue.)

2. As to Federal Reserve structure:

a. "The FRB Chairman and Vice-Chairman should be designated by the President . . . to serve for four-year terms coterminous with the President's" (p. 87).

b. "The FRB should consist of five members, with overlapping ten-year terms; . . . members should be eligible for reappointment" (p. 87).

c. The determination of open-market policies, rediscount rates, and reserve requirements should be vested in the Board; the Federal Open Market Committee would thus be abolished (p. 90).

d. "The Comptroller of the Currency and his functions and the FDIC should be transferred to the Federal Reserve System" (p. 174). The Commission opposes, however, the consolidation of the Treasury and the Federal Reserve (p. 109).

e. "The present form of capital stock of the Federal Reserve banks should be retired. Instead, membership in the System should be evidenced by a nonearning certificate of, say, $500, the same for each member bank" (p. 91).

f. "All insured commercial banks should be required to become members of the Federal Reserve System" (p. 77).

3. As to nonbank intermediaries:

[21] Commission on Money and Credit, *Money and Credit* (Prentice-Hall, Inc., Englewood Cliffs, N.J., 1961). In this summary of recommendations the numbers in parentheses refer to the page numbers in this report.

   a. "There should be no extension of direct Federal Reserve controls over nonbank financial institutions" (p. 81).
   b. "Federal charters [should] be made available for mutual savings banks" (p. 164).
4. As to international finance:
   a. "The present dollar price of gold should be retained" (p. 231).
   b. Gold reserve requirements should be eliminated (p. 234).

The Commission also made a number of recommendations, many of them procedural, in the general areas of taxation, fiscal policy, and the supervision of financial institutions. Although its report is interesting for its careful consideration of conflicting policies and possibilities, it uncovered no unknown problems, presented no new solutions, and is basically pedestrian rather than imaginative.

Summary

The debate over the wisdom and effectiveness of Federal Reserve policy goes on and will continue to go on indefinitely. It changes its form and emphasis from time to time, but frequently the new words merely disguise the old concepts. In brief summary the complaints against the Federal Reserve (each of which can be matched by counterclaims) are that its policies are:

1. Aimed at the wrong goals
2. Ineffective because:
   a. It cannot control velocity
   b. It covers too small a sector of the economy
   c. Interest rates are not that important
3. Ill-timed because of:
   a. The lag in gathering data
   b. Poor judgment
4. Discriminatory (whether this is good or bad is also in dispute)

Some of the arguments involve differences in philosophy or political outlook and will never be finally settled. Some, however, could be eliminated with an increase in our knowledge of the facts or of the theoretical relationships involved. There are a great many aspects of our economy about which our knowledge is not as complete as it should be. Some facets we have never fully understood. Some practices have changed so rapidly that we have not been able to keep up with them. A partial list of areas where further light is needed would include the role of the financial intermediaries, the cause and effect of interest rate changes, the effect of monetary policy on the availability of funds as compared with their price, the factors affecting incentives, the significance of policy for the allocation of capital among its various uses, the importance of liquidity and of money substitutes, forecasting procedures, and many others.

Questions for Thought and Discussion

1. Almost all general credit controls revolve around the use of reserve requirements, either directly or as a fulcrum by means of which other policies are made effective. Is there any other way of controlling the quantity of money?

2. What is the advantage of ceiling reserves compared with increased ordinary reserve requirements?

3. Are reserve requirements against deposits any more logical than reserve requirements against assets?

4. Is it fair to penalize banks, as a velocity reserve would do, for the actions of their customers in spending money faster? Is it possible to penalize the customers?

5. Do you agree with the proposals of the American Bankers Association regarding reserves?

6. What would you do if your bank charged you 25 cents per check? What would General Motors do?

7. What do you think of the desirability of 100 per cent reserves?

8. Debate the desirability of controlling only the quantity of money and letting the market determine its distribution versus the conscious control of the volume of money going into particular areas (e.g., stock market, consumption, housing, government securities, agriculture, small business, steel manufacturing, local governments, Los Angeles, New England, Joe's barber shop).

9. Why is it not possible to affect the quantity of money by regulating the financial intermediaries? Do they have any effect on the monetary aspects of the economy? Can this be controlled?

10. Should savings banks and savings and loan associations be subject to minimum reserve requirements?

11. Why are savings institutions generally forbidden to own common stocks? Is this a desirable type of regulation?

12. If you were rewriting the Federal Reserve Act, what control powers would you give to the Reserve authorities?

13. What monetary problems, other than those mentioned, do you think need further investigation?

Selected Bibliography

See references listed under Chapter 33.

Chapter 35 Fiscal Policy

He hath not money for these Irish wars,
His burdenous taxation notwithstanding.

The Tragedy of King Richard II
Act II, scene 1, line 260

No matter what the Federal Reserve does, it certainly isn't going to lick the business cycle all by itself. That requires the coordinated effort of many governmental agencies as well as the whole business community. The business cycle is by no means solely a monetary phenomenon, and to examine the whole paraphernalia of anticyclical policy would take us far afield. It may be in order, however, to make a brief survey of some of the most important areas of government action that affect aggregate purchasing power and are quasi-monetary. Omission of more specific policies does not mean that they are unimportant but rather that they lie outside the scope of our present study.

Here we will concern ourselves primarily with fiscal policy. This has two aspects: (1) the government budget, concerned with tax and expenditure policy, and (2) the management of the public debt.

Government Taxation and Expenditure

The basic effect of governmental activity on national income was indicated in our discussion of the circuit flow of money and pictured in Figure 25-1 (page 491).

If the government receives more money in taxes than it puts back into the income stream in the form of government expenditures, national income tends to fall. Such a policy would help to restrain inflation. If government expenditures exceed tax receipts, the tendency is to raise national income. This would be an appropriate policy for countering recession. It may, in fact, be the only effective way of raising income if business is too pessimistic to take the initiative in expansion. In such a situation Federal Reserve policy may be utterly futile.

In inflation the Reserve authorities, by reducing excess reserves to zero—or even below—can *force* banks to contract credit. This may be difficult if public opinion is strongly opposed to control or if other agencies of the government are unleasing inflationary forces. But it is *possible.* In depression the Federal Reserve may be helpless. It can provide large amounts of excess reserves, but it cannot require banks to make loans, nor can it force business to borrow. As Federal Reserve officials are fond of saying, you can't push on a string. It is possible to tighten money by pulling, but pushing expands credit only if both banks and borrowers want to take up the slack.

If business doesn't want to invest, the government can make monetary policy effective by doing the borrowing and spending itself. It thus puts money into the pockets of its workers and suppliers, and national income tends to rise just as it would if investment were to increase in the private sector. Fiscal policy is therefore an important supplement to monetary policy.

Automatic Stabilizers. Among the most interesting tools in the government's anticyclical kit are *automatic* (or built-in) *stabilizers,* those ingenious devices that help to bring the economy back to an even keel without any deliberate action on the part of anyone. Their prime advantage lies in the fact that they do not require judgment as to the future course of economic activity or deliberative action on the part of any man or agency, both of which are subject to the pitfalls of prediction and the delays of legislative or administrative machinery. Like automatic sprinklers they do not wait for someone to realize that there is a fire and for the fire department to get there. They detect the fire themselves and immediately go to work.

Automatic stabilizers are not new. The gold standard—under the old "rules of the game"—was one, but we finally decided that it didn't stabilize quite the right thing. The search for automatic substitutes in the monetary field has not been very rewarding, but in other areas several built-in stabilizers have already proved useful.

Federal Income Tax. One such automatic stabilizer is the progressive, pay-as-you-go income tax. As soon as wage payments drop, before any statistics on the subject are available, the actual tax paid is reduced. And because the tax is progressive (at higher rates for higher income), the tax reduction is more than proportional to the drop in income if a wage cut puts the worker into a lower tax bracket. This means more money to spend than he otherwise would have, and the downturn is cushioned as the government absorbs, in reduced tax receipts, part of the force of depression.

When income rises, the reverse happens. The government takes a larger share, and inflationary forces are dulled.

Social Security. Even more directly pointed at the heart of depression is the unemployment-compensation section of the Social Security Act. This works in two ways at once. Since the social security tax is levied on wages, any drop in wage payments immediately reduces tax obligations. At the same time a drop in employment will increase the sums paid to the unemployed, who are then able to maintain their consumption at a higher level than would otherwise be possible. This maintenance of spending power helps to restrict the downturn and to keep it from spreading through the economy.

To a more limited extent the same thing is true of old-age and survivors' insurance. Since old-age benefits depend partly on how much the pensioner earns, a drop in business activity may have some effect on increasing these payments.

Corporate Income Taxes. Corporate income taxes have some of the same effects as personal income taxes, particularly now that they are on a modified pay-as-you-go basis. Since corporate profits vary more than wage payments or other personal income, the variation in corporate income taxes is likely to be greater than that in personal taxes, but the effect on consumption is not quite so direct. The effect on investment, however, may be important.

The Farm Program. Farm price supports are often considered to be stabilizing, but their effect is not entirely clear. In the first place, present supports are determined by the *ratio* between two sets of prices: the prices farmers pay and the prices at which they sell their products. If both sets of prices fall together, payments would not be increased. In addition, the support level is flexible and subject to administrative discretion, so that policy is not completely automatic. The soil-bank program creates even further uncertainty in the farm picture, and the political ramifications of the problem are bound to produce constant revisions in "farm policy." It is doubtful therefore whether the farm program is either truly automatic or even stabilizing. It was destabilizing during much of the postwar period, when large payments to farmers added fuel to an already inflationary situation.

Private Automatic Stabilizers. Many corporations maintain dividends even when profits drop, cutting into their saving to do so. While hardly a matter of fiscal policy, this traditional practice is nevertheless a quasi-automatic stabilizer that has been with us for a long time, helping to maintain personal income when national income falls. Thus, while corporate profits dropped $11.0 billion in the 1958 recession, dividends declined only $0.2 billion.

A similar tendency on the part of consumers to reduce saving as their income falls is also a quasi-automatic stabilizer, for it means that consumption drops less than income.

Summary. The importance of each of these stabilizers (except farm payments) in the recession of 1958 is indicated in Table 35-1. Their combined effect was to cushion a drop of over $16 billion in GNP to a fall of only $2½ billion in personal income and a reduction of only $1 billion in consumption. The high level of consumption in turn encouraged business and thereby helped to stem the tide of depression.

Table 35-1. Changes in GNP and Selected Subclassifications, Third Quarter, 1957, to First Quarter, 1958

Billions of Dollars, Seasonally Adjusted at Annual Rates

Gross national product		−16.3
Corporate profits tax	−5.0	
Undistributed corporate profits	−5.8	
Contributions for social insurance	−0.1	
Government transfer payments	+2.6	
Other factors, net	−0.3	
Personal income		−2.5
Personal taxes	−1.2	
Disposable personal income		−1.3
Personal saving	−0.3	
Personal consumption expenditure		−1.0

Source: Computed from *Survey of Current Business*, vol. 40, no. 7 (July, 1960), pp. 9–11.

In the very mild recession of 1960–1961, GNP fell by only $2.7 billion, while both personal income and personal consumption rose.

Taxation, Redistribution, and Incentives. But while automatic stabilizers may help, they certainly do not guarantee stability. Even in conjunction with monetary policy they may be insufficient to counter the forces of severe depression. Under such conditions discretionary fiscal policy may be needed to reinforce other actions.

Tax policy is half of this area. Other things remaining the same, a reduction in taxes will increase disposable income, will induce people to spend more, and will help offset deflationary forces in the economy. When inflation is the problem, increased taxation will absorb some of the excess purchasing power and reduce the pressure.

This does not mean that the use of taxation policy as a countercyclical device is easy. The very concept of discretionary action implies that it must be consciously *timed* to counteract destabilizing forces, that it must be of the proper magnitude, and that it must be reversed when the situation changes. Difficulties are inevitable.

Any program that has to survive the congressional process cannot be applied rapidly. If the depression (or inflation) is short-lived, a tax reduction (or increase) may take so long to obtain legislative approval that it is applied just in time to meet the economy coming back. If the disturbing forces are strong and lasting, however, tax policy can be very effective.

A similar problem arises from the fact that tax policies, once adopted, are a bit difficult to change. Both the government and the public find it easier to live with established patterns than to adapt to shifting ones. A tax reduction, for instance, designed to counter a recession, may be kept on the books through inertia after the need for it has passed. One way of preventing this is to provide that any tax change designed purely for countercyclical purposes shall automatically expire at the end of a specified and relatively short period. It could be extended if a positive need for its continuation existed, but at least it wouldn't remain merely because of failure to repeal it.

The overall level of tax receipts is by no means the only significant characteristic of tax policy, even from the viewpoint of national income (and there are, of course, many other considerations that must enter into any decision regarding taxes). It is possible to expand or contract national income by changing the *kind* of taxation without affecting its total amount. This can occur either because the shift redistributes income between groups with different propensities to save or because it alters incentives to save or invest.

For example, if a sales tax is substituted for an income tax of the same yield, the result is likely to be depressive. The income tax, being progressive, takes a larger proportion of the income of higher-income groups than of lower, while the sales tax, being regressive, reverses the process. Thus the substitution redistributes some disposable income from the poor, who spend most of their income, to the more wealthy, who save a larger proportion of it. The result is an increase in saving at the expense of consumption, and this tends to depress national income. For this reason a sales tax might be considered desirable in inflation, but it is one of the worst forms of taxation in depression because of its direct discouragement of consumption.

A similar depressive effect would follow the imposition of any tax that reduces incentives to produce or consume. Unfortunately we are not too sure of the actual effect on incentives of various taxes. It is often suggested that the corporate profits tax has serious repercussions on the willingness of corporations to expand and to take risks. If this is true, a reduction of the profits tax would have a more significant expansionary effect than is indicated by the simple numerical effect on government receipts. This area of incentives is one that needs more knowledge than we presently possess, and we raise the point here to indicate the nature of the problem rather than to provide answers to it.

Fiscal policy as a means of economic stabilization suffered the same eclipse as monetary policy during and following the war, but it has also reemerged as an instrument of economic control, particularly in the tax cut of 1964. This reduction of both personal and corporate income tax rates is notable in a number of respects. It was based, more than any other postwar policy, on a deliberate attempt to use the government budget as a stabilizing tool. Yet it did not follow traditional fiscal policy in that the purpose was not to pull the economy out of a recession, but rather to prevent it from falling into one. The economy had been moving upward for three years and was still going strong, but the feeling was that the rise could not last without some stimulus, and the tax cut was to do the job. This measure, although based squarely on Keynesian concepts that have not always had the support of conservative businessmen, received almost unanimous approval from business as well as from economists and government leaders of almost every shade of political opinion. And finally, it was almost perfectly successful. GNP continued its uninterrupted rise, unemployment fell from 5.6 to 4.9 per cent, prices remained relatively stable, and the economy failed to develop the inflationary tendencies or structural maladjustments that a few people feared would result from further expansionary stimulus when the economy was already doing well. These results are at least partly luck, and certainly we cannot say that in this experience we have found the magic formula for continuous prosperity. For one thing, it took Congress over a year to get the tax cut through, and it is highly possible that if it had been passed more quickly, its effect would have come at the wrong time—one example of congressional dawdling turning out to be advantageous. Nevertheless the use of fiscal policy as a stabilizing device has been strongly vindicated, and further efforts of this kind are certain.

This experiment in tax policy both results from, and gives further support to, suggestions that in a period in which unemployment is high but inflation poses a threat to price stability (including the problem of the balance of international payments) it may be possible to fight the stabilization battle on two fronts by directing fiscal policy toward the unemployment problem (as by the tax cut), while monetary policy is used to counter the inflationary pressures in the economy (through increase of the discount rate or otherwise). While we must caution again that all the success of 1964 cannot be attributed to stabilization policies alone, nevertheless there is little doubt that they played an important role. The major question is how we can apply such policies to other and different conditions in order to achieve similar results.

Government Expenditures. On the side of expenditures the problem of timing again arises. Any government project to spend money takes time to get under way; congressional action is ponderous. One solution commonly suggested is for Congress to authorize projects in advance so that they may be put into action by administrative decision as soon as the economy sees the need for them. Some progress has been made along these lines, but Congress tends to look askance on too much delegation of its authority.

Once started, expenditure programs are hard to reverse. This is particularly true of public works projects, such as roads, dams, and public buildings. There is little point in building half a dam and then stopping because the economy is picking up. So it is continued even though its expansionary pressure is no longer needed. In fact the lengthy nature of many public expenditures, coupled with the time it takes to get them started, may turn public works from a stabilizing to a destabilizing influence. Suppose the economy starts downward. Congress initiates a new project. Weeks of legislative action are followed by months of preliminary surveys, engineering studies, and land acquisition, and finally work begins. If the recession is short-lived, the economy is moving up by this time, and the payments now going to workers and suppliers add to inflationary pressure. The problem may be lessened by careful planning, and there are some types of expenditures that do not suffer from such ponderousness, but many projects frequently advocated have this basic defect.

Public works, as well as many other types of government expenditures, may also be difficult to fit into a countercyclical pattern simply because government projects cannot always wait on business conditions. New schools are needed today; new highways are needed today—not at some future time when their construction would aid business recovery. Some projects can be postponed, but by no means all.

As with taxes, the effectiveness of government expenditures in supporting the economy depends not only on their amount but also on their type. Unemployment compensation goes directly to those who are most likely to spend it. Payments for military aircraft filter more slowly to income recipients.

The problem of incentive is also important, for if the government expands its operations into fields normally reserved to private enterprise, there may be an adverse effect on private investment decisions, and an increase in government expenditures is not very helpful if it causes an even greater retrenchment on the part of private business. Any government program, therefore, must take into account *all* its effects on the economy, and here again we need greater understanding of the relation of government programs to incentives.

This discussion of government tax and expenditure problems has been much too brief to cover the subject at all adequately, but we need to move on to those aspects of fiscal policy more directly concerned with monetary matters.

Debt Management

Under normal circumstances (and subject to the qualifications just discussed) a government deficit tends to expand national income, and a surplus tends to restrict it. But the general effect is influenced by the way in which the resulting debt or its retirement is handled.

Financing a Deficit. If government expenditures exceed receipts, it means that the government is putting more money into circulation than it receives in taxes. The rest of the money must come from somewhere, and it makes considerable difference how the deficit is financed. The means of financing fall into four major categories (listed roughly in increasing order of inflationary impact, with the components of the circuit flow that may be affected also indicated):

1. Borrowing from the nonbank public
   a. From consumption
   b. From private investment
   c. From hoarding
2. Borrowing from commercial banks

   a. From private investment
   b. From money creation
3. Drawing down the Treasury's general fund
   a. From hoarding
4. Printing money
   a. From money creation

Borrowing from the Nonbank Public. When the government borrows directly from consumers, it appears from the circuit-flow diagram that the money comes out of saving, but this is by no means the end of our investigation. What would the consumer have done if he had not bought the government securities? Would he have saved just as much? If so, what form would this saving have taken?

Under most circumstances we can assume that people do not save simply in order to buy government bonds. Rather their purchase of bonds is an outlet for savings already accumulated. But this is not always the case, and the government has used considerable ingenuity in devising bond-selling schemes that will increase saving. The most effective is the payroll-deduction plan for buying Series E bonds. While such an agreement is voluntary, there is little doubt that most people force themselves to save more that way than they would be able to do by themselves.

Any additional saving produced this way must come out of reduced consumption. To the extent that a government finances increased expenditures in this manner, the process is not inflationary since the larger government contribution to national income is offset by a smaller flow from private spending.

When the Federal government instituted the payroll saving plan in World War II, it reinforced its noninflationary force by two additional campaigns. One was pressure to get *everyone* to sign up, exemplified in special awards to plants that had 100 per cent participation. The social pressure to conform brought many people in who otherwise wouldn't have bought bonds at all. It is likely that they had to cut expenditures somewhat to participate.

The other campaign was designed to play on patriotic motives. The general theme was: "The boys in foxholes need ammunition—Buy a bond." This is a complete *non sequitur* in the best (or worst) Madison Avenue tradition. If soldiers needed bullets, they would be provided if there were any *physical* way of doing it. A lack of money would not have hampered a government that has the sovereign right to print it. But printing money is inflationary, while persuading people to reduce consumption in order to lend to the government is not. Increased sales of Series E bonds didn't help the United States win the war, but they did help us to get through it with less inflationary pressure than would otherwise have been generated. If *all* the deficit could have been financed this way, inflation would have been no problem.

But even during a war patriotic motives are insufficient to induce consumers to withhold any substantial sums from consumption, and in peacetime the amount must be small indeed.

Most nonbank investors, whether individuals or institutions, buy government bonds out of savings that are already in existence. What would they have done with these savings if the government weren't borrowing money? In most cases they would have bought some other kind of security. Put more simply, the funds would have gone into private investment. If the government diverts funds from private investment, the deficit is also noninflationary, for the increased government expenditure offsets the drop in the private economy. The funds go through a different channel but with the same quantitative effect on national income.

There is, however, another alternative, for it is possible that some people may not trust other kinds of securities and in the absence of government bonds would simply hoard their money. The same result would occur if the absence of sufficient new securities to absorb current saving caused security prices to be bid up (interest yields to drop) to the point that people preferred to hold cash. To the extent that a government deficit calls these funds out of hiding, it is inflationary, for it puts back into circulation money that had not been previously available in the income stream. It is not likely that funds from this source are large.

Since (except for the small amount of funds that may be drawn out of hoards) government sales to the nonbank public are noninflationary, the government has emphasized this type of borrowing during wartime, when a deficit seems necessary but the economy needs no further stimulus. It is for this reason that savings bonds are sold only to individuals, are nontransferable, and cannot be used as collateral for a loan. Another device is the non-bank-eligible bond, which can be bought by ordinary corporations and financial intermediaries but not by commercial banks.

On the other hand, the very advantages of sales to individuals in an inflationary period make them undesirable for use in a depression, when the government is trying to raise national income.

Borrowing from Commercial Banks. Under these circumstances borrowing from commercial banks may be more effective, but even this depends on conditions. If the banks are already loaned up—if they have no excess reserves on which to base additional loans—they cannot lend to the government unless they reduce their loans elsewhere. This would mean a fall in private investment to offset the government expenditure.

Such a situation would be highly unusual, however, at a time when the government was trying to combat a depression. This is normally just the time when banks have excess reserves because business is in no mood to borrow. If they don't, this is the time for monetary and fiscal policy to join forces, with the Federal Reserve promoting easy money to provide the banks with excess reserves on the basis of which they can lend to the Treasury. This new money represents a net addition to the circuit flow and tends to raise national income.

If the Federal Reserve is using open-market purchases to create easy-money conditions, the ultimate—though indirect—effect is that the Federal Reserve becomes the holder of the new securities (or their equivalent). Thus the Federal Reserve creates the funds paid by the government to its employees and suppliers. There is no necessity for banks to restrict their other loans, for under these conditions their reserves would be rising rather than falling. The increased money supply, the higher reserves, the greater liquidity of the public, and the enhanced income level all tend to lift the economy upward.

Using Idle Cash. If there is a sizable balance in the Treasury's general fund, some part of the deficit may be met by reducing this balance to lower levels. This represents dishoarding and has the same inflationary potential as private dishoarding. The amount involved is limited to the Treasury's current balance, and this is not normally much more than adequate for ordinary day-to-day operations.

Using the Printing Press. The most direct and certain method of obtaining money is for the government to print additional currency. This is a time-honored custom (if "honored" is the proper word), a direct descendant of the metallic debasement practiced by kings two millennia ago when they found taxes insufficient to meet their royal needs. But because the practice is subject to considerable abuse and because it is so obviously an inflationary device, the use of the printing press to meet a government deficit has sunk into disrepute, and in this country it does not appear to be a practical possibility. In 1933 Congress gave the President the authority to issue $3 billion worth of greenbacks, but the power was never used and was finally allowed to lapse.

In practice, borrowing from commercial banks to meet a deficit may be fully as inflationary as printing currency, but it has several safeguards that make it less amenable to abuse:

1. Since loans must be repaid,[1] borrowing involves a future commitment whose restraining influence is absent when currency is printed.

2. Since interest on loans is a continuing charge, the cost must be weighed against the advantages, and this is a further sobering consideration.

3. In order to lend, commercial banks must have excess reserves, and this means that the Federal Reserve must give at least passive approval to the government borrowing program. It is possible for the government to suppress the qualms of the Federal Reserve, as it did during World War II, but, like Jiminy Cricket, the Reserve, acting on the government's conscience in this respect, cannot be completely forgotten.

4. In order to borrow, the government must find willing lenders. If it borrows too much, it will find its credit rating deteriorating and will experience greater and greater difficulty in marketing its securities, evidenced most clearly in a rising interest rate.

None of these considerations will prevent a government from borrowing when it feels the need, but they are likely to keep that borrowing within more reasonable limits than would be imposed if the printing press were the ac-

[1] They may also be refunded almost indefinitely, but at least the obligation to face repayment at *some* future time remains.

cepted method of financing a deficit. On the other hand, it should be quite clear that refraining from the issue of additional currency does not relieve the government of responsibility for the inflationary effects of a government deficit.

In a depression, of course, the lift given the economy by a deficit is highly desirable. If both consumers and businessmen are holding back on their expenditures, the government is the only sector of the economy left to raise national income payments. Under these circumstances, as we have already pointed out, some rise in prices may be an inevitable and reasonable price to pay for a substantial increase in employment. But countercyclical policy requires that once full employment is approached, the government should reverse its policy, operate on a budget surplus, and reduce its outstanding debt. Countercyclical policy is not a one-way street, always pushing the economy upward. It should also restrain the undue exuberance of boom conditions.

Repayment of Debt. Fiscal policy, therefore, does not imply a constantly rising national debt. When the economy is running at full blast, it is desirable for the government to reduce its expenditures not only to curb inflationary pressures but also to release needed factors of production to industry in order to give support to physical expansion of output through private investment. To the extent that government expenditures cannot be reduced (and there are many areas of government activity that are vital to the economy at all times), it may be necessary to raise taxes in order to absorb additional purchasing power whose only effect on the economy is to press upward on prices. In either case the government will have a surplus—more tax income than is needed to meet its payments. This is basically deflationary, but how deflationary depends on the way in which the surplus is used. Here there are five possibilities, roughly in order of their increasing deflationary effect:

1. Retirement of nonbank-held debt
   a. Funds flow into consumption
   b. Funds flow into investment
   c. Funds are hoarded
2. Retirement of bank-held debt
   a. Funds are made available for investment
   b. Funds are destroyed
3. Retirement of Federal Reserve-held debt
   a. Funds are destroyed
4. Retaining the surplus in the Treasury account
   a. In commercial banks
   b. In the Federal Reserve (or in vault)
5. Destruction of currency

Since savings bonds can be redeemed at any time the holder wishes, the amount redeemed cannot be controlled by the government. Nor can the Treasury call its securities prior to maturity except for a number of long-term bonds that specifically provide for such earlier repayment (never sooner than ten years prior to maturity). The process of reducing the public debt is primarily one of paying off securities when they mature, without floating new loans. Since the government's discretion is limited to choosing which issues currently maturing will not be replaced, and since any issue is likely to be held by many different kinds of investors among whom no discrimination can be made, the Treasury is restricted in its ability to choose which type of holder is to be reimbursed. But certain institutions (the Federal Reserve, for instance) frequently hold more of certain issues than of others, and if, therefore, it is desired to repay, say, Federal Reserve–held debt primarily, those issues held predominantly by the Reserve will be redeemed as they mature, while others are refunded.

Nonbank-held Debt. When individuals receive repayment for government bonds that they hold, they could use the money to increase their consumption. Thus the money that the government refrained from putting into national income through its own expenditures may reach the same destination through consumption expenditures.

It is much more likely that funds received from redemption will be channeled into other investment outlets. This is almost bound to be true of the large volume of government securities held by institutional investors—savings banks, life insurance companies, trust funds, and so on. If the government is not borrowing, these investors will put their funds to work in corporation bonds or other private loans, thus shifting them to national income via the private investment route. The result will be no reduction in total income.

There is a possibility that some funds received from redemption will be hoarded, particularly if the reduction in the supply of government securities outstanding tends to raise the price of securities and to lower interest yields. To the extent that this occurs, the upward pressure on national income will be decreased, since hoarded funds do not circulate in the payments stream. The volume of hoarding, however, is likely to be small, and the net effect of repayment of public debt held by nonbank investors is therefore likely to be only a small reduction in inflationary pressures, although it will entail a shift in the composition of national output as government expenditure is reduced and private investment and consumption rise.

Bank-held Debt. Strangely enough the repayment of securities held by the commercial banks may have very similar consequences. While it is frequently stated that repayment of bank-held debt is deflationary because it reduces the total amount of money (demand deposits) in existence,[2] this is likely to be temporary, for at the same time it increases excess reserves. If the banking system were loaned up prior to the repayment, it is now no longer loaned up.

[2] The full transaction is as follows: Jones, who has a deposit of $100, pays taxes in that amount by giving the government a check. The government now has $100 on deposit, and Jones has nothing. The government then writes a check for $100 to repay a bank that holds a maturing bond. The bank loses an asset (the bond) worth $100, and the deposit of the government is reduced by the same amount. Nobody owns the deposit; it has been destroyed.

The reduction in deposits has released a fractional amount of required reserves, and on the basis of these excess reserves the banking system can create additional loans equal in amount to those redeemed by the government. If they do so, the additional private investment made possible in this way will equal the reduction in government expenditures, and no deflationary effect will be felt.

Whether the banks *will* use these excess reserves depends on the circumstances. Since we are assuming boom conditions, which suggest that business is trying to borrow as much as is available, it is highly likely that banks will want to lend as much as they can. Here again is an opportunity for monetary and fiscal policy to work together. For if the Federal Reserve uses its various powers to sop up these excess reserves, the banks will be unable to turn around and increase their loans to business. In this case the full deflationary effect of the government surplus will be felt. Not only is money destroyed, but its resurrection is prevented. If the Federal Reserve sells an amount of securities equal to the redemption, the effect will be the same as if securities held by the Federal Reserve had been redeemed.

Redemption of Federal Reserve–held Debt. In this case as money is destroyed bank reserves are reduced by an equal amount, and this forces the banks to contract by a multiple of their loss of reserves. We can review our knowledge of bank operation by following this transaction in detail, using simplified and nominal figures.

Suppose that bank A has the following balance sheet at the beginning of the period (in dollars):

Bank A

Assets		*Liabilities*	
Reserves	20,000	Deposits, individuals	100,000
Loans	60,000	Capital	10,000
Securities	30,000		
	110,000		110,000

Suppose also that its legal reserve requirement is 20 per cent. It is therefore loaned up.

At the same time the Federal Reserve bank of its district has the following balance sheet:

Federal Reserve Bank

Assets		*Liabilities*	
Gold	200,000	Deposits, member banks	180,000
Government securities	200,000	Federal Reserve notes	215,000
		Capital	5,000
	400,000		400,000

Various depositors now pay $4,000 in taxes by sending checks to the government, and these checks are returned to the bank for credit to the Treasury's tax and loan account.

Bank A

Assets		*Liabilities*		
Reserves	20,000	Deposits,		
Loans	60,000	individuals	96,000	(−4,000)
Securities	30,000	Deposits, tax and		
		loan	4,000	(+4,000)
		Capital	10,000	
	110,000		110,000	

The bank's total deposits remain unchanged; only their internal composition has been altered.

The government now wishes to use (part of) this tax income to redeem bonds held by the Federal Reserve bank. It first exercises a *call* on all banks to transfer, say, 50 per cent of all tax and loan deposits to the Federal Reserve. This means that the Reserve bank will charge $2,000 against bank A's reserve account and credit it to the Treasury.

Bank A

Assets			*Liabilities*		
Reserves	18,000	(−2,000)	Deposits,		
Loans	60,000		individuals	96,000	
Securities	30,000		Deposits, tax and		
			loan	2,000	(−2,000)
	110,000		Capital	10,000	
	108,000			108,000	

Federal Reserve Bank

Assets		*Liabilities*		
Gold	200,000	Deposits, member		
Government securities	200,000	banks	178,000	(−2,000)
		Deposits, treasury	2,000	(+2,000)
		Federal Reserve		
		notes	215,000	
		Capital	5,000	
	400,000		400,000	

The government then uses its treasury deposit to redeem $2,000 of securities held by the Federal Reserve. This affects only the Reserve bank.

Federal Reserve Bank

Assets			*Liabilities*		
Gold	200,000		Deposits, member		
Government			banks	178,000	
securities	198,000	(−2,000)	Deposits, treasury	0	(−2,000)
			Federal Reserve		
			notes	215,000	
			Capital	5,000	
	398,000			398,000	

If we examine the last balance sheet of bank A, we find a critical condition. Deposits total $98,000, while reserves are only $18,000—18.4 per cent of deposits. Not only has the $2,000 that was paid in taxes been destroyed, but in the process bank A's reserves have fallen below the required 20 per cent. Bank A must therefore raise its reserves or reduce its deposits. It could do the first by selling securities, the second by letting loans run off until it gets back into balance. If it chooses the latter course, loans would have to fall by $8,000:

Bank A

	Assets		*Liabilities*
Reserves	18,000	Deposits, individuals	88,000 (−8,000)
Loans	52,000 (−8,000)	Deposits, tax and loan	2,000
Securities	30,000	Capital	10,000
	100,000		100,000

Thus if banks are loaned up, as they are likely to be in a boom period, the repayment of Federal Reserve–held debt will create anti-inflationary forces several times the amount of repayment, the exact multiple depending on the average required reserve ratio. The effect is just the same as if the Federal Reserve sold an equal amount of securities to private holders. Or, if it wanted to, the Reserve could offset the effect of redemption by buying an equivalent amount of securities in the open market. In this case, as in others, action is most effective when the Federal Reserve and the Treasury are working together rather than at cross purposes.

Retaining Funds in the Treasury Account. The Treasury could accomplish exactly the same result as that just discussed by hoarding money, that is, by holding unused deposits in the Federal Reserve banks. As the balance sheets show, the restrictive effect is felt at the time the Treasury transfers its funds from the commercial bank to the Federal Reserve rather than at the time it actually redeems its securities.

If, on the other hand, the Treasury hoarded balances in the commercial banks, it would reduce moneyflows by the amount of the funds so immobilized but not by a multiple. It would not reduce bank reserves, but it would remove the amount of the unspent tax receipts from active circulation.

As an anti-inflationary measure there is one minor advantage in the Treasury's holding idle balances and two major disadvantages. On the one hand, it means that the government is building up a cash reserve that can be used immediately when a downturn materializes without the uncertainties of borrowing. On the other hand, keeping idle cash is expensive in terms of the interest that could be saved by using it to pay off debt. In addition, the very fact that the Treasury has a sizable balance may induce Congress to spend it even though inflationary pressures still predominate. Building up such a balance therefore seems on the whole to be more of a theoretical than a practical possibility.

Destruction of Currency. If the government had previously printed large amounts of currency, it might later counteract this move by withdrawing such currency and destroying it. This has sometimes been done by nations attempting to arrest a hyperinflation, but it is not a very practical process under more normal circumstances since it requires some means of *forcing* the public to give up cash (as by the redemption of the old currency in new money of lower denomination).

The Maturity Structure of Debt. Just as the effect of a given volume of government debt depends partly on who owns it, so it depends partly on the maturity of the securities issued. For one thing, savings institutions are more likely to buy bonds, while commercial banks are usually more interested in shorter-dated securities. Thus the maturity structure affects ownership.

In addition, short-term debt is much more liquid than long-term, and an issue of treasury bills, for instance, will therefore have a less restrictive effect on expenditures (both consumption and investment) than the same amount of 20-year bonds, since many individuals and institutions will consider the bills the equivalent of cash, particularly for precautionary purposes. The issue of short-term obligations thus has the greater expansionary potential and would be most effective in a depression, when the economy needs a lift.

In a boom, on the other hand, "spreading out the debt"—that is, increasing its average maturity by refunding bills through the sale of longer-term obligations—reduces the public's liquidity. With falling liquidity people will tend to hold more cash, and this reduction in the velocity of circulation of money will help to damp the inflation even if the total size of the debt is not changed.

Spreading out the debt has been a declared objective of fiscal policy throughout much of the inflationary portion of the postwar period, but in practice the authorities have not accomplished very much in this direction. For one thing it means that long-term bonds must be sold at the very time when interest rates are highest, and this conflicts with the Treasury's attempt to keep interest costs down. In addition there is some feeling that competing with private issues of bonds in a tight money market may interfere with the growth of industry. Although a dearth of funds under such conditions is merely a symptom of an underlying scarcity of resources and although a reduction in corporate borrowing would ease inflationary pressures, this argument seems to carry weight with the Treasury. Admittedly spreading out the debt is a more complex process than it might appear to be on the surface, but it is certainly not an impossible task.

Interest Rates. Interest rates must always be one of the basic concerns of the Treasury, and the structure of rates on government securities in turn has important repercussions throughout the economy. In some respects the level of interest rates is the focal point where monetary and fiscal policy meet. We have already examined several aspects of this problem, and a summary may serve as a fitting conclusion to our discussion of policy.

There are some who think that the Treasury can set any interest rate it wants on securities and thus can determine the market rate of interest on other types of loans. As we have seen, this is not true. If the Treasury pays too low a rate, nobody is going to buy the securities. A government bond selling at 90 per cent of par is not an indication of a lack of faith in the eventual repayment of the bond, but rather of the fact that the bond carries an interest coupon of, say, 2½ per cent when the market thinks securities of this type should be yielding 3 per cent.

But while the Treasury cannot *set* the market interest rate, it does have an important influence on it. As the nation's largest borrower it is a vital factor in the demand for loanable funds, and it does most certainly *influence* the rate by the kind and amount of securities it offers.

The Federal Reserve, on the other hand, is the most important influence on the supply side of the market for loanable funds, and in this role it undoubtedly has even more effect on interest rates than the Treasury has. If they are willing to work together, the two of them *can* set the rate (at least within limits), as they did during World War II and for five years afterward. But as the latter part of this period shows, cooperation in the wrong direction can be seriously detrimental to the economy, while a dispute between them (such as occurred in 1950) is also upsetting. This is why it is important that the Treasury and the Federal Reserve work in harmony, but without either infringing on the prerogatives of the other. While the Federal Reserve has primary responsibility for stabilizing the economy, the Treasury cannot help but play a major role in supplementing the Reserve's activities. Whether this marriage of monetary and fiscal policy will in fact prove adequate to prevent the excesses of either extreme inflation or disastrous depression only the future can tell. The potential would seem to be there.

Questions for Thought and Discussion

1. Are there automatic stabilizers in the economy that we have not listed? Are there some that we don't have that would be desirable?
2. If the progressive income tax is an automatic stabilizer, would it help to make it more progressive?
3. Why does current thought tend to approve of automatic stabilizers in the field of fiscal policy but to reject them for monetary policy? Would it be possible to cure business fluctuations completely by extending automatic stabilizers to all areas of the economy?
4. Suppose the government reduced taxes in the upper-income brackets, thereby incurring a deficit, and sold the bonds to finance it to the very people whose taxes had been reduced. Would this raise national income?

5. If the tax reduction of 1964 was helpful in keeping the economy moving upward, why shouldn't we repeat the process every year?
6. Is a reduction in taxes or an increase in expenditures more desirable as a means of raising national income from depression levels? What taxes? What expenditures?
7. Explain the differing effects on total bank deposits and bank reserves of government borrowing (*a*) from savings institutions, (*b*) from commercial banks, and (*c*) indirectly from the Federal Reserve.
8. If the government has the power to create money, why should it pay interest to borrow it from others? Does the answer have anything to do with debasement?
9. If countercyclical fiscal policy means repaying at least part of the national debt during boom periods, why is the debt higher now than it has been at any other time in history?

Selected Bibliography

American Economic Association: *Readings in Fiscal Policy,* Richard D. Irwin, Inc., Homewood, Ill., 1955.
Buchanan, James M.: *Public Principles of Public Debt,* Richard D. Irwin, Inc., Homewood, Ill., 1958.
———: *The Public Finances,* Richard D. Irwin, Inc., Homewood, Ill., 1960.
Commission on Money and Credit: *Fiscal and Debt Management Policies,* Prentice-Hall, Inc., Englewood Cliffs, N.J., 1963.
Federal Reserve Bank of New York: *The Treasury and the Money Market,* 1954.
Gaines, Tilford C.: *Techniques of Treasury Debt Management,* joint publication of the Graduate School of Business, Columbia University, New York, and The Free Press of Glencoe, New York, 1962.
Groves, Harold M.: *Financing Government,* 6th ed., Holt, Rinehart and Winston, Inc., New York, 1964.
Hall, Challis A., Jr.: *Fiscal Policy for Stable Growth,* Holt, Rinehart and Winston, Inc., New York, 1960.
Hamovitch, William (ed.): *The Federal Deficit: Fiscal Imprudence or Policy Weapon?* D. C. Heath and Company, Boston, 1965.
Hansen, Brent: *The Economic Theory of Fiscal Policy,* Harvard University Press, Cambridge, Mass., 1959.
Kimmel, Lewis H.: *Federal Budget and Fiscal Policy, 1789–1958,* The Brookings Institution, Washington, 1959.
Poole, Kenyon E.: *Public Finance and Economic Welfare,* Holt, Rinehart and Winston, Inc., New York, 1956.
Reuss, Frederick G.: *Fiscal Policy for Growth without Inflation: The German Experiment,* The Johns Hopkins Press, Baltimore, 1963.

U.S. Congress, Joint Economic Committee: *Fiscal Policy Implications of the Economic Outlook and Budget Developments,* Hearings before the Subcommittee on Fiscal Policy, 1957.

———: *Fiscal Policy Implications of the Current Economic Outlook,* Hearings before the Subcommittee on Fiscal Policy, 1958.

———: *The Federal Budget as an Economic Document,* Staff Study, Hearings, and Report of the Subcommittee on Economic Statistics, 1962–1963.

U.S. Congress, Senate Committee on Finance: *Investigation of the Financial Condition of the United States,* Compendium of Comments and Hearings, 1957–1958.

Part Nine
International Monetary Relations

Chapter 36 International Payments

For I have bills for money by exchange
From Florence, and must here deliver them.

The Taming of the Shrew
Act IV, scene 2, line 89

So far we have been examining our monetary system as if it operated in a vacuum, as if it were not affected by events occurring outside the country, as if stabilization were possible on a purely domestic basis. The United States is more nearly self-contained than almost any other country in the world, but we do not quite live in majestic isolation, and an examination of our international activities shows operations, procedures, and problems that differ markedly from the domestic variety.

International trade shows considerable similarity to internal trade in many respects, but it differs in two important ways: (1) International trade must cross a political boundary line and in so doing is subject to innumerable forms of harassment, such as tariffs, quotas, and exchange restrictions. (2) Almost all international trade involves two currencies—one for the buyer and another for the seller—and it therefore necessitates some kind of machinery for transferring francs into pesos at a fair price. It is this second problem that concerns us here.

The Balance of International Payments

Before we attack this problem frontally, let's make sure we understand all the types of transactions that enter into international trade, for every one affects the monetary machinery. We are probably all aware that trade between nations is not restricted to trade between governments. In the Soviet Union the government is the only trader, but in most other countries private individuals—exporters and importers—carry on the bulk of foreign transactions. It is particularly important to remember that when we speak of a country's "balance of international payments," we are including all transactions of all nationals of that country (individuals and institutions as well as government) with foreigners. The balance of international payments is a summary statement of all these transactions. It is, in fact, essentially the "rest-of-the-world" sector of the flow of funds, which we studied in Chapter 28. Since each transaction in double-entry bookkeeping has two sides (every purchase is a transfer of goods for money—every import of merchandise is an export of payment), the balance of payments must always balance if all the necessary information is included.

There is no universal form for classifying the various transactions in which nations engage, but the one shown in Table 36-1 will suffice for our purposes.

Table 36-1. Balance-of-international-payments Classification

	Typical examples of imports and exports (from the point of view of the United States)	
Classification	Imports (debits)	Exports (credits)
Merchandise	A & P buys coffee from Brazil	Chrysler sells a Dodge to Burma
Services:		
Transportation and travel	Americans travel in Japan	The Dodge is shipped via American Export Lines
Capital service (interest, dividends, profits)	AT & T pays interest to a German bondholder	Texaco receives profits from a plant in Iraq
Other services	The U.S. supports an embassy in Chile	Fiat buys insurance from the Hartford Insurance Group
Unilateral transfers (gifts):		
Personal (immigrant remittances)	Joe sends $10 to his mother in Italy	Fred receives a gift of tea from a friend in Ceylon
Institutional (mission work, CARE)	The Baptist Church supports a mission in Ghana	Oxford grants a scholarship to a U.S. student
Governmental (foreign aid, reparations)	U.S. aid is given to Korea	Reverse Lend-Lease payments are received from Belgium
Capital claims:		
Long-term (stocks, bonds, direct investment)	Sam buys stock in Imperial Chemicals, Ltd.	Ford sells an assembly plant that it owned in India
Short-term (open account, bank deposits)	Chase receives deposit credit from the Bank of Milan	Bank of America draws a bank draft against its Paris account
Gold and currency	Spain ships gold to the United States	Paul pays for a Canadian purchase with U.S. coins

Some of these transactions are obvious, while others may seem odd at first glance. Merchandise transactions represent the greater part (by value) of international trade, and it is easy to understand the import and export columns for commodities. It may help us to sort out some of the other items if we remember that when we buy coffee (import), we must pay for it in some way.

Any transaction that involves a United States payment abroad or the obligation to make payment is similarly an import, while any item that obligates a foreigner to pay us (as Chrysler's sale of a car) is an export. This rule will not solve all problems of import and export, but it will help in most cases.

When we support an embassy in a foreign country, we are obligated to pay for its upkeep, and this is an import. When we travel abroad, we must pay for our hotel room, meals, and so on, and this is an import. German bondholders who have lent money to AT & T are providing that corporation with the services of their capital funds, for which AT & T must pay them interest. The interest is a payment to foreigners for a service (the use of their funds) rendered by them to a United States national (AT & T). The terminology causes some confusion here, for when we speak of merchandise, we list the *thing* for which payment is made (a car), while when we come to capital service (and a number of other categories), we list the payment (interest) rather than the thing for which the payment is made (service of capital).[1] If we remember, however, that any transaction involving an outpayment is an import, regardless of how it is named, it will help to keep the nature of imports and exports clear.

This basic principle will explain the seeming inconsistency of unilateral transfers, which by their very nature as gifts involve only a one-way movement. But in double-entry bookkeeping all transactions *must* have two entries. The $10 that Joe sends to his mother is an outpayment, and the reason why he made it (immigrant remittances) must therefore be an import. We are not here concerned with the *$10* he sent (if, for instance, it were a $10 bill, it would appear below under gold and currency), but rather with the *reason* he sent it. Some people find it easier to understand unilateral transfers if they think of them as imports of goodwill. If this clears up the point, fine, but in some cases it is not a wholly accurate description, particularly when used to describe government remittances.[2]

The capital account also frequently causes confusion because the word "capital" is used in two diametrically opposed meanings in this connection. In balance-of-payments statistics capital means capital *claims,* while in common terminology capital means capital *funds.* When Sam buys stock in Imperial Chemicals, he is importing a stock certificate (capital claims) and exporting capital funds. In one place you will find this called a *capital import,* while in another it is described as a *capital export.* The confusion would disappear if the longer phrase were used in each case.

In balance-of-payments terms capital always means capital claims. Any transfer of securities or ownership rights into this country is a capital-claims import, while any transfer of securities or ownership rights to foreigners is

[1] The Department of Commerce in its official statistics lists capital service under the heading "Income on Investments."

[2] United States foreign aid, for instance, has in many cases resulted in ill will because of the way in which it has been administered. Among nations as among individuals you can't *buy* friends, particularly when the gifts have strings attached. Reparations are even less likely to bring goodwill.

a capital-claims export. Thus, when we are investing in other countries by making funds available to them, we are *importing capital* (claims) in spite of the fact that the newspapers will refer to it as an export of capital (funds).

Although the transaction is not so obvious, exactly the same reasoning applies to international bank credits, the most common short-term capital movements. When Chase receives a deposit credit from the Bank of Milan, although it obviously must have deposited something in exchange, the deposit credit itself is an obligation of the Italian bank to pay, and this represents a capital claim of Chase against it. This is an import. As a simplification perhaps it helps to think of it as the importation of a bankbook. As we shall see presently, it is primarily through such transfers of bank credit that international payments are normally made.

Gold and currency movements should cause no trouble. Gold is actually a commodity and is treated as such: when gold moves into the country, this is an import. It is entered separately because it is a very special commodity. It is, in fact, an international money, generally accepted as a means of payment between nations. Currency movements are of very small magnitude. Such as they are, they are accounted for in the same way as gold.

The balance of payments always balances simply because every transaction is entered twice: once as the reason for payment (e.g., automobile exports) and once as the payment itself (e.g., gold imports). This can be illustrated by a simplified and somewhat unreal example, which nevertheless illustrates the basic principles.

Suppose Jones in the United States ships a set of books to Sabini in Italy. Sabini promises to pay within a month. At the moment of shipment the balance of payments of the United States shows:

Imports (debits)	*Exports (credits)*
1*a* Short-term capital (open account)	1*b* Books

Later Sabini sends Jones a check drawn on his own bank in Italy, and Jones now has a claim against the bank in place of his claim against Sabini. The receipt of the check is a (capital-claims) import, while the relinquishment of the open-account claim against Sabini is a (capital-claims) export.

Imports (debits)	*Exports (credits)*
2*a* Short-term capital (bank credit)	2*b* Short-term capital (open account)

Finally Jones finds that Brown wants to buy vases in Italy and needs Italian funds. Jones sells him his check on the Italian bank, and Brown uses this to pay for the vases.

Imports (debits)	*Exports (credits)*
3*a* Vases	3*b* Short-term capital (bank credit)

At each step in the process imports and exports balance. Short-term capital has been used to finance two merchandise transactions, but if we cancel out offsetting transactions (the opening and settlement of Sabini's open account, for one, and the drawing and collection of the check, for another), our net balance of payments would show:

Imports (debits)	*Exports (credits)*
Vases	Books

Although short-term capital movements finance a vast amount of trade, the net movements of such claims are quite small.

While the whole balance of payments must necessarily balance, its subclassifications need not and seldom do. Thus an import *balance of trade* (also called an *unfavorable balance, negative balance,* or *passive balance of trade*) means that a nation's *merchandise* imports exceed its merchandise exports. An export balance of trade (also called a *favorable balance, positive balance,* or *active balance of trade*) means that its exports of merchandise exceed its imports of merchandise.

When services are added to merchandise, we have the *balance of goods and services.* This also may show either an import or an export balance.

Then there is the *balance on current account,* usually defined as the total of merchandise, services, and unilateral transfers. Since this includes everything except capital and gold movements, it is clear that if we have an *import* balance on current account, this must be exactly equaled by an *export* balance on capital claims and gold account. Otherwise the balance of payments as a whole would be out of balance, and this is impossible.

The *balance of payments* is an awkward term, not to be confused with the balance of international payments and not even subject to a generally accepted definition. Basically it is intended to measure the amount of *disequilibrium* in a country's foreign trade, that is, the gap between payments to foreigners that arise from "normal" or "regular" transactions (*autonomous* payments) and similar autonomous receipts. If there is such a gap, it must be covered by some type of *compensatory* financing, such as gold flows or changes in international bank balances.

For some time the Department of Commerce defined the balance of payments for this country as consisting of gold movements plus changes in *foreign* holdings of United States government securities and short-term capital claims against the United States (mostly balances in commercial and Federal Reserve banks). This measured changes in liquid claims that foreigners could use at any time to buy our goods. In the early 1960s certain special transactions were included (such as the sale of nonmarketable securities directly to foreign central banks, prepayments by foreign countries on debts owed to the United States government, and advance payments by such countries for military equipment) on the grounds that such items were not "normal" and were in fact a substitute for gold outpayments.

In 1965 a Bureau of the Budget review committee (the Bernstein Committee) recommended an "official settlements" concept of the payments deficit that would count changes in *private* foreign holdings of claims against the United States as part of the "normal" transactions and leave only changes in the holdings of monetary authorities (treasuries, central banks, and the IMF) of claims against the United States (plus advance repayments of foreign loans) as part of the balance of payments deficit. Because of the amount of controversy involved, the precise statistical content of the "balance of payments" is likely to continue to change. Conceptually it will remain as the amount of disequilibrium in foreign transactions.

The Mechanism of International Payments

Very little currency flows from one country to another. Why is that? Partly because it is easier to make payments through banking facilities. A more significant reason is the fact that currency is money only in its own country. When a United States exporter sells goods to Brazil he has no use for the Brazilian's cruzeiros, while the Brazilian has no dollars in his possession. Some way must be found of changing one currency into the other.

This job is tackled by the banking system, and the larger city banks have specialized foreign exchange departments that can accommodate almost any type of monetary transaction with foreign countries. The process is somewhat similar to check clearing, but much more complicated.

It starts with a network of worldwide correspondent relationships. The Chase Manhattan Bank, for example, has several thousand foreign correspondents in over 150 foreign countries from Aden to Zambia. This network enables such a bank to do business all over the world and in practically any currency used.[3]

There is an almost infinite number of ways in which the technical process of transferring funds from one country to another may be carried out, but most of them are variations of two basic procedures, which we will illustrate here. These are the bill of exchange drawn by the exporter on the importer (or his bank) and the bank draft written by a bank on its correspondent.

Bill of Exchange Drawn under a Letter of Credit. A bill of exchange may be used without the added formality of a letter of credit, but since the latter is by far the most common method of financing international trade, we will concentrate on that. And since we are interested in principles rather than precise operations, we will use only one example and point out in advance that the transaction may differ in any number of details—including the type of letter of credit, the security required by the issuing bank, the means of notification, the tenor of the bill of exchange, the currency in which it is stated, the documents required, the method of collection (at each of several stages), and the handling of interest and other charges.

[3] In the field of foreign trade the word "currency" has a wider meaning than in ordinary domestic use. *Foreign currency* refers to any form of the monetary unit of the country concerned (such as pounds sterling or French francs) and is not limited to bank notes and coins. A foreign currency transaction is usually carried out in terms of bank credits. Foreign currency is also referred to as *foreign exchange.*

Suppose Morris Garages has agreed to sell one MG car to Ace Motors in New York. Morris wants to receive £1,000 for the car, but Ace insists on paying in dollars. Morris looks up the current exchange rate and finds that it is, say, $4 per pound sterling. This means that £1,000 is the equivalent of $4,000, so the contract is written for that amount. But Morris is not quite sure of Ace's credit standing and wants to be absolutely certain that Ace will pay. It is therefore agreed that before the car is shipped Ace will obtain a letter of credit from his bank.[4]

1. A *letter of credit* is a promise by a bank to pay all bills of exchange drawn against it under the conditions stated in the letter. In this case Ace goes to, say, the Irving Trust Company and applies for a letter of credit, which—if Irving agrees to issue it—would read like that shown in Figure 36-1.

The basic meaning of this document is that Irving Trust is promising to pay for the car that Ace has ordered provided the bank is assured that it has been properly shipped. In exchange for this letter Ace signs an agreement promising to pay the bank the sum of money involved ($4,000) the day before it must be paid by Irving Trust, and in addition Ace pays a commission to the bank for rendering this service. This is not an interest charge, since Irving is not lending any money (it is lending only its name and prestige), but the bank must be reimbursed for its expenses in connection with the transaction and for the risk that it runs that Ace may be unable to pay when the time comes. Naturally the bank will not issue a letter of credit unless it has approved Ace's credit standing, but even so a loss is possible.

2. The letter of credit is sent to Morris, assuring payment.

3. Morris delivers the car to the Cunard Lines for shipment to Ace in New York. Cunard acknowledges receipt of the merchandise with an *order bill of lading.* In its simplest form a bill of lading does nothing more than show that the goods have been delivered to the shipping company. The *order* bill of lading, however, which is used almost exclusively in international trade, is, in addition, a document of title. When such a bill is issued, the transportation company will not deliver the goods even to the person to whom they are addressed (the consignee) unless he surrenders the bill of lading—"No tickee, no shirtee."

4. Although the car is now crossing the ocean to New York addressed to Ace, Ace cannot get it from Cunard without the bill of lading, and at this moment Morris has it.

5. With the letter of credit and bill of lading in his possession, Morris is ready to claim payment. His claim takes the form of a bill of exchange drawn on Irving Trust under the terms of the letter of credit. This document is shown in Figure 36-3.

What Morris wants, in spite of what the bill of exchange says, is immediate payment in pounds. This he can get by selling (discounting) the bill to his own bank (say, the Midland Bank). In doing so he must endorse it and offer it to Midland along with the letter of credit, the bill of lading, and the other docu-

[4] The following paragraphs are numbered to correspond with Fig. 36-2, which summarizes this transaction.

IRVING TRUST COMPANY

ONE WALL STREET
NEW YORK 15. N. Y.

IRREVOCABLE CREDIT
NO. 0000

DATE April 1, 19—

Morris Garages
London, England

SPECIMEN

GENTLEMEN:

FOR THE ACCOUNT OF { Ace Motors
New York, N.Y. }

WE HEREBY AUTHORIZE YOU TO DRAW AT 60 days sight TO THE EXTENT OF
$4,000.00 (Four Thousand Dollars) -
ON us.
YOUR DRAFTS MUST BE ACCOMPANIED BY THE FOLLOWING DOCUMENTS (COMPLETE SETS UNLESS OTHERWISE STATED) EVIDENCING SHIPMENT(S) OF:

One automobile, CIF New York, from London to New York.

Commercial Invoices.

Customs Invoice.

Insurance Policy/Certificate in negotiable form covering marine and war risks.

Onboard Ocean Bills of Lading issued to the order of Irving Trust Company, New York, marked "Notify Ace Motors, New York" and "Freight Prepaid".

Negotiation charges are for your account.

Drafts must be negotiated not later than May 10, 19—.

ALL DRAFTS MUST BE MARKED: "DRAWN UNDER IRVING TRUST COMPANY; NEW YORK, CREDIT . . . . . (INDICATING THE NUMBER AND DATE OF THIS CREDIT) . . . . ." AND THE AMOUNTS DRAWN ENDORSED ON THE REVERSE HEREOF BY THE NEGOTIATING BANK.

WE HEREBY ENGAGE WITH THE DRAWERS, ENDORSERS AND BONAFIDE HOLDERS OF THE DRAFTS DRAWN UNDER AND IN COMPLIANCE WITH THE TERMS OF THIS CREDIT THAT THESE DRAFTS WILL BE DULY HONORED BY THE ABOVE DRAWEE.

YOURS VERY TRULY

AUTHORIZED SIGNATURE

*A-756/00 M (3-59)

Figure 36-1. Specimen letter of credit. (*Courtesy of Irving Trust Company, New York.*)

ments called for. The letter of credit accompanied by the proper documents is Midland's guarantee of eventual payment. But by providing pounds now against dollars later Midland incurs two costs: (1) the interest lost on the money advanced (since payment is not called for on the bill until some sixty days in the future) and (2) clerical expenses plus the risk of fluctuation in the exchange rate.

Both costs will be passed on to Morris, who will get perhaps £994 instead

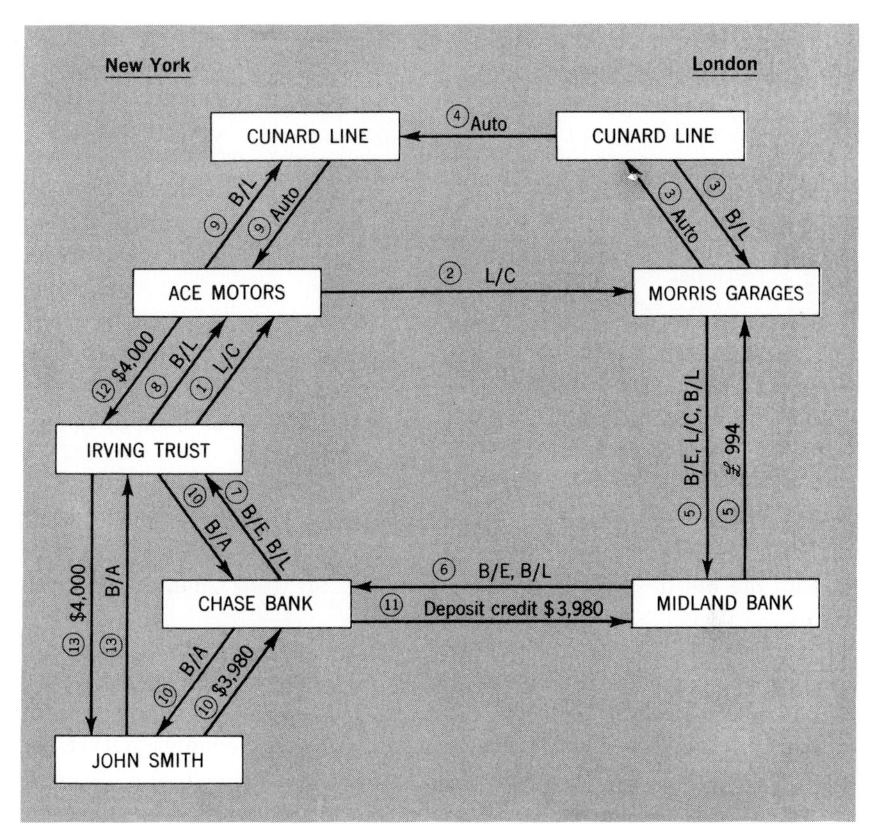

Figure 36-2. Financing international trade with a letter of credit. B/A, bank acceptance; B/E, bill of exchange; B/L, bill of lading; L/C, letter of credit.

of the full £1,000. To Morris this is just another cost of doing business, which he took into account when pricing his cars for export. If he were willing to wait for his money until the bill fell due, he would get perhaps £999 or more, but he prefers to take the smaller amount now and charge the rest up to interest expense.

6. Midland now has what is, in effect, a claim on the Irving Trust. It sends the bill of exchange (accompanied by the other documents) to its New York correspondent (which we will assume to be the Chase Manhattan Bank) for collection.

7. When Chase receives the bill, it sends it to Irving for acceptance. Irving, having satisfied itself that all the documents are in order as required in its letter of credit, *accepts* the bill by writing the word "accepted" with the date and an official signature across its face. The bill is now rechristened a *bank acceptance.* Irving has accepted its obligation to pay the amount stated sixty days after the date on which it first saw the bill as just written on its face. Suppose this date is April 25. The bill is then due on June 24.

8. At the time of acceptance Irving is given the various documents needed to

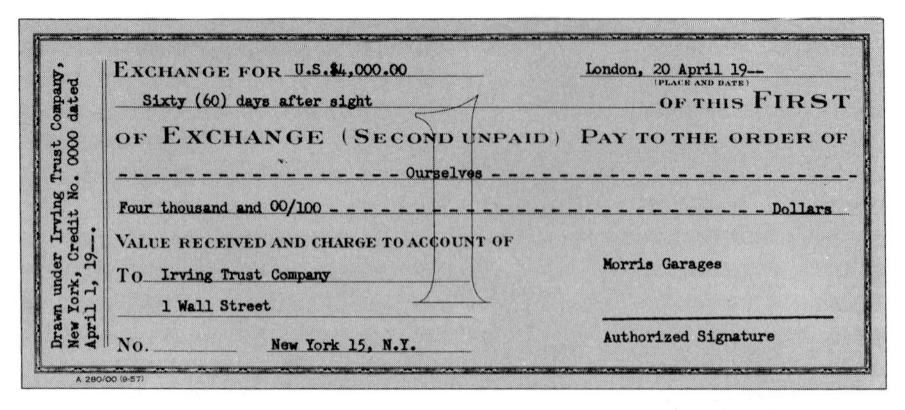
Drawn under Irving Trust Company, New York, Credit No. 0000 dated April 1, 19—.

EXCHANGE FOR U.S.$4,000.00 London, 20 April 19—
(PLACE AND DATE)
Sixty (60) days after sight OF THIS FIRST
OF EXCHANGE (SECOND UNPAID) PAY TO THE ORDER OF
Ourselves
Four thousand and 00/100 Dollars
VALUE RECEIVED AND CHARGE TO ACCOUNT OF
Morris Garages
TO Irving Trust Company
1 Wall Street
Authorized Signature
NO. New York 15, N.Y.
A 280/00 (9-57)

Figure 36-3. Specimen bill of exchange drawn under a letter of credit. (*Courtesy of Irving Trust Company, New York.*)

complete the commercial part of the transaction, of which the bill of lading is the most important. These documents it hands over in turn to Ace Motors.
9. With the bill of lading Ace can claim the auto from Cunard as soon as it arrives.
10. The bank acceptance is returned to Chase. If Chase does not want to hold it for either its own account or that of Midland, it will sell it in the *bill market,* an informal arrangement of buyers and sellers of acceptances similar to the market for government securities or the over-the-counter market. Some investor (we'll call him John Smith, though it may very well be a bank) buys the bill at its discounted value, that is, its face value minus interest to maturity (sixty days) at the going rate (let's say 3 per cent).
11. Chase credits the amount received from the sale ($3,980) to the account of Midland Bank. Midland thus receives a dollar bank balance in exchange for the pounds that it paid Morris.[5]
12. The day before the acceptance falls due (June 23) Ace must pay Irving $4,000.
13. John Smith presents the acceptance to Irving on June 24 and receives his $4,000, and the whole transaction is completed.

This machinery may seem cumbersome compared with domestic transactions, where a seller usually ships goods on open account and the buyer returns a check in due season. Its primary purpose is to make the whole operation as foolproof and as fraudproof as possible. Domestically it is fairly easy to check the credit rating of potential customers, and if they default, legal redress is normally fairly uncomplicated (though of course losses cannot be completely avoided). In international trade, however, it is much more difficult to check credit ratings, and an international lawsuit for nonpayment would be an almost impossible undertaking.

[5] Since $3,980 is the equivalent of £995 at the rate of $4 per pound sterling, we see that Midland has earned £1 for its share in the transaction. Chase has not earned any commission directly but has the benefit of Midland's deposit business.

The use of a letter of credit provides certainty to the seller that he will be paid, and this is reinforced by the fact that ownership of the merchandise in the form of the order bill of lading does not pass to the buyer until the bill is actually accepted. On the other hand, the buyer is protected to the extent that the seller can't get payment until he has produced evidence that the goods are actually shipped.

Bank Draft. When one party trusts the other, however, the procedure can be greatly simplified.

Suppose, for instance, that General Electric has agreed to ship $4,000 worth of appliances to the Big Ben Store in London. Without bothering about letters of credit or order bills of lading the goods are just shipped, and Big Ben is expected to pay (see Figure 36-4):

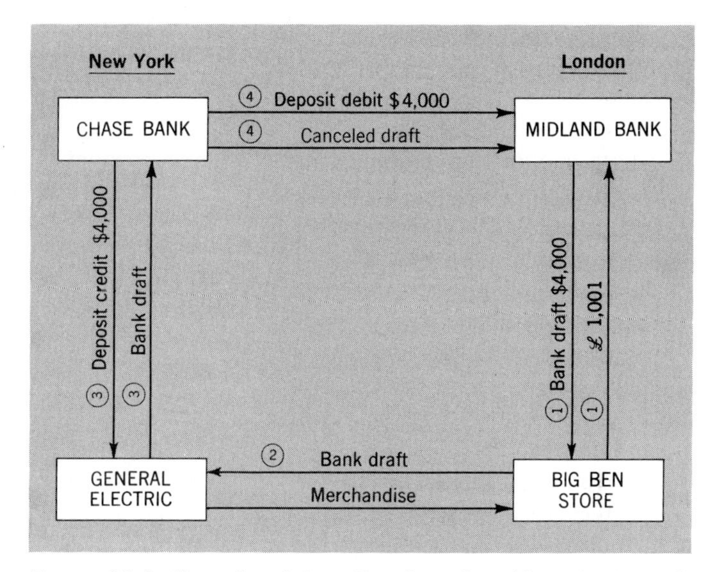

Figure 36-4. Financing international trade with a bank draft.

1. There is still the problem of foreign exchange, for Big Ben has to pay in dollars, which it doesn't have. To get them it goes to its bank (let's assume this is also the Midland Bank) and buys a bank draft. This is simply a check written by one bank on another bank. In this case Midland is writing it against Chase, where it has a dollar account (see Figure 36-5).

If the exchange rate is still $4 per pound sterling, Big Ben will pay Midland £1,000 plus a small service charge for this check.

2. The check is then mailed as full payment to General Electric.

3. General Electric deposits this check, like any other, in its own bank account and receives deposit credit. If it is not deposited directly in Chase, it will be presented for payment through the regular domestic clearing machinery.

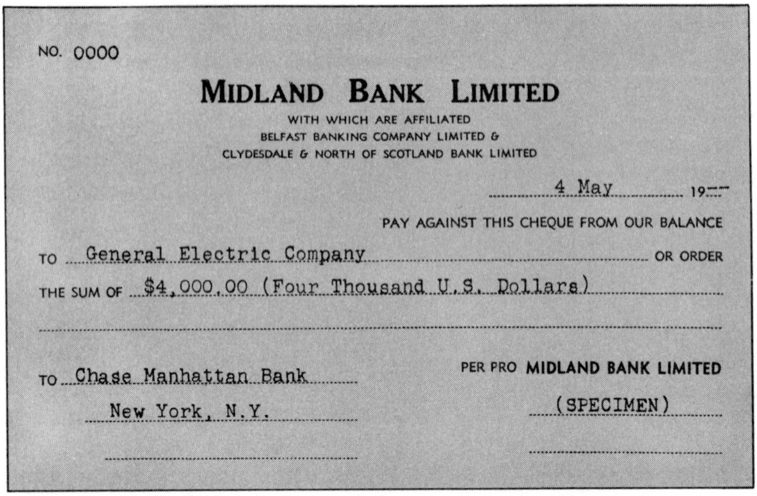

NO. 0000

MIDLAND BANK LIMITED

WITH WHICH ARE AFFILIATED
BELFAST BANKING COMPANY LIMITED &
CLYDESDALE & NORTH OF SCOTLAND BANK LIMITED

4 May 19__

PAY AGAINST THIS CHEQUE FROM OUR BALANCE

TO General Electric Company OR ORDER

THE SUM OF $4,000.00 (Four Thousand U.S. Dollars)

TO Chase Manhattan Bank
New York, N.Y.

PER PRO MIDLAND BANK LIMITED
(SPECIMEN)

Figure 36-5. Specimen bank draft. (*Courtesy of Midland Bank Limited, London.*)

4. Chase deducts this amount from Midland's account and returns the canceled check to Midland. Midland has lost $4,000 of dollar assets and has gained £1,000 plus a commission.

It's so simple. Why isn't it used all the time? The answer has already been given: it doesn't provide the guarantees that foreign traders seem to need. There are two, diametrically opposed, cases in which it is used.

1. Where the buyer has such a *good* credit rating that there is no question of his paying. In this case the goods are shipped on open account, and the buyer pays for them after they are received. This is similar to the normal case in domestic trade.

2. Where the buyer has such a *bad* credit rating that he can't be trusted even under the procedures of a letter of credit. Such a case would arise, for instance, if the buyer couldn't get a letter of credit from his own bank. In this case the seller requires that he be paid *before* the goods are shipped so that he is absolutely certain of payment. But here the buyer has to trust the seller, for once he remits payment he has no guarantee except the honesty of the seller that he will ever get what he has paid for.

The Exchange Risk. It should be noted that under both types of payment procedure the exchange risk is taken by a bank—in our example the Midland Bank.[6] The buyer pays in his own currency; the seller is paid in *his* own currency. The bank exchanges one for the other. Ignoring the arithmetical niceties of service and interest charges, Midland bought $4,000 for £1,000 on April 20 and sold these dollars for the same amount on May 4.

This is fine as long as the exchange rate remains constant. But what would have happened if the value of pounds had risen to, say, $4.08 between April

[6] Under different assumptions it could just as well have been a United States bank.

20 and May 4? This, of course, means that the value of the dollar has fallen, and dollars are the assets that Midland is holding. Then the $4,000 that Midland paid £1,000 for could be sold for only £980, a loss of £20. If the value of pounds had fallen, on the other hand, the bank would have made a profit. This is the exchange risk that any foreign exchange bank has to take as part of its business. The bank reduces this risk as much as possible by keeping well informed of movements and potential movements in exchange rates and by holding a minimum balance in those currencies whose future rates appear to be unpredictable, but the risk cannot be avoided completely.

Triangular Payments. One additional way of reducing risk when the countries involved are small is to carry out payments in the currency of some third, more stable, country. Suppose a dealer in Peru is buying olives in Greece. The Greek merchant's bank may not wish to acquire Peruvian sols, and the contract may therefore call for payment in British pounds.

The Peruvian buyer must then obtain a letter of credit from a British bank (arranged through its Peruvian correspondent, who certifies the credit of the buyer). The Greek exporter draws a sterling bill of exchange (that is, one calling for payment in pounds) under the letter of credit and sells it to a Greek bank, which deposits it for credit in London. The London bank is reimbursed by the Peruvian importer, who buys a bank draft from his own bank drawn in pounds against its account in London. The results of this process are as follows: (1) The Peruvian importer pays his bank in sols; (2) the Peruvian bank gives up a pound deposit of equal value, which it held in a London bank; (3) the London bank transfers this amount to the account of the Greek bank; and (4) the Greek bank, having gained a pound deposit, pays its equivalent in drachmas to the Greek exporter.

The process may sound complicated, but it actually simplifies the whole structure of financial payments by reducing the number of interlacing correspondent relationships and by concentrating a large number of transactions in a few banks in financial centers. These specialists in foreign exchange have developed highly efficient machinery for carrying out transfers all over the world.

For over a hundred years London acted as the world's banker in this manner, and the gold standard of that period has sometimes been nicknamed the "sterling standard," for as long as most payments from and to small countries took place through London, what their currencies were worth in gold was not as important as what they were worth in pounds sterling.

Two world wars have shaken London's preeminence as a banking center, and the growth of United States financial institutions as well as the continuing stability of the dollar have transferred much of the financing of world trade to New York. Simultaneously the dollar standard has partly replaced the sterling standard. The transition is not complete, however, and London is slowly regaining some of its lost prestige as the pound becomes stronger.

Other International Banking Services. While our two case histories indicate the basic principles of international payments, we do not want to leave the impression that this is all that banks engaged in international finance do. On the contrary, their foreign work is just as varied as their domestic operations.

They sell not only drafts, but also cable transfers, which make it possible to have funds delivered to a bank or individual abroad in a matter of minutes. They collect foreign funds due to creditors (bond coupons and checks drawn on foreign banks, for instance). They buy and sell foreign bank notes and coins. They issue traveler's letters of credit, a kind of cross between a letter of credit and a traveler's check. They obtain credit information on foreign firms. They collect information on trade regulations and currency restrictions. They provide letters of introduction for their customers traveling abroad. They deal in silver and (where the law permits) gold. And all these services they make available to their domestic correspondents so that anyone anywhere in the United States can obtain these foreign services from his local bank even though that bank does not itself have any overseas correspondents.

Banks make loans to their foreign correspondents and to foreign corporations and governments. They facilitate the exchange of foreign securities. They act as agents for foreign banks and corporations. They buy and sell foreign exchange among themselves and on foreign markets, thus evening out any temporary differences that might arise in exchange rate quotations and achieving a single worldwide market for all freely convertible currencies.

In other words they facilitate the flow of money and of monetary instruments in such a way as to link the monetary systems of the world as closely together as geography, economic conditions, and legal restrictions will allow. While governmental controls have added to the many complexities inherent in foreign exchange, the international financial mechanism works remarkably well in carrying through the varied transactions among currencies that arise from world trade.

Questions for Thought and Discussion

1. If gold is used to buy foreign securities, which is the export and which the import? Which would be referred to as capital *funds?*

2. When an American holding British securities is repaid their principal value on maturity by a check drawn on a British account in a United States bank, what are the two entries on the balance of international payments?

3. Why do we talk about *total* exports and imports of merchandise, while we are concerned with only the *net* movements of capital claims? (Does our analysis of flow-of-funds accounts shed any light on this problem?)

4. Distinguish between the bill of exchange, the bill of lading, and the letter of credit.

5. Why is it impossible, under the use of a letter of credit, for an importer to obtain goods until he has made satisfactory arrangements *with his own bank* for paying for them?

6. After Irving Trust has accepted a bill drawn against it, what will happen if the importer for whose account it was drawn can't make payment?

7. If you wanted to order a book from a British publisher, how would you make payment? Trace the effect of such payment on all the parties, including the banks, involved.
8. If United States *manufacturers* do not want, say, francs, why should United States *banks* be willing to buy them?
9. Are there any similarities between triangular payments and the Federal Reserve clearing machinery? What are the principal differences?

Selected Bibliography

Crump, Norman: *The ABC of the Foreign Exchanges,* 13th ed., Macmillan & Co., Ltd., London, 1963.

Ellsworth, P. T.: *The International Economy,* 3d ed., The Macmillan Company, New York, 1964.

Evitt, H. E.: *Manual of Foreign Exchange,* 5th ed., Sir Isaac Pitman & Sons, Ltd., London, 1960.

Holmes, Alan R., and Francis H. Schott: *The New York Foreign Exchange Market,* Federal Reserve Bank of New York, 1965.

Lary, Hal B., and Associates: *The United States in the World Economy,* U.S. Government Printing Office, 1943.

McCracken, Paul W., and Emile Benoit: *The Balance of Payments and Domestic Prosperity,* Bureau of Business Research, University of Michigan, Ann Arbor, Mich., 1963.

Madden, John T., and Marcus Nadler: *The International Money Markets,* Prentice-Hall, Inc., Englewood Cliffs, N.J., 1935.

Meade, James E.: *The Balance of Payments,* Oxford University Press, London, 1951.

Salant, Walter S., et al.: *The U.S. Balance of Payments in 1968,* The Brookings Institution, Washington, 1962.

Shaw, Ernest D.: *Practical Aspects of Commercial Letters of Credit,* Irving Trust Company, New York, 1958.

Snider, Delbert A.: *Introduction to International Economics,* 3d ed., Richard D. Irwin, Inc., Homewood, Ill., 1963.

Southard, Frank A.: *Foreign Exchange Practice and Policy,* McGraw-Hill Book Company, New York, 1940.

Stern, Siegfried: *The United States in International Banking,* Columbia University Press, New York, 1951.

U.S. Office of Business Economics: *Balance of Payments Statistical Supplement,* rev. ed., 1963.

Wasserman, Max J., Charles W. Hultman, and L. Zsoldas: *International Finance: Theory, Practice, Institutions,* Simmons-Boardman Publishing Corporation, New York, 1963.

Whitaker, Albert C.: *Foreign Exchange,* Appleton-Century-Crofts, Inc., New York, 1933.

Young, John Parke: *The International Economy,* 4th ed., The Ronald Press Company, New York, 1963.

Chapter 37 Exchange Rates

We can afford no more at such a price.

Love's Labour's Lost
Act V, scene 2, line 224

In carrying on its business the foreign department of the bank is constantly buying and selling foreign money, usually in the form of bank balances held abroad. What determines the rate at which currencies are traded?

The exchange rate—the ratio between the values of two currencies—is actually a price, or, more accurately, two prices simultaneously. Both the thing bought and the thing sold are money. When we speak of the relationship between bread and dollars, we say that the price of bread is 20 cents, not that $1 is worth five loaves of bread (although both statements mean the same thing). In the case of the relationship between dollars and Mexican pesos, however, it is immaterial whether we say that $1 is worth 12½ pesos or that the peso is worth 8 cents.

In some cases we have gotten into the habit of stating the relationship one way rather than the other, but this is a matter of convenience rather than of principle. It is easier to say that £1 equals $2.80 than to turn it around and say that $1 equals £0.357 (or that $1 equals 7 shillings, 1¾ pence). On the other hand it is simpler to say that there are 360 Japanese yen to the dollar than to say that the yen is worth 0.278 cents.

One thing to guard against is the ambiguous statement that a particular exchange rate (say, the pound-dollar rate) rose—or fell. The *price of pounds* can rise, say, from $2.80 to $2.85. But this is the same thing as saying that the price of dollars has *fallen* from £0.357 to £0.351. A rise in the price of one currency must necessarily mean a fall in the price of another.

The exchange rate, then, is the price of one currency stated in terms of another currency. Like any other price it is determined by the forces of supply and demand. But governments very seldom allow these forces to work by themselves, with the result that in actual practice the rate may be drastically influenced or even precisely determined by the way in which the government interferes in the exchange markets.

Freely Fluctuating Exchange Rates

The forces underlying the market can be seen most clearly when the government keeps hands off. In order to study these forces we will start with an analysis of a *freely fluctuating exchange market,* one in which the government takes no steps whatsoever to influence exchange rates. Such a case is extremely rare in practice. But the forces at work in such a market are still operating in other markets as well, although they may be suppressed or diverted by government action.

In a freely fluctuating exchange market the exchange rate is determined by the way in which supply and demand affect the foreign balances held by banks. This can be seen in terms of the transactions examined in Chapter 36. Let us assume that Great Britain and the United States are on a freely fluctuating exchange standard and that the transactions there illustrated are typical of the many kinds of trade carried on between them. We originally assumed that the exchange rate was £1 = $4. We are now ready to see whether this is a proper rate and, if not, how the rate will be changed.

If we ignore, for simplicity, the effect of interest charges and if we ignore further the effect of trade that either of these nations may be carrying on with other countries (which would be extremely important in practice since no nation needs to balance its payments on a bilateral basis), we see that the trade of the United States and Britain is in balance: we export $4,000 worth of appliances and import $4,000 worth of cars. Britain exports £1,000 worth of cars and imports £1,000 worth of appliances. The Midland Bank builds up its dollar balance by buying bills of exchange from Morris and then sells these same balances to Big Ben. If everybody is satisfied with these arrangements, then the exchange rate we assumed *is* the proper one, for there will be no pressure on it to change.

But suppose that the British decide to buy more of our appliances while their exports of cars remain the same. For every bill of exchange worth $4,000 that Midland buys from Morris, Big Ben wants bank drafts for, say, $5,000 to pay for its larger appliance orders. At this rate Midland is soon going to run out of dollars, and it certainly can't sell more than it owns.

Dollars are the Midland Bank's stock-in-trade. It has no use for them except to sell them to customers. It has no source of dollars except those offered to it by other customers. Midland can't create dollars. It can create pounds (just as United States banks can create dollars), but a bank cannot create a *foreign* money. Its promises to pay, which are money, must be promises of its own currency. The only dollars Midland has are those which it has purchased and deposited in United States banks. When its customers want more dollars than are offered to it, then for Midland dollars have become scarce (the dollar shortage in microcosm).

Faced with a shortage of its stock-in-trade, its reaction is that of any seller faced with a booming market for his goods; it will raise the price. Changes in the exchange rate on a freely fluctuating market would normally move in very small steps, but let's imagine a whopping shift from £1 = $4 to £1 = $3. This is a *rise* in the price of dollars from $1 = £0.25 (5 shillings) to $1 = £0.333 (6 shillings, 8 pence).

This has two effects. Since Big Ben has to pay more pounds to buy the same amount of appliances, it will curtail its purchases. A United States product priced at $24 would have cost £6 at the old rate, but £8 at the new. At the higher price fewer will be bought. As far as Midland is concerned this will reduce the quantity of dollars that importers are trying to buy.

On the other hand, Morris, now finding that it can get more pounds for its dollar bills of exchange, is encouraged to lower the dollar price it quotes to United States buyers in the hope of increasing sales. It wants £1,000 per car, but now it can get this amount by charging $3,000 instead of $4,000. At the lower price more MG's will be sold in the United States, and Morris will have more bills to sell to Midland.[1]

This increase in dollars available from exporters and decrease in dollars bought by importers is precisely what Midland wanted when it raised its price for dollars. Perhaps at this new rate the amount purchased and sold will again be in equilibrium. If not, the rate will continue to change until equilibrium is reached.

We can summarize the operation of exchange rates in a freely fluctuating exchange market as follows:

1. As long as a country's imports and exports (including services, invisibles, and long-term capital as well as merchandise) are in equilibrium, the exchange rate will remain unchanged.

2. If such trade is not in equilibrium, the result will be a change in the amount of foreign exchange deposits held by that country's banks.

3. This shift in foreign deposits will cause the banks to alter their exchange rate quotations—raising the price of foreign currencies if the balances are falling, lowering it if balances are rising.

4. The new exchange rate will alter the price of that country's exports abroad and of its imports at home, thereby affecting both its desire to buy and its ability to sell.

[1] If the United States demand for MG's is inelastic, the increased quantity sold will not be sufficient to make up for the drop in price, and the total dollars earned will fall (although the total pounds earned must necessarily rise since the pound price has not changed). If this were true of *all* a country's exports (which does not seem likely under most circumstances), the attainment of equilibrium would be more difficult.

5. This shift will continue until a new equilibrium is reached at *some* exchange rate where imports and exports are again equal. Fluctuating exchange rates are the primary medium through which such equilibrium is restored.

The process of adjustment is described graphically in the appendix to this chapter.

Purchasing Power Parity. While we are on this subject we should mention a theory that has been used to explain the "proper" rate of exchange between two currencies. The purchasing power parity theory leaves much to be desired, but it does have an element of validity to it. This theory says that the exchange rate between two countries should be in the same ratio as the price levels of those countries. Suppose, for instance, that a representative bundle of goods costs 100 schillings in Austria and that the same goods cost 200 pesetas in Spain. Then the exchange rate should be 1 schilling equals 2 pesetas.

The underlying logic of the theory is fairly obvious. If goods in Austria cost half as many schillings as they cost in pesetas in Spain but if the exchange rate were 1 for 1, then everyone who had pesetas would exchange them for an equal number of schillings, which would buy twice as many goods. The demand for schillings would push up their price in pesetas until it reached 1 for 2. At that rate a peseta spent in Spain would buy precisely as much as it would if changed into schillings and spent in Austria, and the pressure on the exchange rate would stop.

If all commodities entered into international trade, and nothing other than commodities did, then the purchasing power parity theory might come close to the truth. But many things are never traded because of their cumbersome nature (houses, for instance) or for other reasons and therefore do not affect exchange rates. At the same time, the exchange rate is influenced by a number of transactions that are not included in any price index. The demand for pounds represents the demand for everything for which pounds must be used in payment: not only merchandise, ordinary services, and tourist expenditures (which may be related to purchasing power parity), but also unilateral transfers, capital service, and capital claims (which are not). Contractual payments must be met regardless of the exchange rate and regardless of prices in the two countries. Immigrant remittances may be made *because* prices in the other country are high (sister Rita in the old country is having a hard time making ends meet). Similarly, investments may be made in other countries (capital-claims imports) because prices are high, yielding higher interest rates and perhaps higher profits. In such cases the effect on exchange rates would be the opposite of that suggested by purchasing power parity, although their influence may be minor.

In spite of these qualifications the basic principle remains that *generally speaking* a rise of prices in any country will reduce the demand for its currency (since fewer people want to buy its goods at the higher prices) and therefore will tend to reduce the price of its currency on the foreign exchange markets. This is the kernel of the purchasing power parity theory.

The International Gold Standard

We have already defined the (pure) gold standard as a situation in which a country (1) defines its currency as a given weight of gold, (2) maintains convertibility at par between gold and all other forms of domestic currency, and (3) permits free movement of gold both domestically and internationally. The international gold standard exists between any two or more countries that are individually on the gold standard. The international gold standard is not the result of any treaty or other agreement between the nations involved. Any nation joins it by supporting a gold value for its currency and leaves it by refusing to support such a value.

Although the adoption of a gold standard does not directly involve the government in the foreign exchange market, the automatic result is to establish an exchange rate with all other gold-standard countries. Thus the gold standard is almost the complete opposite of a freely fluctuating exchange market.

Almost all large trading nations operated on the gold standard from the last quarter of the nineteenth century to World War I and again for a short period thereafter, but no nation has been on a pure gold standard since 1936.

For an illustration of how the standard works let us go back to that earlier period prior to, and just subsequent to, World War I. At that time the United States defined the dollar as 23.22 grains of fine gold. Independently Great Britain defined the pound sterling as 113 grains of fine gold. The pound therefore contained 4.86 (that is, 113/23.22) times as much gold as the dollar, or £1 = $2.86. This is known as *mint parity,* the exchange rate between two currencies determined by the ratio of their respective gold contents.

The government does nothing to enforce this rate, and yet the market cannot depart from it by more than a small amount. If it so happened that supply and demand were such that a country's trade was in equilibrium at the mint parity, fine. But this would be somewhat coincidental.

Suppose we start again with the example we have been using throughout our discussion of international trade but assume that Britain's export and import values were equal at $4.86 per pound sterling. Then Midland would be selling the same amount of dollars that it was buying at that rate. Suppose again that England starts importing more without any change in exports. Midland finds its stock of dollars dwindling as importers buy more to meet their bills. Midland's first impulse is to raise the price at which it sells (and buys) dollars. The price of pounds consequently falls. It goes from $4.86 to $4.85 to $4.84. But (under conditions existing in the twenties) it stops there. It can't fall any further. Why? Because at that point Midland can buy all the dollars it wants with gold; it doesn't have to depend on exporters selling bills of exchange to it.

Under pure gold-standard conditions Midland could take £1 to the Bank of England and get 113 grains of gold for it.[2] It could ship this gold to the United States and through a correspondent could get $4.86 from the Treasury

[2] Not in £1 lots, of course, but in terms of thousands of pounds.

for it. The process, however, is not costless, for the gold must be shipped and insured and other expenses of the transfer met. During the twenties these costs totaled roughly 2 cents per pound sterling (in large shipments, of course). The Midland Bank would receive a *net* amount of $4.84 per pound ($4.86 less 2 cents expenses), and the price of dollars would therefore have to rise (the price of pounds to fall) to £1 = $4.84 before gold shipments would be profitable. But at this price any quantity of dollars could be obtained by gold shipments, and the rate, therefore, would not move any further.

The rate at which it becomes profitable to ship gold is called the *gold point*. In our illustration $4.84 is the British *gold export point*. It is simultaneously the United States *gold import point*.

Under a freely fluctuating exchange standard any deviation from equilibrium is corrected by a shift in exchange rates. Under the gold standard rates are prevented from shifting by more than a token amount. What, then, restores equilibrium?

Theoretically at least, gold movements produce their own corrective through what classical economists called the *price-specie flow mechanism* and the *rules of the game*. These two together constitute the *automatic* gold standard, which, unfortunately, probably worked better in theory than in practice.

Suppose England has an import surplus. British banks run short of dollars, the price of pounds falls to $4.84, and gold is shipped to the United States. Since gold represents the monetary base in Britain, this loss of gold means that the quantity of money in circulation must fall (provided the monetary authorities don't interfere—which would be against the "rules"). And, to the extent that the quantity theory is correct,[3] a reduction in money supply will force down prices. The reduction in British prices makes her goods more desirable abroad, and her exports rise from their depressed levels.

In the United States the reverse is true. We are gaining gold, which is added to the monetary base and permits an expansion of the quantity of money. This pushes up prices and makes United States goods more expensive in Britain as well as at home. Britain will reduce her imports from us.

As her imports fall and exports rise, they will eventually meet, and at that point of equilibrium the downward pressure on the British pound will cease, gold will stop moving, and the internal price level will tend to stabilize—until some new disequilibrating force arises.

Suppose, on the other hand, that Britain moves into a position of export surplus. The whole process is reversed. Britain will buy more dollars from exporters than she can sell to importers. The price of dollars will fall (price of pounds rise) to £1 = $4.88. This is Great Britain's gold import point. The Midland Bank will have its New York correspondent buy gold with dollars at the rate of 113 grains for every $4.86. This gold will be shipped to England and exchanged for £1. In the process Midland will incur expenses of 2 cents per pound sterling, making the total cost $4.88 per pound. The movement of gold in this case will be from the United States to Britain. Our prices will

[3] See Chap. 23.

tend to fall, Britain's to rise; Britain will increase her imports and reduce her exports (we will buy less at the higher prices); and this will tend to correct the original British export surplus.

The final result of gold movements on a country's *external* balance is therefore essentially similar to that produced under a freely fluctuating exchange market. An import balance will set in motion forces that tend to reduce imports and increase exports. The two standards reach this result by different means, however. A freely fluctuating exchange standard promotes equilibrium through a change in the value of the country's currency abroad with minimal effects on its domestic prices. A gold standard, on the other hand, maintains exchange rates within narrow limits and promotes equilibrium through a shift of the country's whole internal price structure.

It is precisely this method of correcting disequilibrium that has put the international gold standard in the doghouse. As early as the twenties the major trading nations had come to the conclusion that they were unwilling to let the vagaries of international trade determine the level of their domestic prices. With the years this conviction has steadily grown as nations have become more and more concerned with domestic control of internal price levels in order to achieve economic stability. President Roosevelt put the matter bluntly and rather undiplomatically when he told the London Monetary Conference of 1933, which had been called to consider the best means of restoring the world gold standard:

> The revaluation of the dollar in terms of American commodities is an end from which the government and the people of the United States cannot be diverted. We wish to make this perfectly clear; we are interested in American commodity prices. What is to be the value of the dollar in terms of foreign currencies is not and cannot be our immediate concern.[4]

This message probably sounded the death knell of the gold standard. In the absence of United States agreement the rest of the world could not see its way clear to a return to gold, and the subsequent history of monetary standards reveals a series of attempts to achieve a workable system that avoids two evils: (1) the uncertainties of a fluctuating exchange rate and (2) the fluctuations of domestic price levels that follow the operation of the automatic gold standard. That search is not yet concluded, for short of stringent government control of international trade, the twin goals—stable domestic prices and stable exchange rates—seem to be mutually incompatible in a world where dynamic economic forces continually require some kind of adjustment to changing conditions.

Nevertheless the attempt continues. It has taken three forms so far: exchange stabilization funds, exchange control, and the modified form of the gold standard adopted by the International Monetary Fund.

[4] Message to the London Monetary and Economic Conference, July 3, 1933. Reproduced in *The Public Papers and Addresses of Franklin D. Roosevelt* (Random House, Inc., New York, 1938), p. 265.

Exchange Stabilization Funds

The gold standard broke down in the thirties precisely because gold-standard countries refused to let international gold movements exercise their "automatic" effect on internal prices. For example, when Great Britain returned to her old gold parity in 1925 after the dislocation of World War I, her goods were overpriced in foreign markets. Disequilibrium in her balance of payments put downward pressure on the world price of pounds, and gold tended to flow out. But Great Britain was unwilling to accept the lower internal price structure that would have developed under the automatic gold standard. Lower prices would discourage businessmen; lower wages (the price of labor) would stir up labor resentment, and she was fearful of another general strike. So the Bank of England and the Treasury took steps to maintain prices contrary to the "rules of the game."

In the United States we found ourselves in the opposite position with an export balance on current account and a moderate gold inflow. But we no more wanted inflation than Britain wanted deflation. The Federal Reserve took steps to tighten money to prevent prices from rising. This is in line with the goal of price stability, and in terms of domestic policy the skyrocketing of stock prices suggests that, if anything, the Federal Reserve did not tighten money sufficiently. This in spite of the fact that according to the rules of the automatic gold standard we should have let inflation take its course.

The net result, here as in Britain, was to frustrate the normal equilibrating force of gold movements. Britain's import surplus continued, as did our export surplus, and the strain on her gold reserves was therefore not relieved. The situation was aggravated by the financial repercussions accompanying the worldwide depression, until finally Great Britain decided that she could no longer stand ready to pay out gold in unlimited amounts. She abandoned the gold standard in September, 1931, setting off a series of similar actions throughout the world.

For a short time the pound sterling was traded on a freely fluctuating exchange market. Almost immediately its value fell from $4.85 to the neighborhood of $3.50, fluctuating from day to day in a wide range around that figure. After a few months of this instability Britain established an Exchange Equalisation Account to minimize these variations. The Account was provided with a fund of foreign assets and treasury bills (which could be sold for sterling in the London market), and it was thus in a position to buy or sell foreign currencies for the purpose of maintaining "order" in the foreign exchange market.

If the price of pounds tended to fall in terms of francs, for instance, the Account would enter the market to buy pounds with francs, thus supporting the price of pounds. If the price of pounds rose, the Account would sell sterling against foreign currencies. In this way the Account could steady the market, eliminating day-to-day fluctuations, but it could not establish a rate very far from that dictated by free supply and demand forces. If it tried to establish a price of sterling substantially above the market, it would be forced to sell foreign currencies continuously, and since its supply of such currencies was limited, it could not pursue this course for very long.

Exchange stabilization funds were established in several other countries, including the United States. It is clear that their activities can *modify* temporary abrupt fluctuations in rates but are completely unable to *establish* a given rate. Following the inauguration of the United States Exchange Stabilization Fund (after the devaluation of the dollar by 40 per cent), the exchange rate for the pound fluctuated between $5.15 and $4.60 until the outbreak of war in 1939 pushed it down below $4.

Exchange Control

Another device developed in the thirties to replace the gold standard was much more effective in determining exchange rates, but at the cost of extensive government interference in all aspects of international trade. Exchange control was first introduced in 1930 and spread rapidly through the world. It took as many guises as a chameleon, reached its highest degree of intricacy in Hitler's Germany, and became almost universal during World War II. The United States is the only large country in the world that has not introduced some type of exchange control at some time.

Regardless of form, the essence of exchange control is a government monopoly of foreign exchange transactions through the licensing of authorized foreign exchange dealers (who would normally be the same banks that have always carried on a foreign business), and the prohibition of any purchase or sale of foreign funds except through such dealers. The dealers in turn are forbidden to carry out any transactions except at prices and under conditions prescribed by the government.

The government can then set any price it wants for any foreign currency. Sometimes the government sets a single exchange rate, sometimes it establishes a selling rate substantially higher than the buying rate, and sometimes it prescribes several rates for the same currency depending on the nature of the transactions involved. Germany at one time had over forty different rates for the mark.

Table 37-1, which shows the official values for the Paraguay currency in 1956,[5] represents a relatively simple case of multiple exchange rates. If exporters shipped merchandise to the United States, they could sell the resulting bills of exchange drawn on us at the rate of 60 guaraníes per dollar. But if they were able to sell bonds to United States investors (capital-claim exports from Paraguay), they could get 109.85 guaraníes per dollar. This encouraged the export of capital claims and services that normally would have a hard time finding markets abroad.

On the other side, importers of essential merchandise could obtain dollars to pay for such goods at 60 guaraníes per dollar. But if they wanted to buy

[5] Paraguay abolished multiple exchange rates in 1957.

Table 37-1. Official Exchange Rates of Paraguay, December 31, 1956
Guaraníes per U.S. Dollar

Buying rate		*Selling rate*	
60.00	Merchandise exports, government receipts, some service items	60.00	Essential merchandise imports, government payments, authorized services
109.85	Other service items, capital-claim exports	85.00	Nonessential merchandise imports
		112.00	Other service items, capital-claim imports

Source: Adapted from International Monetary Fund, *Eighth Annual Report on Exchange Restrictions* (Washington, 1957), p. 250.

nonessential goods, it cost them more (85 guaraníes per dollar), while the purchase of United States securities was even more expensive. This was an obvious attempt to save scarce dollars by making them expensive for what the government considered nonessential uses.

Whether exchange control involves multiple rates or a single rate, it almost inevitably runs into problems in matching up supply and demand. If Great Britain says that the pound is worth $4.03 (as it did from 1940 to 1949) and requires that all dollar transactions take place at that price, what happens if more dollars are wanted at that price than are available? Under a freely fluctuating exchange system the price of dollars would rise (the price of pounds would fall), discouraging buyers and encouraging sellers. Under a gold standard additional dollars could be purchased with gold. Under exchange control neither of these things can happen. There is, in fact, no mechanism for adjusting supply to demand except by rationing the scarce dollars.

The British government then must lay down rules as to who shall get dollars and who shall not. The privileged importer is given a license to buy exchange, while those without licenses cannot obtain dollars (legally) no matter how badly they want them. The government must determine what shall be imported and who shall import it. This gives rise to a mountain of red tape and to the substitution of some official's discretion for the impersonal forces of the marketplace. It gives rise also to inevitable dissatisfaction among those turned down, to bribery, to favoritism, and to the black market.

Under exchange control the tendency for imports to exceed exports is combated by decreeing a reduction in certain imports. The pressure of demand is still there, unsatisfied. Under these conditions a country's trade may be in balance, but it is not in equilibrium.

Theoretically the opposite case of an export surplus could be combated either by hoarding foreign funds received from the excess exports or by cutting exports arbitrarily. Historically, however, no exchange-control country has been faced with this problem for more than a brief period; the universal tendency seems to be for any country adopting exchange control to price its currency too high, thus inviting an import surplus. Even when Great Britain devalued her pound from $4.03 to $2.80 in 1949, it was still overvalued, and though her dollar shortage was relieved considerably, it was not entirely eliminated.

Almost everyone seems to agree that exchange control is undesirable, and most nations have gradually taken steps to eliminate it, but the process is a slow and painful one in view of the general reluctance to let one's currency find its own level in a freely fluctuating market. Considerable progress has been made, however, and the 1958 decision of most European countries to permit free nonresident convertibility for current transactions left only a small residue of exchange-control restrictions.

The movement away from exchange control, however, has not restored either the old gold standard or a freely fluctuating exchange market. The present international monetary system is a new variety under the aegis of the International Monetary Fund and will be discussed in Chapter 39.

Appendix: Graphical Analysis of Exchange Rate Determination

Since any exchange rate is a price, the forces determining it can be plotted on the same kind of graph used in ordinary price analysis.

Freely Fluctuating Exchange Market. Suppose we examine the dollar price of pounds sterling. Looked at from this point of view pounds are the object bought and sold, while dollars are the unit of account in which the price of pounds is expressed.

The dollar demand for pounds is the demand on the part of those who hold dollars for everything for which pounds can be used. It is the demand for British merchandise, British services, travel in Britain, British securities, pounds needed to pay interest to British bondholders, and so on—it is, in fact, the demand for every kind of item entering into our balance of payments with Britain. For simplicity of exposition let us refer to this as the *demand for British goods*.

It is quite obvious that the demand for British goods (and therefore for British pounds) conforms to the same characteristics that influence the demand for anything else; the lower the price, the more prospective purchasers are willing to buy. The demand for pounds therefore slopes downward to the right, or, in the language of the law of demand, the quantity of pounds demanded varies inversely with the price.

What about supply? It must be made clear that the supply of pounds in the sense here considered has nothing to do with the quantity of money in Great Britain. We are concerned only with the supply of pounds in the foreign exchange market that would be *available for purchase with dollars*. Pounds will be offered in this market only to the extent that their owners want dollars instead. The supply of pounds is thus the *pound demand for dollars*. This in turn is the demand for everything for which dollars must be used or (remembering that the phrase is a kind of shorthand) the demand for United States goods. This demand also slopes downward to the right. But our graph (Figure 37-1) shows supply sloping in the opposite direction. If they are the same thing, how can they look completely different?

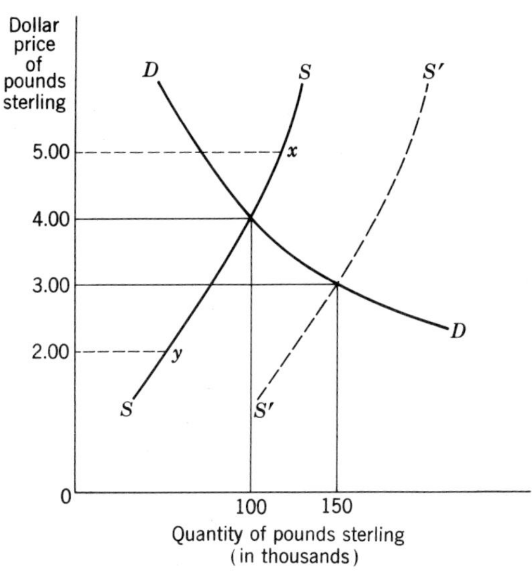

Figure 37-1. Dollar-pound exchange rate on a freely fluctuating exchange market.

The answer lies in the fact that the price scale of Figure 37-1 is in terms of the *dollar price of pounds,* and the higher the dollar price of pounds, the lower the pound price of dollars. From the point of view of the British holder of pounds, point *x* ($5 per pound) represents a *low* price of dollars (£0.2 per dollar) compared with point *y* ($2 per pound, or £0.5 per dollar). Thus while the demand for dollars slopes downward to the right when plotted on a scale showing the pound price of dollars, when it is plotted on a dollar price scale, as here, it is mathematically inverted and slopes up, as curve *SS*.

Figure 37-1 then shows the demand for sterling (*DD*) plotted against the demand for dollars (*SS*), and the intersection of the two curves indicates the equilibrium exchange rate as well as the quantities of the two currencies exchanged. In this graph equilibrium is shown at $4 per pound, and at that rate £100,000 will be bought and sold. If this £100,000 is exchanged at $4 per £1, then $400,000 must be exchanged against it.

If British importers decide to buy more United States goods, the demand for dollars rises. Or, putting it the other way around, the supply of pounds offered against dollars increases, and the supply curve moves to the right. At $4 (or at any other price) importers want to buy more dollars than formerly, as shown in curve *S′S′*. This shift establishes a new equilibrium rate of $3 per £1, and £150,000 is exchanged. At a rate of 3 to 1 this means that $450,000 is sold to obtain £150,000.

The increase in British demand for United States goods has reduced the value of the pound (raised the value of the dollar) and has in the process increased British exports as well as imports by a value of £50,000.

Gold Standard. Under the gold standard the basic forces of supply and demand still underlie the market, but the effect of the gold mechanism is to superimpose a new demand and a new supply on top of the freely fluctuating market curves. Figure 37-2 reproduces curves *DD* and *SS* exactly as drawn in Figure 37-1 (but on a different scale) with the effect of the gold standard added, assuming the conditions of the twenties, when the mint parity was $4.86 = £1 and the gold points were 2 cents away from parity on either side.

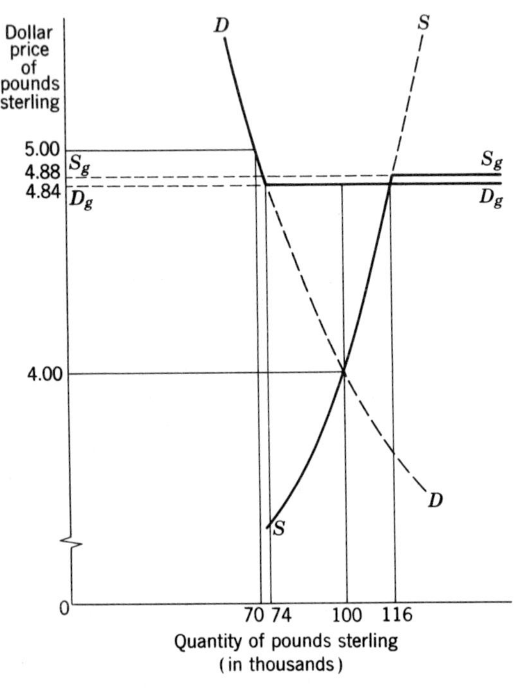

Figure 37-2. Dollar-pound exchange rate under a gold standard (case 1).

Since American holders of sterling can always sell pounds through the gold mechanism for a net price of $4.84, there is for all practical purposes an infinite demand for pounds at this price; as long as the gold standard remains unchanged the gold mechanism will absorb any number of pounds at this price. This is indicated by D_gD_g in Figure 37-2. Similarly anyone can buy pounds with gold at a gross cost of $4.88 each, and there is therefore an apparently unlimited supply of pounds available at this price (S_gS_g).

There appear to be two supplies and two demands: *SS* and *DD* for foreign exchange traded through normal channels and S_gS_g and D_gD_g for exchange purchased through gold movements. Suppose holders of pounds wished to sell £70,000. They could sell them for gold at a price of $4.84 ($D_gD_g$), but they could sell them to private traders for $5 each. Obviously they will sell at the higher price if they can, and so for £70,000 the demand created by gold movements doesn't have any influence on the market. It might just as well not exist, so it is shown dashed. For that quantity of pounds the only demand curve of significance is *DD*. But at £100,000 private dealers will offer only \$4, while shipping gold will yield \$4.84. For that part of the diagram the private demand has no significance and is shown dashed. The demand that matters consists of private demand for small quantities and the gold mechanism demand for larger quantities, that is, the composite heavy line DD_g.

Just as holders want to sell at the highest price, so buyers want to buy at the lowest price. For small quantities they would buy from private suppliers (*SS*); for larger quantities it is cheaper to buy through shipping gold (S_gS_g), and so the significant supply curve is the heavy line SS_g.

Equilibrium in this case as in any other is achieved at the intersection of supply and demand. This is no longer at \$4, for the demand curve that crosses supply at that price is a phantom curve of no practical significance. The real intersection of supply and demand is at \$4.84. At that price private holders are willing to supply £116,000, but private buyers are willing to buy only £74,000. The difference (£42,000) must be sold through the gold mechanism. Holders of pounds will convert £42,000 into gold, ship it to the United States, and sell the gold to the Treasury for dollars. This then is Britain's gold export point.

Suppose the demand for British goods and hence for British pounds increases. Figure 37-3 shows the same initial DD_g and SS_g curves as Figure 37-2 along with a new, increased demand curve $D'D_g$. The gold portion of this curve is the same as ever, but the private demand has increased. Equilibrium is now achieved at \$4.88. Here private traders will buy £120,000, but sellers are willing to sell only £116,500. Buyers must obtain the other £3,500 by shipping gold to England for transfer into sterling.

It is, of course, possible for the curves to intersect within the gold points as indicated by $D''D_g$, with an exchange rate of, say, \$4.86 and with £116,250 exchanged. Under these conditions private demand intersects private supply,

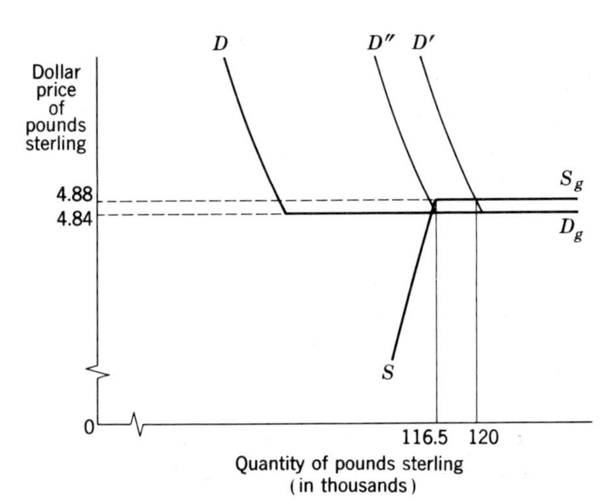

Figure 37-3. Dollar-pound exchange rate under a gold standard (case 2).

and no gold moves. Temporarily at least it is as if the gold standard didn't exist.

Exchange Stabilization Funds. Under an exchange stabilization fund private supply and demand come back into their own. There are no absolute limits to exchange rate fluctuations, but the fund enters the market from time to time on the side of either supply or demand to steady the rate.

Perhaps the market situation is as illustrated by curves *DD* and *SS* in Figure 37-4. Suppose also that the fund considers this an acceptable rate; it will

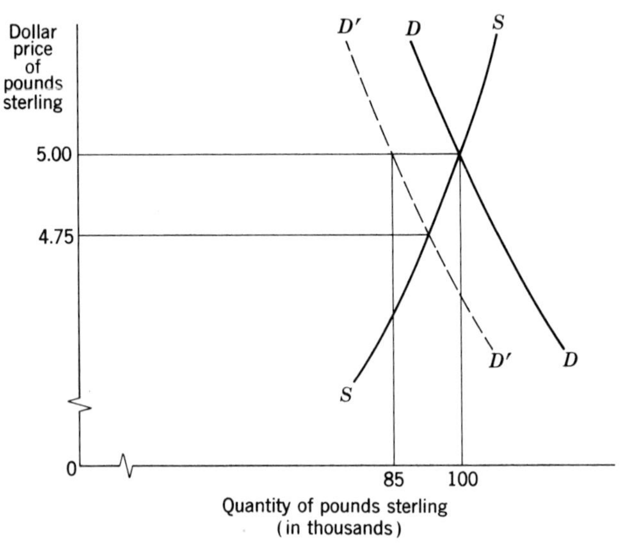

Figure 37-4. Dollar-pound exchange rate with an exchange stabilization fund.

not interfere in the market. Private traders will exchange £100,000 for $500,000 at a rate of $5 = £1. Suppose then that the demand for pounds drops to *D′D′* but that the fund does not want to let the pound rate fall to the new equilibrium. It can enter the market by buying pounds with dollars, adding its own demand to the regular market demand in order to make up the difference between *D′D′* and *DD*. In other words, if private traders are now willing to buy only £85,000 at $5, while sellers are offering £100,000, the fund can keep the price at $5 by buying the other £15,000 itself.

It can do this, however, only as long as it has dollars with which to buy, and when it runs out of dollars, it is going to have to let the rate fall to the new equilibrium of $4.75 unless conditions change in the meantime.

Exchange Control. At least in its simpler forms exchange control is nothing more than a price ceiling or a price floor, depending on which way one looks at it.

Suppose the equilibrium rate in a freely fluctuating market is $2.50 = £1, as in Figure 37-5, but the British government wishes to maintain by decree a

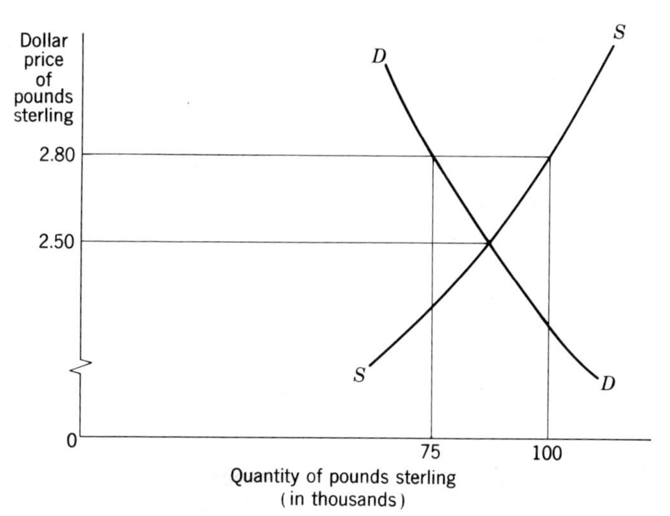

Figure 37-5. Dollar-pound exchange rate under exchange control.

rate of $2.80. At this high price of pounds United States importers wish to buy only £75,000, but the British wish to sell £100,000 against dollars. There is an oversupply of pounds. Turned around, this is the dollar shortage. The British wish to buy $280,000 (£100,000 offered against dollars at $2.80 each), but we wish to sell only $210,000 (the number needed to buy £75,000 at $2.80).

Since the British can get only $210,000, this short supply must be rationed by some means (e.g., import licenses), and Britons who want some $70,000 (equivalent to £25,000 at the controlled rate) must go without. Thus exchange control, like price control, having destroyed the free pricing mechanism, must find some other means of allocating scarce resources.

Questions for Thought and Discussion

1. If the price of francs is falling in world exchange markets, what does this suggest about the price of dollars?

2. Why should the exchange value of a nation's currency fluctuate?

3. Is it correct to say that under a freely fluctuating exchange standard international trade will have *no* effect on a nation's internal price structure? (What about the price of imports?)

4. What effect would a general fall in United States prices have on the foreign demand for dollars? What repercussions would this have under the gold standard? Under a freely fluctuating exchange standard?

5. The most common argument against freely fluctuating exchange markets is that they produce uncertainty. Does this suggest that domestically producers are always certain of the price they will get for their product or have to pay for their raw materials?

6. Explain clearly why, under a gold standard, exchange rates cannot move outside the gold points.

7. If the British Exchange Equalisation Account were trying to maintain a rate of £1 = $5 and the United States Exchange Stabilization Fund were simultaneously trying to maintain a rate of £1 = $4.50, what would happen?

8. Why would an underdeveloped nation want to encourage the sale of securities abroad and discourage the purchase of foreign securities? How does a high price of dollars for both imports and exports of capital claims accomplish this?

9. Using Figure 37-1 as a base, illustrate the effect of an increase in the demand for pounds.

10. Using Figure 37-2 as a base, illustrate the effect of a devaluation of the gold content of the British pound to a mint parity of £1 = $3.80.

Selected Bibliography

Brown, William A.: *The International Gold Standard Reinterpreted, 1914–1934,* 2 vols., National Bureau of Economic Research, Inc., New York, 1940.

Cassel, Gustav: *Money and Exchange after 1914,* The Macmillan Company, New York, 1922.

———: *The Downfall of the Gold Standard,* Oxford University Press, Fair Lawn, N.J., 1936.

Einzig, Paul: *The History of Foreign Exchange,* Macmillan & Co., Ltd., London, 1962.

Gregory, T. E.: *The Gold Standard and Its Future,* 3d ed., E. P. Dutton & Co., Inc., New York, 1935.

Hall, N. F.: *The Exchange Equalisation Account,* Macmillan & Co., Ltd., London, 1935.

Harrod, Roy: *The Dollar,* 2d ed., W. W. Norton & Company, Inc., New York, 1963.

Hawtrey, Ralph G.: *The Gold Standard in Theory and Practice,* 5th ed., Longmans, Green & Co., Ltd., London, 1947.

Heilperin, Michael A.: *International Monetary Economics,* Longmans, Green & Co., Ltd., London, 1939.

International Monetary Fund: *Annual Report on Exchange Restrictions,* Washington.

League of Nations: *International Currency Experience,* Geneva, 1944.

Mikesell, Raymond F.: *Foreign Exchange in the Postwar World,* The Twentieth Century Fund, New York, 1954.

Ropke, Wilhelm: *International Economic Disintegration,* William Hodge & Co., London, 1942.

Sohmen, Egon: *Flexible Exchange Rates,* The University of Chicago Press, Chicago, 1961.

Chapter 38 World Monetary Problems

But, in this troublous time what's to be done?

The Third Part of King Henry VI
Act II, scene 1, line 159

While international monetary problems cannot be divorced from general problems of trade or of international relations, we must in the limited space here available attempt to treat them separately. There are three international aspects of money that we will examine: (1) the effect of international moneyflows on national income; (2) the problem of obtaining a satisfactory monetary standard; and (3) machinery for facilitating the international movement of savings.

The Circuit Flow and International Trade

In Chapter 25 we looked at the circuit flow of money primarily in terms of its domestic effects. Here we are concerned with its international repercussions.

Figure 38-1 is a reproduction of our original flow diagram except that the flow of country A has been linked directly to a similar flow in country B. Since no two countries trade exclusively with each other, it would be more realistic to think of country A as the United States (or any other specific country) and country B as *all other countries together* (the rest of the world).

To the extent that we in the United States buy imports, the price we pay is a leakage from our income stream. Simultaneously, however, it is

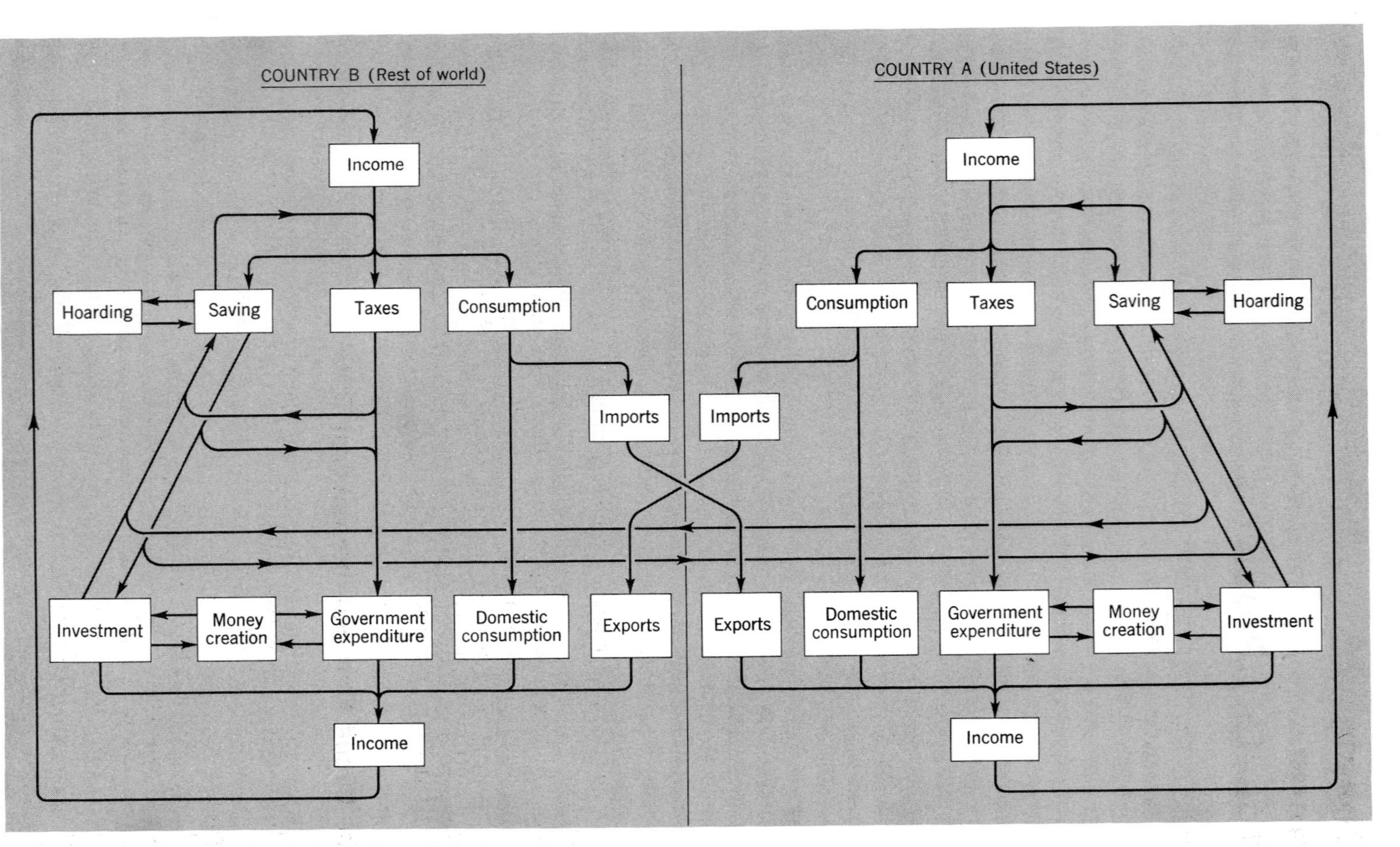

Figure 38-1. The international circuit flow of money.

earned by foreign export firms, which in turn pay their workers and other factors of production, thus adding to *their* national income. We raise their income at the expense of our own.

But this is only half of the story. To the extent that they import our goods, the money comes out of their income stream into ours. This reverses the process. As long as our imports equal our exports, the dollars we pay circle through other countries and come back again. This circuit is not significantly different from that in which consumers buy goods from domestic firms that in turn pass the money through the chain of business payments to income recipients. Under conditions of balanced imports and exports international trade would present no new problem for national income analysis.

Net Foreign Investment. Suppose, however, that exports exceed imports. We are receiving more money than we are sending abroad. But the total of international payments must balance. Where does this "extra money" come from? To understand this we should first clarify what we mean by imports and exports.

As used in national income analysis imports and exports refer to flows of merchandise, services, and unilateral remittances, or what we have already referred to as the balance on current account. If we have an export balance on current account, then the rest of the international account must show an import balance; that is, we must import more capital claims and gold than we export. This is why the excess of exports over imports on current account is referred to as *net foreign investment.* We are investing abroad by buying claims against foreigners, or by redeeming claims formerly held by foreigners, or by acquiring gold. Thus we are financing our export balance by making our savings available to foreigners to enable them to buy goods they otherwise wouldn't have dollars to pay for.

Consumer Saving. This situation would be illustrated in the circuit flow by a movement of funds through rest-of-the-world imports into United States exports, balanced by an equal flow from our saving into foreign investment. This represents dissaving for the rest of the world. It enables them to buy more than their income would permit, just as when a consumer borrows in order to increase his consumption.

Figure 38-2 illustrates this flow by showing only those portions of the complete circuit that are applicable to this transaction (solid line). The net result is that foreign nations are enabled to buy more than they can afford. The extra purchases are financed by our saving and by their dissaving, the funds in essence flowing from our savers back to our export industries.

Money Creation. An export surplus could also be financed if our *banks* lent the money abroad. In this case instead of the funds coming out of saving, they would come from newly created money. The result would be expansionary in the same way as if the banks had lent the money to domestic industries. In the international case the upward pressure comes when the created funds flow back as income for the export industries. The same upward pressure would

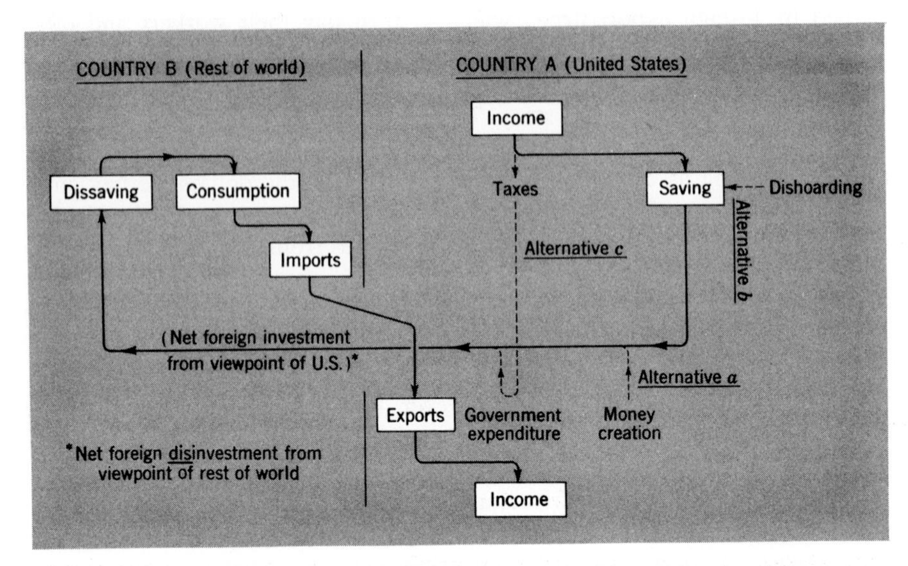

Figure 38-2. The effect of a United States export balance on the circuit flow.

result if private savers dishoarded in order to invest abroad. These two cases are indicated in Figure 38-2 by dashed lines as alternatives *a* and *b*.

Foreign Dissaving. Instead of borrowing, foreign nations may finance an import balance by using savings accumulated in the past. They may draw on dollar balances built up as reserves, or they may sell securities bought at some former period. Thus Great Britain paid for substantial imports from the United States in the early stages of World War II by selling back to us dollar securities (bonds and stocks issued by United States corporations) that the British had accumulated during earlier years when they were able to invest abroad by reason of an export balance.

In terms of our diagram these possibilities are equivalent to those already discussed. It makes no difference as far as the circuit flow is concerned whether Great Britain offers newly issued securities of her own or sells those she already owns. In both cases she is dissaving, though in the first case she is dissaving out of future income (since the obligation must be repaid), while in the second she is dissaving out of past accumulations. A consumer may purchase an automobile by saving up the money over a period of years before buying or by borrowing the money and paying back the debt out of future earnings. In either case he is living beyond his current income at the time of purchase and therefore dissaving.

Government Lending. It is also possible that the *government* may finance an export balance by direct foreign lending. In Figure 38-2 alternative *c* indicates how this would affect the circuit flow if it were financed by taxes. However, the government might obtain the funds by borrowing either from the banks or from savers. We should by now have sufficient understanding of the circuit flow to evaluate the varying effects of these different methods on the level of national income in the United States.

Gold Movement. Another possibility is that the United States might accept gold in payment of the export balance. This represents investment in gold stock and is counted as part of net foreign investment because gold represents a claim on foreign goods that can be exercised any time we want to use it. Since the gold becomes part of our monetary base, this method of financing represents a creation of new money.

Foreign Aid. If the government *gives* the foreign nation the dollars needed to meet its purchases from us, the effect on the flow would be shown differently, for in this case we are not building up any claims against foreigners. They do not have to return a gift, and though its immediate effect may be the same as that of a loan, its long-run result is quite different. For that reason foreign aid (such as that channeled through the Agency for International Development) is included in the *current* account rather than in the capital account. That is, government gifts are recorded as purchases of current services (unilateral remittances) and are therefore counted as imports into the United States in precisely the same way as if the government bought goods (tin for government stockpile, for instance) with the money.

Where government aid balances other current account items, there is no net foreign investment. Figure 38-3 shows those portions of the circuit flow

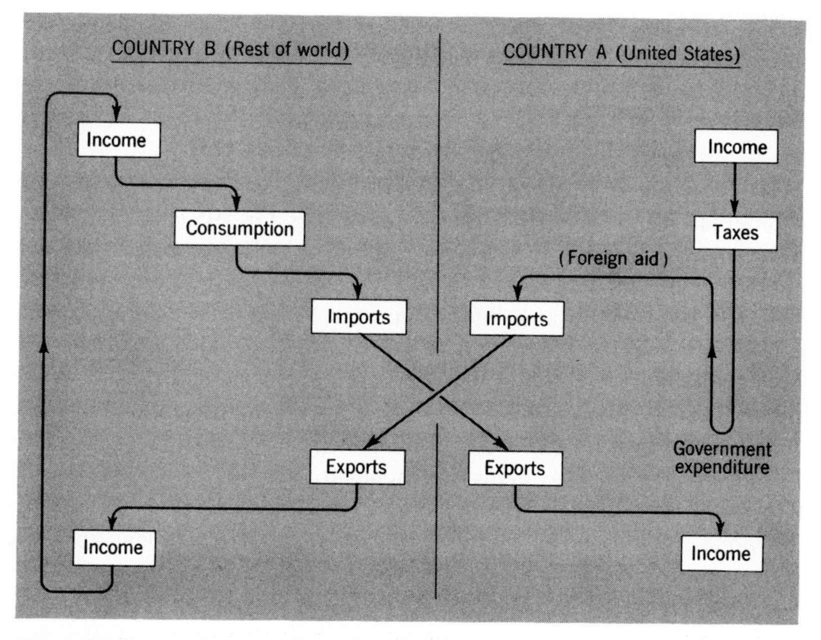

Figure 38-3. The effect of government grants on the circuit flow.

that would be affected by such a situation. Foreign aid is shown as income to the recipient rather than as dissaving since he is under no obligation to repay the money he receives. It therefore allows him to raise his consumption (imports) in the present without lowering it in the future. In this respect it is similar to domestic transfer payments, such as unemployment compensation, which are part of the personal income of the recipients.

The difference in national income accounts between foreign aid and governmental loans can also be shown by a simple numerical example, as indicated in Table 38-1, which assumes no private unilateral transfers, no private capital investment, and no gold movements.

Table 38-1. Illustration of Government Effect on the Balance of International Payments

	Case A: Balancing by foreign grants		Case B: Balancing by foreign loans	
	Imports	Exports	Imports	Exports
Current account:				
Merchandise	11,000	15,000	11,000	15,000
Transportation and travel	900	400	900	400
Income on investments	400	2,000	400	2,000
Other services	2,200	2,000	2,200	2,000
Unilateral transfers, government	4,900			
	19,400	19,400	14,500	19,400
Balance on current account	*0*			*4,900*
Capital account:				
Government loans			4,900	
			19,400	19,400
Net foreign investment	*0*		*4,900*	

The United States Balance of Payments. Table 38-2 gives the actual balance of international payments of the United States for 1957 (a year in which net foreign investment was positive), indicating how both government and private individuals contributed to both unilateral transfers and net foreign investment. Table 38-3 gives the same information for 1959 (in which net foreign investment was negative).

In 1957 foreigners bought $5.7 billion more goods and services from us than they sold to us. Where did they get the funds to pay for this excess? Private persons gave them $0.5 billion, while government aid provided $1.8 billion. Since these two items are included in the current account, this left a balance of $3.4 billion to be financed by net foreign investment. Private individuals and organizations in the United States made loans abroad of $3.6 billion, partly offset by $0.8 billion loaned to us by foreigners. The United States government lent $1.0 billion, and foreigners sent us $0.8 billion of gold. On the other hand, the compilers admit that their statistics are unable

Table 38-2. Balance of International Payments of the United States, 1957*
Billions of Dollars

	Imports	Exports	Import balance	Export balance
Merchandise	13.3	19.4		
Transportation and travel	2.9	2.8		
Income on investments	0.6	2.8		
Other services	3.9†	1.5		
	20.8	26.5		
Balance on goods and service account				5.7
Unilateral transfers (net):				
Private	0.5			
Government	1.8			
	2.3			
Balance on unilateral account			2.3	
Balance on current account				3.4
Capital-claims transfers (net):				
U.S. private	3.6			
U.S. government	1.0			
Foreign nonliquid		0.5		
Foreign liquid		0.3‡		
Monetary gold	0.8‡			
Errors and omissions		1.2		
	5.3	1.9		
Net foreign investment			3.4	

* Excluding transfers under military grants of $2.4 billion.
† Including military expenditures of $3.2 billion.
‡ These two items added together (algebraically) yield a balance-of-payments surplus (Department of Commerce definition) of $0.5 billion.
Source: Adapted from U.S. Department of Commerce, *Balance of Payments, Statistical Supplement, Revised Edition* (1963), p. 4. Detail may not add to totals because of rounding.

to account for an amount of $1.2 billion of exports, and while it is not certain where these omissions occurred, it is assumed that they were primarily on capital account. With this adjustment the net increase in United States claims against foreigners ($3.4 billion) is equal to their excess of purchases on current account.

By 1959 the picture had changed considerably. Imports had risen and exports had fallen, leaving the United States with a net export on goods and service account of only $0.1 billion. Our gifts abroad more than compensated for this figure, and we consequently had an *import* balance on current account of $2.3 billion. United States acquisition of claims against foreigners ($2.8 billion) was actually less than the increase in their claims against us of $3.9 billion—mostly in the form of increases in their dollar balances in United States banks. In addition they acquired $0.7 billion of our gold, while errors and omissions accounted for another $0.4 billion of exports. Thus our net foreign investment was—as it must always be—equal to the balance on current account ($2.3 billion). But in this year, since we had an import balance

Table 38.3. Balance of International Payments of the United States, 1959*

Billions of Dollars

	Imports	Exports	Import balance	Export balance
Merchandise	15.3	16.3		
Transportation and travel	3.4	2.5		
Income on investments	0.8	3.0		
Other services	3.8†	1.6		
	23.3	23.5		
Balance on goods and service account				0.1
Unilateral transfers (net):				
Private	0.6			
Government	1.8			
	2.4			
Balance on unilateral account			2.4	
Balance on current account			2.3	
Capital-claims transfers (net):				
U.S. private	2.4			
U.S. government	0.4			
Foreign nonliquid		0.9		
Foreign liquid		3.0‡		
Monetary gold		0.7‡		
Errors and omissions		0.4		
	2.7	5.0		
Net foreign investment				2.3

* Excluding transfers under military grants of $2.0 billion.
† Including military expenditures of $3.1 billion.
‡ These two items added together yield a balance-of-payments deficit (Department of Commerce definition) of $3.7 billion.
Source: Adapted from U.S. Department of Commerce, *Balance of Payments: Statistical Supplement, Revised Edition* (1963), p. 4.

on current account, the capital accounts show a surplus of exports, that is, net foreign *dis*investment. This ability of foreign countries to increase their net claims against the United States was, among other things, a symbol of improvement in general economic conditions abroad.

It was also an indication of a deteriorating United States position in international trade, which first showed up seriously in 1958 and which has continued into 1965. The nature of the imbalance, however, has shifted over time, and the figures for 1964, for instance (see Table 38-4), are very different from those for 1959. In 1964 our export balance on goods and service account had risen to $8.6 billion with little change in the unilateral transfer account, so that we had an *export* balance on current account (and positive net foreign investment) of $5.8 billion. But a drop in investment by foreigners in this country (export of capital claims) and an increase in our private investment abroad, along with an adverse shift of $0.8 billion in the unrecorded items that appear as errors and omissions, ate up most of the improvement in trade account and left us with a continuing gold and currency drain of $0.2 billion.

Table 38-4. Balance of International Payments of the United States, 1964 *
Billions of Dollars

	Imports	Exports	Import balance	Export balance
Merchandise	18.6	25.3		
Transportation and travel	4.7	3.4		
Income on investments	1.4	5.5		
Other services	3.8†	2.9		
	28.5	37.0		
Balance on goods and service account				8.6
Unilateral transfers (net):				
Private	0.6			
Government	2.2			
	2.7			
Balance on unilateral account			2.7	
Balance on current account				5.8
Capital-claims transfers (net):				
U.S. private	6.5			
U.S. government	1.7			
Foreign nonliquid		0.7		
Foreign liquid		2.6‡		
Monetary reserve assets (net)§		0.2‡		
Errors and omissions	1.2			
	9.3	3.5		
Net foreign investment			5.8	

* Excluding transfers under military grants of $1.3 billion.
† Including military expenditures of $2.8 billion.
‡ These two items added together (plus special transactions of $0.3 billion on capital-claims account) yield a balance-of-payments deficit (Department of Commerce definition) of $3.1 billion.
§ Includes gold, convertible foreign currencies, and IMF gold tranche position.
Source: Adapted from *Survey of Current Business*, vol. 45, no. 6 (June, 1965), p. 16. Detail may not add to totals because of rounding.

The Export of Depression. The international repercussions of trade and of moneyflows mean that business changes in one country will affect other countries as well. The simplest example of this is the drop in a nation's exports that results from a depression among its customers. If business conditions in the United States deteriorate, our national income falls, and consumers buy fewer goods—including fewer imports. Foreign nations see their receipts from exports fall, lowering production and employment in the export industries. The resultant fall in national income in these nations lowers consumption and investment. In its turn, economic distress abroad reduces the markets for our exports, turning the screw tighter in this country. The diminishing foreign trade of the thirties was both a result and a cause of worldwide business collapse.

How strongly a depression in one country will affect its neighbors depends on how important that country is in world trade. A decline in Portugal is likely to have relatively little effect elsewhere. The United States, however, is one of the largest customers of many countries, so that a drop in our imports may have sizable repercussions throughout the world. It used to be accepted as dictum that when the United States sneezed, Europe caught pneumonia. The ability of Europe to weather our recession of 1958 indicates that this is not always so, but there is more than a grain of truth in the general principle.

An Export Balance to Cure Unemployment. Because depressions can be exported, it is sometimes suggested that a nation may pull itself out of a state of collapse by pushing the depression off onto some other country. Since imports represent a leakage from the circuit flow and—other things being equal—reduce national income, while exports are a "seepage" into the circuit flow and tend to raise income, the oversimplified conclusion is sometimes reached that national income can be raised by reducing imports relative to exports, a result that can be achieved by increasing tariffs or other barriers to imports. There is some evidence that this was at least one consideration in the minds of congressmen when they passed the Smoot-Hawley Tariff of 1930.

As a first approximation the reasoning is correct. *All other things remaining the same,* a reduction in imports forced by a rise in tariffs will raise national income by transferring demand away from foreign goods toward domestic goods, thereby shifting unemployment from domestic industries to foreign ones.

What are the chances of all other things remaining the same in these circumstances? Not very good. Since the effect here is that of raising one's own income at the expense of another country, it is somewhat like trying to avoid drowning by standing on someone else's shoulders. The result is hardly likely to be one of stable equilibrium.

For the sake of illustration suppose it is the United States that raises tariffs to increase its income. What is likely to happen?

1. As already noted, the drop in income in the rest of the world will reduce United States exports (though by less than the fall in imports). Our export industries lose by the general impoverishment of their customers.

2. Unless foreign countries have some other source of dollars (such as gold or dollar reserves of substantial size) their imports from the United States will drop not only by reason of a fall in income, but also because—since they are earning fewer dollars—they don't have the funds to buy United States goods. Germany, for instance, may have marks to buy her own goods, but she needs dollars to buy ours.

3. If foreigners borrow the needed dollars from us, funds that might have been used to finance our own business are diverted into foreign investment. This might represent a net gain if our businessmen refuse to borrow, for in this case the foreign investment represents a use of funds otherwise idle. But the gain would be even greater if tariffs had not been used to block trade in the first place.

4. Since a tariff program of this type is designed to hurt foreign nations, it is understandable that they will attempt to retaliate by discriminating against *our* goods. What is sauce for the goose is sauce for the gander. Their retaliation may in turn produce counterretaliation, and everybody is fighting a battle in which everybody loses. The period of the thirties is a depressing example of a continuously rising spiral of trade restrictions and an equally continuous spiral of falling world trade. No nation managed to pull itself out of the mess this way, and everybody drowned.

So while this type of attack on depression seems possible on paper, it doesn't appear to work very well in practice. Surely it would be better for a nation to concentrate on domestic measures to raise its national income. As these measures become effective, they help pull other nations up rather than pushing them down. This is so because our rising income induces larger imports, thus helping to raise the income of exporting nations. Their increase in income in turn tends to raise their imports from us, which reinforces our own efforts to overcome the depression. Surely this type of mutual aid is preferable to the self-defeating "beggar-my-neighbor" policies of mutual retaliation.

Dollar Shortage. In addition to problems associated with the business cycle, the international flow of income has some baffling aspects of a more persistent nature. For a decade after World War II, for instance, most of the world was suffering from a "dollar shortage." Stripped of its technical ramifications this term refers to a situation in which a foreign nation has an import surplus on goods and service account with particular reference to its trade with the United States. Since the rest of the world as a whole wished to buy more goods from us than we wanted to buy from it, a practical problem arose as to where it could get the additional dollars necessary to pay for the excess imports.

Although the phrase was invented in the postwar period, the dollar shortage is of much older vintage than that. The United States has had an export surplus on *merchandise* account in every year but one since 1894 and an export surplus on *goods and service* account in every year since accurate statistics first became available in 1919. Table 38-4 shows the magnitude of this surplus since 1919 and indicates which major items in the balance of payments have offset our excess exports throughout the period.[1]

Since 1919 there have been three basic shifts in these balancing items. During the twenties our export balance on current account was offset primarily by purchases of foreign securities (as indicated by the negative figures for United States capital; the positive figures for foreign capital show that foreigners were also buying our securities but in much smaller amounts).

The stock market collapse put an end to that type of financing, and in 1931 we actually began disposing of our foreign security holdings (the pluses under private United States capital). Foreign nations were then forced to dip into their reserves to finance imports, selling capital assets until 1933 (the minuses

[1] Although the table shows a negative (import) balance on merchandise (and goods and service) account for 1942 through 1944, this is because the figures given exclude transfers under military grants. If the exports of military supplies and equipment are added, these three years would show an *export* balance on merchandise account of $5.7 billion, $10.5 billion, and $11.9 billion, respectively. Government transfer payments would also be higher by equivalent amounts, leaving the total current account unchanged. Military grants (not shown in the table) have continued in varying amounts in subsequent years. In 1964 they amounted to $1.3 billion.

Table 38.5. International Transactions of the United States, 1919 to 1964[a]

Import (−) or Export (+) Balance; Billions of Dollars

Year	Merchandise	Services	Unilateral transfers: Private	Unilateral transfers: Government	Total current account = net foreign investment	Capital: United States: Private	Capital: United States: Government	Capital: Foreign	Gold[b]	Errors and omissions	Deficit[c]
1919	+4.9	−*	−0.8	−0.2	+3.8	−0.2	−2.3	−0.2	+0.2	−1.3	+0.2
1920	+3.1	+0.4	−0.6	−*	+2.8	−0.6	−0.2	−0.3	+0.1	−1.9	+0.1
1921	+2.0	+0.1	−0.5	−0.1	+1.6	−0.6	+*	−*	−0.7	−0.3	−0.7
1922	+0.7	+0.3	−0.3	−*	+0.4	−0.8	+*	+*	−0.3	+0.4	−0.3
1923	+0.4	+0.4	−0.3	−*	+0.5	−0.5	+0.1	+0.4	−0.3	−0.2	−0.3
1924	+1.1	+0.3	−0.3	−*	+1.0	−1.0	+*	+0.4	−0.3	−0.2	−*
1925	+0.7	+0.4	−0.4	−*	+0.7	−0.9	+*	+0.2	+0.1	−0.1	+*
1926	+0.4	+0.4	−0.4	−*	+0.4	−0.9	+*	+0.6	−0.1	−0.1	+0.4
1927	+0.7	+0.3	−0.4	−*	+0.7	−1.3	+*	+0.9	+0.1	−0.4	+1.0
1928	+1.1	+0.3	−0.3	−*	+1.0	−1.5	+*	+0.3	+0.2	−0.1	+0.1
1929	+0.8	+0.3	−0.3	−*	+0.8	−0.8	+*	+0.6	−0.1	−0.4	+0.1
1930	+0.8	+0.2	−0.3	−*	+0.7	−0.6	+0.1	−0.2	−0.3	+0.3	−0.6
1931	+0.4	+0.1	−0.3	−*	+0.2	+0.8	+*	−1.2	+0.1	+0.1	−1.1
1932	+0.3	+0.1	−0.2	−*	+0.2	+0.5	+*	−0.7	−0.1	+0.1	−0.7
1933	+0.2	+0.1	−0.2	−*	+0.2	−*	−*	−0.3	+0.1	+0.1	−0.3
1934	+0.5	+0.1	−0.2	−*	+0.4	+0.3	−*	+0.1	−1.3	+0.4	−1.1
1935	−0.1	+0.2	−0.2	−*	−0.1	+0.3	+*	+1.0	−1.8	+0.4	−1.2
1936	+*	+0.1	−0.2	−*	−0.1	+0.2	+*	+1.0	−1.3	+0.2	−0.9
1937	+0.3	+*	−0.2	−0.1	+0.1	+0.3	+*	+0.6	−1.4	+0.4	−1.1
1938	+1.1	+0.2	−0.2	−*	+1.1	+0.1	−*	+0.4	−1.8	+0.2	−1.5
1939	+0.9	+0.1	−0.2	−*	+0.9	+0.3	−*	+1.2	−3.2	+0.8	−1.9
1940	+1.4	+0.3	−0.2	−*	+1.5	+0.2	−0.1	+1.3	−4.2	+1.3	−2.9
1941	+0.9	+0.3	−0.2	+*	+1.1	+0.1	−0.4	−0.7	−0.7	+0.7	−1.1
1942	−0.4	+0.4	−0.1	−0.1	−0.2	+*	−0.2	+0.1	+*	+0.3	+0.2
1943	−2.1	+*	−0.2	+0.1	−2.2	+*	−0.1	+1.2	+0.8	+0.3	+2.0
1944	−1.8	+0.1	−0.4	+0.1	−2.1	−0.1	−0.2	+0.7	+1.4	+0.4	+1.9
1945	+1.0	−1.5	−0.5	−0.4	−1.4	−0.6	−1.0	+2.1	+0.5	+0.3	+2.7
1946	+6.6	+0.9	−0.7	−2.2	+4.6	−0.4	−3.0	−1.0	−0.6	+0.4	−1.3
1947	+10.0	+1.5	−0.7	−1.9	+8.9	−1.0	−4.2	−1.8	−2.9	+0.9	−4.6
1948	+5.6	+0.8	−0.7	−3.8	+1.9	−0.9	−1.0	+0.4	−1.5	+1.2	−1.0
1949	+5.3	+0.9	−0.5	−5.1	+0.5	−0.6	−0.7	+0.1	−0.2	+0.8	−0.2
1950	+1.0	+0.8	−0.4	−3.6	−2.2	−1.3	−0.2	+1.9	+1.7	−*	+3.6
1951	+2.9	+0.8	−0.4	−3.1	+0.2	−1.0	−0.2	+0.6	−0.1	+0.5	+0.3
1952	+2.5	−0.3	−0.4	−2.1	−0.3	−1.2	−0.4	+1.6	−0.4	+0.6	+1.0
1953	+1.3	−0.9	−0.5	−2.0	−2.1	−0.4	−0.2	+1.2	+1.2	+0.3	+2.2
1954	+2.4	−0.6	−0.5	−1.8	−0.4	−1.6	+0.1	+1.5	+0.3	+0.2	+1.6
1955	+2.8	−0.7	−0.4	−2.0	−0.5	−1.3	−0.3	+1.5	+*	+0.5	+1.1
1956	+4.6	−0.6	−0.5	−1.9	+1.6	−3.1	−0.6	+1.9	−0.3	+0.5	+0.9
1957	+6.1	−0.4	−0.5	−1.8	+3.4	−3.6	−1.0	+0.8	−0.8	+1.2	−0.5
1958	+3.3	−1.1	−0.5	−1.8	−0.1	−2.9	−1.0	+1.3	+2.3	+0.5	+3.5
1959	+1.0	−0.8	−0.6	−1.8	−2.3	−2.4	−0.4	+3.9	+0.7	+0.4	+3.7
1960	+4.8	−0.7	−0.5	−1.9	+1.7	−3.9	−1.1	+2.1	+2.1	−1.0	+3.9
1961	+5.4	+0.2	−0.5	−2.1	+3.1	−4.2	−0.9	+2.5	+0.6	−1.0	+3.1
1962	+4.4	+0.7	−0.5	−2.2	+2.5	−3.4	−1.1	+1.7	+1.5	−1.2	+3.6
1963	+5.1	+0.8	−0.6	−2.2	+3.2	−4.5	−1.7	+3.0	+0.4	−0.4	+3.3
1964	+6.7	+1.9	−0.6	−2.2	+5.8	−6.5	−1.7	+3.3	+0.2	−1.2	+3.1

[a] Excluding transfers under military grants.
[b] Beginning in 1960 includes convertible currency reserves and IMF gold tranche position.
[c] Department of Commerce definition; there are alternative ways of measuring the deficit, which would lead to different results.
* Less than $50 million.
Source: Adapted from U.S. Department of Commerce, *Balance of Payments Statistical Supplement, Revised Edition* (1963), pp. 1–4; *Survey of Current Business,* vol. 45, no. 6 (June, 1965), pp. 10, 12, 16; vol. 45, no. 8 (August, 1965), pp. 34, 35. Detail may not add to totals because of rounding. Figures for 1941–1946 are partly estimated.

under foreign capital), and then shifting to gold exports. The greater part of our large postwar gold stock was acquired in this period.

Since World War II our export surplus on merchandise account has been balanced to some extent by government transfer payments under such programs as UNRRA, Marshall Plan, and the present Agency for International Development (AID). An even greater source of dollars for foreign countries has been private United States investment abroad, which revived during the war and reached a level of $6.5 billion in 1964, a figure four times as high as the prewar peak in 1928.

Dollar Glut. Since 1958 the combination of high (though decreasing) foreign aid expenditures and rising investment abroad has more than offset a substantial trade surplus, and the result has been a deficit in the United States balance of payments of substantial magnitude. The dollar shortage, which some people once thought of as a permanent aspect of international trade, has now given way to a dollar glut and a gold loss of over $9 billion, or more than one-third of our 1957 gold stock.

What to do about it? We might be able to increase exports or decrease imports, but our sizable export balance of trade ($6.7 billion in 1964) shows that on merchandise account we are already doing extremely well. We also have had an export balance on service account for the last four years covered in the table, reflecting primarily a high level of earnings on our foreign investments. Private gifts abroad have been running fairly steadily at half a billion dollars annually, and are probably not subject to much control.

Government foreign aid has sometimes been singled out as the most likely item to cut. But any reduction of aid is likely to result in an almost equal drop in exports. Not only is most foreign aid extended to underdeveloped countries, who generally find themselves short of dollars (as opposed to the developed countries of Europe plus Japan, with whom we are in deficit), but also in recent years the government, conscious of the balance-of-payments problem, has *tied* almost all loans and grants. This means that the recipient is obligated by the terms of the aid agreement to spend the funds exclusively in the United States, thus making the connection between aid and exports clear and direct. By 1965 approximately 85 per cent of all foreign aid was tied.

This leaves only the capital account. One major step that the government has taken has been an "equalization" tax on the income from foreign investments, enacted in 1964 but retroactive to 1963, when it was first proposed. This has discouraged some foreign investment, but not enough to make more than a slight dent in the statistics, partly because it applied only to securities and not to bank loans or to direct investment. In the spring of 1965 President Johnson tried to plug these loopholes by pushing a voluntary program under which both banks and nonfinancial corporations would reduce their foreign expenditures, principally on capital account. Compliance during the early months of this program was remarkably good, but whether it will continue for an extended period is somewhat more questionable.

On the other side of the coin, foreign capital has been attracted to this country by higher interest rates on short-term funds, by reduction of taxes on interest earned here by foreigners, and by attractive issues of United States government securities, some denominated in foreign currencies, which have been sold to foreign central banks. The result of these efforts is apparent in the high rate of foreign capital investment in this country.

But all these actions together have not brought the deficit down to manageable proportions, while the *long-run* effects of the shift in capital movements will be adverse in the sense that it tends to reduce our earnings from investments abroad, while increasing our payments to foreign creditors.

For the long run, therefore, the answer seems to lie in a further increase of the already large export balance of trade. That in turn means keeping our export products competitive in world markets and avoiding inflationary tendencies which would make them less attractive.

Meanwhile on the short-run front, not only have we taken a number of small actions ourselves, but also a considerable amount of international machinery has been established to strengthen the monetary mechanism in order to protect any currency, including the dollar, that finds itself in difficulty. These devices will be discussed in the next chapter.

We need always to bear in mind, however, that the underlying bases of world trade are real commodities and services and that no amount of monetary tinkering will be effective in the long run unless it corrects, or gives time to correct by other means, the physical aspects of trade. Any action that prevents necessary corrective steps from taking place will only perpetuate disequilibrium, though it may disguise it for the time being. The gold standard, for example, broke down primarily because nations were unwilling to let their internal prices adjust to the levels required to maintain international equilibrium. Nevertheless the proper monetary arrangements, effectively utilized, will provide a climate in which other forces can work most satisfactorily.

The Question of the Standard

There may be some advantage in attacking the problem of monetary standards negatively rather than positively. What is the matter with the devices that have so far been tried?

Exchange Controls and Convertibility. Perhaps the worst type of monetary system in terms of its interference with equilibrium is exchange control. Fortunately most countries have moved away from the depression-born and war-encouraged restrictions on foreign exchange transactions, but controls remain in a number of areas. Why?

Under exchange control any tendency toward an import surplus is combated by governmental rationing of scarce foreign exchange. When a nation abolishes the last vestiges of control, its currency becomes fully *convertible,* and any holder of that currency can exchange it for any foreign currency he wants, and vice versa. However, if such a nation continues to have a deficit in its foreign balance, the quantity of foreign currencies demanded will exceed the supply of them available at the current exchange rate, and most countries are not too happy at the alternatives that would face them under such circumstances: (1) If they maintain the value of their currency at its old level and support that par value by permitting holders of their currency to buy gold with it (thus in effect paying for their excess imports with gold), they are afraid of running out of gold; (2) they are unwilling to lower domestic prices to encourage exports; and (3) they do not wish to reduce the par value of their currency for several reasons. Devaluation may lower the esteem in which a nation is held. It upsets contractual obligations based on the former value and changes the patterns of trade. And perhaps most important of all, it worsens the *terms of trade*. This means that it will take more exports (physical volume) to buy fewer imports.

An example using assumed conditions will make this clear. Suppose that in Argentina the peso-dollar exchange rate is pegged at $1 = 20 pesos and that at this rate Argentina has a dollar shortage: there is a tendency for imports to exceed exports. By licensing imports under exchange control, however, the government limits their value to the value of exports. Suppose imports are homogeneous in nature and licenses are issued for 100 units costing $1 each in the United States. Assume also that exports are homogeneous and consist of 100 units costing 20 pesos each. Imports equal exports at $100 (or 2,000 pesos). Argentine importers would be willing to buy, say, 150 units at 20 pesos each if they could get the necessary exchange, but this they are prevented from doing by government controls.

Suppose then that exchange controls are removed. Importers rush to buy 150 units of imports, but this requires $150, while only $100 is available at the old rate, and the resulting pressure forces a devaluation of the peso to, say, $1 = 25 pesos. An imported article costing $1 in the United States, which used to be obtainable for 20 pesos, now costs 25. At this higher price the quantity bought falls; Argentina now imports, say, 120 units with a total value of $120 (or 3,000 pesos). At the same time the fall in price of pesos makes Argentine goods cheaper in the United States. An article costing 20 pesos can now be bought for 80 cents instead of $1. We increase our purchases to 150 units at 20 pesos each, a total value of 3,000 pesos (or $120). Trade is in equilibrium; no controls are needed. But the terms of trade have moved against Argentina. Where formerly she imported 100 units and paid for them by exporting 100 units, a relationship of 1 to 1, she now has to export 150 units to pay for an import of 120, so that it now takes 1¼ export units to buy one import unit. On the other hand, however, she would be increasing her consumption of imports by 20 per cent.

Exchange control with an artificially high exchange rate is therefore a device for raising the real-goods price that foreigners have to pay for a nation's exports. But in the process it denies importers the right to buy goods they want and therefore pushes consumption into channels that yield less satisfaction to the consumer. At the same time the governmental red tape involved is a burden that gives rise to considerable dissatisfaction as well as interference with the productive process.

On balance, therefore, even those few countries still clinging to controls are attempting to break away from them. But to what sort of a standard would they go?

A Return to Gold. Some nostalgic souls, including General de Gaulle, look wistfully back on the good old days of the gold standard and wish for its return. Not only does it seem to provide a real, hard base to the monetary system, something one can clutch in his hand, but it also presumably worked automatically, independently of the decisions of monetary authorities, via the price-specie flow mechanism.

The gold standard, however, is probably as dead as the dodo, and the plaintive voices calling for its resurrection sound like ghosts clanking their chains in the attic. The reasons for its demise, which have been examined at various places throughout this book, may be summarized briefly:

1. It is not as "traditional" as it is often assumed to be and has no more claim to be considered the "right" standard than any other. The test must be its usefulness, not its antiquity.
2. Its historical use is not an unbroken record of success. It has prevented neither depression (1929–1933) nor inflation (1918–1921).
3. It is therefore not automatic, since any program aimed at stability could not count on the gold mechanism alone to achieve it.
4. Domestically no nation is willing to entrust its monetary destiny to the vagaries of gold output and the discovery of new veins.
5. Internationally no nation is willing to relinquish control of its price structure to a mechanical force requiring adjustment to the ebbs and flows of world trade.

If the standard must be managed anyway, and if the managers can be trusted, it is better to remove the inhibitions that the gold standard produces. If the managers can't be trusted, then the system doesn't matter, since the record shows that they will debase gold coinage as readily as paper.

This is not to say that gold is useless. On the contrary it is still generally accepted for final payment of debt in international trade. It is valuable to have such an international money, and there seems to be no reason at present for interfering with this use. But gold movements do not require a gold standard. They are used even for countries that have a freely fluctuating exchange currency. Perhaps in time more satisfactory alternatives for settling final balances will be developed. *Gold earmark* (where ownership is transferred without the physical movement of gold) is a slight trend in that direction. This suggests the possibility of an international gold fund with custody of the world's monetary stocks, all "shipments" taking place through transfers on its books. But there is no point in hurrying the process just for the sake of change. Even without a gold standard, gold will be with us for a long time yet.

World Currency. Although they would consider themselves strange bedfellows, those who advocate a single world currency are very close in concept to the gold-standard devotees. They would substitute a single common money for the gold link that ties national moneys together. Their reasoning is that one cause of the preeminent industrial position of the United States is its single currency. They suggest that a single world currency would break down trade barriers and would facilitate trade throughout the world. The idea is attractive, but in the present state of world tension it is politically hopeless. We have enough trouble in this country deciding on what our monetary policy should be. Imagine the uproar that would ensue if the money supply and its control were in the hands of an international board.

A world federation might naturally produce a universal money, but as long as national antagonisms are as strong as they are (even between presumed friends), a common currency is too much to expect. Improving the political climate is a necessary preliminary task.

Freely Fluctuating Exchanges. At the other extreme are those who maintain that each country should mind its own currency and leave its neighbors alone, that the rate of exchange should be free to fluctuate like any other price according to the forces of supply and demand. The basic argument is that foreign traders, like any other buyers or sellers, are the best judges of their own market and that any governmental interference will introduce undesirable rigidities into the market.

The great advantage of a freely fluctuating rate is that it permits disequilibrating forces to be absorbed where they originate—on the foreign exchange market. It therefore does not transmit them to the price structure of the country except in the prices of specific import or export goods, and it consequently does not interfere with domestic price or employment policy. At the same time it requires no machinery for maintenance and no tinkering to keep it in adjustment.

To the argument that freely fluctuating exchange rates introduce uncertainty into foreign transactions, the advocates of freedom reply (1) that these fluctuations are not essentially different from the fluctuations of other prices such as those of rubber, wheat, or corporate stocks and (2) that the foreign trader as a specialist is adequately equipped to deal with such uncertainties by hedging or otherwise. Although freely fluctuating exchange markets are quite rare, Canada operated under one very satisfactorily for over a decade.

Whatever the validity of these arguments, very few people are willing to accept them. Perhaps the antipathy to a freely fluctuating exchange standard is traditional rather than intelligent, but it is nevertheless strong. The possibility needs much more discussion than it has had, but meanwhile it seems clear that such a standard does not stand much chance of general adoption in the foreseeable future.

Modified Gold Standard. What does that leave? Most of the world today is on a domestically inconvertible, international gold bullion standard under the supervision of the International Monetary Fund. This was designed in an attempt to provide much of the stability of the gold standard without its undesired interference with domestic price structures, and we will examine it in detail in the next chapter. One of its greatest assets is its almost universal acceptance, for any standard works more effectively if nations are determined to cooperate to ensure its success.

Economic Development

Economic development and international investment are more than casually related to monetary standards. The desire to live beyond one's income is widespread, and exchange control sometimes seems on the surface to offer an opportunity to do just that—to solve the dollar shortage more or less painlessly. But the long-run solution must lie in other directions. Economic development is the best answer, not only to the dollar shortage, but to poverty and hunger as well.

For underdeveloped countries poverty and lack of productive facilities are a vicious circle. With a standard of living that presses on physical subsistence it is almost impossible for such a nation to save. Without saving there is no means of obtaining funds for investment. In the absence of investment, industrial development proceeds at a crawl, and without increased productivity the standard of living of the country remains low.

It is obviously possible to squeeze out of this circle—as is demonstrated by the fact that we don't all still live in caves—but the process may be slow or painful or both. The Industrial Revolution took over a century to change the face of England. In the Soviet Union the process has been speeded up by forced saving—by the government taxing away from the people the necessary funds. These sums are then channeled into heavy industry, which will eventually produce a much higher standard of living but which, through six Five-Year Plans, kept the populace in relative poverty, out of which they began to emerge only in the sixties.

There is, however, another way in which the circle can be broken. If the savings can be borrowed from abroad, the process of industrialization can be financed out of *future* saving rather than from past (or present) accumulations; and in the future, saving will be easier as industrialization raises the level of income. We sometimes forget that the United States grew this way. A fair amount of capital for our development came from Britain and France, financing our import balance of goods and services during much of the nineteenth century. The railroads are perhaps the most striking example of foreign capital participation, but they are by no means the only one.

The underdeveloped nations of Asia, Africa, and South America hope to be able to do the same thing. Loans from the more developed nations would not correct their shortage of foreign exchange today but would help to eliminate it in the future by contributing to increased production. With more goods produced domestically the nations involved would be less dependent on foreign products and could reduce their imports without tightening their belts still further. At the same time they would probably be able to expand their export markets, thus squeezing their adverse balance of payments from both ends. In the process their national income would rise, making more saving possible and thus permitting internal financing to take the place of foreign loans.

The problems that arise in economic development are exceedingly complex ones about which volumes could be (and have been) written. We can barely scratch the surface here.

Development projects themselves present many difficulties. It is not enough to want a steel mill. Power and raw materials must be obtained; transportation facilities must be available; a work force must be recruited and trained to do a new, sometimes socially revolutionary, sort of work. The whole economic and social structure must be reoriented toward a different manner of living. This is no easy task; in some cases it may not even be desirable. Various aspects of these structural problems are currently receiving considerable attention, not only from the underdeveloped countries themselves, but also from various other agencies, national and international.

Assuming that certain projects have been accepted as both desirable and feasible, the next step is obtaining the funds. Theoretically this is easy. In terms of supply and demand, investors will make their funds available to borrowers offering the highest interest rate—other things being equal. In international lending other things are never equal, and there are many barriers to the international flow of capital just as there are to the international flow of goods. Some of these are technical, such as the difficulties of language, the lack of institutions for channeling funds into their most useful job, the differences in the types of securities to which nationals of different countries are accustomed, and the complexities of overlapping tax jurisdictions.

Sometimes the difficulties arise from a fear on the part of the borrowing nation that investment will mean exploitation. This has frequently led to restrictions on the form that investment may take. In particular the underdeveloped nations prefer bond financing to stock issues or direct investment in order to assure themselves that control will remain with their own nationals rather than with foreigners. Where stock ownership is permitted, it is often limited to a minority interest for the same reason. These arrangements may discourage certain types of investors.

A third set of barriers lies in the risk of loss. Any kind of investment is risky, but foreign investment has more than its share of uncertainties. The risk of expropriation is perhaps the greatest. Others include restrictions on transfer of profits under exchange-control legislation, the possibility of exchange depreciation, the difficulties of protecting one's rights through an international lawsuit, and misunderstandings that arise from differing laws and customs. At the same time many underdeveloped nations are unwilling or unable to pay the higher interest costs that the greater risk requires.

To some extent governments have attempted to overcome these various difficulties. On occasion the governments of underdeveloped countries have given special concessions to foreign investors or have guaranteed them against expropriation. The United States has provided a measure of tax relief for income earned abroad and has also established an insurance program under which, for a fee, United States investors can under certain circumstances insure themselves against losses due to expropriation or exchange depreciation. All these measures, however, have been of relatively minor importance.

As a result private investment in underdeveloped countries has not met the needs and aspirations of the peoples involved. The tremendous growth of communications has brought home to them the grave disparity between their living standards and those of their neighbors, and they want to share in this prosperity. Private investment has helped some. It has been supplemented by vast amounts of governmental assistance, not only from the United States but also from other industrialized nations, and by various international agencies. These also we will examine in the following chapter.

Questions for Thought and Discussion

1. Under what circumstances will a rise in the national income of the United States cause a fall in national income abroad? Under what circumstances will it cause a rise in national income abroad?

2. Why are government loans abroad counted as part of net foreign investment, while government gifts are not? Are the sources of the funds different?

3. In what ways is the purchase of a foreign bond similar to the construction of a domestic factory?

4. Wesley Mitchell found a correlation between business cycles in the United States and those in other countries as far back as 1800. Why should this be so?

5. It has been suggested that a country might cure an import surplus by emigration. How would this help?

6. Do you see any possibility of ever returning to a pure gold standard?

7. Under a single world government what would happen to international trade? To exchange rates? Would there be any net foreign investment? Why?

8. Are the disadvantages of a freely fluctuating exchange market confined to the fact that it produces uncertainty in trade? Is this a really serious drawback?

9. Why should the richest nation in the world be worried about a deficit in its balance of payments? Would a freely fluctuating exchange rate cure the deficit? How? Would this be desirable?

10. One theory of economic development says that it is impossible without exploitation: in the United States the "robber barons" exploited both labor and consumers to build up industrial empires, while the Soviet Union does it by overtaxing the consumer. Are these descriptions accurate? Are there other ways in which development may be financed? Where will the savings come from?

11. Suppose one wanted to build a steel mill on the upper reaches of the Amazon. What problems would have to be solved first?

12. What ways might be used to stimulate private investment in underdeveloped nations? Why isn't a high interest rate sufficient inducement?

Selected Bibliography

Aubrey, Henry C.: *The Dollar in World Affairs: An Essay in International Financial Policy,* published for the Council on Foreign Relations by Harper & Row, Publishers, Incorporated, New York, 1964.

Basch, Antonin: *Financing Economic Development,* The Macmillan Company, New York, 1964.

Buchanan, Norman S., and Howard S. Ellis: *Approaches to Economic Development,* The Twentieth Century Fund, New York, 1955.

Chandler, Lester V.: *Central Banking and Economic Development,* Allied Publishers Private, Ltd., Bombay, 1962.

Einzig, Paul: *The Euro-dollar System: Practice and Theory of International Interest Rates,* Macmillan & Co., Ltd., London, 1964.

Hansen, Alvin H.: *America's Role in the World Economy,* W. W. Norton & Company, Inc., New York, 1945.

Harris, Seymour E. (ed.): *The Dollar in Crisis,* Harcourt, Brace & World, Inc., New York, 1961.

Hinshaw, Randall: *Toward European Convertibility,* International Finance Section, Princeton University, Princeton, N.J., 1958.

Jacobsson, Per: *International Monetary Problems, 1952–63: Selected Speeches,* International Monetary Fund, Washington, 1964.

Johnson, Harry G.: *International Trade and Economic Growth: Studies in Pure Theory,* Harvard University Press, Cambridge, Mass., 1959.

Kenen, Peter B.: *British Monetary Policy and the Balance of Payments, 1951–1957,* Harvard University Press, Cambridge, Mass., 1960.

Kindleberger, Charles P.: *The Dollar Shortage,* John Wiley & Sons, Inc., New York, 1950.

Lewis, Cleona: *The United States and Foreign Investment Problems,* The Brookings Institution, Washington, 1948.

Machlup, Fritz: *International Trade and the National Income Multiplier,* McGraw-Hill Book Company, New York, 1943.

Mason, Edward H.: *Economic Planning in Underdeveloped Areas,* Fordham University Press, New York, 1958.

Nevin, E.: *Capital Funds in Underdeveloped Countries: The Role of Financial Institutions,* St Martin's Press, Inc., New York, 1961.

Nurkse, Ragnar: *Problems of Capital Formation in Underdeveloped Countries,* Basil Blackwell & Mott, Ltd., Oxford, 1953.

Sohmen, Egon: *International Monetary Problems and the Foreign Exchanges,* International Finance Section, Princeton University, Princeton, N.J., 1963.

Tinbergen, Jan: *The Design of Development,* The Johns Hopkins Press, Baltimore, 1958.

Villard, Henry: *Economic Development,* Holt, Rinehart and Winston, Inc., New York, 1959.

Chapter 39 International Economic Cooperation

Nation shall not lift up sword against nation,
neither shall they learn war any more.

Isaiah 2: 4

The growing interdependence of the world and the increasing complexity of financial processes suggest the need for finding new ways of facilitating international cooperation for the solution of mutual problems. Wars in particular leave their aftermath of confusion and indirectly encourage the search for better financial arrangements—to clear up the mess left by the last war and perhaps to help prevent the next one.

Bank for International Settlements

Such an institution is the Bank for International Settlements (BIS), a regional European attempt to improve monetary relationships. Formed ostensibly to solve the problem of German reparations left over from World War I, the BIS grew out of a widespread concern over the failure of the gold standard to work as well as it should and a belief that greater cooperation among central banks was necessary.

The Bank was established by an international conference in 1929 not only to act as trustee for the handling of German reparations funds, but also to serve as a central bank for central banks, accepting and transferring deposits of gold and currencies and making loans to countries temporarily in need of foreign exchange.

Although the Bank's statutes are a matter of international treaty,[1] it is technically a corporation chartered under Swiss law and having its office in Basel, Switzerland. It is a commercial organization in that it must remain solvent through its own activities, and it pays dividends to its stockholders. Yet its primary objective is not profit, but the maintenance of sound international monetary relationships.

Its stockholders include all the central banks of Europe with the exception of Spain and the Soviet Union.[2] Five of its thirteen directors are, by statute, the governors of the central banks of Belgium, France, Germany, Great Britain, and Italy. An additional five are chosen by these governors from among their compatriots, and there are three further directors from the Netherlands, Sweden, and Switzerland.

The United States was invited to join and to provide two directors, but the Federal Reserve has failed to do so. Certain United States nationals have served on the board in an unofficial capacity, and during 1930–1935 and 1940–1946 the president of the Bank was an American. Lately even this unofficial link between the Bank and the United States has been lacking. The Federal Reserve, however, carries on business relations with the Bank and now regularly sends observers to its meetings.

Perhaps the greatest contribution the BIS has made is through the monthly meetings of its board of directors, consisting as it does of the most important central bankers of Europe. The informal consultations of these men may well be more important in molding the course of European banking than the official actions of the board.

The Bank is small. Its original capital was 500 million Swiss gold francs (a unit of account for which there is no present coined equivalent, currently worth 33 cents), of which only 25 per cent was paid in. In current dollars its total assets are about $2 billion—less than that of any one of half a dozen commercial banks in New York.

All member banks keep accounts of one kind or another with the BIS, either in gold or in their own currencies. It was originally hoped that most of the world's gold would be deposited with the BIS as international custodian of the gold standard. In order to facilitate this movement a large number of governments provided by treaty that they would maintain inviolate any assets of the BIS within their territory in peace or war.

The breakdown of the gold standard little more than a year after the Bank began operations in May, 1930, blasted any hope of much progress in this direction. However, the Bank devised a number of ingenious schemes for transferring currencies, and although its role was curtailed by the avalanche of exchange controls that characterized the thirties, it proved its value in facilitating certain kinds of payments. The Bank became, for instance, the agent of the Universal Postal Union and of the International Committee of

[1] Among Germany and the principal reparations creditors—Belgium, France, Great Britain, Italy, and Japan—plus Switzerland as the host country.

[2] Some of the stock (about 25 per cent) has been sold to private individuals, but the right to vote remains with the central bank that originally subscribed to the stock.

the Red Cross, effecting transfers for those agencies according to their rules. It also loaned funds to central banks faced with temporary shortages of foreign exchange. The war further restricted its activity, but its postwar expansion has been substantial.

BIS operations still center on its role as a bank for central banks. Its deposits, mostly for the accounts of central banks, amounted to $1.8 billion in 1964.[3] Its assets include $0.8 billion in gold and $1.1 billion in loans and investments. Total assets have doubled since 1959 and are twenty times their level in 1947.

The Bank's activities as agent for various international organizations are also growing. Since the war, new agency activities include those for the Marshall Plan and its successor programs in Europe, the Organization for European Economic Cooperation (now the Organization for Economic Cooperation and Development), and the European Community (Coal and Steel, Euratom, and the Common Market). More recently the BIS has been the focal point for a number of cooperative actions designed to strengthen the international monetary system, particularly the currency swap arrangements discussed later in this chapter.

The Bank also has a strong research department that prepares special studies for member banks as well as keeping its finger steadily on the pulse of the world's business. Yearly this knowledge is distilled in the Bank's *Annual Report,* which is widely read as a penetrating analysis of current world economic conditions.

Although small, the BIS is growing, and its influence is unlikely to diminish in the foreseeable future. Conceivably it could form the prototype of a world central bank, but such a development is hardly possible under present political conditions.

The Postwar Muddle

While the BIS grew out of one world war, a second brought an even greater legacy of monetary confusion, following, as it did, on the heels of grave depression. Starting in 1930 nationalism and acute depression wove a spiral of increasing restrictions and decreasing trade. The war intensified the process, and almost everyone agreed that drastic action was needed after the war to reverse this gloomy trend.

Lord Keynes pointed out in 1943 that the attack on the problem would have to be mounted along four fronts simultaneously:

1. The mechanism of currency and exchange.
2. The framework of a commercial policy regulating conditions for exchange of goods, tariffs, preferences, subsidies, import regulations and the like.

[3] The Bank's balance sheet excludes gold held under earmark, securities held in custody for the account of others, and funds held under trust agreements. These items amount to some $0.8 billion.

3. Orderly conduct of production, distribution and price of primary products so as to protect both producers and consumers from the loss and risk for which extravagant fluctuations of market conditions have been responsible in recent times.
4. Investment aid, both medium and long term, for countries whose economic development needs assistance from outside.[4]

All four approaches have been pressed. The International Monetary Fund is concerned with the first; the General Agreement on Tariffs and Trade with the second. Progress in the third has been limited, but some work has been done with commodity agreements. The last job has been tackled by the International Bank for Reconstruction and Development and a growing number of other governmental and private agencies.

While all approaches are necessarily interrelated, we have time here to examine only the predominantly monetary ones, the first and the last.

International Monetary Policy

The automatic gold standard collapsed, and not many mourners pray for its resurrection. A freely fluctuating exchange standard has never had many admirers. Exchange control, almost universal at the close of the war, was snatched at in desperation and satisfied no one, for it places the heavy hand of government control on trade and reduces much of the economic advantage of multilateral exchange.

International Monetary Fund. The primary purpose of the International Monetary Fund (IMF) was to produce some order out of this chaos by establishing a stable exchange market and at the same time helping countries with an adverse balance of trade to finance their purchases without the need for exchange control.

Structure. The Fund was established by international treaty signed by forty-three nations at Bretton Woods in July, 1944. It is an international organization subject to the will of the governments that are its members. The Soviet Union, which signed the original treaty, never ratified it, Poland withdrew (1950) in a dispute over the policies of the Fund, and Czechoslovakia was expelled (1954) for failure to provide information required by the Articles of Agreement. On the other hand, each year has seen additions to membership. As of June, 1965, there were 102 member nations, including all the major countries of the world outside the Soviet sphere of influence.[5]

Each member is assigned a quota, which measures roughly (very roughly since considerable political horse trading entered into the actual determination) the relative importance of each nation in world trade. These quotas are shown in Table 39-1 (pages 776–779). They serve three functions:

[4] *International Clearing Union* (British Information Services, Apr. 8, 1943), p. 3.
[5] The outstanding exception is Switzerland.

1. They represent the amount of the member's subscription to the Fund. The total of $16 billion is therefore the amount of money that the Fund has as working capital.[6] Each country must pay 25 per cent of its quota in gold[7] and the remainder in its own currency. This gives the Fund a stock of currencies of all members plus a large pool of gold that can be exchanged for any currency.[8]
2. The quotas determine approximately the number of votes that the member has in the affairs of the Fund. The correlation is not exact, for voting is weighted somewhat in favor of the smaller countries. Thus the United States quota of $4,125 million is 26 per cent of the total, but our voting power is only 23 per cent of the entire vote.
3. Quotas determine the borrowing limits of members, a matter to be discussed presently.

Member governments select governors, who attend the annual meeting of the Fund in September and constitute its highest governing body. Between meetings power is vested in a board of executive directors. There are nineteen at present: five representing the five nations with the largest quotas,[9] and the other fourteen elected by member nations grouped geographically. Thus Burma, Ceylon, Japan, Nepal, and Thailand elect one executive director; Central America is entitled to one; and so on. The post of executive director is a full-time paid job. Day-to-day operation of the Fund is carried on by a managing director and a professional staff, numbering almost six hundred and representing fifty-nine nationalities. The main office is in Washington.

Operations. The work of the Fund falls into the following categories:

1. Financial machinery
   a. Establishing par values
   b. Lending of currencies
   c. Changes in par values
2. Consultation and cooperation

1*a. Initial par values.* As a first step in providing the kind of exchange stability that existed under the gold standard, the Fund establishes, in consultation with the member involved, an initial par value for each member's currency

[6] The figure was raised 50 per cent (from $9¼ billion) in 1959 because of the growing volume of world trade. Other increases have resulted as new members have joined.
[7] Or 10 per cent of its holdings of gold and United States dollars, whichever is less.
[8] It must be remembered that in international finance "currency" does not mean bills and coin. The Fund's currency holdings consist of balances on deposit to its account in the central banks of the countries concerned, plus non-interest-bearing securities payable in such deposits on demand.
[9] United States, United Kingdom, France, Germany, and India.

as a given weight of gold.[10] This automatically provides a mint parity between any pair of member currencies. Thus the dollar is defined as 0.888,671 *grams* of fine gold,[11] while the British pound contains 2.488,28 grams of gold. The ratio between the two is thus 0.888,671:2.488,28, or £1 = $2.80.[12]

Members of the Fund therefore adhere to the first requirement of the gold standard. They do not, however, necessarily provide internal convertibility between their currencies and gold nor permit gold movements to take place freely. Because gold movements are in many cases not free and because such movements as do take place are not permitted to affect domestic price levels as they were supposed to do under the automatic gold standard, they are not the means of restoring equilibrium once it is disturbed. For this the Fund provides two remedies, one short-run and one long-run.

1*b*. *Lending foreign exchange.* In order to enable a member to meet an adverse (import) balance of trade when the nation involved does not have sufficient foreign reserves to pay for its imports, the Fund makes its own stock of currencies available under specified conditions. The articles refer to this transaction as a *sale,* but it has most of the characteristics of a loan and is frequently so called.

Suppose Italy finds that, because of seasonal or other temporary factors, her exports are insufficient to pay for her imports. She needs additional foreign exchange, let us say dollars. She can buy dollars from the Fund with lire, paying for them at the mint parity plus a service charge of ½ per cent. But once having obtained the dollars she must pay interest on them and eventually pay them back. In practice, therefore, the transaction resembles a loan for which she has to put up lire as collateral.

The quantity of funds that a nation may borrow and the interest rate she has to pay depend on her quota. Basically the rule is that no member may borrow more than 25 per cent of its quota in any one year nor may its total outstanding loans exceed its full quota plus the amount of its initial gold contribution.[13] The Fund has the right to waive these limitations under special circumstances and has done so in a large number of recent cases.

Because the purpose of these Fund transactions is to tide a nation over temporary difficulties, it is expected that the currencies borrowed will be repaid fairly soon. The interest rate charged increases progressively the longer the loan remains unpaid. It rises also as the loan increases in size relative to the quota. Thus the larger the loan and the longer it is kept, the higher the cost to the borrower. In addition to this pressure on the pocketbook the Fund

[10] The Articles of Agreement read "in terms of gold as a common denominator or in terms of the United States dollar of the weight and fineness in effect on July 1, 1944" (art. 4, sec. 1), but since the dollar was itself defined as a given weight of gold, definitions in gold and in dollars are mathematically equivalent.

[11] This is the same as 13⅐ *grains.*

[12] One ounce of gold = $35 = £12½.

[13] The limit may be increased if other nations are simultaneously borrowing its currency. The technicalities are not important enough to examine here.

Table 39-1. Structure and Operation of International Financial Agencies, December 31, 1964

Millions of U.S. Dollars

Member	International Monetary Fund				International Bank for Reconstruction and Development			International Finance Corporation		International Development Association	
	Quota*	Total drawings by member	Member's currency drawn by others	Member's net fund position†	Subscription	Loans made	Loans outstanding	Subscription	Total commitments	Subscription	Credits extended
Afghanistan	29.0	11.2		−11.2	30.0			.111		1.01	3.50
Algeria	75.0				80.0	20.5	20.2			4.03	
Argentina	350.0	377.5	16.0	−190.0	373.3	143.5	142.6	1.662	13.710	18.83	
Australia	500.0	225.0		0.0	533.0	417.7	194.5	2.215	.975	20.18‡	
Austria	175.0		73.0	+53.5	100.0	106.3	70.0	.554		5.04‡	
Belgium	422.0	83.0	236.4	+116.5	450.0	200.8	40.7	2.492			
Bolivia	29.0	22.4		−5.0	21.0			.078		1.06	15.00
Brazil	350.0	428.4		−139.0	373.3	292.1	184.8	1.163	11.300	18.83	
Burma	38.0	15.0		0.0	40.0	33.4	25.8	.166		2.02	
Burundi	15.0				15.0					.76	
Cameroon	19.0				20.0					1.01	
Canada	740.0	300.0	199.0	+60.0	750.0			3.600		37.83‡	
Central African Rep.	10.0				10.0					.50	
Ceylon	78.0	22.5		−22.5	60.0	41.5	33.2	.166		3.03	
Chad	10.0				10.0					.50	
Chile	125.0	199.7		−126.0	93.3	136.6	107.6	.388	8.954	3.53	19.00
China, Rep. of	690.0				750.0	22.8	6.8			30.26	15.30
Colombia	125.0	168.5		−108.5	93.3	389.0	318.1	.388	11.870	3.53	19.50
Congo (Brazzaville)	10.0				10.0					.50	
Congo (Leopoldville)	57.0				60.0					3.02	
Costa Rica	25.0	21.2		−11.7	8.0§	47.8	40.4	.022	.270	.20	5.50
Cyprus	15.0	2.0		−2.0	15.0	21.0	19.3	.083		.76	
Dahomey	10.0				10.0					.50	
Denmark	163.0	44.2	0.8	+0.8	173.3	85.0	44.7	.753		8.74‡	
Dominican Republic	32.0	24.0		−15.0	8.0§			.022		.40	

Ecuador	25.0	23.0		−2.0	17.0	55.6	41.8	.035		.65	8.00
El Salvador	25.0	29.2		0.0	10.7	51.0	35.9	.011	.140	.30	8.00
Ethiopia	19.0	0.6		0.0	10.0	51.9	44.0	.033	2.500	.50	13.50
Finland	125.0	9.5		0.0	76.0	187.8	119.2	.421	2.348	3.83‡	
France	985.0	518.8	835.8	+421.9	1,050.0	418.5	49.3	5.815		52.96‡	
Gabon	10.0				10.0	12.0	0.0			.50	
Germany, Fed. Rep. of	1,200.0		1,490.9	+715.6	1,050.0			3.655		52.96‡	
Ghana	69.0	14.2		−14.2	46.7	47.0	46.9	.166		2.36	
Greece	75.0				50.0			.277	2.101	2.52	
Guatemala	25.0	5.0		0.0	8.0	18.2	8.8	.022	.200	.40	
Guinea	19.0				20.0						
Haiti	15.0	18.2		−8.8	15.0	2.6	1.5	.022		.76	.35
Honduras	19.0	30.0		−10.0	6.0§	20.0	14.2	.011	.350	.30	9.00
Iceland	15.0	6.8		0.0	15.0	7.9	5.2	.011		.10	
India	750.0	575.0		−200.1	800.0	876.1	629.1	4.431	10.865	40.35	485.00
Indonesia	207.0	172.5		−102.5	220.0						
Iran	125.0	121.0		−17.5	90.0	212.7	118.8	.372	.300	4.54	
Iraq	69.0				15.0	12.8	0.0	.067		.76	
Ireland	80.0				60.0			.332		3.03	
Israel	90.0	16.2		0.0	66.6	74.5	70.6	.050		1.68	
Italy	625.0	225.0	279.6	+21.4	360.0§	299.6	131.7	1.994	.960	18.16‡	
Ivory Coast	19.0				20.0			.111		1.01	
Jamaica	25.0				26.7			.148	.224		
Japan	725.0	249.0	134.0	+95.0	666.0	637.9	522.5	2.769		33.59‡	
Jordan	15.0				15.0			.033		.30	8.50
Kenya	32.0				33.3			.184		1.68	7.30
Korea	24.0				25.0			.139		1.26	14.00
Kuwait	63.0				66.7			.369		3.36‡	
Laos	10.0				10.0					.50	
Lebanon	9.0				9.0	27.0	23.6	.050		.45	
Liberia	15.0	7.4		−7.4	15.0	3.3	3.3	.083		.76	
Libya	19.0				20.0			.055		1.01	
Luxembourg	19.0				20.0	12.0	0.0	.111		.38‡	
Malagasy Republic	19.0				20.0	95.5	84.1	.111		1.01	
Malaysia	125.0				50.0			.277	1.308	2.52	
Mali	17.0	5.0		−5.0	17.3					.87	
Mauritania	10.0				10.0					.50	6.70

(*Table continues*)

Table 39-1. Structure and Operation of International Financial Agencies, December 31, 1964 ***Continued***

Millions of U.S. Dollars

	International Monetary Fund				International Bank for Reconstruction and Development			International Finance Corporation		International Development Association	
Member	Quota*	Total drawings by member	Member's currency drawn by others	Member's net fund position†	Subscription	Loans made	Loans outstanding	Subscription	Total commitments	Subscription	Credits extended
Mexico	270.0	112.5		0.0	173.3	458.8	364.1	.720	15.470	8.74	
Morocco	66.0	13.1		−13.1	70.0	32.5	15.0	.388	1.496	3.53	
Nepal	10.0				10.0					.50	
Netherlands	520.0	144.1	363.0	+161.7	550.0	244.0	0.0	3.046		27.74‡	
New Zealand	157.0				166.7	40.3	33.6	.923			
Nicaragua	15.0	37.4		−11.2	6.0	38.1	23.4	.009		.30	3.00
Niger	10.0				10.0					.50	1.50
Nigeria	63.0				66.7	125.5	40.7	.369	2.170	3.36	
Norway	150.0	9.6		0.0	133.3	145.0	96.8	.554		6.72‡	
Pakistan	188.0	12.5		0.0	200.0	361.4	285.9	1.108	7.506	10.09	242.79
Panama	15.0				.4§	18.6	10.4	.002		.02	
Paraguay	15.0	8.1		−0.5	6.0	7.2	0.0	.016		.30	9.60
Peru	47.0	14.5		0.0	35.0	138.4	93.7	.194	8.913	1.77	
Philippines	110.0	58.3		−28.3	100.0	108.4	92.8	.166	4.359	5.04	
Portugal	75.0				80.0	12.5	11.8				
Rwanda	15.0				15.0					.76	
Saudi Arabia	90.0				73.3			.111		3.70	
Senegal	32.0				33.3			.184		1.68	
Sierra Leone	15.0				15.0	3.8	3.6	.083		.76	
Somalia	15.0	4.7		−4.7	15.0			.083		.76	
South Africa	200.0	83.7		0.0	200.0	221.8	50.5	1.108		10.09‡	
Spain	250.0	50.0	79.0	+69.0	200.0	98.0	31.3	1.108	3.812	10.09	
Sudan	57.0	11.7		−5.4	20.0	74.0	66.7	.111	.689	1.01	13.00
Sweden	188.0		89.5	+50.0	200.0			1.108		10.09‡	
Syrian Arab Republic	38.0	39.1		−31.1	33.3			.072		.95	8.50

Tanzania	32.0				33.3			.184	4.731	1.68	18.60
Thailand	95.0				60.0	203.9	133.8	.139	.493	3.03	
Togo	15.0				15.0			.083		.76	
Trinidad and Tobago	25.0				26.7						
Tunisia	29.0	5.2		−5.2	30.0	7.0	0.0	.133	3.500	1.51	5.00
Turkey	108.0	145.0		−55.5	115.0	63.4	35.0	.476	.917	5.80	
Uganda	32.0				33.3			.184		1.68	55.70
United Arab Republic	150.0	191.2		−138.7	106.6§	56.5	47.2	.590		5.08	
United Kingdom	2,440.0	3,361.5	622.0	−998.4	2,600.0	287.2	125.5	14.400		131.14‡	6.40
United States	5,160.0	525.0	4,609.9	−230.8	6,350.0			35.168		320.29‡	
Upper Volta	10.0				10.0					.50	
Uruguay	38.0	15.0		−15.0	10.5§	89.5	67.7				
Venezuela	250.0				140.0	174.0	165.1	.116	4.979		
Vietnam	29.0				30.0					1.51	
Yugoslavia	150.0	136.9		−75.0	106.7	260.7	168.7			4.04	
	20,984.0	9,028.9	9,028.9	−2,621.4 +1,765.4	21,186.0	8,352.2	5,162.7	98.964	127.408	987.45	1,002.24

* These are the new quotas proposed in 1965. They will go into effect individually when each country approves of the increase in its own quota. In most cases the new quota is 25 per cent higher than the former quota; in others it is somewhat larger than this. The total of the former quotas (Dec. 31, 1964) was $16,092.75 million.
† Negative amounts represent member's drawings less both repayments and drawings of the member's currency by others. Positive amounts represent drawings by others in that member's currency less repayments. Total negative and positive positions are unequal primarily because of transactions in gold.
‡ Additional subscriptions in a total amount of $377.6 million are in process of completion for these countries.
§Part I members; the others are Part II members.

Sources: *International Financial News Survey* (IMF), vol. 17, no. 9 (Mar. 5, 1965), p. 87; *International Financial Statistics*, vol. 18, no. 2 (February, 1965), pp. 6, 7; International Bank for Reconstruction and Development, *Annual Report: 1963-64*, pp. 66–67, 82–83; International Bank for Reconstruction and Development, "Statement of Loans, December 31, 1964" (mimeographed); International Development Association, "Statement of Development Credits, December 31, 1964" (mimeographed); International Finance Corporation, *Eighth Annual Report: 1963-1964*, p. 52; International Finance Corporation, "Facts about IFC as of December 31, 1964" (mimeographed).

adds moral suasion in an attempt to prevent nations from using its facilities as a source of long-term capital.

The disequilibrium bred by the war (predominantly the "dollar shortage") provided wide scope for the Fund's lending operations, and it rushed into the battle with great energy only to find that the forces of disequilibrium were too great to be conquered in one blow. Exhausted it sank into a state of quiescence, abandoning almost all economic activity for several years. During this period its basic policy was to refuse all help to any nation still maintaining exchange controls, and this meant just about every one that needed help. In 1956 Per Jacobsson, former economic adviser to the Bank for International Settlements, came to the Fund as managing director and inaugurated a policy of active aid to any nation seriously trying to eliminate controls. As a result the Fund is now playing a much more positive role in international finance. Table 39-1 shows that members had "purchased" (borrowed) $7.5 billion of foreign currencies since the Fund began operations; five-sixths of this was obtained after 1955.

But, as already mentioned, these loans are intended to be temporary, and in fact borrowers have already paid back over 70 per cent of the amount borrowed, thus making funds available for relending to others. Repayment assumes that the disequilibrium that led to the borrowing has been corrected, allowing the member to accumulate a stock of the borrowed currency. What if disequilibrium persists?

1*c. Changes in par values.* In case of a "fundamental disequilibrium"—a phrase never defined but roughly equivalent to a permanent imbalance in trade under existing exchange rates—the articles permit a nation to change the par value of its currency. Before doing so the member must consult with the Fund, and if the change is more than 10 per cent from the initial par value, the Fund must give its consent.

Suppose Italy's import balance appears to be chronic. There is downward pressure on the foreign value of the lira, but since it is tied to all other currencies through its gold parity, the price can't fall. Italy will lose gold, but domestic policies prevent a fall of internal prices. The gap is temporarily closed by borrowing. This doesn't solve the underlying problem, which is that Italian prices are too high to make her goods attractive abroad. The lira is overvalued, and devaluation seems called for. By making lire cheaper, devaluation reduces the price of Italian goods in all other countries at the same time that it makes imports into Italy more expensive. The resulting increase in exports and decrease in imports should reduce the disequilibrium.

A number of devaluations have been approved by the Fund, the most notable occurring in 1949, when Great Britain devalued the pound by 30 per cent, and many other countries followed. This didn't eliminate the dollar shortage—perhaps because the new rates were not the "right" ones—but it certainly reduced it.

Devaluation is a drastic step, but it is felt that under the control of the Fund its disadvantages can be kept to a minimum, it will be employed only as a last resort, and it will take place within a framework of international cooperation and consultation instead of at the whim of a single nation. The idea has not worked perfectly in practice,[14] but what system is perfect? In view of the almost universal dislike of both the uncertainties of a freely fluctuating exchange market and the internal price adjustments forced by an automatic gold standard, the Fund is generally accepted today as a reasonable compromise.

2. *Consultation.* In some respects the financial transactions of the Fund may be less important than the principles for which it stands and the cooperation that it elicits from members. Each nation promised in signing the agreement that it would not increase its monetary barriers to trade and that it would attempt to eliminate all exchange control as soon as possible. The articles assumed that a transition period of five years after the war would be sufficient for nations to overcome the abnormal strains of the war and to return to a pattern of freer multilateral trade.

It has taken considerably longer than that, but control has become progressively less rigorous. Annually since 1950 the Fund has consulted with members concerning the advisability and possibility of moving toward freer markets. These consultations have undoubtedly been one factor in the movement away from exchange control, and today only a few countries maintain more than a small remnant of the previous vast fabric of restrictions.

The general return of convertibility is itself a sign of improvement in both monetary and general economic conditions throughout the world. As inflation has been licked in one country after another—partly through increased production, partly through more effective monetary controls and a determined attempt to bring government budgets more nearly into balance—exports of the former deficit countries have expanded, and they have felt less need for the rigorous limitation of imports inherent in exchange control.

International Liquidity. On the other hand, progress has not been as smooth as might be hoped. Many of the underdeveloped countries have never achieved international balance, and even the industrialized countries have their problems. Britain continues to suffer from crises of confidence in sterling every few years, several other European countries have developed weaknesses at one time or another, and the United States deficit since 1958 has already been mentioned.

There has never been a time when steps to strengthen the international monetary system have not been discussed. One of the basic fears at the present time is that there simply isn't enough international money to transact the world's business. Although in the first instance international payments are made primarily through bank credits, as explained in Chapter 36, there must be some ultimate internationally accepted means of settling net balances for countries whose trade is not in equilibrium.[15] Or, to put the matter another

[14] Several nations have failed to live up to the Articles of Agreement. For instance, France devalued the franc in 1948 in the face of Fund disapproval, and Canada set her dollar free in 1951 with no par value at all.

[15] At least as long as exchange rates are not freely fluctuating.

way, a nation that accumulates sizable quantities of a foreign currency (through an export balance) will want to redeem it in some more desirable form. The fundamental international money, and therefore the base of any nation's international reserves, is gold. But the world's gold stock has been growing much less rapidly than world trade. So nations, like banks, have developed a secondary line of defense in the form of liquid assets (in the international sense) to supplement their gold stock. The emphasis these days, then, has shifted from gold alone to the more inclusive concept of *international liquidity,* which "consists of all the resources that are available to the monetary authorities of countries for the purpose of meeting balance of payments deficits."[16]

Although there is no complete agreement as to what should be included as part of international liquidity and although the data on actual amounts of some types of reserves are incomplete, Table 39-2 gives one analysis of the world's total liquidity (on a somewhat conservative definition) in 1953 and 1963. It is interesting to note that four of the categories listed did not even exist in 1953. Not only has each of the remaining four increased in quantity, but there have been qualitative changes as well.

Table 39-2. Official Reserves and Credit Facilities of All Countries, 1953 and 1963

Billions of U.S. Dollars Equivalent

	Dec. 31, 1953		Dec. 31, 1963		Change	
Reserves:						
Gold	34.32		40.20		+5.88	
Foreign exchange	17.11		25.07		+7.96	
IMF gold tranche	1.89		3.94		+2.05	
Special U.S. bonds	0		0.71		+0.71	
Swaps used	0		0.29		+0.29	
Total reserves		53.32		70.21		+16.89
Credit facilities:						
Assured:						
Swaps unused	0		3.16		+3.16	
IMF standby credits	0		0.51		+0.51	
Subject to negotiation:						
Other IMF tranches	7.14		13.48		+6.34	
Total credit		7.14		17.15		+10.01
Total reserves and credit		60.46		87.36		+26.90

Source: "Ministerial Statement of the Group of Ten and Annex Prepared by Deputies," *Federal Reserve Bulletin*, vol. 50, no. 8 (August, 1964), p. 995.

Gold. Long the traditional form of monetary reserves, official gold holdings have increased substantially in the ten years covered by the figures. A large part of the increase has been due to extraordinary efforts of various governments (France in particular) to draw gold out of hoards into government stocks. On the international level an informal gold pool has been formed by

[16] International Monetary Fund, *Annual Report* (Washington, 1964), p. 25.

the central banks of Belgium, France, Germany, Italy, the Netherlands, Switzerland, the United Kingdom, and the United States. Operated by the Bank of England as agent for the group, the gold pool has two functions: (1) to provide gold for sale when necessary to prevent speculation from driving the price abnormally high and (2) to coordinate the buying activities of the participating nations in order to time purchases in such a way as to steady the market. Both activities, by narrowing the range within which prices on the London gold market fluctuate, have discouraged speculation and have thereby increased the amount of gold flowing into official reserves. The gold pool was first established in October, 1961, and has continued on an informal month-to-month basis.

Foreign Exchange. Many countries have for years considered their holdings of pounds sterling (that is, deposits maintained with the Bank of England) as part of their reserves. This is particularly true of the sterling area, an informal and somewhat changing group which includes the members of the British Commonwealth (except Canada) and a few other countries that carry on a large proportion of their trade with Britain. The sterling-bloc countries tend to tie their currencies to the pound rather than to gold and therefore tend to count sterling as part of their reserves, after the fashion of the gold exchange standard. During World War II the sterling area was strengthened by formal agreement whereby the gold and foreign exchange of all members were held in a common pool for the use of the whole group. More recently the area has reverted to its prewar informal status.

Many countries outside the sterling area also hold sterling reserves because of the historical, and continuing, importance of Britain in world trade and the strength and efficiency of the London money market. As sterling has lost some of its international luster and as Britain's financial status has suffered from strains of various sorts, the dollar has partly replaced the pound as an important international reserve currency. Other strong currencies that enjoy convertibility and hence wide acceptance throughout the world are also counted by some countries as part of their reserves, but the prevalence of sterling and dollar holdings has led to their designation as *key currencies.*

The very large increase in foreign exchange holdings in the ten years prior to 1963 (Table 39-2) is due almost entirely to increases in dollar holdings. This in turn is the reverse die of the adverse balance of payments of the United States. As foreign countries receive payments from us, they hold sizable amounts of these payments in dollars (accounts with the Federal Reserve banks or even commercial banks, or in United States treasury bills), thus increasing their reserves—and total world liquidity. This is one of the paradoxes of the present world monetary system: if the United States cures its balance-of-payments problem, it will cease adding to the foreign stock of dollars and thereby cease to contribute to the desirable, and perhaps even necessary, increase in international liquidity.

On the other side of the picture the United States, which formerly counted only gold as reserves, began in 1961 to acquire small amounts of foreign currency reserves. At one time or another since then it has counted as part of its official reserve holdings a half dozen different European currencies as well as Canadian dollars.

IMF Gold Tranche. Also for the first time in 1963 the United States began to count its *net IMF position* as part of its monetary reserve assets. The 25 per cent of a country's IMF quota that is paid in gold is referred to as its *gold tranche.* Any member may automatically borrow ("buy foreign currencies") up to the amount of the gold tranche. Or, to put it another way, the gold that a country deposits with the IMF is available to it at any time to acquire foreign currencies to meet a balance-of-payments deficit in a similar way to that in which the gold itself might have been used if the IMF didn't exist. It seems only reasonable that such an asset should be included in reserves.[17]

Special United States Bonds. In an effort to finance its balance-of-payments deficit, the United States began in 1961 to issue special medium-term bonds for purchase by foreign central banks. Some of them, denominated in dollars, funded the dollar holdings of the purchasers and thus forestalled the possible conversion of such dollars into gold. Others, denominated in foreign currencies, gave the United States the exchange needed to meet some of its overseas debts. Most of these bonds are redeemable by the holder in case of need and hence represent liquid assets for the central banks that own them.

Swap Arrangements. In 1962 the Federal Reserve inaugurated a series of negotiations with European central banks which culminated in bilateral reciprocal currency agreements, commonly called *swap arrangements.* Under a swap arrangement the Federal Reserve agrees with, say, the Bank of France that either bank will provide its own currency on request in exchange for the currency of the other bank, up to a specified maximum amount.

If the United States is short of francs, it can ask the Bank of France to provide them in exchange for dollars. Or the Bank of France can ask for dollars. In either case the result is the same: the United States gets francs, and France gets dollars. But the country requesting the swap is likely to use the currency it gets to meet international obligations, while the other country will probably hold the currency it gets in return as reserves. Swaps are intended to even out relatively short-term disequilibrium and must be repaid (reversed) at a specified date within a period of three to twelve months.

Table 39-2 shows swaps in two places: (1) The amount actually exchanged is recorded under reserves, and (2) the maximum amount permitted (minus

[17] For some countries, including the United States, the net IMF position includes another item in addition to the gold tranche. If the amount of a member's currency held by the Fund is reduced below the original 75 per cent of its subscription paid in its own currency (by reason of another country's borrowing that currency), the first country's right to borrow is increased by the amount of the drawing. This additional automatic drawing right is called the *net creditor position* or *super gold tranche.* It is included in Table 39-2 as part of the figures for gold tranche.

any amount actually used) is included under credit facilities. The total swap facilities available to the United States as of September, 1965, are shown in Table 39-3.

Table 39-3. Federal Reserve Reciprocal Currency Arrangements, September 1, 1965

Millions of Dollars

Other party to agreement	*Amount of facility*
Austrian National Bank	50
National Bank of Belgium	100
Bank of Canada	250
Bank of England	750
Bank of France	100
German Federal Bank	250
Bank of Italy	450
Bank of Japan	250
Netherlands Bank	100
Bank of Sweden	50
Swiss National Bank	150
Bank for International Settlements	300
	2,800

Source: Federal Reserve Bank of New York, *Monthly Review*, vol. 47, no. 9 (September, 1965), p. 1224.

IMF Standby Credits. There are times when a country may wish to be certain that it can borrow from the IMF, but yet it doesn't need the money immediately. It may then negotiate a line of credit (*standby credit*), which means that it is assured of a loan (or drawing) whenever it wishes the funds within a specified time period. Such funds are then assured and can be drawn upon at will. Frequently standby credits have been negotiated when a country's currency was under speculative attack on world markets. And often the mere knowledge that a country *can* obtain funds with which to support its currency is enough to remove the speculative threat.

Other IMF Tranches. Unless a standby credit has been opened, a member can borrow from the IMF only with IMF approval. Such borrowing rights are therefore conditional and cannot be counted on with certainty. Nevertheless a country that is willing to take the necessary steps to assure its monetary soundness can usually obtain such loans, and hence the access to IMF credit is of substantial value even though something less than certain.

The increase in IMF credit from 1953 to 1963 is primarily the result of a rise of approximately 50 per cent in most members' quotas in 1959. There will be a similar rise of 25 per cent in 1966.

General Arrangements to Borrow. Still further down the liquidity ladder, and not shown in the table, are the General Arrangements to Borrow, instituted between the IMF and ten of its members in 1962. Under these arrangements the members stand ready to lend a total of $6 billion to the Fund "when the Fund and these countries consider that supplementary resources are needed to forestall or cope with an impairment of the international monetary system."[18]

Table 39-4 shows the countries concerned and the amounts they have promised to provide in case of need. These countries are known as the *Group of Ten.* In 1964 Switzerland joined the group as an associate and agreed to make resources available up to a total of $200 million. But since Switzerland is not a member of the IMF, it will make financial arrangements directly with the countries involved under the supervision of the Fund.

Table 39-4. General Arrangements to Borrow

Millions of U.S. Dollars Equivalent

Country	*Amount pledged*
Belgium	150
Canada	200
France	550
Germany	1,000
Italy	550
Japan	250
Netherlands	200
Sweden	100
United Kingdom	1,000
United States	2,000
Total	6,000

Source: *International Financial Statistics*, vol. 18, no. 2 (February, 1965), p. 9.

Ad Hoc Arrangements. In addition to these more or less formal undertakings, the major financial powers stand ready to undertake whatever action seems called for to stabilize the important foreign exchange markets. This attitude of cooperation was formally enunciated by the Basel Agreements of March, 1961, in which the major central banks in the BIS stated their intention of cooperating to discourage speculation on exchange markets. This statement was the initial impetus for several of the organized arrangements already discussed, but it is also evidenced in other actions directed toward specific situations. Close central bank cooperation, for instance, was at least partly responsible for preventing wild speculation in foreign exchange following the death of President Kennedy in November, 1963. It also resulted in the unusual pledge of $3 billion in aid to Britain when the pound experienced a serious crisis in December, 1964. This vast sum, over and above a $1 billion credit from the IMF and not a part of any formal arrangements, was rounded up in

[18] *International Financial News Survey* (International Monetary Fund), vol. 14, no. 1 (Jan. 12, 1962), p. 1.

a period of less than twenty-four hours and is tangible evidence that the reserves and facilities listed in Table 39-2 by no means exhaust the possible sources of funds for nations in difficulty.

Proposals for Reform. All the above, however, fail to convince some economists that world finance is in healthy shape. In fact the very number of arrangements involved suggests to some that the whole fabric is a patchwork rather than a rational, unified system. Consequently the air has been filled with proposals for change. Their number is legion, and they defy description in a short compass.[19]

Among the more widely discussed is one by Robert Triffin, of Yale, who wishes to convert the IMF into a world central bank that would accept for deposit both gold and foreign exchange (primarily dollar and sterling balances) held by any nation.[20] These balances would be guaranteed against devaluation or inconvertibility and would be fully acceptable by all countries in payment of international obligations through a simple clearing mechanism on the Fund's books, or they could be withdrawn at any time. All deposits would be fully convertible into any currency at the official rate of exchange so that deposits with the Fund could be used to make any payments necessary.

In addition the Fund would continue to lend to countries in need of foreign exchange. Such lending (as is true of a commercial bank) would result in a deposit creation for the borrowing country, which, like any deposit, could be withdrawn in any form needed. In the process of lending, the Fund would be creating international reserves, and it could therefore provide any degree of international liquidity needed. It could also buy securities (make investments) in particular areas in a manner similar to open-market operations.

In short, Triffin is suggesting that the IMF utilize the normal procedures of commercial and central banking to create a form of international money that will suffice to satisfy the growing needs of trade. Or, to put it differently, he is suggesting that the procedures now used by the Bank for International Settlements on a purely European basis be refined and extended by the International Monetary Fund to cover the whole world. A number of economists have been favorably impressed by the Triffin proposal, but it appears too drastic for the highly conservative minds of international bankers, and many rival proposals suggest going neither so far nor so fast. Somewhere in this direction, however, lies the route that international finance must eventually take.

Monetary Unions. Another direction of possible change, more limited in

[19] For a survey of such plans see Fritz Machlup, *Plans for Reform of the International Monetary System,* rev. ed. (International Finance Section, Princeton University, Princeton, N.J., 1964); this has been reproduced as chap. 4 in his *International Payments, Debts, and Gold* (Charles Scribner's Sons, New York, 1964).

[20] See Robert Triffin, *Gold and the Dollar Crisis* (Yale University Press, New Haven, Conn., 1960). There are many details and refinements in his plan which we cannot cover in the space here available.

geographical scope, is the monetary union, a cooperative arrangement among countries in which two or more nations join their currency systems by providing for a single currency to be used by all members of the union. A number of such unions have existed in various periods of history, particularly in medieval Europe. More recently some of the most successful unions have involved small countries that have accepted the monetary system of large neighbors.[21]

A more ambitious project was the Latin Monetary Union, established in 1865 among Belgium, France, Italy, and Switzerland, and joined three years later by Greece. Each country accepted at face value the coins of the others, which were minted according to a uniform standard. It was hoped that this might be the start of a worldwide monetary union, but the Latin Union was bimetallic at a period when the movement was away from bimetallism and toward gold. The Union itself had serious difficulties with Gresham's law, and the coinage of standard silver was abandoned in 1878, although the use of token coins continued. This token currency was issued in excessive amounts by Greece and Italy, resulting in a series of crises that were intensified by the introduction of paper currencies during World War I. Although beset with many difficulties, the Union limped along from one expedient to another until its final death in 1927.

The Scandinavian Monetary Union was established in 1873 between Sweden and Denmark. Norway joined in 1875. This union also foundered on the problems of wartime paper currencies. In both cases the primary reason for failure was a degree of inflation in some member nations that was not matched by others. The inflated currency then tended to displace the sounder currencies (Gresham's law again), thereby lowering the value of money of all countries to the inflationary level of the weakest. A monetary union in the absence of a single monetary authority is somewhat like a man with several heads, each telling his muscles what to do.

At the present time the Benelux countries (Belgium, the Netherlands, and Luxembourg) are progressing on an economic union that may eventually produce a single currency. The European Community (the Benelux countries plus France, Italy, and Germany) is discussing the possibility of moving in the same direction. In these cases the monetary union would be a late step in a general economic integration, which might in turn be the predecessor of political union. Monetary policy is so closely tied up with political sovereignty that it is difficult to integrate one without the other.

International Investment

In discussing the International Monetary Fund we implied that its primary function was to mitigate short-run disequilibrium in trade but that its funds were not intended to provide long-term capital. Yet a nation's inability to

[21] E.g., Monaco-France, Lichtenstein-Switzerland, Luxembourg-Belgium, Colombia–United States.

export may be based at least partly on its inability to produce efficiently, which in turn may be the result of a lack of capital equipment. The long-run solution to such a country's problem often depends on long-term funds.

International Bank for Reconstruction and Development. The International Bank for Reconstruction and Development (IBRD, or World Bank) was set up at the same time as the Fund precisely because this need was recognized. At that time the Bank received much less attention than the Fund, and many people thought of it as a more or less useless appendage. Over the years the Bank has steadily broadened its operations and has proved that it also has a vital part to play in the improvement of world economic conditions.

Structure. The members of the Bank are identical with those of the Fund. Each member has a capital subscription that is similar to, but not identical with, its quota in the Fund. The total capital is $21 billion, as shown in Table 39-1.[22] The member's subscription also measures roughly its voting power, but again the smaller nations have a slightly higher vote. The United States subscription is $6,350 million, or 30 per cent of the total, while its vote is 27 per cent.

Of the capital subscription only 10 per cent has been paid in, of which 1 per cent was paid in gold and 9 per cent in the member's own currency.[23] The remainder of the subscription is subject to call only if needed to cover default by borrowers.

The Bank is managed in the same way as the Fund (the governors and executive directors of the two organizations are frequently the same men) except that the head officer is called "president."

Operations. While one of the early objectives of the Bank was to aid reconstruction of war-torn nations, that job is now a matter of history. Its current task is to facilitate the flow of funds for the capital development of the less industrialized countries. It does not compete with private lenders, but rather helps to place loans with them and makes its own loans only when other financing is not available.

The Bank makes loans to member governments or to private enterprises where the government involved is willing to guarantee repayment. Its loans are for specific projects and are made only after extensive investigation by the Bank of the feasibility and economic importance of the project. Loans are nonpolitical. They are also based on sound business procedures. While the Bank was not created to make money, it is not intended to lose any either, and it has so far been successful in avoiding loss on any loan.

In the early days of its operation the Bank received many calls for loans which were hastily drawn up and which proved on investigation to be ill-conceived.

[22] Capital subscriptions were doubled for most countries in 1959, but there was no increase in the *paid-in* portion.

[23] These percentages were originally 20, 2, and 18, respectively, but doubling subscriptions without changing the paid-in portion cut the percentages in half.

The greatest difficulty has been the desire of underdeveloped countries to advance too rapidly and to underestimate the amount of spadework that needs to be done before finished goods can roll off the assembly line. One of the Bank's significant contributions has been the effective work that many of its technical missions have done in exploring the basic economic situation of various member nations at their request and in demonstrating the interdependence of such things as natural resources, agriculture, climate, health, education, land-tenure systems, government fiscal policy, and social conditions.[24]

Only when the Bank feels that a project has a reasonable chance of success within the total framework of the country's structure is credit granted. This need for initial spadework was the primary reason for the low volume of loans during the Bank's early years. Now that a good deal of preliminary planning has been completed, loans are being made much more rapidly.

While loans have been made for a great variety of purposes, it is not surprising that most encompass basic economic services rather than advanced industry (see Table 39-5). One-third of the development loans have been for electric power and another third for transportation.

The loan functions of the Bank fall into three categories:

1. Direct loans
2. Guaranteed loans
3. Joint loans

1. *Direct loans.* The Bank lends its own funds when the project is approved, but the borrower cannot obtain funds elsewhere at reasonable rates. The funds available to the Bank come from the capital subscriptions of members (see Table 39-1) and from its own borrowings. Paid-in subscriptions total $2 billion, most of which is in the various currencies of members. Since the greatest need is for dollars and the currencies of a few other industrialized countries, the Bank has supplemented this source of funds by borrowing on the open market through the issue of its own bonds. The largest offerings, as might be expected, have been in the United States, but securities have also been sold in Belgium, Canada, Germany, Italy, the Netherlands, Switzerland, and the United Kingdom, as shown in Table 39-6. It is interesting to note that the Bank for International Settlements subscribed to the whole of the first bond issue in Switzerland.

Loans made from the Bank's own funds must carry an interest rate high enough to cover its own cost of borrowing, its general expenses, and a special reserve for bad debts (though the Bank is too diplomatic to call it that). Interest rates have ranged from 3 to 6¼ per cent. The lowest rates were on loans made in the early years of operation, when interest rates generally were very low, while 6¼ per cent marks the tight-money period of early 1960, when the Bank had to pay 5 per cent to borrow on its own bonds.[25]

[24] The reports of several of these missions have been published for the Bank by The Johns Hopkins Press, Baltimore.

[25] If funds cost the Bank 5 per cent and it puts aside 1 per cent as a reserve, a 6¼ per cent interest rate leaves only ¼ per cent to meet operating expenses.

Table 39-5. Loans Made by the International Bank for Reconstruction and Development,† Classified by Purpose and Area, June 30, 1964

Millions of U.S. Dollars

Purpose	Total	Areas				
		Africa	Asia	Australia	Europe	Western Hemisphere
Electric power:						
Generation and distribution	2,768	312	624	162	533	1,136
Transportation:						
Railroads	1,241	274	717	37	37	176
Roads	1,159	106	451	51	68	483
Shipping	12				12	
Ports and waterways	349	33	233	8	47	29
Airlines and airports	57		6	44	7	
Pipelines	79	50	29			
	2,898	464	1,435	140	171	688
Telecommunications:						
Telephone, telegraph, and radio	88	4	42		*	42
Agriculture, forestry, and fishing:						
Farm mechanization	121			89	2	29
Irrigation and flood control	458	48	259	6	93	52
Land clearance, farm improvement	46	17	15	6	2	6
Crop processing and storage	6	*			4	2
Livestock improvement	34		1			33
Forestry and fishing	16		8	2	6	
	681	65	283	103	108	122
Industry:						
Iron and steel	380		314	13	23	30
Paper and pulp	139		4	1	113	20
Fertilizer and other chemicals	82		25	*	57	
Other industries	219	21	102	24	59	14
Mining	204	101	55	14	12	22
Development finance companies	283	19	205		59	1
	1,306	141	704	53	322	87
Water supply	67		60		4	3
Education projects	23	10	13			
General development	205	40	75		90	
Postwar reconstruction	497				497	
Grand total, all loans	8,533	1,036	3,235	458	1,726	2,078

† Including credits extended by the International Development Association in a total amount of $778 million.
* Less than $500,000.
Source: International Bank for Reconstruction and Development and International Development Association, *Annual Report, 1963–64,* p. 20. Detail may not add to totals because of rounding.

Loans are made for varying periods up to twenty-five years, and in most cases they are amortized—the principal is paid back in annual installments.

Since loans are evidenced by negotiable securities, the Bank does not have to hold them until maturity if it can find some other lender willing to buy the securities. As loans approach maturity, as the projects involved show greater

Table 39-6. Outstanding Funded Debt of the International Bank for Reconstruction and Development, June 30, 1964
Millions of U.S. Dollars

Debt payable in:	
United States dollars	1,885
Belgian francs	10
Canadian dollars	29
Deutsche marks	275
Italian lire	24
Netherlands guilders	38
Pounds sterling	49
Swiss francs	182
	2,492

Source: International Bank for Reconstruction and Development and International Development Association, *Annual Report, 1963–64,* pp. 70–71.

evidence of being self-supporting, or as the international climate improves, investors who were afraid to trust their funds earlier now feel that it is safe to do so. The Bank can then sell some of the securities that it holds and thus replenish its supply of currency available for new loans.

2. *Guaranteed loans.* In many cases private lenders are willing to provide funds for development projects if the risk is reduced by means of the Bank's guarantee of repayment in case the original borrower defaults. The Bank charges 1 per cent for its guarantee since it is incurring a contingent liability, and this fee must be paid by the borrower. Even with this extra payment the cost of borrowing may be less than it would be if the borrower attempted to obtain funds on its own signature alone.

The Articles of Agreement of the Bank prohibit it from making and guaranteeing loans in an aggregate amount in excess of its *subscribed* capital (currently $19 billion). The unpaid portion of members' subscriptions is a cushion against default, whether of direct or guaranteed loans, and in case of such default in excess of its special reserve fund the members would be called upon to make up the loss by paying in additional portions of their subscribed capital. Fortunately no default has yet occurred.

3. *Joint loans.* A third device effectively used by the bank is to induce private lenders to participate with it in making a loan jointly. A perspective borrower may want more money than private lenders are willing to provide, or it may need longer terms for repayment than private lenders can allow. Frequently the Bank has made loans in conjunction with commercial banks, in which the commercial banks provide credit for short maturities, while the International Bank takes the long maturities. Thus the Bank made a $50 million loan to India in July, 1959, for a railway-expansion program. Seven private banks participated in an aggregate of $3.75 million, covering maturities falling due from 1963 to 1965.[26] In April, 1959, the Bank made a loan of $20 million

[26] The participating banks are Lloyds Bank, Ltd., London; The Chase Manhattan Bank; the Chartered Bank, New York Agency; Bank of America; Irving Trust Company; The Hanover Bank; and The Riggs National Bank of Washington, D.C.

to the Southern Italy Development Fund at the same time that the European Investment Bank (of the Common Market) loaned it $20 million, and an issue of $30 million of its bonds was sold in New York.

This kind of cooperation in making loans is now the rule rather than the exception. It not only permits the Bank's resources to stretch further, but also fulfills its objective of acting as a supplement to private capital rather than as a substitute for it.

International Finance Corporation. In spite of its success in aiding the development of the less industrialized countries, the Bank is rather restricted in its approach by two provisions in its Articles of Agreement. One is that it is limited to loans made to, or guaranteed by, governments. The other is that its investments must be in the form of conservative, interest-bearing bonds. Thus it cannot make loans directly to private firms, nor can it take much risk.

The need for broadening the base of capital participation led to the formation of the International Finance Corporation (IFC) in 1956. This organization is somewhat of a hybrid, both connected with, and dissociated from, the International Bank. The Board of Governors, the executive directors, the annual meeting, and the offices of the two organizations are the same, but the officers and staff, the structural organization, and the accounts are separate. Not only are the books of the International Finance Corporation exclusively its own, but it is forbidden to borrow from, or lend to, the International Bank. The purpose of this somewhat ambivalent nature is to permit the Corporation to benefit from the experience of the Bank without confusing their separate operations.

Membership in the Corporation is open to members of the International Bank. Each member is assigned a capital subscription that is proportional to its subscription to the Bank. The Corporation is much smaller than the Bank, however, with a total authorized capital of $100 million. As of 1965, 78 nations had joined and had paid in $99 million. All subscriptions must be paid in gold or United States dollars.

The purpose of the Corporation is to promote economic development in member nations by means of investments made directly to private firms. It does not lend to governments or to government-controlled enterprises. It provides risk capital through equity investment, but it may also make loans.

The Corporation, like the Bank, does not invest unless funds are not available elsewhere on reasonable terms. It will not provide more than 50 per cent of the cost of an enterprise and attempts to sell its securities to private investors whenever this can be done satisfactorily. It hopes that in this manner its relatively small capital may operate as a revolving fund to be used by firms negotiating the first difficult years of an uncertain venture. If the venture succeeds, the Corporation will surrender its participation to others who are then willing to take it and will turn to other projects in need of a supporting hand. By the very nature of its operation the Corporation is bound to suffer loss on some projects, but it hopes that its gains will exceed its losses over the long run and that it will therefore be able to pay dividends to its own stockholders.

By 1964 the Corporation had made investments of $120 million in businesses in thirty-two countries. Almost 50 per cent of its investments had been either repaid or sold, so that as of June 30, 1965, it held $42 million of loans and $21 million of equity capital.

International Development Association. In 1960 a second affiliate of the IBRD was established. The International Development Association (IDA) has the same executive directors, officers, and staff as the IBRD but keeps separate financial accounts. It has an authorized capital of $1 billion, of which the United States has provided $320 million (see Table 39-1). As of 1965 the Association had ninety-three members divided into two groups. The seventeen "Part I countries," consisting of the more advanced nations, pay their subscriptions in fully convertible funds that may be used at any time by the IDA for development credits. The less advanced "Part II countries" need pay in only 10 per cent of their subscription in convertible funds; the remainder may be paid in their own currency and cannot be used without the member's consent. Part I countries are thought of as contributors, while Part II countries are eligible for credits. In 1964 the Part I countries agreed to provide an additional $750 million in contributions over and above the normal subscriptions in order to provide additional funds to meet the continuing activity of the Association. At the same time the IBRD itself made a grant of $50 million to the IDA.

The primary purpose of the IDA is to provide funds "for countries whose balance of payments prospects would not justify their incurring or continuing to incur, external debt entirely on conventional terms."[27] The credits granted so far have been for a period of fifty years and carry no interest but are subject to a service charge of ¾ of 1 per cent per annum to meet the Association's administrative cost. No repayment is required during the first ten years, 1 per cent is repaid annually during the next ten years, and 3 per cent per year is required for the remainder of the credit. Because terms are lenient, these credits are frequently referred to as *soft loans*. In a number of cases the Association has made loans jointly with the International Bank.

Up to June 30, 1965, the IDA had made commitments to twenty-eight countries in a total amount of $995 million, but only $414 million had actually been disbursed. The amounts involved are included along with IBRD loans in Table 39-5.

Other International Investment Agencies. These world financial institutions are by no means the only ones active in international investment. Private individuals, banks, and other corporations are today, as they have always been, the primary lenders on international account, and several private corporations have been established for the primary purpose of promoting foreign lending.

Governments make many loans directly on a bilateral or multilateral basis. The Soviet Union has made substantial loans to countries in Asia and the Middle East. The Colombo Plan bands together the nations of Southeast Asia

[27] International Development Association, *Annual Report, 1961–62,* p. 6.

for mutual economic assistance. The Common Market has established a European Investment Bank to aid its less advanced regions. An Arab Financial Institution for Economic Development was set up in 1959, and a billion-dollar Inter-American Development Bank in 1960. In 1964, thirty African nations organized the African Development Bank with a capital of $250 million. In 1965 the Asian Development Bank was founded with an initial capital of $1 billion, of which 60 per cent is to be subscribed by Asian member countries and 40 per cent by non-Asian developed countries.

In the United States the Export-Import Bank has been active in the field of foreign loans for many years. The Agency for International Development makes development loans totaling close to $1 billion a year, including those extended through the Alliance for Progress.

At the United Nations level the technical assistance program might be noted, although its primary purpose is the sharing of knowledge rather than of cash. In 1959 the United Nations Special Fund was established to carry on this work on an expanded scale. The more ambitious Special United Nations Fund for Economic Development (SUNFED), which has been discussed for years, has never received substantial support from the nations that would provide most of its money.

Conclusion. The very multiplicity of agencies that have grown up in this area suggests that unfinished tasks still remain. The problem of economic development is indeed vaster than any solutions so far devised. It is perhaps the most important economic problem facing the world in the next several decades. Differing cultures and differing points of view have hindered a common attack on it in the past. It is a job that men of goodwill must tackle in the cause of a common humanity.

But one caution on the role of money. It is not money that the impoverished nations lack; it is goods. Hunger is not conquered by money, but by food. An inappropriate structure of exchange rates is not what makes people poor, though it may be a minor contributing cause of an inefficient organization of industry. Poverty—national and international—can be cured only by greater productivity. A well-designed monetary system is useful in facilitating the production and distribution of goods, but money is a means to an end, not the end itself, and its effect is measured by its efficiency, not by its quantity. Money oils the wheels of progress; too much oil can be as disastrous as too little.

Questions for Thought and Discussion

1. Is there any reason why central banks might be more interested in keeping the BIS than treasuries would be?

2. In what ways does the ability of a country to borrow from the IMF affect its balance of payments in the short run? In the long run?

3. Will devaluation always solve a country's balance-of-payments problems?

Is it possible that there may be *no* way of balancing a nation's imports and exports on current account? If so, how would its balance of international payments balance?

4. In what ways does the present world monetary system resemble the gold standard? In what ways does it differ?

5. What is the relationship between the United States balance-of-payments deficit and the growth of international liquidity? Could other nations increase their holdings of dollars if our payments were in equilibrium?

6. If the United States were to abandon the gold standard, would the dollar remain as a key currency?

7. What do you think are the chances of establishing a world central bank along the lines of the Triffin (or some similar) plan?

8. In what ways does the ability of a country to borrow from the International Bank affect its balance of payments in the short run? in the long run?

9. Why should the United States want to make international loans directly (such as through the Development Loan Fund) rather than through international agencies?

10. Why is it more difficult for a borrowing country to repay a loan in gold or dollars than with its own currency?

11. How can one justify making loans to underdeveloped countries free of interest cost, as is done by the IDA?

12. What new developments have occurred in the international monetary sphere since 1965?

Selected Bibliography

Auboin, Roger: *The Bank for International Settlements, 1930–1955,* International Finance Section, Princeton University, Princeton, N.J., May, 1955.

Aufricht, Hans: *The International Monetary Fund: Legal Aspects, Structure, Functions, 1945–63,* Frederick A. Praeger, Inc., New York, 1964.

Bank for International Settlements: *Annual Reports,* Basel, Switzerland.

Bell, Philip W.: *The Sterling Area in the Postwar World,* Oxford University Press, Fair Lawn, N.J., 1956.

Beyen, J. W.: *Money in a Maelstrom,* The Macmillan Company, New York, 1949.

Boskey, Shirley: *Problems and Practices of Development Banks,* The Johns Hopkins Press, Baltimore, 1959.

Cairncross, Alec: *The International Bank for Reconstruction and Development,* International Finance Section, Princeton University, Princeton, N.J., 1959.

Diamond, William: *Development Banks,* The Johns Hopkins Press, Baltimore, 1957.

Dulles, Eleanor Lansing: *The Bank for International Settlements at Work,* The Macmillan Company, New York, 1932.

Grubel, Herbert G. (ed.): *World Monetary Reform: Plans and Issues,* Stanford University Press, Stanford, Calif., 1963.

Hansen, Alvin H.: *The Dollar and the International Monetary System,* McGraw-Hill Book Company, New York, 1965.

Horie, Shigeo: *The International Monetary Fund,* St Martin's Press, Inc., New York, 1964.

International Bank for Reconstruction and Development: *Annual Reports,* Washington.

———: *The International Bank for Reconstruction and Development, 1946–1953,* The Johns Hopkins Press, Baltimore, 1954.

———: *The World Bank Group in Asia: A Summary of Activities,* 1963.

International Finance Corporation: *Annual Reports,* Washington.

International Monetary Fund: *Annual Reports,* Washington.

———: *The Revival of Monetary Policy,* Washington, 1953.

MacDougall, Donald: *The World Dollar Problem,* St Martin's Press, Inc., New York, 1958.

Machlup, Fritz: *International Payments, Debts, and Gold: Collected Essays,* Charles Scribner's Sons, New York, 1964.

Morris, James: *The Road to Huddersfield: A Journey to Five Continents,* Pantheon Books, a Division of Random House, Inc., New York, 1963.

Robertson, Dennis H.: *Britain in the World Economy,* George Allen & Unwin, Ltd., London, 1954.

Scammell, William M.: *International Monetary Policy,* 2d ed., St Martin's Press, Inc., New York, 1961.

Schloss, H. H.: *The Bank for International Settlements,* North Holland Publishing Company, Amsterdam, 1958.

Tew, Brian: *International Monetary Co-operation, 1945–63,* 7th ed., Hutchinson's University Library, London, 1963.

Triffin, Robert: *Gold and the Dollar Crisis,* Yale University Press, New Haven, Conn., 1960.

Weaver, James H.: *The International Development Association,* Frederick A. Praeger, Inc., New York, 1965.

Williams, John H.: *Postwar Monetary Plans and Other Essays,* Alfred A. Knopf, Inc., New York, 1945.

Willis, Henry Parker: *A History of the Latin Monetary Union,* The University of Chicago Press, Chicago, 1901.

Part Ten
Conclusion

Chapter 40 The Veil of Money

The world is still deceiv'd with ornament.

. . .

Thus ornament is but the guiled shore
To a most dangerous sea; . . . in a word
The seeming truth which cunning times put on
To entrap the wisest. Therefore, thou gaudy gold,
Hard food for Midas, I will none of thee.

The Merchant of Venice
Act III, scene 2, line 74

We have been immersed in a study of money for a long time now. We have discovered—if we did not already know—that it is a vital element of the economy for good or ill. But we need to keep our perspective. Money is important, but not all-important.

The Mercantilist Love of Money

The idea that money can solve all problems is an ancient one. The mercantilists indeed built most of their economics around it, and these theories held the center of the stage in European economic thought for some three hundred years. Mercantilism emerged toward the end of the fourteenth century and grew in favor, if not in wisdom, until it was adopted as the basis for much national policy. Both the physiocrats and Adam Smith tore it apart, but it is not dead. It still appeals to the man in the street, and no less an authority than John Maynard Keynes pays subdued homage to a portion of its doctrine.[1]

No theory that covered as wide a range both geographically and chronologically as mercantilism can be encapsuled in a single sentence, but the

[1] John Maynard Keynes, "Notes on Mercantilism . . . ," in *The General Theory of Employment, Interest and Money* (Harcourt, Brace & World. Inc., New York, 1936), chap. 23.

central core of mercantilism is that money is wealth; nay more, that money is the most desirable form of wealth. Before casting too cruel a judgment on this doctrine, we should recall that in the period involved money consisted predominantly of the precious metals, which were desirable commodities for their own sake.

But to call specie the most desirable form of wealth confuses means and ends, for the whole purpose of money is to buy other, more desirable things. The mercantilists seemed to forget this. "The great and ultimate effect of trade is not wealth at large, but particularly abundance of silver, gold, and jewels, which are not perishable, nor so mutable as other commodities, but are wealth at all times, and all places."[2] As if wheat weren't!

If money is desired above all else, then practical policy should be directed toward the accumulation of money, the building up of hoards. This the nations in the grip of mercantilism tried to accomplish by prohibiting export of precious metals or by the more sophisticated device of encouraging an export balance of trade "because that part of our stock which is not returned to us in wares must necessarily be brought home in treasure."[3] And the more money we have, the better.

Much of the early development of the New World itself was a result of the mercantilist desire for the precious metals. The Spaniards exploited the Incas and the Aztecs both by plundering their stores and by forcing their people to slave in the mines bringing forth new metal. The English, failing to find much treasure in their area of the new continent, accomplished the same result by plundering the Spanish ships. All to the greater glory of gold.

The Classical View of Money

The classical economists paid no such homage to gold. It is probably no exaggeration to say that classical economics was born on a refutation of the mercantilist doctrine. Adam Smith wrote his book—*An Inquiry into the Nature and Causes of the Wealth of Nations* (1776)—to prove that a country was not wealthy by virtue of its stock of money, but because of its production.

Referring to the mercantilists he writes:

> Consumable commodities, it is said, are soon destroyed; whereas gold and silver are of a more durable nature, and, were it not for this continual exportation, might be accumulated for ages together, to the incredible augmentation of the real wealth of the country. . . . We do not, however, reckon that trade disadvantageous which

[2] Sir William Petty, *Essays in Political Arithmetick* (1655), p. 113; quoted in Lewis H. Haney, *History of Economic Thought,* 4th ed. (The Macmillan Company, New York, 1949), p. 119.

[3] Thomas Mun, *England's Treasure by Forraign Trade* (1664); quoted in Leonard Dalton Abbott, *Masterworks of Economics* (Doubleday & Company, Inc., Garden City, N.Y., 1946), p. 16.

consists in the exchange of the hard-ware of England for the wines of France; and yet hard-ware is a very durable commodity, and were it not for this continual exportation, might be accumulated for ages together, to the incredible augmentation of the pots and pans of the country.[4]

The classicists generally relegated money to a distinctly inferior place in the economy. Their theory was essentially a real-goods theory, concerned with corn and cloth and cantaloupes—those things that satisfied man's wants. Yes, money was useful, but it was only a means of facilitating exchange, and, in their opinion, it altered neither the level of output nor the structure of industry. And so, for the most part, they ignored it.

Say's Law. The most explicit formulation of this theory was the law of markets of Jean Baptiste Say. Interestingly enough Say begins his discussion in rebuttal of a common fallacy that still persists today. Speaking of businessmen ("adventurers in the different channels of industry"), Say writes: "When the vent [market] for their commodities is slow, difficult, and productive of little advantage, they pronounce money to be scarce."[5] It is not money that is scarce, he says, but the demand for the product that has fallen. Of what does this demand consist? Of the goods produced by potential customers, which are their source of income. "Yonder farmer," the woollen merchant is told, "will buy your woollens, if his crops be good, and will buy more or less according to their abundance or scantiness; he can buy none at all, if his crops fail altogether."[6]

Thus the demand for one product is the supply of others.

A product is no sooner created, than it, from that instant, affords a market for other products to the full extent of its own value. When the producer has put the finishing hand to his product, he is most anxious to sell it immediately, lest its value should vanish in his hands. Nor is he less anxious to dispose of the money he may get for it; for the value of money is also perishable. But the only way of getting rid of money is in the purchase of some product or other. Thus the mere circumstance of the creation of one product immediately opens a vent for other products.[7]

This is not to say that all products will always find a market, for it is possible to produce too much of one thing and not enough of another. This represents at the same time both an oversupply and a scarcity. Total production has not been too great; it has been directed into the wrong channels. But this has nothing to do with money:

[4] Adam Smith, *An Inquiry into the Nature and Causes of the Wealth of Nations,* ed. by Edwin Cannan (Modern Library, Inc., New York, 1937), pp. 407–408.

[5] Jean Baptiste Say, *A Treatise on Political Economy,* trans. from the 4th ed. of the French by C. R. Prinsep, 5th Amer. ed. (Grigg and Elliott, Philadelphia, 1832), book 1, chap. 15, p. 76.

[6] *Ibid.,* p. 77.

[7] *Ibid.,* pp. 78–79.

Sales can not be said to be dull because money is scarce, but because other products are so. There is always money enough to conduct the circulation and mutual exchange of other values, when those values really exist. Should the increase of traffic require more money to finance it, the want is easily supplied, and is a strong indication of prosperity—a proof that a great abundance of values has been created, which it is wished to exchange for other values.[8]

On the other hand, however, Say was well aware of the dislocations that may be introduced into business by tinkering with the currency, and he spends many pages in illustrating the evils of debasement, which is

. . . destructive of national welfare and prosperity.

It occasions a violent dislocation of the money-prices of commodities, operating in a thousand different ways, according to the particular circumstances of each respectively, and thereby disconcerting the best planned and most useful speculations, and destroying all confidence between lender and borrower. Nobody will willingly lend when he runs the risk of receiving a less sum than he has advanced; nor will any one be in a hurry to borrow, if he is in danger of paying more than he gets. Capital is, consequently, diverted from productive investment; and the blow, given to production by deterioration of the coin, is commonly followed up by the still more fatal ones of taxation upon commodities and the establishment of a maximum of price [price control].

Nor is the effect less serious in respect to national morality. People's ideas of value are kept in a state of confusion for a length of time, during which knavery has an advantage over honest simplicity, in the conduct of pecuniary matters. Moreover, robbery and spoliation are sanctioned by public practice and example; personal interest is set in opposition to integrity; and the voice of the law to the impulse of conscience.[9]

What could be added to this indictment of inflation!

The classicists were not, then, completely ignorant of the havoc that mismanagement of money might produce on the economy, but on the whole they paid less attention to it than the subject deserved. Whatever they might say in asides, their basic attitude is pretty much that of Mill when he says, "There cannot, in short, be intrinsically a more insignificant thing, in the economy of a society, than money; except in the character of a contrivance for sparing time and labour."[10]

The Classical View Disputed

Most of the present generation would disagree with this statement of Mill, though the disagreement in turn uncovers a variety of views among the disputants.

[8] *Ibid.*, p. 78.

[9] *Ibid.*, p. 188.

[10] John Stuart Mill, *Principles of Political Economy*, ed. by W. J. Ashley (Longmans, Green & Co., Ltd., London, 1909), p. 488.

Money as Villain. For one thing we find that money has a positive effect on the structure of industry and on the production and distribution of goods. It is not neutral. In fact it seems to have some inherent tendency to mess things up. Instead of oil in the machinery it has become sand.

The business cycle, as we have seen, is at least partly a monetary phenomenon. Say's law, as Say himself would admit, does not always work. When producers bring goods to market, sell them for money, and then hoard the proceeds or use them to repay bank loans that are not replaced with others, there is a leakage from the circuit flow. Incomes fall, production is slowed, workers are fired, and the economy grinds along in second gear. Money is by no means the only culprit, but it is certainly an accessory before the fact.

Money as Hero. But if money can help get us into trouble, it can also help get us out. This is the role that Keynes stressed. His monetary theory emphasized the importance of lower interest rates in stimulating investment and of a government deficit in raising national income.

A few economists and a number of politicians, going even further, seem to believe that proper manipulation of money will provide maximum production and well-being almost regardless of what the rest of the economy does. Money, they say, is the root of all good. It is the "miracle ingredient" in the economic system that at all seasons can keep the machinery running at high speed. This seems to be the position of the inflationists, who proclaim the gospel of eternal prosperity based on an expanding money supply. It lies behind William Jennings Bryan and his "cross of gold." It cropped up in Upton Sinclair's EPIC plan. Major Douglas, Francis Townsend, and others preach the same doctrine, but from different texts. Even Keynes is sometimes misinterpreted as espousing purely monetary answers to basic problems.

Money as Popular God. The man in the street frequently shares this view with little theoretical knowledge but much fervor. The high priests may dispute among themselves the mysteries of their theology; their followers simply accept the primacy of money as divine revelation. Their creed seems to be: "There is no God but Gold, and six per cent is his profit."

This reverence of the average citizen for money is not merely absorbed from what others tell him. It is the result of his own experience. For him money is a great blessing. He knows perfectly well that *he* is better off if he has more money. Who wouldn't be able to live a little better if his income were boosted a few notches? So let's have more money all around.

If Adam Smith, professor of philosophy, is guilty of the fallacy of composition,[11] who can blame the average citizen for falling into the same trap and thinking that what is good for him must be good for everybody? If a little money is good, more must be even better. If it's good for one person, it must be good for all. Let's eliminate poverty by giving everyone more money.

[11] "What is prudence in the conduct of every private family, can scarce be folly in that of a great kingdom." Smith, *op. cit.,* p. 424.

How about a ten-spot for each citizen every birthday. But if ten is good, a thousand is better. Paper's cheap; why not make it a million?

The Money Illusion

We all know the fallacy, particularly when presented in this blatant form. We recall the German experience of 1923, when a million marks wouldn't buy a postage stamp. When the case is expressed in these terms, it is perfectly clear that it isn't money that makes us rich. Who wants a million dollars if it won't buy anything?

Yet sometimes the situation involves such subtle concepts that even economists are misled. While we know that money is a veil behind which lie real production and consumption, we are so accustomed to seeing the pattern on that veil that sometimes we confuse it with the reality underneath. In fact it might be more apt to speak of money not as a veil, but as a pair of glasses through which we continually view the world around us. The glasses themselves are somewhat distorted, but we've been wearing them so long that we see the distortion as if it were an integral part of the landscape.

Almost everything we do has a money value of one kind or another. Maybe the best things in life are free, but the ones we constantly worry about are the ones we have to pay for—in dollars spent or in dollars we might have earned but didn't.

A lot of us are probably much too concerned about these material problems. Like Oscar Wilde's cynic, we know the price of everything and the value of nothing. Our two most common questions are: "What's in it for me?" and "How much will it cost?" To the philosopher's comment that "money won't buy happiness," the average American answers, "No, but it will buy the things that keep me from being miserable." We would probably be better off as individuals and as a nation if we didn't wear ourselves out trying to keep up (or surpass) the Joneses. But whether desirable or not, it is a fact we can't ignore that in the United States today we see the dollar sign almost everywhere we look. It is therefore hardly surprising that we sometimes mistake the shadow for the substance.

Wages. For most of us our wages determine our standard of living. The number of dollars in the pay envelope is therefore of major importance to each individual. The more dollars, the better. We need no esoteric theory to explain why labor unions fight for higher pay.

But where does the extra money come from if it is won? Since a wage rise by itself does not increase the quantity of goods available to the economy, the worker involved must raise his status at the expense of someone else. Labor unions like to think that the someone else is the "capitalist boss." To a certain extent he may have to meet his increased payroll out of his own pocket, particularly in the early stages of union development when workers are able to pull themselves up from a previous level of exploitation. But once this has been done, little more can be expected from this source, for statistics show that profits are (and always have been) a relatively small fraction of national income.[12]

If the increase doesn't come from profits, it may come from other workers. For if one union gets a raise *and others don't,* it may be that prices rise in the industry affected so that consumers (workers in other industries) have their standard of living lowered by the higher prices they must pay.

If *all* workers get higher pay, and *all* prices go up, then nobody is better off. The larger number of dollars will buy the same old quantity of goods. Money wages have risen, but real wages haven't. Perhaps the money illusion will make workers think they have gotten something, but they haven't.

There is a fourth possibility, a very important one. The rise in wages may be offset by increased productivity, so that it neither reduces profits nor pushes up prices. In this case workers as a whole are really better off. As the economy has progressed, this is actually what has happened. Increased output has meant more pie to be distributed to everyone. But it wasn't the wage increase that did it. The same aggregate result would have been achieved if money wages had remained the same and prices had been reduced. This raises real income just as surely as the other way. Undoubtedly the *distribution* of income would be different in the two cases, and which is preferable on this basis is a moot question. But the *total* increase in living standards would be the same.

Assets. Just as a man's income is measured in dollars, so is his wealth. His assets may consist of a house, furniture, clothing, a car, cash in the bank, and perhaps some securities, but the only way the magnitude of these possessions can be assessed in comparable figures is in terms of their money value. So we say that Tom Brown is worth $20,000, which is the total monetary value of his assets (minus his liabilities, if any).

Now surely if Brown was worth only $10,000 ten years ago, his wealth has doubled. Or has it? Not if the value of the dollar has shrunk in the same period and if he values his assets at their *current* price. If prices have more than doubled, his actual wealth has diminished.

In fact Smith, who values his assets at $15,000, may actually be better off than Brown with $20,000. To take a simple case, suppose that Brown's total assets consist of a house he has just bought and for which he paid cash, hocking all his other assets to do so. Smith's assets consist of (1) an identical house built ten years ago for $10,000, which he now lists as worth $8,000 (because of depreciation), and (2) $7,000 in cash. Suppose further that prices have doubled in the last ten years. Smith's house then is worth 16,000 of *today's* dollars, and this together with his $7,000 in cash indicates a worth of $23,000 in current prices—substantially more than Brown's. Of course Smith could

[12] Since the Department of Commerce series was first compiled in 1929, corporate profits after tax as a proportion of national income have ranged from a negative figure (1931 and 1932) to a maximum of 9.9 per cent in 1929. In 1964 the figure was 7.2 per cent. [*Survey of Current Business,* vol. 45, no. 8 (August, 1965), pp. 28–29.]

use current market values instead of the original cost figure to value his assets, but conservative accounting practice generally discourages this.

When comparing corporate balance sheets it is frequently important to know when the assets were acquired in order to avoid being misled by artificial differences that are introduced by the money illusion. Similar problems arise in buying fire insurance. A policy covering original cost will not replace the building in an inflationary period. And in life insurance a policy that was originally sufficient may need to be supplemented to match price increases.

Costs. Although businessmen are more apt to be aware of the pitfalls of the money illusion than consumers, it does raise many problems for them. If depreciation allowances are figured (as they almost always are) on the original cost of the building or equipment, they understate, in a period of rising prices, the real cost of producing goods. The contribution of the equipment to the production process is valued at less than its real current worth. This both overstates profits and fails to provide for replacement of the facilities when they wear out.

The same problem arises with inventories. As prices rise, materials can be bought only at a higher cost. What then is the material cost of goods produced? Is it the original cost of early, cheaper inventories of supplies on hand at the beginning of the accounting period, or is it the higher cost of replacing these stocks? Accountants are still fighting the battle of "fifo" and "lifo," the two alternative methods of pricing inventories, but neither is wholly satisfactory. Manufacturers know the *physical* volume of materials used, but variations in the value of money play havoc with their attempt to describe this fact accurately in monetary terms. Those who read the resulting accounting statements are as likely as not to be misled by the figures put before them. Few realize that a statement of profit and loss is only a tentative statement because the yardstick used—the dollar—changed its size in the process of measurement. It's like trying to measure the growth in height of a child with a column of mercury.

Foreign Trade. The mercantilist illusion still persists in foreign trade, even in the terminology we use. The mercantilists referred to an export balance of trade as a favorable balance because it must be settled in gold. The phrase still sticks, although a "favorable" balance may be quite undesirable under certain circumstances. A favorable balance means that a country is exporting goods of a higher value than those it is importing. In real terms, therefore, such a balance reduces the total amount of goods available to the community and, in the short run at least, reduces the standard of living.

This is not necessarily bad. Just as a saver reduces his current standard of living in order to have more in the future, a nation may make foreign loans in anticipation of interest earnings later. But if the interest is to be of *real* benefit, it can be paid only in goods, and a mature creditor nation earning interest on past loans will have an import ("unfavorable") balance on goods and service account. A perpetual export balance therefore prevents the nation from ever enjoying the higher standard of living to which its loans should entitle it.

And of course an export balance would be folly for an underdeveloped nation trying to build up its economy. The foreign loans that it receives enable it to import the machinery and other goods that its industrialization requires. Yet the money illusion prevents many people from realizing the advantages to be gained from an import ("unfavorable") balance of trade. Perhaps mercantilism is officially dead, but its ghost still haunts the world.

National Policy. In its most virulent form the money illusion takes the guise of the belief that full employment can be assured by perpetual inflation, that here is the golden key to the conquest of the business cycle. In one of its aspects this is a belief in the efficacy of the illusion itself. Optimism is supposed to reign forever as long as money incomes rise. No one is supposed to notice the rise in costs or the vanishing value of monetary assets. This optimism will keep the wheels of business turning at maximum speed.

While the illusion is widespread, it is not (unfortunately?) that deeply rooted in the nation's consciousness. The longer inflation lasts and the more rapidly it progresses, the greater attention it receives. As Lincoln said, "You can't fool all of the people all of the time." While the illusion, like dark glasses, may hide the real situation in obscure corners of the economy where relationships are not too clear to begin with, it cannot mislead us completely in the bright light of the obvious.

Saving, Investment, and Economic Progress

One of the darkest corners, currently, seems to be the relationship between saving and investment. We have spent some time demonstrating the equality of these two concepts. Yet even economists who accept this equality without question sometimes do not realize all the implications of the equation. The amount of money saved equals the amount invested. But this is only superficial. Underneath we find that the real value of saving must equal the real value of investment.

Let's remember what we mean by these two terms. Saving is the excess of income over consumption (including taxes). Investment is the increase in the physical assets of business. Saving therefore represents the foregoing of current consumption. Investment represents the acquisition of real assets. The identity of these two cannot be overemphasized. Except for foreign investment, *it is absolutely impossible for a nation to save without equivalent investment; it is absolutely impossible to invest without equivalent saving*. This is more than a semantic or algebraic exercise in logic. It is a hard fact of existence, obvious to the aboriginal savage and equally true today, although the processes are overlaid with so many intervening transactions that it is not so evident.

Suppose we start with the cave man (let's call him Og) at a subsistence level of living and completely without tools. He has never saved; therefore he has no capital. He gets his living by picking berries, roots, or whatever else he can get by hand. This is tedious and inefficient. He could do so much better if he had a spear to catch fish or a trap to catch animals. But he can't make these things without devoting time to it, time that otherwise would be spent in getting his food. He has two alternatives if he wishes to invest (to increase his stock of durable goods): (1) He can go hungry while he takes time from food gathering to make his spear, or (2) he can put in longer hours, working more in order to produce the spear while spending the same amount of time meeting his immediate needs. In the first case he has reduced his consumption below his production (income); in the second he has raised his production above his consumption. In either case he has saved. The result is investment. He now has a spear he didn't have before. The spear is precisely what he has produced and not consumed.

Suppose that instead of making the spear himself, Og had commissioned a neighbor to do it, paying him with food he gathered. Og did not produce the spear, but it still represents in value the difference between his production (of food) and his consumption, this difference being equal to the food paid for the spear. Saving still equals investment.

Suppose a third case in which Og can neither reduce his food consumption without starvation nor increase his output without collapse. But he knows that he could get the same amount of food with less effort if he had a spear. He arranges with a neighbor who is better off than he is to borrow enough food for a week and to repay it gradually over a period of time. During the week that he is freed from food gathering he makes a spear. This enables him not only to provide enough food for himself, but also to get enough more to pay back his loan. His increased productivity allows him to save enough food to pay interest on the loan and to raise his own standard of living at the same time.

The time saved now in gathering food can be used to make other tools—a trap, a bucket for carrying water, a knife, a plow, a spinning wheel, a loom, a house, a blacksmith shop, an iron furnace, an automobile plant. It is precisely by this method that industrialization has been introduced.

Frugality, in the sense of not consuming all one's output (or all the income representing that output) permits the acquisition (directly or through others) of capital equipment, which in turn raises income and permits a higher consumption level. At the same time increased income also permits greater saving, which in turn pushes income still higher through the greater investment it makes possible. To him that hath shall be given—if he saves part of it.

The ultimate fact remains that no investment can occur—no capital goods can be accumulated—unless these goods are both (1) produced and (2) not immediately consumed. Somebody has to save.

Voluntary versus Forced Saving. Saving may take many forms and is often disguised. We don't need to dwell on the obvious forms: a proprietor puts his own money into his business; individuals provide corporate capital through the purchase of stocks and bonds; financial intermediaries make loans from the savings entrusted to them by others.

On the other hand, saving may be less than voluntary, and there are at least three ways in which forced saving may be obtained.

Reinvested Earnings. When a corporation fails to pay out all its earnings (after taxes) to its stockholders, it is forcing those stockholders to save. This is true whether it pays stock dividends or not. As long as payments are not made in cash, the stockholder has earned (through his corporation) an income that he cannot spend. This saving is reflected in an increase in his assets (as is all saving) through the increased value of his ownership interest in the corporation, and this is true whether a stock dividend gives him another piece of paper to represent this greater value or whether it is represented simply by an increase in the book value of the same old stock. But his consumption will be less than if he had a cash dividend to spend.

Government Saving. The government may take taxes from its citizens and make the funds available, through its various lending agencies, to others who will use them for investment. The taxpayers are forced to save indirectly.

Or the government may produce public works—dams, roads, schools, post offices, and so on—itself. In this country statisticians do not count such projects as investment even though they add to the wealth of the country. But there is certainly a sound economic reason for treating them on a par with factories, and perhaps the statistical series may be altered in the future to take account of the similarity. They certainly increase the real wealth of the country though not its privately owned wealth.

Many other governments go much further than the United States in the amount of saving put to work in this way. The Soviet Union obtains the largest part of its saving from taxation, these funds being used to construct government factories. Consumption is kept lower than it otherwise would be simply because the consumer never receives all his income. The high rate of investment in the Soviet Union could not exist without this high rate of (forced) saving.

Inflation. Businessmen can get the money for expansion not only from voluntary savers, reinvested earnings, or the government, but, as we well know, also from banks, which create it out of nothing. Surely this represents investment without saving. Unfortunately not! It is still impossible to get anything for nothing.

There are two possibilities. Suppose in the first case that the economy is in a depression. The result of the increased investment will be more men at work, higher income, and a higher level of saving to match the greater investment. Obviously if the borrower is building a factory or producing equipment, these things can't be consumed. The higher income can result in greater consumption only if more *consumer* goods are made available. If the newly employed workers try to spend all their money for consumption goods, this will raise the output of consumption goods, and hence of income, until the economy as a whole is willing to refrain from consuming an amount equal to the value of the investment. This is the essence of the multiplier, already described at some length. The ultimate result is that higher income levels produce voluntary saving equal to the new investment.

The second case is that in which the economy is already at full employment.

The Zero Corporation borrows from a bank in order to expand output. But if there are no unemployed resources in the economy, the only way the Zero Corporation can get additional men and materials is to bid them away from some other employment. Zero can increase output only by reducing output somewhere else. If the alternative from which resources come is one of the capital goods industries, then investment is reduced in one area to permit its expansion elsewhere, and there is no net new investment. If the alternative is a consumer goods industry, then the absolute volume of goods available to consumers is reduced. If real income cannot rise (full employment) and real investment is increased, then obviously real consumption must fall whether consumers want it to or not. Consequently real saving must rise.

The mechanism by which this result is produced is inflation. Consumers, attempting to buy the same amount of goods when less is available, force prices up. Money incomes rise, but more consumer goods are still not on the market. If consumers continue to try to buy more, prices will keep on rising to ration the scarce supply of goods. Only when consumers withdraw from the market (save) an amount of funds equal to current investment will the price pressure ease and the upward price spiral cease.

The fact that the monetary value of consumption may not fall and is, in fact, more likely to rise is not significant from the point of view of real consumption. This is the money illusion. Real consumption has dropped; real saving has increased. The economy has shifted its direction toward less consumer goods and more capital goods. The investment means less goods to consume.

Forced saving under these circumstances may well result in serious distortions in the economy, for the use of resources is not in line with the desired patterns as indicated by free consumer decisions between present consumption and future consumption (saving). The banks, by creating additional money, have given business investors control over a larger portion of the economy (through enlarged purchasing power) than they could obtain under the free play of the market. The result is likely to be an undesirable volume of business investment, which in turn may later create problems when the economy loses its buoyancy and is unable to support the topheavy structure of industry. How serious such distortion will be depends on a great number of factors. It may be absorbed in a rapidly growing economy without serious disturbance. Under less favorable circumstances it may be an important contributing cause of later depression.

Dissaving. A rather different problem arises from the ultimate objective of saving—dissaving. As far as individuals are concerned, most of them save today in order to be able to spend tomorrow. This is particularly true of the increasingly popular pension plans. On retirement the pensioner expects to enjoy the fruits of his former labor.

But one doesn't save food, clothing, shelter, or the other things he wants to consume later (except when he buys a house). One normally saves money. This means that when the time comes to retire or to use savings in any other way, the savings must be turned into real goods. Dissaving means consuming more than one produces. At the same time someone else must be saving an equal amount, or else the economy as a whole will be disinvesting—will be using up its capital.

Someone must produce the food, clothing, and other goods that retired persons consume. These producers therefore must consume less than they themselves produce. If the whole nation were to retire at the same time, everyone would starve to death even if he had plenty of monetary assets. Here is the money illusion again. We think that we are guaranteeing our future by our present saving. Perhaps we are, but only if in that future others are willing to support us by exchanging real goods for our savings.

This problem suggests two lines of thought. First is the possibility of inflation, mentioned so repeatedly because it is so important. If our savings lose value over time, we may discover that we are paupers when we finally want to use them.

The second concerns the volume of production itself. At the same time that the doctors are lengthening our life span, at the same time that young people are staying in school longer, at the same time that many people are retiring earlier, the actual workweek of the remaining labor force is being reduced. There is no monetary legerdemain by which we can avoid the fact that a shorter workweek for fewer workers (proportionately) must support a larger nonworking population. If productivity does not rise, the nation's standard of living must fall.

Current consumption must come from current production or from disinvestment. There is no other source. Each worker in the future therefore must save more in order to let the growing nonworking population consume more. This does not necessarily mean that he must consume less in absolute terms. A growing real income based on technological advances may permit him both to save more *and* to consume more. But it is necessary that saving on the part of the working force make up a larger *proportion* of income in order to offset the dissaving of others, or else the productive capacity of the nation will suffer.

Some of the laws of economics are as inexorable as those of physics. We cannot consume what we do not produce. We cannot invest what we have not saved. We cannot dissave without disinvesting. No monetary manipulation in the world can invalidate those facts. The study of money, therefore, can never supplant the study of production and distribution; it can only supplement these other, more basic fields.

Wealth and Welfare

And one final word on the veils that hide our understanding of basic relationships. Without belittling the importance of money, we have tried to point out that undue concentration on monetary values may obscure the real facts of economic life. We could go one step further and suggest that just as monetary economists may become so wrapped up in their subject that they forget the broader implications of economics, so economists in general frequently allow their specialization to narrow their interest to the confines of their single field.

But material well-being is not the ultimate goal of life, and if we have concentrated on material goods in this book, it is because no book, no course, indeed no life can comprehend everything. Specialization is necessary in this complicated day and age, but specialization sometimes has its drawbacks in narrowing our perspective.

In our saner moments all of us realize that wealth is not everything. We commiserate with the poor little rich girl and the bird in the gilded cage. We often speak of the "finer things of life," and they are not economic. But our saner moments are all too few, and in the United States we sometimes emphasize material goods to the relative exclusion of culture, neighborliness, or even plain fun. Economists in particular need to be reminded frequently that their professional specialty is not the be-all and end-all of life. Contentment does not consist solely in the possession of the latest in electric toothbrushes.

Questions for Thought and Discussion

1. Does the fact that wars were fought to a large extent with mercenaries during the mercantilist period shed any light on their doctrines?
2. What did Say mean when he said that supply creates its own demand?
3. Does Say's statement that "the value of money is also perishable" shed any light on inflationary conditions in his time? What does this remark suggest about velocity?
4. If classical economists were aware of the problems of inflation, why did they pay so little attention to money?
5. If each individual is better off with more money, why isn't everybody?
6. Are wage earners showing more understanding of the importance of *real* wages than they formerly did? What do "escalator clauses" in wage contracts suggest on this score?
7. To what extent can workers better their position by make-work rules?
8. If money is such a poor yardstick in measuring values (such as assets and costs), why do we use it? What alternatives are there?
9. What is the effect on the economy of a concentrated advertising campaign that induces people to buy goods now rather than save for the future?
10. If saving is necessary to capital accumulation, what is the meaning of the "paradox of thrift"? Can saving be too great? (Remember *ex post* and *ex ante.*)
11. Is voluntary saving more desirable than forced saving? Always? What forms of forced saving are most desirable (or least undesirable)?
12. Why should building a Railway Express office constitute investment, while building a post office is not so classified?
13. Why, in assessing the economic effect of a given policy, do we almost

always have to ask first whether it will be applied under conditions of depression or full employment?

14. Suppose the United States is making net foreign investments. What is the effect on our immediate real consumption? On our long-run real income? On the borrower's immediate real consumption? On his long-run real income?

15. In what sense does the government support retired workers on social security? In what sense do other workers support them?

16. In what ways does an agricultural economy in which each family is (relatively) self-sufficient differ from an industrialized economy in its treatment of saving, investment, and retirement?

17. Would it be possible for the whole nation to live for, say, two weeks on unemployment insurance? (Who would deliver the checks? Who would cash them?)

18. Why does the United States seem to be more materialistically minded than most of the rest of the world?

19. Is it possible for a nation to have too much money? Too little? What is the "right" amount?

20. Has this course altered any of your basic views on the role of money in the economy?

Selected Bibliography

Bresciani-Turroni, Constantino: *The Economics of Inflation: A Study of Currency Depreciation in Post-war Germany, 1914–1923,* trans. by Millicent E. Sayers, Barnes & Noble, Inc., New York, 1937.

Clark, John Maurice: *Economic Institutions and Human Welfare,* Alfred A. Knopf, Inc., New York, 1957.

Fisher, Irving: *The Money Illusion,* The Adelphi Company, New York, 1928.

Graham, Frank D.: *Exchange, Prices, and Production in Hyper-inflation Germany, 1920–1923,* Princeton University Press, Princeton, N.J., 1930.

Hobson, John A.: *Work and Wealth: A Human Valuation,* The Macmillan Company, New York, 1914.

Knight, Frank H.: *Freedom and Reform,* Harper & Row, Publishers, Incorporated, New York, 1947.

Pigou, A. C.: *The Veil of Money,* Macmillan & Co., Ltd., London, 1949.

Rogers, James Harvey: *The Process of Inflation in France, 1914–1927,* Columbia University Press, New York, 1929.

White, Andrew Dickson: *Fiat Money Inflation in France,* Appleton-Century-Crofts, Inc., New York, 1933.

Willis, H. Parker, and John M. Chapman: *The Economics of Inflation,* Columbia University Press, New York, 1935.

Glossary

Many of the words defined here have more than one meaning. I have given only that meaning most commonly used in this book. The page references in parentheses indicate where the primary discussion of the concept may be found. For other references and for concepts and institutions not included here see the Index.

Accelerator. A numerical expression of the relation between a given increase in consumption and the increase in investment that it will cause (525).

Accord. *See* Treasury–Federal Reserve Accord.

Advances. *See* discounts and advances.

Assay. Testing the fineness (purity) of the metal in a coin (30).

Asset. Anything of value owned by an individual or organization (142).

Asset reserves. A proposal that legal reserves be computed as a given percentage of loans and securities rather than of deposits (678).

Automatic (built-in) stabilizers. Governmental policies that react to a change in movement of business without the need for any conscious action on the part of the government (697).

Balance of international payments. A summary of all transactions carried out by nationals of a given country with foreigners. It comprises (1) merchandise, (2) services, (3) unilateral transfers, and (4) capital claims, including gold (718). The **balance of trade** concerns the relation of imports to exports of merchandise (item 1). The **balance of goods and services** adds item 2. The **balance on current account** adds item 3. The **balance on capital account** consists of item 4 (721).

Balance sheet. A statement of the financial position of an individual or organization at a particular point in time as indicated by the value of his assets and liabilities (142).

Balance sheet equation. Assets − liabilities = net worth *or* assets = liabilities + net worth (143).

Bank, commercial. An institution, or that part of an institution, that concerns itself with the receipt, creation, and transfer of demand deposits for the accommodation of the general public (140).

Bank (banker's) acceptance. A bill of exchange drawn on a bank, which the bank has agreed to pay by writing "accepted" across its face (725).

Bank draft. A check written by a bank on its account in a correspondent bank (727).

Bank of deposit (giro bank). An institution (seventeenth to nineteenth centuries) that accepted silver for deposit on the basis of weight, issued its own bank credits in exchange, and kept a 100 per cent silver reserve (85).

Bank of issue. A bank (now usually a central bank) that issues bank notes.

Bank rate. British terminology for what we would call the **discount rate** (364).

Base period. In index numbers, a period chosen arbitrarily to be set equal to 100 (385).

Bill broker. A firm that specializes in buying, selling, and trading bills of exchange (329).

Bill of credit. Fiat currency issued by the American colonies (107).

Bill of exchange. An unconditional order, requiring a certain individual to pay a certain sum of money to the order of a certain individual at a certain time (70).

Bill of lading. A receipt for merchandise for shipment given by a transportation company. In its **order** form used in international trade it also represents title to the merchandise (723).

"Bills-only" policy. A practice of the Federal Reserve System of conducting open-market operations only in Treasury bills and not in longer-term government securities (687).

Bimetallism. A monetary system in which two metals serve equally as the standard money with a legal ratio fixed between them (36).

Bond. A promissory note of a corporation or government issued for a period of five years or more (295).

Book value. The value of assets as they are carried on the balance sheet.

Bullion. Monetary metal in an uncoined form (113).

Business cycle. A general movement of business activity up and down through expansion, recession, contraction, and revival over a period of time longer than one year from peak to peak or trough to trough (416).

Call. A demand issued by the Treasury to those commercial banks in which it has tax and loan accounts requiring them to transfer a certain portion of these accounts to its credit with the Federal Reserve banks (235).

Call loan. An old form of loan on a day-to-day basis (usually on stock collateral) on which the bank could demand payment at any time (189).

Capital. (1) The original contribution of stockholders to the financial structure of a business (142). (2) More generally, funds received from either stockholders or creditors (719). (3) In real terms, the physical plant, equipment, and materials used in production (485). (4) In international trade, securities or other claims against foreigners—more accurately called **capital claims** (719–720).

Capital market. The various institutions and arrangements concerned with the purchase, sale, and transfer of stocks and bonds (294).

Cash. (1) Currency. (2) Less commonly, money.

Cash items in process of collection. Checks received by a bank from its depositors that it has not yet had time to collect from the banks on which they are drawn (182).

Ceiling reserves. A proposal to put additional reserve requirements on all deposits in excess of some specified amount (677).

Central bank. A bank (usually quasi-governmental) that provides services for, and some degree of supervision over, commercial banks. Today it is usually the primary issuer of paper currency (206).

Certified check. A check drawn by an individual on his account, on the face of which the bank has certified that the check is valid and will be paid on presentation (180).

Chain banking. A situation in which an individual maintains stock ownership and control of two or more banks (283).

Clearing. The process by which a check is collected from the bank on which it is drawn when deposited in some other bank (113).

Coin. A piece of metal whose value is certified upon its face (30).

Commercial paper. The promissory notes of businessmen given in exchange for short-term (commercial) loans from banks (147). **Eligible commercial paper** is such paper that the Federal Reserve banks are willing to accept for rediscount (209). **Open-market commercial paper** represents large-scale issues of promissory notes of a corporation, similar to bonds but of short term (329).

Commodity money. An article that is used as money but that has just as great a value in its nonmonetary uses (34).

Compensating balance. An amount that a bank may require a borrower to retain in his deposit account as a condition of the loan (167*n.*).

Consumption. The purchase of goods for one's own use (481).

Continental currency. Fiat money issued by the Continental Congress from 1775 to 1781 (110).

Convenience motive. The holding of money because it is too much trouble to do anything else with it (462).

Correspondent. A bank that maintains deposit and other relations with another bank (145).

Cost push. The theory that prices are pushed up by an increase in costs, particularly labor costs (468).

Credit. The present acquisition of anything of value in exchange for the promise to return an equivalent at some future time (62).

Credit instrument. The document that evidences the terms of a credit transaction (67).

Credit standing. The ability of a person to obtain credit based on the lender's belief in his capacity and willingness to make repayment (64).

Currency. Coins and paper bills used as money (45). In international trade, currency refers to *any* form of foreign money; most foreign currency transactions involve bank deposits (722*n.*).

Currency in circulation. The amount of currency issued minus that portion held by the monetary authorities: Treasury and Federal Reserve banks (46).

Currency outside banks. The currency portion of purchasing power in the hands of the public. It consists of currency in circulation minus vault cash held by banks (46).

Customary reserves (working reserves). The amount of liquid assets that a bank holds as a matter of prudence in addition to any assets required by law (172).

Debasement. The issue of coins containing less precious metal than they are alleged to contain (32).

Debt. The promise to repay at some future time the equivalent of something of value previously received (23).

Deficit, government. A situation in which government expenditures exceed tax receipts (702).

Deflation. A fall in the general price level.

Demand deposits, adjusted. The checking account portion of purchasing power in the hands of the public. It consists of gross deposits minus the following four items: cash items in process of collection, interbank deposits, government deposits, and time deposits (52).

Demand loan. A loan on a day-to-day basis (usually on stock collateral) which the bank could terminate at any time but which it is more likely merely to discourage by raising the interest rate (189).

Demand pull. The theory that prices are pulled up by an increase in demand, usually due to an increase in the quantity of money (467).

Deposit. A bank's obligation to pay a sum of money on demand (demand deposit) or after a certain period of notice (time deposit). The use of the word "deposit" to mean the payment of money into a bank for credit to one's account, while common, is apt to be confusing (144).

Direct controls. Regulations of the monetary authorities that restrict the terms under which loans may be made for specific purposes, such as consumer installment purchases (250).

Discount. *See* loans and discounts; also interest and discount.

Discount (rediscount) rate. The charge levied by the Federal Reserve banks on loans to member banks (245).

Discounts and advances. The process by which a Federal Reserve bank lends to member banks; also the asset that the Reserve bank acquires in exchange for the funds advanced. When a bank borrows on the basis of commercial paper that it holds, it is a **discount;** when a bank borrows on its own note, it is an **advance** (227).

Disposable personal income. Personal income minus personal taxes (479).

Dollar glut. A situation in which foreign nationals hold more dollars than they want to use to obtain United States goods, so that they either demand gold or hold the dollars as a liquid claim against the United States (761).

Dollar shortage. A situation in which foreign nationals wish to obtain more dollars to buy United States goods than are available at current exchange rates, so that the scarce dollars must be rationed (759).

Drawee. The person or bank on whom a bill of exchange is drawn and who is ordered to make payment; also called the **payer** (71).

Drawer. The person who writes a bill of exchange or promissory note; also called the **maker** (71).

Dual banking system. A situation in which a bank may be chartered and supervised by either state or Federal agencies (281).

Effective money supply. The total ready purchasing power in the hands of the public. It consists of currency outside banks and demand deposits, adjusted (45).

Eligible commercial paper. *See* commercial paper.

Equation of exchange. The value of goods sold is equal to the money spent for them; $PT = MV$ (438).

Equilibrium. A situation that contains within itself no forces tending to cause change.

Equity. *See* net worth.

Ex ante. Looked at in anticipation; the expectation of what is to come (513).

Ex post. Looked at from hindsight; the record of what has already happened (495).

Excess reserves. The amount of reserves (usually currency plus amounts owed by other banks) held by a bank minus the amount it is required to hold by law or custom (165).

Exchange control. A situation in which the government prohibits all transactions in foreign exchange except under prescribed conditions and at predetermined rates (740).

Exchange rate. The price of one nation's money expressed in terms of a second nation's monetary unit (732).

Face value. The value in terms of the monetary unit stamped on a coin or written on a credit instrument (30).

Federal funds. Reserve balances held by a member bank with its Federal Reserve bank (189).

Fiat currency. Paper money issued with no specific backing and no promise of redemption.

Finance paper. Open-market commercial paper issued by a sales finance company (329).

Financial intermediary. An institution that transmits, or aids in the transmission of, funds between those who supply them and those who wish to use them (292).

Fiscal policy. Governmental actions that affect the economy in the form of government expenditures, taxation, and debt management (696).

Float. On the balance sheet of a Federal Reserve bank, the difference between cash items in process of collection and deferred availability cash items, representing credit given to member banks for deposited checks before the Reserve has had time to collect them (232).

Forced saving. An involuntary reduction in consumption due to reduced purchasing power. It may be caused by corporate saving, government saving, or inflation (810).

Foreign exchange. Foreign money; money denominated in a foreign monetary unit (722*n.*).

Fractional-reserve banking. The issue of demand deposits in excess of the amount of reserves held against them (156).

Free banking. The principle that any group could establish a bank under a general incorporation law by meeting prescribed requirements (126).

Free coinage. The right of an individual to take the standard monetary metal to the mint and have it coined (113).

Freely fluctuating exchange market. A market for foreign exchange in which the government does not interfere in any way (733).

Full employment. (1) A situation where there are more job openings than unemployed workers. (2) More commonly in the United States, a situation where not more than 5 (or 4 or 3) per cent of the work force is unemployed (605).

Giro bank. *See* bank of deposit.

Giro order. An order to a bank to pay a certain sum of money to a certain individual, but unlike a check sent directly to the bank rather than to the payee (371).

Gold drain. A flow of gold abroad, which has a tendency to restrict the ability of the monetary system to expand (174).

Gold points. Under the international gold standard, the exchange rate at which gold tends to flow from one country to another (737).

Gold standard. A situation in which a country (1) defines its currency as a given weight of gold, (2) provides convertibility between gold and all other forms of currency, and (3) permits free movement of gold (37). The **gold coin standard** requires in addition the free coinage of gold (37). Under the **gold bullion standard** convertibility is maintained only in terms of standard bullion bars (39). Under the **gold exchange standard** the government may provide convertibility in either gold or foreign exchange on a gold-standard country at its option (39). Under a **gold reserve standard** a nation restricts either convertibility or free movement or both (40).

Gold tranche. The portion of a member's subscription to the International Monetary Fund that is paid in the form of gold (784).

Goldsmiths. Originally craftsmen in jewels and precious metals (working goldsmiths), who developed in the seventeenth century the modern technique of fractional-reserve banking (goldsmith bankers) (86).

Goldsmith's note. A promise by a goldsmith to pay specie to the bearer on demand; an early form of paper money (88).

Government expenditures. Government purchases of goods and services, transfer payments, and net government interest (484).

Greenbacks (United States notes). Fiat currency originally issued during the Civil War (48).

Gresham's law. Bad money (debased, worn, or overvalued coins or irredeemable paper currency) tends to drive good money out of circulation (33).

Gross national product (GNP). The market value of all commodities and services produced by an economy in a year (or other period of time) (474).

Group of Ten. Ten countries that cooperate closely on international monetary matters. They consist of Belgium, Canada, France, West Germany, Italy, Japan, Netherlands, Sweden, United Kingdom, and United States. Switzerland is an associate member (786).

Group banking. A situation in which a holding company maintains stock ownership and control of two or more banks (283).

Hoarding. All saving not made available for investment (486). *See also* liquidity preference.

Hoards. The accumulated stocks of money resulting from past hoarding, net (486).

Independent Treasury. A system of subtreasuries for the receipt and payment of money on behalf of the government, 1840 to 1921 (128).

Index. A list of numbers showing the relative change over time of a given series (such as prices) by relating the value of the series in each year to a conventional value of 100 in an arbitrarily chosen base period (385).

Inflation. A rise in the general price level.

Interest and discount. The charge made by a lender for advancing funds. When the charge is paid at maturity, it is **interest;** when it is deducted in advance, it is **discount** (147).

Interest rate. The charge for a loan stated as a percentage of the amount actually borrowed per year. It may be calculated by the formula $i = \frac{2MC}{P(N+1)}$ (73–74).

International liquidity. All resources available to the world's monetary authorities for the purpose of meeting balance of payments deficits (782).

Inventories. Stocks of merchandise held by a businessman for sale or for use in the productive process.

Investment, domestic. An increase in the physical assets (real capital) of business (485).

Investment, net foreign. Exports on current account minus imports on current account ($Ex - Im$). It is equal to both the export balance on current account and the import balance on capital-claims account (751).

Investment, total. Domestic investment plus net foreign investment (502).

Investments. *See* loans and investments.

IOU. A promissory note.

Key currency. The currency of any country that is widely used as a means of international payment and as a pool of international liquidity (783).

Legal reserves. The amount of assets in whatever form that a bank is required to hold by law (172).

Legal tender. Currency that the law says *must* be accepted at face value in payment of debt (41).

Letter of credit. A letter from a bank promising (on behalf of an importer) to pay for merchandise provided the exporter fulfills certain specified conditions (723).

Liability. Any debt owed to another (142).

Liquidity. The speed and certainty with which assets can be turned into money (54).

Liquidity preference. The desire to hold money rather than less liquid earning assets (457).

Liquidity trap. The situation that exists if the people wish to hoard an indefinite quantity of money at low interest rates, so that an increase in the money supply will be absorbed into these holdings without exerting any upward push on the economy (565).

Loanable funds. The amount of funds that would be supplied by lenders or demanded by borrowers in a given period at various rates of interest (554).

Loans and discounts. The process by which a bank lends to its customers; also the asset that the bank acquires in exchange for the funds advanced. If interest is paid when the debt is repaid, it is a **loan;** if the charge is deducted in advance, it is a **discount** (147).

Loans and investments. The earning assets of a bank. **Loans** (and discounts) are usually personally negotiated with each borrower; **investments** are generally securities purchased on the open market (146).

Margin requirements. Limits set by the Federal Reserve on the amount that can be borrowed for purchasing or carrying securities (250).

Maturity. The time at which a loan falls due for repayment (66).

Member bank. A bank that has accepted the obligations and privileges of membership in the Federal Reserve System (220).

Mercantilism. A school of thought of the fifteenth to eighteenth centuries that emphasized the importance of money as the most desirable form of wealth (801–802).

Mint parity. The exchange rate between two currencies that is precisely equal to the ratio of their gold contents (736).

Monetary union. A group of countries that agree either to establish a common currency or to accept one another's currencies at a par with their own in domestic trade (787–788).

Monetary unit (money of account). An accounting standard in which the value (price) of all other goods is measured (19).

Monetization of debt. The process by which a borrower gives his promissory note to a bank in exchange for the bank's promise to honor his checks, a promise that he can use as money (160).

Money. Anything that is generally acceptable as a means of payment (medium of exchange) at a given time and place (15).

Money creation. The injection of new money into the circuit flow either by banks or by the government (489–490).

Money market. The various arrangements and institutions concerned with the purchase, sale, and transfer of short-term credit instruments (294).

Moral suasion. Pressure exerted by the Federal Reserve on the banking system without any attempt to compel compliance (247).

Multiplier. A numerical expression of the relation between a given increase in investment and the (greater) increase in national income that results; $K = \frac{1}{1 - C}$ (580).

National income. (1) The sum of all income earned by the factors of production for their share in the productive process during a year (or other period of time) (477). (2) In a broader sense, *any* measure of national output or receipts, such as GNP, NNP, or personal income (474).

Near-money. Anything that can be readily turned into money at a known value; predominantly savings accounts and savings bonds (54).

Negotiable instrument. A promissory note or bill of exchange that conforms to certain legal requirements and is readily transferred (negotiated) from one holder to another with maximum safety (69).

Net foreign investment. *See* investment, net foreign.

Net national product (NNP). Gross national product minus capital consumption allowances (primarily depreciation) (477).

Net worth (equity). The value of an individual's (or organization's) assets after deducting the claims of creditors (liabilities) (142).

Nonmember clearing bank. A bank that is not a member of the Federal Reserve System but that maintains with its Federal Reserve bank a sufficient deposit balance to permit checks drawn on it to be cleared through the Federal Reserve clearing machinery (151).

Nonpar bank. A bank that levies a special charge (exchange charge) on checks that are presented for payment through the mail rather than over the counter; that is, it refuses to pay such checks at par (face value) (151).

Officer's check. A check drawn by an officer of a bank on the bank itself (180).

100 per cent reserves. A proposal that the reserve requirement against demand deposits be raised to 100 per cent (681).

Open-market operations. The purchase and sale by the Federal Reserve of government securities and bank acceptances through the normal channels of such trade (229).

Operation nudge. Another name for **operation twist.**

Operation twist. An attempt by the Federal Reserve to raise short-term interest rates without raising long-term rates in order to attract international funds without discouraging domestic investment (648).

Optimum production. The greatest output that can reasonably be achieved, given the general social and organizational structure of the economy (603).

Payee. The person to whom payment is to be made on a promissory note or bill of exchange (68).

Pecuniary. Monetary. A **pecuniary society** is one accustomed to using money.

Personal income. The amount of money actually received as income or transfer payments by the residents of a nation during a year (or other period) (478).

Portfolio management. The science (or art) of balancing the various types of assets in a bank's portfolio so as to maximize income without incurring the danger of insolvency (186).

Precautionary motive. The desire to hold money to meet unforeseen emergencies or opportunities (459).

Price. The value of a good expressed in the monetary unit (384).

Price-specie flow mechanism. Under the gold standard, the mechanism by which abnormally high prices in one country would result in a loss of gold, hence a reduction in the quantity of money and a drop in prices; and the opposite if prices were too low (737).

Primary reserves. Assets held by a bank that are completely liquid. They include cash and due from banks (186).

Progressive tax. One that takes a larger percentage of the income of the rich than of the poor (700).

Promissory note. An unconditional promise to pay a certain sum of money to the order of a certain individual at a certain time (68).

Purchasing power parity theory. A theory that says that the foreign exchange value of any two countries' currencies should be in the same ratio as their price levels (735).

Pure (net) interest. The amount of interest charged on a loan minus the risk premium and all costs (569).

Quantity theory. A theory that says that a change in the quantity of money will produce an equal proportionate change in the price level (444).

Real-bills doctrine. The belief that loans should be made by a commercial bank only to finance the distribution of goods actually in existence (183).

Rediscount. *See* discount rate; discounts and advances.

Regressive tax. One that takes a larger percentage of the income of the poor than of the rich (700).

Repressed inflation. A situation where excess purchasing power tends to force prices up but where the price rise is prevented by artificial means such as price control (637).

Risk premium. That part of an interest charge estimated to cover the possibility of the loan being defaulted in whole or in part (568).

Saving, government (government surplus). Government receipts minus government expenditures ($T - G$) (501).

Saving, personal. All income not used for consumption or taxes (481).

Saving, total. Personal saving plus government saving (502).

Savings. The accumulated assets resulting from past saving, net (483).

Say's law. Jean Baptiste Say (1767–1832) suggested that supply creates its own demand (803).

Scrip. "Money" issued by local governments, to which a tax stamp must be attached each week in order to maintain its validity (662).

Seasonal variation. Fluctuations in any component of business activity that recur fairly regularly at the same period each year (416).

Secondary reserves. Assets held by a bank that are convertible into cash on short notice. They include treasury bills, bank acceptances, and other highly liquid assets (188).

Secular trend. A long-term, persistent (but necessarily steady) movement of any component of business activity in one direction (413).

Securities. Claims to wealth, such as stocks and bonds.

Security reserves. A proposal that banks be required to hold a certain amount of government securities in addition to their other reserves (676).

Specie. Coin, usually full-bodied gold or silver; sometimes also gold or silver bullion (40).

Speculative motive. The desire to hold money because its value is expected to rise; that is, prices of goods or securities are expected to fall (462).

Stock. An evidence of the holder's part ownership in a corporation (295).

Surplus. (Roughly) the net worth of a business in excess of the amount originally contributed by stockholders (capital).

Surplus, government. *See* saving, government.

Tax and loan accounts. Demand deposit accounts of the United States Treasury held in commercial banks (234).

Tenor. *See* usance.

Term loan. A loan made by a commercial bank for a period of a year or longer (184).

Tight money market. A situation in which loans are more difficult to get than usual. It is generally characterized by both rising interest rates and credit rationing (192).

Time preference. The theory that if given a choice, people will always prefer consumption now to consumption later (569).

Token. Currency whose intrinsic value is less than its face value (42).

Transactions motive. The desire to hold money to meet ordinary or known expenditures (458).

Transfer payments. Payments received by individuals that are not the result of their productive effort in the period in which they are received, such as unemployment insurance, pensions, gifts, and so on (478).

Treasury–Federal Reserve Accord. An agreement between the two agencies in March, 1951, whereby the Federal Reserve won its right to abandon market support of government securities in the interest of more effective monetary control (642).

Trustee. An individual or institution who manages the funds of someone else (the **trustor**) for the benefit of either the trustor or someone whom he has named (the **beneficiary**) under a written understanding (the **trust agreement**) (335).
Twist. *See* operation twist.

Unit banking. A situation in which a bank does not operate any branches. A **unit banking system** is one in which most banks do not operate branches (271).
United States notes. *See* greenbacks.
Usance (tenor). The length of time a loan has to run until maturity (66).
Usury. Originally, any interest charge; now, an exorbitant interest charge, usually defined by law (82).

Valuation reserves. An amount deducted by a creditor from the book value of debts due him, in the expectation that some of them are likely to be defaulted (185).
Value of money. The power of money to buy goods (383–384).
Vault cash. Currency held by a bank to meet the demands of its customers (165).
Velocity of circulation. The speed with which money moves through the economy (438). **Income velocity** is the number of times per year (or other period) that an average dollar moves from one income recipient to another (442). **Transactions velocity** is the number of times per year (or other period) that an average dollar changes hands (439).
Velocity reserves. A proposal that reserve requirements be based not only on deposits, but also on the velocity of their turnover (679).

Wealth. The sum total of all physical goods of value (23).
Working reserves. *See* customary reserves.

Index